Wellington's Men Remembered

Wellington's Men Remembered

A Register Of Memorials To Soldiers
Who Served In The Peninsular War
And At Waterloo 1808 – 1815

Volume I

A – L

Janet and David Bromley

Foreword By His Grace The Duke Of Wellington

First published in Great Britain in 2012 by
The Praetorian Press
an imprint of
Pen & Sword Books Ltd
47 Church Street
Barnsley
South Yorkshire
S70 2AS

ISBN 978 1 84884 675 3

Typeset in Sabon by
Phoenix Typesetting, Auldgirth, Dumfriesshire

Printed and bound in England by
CPI Group (UK) Ltd, Croydon, CR0 4YY

Pen & Sword Books Ltd incorporates the Imprints of Pen & Sword Aviation, Pen
& Sword Family History, Pen & Sword Maritime, Pen & Sword Military, Pen &
Sword Discovery, Wharncliffe Local History, Wharncliffe True Crime,
Wharncliffe Transport, Pen & Sword Select, Pen & Sword Military Classics, Leo
Cooper, The Praetorian Press, Remember When, Seaforth Publishing and
Frontline Publishing

For a complete list of Pen & Sword titles please contact
PEN & SWORD BOOKS LIMITED
47 Church Street, Barnsley, South Yorkshire, S70 2AS, England
E-mail: enquiries@pen-and-sword.co.uk
Website: www.pen-and-sword.co.uk

Contents

FOREWORD BY

**HIS GRACE THE DUKE OF WELLINGTON
KG., LVO., OBE., MC., DL**

Some twelve years or so ago the Association of Friends of the Waterloo Committee conceived the idea of a "Register of Memorials" to record the existence of over 3000 memorials to British and Allied Soldiers who fought in the Peninsular War and at Waterloo. These exist in no less than 24 countries in the world. The concept was originally initiated by Bob Elmer of Australia but was taken over by Janet and David Bromley ten years ago.

Many memorials are now lost due to the closure of churches, decay, age and the removal of headstones to ensure ease of maintenance for churchyards and cemeteries. "Wellington's Men Remembered" will provide a permanent record of the memorials to so many men who served in the defeat of Napoleon two hundred years ago.

I commend the huge amount of time and effort dedicated to the research by Janet and David Bromley and also more than 400 contributors who have helped with the project for so many years.

Wellington

6th April 2011

"The Paths To Glory Lead But To The Grave"

Elegy Written in a Country Churchyard
Thomas Grey

Dedicated To All The
Peninsular And Waterloo Men
Who Lie In
Unmarked Graves

Preface

Wellington's Men Remembered originated as the *Register of Memorials* under which title it was known during the twelve years of compilation. The idea was conceived by John Morewood and his late father, Alan Walter Morewood, when they found the memorial tablet at St Bega's Church, Bassenthwaite, Cumbria to Lieutenant and Captain Walter Vane of the 1st Regiment of Foot Guards, who died of his wounds received at the Sortie from Bayonne in 1814.

The Waterloo Association, (formerly the Association of Friends of the Waterloo Committee) adopted the project as a contribution to the Millennium celebrations, but did not appreciate at the time the potential size and scope of the work. Association members were invited to research memorials by visiting churches, cemeteries and other likely locations and submit their findings to Bob Elmer in Australia who initially undertook the collection and filing of data until he handed the 300 records then collected to Janet and David Bromley in 2000. They redefined the scope limiting it to memorials to British and allied soldiers who fought in the Peninsular War and at Waterloo.

The objective agreed by the Council of the Association was:

> To publish a volume recording all known memorials to British and Allied soldiers in the form of memorial tablets, headstones, graves etc in churches and cemeteries, together with statues, columns, and other memorials commemorating soldiers who fought in the Peninsular War and at Waterloo, wherever they may be located, supported with details of inscriptions on memorials and a photograph wherever possible.

The help and support of over 400 contributors, many of them members of the Waterloo Association, and other interested individuals in finding, recording and photographing memorials is most appreciated, and the book would not have been produced without their continual interest and support. Their names are acknowledged in the List of Contributors. They have enabled a database to be compiled that will serve as a definitive source book for many years to come and enable military historians, genealogists and others to locate and visit these important historical memorials to the endeavours of so many men who served in the Army during the Peninsular War and at Waterloo between 1808 and 1815.

The Waterloo Association has contributed funds on an annual basis to support the publication of the work, and this has been generously supplemented by donations from members and others, from fundraising activities and, in one case, very generous sponsorship. In addition the research gained the AVB Norman Trust Research Grant in 2008. The support and encouragement of Ian Fletcher is particularly appreciated, together with the help and advice from Jamie Wilson, Lisa Hooson, Richard Doherty and staff at Pen and Sword Ltd. and Malcolm Bates of Phoenix Typesetting.

Wellington's Men Remembered has been compiled over a period of twelve years by Janet and David Bromley who are the Honorary Archivists to the Waterloo Association and members of the Council.

Introduction

Wellington's Men Remembered will be published in two volumes, A - L and M - Z, containing memorials to about 3,000 men who served in the Peninsular War and at Waterloo together with 150 regimental and battlefield memorials in twenty-four countries worldwide. Many are supported with photographs. Some men are represented by multiple memorials in different geographical locations.

Most have been found on site visits. Others which have not yet been found or are no longer extant have been traced by means of documentary research in libraries and archives and have been recorded from published memorial inscriptions. Many of the latter represent memorials that have long been lost, others still remain to be visited and recorded. Some men have been entered into the Register on the strength of church burial records.

The addition of biographical summaries of the service records, appointments, honours, awards and other personal records of the achievements of the men concerned will be of additional value and complements other sources of biographical information. These include their service in the Peninsula and at Waterloo and some records of service before and after those campaigns. Service records for NCOs and other ranks are not as comprehensive as for officers. Honours and awards are identified with the exception of the Waterloo Medal as it was presented to all ranks present on the 16th, 17th and 18th June 1815 and those in reserve.

Memorials are recorded for officers and men under their name, rank and regiment in 1815 or earlier if they served in the Peninsula but were not at Waterloo. In a small number of cases men changed their names and any subsequent or former names are recorded with a reference to the name under which the main entry is recorded.

Ranks and details of service are recorded from various sources, including the *Challis Index*, the *Army List*, *Hart's Army List*, regimental histories and the *London Gazette*. Comparison of data from these various sources reveals that records of dates of service and appointments vary slightly. Every effort has been made to ensure accuracy, but in a minority of cases it has been difficult to reconcile conflicting records. This applies particularly to ranks from the eighteenth century.

Full inscriptions of memorials are recorded, compacted to reduce space and set in capitals for consistency of presentation. The actual layout of style can normally be seen in the photograph. Locations of memorials are included in the heading to Church, Cemetery, Town, County and Country for overseas records. In the case of memorials to families, on which the soldier is mentioned together with other family members, only an extract of the relevant part is normally included. Omissions are identified by (...............) and refer to other members of the family or unrelated detail. These can be seen from the photograph.

Family relationships between men are recorded, with reference to the rank that they held at the time of Waterloo or at the end of their Peninsular service if they did not serve at Waterloo, in the same way as ranks are recorded in the heading. Memorials to wives which refer to their husband are not included unless the memorial includes a specific note of her husband's service record in addition to his rank and regiment.

Each entry comprises:

Full name
Rank and Regiment
Location of memorial and indication of a photograph in the DVD
Ranks and dates of appointment
Service in the Peninsula and at Waterloo
Other service records before 1808 and after 1815
Honours medal and awards

Family links
Bibliographical references

Where a memorial inscription has been recorded from a published source and the grave has not been found, the details are included in the form in the published list of memorial inscriptions, and indicated by the abbreviation (M.I.). These are shown within "........". Such memorial inscriptions are sometimes abstracts of the full memorial record as they were produced mainly for genealogical research.

A small number of memorials which indicate presence in the Peninsular War and Waterloo have been omitted if it has not been possible to authenticate the claims made on the memorial inscription. These will be subject to further research and incorporated into a Supplement contained within Volume Two.

The technical description of memorials has follows a simplified version of the classification in *Recording and Analysing Graveyards* by Harold Mytum published in 2000. The following broad classification has been adopted:

Altar Box/Chest tomb	Brass memorial tablet
Column	Cross
Headstone	Ledger stone
Low monument	Mausoleum
Memorial tablet	Monument
Obelisk	Pedestal tomb
Sarcophagus	Statue
Table tomb	

If a search failed to locate a memorial which has been traced from a memorial inscription it is marked as 'No longer extant'. It is always possible that a search has failed to reveal the memorial or it was not found because it is seriously eroded or buried beneath dense and impenetrable undergrowth. Other memorials have been destroyed as a result of war damage, the clearance of churchyards, or decay caused by weathering and vandalism. Some headstones have been arranged around cemetery walls or used as paving stones in order to ease ground maintenance.

Generally a memorial tablet will be found inside a church, while graves and headstones will obviously be located in the churchyard or cemetery. Many memorials, particularly gravestones carved in soft stone such as sandstone, have deteriorated over the years, and it has not always been possible to identify the entire inscription. Where this is the case, all the words identifiable have been included, and missing words or letters marked ********.

Where there is documentary evidence of the precise location of the burial place of a man, but no evidence of the existence of a grave or memorial, an entry is occasionally made in the form of 'buried at' and the grave number recorded. In some cases monumental masons have made errors of spelling, and these have been reproduced as they appear on the memorial.

Photographs of memorials appear on a DVD inserted into each volume and are noted after the location of the memorial. In the case of regimental and battlefield memorials, photographs will appear on the DVD in Volume Two.

Unfortunately it has not been possible to obtain permission to take photographs or receive permission to reproduce a photograph for copyright reasons in a small number of cases.

Over the period of the survey, the quality of cameras has improved significantly. The photographic skills of contributors and their equipment has also improved over the years. Consequently the photographs reproduced in the illustrations database vary widely in quality from high-definition digital images to poor quality camera images taken on less sophisticated equipment. All have been included as representing the best available image of the memorial. Where better images become available, they will be added to the ongoing database.

Bibliographical references are included for each man where they have been found, including monographs, biographies from the *Dictionary of National Biography* and other national biographies, *Royal Military Calendar*, *Household Brigade Journal*, *United Service Journal* (later *United Service Magazine*), *Gentleman's Magazine*, *Annual Register*, and regimental histories. Occasionally obituaries published in newspapers are noted. Bibliographical references of a more general nature which are not specific to an individual will appear in the Bibliography in Volume Two.

The Place Index records memorials under the name of the county in England and Scotland, as found in contemporary published gazetteers of the mid-nineteenth century. The exception is Cumbria, which includes places previously in Lancashire, Cumberland and Westmoreland. *Fullerton's Parliamentary Gazetteer - 1845* is used as the definitive source for English and Welsh place names. In Scotland, Fullerton's *Topographical and Historical Gazetteer of Scotland* 1842 and for Ireland, *Fullerton's Parliamentary Gazetteer 1844-45* have been used for verification. Many towns have been transferred from county to county over the years. For instance, Slough, now in Berkshire, was previously in Buckinghamshire, and there are many examples of this kind. If in doubt, it is recommended to check adjacent counties.

The Regimental Index records the rank of the man at the time of Waterloo, or earlier if he did not serve there. Regiments are indexed following the order of regiments in the annual Army List for 1815. Where an entry contains more than one given name, the first name is recorded, with other names sometimes represented by initials to contain the index entry to one line.

There are still many unrecorded memorials and readers are requested to notify the editors of new records and also to report any errors and discrepancies in order to maintain the database with a view to recording them in a Supplement and possibly a future edition.

The editors acknowledge that there are inevitably inconsistencies in the text caused by transcription and typing errors, and the problem of transcribing contributions from many diverse sources and information supplied in photographic form in various levels of quality.

Abbreviations

AAG	Assistant Adjutant General	KCH	Knight Commander of the Royal Hanoverian Guelphic Order
Asst	Assistant		
ADC	Aide de Camp		
Adjt	Adjutant	KCTS	Knight Commander of the Tower and Sword
AG	Adjutant General		
AQMG	Assistant Quartermaster General	KG	Knight of the Garter
		KGL	King's German Legion
Bart	Baronet	KH	Knight of the Royal Hanoverian Guelphic Order
Bt	Brevet		
CB	Companion of the Order of the Bath	KMB	Knight of Maximilian of Bavaria
CMG	Companion of the Order of St Michael and St George	KMM	Knight of Military Order of Merit of Prussia
CO	Commanding Officer	KMT	Knight of Maria Theresa of Austria
COMM	Commissary		
DAAG	Deputy Assistant Adjutant General	KOYLI	King's Own Yorkshire Light Infantry
DAG	Deputy Adjutant General	KP	Knight of the Order of St Patrick
DAQMG	Deputy Assistant Quartermaster General	KSA	Knight of St Anne of Russia
DQMG	Deputy Quartermaster General	KSF	Knight of St Ferdinand
EOPS	Engaged on a Particular Service	KSG	Knight of St George of Russia
GCB	Knight Grand Cross of the Order of the Bath	KTS	Knight of the Tower and Sword of Portugal
GCH	Knight Grand Cross of Hanover	KW	Knight of William of Holland
		MGS	Military General Service medal
GCMG	Knight Grand Cross of the Order of St Michael and St George	MI	Memorial inscription
		MKW	Military Knight of Windsor
		NCO	Non Commissioned Officer
GCMM	Grand Cross of the Royal Order of Military Merit of France	NGS	Naval General Service medal
		Obit	Obituary
		OC	Officer Commanding
GCSI	Knight Grand Commander of the Star of India	PC	Privy Councillor
		QMG	Quartermaster General
GOC	General Officer Commanding	RA	Royal Artillery
KB	Knight Companion of the Order of the Bath (pre-1815)	RE	Royal Engineers
		RHA	Royal Horse Artillery
KC	Knight Commander of the Order of the Bath (pre-1815)	RHG	Royal Horse Guards
		RN	Royal Navy
KCB	Knight Commander of the Order of the Bath		

Acknowledgements

His Grace the Duke of Wellington, Jack Abernethy, Henry and Catherine Adams, Marmaduke Alderson, Kerrie Alexander, Charles Anderson, Roger Ansell, Peter Applebee (Adelaide Northern Districts Family History Group), José Manuel Ariza, Garry Ashby, C. E. John Ashton, Wendy Atkin, Linda Attrell, Terry Babbage, John Backhouse, Ken A. Baddeley, Diane and Keith Baines, Joe Baker, Mrs M. Baker, Derek Barber, R. W. Barber, Rev Lee Bastion, Cynthia and Roger Bayliss, Bedfordshire Libraries, Eva Beech, Christopher Bell, Phil Bendall, Alice Berkeley, Paul J. Bennett, Stephen Best, Tony Bibby, Tony and Jill Birch, Gillian Blake, Peter Blakebrough, Frank Bland, Allan Boldero, Michael Bond, Alison Boreham, Chris Bray, Brian Bridges, British Association for Cemeteries in South Asia, Derek Broadhurst, Stephen Bromley, Brompton Cemetery, Brookwood Cemetery Society, Peter and Audrey Brown, Kathleen Brown, Freda Browne, Andrew Browning, Suzanne Brunt, Norman H. Brunyee, Paul F. Brunyee, Philip Brunyee, Buckinghamshire Libraries, Father Ian Bullock, Alan Bullwinkle, George Burley, Ron Burrows, Barbara Capel, Count Emo Capodilista, Barry Cargill, Carlisle Reference Library, David Carpenter, Jo Carter, Frances Carver, Peter Catley, R. Gordon Champ, Barrie and Margaret Chapman, Alain Chappet, John Checketts, John A. Christie, Frank A. O. Clarke, John Clarke, Clash-of-Steel.com, John Clements, Delphine Coleman, William Colfer, Rosemary Collins, Reg W. Connor, Tim Cooke, Graeme Cooper, Robin E. Cousins, Lynn Craig, Bruce Cripps, J. Barry Crisp, Jonathan Crook, Allen Crosbie, Michael Crumplin, Des Cummins, Raymond Cusick, Margaret Daniel, John Darwent, Rosemary Davidson, Bruce Davies, Eddy Davis, Catherine Delahunty, Margaret Denton, Elizabeth Deverell, Carole and John Divall, Nimrod Dix, Peter Donnelly, Jean Downer, John Downham, Robert Dows-Miller, Derek Drake, E. J. Draper, Andrew Driver, Duke of Wellington's Regimental Museum and Archives, Robin Dunbar, Dundee Library and Information Services, Michael B. Dunn, Craig Durham, Paddy Earp, Stuart Eastwood, Gabrielle and Hans Ebke, Steven Ede-Borrett, Dudley Edwards, Roger Edwards, John Ellis, Bob Elmer, Otto Ludwig Engelbrecht, George Evelyn, Stuart Fagan, Jean Fanthorpe, Gary Farmer, Susan M. Farrington, Leo Favret, Dan FitzGerald, Scott Flaving, Ian Fletcher, the Revd Stephen and Will Fletcher, Andrew Floyd, Peter Foden, John Foreman, S. L. Forster, Friends of Highgate Cemetery, Friends of Kensal Green Cemetery, Friends of Nunhead Cemetery, Friends of Sheffield General Cemetery, Friends of Southampton Old Cemetery, Friends of York Cemetery, Patricia Frykberg, Tom Fulton, Jane Furlong, Stephen Furrness, Gail Fynes, Ted Gale, Basil Garratt, Steve Geary, Lucien Gerke, William Gervais, Alan Gibb, John Gierke, Derek Glen, Gareth Glover, J. Godley, Richard Goodridge, Kevin Gorman, Lou Gotfreund, Mary Gough, Russell Granger, Jim Grant, Peter Gratton, Rev Alastair Gray, Ken Gray, Barry Greenwood, Barry Gregson, John Grehan, Ieuan Griffiths, Anne Grimshaw, Colette Grosjean, Guards Museum, Joan and Prodip Guha, Richard and Trisha Gunn, Rosemary Hales, Halifax Public Library Nova Scotia, Sandy and Elizabeth Hall, David Hallewell, William Hallewell, Nick Hallidie, Clive Hamilton, David Hammersley, Peter Hammersley, William Hanna, Clare Harding, David and Hilary Harris, Hank Harris, Mrs Hattrell, Shirley M. Hay, Philip Haythornthwaite, Rod Henley, Peter Helmore, Andrew Hepworth, George Hewitt, Dennis Hill, Malcolm Hill, Richard Hill, Derek Hindle, Peter Hoare, Alan and Natasha Holliday, Ellie and Chris Hollings, David Hooper, Lisa Hooson, David Horn, Ben Hughes, John R. Hughes, Merrion Hughes, Ed Humphreys, Katie Hyde, Mike Hyde, Imperial War Museum, Dennis and Denise Ireland, Cheryl and Michel Itthurraide, Alan Jackson, Janice Jackson, Jocelyn Jackson, Judith Jackson, Dr Gordon James, R. H. James, Jarrold Publishing, Canon Johnson, Mrs B. Johnson, Jane Johnson, Janice Johnson, Bruce Jones, Colin Jones, Derek and Jean Jones, Jane Jones, Louise Jones, S. Jones, Sean Jones, Trevor Jones, Ronald Kay, Andrew Kemel, Kensal Green Cemetery staff, Mrs Ketley, Glen Kilday, J. Bishop King, Robin and Sarah King, Chris Kirk, Alan Lagden, Elizabeth and Jim Laidlaw, Paul Lanagan, Gordon Lane, Larry Leone, Last Post Fund Montreal, Rose La Terriere, Bernard Lavell, Edgar Lawrence, Jim Lees, Miss D. G. Le Faye, Leona Lefoley, Victoria Lendrum, John Lester, M. I.

Lindley, Bill Little, Duncan Lodge, Bob Longden, Francisco José Martinez Lopez, Patricia Luxford, Maurice McCabe, Terry McCabe, Joanne McCarthy, Craig McCauley, J. M. McClaren, Jean McCulloch, Donald MacEwan, Michael Maguire, Michael MacMahon, Elizabeth Manneke, Roger Manning, J. David Markham, Andrew Martin, Angela Martin, Robin Martin, Helen Meddings, Gloria Miles, Sir Stephen Miller, Brian Milhench, Bob Millward, Colin Milne, David and Maureen Milner, Richard Milsom, Yves Moerman, Judith Monk, John Montgomery (RUSI), Mike Moody, John Morewood, Tony Morisset, Clive Morris, Dorothy and Ron Morris, Brenda Morrison, Bob Moulder, Norman Murphy, National Trust of Australia, Tony Negus, Niagara Historical Society and Museum, Dean and Chapter of Newcastle upon-Tyne Cathedral, Bob Nicholls, Thomas Nielsen, Bill Norman, North Staffordshire Victorian Military History and Research Society, John O'Brien, John Ogden, Keith Oliver, Orders & Medals Society, Oxfordshire and Buckinghamshire Light Infantry Museum, Julia Page, Jane and Gary Parker, Michael Parroy, Steven Payne, Anne Pealing, Johanna Peebes, Dennis Perriam, Perth and Kinross Heritage Trust, Doug Peters, Audrey Phillips, Ben Phillips, Gill Picken, Ron Pigram, Fulvio Poli, David Poole, Portsmouth Napoleonic Society, Victor Powell, Terry Pratt, Isobel Pridmore, Andrew Prince, John Provan, Christine Pullen, Emma, Guy, James and Katharine Purchon, Queen's Lancashire Regimental Museum, Frances Radley, Mrs V. H. Ramage, Helen and John Ratcliffe, Frederick and Joyce Ratcliffe, Susan Ratcliffe, Ken Ray, Dinah Read, Redcoats website, Tony Redsell, Wilson Reid, Fiona Reynoldson, Nettie Rice, Colin Richardson, Mr and Mrs Ryder-Richardson, Paul Ridgley, Cynthia and Derek Ringrose, Hilary Robinson, Mark Robinson, Michael Robinson, Peter Robinson, Peter Robson, David Rogers, Ken A. Rowley, K. Rowley-Brecon, Elizabeth Roy, Royal Green Jackets Museum, John Rumsby, Ailsa Rushbrooke, His Grace the Duke of Rutland, Trevor Rutter, Charles Sale, Salford Local History Library, Michaela Salmon, Chris Sanham, Mrs E. Saunders, Tanya Schmoller, Scots Guards Archives, Valerie Scott, Ken Sears, Bill Sidgwick, Terry Senior, John Sewell, T. Sewell, Chris Shaw, George Shaw, Matthew Shaw (Brompton Cemetery), Maya Sheridan, Geoffrey Skeet, Anne Slack, Iain Small, Ken Smallwood, Nicol Smith, Peter Smith, Diane Snowden, Bryan Somers, Alan Sorenson, (Libraries Northern Ireland), John and Jeremy Spikens, Julian Spilsbury, Barry Stephenson, the Revd Brian H. Stevens, Peter and Judith Stevens, Theo Steward, Felix Stirling, Klaus Stolze, Alison J. Stratton, Beverley and Gordon Stroud, Duncan Sutton (Surrey History Centre), G. Symes, Michael Symington, Clive Symons, Lawrence Taylor, Patricia A. Taylor, Liz Teall, Richard Tennant, Ron and Margaret Thompson, Peter G. Thompson, Ray Thorburn, Carys Thorn, Peter Thorn, D. Timmermans, Alan Tod, Thelma Todd (Institute of Directors), Malcolm Toes, Gabor Toth (Wellington City Library, New Zealand), Robert Tripp, Paul Tritton, C. L. Tweedale, David Verran, Mr and Mrs Waddelow, Martin Wade, Alan Walker, Valerie M. Walker, Douglas Walshe, John Walters, Karen Walton, P. W. Ward, Robert Wareham, Philip, Nicholas and Edmund Wareham, William Warre, Winifred Waterall, Dr A. W. Webb, Sir Evelyn Webb-Carter, Lady Jane Wellesley, Westminster Abbey Dean and Chapter, John White, Stephen White, Betty Whitehouse, Mr and Mrs D. A. Whitehouse, the Revd David Whiteman, Libby and Rob Whitethread, Mark Whyman, Peter Wigan, Tony Wilks, Sheila and Martin Wills, Doug Wilson, Edward and Primrose Wilson, Jennifer Wilson, Tom Winks, C. John Wood, Ron Woollacott, C. S. Worthington, Christine Wright, Evan Wright, Paul and Ann Wylie, Alan, Ian and Jane Yonge, Colin Yorke, Frank and Joan Young, Geoffrey Young.

Register Of Names

ABELL, Charles

Lieutenant. 83rd Regiment of Foot.

Gravestone: Galle Face Burial Ground, Colombo, Ceylon. (Burial ground no longer extant). (M.I.)

'SACRED TO THE MEMORY OF / LIEUT CHARLES ABELL OF / H. M. 83RD REGT., / WHO DEPARTED THIS LIFE / 5TH FEB 1822, / AGED 32 YEARS.'

Ensign 8 May 1805. Lt 11 Mar 1808.

Served in the Peninsula Apr 1809 – Apr 1814. Present at Douro and Talavera (severely wounded, taken prisoner and remained in prison until the end of the war). Also served in Ceylon 1817 (Commandant at Chilaw 1819 – 1820 and afterwards stationed at Kurunegalla). In 1822, whilst out hunting and on a tour of inspection with the Commandant he succumbed to a fever and died a few days later. Changed his name from Francis to Charles 1814.

REFERENCE: Lewis, J. Penry, *List of inscriptions on tombstones and monuments in Ceylon, 1913, reprint 1994, p. 33.*

ABERCROMBY, Hon. Alexander

Captain and Lieutenant Colonel. Coldstream Regiment of Foot Guards.

Memorial: St John's Episcopal Churchyard, (Division 10). Edinburgh, Scotland. (M.I.)

"RT. HON RALPH ABERCROMBY .... FOURTH SON, ALEXANDER, CB. BORN 1784, ENTERED THE ARMY 1799, SERVED IN THE EXPEDITION TO HOLLAND, THROUGHOUT THE PENINSULAR WAR AND AT WATERLOO. DIED 27TH AUGUST 1853."

Cornet 2nd Dragoon Guards 16 Aug 1799. Lt 52nd Foot 19 Mar 1800. Capt 23rd Foot Jul 1801. Major 100th Foot 22 Jul 1806. Major 81st Foot 7 Jan 1807. Bt Lt Colonel 28 Feb 1808. Lt Colonel 28th Foot 10 Dec 1808. Bt Colonel 4 Jun 1814. Capt and Lt Colonel Coldstream Guards 25 Jul 1814.

Served in the Peninsula with 2/28th Jul 1809 – Aug 1811, 1/28th Sep 1811 – Jan 1813 and on Staff Feb 1813 – Apr 1814 (AQMG). Present at Busaco, Albuera (Commanded 3 Brigade 2nd Division), Arroyo dos Molinos, Almarez, Vittoria, Pyrenees, Orthes and Bordeaux. He was mentioned in Beresford's Despatch at Albuera – 'The conduct of the brigade was most conspicuously gallant and that of the third brigade under the command of the Hon. Lieut Col Alexander Abercromby was not less so.' Gold Cross for Albuera, Vittoria, Pyrenees and Orthes. KTS. Present at Quatre Bras and Waterloo as AQMG (wounded). CB. Also served at the Helder 1799, Ferrol 1800 and Sicily 1806–1807. Son of Sir Ralph Abercromby killed in the Egyptian campaign 1801.

REFERENCE: *Dictionary of National Biography. Royal Military Calendar, Vol 4, p. 188.*

ACKLAND, Dudley

Major. 57th (West Middlesex) Regiment of Foot.

Named on the Memorial: St Andrew's Church, (now Musée Historique), Biarritz, France. (Photograph)

Ensign 22 Oct 1802. Lt 5 Mar 1803. Capt 8 Dec 1804. Major 13 Dec 1810.

Served in the Peninsula Jul 1809 – Feb 1811 and Jun 1812 – Nov 1813. Present at Vittoria, Pyrenees and Nivelle where he was killed Nov 1813. Gold Medal for Nivelle.

1

ACLAND, Sir Wroth Palmer
Captain and Lieutenant Colonel. Coldstream Regiment of Foot Guards.
Memorial tablet: Bath Abbey, Bath, Somerset. (Photograph)

SACRED TO THE MEMORY OF / LIEU^T. GENERAL SIR WROTH PALMER ACLAND, / COL^L.
COMM^T OF 60TH REG^T OF INFANTRY, KNIGHT COMMANDER OF THE BATH. / HIS LIFE WAS
DEVOTED TO THE DUTIES OF HIS PROFESSION, / HIS CONDUCT APPROVED IN THE VARIOUS
EXPEDITIONS / IN WHICH HE WAS ACTIVELY EMPLOYED IN THE EAST INDIES, / IN SOUTH
AMERICA, IN HOLLAND, IN THE PENINSULA, AND IN ITALY: / WHERE FOR HIS GALLANT
CONDUCT AT THE BATTLE OF MAIDA, / HE RECEIVED THE THANKS OF BOTH HOUSES OF
PARLIAMENT. / HE WAS THE YOUNGEST SON / OF ARTHUR ACLAND ESQ^R. OF FAIRFIELD IN
THIS COUNTY / AND DIED LAMENTED BY ALL WHO KNEW HIM, / MARCH 8TH 1816, IN THE
46TH YEAR OF HIS AGE; / AND IS BURIED IN THIS CHURCH.

Ensign 17th Foot 28 Apr 1787. Lieutenant 10 Jul 1790. Capt 27 Jan 1791. Capt 3rd Foot May 1793. Major
19th Foot 1794. Lt Colonel 1 Jan 1795. Capt and Lt Colonel Coldstream Guards 10 May 1800. Bt Colonel
25 Sep 1803. Major General 25 Jul 1810. Lt General 4 Jun 1814.
   Served in the Peninsula Aug – Nov 1808 (Commanded 8 Brigade). Present at Vimeiro (Mentioned in
Despatches – owing to ill health had to return to England). Also served in Flanders 1793–1794, India,
Mediterranean 1804 – 1806 (present at Malta, Naples), Sicily 1806 (present at Maida), South America
1807 (present at Montevideo) and Walcheren 1809 (present at Flushing). Gold Medal for Maida and
Vimeiro. KCB 2 Jan 1815. Colonel 60th Foot.
Note: Surname spelt as Ackland in regimental records.

ACOMB, John
Corporal. 2nd Life Guards.
Headstone: St Mary's Churchyard, Sand Hutton, Yorkshire. (Photograph)

IN MEMORY OF / JOHN ACOMB / CORPORAL 2ND LIFE GUARDS / WHO IS BURIED IN THIS
CHURCHYARD / HE FOUGHT AT THE / BATTLE OF WATERLOO / AND DIED AT SAND
HUTTON / 1849

Pte 10 Nov 1809. Cpl 1814.
   Served in the Peninsula Nov 1812 – Apr 1814. Present at Vittoria. Served at Waterloo. Discharged 10
Mar 1821 owing to ill health. MGS medal for Vittoria.

ADAIR, James
Captain. 27th (Inniskilling) Regiment of Foot.
Ledger stone within Family railed enclosure: St Mary's Churchyard, Dumfries, Dumfriesshire, Scotland.
(Photograph)

" .... / MAJOR JAMES ADAIR / OF THE 24TH AND 27TH REGIMENT / BORN AT
HARVIESTON / CLACKMANNANSHIRE 1792. DIED AT / TETCHEN IN BOHEMIA 1871. /
..................."

Ensign 27th Foot 7 Mar 1810. Lt 102nd Ft 10 Oct 1811. Lt 27th Foot 13 Feb 1812. Capt 27th Foot 25 Mar
1815. Capt 24th Foot 1818. Major 24th Foot 12 Dec 1826.
   Served in the Peninsula Nov 1812 – Apr 1814. Present at Alcoy, Biar, Castalla, Tarragona and Villa
Franca. Served with the Army of Occupation. Also served in Sicily 1810 – 1811. Half pay 1 Feb 1827.

ADAIR, Robert
Lieutenant and Captain. 1st Regiment of Foot Guards.
Named on the Regimental Memorial: St Joseph's Church, Waterloo, Belgium. (Photograph)
Named on Memorial Panel VIII for Quatre Bras: Royal Military Chapel, Wellington Barracks, London.
(M.I.) (Destroyed by a Flying Bomb 1944.)

Ensign 14 May 1804. Lt and Capt 26 Oct 1809.
    Served in the Peninsula Oct 1808 – Jan 1809, Apr 1810 – May 1811 and Apr 1813 – Apr 1814. Present at Corunna, Cadiz, Barrosa (wounded), Bidassoa, Nivelle, Nive, Adour and Bayonne. Present at Quatre Bras where he was severely wounded and died of his wounds 16 Jun 1815.

ADAIR, Walter William
Captain. 88th (Connaught Rangers) Regiment of Foot.
Memorial tablet: All Saints Church, Newland, Gloucestershire. (In floor). (Photograph)

SACRED / TO THE MEMORY / OF CAPTAIN W / WILLIAM ADAIR / OF THE 88 REG / WHO DIED 15 MAY / 1815, AGED 45 / IN CONSEQUENCE / OF A WOUND RECEIVED / AT THE BATTLE OF / SALAMANCA UNDER / THE COMMAND OF / THE DUKE OF / WELLINGTON.

Ensign 12 Nov 1799. Lt 3 Nov 1803. Captain 30 Jun 1808.
    Served in the Peninsula with 2/88th Apr 1810 – Jun 1811 and 1/88th Jul 1811 – Nov 1812. Present at Cadiz, Sabugal, Fuentes d'Onoro, Ciudad Rodrigo, Badajoz and Salamanca where he was severely wounded. This wound caused his death in 1815. Also served in Egypt 1801 (awarded Sultan's Gold medal for Egypt), South America 1807 (present at Buenos Ayres, where he was wounded).

ADAM, Frederick William
Lieutenant Colonel. 21st (Royal North British Fusiliers) Regiment of Foot.
Statue: Corfu, Greece. (In front of the Palace of St Michael and St George). No inscription on Statue. (Photograph)

Ensign 26th Foot 4 Nov 1795. Lt 2 Feb 1796. Lt 27th Foot Jul 1799. Capt 9th Foot 30 Aug 1799. Lt and Capt Coldstream Guards 8 Dec 1799. Major 5th Battalion of Reserve 9 Jul 1803. Lt Colonel 5th Garrison Battalion 28 Aug 1804. Lt Colonel 21st Foot 5 Jan 1805. Bt Colonel 20 Feb 1812. Major General 4 Jun 1814. Lt General 22 Jul 1830.
    Served in the Peninsula on East coast of Spain Jan 1813 – Apr 1814 (Brigade commander under Lt Gen Sir John Murray). Present at Alicante (wounded), Castalla (mentioned in Murray's Despatches), Tarragona and Ordal (wounded and awarded pension of £300 per annum). Present at Waterloo (Commanded 3 Brigade (52nd, 71st and 95th), in Lt General Sir Henry Clinton's division, where they decisively routed the final assault of the French and Adam was severely wounded).
    Also served at the Helder 1799, Egypt 1801, Sicily 1806 – 1812 (DAG). Ionian Islands 1824–1832 (High Commissioner), India 1832–1837 (Governor of Madras). MGS medal for Egypt. KCB 22 Jun 1815. Russian Order of St Anne and Austrian Order of Maria Theresa for Waterloo. GCMG 1833, GCB 1840. Colonel 73rd Foot 22 May 1829. Colonel 57th Foot 4 Dec 1835. Colonel 21st Foot 1843. Died 17 Aug 1853.
REFERENCE: *Dictionary of National Biography. Royal Military Calendar Vol 3, pp. 384–9. Gentleman's Magazine, Nov 1853, pp. 527–8. Annual Register, 1853, Appx, pp. 241–2.*

ADAMS, John
Lieutenant. 2nd (Queen's Royal) Regiment of Foot.
Named on the Regimental Memorial: St Michael's Cathedral, Bridgetown, Barbados, West Indies. (Photograph)

Ensign 11 Apr 1809. Lt 22 Aug 1811.

Served in the Peninsula Mar 1811 – Dec 1812. Present at Almeida, Salamanca and the retreat from Burgos. Also served at Walcheren 1809 and West Indies, where he died in Barbados during a yellow fever epidemic 14 Apr 1818.

ADAMS, John

Sergeant. 1st (King's) Dragoon Guards.
Headstone: Tonge Cemetery, Bolton, Lancashire. (Photograph)

.... / ALSO OF THE ABOVE NAMED / JOHN ADAMS / WHO DIED OCTR 14TH 1876 IN THE 93RD / YEAR OF HIS AGE.

Pte 25 Apr 1801. Cpl 1809. Sgt 1912.

Served at Waterloo where he was wounded three times and his horse was killed under him, but he seized another and continued fighting. For his services at Waterloo he was promoted to Sergeant. Served in France with the Army of Occupation. Also served in Ireland. By the time he retired in 1827 he had become Troop Sergeant.

Joined the Bolton troop of the Duke of Lancaster's Own Yeomanry 1828. Transferred to the Worsley troop in 1849 as Troop Sergeant Major and later became Regimental Sergeant Major. He never missed one annual drill at Preston and elsewhere up to his death even though he was 92 when he died. Served his country for 72 years. Awarded a good conduct and long service medal 1863.

ADYE, Stephen Galway

Lieutenant Colonel. Royal Artillery.
Memorial: St Mary's Churchyard, Woolwich, Kent. (No longer extant. Church bombed in the Second World War). (M.I.)

"BENEATH THIS STONE ARE DEPOSITED THE MORTAL REMAINS OF MARY, WIFE OF BRIGADE MAJOR ADYE, WHO DIED 20 SEPTEMBER 1809 AGED 37. ALSO OF MAJOR GENERAL STEPHEN GALWAY ADYE CB HUSBAND TO THE ABOVE MARY ADYE WHO DIED ON 13 SEPTEMBER 1838 AGED 66. .... "

2nd Lt 24 Apr 1793. 1st Lt 1 Jun 1794. Capt-Lieut 7 Nov 1798. Capt 1 May 1803. Bt Major 25 Jul 1810. Major 1 Oct 1812. Lt Colonel 20 Dec 1817. Colonel 29 Jul 1825. Major General 10 Jan 1837.

Served in the Peninsula Apr 1813 – Apr 1814. Present at Cadiz. Present at Waterloo (commanding Artillery of 1st Division). CB. Also served at Ferrol 1800, Egypt 1801 (present at Alexandria – awarded Gold Medal by the Sultan) and Walcheren 1809 (Mentioned in Despatches). Superintendent of Royal Laboratory Jun 1835.
REFERENCE: *Gentleman's Magazine, Dec 1838, p. 659.*

AINSLIE, George

Assistant Commissary General. Commissariat Department.
Grave: British Cemetery, Lisbon, Portugal. (M.I.)

"GEORGE AINSLIE – ASSISTANT COMMISSARY BRITISH ARMY. DIED FEB 15TH 1821."

Dep Asst Comm Gen 28 May 1810. Asst Comm Gen 29 Mar 1813.

Served in the Peninsula Apr 1809 – Apr 1814 (in accounts department in Lisbon).

AINSLIE, George Simon Harcourt
Ensign. 69th (South Lincolnshire) Regiment of Foot.
Buried in Foster Hill Road Cemetery, Bedford, Bedfordshire. (No longer extant: Grave number 157 IG8)

Ensign 69th Foot 10 Nov 1814. Cornet 1st Dragoons 22 Jun 1815.
    Served at Waterloo with 69th Foot. Joined 1st Dragoons and took the name of Harcourt, the name under which he is buried. Half pay 21 Mar 1822. Educated at Eton, he became one of the co-founders of Cheltenham College, and by 1841 was Honorary Secretary to the College. Died at Bedford 28 Dec 1868 aged 72 years.

AIRD, Thomas
Lieutenant Colonel. Royal Waggon Train.
Memorial tablet: Maybole Parish Church, Maybole, Ayrshire, Scotland. (Photograph)

SACRED TO THE MEMORY OF / (MY BELOVED PARENTS) / LIEUT-COLONEL THOMAS AIRD, / WHO PASSED 56 YEARS OF HIS LIFE IN THE SERVICE OF HIS COUNTRY, / 28 YEARS IN THE SCOTS GREYS, / AND COMMANDED A CORPS THROUGH THE PENINSULA, UNTIL WATERLOO. / HE WAS BORN IN MAYBOLE, DECEMBER 21ST DEC 1760, / DIED SUNDERLAND, CO. DURHAM, NOVEMBER 1ST 1839, AGED 79 YEARS, / HONORED AND RESPECTED BY ALL WHO KNEW HIM. / LUKE, CHAP. VII – VERSE 8 / ALSO TO THE MEMORY OF A MOST EXEM-PLARY MOTHER, / MARGARET, NÉE WALLACE, / BORN IN AYR, MARCH 3RD 1768, / DIED IN PORTOBELLO, NEAR EDINBURGH, OCTOBER 5TH 1834, AGED 66. / "BLESSED ARE THE DEAD THAT DIE IN THE LORD." REV. CHAP. IV – VERSE 13 / THIS RECORD IS PLACED BY THEIR SECOND DAUGHTER SUSAN MARGARETTA AIRD, / JUNE 1ST 1864. / THE FATHER'S REMAINS LIE AT HOUGHTON-LE-SPRING CO, DURHAM; / THE MOTHER'S AT PORTOBELLO.

Buried In St Michael and All Angels Churchyard, Houghton-le-Spring, Durham.

Cornet 2nd Dragoons 20 Aug 1784. Lt 20 Aug 1799. Capt Royal Waggon Train 2 May 1800. Major 27 Oct 1808. Bt Lt Colonel 2 Jun 1814. Lt Colonel 4 May 1815.
    Served in the Peninsula Jun 1809 – Apr 1814 (attached to HQ Jun – Jul 1813). Present at Waterloo. His son-in-law Lt John Elwes 71st Foot was fatally wounded at Waterloo a few weeks after his marriage. Half pay 25 Dec 1818. Also served in Flanders 1793–1795 and Hanover 1805.

AITCHISON, Sir John
Captain and Lieutenant Colonel. 3rd Regiment of Foot Guards.
Mausoleum: Kensal Green Cemetery, London. (22621/140/RS). (Photograph)

IN THE VAULT OF THIS MAUSOLEUM REPOSE THE MORTAL REMAINS / OF / GENERAL SIR JOHN AITCHISON G.C.B. / BORN ON 27TH APRIL 1789, DIED ON 12TH MAY 1875. / ENTERING THE 3RD GUARDS, NOW STYLED SCOTS GUARDS, AT THE AGE OF 16 IN 1805 / HE SERVED IN 1807 AT THE SEIGE AND CAPTURE OF COPENHAGEN. / HAVING EMBARKED IN 1808 FOR THE PENINSULA HE WAS IN 1809 PRESENT AT THE PASSAGE OF THE / DOURO, CAPTURE OF OPORTO, AND SUBSEQUENT PURSUIT OF SOULT'S ARMY TO SALAMONDE. / AT THE BATTLE OF TALAVERA IN 1809 HE WAS WOUNDED IN THE ARM / WHILE CARRYING THE KING'S COLOUR WHICH WAS ALSO SHOT THROUGH. / HE SERVED IN THE CAMPAIGNS OF 1810, 12, 13 AND 14 / AND WAS PRESENT AT THE BATTLE OF BUSACO, AND RETREAT TO THE LINES OF TORRES VEDRAS / ALSO AT THE BATTLE OF SALAMANCA, SEIGE OF BURGOS / AND THE RETREAT FROM THENCE INTO PORTUGAL. / HE WAS PRESENT AT THE AFFAIR AT OSMA, BATTLE OF VITTORIA, AFFAIR AT TOLOSA, / SEIGE OF SAN SEBASTIAN, BATTLES OF NIVELLE, INVESTMENT OF BAYONNE, / SEIGE OF THE CITADEL AND REPULSE OF THE SORTIE. / HE

RECEIVED THE WAR MEDAL WITH SIX CLASPS. / HE WAS COLONEL OF THE 3ᴿᴰ GUARDS WHEN PROMOTED TO MAJOR GENERAL ON 9ᵀᴴ NOVᴿ 1841 / AFTER HAVING COMMANDED THAT REGIMENT FOR UPWARDS OF FOUR YEARS. / FROM JUNE 1845 TO NOVᴿ 1851 HE SERVED WITH MUCH DISTINCTION IN INDIA / AS MAJOR GENERAL ON THE STAFF OF THE MADRAS PRESIDENCY, BEING IN COMMAND / OF THE MYSORE DIVISION, INCLUDING COORG AND OF THE PROVINCES OF MALABAR AND CANARA. / FROM 1867 HE WAS COLONEL OF THE 72ᴺᴰ HIGHLANDERS NOW STYLED SEAFORTH HIGHLANDERS / UNTIL 1870 WHEN HE WAS APPOINTED COLONEL OF THE SCOTS FUSILIER GUARDS, / WHICH COMMAND HE HELD UNTIL HIS DEATH IN 1875. / IN 1868 HE WAS MADE A GRAND CROSS OF THE BATH.

Memorial: Royal Military Chapel, Wellington Barracks, London. (M.I.) (Destroyed by a Flying Bomb 1944.)

"PLACED BY GENERAL HENRY LORD ROKEBY, G.C.B., IN MEMORY OF / GENERAL SIR JOHN AITCHISON, G.C.B., / 3ᴿᴰ GUARDS, 1805. LIEUT.-COLONEL SCOTS FUSILIER GUARDS, 1837–41; COLONEL SCOTS FUSILIER GUARDS, 1870–75. HE SERVED AT COPENHAGEN, 1807; AND IN THE FIELD, UNDER THE GREAT DUKE OF WELLINGTON, 1808–14, RECEIVING THE WAR MEDAL WITH 6 CLASPS; MAJOR- GENERAL IN INDIA, 1845–51."

Ensign 25 Oct 1805. Lt and Capt 22 Nov 1810. Capt and Lt Colonel 15 Dec 1814. Major with rank of Colonel 20 May 1836. Major General 23 Nov 1841. Lt General 11 Nov 1851. General 30 Jul 1860.

Served in the Peninsula Mar 1809 – Oct 1810 and May 1812 – Apr 1814. Present at Douro, Talavera (wounded while carrying the King's colour), Busaco, Salamanca, Burgos and retreat from Burgos, Osma, Vittoria, Tolosa, Nivelle, Nive, Adour and Bayonne. Also served in the Baltic 1807, India 1845–1851 (on Staff at Madras in command of the Mysore Division). MGS medal for Talavera, Busaco, Salamanca, Vittoria, Nivelle and Nive. GCB. Colonel 72ⁿᵈ Foot 20 Dec 1851. Colonel Scots Fusilier Guards 27 Aug 1870.

REFERENCE: Thompson, W. F. K., *An Ensign in the Peninsular War: the letters of John Aitchison*, 1981. *Dictionary of National Biography. Household Brigade Journal*, 1875, pp. 301–3.

AKENSIDE, William
Lieutenant. 14ᵗʰ (Buckinghamshire) Regiment of Foot.
Memorial tablet: St Andrew's Church, Heddon on the Wall, Northumberland. (Photograph)

SACRED TO THE MEMORY OF / CAPTAIN WILLIAM AKENSIDE / OF THE 14ᵀᴴ REGᵀ OF FOOT SON OF / WILLIAM AKENSIDE / LATE OF EACHWICK / WHO DEPARTED THIS LIFE / THE 22ᴺᴰ OF OCTᴿ 1830 / AGED 49 YEARS. / ...."

Ensign Royal Lancashire Militia 4 May 1803. Ensign 28ᵗʰ Foot 9 Sep 1806. Lt 14ᵗʰ Foot 6 Aug 1807. Capt 6 Sep 1821.

Served in the Peninsula Nov 1808 – Jan 1809. Present at Corunna. Present at Waterloo in Capt John Maxwell's Company, storming of Cambrai and the Occupation of Paris. Also served at Walcheren 1809.

ALBERT, Anton
Lieutenant: 1ˢᵗ Battalion Light Infantry, King's German Legion.
Named on the Regimental Memorial: La Haye Sainte, Waterloo, Belgium. (Photograph)

Ensign 21 May 1809. Lt 27 Jan 1811.

Served in the Peninsula Mar 1811 – Apr 1814. Present at Albuera, second siege of Badajoz, siege of Salamanca Forts, Moriscos, Salamanca, Venta del Poza, Vittoria, Tolosa, Bidassoa, Nivelle, Nive, St

Etienne and Bayonne. Present at Waterloo where he was killed. Also served at Walcheren 1809 and Netherlands 1814.

ALCORN, William
Private. 2nd (Royal North British) Regiment of Dragoons.
Family Headstone: Fogo Cemetery, Berwickshire, Scotland. (Photograph)

ERECTED / TO THE MEMORY OF / WILLIAM ALCORN WHO DIED / AT FOGO 1825 AGED 71 YEARS / .... / ALSO / WILLIAM ALCORN HIS SON WHO FELL / AT WATERLOO AGED 26 YEARS.

Served at Waterloo where he was killed in the Cavalry charge.

ALEXANDER, Henry
Lieutenant. 28th (North Gloucestershire) Regiment of Foot.
Low monument: St George's Churchyard, Beckenham, Kent. (Photograph)

SACRED TO THE MEMORY OF HENRY ALEXANDER LATE LIEUT COL 96TH FOOT AND FORMERLY LIEUT OF 28TH FOOT WITH WHICH REGIMENT HE SERVED IN THE PENINSULAR WAR. DIED 4 OCT 1863 AGED 70.

Ensign 13 Jun 1811. Lt 26 Aug 1813. Capt Staff Corps 13 Aug 1825. Bt Lt Colonel 11 Nov 1851.
    Served in the Peninsula with 1/28th Jan 1813 – Apr 1814. Present at Vittoria (wounded), Maya, Pyrenees, Nivelle, Nive, Garris, Orthes, Aire, Tarbes and Toulouse. Half pay 15 Jan 1829. MGS medal for Vittoria, Pyrenees, Nivelle, Nive, Orthes and Toulouse.

ALGEO, James
Lieutenant. 77th (East Middlesex) Regiment of Foot.
Headstone laid flat: Kensal Green Cemetery, London. (15115/132/RS). Seriously eroded. (Photograph)

IN MEMORY OF / COLONEL JAMES ALGEO / ....

Ensign 2 Sept 1806. Lt 4 Jun 1811. Capt 21 Feb 1825. Bt Major 28 Jun 1838. Bt Lt Colonel 11 Nov 1851.
    Served in the Peninsula Aug 1813 – Apr 1814. Present at Bayonne. Buried in Kensal Green 11 Mar 1850 aged 73.

ALLEN, George Augustus
Ensign. 1st Regiment of Foot Guards.
Memorial tablet: Exeter Cathedral, Devon. (Photograph)

BENEATH THIS TABLET / LIE THE REMAINS / OF GEORGE AUGUSTUS ALLEN ESQ. / LATE LIEUT. & CAPTAIN IN THE GRENADIER REGIMENT / OF FOOT GUARDS. / HE WAS THE FOURTH SON OF MAJOR ALLEN / OF BROOMSGROVE IN WORCESTERSHIRE / AND OF / LOUISA, FIFTH DAUGHTER OF CHARLES FITZ ROY / THE FIRST LORD SOUTHAMPTON. / HE SERVED HONORABLY IN THE ABOVE CORPS / UPWARDS OF TWELVE YEARS / AND WAS PRESENT AT THE MEMORABLE / BATTLE OF WATERLOO. / AT THE EARLY AGE OF TWENTY EIGHT / ON THE 9TH MAY 1826 / HE DIED OF CONSUMPTION / AT SIDMOUTH / SINCERELY AND DESERVEDLY REGRETTED / BY HIS FAMILY AND FRIENDS.

Memorial: Royal Military Chapel, Wellington Barracks, London. (M.I.) (Destroyed by a Flying Bomb 1944.)

"CAPTAIN GEORGE ALLEN. / 1ST GUARDS, 1814–26; CARRIED THE REGIMENTAL COLOURS OF THE 2ND BATTALION AT WATERLOO."

Ensign 21 Apr 1814. Lt and Capt 25 Jul 1822.
    Present at Waterloo where he carried the Regimental colours and served at the defence of Hougoumont. Half pay 6 Apr 1826 owing to ill health and died a month later.

ALLEN, James
Captain. 23rd Regiment of Light Dragoons.
Chest tomb: St Mary's Churchyard, Prestbury, Cheltenham, Gloucestershire. (Photograph)

SACRED / TO THE MEMORY OF / LIEUT COL JAMES ALLEN / OF INCHMARTIN PERTHSHIRE / LATE OF THE 23RD LIGHT DRAGOONS / HE DIED AT LEAMINGTON PRIORS / ON THE 9TH OF FEB 1839 / AGED ** YEARS

Lt 25th Foot 22 Aug 1798. Capt 18th Lt Dragoons 2 Oct 1800. Capt 32nd Foot 14 Feb 1803. Capt 23rd Lt Dragoons 3 Feb 1804. Bt Major 4 Jun 1811. Bt Lt Colonel 12 Aug 1819.
    Served in the Peninsula Jun 1809 – Apr 1814. Present at Talavera where he was taken prisoner until Apr 1814. Half pay 6 Oct 1814.

ALLEN, John
Ensign. 1st (Royal Scots) Regiment of Foot.
Memorial Tablet: St George's Chapel, Windsor, Berkshire. (West wall of Deanery cloisters). (Photograph)

SACRED / TO THE MEMORY OF / JOHN ALLEN ESQUIRE, / MILITARY KNIGHT OF WINDSOR, / WHO DIED APRIL 15TH 1850: / AGED 74 YEARS.

Ensign 1st West India Regiment 8 Mar 1810. Ensign 1st Foot 19 Mar 1811.
    Served in the Peninsula 1811 – 1812. Present at Ciudad Rodrigo. Half pay 6 May 1816. Military Knight of Windsor 16 Mar 1836.

ALLEN, Thomas
Lieutenant. 1st Line Battalion, King's German Legion.
Ledger stone: All Saint's Churchyard, Springfield, Chelmsford, Essex. (Photograph)

LIEUTENANT THOMAS ALLEN / SON OF THE LATE THOMAS ALLEN OF CRANE HALL / NEAR IPSWICH / HAVING SERVED / HIS COUNTRY IN THE KING'S GERMAN LEGION / IN THE PENINSULAR AND AT WATERLOO / DIED IN PEACE AT SPRINGFIELD / NOV 12TH 1833 AGED 46.

Ensign 1 Feb 1809. Lt 8 Sep 1809.
    Served in the Peninsula Jun 1809 – Apr 1814. Present at Talavera (wounded), Busaco, Fuentes d'Onoro, Ciudad Rodrigo, Moriscos, Salamanca, Burgos, Vittoria, Tolosa, San Sebastian, Bidassoa, Nivelle, Nive, St Etienne and Bayonne. Present at Waterloo. Also served in the Netherlands 1814.

ALLIX, Charles
Lieutenant and Captain. 1st Regiment of Foot Guards.
Memorial window and Brass memorial tablet: St Mary's Church, Swaffham Prior, Cambridgeshire. (Photograph)

"THIS WINDOW WAS ERECTED BY / CHARLES PETER ALLIX, TO THE GLORY OF GOD, / AND IN LOVING MEMORY OF HIS FATHER / COLONEL CHARLES ALLIX OF SWAFFHAM HOUSE,

/ LATE OF THE GRENADIER GUARDS IN WHICH / REGIMENT HE SERVED IN THE WALCHEREN EXPEDITION, / THE PENINSULAR WAR, AND AT WATERLOO. / BORN AP. 24 1787. DIED AP. 24 1862 A.D. R.I.P. / THIS WINDOW WAS MOVED FROM THE CHURCH OF ST CYRIAC / TOGETHER WITH THE OTHER SOUTH CHANCEL WINDOW. XMAS 1878 / A.D."

Family Memorial tablet: St Mary's Church, Swaffham Prior, Cambridgeshire. (South wall). (M.I.)

"LIEUTENANT AND CAPTAIN (LATER COLONEL) CHARLES ALLIX (1787–1862) OF THE GRENADIER GUARDS, IN WHICH HE SERVED IN THE WALCHEREN EXPEDITION, THE PENINSULAR WARS, AND AT WATERLOO."

Ensign 28 Apr 1804. Lt and Capt 1 Dec 1810. Adjutant 1813. Capt and Lt Colonel 1 Jul 1815. Bt Colonel 10 Jan 1837.

Served in the Peninsula Oct 1808 – Jan 1809, Jun 1811 – Oct 1812 (ADC to Major General H. Campbell) and Aug – Dec 1813 (Brigade Major 1 Brigade 4th Division). Present at Corunna, Ciudad Rodrigo, Badajoz, Salamanca, Pyrenees and Nivelle (severely wounded). Present at Waterloo. MGS medal for Corunna, Ciudad Rodrigo, Badajoz, Salamanca, Pyrenees and Nivelle. Also served at Walcheren 1809. Retired on half pay 12 Apr 1827. Died 24 Apr 1862. Brother of Lt William Allix 95th Foot.

ALLIX, William
1st Lieutenant. 95th Regiment of Foot.
Family Memorial tablet: St Mary's Church, Swaffham Prior, Cambridgeshire. (South wall). (M.I.)

"..................... / WILLIAM, AGED 23, / A LIEUTENANT IN THE 95 REGT / FELL AT THE SIEGE OF BADAJOZ IN SPAIN / THE 6TH OF APRIL 1812 / BRAVELY VINDICATING THE INSULTED RIGHTS / OF ALL NATIONS / AGAINST THE TYRANNY & OPPRESSION / OF THE FRENCH / ...."

Ensign 18th Foot 20 Jul 1809. Lt 34th Foot 12 Apr 1810. Lt 95th Foot 17 May 1810.

Served in the Peninsula with 3/95th Dec 1811 – Apr 1812. Present at Ciudad Rodrigo and Badajoz where he was killed at the storming of the Fort 6 Apr 1812. Brother of Lt and Capt Charles Allix 1st Foot Guards.

ALLMAN, Francis
Captain. 48th (Northamptonshire) Regiment of Foot.
Buried in Church of England Cemetery, Yass, New South Wales, Australia. Inscription not recorded.

Ensign 2nd Foot 1794. Lt 48th Foot 9 Jul 1803. Capt 1 Jun 1809.

Served in the Peninsula Jul 1809 – Apr 1814. Present at Douro, Talavera, Busaco and Albuera (wounded, listed as missing, but had been taken prisoner and remained in prison until the end of the war. Awarded pension of £100 per annum for his wound). After the war he went to Australia with the 48th Foot. Posted to Port Macquarie as Commandant, to establish a settlement in 1821. When the regiment left for India in 1825 he decided to remain in Australia and went on half pay 5 Dec 1825, resigning in 1829. Served as magistrate and in other public offices, retiring in 1844 to Yass, where he died 24 Oct 1860. Also served at the Helder 1799, Egypt 1801 (present at Alexandria where he was wounded). MGS medal for Egypt, Talavera, Busaco and Albuera.
REFERENCE: *Australian Dictionary of Biography*. Obit. *Yass Chronicle, (New South Wales), 27 Oct 1860*.

ALTEN, Count Charles von
Colonel Commandant. 1st Battalion Light Infantry, King's German Legion.
Statue: Waterloo Place, Hanover, Germany. Inscription not recorded. (Photograph)

Ensign Hanoverian Foot Guards 1781. Lt 1785. Capt 1790. Major 1795. Bt Lt Colonel 1800 (Hanoverian Corps disbanded in 1803). Lt Colonel 1st Battalion Lt Infantry King's German Legion Nov 1803. Colonel Commandant 22 Dec 1804. Major General 25 Jul 1810. Lt General Hanoverian Army 1814. General Hanoverian Service 1816.

Served in the Peninsula Aug 1808 – Jan 1809, Feb 1811 – Apr 1812 (Commanded 1 Brigade 7th Division) and Apr 1812 -Apr 1814 (GOC Lt Division after the death of Major General Robert Craufurd). Present in the Corunna campaign, Vigo, Albuera (Mentioned in Despatches), second siege of Badajoz, Salamanca, San Munos, Hormaza (Mentioned in Despatches), San Millan (Mentioned in Despatches), Vittoria (Mentioned in Despatches), Pyrenees, Bidassoa (Mentioned in Despatches), Nivelle (Mentioned in Despatches) Nive (Mentioned in Despatches), Orthes (Mentioned in Despatches), Tarbes and Toulouse.

Gold Cross for Albuera, Salamanca, Vittoria, Nivelle, Nive, Orthes and Toulouse. KCB 2 Jan 1815. Present at Waterloo (severely wounded) where he commanded the 3rd Division which was made up of one British brigade, one from the King's German Legion and one from Hanoverian troops. At Quatre Bras and at Waterloo the 3rd Division were in the thick of the fighting. Served with the Army of Occupation (in command of the Hanoverian troops with the rank of General in the Hanoverian service).

Also served in Flanders 1793–1795 with Hanoverian Army (present at Famars, Valenciennes, Hondschotte where he was placed in command of a battalion of Light troops along the River Lys and showed his skill at organising Light companies), Baltic 1807–1808, Walcheren 1809 and Netherlands 1814. After Waterloo returned to Hanover and was appointed Inspector General of Infantry and later Minister of War 1831. Died 20 Apr 1844 at Botzen in the Tyrol where he had gone for his health. Awarded honours from Britain and many of the European nations including GCB, GCH, Grand Cross of the Imperial Austrian Order of St Stephen, Grand Cross of the Imperial Russian Order of St Alexander Newsky, Grand Cross of the Royal Prussian Order of the Red Eagle, Knight Commander of Tower and Sword of Portugal and Knight's Cross of the Royal Order of William of the Netherlands.

REFERENCE: *Dictionary of National Biography. United Service Journal, Jun 1840, pp. 244–6. Royal Military Calendar, Vol 3, p 103–12.*

AMOS, John Greene
Captain. 40th (2nd Somersetshire) Regiment of Foot.
Grave: St John's Churchyard, Bedford, Bedfordshire. (South side of church). (No longer extant). (M.I.)

"SACRED TO THE MEMORY / OF / MARY THE WIFE OF / CAPTAIN JOHN GREENE AMOS / .... / ALSO OF / CAPT JOHN GREENE AMOS / WHO DEPARTED THIS LIFE / ON THE 23RD OF MARCH 1846 / AGED 69 YEARS."

Ensign Bedfordshire Militia 12 Sep 1803. Capt 24 Oct 1807. Capt 40th Foot 25 Dec 1813.
Served in the Peninsula Apr 1814. Present at Toulouse.

ANDERSON, Alexander
Captain. 42nd (Royal Highland) Regiment of Foot.
Flat slab raised on four plain short pillars: New Calton Burial Ground, Edinburgh, Scotland. (South side of the entrance walk that runs east and west near north wall). (M.I.)

"IN MEMORY OF COLONEL SIR ALEXANDER ANDERSON, C.B., K.T.S., ETC., WHO BY DIVINE GRACE, DIED IN THE HOPE OF ETERNAL GLORY, THROUGH HIS LORD AND SAVIOUR JESUS CHRIST, ON THE 26TH DAY OF JULY 1842 IN THE 55TH YEAR OF HIS AGE."

Ensign 92nd Foot 9 Oct 1799. Lt 42nd Foot 9 Apr 1801. Re-appointed after half pay to Lt 42nd 9 Jul 1803. Capt 8 Feb 1809. Bt Major 21 Jun 1813. Bt Lt Colonel 2 Nov 1816. Bt Colonel 10 Jan 1837. Portuguese Army: Major 24 Oct 1810. Lt Colonel 14 Apr 1812.

Served in the Peninsula with 42nd Foot Aug 1808 – Jan 1809 and with Portuguese Army May 1810 – Apr 1814 (commanded 11th Portuguese Infantry). Present at Corunna (wounded), Busaco, Redinha, Campo Mayor, Olivencia, first siege of Badajoz, Albuera, Fuente Guinaldo, Ciudad Rodrigo, Badajoz (wounded and Mentioned in Beresford's Despatches), Canizal, Salamanca (wounded), Alba de Tormes, Vittoria, Pyrenees, Nivelle, Orthes (Mentioned in Beresford's Despatches) and Toulouse (Mentioned in Beresford's Despatches). Also served in Egypt 1801. Gold Cross for Badajoz, Salamanca, Vittoria, Pyrenees, Nivelle, Orthes and Toulouse. Half pay 29 Aug 1826. CB and KTS. Awarded Portuguese Command medal for seven battles and Cross for five campaigns, Spanish medal for Albuera, Knight of St Bento de Avis of Portugal, St Anne of Russia, Wilhelm of the Netherlands and Crescent of Turkey.

ANDERSON, Andrew
Surgeon. 61st (South Gloucestershire) Regiment of Foot.
Grave: Grange Cemetery, Edinburgh, Midlothian, Scotland. (Section 1. Grave number 23). (M.I.)

" IN MEMORY OF ANDREW ANDERSON ESQ. M.D. LATE SURGEON 92ND HIGHLANDERS. DIED AT EDINBURGH 19TH JULY 1860, AGED 75. BORN AT SELKIRK OCT 1784. ENTERED THE ARMY 1805 AND SERVED 28 YEARS IN ITALY, SICILY, HOLLAND THE PENINSULA AND WEST INDIES. HE RECEIVE THE WAR MEDAL WITH FIVE CLASPS ...."

Family Headstone: Old Kirkyard, Selkirk, Selkirkshire, Scotland. (M.I.)

"SACRED TO THE MEMORY OF HIM WHOSE REMAINS ARE HERE DEPOSITED. THOMAS ANDERSON, LATE SURGEON SELKIRK .... CHILDREN ANDREW ANDERSON, SURGEON HER MAJESTY'S 92ND HIGHLANDERS WHO DIED IN THE YEAR 1860 AGED 75 YEARS."

Hospital Mate 4 Mar 1805. Asst Surgeon 79th Foot 4 Feb 1808. Surgeon 61st Foot 25 Jun 1812. Surgeon 92 Foot 1 Jan 1818.
    Served in the Peninsula Jan 1810 – Jun 1812 and Jul 1812 – Aug 1815. Present at Cadiz, Busaco, Foz d'Arouce, Fuentes d'Onoro, Salamanca, Burgos and Pyrenees. Also served in Sicily 1806 (present at Maida) and Walcheren 1809 (present at siege of Flushing). MD Edinburgh 1818. Retired on half pay 23 Aug 1833. MGS medal for Maida, Busaco, Fuentes d'Onoro, Salamanca and Pyrenees. Died 19 Jun 1860.

ANDERSON, James
Lieutenant. 71st (Highland Light Infantry) Regiment of Foot.
Pedestal tomb: St, Mary's Churchyard, Kilkenny, Ireland. (Photograph)

SACRED / TO THE MEMORY OF / LIEUT JAMES ANDERSON OF THE 71ST REG. OF FOOT / WHO FELL / IN THE CAUSE OF HIS COUNTRY AND OF EUROPE / IN THE ACTION AT THE TOWN OF AIRE IN FRANCE / ON THE 2ND MARCH / 1814.

Named on the Memorial: St Andrew's Church, (now Musée Historique), Biarritz, France. (Photograph)

Ensign 22 Mar 1810. Lieutenant 6 Aug 1812.
    Served in the Peninsula Jan – Mar 1814. Present at Orthes and Aire where he was killed 2 Mar 1814.

ANDERSON, James
Private. Royal Artillery Drivers.
Headstone: Migvie Churchyard, Aberdeenshire, Scotland. (Photograph)

TO THE MEMORY OF / JAMES ANDERSON OF THE / ROYAL ARTILLERY, / WHO DIED AT NEWKIRK COLDSTONE, / 5. OCT^R. 1853. AGED 60. / ....

Served in the Peninsula. Present at Vittoria and Pyrenees. MGS medal for Vittoria and Pyrenees.

ANDERSON, Joseph
Captain. York Chasseurs.
Pedestal tomb with Cross in a railed enclosure: St Kilda Cemetery, Melbourne, Victoria, Australia. (Compt. B Grave 0115). (Photograph)

SACRED TO THE MEMORY OF / COLONEL JOSEPH ANDERSON / LATE OF HM 50TH QUEEN'S OWN REG. / A COMPANION OF THE BATH AND A KNIGHT OF HANOVER / BORN JULY 1 1790 DIED JULY 18 1877 / AFTER A MILITARY SERVICE OF / OVER HALF A CENTURY

Ensign 78th Foot 1806. Lt 24th Foot 6 Oct 1808. Capt York Chasseurs 20 Jan 1814. Capt 50th Foot 3 May 1821. Major 16 Feb 1826. Lt Colonel 1 Apr 1841.

Served in the Peninsula Apr 1809 – Jan 1812. Present at Talavera (wounded), Busaco, retreat to Torres Vedras and Fuentes d'Onoro. Also served in Sicily 1806 (present at Maida), Egypt 1807, Guadeloupe 1815 and India 1843–1844 (present at the battle of Punniar where he was severely wounded in the head while charging enemy guns – awarded Medal). MGS medal for Maida, Talavera, Busaco and Fuentes d'Onoro. CB. KH.

Went to Australia in 1834 with 50th Foot and appointed Governor of Norfolk Island to suppress riot of convicts there. Remained there until 1839 and the island remained quiet under his governorship. While there he acquired land in Victoria with his brother. After his return from India in 1844 settled in Australia. Died in Melbourne 18 Jul 1877.

REFERENCE: Australian Dictionary of Biography. Anderson, Joseph Jocelyn, Recollections of a Peninsula veteran, 1913, reprint 2010.

ANDERSON, Paul
Lieutenant Colonel. 60th (Royal American) Regiment of Foot.
Chest tomb: Abbey Cemetery, Bath, Somerset. (Photograph)

IN MEMORY OF / GENERAL PAUL ANDERSON, C.B. K.C. / SECOND SON OF JAMES ANDERSON / OF GRACE DIEU C^O OF WATERFORD, ESQ^{RE} / COL OF 78TH HIGHLANDERS / AND LATE GOVERNOR OF PENDENNIS CASTLE / WHO DIED IN THIS CITY, / ON THE 17TH OF DECEMBER 1851 / IN THE 86TH YEAR OF HIS AGE.

Ensign 51st Foot 31 Mar 1788. Lt 31 Mar 1791. Capt 4th West India Regt 1 Jul 1795. Capt 31st Foot 25 May 1796. Major 9th Foot 25 Jun 1801. Lt Colonel Nova Scotia Fencibles 17 Oct 1805. Lt Colonel 60th Foot 14 Jan 1808. Bt Colonel 4 Jun 1813. Major General 12 Aug 1819. Lt General 10 Jan 1837.

Served in the Peninsula Aug 1808 – Jan 1809 (DAG). Present at Corunna. Also served in Corsica 1795, West Indies 1795–1796 (wounded), Irish Rebellion 1798, the Helder 1799, Egypt 1801 (wounded and awarded pension of £300 per annum), Sicily 1806, Sweden 1808, Walcheren 1809 (AAG – present at Flushing) Malta 1811–1815 (DAG). Gold Medal for Corunna and MGS medal for Egypt. CB and KC.

A friend of Sir John Moore for 21 years, he served with him in the West Indies, Ireland, the Helder, Egypt, Sicily, Sweden and Corunna. He saved Moore's life twice. Once when the surgeon would not visit Moore when he had yellow fever. Despite this infectious disease Anderson tended him and saved his life. He was with him as Moore lay dying in Corunna and Moore asked him not to leave him so he stayed with him to the end. The next day Anderson wrote an account of everything that Moore said on his death bed. Moore stated that he had never known any man so perfectly self possessed and unconscious of danger under a hot fire as Anderson. A very modest man, he never pressed his claims for advancement but

Wellington appointed him Governor of Gravesend and Tilbury Fort 1827, and Governor of Pendennis Castle 1832–1837. Colonel 78th Foot 9 Feb 1837.

REFERENCE: *Gentleman's Magazine, Mar 1852, pp. 299–300. Royal Military Calendar Vol 4, pp. 125–7. United Service Magazine, Feb 1852, pp. 316–7. Annual Register, 1851, Appx, p 364.*

ANDERSON, William

Ensign. 1st (Royal Scots) Regiment of Foot.
Named on the Regimental Memorial: St Joseph's Church, Waterloo, Belgium. (Photograph)

Ensign 27 Oct 1814.

Served with 3rd Battalion at Quatre Bras, where he was killed carrying the colours. His brother Lt John Anderson, 1st Foot died from his wounds at the siege of San Sebastian 1813.

ANDREW, Donald

Private. 79th (Cameron Highlanders) Regiment of Foot.
Memorial: Olrig Churchyard, Caithness, Scotland. (Photograph)

IN MEMORY / OF / DONALD ANDREW / WHO DIED DEC 16TH 1869 / AGED 95 / A VETERAN WHO FOUGHT IN / EGYPT, SPAIN, AND WATERLOO / UNDER ABERCROMBY, MOORE / AND WELLINGTON TAKING PART / IN 27 ENGAGEMENTS. / ....

Served in the Peninsula Mar 1810 – Apr 1814. Present at Fuentes d'Onoro, Salamanca, Pyrenees, Nivelle, Nive and Orthes. Served at Waterloo in Capt A. McLean's Company of Grenadiers (severely wounded). He had a strong constitution and was one of the 84 men of the 79th who answered roll call on the morning after Waterloo. Also present at Egypt 1801. MGS medal for Egypt, Fuentes d'Onoro, Salamanca, Pyrenees, Nivelle, Nive and Toulouse.

REFERENCE: *Obit. John O'Groats Journal, 23 Dec 1869.*

ANDREWS, Thomas

Captain. 74th (Highland) Regiment of Foot.
Memorial: Porch of St Andrew's Church, (now Musée Historique), Biarritz, France. (Photograph)
Named on the Regimental Memorial. St Giles's Cathedral, Edinburgh, Scotland. (Photograph)

Lt 75th Foot 5 Nov 1800. Capt 35th Foot 23 Jun 1808. Capt 74th Foot 11 Mar 1813.

Served in the Peninsula Jul 1813 – Apr 1814. Present at Pyrenees, Nivelle, Orthes, Vic Bigorre, Tarbes and Toulouse where he was severely wounded and died of his wounds 10 Apr 1814.

ANGLESEY, Henry William Marquis of see UXBRIDGE, Henry William Earl of

ANGROVE, John George

Lieutenant. 43rd (Monmouthshire) Light Infantry Regiment of Foot.
Named on the Memorial: St Andrew's Church, (now Musée Historique), Biarritz, France. (Photograph)

Ensign 16 Apr 1809 (from Royal Cornwall Militia). Lt 24 May 1810.

Served in the Peninsula with 1/43rd Aug 1812 – Nov 1813. Present at San Munos, Vittoria, Pyrenees, Heights of Vera, Bidassoa and Nivelle where he was severely wounded and died of his wounds 13 Nov 1813.

ANNESLEY, Marcus
Captain. 61st (South Gloucestershire) Regiment of Foot.
Ledger stone: St Mary and St Michael Abbey, Churchyard, Malvern, Worcestershire. Inscription illegible. (Photograph)

Ensign 67th Foot 16 Jan 1798. Lt 61st Foot 26 Apr 1798. Capt 24 Dec 1807. Major 19 Jul 1821.

Served in the Peninsula Oct 1811 – Mar 1814. Present at the siege of Salamanca Forts, Salamanca (took command of the regiment when all the senior officers were killed or wounded), Burgos, Pyrenees (wounded) and Nivelle (severely wounded and awarded pension of £70 per annum). Gold Medal for Salamanca, but did not receive the promotion that usually followed. Also served in Egypt 1801, Sicily 1805–1806 (present at Maida) and West Indies 1817–1820. Half pay 5 Jul 1833. He had served for 44 years. Died in Great Malvern 2 Oct 1843.
REFERENCE: *Gentleman's Magazine, Apr 1843, pp. 428–9.*

ANSELL, Francis Hutchings
Captain. 74th (Highland) Regiment of Foot.
Memorial tablet: St Mark's Episcopalian Churchyard, Portobello, Edinburgh, Scotland. (Photograph)

SACRED / TO THE MEMORY OF / FRANCIS HUTCHINGS ANSELL / LATE CAPTAIN / 74TH REG. OF FOOT / WHO DIED AT PORTOBELLO / 20 AUGST 1835 / AGED ** / 28 YEARS OF WHICH HE / DEDICATED TO THE SERVICE OF / HIS COUNTRY

Ensign 69th Foot 27 Mar 1804. Lt 74th Foot 1 Jan 1806. Capt 15 Jun 1815.

Served in the Peninsula Sep 1812 – Apr 1814. Present at Pyrenees, Nivelle, Nive, Orthes, Tarbes and Toulouse. Also served at Walcheren 1809, North America 1818 and West Indies until 1830.

ANSLEY, Benjamin
Lieutenant Colonel. Royal Corsican Rangers.
Tombstone: Protestant Cemetery, Naples, Italy. (M.I.)

"COL. BENJAMIN ANSLEY, SCOTS FUSILIER GUARDS, / K.H., OBIT 26 AUG 1846."

Ensign 3rd Foot Guards 21 Mar 1798. Lt and Capt 25 Nov 1809. Bt Lt Colonel 28 Mar 1811. Lt Colonel Royal Corsican Rangers 28 Feb 1812. Bt Colonel 19 Jul 1821.

Served in the Peninsula Mar 1809 – Jul 1809. Present at Douro and pursuit of the French to Salamonde. Returned to England as the wound he sustained in the Egyptian campaign was again causing him pain. Half pay 1812. KH. Also served at the Helder 1799, Ireland 1800, Egypt 1801 (present at Aboukir, Grand Cairo and Alexandria where he was severely wounded and awarded pension of £300 per annum) and Copenhagen 1807.
REFERENCE: *Gentleman's Magazine, Jan 1847, pp. 86–7. Annual Register, 1846, Appx, p. 286.*

ANSON, Sir George
Colonel. 23rd Regiment of Light Dragoons.
Interred in Catacomb A (v47 c10&11) Kensal Green Cemetery, London.

Cornet 16th Lt Dragoons 3 May 1786. Lt 16 Mar 1791. Capt 20th Lt Dragoons 9 Sep 1792. Major 25 Dec 1794. Major 16th Lt Dragoons Sep 1797. Lt Colonel 20th Lt Dragoons 21 Dec 1797. Lt Colonel 15th Lt Dragoons 6 Sep 1798. Bt Colonel 1 Jan 1805. Lt Colonel 16th Lt Dragoons 12 Dec 1805. Major General 25 Jul 1810. Colonel 23rd Lt Dragoons 3 Aug 1814. Lt General 12 Aug 1819. General 10 Jun 1837.

Served in the Peninsula Apr 1809 – Jan 1810, May 1810 – Feb 1811, May 1811 – Jan 1812 and Jun 1812 – Jul 1813 (Commanded C Cavalry Brigade). Present at Douro, Talavera (Mentioned in Despatches),

Busaco, El Bodon (Mentioned in Despatches), Llerena, Castrejon (Mentioned in Despatches), Salamanca (Mentioned in Despatches), retreat from Burgos (Mentioned in Despatches), Venta del Poza, Tolosa (Mentioned in Despatches), and Vittoria (Mentioned in Despatches). Gold Medal for Talavera, Salamanca and Vittoria. KCB 2 Jan 1815. KCTS. Also served in Flanders 1795 and the Helder 1799. Colonel 4th Dragoon Guards 24 Feb 1827. MP for Lichfield 1806 – 1841. Brother of Capt and Lt Colonel Sir William Anson 1st Foot Guards. Died 4 Nov 1849.
REFERENCE: *Royal Military Calendar, Vol 3, pp. 29–32. Gentleman's Magazine, Jan 1850, pp. 87–8. Annual Register, 1849, Appx, pp. 283–4.*

ANSON, Hon. George
Ensign. 3rd Regiment of Foot Guards.
Ledger stone: Kensal Green Cemetery, London. (6361/77/IC). (Photograph)

IN MEMORY OF / GENERAL HONBLE GEORGE ANSON / COMMANDER IN CHIEF IN INDIA / BORN 13TH OCTOBER 1797 / DIED AT KARNAL, INDIA / WHEN ON THE MARCH TO DELHI / 27TH MAY 1857 / HIS REMAINS HAVING BEEN BROUGHT FROM INDIA / WERE INTERRED IN KENSAL GREEN / CEMETERY / 5TH FEBRUARY 1860.

Ensign 8 Jan 1814. Lt and Capt 20 Jun 1820. Capt 52nd 26 Sep 1822. Capt 14th Lt Dragoons 10 May 1823. Major 7th Dragoon Guards 1 Apr 1824. Lt Colonel 19 May 1825. Colonel 28 Jun 1838. Major General 11 Nov 1851.
Present at Waterloo. After Waterloo held various seats in Parliament at Great Yarmouth, Stoke-on-Trent and South Staffordshire from 1841–53. During that time he was Principal Storekeeper of the Ordnance and also a prominent member of the Turf, winning the Derby and Oaks. Went to India Jul 1853 as officer in charge of the Bengal Army, the largest of the three armies in India. Commander in Chief in India Dec 1855, during the turbulent build up to the Indian Mutiny. Colonel 55th Foot 1856. In 1857 he was in the hills at Simla due to ill health when the Mutiny broke out and died on his way to Delhi.
REFERENCE: *Dictionary of National Biography. Gentleman's Magazine, Aug 1857, p. 216. Annual Register, 1857, Appx, p. 357.*

ANSON, Sir William
Captain and Lieutenant Colonel. 1st Regiment of Foot Guards.
Interred in Catacomb A (v18 c3 – 4). Kensal Green Cemetery, London.

Ensign 1st Foot Guards 13 Jun 1789. Lt and Capt 25 Apr 1793. Capt and Lt Col 28 Sep 1797. Bt Colonel 30 Oct 1805. Major General 4 Jun 1811. Lt General 12 Aug 1819. General 10 Jan 1837.
Served in the Peninsula Oct 1808 – Jan 1809 and Apr 1812 – Apr 1814 (Commanded 1 Brigade 4th Division). Present at Corunna, Castrejon (Mentioned in Despatches), Salamanca (Mentioned in Despatches), Burgos (Mentioned in Despatches), Vittoria, Pyrenees (Mentioned in Despatches), Nivelle (Mentioned in Despatches), Orthes (Mentioned in Despatches) and Toulouse. Gold Cross for Corunna, Salamanca, Vittoria, Pyrenees, Nivelle, Orthes and Toulouse. KCB 2 Jan 1815. Colonel 66th Foot 7 Dec 1829. Colonel 47th Foot 25 Mar 1835. Also served in Flanders 1793–1795 (present at Famars and Valenciennes), Sicily 1806 and Walcheren 1809. Served 58 years in the army. Died 13 Jan 1847. Brother of Colonel Sir George Anson 23rd Lt Dragoons.
REFERENCE: *Gentleman's Magazine, Apr 1847, pp. 423–4. Annual Register, 1847, Appx, pp. 200–1.*

ANSTRUTHER, Robert
Captain and Lieutenant Colonel. 3rd Regiment of Foot Guards.
Memorial tablet: Abercrombie Kirk, Balcaskie House, Fife, Scotland. (Photograph)
Abercrombie Kirk is on private land. Permission and an appointment from the owner at Balcaskie House should be sought in order to view the memorial.

SACRED / TO THE MEMORY OF / BRIG^R GEN^L ROBERT ANSTRUTHER / ELDEST SON OF / SIR ROBERT ANSTRUTHER BART. / OF BALCASKIE, / BORN 3^D MARCH 1768. / DIED 11TH JANY 1809. / HE SERVED IN THE CAMPAIGNS OF FLANDERS 1795, / IN THE EXPEDITION TO THE HELDER 1799, / IN EGYPT, 1800–1, WHERE HE ACTED AS / Q^R. M^R. GENERAL TO THE ARMY, / AND AT THE BATTLE OF VIMIERA 1808, / WHERE HE COMMANDED A BRIGADE. / HE DIED FROM FATIGUE / CONSEQUENT UPON HIS EXERTIONS IN / BRINGING UP THE REAR OF THE BRITISH ARMY / IN THEIR RETREAT TO CORUNNA. / WITH GREAT ABILITIES IN HIS PROFESSION / HE WAS AN ELEGANT WRITER, / A PROFOUND SCHOLAR, / AND AN ACCOMPLISHED GENTLEMAN. / HE WAS BURIED ON THE N.E. BASTION / OF THE CITADEL OF CORUNNA, / WHERE HIS FRIEND AND COMMANDER, / SIR JOHN MOORE, / IN COMPLIANCE WITH HIS WISH, / LIES BY HIS SIDE.

Memorial tablet: San Vicente, Elvina, Corunna, Spain. (Photograph)

ROLICA – BUSSACO / TALAVEA – LA ALBUERA / VIMIERO – FUENTES DE O ORO / BADAJOZ – PIRINEOS / SAHUGUN – ALMAREZ / SALAMANCA – ORTHEZ / CORU A – CIUDAD RODRIGO / VICTORIA – TOULOUSE / PENINSULAR WAR 1808 – 1814 / EN MEMORIA / DEL GENERAL DE BRIGADE ROBERT ANSTRUTHER, QUE FORMABA PARTE / DE LA RESERVA BAJO LAS ORDENES DEL GENERAL SIR JOHN MOORE. / MURIO EN A CORUNA, EL 14 DE ENERO DO 1809. / Y DEL TENIENTE CORONEL JOHN MACKENZIE DEL 5º DE INFANTERIA. / MURIO EN PALAVEA DE ABAIXO, A CORUNA, EL 15 DE ENERO DE 1809. / 200º ANNIVERSARIO DE LA BATALLA DE A CORUNA 1809 – 2009. / IN MEMORY / OF BRIGADIER GENERAL ROBERT ANSTRUTHER, WHO FORMED PART / OF THE RESERVE UNDER GENERAL SIR JOHN MOORE, / AND DIED IN CORUNNA ON 14 JANUARY 1808, / AND LIEUTENANT COLONEL JOHN MACKENZIE, 5TH FOOT / WHO DIED IN PALAVEA DE ADAGIO, CORUNNA, ON 15 JANUARY 1809. / 200TH ANNIVERSARY OF THE BATTLE OF CORUNNA 1809–2009 / EXCMO. AYUNTAMIENTO DE A CORUNA / ASSOCIATI N HIST RICO CULTURAL "THE ROYAL GREEN JACKETS" / EMBAJADA DE S. M. BRITANICA EN ESPANA. / ASSOCIACI N NAP LEONICA ESPA OLA.

Named on Memorial Panel VI for Corunna: Royal Military Chapel, Wellington Barracks, London. (M.I.) (Destroyed by a Flying Bomb 1944)

Ensign 1788. Lt and Capt 3rd Foot Guards 1792. Major 68th Foot Mar 1797. Lt Colonel Aug 1797. Capt and Lt Colonel 3rd Foot Guards Aug 1799. Bt Colonel 1 Jan 1805.
    Served in the Peninsula Aug 1808 – Jan 1809. (Commanded a Brigade Aug – Oct 1808 and Commanded a Brigade of Reserve Division Oct 1808 – Jan 1809). Present at Vimeiro (Mentioned in Despatches) and the Corunna campaign. Gold Medal for Vimeiro. Died of dysentery at Corunna 14 Jan 1809. Also served in Flanders 1793–1794, West Indies 1798, the Helder 1799 and Egypt 1800–1801 (QMG). Educated at Winchester.
REFERENCE: *Dictionary of National Biography.*

ANSTRUTHER, Windham Carmichael
Lieutenant and Captain. Coldstream Regiment of Foot Guards.
Monument: Kensal Green Cemetery, London. (13261/88/IC). (Photograph)

SACRED TO THE MEMORY / OF / .... / ALSO OF THE ABOVE NAMED / SIR WINDHAM CARMICHAEL / ANSTRUTHER, / BARONET OF NOVA SCOTIA / AND GREAT BRITAIN. / BORN 6TH MARCH 1793, / DIED 8TH SEPTEMBER 1869

Ensign 5 Jul 1810. Lt and Capt 17 Mar 1814.
    Served in the Peninsula Jul 1812 – Feb 1814. Present at Salamanca, Burgos, Bidassoa and Nivelle

(severely wounded and awarded pension of £50 per annum). MGS medal for Salamanca and Nivelle. Retired 26 Feb 1817.

ANWYL, Robert
Captain. 4th (King's Own) Regiment of Foot.
Memorial tablet: St George's Church, Arreton, Isle of Wight. (Photograph)

IN MEMORY OF / LIEUT COLL ROBERT ANWYL, / OF VRON, IN MERIONETHSHIRE: / WHO AFTER 32 YEARS OF DISTINGUISHED SERVICE (28 OF WHICH / HE SERVED IN THE 4TH OR KINGS OWN REGIMENT.) / ON HIS RETURN TO HIS NATIVE PLACE / HAVING RESIGNED THE COMMAND OF THE 95TH REGT AT MALTA / DIED AT NEWPORT IN THIS ISLAND. / JUNE 27TH 1831, AGED 51 YEARS. / HIS REMAINS ARE DEPOSITED IN A VAULT WITHIN THE RAILINGS ON THE / SOUTH SIDE OF THE PORCH OF THIS CHURCH. / ....

Chest tomb in railed enclosure: St George's Churchyard, Arreton, Isle of Wight. Seriously eroded. (Photograph)

Ensign 27 Jul 1799. Lt 27 Oct 1799. Capt 14 Aug 1804. Bt Major 21 Jun 1813. Bt Lt Colonel 21 Jun 1817. Major 4th Foot 3 Aug 1820. Lt Colonel 95th Foot 13 Dec 1827.
    Served in the Peninsula Jan 1811 – Apr 1814 (from Oct 1812 Brigade Major 2 Brigade 5th Division). Present at Barba del Puerco, Fuentes d'Onoro, Badajoz (wounded), Salamanca, retreat from Burgos, Villa Muriel, Vittoria, San Sebastian, Bidassoa, Nivelle, Nive (wounded) and Bayonne. AAG to General Colville 1814. Gold Medal for San Sebastian. Also served at the Helder 1799, Walcheren 1809, North America 1814 and Malta. Retired on half pay 15 Jun 1830.

ARABIN, Frederick
2nd Captain. Royal Artillery.
Memorial tablet: St Faith's Church, Havant, Hampshire. (Photograph)

TO THE MEMORY / OF / LIEUTENANT COLONEL / FREDERICK ARABIN, R.A., / BORN IN DUBLIN NOVEMBER 23RD 1785, / DIED AT BERMUDA AUGUST 17TH 1843. / ....

2nd Lt 8 Sep 1803. 1st Lt 12 Sep 1803. 2nd Capt 11 Jul 1811. Capt 29 Jul 1825. Bt Major 22 Jul 1830. Lt Col 18 Dec 1837.
    Served in the Peninsula Apr 1812 – Apr 1814. Present at Biar, Castalla (Mentioned in Despatches), Tarragona (Mentioned in Despatches) and Ordal (Mentioned in Despatches). At Tarragona he commanded the artillery at the siege and capture of Fort San Felipe, the whole operation lasting four days. Served with the Army of Occupation 1815–1816. Also served in Martinique 1808–1809, Canada 1820–1824, Halifax 1832–1838 and Bermuda 1841–1843 where he died 17 Aug 1843.

ARBUTHNOT, Sir Robert
Captain and Lieutenant Colonel. Coldstream Regiment of Foot Guards.
Memorial tablet: Church of St Boniface, Bonchurch, Isle of Wight. (Photograph)

IN / MEMORY OF / LIEUTENANT GENERAL / SIR ROBERT ARBUTHNOT, / K.C.B. AND K.T.S. / WHO AFTER AN ACTIVE LIFE SPENT IN / THE SERVICE OF HIS COUNTRY IN THE / FOUR QUARTERS OF THE GLOBE, / DIED IN PEACE IN BONCHURCH ON / THE 6TH MAY 1853, / IN THE 80TH YEAR OF HIS AGE. / SINCERELY REGRETTED.

Cornet 23rd Lt Dragoons 1 Jan 1797. Lt 1 Jun 1797. Adjt Jul 1798. Capt 20 Aug 1802. Capt 20 Lt Dragoons 24 Mar 1805. Major 13 Apr 1809. Bt Lt Colonel 24 Mar 1809. Capt and Lt Colonel Coldstream

Guards 25 Jul 1814. Bt Colonel 19 Jul 1821. Major General 22 Jul 1830. Lt General 23 Nov 1841. Portuguese Army: Major 13 Apr 1809. Bt Lt Colonel 22 May 1811. Lt Colonel 25 Feb 1813.

Served in the Peninsula Aug 1808 – Jan 1809 (on Staff as ADC to General Beresford), Mar 1809 – Apr 1814 (with Portuguese Army and Military Secretary to Beresford). Present at Corunna, Douro, Busaco, Olivencia, first siege of Badajoz (Mentioned in Despatches), Albuera (Mentioned in Despatches and brought home the despatches for the battle), Ciudad Rodrigo, Badajoz, Salamanca, Nivelle, Nive (Mentioned in Beresford's Despatches), Adour, Orthes (Mentioned in Beresford's Despatches) and Toulouse. Gold Cross for Busaco, Albuera, Badajoz, Nivelle, Nive, Orthes and Toulouse. MGS medal for Corunna and Ciudad Rodrigo. KCB 2 Jan 1815 and KTS.

Also served in the Irish Rebellion 1798 (present at Ballynahinch), Cape of Good Hope 1806, South America 1807 (present at Buenos Ayres and taken prisoner for 13 months). On his return home was appointed Military Secretary to Beresford in Madeira and then Portugal, Ceylon 1838 (in command of the troops on the island) and India (commanded a division in Bengal until 1841). Colonel 76th Foot 31 May 1843. Brother of Lt Colonel Sir Thomas Arbuthnot 57th Foot who also served in the Peninsula.
REFERENCE: *Dictionary of National Biography. Royal Military Calendar, Vol 4, pp. 34–6. Gentleman's Magazine, Jul 1853, pp. 90–1. Annual Register 1853, Appx, pp. 227–8.*

ARBUTHNOT, Sir Thomas
Lieutenant Colonel. 57th (West Middlesex) Regiment of Foot.
Memorial tablet: St Philip's Church, Salford, Lancashire. (Photograph)

SACRED TO THE MEMORY OF / LIEUT GENERAL SIR THOMAS ARBUTHNOT K.C.B. / WHO DIED AT MANCHESTER WHEN IN COMMAND OF THE / NORTHERN AND MIDLAND / DISTRICTS / ON THE 26TH DAY OF JANUARY 1849, / AGED 72 YEARS. / REQUIESCAT IN PACE

Memorial tablet: Kinsale, County Cork, Ireland. ("The old colours of the 71st Foot were placed over a tablet erected at Kinsale to the memory of the late Lt General Sir Thomas Arbuthnot a native of that place who commanded the regiment for many years.")

Ensign 29th Foot 23 Nov 1795. Lt 40th Foot 1 May 1796. Capt 8th West India Regt 25 Jun 1798. Capt Royal Staff Corps 26 May 1803. Major 5th West India Regt 7 Apr 1808. Bt Lt Colonel 24 May 1810. Lt Colonel 57th Foot 24 Mar 1814. Bt Colonel 4 Jun 1814. Lt Colonel 71st Foot 12 Aug 1819. Major General 27 May 1825. Lt General 28 Jun 1838.

Served in the Peninsula Aug 1808 - Jan 1809 (AAG) and Jul 1813 - Apr 1815 (AQMG 3 Division). Present at Rolica, Vimiero, Corunna, Pyrenees, Nivelle, Nive, Orthes and Tarbes (severely wounded). Gold Cross for Rolica, Vimiero, Corunna, Pyrenees, Nivelle and Orthes. KCB Jan 1815. Also served at the Cape of Good Hope 1813 (DQMG), Canada 1814, Portugal 1826, Ireland 1828 and Manchester 1842 (in command of the Northern and Midland Districts during the disturbances in 1840's). Colonel 52nd Foot 23 Dec 1839. Colonel 71st Foot 18 Feb 1848. Brother of Capt and Lt Colonel Robert Arbuthnot Coldstream Guards.
REFERENCE: *Dictionary of National Biography. Gentleman's Magazine, Apr 1849, pp.425-6. Annual Register, 1849, Appx p.220.*

ARCHDALL, Richard
Lieutenant. 60th (Royal American) Regiment of Foot.
Headstone: Green Street Cemetery, St Helier, Jersey, Channel Islands. (Plot 14 North stone). Seriously eroded and inscription recorded from memorial inscription. (Photograph)

"SACRED TO THE MEMORY OF / RICHARD ARCHDALL, ESQ. / LATE LIEUT COL IN THE 40TH REGT OF FOOT / WHO DIED JAN 25TH 1829 AGED 45 YEARS."

Ensign 40th Foot 18 Apr 1800. Lt 29 Oct 1802. Capt 17 Dec 1803. Major 21 Aug 1806. Bt Lt Colonel 17 Aug 1812. Rejoined army as Cornet 3rd Lt Dragoons 3 Mar 1814. Lt 60th Foot 24 Apr 1814. Lt 11th Lt Dragoons 12 Nov 1818.

Served in the Peninsula with 40th Foot Aug – Nov 1808 and Apr 1810 – Jul 1813. Present at Rolica, Vimeiro, Busaco, Redinha, first siege of Badajoz, Castrejon (Mentioned in Despatches), Salamanca and Vittoria. Gold Medal for Salamanca (in command of his battalion and awarded Lt Colonelcy).

Appeared before a Court Martial 1813, found guilty of various offences and dismissed from the service of the 40th Foot. Later rejoined 3rd Lt Dragoons 1814. Assistant Inspector General Barrack Department 1818–1828. Retired on half pay 25 Dec 1822.
REFERENCE: *United Service Journal, Feb 1829, p. 520.*

ARCHER, Clement
Lieutenant Colonel. 16th (Queen's) Regiment of Light Dragoons.
Memorial tablet: St Peter's Church, Boughton Monchelsea, Kent. (Photograph)

IN A VAULT NEAR THIS SPOT, / ARE DEPOSITED THE REMAINS OF: / CLEMENT ARCHER ESQUIRE. / DEEPLY REGRETTED BY HIS FAMILY AND FRIENDS; / LATE LIEUTT COLONEL OF H. M. 16TH REGT OF LIGHT DRAGNS / IN WHICH REGIMENT HE WAS BELOVED AND RESPECTED / DURING A PERIOD OF / TWENTY YEARS; / HE WAS BORN AUGT 16TH 1765 AND DIED NOVR 1817. / HE MARRIED MARIANNE (DAUGHTER OF / ROBERT WRIGHT ESQRE OF WIMBLEDON) / BY WHOM HE LEFT THREE CHILDREN.

Memorial vault: St Peter's Church, Boughton Monchelsea, Kent. (Photograph)

SACRED TO THE MEMORY OF / CLEMENT ARCHER ESQR LATE LIEUT COLONEL IN THE 16TH / REGIMENT OF LT DRAGOONS WHO DEPARTED THIS LIFE AT / BOUGHTON ON THE 8TH NOVR 1817 IN THE 53 YEAR OF HIS AGE.

Cornet 8 Apr 1794. Lt 17 Jun 1794. Capt 15 Sep 1796. Major 13 Nov 1806. Lt Colonel 1 Nov 1810.

Served in the Peninsula Sep 1809 – Jun 1811 and Dec 1811 – May 1812. Present at Coa, Busaco, Sabugal, Fuentes d'Onoro and Llerena. Gold Medal for Fuentes d'Onoro. Also served in Flanders 1794–1795. Commanded the regiment from 2 Apr 1811, but had to retire in 1812 owing to ill health.

ARDEN, Henry
Lieutenant. 61st (South Gloucestershire) Regiment of Foot.
Named on the Memorial: St Andrew's Church, (now Musée Historique), Biarritz, France. (Photograph)

Lt 3 Nov 1808.

Served in the Peninsula Oct 1811 – Apr 1814. Present at the siege of Salamanca Forts, Orthes, Tarbes and Toulouse where he was severely wounded and died of his wounds on 11 Apr 1814.

ARMSTRONG, Andrew
Assistant Surgeon. 1st Regiment of Foot Guards.
Headstone: St James's Churchyard, Appleby, Cumbria. (Photograph)

.... / JANE ARMSTRONG / WIDOW OF ANDREW ARMSTRONG SURGEON GRENADIER / GUARDS WHO TOOK PART IN THE / BATTLE OF WATERLOO. / ....

Hospital Mate General Service 12 Jul 1810. Asst Surgeon 1st Foot Guards 18 Jul 1811. Surgeon 11 Nov 1824.

Served in the Peninsula with 3rd Battalion Sep 1811 – Mar 1812 and 1st Battalion Sep 1812 – Apr 1814.

Present at Cadiz, Bidassoa, Nivelle, Nive, Adour and Bayonne. Present at Waterloo. Died in Edinburgh 23 Feb 1828.

ARMSTRONG, Henry Bruere
Lieutenant. 14th (Buckinghamshire) Regiment of Foot.
Memorial tablet: St John's Church, Meerut Cantonment, Meerut, India. (M.I.)

"SACRED TO THE MEMORY OF BRIGADIER GENERAL W. T. EDWARDS, HIS MAJESTY'S 14TH REGIMENT AND CAPTAIN H. B. ARMSTRONG OF THE SAME CORPS, WHO IN THE SUCCESSFUL ASSAULT ON THE FORTRESS OF BHARATPUR ON THE MORNING OF 18TH JANY 1825 FELL ON THE RAMPARTS IN THE GALLANT DISCHARGE OF HIS DUTY. GENERAL EDWARDS LEADING THE LEFT COLUMN OF ATTACK."

Ensign Nova Scotia Fencibles 24 Aug 1804. Lt 23 Jan 1806. Lt and Adjt 14th Foot 29 Oct 1808. Capt 1825.
   Served in the Peninsula May 1810. Present at Tarifa (from service in Gibraltar). Also served in India (present in the siege of Bhurtpore where he was killed in the assault on the fort on 18 Jan 1825).

ARMSTRONG, John
Lieutenant. 1st (Royal Scots) Regiment of Foot.
Named on the Regimental Memorial: St Joseph's Church, Waterloo, Belgium. (Photograph)

Ensign 3 Feb 1807. Lt 27 Apr 1809.
   Served in the Peninsula Nov 1810 – Nov 1813. Present at Fuentes d'Onoro, Badajoz, Castrejon, Salamanca, Burgos, Villa Muriel, Vittoria (wounded), and the capture of San Sebastian (wounded). Present at Quatre Bras and Waterloo where he was killed 18 Jun 1815.

ARMSTRONG, Richard
Major. Staff Appointment in Spain and Portugal.
Memorial window: St Mary's Cathedral, Lincoln, Lincolnshire. (Photograph)

IN MEMORIAM RICARDI ARMSTRONG, EQUITIS AURATI QUI MORTEM OBIIT /IIID DIE MARTII A.D. MDCCCLIV. AETATIS SUA LXXII ....

Ensign 32nd Foot 23 Jun 1796. Lt 5 Nov 1799. Capt 9th Battalion of Reserve 9 Jul 1803. Capt 8th Veteran Battalion 31 Jan 1805. Capt 97th Foot 7 Jul 1808. Major 97th Foot 30 May 1811. Bt Lt Colonel 26 Aug 1813. Bt Colonel 22 Jul 1830. Major General 23 Nov 1841. Lt General 11 Nov 1851. Portuguese Army: Major 7th Line 14 Jun 1809. Major 16th Line 3 Sep 1810. Lt Col 10th Caçadores 3 Jul 1811. Lt Col 4th Line 18 Sep 1813.
   Served in the Peninsula with 97th Foot Aug 1808 – Jun 1809. With Portuguese Army: Jun 1809 – Sep 1813 and Jan – Apr 1814. Present at Oporto, Busaco (Mentioned in Despatches), Pombal, Redinha, Alba de Tormes, Vittoria, Pyrenees (severely wounded) and Toulouse. Gold Medal for Busaco, Vittoria and Pyrenees. MGS medal for Toulouse. KTS. KCB. Served in Portugal for six years at the end of the war and retired in 1821 from the Portuguese service.
   Also served in the Burma campaign 1824–1826 (present at Prome 1 Dec 1825. Awarded Army of India medal for Ava), Canada 1841 and India 1851–1854 (Commander in Chief at Madras). Colonel 32nd Foot 25 Jun 1850. Died 3 Mar 1854 on voyage home from India.
REFERENCE: *Annual Register, 1854, Appx, pp. 273–4.*

ARNOLD, Edward John Richard

Lieutenant. 12th (Prince of Wales's) Regiment of Light Dragoons.
Memorial tablet: St Anne's Church, Soho, London. (No longer extant). The church was bombed 24 Sep 1940. (M.I.)

"IN MEMORY OF / EDWARD JOHN RICHARD ARNOLD / LATE OF THE 11TH LT DRAGNS / WHO DIED AT MEERUT IN BENGAL / WHILE ON SERVICE WITH THE REGT / THE 31ST AUG 1836. BORN 3RD FEBRY 1794"

Buried in Meerut Cantonment, Meerut, India. (Burial register)

"CAPT EDWARD ARNOLD 11TH DRAGOONS DIED 31 AUG 1836 AGED 42".

Cornet 15th Lt Dragoons 22 Feb 1810. Lt 15th Lt Dragoons 25 Jul 1811. Lt 12th Lt Dragoons 31 Oct 1811. Lt 11th Lt Dragoons 29 Mar 1827.
    Served in the Peninsula May – Jun 1812 and Jul – Nov 1813. Half pay 1814. Later rejoined the 11th Lt Dragoons and served in India until his death in 1836. Held the local rank of Captain in India.

ARNOLD, Robert

Lieutenant. 10th (Prince of Wales's Own) Regiment of Light Dragoons.
Memorial tablet: St Mary Magdalene Church, South Holmwood, Surrey. (Photograph)

TO THE MEMORY / OF / LIEUT COLONEL ROBERT ARNOLD / 16TH QUEEN'S LANCERS, / WHO AFTER HAVING SERVED / WITH DISTINCTION IN SPAIN, PORTUGAL, FRANCE / AND AT WATERLOO, / DIED AT CABUL, / WHEN BRIGADIER COMMANDING / THE BENGAL CAVALRY / OF THE ARMY OF INDIA, / ON THE 20TH AUGUST 1839. / .... / THIS MONUMENT IS ERECTED BY THE OFFICERS, NON-COMMISSIONED / OFFICERS AND PRIVATES OF THE 16TH QUEEN'S LANCERS AS A / TESTIMONY OF THEIR REGARD FOR A GALLANT SOLDIER AND BELOVED COMRADE.

Memorial tablet: St John's Church, Meerut Cantonment, Meerut, India. (Photograph)

SACRED TO THE MEMORY OF / LIEUTENANT-COLONEL ROBERT ARNOLD / 16TH LANCERS, BRIGADIER COMMANDING THE BENGAL CAVALRY OF THE / ARMY OF THE INDUS; / WHO DIED AT CAUBUL 20TH AUGUST 1839. / .... / THIS TABLET IS ERECTED BY THE / REGIMENTAL OFFICERS AND MEN AS A RECORD OF THEIR / AFFECTION AND ESTEEM FOR THEIR COMMANDING OFFICER

Named on the Memorial tablet to 16th Lancers: Afghan Memorial Church, St John the Evangelist, Colaba, Bombay, India. (M.I.)

Ensign 4th Foot 21 Nov 1809. Lt 13 May 1812. Lt 16th Lt Dragoons 30 May 1812. Lt 10th Lt Dragoons 12 Nov 1814. Capt 9 Jul 1818. Major 14 Apr 1825. Lt Colonel 16th Lt Dragoons 22 Jun 1826.
    Served in the Peninsula with 1/4th Jan 1811 – Jun 1812, 2/4th Jul 1812 – Aug 1812 and 16th Lt Dragoons Sep 1812 – Apr 1814. Present at Fuentes d'Onoro, Barba del Puerco, Badajoz (wounded), Salamanca, Venta del Poza, Vittoria (wounded), Nivelle, Nive and Bayonne. Present at Waterloo with 10th Lt Dragoons (severely wounded – shot through lungs while charging a French square at the head of his troop). Also served in India. Commanded a brigade of cavalry sent to Afghanistan under Sir John Keane 1838 (present at capture of Ghuznee and occupation of Kabul). Considered to be one of the best cavalry officers in the service, especially on outpost duty. Educated at Winchester. Died at Kabul 20 Aug 1839.
REFERENCE: *Gentleman's Magazine, Apr 1840, p. 435. Annual Register, 1839, Appx, p. 359.*

ARNOTT, Archibald

Surgeon. 20th (East Devonshire) Regiment of Foot.
Headstone in railed enclosure: Parish Churchyard, Ecclefechan, Dumfriesshire, Scotland. (Photograph)

SACRED TO THE MEMORY OF / ARCHIBALD ARNOTT, ESQUIRE / KIRKCONNEL HALL. / BORN 18TH APRIL 1772. / DIED 6TH JULY 1855. / DR ARNOTT WAS FOR MANY YEARS. / SURGEON OF THE 20TH FOOT AND / SERVED IN EGYPT, AT MAIDA, WALCHEREN, / THROUGHOUT THE PENINSULAR WAR, / AND IN INDIA. / AT ST HELENA HE WAS THE MEDICAL / ATTENDANT OF / NAPOLEON BUONAPARTE, / WHOSE ESTEEM HE WON AND WHOSE / LAST MOMENTS HE SOOTHED. / THE REMAINDER OF HIS MOST USEFUL / AND EXEMPLARY LIFE. / HE SPENT IN THE RETIREMENT / OF HIS NATIVE PLACE, / HONOURED / AND BELOVED BY ALL THAT KNEW HIM

Regimental Mate 11th Dragoons 14 Apr 1795. Asst Surgeon 25 Dec 1796. Surgeon 20th Regiment 23 Aug 1799.

Served in the Peninsula Aug 1808 – Jan 1809 and Nov 1812 – Apr 1814. Present at Vimeiro, Corunna, Vittoria, Pyrenees, Nivelle, Nive, Orthes and Toulouse. Also served at the Helder 1799, Egypt 1801, Maida 1806 and Walcheren 1809. MD Edinburgh 1815. Appointed Surgeon to Napoleon on St Helena in 1819 and present at his autopsy 6 May 1821. Author of *An account of the last illness of Napoleon*, 1822. Retired on half pay 25 Dec 1826. MGS medal for Egypt, Maida, Vimeiro, Corunna, Vittoria, Pyrenees, Nivelle, Nive, Orthes and Toulouse

REFERENCE: *Annual Register, 1855, Appx, p. 292. Wilson, J. B., Dr Archibald Arnott, Surgeon to the 20th Foot and Physician to Napoleon, British Medical Journal, 1975, Marsh, Kenneth, Boney's doctor, Medal News, June/July 2011, pp. 17–20.*

ASHBURNHAM, Hon. John

Ensign. Coldstream Regiment of Foot Guards.
Named on Memorial Panel VI: Royal Military Chapel, Wellington Barracks, London. (M.I.) (Destroyed by a Flying Bomb 1944)

Lt 7th Foot 20 Feb 1806. Ensign Coldstream Guards 1 Jan 1807.

Served in the Peninsula Mar- Dec 1809. Present at Douro and Talavera. Also served at Copenhagen 1807. Reported to have drowned on passage to England from Portugal Dec 1809.

ASHCROFT, Timothy

Private. 1st Regiment of Foot Guards.
Gravestone: St Oswald's Churchyard, Winwick, Cheshire. Seriously eroded. (M.I.)

"TIMOTHY ASHCROFT AGED 84 YEARS. / DIED APRIL 18TH 1861".

Pte 24 Apr 1801

Served in the Peninsula 1808 – Jan 1809. Present at Corunna. Served at Waterloo. MGS medal for Corunna. Served for 24 years and one day. Discharged 25 Mar 1825 aged 48 in consequence of length of service, defective sight and bad health. Chelsea out-pensioner. Pension 1/1½ d per day.

ASHTON, Henry

Clerk. Commissariat Department.
Mural Headstone: Memorial wall, Anglesea Barracks, Hobart, Tasmania, Australia. (Relocated from St David's Park, Hobart in 1974). (Photograph)

SACRED / TO THE MEMORY OF / HENRY ASHTON, SENIOR, / DEPUTY ASSISTANT COM-MISSARY GENERAL, / WHO DEPARTED THIS LIFE 19 AUGUST 1828 / AGED 42 YEARS. /
…………………..

Clerk Commissariat Dept 31 Mar 1813. Dep Asst Comm Gen 19 Jul 1821.

Present in the Peninsula (Lisbon Commissariat Office 1813–1817). Also served as Clerk in office of Sir Robert Hugh Kennedy, Commissary General in London 1817–1823 and Barbados, West Indies 1823–1826. Posted to Hobart, Tasmania, where he was employed in the Commissariat of Accounts Dec 1827 – Aug 1828.

ASHTON, John
Lieutenant and Captain. 3rd Regiment of Foot Guards.
Named on the Regimental Memorial: St Joseph's Church, Waterloo, Belgium. (Photograph)

Named on Memorial Panel VIII for Waterloo: Royal Military Chapel, Wellington Barracks, London. (M.I.) (Destroyed by a Flying Bomb 1944)

Ensign 29 May 1811. Lt and Capt 2 Sep 1814.
Served in the Peninsula Sep 1813 – Apr 1814. Present at Bidassoa, Nivelle, Nive, Adour and Bayonne. Present at Waterloo in 2nd Battalion where he was killed.

ASKEW, Henry
2nd Major. 1st Regiment of Foot Guards.
Memorial: Royal Military Chapel, Wellington Barracks, London. (M.I.) (Destroyed by a Flying Bomb 1944)

"THESE COLOURS BELONGED TO THE 2ND BATTALION 1ST GUARDS, AND WERE CARRIED THROUGH THE WATERLOO CAMPAIGN. THEY CAME INTO THE POSSESSION OF LIEUT.-GENERAL, SIR HENRY ASKEW, KT., C.B., WHO COMMANDED THE BATTALION AT QUATRE BRAS, WHERE HE WAS WOUNDED. HIS NEPHEW, MR. WATSON ASKEW, OF PALLINSBURN, NORTHUMBERLAND, RESTORED THEM TO THE REGIMENT. THEY WERE PLACED IN THIS CHAPEL, NOVEMBER 18, 1881. SIR HENRY ASKEW JOINED THE REGIMENT IN 1793. HE SERVED IN HOLLAND IN 1794-6, IN SICILY IN 1806-7, AND IN THE PENINSULA IN 1812. HE COMMANDED THE 1ST BATTALION DURING THE OPERATIONS IN THE SOUTH OF FRANCE, 1813-14; IN AUGUST, 1814, WAS APPOINTED MAJOR OF THE 2ND BATTALION WHEN QUAR-TERED IN HOLLAND, AND REMAINED ABROAD UNTIL JANUARY, 1816, WHEN THE BATTALION RETURNED HOME FROM PARIS. HE CONTINUED IN COMMAND TILL PROMOTED TO BE MAJOR-GENERAL IN 1821."

Ensign 19 Jun 1793. Lt and Capt 18 Mar 1795. Capt and Lt Colonel 27 Aug 1807. Bt Colonel 4 Jun 1814. 2nd Major 25 Jul 1814. Major General 19 Jul 1821. Lt General 10 Jan 1837.
Served in the Peninsula with 1st Battalion Sep 1812 – Apr 1814. Present at Bidassoa, Nivelle, Nive, Adour and Bayonne. Gold Medal for Nive. CB. Present at Quatre Bras (wounded), Waterloo in command of 1st Foot Guards and with the Army of Occupation until 1816. Also served in Flanders 1794–1795, Sicily 1806–1807 and Walcheren 1809. Knighted 1821. Died in Cologne 25 Jun 1847.
REFERENCE: *Gentleman's Magazine, Oct 1847, p. 432. Annual Register, 1847, Appx, p. 240.*

ATKINSON, Abraham
Lieutenant. 74th (Highland) Regiment of Foot.
Memorial tablet: Waringstown Church, Waringstown, County Down, Northern Ireland. (North wall of Nave). (Photograph)

TO THE MEMORY / OF / LIEUT ATKINSON, / LATE OF THE 74TH REGT OF INFANTRY / WHO DIED THE 13TH OCTR 1830 AGED 45 YEARS. / THIS MONUMENT IS ERECTED / BY HIS BROTHER OFFICERS / AS A TESTIMONIAL OF THEIR / HIGH SENSE OF HIS WORTH AS / A MAN AND A SOLDIER"

Ensign 21 Dec 1809. Lt 28 Apr 1812.

Served in the Peninsula May 1810 – Apr 1814. Present at Busaco, Casal Nova, Foz d'Arouce, Fuentes d'Onoro, second siege of Badajoz, El Bodon, Ciudad Rodrigo (wounded), Badajoz (wounded 19 Mar 1812), Salamanca, Vittoria, Pyrenees, Nivelle, Nive, Orthes and Vic Bigorre (wounded). Also served in North America 1818–1828. Retired on half pay Sep 1830.

AUBIN, Phillip

Lieutenant. 57th (West Middlesex) Regiment of Foot.
Chest tomb: Mont l'Abbaye Cemetery, St Helier, Jersey, Channel Islands. (Photograph)

SACRED TO THE MEMORY OF / PHILIP AUBIN / LATE LIEUTENANT COLONEL / OF HER MAJESTY'S 57TH REGIMENT / WHO DEPARTED THIS LIFE / AT ROCKINGHAM HOUSE, ST HELIER, JERSEY / ON THE 7TH DAY OF MAY 1863 / AGED 67 YEARS.

Ensign 14 Feb 1811. Lt 29 Apr 1813. Capt 22 Jun 1826. Major 12 Apr 1831. Lt Colonel 28 Nov 1854.

Served in the Peninsula Jan 1812 – Apr 1814. Present at Vittoria, Pyrenees, Nivelle, Nive, Adour (wounded), Orthes and Vic Bigorre (severely wounded). Also served in North America 1814–1815, Australia 1830 – Jul 1831 and India Aug 1831 – 1840. Retired on full pay 11 Feb 1842. MGS medal for Vittoria, Pyrenees, Nivelle, Nive and Orthes.

AUCHMUTY, Samuel Benjamin

Major. 7th (Royal Fusiliers) Regiment of Foot.
Tomb: Pau Cemetery, Pau, Basses Pyrenees, France. (Photograph)

SACRED TO THE MEMORY OF / SIR SAMUEL BENJAMIN AUCHMUTY G.C.B. / GENERAL IN H.B.MS. ARMY. / COLONEL OF THE 7TH ROYAL FUSILIERS. / BORN AT BRIENSTOWN HOUSE CO. / LONGFORD / APRIL 28TH 1780 / DIED AT PAU APRIL 30TH 1868.

Ensign 60th Foot 15 Oct 1797. Lt 68th Foot 13 Mar 1800. Capt 14 Nov 1805. Capt 70th Foot 5 Jul 1806. Capt 7th Foot 22 Oct 1807. Bt Major 26 Aug 1813. Major 28 Oct 1813. Bt Lt Colonel 12 Apr 1814. Bt Colonel 6 May 1831. Major General 23 Nov 1841. Lt General 11 Nov 1851. General 19 Jun 1860.

Served in the Peninsula Apr 1809 – Nov 1810 (Brigade Major to General Alex Campbell), Dec 1810 – Jul 1812 (DAAG 6th Division), Mar – Nov 1813 (ADC to Sir Lowry Cole) and Dec 1813 – Apr 1814 (in command of the Light Companies of Major General Ross's Brigade). Present at Douro, Talavera, Busaco, Torres Vedras, the pursuit of Massena, Fuentes d'Onoro, Vittoria, Pyrenees (awarded Bt Majority), Orthes and Toulouse (awarded Bt Lt Colonelcy). Gold Medal for Orthes and Toulouse. Also served in the West Indies (present at St Lucia). MGS medal for Talavera, Busaco, Fuentes d'Onoro, Vittoria and Toulouse. GCB. Colonel 65th Foot 31 Jan 1851. Colonel 7th Foot 18 Jan 1855. Also served in North America 1814–1815. Retired on half pay 1 Aug 1832. Son of Lt General Sir Samuel Auchmuty.
REFERENCE: *Gentleman's Magazine, May 1868, pp. 788–9.*

AUSTIN, John

Captain. 58th (Rutlandshire) Regiment of Foot.
Headstone: Smallcombe Cemetery, Bath, Somerset. (Photograph)

HERE RESTETH / JOHN AUSTIN / BRIGADIER GENERAL IN THE ARMY OF PORTUGAL / BORN 17TH JUNE 1775 DIED 25TH MARCH 1860

Ensign 85th Foot 30 Jan 1800. Lt 22 Jul 1800. Lt 69th Foot 13 Nov 1805. Capt 58th Foot 28 Nov 1805. Bt Major 4 Sep 1807. Bt Lt Colonel 25 Feb 1813. Lt Colonel (unattached) 8 Jun 1826. Lt Colonel 17th Foot 30 Jun 1829.

Served in the Peninsula Jul 1809 – Mar 1810 (on staff as DAG), and Apr 1810 – Apr 1814 (with Portuguese Army). Military Governor of the Algarve 11 Apr 1810. Also served in the Irish Rebellion 1798, Madeira 1801–1802, West Indies (present in Jamaica 1802–1803. Deputy Judge Advocate), Ireland 1806–1807 (Brigade Major) and Madeira 1807 (DAG). Retired 13 Aug 1829.
REFERENCE: *Royal Military Calendar, Vol 4, pp. 441–2.*

AUSTIN, Thomas
Lieutenant. 35th (Sussex) Regiment of Foot.
Grave: St Arnos Vale Cemetery, Bristol, Somerset. (Grave G 116).

Ensign 17 May 1810. Lt 6 Dec 1813.

Served in the Netherlands 1814 (present at Antwerp where he was severely wounded, his leg amputated and awarded pension of £70 per annum). Known as 'Old Stick Leg'. Prussian medal for the campaign of 1813. Also served in Ireland 1820 (present at Duncannon Fort, Wexford Harbour and County Wexford where he was wounded by a rebel sympathiser).
REFERENCE: *Austin, H. H., Old Stick Leg: extracts from the diaries of Major Thomas Austin, 1926.*

AUSTIN, William
Lieutenant, 52nd (Oxfordshire) Light Infantry Regiment of Foot.
Headstone: Smallcombe Cemetery, Bath, Somerset. (The original headstone has been replaced by a new headstone with the same wording, erected by the Oxford and Buckinghamshire Regimental Association). (Photograph)

IN MEMORY OF / MAJOR WILLIAM AUSTIN / WHO DIED AT BATH / ON THE 2ND NOVEMBER 1877 / IN THE 83RD YEAR OF HIS AGE / IN THE HOPE OF A JOYFUL RESURRECTION / THROUGH OUR LORD JESUS CHRIST AMEN / HE SERVED IN THE 52ND REGIMENT / IN THE PENINSULAR WAR / AND AT THE BATTLE OF WATERLOO

Ensign 52nd Foot 5 Sep 1811. Lt 6 Apr 1813. Lt 97th Foot 25 Mar 1824. Capt 51st Foot 26 Sep 1834. Major 42nd Foot 4 Jul 1845.

Served in the Peninsula with 2/52nd Oct 1811 – Apr 1812. Present at Ciudad Rodrigo. Present at Waterloo with 1/52nd. Also served in the Netherlands (present at Merxem). Retired 25 Jul 1845. MGS medal for Ciudad Rodrigo.

AYLING, John
Lieutenant. 40th (2nd Somersetshire) Regiment of Foot.
Memorial tablet: All Hallows Church, Tillington, Sussex. (Photograph)

SACRED TO THE MEMORY OF / LIEUT. JOHN AYLING, / OF THE 40TH REGT / SLAIN IN THE TRENCHES BEFORE BADAJOZ, / ON THE NIGHT OF THE 6TH APRIL 1812, / AGED 23 YEARS.

Ensign 10 Dec 1805. Lt Foot 9 Feb 1807.

Served in the Peninsula Aug 1808 – Apr 1812. Present at Rolica, Vimeiro, Talavera, Busaco, Redinha, first siege of Badajoz (wounded), and affairs near Badajoz 20 Jun 1811 (Mentioned in Despatches) and Badajoz where he was killed in the trenches before the assault 6 Apr 1812. He was found at the breach wounded in the thigh by Pte Charles Filer who carried him to seek medical help. During this journey a cannon ball took off his head which in the noise and confusion was unknown to Filer. Upon delivery Filer was asked why he carried in a corpse and declared, "that the Lieutenant had a head on when he took him up."

BABINGTON, John
Captain. 14th (Duchess of York's Own) Regiment of Light Dragoons.
Memorial: Highgate Cemetery, London. (Photograph)

.... / ALSO IN MEMORY OF / LIEUT.-COLONEL BABINGTON, / LATE OF THE 14TH L^T DRAGOONS, / HUSBAND OF THE ABOVE, / WHO DEPARTED THIS LIFE ON THE / 1ST OF JANUARY, 1848, AGED 70. / HE HAD SERVED WITH THAT REGIMENT / THROUGHOUT HIS WHOLE CAREER, / FIRST IN THE EXPEDITION TO QUIBERON BAY, / AND THE ISLE OF DIEU IN THE COAST OF / LA VENDÉE IN 1795, / HE WAS SUBSEQUENTLY TWO YEARS IN / ST DOMINGO AFTER ITS REVOLT FROM THE FRENCH. / HE SERVED IN THE PENINSULA AND / SOUTH OF FRANCE FROM 1808 TO MARCH, 1814, / INCLUDING THE PASSAGE TO THE DOURO, / THE BATTLE OF TALAVERA, THE AFFAIR IN / FRONT OF CIUDAD RODRIGO, THE PASSAGE OF THE COA, / AND THE VARIOUS ACTIONS COVERING THE RETREAT / FROM ALMEIDA TO TORRES VEDRAS, THE BATTLE OF BUSACO, / AND IN ALL THE ACTIONS FROM SANTAREM TO THE / FRONTIERS OF SPAIN.

Pte 1795. Cornet 25 Jun 1802. Lt 19 Jul 1804. Capt 27 Dec 1809. Bt Major 21 Jun 1817. Bt Lt Colonel 10 Jan 1837.
     Served in the Peninsula Dec 1808 – Apr 1811 and Sep 1813 – Apr 1814. Present at Douro, Talavera, Sexmiro, Coa, Busaco, Sobral, Nivelle, Nive and Orthes (wounded and taken prisoner 14 Mar 1814 until Apr 1814). Also served at Quiberon Bay 1795 and the West Indies 1798 (present at St Domingo). Sailed for the West Indies en route to North America after Apr 1814. While there he was recalled to Europe on the news that Napoleon had escaped from Elba. By the time he reached Belgium the battle of Waterloo was over. MGS medal for Talavera, Busaco, Nivelle, Nive and Orthes. Retired on half pay 21 Mar 1822. REFERENCE: *Gentleman's Magazine, Feb 1848, p. 200. Annual Register, 1848, Appx, p. 200.*

BACKHOUSE, John William
1st Lieutenant. 95th Regiment of Foot.
Memorial tablet: St Leonard's Church, Deal, Kent. (North wall of chancel). (M.I.)

"SACRED TO THE MEMORY OF LIEUT J. W. BACKHOUSE / OF HIS MAJESTY'S 95TH OR RIFLE REGIMENT / ELDEST SON OF THE REV^D J. B. BACKHOUSE, A.M. / RECTOR OF THIS PARISH, BY SARAH HIS WIFE, / WHO AFTER SERVING THREE CAMPAIGNS / IN SPAIN AND PORTUGAL WAS WOUNDED IN THE / BATTLE BEFORE NEW ORLEANS IN / AMERICA / ON THE 8TH OF JANUARY 1815 AND DIED THE NEXT DAY / IN THE 21ST YEAR OF HIS AGE. / THIS GOOD YOUNG MAN AND GALLANT SOLDIER / FELL SINCERELY LAMENTED BY HIS FRIENDS / AND HIGHLY RESPECTED BY HIS BROTHER OFFICERS."

2nd Lt 9 May 1811. Lt 26 Aug 1813.
     Served in the Peninsula with 3rd Battalion Jul – Dec 1812 and May 1813 – Apr 1814. Present at Salamanca, Pyrenees, Vera, Bidassoa, Nivelle, Nive, Orthes, Tarbes and Toulouse. Also served in North America 1814–1815 where he was present at New Orleans, severely wounded and died of his wounds 8 Jan 1815.

BACON, Anthony

Lieutenant. 10th (Prince of Wales's Own) Regiment of Light Dragoons.
Headstone: Kensal Green Cemetery, London. (12759/22/3). (Photograph)

.... / ALSO HER FATHER / GENERAL ANTHONY BACON, / LATE 17TH LANCERS. / HE SERVED IN THE PENINSULA WITH THE 16TH / LIGHT DRAGOONS DURING THE YEARS 1813 AND 1814. / HE WAS PRESENT AT THE BATTLE OF THE PYRENEES, WITH / THE COVERING PARTY DURING THE SIEGE OF SAN SEBASTIAN, / AT THE DIFFERENT AFFAIRS ON THE BIDASSOA AND THE / PASSAGE OF THAT RIVER AT THE BATTLE OF THE NIVELLE, / THE ACTIONS OF 9TH 10TH 11TH 12TH AND 13TH DECEMBER / CONSEQUENT ON THE PASSAGE OF THE NIVE AND AT THE / PASSAGE OF THE ADOUR. HE WAS AWARDED THE WAR MEDAL / WITH TWO CLASPS. IN THE CAMPAIGN OF 1815. HE SERVED / WITH THE 10TH HUSSARS AT THE BATTLE OF QUATRE BRAS / RETREAT ON THE 17TH JUNE AND BATTLE OF WATERLOO / IN WHICH HE HAD TWO HORSES SHOT UNDER HIM AND WAS / SEVERELY WOUNDED IN THE LAST CHARGE. IN 1832 HE / WAS APPOINTED TO THE COMMAND OF THE PORTUGUESE / CAVALRY AND WAS PROMOTED TO THE RANK OF GENERAL / OFFICER UPON THE FIELD BY SWORD IN 1833 BY THE / EMPEROR DON PEDRO IN PERSON FOR SPECIAL SERVICES. / HE WAS CREATED A KNIGHT COMMANDER OF THE TOWER / AND SWORD AND AWARDED THE PORTUGUESE CROSS. / HE DIED 2 JULY 1864 AGED 68 YEARS. / ....

Cornet 16th Lt Dragoons 13 Aug 1812. Lt 11 Mar 1813. Lt 10th Lt Dragoons 9 Feb 1815. Lt 13th Lt Dragoons 5 Nov 1818. Capt 11 Oct 1821. Capt 94th Foot 1 Dec 1823. Major 31 Dec 1825 (unattached). Major 17th Lancers 8 Apr 1826.

   Served in the Peninsula with 16th Lt Dragoons Aug 1813 – Apr 1814. Present at Nivelle, Nive and Bayonne. MGS medal for Nivelle and Nive. Present at Waterloo with 10th Lt Dragoons. He was badly wounded in the final charge led by Major Hon. Frederick Howard and lay all night on the field of battle. Lord Anglesey regarded him as the best cavalry officer that he had ever known. Also served in India 1818–1821 with 13th Lt Dragoons and Gibraltar 1823 with 94th Foot. Retired 31 Dec 1827. Served in the Portuguese Army 1832–1833 and was Colonel Commandant of their cavalry. Promoted to General 12 Oct 1833 by the Emperor Don Pedro at the battle of Loures. KTS.
REFERENCE: Boger, A. T., The story of General Bacon; being a short biography of a Peninsular and Waterloo veteran, 1903. Gentleman's Magazine, Aug 1864, p. 261. United Service Magazine, Aug 1864, p. 596.

BADDELEY, Benjamin

Private. 23rd (Royal Welch Fusiliers) Regiment of Foot.
Headstone: Leigh Cemetery, Lancashire. (Photograph)

OF YOUR CHARITY PRAY FOR THE SOUL / OF / BENJAMIN BADDELEY, / WHO DIED APRIL 12TH 1873, AGED 79 YEARS. / HE FOUGHT THE BATTLES OF HIS COUNTRY AT / VITTORIA, PYRENEES, NIVELLE, NIVE, / ORTHES, PAMPELUNA, TOULOUSE, / CAMBRAY AND WATERLOO. / ....

Pte 21 Nov 1811. Cpl 18 Jul 1818. Pte Oct 1818 (reduction in rank owing to his desertion from Oct 1818 – Apr 1819).

   Served in the Peninsula 1812 – Apr 1814. Present at Vittoria, Pyrenees, Nivelle, Nive, Orthes and Toulouse. Present at Waterloo, siege of Cambrai and with the Army of Occupation. Also served in Gibraltar and West Indies. Retired from the army 10 Jul 1833. MGS medal for Vittoria, Pyrenees, Nivelle, Nive, Orthes and Toulouse. After he left the army became a railway station master.

BADDELEY, Frederick Henry
Lieutenant. Royal Engineers.
Named on the Regimental Memorial: Rochester Cathedral, Rochester, Kent. (Photograph)

2nd Lt 1 Jan 1814. Lt 1 Aug 1814. 2nd Capt 25 Jun 1835. Capt 23 Nov 1841. Bt Major 9 Nov 1846. Lt Colonel 6 Sep 1849. Bt Colonel 28 Nov 1854. Colonel 21 May 1855. Major General 10 Jun 1856.
   Served in the Netherlands and France with the Army of Occupation 1815–1816. Retired on full pay 10 Jun 1850. Died in Jersey 4 May 1879.

BAILEY, Morris William
Major. 30th (Cambridgeshire) Regiment of Foot.
Memorial tablet: St Stephen's Church, Charlton Musgrove, Somerset. (Photograph)

TO THE / DEAR AND HONOURABLE MEMORY OF / L. COL MORRIS WILLIAM BAILEY, / COMPANION OF / THE MOST HONOURABLE ORDER OF THE BATH, / LATE OF HER MAJESTY'S 30TH REGIMENT OF FOOT, / AND MAGISTRATE / FOR THE COUNTY OF SOMERSET, / WHO DIED ON THE MORNING OF THE 28TH NOVR 1845, / AGED 65. / DEEPLY LAMENTED BY THOSE HE HAS LEFT / TO DEPLORE HIS IRREPARABLE LOSS, / AND EQUALLY ESTEEMED AND RESPECTED IN HIS / PROFESSIONAL, AS WELL AS HIS DOMESTIC CAREER. / IN ADDITION TO THE SERVICE RENDERED TO / HIS COUNTRY IN ALMOST EVERY QUARTER OF THE / GLOBE, HE COMMANDED HIS REGT, / AT THE MEMORABLE BATTLE OF WATERLOO, / AND WAS SEVERELY WOUNDED / AT THE CLOSE OF THAT EVENTFUL CONFLICT. / TO THOSE WHO SURVIVE HIM MAY GOD IN HIS MERCY / VOUCHSAFE A HAPPY MEETING IN HEAVEN / THROUGH THE MERITS OF OUR SAVIOUR / JESUS CHRIST.

Lt 10th Foot 11 Sep 1795. Capt 21 Feb 1798. Major Meuron's Regiment 17 Jan 1809. Major 30th Foot 25 Jul 1811. Bt Lt Colonel 4 Jun 1814. Major 80th Foot 25 Dec 1817. Lt Colonel 64th Foot 26 Oct 1820.
   Present at Quatre Bras and Waterloo. At Quatre Bras the commanding officer of the 30th, Lt Colonel Hamilton was severely wounded, so Bailey, then a Bt Lt Colonel took command of the regiment. He, himself, was severely wounded at the end of the Battle of Waterloo, but continued to the Capture of Paris and the Army of Occupation. CB.
   Also served in India 1798 (extra ADC to Governor General Lord Wellesley), Egypt 1801, Malta, Gibraltar and the Netherlands 1814–1815. Retired in 1822 and devoted his time to magisterial duties.
REFERENCE: *Gentleman's Magazine, Feb 1846, p. 210. Annual Register, 1845, Appx, p. 318.*

BAILLIE, Mackay Hugh
Lieutenant. 43rd (Monmouthshire) Light Infantry Regiment of Foot.
Named on the Memorial: St Andrew's Church, (now Musée Historique), Biarritz, France. (Photograph)

Ensign 9 Nov 1809. Lt 18 Jul 1811.
   Served in the Peninsula with the 1/43rd Jul 1810 – Dec 1812 and Aug – Nov 1813. Present at Coa, Busaco, Pombal, Redinha, Foz d'Arouce, Casal Nova, Sabugal, Fuentes d'Onoro, Ciudad Rodrigo, Badajoz (severely wounded), Salamanca, San Munos (wounded), Vittoria, Pyrenees, Bidassoa and Nivelle. Killed at Arcangues in the action before Bayonne 23 Nov 1813.

BAIN, William
Ensign. 33rd (1st Yorkshire West Riding) Regiment of Foot.
Grave: New Calton Burial Ground, (Grave 406 stone placed under no 405), Edinburgh, Scotland. (Photograph of site of grave). (M.I.)

"ERECTED BY STAFF SURGEON DAVID BAIN MD TO HIS UNCLE LT WM BAIN, LATE OF 33RD

REGT. HE WAS SEVERELY WOUNDED AT BATTLE OF WATERLOO AND DIED AT EDINBURGH 23 JUNE 1860 AGED 66."

Ensign 22 Apr 1813. Lt 14 Aug 1815. Present at Waterloo where he was severely wounded and awarded pension of £70 per annum. Half pay 25 Mar 1817.

BAINBRIGGE, John Hankey
Captain. 41st Regiment of Foot.
Monument: St Andrew's Churchyard, St Andrew, Guernsey, Channel Islands. (Photograph)

IN MEMORY OF GENERAL JOHN HANKEY BAINBRIGGE / WHO DIED AT HIS RESIDENCE ROHAIS MANOR ON THE 15TH MARCH 1881, / IN THE 90TH YEAR OF HIS AGE. HE LOST HIS LEFT ARM IN THE PENIN – / SULAR WAR: RECEIVING THE WAR MEDAL WITH CLASPS FOR VIMIERO, / CORUNNA, VITTORIA AND PYRENEES TOGETHER WITH THE / REWARD FOR DISTINGUISHED AND MERITORIOUS SERVICE.

Ensign 20th Foot 25 Mar 1808. Lt 9 Mar 1809. Capt 41st Foot 9 Dec 1813. Bt Major 10 Jan 1837. Bt Lt Colonel 20 Oct 1846. Bt Colonel 20 Jun 1854. Major General 16 Aug 1861. Lt General 22 Oct 1870. General 1 Oct 1877.
   Served in the Peninsula Aug 1808 – Jan 1809 and Nov 1812 – Sep 1813. Present at Vimeiro, Corunna, Vittoria and Pyrenees (severely wounded at Sorauren – twice wounded, lost his left arm and awarded pension of £100 per annum). MGS medal for Vimeiro, Corunna, Vittoria and Pyrenees. Also served at Walcheren 1809. Fort Major and Adjutant of Guernsey. Retired in 1861. Younger brother of Major Philip Bainbrigge AQMG.

BAINBRIGGE, Philip
Major. Permanent Assistant Quartermaster General.
Grave: St Peter's Churchyard, Titchfield, Hampshire. (Section E 51). (M.I.)

"IN MEMORY OF GENERAL SIR PHILIP BAINBRIGGE KCB WHO SERVED WITH DISTINCTION DURING THE PENINSULAR WAR AND WAS COMMANDER OF THE FORCES IN CEYLON. HE DIED AT THE PARISH OF ST MARGARET'S 20TH DECEMBER 1862 AGED 76."

Memorial tablet: St Peter's Church, Titchfield, Hampshire. (In Chancel). (M.I.)

"ERECTED TO THE GLORY OF GOD AND IN MEMORY OF GENERAL SIR PHILIP BAINBRIGGE KCB WHO DIED DECEMBER 20TH 1862 AGED 76. ...."

Midshipman in Royal Navy 1799. Ensign 20th Foot 30 Jun 1800. Lt 13 Nov 1800. Lt 7th Foot 1803. Capt 18th Foot 17 Oct 1805. Capt 93rd Foot 4 Jun 1807. Major and Permanent AQMG 15 Oct 1812. Bt Lt Colonel 21 Jun 1817. Lt Colonel Staff 2 Aug 1827. Bt Colonel 10 Jun 1837. Major General 9 Nov 1846. Lt General 20 Jun 1854. General 24 Aug 1861.
   Served in the Peninsula Oct 1810 – Dec 1812 (on Staff as DAQMG) and Jan 1813 – Apr 1814 (AQMG). Present at Olivencia, Ciudad Rodrigo, Badajoz, Castrejon, siege of Salamanca Forts, Salamanca, Burgos and retreat from Burgos, Villa Muriel, Vittoria, Pyrenees, Nive, Garris, Tarbes, Vic Bigorre and Toulouse. Returned to France in 1815 and joined the Army in the advance on Paris (organised the Army of Occupation). Also served in Malta 1801, West Indies 1805 (Inspector of Fortifications), Ireland 1841 (DQMG), Ceylon 1852–1854 (in command of the Forces there).
   His father, commanding the 20th Foot, was killed at Egmont-op-Zee 1799 and Philip was given a commission in the Army as Ensign in the 20th Foot. As he was only 14 years old he was given a year's absence and joined in 1801. During his service in the West Indies in 1805 he made plans of forts and

defences and in 1809 was advised to go the Royal Military College at High Wycombe. He passed all the examinations with distinction, even inventing a Protracting Pocket Sextant, which he used to make surveys more accurate.

In 1810 went to Portugal on the Staff, employed in sketching the ground and reporting on positions. Wellington used him to sketch out the ground at Salamanca for the forthcoming battle. These sketches were made in 2½ hours with enemy skirmishers in the vicinity. Present at the siege of Burgos and assisted in the retreat having made a careful study of the countryside. Did not receive any awards at the end of the War. As he had worked under senior officers at Headquarters he did not qualify for a Gold Medal and therefore not eligible for a CB. However he was rewarded in 1838 with a CB and KCB 1860. MGS medal for Ciudad Rodrigo, Badajoz, Salamanca, Vittoria, Pyrenees, Nive and Toulouse.

Philip Bainbrigge was one of the officers who benefited from going to the Royal Military College. He proved the advantage of having a scientifically trained mind to carry out Staff duties. He was a highly talented man and Wellington acknowledged this even in 1811. Colonel 26th Cameronian Regt 1854. Elder brother of Capt John Hankey Bainbrigge 41st Foot.

REFERENCE: *Royal Military Calendar, Vol 5, p 134. Gentleman's Magazine, Feb 1863, pp. 237–238. United Service Magazine, Feb 1863, pp. 271–4.*

BAIRD, Sir David
Colonel. 24th (Warwickshire) Regiment of Foot.
Obelisk: Summit of Tom a'Chasteil, near Crieff, Perthshire, Scotland. (Photograph)

IN HONOUR AND TO THE MEMORY OF / GENERAL SIR DAVID BAIRD, / BARᵀ, G.C.B. & K.C., / THIS COLUMN WAS ERECTED / A.D. 1832. / TO THE INDOMITABLE COURAGE IN THE FIELD / HE UNITED / WISDOM AND PRUDENCE / IN THE COUNCIL. / A BRAVE BUT GENEROUS ENEMY, / HIS VICTORIES WERE EVER TEMPERED BY MERCY: / AND WITH HIS ARDENT LOVE OF GLORY / WAS BLENDED / THE TENDEREST CARE FOR HIS GALLANT AND DEVOTED FOLLOWERS. / THE DETAILS OF HIS PUBLIC SERVICE ARE RECORDED / IN THE ANNALS OF HIS COUNTRY. / HIS PRIVATE VIRTUES ARE EMBALMED IN THE HEARTS OF HIS FRIENDS. / HONOUR AND DUTY WERE THE GUIDING STARS OF HIS DESTINY: / PIETY AND CHARITY THE LEADING CHARACTERISTICS OF HIS MIND. / HE FELT NO JEALOUSIES HE HARBOURED NO RESENTMENTS. / HE KNEW NO GUILE. / IN THE LAND OF HIS FATHERS / HE AT LAST FOUND / REPOSE AND HAPPINESS IN DOMESTIC LIFE: / FORGETTING THE CARES AND TURMOILS OF HIS EVENTFUL & BRILLIANT CAREER, / AND IN THE EXERCISE OF EVERY SOCIAL AND CHRISTIAN VIRTUE / HE DIED BELOVED AND LAMENTED, / AS HE HAD LIVED / HONOURED AND RENOWNED.

Memorial tablet, Parish Church, Crieff, Perthshire, Scotland. (Photograph)

TO THE MEMORY / OF / GENERAL, THE RIGHT HON. / SIR DAVID BAIRD, BARᵀ, G.C.B., K.C., / THIS TABLET / IS GRATEFULLY INSCRIBED BY THE INHABITANTS OF THE / PARISH OF CRIEFF AND ITS NEIGHBOURHOOD, / NOT TO COMMEMORATE HIS MARTIAL ACHIEVE-MENTS, FOR / THESE ARE RECORDED IN THE / ANNALS OF HIS COUNTRY, / BUT AS THEIR HUMBLE TESTIMONY TO THOSE EXCELLENCES IN / HIS CHARACTER, WHICH THEY DESIRE TO SEE HANDED DOWN TO / POSTERITY, AND WHICH WILL BE HELD IN REMEMBRANCE, / "IF THERE BE ANY VIRTUE, OR ANY PRAISE IN THINGS / "THAT ARE TRUE, AND HONEST, AND JUST, AND PURE, / "AND LOVELY AND OF GOOD REPORT." / IN HIM THE STERNER VIRTUES OF UPRIGHTNESS AND / UNBENDING INTEGRITY WERE BLENDED WITH ALL THE / CHARITIES OF THE KINDLIEST AND MOST GENEROUS NATURE. / "HE WAS THE FATHER OF THE POOR, AND THE CAUSE / "WHICH HE KNEW NOT HE SEARCHED OUT." / NOR WAS THE DISINTERESTEDNESS OF HIS BENEVOLENCE / MORE SINCERE THAN HIS RESPECT FOR RELIGION AND ITS / ORDINANCES: AND TO HIS INCREASING EXERTIONS ARE THIS /

CONGREGATION CHIEFLY INDEBTED FOR THE COMFORT AND / ACCOMMODATION WHICH THEY ENJOY, IN HAVING NOW A FIT / TEMPLE IN WHICH TO WORSHIP THE GOD OF THEIR FATHERS. / OB. AUG. 18, 1829. / REMOVED FROM OLD CHURCH 1862.

Ensign 2nd Foot 16 Dec 1772. Lt 10 Mar 1778. Capt 73rd Foot 24 Sep 1778. (In 1785 the 73rd Regiment became the 71st Regiment). Major 71st Foot 5 Jun 1787. Lt Colonel 8 Dec 1790. Major General 18 Jun 1798. Lt General 30 Oct 1805. General 4 Jun 1814.

Served in the Peninsula Oct 1808 – Jan 1809. Present in the Corunna campaign (second in Command to Sir John Moore. Baird was wounded, lost an arm and awarded pension of £450 per annum). Gold Medal for Corunna. Also served in India 1779–1784 (present at battle of Perimbancum. Wounded and taken prisoner by Hyder Ali for three and a half years, chained to another prisoner). Released Mar 1784. Returned to India 1791 (present at the reduction of the hill forts of Mysore), Cape of Good Hope 1797–1798. Returned to India again in 1799 (led the storming party at Seringapatam – death of Tippoo Sultan).

Baird felt that he should have been made Governor of Seringapatam but Arthur Wellesley was chosen instead. Baird led the forces from India across the desert to reach the Nile to help Abercromby in Egypt 1801. Returned across the desert to India but on his return found that the future Duke of Wellington was in command of the greater part of the Army and so he obtained permission to return to Britain. Was very popular with his men in India and Egypt. KCB 4 May 1801.

Also served at the Cape of Good Hope 1805 and Copenhagen 1807 (wounded). Governor of Kinsale 1819. Commander of Forces in Ireland 1820. Governor of Fort George 1829. Colonel 54th Foot 8 May 1801. Colonel 24th Foot 19 Jul 1807. Died 18 Aug 1829 and buried at Culcross. Uncle of Capt and Lt Colonel Hon Alexander Gordon 3rd Foot Guards, Capt James Baird 66th Foot and Capt Patrick Baird 77th Foot.

REFERENCE: *Dictionary of National Biography. Gentleman's Magazine, Sep 1829, pp. 271–4. Haley, A. H., Our Davy: General Sir David Baird, K. B., 1757–1829, 1849. Hook, Theodore Edward, Life of Sir David Baird, 2 vols, 1832. Wilkin, Walter Howard, Life of Sir David Baird, George Allen, 1912. Cole, John William, Memoirs of British Generals, Vol 1, 1856, pp. 61–106.*

BAIRD, James
Captain. 66th (Berkshire) Regiment.
Obelisk: Holy Rood Churchyard, Stirling, Stirlingshire, Scotland. (Photograph)

LT COLONEL JAMES BAIRD / LATE OF 66TH REGT / WHO DIED 5TH SEPT 1848 / AGED 70 YEARS.

Ensign 17 May 1798. Lt 17 Sep 1800. Capt 14 Jul 1806. Bt Major 12 Aug 1819. Major 13 Jan 1825. Bt Lt Colonel 10 Jan 1837.

Served in the Peninsula Nov 1808 – Jan 1809 and Jun – Aug 1810 (ADC to his uncle Sir David Baird). Present at Corunna. Brother of Capt Patrick Baird 77th Foot and nephew of Colonel Sir David Baird 24th Foot.

BAIRD, Patrick
Captain. 77th (East Middlesex) Regiment of Foot.
Obelisk: Holy Rood Churchyard, Stirling, Stirlingshire, Scotland. (Photograph)

.... / MAJOR PATRICK BAIRD / LATE OF 77TH REGT / WHO DIED 21ST / OCTR 1842 / AGED 61 YEARS.

Ensign 22 Jan 1801. Lt 22 Sep 1803. Capt 6 Jun 1811. Major 13 Aug 1822.

Served in the Peninsula Jul 1811 – Jan 1812. Present at Ciudad Rodrigo (severely wounded). Also served at Walcheren 1809. Brother of Capt James Baird 66th Foot and nephew of Colonel Sir David Baird 24th Foot.

BAIRD, William

Quartermaster. 59th (2nd Nottinghamshire) Regiment of Foot.
Named on the Regimental Memorial monument: Christ Church Churchyard, Tramore, County Waterford, Ireland. (Photograph)

Quartermaster 31 May 1810.
    Served in the Peninsula with 2nd Battalion Sep 1812 – Apr 1814. Present at Cadiz, Vittoria, San Sebastian and Bayonne. Present at Waterloo in the reserve at Hal, siege of Cambrai and the Army of Occupation. Drowned with his wife and children when the *Sea Horse* transport was wrecked in a storm in Tramore Bay off the coast of Ireland 30 Jan 1816.

BAIRD, William

Sergeant. 12th (Prince of Wales's) Regiment of Light Dragoons.
Named on the Regimental Memorial: St Joseph's Church, Waterloo, Belgium. (Photograph)
    Killed at Waterloo.

BAKER, James Harrison

Captain. 34th (Cumberland) Regiment of Foot.
Memorial tablet: St Agnes' Church, Cawston, Norfolk. (North wall of chancel). (Photograph)

WATCH / AND PRAY / TO THE MEMORY OF / JAMES HARRISON BAKER / MAJOR OF THE 34TH REGIMENT. / SECOND SON OF RICHARD BAKER D.D. RECTOR OF THIS PARISH / AND ELIZABETH HIS WIFE / WHO FELL IN THE BATTLE OF TOULOUSE ON THE 10TH APRIL, 1814 / AS HE WAS GALLANTLY LEADING IN HIS REGIMENT INTO AN INTRENCHMENT / IN THE 33RD YEAR OF HIS AGE. / THE EXCELLENT CONDUCT OF THIS DESERVING OFFICER DURING 16 YEARS / SERVICE IN JERSEY THE CAPE AND INDIA ALWAYS GAINED HIM / THE COMMENDATION OF HIS SUPERIORS AND IN THE PENINSULA / HIS COURAGE – ENTERPRISE AND ABILITY WERE SO CONSPICUOUS / THAT THEY WERE ACKNOWLEDGED AND RECORDED. / HE LIVED 28 HOURS TO HEAR OF THE GLORIOUS DELIVERANCE OF / EUROPE FROM A DESOLATING AND DEGRADING TYRANNY. / NOR WAS HE LESS DISTINGUISHED IN PRIVATE LIFE FOR HIS / AMIABLE AND ATTRACTIVE VIRTUES. MODEST, HUMBLE, GENTLE. / HIS FEELING HEART AND ACTIVE HAND WERE EVER READY FOR THE / SERVICE OF THOSE IN EVERY STATION WITH WHOM HE LIVED.

Memorial tablet: St Mary's Church, Bury St Edmunds, Suffolk. (M.I.)

"SACRED TO THE MEMORY OF JAMES HARRISON BAKER, MAJOR IN THE 34TH REGIMENT OF FOOT, SECOND SON OF THE REV. RICHARD BAKER, D. D., OF CAWSTON, IN THE COUNTY OF NORFOLK, AND ELIZABETH, HIS WIFE. THIS AMIABLE AND SPIRITED YOUNG OFFICER RECEIVED A MORTAL WOUND AT THE BATTLE OF TOULOUSE, APRIL 10, 1814, AND EXPIRED THE FOLLOWING DAY, IN THE 33RD YEAR OF HIS AGE. THE GALLANTRY, ACTIVE ZEAL, AND COOL COURAGE WHICH HE DISPLAYED IN THIS LAST ACTION WITH THE ENEMY ATTRACTED THE PARTICULAR NOTICE OF HIS COMMANDING OFFICERS, EXPRESSED BY HIGH COMMENDATIONS OF HIS MANLY AND GALLANT CONDUCT ON THE MEMORABLE OCCASION. IN PRIVATE LIFE HE WAS DESERVEDLY ESTEEMED FOR THE ESTIMABLE QUALITIES OF THE FRIEND AND CHRISTIAN. THIS TABLET WAS ERECTED BY HIS MATERNAL UNCLE, JAMES OAKES, ESQ, IN TESTIMONY OF HIS SINCERE REGARD AND AFFECTION".

Named on the Memorial: St Andrew's Church, (now Musée Historique), Biarritz, France. (Photograph)

Ensign 66th Foot 6 Feb 1798. Lt 34th Foot 10 Mar 1798. Capt 8 Jul 1806. Bt Major 10 Mar 1814.

Served in the Peninsula Dec 1812 – Apr 1814. Present at Pyrenees, Nivelle, Nive, Orthes and Toulouse where he was wounded 10 Apr 1814 and died of his wounds 11 Apr 1814. Also served in Jersey, Cape of Good Hope 1805 and India 1806.

BALDWIN, George
Lieutenant. 14th (Buckinghamshire) Regiment of Foot.
Grave: Civil Cemetery, Ferozepore, India. (M.I.)

Named on the Monument to the Fallen, Ferozepore, India (M.I.)

"IN MEMORY OF THE FOLLOWING OFFICERS OF H. M. 31ST REGIMENT / WHO FELL IN THE ACTIONS OF MOODKIE, FEROZESHAH AND SOBRAON, / DURING THE CAMPAIGN AGAINST THE SIKHS IN THE YEARS 1845 – 46 / AND WHO ARE INTERRED AT OR NEAR THIS SPOT. / MAJOR GEORGE BALDWIN, 21ST DEC^R 1845. / ...."

Ensign 36th Foot 2 Jun 1808. 2nd Lt 3rd Ceylon Regt 4 Apr 1811. Lt 14th Foot 9 Nov 1814. Lt 75th Foot 19 Oct 1820. Lt 31st Foot 14 Mar 1822. Capt 14 Jun 1833. Bt Major 23 Dec 1842 Major 31st Foot 8 Oct 1844.

Served with 3/14th Foot at Waterloo, siege of Cambrai, the Capture of Paris and with the Army of Occupation. Also served at Walcheren 1809 (present with 36th Foot at siege of Flushing), Malta and Ionian Islands 1816–1817 and Ireland 1822–1824. Returned to England 1825 for embarkation for India on board the *Kent* and was present on 1 March when the vessel caught fire and sank in the Bay of Biscay. Baldwin was one of the few survivors, but severely injured so did not arrive in India until 1826.

Also served in India and Afghanistan 1826–1845 (present with the relief column in 1842 after the first invasion of Afghanistan). Awarded Brevet Majority and medal (present at Mazina, Jagdalak and Tezin). Also present in the first Sikh War Dec 1845 (present at Mudki, and three days later at the battle of Ferozeshah 21 Dec where he was severely wounded and died from his wounds at Ferozepore 30 Dec 1845).
REFERENCE: *Gentleman's Magazine, May 1846, p. 538.*

BALE, John
Private. 40th (2nd Somersetshire) Regiment of Foot.
Headstone: St Andrew's Churchyard, Wiveliscombe, Somerset. (South side of Church, Section D, Grave number 174). (Photograph)

IN LOVING MEMORY OF / OUR DEAR FATHER / JOHN BALE, / (WHO FOUGHT IN THE BATTLE OF WATERLOO) / DIED DECEMBER 8TH 1861, AGED 72 YEARS. / ....

Pte 10 Dec 1813.
Served at Waterloo in Captain S. Stretton's Company. Also served in North America, Australia (New South Wales and Van Diemen's Land) and India. Discharged 30 Nov 1831.

BALFOUR, William
Major. 40th (2nd Somersetshire) Regiment of Foot.
Interred in Catacomb A 1322 (v15 c4) Kensal Green Cemetery, London.

Ensign Hanger's Recruiting Corps 31 Aug 1798. Ensign 40th Foot 25 Jul 1799. Lt 8 Aug 1800. Capt 22 Sep 1804. Major 4 Feb 1808. Bt Lt Colonel 12 Apr 1814. Major 3rd Foot 8 Jul 1819. Major 40th Foot 22 Jun 1820. Lt Colonel 82nd Foot 17 Jan 1829.

Served in the Peninsula with 1/40th Oct 1813 – Apr 1814. Present at Nivelle (commanded the 40th Foot), Nive, Orthes and Toulouse. Gold Medal for Nivelle. Also served at the Helder 1799, Copenhagen 1807

(ADC to Major General Brent Spencer), Ireland 1808 and Mauritius 1827–1833. Half pay 1814–1817. In 1820 went with 40th Regt to Australia until 1827. On his return to England he joined the 82nd Regt, serving in Mauritius (commandant of Port Louis). Retired in 1833. Died 10 Feb 1838.
REFERENCE: *Dictionary of National Biography. Australian Dictionary of Biography. Gentleman's Magazine, Jun 1838, p. 661.*

BALL, James
Sergeant. 51st (2nd Yorkshire West Riding) Light Infantry.
Named on the Regimental Memorial: KOYLI Chapel, York Minster, Yorkshire. (Photograph)
   Killed in the Peninsula.

BALLER, George
Sergeant. 95th Regiment of Foot.
Ledger stone: Brompton Cemetery, London. (Photograph)

COLOUR SERGEANT / GEORGE BALLER / 1ST BATTALION / 95TH REGIMENT OF FOOT / RIFLES / 1787 – 1868 / A GALLANT RIFLEMAN OF / THE PENINSULAR CAMPAIGN / AND WATERLOO

Pte 12 May 1809. Cpl 1811. Sgt 1813.
   Served in the Peninsula. Present at Almeida (wounded and taken prisoner, escorted to Vittoria, escaped from prison and joined the guerrillas. Severely wounded in a fight with French but managed to get to Gibraltar, sailed for Portugal and rejoined his regiment), Fuentes d'Onoro, Ciudad Rodrigo, Badajoz and Salamanca. Returned to England 1812. Present at Quatre Bras (wounded) and Waterloo in Capt F. Glass's Company where he was wounded. Also served in the Netherlands 1814–1815 (present at Merxem where he was wounded). Discharged 25 May 1816. MGS medal for Fuentes d'Onoro, Ciudad Rodrigo, Badajoz and Salamanca. Chelsea pensioner.
   Buried in a common grave at Brompton Cemetery 14 Jul 1868. Memorial erected and dedicated 14 Jul 2007.

BALVAIRD, William
Major. 95th Regiment of Foot.
Family Headstone: St Mary's Churchyard, Tibbermore, Perthshire, Scotland. (Grave number 84 – on path). (Photograph)

IN MEMORIAM / .... / COLONEL WILLIAM BALVAIRD KCB. / DIED 6TH FEBRUARY 1853 AGED 78.

Ensign 94th Foot 24 Mar 1803. Lt 78th Foot 17 Apr 1804. Capt 100th Foot 16 May 1805. Capt 95th Foot 15 Aug 1805. Bt Major 22 Nov 1813. Major 21 Jul 1814. Bt Lt Colonel 21 Jun 1817. Major 99th Foot 25 Mar 1824. Bt Colonel 10 Jan 1837. Lt Colonel 37th Foot 27 Aug 1841.
   Served in the Peninsula with 1/95th Jul 1809 – Oct 1812 and 3/95th Jul 1813 – Apr 1814. Present at Coa, Busaco, Pombal, Redinha, Casal Nova, Foz d'Arouce, Sabugal, Fuentes d'Onoro, Ciudad Rodrigo, Badajoz (severely wounded), Salamanca, Pyrenees, Vera, Bidassoa, Nivelle and Nive. Gold Medal for Nivelle and Nive. MGS medal for Busaco, Fuentes d'Onoro, Ciudad Rodrigo, Badajoz, Salamanca and Pyrenees. CB. Retired 29 Aug 1841.

BAMBRICK, Robert
Private. 11th Regiment of Light Dragoons.
Memorial tablet: St Michael and St George Cathedral, Grahamstown, South Africa. (Photograph)

SACRED / TO THE MEMORY OF / CAPTAIN ROBERT BAMBRICK, / 7TH DRAGOON GUARDS,

AGED 48 YEARS / WHO FELL IN ACTION WITH THE KAFFIRS NEAR BURNSHILL, / 16TH APRIL 1846. / SERVICES (WITH 11TH LIGHT DRAGOONS) / "WATERLOO" "BHURTPORE." / THIS TABLET HAS BEEN ERECTED / BY HIS BROTHER OFFICERS, / IN TOKEN OF THEIR ESTEEM AND REGRET.

Note: The three words 'WITH THE KAFFIRS' have been erased from the memorial tablet.

Private Aug 1814. Sgt Jun 1815. Commissioned from the ranks 1820. Cornet 11th Lt Dragoons 14 Dec 1820. Lt 12 Oct 1825. Riding Master 1833–1843. Capt 7th Dragoon Guards 25 Feb 1843.

Present at Waterloo with 11th Lt Dragoons in Capt J. A. Schreiber's Troop (promoted to Sergeant for his bravery). Also served in India (present at the siege and capture of Bhurtpore 1825–1826) and Cape of Good Hope with 7th Dragoon Guards 1843–1846 (present in the Kaffir War of 1846 (War of the Axe). The camp at Burns Hill had been attacked by Kaffirs who captured the cattle. Cavalry was sent out under Capt Bambrick to retrieve them. However they were attacked with such force that the soldiers had to retreat without the cattle, but not before Capt Bambrick had been killed. He is buried at the Burn's Hill mission station with Capt John Sands of the Cape Mounted Riflemen).
REFERENCE: *Tambling, Victor R. S., The Bambrick brothers. Waterloo Journal, Aug 1999, pp. 27–8.*

BARCLAY, Delancey

Captain and Lieutenant Colonel. 1st Regiment of Foot Guards.
Memorial tablet: St John's Church, Wooton, Surrey. (South side of Chancel). Inscription from Memorial Inscription record. (Photograph)

"SACRED TO THE MEMORY OF COLONEL DELANCEY BARCLAY C.B. OF THE GRENADIER GUARDS, MANY YEARS AIDE DE CAMP TO HRH DUKE OF YORK, AND SUBSEQUENTLY TO HRH KING GEORGE IV. HE WAS SECOND SON OF COLONEL THOMAS BARCLAY; AND HAVING EARLY ENTERED THE ARMY, HE RECOMMENDED HIMSELF BY SERVICES AND CONDUCT TO THE ABOVE HONOURABLE RANK AND APPOINTMENT AND TWICE ENTERED PARIS WITH THE ALLIED FORCES IN 1814, AND AGAIN AS ASST ADJUTANT GEN. TO THE ARMY UNDER THE DUKE OF WELLINGTON IN 1815; AFTER HAVING SHARED WITH DISTINCTION IN THE DANGERS AND HONORS IN THE FIELD OF WATERLOO. HE DIED ON THE 29TH MARCH, 1826, IN THE 46TH YEAR OF HIS AGE. HIS REMAINS REPOSE IN THE FAMILY VAULT OF ROBERT BARCLAY, ESQ., OF BURY HILL, OPPOSITE TO THE NORTH WEST ANGLE OF THIS CHURCH. "

Ensign 41st Foot 11 Jan 1800. Cornet 17th Dragoons 29 Aug 1801. Lt 9 Jul 1802. Capt 56th Foot 24 Apr 1805. Major Royal York Rangers 23 Aug 1810. Lt Col Royal Corsican Rangers 28 Feb 1812. Capt and Lt Colonel 1st Regt of Foot Guards 25 Jul 1814. Bt Colonel 29 May 1825.

Present at Waterloo (AAG). For many years ADC to Duke of York and George IV. Also served in Flanders. CB.
REFERENCE: *Gentleman's Magazine, May 1826, p. 465.*

BARING, Baron Georg von

Major. 2nd Battalion Light Infantry, King's German Legion.
Memorial: Waterloo Place, Hanover, Germany. (Photograph)

GEORG FREIHERR VON BARING / GEBOREN ZU HANNOVER DEN 8TEN MARZ 1773 / SEIT 1786 IN DER HANNÖVERISCHEN ARMEE / SPÄTET IN DER KÖNIGL: DEUTSCHEN LEGION / VERTHEIDIGER VON LA HAYE SAINTE / IN DER SCHLACHT VON WATERLOO / GESTORBEN ZU WIESBADEN ALS KÖNLGL: HANNÖVER: / GENERALLIEUTENANT DEN 27TEN FEBRUAR 1848.

Hanoverian Army from 1786. Capt 1st Battalion Lt Infantry King's German Legion 10 Nov 1803. Bt Major 21 Jun 1813. Major 2nd Battalion Lt Infantry 4 Apr 1814.

Served in the Peninsula Aug 1808 – Jan 1809 and Mar 1811 – Apr 1814 (ADC to Major General Charles Alten). Present at Vigo, Albuera (wounded), Ciudad Rodrigo, first siege of Badajoz, Salamanca, Vittoria, Pyrenees, Bidassoa, Nivelle, Nive, Orthes, Tarbes and Toulouse. Also served at Hanover 1805, Baltic 1807–1808, Walcheren 1809 and Netherlands 1814. Present at Waterloo (defender of La Haye Sainte Farm from 1.30pm until they ran out of ammunition around 6pm and had to abandon the farm. The battalion had nearly 50% casualties). CB. KH. Military Order of William of the Netherlands, King William's Cross of Hanover. Later became Major General in the Hanoverian Army and Commandant at Hanover.

BARKER, Collet
Lieutenant. 39th (Dorsetshire) Regiment of Foot.
Memorial tablet: St James's Church, Sydney, New South Wales, Australia. (Photograph)

SACRED / TO THE MEMORY OF, / CAPTAIN COLLET BARKER, / OF HER MAJESTY'S 39TH REGIMENT OF FOOT, / WHO WAS TREACHEROUSLY MURDERED BY / ABORIGINAL NATIVES, / ON THE 30TH APRIL 1851 / WHILE ENDEAVOURING IN THE PERFORMANCE OF HIS DUTY / TO ASCERTAIN THE COMMUNICATION BETWEEN / LAKE ALEXANDRINA AND THE GULF OF ST VINCENT / ON THE SOUTH WEST COAST OF NEW HOLLAND. / IN TOKEN OF ESTEEM FOR THE SINGULAR WORTH / AND IN AFFECTIONATE REMEMBRANCE OF THE MANY VIRTUES / OF THE DECEASED, / THIS TABLET IS ERECTED BY / COLONEL LINDSAY C. B. AND HIS BROTHER OFFICERS.

Obelisk: Mount Barker, South Australia, Australia. (Photograph)

ERECTED / TO THE MEMORY OF / CAPTAIN COLLET / BARKER / OF H.M. 39TH REGIMENT OF FOOT / WHO DISCOVERED THE DISTRICT AND / MOUNT WHICH BEARS HIS NAME. / HE WAS KILLED BY THE BLACKS ON THE / 30TH APRIL 1831 WHILE ENDEAVOURING / TO ASCERTAIN THE COMMUNICATION / BETWEEN LAKE ALEXANDRINA / AND ENCOUNTER BAY.

Ensign 23 Jan 1806. Lt 18 May 1809. Capt 16 Jun 1825.

Served in the Peninsula with 1/39th Jan 1812 – Apr 1814. Present at Vittoria, Pyrenees, Nivelle, Nive, Garris, Orthes, Aire and Toulouse. Also served in Sicily 1807–1811, North America 1814 and Ireland 1816. Went to Sydney Feb 1828 with the regiment and was appointed commandant of Fort Wellington settlement on Raffles Bay in the North of Australia. Took command of a penal settlement at King George Sound which closed in 1831 and returned to Sydney. In both settlements he improved conditions for the convicts and insisted on humane treatment for the Aborigines who began to trust him. Unfortunately while exploring part of South Australia in 1831 en route to a new posting in New Zealand, he met some hostile Aborigines who speared him to death.
REFERENCE: *Dictionary of National Biography. Australian Dictionary of Biography.*

BARKER, Robert
2nd Lieutenant. 95th Regiment of Foot.
Box tomb within railings: St Bride's Churchyard, Sanquhar, Dumfriesshire, Scotland. (Photograph)

.... / ALSO ROBERT BARKER, LATE CAPTAIN IN THE / 20TH REGIMENT OF FOOT WHO DIED HERE 23 FEB. / 1840, AGED 42 YEARS. / ....

2nd Lt 16 Sep 1813. Lt 20 Feb 1817. Lt 58th Foot 14 Jun 1821. Lt 20th Regt 10 Oct 1822. Capt 3 Jun 1835.

Served in the Peninsula Dec 1813 – Apr 1814 (aged 16). Present at Pyrenees, Nivelle, Nive and Orthes.

Served in France with the Army of Occupation. Also served in North America 1814–1815 (present at New Orleans where he was severely wounded and awarded pension of £50 per annum), and India with 20th Foot. Returned home on recruiting duties but retired 31 Dec 1839 owing to ill health and died a few weeks later.

BARLOW, James
Surgeon. 32nd (Cornwall) Regiment of Foot.
Headstone: Mount Jerome Cemetery, Dublin, Ireland. (Grave number C81 –1644). (Photograph)

IN MEMORY OF / JAMES BARLOW M.D / LATE SURGEON / 5TH DRAGOON GUARDS / WHO DIED / ON THE 3RD DAY OF OCTOBER 1852 / AGED 70 YEARS

Hospital Mate Jun 1803. Asst Surgeon 8th Foot 5 Mar 1807. Asst Surgeon 19th Lt Dragoons 11 Feb 1808. Surgeon 32nd Foot 29 Jul 1813. Surgeon 3rd Dragoons 12 Jun 1828. Surgeon 5th Dragoon Guards 18 Mar 1836.
  Present at Copenhagen 1807, Martinique 1809 and Netherlands 1814–1815. FRCS. MD Glasgow 1833. Retired 15 Mar 1850.

BARNARD, Sir Andrew Francis
Lieutenant Colonel. 95th Regiment of Foot.
Memorial window: Sir John Moore Library, Shorncliffe, Kent. (Photograph)

ANDREW BARNARD

Named on the Regimental Memorial: Winchester Cathedral, Winchester, Hampshire. (Photograph)

Buried in the Royal Hospital, Chelsea, London.

Ensign 90th Foot 26 Aug 1794. Lt 81st Foot 23 Sep 1794. Capt-Lieut 13 Nov 1794. Capt 29 Sep 1795. Capt 55th Foot 2 Dec 1795. Lt and Capt 1st Foot Guards 19 Dec 1799. Bt Major 1 Jan 1805. Major 7th West India Regt 2 Jan 1808. Lt Colonel on Staff as Inspecting Field Officer of Militia in Canada 28 Jan 1808. Lt Colonel 1st Foot 16 Dec 1808. Lt Colonel 95th Foot 29 Mar 1810. Bt Colonel 4 Jun 1813. Major General 12 Aug 1819. Colonel Commandant 1st Battalion Rifle Brigade 25 Aug 1822. Lt General 13 Jan 1837. General 11 Nov 1851.
  Served in the Peninsula with 3/95th Aug 1810 – May 1813, 1/95th May 1813 – Apr 1814. (Commanded 1 Brigade Lt Division Dec 1811 – Jan 1812 and Jul 1812 – May 1813. Commanded 2 Brigade Lt Division Feb – Apr 1814). Present at Cadiz, Barrosa (severely wounded and Mentioned in Despatches), Ciudad Rodrigo (Mentioned in Despatches), Badajoz, Salamanca, San Millan, Vittoria, Pyrenees, Vera, Bidassoa, Nivelle (severely wounded and Mentioned in Despatches), Orthes, Tarbes and Toulouse. Gold Cross for Barrosa, Ciudad Rodrigo, Badajoz, Salamanca, Vittoria, Nivelle, Orthes, Tarbes and Toulouse. Served at Waterloo (wounded and awarded the Russian Order of St George and Austrian Order of Maria Theresa). GCB. GCH. Present with the Army of Occupation (Commandant of the British Division occupying Paris). Also served in the West Indies 1795 (present at St Lucia) and the Helder 1799. Lt Governor of Chelsea Hospital 26 Nov 1849. Died 17 Jan 1855.
REFERENCE: *Dictionary of National Biography. Royal Military Calendar, Vol 4, p. 31. Gentleman's Magazine, Mar 1855, pp. 309–10. Annual Register, 1855, Appx, p. 243.*

BARNARD, Charles Lewyns
Captain. 2nd (Royal North British) Regiment of Dragoons.
Memorial: All Saints Church, South Cave, Beverley, Yorkshire. (Above vestry door). (Photograph)

THIS TABLET IS ERECTED TO THE MEMORY / OF CAPT[N] CHARLES LEWYNS BARNARD, OF THE 2[D] R. N. B. DRAGOONS / WHO DIED AT WATERLOO, 18TH JUNE AGED 25 YEARS, / AND WAS BURIED ON THE FIELD OF BATTLE. / HE SERVED A CAMPAIGN IN GERMANY & NEARLY THE WHOLE / OF THE SPANISH WAR, IN WHICH HE WAS SEVERELY WOUNDED. / AT THE BATTLE OF WATERLOO / HE LED INTO ACTION THE RIGHT SQUADRON OF HIS HIGHLY / DISTINGUISHED REGIMENT & DISPLAYED BEFORE HE FELL, / TALENTS AND COURAGE THAT GAINED HIM THE ADMIRATION / OF ALL HIS BROTHER SOLDIERS. / YE THAT RESPECT THE UNION OF VIRTUE, VALOUR & ABILITY, / PAUSE, ERE YE PASS THIS TABLET, / AND IF YE HAVE SONS OR BROTHERS, PRAY THAT THEIR LIVES / MAY BE AS FAIR & THEIR DEATHS AS GLORIOUS AS HIS.

Capt 38th Foot 18 Jun 1807. Capt 1st Dragoon Guards 16 Sep 1813. Capt 2nd Regiment of Dragoons 2 Feb 1815.

Served in the Peninsula with 2nd Battalion 38th Foot Apr 1810 – Jan 1813. Present at Busaco, first siege of Badajoz, Fuentes d'Onoro, Badajoz (wounded), Castrejon, Salamanca, Burgos and Villa Muriel. Present at Waterloo where he was killed in the charge of the Scots Greys. He was one of the few officers of the Scots Greys who had served in the Peninsula.
REFERENCE: *Carman, W. Y., A Captain of the Royal North British Dragoons, 1813. Journal of the Society for Army Historical Research, Vol 32, No. 131, Autumn 1954, pp. 118–9. (Commentary on portrait)*

BARNES, James Stevenson
Lieutenant Colonel. 1st (Royal Scots) Regiment of Foot.
Interred in Catacomb B (v92 c3) Kensal Green Cemetery, London.

Ensign 11 Jul 1792. Lt 9 Jan 1794. Capt 27 Feb 1796. Major 17 Sep 1802. Lt Col Fribourg Regt 6 Nov 1806. Lt Colonel Chasseurs Britanniques 11 Jun 1807. Lt Col 1st Foot 21 Apr 1808. Bt Colonel 4 Jun 1814. Major General 19 Jul 1821. Lt General 10 Jan 1837.

Served in the Peninsula Apr 1810 – Sep 1812 and Jul 1813 – Apr 1814. (Commanded 1 Brigade 5th Division Aug – Sep 1810). Present at Busaco, Fuentes d'Onoro, Badajoz, Castrejon, Salamanca (severely wounded) San Sebastian (Mentioned in Despatches), Bidassoa, Nivelle, Nive and Bayonne. At San Sebastian, although in command of a Brigade he led the Royals in the attack. Gold Cross for Busaco, Salamanca, San Sebastian and Nive. MGS medal for Egypt, Fuentes d'Onoro, Badajoz and Nivelle. KCB and KTS. Also served at Toulon 1793, Corsica 1794, the Helder 1799 (present at Alkmaar where he was wounded), Ferrol 1800, Egypt 1801, West Indies 1804–1805, Malta 1806 and Walcheren 1809. Colonel Commandant 2nd Battalion Rifle Brigade 7 Jan 1833. Colonel 20th Foot 25 Apr 1842. Died 6 Oct 1850 aged 74.
REFERENCE: *Royal Military Calendar, Vol 4, pp. 158–60. Gentleman's Magazine, Nov 1850, pp. 548–9 (under Barns). Annual Register, 1850, Appx, pp. 269–70 (under Barns).*

BARNETT, Charles John
Lieutenant and Captain. 3rd Regiment of Foot Guards.
Memorial: Royal Military Chapel, Wellington Barracks, London. (M.I.) (Destroyed by a Flying Bomb 1944)

"IN MEMORY OF / LIEUT.-COLONEL CHARLES JOHN BARNETT, / BORN, 1790. 3RD GUARDS 1807–26. / "BUSACO," "FUENTES D'ONOR," "CIUDAD RODRIGO," "WATERLOO." / DIED 4TH AUGUST, 1856. / PLACED BY HIS NEPHEWS – HENRY BARNETT, CHARLES BARNETT, 1881."

2nd Lt 23rd Foot 19 Feb 1807. Ensign 3rd Foot Guards 5 Mar 1807. Lt and Capt 16 Apr 1812. Capt and Lt Colonel 26 Oct 1820.

Served in the Peninsula Nov 1809 – May 1812 and Dec 1813. Present at Busaco, Fuentes d'Onoro,

Ciudad Rodrigo and Nive. Present at Waterloo. MGS medal for Busaco, Fuentes d'Onoro, Ciudad Rodrigo and Nive. Retired 26 Oct 1826. Appointed Consul General in Egypt 1841.

BARNEY, George
2nd Captain. Royal Engineers.
Headstone: St Thomas's Cemetery, St Leonard's, Sydney, New South Wales, Australia. (Row 8 S). (Photograph)

IN LOVING REMEMBRANCE / OF / LT COL^L BARNEY, R. E. / WHO DIED ON 16TH APRIL 1862

Memorial: Near Cadman's Cottage, The Rocks, Sydney, New South Wales, Australia. (Photograph)

LIEUTENANT COLONEL GEORGE BARNEY R. E. / COMMANDING ROYAL ENGINEERS 1835 – 1843 / COLONEL ENGINEER 1835 – 1844 / SUPERINTENDENT NORTH AUSTRALIA 1846 – 1847 / CHIEF COMMISSIONER CROWN LANDS 1849 – 1855 / MEMBER LEGISLATIVE COUNCIL 1851 – 1856 / SURVEYOR GENERAL 1855 – 1859 / DURING HIS TERM OF OFFICE WAS RESPONSIBLE FOR FORTIFICATIONS / MARITIME BUILDING AND ROAD WORKS CONSTRUCTED IN THE COLONY / OF NEW SOUTH WALES. / AMONG THE MORE IMPORTANT WERE: / FORTIFICA-TIONS AT MIDDLE, SOUTH, BRADLEYS AND GEORGES HEADS / DAWES POINT BATTERY AND FORT DENISON, CIRCULAR QUAY, CUSTOMS / HOUSE, GARRISON CHURCH, NEWCASTLE BREAKWATER, ADMIRALTY / HOUSE, NEW GOVERNMENT HOUSE AND VICTORIA BARRACKS, FROM WHENCE / CAME THESE STONES.

2nd Lt 11 Jul 1808. 1st Lt 24 Jun 1809. 2nd Captain 1 Sep 1813. Capt 29 Jul 1825. Bt Major 10 Jan 1837. Lt Colonel 15 Aug 1840.
Served in the Peninsula 1811–1813. Present at Tarifa, Cadiz and San Sebastian (severely wounded). Also served at Guadeloupe 1815.
Went to Australia and served in Sydney with a detachment of Royal Engineers 1835. Appointed Colonial Engineer, superintending public works. Returned to England and went on half pay, but in 1846 sold his commission and returned to Sydney. Superintendent of a new convict colony in Northern Australia. Chief Commissioner of Crown Lands 1849. Surveyor-General 1855.
REFERENCE: *Australian Dictionary of Biography. Jobat, K., The Barneys 1835–1865: a pioneer family of Queensland, 1997.*

BAROU, Richard John
Lieutenant. Royal Engineers.
Named on the Regimental Memorial: Rochester Cathedral, Rochester, Kent. (Photograph)

2nd Lt 1 Jun 1810. Lt 1 May 1811. 2nd Capt 20 Dec 1822. Capt 25 Jun 1835. Bt Major 10 Jan 1837. Bt Lt Colonel 28 Nov 1854.
Served in the Peninsula Feb 1813 – Apr 1814. Present at Torres Vedras. Retired on full pay 13 Sep 1818. Died in London 12 Apr 1871.

BARRA, Joseph
Lieutenant and Adjutant. 16th (Queen's) Regiment of Light Dragoons.
Ledger stone: St John's Churchyard, Knutsford, Cheshire. (Photograph)

SACRED TO THE MEMORY / OF CAPTAIN J. BARRA, LATE OF THE / 16TH QUEENS DRAGOONS. HE FOUGHT / IN MANY BATTLES AND DIED JULY 12 / 1839 IN THE 59TH YEAR OF HIS AGE. /
………………..

Private 11th Lt Dragoons 1797. Sgt 1801. Cornet 16th Lt Dragoons 27 Aug 1807. Lt and Adjutant 4 Oct 1808. Capt 29 Jul 1815.

Served in the Peninsula Apr 1809 – Apr 1814. Present at Douro, Talavera, Coa, Busaco, Redinha, Casal Nova, Foz d'Arouce, Sabugal, Fuentes d'Onoro, El Bodon, Llerena, Castrejon, Salamanca, Venta del Poza, Vittoria (wounded), Nivelle, Nive and Bayonne.

Present at Waterloo. Covered the retreat of the infantry from Quatre Bras. After the heavy Cavalry charge on the 18th June their retreat was covered by the 16th Lt Dragoons. Towards the end of the day they were attacking French infantry when Capt Buchanan was killed and Barra took command of his troop. Promoted Captain Jul 1815. Present at the Capture of Paris and with the Army of Occupation until Dec 1815. Also served at the Helder 1799 (present at Egmont-op-Zee), Egypt 1801 and Ireland 1816. Retired on half pay 1819. Adjutant of the Cheshire Yeomanry Cavalry.

He was held in such high esteem by his fellow officers that after the Peninsular War he was presented with a sword inscribed: 'To Lieut & Adjt Barra, 16th or Queen's Light Dragoons – this sword was presented by the officers of his regiment as a token of their high esteem and approbation of his services both at home and abroad'. Buried in Knutsford with full military honours.

REFERENCE: *Barra, Joseph, Waterloo to Peterloo: a biographical note on Captain Joseph Barra (1780 – 1839), 16th Light Dragoons, (Mss in Cheshire Record Office. SF/920/BAR/1). Gentleman's Magazine, Sep 1839, p. 322. Annual Register, 1839, Appx, p. 353.*

BARRINGTON, Edward George
Lieutenant. 5th (Princess Charlotte of Wales's) Dragoon Guards.
Headstone: Green Street Cemetery, St Helier, Jersey, Channel Islands. (South Wall). (No longer extant). Photograph of site). (M.I.)

"FRANCIS EDWARD ROWEN ………………… AND TO THE MEMORY OF EDWARD GEORGE BARRINGTON ESQ., LATE OF 5TH DRAGOON GUARDS AND BROTHER IN LAW OF THE ABOVE, WHO DEPARTED THIS LIFE IN ST HELIER THE 4TH DAY OF DEC 1844, AGED 51 YEARS."

Cornet 28 Mar 1811. Lt 13 Feb 1812.

Served in the Peninsula Aug 1812 – Apr 1814. Present at Vittoria and Toulouse. Retired on half pay 12 Dec 1825.

BARRINGTON, Hon. Samuel Shute P.
Ensign. 1st Regiment of Foot Guards.
Named on the Regimental Memorial: St Joseph's Church, Waterloo, Belgium. (Photograph)

Memorial tablet: Inside Mausoleum, Evere Cemetery, Brussels, Belgium. (M.I.)

"LIEUTENANT THE HONORABLE SAMUEL SHUTE BARRINGTON 2ND BATTALION 1ST FOOT GUARDS"

Named on Memorial Panel VIII for Quatre Bras: Royal Military Chapel, Wellington Barracks, London. (M.I.) (Destroyed by a Flying Bomb 1944)

Ensign 24 Nov 1814.

Present at Quatre Bras where he was killed. One of the select band of soldiers buried in the Mausoleum at Evere.

BARRY, Philip
Lieutenant. Royal Engineers.
Chest tomb: Candie Cemetery, St Peter Port, Guernsey, Channel Islands. (Photograph)

SACRED / TO THE MEMORY OF / PHILIP BARRY / MAJOR GENERAL ROYAL ENGINEERS / BORN IN CO. MEATH 18TH JUNE 1789 / DIED AT GUERNSEY 17TH APRIL 1861 / DEEPLY REGRETTED.

2nd Lt 10 Feb 1809. 1st Lt 1 Mar 1810. Capt 1 Oct 1814. Bt Major 10 Jan 1837. Lt Col 23 Nov 1841. Colonel 17 Feb 1854. Major General 13 Jan 1855.
   Served in the Peninsula Sep 1812 – Oct 1813. Present at the siege of San Sebastian Aug 1813 where he was severely wounded when leading a party to the breach. MGS medal for San Sebastian.

BARRY, William
Assistant Surgeon. 40th (2nd Somersetshire) Regiment of Foot.
Ledger stone: Abbey Cemetery, Bath, Somerset. (Photograph)

IN MEMORY OF / WILLIAM BARRY M.D / OF THE 40TH REGIMENT / DEPUTY INSPECTOR GENERAL. / SECOND SON OF / THE REVD HENRY WILLIAM BARRY / VICAR OF ALL SAINTS HEREFORD. / HE SERVED IN AFRICA AND AMERICA, / THE PENINSULAR AND AT WATERLOO / AND DIED AT BATH. / ON THE 2ND JUNE 1863. / IN THE 80TH YEAR OF HIS AGE.

Hospital Assistant 15 Apr 1808. Asst Surgeon 40th Foot 4 Jan 1810. Staff Surgeon 19 Nov 1821. Deputy Inspector of Hospitals 10 Nov 1825.
   Served in the Peninsula Aug 1808 – Dec 1809, Jan 1810 – Aug 1811 and Sep 1813 – Apr 1814. Present at Busaco, Redinha, first siege of Badajoz, Olivencia, Bidassoa, Nivelle, Orthes and Toulouse. Present at Waterloo. Also served in North America 1814–1815 (present at New Orleans). MGS medal for Busaco, Nivelle, Orthes and Toulouse. MD Glasgow 1818. Retired on half pay 25 Jun 1828.

BARTON, Alexander
Captain. 12th (Prince of Wales's) Regiment of Light Dragoons.
Grave: Colmonell Kirkyard, Colmonell, Ayrshire, Scotland. (Grave number 272). (M.I.)

"JOHN BARTON FARQUHAR GRAY .... ALSO IN AFFECTIONATE REMEMBRANCE OF LIEUT COL ALEXANDER BARTON, K.H. OF BALLAIRD, WHO DIED AT KIRKHILL CASTLE 20 JAN 1864 AGED 77 YEARS."

Cornet 1 Aug 1805. Lt 7 May 1807. Capt 17 Jan 1811. Bt Major 21 Jan 1819. Major 19 Feb 1824. Bt Lt Colonel 10 Jan 1837.
   Served in the Peninsula May 1812 – Aug 1813. Present at Aldea da Ponte, Castrejon, Salamanca, Venta del Poza and Vittoria. Present at Waterloo. Also served at Walcheren 1809 and Portugal 1826 (in command of four troops of 12th Lt Dragoons sent to aid the Portuguese government). MGS medal for Salamanca and Vittoria. KH.

BARTTELOT, George see SMYTH, George Barttelot.

BARWICK, Thomas
Private. 2nd Life Guards.
Memorial: St Peter's Cathedral, Bradford, Yorkshire. (M.I.)

"................ THOMAS BARWICK, TRUMPETER, 2ND LIFE GUARDS AT THE BATTLE OF /

WATERLOO FOUGHT ON SUNDAY, JUNE 18TH, 1815, OWNER OF THIS STONE, ANNO DOMINI 1822."

Enlisted 1813 aged 21 years. Served at Waterloo as trumpeter with 2nd Life Guards. Discharged as a consequence of an injury 1816.

BATHURST, James
Major. 60th (Royal American) Regiment of Foot.
Interred in Catacomb B (v128 c8) Kensal Green Cemetery, London.

Ensign 70th Foot 10 May 1794. Lt 16 Nov 1794. Capt 7th West India Regt 25 Dec 1799. Major 60th Foot 1 Oct 1803. Bt Lt Colonel 10 Oct 1805. Bt Colonel 4 Jun 1813. Major General 12 Aug 1819. Lt General 10 Jan 1837.

Served in the Peninsula Aug 1808 – Jan 1809 (AQMG), May 1809 – Mar 1810 and Jul – Dec 1810 (AQMG and Military Secretary to Wellington). Present at Rolica (Mentioned in Despatches), Vimeiro (Mentioned in Despatches), Corunna, Douro (Mentioned in Despatches), Talavera (Mentioned in Despatches) and Busaco (Mentioned in Despatches). Gold Cross for Rolica, Vimeiro, Corunna, Talavera and Busaco. KCB 1833. Also served in Surinam 1800, Egypt 1801 (present at Alexandria), Hanover 1805 (appointed to the Staff of the King's German Legion as Military Commissary and served with Russian and Prussian armies in Poland) and the Baltic 1807. Later Governor of Berwick. Died 13 Apr 1850.
REFERENCE: *Royal Military Calendar, Vol 4, p. 124. Gentleman's Magazine, Jun 1850, p. 660. Annual Register, 1850, Appx, pp. 220–1.*

BATHURST, Hon Thomas Seymour
Ensign. 1st Regiment of Foot Guards.
Memorial tablet: St John the Baptist Church, Cirencester, Gloucestershire. (In Trinity Chapel, over door leading to North Porch). (Photograph)

TO THE MEMORY OF / LIEUT. COL. THE HONBLE SEYMOUR THOMAS BATHURST / THIRD SON OF HENRY III EARL BATHURST K. G. / BORN OCTOBER XXVII MDCCXCV. DIED APRIL X MDCCCXXXIV.

Memorial: Royal Military Chapel, Wellington Barracks, London. (M.I.) (Destroyed by a Flying Bomb 1944)

"THE HON. THOMAS SEYMOUR BATHURST, / GRENADIER GUARDS, 1814–23. PRESENT AT WATERLOO. / D.D. HIS SON, ALLEN, SIXTH EARL BATHURST"

Ensign 11 Jan 1814. Lt 80th Foot 4 Jan 1821. Lt and Capt 1st Foot Guards 25 Jan 1821. Capt Cape Corps 11 Jul 1823. Lt Col 9 Jun 1825.

Present at Waterloo. Also served in the Ionian Islands (Inspecting Field Officer of Militia 9 Jun 1825). Retired on half pay 1828.

BATTERSBY, George
Captain. 1st (King's) Dragoon Guards.
Memorial tablet: St Joseph's Church, Waterloo, Belgium. (Photograph)

SACRED TO THE MEMORY / OF CAPT GEORGE BATTERSBY 1ST KINGS REGT OF DRAGOON GUARDS / IN THE ROYAL HORSE GUARDS BRIGADE / WHO FELL IN THE FIELD OF GLORY IN A DISTINGUISH'D CHARGE OF / HEAVY CAVALRY JUNE 18TH 1815 AT THE BATTLE OF WATERLOO, / AGED 25 YEARS. / HE HAD ALREADY SERV'D WITH GREAT CREDIT IN SEVERAL

CAMPAIGNS / IN SPAIN AND IN FRANCE AS AID DE CAMP TO M. GENERAL HOWARD K.C.B. / HIS WAS AN ARDENT, A SUPERIOR AND A NOBLE SPIRIT. / IN LASTING REMEMBRANCE OF HIM, AND OF HIS HEROIC END, THIS TABLET / IS RAIS'D BY A MOURNING AND AN ATTACHED FRIEND.

Memorial tablet: Formerly in redundant Loughcrew Church, Loughcrew, County Meath, Ireland. Currently in possession of a Battersby descendant. (Photograph)

SACRED / TO THE / MEMORY / OF / GEORGE BATTERSBY ESQ^R / LATE CAPTAIN / IN / HIS MAJESTY'S FIRST REGIMENT / OF / DRAGOON GUARDS / WHO FELL / IN THE EVER MEMO-RABLE BATTLE / OF / WATERLOO / ON THE 18TH OF JUNE / MDCCCXV / AGED / 26 YEARS.

Cornet 23rd Lt Dragoons 4 Aug 1808. Lt 18 May 1809. Capt 2 Sep 1813. Capt 1st Dragoon Guards 1815.
    Served in the Peninsula Jun 1809 – Dec 1810 and Jan 1811 – Apr 1814 (ADC to Major General Howard). Present at Talavera, Fuentes d'Onoro, Arroyo dos Molinos, Almarez (Mentioned in Despatches), Vittoria, Nive, Bayonne (severely wounded). On the disbanding of 23rd Dragoons in 1815 joined the 1st Dragoon Guards and served with them at Waterloo where he was killed in the last cavalry charge.

BATTERSBY, James
Lieutenant. 20th (East Devonshire) Regiment of Foot.
Ledger stone: St Nicholas Churchyard, Dundalk, County Louth, Ireland. (Photograph)

TO THE MEMORY OF / JAMES BATTERSBY / LATE OF H. M. XX REG^T OF FOOT / AND FOR UPWARDS OF 30 YEARS / COUNTY INSPECTOR OF CONSTABULARY. / HE DIED AT DUNDALK ON THE / 27TH OF MAY 1853 / IN THE 63RD YEAR OF HIS AGE. / (VERSE)

Ensign 13 May 1813. Lt 30 Mar 1814.
    Served in the Peninsula Aug 1813 – Apr 1814. Present at Nivelle, Nive, Orthes and Toulouse. Retired on half pay 25 Jun 1817. Afterwards served 30 years in the police force rising to the rank of County Inspector of Constabulary. MGS medal for Nivelle, Nive, Orthes and Toulouse.

BATTY, Robert
Ensign. 1st Regiment of Foot Guards.
Obelisk: St Martin's Cemetery, Camden Town, London. (Photocopy image)
Note: The obelisk has been vandalised and removed in parts for safe keeping to the Camden Council work-shop. Investigations are currently taking place to consider refurbishment and restoration. (Photograph)

SACRED TO THE MEMORY OF / LT-COL ROBERT BATTY. / BORN 5TH AUGUST 1787 / DEPARTED THIS LIFE 20TH NOV^R. 1848, / IN THE 60TH YEAR OF HIS AGE / AFTER A LONG AND PAINFUL ILLNESS.

Ensign 14 Jan 1813. Lt and Capt 29 Jun 1815. Lt Colonel (unattached) 30 Dec1828.
    Served in the Peninsula with 3rd Battalion Oct 1813 – Apr 1814. Present at Nivelle, Nive, Adour and Bayonne. MGS medal for Nivelle and Nive. Present at Waterloo (wounded), the siege of Péronne and with the Army of Occupation). Also served in the Netherlands 1814 (present at Bergen-op-Zoom) and the expe-dition to Portugal 1826–1827 (ADC to Sir William Clinton). Educated at Caius College Cambridge. He became an eminent amateur draughtsman. FRS. Wrote an account of the campaign in the Netherlands, 1815, illustrated with plates of Waterloo drawn by himself.
REFERENCE: *Dictionary of National Biography. Gentleman's Magazine, Feb 1849, pp. 207–8. Annual Register, 1848, Appx, p. 201. Batty, Captain Robert, An historical sketch of the campaign of 1815, illus-*

trated by plans of the operations, and of Quatre Bras, Ligny, and Waterloo, 2ⁿᵈ edition, London 1820, reprint 1981. Batty, Captain Robert, Campaign of the left wing of the Allied Army in the western Pyrenees and south of France, 1813–1814, 1823, reprint 1983.

BAXTER, Alexander
Staff Surgeon. Medical Department.
Interred in Catacomb B 3208 (v90 c14) Kensal Green Cemetery, London.

Hospital Mate 31 Aug 1798. Asst Surgeon 35th Foot 30 Aug 1799. Surgeon Royal Corsican Rangers 12 Apr 1805. Surgeon 48th Foot 13 Apr 1809. Staff Surgeon 3 Sep 1812. Deputy Inspector of Hospitals 3 Aug 1815.
    Served in the Peninsula Jun 1810 – Sep 1812 and Oct 1812 – Apr 1814. Present at Busaco, Albuera, Aldea da Ponte, Ciudad Rodrigo, Badajoz and Salamanca. Also served at the Helder 1799 and North America 1814. Accompanied Sir Hudson Lowe to St Helena in 1816 as Principal Medical Officer, returning in 1819. MD Edinburgh 1820. Retired on full pay 1823. Died in London 19 Sep 1841.

BAXTER, John
Private. 12th (Prince of Wales's) Regiment of Light Dragoons.
Named on the Regimental Memorial: St Joseph's Church, Waterloo, Belgium. (Photograph)
    Killed at Waterloo.

BAXTER, Robert
Private. 5th (Northumberland) Regiment of Foot.
Buried in the Abbey Burial Ground, Bury St Edmund's, Suffolk. (No longer extant). (M.I.)

"ROBERT BAXTER DIED 18.4.1846 AGED 62 YEARS AND SARAH BAXTER (HIS WIFE) DIED 22.8.1849 AGED 66 YEARS."

Pte 24 Apr 1805.
    Served in the Peninsula with 1/5th Jul 1808 – Jan 1809 and Jun 1812 – Apr 1814. Present at Corunna, Madrid, retreat from Madrid (missing and taken prisoner until Sep 1814). Served in France with the Army of Occupation Jun 1815 – Jul 1817 (present at Valenciennes). Also served in Hanover 1805 (shipwrecked off coast of Holland and taken prisoner), Walcheren 1809 (present at Flushing). Awarded medal for good conduct. Served for 13 years and 317 days. Discharged 15 Jan 1816. Chelsea Out Pensioner.

BAYE, Benjamin
Private. 5th (Northumberland) Regiment of Foot.
Ringed Cross on headstone: St Matthews Churchyard, Adelaide, South Australia, Australia. (Photograph)

BENJAMIN BAYE. / DIED 14TH JUNE 1856. / AGED / 70 / YEARS / HE SERVED HIS COUNTRY IN GENERAL / ENGAGEMENTS AND WAS WITH THE BRITISH / ARMY DURING THE MEMORABLE / RETREAT TO / CORUNNA / HE WAS A KIND HUSBAND, / FATHER AND FAITHFUL / FRIEND AND SERVANT. / THIS STONE IS ERECTED / AS A TOKEN OF REGARD / BY THE GOVERNORS, / MASTERS AND SCHOLARS / OF THE / COLLEGIATE SCHOOL / OF ST. PETER'S / ADELAIDE.

Served in the Peninsula with 1/5th 1808 – Jan 1809 and Jun 1812 – Apr 1814. Present at Corunna, Pyrenees, Nivelle, Nive and Toulouse. Later went to Australia where he died 1856. MGS medal for Corunna, Pyrenees, Nivelle, Nive and Toulouse.

BAYLY, Frederick
1st Lieutenant. Royal Artillery.
Low monument: Abbey Cemetery, Bath, Somerset. (Photograph)

IN MEMORY OF / LIEUT FREDERICK BAYLY, / (LATE ROYAL ARTILLERY) / BORN JULY 14TH 1791, DIED NOVEMBER 16TH 1891. / R.I.P.

2nd Lt 5 Jun 1809. 1st Lt 21 Jun 1812.
    Served in the Peninsula Jun 1810 – Apr 1814. Present at Busaco, Castalla and Tarragona. At Busaco Capt Lane describes Bayly's conduct as admirable 'It was the first time he had been in action and no old soldier could have acted better'. Served in the Waterloo campaign under Sir Alexander Dickson with the Prussian Army (present at Mauberge, Landrecy, Philipville and Rocroy). Also served in North America 1814 (present at Washington, Baltimore and New Orleans where he was wounded). Retired on half pay 20 Jun 1829. Died 16 Nov 1891 aged 100 – the last but one surviving Peninsular War officer.

BAYNES, George Macleod
1st Lieutenant. Royal Artillery.
Buried in Candie Cemetery, St Peter Port, Guernsey, Channel Islands. (Burial register)

2nd Lt 4 Apr 1807. 1st Lt 1 Feb 1808. 2nd Capt 1 Aug 1827.
    Served in the Peninsula Sep 1812 – Apr 1814. Present at Pyrenees, Nivelle and Toulouse. Present at Quatre Bras and Waterloo in Captain Sandham's Brigade and with the Army of Occupation until Dec 1818. Also served in North America 1822–1827 and the Ionian Islands 1827–1830. Retired on half pay 25 Sep 1834. Died in Guernsey 28 Oct 1874. Brother of Captain Henry Baynes R.A.

BAYNES, Henry
2nd Captain. Royal Artillery.
Obelisk: Candie Cemetery, St Peter Port, Guernsey, Channel Islands. Seriously eroded. (Photograph)

SACRED TO THE MEMORY OF / LIEUT COLONEL HENRY BAYNES / .... / ROYAL REGIMENT ARTILLERY / BORN IN ***** 1 ***** / DIED 15 JULY 1844

2nd Lt 23 Feb 1801. 1st Lt 1 Nov 1802. 2nd Capt 1 Feb 1808. Bt Major 21 Jan 1819. Capt 24 Jul 1823. Lt Colonel 10 Jan 1837.
    Served in the Peninsula Mar 1809 – Jan 1813. Present at Douro, Talavera (wounded), Busaco, Ciudad Rodrigo, siege of Salamanca Forts and Salamanca. Gold Medal for Talavera. KH. Present at Waterloo on staff of Royal Artillery as Brigade Major (wounded). Also served at Naples 1805 and the Netherlands 1814–1815 (present at Antwerp). Brother of 1st Lt George Macleod Baynes R.A.
REFERENCE: Carman, W. Y. and Abbott, P. E., *Major Henry Baynes, Royal Artillery, c. 1826, Journal of the Society for Army Historical Research, Vol 39, No 160, Dec 1961, pp. 205–12.*

BEAN, George
Captain. Royal Artillery.
Memorial tablet: St Mary the Magdalene Church, Richmond, Surrey. (Photograph)

SACRED TO THE MEMORY OF MAJOR GEORGE BEAN, / OF THE ROYAL HORSE ARTILLERY; / WHO WAS KILLED BY A CANNON BALL IN THE 36TH YEAR OF HIS AGE, AT THE HEAD OF HIS TROOP / ON THE 18TH OF JUNE, 1815, IN THE GLORIOUS BATTLE OF / WATERLOO. / AT THE AGE OF SEVENTEEN, HE WAS, AT HIS OWN REQUEST, / PLACED IN THE ROYAL REGIMENT OF ARTILLERY; / SERVED UNDER LORD NELSON, IN THE BATTLE OF COPENHAGEN / AND VOLUNTEERED TO ACCOMPANY THE EXPEDITION / WHICH WAS SENT TO CUT OUT

THE BOATS AT BOULOGNE, / FOR WHICH HE RECEIVED HIS LORDSHIP'S PUBLIC THANKS. / HE ALSO PECULIARLY DISTINGUISHED HIMSELF / UNDER SIR DAVID BAIRD, AND THE DUKE OF WELLINGTON, IN SPAIN / WHERE HE WAS SEVENTEEN TIMES SUCCESSFULLY ENGAGED WITH THE ENEMY; / BUT SIGNALIZED HIMSELF PRINCIPALLY AT THE BATTLES OF / VITTORIA, ORTHES, AND THOULOUSE. / UNHAPPILY HIS MILITARY CAREER TERMINATED PREMATURELY; / HE FELL, IT IS TRUE, IN THE FIELD OF GLORY, / LAMENTED BY HIS SURVIVING OFFICERS AND MEN; / BUT ALAS! HAS LEFT A WIDOWED MOTHER, AND AN AFFECTIONATE WIFE, WITH TWO INFANT CHILDREN / TO LAMENT THEIR IRREPARABLE LOSS. / THIS MONUMENT IS ERECTED / AS A WELL-MERITED TRIBUTE OF MATERNAL, CONJUGAL, AND FRATERNAL AFFECTION / AND AS A MEMORIAL OF HIS PUBLIC AND PRIVATE WORTH.

Named on the Regimental Memorial: St Joseph's Church, Waterloo, Belgium. (Photograph)

2nd Lt 14 Apr 1795. 1st Lt 9 Jan 1797. Capt-Lieut 12 Sep 1803. 1st Capt 1 Feb 1808. Bt Major 12 Apr 1814.
    Served in the Peninsula Oct 1808 – Jan 1809 and Feb 1813 – Apr 1814. Present at Corunna, Vittoria, Pyrenees, Garris, Orthes, Aire (wounded and Mentioned in Despatches), Tarbes and Toulouse. Gold Medal for Vittoria and Orthes. Present at Waterloo where he was killed in command of 'D' troop, which he had commanded since 1813. Also served with Royal Navy at the Battle of Copenhagen 1801.

BEATTY, John Walwyn
Major. 7th (Royal Fusiliers) Regiment of Foot.
Memorial tablet: St George's Chapel, Windsor, Berkshire. (Wall of Rutland Chapel). (Photograph)

TO THE MEMORY OF / LIEUTENANT COLONEL / JOHN WALWYN BEATTY / COMPANION OF THE BATH / MAJOR IN THE ROYAL FUSILIERS, / WHO DIED AT WINDSOR / JULY 2D 1823 AND IS BURIED IN / THE GROUNDS OF ST GEORGES CHAPEL. / HE HAD SERVED IN THE ARMY 28 / YEARS, SEVENTEEN OF WHICH / IN THE FUSILIERS. AET 46. / THIS TABLET IS ERECTED BY / HIS BROTHER OFFICERS / AS A TRIBUTE OF / THEIR ESTEEM / AND REGARD.

Ensign 2nd Foot 3 Jun 1795. Lt 14 Jun 1796. Capt 7th Foot 19 Aug 1804. Major 2 Jan 1812. Bt Lt Colonel 12 Apr 1814.
    Served in the Peninsula with 1/7th Jul – Dec 1810, Jun – Oct 1812 and Aug 1813 – Apr 1814. With Portuguese Army: Jan 1811 – May 1812 and Nov 1812 – Jul 1813 as Major 24th Line. Present at Busaco, Salamanca, Burgos, Osma, Vittoria, Orthes and Toulouse. Gold Medal for Salamanca, Orthes and Toulouse. Served in France with the Army of Occupation. CB. Also served in the West Indies 1796–1797, Irish Rebellion 1798, the Helder 1799, Egypt 1801, Copenhagen 1807, West Indies 1808–1809, Martinique 1809, North America 1814–1815 (present at New Orleans). Retired 26 Jun 1823.

BEAUCHAMP, General Earl see LYGON, Hon Henry Beauchamp

BEAUFOY, John Henry
Lieutenant. 7th (Royal Fusiliers) Regiment of Foot.
Memorial tablet: St Mary's Church, Upton Grey, Hampshire. (Photograph)

TO THE MEMORY OF / LIEUTENANT JOHN HENRY BEAUFOY, / OF THE 7TH REGIMENT, OR ROYAL FUSILEERS: / WHO FELL GLORIOUSLY, ON THE 28TH OF JULY,1809, / (AGED 19 YEARS AND 11 MONTHS,) / IN THE BATTLE OF TALAVERA; / WHERE THE BATTALION TO WHICH HE BELONGED / PARTICULARLY DISTINGUISHED ITSELF: / THIS MONUMENT IS ERECTED, / BY JOHN HANBURY BEAUFOY, HIS AFFLICTED FATHER.

Ensign 46th Foot Nov 1807. Lt 7th Foot 17 Dec 1807.

Served in the Peninsula with 2/7th Apr – Jul 1809. Present at Douro and Talavera where the regiment was mentioned in Wellington's despatches for bravery. Beaufoy was killed in the action, the only officer of the 7th Foot to lose his life.

BEAUFOY, Mark

Ensign. Coldstream Regiment of Foot Guards.
Headstone: St Martin's Churchyard, Bowness-on-Windermere, Cumbria. (Photograph)

HERE LIES / MARK BEAUFOY ESQRE. / FORMERLY IN THE / COLDSTREAM REGIMENT OF GUARDS, / BUT FOR NEARLY THIRTY YEARS / A RESIDENT IN THIS PARISH / OF WINDER-MERE: / HE DIED ON THE 31ST DAY OF MAY / 1854, / IN HIS 61ST YEAR.

Memorial tablet: St Martin's Church, Bowness-on-Windermere, Cumbria. (Photograph)

CAPTAIN MARK BEAUFOY, / FORMERLY OF THE COLDSTREAM GUARDS, / WITH WHICH REGIMENT HE SERVED / AT THE BATTLE OF WATERLOO. / HE DIED AT WINDERMERE, MAY 31ST 1854. / AGED 60 YEARS.

Ensign 12 Nov 1812. Lt and Capt 15 May 1817. Half pay 25 Dec 1818. Exchanged back to full pay 14 Oct 1819.

Present at Waterloo. Adjutant 17 Apr 1823 – 9 Feb 1825 when he retired. Educated at Eton.

BECKETT, Richard

Lieutenant and Captain. Coldstream Regiment of Foot Guards.
Memorial tablet: St Laurence's Church, Corringham, Lincolnshire. (Photograph)

SACRED / TO THE MEMORY OF / RICHARD BECKETT, / OF THE COLDSTREAM REGIMENT OF GUARDS / WHO FELL AT THE BATTLE OF / TALAVERA DE LA REYNA IN SPAIN, / ON THE 28TH OF JULY 1809, / AGED 27 YEARS. / HE WAS KILLED BY A MUSKET SHOT / WHILE ACTIVELY DISCHARGING HIS DUTY AS / BRIGADE MAJOR TO THE BRIGADE OF GUARDS / WHICH FORMED PART OF THE BRITISH ARMY / IN THAT MEMORABLE ENGAGEMENT. / "DULCE ET DECORUM EST PRO PATRIA MORI" / THIS TABLET IS ERECTED BY THE AFFLICTED FATHER / OF A DUTIFUL AND DEARLY / BELOVED SON.

Memorial tablet: St Peter's Church, Leeds, Yorkshire. (Photograph)

TO THE MEMORY OF / CAPTAIN SAMUEL WALKER OF THE 3RD REGT OF GUARDS / AND / RICHARD BECKETT OF THE COLDSTREAM REGT OF GUARDS / NATIVES OF LEEDS / WHO / HAVING BRAVELY SERVED THEIR COUNTRY TOGETHER / IN EGYPT, GERMANY, DENMARK AND PORTUGAL / FELL IN THE PRIME OF LIFE / AT THE GLORIOUS BATTLE OF TALAVERA, SPAIN / ON THE 28TH JULY 1809. / THEIR FELLOW TOWNSMEN DEDICATED THIS MONUMENT.

Named on Memorial Panel VI for Talavera: Royal Military Chapel, Wellington Barracks, London. (M.I.) (Destroyed by a Flying Bomb 1944)

Ensign 23 Jan 1800. Lt and Capt 16 Jul 1801.
Served in the Peninsula Mar – Jul 1809 as Brigade Major. Present at Douro and Talavera where he was killed 28 Jul 1809. Also served in Egypt 1801, Hanover 1805 and Copenhagen 1807. Educated at Eton. Played cricket for MCC 1804–1807.

BECKFORD, Francis Love

Ensign. Coldstream Regiment of Foot Guards.
Memorial: Royal Military Chapel, Wellington Barracks, London. (M.I.) (Destroyed by a Flying Bomb 1944)

"FRANCIS LOVE BECKFORD. / BORN FEBRUARY 15TH, 1789; DIED JUNE 1ST, 1875. / COLD-STREAM GUARDS FROM JANUARY 25TH, 1810, TO DECEMBER 29TH, 1813. HE SERVED WITH THE 1ST BATTALION IN THE PENINSULA FROM OCTOBER 11, 1811, TO OCTOBER 3, 1812, AND RECEIVED THE WAR MEDAL, WITH CLASP FOR CIUDAD RODRIGO. / PLACED TO HIS MEMORY BY HIS NIECES, MARIA BECKFORD, JOANNA BECKFORD, HARRIETTE BECK-FORD."

Ensign 25 Jan 1810.
   Served in the Peninsula Sep 1811 – Sep 1812. Present at Ciudad Rodrigo. MGS medal for Ciudad Rodrigo. Resigned 29 Dec 1813.

BECKWITH, Sir Thomas Sidney

Lieutenant Colonel. 95th Regiment of Foot.
Tombstone: Church of Mahableshwar, Bombay, India. (M.I.)

"SACRED TO THE MEMORY OF LIEUTENANT-GENERAL / SIR. T. SIDNEY BECKWITH, KCB, GOVERNOR / AND COMMANDER-IN-CHIEF OF BOMBAY, / AND COLONEL OF HIS MAJESTY'S RIFLE BRIGADE, / WHO AFTER A LONG COURSE OF DISTINGUISHED SERVICES / EXPIRED AT HIS RESIDENCE ON THESE HILLS ON / THE 15TH DAY OF JANUARY 1831 AGED SIXTY YEARS. / ERECTED BY A SMALL CIRCLE OF HIS FRIENDS / IN TESTIMONY OF THEIR ADMIRATION FOR HIS / NOBLE CHARACTER AND TO PERPETUATE THE / NAME OF SO GOOD AND AMIABLE A MAN."

Memorial window: Sir John Moore Library, Shorncliffe, Kent. (Photograph)

SYDNEY BECKWITH

Named on the Regimental Memorial: Winchester Cathedral, Winchester, Hampshire. (Photograph)

Lt 71st Foot 2 Feb 1791. Capt 4 Oct 1797. Capt Rifle Corps 29 Aug 1800. Bt Major 11 Mar 1802. Major 28 Apr 1802. Lt Colonel 95th Foot 20 Jan 1803. Bt Colonel 4 Jun 1811. Major General 4 Jun 1814. Lt General 22 Jul 1830.
   Served in the Peninsula with 1/95th Aug – Jan 1809 and Jul 1809 – Jul 1811. Commanded 1 Brigade Lt Division from Aug 1810. Present at Vimeiro, Cacabellos, Corunna, Barba del Puerco (Mentioned in Despatches), Coa (Mentioned in Despatches), Busaco (Mentioned in Despatches), Pombal, Redinha, Casal Nova (Mentioned in Despatches), Foz d'Arouce, Sabugal (wounded and Mentioned in Despatches) and Fuentes d'Onoro. After Fuentes d'Onoro returned to England owing to ill health and Colonel Barnard succeeded him. Beckwith had successfully commanded the regiment from its creation in 1802 under the supervision of Sir John Moore. He was much admired by his officers and men to whose welfare he always paid attention. Kincaid said 'He was one of the ablest outpost generals, and few officers knew so well how to make the most of a small force'. Gold Medal for Vimeiro, Corunna and Busaco. KCB 2 Jan 1815 and KTS. Also served in India (present at Seringapatam and Pondicherry 1793), Ceylon 1795, Copenhagen 1801 (with Nelson), Hanover 1805, Baltic 1807, Walcheren 1809, Canada 1811–1814 (QMG. Present at Plattsburgh 1814) and India (Commander in Chief at Bombay May 1829). Colonel Commandant 2nd Battalion Rifle Brigade 27 Jan 1822.

REFERENCE: *Dictionary of National Biography. Dictionary of Canadian Biography. Gentleman's Magazine, Aug 1831, p. 83.*

BECKWITH, William
Cornet. 16th (Queen's) Regiment of Light Dragoons.
Family vault and Coat of Arms: Houghton Hillside Cemetery, Houghton-Le-Spring, County Durham. (In rock face on higher level plateau). (Photograph)

IN MEMORY OF / GENERAL WILLIAM BECKWITH KCH, / OF SILKSWORTH AND TRIMDON, / COLONEL 14TH HUSSARS, / WHO DIED FEB 23RD 1871, / AGED 75 YEARS. / ....

Cornet 7 Jan 1813. Lt 12 Dec 1815. Capt 14th Lt Dragoons 9 May 1822. Major 14 Feb 1828. Lt Colonel 6 Dec 1833. Bt Colonel 9 Nov 1846. Major General 20 Jun 1854. Lt General 26 Nov 1861. General 28 Oct 1869.
    Served in the Peninsula with 16th Lt Dragoons Jul 1813 – Apr 1814. Present at Nivelle, Nive and Bayonne. Present at Quatre Bras covering the retreat of the infantry on 17 June and at Waterloo. Also served in India 1822 (present at Bhurtpore where they were the first regiment to use the lance) and Bristol 1831 to quell the riots there. This was a serious disturbance as the rioters set fire to the city. Most of them died in the flames or were killed in the cavalry charges of the 14th Lt Dragoons led by William Beckwith. MGS medal for Nivelle and Nive. KH. Half pay 6 Dec 1833. Colonel 14th Hussars 12 Nov 1860.

BEECHAM, Joseph
Sergeant 51st (2nd Yorkshire West Riding) Light Infantry.
Named on the Regimental Memorial: KOYLI Chapel, York Minster, Yorkshire. (Photograph)
    Killed in the Peninsula.

BEERE, Henry
Lieutenant. 30th (Cambridgeshire) Regiment of Foot.
Named on the Regimental Memorial: St Joseph's Church, Waterloo, Belgium. (Photograph)
Memorial tablet: Littleton Church, Littleton, County Tipperary, Ireland. (Photograph)

See entry below for Hercules Beere for details of the inscription

Volunteer Tipperary Militia. Ensign 30th Foot 28 Feb 1812. Lt 7 Sep 1814.
    Served in the Peninsula Jul 1812 – Feb 1813. Present at Salamanca, retreat from Burgos (wounded at Villa Muriel 25 Oct 1812 while carrying the Colours). Present at Waterloo where he was killed aged 20. Also served in the Netherlands 1814. Volunteered from the Tipperary Militia at the age of 17. His brother Ensign Hercules Beere of 61st Foot also served in the Peninsula and they were both at Salamanca where Hercules died from his wounds.

BEERE, Hercules
Ensign. 61st (South Gloucestershire) Regiment of Foot.
Memorial tablet: Littleton Church, Littleton, County Tipperary, Ireland. (Photograph)

SACRED TO THE MEMORY OF / HERCULES AND HENRY BEERE / LATE OF LISKEVEEN CASTLE / HERCULES BEERE / LIEUTENANT IN THE 61ST REGIMENT / SERVED IN THE SPANISH CAMPAIGN / WAS SEVERELY WOUNDED AT TALAVERA / AND KILLED AT SALAMANCA ON THE 22ND DAY OF JULY 1812 / AGED 31 YEARS / HENRY BEERE / LIEUTENANT IN THE 30TH REGIMENT / VOLUNTEERED FROM THE TIPPERARY MILITIA / WAS WOUNDED AT SALA-MANCA / AND KILLED AT WATERLOO ON THE 18TH DAY OF JUNE 1815 / AGED 20 YEARS / THEY WERE BELOVED AS WELL BY THEIR BROTHER OFFICERS / AS BY THE BRAVE MEN

UNDER THEIR COMMAND / WHOM THEY HAD SO OFTEN LED TO VICTORY / AND IN CONSIDERATION OF THEIR DISTINGUISHED SERVICES / HIS ROYAL HIGHNESS THE DUKE OF YORK HAD A / LIBERAL ANNUITY GRANTED TO EACH OF THEIR SIX SISTERS / THIS MONUMENT / IS ERECTED BY THEIR AFFECTIONATE BROTHER / RICHARD BEERE

Ensign 15 Aug 1809.
    Served in the Peninsula Sep – Nov 1809 and Oct 1811 – Jul 1812. Present at Salamanca (severely wounded and died of his wounds 22 Jul 1812) His younger brother Lt Henry Beere also fought at Salamanca with the 30th Foot and was killed at Waterloo.

BEGGS, John
Private. 31st (Huntingdonshire) Regiment of Foot.
Tombstone: Cemetery No 2, Dinapore, India. (M.I.)

"SACRED / TO THE MEMORY OF / JOHN BEGGS LATE A PRIVATE / IN NO 5 OR CAPTN J. SPENCER'S COM / PANY HS MS 31ST REGT. A NATIVE / OF THE PARISH OF AGHAFATES / COUNTY ANTRIM WHO DEPARTED / THIS LIFE 1ST JUNE 1837 / AGED 43 YEARS / WHO HAVING SERVED IN THE ABOVE / REGT UPWARDS 25 YEARS, A PART OF / WHICH WAS DURING THE PENINSULAR WAR IN EUROPE. / THE DECEASED WAS IN 11 GENERAL ENGAGE-MENTS AND 18 SKIRMISHES / THIS TOMB WAS ERECTED BY A FEW SELECTED FRIENDS / WHO KNEW HIS WORTH WHEN LIVING AND MOURN HIM NOW DEAD."

Served in the Peninsula 1812 – Apr 1814. Present at Vittoria, Pyrenees, Nivelle, Nive, Garris, Orthes, Aire and Toulouse. Also served in India.

BELL, Edward Wells
Lieutenant. 7th (Royal Fusiliers) Regiment of Foot.
Ledger stone on a base: St Mary's Churchyard, Kempsey, Worcestershire. (Photograph)

IN THE VAULT / ARE DEPOSITED THE REMAINS OF / GEN. EDWARD WELLS BELL / COLONEL OF THE 7TH REGIMENT / WHO DEPARTED THIS LIFE / AT KEMPSEY 9TH OCT 1870 / AGED 81 YEARS

Lt 16 May 1811. Capt 20 Jun 1822. Major 19 Dec 1826. Lt Colonel 29 Jun 1830. Colonel 9 Nov 1846. Major General 20 Jun 1854. Lt General 27 Dec 1860. General 12 Jul 1868.
    Served in the Peninsula with 1/7th Oct 1811 – Apr 1814. Present at Fuente Guinaldo, Aldea da Ponte, Castrejon, Salamanca, Vittoria, Bidassoa, Nivelle and Nive. Served in France with the Army of Occupation 1815–1818. Also served in North America 1814–1815 (present at New Orleans), and Jamaica (in command of the troops). MGS medal for Salamanca, Vittoria, Nivelle and Nive. Colonel 66th Foot 26 Dec 1859.

BELL, George
Lieutenant. 34th (Cumberland) Regiment of Foot.
Monument: Kensal Green Cemetery, London. (24010/126/2). (Photograph)

IN MEMORY OF THE BRAVE / BENEATH THIS MEMORIAL / REST THE MORTAL REMAINS OF / GENERAL SIR GEORGE BELL KCB / DIED 10TH JULY 1877. / AGED 83. / ....

Ensign 14 Mar 1811. Lt 17 Feb 1814. Lt 45th Foot 17 Feb 1825. Lt 1st Foot 1826. Capt 7 Aug 1828. Bt Major 29 Mar 1839. Major 14 Jul 1843. Lt Colonel 5 Dec 1843. Bt Colonel 20 Jun 1854. Major General 9 Apr 1859. Lt General 28 Jan 1869. General 8 Mar 1873.

Served in the Peninsula Sep 1811 – Apr 1814. Present at Arroyo dos Molinos (carried the colours), second siege of Badajoz, retreat from Burgos, Vittoria, Pyrenees, Nivelle, Nive, Orthes, Aire, Tarbes and Toulouse (wounded). MGS medal for Vittoria, Pyrenees, Nivelle, Nive, Orthes and Toulouse. Also served in Burma 1824–1826 (awarded the Army of India medal for Ava), Canada 1837–1838 (in Canadian Rebellion and awarded Bt Majority) and in the Crimea 1854–1855 (commanded the 1st Foot at Alma, Inkerman and Sebastopol where he was wounded. Later commanded a Brigade in the Crimea. Awarded medal with three clasps for Alma, Inkerman and Sebastopol, Knight of Legion of Honour and 4th Class of the Medjidie). KCB 1867. Colonel 104th Foot 23 Oct 1863. Colonel 32nd Foot 2 Feb 1867. Colonel 1st Foot 3 Aug 1868.

REFERENCE: *Dictionary of National Biography. Bell, Sir George, Soldiers' glory: being 'Rough notes of an old soldier', 1867, reprint 1991. Annual Register, 1877, Appx, p. 153.*

BELL, John
Captain. 4th (King's Own) Regiment of Foot.
Low monument: Kensal Green Cemetery, London. (12881/144/PS). (Photograph)

GENERAL / SIR JOHN BELL GCB. / DIED 20TH NOVEMBER 1876 / IN HIS 95TH YEAR

Ensign 52nd Foot 1 Aug 1805. Lt 1 Oct 1807. Capt 4th Foot 12 Mar 1812. Bt Major 21 Jun 1813. Bt Lt Colonel 12 Apr 1814. Colonel 6 May 1831. Major General 23 Nov 1841. Lt General 11 Nov 1851. General 15 Jun 1860.

Served in the Peninsula with 2/52nd Aug 1808 – Jan 1809, Jul 1809 – Jul 1810 (with Staff as DQMG, 3rd Division), Aug 1810 – Jul 1813 (DAQMG, Lt Divison) and Aug 1813 – Apr 1814 (AQMG).

Present at Vimeiro (wounded), Corunna, Coa, Busaco, Ciudad Rodrigo, Badajoz, Castrejon, Salamanca, Subijana de Morillos, Vittoria, Pyrenees, Nivelle, Orthes and Toulouse. Gold Cross for Pyrenees, Nivelle, Orthes and Toulouse. MGS medal for Vimeiro, Busaco, Ciudad Rodrigo, Badajoz, Salamanca and Vittoria. GCB. Also served in Sicily 1806–1807, North America 1814–1815, Cape of Good Hope 1828–1841 (Chief Secretary to the Government) and Guernsey (Lt Governor 1848–1854). Colonel 4th Foot 26 Dec 1853.

REFERENCE: *Dictionary of National Biography. Annual Register, 1876, Appx, p. 159.*

BELL, Thomas
Lieutenant. 1st (Royal Scots) Regiment of Foot.
Buried in Sitabaldi Cemetery, India.

Ensign 2 Nov 1809. Lt 13 Dec 1810.

Served in the Peninsula with 3rd Battalion Dec 1812 – Apr 1814. Present at Osma, Vittoria, first and second sieges of San Sebastian, Bidassoa, Nivelle, Nive and Bayonne. Also served in India (present at Juma Darwaya where he was killed 24 Dec 1817 at the breach). His conduct was so gallant that it was said that if everyone had behaved as he did, the outcome would have been different. The enemy sent a flag of truce so that his body might be removed for burial.

BELL, William
1st Lieutenant. Royal Artillery.
Headstone in railed enclosure: St Nicholas Churchyard, West Tanfield, Yorkshire. (Photograph)

IN MEMORY OF / GENERAL SIR WILLIAM BELL KCB / COLONEL COMMANDANT / ROYAL HORSE ARTILLERY. / BORN 28TH NOV 1788. DIED 28TH MARCH 1873 / AGED 84. / HE SERVED IN THE WEST INDIES FROM 1806–1810. / IN THE PENINSULA IN 1813 AND 1814, AND WAS / ADJUTANT OF THE ROYAL HORSE ARTILLERY AT / QUATRE BRAS AND WATERLOO.

Stained glass window: St Nicholas Church, West Tanfield, Yorkshire. (Photograph)

TO THE GLORY OF GOD IN MEMORY OF GENERAL SIR WILLIAM BELL KCB / DECEASED 28 MARCH 1875 AGED 84 HE WAS ADJUTANT OF / ROYAL HORSE ARTILLERY IN THE PENINSULAR AND AT WATERLOO / THIS WINDOW IS ERECTED BY HIS RELATIONS & FRIENDS

2nd Lt 23 Nov 1804. 1st Lt 2 Dec 1805. 2nd Capt 3 Jul 1815. Capt 22 Jul 1830. Bt Major 10 Jan 1837. Lt Colonel 13 Apr 1842. Colonel 18 Mar 1852. Major General 29 Aug 1857. Lt General 27 Feb 1866. General 31 Jun 1872.

Served in the Peninsula Jul 1813 – Apr 1814 (Adjutant Royal Horse Artillery). Present at Bidassoa, Nivelle, Nive, Adour, Bayonne, Vic Bigorre, Tarbes and Toulouse (wounded). Present at Quatre Bras and Waterloo (Staff Adjutant to Sir Augustus Frazer, who commanded the Royal Horse Artillery). Bell was employed on the dangerous task of conveying instructions and orders to officers commanding batteries in all parts of the field. Present at the Capture of Paris and with the Army of Occupation. MGS medal for Martinique, Guadeloupe, Nivelle, Nive and Toulouse. CB. Colonel Commandant 'B' Brigade Royal Horse Artillery 26 Dec 1865. KCB 1867. Also served in the West Indies 1806–1810 (present at St Thomas and St Croix 1807), Martinique 1809 (present at Fort Desaix) and Guadeloupe 1810 (present at Les Saintes).

BELLINGHAM, Henry Tenison
Captain. 4th (King's Own) Regiment of Foot.
Memorial: St Mary's Church, Castlebellingham, County Louth, Ireland. (Photograph)

IN MEMORY OF / HENRY TENISON BELLINGHAM ESQ / SECOND SON OF HENRY BELLINGHAM / OF CASTLE BELLINGHAM ESQ. / AND CAPTAIN OF HIS MAJESTY'S 4TH / OR KING'S OWN REGT OF FOOT, / AT THE STORMING OF BADAJOS IN SPAIN / ON THE 6TH OF APRIL 1812 / HE FELL GALLANTLY LEADING HIS MEN. / BELOVED AND LAMENTED / BY ALL HIS BROTHER OFFICERS / AGED 26 YEARS.

Lt 21 Apr 1804. Capt 14 Feb 1811.

Served in the Peninsula Aug 1808 – Jan 1809 and Nov 1810 – Apr 1812. Present at Corunna, Fuentes d'Onoro, Barba del Puerco and Badajoz where he was killed at the siege 6 Apr 1812. Also served at Walcheren 1809.

BENNETT, Joseph
Lieutenant. 28th (North Gloucestershire) Regiment of Foot.
Memorial tablet: King's Chapel, Gibraltar. (North wall). (Photograph)

TO THE MEMORY OF / LIEUTENANTS JOSEPH BENNETT & JOHN LIGHT / OF THE LIGHT INFANTRY & GRENADIER COMPANIES / OF THE 28TH REGIMENT. / COMMANDED BY LIEUTENANT COLONEL BELSON, / WHICH, TOGETHER WITH THE FLANK COMPANIES OF THIS GARRISON / WERE DETACHED TO TARIFA, WHERE A FORCE WAS ASSEMBLED BY / LIEUTENANT GENERAL GRAHAM / TO ATTACK, IN CONJUNCTION WITH THE SPANISH ARMY; / THE FRENCH BEFORE CADIZ. / AT THE MEMORABLE BATTLE OF BARROSA, / FOUGHT ON THE 5TH MARCH 1811, THOSE TWO PROMISING YOUNG / OFFICERS, AT THE HEAD OF THEIR RESPECTIVE COMPANIES, (THEIR / CAPTAINS HAVING BOTH QUITTED THE FIELD FROM SHOTS EARLY / IN THE ACTION) RECEIVED THEIR MORTAL WOUNDS. / THIS TABLET IS ERECTED BY THEIR BROTHER OFFICERS / IN TESTIMONY OF THEIR ESTEEM FOR THEM.

Ensign 23 Aug 1803. Lt 29 Mar 1805.

Served in the Peninsula with 1/28th Jul 1808 – Jan 1809 and Sep 1810 – Mar 1811. Present at Corunna,

Tarifa and Barrosa where he was severely wounded 5 Mar and died of his wounds 7 Mar 1811. Also present at Walcheren 1809.

BENT, James
Major. 20th (East Devonshire) Regiment of Foot.
Named on the Memorial: St Andrew's Church, (now Musée Historique), Biarritz, France. (Photograph)

Ensign 92nd Foot 16 Apr 1798. Lt 19 Oct 1799. Capt 31 Mar 1803. Bt Major 4 Jun 1813. Major 20th Foot 23 Sep 1813.
  Served in the Peninsula Aug 1808 – Jan 1809 and Nov 1812 – Feb 1814. Present at Vimeiro, Corunna, Vittoria, Pyrenees (wounded at Roncesvalles), Nive and Orthes where he was killed Feb 1814. Gold Medal for Orthes. Also served at the Helder 1799 (present at Egmont-op-Zee), Egypt 1801, Sicily (present at Maida 1806) and Walcheren 1809.

BENTHAM, William
2nd Captain. Royal Artillery.
Headstone: St Luke's Churchyard, Charlton, Kent. (Grave number 143). (Photograph)

IN MEMORY OF / MAJOR WILLIAM BENTHAM / ROYAL ARTILLERY / BORN 1786, DIED 1832. / A TRIBUTE OF RESPECT / FROM HIS FRIENDS IN THE REGIMENT. / ....

2nd Lt 15 Mar 1803. 1st Lt 12 Sep 1803. 2nd Capt 30 Apr 1809. Capt 29 Jul 1825. Bt Major 22 Jul 1830.
  Served in the Peninsula Feb 1813 – Apr 1814. Present at Bayonne. Served in France with the Army of Occupation 1815–1818. Also served in Malta, Sicily and Calabria 1803–1808 and Canada May – Dec 1830.

BENTINCK, Charles Anthony F.
Lieutenant and Captain. Coldstream Regiment of Foot Guards.
Memorial: Royal Military Chapel, Wellington Barracks, London. (M.I.) (Destroyed by a Flying Bomb 1944)

"LIEUT.-GENERAL BENTINCK, / BORN 4TH MARCH, 1792. / COLDSTREAM GUARDS, 1808–48. SERVED IN THE PENINSULA, 1810–11, AND WAS WOUNDED AT BARROSA. IN 1813 HE ACCOMPANIED THE EXPEDITION TO HOLLAND AS ADJUTANT, AND WAS ENGAGED AT MERXEM, ANTWERP, AND BERGEN-OP-ZOOM. HE WAS ASSISTANT ADJUTANT-GENERAL TO THE 2ND / DIVISION AT WATERLOO. DIED 28TH OCTOBER, 1864."

Ensign 16 Nov 1808. Lt and Capt 24 Sep 1812. Bt Major 18 Jun 1815. Capt and Lt Colonel 27 May 1825. Bt Colonel 28 Jun 1838. Major General 11 Nov 1851. Lt General 15 Jan 1858.
  Served in the Peninsula Apr 1810 – Apr 1811. Present at Cadiz and Barrosa (wounded). Also served in the Netherlands 1813–1814. Appointed Adjutant to 2nd Battalion and went to Holland under Lord Lynedoch (present at Merxem, Antwerp and Bergen-op-Zoom). Present at Waterloo (DAAG to 2nd Divison under Sir Henry Clinton), the Capture of Paris and with the Army of Occupation. MGS medal for Barrosa. Colonel 12th Foot 14 Apr 1857. Brother of Colonel Lord William Henry Cavendish Bentinck 11th Lt Dragoons.
REFERENCE: *Gentleman's Magazine, Dec 1864, p. 805. Household Brigade Journal, 1864, pp. 334–5.*

BENTINCK, Richard
Drummer. 23rd (Royal Welch Fusiliers) Regiment of Foot.
Headstone: Heywood Cemetery, Heywood, Lancashire. (Section E 293). (Photograph)

IN / REMEMBRANCE / OF / RICHARD BENTINCK / OF HAYWOOD / A WATERLOO HERO, / OF THE 24TH REGIMENT OF FOOT. / BORN 1786. DIED 1874. / ....

Served in the Peninsula Dec 1810 – Apr 1814. Present at Albuera, Badajoz, Salamanca, Vittoria, Pyrenees, Orthes and Toulouse (Served under the name of Nichol Bentick. Regimental rolls indicate that Richard and Nichol are the same man). Present at Waterloo with Captain Hawtyn's Company of Grenadiers. MGS medal for Albuera, Badajoz, Salamanca, Vittoria, Pyrenees, Orthes and Toulouse. Note: Headstone incorrectly names 24th Foot.
REFERENCE: *Crook, Jonathan, The very thing: the recollections of Drummer Bentinck, 1807–1823, 2011.*

BENTINCK, Lord William Henry Cavendish
Colonel. 11th Regiment of Light Dragoons.
Buried in the Family vault of the Dukes of Portland, Trinity Chapel, Marylebone, London.

Statue: Calcutta, India. (South west side of the Victoria memorial). (Epitaph written by Thomas Babington Macaulay). (Photograph)

TO / WILLIAM CAVENDISH BENTINCK, / WHO, DURING SEVEN YEARS, RULED INDIA WITH EMINENT PRUDENCE, / INTEGRITY, AND BENEVOLENCE; / WHO, PLACED AT THE HEAD OF A GREAT EMPIRE, NEVER LAID ASIDE / THE SIMPLICITY AND MODERATION OF / A PRIVATE CITIZEN; WHO INFUSED INTO ORIENTAL DESPOTISM THE SPIRIT OF / BRITISH FREEDOM; / WHO NEVER FORGOT THAT THE END OF GOVERNMENT / IS THE WELFARE OF THE GOVERNED; / WHO ABOLISHED CRUEL RITES; / WHO EFFACED HUMILIATING DISTINCTION; / WHO ALLOWED LIBERTY TO THE EXPRESSION OF PUBLIC OPINIONS / WHOSE CONSTANT STUDY IT WAS TO ELEVATE / THE MORAL AND INTELLECTUAL CHARACTER OF THE NATION / COMMITTED TO HIS CHARGE. / THIS MONUMENT WAS ERECTED / BY MEN; / WHO DIFFERING FROM EACH OTHER / IN RACE, IN MANNERS, IN LANGUAGE, AND IN RELIGION / CHERISH WITH EQUAL VENERATION AND GRATITUDE / THE MEMORY OF HIS WISE, UPRIGHT / AND PATERNAL ADMINISTRATION. / CALCUTTA, 4TH FEBRUARY 1835.

Ensign Coldstream Guards 27 Jan 1791. Captain-Lieutenant and Captain 2nd Lt Dragoons 1 Aug 1792. Capt 11th Lt Dragoons 20 Feb 1793. Major 28th Foot 21 Feb 1794. Lt Colonel 24th Lt Dragoons 20 Mar 1794. Bt Colonel 1 Jan 1798. Major General 1 Jan 1805. Colonel 20th Lt Dragoons 4 Jan 1810. Lt General 4 Jun 1811. Colonel 11th Lt Dragoons 27 Jan 1813. General 27 May 1825.

Served in the Peninsula Sep 1808 – Jan 1809 (Commanded 1 Brigade 1st Division) and Jun – Sep 1813 (GOC Eastern Spain). Present at Corunna. After Corunna returned to England 1809. Appointed Envoy to the Court of Sicily and Commander-in-Chief of all H.M.'s forces in the island 1811. Commanded the forces from Sicily sent to Eastern Spain 1813. Present at Ordal and Tarragona. GCB. GCH.

Also served in Flanders 1794, Italy (present at Trebbia 1799 and Marengo 1800. Liaison officer with the Austro-Hungarian forces), Egypt 1801 (sent to command cavalry but arrived too late) and Madras 1803 (Governor). After the mutiny at Vellore, Bentinck was sent home in disgrace, possibly chosen as a scapegoat. On his return to India in 1827 as Governor General he was responsible for sound, economic and political reforms which were not always acceptable to the government of the day. Commander in Chief of the Army of India 1833. Returned to England 1837 and became MP for Glasgow. Died in Paris 17 Jan 1839.

Wellington said that Bentinck 'did everything with the best intention but he was a wrong-headed man, and if he went wrong he would continue to do the wrong thing'. Educated at Winchester. Died in Paris 17 Jun 1839 aged 68. Brother of Lt and Capt Charles Anthony Frederick Bentinck Coldstream Guards.
REFERENCE: *Dictionary of National Biography. Royal Military Calendar, Vol 2, pp. 200–4. Gentleman's Magazine, Aug 1839, pp. 198–200. Annual Register, 1839, Appx, pp. 344–5.*

BERESFORD, John Theophilus
Lieutenant. 88th (Connaught Rangers) Regiment of Foot.
Memorial tablet: Westminster Abbey, London. (Photograph)

SACRED TO THE MEMORY OF JOHN THEOPHILUS BERESFORD, / ELDEST SON OF MARCUS BERESFORD, AND THE LADY FRANCES, HIS WIFE. / LIEUTENANT IN THE 88TH REGIMENT OF FOOT / WHO DIED IN THE 21ST YEAR OF HIS AGE, AT VILLA FORMOSA IN SPAIN / OF WOUNDS RECEIVED FROM THE EXPLODING OF A POWDER MAGAZINE / AT CUIDAD RODRIGO; AFTER HE HAD PASSED UNHURT THROUGH EIGHT / DAYS OF VOLUNTARY SERVICE OF THE GREATEST DANGER DURING THE / SIEGE; FOR WHICH HE RECEIVED THE THANKS OF THE COMMANDER IN CHIEF. / BRAVE AND ZEALOUS IN HIS MILITARY DUTIES, ANIMATED BY A STRONG / FEELING OF PIETY TO GOD! AND DISTINGUISHED BY HIS ARDENT FILIAL / AFFECTION AND DUTY TOWARDS A WIDOWED MOTHER; HE HAS LEFT TO HER / THE RECOLLECTION OF HIS RISING VIRTUES, AS HER ONLY CONSOLATION / UNDER THE IRREPARABLE LOSS SHE HAS SUSTAINED / BY HIS DEATH. / BORN JANUARY 16TH 1792, DIED JANUARY 29TH 1812. / INTERRED WITH MILITARY HONOURS IN THE FORT OF ALMEIDA.

Headstone: Almeida, Portugal. (Photograph)

JOHN BERESFORD LIEUTENANT / IN THE 88TH REG[T]. RECEIVED A MORTAL WOUND / BY THE EXPLOSION OF A MINE ON THE / BREACH OF CUIDAD RODRIGO / THE / 19TH JANUARY 1812. / O TENENTE JOAO BERESFORD DO / REG[T] BRIT NO 88 P O CFLECIO D'BUMA / MINA QUE VOON NA BRECHA DE / CIUDAD RODRIGO; E QUE ELLE ENTRE / OS PREMEIROS MONTOU E NA NOITE / DE 19[D] JANEIRO 1812 / MORREO NA EDADE DE 21 ANNOS / SSEOS. MARQUEZ DE CAMPO MAIOR / DE ESTE MODO MANDOU / COMMEMORAR / A MORTE D'BUM PARENTE ESTIMADO.

2nd Lt 23rd Foot 7 Dec 1808. Lt 88th Foot 28 Jun 1810.
      Served in the Peninsula Jul 1811 – Jan 1812. Present at El Bodon and Ciudad Rodrigo. Severely wounded by an explosion of a powder magazine at Ciudad Rodrigo 19 Jan 1812, after having spent eight days of dangerous voluntary service at the siege (Mentioned in Despatches). Died at Villa Formosa 29 Jan 1812, and was buried in the Fort of Almeida. Nephew of Colonel William Carr Beresford 88th Foot.

BERESFORD, Sir William Carr
Colonel. 88th (Connaught Rangers) Regiment of Foot.
Chest tomb: Christ Church, Kilndown, Goudhurst, Kent. (Photograph)
The tomb, together with the adjacent tomb to his wife, were originally surmounted by a canopy described as 'the vault was surmounted by a mausoleum of singular beauty and almost unique in design – the only other one like it being the tomb of the Scalgia family in Verona. The canopy, borne by light columns of granite was found unsafe in the early 1920's and removed.' (Photograph)

HERE LIES WILLIAM CARR BERESFORD – VISCOUNT BERESFORD GCB / GENERAL FIELD MARSHAL CAPTAIN GENERAL OF / ENGLAND PORTUGAL SPAIN. WHO DECEASED 8 JAN 1854 AGED 86. / LORD HAVE MERCY ON ME

Ensign 6th Foot 20 Aug 1785. Lt 16th Foot 25 Jun 1789. Capt Independent Company 24 Jan 1791. Capt 69th Foot 31 May 1791. Major 1 Mar 1794. Lt Colonel 124th Foot 11 Aug 1794. Lt Colonel 88th Foot 16 Sep 1795. Bt Colonel 1 Jan 1800. Colonel 88th Foot 9 Feb 1807. Major General 25 Apr 1808. Lt General 1 Jun 1812. General 27 May 1825. Portuguese Army: Commander in Chief Mar 1809.
      Served in the Peninsula Aug 1808 – Jan 1809 (Commanded 1 Brigade 3rd Division), Mar 1809 – Aug 1813 and Oct 1813 – Apr 1814 (Portuguese Army). Present at Corunna, Busaco, Campo Mayor, first siege

of Badajoz, Albuera, Ciudad Rodrigo, Badajoz, Salamanca (severely wounded), Vittoria, Pyrenees, Nivelle, Nive, Orthes, Bordeaux and Toulouse.

Wellington recognised the need to reform the Portuguese Army and realised that Beresford was the ideal person to carry out this task. In 1809 Beresford was appointed Commander in Chief of the Portuguese Army. Gold Cross for Corunna, Busaco, Albuera, Badajoz, Salamanca, Vittoria, Pyrenees, Nivelle, Nive, Orthes and Toulouse. MGS medal for Egypt and Ciudad Rodrigo. GCH. GCB 2 Jan 1815. Grand Cross of the Tower and Sword, Grand Cross of St Fernando, Grand Cross of St Ferdinand and Merit, Grand Cross of St Herminigilda. Duke of Elvas. Field Marshal of Portugal.

Also served in Nova Scotia 1786 (wounded in a shooting accident and lost sight in his left eye), Toulon 1793 (with 69th Foot serving as marines), Corsica, Bastia and Calvi 1794, West Indies 1795, Egypt 1801, Cape of Good Hope 1806 and South America 1807 (present at Buenos Ayres, where he was taken prisoner and escaped after six months).

Remained in Portugal from 1814–1819 in command of the Army and then returned to England where he entered politics, but did not take an active part. Colonel 69th Foot 11 Mar 1819. Colonel 16th Foot 15 Mar 1823. Colonel 60th Foot 23 Sep 1852. Governor of Cork 1818–1820. Created Viscount Beresford of Beresford (Staffordshire) 1823. Appointed by Wellington as Master General of Ordnance 1828. In the 1830's there was a dispute between Beresford and Charles Edward Long, nephew of Lt General Robert Ballard Long. He was trying to clear his uncle's name over the handling of troops at the battle of Campo Mayor. Uncle of Lt John Theophilus Beresford 88th Foot.

REFERENCE: *Dictionary of National Biography. Vickness, S. E., Marshal of Portugal: the military career of William Carr Beresford, 1976. Gentleman's Magazine, Mar 1854, pp. 311–4. Annual Register, 1854, Appx, pp. 258–61. Cole, John William, Memoirs of British Generals, Vol 1, 1856, pp. 163–218.*

BERFORD, Richard
Lieutenant. 2nd (Queen's Royal) Regiment of Foot.
Grave: Christ Churchyard, Worthing, Sussex. (M.I.)

"CAPTAIN BERFORD OF THE QUEEN'S ROYALS, LATE OF WESTERFIELD HOUSE, DIED DECEMBER 15TH 1855 IN THE 70TH YEAR OF HIS AGE."

Ensign 5th Foot 25 Oct 1807. Lt 2nd Foot 12 Sep 1809. Capt 30 Sep 1819.

Served in the Peninsula with 1/5th Foot Aug 1808 – Jan 1809 and 2nd Foot Jan 1813 – Apr 1814. Present at Rolica, Vimeiro, Lugo, Corunna, Vittoria, Pyrenees, Nivelle, Nive, Adour, Orthes and Toulouse. Also served at Walcheren 1809 (present at Flushing). Retired on half pay 30 Sep 1819. MGS medal for Rolica, Vimeiro, Corunna, Vittoria, Pyrenees, Nivelle, Nive, Orthes and Toulouse.

BERKELEY, Sir George Henry Frederick
Lieutenant Colonel. 35th (Sussex) Regiment of Foot.
Memorial tablet: St Peter's Church, West Molesey, Surrey. (Photograph)

SACRED TO THE MEMORY OF / GENERAL SIR GEORGE H. F. BERKELEY, KCB, KTS, KW &c., / WHO SERVED IN EGYPT IN THE 35TH FOOT IN 1807 / AND AFTERWARDS THROUGH THE PENINSULAR WAR / AS ASSISTANT ADJUTANT GENERAL FROM 1809 TO 1814, / AND AGAIN AT THE BATTLE OF WATERLOO, / WHERE HE WAS SEVERELY WOUNDED. / AS A GENERAL OFFICER HE COMMANDED H. M. FORCES / IN CAFFRARIA, / AND BROUGHT THE WAR TO A SUCCESSFUL CLOSE IN 1847, / AND WAS AFTERWARDS COMMANDER IN CHIEF AT MADRAS. / HIGHLY ESTEEMED IN HIS PUBLIC CAREER, / HE WAS UNIVERSALLY BELOVED IN PRIVATE LIFE, / HIS GREAT DESIRE BEING TO MAKE ALL AROUND HIM HAPPY. / HE MARRIED MARCH 27TH 1815, LUCY, DAUGHTER OF / SIR THOMAS SUTTON, BART., OF MOULSEY HURST HOUSE. / HE DIED ON THE 26TH OF SEPTEMBER 1857, IN HIS 73RD YEAR.

Buried in the Family vault: St Peter's Churchyard, West Molesey, Surrey. (Photograph)

Cornet Royal Horse Guards Jan 1802. Lt Aug 1803. Capt 35th Foot 1 May 1805. Bt Major 28 Jan 1808. Major 25 Mar 1808. Lt Colonel 13 Jun 1811. Lt Colonel 44th Foot 12 Aug 1819. Capt and Lt Colonel 3rd Foot Guards 22 Feb 1821. Bt Colonel 27 May 1825. Major General 10 Jan 1837. Lt General 9 Nov 1846. General 20 Jun 1854.

Served in the Peninsula Apr 1809 – Apr 1814 (on Staff as AQMG). Present at Douro, Talavera, Busaco, first siege of Badajoz, Fuentes d'Onoro, Badajoz, Salamanca, Burgos, Villa Muriel, Vittoria, San Sebastian, Bidassoa, Nivelle, Nive and Bayonne. Gold Cross for Busaco, Fuentes d'Onoro, Badajoz, Salamanca, Vittoria, San Sebastian and Nive. MGS medal for Talavera. KCB 2 Jan 1815 and KTS. Present at Waterloo as AAG (wounded). Awarded 4th Class of St Vladimir of Russia and 4th Class of King Wilhelm of the Netherlands. Also served in Sicily 1807, Egypt 1807 (present at Alexandria), Cape of Good Hope Jan – Oct 1847 (in command of the troops at the Cape who fought in the Kaffir Wars). Colonel 35th Foot 11 Jul 1845.
REFERENCE: *Royal Military Calendar, Vol 4, p. 367. Annual Register, 1857, Appx, p. 337.*

BERNARD, Hon Francis
Lieutenant. 9th Light Dragoons.
Memorial tablet: St Peter's Church, Bandon, County Cork, Ireland. (Photograph)

SACRED / TO THE MEMORY OF / THE HON FRANCIS BERNARD / THIRD SON OF / FRANCIS EARL OF BANDON / AND / CATHERINE HENRIETTA COUNTESS OF BANDON / BORN FEBR 27TH 1789 / LIEUTENANT 9TH LIGHT DRAGOONS / DIED IN HIS COUNTRY'S SERVICE / AT ALTER DO CHAO / IN PORTUGAL / JAN 24TH 1813

Cornet 3rd Dragoon Guards 9 Oct 1806. Ensign 1st Foot Guards 4 Apr 1807. Lt 9th Lt Dragoons 23 Jun 1808.

Served in the Peninsula Aug 1811 – Jan 1813. Died from fever at Alter do Chao in Portugal, 24 Jan 1813. Brother of Cornet Henry Boyle Bernard 1st Dragoon Guards who was killed at Waterloo.
REFERENCE: *Gentleman's Magazine, Mar 1813, p. 286.*

BERNARD, Hon. Henry Boyle
Cornet. 1st (King's) Dragoon Guards.
Memorial tablet: St Peter's Church, Bandon, County Cork, Ireland. (Photograph)

SACRED / TO THE MEMORY OF / THE HON. HENRY BOYLE BERNARD, / FIFTH SON OF / FRANCIS EARL OF BANDON / AND / CATHERINE HENRIETTA COUNTESS OF BANDON / BORN DECR 5TH 1797 / CORNET 1ST DRAGOON GUARDS, / KILLED AT THE BATTLE OF / WATERLOO / JUNE 18TH 1815.

Cornet 15 Jun 1814.

Present at Waterloo. Covered the retreat of the infantry from Quatre Bras. Took part in the charge of the Household Brigade at Waterloo aged 18, where he was wounded, taken prisoner by the French and never seen again. In one of John Hibbert's letters home he wrote: 'We know pretty well what became of him, he was taken prisoner after having been wounded, and not being able to keep up with the French, they killed him on the road. They served a great many English officers in the same way; their retreat was extremely rapid.' His mother died of grief at hearing the news of his death. His brother Lt Francis Bernard 9th Lt Dragoons died in the Peninsula.

BERTIE, Lindsey James
Lieutenant. 12th (Prince of Wales's) Regiment of Light Dragoons.
Named on the Regimental Memorial: St Joseph's Church, Waterloo, Belgium. (Photograph)

Cornet 17 Oct 1811. Lt 7 May 1812.
   Served in the Peninsula Apr 1812 – Apr 1814. Present at Castrejon, Salamanca, Venta del Poza, Vittoria, Nivelle, Nive and Adour. Present at Waterloo where he was killed.

BETTON, John
Captain. 3rd (Prince of Wales's) Dragoon Guards.
Memorial tablet: Abbey Church, Shrewsbury, Shropshire. (Photograph)

SACRED TO THE MEMORY / OF / .... / ALSO THEIR SON / JOHN BETTON / CAPTAIN IN HIS MAJESTY'S 3RD DRAGOON GUARDS / WHO DIED NOVR 20TH 1809 / AT MERIDA IN SPAIN, AGED 31 YEARS.

Cornet 9 Jun 1798. Lt 10 May 1800. Capt 28 Feb 1805.
   Served in the Peninsula May 1809 – Nov 1809. Present at Talavera. Died of fever at Merida 20 Nov 1809.
REFERENCE: *Letters written whilst serving in the Peninsular War, 1805 – 1809. Manuscript records in Bodleian Library, University of Oxford.*

BETTY, Christopher Stewart
Ensign. 27th (Inniskilling) Regiment of Foot.
Memorial tablet: St Macartin's Cathedral, Enniskillen, County Fermanagh, Northern Ireland. (Photograph)

SACRED / TO THE MEMORY OF / CHRISTOPHER STEWART BETTY / LIEUTENANT 35TH REGIMENT / WHO DIED AT ENNISKILLEN / ON 6TH DAY OF AUGUST AD 1838. / THIS TABLET HAS BEEN ERECTED / AS A TRIBUTE OF ESTEEM AND RESPECT / BY THE OFFICERS OF THE 35TH REGIMENT.

Ensign 27th Foot 13 Aug 1812. Lt 6 Jul 1814. Lt 35th Foot 5 May 1825.
   Served in the Peninsula with 3/27th Mar – Apr 1814. Present at Toulouse. Also served in North America 1814. His brother Lt John Betty 1/27th Foot also served in the Peninsula and at Waterloo.

BEVAN, Charles
Lieutenant Colonel. 4th (King's Own) Regiment of Foot.
Memorial tablet: British Cemetery, Elvas, Portugal. (Photograph)

LIEUT COL CHARLES BEVAN, 4TH OR KING'S OWN REGT / THIS STONE IS ERECTED TO THE MEMORY / OF CHARLES BEVAN, LATE LIEUT. / COL. OF THE 4TH OR KING'S OWN REGT, WITH / THE INTENTION OF RECORDING HIS / VIRTUES. THEY ARE DEEPLY ENGRAVEN ON THE / HEARTS OF THOSE WHO KNEW HIM / AND WILL EVER LIVE IN THEIR REMEMBRANCE. / A STONE WITH THIS INSCRIPTION WAS / ERECTED OVER THE GRAVE OF COL / BEVAN IN PORTALEGRE CASTLE WHERE HE WAS / BURIED ON 11 JULY 1811. THAT / STONE HAVING BEEN REMOVED WHEN A ROAD / WAS BUILT THERE, THIS REPLACEMENT / IS PLACED BY HIS DESCENDANTS TO HONOUR THE / MEMORY OF AN OFFICER WHO PUT / REGIMENTAL HONOUR BEFORE HIS OWN LIFE. / ERECTED ON BEHALF OF ANN COLFER / (D 1980) AND SARA CAVALEIRO, DAUGHTERS / OF MAJOR JAMES BEVAN WHO / CARRIED CHARLES SWORD DURING HIS OWN / SERVICE IN THE KING'S OWN 1913 – 1935 / AND OF MRS. R.

STAFFORD, HUGH STAFFORD, / MARGARET SMITH AND DIANA / THOMAS AND THEIR CHILDREN. / WILLIAM COLFER CB, 14 OCTOBER 2000

Ensign 37th Foot Apr 1795. Lt 12 Sep 1795. Capt 28th Foot Mar 1800. Major 1 Dec 1804. Lt Colonel 4th Foot 18 Jan 1810.

Served in the Peninsula with 1/28th Aug 1808 – Jan 1809 and 4th Foot Jan – Jul 1811. Present at Corunna, Fuentes d'Onoro and Barba del Puerco. Major General Erskine delayed giving Bevan the order to march to defend the bridge at Barba del Puerco until it was too late. Bevan was accused of letting the French escape from Almeida over the bridge at Barba del Puerco, and shot himself at Portalegre 8 Jul 1811.

Also served in Gibraltar 1795–1798 (ADC to Lt General Grinfield), Minorca 1800, Egypt 1801 (present at Aboukir and Mandora Mar 1801 where he was severely wounded), Ireland 1801–1804, Hanover 1805, Copenhagen 1807, Sweden 1808 and Walcheren 1809.
REFERENCE: Hunter, Archie, *Wellington's scapegoat: the tragedy of Lieutenant Colonel Charles Bevan*, 2003.

BIGNALL, Francis
Captain. 27th (Inniskilling) Regiment of Foot.
Named on the Memorial: St Andrew's Church, (now Musée Historique), Biarritz, France. (Photograph)

Ensign 21 Apr 1804. Lt 3 Jun 1805. Capt 14 Nov 1811.

Served in the Peninsula with 2/27th Dec 1812 – Feb 1813 and 3/27th Mar 1813 – Apr 1814. Present at East Coast of Spain, Nivelle, Nive, Orthes and Toulouse where he was killed 10 Apr 1814.

BIRCH, James
2nd Captain. Royal Engineers.
Named on the Regimental Memorial: Rochester Cathedral, Rochester, Kent. (Photograph)

2nd Lt 12 Jul 1809. Lt 1 May 1811. 2nd Capt 20 Dec 1814.

Served in the Peninsula Oct 1810 – Apr 1814. Present at Cadiz, Tarifa, Carthagena and Tarragona. Also served at Genoa 1814. Half pay 24 Sep 1825. Died at St Leonards-on-Sea 20 Jun 1866.

BIRCH, John Francis
Lieutenant Colonel. Royal Engineers.
Named on the Regimental Memorial: Rochester Cathedral, Rochester, Kent. (Photograph)

2nd Lt Royal Artillery 18 Sep 1793. 2nd Lt Royal Engineers 1 Jan 1794. Lt 20 Nov 1796. Capt-Lt 18 Apr 1801. 2nd Capt 19 Jul 1804. Capt 1 Mar 1805. Bt Major 6 Mar 1811. Lt Colonel 21 Jul 1813. Colonel 29 Jul 1825. Major General 10 Jan 1837. Lt General 9 Nov 1846. Colonel Commandant 12 Oct 1847. General 20 Jun 1854.

Served in the Peninsula Aug 1808 – Jan 1809 and Mar 1810 – Mar 1811. Present in the Corunna campaign (wounded at Valmesada 7 Nov 1808), Cadiz, Barrosa (Mentioned in Despatches and awarded Brevet Majority). Also served in Flanders 1793–1795, Minorca 1798, Egypt 1801, Copenhagen 1807 and Walcheren 1809. MGS medal for Egypt and Barrosa. CB. Died in Folkestone 29 May 1856.

BIRCH, Robert Henry
Captain. Royal Artillery.
Headstone: Mount Jerome Cemetery, Dublin, Ireland. (Grave number C14–250). (Photograph)

IN REMEMBRANCE / OF A KIND AND / AFFECTIONATE HUSBAND / THIS / MONUMENT HAS BEEN ERECTED / BY GEORGINA WIFE OF / ROBERT HENRY BIRCH / MAJOR GENERAL / OF

THE ROYAL ARTILLERY / WHO DIED / ON THE 29TH DAY OF JUNE 1851 / HAVING ATTAINED HIS 80TH YEAR

2nd Lt 9 Mar 1795. 1st Lt 25 Jul 1795. Capt-Lieut 12 Sep 1803. Capt 27 Jun 1807. Bt Major 4 Jun 1814. Major 29 Jul 1825. Lt Colonel 12 Dec 1826. Colonel 10 Jan 1837. Major General 9 Nov 1846.

Served in the Peninsula Apr 1810 – Dec 1812. Present at Cadiz and Seville. Also served in the Irish Rebellion 1798, a secret expedition to the Mediterranean under Sir James Craig 1805, Sicily 1806, Walcheren 1809 and West Indies 1829–1833. Colonel Commandant 12 Aug 1849.

BIRD, Henry
Major. 5th (Northumberland) Regiment of Foot.
Memorial tablet: St Peter's Church, Goytre, Monmouthshire, Wales. (Photograph)

IN MEMORY OF / COLONEL HENRY BIRD, / BORN AT DETROIT, U.S. APRIL 24TH 1780. / COL. BIRD ENTERED THE ARMY IN THE 29TH REGT, / WAS LIEUT IN THE 94TH AND CAPTAIN IN THE 5TH REGT. / SERVED AS MAJOR IN THE EXPEDITION TO HANOVER / IN 1805, AND AT THE STORMING OF BUENOS AYRES, IN 1807, / AND IN THE BATTLES OF ROLEIA, AND VIMIERA, IN 1808. / IN 1809 HE SERVED UNDER SIR JOHN MOORE, IN SPAIN, / AFTERWARDS IN THE EXPEDITION TO WALCHEREN; / AT THE SIEGE OF FLUSHING HE WAS MADE PRISONER, / WHILST CHARGING A FRENCH COLUMN, AND ON BEING / RESTORED TO LIBERTY AT THE SURRENDER OF THAT / FORTRESS, HE SERVED IN THE PENINSULAR UNDER / LORD WELLINGTON, AND DISTINGUISHED HIMSELF AT THE / BATTLES OF SALAMANCA, AND VITTORIA; / AT THE CLOSE OF THE PENINSULAR WAR IN 1815 / HE RETURNED HOME TO GOYTRE HOUSE, IN THIS PARISH. / IN 1822, HE WAS APPOINTED TO THE 16TH REGT IN CEYLON, / AND WAS DEPUTY COMMISSARY GENERAL / OF THAT ISLAND. / ON THE 2ND APRIL 1829, HE WAS SEIZED WITH CHOLERA / AND DIED THE FOLLOWING DAY, LEAVING A WIDOW, / AND FOUR CHILDREN, AND LAMENTED BY A WIDE / CIRCLE OF FRIENDS. / ....

Ensign 29th Foot 16 Aug 1794. Lt 94th Foot 6 Sep 1794. Capt 112th Foot 1795. Capt 5th Foot 10 Sep 1803. Bt Major 1 Jan 1805. Major 10 Jun 1813. Bt Lt Colonel 1 Jan 1812. Major 87th Foot 28 Mar 1816. Major 16th Foot 7 Feb 1822. Lt Colonel 25 Apr 1828. Lt Colonel Ceylon Corps 1829.

Served in the Peninsula with 1/5th Jul 1808 – Jan 1809 and Jun 1812 – Aug 1813. Present at Rolica, Vimeiro, Corunna, Salamanca, retreat from Burgos and Vittoria. Also served at Hanover 1805, South America 1807 (present at Buenos Ayres), Walcheren 1809 (taken prisoner at Flushing) and Ceylon 1822–1829 (with 16th Foot) In 1829 appointed Lt Colonel of the Ceylon Corps with the post of Deputy Commissary General for the island. Before he could take up his position he died suddenly of cholera 2 Apr 1829.
REFERENCE: *Gentleman's Magazine*, Oct 1829, p. 370 and Nov 1829, pp. 467–8.

BIRNES, Joseph
Private. Royal Sappers and Miners.
Buried in the Private Soldiers Burial Ground, Royal Hospital, Kilmainham, Dublin, Ireland.

Served in the Peninsula 1812 – Apr 1814. Present at Vittoria and San Sebastian. Awarded MGS medal for Vittoria and San Sebastian.

BIRTWHISTLE, John
Ensign. 32nd (Cornwall) Regiment of Foot.
Grave: Borough Cemetery, Cheltenham, Gloucestershire. (M.I.)

"SACRED TO THE MEMORY OF MAJOR GENERAL JOHN BIRTWHISTLE. LATE HM 32ND LIGHT INFANTRY WHO DIED OCTOBER 6TH 1867 AGED 75"

Ensign 14 Apr 1813. Lt 14 Jan 1819. Capt 13 May 1824. Bt Major 28 Jun 1838. Major 19 Jan 1839. Bt Lt Colonel 11 Nov 1851. Bt Colonel 28 Nov 1854. Major General 28 Aug 1865.

Served in the Peninsula Apr 1814. Present at Quatre Bras (wounded) and Waterloo (severely wounded carrying the colours of the 32nd Foot). Also served in Canada 1830–1842 (present during the Canadian Rebellion 1837–1838 for which he received a Brevet Majority for his conduct). Retired on half pay 12 Mar 1841.

BISDOM, D. R.
Major. 1st Carabineers Regiment, Dutch Cavalry.
Named on the Memorial to Dutch officers killed at Waterloo: St Joseph's Church, Waterloo, Belgium. (Photograph)

BISHOP, Isaac
Private. 12th (Prince of Wales's) Regiment of Light Dragoons.
Named on the Regimental Memorial: St Joseph's Church, Waterloo, Belgium. (Photograph)
    Killed at Waterloo.

BISHOP, William Bradshaw
Corporal Major. 1st Life Guards.
Headstone: Old Town Cemetery, Bideford, Devon. (Photograph)

SACRED / TO THE MEMORY OF / WILLIAM BRADSHAW BISHOP, / OF DISTINGUISHED MILI-TARY / REPUTATION, HAVING FOUGHT THROUGH / THE PENINSULA, AND AT WATERLOO: / WHO DEPARTED THIS LIFE / ON THE 11TH SEPTEMBER 1862, / IN HIS 86TH YEAR. / (VERSE)

Cpl Major. Quartermaster 1st Life Guards 19 Jun 1815.
    Served in the Peninsula Nov 1812 – Apr 1814. Present at Vittoria and Toulouse. Served at Waterloo (wounded and made Quartermaster of the regiment the day after the battle). MGS medal for Vittoria and Toulouse. Retired on full pay 27 May 1825.

BISHOPP, Cecil
Major. 98th Regiment of Foot.
Low monument in railed enclosure: Drummond Hill Cemetery, Lundy's Lane, Niagara, Canada. (Plot 325). (Photograph)

SACRED / TO THE MEMORY OF / LIEUTT COLL THE / HONBLE CECIL BISHOPP / 1ST FOOT GUARDS AND / INSPECTING FIELD / OFFICER IN UPPER / CANADA. ELDEST AND / ONLY SURVIVING SON / OF SIR CECIL BISHOPP / BART; BARON DE LA / ZOUCH IN ENGLAND. / AFTER HAVING SERVED WITH DIS – / TINCTION IN THE BRITISH ARMY / IN HOLLAND SPAIN AND PORTUGAL / HE DIED ON THE 16 JULY 1813 AGED / 30 IN CONSEQUENCE OF WOUNDS / RECEIVED IN ACTION WITH THE EN / EMY AT BLACK ROCK ON THE 11TH / OF THE SAME MONTH TO THE / GREAT GRIEF OF HIS FAMILY AND / FRIENDS AND IS BURIED HERE. / THIS TOMB ERECTED AT THE TIME / BY HIS BROTHER OFFICERS BECOM – / ING MUCH DILAPI-DATED IS NOW IN / 1846 RENEWED BY HIS AFFECTION / ATE SISTERS THE BARONESS DE LA / ZOUCHE, AND THE HON M. / PECHELL IN MEMORIAL OF AN EX – / CELLENT MAN AND BELOVED / BROTHER.

Memorial: St Peter's Church, Parham Park, Storrington, Sussex. (In vestry). (Photograph)

SACRED TO THE MEMORY OF / LIEUT. COL. CECIL BISHOPP LIEUT & CAPT. 1ST FOOT GUARDS / ELDEST SON OF SIR CECIL BISSHOPP BT, BARON DE LA ZOUCH, / AND HARRIET ANNE HIS WIFE. / AFTER HAVING SERVED WITH DISTINCTION / IN FLANDERS, SPAIN AND PORTUGAL / HE DIED, TO THE GREAT GRIEF OF HIS FAMILY, AND ALL WHO KNEW HIM / OF WOUNDS RECEIVED IN BATTLE AT ERIE NORTH AMERICA, 12TH JULY 1812, AGED 30, / AND IS BURIED UNDER AN OAK TREE AT STAMFORD / NEAR THE FALLS OF NIAGARA .... / HIS PILLOW ROOT OF STURDY OAK, / HIS SHROUD A SOLDIER'S SIMPLE CLOAK, / HIS DIRGE 'TWILL SOUND 'TILL TIME'S NO MORE. / NIAGARA'S LOUD DEEP SOLEMN ROAR, / THERE CECIL LIES; SAY WHERE THE GRAVE, / MORE WORTHY OF A BRITON BRAVE.

Ensign 1st Foot Guards 20 Sep 1799. Lt and Capt 16 Oct 1800. Capt 47th Foot Aug 1803. Lt and Capt 1st Foot Guards 3 Sep 1803. Bt Major 1 Jan 1812. Major 98th Foot 9 Apr 1812. Bt Lt Colonel and Inspecting Field Officer of Militia in Canada 25 Apr 1812.

Served in the Peninsula Oct 1808 – Jan 1809. Present at Corunna. Also served at Walcheren 1809 and Canada 1812–1813 (wounded at Black Rock and died of his wounds 16 Jul 1813). Bishopp commanded the regular troops between Chippewa and Fort Erie. On 11 Jul 1813 he led a raid on Black Rock New York, storming the fort and capturing large quantities of stores and artillery. He delayed his return to Canada as he wanted to take barrels of salt which was scarce in Upper Canada. The Americans had time to regroup and attacked again and Bishopp was wounded and died of his wounds 16 Jul 1813.
REFERENCE: *Dictionary of Canadian Biography.*

BLACHLEY, Charles
2nd Captain. Royal Artillery.
Low monument: St Andrew's Churchyard, Banwell, Somerset. (Photograph)

MAJOR GENERAL CHARLES BLACHLEY, ROYAL HORSE ARTILLERY / ELDEST SON OF CHARLES BLACHLEY ESQR OF BURY ST EDMUNDS AND HIS WIFE ANNE / DAUGHTER OF PELL HEIGHAM ESQUIRE OF HUNSTON HALL, SUFFOLK / BORN NOVR 28TH 1787, DIED FEBRY 16TH 1857.

2nd Lt 3 Dec 1803. 1st Lt 1 Mar 1804. 2nd Capt 21 Jun 1812. Capt 12 Dec 1826. Bt Major 22 Jul 1830. Lt Colonel 20 Jul 1840. Major General 14 Jun 1856.

Served in the Peninsula Sep 1809 – Dec 1812. Present at Busaco, Pombal, Redinha, Casal Nova, Foz d'Arouce, Fuentes d'Onoro, Aldea da Ponte, Castrejon, Salamanca and Burgos. MGS medal for Busaco, Fuentes d'Onoro and Salamanca. Retired on full pay Nov 1846. Shares the same grave with his brother 2nd Capt Henry Blachley Royal Artillery.

BLACHLEY, Henry
2nd Captain. Royal Artillery.
Low monument: St Andrew's Churchyard, Banwell, Somerset. (Photograph)

IN MEMORY OF / LIEUT GENERAL HENRY BLACHLEY, ROYAL ARTILLERY / SECOND SON OF / CHARLES BLACHLEY ESQ AND HIS WIFE ANNE DAUGHTER OF / PELL HEIGHAM ESQ OF HUNSTON HALL / BORN JAN'Y 1 1789 DIED AUG 13 1868 / AGED 79

2nd Lt 10 Aug 1804. 1st Lt 18 Feb 1805. 2nd Capt 20 Dec 1814. Capt 30 Dec 1828. Bt. Major 10 Jan 1837. Lt Colonel 23 Nov 1841. Major General 29 Aug 1857. Lt General 27 Feb 1866.

Served in the Peninsula Feb 1812 – Apr 1814. Present at Badajoz, Castrejon, Salamanca, Madrid, Burgos (conduct of his troop especially noted), Osma, Vittoria, first and second sieges of San Sebastian, Bidassoa, Nivelle, Nive, Adour and Sortie from Bayonne (wounded). MGS medal for Salamanca, Vittoria, San

Sebastian, Nivelle and Nive. Also served in France with the Army of Occupation 1817–1818 and Corfu 1829–1834. Shares the same grave with his brother 2nd Capt Charles Blachley Royal Artillery.

BLACK, John Lewis
Lieutenant. 1st (Royal Scots) Regiment of Foot.
Low monument: Walcot Cemetery, Lansdown, Bath, Somerset. (Photograph)

SACRED / TO THE MEMORY OF / Lᵀ COLONEL JOHN LEWIS BLACK / LATE OF H. M. 53ᴿᴰ REGI-MENT. / SERVED THE CAMPAIGN OF 1815 / INCLUDING THE BATTLES OF / QUATRE BRAS & WATERLOO / AT WHICH LAST HE WAS SLIGHTLY WOUNDED. / ALSO THE CAMPAIGN OF THE SUTLEJ / INCLUDING THE BATTLES OF / BUNDEERWAL, ALIWAL AND SOBRAON / DIED FEB 3 1859 / AGED 81 YEARS.

Ensign 49th Foot 22 Apr 1813. Lt 10 Mar 1814. Lt 1st Foot 23 Feb 1815. Capt 53rd Foot 16 Jun 1825. Bt Major 28 Jun 1838. Bt Lt Colonel 11 Nov 1851.
    Present at Quatre Bras and Waterloo (wounded). Also served in India in the Sikh Wars 1845–1846 (present at Buddiwal, Aliwal and Sobraon). Awarded Sutlej medal. Retired on half pay 3 Dec 1847.
REFERENCE: *Gentleman's Magazine, Mar 1859, p. 332. Annual Register, 1859, Appx, p. 410.*

BLACKLIN, Richard
Volunteer. 1st (Royal Scots) Regiment of Foot.
Memorial tablet: St George's Chapel, Windsor, Berkshire. (North wall of Dean's Cloister). (Photograph)

IN MEMORY / OF RICHARD BLACKLIN / OF THE 1ST ROYALS / DIED MAY 18TH 1867 / AGED 77 YEARS. / ABOVE SERVED UPWARDS / OF HALF A CENTURY / IN H. M. ARMY

Volunteer May 1815. Ensign 1st Foot 18 Jul 1815. Lt 13 Jul 1820. Capt 8 Aug 1833. Major 9 Nov 1846. Lt Colonel 20 Jun 1854. Colonel 1 Nov 1858.
    Served as a Volunteer with 3/1st at Quatre Bras and Waterloo (after four officers had been killed he carried the King's Colours at Waterloo where he was wounded), the Capture of Paris and with the Army of Occupation 1815–1816. One of only five surviving officers who marched with the regiment to Paris. Commissioned after Waterloo. Also served in India 1817 in 2nd Battalion and took part in campaigns in Deccan 1817–1818 (present at battle of Nagpore and the siege of Asseerghur 1819 in command of the leading company at the assault. Awarded medal), West Indies and Turkey. Military Knight of Windsor 3 Apr 1865.

BLACKMAN, John Lucie
Lieutenant and Captain. Coldstream Regiment of Foot Guards.
Low monument: Orchard at Hougoumont, Waterloo, Belgium. (Photograph)

JOHN LUCIE BLACKMAN WATERLOO 1815

Memorial tablet: Inside Mausoleum, Evere Cemetery, Brussels, Belgium. (Photograph)

CAPTAIN / JOHN LUCIE / BLACKMAN / COLDSTREAM GUARDS / AGED 21

Named on Memorial Panel VIII for Waterloo: Royal Military Chapel, Wellington Barracks, London. (M.I.) (Destroyed by a Flying Bomb 1944)

Ensign 5 Apr 1810. Lt and Capt 11 Jan 1814.
    Served in the Peninsula Feb 1812 – Mar 1814. Present at Salamanca, Burgos, Vittoria, Bidassoa, Nivelle, Nive, Adour and Bayonne. Present at Waterloo where he was killed in the orchard while defending

Hougoumont aged 21 years. Also served at Walcheren 1809 and the Netherlands 1814. Originally buried in the orchard of Hougoumont. Later one of the select band of soldiers buried in the Mausoleum at Evere.
REFERENCE: *Glover, Gareth, It all culminated at Hougoumont – the letters of Captain John Lucie Blackman, Coldstream Guards, 1812–1815, 2009.*

BLACKWELL, Nathaniel Shephard Freeman
Lieutenant Colonel. 62nd (Wiltshire) Regiment of Foot.
Ledger stone: Holy Trinity Churchyard, Cheltenham, Gloucestershire. (Photograph)

UNDERNEATH / ARE DEPOSITED THE REMAINS OF / MAJOR GENERAL / NATHANIEL SHEPHARD / FREEMAN BLACKWELL CB / LATE GOVERNOR / OF THE ISLAND OF TOBAGO / WHO DIED AT CHELTENHAM / 28TH AUGUST 1833 / AGED 55 YEARS

Ensign 94th Foot 1794. Lt 9 Sep 1795. Capt 60th Foot 11 Dec 1800. Capt 41st Foot 25 Dec 1802. Major 1st West India Regt 27 Feb 1806. Lt Colonel 4th West India Regt 4th Apr 1808. Lt Colonel 62nd Foot 13 Jun 1811. Bt Colonel 4 Jun 1814. Major General 27 May 1825.
  Served in the Peninsula Oct 1813 – Apr 1814. Present at Bidassoa, Nivelle, Nive and Bayonne. Present in France with the Army of Occupation 30 Jun – Dec 1815. Also served in the Cape of Good Hope, India 1795–1799 (the Mysore Wars 1799, present at Malavelly and Seringapatam), Canada 1802–1805, West Indies 1806–1812 (present at the capture of St Thomas and Santa Cruz 1807, Martinique and Guadeloupe 1809). Gold Medal for Martinique, Guadeloupe and Nive. CB. Commandant of the Hibernian School, Dublin 1819. Governor of Tobago 1828–1832. Educated at Charterhouse.
REFERENCE: *Royal Military Calendar, Vol 4, p. 196.*

BLACKWOOD, Robert Temple
Captain. 69th (South Lincolnshire) Regiment of Foot.
Memorial tablet: St John the Evangelist Church, Killyleagh, County Down, Northern Ireland. (South side of west doorway). (Photograph)

THIS MONUMENT IS PIOUSLY ERECTED BY / THE HONBLE AND REVD JOHN BLACKWOOD / RECTOR OF RATHCORMICK, CO OF CORK TO THE MEMORY OF HIS NEPHEW / THE GALLANT AND THE GOOD ROBERT TEMPLE BLACKWOOD, ESQRE / LATE CAPTAIN IN HIS MAJESTY'S 69TH REGIMENT OF FOOT / WHO FELL IN THE BATTLE OF WATERLOO, ON THE 18TH JUNE 1815 / IN THE 24TH YEAR OF HIS AGE, DEEPLY AND SINCERELY REGRETTED BY HIS FAMILY AND FRIENDS / TO WHOM HIS MANY AMIABLE QUALITIES, AFFECTIONATE DISPO-SITION / AND CHEERFUL TEMPER HAD HIGHLY ENDEARED HIM. / HE WAS THE GRANDSON OF SIR JOHN BLACKWOOD OF BALLYLEIDY, BART / AND BARONESS DUFFERIN AND CLONEBOYE OF KILLYLEAGH / BY THEIR FOURTH SON, THE HONBLE HANS BLACKWOOD AND HESTER MEHITABLE / TEMPLE, DAUGHTER OF ROBERT TEMPLE ESQRE OF TEN HILLY NEAR BOSTON, NORTH AMERICA. / CAPTAIN BLACKWOOD HAD PREVIOUSLY SERVED IN THE 52ND REGIMENT IN ALL THE CAMPAIGNS / IN WHICH IT WAS ENGAGED FROM 1807 TO THE CONCLUSION OF THE PEACE IN 1814 IN THE COURSE / OF WHICH PERIOD HE WAS SEVERELY WOUNDED IN THE STORMING OF BADAJOS UNDER / THE COMMAND OF FIELD MARSHAL HIS GRACE THE DUKE OF WELLINGTON.

Ensign 52nd Foot 18 Dec 1806. Lt 20 Jul 1808. Capt 86th Foot 8 Nov 1813. Capt 69th Foot Mar 1815.
  Served in the Peninsula with 1/52nd Aug – Sep 1808, 2/52nd Oct 1808 – Jan 1809 and Mar – Oct 1811 and 1/52nd Nov 1811 – Jun 1812 and Sep – Dec 1813. Present at Vigo, Sabugal, Fuentes d'Onoro, Ciudad Rodrigo, Badajoz (severely wounded) and Nivelle. Attained a captaincy in the 86th (County Down) Regiment of Foot Nov 1813 but the regiment was reduced in April 1814 and he went on half pay. Joined the 69th at the outbreak of the Waterloo campaign and was present at Quatre Bras. He survived the attack

by the French cavalry when the regiment was in line instead of square, but was killed at Waterloo 18 Jun. Also served at Walcheren 1809.

BLAIR, Thomas Hunter
Captain. 91st Regiment of Foot.
Mural Memorial tablet: Greyfriars Churchyard, Edinburgh, Scotland. (In walled enclosure). (Photograph)

UNDERNEATH / ARE INTERRED THE REMAINS OF / THOMAS HUNTER BLAIR, ESQ. / OF DUNSKEY, WIGTONSHIRE / MAJOR GENERAL / IN HER MAJESTY'S SERVICE. / COMMANDER OF THE BATH / AND DEPUTY LIEUTENANT OF THE / COUNTY OF WIGTON. / BORN 5TH OCTOBER 1782, DIED 31ST AUGUST 1849. / HE WAS THE SIXTH SON OF / JAMES HUNTER BLAIR, BART. OF DUNSKEY / DISTINGUISHED FOR HIS SERVICES / IN THE PENINSULA, BELGIUM AND AVA. / HE WAS PRESENT AT THE BATTLES OF / ROLEIA, VIMIERO, LUGO, CORUNNA, OPORTO, / TALAVERA, WATERLOO AND MELLOON, / FOR MOST OF WHICH ACTIONS HE HAD MEDALS, / AND HE WAS SEVERELY WOUNDED / AT TALAVERA AND AT WATERLOO. / AS A GALLANT SOLDIER, / BENEVOLENT, GENEROUS AND BELOVED MEMBER OF SOCIETY / HE WAS SINCERELY AND UNIVERSALLY LAMENTED. / ....

Ensign 24 Jul 1802. Lt 14 Sep 1804. Capt 28 Mar 1805. Bt Major 4 Jun 1814. Bt Lt Colonel 18 Jun 1815. Major 8 Jun 1818. Major 87th Foot 1 Apr 1819. Bt Colonel 10 Jan 1837. Major General 9 Nov 1846.

Served in the Peninsula Aug 1808 – Jan 1809 (ADC to Lt General Dalrymple Aug 1808, Brigade Major to Lt General Beresford Sep – Dec 1808, ADC to Major General Hill Dec 1808 – Jan 1809). Brigade Major to Major General Cameron May – Jul 1809). Present at Obidos, Rolica, Vimeiro, Lugo, Corunna, Oporto, Salamonde and Talavera (severely wounded, taken prisoner while in hospital and remained a prisoner until Apr 1814).

Present at Waterloo as Brigade Major to Major General Adams (severely wounded). Awarded Brevet Lt Colonelcy for his actions. Also served in India 1819–1831 (present at Ava where he commanded a brigade at the capture of Melloon). MGS medal for Rolica, Vimeiro, Corunna and Talavera. CB. Retired on half pay 25 Feb 1831.

REFERENCE: *Gentleman's Magazine, Nov 1849, p. 539. Annual Register, 1849, Appx, p. 265.*

BLAIR, William
Ensign. 67th (South Hampshire) Regiment of Foot.
Ledger stone: Cromdale Churchyard, Morayshire, Scotland. (M.I.)

"CAPT. WILLIAM BLAIR 67TH REGT. DIED FORRES 21ST SEPT 1838, AGED 65."

Sgt Major 67th Foot. Ensign 5th West India Regt 15 May 1811. Ensign 67th Foot 2 Apr 1812. Lt 15 Sep 1815. Paymaster 15 May 1823.

Served in the Peninsula Dec 1810 – Apr 1814. Present at Cadiz, Barrosa (commissioned after the battle for his bravery) and Tarragona.

BLAKE, Robert
Lieutenant. 3rd (East Kent) Regiment of Foot.
Memorial tablet: St Mary the Virgin Church, Wroxham, Norfolk. (Photograph)

IN MEMORY OF / ROBERT BLAKE HUMFREY / OF THIS PARISH ESQUIRE, / DEPUTY LIEU-TENANT AND JUSTICE OF THE PEACE. / AS AN OFFICER OF THE 3RD REGIMENT THE BUFFS / AT THE AGE OF 17 HE SERVED IN THE / PENINSULAR WAR UNDER WELLINGTON, / AND LOST HIS LEFT LEG AT THE PASSAGE OF THE NIVE / WHEN IN COMMAND OF THE 3RD / HE MARRIED CHARLOTTE, DAUGHTER OF COL HARVEY, / OF THORPE, AND IS SURVIVED BY

HIS SEVEN CHILDREN. / HE LIVED TO A GOOD OLD AGE / RESPECTED HONOURED AND BELOVED. / BORN 23ʀᴅ NOVEMBER 1795. / DIED 15ᴛʜ OCTOBER 1886.

Ensign 30 Apr 1812. Lt 23 Sep 1813.
    Served in the Peninsula Sep 1813 – Mar 1814. Present at Nivelle and Nive (severely wounded at St Pierre 13 Dec 1813 where his left leg was amputated). Awarded £100 pension per annum for loss of his leg. Half pay 1816. Retired on full pay as Lt in 9ᵗʰ Royal Veteran Battalion. Later became Deputy Lieutenant of Norfolk and Justice of the Peace. MGS medal for Nivelle and Nive. Changed name to Robert Blake Humfrey.

BLAKE, William Williams
Major. 20ᵗʰ Regiment of Light Dragoons.
Box tomb: St Andrew's Old Churchyard, Hove, Sussex. (Photograph)

COLONEL WILLIAM WILLIAMS BLAKE C.B. / LATE OF THE 20ᵀᴴ LIGHT DRAGOONS. / BORN MARCH 14 1779. DIED FEBRUARY 21 1863. / ....

Cornet 26 Apr 1797. Lt 31 Oct 1799. Capt 18 Feb 1802. Major 21 Mar 1805. Bt Lt Col 1 Jan 1812. Bt Colonel 22 Jul 1830.
    Served in the Peninsula Aug 1808 – Sep 1809 and Jan – Nov 1813. Present at Rolica, Vimeiro, Douro (Mentioned in Despatches), Castalla and Ordal. Gold Medal for Rolica and Vimeiro. CB. Also served in the West Indies 1797–1802, Cape of Good Hope 1806, South America 1807 (present at Maldonado and siege of Montevideo) and Sicily 1810–1811. Retired 22 Jul 1830.

BLAKENEY, Sir Edward
Lieutenant Colonel. 7ᵗʰ (Royal Fusiliers) Regiment of Foot.
Chest tomb: Oak Lane Cemetery, Twickenham, Middlesex, London. (Photograph)

TO THE MEMORY OF / FIELD – MARSHAL / THE RIGHT HONᴮᴸᴱ SIR EDWARD BLAKENEY, / G.C.B. & G.C.H. / GOVERNOR OF THE ROYAL HOSPITAL CHELSEA, / WHO DIED THE 2ᴺᴰ AUGUST 1868 / AGED 90.

Cornet 8ᵗʰ Lt Dragoons 28 Feb 1794. Lt 121ˢᵗ Foot 24 Feb 1794. Capt 99ᵗʰ Foot 24 Dec 1794. Capt 17ᵗʰ Foot 8 Mar 1798. Major 17 Sep 1801. Major 47ᵗʰ Foot 9 Jul 1803. Major 7ᵗʰ Foot 24 Mar 1804. Bt Lt Colonel 25 Apr 1808. Lt Colonel 20 Jul 1811. Bt Colonel 4 Jun 1814. Major General 27 Mar 1825. Lt General 28 Jun 1838. General 20 Jun 1854. Field Marshal 9 Nov 1862.
    Served in the Peninsula with 1/7ᵗʰ Aug – Oct 1810, 2/7ᵗʰ Nov 1810 – Jun 1811 and 1/7ᵗʰ Jul 1811 – May 1812 and Jan 1813 – Jan 1814. Present at Busaco, Pombal, Condeixa, first siege of Badajoz, Albuera (wounded), Aldea da Ponte, Ciudad Rodrigo, Badajoz (severely wounded), Vittoria, Pyrenees, Bidassoa, Nivelle and Nive. Present at the Capture of Paris and with the Army of Occupation. KCB 2 Jan 1815. Also served in the West Indies 1794–1796 (present at Demerara, Berbice, Essiquibo – three times taken prisoner by pirates), the Helder 1799, Copenhagen 1807, Martinique 1809, North America 1814–1815 (present at New Orleans), Portugal 1826 (commanded the 1ˢᵗ Brigade in the expedition to Portugal), Ireland Aug 1836 – Mar 1855 (Commander in Chief). Gold Cross for Martinique, Albuera, Badajoz, Vittoria and Pyrenees. MGS medal for Busaco, Ciudad Rodrigo, Nivelle and Nive. GCB. GCH. Colonel 7ᵗʰ Foot 20 Sep 1832. Colonel 1ˢᵗ Foot 21 Dec 1854. Lt Governor Chelsea Hospital 6 Feb 1855. Governor Chelsea Hospital 25 Sep 1856. Colonel Rifle Brigade 28 Aug 1865.
Rᴇғᴇʀᴇɴᴄᴇ: *Dictionary of National Biography. United Service Magazine, Sep 1868, pp. 130–1. Gentleman's Magazine, Sep 1868, pp. 567–8.*

BLAKISTON, John
Captain. 27th (Inniskilling) Regiment of Foot.
Memorial tablet: St Wilfred's Church, Mobberley, Cheshire. (M.I.)

IN MEMORY OF / MAJOR JOHN BLAKISTON OF MOBBERLEY / WHO DIED ON JUNE 4TH 1867
AGED 82 YEARS. / .... / IN YOUTH HE WAS A DISTINGUISHED SOLDIER / IN MIDDLE AGE
AN ACTIVE POLITICIAN. / THEY PASSED THE EVENINGS OF THEIR DAYS IN RETIREMENT /
IN THIS PARISH, LOVED AND RESPECTED BY THEIR FAMILY AND NEIGHBOURS.

Low monument: St Wilfred's Churchyard, Mobberley, Cheshire. (Photograph)

IN MEMORY OF MAJOR JOHN BLAKISTON OF MOBBERLY / WHO DIED ON JUNE 4TH 1867
AGED 82 YEARS.

Named on the Regimental Memorial: Rochester Cathedral, Rochester, Kent. (Photograph)

Ensign 71st Foot May 1794. Lt Madras Engineers Jul 1794–1812. Capt 27th Foot 30 Sep 1813. Portuguese
Army: Capt 17th Line 22 Apr 1813.
    Served in the Peninsula Apr 1813 – Apr 1814 with the Portuguese Army. Present at Vittoria, San
Sebastian (severely wounded when serving as an Engineer during the siege), Nivelle, Orthes and Toulouse.
Also served in India 1794–1812 in the Madras Engineers (present at Assaye, Argaum. Ahmednuggar,
Gawilghur and Vellore) and Java 1811. Retired to England 1812 owing to ill health, but returned to the
Army in the Peninsula Apr 1813. Half pay 1816. MGS medal for Java, Vittoria, San Sebastian, Nivelle,
Orthes and Toulouse. Army of India medal for Assaye, Argaum and Gawilghur.
    Appointed one of the Honourable Corps of Gentlemen at Arms on Wellington's recommendation
1843–1865. Magistrate in Cheshire and Hampshire.
REFERENCE: Blakiston, John, Twelve years military adventures in three quarters of the Globe; or, Memoirs
of an officer who served in the armies of His Majesty and of the East India Company, between the years
1804 and 1814, in which are contained the campaigns of the Duke of Wellington in India, and his last in
Spain and the south of France, 2 vols, 1829. Gentleman's Magazine, Aug 1867, pp. 249–50.

BLANCKLEY, Henry Stanyford
Captain. 23rd (Royal Welch Fusiliers) Regiment of Foot.
Memorial: Ranipet Cemetery, North Arcot, India. (M.I.)

"TO THE MEMORY OF MAJOR HENRY STANYFORD BLANCKLEY, 13TH LT DRAGOONS, AGED
34 WHO DIED 2 NOV 1819. ERECTED BY HIS SURVIVING BROTHER OFFICERS."

Ensign 16 Oct 1805. Lt 31 Jul 1806. Capt 21 May 1812. Capt 13th Lt Dragoons 30 Jun 1815. Bt Major
21 Jul 1817.
    Served in the Peninsula with 1/23rd Dec 1810 – Sep 1811 and Oct 1811 – Sep 1813 (engaged on
Particular Services). Present at Redinha, Olivencia, first siege of Badajoz and Albuera. Present at Waterloo
(DAAG). Also served at Martinique 1809 and India 1819 with 13th Lt Dragoons (drowned in a boating
accident on the Cauveryparck tank along with another officer and their female companion.

BLANCO, Thomas
Private. 51st (2nd Yorkshire West Riding) Light Infantry.
Memorial tablet: St Giles Church, Pontefract, Yorkshire. (Photograph)

IN MEMORY OF / THOMAS BLANCO / WHO SERVED WITH THE / 51ST KING'S OWN LIGHT
INFANTRY, / THROUGHOUT THE PENINSULAR CAMPAIGN / AND WAS ONE OF A PARTY

WHO STAYED / TO BURY SIR JOHN MOORE AT CORUNNA. / HE DIED AT PONTEFRACT JULY 11 1873 / AGED 90 YEARS. / THIS MONUMENT IS ERECTED BY THE OFFICERS, / NON COMMISSIONED OFFICERS AND PRIVATE SOLDIERS / OF THE 51ST REGIMENT AS A MARK OF RESPECT FOR THE / VETERAN'S GALLANT SERVICES.

Served in the Peninsula 1808 – Jan 1809. Present at Corunna. One of the party who buried Sir John Moore after the battle.

BLANE, Hugh Seymour
Ensign. 3rd Regiment of Foot Guards.
Memorial: Royal Military Chapel, Wellington Barracks, London. (M.I.) (Destroyed by a Flying Bomb 1944)

"IN MEMORY OF / JOHN HAMILTON ELRINGTON, GEORGE DOUGLAS STANDEN, AND SIR / HUGH SEYMOUR BLANE, BART., / OF THE LIGHT COMPANY 3RD GUARDS, DURING THE DEFENCE OF HOUGOUMONT AT / THE BATTLE OF WATERLOO. / PLACED BY THE REVEREND WILLIAM FREDERICK ELRINGTON, B.A., / LATE LIEUT.-COLONEL SCOTS FUSILIER GUARDS".

Ensign 31 Mar 1814. Lt and Capt 15 Mar 1821.
   Served at Waterloo in the defence of Hougoumont. Retired Aug 1831 to his estate in Blanefield, north of Glasgow. Second Baronet 1834. Died 1869.
REFERENCE: *Household Brigade Journal, 1869, p. 321.*

BLANSHARD, Thomas
2nd Captain. Royal Engineers.
Named on the Regimental Memorial: Rochester Cathedral, Rochester, Kent. (Photograph)

2nd Lt 28 Sep 1807. Lt 1 Apr 1808. 2nd Capt 21 Jul 1813. Bt Major 29 Sep 1814. Capt 23 Mar 1825. Lt Colonel 10 Jan 1837. Colonel 5 Jul 1851. Major General 16 Dec 1854.
   Served in the Peninsula Mar – Apr 1814. Present at the siege of Bayonne and Sortie from Bayonne. Also served in North America 1814–1815 (present at Washington, Baltimore, New Orleans and Fort Bowyer) and in France with the Army of Occupation 1815–1817. CB. Died 19 Jun 1859.

BLANTYRE, Lord Robert
Lieutenant Colonel. 42nd (Royal Highland) Regiment of Foot.
Memorial tablet inside Mausoleum: Bolton Church, East Lothian, Scotland. (Inscription from Memorial Inscription record). (Photograph of exterior of mausoleum)

"ROBERT WALTER STUART, 11TH LORD BLANTYRE, MAJOR GENERAL IN THE ARMY, SERVED IN HOLLAND AND IN THE PENINSULAR WAR. BORN 26TH DECEMBER 1775, ACCIDENTALLY KILLED IN BRUSSELS DURING THE REVOLUTION ON THE 23RD SEPTEMBER 1830, AGED 54. HIS REMAINS WERE BROUGHT FROM BRUSSELS AND LAID HERE. THIS TABLET IS PLACED IN LOVING MEMORY BY HIS WIFE, FANNY MARY, DAUGHTER OF THE HON. JOHN RODNEY, BORN 26 JULY 1792, DIED 19 NOVEMBER 1875".

Obelisk: Ferry Road, Bishopton, Renfrewshire, Scotland. (Photograph)

ERECTED / BY / THE COUNTY OF RENFREW, / TO / THE MEMORY OF / THE RIGHT HONOURABLE ROBERT WALTER, / 11TH LORD BLANTYRE. / A MAJOR GENERAL IN THE

BRITISH ARMY, / AND FORMERLY / LORD LIEUTENANT / OF / RENFREWSHIRE. / IN TESTI-
MONY OF RESPECT FOR HIS PUBLIC / SERVICES AND AS A TRIBUTE OF ESTEEM / FOR HIS
PRIVATE WORTH. / DIED 23ᴰ SEP 1830.

Ensign 3ʳᵈ Foot Guards 13 Mar 1795. Lt 31ˢᵗ Foot 19 May 1798. Capt 12ᵗʰ Lt Dragoons 1798. Capt 7ᵗʰ
Lt Dragoons Jul 1799. Major 17ᵗʰ Lt Dragoons Apr 1804. Lt Colonel 42ⁿᵈ Foot 19 Sep 1804. Bt Colonel
4 Jun 1813. Major General 12 Aug 1819.
    Served in the Peninsula Jul 1809 – Apr 1812 (Commanded 2 Brigade 1ˢᵗ Division Aug 1810 – Jan 1812).
Present at Busaco, Fuentes d'Onoro (Mentioned in Despatches) and Ciudad Rodrigo. In command of
2/42ⁿᵈ in the Peninsula. When the 2ⁿᵈ Battalion was used to fill up the ranks in the 1ˢᵗ Battalion Blantyre
was ordered home with the remaining men in 1812. Half pay 1813. Also served in Portugal 1798, the
Helder 1799, Egypt 1801 (ADC to Sir John Stuart) and the Baltic 1807 (AAG). Gold Medal for Fuentes
d'Onoro. KTS. CB. Educated at Eton. Lord Lieutenant of Renfrewshire 1820 – 1822. Accidentally shot
as he leant out of his hotel window during the Revolution in Brussels 1830.
REFERENCE: *Royal Military Calendar, Vol 3, pp. 415–6.*

BLATHWAYT, George William
Lieutenant. 23ʳᵈ Regiment of Light Dragoons.
Headstone: St Peter's Churchyard, Dyrham, Gloucestershire. (Photograph)

GEORGE WILLIAM BLATHWAYT / OF DYRHAM PARK / LIEUT COLONEL IN THE ARMY /
BORN 25ᵀᴴ FEB 1797 / DIED 14ᵀᴴ MAY 1871

Brass memorial tablet: St Peter's Church, Dyrham, Gloucestershire. (Photograph)

IN MEMORY OF / GEORGE WILLIAM BLATHWAYT OF DYRHAM PARK / LATE 23ᴿᴰ LIGHT
DRAGOONS & KINGS DRAGOON GUARDS. / BORN FEB 25 1797. DIED MAY 14 1871.

Memorial tablet: Clock Tower, Chipping Sodbury, Gloucestershire. (Photograph)

THIS CLOCK TOWER WAS / ERECTED BY FRIENDS AND NEIGHBOURS / TO THE MEMORY OF
/ LIEUᵀ COLONEL GEORGE WILLIAM BLATHWAYT / OF DYRHAM PARK IN THIS COUNTY /
JUSTICE OF THE PEACE FOR THE COUNTIES OF / GLOUCESTER WILTS AND SOMERSET /
SERVED IN THE WATERLOO CAMPAIGN 1815 / MAJOR ROYAL GLOUCESTERSHIRE
YEOMANRY 1854 / BORN FEBRUARY 25ᵀᴴ 1797 DIED MAY 14ᵀᴴ 1871.

Cornet 25 Nov 1813. Lt 23ʳᵈ Lt Dragoons 4 May 1815. Capt 9 Jun 1825. Major Gloucestershire Yeomanry
1854. Half pay 9 Jun 1825.
    Present at Waterloo. Buried under a willow tree from a cutting taken from St Helena. Served in the
Royal Gloucestershire Yeomanry. Justice of the Peace for Gloucestershire, Wiltshire and Somerset.
REFERENCE: *Blathwayt, George W., Recollections of my life including military service at Waterloo by
Colonel George Blathwayt, 23ʳᵈ Lt Dragoons, edited by Gareth Glover, 2004.*

BLOMER, Charles
Captain. 31ˢᵗ (Huntingdonshire) Regiment of Foot.
Box tomb: St Mary the Virgin Churchyard, Carisbrooke, Isle of Wight. (Grave number 314). Seriously
eroded and inscription recorded from memorial inscription. (Photograph)

"CAPT CHARLES BLOMER, LATE OF THE 31ˢᵗ REGT, DIED 11 MAY 1835, AGED 52 YEARS."

Ensign 20ᵗʰ Foot 12 May 1795. Adjutant 29 Oct 1799. Lt 31ˢᵗ Foot 5 Sep 1801. Capt 7 Feb 1807.

Served in the Peninsula Apr – Jul 1809 and Sep 1811 – Apr 1814. Present at Vittoria, Pyrenees, Nivelle and Nive. Also served in Egypt 1801 (wounded and awarded pension of £100 per annum).

BLOMFIELD, Thomas Valentine
Lieutenant. 48th (Northamptonshire) Regiment of Foot.
Headstone in railed enclosure: Denham Court Churchyard, Denham Court, Sydney, New South Wales, Australia. (Photograph)

THOMAS VALENTINE / BLOMFIELD. / BORN / FEBRUARY 14, 1793, / DIED MAY 19, 1857.

Ensign 8 Jun 1809. Lt 17 Jun 1811.
   Served in the Peninsula Oct 1809 – Apr 1814. Present at Busaco, Albuera, Aldea da Ponte, Ciudad Rodrigo, Badajoz, Salamanca, Vittoria, Orthes and Toulouse. Went with his regiment to New South Wales, Australia in 1817. Retired from the army in 1824 and settled on his grant of 2,000 acres of land and acquired further land in the Hunter River district. Held various appointments as a Magistrate. Awarded MGS medal for Busaco, Albuera, Ciudad Rodrigo, Badajoz, Salamanca, Vittoria, Orthes and Toulouse. Died 19 May 1857 at Denham Court, near Liverpool in Australia.

BLOOD, John Aylward
Ensign. 68th (Durham) Regiment of Foot.
Low monument: Abbey Cemetery, Bath, Somerset. (Photograph)

BENEATH / ARE DEPOSITED THE REMAINS OF / LIEUTᵀ COLONEL JOHN AYLWARD BLOOD, / WHO DIED 22ᴺᴰ JULY 1847 / AGED 48.

Volunteer 59th Foot 1813. Ensign 68th Foot 3 Mar 1814. Lt 7th Foot 26 Mar 1825. Lt 68th Foot 8 Apr 1825. Capt 6 Aug 1829. Major 3 May 1833. Lt Colonel 9 Nov 1846.
   Served in the Peninsula Oct 1813 – Apr 1814. Present at Nivelle (wounded), Nive and Bayonne. MGS medal for Nivelle and Nive. Half pay 12 Oct 1838.

BLOOD, Thomas
Sergeant Major. 16th (Queen's) Regiment of Light Dragoons.
Pedestal tomb: St Giles the Abbot Churchyard, Cheadle, Staffordshire. (Photograph)

TO THE MEMORY OF LIEUTENANT THOMAS BLOOD OF THE 16TH LANCERS. HE ENTERED THE ARMY IN 1793 AT THE AGE OF 18; AND WENT THROUGH THE ARDUOUS AND DISAS-TROUS CAMPAIGNS IN FLANDERS, UNDER THE DUKE OF YORK AND WAS IN THE ACTIONS OF THE CATEAU PLAINS, TOURNAY, AND LISLE; WHERE FOR HIS GALLANTRY HE WAS APPOINTED REGIMENTAL RIDING MASTER. HE WAS NEXT ENGAGED IN HONOURABLE SERVICE IN DIFFERENT CLIMES UNTIL HE WAS CALLED TO SHARE IN THE GLORIES OF THE PENINSULAR WAR; WHERE HIS UNDAUNTED BRAVERY, HIS ENTHUSIASTIC GALLANTRY, HIS SKILFUL AND DARING EXPLOITS, SHONE FORTH WITH CONSPICUOUS LUSTRE. HE DISTINGUISHED HIMSELF AT TALAVERA, BUSACO, FUENTES ONORO, SALAMANCA, THE PYRENEES AND TOULOUSE; / AND EARNED NEVER FADING LAURELS ON THE PLAINS OF WATERLOO. AFTER GENERAL PEACE HE EMBARKED FOR THE EAST INDIES AND AGAIN WAS DISTINGUISHED FOR HIS SKILL AND GALLANTRY, ESPECIALLY AT THE CAPTURE OF BHURTPORE. AFTER UNREMITTINGLY SERVING HIS COUNTRY FOR 40 YEARS, WITH A ZEAL RARELY EQUALLED, AND WITH A COURAGE NEVER SURPASSED, THE INCREASING PRES-SURE OF INFIRMITIES COMPELLED HIM TO RETIRE FROM ACTIVE SERVICE. THE FEW REMAINING YEARS OF HIS LIFE WERE YEARS OF PAIN. WORN OUT BY THE ENERVATING EFFECTS OF THE EASTERN CLIMATE, HE DIED JUNE 20TH, 1840, AGED 65 YEARS.

TESTIMONIALS TO HIS SERVICE AND ABILITIES:-
"A BETTER OR MORE GALLANT SOLDIER IS NOT TO BE FOUND IN THE ARMY. I HAD SO MANY OPPORTUNITIES OF WITNESSING YOUR GALLANTRY, INTELLIGENCE AND CONDUCT IN THE PENINSULAR THAT I AM BOUND TO GIVE THE STRONGEST TESTIMONY IN YOUR FAVOUR." / SIR F. PONSONBY.

"LIEUTENANT BLOOD HAS BEEN KNOWN TO ME 33 YEARS, AND WAS FOR HIS GOOD CONDUCT AND BRAVERY PROMOTED BY ME CORPORAL, SERJEANT, AND RIDING MASTER. HE WAS FREQUENTLY FOR HIS GALLANTRY AND GOOD SERVICES IN THE PENIN-SULAR BROUGHT TO THE NOTICE OF THE DUKE OF WELLINGTON. IN THE EAST INDIES. I HAD MANY OPPORTUNITIES OF WITNESSING HIS INVALUABLE SERVICES." / LORD COMBERMERE.

"I AM ANXIOUS TO TESTIFY THAT THE MANY GALLANT EXPLOITS PERFORMED BY YOU IN THE FIELD; THE MANY RECORDED INSTANCES OF YOUR UNDAUNTED BRAVERY; THE ENTHUSIASTIC ZEAL AND ATTACHMENT EVER EVINCED BY YOU IN THE SERVICE, SHINE FORTH NOT ONLY AS THE DEEDS OF THE BRAVEST OF THE BRAVE, BUT HAVE RECEIVED ADDITIONAL LUSTRE FROM THE REPUTATION YOU HAVE MAINTAINED AS AN OFFICER, WHOSE CONDUCT HAS BEEN DISTINGUISHED FOR CANDOUR, INTEGRITY AND HONOUR." / R. ARNOLD, COLONEL, 16TH LANCERS.

"HIS ROYAL HIGHNESS THINKS IT RIGHT TO STATE THAT MR BLOOD IS ONE OF THE MOST MERITORIOUS OLD OFFICERS IN THE KING'S SERVICE." / DUKE OF YORK.

Private 1793. Corporal and Roughrider 1798. Sergeant and Roughrider 1799. Sgt Major 1813. Cornet and Riding Master 25 Oct 1822. Lt 18 Jul 1826.

Served in the Peninsula 1809–1814. Present at Talavera, Busaco, Fuentes d'Onoro, Salamanca, retreat from Burgos, Vittoria, Nive and Bayonne. Present at Waterloo. Also served in Flanders 1793–1794 (present at Le Cateau, Tournai and Lille), and in India 1822–1831 (present at the siege of Bhurtpore. Commissioned to Lieutenant 18 Jul 1826). Half pay 28 Mar 1834. Retired in 1835 and died 20 Jun 1840, aged 65.

BLOOMFIELD, David
Sergeant. 32nd (Cornwall) Regiment of Foot.
Ledger stone: St Macartan's Cathedral Cemetery, Clogher, County Tyrone, Northern Ireland.
(Photograph)

ERECTED BY SERGT. DAVID BLOOMFIELD, 32ND FOOT, WHO SERVED IN THE PENINSULA UNDER THE DUKE OF WELLINGTON. AND WAS PRESENT AT ROLICA 17TH AUG. 1808, VIMIERO 21ST AUG. 1808, TALAVERA 27TH AND 28TH JULY 1809, SALAMANCA 22ND JULY 1812, VITTORIA 21ST JUNE 1813, PYRENEES 28TH 29TH AND 30TH JULY 1813, NIVELLE 10TH NOV 1813 AT WHICH DATE HE WAS SEVERELY WOUNDED. AND HAS NOW BEEN 82 YEARS IN HER MAJESTY'S SERVICE. UNDERNEATH ARE THE REMAINS OF ANNE BLOOMFIELD, HIS WIFE, WHO DEPARTED THIS LIFE 3RD JUNE 1870 AGED 88 YEARS. ALSO SERGT. DAVID BLOOMFIELD OF SLATMORE WHO DEPARTED THIS LIFE 21ST MAY 1882 AGED 100 YEARS.

Pte 1800.

Served in the Peninsula Aug 1808 – Jan 1809, Feb 1809 – Aug 1809 and Sep 1809 – Apr 1814. Present at Rolica, Vimeiro, Douro, Talavera, siege of Salamanca Forts, Salamanca, Vittoria, Pyrenees and Nivelle (severely wounded 10 Nov 1813). Did not go to Corunna with rest of the regiment, but stayed behind at Lisbon. Then joined 2nd Battalion of Detachments and fought at Douro and Talavera. MGS medal for Rolica, Talavera, Salamanca, Vittoria and Nivelle.

BLOOMFIELD, James Henry
Captain. 51st (2nd Yorkshire West Riding) Light Infantry.
Named on the Regimental Memorial: KOYLI Chapel, York Minster, Yorkshire. (Photograph)

Ensign 1801. Lt 1803. Capt 5 Nov 1805.
   Served in the Peninsula Oct 1808 – Jan 1809. Present at Corunna. Also served in Ceylon 1803 and Walcheren 1809 where he died of fever 13 Sep 1809.

BLUMENBACH, Carl Edward
Lieutenant. Artillery, King's German Legion.
Named on the Memorial: St Andrew's Church, (now Musée Historique), Biarritz, France. (Photograph)

Lt 21 Jan 1806.
   Served in the Peninsula 1808–1814. Present at Albuera (wounded) and Toulouse where he was killed 10 Apr 1814. Also served in the Baltic 1807–1808.

BLUNT, Richard
Lieutenant Colonel. 3rd (East Kent) Regiment of Foot.
Grave: St James's Churchyard, Shirley, Southampton, Hampshire. (M.I.)

"RICHARD BLUNT, GENERAL, HUSBAND OF POLLY BLUNT, COLONEL OF 66TH REGT OF FOOT. COMMANDER OF THE TOWER AND SWORD OF PORTUGAL. DIED 25 DECEMBER 1859 AGED 90."

Ensign 3rd Foot 31 Jan 1787. Lt 23 Feb 1791. Capt 11 Jul 1793. Major 17 May 1796. Lt Colonel 23 Aug 1797. Bt Colonel 28 Oct 1809. Major General 1 Jan 1812. Lt General 27 May 1825. General 23 Nov 1841. Portuguese Army: Colonel 4th Line 25 Mar 1809. Field Marshal 5 Feb 1812.
   Served in the Peninsula with 3rd Foot Sep 1808 – Mar 1809 and with Portuguese Army Mar 1809 – Apr 1814 (Governor of Peniche and Inspector General of Recruits). Also served in the West Indies 1787–1790, Flanders 1794–1795, West Indies 1795–1802, Hanover 1805 and Madeira 1807. KTS. Colonel 66th Foot 25 Mar 1835.

BLYTH, John Willes
1st Lieutenant Commissaries. Royal Artillery Drivers.
Headstone: St Mary's Churchyard, Appledore, Devonshire. (Photograph)

SACRED / TO THE MEMORY OF / CAPT. JOHN WILLES BLYTH / OF H.M. ROYAL HORSE ARTILLERY, / OBIT 13TH JULY 1857. / AETAT 73.

1st Lt Commissaries 24 Oct 1803.
   Served in the Peninsula Apr 1811 – Jul 1812 and Jan 1813 – Apr 1814. Present at the first siege of Badajoz and Albuera (wounded). MGS medal for Albuera. Retired on half pay 1 Aug 1816.

BLYTHMAN, Augustus
Private. 95th Regiment of Foot.
Headstone: St Mary with Holy Trinity Churchyard, Richmond, Yorkshire. (Photograph)

SACRED / TO THE / MEMORY OF / AUGUSTUS BLYTHMAN / WHO DIED DECR 15TH 1847 AGED 57 YEARS. / HE WAS A NATIVE OF THE COUNTY OF SURREY AND / SERVED SEVERAL YEARS IN THE 95 RIFLE CORPS / DURING THE PENINSULAR WAR UNDER HIS / GRACE THE DUKE OF WELLINGTON; / HE WAS PRESENT AT THE ACTION OF / NIVE ORTHES AND TOULOUSE

AND / THE MEMORABLE BATTLE OF WATERLOO. / HE WAS 35 YEARS A FAITHFUL SERVANT / TO T. T. WORSLEY / **********

Served in the Peninsula 1812 – Apr 1814. Present at Nive, Orthes and Toulouse. Also served at Waterloo. MGS medal for Nive, Orthes and Toulouse. He was the servant to Thomas Taylor Worsley, a member of a prominent family in Yorkshire, who was a Lieutenant in the 95th Foot and served in the Peninsula Jan 1812 – Apr 1814 and at Waterloo. Blythman continued in his service after the war.

BOASE, John
Lieutenant. 32nd (Cornwall) Regiment of Foot.
Headstone: Falmouth Churchyard, Falmouth, Cornwall. (Photograph)

IN / MEMORY OF / LIEUT JOHN BOASE. / OBIT SEPR 11TH 1854; / AGED 71 YEARS. / FOR MANY YEARS / BARRACK MASTER / AT PENDENNIS CASTLE.

Ensign Aug 1807. Lt 9 Jun 1808.
    Served in the Peninsula Aug 1808 – Jan 1809 and Jul 1811 – Apr 1814. Present at Rolica, Vimeiro, Corunna, siege of Salamanca Forts, Salamanca (severely wounded), Pyrenees, Bidassoa, Nivelle, (wounded), Nive and Orthes. Present at Quatre Bras (severely wounded). MGS medal for Rolica, Vimeiro, Corunna, Salamanca, Pyrenees, Nivelle, Nive and Orthes. Barrack Master at Pendennis Castle.

BOATES, Henry Ellis
Lieutenant. Royal Regiment of Horse Guards.
Low monument: St Hilary's Churchyard, Erbistock, Denbighshire, Wales. (Photograph)

HENRY ELLIS BOATES DECR 3 1858

Memorial brass: St Hilary's Church, Erbistock, Denbighshire, Wales. (Photograph)

IN A VAULT TO THE NORTH SIDE OF THE CHURCH LIE ALL THAT IS EARTHLY OF / LIEUT-COLONEL HENRY ELLIS BOATES OF ROSEHILL IN THIS PARISH FORMERLY OF THE ROYAL / HORSE GUARDS BLUE. HE DIED BY A FALL FROM HIS HORSE DEC 1858 AGED 64. /
....

Stained glass window: St Hilary's Church, Erbistock, Denbighshire, Wales. (Photograph)

THIS WINDOW IS TO THE GLORY OF GOD AND IN MEMORY OF LIEUT. COLONEL HENRY ELLIS BOATES & OF CAROLINE BOATES HIS WIFE ....

Cornet 16 Jul 1812. Lt 28 Jan 1813. Capt 4 May 1820. Lt Colonel (unattached) 21 Nov 1828. Capt and Lt Colonel 1st Foot Guards 11 Nov 1836.
    Served in the Peninsula Jan – Apr 1814. Present at Toulouse. Present at Waterloo. MGS medal for Toulouse. Retired 2 Dec 1836. High Sheriff of Denbighshire 1841.

BOBERS, Carl von
Captain and Brigade Major. Staff Corps, King's German Legion.
Named on the Regimental Memorial: La Haye Sainte, Waterloo, Belgium. (Photograph)

Cornet 1st Hussars 10 Sep 1808. Lt 12 Jul 1811. Capt 13 Sep 1814.
    Served in the Peninsula Jun 1809 – Apr 1814. Present at Talavera, Coa, Busaco, Pombal, Sabugal,

Fuentes d'Onoro, El Bodon, Morales, Castalla, Salamanca, Vittoria, Pyrenees, Nivelle, Orthes and Toulouse. Present at Waterloo where he was killed. Also served in the Netherlands 1814.

BOELTJES, K.
Lieutenant. 5th National Militia Battalion, Dutch Infantry.
Named on the Memorial to Dutch officers killed at Quatre Bras: St Joseph's Church, Waterloo, Belgium..
(Photograph)

BOGUE, Richard
Captain. Royal Artillery.
Memorial tablet: St Peter's Church, Titchfield, Hampshire. (Photograph)

THE MEMORIAL / OF PRIVATE WORTH AND MILITARY GLORY / SACRED TO / CAPTAIN RICHARD BOGUE / OF THE ROYAL HORSE ARTILLERY; / WHO FELL BY A RIFLE SHOT, IN THE BATTLE OF LEIPSIC / ON THE 18TH OCTOBER 1813 / WHILE COMMANDING THE BRITISH ROCKET BRIGADE IN / THE GLORIOUS VICTORY OF THAT MEMORABLE DAY. / HE HAD A MOMENT BEFORE RECEIVED THE THANKS OF THE PRINCE, / AND ALLIED GENERALS, UNDER WHOM HE SERVED / FOR COMPELLING THE SURRENDER OF FIVE FRENCH BATTAL-IONS AT PAUNSDORF / TO HIS OWN SMALL FORCE, NOT EXCEEDING TWO HUNDRED MEN. / HIS REMAINS WERE INTERRED AT TAUCHA, NEAR LEIPSIC, IN THE 31ST YEAR OF HIS AGE. / AS AN OFFICER, HE EMINENTLY COMBINED PROFESSIONAL SCIENCE / WITH THE MOST ARDENT VALOUR. / BY HIS INDEFATIGABLE ATTENTION, THAT FORMIDABLE WEAPON THE CONGREVE ROCKET WAS APPLIED / WITH A PRECISION AND SUCCESS / PROPORTIONATE TO ITS IMPORTANCE AS AN INVENTION OF DESTRUCTIVE WARFARE. / AS A HUSBAND, A FATHER AND A FRIEND, / THE PRACTICE OF EVERY DOMESTIC VIRTUE, RESULTING ALIKE FROM A RECTITUDE AND CONSCIOUS / DUTY, RECEIVED A BRIGHTER LUSTRE FROM A FERVENT THOUGH RATIONAL PIETY. / HE WAS THE YOUNGEST SON OF THE LATE DR BOGUE OF FAREHAM IN THIS COUNTY, AND MARRIED MARY ISABELLA, / DAUGHTER OF JOHN HANSON ESQR. OF GREAT BROMLEY HALL, / AND WOODFORD IN ESSEX, WHO AS A SMALL / TRIBUTE TO THE MEMORY OF THE BEST OF HUSBANDS, / AND IN TESTIMONY OF HER AFFECTION AND REGRET / HAS CAUSED THIS TABLET TO BE INSCRIBED TO HIS RESPECTED NAME.

Monument: Taucha Cemetery, near Leipzig, Germany. (Photograph)
The monument was originally erected in 1816, restored in 1896 and restored again in 1930.

SACRED TO / RICHARD BOGUE / NATIVE OF HAMPSHIRE IN ENGLAND AND / CAPTAIN IN HIS BRITANNIC MAJESTY'S / REGIMENT OF ROYAL HORSE ARTILLERY / WHO FELL IN THE 31ST YEAR OF HIS / AGE GLORIOUSLY FIGHTING FOR THE / COMBINED CAUSE OF GERMANY AND HER / ALLIES AT THE BATTLE OF LEIPZIG / ON THE 18TH OF OCTOBER 1813, WHILE / COMMANDING THE CONGREVE ROCKET / BRIGADE, HAVING BY DISTINGUISHED / SERVICES AT THE VILLAGE OF PAUNSDORF / BORNE A MOST CONSPICUOUS PART IN / THE VICTORY OF THAT MEMORABLE DAY.

Monument: Paunsdorf, Germany. (Photograph)
The monument was erected between 1816 and 1863 by Theodor Apel, a Leipzig historian, who erected 44 such marker stones at his own expense. The stone to Bogue is number 40.

North side: CAPTAIN / BOGUE / ENGLISCHE / RAKENBATTERIE

South West side: V / SCHLACHT / BEI / LEIPZIG / AM / 18. OCTOBER / 1813 / 40 / DE THEODER APEL

2nd Lt 14 Jul 1798. 1st Lt 10 Feb 1800. 2nd Capt 18 Mar 1806.

Served in the Peninsula with 'B' Troop Royal Horse Artillery Nov 1808 – Jan 1809. Present at Sahagun, Benevente and the Corunna campaign. In command of the Rocket Brigade attached to the bodyguard of the Crown Prince of Sweden at the battle of Leipzig, where he was killed 18 Oct 1813. Awarded 4th Class Swedish Military Order of the Sword. Brother in law of Capt William Hanson killed at Villa Franca.
REFERENCE: *Gentleman's Magazine*, Nov 1813, p. 507. *Royal Artillery Institution Proceedings, Vol 24, pp. 131–6.*

BOLDERO, Henry
Lieutenant. 14th (Buckinghamshire) Regiment of Foot.
Family Memorial stone in railed enclosure: St Andrew's Churchyard, Nuthurst, Sussex. (M.I.)

"SACRED / TO THE MEMORY OF / HENRY BOLDERO, ESQRE, / OF SOUTH LODGE, ST LEONARDS FOREST / IN THE PARISH OF LOWER BEEDING. / HE WAS BORN ON THE 19TH APRIL 1789, / AND DIED ON THE 1ST OF MARCH 1859, / AGED 69 YEARS. / ...."

Ensign 25 Jan 1813. Lt 13 Apr 1815.
Present at Waterloo, the siege of Cambrai and the Occupation of Paris. Retired on half pay 25 Jun 1818. Elder brother of Lt and Capt Lonsdale Boldero 1st Foot Guards.

BOLDERO, Lonsdale
Lieutenant and Captain. 1st Regiment of Foot Guards.
Family Memorial stone in railed enclosure: St Andrew's Churchyard, Nuthurst, Sussex. (M.I.)

" .... ALSO OF COLONEL LONSDALE BOLDERO OF THE GRENADIER GUARDS, HE WAS BORN ON THE 8TH OF SEPTEMBER 1793, AND DIED AT LOWER BEEDING ON THE 20TH OF JANUARY 1863, AGED 69 YEARS"

Memorial tablet: Holy Trinity Church, Lower Beeding, Sussex. (Photograph)

IN MEMORY OF COLONEL LONSDALE BOLDERO / OF THE GRENADIER GUARDS. BORN SEPTEMBER 1793 / DIED AT LOWER BEEDING JANUARY 20TH 1863.

Stained glass window: Holy Trinity Church, Lower Beeding, Sussex. (Photograph)

FRATER CARISSIMO / LONSDALE BOLDERO AD 1862

Ensign 15 Sep 1809. Lt and Capt 20 Oct 1813. Capt and Lt Colonel 22 Jul 1830. Major 15 Apr 1845.
Served in the Peninsula with 2nd battalion Dec 1810 – May 1811 and 1st battalion Sep 1812 – Oct 1813. Present at Cadiz and Barrosa. Served at Waterloo. MGS medal for Barrosa. Also served in the Netherlands 1814–1815. Retired Oct 1846. Younger brother of Lt Henry Boldero 14th Foot.
Note: Discrepancy in data on starined glass window.

BOLTON, Daniel
Lieutenant. Royal Engineers.
Named on the Regimental Memorial: Rochester Cathedral, Rochester, Kent. (Photograph)

2nd Lt 14 Dec 1811. Lt 1 Jul 1812. 2nd Capt 7 Jun 1825. Capt 10 Jan 1837. Bt Major 28 Jun 1838. Lt Colonel 9 Nov 1846. Bt Colonel 20 Jun 1854. Colonel 13 Dec 1854. Major General 20 Jun 1859.
Served in the Peninsula Oct – Apr 1814. Also served in Holland 1814–1815 and in France with the Army of Occupation 1815–1818. Died at Cape Town 16 May 1860.

BOLTON, George
Ensign. 9th (East Norfolk) Regiment of Foot.
Named on the Memorial: St Andrew's Church, (now Musée Historique), Biarritz, France. (Photograph)

Ensign 22 Oct 1812.
    Served in the Peninsula Nov – Dec 1813. Present at Nivelle and Nive where he was killed 10 Dec 1813.

BOLTON, John
Surgeon. 6th (Inniskilling) Regiment of Dragoons.
Buried in Kensal Green Cemetery, London. ((No longer extant: Grave number 9829/69/-)

Surgeon 6th Dragoons 14 Sep 1791. Surgeon 7th West India Regt 19 Feb 1824.
    Present at Waterloo with 6th Dragoons. Surgeon of the Inniskillings for 32 years. Also served in Flanders 1793–1794. Half pay 19 Feb 1824. Died 14 Oct 1851.

BOLTON, Robert Dawson
Captain. 18th Regiment of Light Dragoons.
Named on the Memorial: St Andrew's Church, (now Musée Historique), Biarritz, France. (Photograph)

Cornet 20 Jun 1801. Lt 24 May 1803. Capt 4 Mar 1807.
    Served in the Peninsula Sep 1808 – Jan 1809 and Feb – Dec 1813. Present at Benevente, Morales, Vittoria, Nivelle and Nive. Severely wounded at the action at Mendionde 18 Dec 1813, taken prisoner and died of his wounds 19 Dec 1813.

BOLTON, Samuel
Captain. Royal Horse Artillery.
Named on the Regimental Memorial: St Joseph's Church, Waterloo, Belgium. (Photograph)

2nd Lt 9 Oct 1799. 1st Lt 14 Oct 1801. 2nd Capt 22 Oct 1806. Capt 20 Dec 1814.
    Served in the Peninsula Feb 1813 – Apr 1814. Present at Vittoria, San Sebastian, Bidassoa, Nivelle, Nive, Adour and Bayonne. Present at Waterloo, where he was killed during the final actions of the battle, when his guns fired on the advancing Imperial Guard and threw them into confusion before the Guards and the 52nd completed the rout. Also served at Copenhagen 1807.

BOLTON, Samuel
Lieutenant. 31st (Huntingdonshire) Regiment of Foot.
Monument to the Fallen: Civil Cemetery, Ferozepore, India. (M.I.)

"IN MEMORY OF THE FOLLOWING OFFICERS OF H. M. 31ST REGIMENT / WHO FELL IN THE ACTIONS OF MOODKIE, FEROZESHAH AND SOBRAON, / DURING THE CAMPAIGNS AGAINST THE SIKHS IN THE YEARS 1845 – 46 / AND WHO ARE INTERRED AT OR NEAR THIS SPOT. / COLONEL SAMUEL BOLTON, CB, 18TH DEC 1845. / ...."

Ensign 5 Feb 1807. Lt 6 Apr 1809. Capt 24 Oct 1822. Major 14 Jun 1833. Lt Colonel 24 Nov 1835. Bt Colonel Dec 1842.
    Served in the Peninsula with 2/31st Nov 1808 – Apr 1814. (Adjutant of the battalion May 1813 – Apr 1814). Present at Talavera, Busaco, Albuera (wounded), Arroyo dos Molinos, Vittoria, Pyrenees, Nive, Garris, Orthes, Aire and Toulouse. Transferred to 1st Battalion when the 2nd battalion was disbanded after the war. Also served in Sicily, Naples and India 1825 – 1846. (in command of the regiment in the first Afghan war 1842. Present at Mazina, Jagdulak, Tezin and Kabul). Awarded Bt Colonelcy and CB. Commanded 1st Brigade of Infantry of the Army of the Sutlej in the first Sikh War Dec 1845. Present at

the first battle at Moodki where he was wounded 18 Dec 1845 and died of his wounds 4 Jan 1846 at Ferozepore.

BOND, Robert
Private. 4th (King's Own) Regiment of Foot.
Headstone: St Mary the Virgin Churchyard, Yaxley, Suffolk. (Photograph)

IN MEMORIAM / ROBERT, KNOWN AS WATERLOO BOND, / FATHER OF A LARGE FAMILY IN THIS PLACE. / AS A SOLDIER HE SAW MUCH ACTIVE SERVICE / WITH THE 4TH REGIMENT, KING'S OWN BETWEEN / THE YEARS 1812 AND 1815 IN THE PENINSULA AND / IN N. AMERICA AND THE NETHERLANDS, WHERE HE WAS / WOUNDED AT THE BATTLE OF WATERLOO. / HE DIED A CHRISTIAN DEATH ON THE NIGHT / OF HIS BIRTHDAY, CHRISTMAS DAY, 1878, AGED / 88, AND LIES BURIED HERE BESIDE HIS WIFE MARY." / "THIS STONE IS SET UP PRO TEM. UNTIL FUNDS ARE FORTHCOMING TO ERECT A PROPER CHURCHYARD CROSS (£60) TO COMMEMORATE ROBERT, KNOWN AS 'WATERLOO' BOND. THE APPEAL FOR FUNDS TOWARDS A MORE IMPOSING MEMORIAL NOT BEING SUFFICIENTLY RESPONDED TO, THE STONE "SET UP PRO TEM." STILL REMAINS.

The note indicates that a more elaborate memorial originally planned was not erected.

Pte 1809.
Served in the Peninsula. Present at Salamanca, Vittoria, San Sebastian and Nive. Present at Waterloo (wounded) in Capt Fletcher's Company No 3. Discharged 1816 with a pension. Also served in North America (present at Bladensburg). (Known as 'Waterloo' Bond)

BONE, Hugh
Staff Surgeon. Medical Department.
Obelisk: Dean Cemetery, Edinburgh, Scotland. (Section F 792). (Photograph)

HUGH BONE M. D. / INSPECTOR GENERAL / OF ARMY HOSPITALS / BORN IN AYR. / DIED 18TH JANUARY 1858 / AGED 81 YEARS.

Hospital Assistant 8 Sep 1803. Asst Surgeon 5th Foot 17 Sep 1803. Surgeon 6th Foot 13 Jul 1809. Staff Surgeon 26 Mar 1812. Asst Inspector of Hospitals 7 Sep 1815. Bt Deputy Inspector of Hospitals 27 May 1825. Deputy Inspector General of Hospitals 1 Nov 1827. Inspector General 2 Oct 1843.
Served in the Peninsula with 1/5th Jul 1808 – Jan 1809 and on Staff May 1812 – Apr 1814. Present at Rolica, Vimeiro and Corunna. MGS medal for Rolica, Vimeiro and Corunna. Also served in South America 1807 and Walcheren 1809. MD Glasgow 1815.

BONE, Peter Joseph
Lieutenant. 36th (Herefordshire) Regiment of Foot.
Named on the Memorial: St Andrew's Church, (now Musée Historique), Biarritz, France. (Photograph)

Ensign 21 Apr 1807. Lt 30 May 1809.
Served in the Peninsula Aug 1808 – Jan 1809, Mar 1811 – Jul 1812 and Dec 1812 – Apr 1814. Present at Rolica, Vimeiro (wounded), Corunna, Barba del Puerco, Pyrenees, Bidassoa, Nivelle, Nive, Orthes, Vic Bigorre, Tarbes and Toulouse where he was severely wounded and died of his wounds Apr 1814.

BONNYCASTLE, Richard
2nd Captain. Royal Engineers.
Memorial: Advanced Battery, Fort Henry, Kingston, Canada. (Photograph – Internet record)

AS AN OFFICER IN THE CORPS OF ROYAL ENGINEERS, BONNYCASTLE WAS TRAINED IN ENGINEERING, MAPMAKING, GEOLOGY AND PAINTING. HE SERVED IN EUROPE AND NOVA SCOTIA BEFORE COMING TO UPPER CANADA IN 1826. THE MILITARY SURVEYS AND RELATED SCIENTIFIC WORK THAT HE PRODUCED WHILE POSTED AT NIAGARA, KINGSTON AND YORK CONTRIBUTED TO THE ECONOMIC DEVELOPMENT OF THE PROVINCE. BONNYCASTLE WAS RECALLED HERE IN 1837 TO SUPERVISE COMPLETION OF THE NEW FORT HENRY. HIS MASTERFUL DEFENCE OF KINGSTON DURING THE REBELLIONS OF 1837–38 EARNED HIM A KNIGHTHOOD. AN INTERESTED OBSERVER OF HUMAN NATURE, SIR RICHARD WROTE FOUR BOOKS DETAILING THE SOCIAL LIFE, HISTORY AND PHYSICAL FEATURES OF BRITISH NORTH AMERICA / MEMORIAL ERECTED BY ONTARIO HERITAGE FOUNDATION, 1957.

2nd Lt 28 Sep 1808. Lt 24 Jun 1809. 2nd Capt 11 Feb 1814. Capt 29 Jul 1825. Bt Major 10 Jun 1837. Lt Colonel 7 Sep 1840.

Served in France with the Army of Occupation 1816–1817. Also served at Walcheren 1809 (present at Flushing) and North America 1812–1815 (present at the capture of Fort Castine as Commanding Engineer of extensive works on Castine Peninsula in Maine, east of the Penobscot river) and Canada where he served during the Rebellion of 1837–1838 and was in command of the militia and volunteers. Supervised work to complete the new Fort Henry and defended Kingston during the Rebellion, for which he was knighted. Commanding Engineer in Newfoundland.

Wrote four books on Canada: *The Canadas in 1841*, 2 volumes, 1842, *Newfoundland in 1842*, 2 volumes, 1842, *Canada and the Canadian in 1846*, 2 volumes 1846 and *Canada as it was, is and may be*, 2 volumes, 1852. These books all attracted immigrants and business to Canada. Died in Kingston 3 Nov 1847.

REFERENCE: *Dictionary of National Biography. Dictionary of Canadian Biography.*

BOOTH, Charles
Lieutenant. 52nd (Oxfordshire) Light Infantry Regiment of Foot.
Memorial stone: St Andrew's Churchyard, Rushmere, near Ipswich, Suffolk. (M.I.)

SACRED / TO THE MEMORY OF / LIEUTENANT / CHARLES BOOTH / IN THE 52ND REGT OF FOOT / DIED 6TH APRIL 1812.

Ensign 1st West Yorkshire Regiment of Militia 7 Aug 1804. Lt 52nd Foot 3 Jul 1805.

Served in the Peninsula with 1/52nd Aug 1808 – Jan 1809 and Jul 1809 – Apr 1812. Present at Corunna, Coa, Busaco, Pombal, Redinha, Casal Nova, Foz d'Arouce, Sabugal, Fuentes d'Onoro, Ciudad Rodrigo and Badajoz (volunteered for the storming party at the siege where he was killed 6 Apr 1812). Also served in Sicily 1806–1807 and the Baltic 1808. Brother of Capt Henry Booth 43rd Foot and Capt William Booth 15th Lt Dragoons.

BOOTH, Henry
Captain. 43rd (Monmouthshire) Light Infantry Regiment of Foot.
Memorial tablet: All Saints Church, Northallerton, Yorkshire. (Photograph)

NEAR THIS PLACE IS INTERRED THE BODY / OF LIEUT: COLONEL HENRY BOOTH ESQR, K H OF / THE 43RD REGIMENT OF LIGHT INFANTRY. / FIFTH SON OF THE LATE WM BOOTH ESQ. OF BRUSH HOUSE, / IN THE PARISH OF ECCLESFIELD, IN THE COUNTY OF YORK, / HE DIED AT NORTHALLERTON MAY 6TH 1841 AGED 51. / HIS MILITARY LIFE WAS PASSED IN THE 43RD REGIMENT. HE ENTERED IT AS ENSIGN / MARCH 6TH 1806, WAS PROMOTED TO BE LIEUT: COLONEL JUNE 29TH 1830, / AND RETAINED THE COMMAND OF IT UNTIL THE DAY OF HIS DEATH. / HE SERVED WITH THE ARMIES IN SPAIN AND PORTUGAL / UNDER SIR JOHN

MOORE AND THE DUKE OF WELLINGTON, AND WAS PRESENT AT / VIMIERO, CORUNNA, THE PASSAGE OF THE COA, BUSACO AND SALAMANCA, / VITTORIA AND THE ATTACK ON THE HEIGHTS OF VERA. / THIS TABLET WAS ERECTED BY THE OFFICERS NON COMMISSIONED OFFICERS / AND PRIVATES OF THE REGIMENT WHO HAD SERVED UNDER HIS COMMAND, / TO RECORD THEIR RESPECT FOR HIS CHARACTER, AND THEIR ESTEEM AND AFFECTION / FOR HIS GALLANT, GENEROUS AND AMIABLE QUALITIES BY WHICH / HE WON THE HEARTS OF ALL WHO SERVED UNDER HIM AND INFUSED THROUGH EVERY RANK / A HIGH AND HONOURABLE FEELING.

Ensign 6 Mar 1806. Lt 11 Jun 1807. Capt 25 Jun 1812. Major 29 Aug 1822. Lt Colonel 29 Jun 1830.

Served in the Peninsula with 2/43rd Aug 1808 – Jan 1809, 1/43rd Jul 1809 – Mar 1811 and Jun 1812 – Oct 1813. Present at Vimiero, Corunna, Coa, Busaco, Salamanca, San Munos, Vittoria, Pyrenees and Vera. Also served in Canada 1837–1838 (commanded the Battalion during the Rebellion). KH 1835. Died 6 May 1841. His brother Lt Charles served in the 52nd Regt and was killed at Badajoz in a storming party. His brother Capt William served with the 95th and then joined the 15th Lt Dragoons in 1809, serving with them in the Peninsula and at Waterloo.

REFERENCE: *The Booth Letters – 43rd and 52nd Chronicle of 1932 and 1933.* and *Three Brothers in the Light Division – 43rd and 52nd Chronicle of 1894. (Regimental Journal).* Portrait in: *Journal of the Society for Army Historical Research, Vol 41, No 166, Jun 1963, pp. 54–5. Gentleman's Magazine, Aug 1841, pp. 206–7.*

BOOTHBY, Charles
Captain. Royal Engineers.
Brass Memorial tablet: St Peter and St Paul Church, Algarkirk, Lincolnshire. (In chancel floor). (Photograph)

BENEATH ARE DEPOSITED THE / MORTAL REMAINS OF THE REV^{D}. / CHARLES BOOTHBY VICAR OF / SUTTERTON AND PREBENDARY OF / SOUTHWELL, FORMERLY CAPTAIN / IN THE ROYAL ENGINEERS, THIRD / SON OF SIR WILLIAM AND DAME / RAFELLA BOOTHBY BORN MDCCLXXXVI / MARRIED MDCCCXX MARIANNE / CATHARINE THIRD DAUGHTER OF THE / REV^{D}. BASIL BURY BERIDGE AND / OF DOROTHY HIS WIFE. HE DIED IN / THE BLESSED HOPE OF MERCY THROUGH / CHRIST ON THE XIXTH OF AUGUST / MDCCCXLVI DEEPLY MOURNED AND / REGRETTED BY HIS WIDOW AND CHILDREN.

2nd Lt 1 Jan 1804. 1st Lt 1 Mar 1805. 2nd Capt 24 Jun 1809. Capt 21 Jul 1813.

Served in the Peninsula 1808 – Jan 1809 and Mar 1809 – Jul 1810. Present at Corunna, Talavera (severely wounded – leg amputated and taken prisoner until Aug 1810). Also served in Calabria 1806 and the Baltic 1808. Later entered the church.

REFERENCE: *Boothby, Charles, A Prisoner in France, the memoirs, diary and correspondence of Charles Boothby, Captain, Royal Engineers, during his last campaign, 1898.*

BORLAND, James
Inspector General of Hospitals. Medical Department.
Memorial tablet: St Mary with St Alban Church, Teddington, Middlesex, London. (Photograph)

IN THIS CHURCHYARD / ARE DEPOSITED THE MORTAL REMAINS OF / JAMES BORLAND, M.D. / INSPECTOR GENERAL OF ARMY HOSPITALS. / BORN APRIL 1ST 1774, / DIED FEB^{Y} 22ND 1863.

Regimental Mate 42nd Foot 19 Oct 1792. Hospital Mate 1793. Surgeon 23rd Foot 2 Apr 1794. Staff Surgeon 16 Sep 1795. Deputy Inspector General of Russian Hospitals 5 Dec 1799 – 1801. Inspector General of Hospitals 22 Jan 1807.

Present at Walcheren 1809. Also served in Flanders 1793, West Indies 1794–1798, the Helder 1799 and Sicily 1810–1816. MD. Retired 25 Dec 1816. Honorary Surgeon to the Duke of Kent.
REFERENCE: *Dictionary of National Biography.*

BORLASE, Charles
Captain. 2nd (Queen's Royal) Regiment of Foot.
Memorial tablet: Holy Trinity Church, Fareham, Hampshire. (Photograph)

IN MEMORY OF / CAPTAIN CHARLES BORLASE, / LATE OF THE 2ND REGT OF FOOT / AND FORMERLY OF PENZANCE, IN THE COUNTY OF CORNWALL, / WHO DIED THE 12TH OF SEPTR 1836. / AGED 50 YEARS. / (VERSE) / THIS TRIBUTE OF AFFECTION IS ERECTED BY HIS WIDOW / WHO WITH TWO CHILDREN IS LEFT TO DEPLORE HIS LOSS.

Lt 19 Mar 1807. Capt 1 Sep 1813.
    Served in the Peninsula Nov 1808 – Jan 1809, May 1811 – Dec 1812 and with 2nd Provisional Battalion Jan 1813 – Apr 1814. Present in the Corunna campaign, siege of Salamanca Forts, Salamanca, Vittoria, Pyrenees, Nivelle, Adour, Orthes and Toulouse. Also served at Walcheren 1809.

BÖSEWIEL, Adolph
Major. 2nd Battalion Light Infantry, King's German Legion.
Named on the Regimental Memorial: La Haye Sainte, Waterloo, Belgium. (Photograph)

Capt 5 May 1804. Major 4 Jun 1814.
    Served in the Peninsula Aug 1808 – Jan 1809 and Mar 1811 – Apr 1814. Present at Vigo and the first siege of Badajoz (wounded and taken prisoner). Remained in prison from Apr 1811 – Apr 1814. Present at Waterloo where he was killed. Also served at Hanover 1805, Copenhagen 1807, Walcheren 1809 and Netherlands 1814.

BOSWELL, John Irvine
Lieutenant and Captain. Coldstream Regiment of Foot Guards.
Monument: On hill of Auchlee, Maryculter, Aberdeenshire. (Photograph)

IN MEMORY OF / JOHN IRVINE BOSWELL / OF / BALMUTO AND KINGCAUSIE / BORN 28TH DECEMBER 1785; DIED 23RD DECEMBER 1860. / A MAN WHO LOVED HIS SAVIOUR, / WALKED STEADFASTLY WITH HIS GOD, / AND WHOSE RULE OF LIFE WAS / WHATSOEVER YE DO IN WORD OR DEED / DO ALL IN THE NAME OF THE LORD JESUS CHRIST. / IN EARLY LIFE HE JOINED THE COLDSTREAM GUARDS AND / CARRIED THEIR COLOURS IN THE BATTLE OF TALAVERA. / RETIRING FROM THE ARMY HE SETTLED AT KINGCAUSIE, / AND LIVED TO TRANSFORM THE NATURAL BARENESS OF / THE ESTATE INTO LUXU-RIANT FERTILITY. HE WILL LONG BE / REMEMBERED IN THE DISTRICT FOR THE ENLIGHTENED ZEAL WHICH / HE DISPLAYED IN THE INTRODUCTION OF ALL THE IMPROVEMENTS / OF MODERN AGRICULTURE; AND HE DID NOT CONFINE HIS / ATTEN-TION TO HIS OWN ESTATES. HIS KNOWLEDGE AND / EXPERIENCE BEING EVER AT THE SERVICE OF HIS / NEIGHBOURS RICH AND POOR ALIKE. IN EVERY POSITION / AND RELA-TION OF LIFE HE MAINTAINED WITH RARE / FIDELITY THE CHARACTER OF A / CHRISTIAN GENTLEMAN / AND HE DIED IN PEACE, TRUSTING SIMPLY IN THE MERITS / OF HIS SAVIOUR FOR ACCEPTANCE WITH HIS GOD. / HIS SORROWING WIDOW / MARGARET IRVINE BOSWELL / ERECTED THIS MONUMENT / AS A SOLACE IN HER BITTER BEREAVE-MENT / A.D. MDCCCLXII.

Ensign 21 Dec 1804. Lt and Capt 8 Mar 1810.

Served in the Peninsula Mar 1809 – Mar 1810. Present at Douro and Talavera (carried the colours). Retired Dec 1810 and devoted his time to improving his estates in Scotland. MGS medal for Talavera.

BOTELER, Richard
Captain. Royal Engineers.
Memorial tablet: St Mary's Church, Eastry, Kent. (M.I.)

"THIS TABLET IS ERECTED TO THE MEMORY OF LIEUT. COLONEL RICHARD BOTELER, OF H.M. CORPS OF ROYAL ENGINEERS, WHO AFTER MANY YEARS OF SERVICE AT HOME, AND IN AFRICA, SOUTH AMERICA, SPAIN, PORTUGAL AND CANADA, AND LAST AS COMMANDING ENGINEER AT HALIFAX IN NOVA SCOTIA, PERISHED AT SEA IN H.M. PACKET CALYPSO ON HIS PASSAGE TO ENGLAND ON LEAVE OF ABSENCE, IN THE BEGINNING OF THE YEAR 1833, AT THE AGE OF 46 YEARS." ....

Named on the Regimental Memorial: Rochester Cathedral, Rochester, Kent. (Photograph)

2nd Lt 1 Jan 1804. 1st Lt 1 Mar 1805. 2nd Capt 26 Jun 1809. Capt 21 Jul 1813. Lt Colonel 29 Oct 1828.
   Served in the Peninsula Aug 1808 – Jul 1809 and Apr 1811 – Apr 1814. Present at Vimeiro, Corunna, first siege of Badajoz (severely wounded 9 May 1811) San Sebastian and Nive. Also served in South America 1807 (present at Buenos Ayres), Walcheren 1809 and Canada (Commanding Engineer at Halifax). Drowned on passage to England on the sinking of HMS *Calypso* 1833.

BOUCHIER, Thomas
Surgeon. 57th (West Middlesex) Regiment of Foot.
Headstone used as a paving stone: St Saviour's Churchyard, Torquay, Devon. (M.I.)

"SACRED / TO THE MEMORY OF / THOMAS BOUCHIER MD / SURGEON OF HER MAJESTY'S 98TH REGT / AND FORMERLY OF THE 36TH REGT / AGED 57 YEARS / DIED 20TH MARCH 1844."

Asst Surgeon 3rd Foot 24 May 1804. Asst Surgeon 34th Foot 21 May 1807. Surgeon 57th Foot 22 Aug 1811. Surgeon 104th Foot 28 Nov 1816. Surgeon 36th Foot 29 May 1817. Surgeon 98th Foot 2 Aug 1831.
   Served in the Peninsula with 34th Foot Jul 1809 – Oct 1811 and 57th Foot Jan – Dec 1812. Present at Busaco, Olivencia, first siege of Badajoz and Albuera. Retired on half pay 29 Dec 1840.

BOULCOTT, Joseph
Sergeant. 1st Regiment of Foot Guards.
Headstone: St Mary's Churchyard, Theydon Bois, Essex. Seriously eroded. (Photograph)

SACRED / TO THE MEMORY OF / JOSEPH BOULCOTT / LATE CLERK OF CHEQUE TOWER, LONDON / WHO DIED OCTOBER 22ND 1850 / AGED 74 YEARS. / SERVED IN HOLLAND UNDER THE LATE / DUKE OF YORK / WITH THE ARMY IN SICILY / AND SIR JOHN MOORE AT THE BATTLE OF CORUNNA / AND ALSO IN SPAIN PORTUGAL AND FRANCE. / HE WAS THE CONFIDENTIAL ADHERENT OF / THE DUKE OF WELLINGTON / FROM THE FIRST VICTORY OF / WATERLOO / UNTIL THE WITHDRAWAL OF THE ALLIES FROM / PARIS, 1818 / ....

Pte 16 Jan 1798. Cpl 25 Jan 1800. Sgt 25 Oct 1803.
   Served in the Peninsula with 3rd Battalion Oct 1808 – Jan 1809 and Apr 1811 – Apr 1814. Present at Corunna, Cadiz, Burgos, Bidassoa, Nivelle, Nive and Bayonne. Present at Waterloo in Lt Colonel Fead's Company, the Capture of Paris and with the Army of Occupation. Also served at the Helder 1799, Sicily 1806 and Walcheren 1809. Discharged 1 Aug 1817 after serving for 21 years, granted a pension of one shilling and ten pence per day. He was then taken on to Wellington's personal staff and became his baggage

master until 1818. Appointed Clerk of the Cheque under the Board of Ordnance in the Tower of London 1818 until he retired in 1849. MGS medal for Corunna, Nivelle and Nive. His brother William was severely wounded at Waterloo and died of his wounds the next day.

REFERENCE: *Beech, H. Eva, Joseph Boulcott of the Grenadier Guards: baggage master to the Duke of Wellington, 1994. Beech, Eva, My Waterloo kinsmen: Sergeants William and Joseph Boulcott, Waterloo Journal, Apr 1982, pp. 8–11. Gentleman's Magazine, Dec 1850, p 672. Annual Register, 1850, Appx, p. 272.*

BOURCHIER, James Claud

Captain. 11th Regiment of Light Dragoons.
Low monument and Cross: St Andrew's Churchyard, Buxton, Norfolk. (Photograph)

LT. GENERAL JAMES CLAUD BOURCHIER / COL. OF THE 3RD DRAGOON GUARDS / DIED FEBRUARY 1859 AGED 78 YEARS / BLESSED ARE THE DEAD, WHICH LIE IN THE LORD.

Cornet 28 Sep 1797. Lt 6 Aug 1799. Capt 29 Jan 1803. Bt Major 4 Jun 1814. Bt Lt Colonel 18 Jun 1815. Major 5 Nov 1818. Bt Colonel 10 Jan 1837. Major General 9 Nov 1846. Lt General 20 Jun 1854.

Served in the Peninsula Jun 1811 – Jun 1812. Present at Morales, Castrejon, Salamanca and Venta del Pozo. Present at Quatre Bras covering the retreat 17 June, Waterloo (awarded Bt Lt Colonelcy), the Capture of Paris and with the Army of Occupation. Also served in Cadiz 1800, Egypt 1801 (with Sir Ralph Abercromby's expedition). MGS medal for Egypt and Salamanca. Gold Medal from the Sultan of Egypt. Retired on half pay 25 Sep 1820. Colonel 3rd Dragoon Guards 9 Jan 1851.

REFERENCE: *Annual Register, 1859, Appx, p. 411.*

BOURKE, Richard

Major. Staff Appointment in Spain and Portugal.
Statue: Sydney, New South Wales, Australia. (Photograph)

THIS STATUE / OF / LIEUTENANT GENERAL / SIR RICHARD BOURKE, K.C.B. / IS ERECTED BY THE PEOPLE OF NEW SOUTH WALES / TO RECORD HIS ABLE HONEST AND BENEVOLENT ADMINISTRATION / FROM 1831 TO 1837. / ELECTED FOR THE GOVERNMENT AT A PERIOD OF SINGULAR DIFFICULTY, / HIS JUDGEMENT, URBANITY, AND FIRMNESS JUSTIFIED THE CHOICE. / COMPREHENDING AT ONCE THE VAST RESOURCES / PECULIAR TO THIS COLONY. / HE APPLIED THEM, FOR THE FIRST TIME, SYSTEMATICALLY TO ITS BENEFIT / HE VOLUNTARILY DIVESTED HIMSELF OF THE PRODIGIOUS INFLUENCE / ARISING FROM THE ASSIGNMENT OF PENAL LABOUR, AND ENACTED / FIRST AND SALUTARY LAWS FOR THE AMELIORATION OF PENAL DISCIPLINE. / HE WAS THE FIRST GOVERNOR, WHO PUBLISHED SATISFACTORY ACCOUNTS / OF THE PUBLIC RECEIPTS AND EXPENDITURE. / WITHOUT OPPRESSION, OR DETRIMENT TO ANY INTEREST, / HE RAISED THE REVENUE TO A VAST AMOUNT, AND FROM ITS SURPLUS, / REALISED EXTENSIVE PLANS OF IMMIGRATION. / HE ESTABLISHED RELIGIOUS EQUALITY ON A JUST AND FIRM BASIS, / AND SOUGHT TO PROVIDE FOR ALL, WITHOUT DISTINCTION OF SECT, / A SOUND AND ADEQUATE SYSTEM OF NATIONAL EDUCATION. / HE CONSTRUCTED VARIOUS PUBLIC WORKS OF PERMANENT UTILITY. / HE FOUNDED THE FLOURISHING SETTLEMENT OF PORT PHILIP, / AND THREW OPEN THE UNLIMITED WILDS OF AUSTRALIA / TO PASTORAL ENTERPRIZE. / HE ESTABLISHED SAVING BANKS, AND WAS THE PATRON OF / THE FIRST MECHANICS' INSTITUTE. HE CREATED AN EQUITABLE TRIBUNAL / FOR DETERMINING UPON CLAIMS FOR LANDS. / HE WAS THE WARMEST FRIEND OF THE LIBERTY OF THE PRESS. HE EXTENDED TRIAL BY JURY / AFTER ITS ALMOST TOTAL SUSPENSION FOR MANY YEARS. / BY THESE AND NUMEROUS OTHER MEASURES / THE MORAL, RELIGIOUS, AND GENERAL IMPROVEMENT OF ALL CLASSES / HE RAISED THE COLONY TO UNEXAMPLED PROSPERITY; / AND RETIRED AMID THE REVERENT AND AFFECTIONATE REGRET / OF THE PEOPLE; HAVING WON

THEIR CONFIDENCE BY HIS INTEGRITY, / GRATITUDE BY HIS SERVICES, THEIR ADMIRA-
TION BY HIS PUBLIC TALENT, / AND THEIR ESTEEM BY HIS PRIVATE WORTH.

Statue erected 11 Apr1842 in front of the Public Library in Sydney by the people of New South Wales to
record his administration 1831–1837.

Family mausoleum: Castleconnell Churchyard, Limerick, Ireland. (Photograph)

THE BURIAL PLACE / OF / GENERAL SIR RICHARD BOURKE KCB / AND OF HIS DESCENDANTS

Ensign 1st Foot Guards 22 Nov 1798. Lt and Capt 25 Nov 1799. Capt 47th Foot 1803. Bt Major 27 Aug
1805. Bt Lt Colonel 16 Sep 1806 (as Superintendent of the junior department of the Royal Military
College). Bt Colonel 4 Jun 1814. Major General 19 Jul 1821. Lt General 10 Jan 1837. General 11 Nov
1851.
    Served in the Peninsula Apr – Jul 1809 (with the Spanish Army) and Jun 1812 – Aug 1814 (British
Military Agent in Galicia owing to his knowledge of Spanish). Also served at the Helder 1799 (severely
wounded and awarded pension of £50 per annum), South America 1807 (QMG. Present at Montevideo
and Buenos Ayres). Lt Governor Eastern District of the Cape of Good Hope 1825–1829. Governor of
New South Wales Jun 1831–1837.
    Proved to be a very competent administrator. In Australia he started the reform to representative govern-
ment with a council made up of 36 members, two thirds of which were to be nominated by the colonists.
Responsible for the development of Port Philip district. During his time as Governor the population
doubled, revenue trebled and trade increased. He brought about improved relations among the people.
Appointed Colonel 64th Foot 29 Nov 1837 on his return to England. KCB. Later went to Ireland and in
1844 edited with Earl Fitzwilliam, four volumes of *Correspondence of Edmund Burke*. Educated at
Winchester. Died 13 Aug 1855.
REFERENCE: *Dictionary of National Biography. Australian Dictionary of Biography. Gentleman's
Magazine, Oct 1855, pp. 428–9. Annual Register, 1855, Appx, pp. 298–9. Royal Military Calendar, Vol
4, pp. 155–6.*

BOUVERIE, Everard William
Lieutenant. Royal Regiment of Horse Guards.
Memorial tablet: St Edmund, King and Martyr Church, Hardingstone, Northampton. (Photograph)

SACRED TO THE MEMORY OF / GENERAL EVERARD WILLIAM BOUVERIE, / ELDEST SON OF
/ EDWARD BOUVERIE ESQRE. / OF DELAPRE ABBEY, / WHO DIED 18TH NOVR 1871, / AGED 82.

Cornet 2 Apr 1812. Lt 15 Oct 1812. Capt 9 Sep 1819. Bt Major 6 May 1831. Lt Colonel 4 Dec 1832.
Colonel 16 Sep 1845. Major General 11 Nov 1851. Lt General 30 Jul 1860. General 9 Apr 1868.
    Served in the Peninsula Nov 1812 – Apr 1814. Present at Vittoria and Toulouse. MGS medal for Vittoria
and Toulouse. Present at Waterloo (wounded). Equerry to Prince Albert 1840 and later Equerry to Queen
Victoria 1853. Colonel 15th Hussars 1859. Brother of Capt and Lt Colonel Henry Frederick Bouverie
Coldstream Guards. Educated at Harrow and St John's College Cambridge.
REFERENCE: *Household Brigade Journal, 1871, p. 315.*

BOUVERIE, Sir Henry Frederick
Captain and Lieutenant Colonel. Coldstream Regiment of Foot Guards.
Memorial tablet: Allhallows Church, Woolbeding, Sussex. (Photograph)

LIEUTENANT GENERAL / SIR HENRY FREDERICK BOUVERIE, / G.C.B., G.C.M.G / DIED
NOVEMBER 14 1852 / AGED 69 YEARS.

Named on the Civil Commissioners and Governors of Malta tablet, Grand Masters Palace, Valletta, Malta. (Photograph)

Ensign 23 Oct 1799. Lt and Capt 19 Nov 1800. Capt and Lt Colonel 28 Jun 1810. Bt Colonel 4 Jun 1814. 2nd Major 18 Jan 1820. Major 25 Jul 1821. Major General 27 May 1825. Lt General 28 Jun 1838.

Served in the Peninsula Mar 1809 – Aug 1814 (ADC and Military Secretary to Lord Wellington May 1809 – Aug 1810), AAG Division 1, Apr 1812 – Oct 1813 and AAG Division 2, Nov 1813 – Apr 1814). Present at Douro, Talavera (wounded), Badajoz, Salamanca, Burgos, Vittoria (Mentioned in Despatches), San Sebastian (Mentioned in Despatches), Nive (Mentioned in Despatches), Orthes, Aire, Tarbes and Toulouse. KCB 2 Jan 1815. Also served in Egypt 1801, Baltic 1807, and the Netherlands 1814. Gold Cross for Salamanca, Vittoria, San Sebastian, Nive, Orthes. MGS medal for Egypt, Talavera and Toulouse. GCB. GCMG.

Governor of Malta 1836–1843. Colonel 1st West India Regt 1842 and Colonel 97th Foot Nov 1843. Educated at Eton. Died the day before his departure to London to take a prominent part in the Duke of Wellington's funeral. Brother of Lt Everard William Bouverie Royal Horse Guards.

REFERENCE: *Gentleman's Magazine, Jan 1853, pp. 92–3. Annual Register, 1852, Appx, pp. 329–30.*

BOWATER, Edward

Captain and Lieutenant Colonel. 3rd Regiment of Foot Guards.
Memorial tablet and Stained glass window: Royal Military Chapel, Wellington Barracks, London. (M.I.) (Destroyed by a Flying Bomb 1944) (Photograph of Stained glass window in the Apse, which is the only original part of the Chapel)

"HIS WIDOW, AND HIS DAUGHTER LADY KNIGHTLY, TO THE MEMORY OF / GENERAL SIR EDWARD BOWATER, K.C.H. / COLONEL OF THE 49TH, THE PRINCESS CHARLOTTE OF WALES OR HERTFORDSHIRE REGIMENT. BORN IN 1787. HE JOINED THE 3RD GUARDS IN 1804. HE WAS PRESENT AT THE SIEGE OF COPENHAGEN, 1807, AND SERVED WITH THE ARMY IN THE PENINSULA FROM DECEMBER, 1808, TO NOVEMBER, 1809, AND FROM DECEMBER, 1811, TILL THE PEACE IN 1814. HE WAS AT THE PASSAGE OF THE DOURO, THE BATTLES OF TALAVERA AND SALAMANCA, THE CAPTURE OF MADRID, THE SIEGE OF BURGOS, THE BATTLE OF VITTORIA, THE PASSAGE OF THE BIDASSOA, THE ASSAULT OF SAN SEBASTIAN, THE BATTLES OF THE NIVE AND THE NIVELLE, AND AT QUATRE BRAS AND WATERLOO. HE WAS WOUNDED AT TALAVERA AND AT WATERLOO. HE WAS MAJOR IN THE REGIMENT IN 1826, AND LIEUT.-COLONEL IN 1836. / HE WAS PROMOTED TO BE MAJOR-GENERAL IN 1837, AND DIED IN 1861, AFTER 57 YEARS SERVICE".

Ensign 31 Mar 1804. Lt and Capt 23 Aug 1809. Capt and Lt Colonel 25 Jul 1814. Bt Colonel 12 Oct 1826 Major General 10 Jan 1837. Lt General 9 Nov 1846. General 20 Jun 1854.

Served in the Peninsula Mar – Oct 1809 and Apr 1812 – Feb 1814. Present at Douro, Talavera (wounded), Salamanca, Burgos, Vittoria, Bidassoa, Nivelle and Nive. Present at Quatre Bras and Waterloo (wounded). Also served at Copenhagen 1807. MGS medal for Talavera, Salamanca, Vittoria, Nivelle and Nive. KCH 1837. Appointed Equerry to Prince Albert 1840. Colonel 49th Foot 24 Apr 1846. Chosen by Queen Victoria to take charge of Prince Leopold on his visit to the South of France. While there Sir Edward Bowater was taken ill and died at Cannes 14 Dec 1861. Educated at Harrow.

REFERENCE: *Dictionary of National Biography. Household Brigade Journal, 1862, p. 236. Gentleman's Magazine, Jan 1862 p. 109. Annual Register, 1861, Appx, p. 405.*

BOWEN, Robert

Ensign. Coldstream Regiment of Foot Guards.
Gravestone: Ta Braxia Cemetery, Ta Braxia, Malta. (M.I.)

"ROBERT BOWEN, LATE LT. COL. IN THE COLDSTREAM GUARDS, DIED AT MALTA 4 JUNE 1874, AGED 77."

Ensign 24 Mar 1814. Capt 55th Foot 30 Jan 1823. Lt and Capt Coldstream Guards 19 Feb 1823. Capt and Lt Colonel 27 Jan 1832.
   Present at Waterloo.

BOWERS, Charles Robert
Lieutenant. 13th Regiment of Light Dragoons.
Low monument in a railed enclosure: St John the Evangelist Churchyard, Little Tew, Oxfordshire. (Photograph)

IN MEMORY OF / LT GENERAL CHARLES ROBERT BOWERS / LATE OF THE 13TH LIGHT DRAGOONS / DIED 9TH OCTOBER 1870 AGED SEVENTY SEVEN YEARS / HE SERVED AND WAS WOUNDED AT THE BATTLE OF WATERLOO.

Cornet 18 Jan 1810. Lt 18 Oct 1810. Capt 23rd Foot 8 Dec 1818. Capt 37th Foot Aug 1825. Major 15 Aug 1826. Bt Lt Colonel 23 Nov 1841. Bt Colonel 20 Jun 1854. Major General 26 Oct 1858. Lt General Mar 1866.
   Present at Waterloo (severely wounded and awarded pension of £70 per annum). His brother Capt Mansell Bowers in the same regiment was also wounded at Waterloo.

BOWES, Barnard Foord
Lieutenant Colonel. 6th (1st Warwickshire) Regiment of Foot.
Memorial tablet: Beverley Minster, Beverley, Yorkshire. (Photograph)

SACRED TO THE MEMORY OF / MAJOR GENERAL. BARNARD FOORD BOWES. / A BELOV'D & LAMENTED HUSBAND, WHOSE VIRTUES ARE RECORDED / IN THE HEARTS OF HIS SORROWING RELATIVES, AND FRIENDS; / HIS DEEDS OF VALOUR IN ARMS, ARE PERPETU- ATED ON / A MONUMENT ERECTED IN THE CATHEDRAL CHURCH OF ST PAUL'S, / BY HIS GRATEFUL COUNTRY, AS A TRIBUTE OF RESPECT / DUE TO HIS MERITORIOUS ACTIONS: PLACING HIM AMONG THE / FOREMOST IN THE LIST OF THOSE GALLANT HEROES, WHO HAVE / BLED IN THE DEFENCE OF THEIR KING AND CONSTITUTION: / HE FELL ON THE 23D OF JUNE 1812, IN THE 43D YEAR OF HIS AGE, / AFTER ALMOST A LIFE DEVOTED TO THE SERVICE / AND WHILE LEADING THE FORLORN HOPE, TO THE ASSAULT / OF THE FORTRESS LA MERCIA SALAMANCA. / SO SLEEP THE BRAVE NOW SUNK TO REST / BY ALL THEIR COUNTRY'S WISHES BLEST.

Memorial tablet: St Paul's Cathedral, London. (North transept). (Photograph)

ERECTED AT THE PUBLIC EXPENSE TO THE MEMORY OF / MAJOR GENERAL BARNARD FOORD BOWES, / WHO FELL GLORIOUSLY ON THE 27TH JUNE 1812, / WHILE LEADING THE TROOPS TO THE ASSAULT ON THE FORTS AT SALAMANCA.

Note discrepancy in date of death on the two memorials.

Ensign 26th Foot 10 Nov 1781. Lt 1783. Capt Independent Co 27 Jan 1791. Capt 26 Foot 5 Feb 1791. Major 85th Foot 21 Jun 1796. Lt Colonel 6th Foot 1 Dec 1796. Bt Colonel 1 Jan 1805. Major General 15 Jul 1810.
   Served in the Peninsula Aug 1808 (Commanded 4 Brigade), Feb – Mar 1812 (Commanded 2 Brigade 4th Division), Apr – Jun 1812 (Commanded 2 Brigade 6th Division). Present at Rolica, Vimeiro, Badajoz

(wounded twice, his ADC Captain Johnson was killed at his side) and siege of the Salamanca Forts (at the siege of Fort St Cayetano he headed his brigade in the storming party but was immediately wounded. While his wounds were being dressed he heard that his men were being repulsed and returned to cheer them on, when he was fatally shot 23 Jun 1812). Gold medal for Rolica, Vimeiro and Badajoz. Also served in Ireland 1796–1798, America 1799–1806 and Gibraltar 1808–1810 (from where he volunteered for Vimeiro). Returned to Gibraltar where he became second in command. Petitioned for leave to serve under Wellington and went to Spain again in 1812.

REFERENCE: *Gentleman's Magazine, Oct 1812, p. 403.*

BOWLES, George

Lieutenant and Captain. Coldstream Regiment of Foot Guards.
Pedestal tomb: Kensal Green Cemetery, London. Inscription illegible. (1736/77/IC). (Photograph)
Memorial: Royal Military Chapel, Wellington Barracks, London. (M.I.) (Destroyed by a Flying Bomb 1944)

"THE WINDOW ABOVE THE GALLERY IS PLACED IN MEMORY OF / GENERAL SIR G. BOWLES, G.C.B. / COLONEL 1ST WEST INDIA REGIMENT; LIEUTENANT OF THE TOWER OF LONDON; COLDSTREAM GUARDS, 1804–43; MAJOR 2ND BATTALION, 1839. HE SERVED IN GERMANY, UNDER LORD CATHCART, 1805–6, AND AT THE SIEGE AND CAPTURE OF COPENHAGEN, 1807. HE WAS PRESENT AT THE PASSAGE OF THE DOURO, AT THE BATTLES OF TALAVERA, SALAMANCA, AND VITTORIA; THE SIEGES OF CIUDAD RODRIGO, BADAJOS, BURGOS, AND SAN SEBASTIAN; AT THE CAPTURE OF MADRID; AT THE PASSAGES OF THE BIDASSOA, THE NIVELLE, THE NIVE, AND THE ADOUR; AND AT THE INVESTMENT OF BAYONNE, AT THE BATTLES OF QUATRE BRAS AND WATERLOO, AND AT THE CAPTURE OF PARIS. DIED 21ST MAY, 1876."

Ensign 20 Dec 1804. Lt and Capt 1st Feb 1810. Bt Major 18 Jun 1815. Lt Col 14 Jun 1821. Bt Colonel 10 Jan 1837. Major General 9 Nov 1846. Lieutenant General 20 Jun 1854. General 9 Nov 1862.

Served in the Peninsula Mar – Dec 1809 and Sep 1811 – Apr 1814. Present at Douro, Talavera, Ciudad Rodrigo, Salamanca, Burgos, Vittoria, Bidassoa, Nivelle, Nive, Adour and Bayonne. Present at Quatre Bras, Waterloo, the capture of Paris and with the Army of Occupation. Awarded Brevet Majority for Waterloo. Also served in Hanover 1805, Baltic 1807, the Netherlands 1814, Canada 1818–1820 (Military Secretary to the Duke of Richmond) and West Indies 1820–1825 (DAG). In command of the troops in the Canadian Rebellion 1838. Half pay 1843. MGS medal for Talavera, Ciudad Rodrigo, Salamanca, Vittoria, Nivelle and Nive. KCB. Colonel 1st West India Regt 9 Sep 1855. Appointed Lieutenant of the Tower of London 1851. GCB 1873.

REFERENCE: *Dictionary of National Biography. Annual Register, 1876, Appx, p. 142. Glover, Gareth, ed., The Peninsular and Waterloo letters of Major George Bowles 1st Foot Guards 1807 – 1819, 2008.*

BOWMAN, David

Captain. 91st Regiment of Foot.
Low monument: Monifieth Churchyard, Angus, Scotland. (Photograph)

SACRED TO THE MEMORY OF / DAVID BOWMAN / CAPTAIN 91ST REGIMENT OF FOOT / WHO DIED AT BROUGHTY FERRY / 28TH AUGUST 1847 AGED 67 YEARS.

Ensign 29 Sep 1804. Lt 19 Jun 1806. Capt 16 Dec 1813.

Served in the Peninsula Oct 1812 – Apr 1814. Present at Pyrenees, Nivelle, Nive, Orthes, Aire and Toulouse. Also served at Walcheren 1809.

BOWMAN, William Flockhart
Deputy Assistant Commissary General. Commissariat Department.
Three tier pennant slab: Maida Bastion Garden of Rest, Floriana, Malta. (Photograph)

SACRED TO THE MEMORY OF / WILLIAM FLOCKHART BOWMAN ESQ. / DEPUTY COMMIS-
SARY GENERAL / WHO DEPARTED THIS LIFE AT MALTA ON THE 11TH APRIL 1855 / AGED 70
YEARS. / THIS MONUMENT HAS BEEN ERECTED OVER HIS REMAINS / BY THE OFFICERS OF
THE / COMMISSARIAT STATIONED AT MALTA / IN TESTIMONY OF THEIR RESPECT FOR HIS
MEMORY.

Dep Asst Comm Gen 4 May 1814. Asst Comm Gen 20 Jun 1837.
    Served in the Peninsula Apr 1814 (stationed in Lisbon).

BOYCE, John
Lieutenant. 33rd (1st Yorkshire West Riding) Regiment of Foot.
Named on the Regimental Memorial: St Joseph's Church, Waterloo, Belgium. (Photograph)

Northumberland Militia. Ensign 33rd Foot 18 Apr 1809. Lt 1 Jan 1811.
    Present at Quatre Bras where he was killed. Also served in the Netherlands 1814–1815

BOYCE, Shapland
Major. 13th Regiment of Light Dragoons.
Memorial: Bannow Church, County Wexford, Ireland. (M.I.)

"BENEATH THIS STONE LIES BURIED SAMUEL BOYCE OF THIS PARISH .... ALSO
THEIR SON SHAPLAND BOYCE WHO DIED FEB 22ND 1833."

Captain 105th Foot 28 Feb 1795. Capt 13th Lt Dragoons 17 Mar 1803. Bt Major 25 Apr 1808. Major 4
Jun 1813. Bt Lt Colonel 4 Jun 1814. Lt Colonel 13th Lt Dragoons 8 Dec 1818.
    Served in the Peninsula Apr 1810 – Apr 1814. Present at Campo Mayor, Albuera, Usagre, Arroyo dos
Molinos, Alba de Tormes, Vittoria, Pyrenees, Nivelle, Nive, Adour, Garris, Orthes, Aire, Tarbes and
Toulouse. Awarded Bt Lt Colonelcy for his services in the Peninsula. Present at Waterloo (wounded). Took
over command of the Regiment on 18th Jun as Patrick Doherty was ill with a fever from his service in the
West Indies after Doherty had commanded the regiment on 16th and 17th June. CB. Educated at Eton.

BOYD, George
Lieutenant. 1st Line Battalion, King's German Legion.
Named on the Memorial: St Andrew's Church, (now Musée Historique), Biarritz, France. (Photograph)

Ensign 29 May 1809. Lt 18 Mar 1812.
    Served in the Peninsula Nov 1809 – Nov 1813. Present at Busaco, Fuentes d'Onoro, Ciudad Rodrigo,
Moriscos, Salamanca, Burgos, Vittoria, Tolosa (wounded), San Sebastian, Bidassoa and Nivelle where he
was killed 10 Nov 1813.

BOYES, Robert Nairne
Ensign. 85th (Buckinghamshire Volunteers) Light Infantry Regiment of Foot.
Headstone: Old Churchyard, Spital, Windsor, Berkshire. (Photograph)

IN / LOVING MEMORY / OF / ROBERT NAIRNE BOYES MKW / CAPTAIN LATE 85TH REGIMENT.
/ DIED NOVEMBER 26TH 1872, / AGED 75 YEARS.

Volunteer 85th Foot. Ensign 6th Foot 26 May 1814. Ensign 85th Foot 13 Oct 1814. Lt 8 Jun 1815. Capt 55th Foot 9 Aug 1831.

Served in the Peninsula Mar – Apr 1814. Present at Bayonne. Also served in North America (present at Bladensburg, Washington, Baltimore and New Orleans) and in South Africa. (Barrack Master at Grahamstown, 1836). Died a Military Knight of Windsor 1872.

BRADBURY, Emmanuel

Sergeant. 1st (Kings) Dragoon Guards.
Grave: St George's Churchyard, Hulme, Manchester, Lancashire. (No longer extant. The church has been made into flats and the churchyard into a car park). (M.I.)

"EMMANUEL BRADBURY / BARRACK HOSPITAL SERGEANT / 1ST K. D. G. / DIED 4TH DECEMBER 1847 / AGED 62 YEARS"

Pte 27 Oct 1799. Cpl 3 Dec 1808. Sgt 28 Mar 1812.
Present at Waterloo. Discharged after 27 years and 41 days service aged 47.

BRADBY, Joseph

Captain. 28th (North Gloucestershire) Regiment of Foot.
Memorial tablet: All Saints Church, Fawley, Hampshire. (Photograph)

THIS MONUMENT IS ERECTED IN MEMORY OF / MAJOR JOSEPH BRADBY / OF THE 28TH REGIMENT OF FOOT, / WHO DIED / ON THE 24TH AUGUST 1813, AT VITTORIA IN SPAIN, / OF THE WOUNDS HE RECEIVED / IN THE BATTLE OF THE PYRENEES, / AGED 33 YEARS. / THUS TERMINATED A BRILLIANT CAREER / OF FIFTEEN YEARS IN ACTUAL SERVICE. / HE WAS SINCERELY REGRETTED / BY HIS RELATIVES AND BROTHER OFFICERS, / TO WHOM HE WAS ENDEARED BY AFFECTION / AND URBANITY OF MANNERS. / HIS REMAINS WERE INTERRED AT VITTORIA, / WITH MILITARY HONOURS.

Capt 20 May 1802. Bt Major Jul 1813.
Served in the Peninsula Aug 1808 – Aug 1813 with 1/28 Aug 1808 – Jan 1809, 1st battalion of Detachments Feb – Sep 1809 and 1/28th Sep 1810 – Aug 1813. Present at Douro, Talavera (wounded), Tarifa, Barrosa (severely wounded), Arroyo dos Molinos, Almarez, retreat from Burgos, Vittoria, Pyrenees (severely wounded at Maya 25 Jul 1813 and died of his wounds 24 Aug 1813). Was left behind in Lisbon owing to a fever during the retreat to Corunna and joined the Battalion of Detachments to fight at Talavera. Gold Medal for Vittoria and awarded Brevet Majority.

BRADFORD, Sir Henry Hollis

Captain and Lieutenant Colonel. 1st Regiment of Foot Guards.
Memorial tablet: St Mary's Church, Storrington, Sussex. (Photograph)

TO THE MEMORY OF / SIR HENRY HOLLIS BRADFORD / KNIGHT COMMANDER / OF THE MOST HONOURABLE MILITARY ORDER OF THE BATH / AND LIEUTENANT-COLONEL / OF THE FIRST OR GRENADIER REGIMENT OF THE FOOT GUARDS / THIS MONUMENT IS ERECTED / BY HIS COMPANIONS IN ARMS / THE WITNESSES OF HIS VALOR / AND SHARERS OF HIS SOCIAL HOURS / HE DIED AT LA VACHERIE NEAR LILLERS IN FRANCE / ON THE 17TH OF DECEMBER 1816 / IN THE 35TH YEAR OF HIS AGE / AND WAS BURIED IN THIS CHURCH YARD

Named on the Family vault: St Mary's Churchyard, Storrington, Sussex. (Photograph)

IN / MEMORY OF / .... / AND OF THEIR THIRD SON / LT. COL. SIR HENRY HOLLIS BRADFORD. KCB / GRENADIER GUARDS / DIED 17TH DECEMBER 1816 FROM / WOUNDS RECEIVED AT / WATERLOO / AGED 36.

Memorial tablet: St Andrew's Church, Hartburn, Northumberland. (Photograph)

IN MEMORY OF LT COLONEL SIR HENRY BRADFORD / KCB OF THE 1ST REGIMENT OF GUARDS WHO WAS / ENGAGED IN MOST OF THE BATTLES AND SIEGES / DURING THE WARS IN PORTUGAL, SPAIN, FRANCE / AND THE NETHERLANDS, FROM 1807 TO 1815, / AND DIED FROM THE EFFECTS OF A WOUND / RECEIVED AT THE BATTLE OF WATERLOO / DEC. 17 1816, AGED 35 YEARS. / HIS REMAINS LIE IN STORRINGTON / CHURCHYARD, SUSSEX.

Memorial: Royal Military Chapel, Wellington Barracks, London. (M.I) (Destroyed by a Flying Bomb 1944)

"IN MEMORY OF / LIEUT–COLONEL SIR HENRY BRADFORD, K.C.B. / 1ST GUARDS, 1814–16. / AIDE-DE-CAMP AT COPENHAGEN, CORUNNA, FLUSHING. / ASSISTANT ADJUTANT-GENERAL AT / SALAMANCA, / VITTORIA, PYRENEES, NIVELLE, ORTHES, TOULOUSE, WATERLOO. / DIED ON 17TH DECEMBER 1816, FROM A WOUND / RECEIVED AT WATERLOO. AGED 35. / PLACED BY HIS NEPHEW, LIEUT-COLONEL RALPH BRADFORD ATKINSON, GRENADIER GUARDS, 1840 TO 1860."

Named on Memorial Panel VIII for Waterloo: Royal Military Chapel, Wellington Barracks, London. (M.I.) (Destroyed by a Flying Bomb 1944)

Ensign 4th Foot 26 Jun 1800. Lt 22 Jan 1801. Capt 4th Foot 1 Oct 1802. Bt Major 8 Sep 1808. Major 11th Foot 20 Sep 1808. Bt Lt Colonel 28 Dec 1809. Capt and Lt Colonel 1st Foot Guards 25 Jul 1814.
    Served in the Peninsula Aug 1808 – Jan 1809 (ADC to General Fraser), Nov 1811 – Apr 1814 (on Staff as AAG 4th Division). Present at Corunna, Salamanca, Vittoria, Pyrenees, Nivelle, Orthes and Toulouse. Present at Waterloo as AQMG (severely wounded and died of his wounds 17 Dec 1816). Gold Cross for Salamanca, Vittoria, Pyrenees, Nivelle, Orthes and Toulouse. KCB 2 Jan 1815. Also served at Hanover 1805, Copenhagen 1807, Sweden 1808 and Walcheren 1809 (present at the siege of Flushing). His brother Lt and Capt Keating Bradford of the 3rd Foot Guards was killed at Rolica in 1808, his brother Lt Colonel Sir Thomas Bradford 82nd Foot also served in the Peninsula and his brother Rev William Bradford was at Corunna.
REFERENCE: *Gentleman's Magazine, 1816, Part 2, Supplement, p. 626.*

BRADFORD, Keating James
Lieutenant and Captain. 3rd Regiment of Foot Guards.
Named on Memorial Panel VI for Vimeiro: Royal Military Chapel, Wellington Barracks, London. (M.I.) (Destroyed by a Flying Bomb 1944)

Ensign 1st Foot 1798. Lt and Capt 3rd Foot Guards 15 Jan 1807.
    Served in the Peninsula Aug 1808 (DAAG). Present at Rolica where he was killed 17 Aug 1808. Also served in Portugal 1798. Brother of Capt and Lt Colonel Henry Hollis Bradford 1st Foot Guards, Lt Colonel Sir Thomas Bradford 82nd Foot and Rev William Bradford.

BRADFORD, Sir Thomas
Lieutenant Colonel. 82nd (Prince of Wales's Volunteers) Regiment of Foot.
Memorial tablet: St Andrew's Church, Hartburn, Northumberland. (Photograph)

IN MEMORY OF GENERAL SIR THOMAS BRADFORD, / GCB, GCH COLONEL, OF THE 4TH REG^{T} OF FOOT, / WHO WAS ENGAGED IN MOST OF THE BATTLES / AND SIEGES DURING THE WARS IN SOUTH / AMERICA, PORTUGAL, SPAIN AND FRANCE, / FROM 1806 TO 1815, AND WAS / SEVERELY WOUNDED AT BAYONNE. / HE DIED NOV^{R} 28 1853. / HIS REMAINS LIE IN THE / VAULT BENEATH.

Memorial window: St Andrew's Church, Hartburn, Northumberland. (Photograph)

TO THE MEMORY OF GENERAL SIR THOMAS BRADFORD, G.C.B. DIED NOV 28 1853. / THE WINDOWS ABOVE ARE DEDICATED BY HIS WIDOW & CHILDREN.

Ensign Independent Company 20 Oct 1793. Lt 9 Dec 1793. Capt 15 Apr 1794. Major Nottingham Fencibles 9 Sep 1795. Bt Lt Colonel 1 Jan 1801. Lt Colonel 3rd Garrison Battalion 25 Feb 1805. Major 87th Foot 30 May 1805. Lt Colonel 34th Foot 18 May 1809. Lt Colonel 82nd Foot 21 Dec 1809. Bt Colonel 25 Jul 1810. Major General 4 Jun 1813. Lt General 29 May 1825. General 23 Nov 1841. Portuguese Army: Brigadier General 19 Dec 1811. Field Marshal 10 Jul 1813.

Served in the Peninsula with 87th Foot Aug 1808 – Jan 1809 (AAG) and with Portuguese Army Dec 1811 – Apr 1814 (Commanded 10 Portuguese Brigade). Present at Vimeiro, Corunna, Salamanca (Mentioned in Despatches), Burgos and retreat from Burgos, Vittoria, San Sebastian (Mentioned in Beresford's Despatches), Nive (Mentioned in Beresford's Despatches), Adour (Mentioned in Beresford's Despatches) and Bayonne (severely wounded and awarded pension of £350 per annum). Gold Cross for Corunna, Salamanca, Vittoria, San Sebastian and Nive. KCB 2 Jan 1815. KTS. Had not recovered from his wound in time to take part at Waterloo, but later joined the Army of Occupation until 1818.

Also served in the Irish Rebellion 1798, Hanover 1805, South America 1807 (present at Montevideo and Buenos Ayres), Scotland 1819–1825, India 1825–1829 (Commander of H. M. Forces and Company Forces in Bombay). GCH 1831. Commissioner of Royal Military College and Commissioner of Royal Military Asylum 1832. GCB 1838.

Colonel 94th Foot 1 Dec 1823. Colonel 30th Foot 16 Apr 1829. Colonel 4th Foot 7 Feb 1846. Brother of Lt and Capt Keating Bradford 3rd Foot Guards, Capt and Lt Colonel Henry Hollis Bradford 1st Foot Guards and Rev William Bradford.

REFERENCE: *United Service Magazine, Jan 1854, pp. 156–8. Gentleman's Magazine, Mar 1854, pp. 315–6. Annual Register, 1853, Appx, p. 272.*

BRADFORD, William
Chaplain to the Forces. Chaplains Department.
Vault: St Mary's Churchyard, Storrington, Sussex. (Photograph)

IN / MEMORY OF / REV. WILLIAM BRADFORD, M.A. / SECOND SON OF / THOMAS AND ELIZABETH BRADFORD, / DIED 19TH JUNE 1857, / AGED 77. / ALSO OF MARTHA, HIS WIFE / DIED 18TH DECEMBER 1873.

Stained glass window: St Mary's Church, Storrington, Sussex. (Behind altar). (Photograph)

IN MEMORY OF WILLIAM BRADFORD 40 YEARS RECTOR OF THE PARISH OF STORRINGTON HE DIED IN JUNE 1857 ALSO IN MEMORY OF MARTHA HIS WIFE WHO DIED DECEMBER 1873

Served in the Peninsula 1808 – Jan 1809. Present in the Corunna Campaign. (Chaplain of Brigade). Author of *Sketches of the country, character and costumes in Portugal and Spain*, 1809. Brother of Capt and Lt Colonel Sir Henry Hollis Bradford, Lt and Capt Keating Bradford and Lt Colonel Sir Thomas Bradford.

BRADNOCK, George
Assistant Commissary and Paymaster. Field Train Department of Ordnance.
Memorial: British Cemetery, Lisbon, Portugal. (No longer extant: Grave number D11). (M.I.)

"ERECTED BY OFFICERS OF THE FIELD TRAIN DEPARTMENT OF THE ORDNANCE IN MEMORY OF GEORGE BRADNOCK, ASST COMMISSARY AND PAYMASTER OF THE FIELD TRAIN OF THE ORDNANCE, WHO DIED AT LISBON 9 JUN 1809 AGED 39. ...."

Conductor of Stores 1 Jun 1794. Clerk of Stores 1 Apr 1803. Asst Comm Gen 21 Mar 1805.
    Served in the Peninsula 1811. Died in Lisbon 13 Jun 1811 (differs from date on memorial). Served for 17 years with the department. Also served at the Helder 1799, Egypt 1801 and Sicily 1806.

BRADSHAWE, George Paris
Lieutenant. 77th (East Middlesex) Regiment of Foot.
Obelisk: Kensal Green Cemetery, London. (11320/54/PS). (Photograph)

M. S. / MAJOR GENERAL / GEORGE PARIS BRADSHAWE K. H. / ELDEST SON OF THE LATE / LIEUT. COL. PARIS BRADSHAWE H.E.I.C.S. / FORMERLY RESIDENT AT LUCKNOW / BORN MAY XI AD MDCCXCL / DIED MAR XI AD MDCCCLIV. / MAJOR GENERAL GEORGE PARIS BRADSHAWE / SERVED IN THE EXPEDITION TO MADEIRA IN / MDCCCVII WALCHEREN IN MDCCCIX INCLUDING / THE LANDING AT TER-VERE, SIEGE AND / BOMBARDMENT OF FLUSHING: PENINSULA / FROM JUNE MDCCCXI TO THE END OF THE WAR / INCLUDING THE SIEGE, ASSAULT AND CAPTURE / OF CUIDAD RODRIGO AND BADAJOZ, / OPERATIONS ON THE BIDASSOA AND ADOUR, / BLOCKADE OF BAYONNE AND REPULSE OF THE / SORTIE. / HE COMMANDED HIS MAJESTY'S SEVENTY / SEVENTH REGIMENT OF FOOT FROM NOV / MDCCCXXXIII TO AUG MDCCCXLVIII / DURING WHICH PERIOD HE ACCOMPANIED / THE REGIMENT AND SERVED WITH IT / AT HOME AND ABROAD IN JAMAICA, MALTA / CORFU AND NORTH AMERICA / H R I P / THIS MONUMENT / IS ERECTED TO HIS MEMORY / BY HIS WIDOW.

Ensign 2 Oct 1806. Lt 16 Jun 1808. Capt 23 May 1816. Major 26 Dec 1822. Lt Col 10 Jun 1826. Major General 11 Nov 1851.
    Served in the Peninsula Jul 1811 – Dec 1812 and Feb 1813 – Apr 1814. Present at Ciudad Rodrigo, Badajoz, Bidassoa, Adour and Bayonne. MGS medal for Ciudad Rodrigo and Badajoz. Also served in Madeira 1807 and Walcheren 1809 (present at the siege of Flushing), West Indies, Malta, Corfu and North America. KH. Died 11 Mar 1854.

BRADY, John James
Hospital Assistant. Medical Department.
Ledger stone: St Mary the Virgin Churchyard, Kirkby Lonsdale, Cumbria. Seriously eroded. (Photograph)

IN MEMORY OF JOHN JAMES BRADY / OF THE 93RD HIGHLANDERS / WHO SERVED AS A MEDICAL OFFICER / IN THE PENINSULAR WAR. / HE DIED ON THE 9TH OF OCTOBER 1830 / AGED 36 YEARS.

Hospital Assistant 7 Apr 1813. Asst Surgeon 93rd Foot 9 Nov 1815.
    Served in the Peninsula Jul 1813 – Apr 1814. Retired on full pay 29 May 1817. Rejoined the 93rd again Jan 1826 and served until his death in Oct 1830.

BRAGGE, William
Captain. 3rd (King's Own) Regiment of Dragoons.
Low monument: St Mary the Virgin Churchyard, Thorncombe, Dorset. (Photograph)

COLONEL WILLIAM BRAGGE OF SADBOROW, WHO DIED APRIL 6TH 1863, AGED 74.

Cornet 24 May 1810. Lt 11 Oct 1810. Capt 24 Jun 1813. Major 10 Jun 1826.
    Served in the Peninsula Nov 1811 – Mar 1814. Present at Salamanca, retreat from Burgos and Vittoria. Returned to England before Toulouse. Served in France with the Army of Occupation Aug 1815 – Nov 1818. MGS medal for Salamanca and Vittoria. Also served in Ireland 1818. Half pay Jun 1826. Retired 1853 and became High Sheriff of Dorset.
REFERENCE: *Cassels, S. A. C., Peninsular portrait 1811 – 1814, the letters of Captain William Bragge, Third (King's Own) Dragoons, 1963.*

BRAMWELL, John
Ensign. 92nd Regiment of Foot.
Family Memorial: Kirkmahoe Churchyard, Kirkton, Dumfriesshire, Scotland. (Photograph)

.... / ALSO OF THE ABOVE JOHN BRAMWELL / LATE LIEUTENANT IN THE 92ND / GORDON HIGHLANDERS REGIMENT, / WHO DIED AT WEST GALLABERRY ON THE / 8TH JUNE 1881, AGED 85.

Ensign 29 Jul 1813. Lt 18 Jul 1815.
    Served at Quatre Bras (carried the colours, was severely wounded, had his right leg amputated and awarded pension of £70 per annum). Half pay 25 Feb 1817. Took an active part in public life in Sanquhar in Dumfriesshire, became Mayor of the Town Council for several years and Treasurer of the Borough.

BRAND, Hon Henry Otway, Lord Dacre see Otway, Henry

BRANFILL, Champion Edward
Captain. 3rd (King's Own) Regiment of Dragoons.
Memorial tablet: St Laurence's Church, Upminster, Essex. (Photograph)

TO THE MEMORY OF / CHAMPION EDWARD BRANFILL, / (ONLY SON OF CHAMPION BRANFILL,) / OF UPMINSTER HALL, ESQUIRE, / WHO WAS BORN ON THE 13TH DAY OF JULY 1789, / AND DECEASED ON THE 7TH DAY OF OCTOBER 1844. / HE SERVED AS A CAPTAIN IN THE 3RD REGIMENT OF DRAGOONS / IN THE PENINSULAR WAR, / AND ON HIS RETIREMENT IN THE YEAR 1816 HE WAS COMMISSIONED / JUSTICE OF THE PEACE AND DEPUTY LIEUTENANT OF THE COUNTY.

Cornet May 1810. Lt 15 Nov 1810. Capt 21 Oct 1813.
    Served in the Peninsula Aug 1811 – Apr 1814. Present at Castrejon (wounded) and Toulouse. Retired 1816. Justice of the Peace and Deputy Lieutenant of Essex.
REFERENCE: *Gentleman's Magazine, Dec 1844, pp. 649–50.*

BRAUND, John
Sergeant. 51st (2nd Yorkshire West Riding) Light Infantry.
Named on the Regimental Memorial: KOYLI Chapel, York Minster, Yorkshire. (Photograph)
    Killed in the Peninsula.

BREDA, Cornelius
Cornet. 6th Hussars, Dutch Cavalry.
Named on the Regimental Memorial to officers of the Dutch 6th Regiment of Hussars killed at Waterloo, St Joseph's Church, Waterloo. (Photograph)

BREDIN, Andrew
Captain. Royal Artillery.
Grave: St Nicholas Churchyard, Plumstead, Kent and named on the Regimental Memorial: St Nicholas Church, Plumstead, Kent. Destroyed by a flying bomb in the Second World War)

2nd Lt 9 Sep 1794. Capt-Lieut 6 Jul 1798. Capt 23 Oct 1804. Bt Major 25 Jul 1810. Bt Lt Colonel 12 Aug 1819. Major 12 Jun 1823. Lt Colonel 17 Oct 1823. Colonel 20 Jul 1834. Major General 23 Nov 1841. Joined the Royal Artillery from the Royal Irish Artillery.
   Served in the Peninsula 1812–1814. Present at Salamanca. Also served in the West Indies 1785–1805 (present at Grenada, St Vincent and St Lucia), Gibraltar 1808–1812, Upper Canada 1819–1824 and Halifax 1828–1833. Died at Plumstead 28 Oct 1845.
REFERENCE: *Gentleman's Magazine, Dec 1845, p. 640. Annual Register, 1845, Appx, p. 309.*

BRERETON, William
1st Lieutenant. Royal Artillery.
Interred in Catacomb B (v153 c7) Kensal Green Cemetery, London.

2nd Lt 1 May 1805. 1st Lt 1 Jun 1806. 2nd Capt 30 Sep 1816. Capt 26 Oct 1831. Lt Col 17 Aug 1843. Colonel 24 Jan 1854. Major General 16 Dec 1854. Lt General 27 Jun 1864.
   Served in the Peninsula Apr 1810 – Dec 1812 and May 1813 – Apr 1814. Present at Cadiz (present at Fort Matagorda, wounded and Mentioned in Despatches), Barrosa (wounded), retreat from Burgos, San Munos, Vittoria, Pyrenees, San Sebastian, Helette, Garris, Sauveterre, Orthes, Aire, Tarbes and Toulouse. Present at Quatre Bras and Waterloo in Major Norman Ramsay's 'H' Troop (severely wounded). MGS medal for Barrosa, Vittoria, Pyrenees, San Sebastian, Orthes and Toulouse. KCB and KH. Also served at Walcheren 1809, China 1846–1847 (second in command in the expedition up the Canton river), and the Crimea (directed naval batteries against Sebastopol during the siege 17 Oct 1854). One of the few men who served in both the Peninsular and Crimean Wars. Appointed Colonel Commandant Royal Artillery 1 Apr 1864. Died 27 Jul 1864 aged 77. Left money in his will to encourage NCOs. at Woolwich to play cricket.
REFERENCE: *Dictionary of National Biography. Gentleman's Magazine, Oct 1864, pp. 526–7.*

BRETON, John Frederick
1st Lieutenant. Royal Artillery.
Low monument: St Michael and All Angels Churchyard, Lyndhurst, Hampshire. Inscription illegible. (Photograph)

2nd Lt 1 Oct 1808. 1st Lt 15 Mar 1811.
   Present at Waterloo in Capt. A. Mercer's Troop. Had three horses killed under him during the battle. Retired on half pay 1823. Died at Lyndhurst Hampshire 17 Mar 1852.

BRIDGEMAN, Orlando
Lieutenant and Captain. 1st Regiment of Foot Guards.
Family Memorial tablet: St Mary with St Alban Church, Teddington, Middlesex, London. (Photograph)

.... / IN THE SAME VAULT ARE DEPOSITED THE REMAINS OF / THE HON^BLE ORLANDO HENRY BRIDGEMAN, / THIRD SON OF ORLANDO, EARL OF BRADFORD, / AND

DESCENDANT OF THE SIXTH GENERATION OF / THE ABOVE NAMED SIR ORLANDO. / HE DECEASED THE 28TH DAY OF AUGUST 1827, / AGED 33 YEARS. / ....

Memorial: Royal Military Chapel, Wellington Barracks, London. (M.I.) (Destroyed by a Flying Bomb 1944)

"CAPTAIN HON. ORLANDO BRIDGEMAN, / SON OF FIRST EARL OF BRADFORD. 1ST GUARDS, 1811 – 1819. / D.D. LIEUT,-COLONEL HON. FRANCIS BRIDGEMAN, SCOTS GUARDS, 1879."

Ensign 1st Foot Guards 14 Feb 1811. Lt and Capt 25 Dec 1813.
    Served in the Peninsula with 3rd Battalion Jun 1812 – Mar 1814. Present at Cadiz, San Sebastian (wounded), Bidassoa, Nivelle, Nive, Adour and Bayonne. Present at Waterloo where he was wounded (extra ADC to Lord Hill). Half pay 25 Feb 1819.
REFERENCE: *Glover, Gareth ed., A young gentleman at war: the letters of Captain the Honourable Orlando Bridgeman, 1st Foot Guards in the Peninsula and at Waterloo 1812–1815, 2008.*

BRIDGES, Edward Jacob
1st Lieutenant. Royal Artillery.
Headstone: Kensal Green Cemetery, London. Inscription illegible. (9512/155/2). (Photograph)

2nd Lt 1 Oct 1808. 1st Lt 14 Mar 1811. 2nd Capt 4 Aug 1829. Capt 20 Nov 1839. Bt Major 23 Nov 1841.
    Served in the Peninsula Sep 1811 – Apr 1814. Present at Cadiz, Carthagena, Vittoria, Pyrenees, Bidassoa, Nivelle, Nive, Adour and Bayonne. Served with the Army of Occupation, attached to the Prussian Corps d'Armèe in 1815 (present at the reduction of Philippeville, Marienbourg and Rocroy). MGS medal for Vittoria, Pyrenees, Nivelle and Nive. Adjutant to Sir Alexander Dickson Jul – Aug 1815. Also served at Walcheren 1809 (present at the siege of Flushing), Portugal 1826 (Adjutant to the Royal Artillery) and Canada 1838 (Brigade Major to Royal Artillery during the Canadian Rebellion). Died 16 Apr 1851.

BRIGGS, James
Lieutenant. 91st Regiment of Foot.
Memorial tablet: Largo Parish Church, Largo, Fife, Scotland. (Photograph)

IN MEMORY OF / LIEUT. WILLIAM BRIGGS, / INTERPRETER AND QUARTER MASTER / 20TH REGT BENGAL NATIVE INFANTRY / MUCH ESTEEMED AND DEEPLY REGRETTED / BY HIS BROTHER OFFICERS, / WHO ERECTED A TABLET / TO HIS MEMORY AT MOORSHEDABAD, / WHERE HE DIED IN 1827. / ALSO OF / MAJOR JAMES BRIGGS, K.H. / IN THE 91ST, 63D AND 50TH REGIMENTS, / AND WAS SEVERELY WOUNDED / AT THE SIEGE OF BERGEN-OP-ZOOM. / DIED 3D APRIL 1855. / THIS MEMORIAL IS ERECTED / AS A TRIBUTE OF AFFECTION / BY THEIR SURVIVING BROTHER, / DAVID BRIGGS COMMANDER R.A.

Ensign 10 Sep 1812. Lt 91st Foot 28 Jul 1814. Lt 50th Foot 22 Jun 1820. Capt 63rd Foot 1 Oct 1825. Major 16 Nov 1832.
    Served in the Netherlands (present at Bergen-op-Zoom, where he was severely wounded, taken prisoner until Apr 1814 and awarded pension of £50 per annum). Half pay 25 Feb 1816.

BRIGGS, James
Private. 95th Regiment of Foot.
Headstone: Bellie Cemetery, Fochabers, Morayshire, Scotland. (Photograph)

TO THE MEMORY OF / .... / AND / JAMES BRIGGS WHO DIED AT THE / LODGES ON 1ST FEB 1871 AGED 74

Pte Nottinghamshire Militia 1813. Pte 95th Foot 5 Apr 1814. Pte 7th Lt Dragoons 1821.

Present at Waterloo with 95th Foot and with the Army of Occupation. Discharged from 7th Lt Dragoons 1831 as no longer fit for service. Became Gatekeeper and porter to the Duke of Gordon at Gordon Castle, Fochabers. Remained there for forty years until his death on 1 Feb 1871 aged 74.
REFERENCE: *Elgin Courant, 3 Feb 1871, p. 5.*

BRIGGS, John Falconer
Major. 28th (North Gloucestershire) Regiment of Foot.
Memorial tablet: Largo Church, Fife, Scotland. (Photograph)

IN MEMORY OF / COL. JOHN FALCONER BRIGGS K.H / OF STRATHAIRLY AND OVER CARNBEE / WHO DIED LAMENTED ON THE / 27TH OF MARCH 1850 AGED 61 YEARS. / HE ENTERED EARLY IN THE SERVICE OF / HIS COUNTRY IN H.M 28TH FOOT / AND FOUGHT UNDER HER BANNERS AT / COPENHAGEN, SWEDEN, HOLLAND, / AND NEARLY ALL THE GLORIOUS ACTIONS / OF THE PENINSULAR WAR, AND WON THE / ESTEEM OF HIS COMPAN-IONS IN ARMS, / AND DISTINGUISHED SHARE IN THE / REWARDS ASSIGNED TO VALOUR BY A / GRATEFUL COUNTRY. / THIS MONUMENT IS ERECTED BY / HIS SORROWING WIDOW AND CHILDREN / TO RECORD THEIR LOVE FOR AN AFFECTIONATE / HUSBAND, A FOND FATHER, A SINCERE / CHRISTIAN, A TRUE PATRIOT AND A GALLANT SOLDIER / ....

Named on the Family Memorial tablet: Upper Largo Churchyard, Fife, Scotland. (Photograph)

HERE REST / THE REMAINS OF / .... / LIEUT. COL J. F. BRIGGS, K.H. / WHO DIED 27TH MARCH 1850, AGED 61. / .... / ERECTED BY LIEUT D. BRIGGS R. N. / 1850

Ensign 9 Jul 1803. Lt 31 Oct 1805. Capt 18 Jan 1810. Major 8 Dec 1814. Bt Lt Colonel 10 Jan 1837.

Served in the Peninsula with 1/28th Jul 1808 – Jan 1809, 1st Battalion of Detachments Feb – Oct 1809, 2/28th Sep 1810 – Sep 1811 and 1/28th Sep 1813 – Apr 1814. Present in the Corunna campaign, Douro, Talavera, Busaco, first siege of Badajoz, Albuera, Nivelle, Nive, Garris, Orthes, Aire and Toulouse. Also served at Copenhagen 1807 and Sweden 1808. Retired on half pay 25 Dec 1814. KH. MGS medal for Talavera, Busaco, Albuera, Nivelle, Nive, Orthes and Toulouse.

BRIGGS, William
Private. 33rd (1st Yorkshire West Riding) Regiment of Foot.
Named on the Family Memorial: Sheffield General Cemetery, Sheffield, Yorkshire. (Plot Hs 160). (M.I.)

"................... ALSO WILLIAM BRIGGS, WHO DIED MAR 12TH 1878, AGED 82 YEARS"

Served at Waterloo.

BRIGHT, Henry
Captain. 87th (Prince of Wales's Own Irish) Regiment of Foot.
Named on the Memorial: St Andrew's Church, (now Musée Historique), Biarritz, France. (Photograph)

Memorial tablet: Chapel in Churchyard at Toulouse, France. (M.I.)

"CE MONUMENT A ÉTÉ CONSACRÉ À LA MEMOIRE / DE HENRY BRIGHT MAJOR DU 87ME REGT DE / H M B QUI A ÉTÉ TUÉ LE 10 AVRIL 1814 / SOUS LES MURS DE TOULOUSE."

Lt 76th Foot 26 Aug 1806. Capt 87th Foot 18 Aug 1808. Bt Major 22 Nov 1813.

Served in the Peninsula Mar 1809 – May 1811 and Nov 1811 – Apr 1814. Present at Douro, Talavera, Cadiz, Barrosa, Tarifa, Vittoria, Pyrenees, Nivelle, Nive, Orthes, Vic Bigorre and Toulouse where he was killed 10 Apr 1814. Gold Medal for Orthes.

BRINE, James
Captain. 39th (Dorsetshire) Regiment of Foot.
Buried in All Saints Churchyard, Chardstock, Dorset.
Memorial window: St Giles and St Nicholas Church, Sidmouth, Devon. (Photograph)

MAJOR JAMES BRINE FORMERLY OF THE 7TH REGIMENT OF FOOT. SECOND SON OF THE LATE ADMIRAL JAMES BRINE OF BLANDFORD IN THE COUNTRY OF DORSET. DIED AT 'CLAREMONT' IN THIS PARISH JULY 9 1859 AGED 75. GRAMINA JULIA PETRINA HIS WIFE .... THEIR REMAINS LIE BURIED AT CHARDSTOCK, 'ALL SAINTS' IN THE COUNTY OF DORSET.

Ensign 53rd Foot 23 Apr 1805. Lt 39th Foot 31 Oct 1805. Capt 3 Mar 1808. Capt 7th Foot 25 Jan 1824. Bt Major 27 May 1825. Major (unattached) 19 Sep 1826.
Served in the Peninsula with 2/39th Jul 1809 – Jun 1811 and 1/39th Sep 1813 – Mar 1814. Present at first siege of Badajoz, Albuera (wounded and awarded pension of £100 per annum), Pyrenees, Nivelle and Nive. Also served in North America 1814–1815. MGS medal for Albuera, Pyrenees, Nivelle and Nive. Retired on half pay 21 May 1825.

BRINGHURST, John Dorset
Captain. 1st (King's) Dragoon Guards.
Memorial tablet: St Augustine's Church, Woodston, Cambridgeshire. (Removed from the old church and is now stored with others in a locked room). (Photograph)

THE REVD J. BRINGHURST / RECTOR OF THIS PARISH / OUT OF PATERNAL AFFECTION / TO A BELOVED SON / ERECTS THIS MONUMENT / TO RECORD THE DEATH OF / MAJOR JOHN DORSET BRINGHURST / OF THE KING'S DRAGOON GUARDS / WHO FELL AT THE HEAD OF HIS TROOP / IN THE EVER MEMORABLE BATTLE / OF WATERLOO IN FLANDERS / JUNE 18TH 1815. AGED 30 YEARS.

Memorial tablet: St Joseph's Church, Waterloo, Belgium. (Photograph)

IN MEMORY OF / MAJOR JOHN DORSET BRINGHURST / IE REGT KING'S DRAGOON GUARDS, / WHO AFTER SERVING SEVEN CAMPAIGNS, AS / AID DE CAMP TO MAJOR GEN SIR H. FANE K.C.B. / IN SPAIN, PORTUGAL & FRANCE, / WAS KILLED, / IN A CHARGE OF CAVALRY AT THE BATTLE OF / WATERLOO / ON THE 18TH OF JUNE 1815. / HE WAS BURIED ON THE SPOT WHERE HE FELL, NEAR THE / WEST ENTRANCE OF THE FARM OF LA HAYE SAINTE.

Cornet 1st Dragoon Guards 27 Mar 1806. Lt 1 Jan 1807. Capt 94th Foot 18 Jul 1811. Capt 1st Dragoon Guards 24 Oct 1811. Bt Major 12 Apr 1814.
Served in the Peninsula Aug 1808 – Jan 1809, Jun 1809 – Dec 1810 and May 1813 – Apr 1814 (ADC to Major General Henry Fane). Present at Rolica, Vimeiro, Corunna, Talavera, Busaco, Vittoria (wounded), Orthes and Aire. Present at Waterloo where he was killed in the cavalry charge of the Household Brigade. One of the few officers in the regiment who had Peninsular experience. Educated at Oundle.

BRISBANE, Sir Thomas Makdougall

Lieutenant Colonel. Royal York Rangers.
Memorial tablet on Family mausoleum: Largs Parish Churchyard, Ayrshire, Scotland. (Photograph)

IN MEMORY OF / GENERAL SIR THOMAS MAKDOUGALL BRISBANE, BART. / GCB GCH / COLONEL OF THE 18TH (CUMBERLAND) REGIMENT OF FOOT / PRESIDENT OF THE ROYAL SOCIETY OF EDINBURGH / DCL OF OXFORD AND CAMBRIDGE / AND FOR SOME YEARS / GOVERNOR GENERAL OF NEW SOUTH WALES / BORN JULY 23RD 1773 / DIED JANUARY 27TH 1860

Ensign 38th Foot 10 Jan 1790. Lt 30 Jul 1791. Capt 53rd Foot 13 Apr 1794. Major 5 Aug 1795. Lt Colonel 69th Foot 4 Apr 1800. Lt Colonel Royal York Rangers 1805. Bt Colonel 25 Jul 1810. Major General 4 Jun 1813. Lt General 27 May 1825. General 23 Nov 1841.

Served in the Peninsula Jan 1813 – Apr 1814. Present at Vittoria, Pyrenees, Nivelle, Nive, Orthes (severely wounded and Mentioned in Despatches), Vic Bigorre and Toulouse (severely wounded and Mentioned in Despatches). Served in France with the Army of Occupation 1815 (commanded a brigade at Paris). Gold Cross for Vittoria, Pyrenees, Nivelle, Orthes and Toulouse. MGS medal for Nive. KCB 2 Jan 1815. GCB. GCH. Also served in Flanders 1793–1795 (present at Valenciennes, Famars (wounded), Dunkirk, Nieuport and Nimwegen), West Indies 1795–1796 (present at the capture of Trinidad - wounded), Jamaica 1801–1803, North America 1814 (present in command of a brigade at Plattsburg).

Governor of New South Wales 1821. While in Australia turned his attention to astronomy and recorded 7,385 stars for which he received the Copley medal of the Royal Society. Founded an observatory in New South Wales. President of the Royal Society of Edinburgh 1832 and President of the British Association 1833. Erected an observatory at Makerstoun, Scotland 1841. Founded two gold medals for scientific merit, one to be awarded by the Royal Society and the other by the Society of Arts. Colonel 34th Foot 16 Dec 1826. Died 27 Jan 1860 aged 87.

REFERENCE: *Dictionary of National Biography. Australian Dictionary of Biography. Royal Military Calendar, Vol 3, pp. 262–3. Brisbane, Sir Thomas Makdougall, Reminiscences of General Sir Thomas Makdougall Brisbane, 1860. Gentleman's Magazine, Mar 1860, pp. 298–302. Annual Register, 1860, Appx, pp 394–5.*

BRISCALL, Samuel

Chaplain to the Forces. Chaplains Department.
Family Memorial: St Mary's Church, Stockport, Cheshire. (In nave, now built over). (M.I.)

"HERE WAS BURIED THE BODY OF / JAMES BRISCALL / OF STOCKPORT WHO DIED SEP 14 1814 / AGED 63 YEARS. / ……………….. / SAMUEL THEIR SON DIED OCT 7TH / 1848. AGED 70 YEARS. / ………………."

Deacon 2 Dec 1805. Chaplain to the Forces 25 Dec 1809.

Served in the Peninsula Aug 1808 – Jan 1809, Jul 1809 – Feb 1812 and May 1813 – Apr 1814. Present at Corunna and Nive. From July 1809 attached to headquarters, and became close to Wellington who described him as 'an excellent young man.'

BRISCOE, Edward

Lieutenant. 97th (Queen's Own) Regiment of Foot.
Memorial tablet: Fiddown Church, County Kilkenny, Ireland. (Photograph)

IN MEMORY OF / EDWARD BRISCOE / LATE CAPTAIN 41ST REGT. (THE WELSH), / SON OF / EDWARD VILLIERS BRISCOE / OF WILLMOUNT, / BORN JUNE 2ND 1792. / ENSIGN 97TH REGT 1809, ENGAGED AT BUSACO, / ALBUHERA, WHERE HE CARRIED THE COLOURS, / AND THE

SIEGE OF BADAJOS. / HE SERVED AS BRIGADE MAJOR 41ST REGT / IN THE BURMESE WAR, 1826. / DIED FEBRUARY 2ND 1881.

Ensign 8 Jun 1809. Lt 23 Nov 1809. Lt 41st Foot 1826. Capt 18 Jan 1828. Capt 59th Foot 29 Oct 1829.
    Served in the Peninsula Oct 1809 – Dec 1811. Present at Busaco, Albuera (carried the colours) and second siege of Badajoz. Also served in North America 1814–1815, India 1824–1826 (present in the Ava campaign – Brigade Major 41st Foot). MGS medal for Busaco and Albuera and Army of India medal for Ava.

BROADBENT, William
Private. Royal Artillery.
Ledger stone: St John the Baptist Churchyard, Kirkheaton, Yorkshire. (Photograph)

IN MEMORY OF / WILLIAM BROADBENT OF WHITLEY HALL SHROG- / -BOTTOM / (BLACK-SMITH) WHO DEPARTED THIS LIFE / OCTOBER 31ST 1856, AGED 84 YEARS. / ………………

Served in the Peninsula. Present at Salamanca where he was severely wounded and lost his leg.

BROCK, Saumarez
Captain. 43rd (Monmouthshire) Light Infantry Regiment of Foot.
Pedestal tomb: Candie Cemetery, St Peter Port, Guernsey, Channel Islands. (Photograph)

SACRED / TO THE MEMORY OF / COLONEL SAUMAREZ BROCK, K.H., / WHO DIED APRIL 23 1854 / AGED 67.

Ensign 96th Foot 25 Nov 1802. Lt 48th Foot 14 Apr 1804. Capt 28 Mar 1805. Capt 43rd Foot 6 Aug 1807. Major 12 Oct 1815. Major 55th Foot 29 Aug 1822. Lt Colonel 12 Jun 1830. Lt Colonel 48th Foot 30 Mar 1833. Bt Colonel 9 Nov 1846.
    Served in the Peninsula with 2/43rd Aug 1808 – Jan 1809 and 1/43rd Jul – Dec 1811 and Feb 1813 – Apr 1814. Present at Vimeiro (wounded and awarded pension of £100 per annum), Vittoria, Pyrenees, Bidassoa, Nivelle, Nive, Tarbes and Toulouse. Served in France 1815 (present at the Capture of Paris) and with the Army of Occupation. Also served in North America 1814–1815 (present at New Orleans) and India (present in the Coorg campaign 1834 with the 48th Foot). Half pay 13 May 1835. MGS medal for Vimeiro, Vittoria, Pyrenees, Nivelle, Nive and Toulouse. KH.
REFERENCE: *United Service Magazine, Jun 1854, pp. 315–6.*

BROKE, Sir Charles
Major. Permanent Assistant Quartermaster General.
Memorial tablet: St Martin's Church, Nacton, Suffolk. (Photograph)

TO THE MEMORY OF / MAJOR GENERAL SIR CHARLES BROKE VERE, K.C.B, / KNIGHT OF THE TOWER AND SWORD OF PORTUGAL, / AND OF SEVERAL OTHER FOREIGN ORDERS. / SECOND SON OF PHILIP BOWES BROKE, ESQRE / AND BROTHER OF / REAR ADMIRAL SIR PHILIP BOWES VERE BROKE, BART K.C.B. / WHO DIED ON THE 1ST APRIL 1843, / IN THE 65TH YEAR OF HIS AGE, / HAVING PASSED THROUGH A LONG / AND DISTINGUISHED MILITARY CAREER / IN DIFFERENT PARTS OF THE WORLD, / AND HAVING RECEIVED FROM HIS SOVEREIGN, / VARIOUS MARKS OF DISTINCTION / FOR HIS CONDUCT IN THE FIELD, / DURING THE WAR IN SPAIN UNDER THE DUKE OF WELLINGTON, / AND IN THE CAMPAIGN OF WATERLOO: / IN THE FORMER OF WHICH HE WAS SEVERELY WOUNDED, / AT THE ASSAULT OF BADAJOS. / HE WAS RETURNED TO PARLIAMENT FOR HIS NATIVE COUNTY / IN 1835, / AND CONTINUED TO REPRESENT IT TILL HIS DEATH, / EVER EVINCING IN THE

DISCHARGE OF HIS DUTIES / THE MOST DEVOTED LOYALTY TO THE THRONE / AND THE WARMEST ATTACHMENT TO THE RELIGION / AND TO THE CONSTITUTION OF HIS COUNTRY, / WHILE IN HIS OWN LIFE HE EXEMPLIFIED / ALL THOSE VIRTUES / WHICH MARK THE CHARACTER / OF / THE CHRISTIAN.

Ensign 5th Foot 23 Jun 1796. Lt 7 Dec 1796. Capt 21 Feb 1799. Major 4 Feb 1808. Bt Lt Colonel 27 Apr 1812. Bt Colonel 27 May 1825. Major General 10 Jun 1837.

Served in the Peninsula with 2/5th Jul – Dec 1809 and on Staff in QMG's Department Jan 1810 – Apr 1814. Present at Busaco, Albuera, Ciudad Rodrigo, Badajoz (severely wounded), Salamanca, Vittoria, Pamplona, Pyrenees, Bidassoa, Nivelle, Nive, Gave d'Oleron, Orthes, Bayonne and Toulouse. Present at Waterloo (AQMG). Also served at the Helder 1799, Hanover 1805 and South America 1807 (present at Buenos Ayres). Gold Cross for Albuera, Badajoz, Salamanca, Vittoria, Pyrenees, Nivelle, Nive, Orthes and Toulouse. KCB 2 Jan 1815. KCH. KTS. Awarded Order of St Vladimir of Russia 4th Class and Order of Wilhelm of the Netherlands. Took the surname of Vere 1822. MP for Suffolk 1835-1843. Elder brother of Capt Horatio George Broke 58th Foot.
REFERENCE: *Royal Military Calendar, Vol 4, p. 411. Dictionary of National Biography (Under Vere). Gentleman's Magazine, Jun 1843, p. 654. (Under Vere). Annual Register, 1843, Appx, pp. 246–7 (Under Vere).*

BROKE, Horatio George
Captain. 58th (Rutlandshire) Regiment of Foot.
Low monument: Kensal Green Cemetery, London. (16132/75/IC). (Photograph)

SACRED TO THE MEMORY OF LIEUTENANT GENERAL HORATIO BROKE / BORN 4TH JANUARY 1790. DIED 30TH AUGUST 1860

Memorial tablet: St Martin's Church, Nacton, Suffolk. (Photograph)

SACRED TO THE MEMORY / OF / LIEUTENANT-GENERAL HORATIO GEORGE BROKE, / COLONEL OF HER MAJESTY'S 88TH REGIMENT; / YOUNGEST SON OF / PHILIP BOWES BROKE, ESQRE OF BROKE HALL, IN THIS PARISH. / BORN JUNE 4TH 1790, DIED AUGUST 30TH 1860. / HIS REMAINS ARE INTERRED IN THE CEMETERY / AT KENSAL GREEN, NEAR LONDON.

Ensign 52nd Foot 29 May 1806. Lt 15 Feb 1808. Capt 58th Foot 18 Mar 1813. Bt Major 28 Jul 1814. Major 12 Jun 1823. Bt Lt Colonel 20 Jul 1830. Colonel 23 Nov 1841. Major General 11 Nov 1851. Lt General 15 Jun 1860.

Served in the Peninsula with 2/52nd Aug 1808 – Jan 1809 and Mar – Jul 1811, 1/52nd Aug 1811 – Aug 1812 and Sep 1812 – Apr 1814 (ADC to Major General Clinton). Present at Vimeiro, Vigo, Sabugal, Salamanca, Burgos (severely wounded), Nive and Orthes (severely wounded). MGS medal for Vimeiro, Salamanca, Nive and Orthes. Served in France with the Army of Occupation until 1818 (again as ADC to Major General Clinton). Also served in the Baltic 1807 and Walcheren 1809. Colonel 88th Foot 24 Dec 1858. Younger brother of Major Charles Broke AQMG.
REFERENCE: *Annual Register, 1860, Appx, pp. 395–6.*

BROMHEAD, Edmund De Gonville
Lieutenant. 54th (West Norfolk) Regiment of Foot.
Low monument: St Firmin's Churchyard, Thurlby, Lincolnshire. (Photograph)

MAJOR SIR EDMUND DE GONVILLE BROMHEAD BART. / SON OF LIEUT-GENERAL SIR GONVILLE BROMHEAD BART / AND THE HONOURABLE JANE FFRENCH, HIS WIFE. / BORN 22 JANUARY 1791. DIED 25 OCTOBER 1870. / SERVED IN THE FRENCH WAR 1813 – 14 – 15.

PRESENT AT WATERLOO.

Ensign 8th Foot 2 Nov 1808. Lt 54th Foot 23 Mar 1809. Capt 19th Foot 27 Jun 1822. Major (unattached) 13 May 1826.

Present at Waterloo in reserve at Hal, siege of Cambrai and with the Army of Occupation.

BROMHEAD, John
Lieutenant Colonel. 77th (East Middlesex) Regiment of Foot.
Grave: St Peter at Gowts with St Andrews Churchyard, Lincoln, Lincolnshire. (M.I.)

"COLONEL JOHN BROMHEAD CB / DIED 14 FEB 1837 / AGED 60."

Ensign 24th Foot 13 Nov 1793. Lt 16 Jun 1795. Capt 31 Oct 1799. Major 34th Foot 16 May 1805. Lt Colonel 77th Foot 26 Jun 1809. Bt Colonel 12 Aug 1819.

Served in the Peninsula Jul 1809, Jul – Oct 1811 and Apr 1812 – Apr 1814. Present in July 1809 with the 34th Foot but on his promotion to the 77th Foot returned home. Returned again to the Peninsula with 77th Foot in July 1811. Present at El Bodon (Mentioned in Despatches), Badajoz and Bayonne. Gold Medal for Badajoz. CB. Also served in Canada, Nova Scotia, Egypt 1801 and Hanover 1805.

BROOKE, Sir Arthur
Lieutenant Colonel. 44th (East Essex) Regiment of Foot.
Interred in Catacomb B 4283 (v102 c5) Kensal Green Cemetery, London.

Ensign 31 Oct 1792. Lt 26 Nov 1793. Capt 19 Sep 1795. Major 26 Dec 1802. Lt Col 15 Jun 1804. Bt Colonel 4 Jun 1813. Major General 12 Aug 1819. Lt General 10 Jan 1837.

Served in the Peninsula Aug 1813 – Apr 1814. Present at Tarragona (Commanded a Brigade). Also served in Germany 1794, West Indies 1795–1796 (present at St Lucia), Egypt 1801 (present at Alexandria), Sicily 1805 and North America (embarked from Bordeaux for North America 1 Jun 1814, where he was second in command under Major General Ross (present at Bladensburg, Baltimore – took command after the death of Ross, and New Orleans). Military Governor of Yarmouth. KCB. Colonel 86th Foot 24 May 1837. Died in London 26 Jul 1843.
REFERENCE: *Gentleman's Magazine, Oct 1843, p. 434. Annual Register, 1843, Appx, pp. 284–5.*

BROOKE, Francis
Lieutenant Colonel. 4th (King's Own) Regiment of Foot.
Memorial tablet: Aghalurcher Parish Church, Colebrooke Park, County Fermanagh, Ireland. (Photograph)

SACRED TO THE MEMORY OF / LIEUT. COLL FRANCIS BROOKE, / LATE OF THE 4TH OR KING'S OWN REGT; / WHO DEPARTED THIS LIFE, / THE 24TH OF JULY 1826; / IN THE 55TH YEAR OF HIS AGE. / HIS MEMORY WILL BE RECORDED, / IN THE ANNALS OF HIS COUNTRY / AND EMBALMED / IN THE HEARTS OF HIS NUMEROUS RELATIVES / AND FRIENDS. / THIS STONE IS DEDICATED BY / HIS AFFLICTED WIDOW / JANE BROOKE.

Ensign 23 Apr 1791. Lt 3 Jun 1794. Capt 16 Aug 1797. Major 18 Aug 1804. Lt Colonel 14 Feb 1811.

Served in the Peninsula with 1/4th Aug 1808 – Jan 1809 and Nov 1810 – Nov 1813. (Commanded 2 Brigade 5th Division Jul – Dec 1812). Present at Corunna, Badajoz, Salamanca, Burgos, retreat from Burgos, Villa Muriel, Vittoria and San Sebastian. Gold Cross for Badajoz, Salamanca, Vittoria and San Sebastian. Present at Waterloo in command of 4th Foot. CB. Also served in North America 1794, the Helder 1799, Baltic 1807 and Walcheren 1809. Uncle of Lt Francis Brooke 1st Dragoon Guards.
REFERENCE: *Royal Military Calendar, Vol 4, p. 330.*

BROOKE, Francis

Lieutenant. 1st (King's) Dragoon Guards.
Memorial tablet: Aghalurcher Parish Church, Colebrooke Park, County Fermanagh, Ireland. (Photograph)

SACRED TO THE MEMORY OF LIEUT FRANCIS BROOKE / OF THE 1ST DRAGOON GUARDS / ELDEST SON OF SIR HENRY BROOKE BART / WHO FELL IN THE 22ND YEAR OF HIS AGE / WHEN GALLANTLY CHARGING THE FRENCH / IN THE EVER MEMORABLE BATTLE OF WATERLOO 18TH JUNE 1815 / THIS MONUMENT IS ERECTED BY HIS PARENTS / AS A MEMORIAL OF THEIR / AFFECTION FOR HIM / AND IN REMEMBRANCE OF HIS MANY VIRTUES.

Cornet 5 Jun 1811. Lt 31 Dec 1812.
    Present at Waterloo where he was killed. Nephew of Lt Colonel Francis Brooke 4th Foot.

BROOKE, Thomas

Lieutenant and Captain. 1st Regiment of Foot Guards.
Headstone: Kensal Green Cemetery, London. (22180/54/RS). Seriously eroded. (Photograph)

TO THE MEMORY OF / COLONEL THOMAS BROOKE / SON OF SIR RICHARD BROOKE / GRENADIER GUARDS / SERVED UNDER SIR JOHN MOORE / IN THE PENINSULA 1808 / AND SUBSEQUENT CAMPAIGNS / UNDER DUKE OF WELLINGTON

Ensign 7 Mar 1805. Lt and Capt 13 Feb 1811. Capt and Lt Colonel 5 Jul 1815.
    Served in the Peninsula with 3rd Battalion Oct 1808 – Jan 1809 and Sep 1812 – Apr 1814. Present at Corunna, Bidassoa, Nivelle, Nive, Adour and Bayonne. MGS medal for Corunna, Nivelle and Nive. Retired 12 Jun 1838. Educated at Eton. Buried in Kensal Green 19 May 1870.

BROOKES, Robert

Lieutenant. 9th (East Norfolk) Regiment of Foot.
Memorial tablet: St James's Church, Piccadilly, London. (On staircase in north-east of the vestibule). (Photograph)

SACRED TO THE MEMORY OF / ROBERT BROOKES, / LIEUTENANT COLONEL IN H. M. 24TH REGIMENT OF FOOT. / BORN 21ST JUNE 1792. / COMMENCED HIS MILITARY CAREER AS AN ENSIGN IN THE 9TH FOOT. / IN THE YEAR 1811 SERVED IN THE PENINSULAR FROM THAT PERIOD / TO THE END OF THE WAR. / SUBSEQUENTLY IN NORTH AMERICA / UNTIL THE TERMINATION OF THE AMERICAN WAR / AND AFTERWARDS WITH THE ARMY OF OCCU-PATION IN FRANCE / AND WAS KILLED AT THE HEAD OF HIS REGIMENT / AT THE BATTLE OF CHILLIAN WALLAH / ON THE 13TH OF JANUARY 1849. / MOST DEEPLY AND DESERVEDLY LAMENTED / BY HIS BROTHER OFFICERS, AND ALL WHO KNEW HIM. / THIS TABLET IS ERECTED / AS A TRIBUTE OF SINCERE AFFECTION BY HIS WIDOW.

Memorial: Named on the Mayo cross on Chillianwala Battlefield, Gujerat, India.

Ensign South Gloucester Militia 1809. Ensign 9th Foot 16 May 1811. Lt 23 Aug 1813. Capt 27 Aug 1825. Capt 69th Foot 30 Aug 1826. Major 3 May 1831. Lt Colonel 24th Foot 28 Apr 1846.
    Served in the Peninsula with 1/9th Sep 1811 – Apr 1814. Present at Castrejon, Salamanca, siege and retreat from Burgos, Villa Muriel, Osma, Vittoria, San Sebastian (wounded whilst acting as an engineer), Bidassoa (wounded), Nivelle, Nive (wounded) and Bayonne. Also served in North America 1814 – Jun 1815, but returned too late for Waterloo. Present in France with the Army of Occupation until Oct 1818. MGS medal for Salamanca, Vittoria, San Sebastian, Nivelle and Nive.
    Also served in the West Indies 1819–1825 and 1831–1838, North America 1838–1842 and India 1846

with 24th Foot where he was killed at Chillianwala whilst leading a charge against Sikh guns 13 Jan 1849. Lord Gough said 'Brookes was an officer not surpassed for sound judgement and military daring during this or any other army.' During his last leave in 1848 he married, and his wife accompanied him back to India. She returned to England on his death in the following year and lived until 1895.

BROTHERTON, Thomas William
Major. 14th (Duchess of York's Own) Regiment of Light Dragoons.
Cross on stepped base: St Andrews Churchyard, Cobham, Surrey. (Photograph)

GENERAL SIR THOMAS WILLIAM BROTHERTON G.C.B. / DIED JANUARY 20TH 1868. AGED 83.

Ensign Coldstream Guards 24 Jan 1800. Lt and Capt 17 Jul 1801. Capt 14th Lt Dragoons 4 Jun 1807. Major 3rd Dragoon Guards 28 Nov 1811. Major 14th Lt Dragoons 26 Mar 1812. Bt Lt Colonel 19 May 1814. Bt Colonel 22 Jul 1830. Major General 23 Nov 1841. Lt General 11 Nov 1851. General 1 Apr 1860.
    Served in the Peninsula Dec 1808 – Dec 1810, Apr – Oct 1811 and Jun 1812 – Apr 1814. Present at Douro, Sexmiro, Coa, Busaco, Fuentes d'Onoro, El Bodon (Mentioned in Beresford's Despatches), Castrejon (wounded), Salamanca (wounded), Vittoria, Pyrenees, Nivelle, Nive (wounded and taken prisoner until Apr 1814). Also served in Egypt 1801 and Hanover 1805. Retired from 14th Lt Dragoons 1820. Commandant of Cavalry at Maidstone 1832. On staff of Northern District at York 1842. Inspecting General of Cavalry in Great Britain 1847. MGS medal for Egypt, Busaco, Fuentes d'Onoro, Salamanca, Vittoria, Pyrenees, Nivelle and Nive. KCB 1855. GCB 1861. Colonel 15th Hussars May 1849. Colonel 1st Dragoon Guards 17 Jul 1859. Educated at Winchester.
REFERENCE: *Dictionary of National Biography. Gentleman's Magazine, Mar 1868, p. 398. United Service Magazine, Mar 1868, pp. 444–5. Perrett, Bryan, editor, A hawk at war: the Peninsular War reminiscences of General Thomas Brotherton, CB., 1986.*

BROUGHTON, Samuel Daniel
Surgeon. 2nd Life Guards.
Interred in Catacomb A (Pub v50) Kensal Green Cemetery, London.

Surgeon Dorset Militia. Asst Surgeon 2nd Life Guards 22 Sep 1812. Surgeon 27 Oct 1812. Surgeon 2nd Life Guards Jul 1821.
    Served in the Peninsula Nov 1812 – Apr 1814 with 2nd Life Guards. Present at Vittoria and Toulouse. Surgeon to the squadrons of the regiment which served in the Peninsula. Sir John Moore's brother was the surgeon to the remaining Life Guards in England. On Mr Moore's retirement in July 1821, Broughton became surgeon to the whole regiment. Present at Waterloo. In 1837, owing to any ankle injury had to have his foot amputated, but died after the operation 20 Aug 1837.
REFERENCE: *Dictionary of National Biography. Annual Register, 1837, Appx, p. 203. Broughton, Samuel, Letters from Portugal, Spain and France in 1812, 1813 and 1814, 1815, reprint 2005.*

BROWN, Ebenezer
Deputy Inspector of Hospitals. Medical Department.
Memorial: St George's Cathedral Cemetery, Madras, India. (M.I.)

"EBENEZER BROWN MD. / INSPECTOR OF HOSPITALS AND / PRINCIPAL MEDICAL OFFICER / OF THE KING'S TROOPS IN THE MADRAS PRESIDENCY. / ERECTED BY THE OFFICERS OF THE DEPARTMENT. / 2ND JULY 1828."

Regimental Mate 79th Foot 24 Apr 1795. Asst Surgeon 24 Dec 1796. Surgeon 30th Foot 4 Apr 1800. Staff Surgeon 22 Oct 1803. Deputy Inspector of Hospitals 25 Dec 1812.

Served in the Peninsula Jul 1812 – Apr 1814. Present at Carthagena and Tarragona. MD Aberdeen 1825. Also served in India.

BROWN, George

Major. 85th (Buckinghamshire Volunteers) Light Infantry Regiment of Foot.
Family Mural Memorial: Holy Trinity Cathedral Churchyard, Elgin, Morayshire, Scotland. (Photograph)

IN MEMORY OF / GENERAL SIR GEORGE BROWN GCB. KH. / THIRD SON OF / GEORGE BROWN AND MARGARET CLERK / BORN AT LINKWOOD JULY 22 1790 / AND DIED THERE AUGUST 27TH 1865, / AGED 75 YEARS. / ....

Ensign 43rd Foot 23 Jan 1806. Lt 8 Sep 1806. Capt 3rd Garrison Battalion 20 Jun 1811. Capt 85th Foot 2 Jul 1812. Major 26 May 1814. Bt Lt Colonel 29 Sep 1814. Lt Colonel Rifle Brigade 5 Feb 1824. Colonel 6 May 1831. Major General 23 Nov 1841. Lt General 11 Nov 1851. General 7 Sep 1855.
    Served in the Peninsula with 2/43rd Aug 1808 – Jan 1809, 1st Battalion detachments Feb – Sep 1809, 1/43rd Oct 1809 – Aug 1811 and 85th Foot Aug 1813 – Apr 1814. Present at Vimeiro, Douro, Talavera (severely wounded), Coa, Busaco, Redinha, Casal Nova, Foz d'Arouce, Sabugal, Fuentes d'Onoro, San Sebastian, Nivelle, Nive and Bayonne. After 1815 mainly served on the Staff as DAAG, then DAG. Also served at Copenhagen 1807, North America 1814–1815 (severely wounded at Bladensburg and awarded pension of £200 per annum), Crimea 1854 in command of the Light Division (present at the Alma and Inkerman where he was severely wounded, Balaclava and Sebastopol). MGS medal for Vimeiro, Talavera, Busaco, Fuentes d'Onoro, San Sebastian, Nivelle and Nive. KH 1831. GCB 1853. Medal and four clasps for the Crimea, Grand Cross of the Legion of Honour and Order of the Medjidie 1856. Deputy Adjutant General Horse Guards 1841. Adjutant General of the Forces 1851 (resigned 1853). Commander in Chief Ireland Apr 1860 – Jun 1865. Colonel Rifle Brigade 18 Apr 1863.
REFERENCE: *Dictionary of National Biography. United Service Magazine, Oct 1865, pp. 285–6. Gentleman's Magazine, Nov 1865, pp. 643–4. Annual Register, 1865, Appx, pp. 186–7. Oxfordshire Light Infantry Chronicle, 1899, p. 148.*

BROWN, James

Private: 2nd (Royal North British) Regiment of Dragoons.
Low monument in railed enclosure: Near Asheville, North Carolina, United States of America. Inscription not recorded. (Photograph)

Present at Waterloo in Capt Vernor's Troop. Died in America 1840 aged 50 years.

BROWN, Stephen

Private. 7th (Queen's Own) Regiment of Light Dragoons.
Headstone: Bathurst Cemetery, Bathurst, Eastern Cape, South Africa. (Photograph)

SACRED / TO THE MEMORY OF / STEPHEN BROWN / BORN JAN. 30, 1771 / AT MIDDLESEX, ENGLAND, / DIED AT BATHURST / OCT 21, 1840 / AND OF / WILLIAM BROWN / BORN AT CHELSEA ENGLAND / FEB. 29, 1816 / TREACHEROUSLY KILLED BY KAFFIRS / IN TIME OF PEACE / JULY 24, 1843.

Pte 7th Lt Dragoons 3 Jul 1812.
    Present at Quatre Bras (covering the retreat of the infantry) and at Waterloo. After Waterloo he returned to England, but employment was hard to find for discharged soldiers. The country was deep in economic recession owing to the cost of the Napoleonic Wars since 1793. Many ideas were discussed on settlements overseas and Stephen Brown and his family sailed to the Cape of Good Hope to a settlement on the Eastern

Cape frontier. He died there in 1840 but his sons followed in his footsteps, joined the army and fought in the Kaffir Wars.

REFERENCE: *Frykberg, P., Stephen Brown 1771–1840 : our Waterloo Hussar, Waterloo Journal, Aug 1999, pp. 9–10.*

BROWN, Thomas
Lieutenant and Captain. 1st Regiment of Foot Guards.
Memorial tablet: Inside Mausoleum, Evere Cemetery, Brussels, Belgium. (M.I.)

"CAPTAIN T. BROWN 1ST FOOT GUARDS"

Named on the Regimental Memorial: St Joseph's Church, Waterloo, Belgium. (Photograph)
Named on Memorial Panel VIII for Quatre Bras: Royal Military Chapel, Wellington Barracks, London. (M.I.) (Destroyed by a Flying Bomb 1944)

Ensign 13 Aug 1812. Lt and Capt 22 Mar 1814.
   Served in the Peninsula with 1st Battalion May 1813 – Apr 1814. Present at Bidassoa, Nivelle, Nive, Adour and Bayonne. Present at Quatre Bras where he was killed 16 Jun 1815. One of the select band of soldiers buried in the Mausoleum at Evere.

BROWN, Thomas
Lieutenant. 79th (Cameron Highlanders) Regiment of Foot.
Memorial: East Preston Street Burial Ground, Edinburgh, Scotland. (East Walk). (M.I.)

"ERECTED BY HUGH AND LUCY BROWN IN MEMORY OF THEIR FATHER AND UNCLE CAPT THOMAS BROWN, LATE 79TH CAMERON HIGHLANDERS, WHO DIED 7 JULY 1863, AGED 79."

Ensign 23 Oct 1806. Lt 15 Dec 1807. Capt 20 Jul 1815.
   Served in the Peninsula Jul 1810 – Apr 1814. Present at Cadiz, Busaco (wounded), Foz d'Arouce, Fuentes d'Onoro, Salamanca, Burgos, Pyrenees, Nivelle, Nive and Toulouse. Present at Quatre Bras (severely wounded and awarded pension of £100 per annum) and Waterloo. Also served in the Baltic 1807. Retired on half pay 25 Feb 1816. MGS medal for Busaco, Fuentes d'Onoro, Salamanca, Pyrenees, Nivelle, Nive and Toulouse.

BROWNE, Barton Parker
Cornet. 11th Regiment of Light Dragoons.
Cross on stepped base: Locksbrook Cemetery, Bath. (Grave number F 274). (Photograph)

SACRED / TO THE MEMORY OF / COLONEL BARTON PARKER BROWNE, / BORN 13 MARCH 1798. DIED 16 JUNE 1889. / FOUGHT AT WATERLOO, / SERVED AT BHURTPORE.

Cornet 8 Apr 1813. Lt 22 Jun 1815. Capt 5 May 1824. Bt Major 28 Jun 1838. Lt Col 11 Nov 1851.
   Present at Quatre Bras (covering the retreat of the infantry), Waterloo, the Capture of Paris and with the Army of Occupation. Also served in India (present at the siege and capture of Bhurtpore 1825–1826. He volunteered for a dismounted cavalry storming party and was awarded a medal). Reputed to be one of the finest swordsmen in the British Army. Retired Nov 1851.
REFERENCE: *Obit. Daily Telegraph, 25 Jun 1889.*

BROWNE, John
Captain. 4th (King's Own) Regiment of Foot.
Memorial tablet: Castlebar Church of Ireland, Castlebar, County Mayo, Ireland. (Photograph)

IN MEMORY OF / LIEUT COLONEL JOHN BROWNE, / OF BREAFFY IN THIS COUNTY; / 4TH KING'S OWN REGIMENT, / THEN OF THE 92ND HIGHLANDERS, AND 98TH FOOT. / HE SERVED HIS KING AND COUNTRY / IN THE EXPEDITION TO SWEDEN, / THE RETREAT ON CORUNNA, THE LINES OF / TORRES VEDRAS, / REDINHA, FUENTES D'ONOR, / CIUDAD RODRIGA AND THE SIEGE OF BADAJOS / WHERE HE WAS SEVERELY WOUNDED; / THE BATTLES OF / QUATRE BRAS AND WATERLOO, / THERE RECEIVED THREE WOUNDS FROM WHICH HE LAY / 48 HOURS FOR DEAD ON THE FIELD OF VICTORY. / HE DIED AT BREAFFY, / 20TH NOVR 1849. / .... / THIS TABLET / IS ERECTED BY THE WIDOW AND CHILDREN OF / LIEUT. COL. JOHN BROWNE.

Headstone: Castlebar Church of Ireland Churchyard, Castlebar, County Mayo, Ireland. (Photograph)

IN MEMORY OF / JOHN BROWNE ESQ / OF BREAFFY / LIEUT COLONEL H.M. 98TH REGT / DIED NOV 20TH 1849 / AGED 57.

Ensign 21 Oct 1804 (aged 14). Lt 28 Feb 1805. Capt 25 May 1815. Capt 92nd Foot 12 Nov 1818. Bt Major 21 Jan 1819. Bt Lt Colonel 10 Jan 1837. Portuguese Army: Capt 1st Line 2 Apr 1809 (retired 3 Nov 1809).
    Served in the Peninsula with 4th Foot Aug 1808 – Jan 1809, 2nd Battalion Detachments Feb – Mar 1809 and 4th Foot Nov 1810 – Jun 1812. Present in the Corunna campaign, Fuentes d'Onoro, Barba del Puerco and Badajoz (severely wounded and awarded pension of £70 per annum). Present at Waterloo (severely wounded, shot through the head and left for dead on the battlefield). His death reported to his family. He was found in time, and by having his head wound trepanned was able to recover. Awarded a second pension of £100 per annum. Also served in the Baltic 1808, West Indies (present in Jamaica with 92nd Foot 1818 when the regiment lost half their strength through yellow fever at Up Park Camp). Half pay 10 Feb 1837.
REFERENCE: *Gentleman's Magazine, Jan 1850, pp. 89–90. Annual Register, 1849, Appx, p. 288.*

BROWNE, Richard Jebb
Staff Surgeon. Medical Department.
Memorial tablet: St Mary's Church, Newry, Northern Ireland. (Photograph)

TO THE MEMORY OF THE LATE LAMENTED / RICHARD JEBB BROWNE ESQR / FORMERLY SURGEON OF THE 59 REGT INFANTRY, / SUBSEQUENTLY ATTACHED / TO THE STAFF OF THE NORTHERN RECRUITING DISTRICT, / AND MANY YEARS RESIDENT IN NEWRY. / COULD THE PRAYERS OF HIS ATTACHED FAMILY AND FRIENDS / AND "THE BLESSING OF THOSE THAT WERE READY TO PERISH" / HAVE AUGHT AVAILED, / THIS TRULY EXCELLENT MAN WOULD HAVE BEEN LENT / A LITTLE LONGER TO THE WORLD, / BUT – "THE WAYS OF GOD ARE NOT OUR WAYS", / ON THE 19TH OF MAY 1832, AGED 57, HE WAS REMOVED / BY CHOLERA, FROM A SPHERE OF GREAT USEFULNESS / ON EARTH, TO "ENDURING HERITAGE IN HEAVEN" / ....

Slate slab in railed enclosure. St Patrick's Churchyard, Newry, Northern Ireland. (M.I.)

"SACRED TO THE MEMORY OF RICHARD JEBB BROWNE, ESQ., SURGEON OF H. M. 59TH REGIMENT OF FOOT WHO DEPARTED THIS LIFE ON 19TH OF MAY 1832, AGED 57 YEARS......."

Regimental Mate 15th Foot 18 Apr 1794. Garrison Mate 24 Sep 1794. Asst Surgeon 12th Battery Reserve 25 Apr 1804. Asst Surgeon 59th Foot 19 Oct 1804. Surgeon 59th Foot 23 Jan 1806. Staff Surgeon 5 Nov 1812.

Served in the Peninsula Sep 1808 – Jan 1809 and Sep – Dec 1812. Present at Corunna and Cadiz. Also served in the West Indies 1794 (present at Dominica) and Walcheren 1809. Retired on half pay Dec 1827.

BROWNE, Thomas Gore
2nd Captain. Royal Artillery.
Ledger stone: Old Common Cemetery, Southampton, Hampshire Southampton. (NO51 002). (Photograph)

IN MEMORY OF / COLONEL / THOMAS GORE BROWNE / OF THE ROYAL ARTILLERY / WHO DEPARTED THIS LIFE / AT SOUTHAMPTON / JANUARY THE 23RD 1854 / AGED 69 YEARS.

Memorial: Sandpits Cemetery, Gibraltar. (M.I.)

"COL. GORE BROWN, COMMANDING ROYAL ARTILLERY".

2nd Lt 23 Feb 1801. 1st Lt 19 Nov 1802. 2nd Capt 1 Feb 1808. Capt 4 Sep 1823. Lt Col 1 Jul 1836. Colonel 9 Nov 1846.
Served at Waterloo in Major George W. Unett's Brigade, siege of Cambrai and with the Army of Occupation until Nov 1818. Also served at Walcheren 1809 (present at the siege of Flushing), Jamaica 1829–1831 and Gibraltar 1839–1844 (commanded the Royal Artillery).

BROWNE, Thomas Henry
Captain. 23rd (Royal Welch Fusiliers) Regiment of Foot.
Memorial tablet: St Asaph Cathedral, St Asaph, Flintshire, Wales. (Photograph)

IN MEMORY OF / LT GENL SIR HENRY BROWNE K.C.H. / COLL OF H.M.S 80TH REGT / OF BRON-WYLFA, IN THIS PARISH, / WHO DIED MARCH 11TH 1855, AGED 69. / THIS TABLET IS ERECTED BY / HIS ELDER SON.

Ensign 28 Oct 1805. Lt 18 Sep 1806. Capt 15 Apr 1813. Bt Major 21 Jun 1817. Bt Lt Colonel 21 Jan 1819. Bt Colonel 10 Jan 1837. Lt General 20 Jun 1854.
Served in the Peninsula with 1/23rd Dec 1810 – Dec 1812 and Jan 1813 – Apr 1814 (on Staff as DAAG). Present at Salamanca, Burgos and the retreat, Vittoria (wounded, captured by the French but rescued by the 15th Lt Dragoons), Pyrenees, Nivelle, Nive, Orthes, Tarbes and Toulouse. Wellington wanted him on his staff at Waterloo, but Horse Guards refused, so he went as ADC to Sir Charles Stewart at Vienna, headquarters of Austrian, Prussian and Russian armies. Present at the Capture of Paris and with the Army of Occupation.
Also served at Copenhagen 1807 and Martinique 1809 (present at Fort Desaix where he was wounded). MGS medal for Martinique, Salamanca, Vittoria, Pyrenees, Nivelle, Nive, Orthes and Toulouse. KCH 1821. KCB 1826. He was fluent in Italian and was appointed a member of the Milan commission to investigate the conduct of Caroline Princess of Wales, to enable the Prince Regent to obtain his divorce. Survived a murder attempt. High Sheriff of Flintshire 1824. Colonel 80th Foot Aug 1854.
REFERENCE: *Dictionary of National Biography. Buckley, Roger Norman ed., The Napoleonic war journal of Captain Thomas Henry Browne, 1808–1816, 1987. Gentleman's Magazine, Apr 1855, p. 421. Annual Register, 1855, Appx, p. 261.*

BROWNRIGG, Sir Robert
Colonel. 9th (East Norfolk) Regiment of Foot.
Memorial tablet: St Maughan's Church, St Maughan, Monmouthshire. (Photograph).

IN A VAULT BENEATH / ARE DEPOSITED THE MORTAL REMAINS OF / GENERAL SIR ROBERT

BROWNRIGG, BARONET / KNIGHT GRAND CROSS / OF THE MOST HONORABLE ORDER OF THE BATH. / GOVERNOR OF LANDGUARD FORT, / AND COLONEL OF THE 9TH REGIMENT OF FOOT; / WHO HAVING SERVED HIS KING AND COUNTRY / IN MANY IMPORTANT SITUATIONS AT HOME AND ABROAD / DIED, FULL OF YEARS AND FULL OF HONOUR / AT HIS SEAT, HILSTONE HOUSE, IN THIS PARISH, / ON THE 27TH DAY OF MAY 1833, / IN THE 76TH YEAR OF HIS AGE.

Ensign 14th Foot 22 Nov 1775. Lt 6 Jun 1778. Capt 100th Foot 1784. Capt 35th Foot Oct 1784. Capt 52nd Foot Jun 1786. Bt Major 19 May 1790. Lt Colonel 88th Foot 25 Sep 1793. Bt Colonel 3 May 1796. Colonel 60th Foot 25 Jun 1799. Major General 29 Apr 1802. Colonel 9th Foot 3 Oct 1805. Lt General 25 Apr 1808. General 12 Aug 1819.

 Served at Walcheren Jul 1809 (present at the siege of Flushing). Also served in America 1776 with 14th Foot, West Indies 1782–1784 and Flanders 1794–1795 (DQMG). Military Secretary to the Duke of York 1795–1803. QMG to the forces 1803. Governor and Commander in Chief of forces in Ceylon 1813–1820 (present at capture of Kandy 1815). GCB 2 Jan 1815. Governor of Landguard Fort 21 Feb 1823.
REFERENCE: Royal Military Calendar Vol 2, pp. 126–7. Annual Register, 1833, Appx, pp. 220–1.

BRUCE, John Robertson
1st Lieutenant. Royal Artillery.
Family mausoleum: Old Dunboe Churchyard, Downhill, County Londonderry, Northern Ireland. (Photograph)

THE FAMILY BURIAL PLACE / OF / SIR H. H. A. BRUCE BARᵀ / BUILT 1810

2nd Lt 1 Mar 1806. 1st Lt 1 Jun 1806.
 Present at Waterloo in Major Beane's Troop. Retired on half pay 16 Jun 1820. Married daughter of Lt and Capt Robert Bamford Hesketh 3rd Foot Guards. Died 22 Apr 1836.

BRUCE, Robert
Ensign. 1st Regiment of Foot Guards.
Ledger stone: Parish Church of Clackmannan, Clackmannanshire, Scotland. (Photograph)

ROBERT BRUCE ESQ. / BORN AT KENNET 8TH DECEMBER 1795. / IN 1813 HE ENTERED THE ARMY / AND SERVED IN THE GRENADIER GUARDS / IN THE PENINSULA AND AT WATERLOO. / BELOVED AND LAMENTED / HE DIED AT KENNET 13TH AUGUST 1864.

Ensign 9 Dec 1813. Lt 60th Foot 25 May 1820. Lt and Capt 15 Jun 1820.
 Present at Waterloo (wounded). Retired 8 Jul 1824. MP for the County of Clackmannan, 1820–1824.

BRUCE, William
Captain. 79th (Cameron Highlanders) Regiment of Foot.
Low monument with convex top: Brompton Cemetery, London. (BR 54289). (Photograph)

IN MEMORY OF / LIEUT. COLONEL WILLIAM BRUCE K.H. / OF THE 79 HIGHLANDERS, / AND 48 REGIMENT, / WHO DIED 28 NOVEMBER 1868, / AGED 78 YEARS. / PENINSULA, / PYRENEES, NIVELLE, / NIVE, TOULOUSE, / WATERLOO.

Ensign 4th Garrison Battalion 1 Dec 1806. Lt 17 Jan 1806. Lt 79th Foot 26 May 1808. Capt 14 Mar 1811. Capt 82nd Foot 10 Jul 1817. Capt 75th Foot 15 Apr 1824. Major 31 Dec 1827. Bt Lt Colonel 23 Nov 1841. Bt Colonel 11 Dec 1849.
 Served in the Peninsula Dec 1812 – Apr 1814. Present at Pyrenees, Pamplona, Nivelle, Nive, Bayonne,

Toulouse. Present at Quatre Bras (severely wounded). MGS medal for Pyrenees, Nivelle, Nive and Toulouse. KH. Half pay 27 Nov 1828.

BRÜGGEMANN, Heinrich
Lieutenant and Adjutant. 3rd Regiment of Hussars, King's German Legion.
Named on the Regimental Memorial: La Haye Sainte, Waterloo, Belgium. (Photograph)

Cornet 30 Nov 1807. Adjt 4 Jan 1810. Lt 16 Feb 1812.
    Served in the Peninsula Aug 1808 – Jan 1809. Present at Benevente (wounded). Present at Waterloo where he was killed. Also served in the Baltic 1807–1808, North Germany 1813–1814 (present at Ghorde where he was wounded) and Netherlands 1814–1815.

BRUMWELL, John
Lieutenant. 43rd (Monmouthshire) Light Infantry Regiment of Foot.
Memorial Tablet: St John's Church, Stanhope, Yorkshire. (Photograph)

TO THE GLORY OF GOD / AND IN MEMORY OF / LIEUTENANT JOHN BRUMWELL, / WHO WAS BORN 1785 / AT WARDEN HILL IN THE PARISH OF STANHOPE. / SERVING WITH / HIS REGIMENT THE 43RD LIGHT INFANTRY, / IN THE PENINSULAR WAR. / HE FOUGHT FOR HIS COUNTRY AND THE LIBERTIES OF EUROPE / AT BUSACO, FUENTES DE ONORO / AND / VOLUNTEERING FOR THE "FORLORN HOPE" / AT THE STORMING OF CIUDAD RODRIGO, / JAN 19TH 1812, / WAS MORTALLY WOUNDED IN SIGHT OF VICTORY / AND EXPIRED IN THE PRIME OF LIFE / A SACRIFICE TO DUTY. / JAN 27TH 1812.

Ensign Royal Cumberland Militia. Ensign 4 Jul 1808. Lt 28 Sep 1809.
    Served in the Peninsula with 2/43rd Oct 1808 – Jan 1809 and 1/43rd Jul 1809 – Jan 1812. Present at Corunna, Coa, Busaco, Redinha, Casal Nova, Foz d'Arouce, Sabugal, Fuentes d'Onoro and Ciudad Rodrigo (severely wounded at the assault, having volunteered for the Forlorn Hope 19 Jan 1812 and died of his wounds 27 Jan 1812).
REFERENCE: *Oxfordshire and Buckinghamshire Light Infantry Chronicle, 1914, pp. 113–22. Egglestone, William Morley, Letters of a Weardale soldier, privately published, 1912.*

BRUNKER, James
Paymaster. 5th (Princess Charlotte of Wales) Dragoon Guards.
Box tomb: St Brigid's Churchyard, Rathaspeck, County Wexford, Ireland. Seriously eroded. (Photograph)

.... / TO THE MEMORY OF / CAPTAIN JAMES BRUNKER /LATE OF THE 5TH DRAGOON GUARDS / WHO DIED THE 17TH OF JULY 1838 / ....

Quartermaster. Cornet 25 Jul 1795. Lt 26 Mar 1796. Capt 6 Jul 1798. Adjutant 1800. Paymaster 26 Jul 1806.
    Served in the Peninsula Sep 1811 – Apr 1814. Present at Llerena, Salamanca, Vittoria and Toulouse.

BRUNSWICK, Frederick William Duke of
Colonel in Chief. Duke of Brunswick's Oels' Corps.
Statue: Quatre Bras, Waterloo, Belgium. (Photograph)

FRIEDRICH WILHELM / HERZOG ZU BRAUNSCHWEIG UND LÜNEBERG / KAMPFTE UND FIEL UNWEIT DIESER STÄATE / AN DER SPITZE SEINER TRUPPEN / AM XVI JUNI MDCCCXV

English translation of German text.

"FREDERICK-WILLIAM, DUKE OF BRUNSWICK AND LUNEBURG, FELL NEAR THIS PLACE WHILE FIGHTING AT THE HEAD OF HIS TROOPS, ON 16 JUNE 1815."

Reverses side of monument:

"IN MEMORY OF THE HERO AND HIS WARRIORS WHO FELL WITH HIM FOR GERMANY. THE GRATEFUL HOMELAND. MDCCCMXXXX."

Statue: Brunswick, Germany. Inscription not recorded. (Photograph)

Capt Prussian Army 1789. Major General 1806. Lt General 1 Jul 1809. Colonel in Chief 25 Sep 1809.
    Served in the Peninsula Sep 1810 – Apr 1814. Present at Quatre Bras where he was killed trying to rally his troops. His men were not the experienced soldiers who served in the Peninsula and who performed well on outpost duties. They were mainly 18 year olds and the officers were not much older. After Frederick's death at Quatre Bras the Brunswickers became demoralised and were kept in reserve on the 18th June. Later in the day Wellington had to use them under his supervision. Also served at Jena and Auerstadt 1806. Frederick was known as the Black Duke dressing all his soldiers in black. He was intent on avenging his father's death at Auerstadt.

BRUNTON, Richard
Captain. 60th (Royal American) Regiment of Foot.
Low monument: Abbey Cemetery, Bath, Somerset. (Photograph)

IN MEMORY OF RICHARD BRUNTON LATE LIEUT COLONEL OF THE 82ND FOOT AND 13TH LIGHT DRAGOONS WHO DIED JULY MDCCCXLVI AGED LVIII YEARS.

Ensign 43rd Foot 10 Nov 1808. Lt 12 Dec 1809. Capt 60th Foot 10 Nov 1813. Capt 13th Lt Dragoons 10 Nov 1819. Major 2 Mar 1826. Lt Colonel 31 Dec 1830. Portuguese Army: Capt 6th Caçadores 6 Mar 1811.
    Served in the Peninsula with 2/43rd Oct 1808 – Jan 1809, 1/43rd Jul 1809 – Jan 1811 and with Portuguese Army Mar 1811 – Jan 1814. Present at Corunna, Coa, Busaco, Fuentes d'Onoro, Arroyo dos Molinos, Almarez, Vittoria, Maya Pass, Pyrenees (wounded), Nivelle and Nive (severely wounded at St Pierre). Present at Waterloo (on Staff as DQMG) and with the Army of Occupation until Feb 1816. Also served in India 1820–1826 and 1828–1840. Retired 23 Jan 1845.

BRUNTON, Thomas
Private. 1st Life Guards.
Memorial: St Cuthbert's Churchyard, Kirkleatham, Yorkshire. (Plot 386). (M.I.)

"THOMAS BRUNTON, LATE OF REGIMENTAL LIFE GUARDS DIED OCT 20TH 1853."

Pte 24 Aug 1810. Cpl of Horse 24 Dec 1818.
    Served in the Peninsula Nov 1812 – Apr 1814. Present at Vittoria and Toulouse. Served at Waterloo. Also served in the Netherlands 1814–1815. MGS medal for Vittoria and Toulouse. Discharged 2 Sep 1833.

BRYAN, George
Lieutenant and Captain. Coldstream Regiment of Foot Guards.
Memorial Monument: Westminster Abbey, London. (Photograph)

SACRED TO THE MEMORY OF / CAPTAIN GEORGE BRYAN, / LATE OF HIS MAJESTY'S COLD-STREAM REGIMENT OF FOOT GUARDS; / SON OF THE REVD JOHN BRYAN AND ELIZA

LOUISE, HIS WIFE, / OF HERTFORD IN THE ISLAND OF JAMAICA. / HE RECEIVED THE EARLY PART OF HIS EDUCATION AT WINCHESTER COLLEGE, / AND FINISHED HIS ACADEMIC STUDIES AT CHRIST CHURCH, OXFORD. / IT WAS HIS HAPPINESS / NOT ONLY TO MERIT THE WARMEST ESTEEM OF THE COMPANIONS OF HIS YOUTHFUL YEARS, / BUT TO OBTAIN THE HIGHEST APPROBATION / OF THOSE WHO GUIDED HIS PROGRESS IN THE PATHS OF SCIENCE, / AND OF ALL WHO WITNESSED HIS UNREMITTING ZEAL IN THE SEVERAL DUTIES / OF A MILITARY LIFE. / HE FELL IN THE MONTH OF JULY, 1809, IN THE 27TH YEAR OF HIS AGE, / AT THE BATTLE OF TALAVERA IN SPAIN, SO GLORIOUS IN THE ANNALS OF BRITISH VALOUR, / BUT SO DEEPLY AFFLICTING TO A WIDOWED MOTHER. / HIS REMAINS WERE INTERRED WITH EVERY MILITARY HONOUR, / IN THE GARDEN OF THE CONVENT OF SAINT JERONIMO, / WHEN EVEN OFFICERS OF THE ENEMY JOINED IN EVINCING RESPECT TO HIS MEMORY, / AND SYMPATHY FOR HIS UNTIMELY FATE.

Named on Memorial Panel VI for Talavera: Royal Military Chapel, Wellington Barracks, London. (M.I.) (Destroyed by a Flying Bomb 1944)

Ensign 6 Dec 1803. Adjutant 1 May 1805. Lt and Capt 24 Jul 1807.
    Served in the Peninsula Mar – Sep 1809. Present at Douro and Talavera (severely wounded, taken prisoner 27 Jul 1809 and died of his wounds 30 Sep 1809). Educated at Winchester School and Oxford University.

BRYCE, Alexander
Colonel. Royal Engineers.
Named on the Regimental Memorial: Rochester Cathedral, Rochester, Kent. (Photograph)

2nd Lt Royal Artillery. 24 Aug 1787. 2nd Lt Royal Engineers. 12 Mar 1789. Lt 16 Jan 1793. Capt-Lt 3 Mar 1797. Capt 28 Feb 1801. Bt Major 25 Dec 1801. Bt Lt Colonel 25 Apr 1808. Lt Colonel 24 Jun 1809. Bt Colonel 4 Jun 1814. Colonel 24 Dec 1814. Colonel Commandant 28 Oct 1829. Major General 27 May 1825.
    Served in the Netherlands on a commission to examine the restoration of fortresses and in France with the Army of Occupation 1815–1816. Also served in Egypt 1801 (present at Aboukir, Rhamanie and Grand Cairo – awarded Bt Majority) and Sicily 1807–1811. CB. Inspector General of Fortifications 1829. Considered one of the most able of Engineers. Died in London 4 Oct 1832.
REFERENCE: *Gentleman's Magazine, Nov 1832, p. 474.*

BUBB, Anthony
Lieutenant. 61st (South Gloucestershire) Regiment of Foot.
Headstone: St Peter's Churchyard, Llanwenarth, Abergavenny, Monmouthshire, Wales. (Photograph)

IN MEMORY OF / LIEUT ANTHONY BUBB / OF CANTREFF, ABERGAVENNY / LATE OF HER MAJESTY'S 61ST REGT / YOUNGEST SON OF THE LATE / MR HENRY BUBB / OF WITCOMB COURT IN THE COUNTY / OF GLOUCESTER / DIED JUNE 21ST 1874 / AGED 82 YEARS.

Ensign 20 Feb 1812. Lt 16 Dec 1813.
    Served in the Peninsula Apr 1813 – Apr 1814. Present at Pyrenees, Nivelle, Nive, Orthes and Tarbes. Retired on half pay 1814. MGS medal for Pyrenees, Nivelle, Nive and Orthes.

BUCHAN, John
Lieutenant Colonel. 4th West India Regiment of Foot.
Monument: Kensal Green Cemetery, London. (8916/90/IC). (Photograph)

TO THE MEMORY OF / LIEUTENANT GENERAL / SIR JOHN BUCHAN, / KNIGHT-COMMANDER OF THE BATH, / KNIGHT COMMANDER OF THE TOWER / AND SWORD OF PORTUGAL. / COLONEL OF HER MAJESTY'S / 32ND REGIMENT OF FOOT. / HE WAS SON OF THE LATE / GEORGE BUCHAN, ESQRE / OF KELSOE BERWICKSHIRE, / AND DIED IN LONDON, / ON THE 2ND OF JUNE 1850 / IN THE 67TH YEAR OF HIS AGE / HAVING SERVED HIS COUNTRY / WITH HONOR AND DISTINCTION / IN MANY ARDUOUS CAMPAIGNS FOR / A PERIOD OF FIFTY FIVE YEARS.

Ensign 94th Foot 29 Jul 1795. Lt Oct 21 1795. Capt 2nd Ceylon Regt 15 Mar 1802. Major 30 Jun 1804. Lt Colonel 4th West India Regt 30 Mar 1809. Bt Colonel 12 Aug 1819. Lt Colonel 29th Foot 28 Feb 1822. Major General 22 Jul 1830. Lt General 23 Nov 1841. Portuguese Army: Colonel 22 Line 1811. Brigadier 1813.
    Served in the Peninsula with Portuguese Army Jun 1811- Apr 1814. (Commanded 2 Portuguese Brigade 1813–1814). Present at Vittoria, Pyrenees, Nivelle (Mentioned in Beresford's Despatches), Nive (Mentioned in Beresford's Despatches), Orthes and Toulouse. Gold Cross for Guadeloupe, Vittoria, Pyrenees, Nivelle and Nive. MGS medal for Orthes and Toulouse. KCB 1837 and KTS. Also served in India (present in the Mysore War – Malavelly and Seringapatam 1799, awarded Gold Medal), Polygar Wars 1801–1802, Kandian War 1803 and Guadeloupe 1810. Colonel 95th (Derbyshire) Regiment 5 Nov 1838. Colonel 32nd Foot 12 Jun 1843.
    REFERENCE: *Gentleman's Magazine, Jul 1850, p. 93 and Oct 1850, p. 437. Annual Register, 1850, Appx, p. 233.*

BUCHANAN, James
Lieutenant and Captain. 3rd Regiment of Foot Guards.
Named on Memorial Panel VI for Talavera: Royal Military Chapel, Wellington Barracks, London. (M.I.) (Destroyed by a Flying Bomb 1944)

Ensign 39th Foot 9 Apr 1796. Lt and Capt 3rd Foot Guards 6 Feb 1800.
    Served in the Peninsula Mar – Jul 1809. Present at Douro and Talavera where he was killed 28 Jul 1809.

BUCHANAN, John
Lieutenant. 43rd (Monmouthshire) Light Infantry Regiment of Foot.
Ledger stone: St Patrick's Church of Ireland, Newry, Northern Ireland. (Photograph)

UNDERNEATH / IS INTERRED THE BODY OF / ELIZABETH, / WIFE OF JOHN BUCHANAN / LATE LIEUT 43RD REGT / WHO DIED ON THE MORNING / OF THE 8TH OF MARCH 1858. / ALSO THE ABOVE NAMED JOHN BUCHANAN / WHO DEPARTED THIS LIFE THE 4TH DAY OF AUGUST 1866 / IN THE 89 YEAR OF HIS AGE.

Ensign 5 Jun 1806. Lt 5 May 1808. Lt 58th Foot 29 Apr 1836.
    Served in the Peninsula with 1/43rd Aug 1812 – Sep 1813. Present at Vittoria (wounded) and Pyrenees. MGS medal for Vittoria and Pyrenees. Also served at Copenhagen 1807. Half pay 24 Aug 1814. Retired 13 May 1836.

BUCHANAN, John Phillips
Captain. 16th (Queen's) Regiment of Light Dragoons.
Memorial tablet: Chester Cathedral, Chester, Cheshire. (South transept). (Photograph)

SACRED TO THE MEMORY, / OF CAPTAIN JOHN PHILLIPS BUCHANAN: / OF THE 16TH OR QUEENS REGIMENT, OF LIGHT DRAGOONS, / WHO, IN THE GLORIOUS & DECISIVE, / BATTLE OF WATERLOO, / ON THE 18TH DAY OF JUNE 1815, / WAS KILL'D BY A MUSKET SHOT, / IN

THE HOUR OF VICTORY! / IN THE 27ᵀᴴ YEAR OF HIS AGE. / ACCOMPLISHED IN ALL THE QUALITIES WHICH DISTINGUISH THE SOLDIER, / OR ADORN THE GENTLEMAN – HIS COURAGE, HIS ZEAL, & DEVOTION / TO HIS PROFESSION, WHILST ACTIVELY, & UNCEASINGLY, ENGAGED IN THE MEMORABLE / CAMPAIGNS, IN PORTUGAL, IN SPAIN, & IN FRANCE, ACQUIRED HIM THE / FRIENDSHIP, THE CONFIDENCE, & JUST ADMIRATION, OF HIS BROTHER OFFICERS. / IN THE MORE RETIRED SCENES, OF PRIVATE LIFE, HE WAS NO LESS EXEMPLARY. / SUPERIOR TO EVERY MEAN AND SELFISH CONSIDERATION HE WAS UNIFORMLY / LIBERAL, AFFECTIONATE, & UNASSUMING. AND WHILST HIS INGENUOUS DIS – / POSITION, & UNAFFECTED MANNERS, SECURED THE KINDNESS, THE ESTEEM OF ALL – / THE LOSS, WHICH HIS FAMILY, & FRIENDS, HAVE SUSTAINED, BY HIS GLORIOUS, / BUT UNTIMELY DEATH, CAN NEVER BE CONTEMPLATED, WITHOUT EMOTIONS OF / DEEP, & SINCERE REGRET. / HIS AFFLICTED MOTHER, & ONLY SURVIVING PARENT, / HAS CAUSED THIS MONUMENT TO BE ERECTED, / TO THE MEMORY, & VIRTUES / OF A BELOVED & LAMENTED SON.

Cornet 11 Apr 1807. Lt 17 Mar 1808. Capt 28 May 1812.

Served in the Peninsula Apr 1809 – Dec 1812 and Jul 1813 – Apr 1814. Present at Douro, Talavera, Coa, Busaco, Redinha, Casal Nova, Foz d'Arouce, Sabugal, Fuentes d'Onoro, El Bodon, Llerena, Castrejon, Salamanca, Venta del Poza, Nivelle, Nive and Bayonne. Also served at Quatre Bras to cover troops retreating to Waterloo and at Waterloo where the 16ᵗʰ were attacking a body of French infantry towards the end of the day when he was killed.

BUCK, Henry Rishton
Lieutenant. 33ʳᵈ (1ˢᵗ Yorkshire West Riding) Regiment of Foot.
Memorial tablet: St Michael's Church, Kirkham, Lancashire. (Photograph)

IN MEMORY OF / HENRY RISHTON BUCK A. B. / LIEUT. 33ᴰ REGT. / WHO FELL IN BATTLE AT / WATERLOO / JUNE 18ᵀᴴ 1815 AEᵀ 27. / ALSO OF / JAMES BUCK / LIEUT 21ˢᵀ LIGHT DRAGOONS WHO DIED / JANʸ 7ᵀᴴ 1815 AEᵀ 19.

Memorial brass: Sedbergh School Chapel, Sedbergh, Yorkshire. (Photograph)

IN MEMORY OF / HENRY RISHTON BUCK BA., / LIEUT: IN THE 33ᴿᴰ FOOT / WHO WAS KILLED AT / THE BATTLE OF WATERLOO. / HE WAS EDUCATED AT / SEDBERGH AND CAMBRIDGE. / 8 JUNE 1915

Carved initials on panel at Sedbergh School, Sedbergh, Yorkshire. (Photograph)

Named on the Regimental Memorial: St Joseph's Church, Waterloo, Belgium. (Photograph)

Ensign 6 Apr 1809. Lt 16 Nov 1809.

Present at Quatre Bras and Waterloo where he was killed late in the day on 18 Jun in the fighting around the farmhouse of La Haye Sainte. Also served in the Netherlands 1814 (present at the siege of Antwerp and Bergen-op-Zoom where he was wounded) After his schooldays at Sedbergh School he entered Cambridge University to take his BA degree in 1809 before joining the 33ʳᵈ Foot. 100 years after Waterloo a plaque to his memory was unveiled in the Sedbergh School Chapel. His brother Lt James Buck, 21ˢᵗ Lt Dragoons died Jan 1815.

BUCKERIDGE, Henry Mark
Lieutenant. Royal Engineers.
Box tomb: Sandpits Cemetery, Gibraltar. (Photograph)

IN MEMORY / OF / HENRY BUCKERIDGE / OF THE CORPS OF ROYAL ENGINEERS / WHO DEPARTED THIS LIFE ON THE / 12TH OF APRIL 1821 / AGED 25

Named on the Regimental Memorial: Rochester Cathedral, Rochester, Kent. (Photograph)

2nd Lt 1 Jan 1814. Lt 1 Aug 1814.
   Served in France with the Army of Occupation 1815–1816. Also served in the Netherlands 1814–1815 and Gibraltar where he died 12th April 1821 aged 25.

BUCKERIDGE, John Charles
Ensign. Coldstream Regiment of Foot Guards.
Memorial: St John Baptist Church, Windsor, Berkshire. (Photograph)

SACRED TO THE MEMORY OF / JOHN CHARLES BUCKERIDGE, / ENSIGN IN THE COLD-STREAM REGT OF FOOT GUARDS. / HE SERVED IN SPAIN / UNDER THE COMMAND OF MARQUIS / WELLINGTON, / WAS AT THE BATTLE OF SALAMANCA, / AND GALLANTLY FELL AT HIS POST / AT THE SIEGE OF THE CASTLE OF BURGOS, / OCTBR THE 9TH 1812, IN THE 18TH YEAR OF HIS AGE.

Named on Memorial Panel VII for Burgos: Royal Military Chapel, Wellington Barracks, London. (M.I.) (Destroyed by a Flying Bomb 1944)

Ensign 29 Mar 1810.
   Served in the Peninsula May – Oct 1812. Present at Salamanca and the siege of Burgos where he was killed Oct 1812, aged 18 years. Educated at Eton.

BUCKLEY, George Richard
Ensign. Coldstream Regiment of Foot Guards.
Memorial tablet: All Saints Church, Minstead, Hampshire. (Photograph)

.... / ALSO TO THE MEMORY OF / GEORGE RICHARD BUCKLEY / SECOND SON OF E. F. BUCKLEY ESQRE AND LADY GEORGINA BUCKLEY / ENSIGN IN THE COLDSTREAM GUARDS / WHO DIED WHILST SERVING WITH THE ARMY AT PARIS / ON THE 15TH OF AUGUST 1815, / IN THE 18TH YEAR OF HIS AGE.

Named on Memorial Panel VIII for Waterloo: Royal Military Chapel, Wellington Barracks, London. (M.I.) (Destroyed by a Flying Bomb 1944)

Ensign 17 Feb 1814.
   Present at Waterloo and with the Army of Occupation. Died from fatigue in Paris 15 Aug 1815 aged 18 years.

BUCKLEY, Henry
Lieutenant. 15th (King's) Regiment of Light Dragoons.
Memorial tablet: St Mary-at-Lambeth Church, Lambeth, London. (In porch. Church is now the Museum of Garden History). (Photograph)

TO THE MEMORY OF / HENRY BUCKLEY / LIEUTENANT IN THE 15TH HUSSARS / WHO DIED AT WATERLOO JUNE 18TH 1815 / IN THE 19TH YEAR OF HIS AGE. / THE REGIMENT HAD BEEN ENGAGED UPON / THE PLAINS OF WATERLOO ON THE 18TH FROM / TEN IN THE MORNING TILL FOUR IN THE AFTERNOON / AND IN THE VARIOUS CHARGES HAD BEHAVED / WITH

DISTINGUISHED COURAGE. / WHEN IN THE ACT OF CHARGING A SOLID SQUARE OF INFANTRY / AND IN FRONT OF HIS TROOP ANIMATING THE MEN HE WAS / STRUCK BY A MUSKET BALL AND MORTALLY WOUNDED. / HIS CONDUCT DURING THE ACTION GAINED HIM THE APPROBATION / OF HIS COMMANDING OFFICER AND THE ADMIRATION / OF HIS COMPANIONS.

Named on the Regimental Memorial: St Joseph's Church, Waterloo, Belgium. (Photograph)

Cornet 24 Feb 1814. Lt 25 Aug 1814.
    Present at Waterloo where he was killed aged 19 years.

BUCKLEY, James Ogden
Captain. 15th (King's) Regiment of Light Dragoons.
Gravestone: St Mary's Churchyard, Cheltenham, Gloucestershire. (No longer extant). (M.I.)

"CAPT J .O. BUCKLEY, 15TH KING'S HUSSARS DIED 5TH MARCH 1823, AGED 45."

Adjutant 21 Aug 1804. Lt 24 Jan 1805. Capt 6 Oct 1813.
    Served in the Peninsula Nov 1808 – Jan 1809 and Feb – Nov 1813. Present in the Corunna campaign, Morales and Vittoria.

BUCKLEY, William
Captain. 1st (Royal Scots) Regiment of Foot.
Named on the Regimental Memorial: St Joseph's Church, Waterloo, Belgium. (Photograph)

Lt 28 Aug 1804. Capt 11 Oct 1810.
    Served in the Peninsula with 3/1st Nov 1812 – Apr 1814. Present at Osma, Vittoria, San Sebastian (wounded), Bidassoa, Nivelle, Nive and Bayonne (wounded). Present at Quatre Bras where he was killed 16 Jun 1815.

BUCKNER, Richard
Lieutenant Colonel. Royal Artillery.
Memorial tablet: Holy Trinity Cathedral, Chichester, Sussex. (Right aisle). (Photograph)

SACRED / TO THE MEMORY OF / RICHARD BUCKNER, ESQ C.B / LATE LT COL IN / THE ROYAL REGIMENT OF ARTILLERY. / A MAGISTRATE AND DEPUTY LIEUTENANT FOR / THE COUNTY OF SUSSEX. / HE DIED AT HIS HOUSE AT WHYKE / 13TH OF MARCH 1837, / IN THE 64TH YEAR OF HIS AGE / AND IS BURIED IN THE FAMILY VAULT / IN THE SOUTH TRANSEPT OF THIS CATHEDRAL.

1st Lt 1 Jan 1794. Capt- Lieut 2 Nov 1797. Capt 9 Sep 1802. Major 27 Sep 1810. Lt Col 20 Dec 1814.
    Served in the Peninsula Jun 1813 – Apr 1814. Present at Vittoria, second siege of San Sebastian and Nivelle. Gold Medal for Vittoria, San Sebastian and Nivelle. C.B. Also served at the Helder 1799, Mediterranean 1807–1808 and Walcheren 1809. Justice of the Peace and Deputy Lieutenant for Sussex.Retired 12 Jun 1823.

BUDGEN, John Robert
1st Lieutenant. 95th Regiment of Foot.
Headstone: Mont l'Abbaye Cemetery, St Helier, Jersey, Channel Islands. Seriously eroded. (Grave number F 146). (Photograph)

2nd Lt 17 Mar 1808. 1st Lt 4 May 1809. Capt 15 Jun 1815. Capt 73rd Foot 9 Aug 1833.

Served in the Peninsula with 1/95th Nov 1808 – Jan 1809 and 2/95th Mar 1810 – Apr 1814. Present at Cacabellos, Corunna, Cadiz, Tarifa, Barrosa, San Millan, Vittoria, Pyrenees, Vera, Bidassoa (wounded), Nivelle, Nive, Orthes, Tarbes and Toulouse. Present at Waterloo. Also served at Walcheren 1809. Half pay 1818 on reduction of the 3rd battalion. Justice of the Peace and Deputy Lieutenant for Surrey, and Justice of the Peace for County Wexford. MGS medal for Corunna, Barrosa, Vittoria, Pyrenees, Nivelle, Nive, Orthes and Toulouse. Retired 23 Aug 1833. Died in Jersey 4 Dec 1866.

BULL, Robert
Captain. Royal Artillery.
Memorial tablet: Church of the Holy Trinity, Bath, Somerset. (Photograph)

SACRED / TO THE MEMORY OF / COLONEL ROBERT BULL, C.B. & K.H. / LATE OF THE ROYAL HORSE ARTILLERY, / WHO DIED IN THIS CITY APRIL 17TH 1835, / AGED 56 YEARS. / HE SERVED HIS KING AND COUNTRY, WITH ZEAL / AND FIDELITY, FOR UPWARDS OF FORTY YEARS: / IN MANY INSTANCES, CALLING FORTH THE PRAISES / AND THANKS OF THOSE IN COMMAND BY HIS / MERITORIOUS AND DISTINGUISHED CONDUCT, / ESPECIALLY IN THE WEST INDIES, IN THE PENINSULA, / AND AT WATERLOO. / HE WAS ESTEEMED AND HONOURED BY HIS BROTHER OFFICERS, / AND BELOVED BY HIS FAMILY AND FRIENDS: / THEIR CHIEF SOLACE FLOWS FROM THE ASSURANCE, / THAT IN HIS CHRISTIAN WARFARE HE FOUGHT, / AND, BY GRACE CONQUERED, UNDER THE BANNERS OF / THE CAPTAIN OF OUR SALVATION. / THIS TRIBUTE OF AFFECTION IS PLACED BY / HIS AFFLICTED WIDOW, WHO HUMBLY HOPES A / BLESSED REUNION. / ....

2nd Lt. 6 Nov 1794. 1st Lt 6 Mar 1795. Capt-Lieut 14 Oct 1801. Capt 28 Jun 1805. Bt Major 31 Dec 1811. Bt Lt Colonel 18 Jun 1815. Major 3 Jul 1823. Lt Colonel 29 Jul 1825.

Served in the Peninsula Aug 1809 – Nov 1812 (Commanded 1 Troop RHA) Present at Celerico, Busaco, Pombal, Redinha, Casal Nova (Mentioned in Despatches), Foz d'Arouce (Mentioned in Despatches), Sabugal (Mentioned in Despatches), Fuentes d'Onoro, second siege of Badajoz, Aldea da Ponte, Ciudad Rodrigo, Fuente Guinaldo, siege of Salamanca Forts, Castrejon, Salamanca, Llerena, Burgos and Tudela. Gold Medal for Busaco, Fuentes d'Onoro and Salamanca. CB. KH.

Present at Waterloo in command of a Troop at the rear of the orchard at Hougoumont. Was able to remove the French infantry in the surrounding areas by accurate firing despite the presence of Allied troops in the wood. Also served with the Army of Occupation until 1818 in spite of being severely wounded. Awarded Bt Colonelcy for actions at Waterloo. Retired on full pay 1834 (permanently disabled from all his wounds, he could no longer walk without assistance). Also served in the West Indies 1796–1798.

BULLEN, James
Ensign. 30th (Cambridgeshire) Regiment of Foot.
Named on the Regimental Memorial: St Joseph's Church, Waterloo, Belgium. (Photograph)

Ensign 23 Nov 1814.
Present at Waterloo where he was killed.

BULLIVANT, John
Lieutenant. 76th Regiment of Foot.
Memorial tablet: All Saints Church, Oakham, Rutland. (Photograph)

IN MEMORY OF / JOHN BULLIVANT ESQR / LATE LIEUTENANT IN THE 76TH REGT, / WHO SERVED UNDER GENL. SIR JOHN MOORE, / WAS ENGAGD. AT THE BATTLE OF CORUNNA. / HE DIED, MAY 2ND 1825, / AGED 40 YEARS.

Lt 26 Nov 1807.
    Served in the Peninsula Nov1808 – Jan 1809. Present at Corunna. Also served at Walcheren 1809. Retired 1813.

BÜLOW, Friedrich von
Captain. 2nd Regiment of Dragoons, King's German Legion.
Named on the Regimental Memorial: La Haye Sainte, Waterloo, Belgium. (Photograph)

Lt 10 May 1810.
    Served in the Peninsula Jan 1812 – Apr 1814. Present at Castrejon, Salamanca, Garcia Hernandez, Majalahonda, Venta del Poza, San Millan, Vittoria, Vic Bigorre and Toulouse. Present at Waterloo where he was killed. Also served in the Netherlands 1814.

BULTEEL, John
Lieutenant and Captain. 1st Regiment of Foot Guards.
Named on Memorial Panel VIII for Bergen-Op-Zoom: Royal Military Chapel, Wellington Barracks, London. (M.I.) (Destroyed by a Flying Bomb 1944)

Ensign 13 Sep 1809. Lt and Capt 22 Jul 1813.
    Served in the Peninsula with 2nd Battalion Mar 1810 – May 1811 and 3rd Battalion May 1811 – Jul 1813. Present at Cadiz, Barrosa and Seville. Also served in the Netherlands 1814 (present at Bergen-op-Zoom, severely wounded and died of his wounds 9 Mar 1814). Educated at Eton.

BUNBURY, Thomas
Lieutenant. 91st Regiment of Foot.
Pedestal tomb: Kensal Green Cemetery, London. (16736/17/2). Seriously eroded. Inscription partly illegible. (Photograph)

IN MEMORY OF / LIEUTENANT COLONEL / THOMAS BUNBURY CB. KTS. / LATE OF THE 80TH REGIMENT / HE DIED 25TH DECEMBER 1861 / AGED 72 YEARS. / ....

Named on the Regimental Memorial to 80th Foot: Lichfield Cathedral, Lichfield, Staffordshire. (Photograph)
(Lt Colonel Bunbury's medals are displayed on the memorial for those who fell in the Sutlej campaign of 1845–1846).

Ensign 3rd Foot 13 Aug 1807. Lt 91st Foot 17 Aug 1809. Capt 25 Oct 1814. Capt 80th Foot 1822. Major 21 Nov 1834. Lt Colonel 20 Jul 1844. Portuguese Army: Capt 20th Line Oct 1809. Capt 5th Caçadores 1813. Major 3rd Caçadores 1813.
    Served in the Peninsula with 3rd Foot Sep 1808 – Oct 1809 and with Portuguese Army 1809 – Apr 1814 (Brigade Major at Cadiz Jul 1811 – Sep 1812). Present at Douro, Talavera, Cadiz, Tarifa, Barrosa (Mentioned in Beresford's Despatches), Seville, Nivelle, Nive (severely wounded), Bayonne and Toulouse (commanded the 6th Caçadores). Also served in Malta 1823, New Zealand (commanded the troops and helped establish a settlement 1840–1844). On returning to England two ships carrying troops and followers were shipwrecked on one of the Andaman Islands. Bunbury was in command there for 51 days and eventually 500 troops and sailors and 104 women and children were rescued.
    Also served in India 1845–1846 (took part in the Sutlej campaign and commanded the 80th Foot at Moodki where he was wounded, Ferozeshah and Sobraon. Awarded medal). MGS medal for Talavera, Barrosa, Nivelle, Nive and Toulouse. CB and KTS. Died 25 Dec 1861.
REFERENCE: Bunbury, Thomas, Reminiscences of a veteran: being personal and military adventures in Portugal, Spain, France, Malta … and India etc., 3 vols, 1861, reprint 2009. Lambourn, Alan, Major

Thomas Bunbury, envoy extraordinary, New Zealand's soldier-treaty-maker, 1995. Gregory, Desmond, No ordinary general: Lt General Sir Henry Bunbury, 1778–1860: the best soldier historian, 1999.

BURBIDGE, Frederick
Private. 95th Regiment of Foot.
Buried in All Saints Churchyard, Gilmorton, Leicestershire. (Burial register)

Pte 1 Apr 1809.
    Served in the Peninsula. Present at Barrosa, Orthes and Toulouse (wounded). Discharged 27 May 1816. MGS medal for Barrosa, Orthes and Toulouse. Died 7 Jan 1867.

BURCH, Thomas
Corporal. 79th (Cameron Highlanders) Regiment of Foot.
Headstone: St Andrew's Churchyard, Presteigne, Powys, Wales. (Photograph)
The headstone was refurbished in 2006 with financial support from the Association of Friends of the Waterloo Committee and the 79th Cameron Highlanders.

IN MEMORY OF / THOMAS BURCH, LATE SERGEANT, / IN THE 79, OR CAMERON HIGH-LANDERS, / HE DIED JANUARY 23, 1850, / AGED 68 YEARS. / HE SERVED IN EGYPT, PENINSULA, AND WATERLOO / AND WAS ENGAGED IN UPWARDS OF THIRTY / BATTLES, SIEGES AND SKIRMISHES.

Sgt 1814. Cpl 1815.
    Served in the Peninsula 1808 – Jan 1809 and Mar 1810 – Apr 1814. Present at Corunna, Cadiz, Busaco, Fuentes d'Onoro, Burgos, Pyrenees, Nivelle and Toulouse. Present at Waterloo in Capt M. Fraser's Company No 8. Also served in Egypt 1807. MGS medal for Corunna, Busaco, Fuentes d'Onoro, Pyrenees, Nivelle and Toulouse.

BURGESS, Wentworth Noel
Ensign. Coldstream Regiment of Foot Guards.
Named on Memorial Panel VII for Burgos: Royal Military Chapel, Wellington Barracks, London. (M.I.) (Destroyed by a Flying Bomb 1944)

Ensign 52nd Foot 18 Aug 1808. Ensign Coldstream Guards 1 Jun 1809.
    Served in the Peninsula with 2/52nd Aug 1808 – Jan 1809 and with Coldstream Guards Dec 1810 – Oct 1812. Present at Vimeiro, Vigo, Fuentes d'Onoro, Ciudad Rodrigo, Salamanca and Burgos where he was killed at the siege 18 Oct 1812.
REFERENCE: *Gentleman's Magazine, 1812, Supplement to Part 2, p. 670.*

BURGOYNE, John Fox
Lieutenant Colonel. Royal Engineers.
Buried in Chapel Royal of St Peter ad Vincula, Tower of London, London.
Statue: Waterloo Place, London. (Photograph)

JOHN FOX BURGOYNE. / FIELD MARSHAL, / G.C.B. / BORN 1782 – DIED 1871. / ERECTED BY HIS BROTHER OFFICERS OF / ROYAL ENGINEERS. / "HOW YOUNGLY HE BEGAN TO SERVE HIS COUNTRY / "HOW LONG CONTINUED" / CORIOLANUS

Family Memorial headstone: Brompton Cemetery, London. (Photograph)

IN MEMORY / OF GENERAL / JOHN FOX BURGOYNE / DIED 7TH OCTOBER 1871 / ....

2nd Lt 29 Aug 1798. 1st Lt 1 Jul 1800. 2nd Capt 1 Mar 1805. Capt 24 Jun 1809. Bt Major 6 Feb 1812. Bt Lt Colonel 27 Apr 1812. Lt Colonel 20 Dec 1814. Colonel 22 Jul 1830. Major General 28 Jun 1838. Lt General 11 Nov 1851. General 5 Sep 1855. Field Marshal 1 Jan 1868.

Served in the Peninsula Aug 1808 – Jan 1809 and May 1809 – Apr 1814. Present at Vigo, Douro, Busaco, second siege of Badajoz, El Bodon, Aldea da Ponte, Ciudad Rodrigo (awarded Bt Majority), Badajoz (awarded Bt Lt Colonelcy), siege of Salamanca Forts, Salamanca (Mentioned in Despatches), Burgos (wounded and Mentioned in Despatches), Vittoria, San Sebastian (wounded and Mentioned in Despatches), Bidassoa, Nivelle, Nive, Adour, and Bayonne (Mentioned in Despatches).

Succeeded in command of Royal Engineers at San Sebastian when Sir Richard Fletcher was killed. Gold Cross for Badajoz, Salamanca, Vittoria, San Sebastian and Nive. Also served at Malta 1800, Egypt 1807, North America 1814–1815 (present at New Orleans and Fort Bowyer). Present at the Capture of Paris and with the Army of Occupation. Returned to Portugal with Lt General Clinton's expedition as Commanding Engineer 1827.

Chairman of Public Works in Ireland 1830–1845. Inspector General of Fortifications 1845. GCB. KTS. Member of various commissions – Sewers, Great Exhibition, Penny Post etc 1849. Served in the Crimea 1854 (present at the Alma, Salamanca, Inkerman and Sebastopol). Promoted to the rank of General and created a Baronet. Awarded medal with four clasps for the Crimea and Turkish medal of Nishid Medjidie. Constable of Tower of London 1865. Active member of the National Red Cross Society for Aiding the Sick and Wounded in War. Died 1 Oct 1871. Wellington said of him: "If Burgoyne only knew his own value no one would equal him."

REFERENCE: *Dictionary of National Biography. Head, Francis Bond, Sketches of the life and death of the late Field Marshal Sir J. Burgoyne, 1872. Wrottesley, G., Life and correspondence of Field Marshal Sir John Burgoyne, 2 vols, 1873. Wrottesley, George ed., The military opinions of General Sir John Fox Burgoyne, 1869. United Service Magazine, Nov 1871, pp. 446–7. Annual Register, 1871, Appx, pp. 160–1. Patterson, A. Temple, Field-Marshal Sir John Fox Burgoyne 1782–1871, Journal of the Society for Army Historical Research, Vol 42, No 172, Dec 1964, pp. 168–74.*

BURKE, James
Lieutenant. 44th (East Essex) Regiment of Foot.
Headstone: St Benet's Catholic Churchyard, Kemerton, Gloucestershire. (Photograph)

PRAY FOR THE SOUL / OF / MAJOR JAMES BURKE, / FORMERLY OF HM 44TH REGT / WITH WHICH HE SERVED / AND WAS WOUNDED AT / WATERLOO. / HE WAS BORN AT ARLAMAN / CO. LIMERICK IRELAND / AND DIED AT CHELTENHAM / ON THE 8TH FEBRUARY 1849 / AGED 63 YEARS. / DEEPLY REGRETTED BY HIS WIDOW / CHILDREN AND FRIENDS / MAY HE REST IN PEACE / AMEN.

Ensign 21 May 1812. Lt 30 Mar 1814. Capt 7 Jul 1825. Bt Major 28 Jun 1838.
Served in the Peninsula Dec 1812 – Jan 1814. Present at Quatre Bras (wounded) and Waterloo (severely wounded). Half pay Mar 1816.

BURLEY, William
Private. 12th (Prince of Wales's) Regiment of Light Dragoons.
Named on the Regimental Memorial: St Joseph's Church, Waterloo, Belgium. (Photograph)
Present at Waterloo where he was killed.

BURNABY, John Dick
Captain and Lieutenant Colonel. 1st Regiment of Foot Guards.
Memorial: Royal Military Chapel, Wellington Barracks, London. (M.I.) (Destroyed by a Flying Bomb 1944)

"A SIMILAR MOSAIC IS GIVEN BY T. F. A. BURNABY, AND OTHER MEMBERS OF THE FAMILY, / IN MEMORY OF THEIR FATHER, / COLONEL JOHN DICK BURNABY, WHO SERVED IN THE 1ST GUARDS FROM 1792 TO 1812. / HE WAS PRESENT DURING THE CAMPAIGN OF 1793, IN HOLLAND; THE EXPEDITION TO SICILY IN 1806; THE CAMPAIGN IN SPAIN UNDER GENERAL SIR JOHN MOORE, K.B., INCLUDING THE BATTLE OF CORUNNA, 1808–9; THE EXPEDITION TO THE SCHELDT, 1809; AND THE DEFENCE OF CADIZ, 1811. HE WAS ADJUTANT TO THE 2ND BATTALION FROM 1797 TO 1803, AND RETIRED WITH THE RANK OF COLONEL, 1812".

Ensign 1 Feb 1792. Lt and Capt 5 Mar 1794. Capt and Lt Colonel 25 Jun 1803. Bt Colonel 1 Jan 1812.
  Served in the Peninsula with 3rd Battalion Oct 1808 – Jan 1809 and Apr – Jul 1811. Present at Corunna and Cadiz. Adjutant 2nd Battalion 1797 – 1803. Also served in Flanders 1793–1794, Sicily 1806 and Walcheren 1809. Retired 11 Jun 1812. Served 30 years as Justice of the Peace and Deputy Lieutenant of Leicestershire. Died 1 Jun 1852.

BURNE, Robert
Colonel. 36th (Herefordshire) Regiment of Foot.
Pedestal tomb: St John the Baptist Churchyard, Aldenham, Hertfordshire. Seriously eroded and inscription recorded from memorial inscription. (Photograph)

"SACRED TO THE MEMORY OF LIEUT GENERAL ROBERT BURNE LATE GOVERNOR OF CARLISLE, LIEUTENANT GENERAL COMMANDANT OF HIS MAJESTY'S GALLANT 36TH REGIMENT OF FOOT. IN THE YEAR 1811 HE COMMANDED THE 6TH DIVISION OF THE BRITISH ARMY IN PORTUGAL, WHO AFTER FORTY ONE YEARS OF MOST ACTIVE SERVICE, DEVOTED TO THE HONOUR OF HIS KING AND COUNTRY, DEPARTED THIS LIFE ON THE 9TH DAY OF JUNE 1825 AT BERKELEY COTTAGE IN THIS COUNTY. / EUROPE, ROLICA, VIMIERO, CORUNNA, FUENTES DE ONORE, FLUSHING. / ASIA, CANANORE, SATTIMUNGOLUM, SHOWERE, STORMING OF BANGALORE, BHUTON, FORT OF BANGALORE, HILL FORT OF NUNDY DROOG, CARRIGATT HILL, SERINGAPATAM, STORMING OF END GAW REDOUBT, PONDICHERRY. / SUBURBS OF BUENOS AYRES, BUENOS AYRES."

Ensign 36 Foot 1773. Lt 13 Jan 1777. Capt 7 May 1784. Bt Major 1 Mar 1794. Major 1796. Bt Lt Colonel 1 Jan 1798. Lt Colonel 36th Foot 13 Nov 1799. Bt Colonel 25 Apr 1808. Major General 4 Jun 1811. Lt General 19 Jul 1821.
  Served in the Peninsula Aug 1808 – Jan 1809 and Mar 1811 – Mar 1812 (Commanded a brigade in the 6th Division). Present at Rolica, Vimeiro (Mentioned in Despatches), Corunna and Fuentes d'Onoro. Gold Medal for Rolica, Vimeiro and Corunna. Also served in India 1783–1799 (present at Sittimungulum, Showere, Pettah, Bangalore, Nundydroog, Seringapatam and Pondicherry), Hanover 1805, South America 1807 (present at Buenos Ayres) and Walcheren 1809 (present at Flushing. Colonel on Staff until the evacuation of the island).
  Wellington wrote to Castlereagh 'I have mentioned Colonel Burne of the 36th Regiment in a very particular manner; and I assure you that there is nothing that will give me so much satisfaction as to hear that something has been done for this old and meritorious soldier. The 36th Regiment are an example to the army' Governor of Carlisle 1809. Commanded 36th Foot from 1799 until 1811.
REFERENCE: *Dictionary of National Biography. Royal Military Calendar, Vol 3, pp. 145–8. Gentleman's Magazine, Aug 1825, pp. 180–1.*

BURNETT, John
Lieutenant. 52nd (Oxfordshire) Light Infantry Regiment of Foot.
Vault with railings: Whitechurch alias Castalane Churchyard, County Kilkenny, Ireland. (M.I.)

"ERECTED BY HELENA BURNETT TO THE MEMORY OF HER BELOVED HUSBAND, JOHN

BURNETT OF COOKESTOUN ESQ, LATE 52ND REGT, WHOSE REMAINS ARE DEPOSITED HERE. HE DEPARTED THIS LIFE AT HIS HOUSE MERRION SQUARE DUBLIN 26 JUN 1861 IN THE 68TH YEAR OF HIS AGE."

Ensign 27 May 1813. Lt 8 May 1815.
　　Present at Waterloo. Half pay 1816 on reduction of the regiment.

BURRARD, Sir Harry
Lieutenant Colonel. 1st Regiment of Foot Guards.
Buried in Lymington Churchyard, Lymington, Hampshire.
Memorial: Royal Military Chapel, Wellington Barracks, London. (M.I.) (Destroyed by a Flying Bomb 1944)

"IN MEMORY OF LIEUT.-GENERAL SIR HARRY BURRARD, BART., M.P.; ENSIGN PAUL HARRY DURELL BURRARD; ENSIGN WILLIAM BURRARD; CAPTAIN EDWARD BURRARD. / SIR HARRY BURRARD, BORN JUNE 1, 1755, WAS TRANSFERRED TO THE 1ST GUARDS MARCH 13, 1789, AND DIED IN ITS COMMAND, OCTOBER 17, 1813. HE TOOK PART IN THE CAMPAIGNS IN FLANDERS DURING 1794 AND 1798, AND LED THE 2ND BRIGADE OF GUARDS AT THE HELDER IN 1799. HE WAS CREATED A BARONET FOR HIS SERVICES AT COPENHAGEN IN 1807, AND COMMANDED THE BRITISH FORCES IN PORTUGAL, AT THE VICTORY OF VIMIERA, 1808. HIS ELDEST SON, PAUL, WAS IN THE 1ST GUARDS, AND AIDE-DE-CAMP TO GENERAL SIR JOHN MOORE, AT CORUNNA WHERE, AT THE AGE OF 19, HE WAS MORTALLY WOUNDED, JANUARY 16, 1809. HIS FOURTH SON, WILLIAM, ALSO IN THE 1ST GUARDS, WAS AT THE AGE OF 19, MORTALLY WOUNDED IN AN ATTACK ON SAN SEBASTIAN, AUGUST 31, 1813. HIS FIFTH SON, EDWARD, SERVED IN THE GRENADIER GUARDS, FROM 1813 TO 1830, AND DIED APRIL 23, 1832. PLACED BY THE SURVIVING MEMBERS OF THE FAMILY."

2nd Lt Royal Artillery 13 Mar 1772. Lt 60th Foot 1776. Capt 18 Sep 1777. Major 14th Foot 21 Dec 1786. Capt and Lt Colonel 1st Foot Guards 13 Mar 1789. 3rd Major 31 Aug 1798. Major General 1 Jan 1798. 2nd Major 25 Nov 1799. 1st Major 21 Aug 1801. Lt Colonel 1st Foot Guards 16 Apr 1804. Lt General 1 Jan 1805.
　　Served in the Peninsula Aug – Oct 1808. Present at Vimeiro only when the fighting was well advanced. He had been sent to Portugal with Sir Hew Dalrymple to take command from Sir Arthur Wellesley. By the time that Burrard had disembarked Wellesley had fought and won at Rolica and was winning at Vimeiro. Burrard would not let Wellington pursue the French when they were beaten after Vimeiro. After the Convention of Cintra, an inquiry was held into the conduct of the three commanders. Burrard was absolved by the court but never again took military command. After that personal tragedy played a part, two of his sons (one in the Navy) were killed in 1809 and a third son, William was killed at San Sebastian 1813. This brought about his own death by grief on 18 Oct 1813. Father of Ensign Paul Burrard and Ensign William Burrard both of 1st Foot Guards.
　　Also served in the American War of Independence 1778–1779, Flanders 1793–1795, the Helder 1799, Copenhagen 1807 (second in command to Cathcart and awarded a baronetcy). M.P. for Lymington 1780–1791. Governor of Calshot Castle 1787–1813.
REFERENCE: *Dictionary of National Biography*.

BURRARD, Paul Harry Durell
Ensign. 1st Regiment of Foot Guards.
Memorial tablet: St Thomas Church, Lymington, Hampshire. (Photograph)

TO THE MEMORY OF PAUL H. D. BURRARD, ELDEST SON OF SIR HARRY BURRARD BART / ENSIGN IN THE FIRST REGIMENT OF FOOT-GUARDS, / AND AID-DE-CAMP TO LIEUTT-

GENERAL SIR JOHN MOORE, OF IMMORTAL MEMORY. / HE DIED ON HIS PASSAGE TO ENGLAND, / ON THE 21ST OF JANUARY 1809; AGED 18 YEARS AND 11 MONTHS; / OF A WOUND HE RECEIVED AT THE BATTLE OF CORUNNA. / AN OFFICER OF HIGH RANK IN THE ARMY DESCRIBED HIM THUS. / "IN EVERY RESPECT YOUNG BURRARD GAVE THE MOST PROMISING EXPECTATIONS. HIS ATTENTION TO / SIR JOHN MOORE WAS UNREMITTING, AND HIS GALLANTRY WENT HAND IN HAND WITH HIS ZEAL. / HE WAS NEAR THE GENERAL WHEN HE FELL; AND HAD HIMSELF A HORSE KILLED UNDER HIM, / BUT IT WAS NOT TILL NEARER THE CLOSE OF THE ACTION, THAT HE RECEIVED HIS WOUND, / WHICH PROVED FATAL TO HIM – HE CARRIED TO THE GRAVE THE / ESTEEM AND AFFECTION OF ALL WHO KNEW HIM" / (VERSE)

Named on Memorial Panel VI for Corunna: Royal Military Chapel, Wellington Barracks, London. (M.I.) (Destroyed by a Flying Bomb 1944)

For inscription see entry above for his father Sir Harry Burrard, for memorial in the Royal Military Chapel.

Ensign 5 Sep 1805.
 Served in the Peninsula Aug 1808 – Jan 1809. (ADC to Lt General Burrard Aug – Oct 1808 and ADC to Sir John Moore Nov 1808 – Jan 1809). Present at Corunna (severely wounded and died of his wounds on 21 Jan 1809 returning to England). Son of Lt Colonel Sir Harry Burrard 1st Foot Guards. His younger brother Ensign William Burrard 1st Foot Guards died at San Sebastian.

BURRARD, William
Ensign. 1st Regiment of Foot Guards.
Named on Memorial Panel VI for San Sebastian:: Royal Military Chapel, Wellington Barracks, London. (M.I.) (Destroyed by a Flying Bomb 1944)

See entry for his father Sir Harry Burrard above, for memorial in the Royal Military Chapel.

Ensign 17 Jan 1811.
 Served in the Peninsula Sep 1812 – Sep 1813. Present at San Sebastian (severely wounded and died of his wounds 2 Sep 1813). Son of Lt Colonel Sir Harry Burrard 1st Foot Guards. Brother of Ensign Paul Burrard 1st Foot Guards who was killed at Corunna.

BURROUGHS, William
Lieutenant and Captain. Coldstream Regiment of Foot Guards.
Ledger stone: Coldstream Guards Cemetery, St Etienne, Bayonne, France. (Photograph)

W. B.

Named on the Memorial: St Andrew's Church, (now Musée Historique), Biarritz, France. (Photograph)
Named on Memorial Panel VII for the Sortie from Bayonne: Royal Military Chapel, Wellington Barracks, London. (M.I.) (Destroyed by a Flying Bomb 1944)

Ensign 26 Jul 1804. Lt and Capt 28 Sep 1809.
 Served in the Peninsula Mar 1809 – Jan 1810 and Jul 1812 – Apr 1814. Present at Douro, Talavera, Salamanca, Burgos, Vittoria, Nivelle, Nive, Adour and Bayonne where he was severely wounded at the Sortie from Bayonne 14 Apr 1814 and died of his wounds 26 Apr 1814. Educated at Eton.

BURROWS, Charles Montague
Volunteer. 14th (Buckinghamshire) Regiment of Foot.
Memorial tablet: Museum, English Harbour Dockyard, Antigua, West Indies. (Photograph)

SACRED TO THE MEMORY OF / LIEUT. CHARLES MONTAGUE BURROWS / LATE OF THE 36TH REGT / WHO DEPARTED THIS LIFE THE 27TH OF JUNE 1835 / AETAT 35, / REGRETTED BY HIS BROTHER OFFICERS / WHO HAVE PLACED THIS TRIBUTE OF RESPECT / TO HIS MEMORY. / LIEUTENANT BURROWS / COMMENCED HIS MILITARY CAREER AT / WATERLOO, / AND ENDED IT IN THE ISLAND OF ANTIGUA.

Volunteer 14th Foot May 1815. Ensign 14th Foot 27 Jun 1815. Lt 36th Foot 28 Jun 1824.
    At the age of 15 volunteered to fight with the regiment at Waterloo. His father was Lt Colonel Montagu Burrows of the 2nd Battalion 14th Foot, but he was not at Waterloo. Also served in the West Indies 1830 until his death in 1835.

BURROWS, John
Sergeant. 20th (East Devonshire) Regiment of Foot.
Headstone: St Leonard's Churchyard, Colchester, Essex. Seriously eroded. (Photograph)

SACRED / TO THE MEMORY OF / JOHN BURROWS / LATE SERGT OF HIS MAJESTY'S FOOT 20TH / OR EAST DEVON REGT OF FOOT / WHO DIED JUNE 3RD 1810 / AETAT 35. / TO THIS SAD SHRINE WHO'ER THOU ART DRAW NEAR / HERE LIES A SOLDIER WHOSE NAME HIS FRIENDS REVERE. / IN BATTLE BRAVE OFT TIMES HE HAS BEEN, / SOUGHT DEATH IN VARIOUS FORMS BUT WAS DENIED. / BUT HERE THAT TYRANT GRIM, GRIEF TO RELATE / UNTIMELY CAME, CLAIMED HIM AND SEALED HIS FATE. / THIS STONE IS ERECTED BY COMRADE SERGEANTS / AS A TOKEN OF THEIR ESTEEM TO THE DECEASED.

Served in the Peninsula 1808 – Jan 1809. Present at Vimeiro and Corunna.

BURTON, Francis
Surgeon. 4th (King's Own) Regiment of Foot.
Memorial tablet: St Nicholas Church, Elstree, Hertfordshire. (Photograph)

SACRED TO THE MEMORY OF / FRANCIS BURTON, M. D. / 12TH ROYAL LANCERS / WHO DIED OCTOBER 24TH 1828 AGED 41. / REGRETTED AND ESTEEMED / BY ALL WHO KNEW HIM / HIS REMAINS ARE DEPOSITED / IN THE VAULT OF HIS FATHER IN LAW / H. BAKER, ESQR LATE OF THIS PARISH.

Buried in the Family vault: St Nicholas Church, Elstree, Hertfordshire. Inscription illegible. (Photograph)

Asst Surgeon North Devon Militia. Asst Surgeon 5th Garrison Battalion 5 May 1807. Asst Surgeon 36th Foot 10 Mar 1808. Surgeon 4th Foot 9 Sep 1813. Surgeon 66th Foot 16 Dec 1819. Surgeon 12th Lancers 30 Jun 1825.
    Served in the Peninsula with 36th Foot Mar 1811 – Sep 1813 and 4th Foot Nov 1813 – Jan 1814. Present at the siege of Salamanca Forts, Salamanca, Pyrenees, Nivelle and Bayonne. Present at Waterloo. Also served at Walcheren 1809 and North America 1814. MD Edinburgh 1820. One of the five Army Medical Officers present at the autopsy on Napoleon.

BURTON, John Curzon
1st Lieutenant. Royal Artillery.
Columnar pedestal tomb: Kensal Green Cemetery, London. (19077/90/PS). (Photograph)

HERE RESTS THE BODY OF / JOHN CURZON BURTON / LATE CAPTAIN ROYAL ARTILLERY / YOUNGEST SON OF / LIEUT^T GENERAL BURTON / ROYAL ARTILLERY / BORN 25TH AUGUST 1790 / DIED 19TH NOVEMBER 1875

2nd Lt 4 Apr 1807. 1st Lt 1 Feb 1808. 2nd Capt 6 Nov 1827.
    Served in the Peninsula Mar 1813 – Apr 1814. Present on the east coast of Spain in Capt Alex Campbell's Company (present at Tarragona). Half pay 25 Nov 1833.

BURY, George
Captain. 6th Garrison Battalion.
Memorial: Mount Jerome Cemetery, Dublin, Ireland. (Grave number C113–545).

Ensign 88th Foot 25 Sep 1804. Lt 11 Jul 1805. Capt 30 Aug 1810. Capt 6th Garrison Battalion 16 Jan 1812.
    Served in the Peninsula with 1/88th Mar 1809 – Nov 1810 and 2/88th Nov 1810 – Jun 1811. Present at Busaco (wounded), Sabugal and Fuentes d'Onoro. Also served in South America 1807 (present at Buenos Ayres where he was wounded). Went on half pay when Garrison Battalion was disbanded in 1814. MGS medal for Busaco and Fuentes d'Onoro. Died in Dublin 24 Jan 1851 aged 70.

BUSSEY, John
Private. 7th (Royal Fusiliers) Regiment of Foot.
Headstone: York Cemetery, York, Yorkshire. (Grave number D/13/08). (Photograph)

IN AFFECTIONATE REMEMBRANCE / OF / JOHN BUSSEY, DIED JULY 24TH 1829, AGED 55. / FOR 20 YEARS HE SERVED HIS COUNTRY AND WAS / WITH THE 9TH REGIMENT IN HOLLAND, AND THE / ROYAL FUSILIERS DURING THE PENINSULAR WAR / 1809 – 1814; AND AFTER SERVING IN AMERICA / RECEIVED HIS DISCHARGE 1815. INTERRED IN / ALL SAINTS CHURCHYARD, HIGH OUSEGATE / ....

Served in the Peninsula with 7th Foot 1809 – Apr 1814. Also served with 9th Foot in Flanders 1794–1795 and North America 1814–1815. Discharged 1815.

BUTCHER, George Kear
Sergeant Major. 11th Regiment of Light Dragoons.
Headstone: St Mildred's Churchyard, Whippingham, Isle of Wight. (Photograph)

GEORGE KEAR BUTCHER / LATE CAPTAIN IN THE / 11TH LIGHT DRAGOONS / IN WHICH REGI-MENT HE / SERVED FOR 37 YEARS AND 3 MONTHS / FROM 1799 TO 1837. / DIED / 14TH MARCH 1858 / IN THE 75TH YEAR OF HIS AGE

Sgt Major. Promoted from the ranks. Cornet and Adjt 12 Oct 1815. Lt 8 Nov 1818. Capt 13 Nov 1834.
    Served in the Peninsula Jun 1811 – Jun 1813. Present at El Bodon, Moriscos, Castrejon, Salamanca, Majalahonda and Venta del Poza. Present at Quatre Bras, Waterloo and the Capture of Paris. Also served in India 1824–1826 (present at the siege of Bhurtpore). Retired 14 May 1837. MGS medal for Salamanca.

BUTCHER, Thomas
Sergeant. 51st (2nd Yorkshire West Riding) Light Infantry.
Named on the Regimental Memorial: KOYLI Chapel, York Minster, Yorkshire. (Photograph)
    Killed in the Peninsula.

BUTLER, Hon. Henry Edward
Major. 4th Garrison Battalion.
Stained glass window: Royal Garrison Church, Portsmouth, Hampshire. (Destroyed in an air raid in the Second World War). (M.I)

"TO THE GLORY OF GOD AND IN PIOUS MEMORY OF LIEUT. GENL THE HON: HENRY EDWARD BUTLER WHO SERVED IN EGYPT AND THE PENINSULAR WAR. DIED IN PARIS DEC 7 1856 AGED 76."

Ensign 85th Foot 15 Feb 1800. Lt 27th Foot 21 Jun 1800. Capt 98th Foot 22 May 1804. Bt Major 30 May 1811. Major 4th Garrison Battalion 19 Mar 1812. Major 67th Foot 21 Dec 1815. Lt Colonel 2nd Garrison Battalion 4 Jul 1816. Bt Colonel 10 Jan 1837. Major General 9 Nov 1846. Lt General 20 Jun 1854. Portuguese Army: Major 9th Line 22 Jun 1810.
    Served in the Peninsula with Portuguese Army Jun 1810 – May 1812. Present at Busaco (wounded). Also served in Egypt 1801. Awarded Turkish Gold Medal. MGS Medal for Egypt and Busaco. Retired 5 May 1812. Appointed Colonel 94th Foot 25 Jul 1854 and Colonel 55th Foot 29 Jan 1855
REFERENCE: *Gentleman's Magazine, Feb 1857, p. 249. Annual Register, 1856, Appx, p. 285.*

BUTLER, John O'Bryan
Ensign. 32nd (Cornwall) Regiment of Foot.
Named on the Memorial: St Andrew's Church, (now Musée Historique), Biarritz, France. (Photograph)

Ensign 24 Aug 1812.
    Served in the Peninsula Sep – Nov 1813. Present at Bidassoa and Nivelle where he was killed 10 Nov 1813.

BUTLER, Pierce
Paymaster. 52nd (Oxfordshire) Light Infantry Regiment of Foot.
Interred in Catacomb B (v120 c15) Kensal Green Cemetery, London.

Paymaster 28 Feb 1805.
    Served in the Peninsula with 2/52nd Aug 1808 – Jan 1809. Present at Vimeiro and Vigo. Also served in the Netherlands 1814. Died 21 Jun 1841 aged 72.

BUTLER, Theobald
Lieutenant. 32nd (Cornwall) Regiment of Foot.
Pedestal tomb: Mount Jerome Cemetery, Dublin, Ireland. (Photograph)

ERECTED TO THE MEMORY OF / MAJOR THEOBALD BUTLER / WHO DIED 26TH DECR 1851, AGED 66 YEARS. / HAVING ENTERED THE BRITISH ARMY AT / AN EARLY AGE HE SERVED UNDER / SIR JOHN MOORE AND SUBSEQUENTLY / UNDER HIS GRACE THE DUKE OF WELLINGTON / THROUGHOUT THE PENINSULAR WARS / FOR WHICH HE RECEIVED A MEDAL AND / SEVEN CLASPS, HE ALSO RECEIVED A / SECOND MEDAL FOR BEING PRESENT AT / THE MEMORABLE BATTLE OF WATERLOO / IN 1815. LATTERLY HE DEVOTED HIMSELF / TO THE PRACTICE OF THOSE CHRISTIAN / VIRTUES WHICH WILL BE THE MEANS OF / PROCURING FOR HIM A HAPPY ETERNITY. / ....

Ensign 8 Oct 1806. Lt 28 Apr 1808. Capt 28 Nov 1834. Bt Major 9 Nov 1846.
    Served in the Peninsula Aug 1808 – Jan 1809 and Jul 1811 – Apr 1814. Present at Rolica, Vimeiro, siege of Salamanca Forts, Salamanca, Burgos and retreat from Burgos, Pyrenees, Bidassoa, Nivelle, Nive

and Orthes. Present at Waterloo. Retired on half pay 28 Nov 1834. MGS medal for Rolica, Vimeiro, Salamanca, Pyrenees, Nivelle, Nive and Orthes.

BUTLER, Theodore
Ensign. 87th (Prince of Wales's Own Irish) Regiment of Foot.
Buried at Verdun Prison, France. (Burial record)

Ensign 25 Aug 1808.
    Served in the Peninsula Jul 1809 – Jul 1813. Present at Talavera (severely wounded and taken prisoner by the French). Died in prison 1 Jul 1813.

BUTTERWORTH, Henry
Lieutenant. 32nd (Cornwall) Regiment of Foot.
Chest Tomb: St John's Churchyard, Smallbridge, Rochdale, Lancashire. (Photograph)

HENRY BUTTERWORTH ESQUIRE A MAGISTRATE FOR THE / COUNTY OF LANCASTER. BORN 18 MARCH 1783 AT GREEN. / DIED 8TH JUNE 1860 AT HEYBROOK. NR ROCHDALE. FORMERLY / LIEUTENANT IN THE 32ND / REGIMENT OF FOOT AND WAS ENGAGED / IN THE BATTLES OF ROLICA. VIMEIRO. SALAMANCA AND TALAVERA. / PYRENEES. NIVELLE. NIVE. ORTHES AND WATERLOO.

Ensign 1st Royal Regiment of Lancashire Militia 1805. Ensign 32nd Foot 25 Aug 1807. Lt 27 Apr 1809.
    Served in the Peninsula with 32nd Foot Aug 1808 – Jan 1809 and Jul 1811 – Apr 1814 and 2nd Battalion detachment Feb – Aug 1809. Present at Rolica, Vimeiro, Douro, Talavera, siege of Salamanca Forts, Salamanca (severely wounded), Pyrenees and Nivelle.
    Present at Waterloo (wounded three times but did not leave the field). He obtained a commission in the 1st Royal Regiment of Lancashire Militia in 1805, volunteered for the regular army and was appointed to the 32nd Foot in 1807. He was well liked by his men and when he was severely wounded at Salamanca, one of his men, Private Ashbridge from Smallbridge carried him to find medical assistance. Half pay 11 May 1820. Became a Magistrate and Deputy Lieutenant of the County. MGS medal for Rolica, Vimeiro, Talavera, Salamanca, Pyrenees and Nivelle. Belonged to a club in Rochdale formed to look after local Peninsular and Waterloo men. In 1856 twenty of the members took a train to Manchester for the unveiling of the statue to the Duke of Wellington and were addressed by General Sir Harry Smith.

BUTTERY, William
Private. 81st Regiment of Foot.
Grave: Mont Cochon, St Helier, Jersey.

Pte 24 Mar 1807
    Served in the Peninsula 7 Nov 1808 – Jan 1809 with 2/81st Foot. Present at Corunna. Also served in Canada. MGS medal for Corunna. Discharged in Guernsey 14 Apr 1829 aged 40. Chelsea Pensioner. Died in Jersey 10 Mar 1870 aged 81 years.

BUXTON, James William
2nd Assistant Surgeon. Ordnance Medical Department, Royal Artillery.
Buried in Messina, Italy. (M.I.)

"SACRED TO THE MEMORY OF / JAMES WILLIAM BUXTON / OF COLCHESTER, ESSEX. / LATE ASSISTANT SURGEON / OF THE ROYAL BRITISH ARTILLERY / WHO DEPARTED THIS LIFE / AUGUST 5TH 1814 / AGED 25 YEARS."

2nd Asst Surgeon Royal Artillery 12 Jun 1811.

Served in the Peninsula Jun 1812 – Apr 1813 in Capt Holcombe's Company. Present at Castalla. Died at Messina 5 Aug 1814.

BY, John
Captain. Royal Engineers.
Monument: St Alban's Churchyard, Frant, Sussex. (Photograph)

IN MEMORY / OF / L^T JOHN BY, ROYAL ENGINEERS, / OF SHERNFIELD PARK IN THIS PARISH / WHO DIED 18TH FEB^Y 1836 AGED 53 / ....

Memorial tablet: St Alban's Church, Frant, Sussex. (M.I.)

"LIEUTENANT COLONEL JOHN BY, ROYAL ENGINEERS, DIED 1ST FEBRUARY 1836, AGED 53. HE WAS THE FOUNDER OF THE CITY OF OTTAWA (ORIGINALLY CALLED 'BY TOWN'). ERECTED BY HIS WIDOW."

Named on the Regimental Memorial, Rochester Cathedral, Rochester, Kent. (Photograph)

2nd Lt Royal Artillery 1 Aug 1799. Lt Royal Engineers 18 Apr 1801. 2nd Capt Royal Engineers 2 Mar 1805. Capt 24 Jun 1809. Bt Major 23 Jun 1814. Lt Colonel 24 Dec 1824.

Served in the Peninsula Apr – Aug 1811. Present at the first and second sieges of Badajoz. Sent to Lisbon due to ill health Aug 1811, returned to England and was too ill to return to the Peninsula. Took charge of the Royal Gunpowder Mills at Faversham, Purfleet and Waltham Abbey from 1812–1821.

Went to Canada to build a waterway to join the military headquarters at Kingston with Ottawa region 1825. This became the Rideau Canal. His construction camp was so well planned that it was named Bytown, having a hospital and barracks. The town grew in size and when in 1867 Canada became self governing, the town was renamed Ottawa and became the capital city. Returned to England in 1832 due to ill health.

REFERENCE: *Dictionary of National Biography. Dictionary of Canadian Biography. Leggett, R., John By, Lieutenant Colonel, Royal Engineers, 1779–1836: Builder of the Rideau Canal, Founder of Ottawa, Ottawa Historical Society, 1982. Hill, H. P., Lieutenant-Colonel John By; a biography, Royal Engineers Journal (New series), 46, 1932, pp. 522–5.*

BYAM, William
Lieutenant. 15th (King's) Regiment of Light Dragoons.
Headstone with low monument: Old Common Cemetery, Southampton, Hampshire. (G044 005). (Photograph)

IN MEMORY OF SIR WILLIAM BYAM / DIED AT WESTWOOD / 5TH JULY 1869, AGED 77. / ALSO OF EDWARD GAMAGE BYAM / HIS SON, LATE CAPT 59TH REGT / DIED 6TH JULY 1875 AGED 52.

Cornet 5 Dec 1811. Lt 17 Sep 1812.

Served in the Peninsula Aug 1813 – Apr 1814. Present at Orthes and Toulouse. Present at Waterloo (severely wounded). Retired 1817. Inherited family estates in Antigua and became President of the Island Council. Knighted in 1859. His brother Lt Edward Byam was in the same regiment at Waterloo.

BYNG, Sir John
Captain and Lieutenant Colonel. 3rd Regiment of Foot Guards.
Memorial: Royal Military Chapel, Wellington Barracks, London. (M.I.) (Destroyed by a Flying Bomb 1944)

"TO THE MEMORY OF / FIELD-MARSHAL, JOHN EARL OF STRAFFORD, G.C.B., G.C.H., K.M.T. / BORN, 1778: DIED, 1860. / COLONEL COLDSTREAM GUARDS, 1850–60. HE ENTERED THE ARMY IN 1793; SERVED IN THE 3RD GUARDS, 1804–14 AND COMMANDED AT WATERLOO THE 2ND BRIGADE OF GUARDS IN THE BRILLIANT DEFENCE OF HOUGOUMONT. HE SERVED IN FLANDERS, IN HOLLAND, AND IN IRELAND; AND TOOK PART IN THE EXPEDITIONS TO HANOVER, TO COPENHAGEN, AND TO WALCHEREN. HE COMMANDED FOR THREE YEARS A BRIGADE IN THE 2ND DIVISION OF THE ARMY IN THE FIELD, UNDER THE DUKE OF WELLINGTON, AND WAS PRESENT IN NEARLY ALL THE BATTLES OF THE PENINSULA. / PLACED BY HIS SON, GEORGE, EARL OF STRAFFORD, 1879"

Ensign 33rd Foot 30 Sep 1793. Lt 1 Dec 1793. Capt 10 Dec 1794. Major 60th Foot 20 Jun 1799. Lt Col 29th Foot 14 Mar 1800. Capt and Lt Colonel 3rd Foot Guards 4 Aug 1804. Bt Colonel 25 Jul 1810. Major General 4 Jun 1813. Lt General 27 Aug 1825. General 23 Nov 1841. Field Marshal 2 Oct 1855.
    Served in the Peninsula Sep 1811 – Apr 1814 (Commanded 2 Brigade 2nd Division). Present at Vittoria, Pyrenees (Mentioned in Despatches), Nivelle (wounded and Mentioned in Despatches), Nive (Mentioned in Despatches), Garris, Orthes, Aire (Mentioned in Despatches), Tarbes and Toulouse. Gold Cross for Vittoria, Pyrenees, Nivelle, Nive and Orthes. MGS medal for Toulouse. KCB 2 Jan 1815. Present at Waterloo (in command of a brigade of Guards at Hougoumont). Present at the siege of Peronne, the Capture of Paris and with the Army of Occupation. GCB. GCH. KMT. KSG. Also served in Flanders 1794–1795, Irish Rebellion 1798, Hanover 1805, Copenhagen 1807 and Walcheren 1809. Colonel 2nd West India Regiment 26 Jul 1822. Colonel 29th Foot 23 Jan 1828. Commander-in-Chief Ireland 1828–1831. Colonel Coldstream Guards 15 Aug 1850. MP for Poole Oct 1831 – May 1835. Died 3 Jun 1860.
    REFERENCE: *Dictionary of National Biography. Annual Register, 1860, Appx, p 492. Royal Military Calendar, Vol 3, pp. 259–2. Gentleman's Magazine, Jul 1860, pp. 88–9.*

BYROM, Ashton Johnson
Lieutenant. 5th (Princess Charlotte of Wales's) Dragoon Guards.
Buried in Meerut Cantonment Cemetery, Meerut, India. (Burial register)

"CAPT A. J. BYROM, 16TH LANCERS DIED ON 15 JULY 1828, AGED 34."

Cornet 4th Dragoons 12 Mar 1812. Lt 25 Feb 1813. Lt 5th Dragoon Guards 22 Sep 1814. Capt 16th Lt Dragoons 27 Apr 1820.
    Served in the Peninsula Dec 1812 – Apr 1814. Present at Vittoria and Toulouse. Also served in India with 16th Lt Dragoons 1824 (present at the siege of Bhurtpore) until his death in India 1828.

CADELL, Charles
Captain. 28th (North Gloucestershire) Regiment of Foot.
Cross on stepped base: St Saviour's Churchyard, St Helier, Jersey, Channel Islands. (Photograph)

IN MEMORY OF / CHARLES CADELL K. H. / LT COLL UNATT. LATE 28TH REGT / WHO DIED AT ST HELIER / ON THE 7TH MARCH 1866 / IN HIS 80TH YEAR.

Ensign 7 Sep 1804. Lt 1 Aug 1805. Capt 9 Mar 1809. Major 14 Dec 1826. Lt Colonel 27 Sep 1833.
    Served in the Peninsula with 1/28th Jul 1808 – Jan 1809, Jul 1810 – Mar 1811 and Jul 1811 – Apr 1814.

Present at Corunna, Tarifa, Barrosa (wounded), Cadiz, Arroyo dos Molinos, Almarez, retreat from Burgos, Vittoria, Pyrenees, Nivelle, Nive, Orthes, Aire and Toulouse. Present at Waterloo (commanded the regiment when senior officers were killed or wounded). Also served at Copenhagen 1807, Sweden 1808 and Walcheren 1809. MGS medal for Corunna, Barrosa, Vittoria, Pyrenees, Nivelle, Nive, Orthes and Toulouse. KH. Half pay 27 Sep 1833. Author of *Narrative of the campaigns of the 28th Regiment since their return from Egypt in 1802, 1835.*

CADOGAN, Hon. Henry

Lieutenant Colonel. 71st (Highland Light Infantry) Regiment of Foot.
Memorial tablet: St Paul's Cathedral, London. (South transept). (Photograph)

ERECTED AT THE PUBLIC EXPENSE TO THE MEMORY OF / COLONEL THE HONBLE HENRY CADOGAN, WHO FELL GLORIOUSLY / IN THE COMMAND OF A BRIGADE AT THE MEMORABLE BATTLE OF VITTORIA 21ST JUNE 1813, / WHEN A COMPLETE VICTORY WAS GAINED OVER THE FRENCH ARMY BY THE ALLIED FORCES / UNDER THE MARQUIS OF WELLINGTON. / COLONEL CADOGAN WAS THE SON OF CHARLES SLOANE, EARL CADOGAN BORN 26TH FEBRUARY 1780.

Monument: St Kentigern's Cathedral, Glasgow, Lanarkshire, Scotland. (Photograph)

SACRED TO THE MEMORY / OF / THE HONOURABLE HENRY CADOGAN, / LIEUT. COLONEL OF THE 71ST, OR GLASGOW REGT, / HONORARY BURGESS OF THIS CITY, / WHO GLORIOUSLY FELL AT THE HEAD OF HIS BATTALION, / IN THE EVER MEMORABLE BATTLE OF VITTORIA, JUNE 21ST 1813, / AGED THIRTY-THREE YEARS. / THIS MONUMENT IS ERECTED / BY A FEW OF HIS FRIENDS IN THE CITY AND NEIGHBOURHOOD / TO PERPETUATE THE REMEMBRANCE / OF HIS WORTH AS A MAN, AND HIS / GALLANTRY AS A SOLDIER.

Memorial tablet: St Luke's Church, Chelsea, London. (Photograph)

TO THE MEMORY OF / LIEUTENANT COLONEL THE HONOURABLE HENRY CADOGAN, / OF HIS MAJESTY'S SEVENTY FIRST REGIMENT / WHO FELL IN THE BATTLE OF VITTORIA, ON THE 21ST OF JUNE 1813, / IN THE 33RD YEAR OF HIS AGE. / THE OFFICERS OF HIS REGIMENT HAVE ERECTED THIS MONUMENT / IN TOKEN OF THEIR ESTEEM AND RESPECT.

Memorial tablet: St Mary the Virgin Church, Santon Downham, Suffolk. (Photograph)

IN MEMORY OF / LIEUTENANT COLONEL THE HONOURABLE HENRY CADOGAN, / OF THE 71T REGIMENT OF HIGHLAND LIGHT INFANTRY / BORN FEBRUARY 2ND 1780 / FELL AT THE BATTLE OF VITTORIA / JUNE 21ST 1813.

Ensign 18th Foot 9 Aug 1797. Lt and Capt Coldstream Guards 9 Dec 1799. Major 53rd Foot 8 Dec 1804. Lt Colonel 18th Foot 22 Aug 1805. Lt Colonel 71st Foot 7 Jan 1808.
    Served in the Peninsula Jun 1809 – Sep 1810 (extra ADC to Wellington), with 71st Foot Sep 1810 – Nov 1812 and Nov 1812 – Jun 1813 (Commanded 2 Brigade 2nd Division). Present at Douro, Talavera, Sobral (Mentioned in Despatches), Fuentes d'Onoro (Mentioned in Despatches), Arroyo dos Molinos (Mentioned in Despatches), Almarez, (Mentioned in Despatches), Alba de Tormes (Mentioned in Despatches) and Vittoria where he was killed and Mentioned in Despatches. Severely wounded leading the 71st Foot up the Pueblo Heights at the battle of Vittoria, he was carried up to a vantage point so that he could see how the battle was progressing and died at 4pm watching his troops fight their way to victory. Gold Medal for Fuentes d'Onoro and Vittoria. Also served in South America 1807 (present at Buenos Ayres). Wellington's *Dispatch* on Vittoria mentions Cadogan – 'and I am concerned to report that Lt. Col.

Cadogan has died of a wound which he received. In him His Majesty has lost an officer of great zeal and tried gallantry, who had already acquired the respect and regard of the whole profession, and of whom it might be expected, that if he had lived he would have rendered the most important services to his country'

Henry Cadogan's sister Charlotte was married to Henry Wellesley, Wellington's brother. In 1809 she eloped with Henry Lord Paget. Cadogan offered to leave the Army and look after her if she would leave Paget but she refused. He also offered to fight Paget in a duel but it was his brother George who fought the duel. Shortly after this Cadogan went to Spain as ADC to Wellington.

REFERENCE: *Dictionary of National Biography. Pearman, R., The Cadogans at war: 1783–1862, 1990.*

CADOUX, Daniel
Captain. 95th Regiment of Foot.
Memorial tablet: Bridge at Vera, Pyrenees, Spain. (Photograph)

TO THE GLORY OF GOD / AND IN MEMORY OF / CAPTAIN DANIEL CADOUX / AND HIS GALLANT RIFLEMEN / OF THE 2ND BN 95TH (RIFLE BRIGADE) / WHO ON 1 SEPTEMBER 1813 / FELL GLORIOUSLY / DEFENDING THIS BRIDGE / AGAINST THE FURIOUS ATTACK / OF A FRENCH DIVISION. / HIS FAME CAN NEVER DIE / (SIR HARRY SMITH) / ERECTED BY THE RIFLE BRIGADE AND HIS RELATIVES MARY HUDSON & HENRY HUDSON / 1921

Lt Oxfordshire Fencible Cavalry. 2nd Lt 95th Foot 2 Feb 1801. Lt 25 Jun 1803. Capt 10 Jul 1807.

Served in the Peninsula Oct 1808 – Jan 1809 and Feb 1810 – Aug 1813. Present at Vigo, Cadiz, Barrosa, Seville (Mentioned in Despatches), San Millan, Vittoria, Pyrenees and Vera where he was killed at the Bridge of Vera 1 Sep 1813 in an heroic action aided by his company of Riflemen to stop a French division from crossing the Bidassoa. Skerrett refused to send reinforcements and 63 were killed from the 100 Rifles. Skerrett was never forgiven by the 95th Foot for this unnecessary loss of life. Also served at Walcheren 1809.

CAIRNCROSS, John
Bombardier. Royal Artillery.
Monument: Holy Trinity Cathedral Churchyard, Brechin, Angus, Scotland. (Photograph)

IN MEMORY OF / JOHN CAIRNCROSS / SOMETIME MERCHANT IN BRECHIN / FORMERLY OF THE ROYAL ARTILLERY / BORN 15TH MAY 1783, DIED 14TH JUNE 1853. / HE SERVED IN THE PENINSULAR CAMPAIGN AND WAS / PRINCIPAL CLERK IN THE ARTILLERY OFFICE AT HEADQUARTERS / UNTIL THE DUKE OF WELLINGTON'S ARMY FINALLY QUITTED / FRANCE. HE WAS PRESENT AT THE BATTLES OF / CORUNNA. BADAJOZ. SAN SEBASTIAN. / OPORTO. SALAMANCA. PYRENEES. / TALAVERA. CUIDAD RODRIGO. ORTHES. / FUENTES D' ONORO. VITTORIA. TOULOUSE. / FOR WHICH HE RECEIVED THE WAR MEDAL WITH CLASPS /
....

Pte 19 May 1801. Bombardier 1806.

Served in the Peninsula 1808 – Jan 1809, Apr 1809 – May 1811 and 1812 – Apr 1814. Present at Corunna, Fuentes d'Onoro, Ciudad Rodrigo, Badajoz, Salamanca, Vittoria, Pyrenees, San Sebastian, Nivelle, Nive and Toulouse. Also served in Java Aug 1811. MGS medal for Corunna, Fuentes d'Onoro, Java, Ciudad Rodrigo, Badajoz, Salamanca, Vittoria, Pyrenees, San Sebastian, Nivelle, Nive and Toulouse. Discharged 1 Oct 1814 with a pension of 1 shilling per day, as a consequence of a sprained ankle in Spain.

CAIRNES, George
Lieutenant. 36th (Herefordshire) Regiment of Foot.
Family grave: St James's Churchyard, Shirley, Southampton, Hampshire. (M.I.)

"GEORGE CAIRNES, LT COLONEL, 36TH FOOT. DIED MAY 1ST 1871."

Ensign 15 Dec 1808. Lt 2 Jan 1812. Capt 4 Nov 1824. Major 4 Dec 1832.
    Served in the Peninsula Mar 1811 – Aug 1812 and Oct 1813 – Apr 1814. Also served at Walcheren 1809 (present at the siege of Flushing). Later Lt Colonel Commandant 4th West Yorkshire Militia.

CAIRNES, Robert Macpherson
2nd Captain. Royal Artillery.
Memorial tablet: Canterbury Cathedral, Kent. (Photograph)

SACRED / TO THE MEMORY / OF / ROBERT MACPHERSON CAIRNES, / MAJOR OF ROYAL HORSE ARTILLERY, / WHO WAS TAKEN FROM THIS SUBLUNARY SCENE / JUNE THE 18TH 1815. / AGED 30. / BRIEF, BUT MOST NOBLE, WAS HIS CAREER, / AND HIS END WAS GLORIOUS, / BRAVELY ASSERTING THE CAUSE OF AN INJURED MONARCH, / HE FELL ON THE PLAINS OF WATERLOO. / HIS RARE ENDOWMENTS, / HIS HIGH QUALITIES, / THE ENDEARING ATTRACTIONS OF HIS CHARACTER / AS SON, AS BROTHER AND AS FRIEND, / ARE INDELIBLY IMPRESSED ON THE HEARTS OF ALL / WHO HAD THE HAPPINESS OF POSSESSING HIS ESTEEM, / AND WHO NOW FEEL THE EXQUISITE ANGUISH / INFLICTED BY HIS EARLY DEATH. / THIS HUMBLE MONUMENT / ERECTED BY THE HAND OF FRIENDSHIP, / IS A FAITHFUL, BUT VERY INADEQUATE TESTIMONY / OF AFFECTION AND GRIEF WHICH NO LANGUAGE CAN EXPRESS, / OF AFFECTION WHICH LIVES BEYOND THE TOMB, / OF GRIEF WHICH WILL NEVER TERMINATE / TILL THOSE WHO NOW DEPLORE HIS LOSS / SHALL REJOIN HIM / IN THE BLEST REALMS / OF / EVERLASTING PEACE.

Memorial tablet: St Joseph's Church, Waterloo, Belgium. (Photograph)

IN MEMORIAM / ROBERTI CAIRNES, / EQUITATUS REGII APUD EXERCITUM BRITANNICUM / SUB DUCE DE WELLINGTON, / BELLICA TORMENTA AGENTIS, LEGATI, / QUI IN CAMPO WATERLOOIENSI, / 18MO CAL. JUHII M. DCCCXV / ACIE FERVENTE / OCCISUS, DEFLETAM COMMILITONIBUS, / ET AMICIS LUCTUOSAM / ANNO ÆTAT SUAE XXXMO. MORTEM OBIIT. / FRATRI OPTIMO ET CARISSIMO, / FRATER, QUI IN PRÆLIO LATERI ADHÆRENS / MORI-BUNDI HALITIUN SUSCEPIT SUPREMUM, / HOC MARMOR, PIETATIS ÆTERNÆ TESTIMONIUM, / MÆRENS PONERE CURAVIT. / BURKE CUPPAGE.

Named on the Regimental Memorial: St Joseph's Church, Waterloo, Belgium. (Photograph)

2nd Lt 1 Jun 1801. 1st Lt 1 May 1803. 2nd Capt 1 Feb 1808. Bt Major 12 Apr 1814.
    Served in the Peninsula Jun 1810 – Jul 1811 and Jan 1812 – Aug 1812, Sep 1812 – Feb 1814 (Commanded 4th Company 10th Battalion) and Mar – Apr 1814 ('I' Troop R.H.A). Present at Cadiz, Barrosa, Seville (wounded by explosion of powder), Vittoria, Nivelle, Pyrenees and Bayonne. Gold Medal for Vittoria and Pyrenees and Bt Majority for his conduct in the Peninsula. While in the Peninsula he improved the organisation of Field Artillery so that each officer had complete control of all his men including drivers. Previously officers in the Drivers Corps had taken responsibility for the drivers, leading to divided loyalties. In 1822 the Drivers Corps was finally abolished. Present at Waterloo in Major Bull's Troop where he was killed early in the action and Lt Louis took his place.

CAIRNS, James
Sergeant. 95th Regiment of Foot.
Headstone: Holy Trinity Churchyard, Berwick-on-Tweed, Northumberland. (Photograph)

John Acomb 2ⁿᵈ Life Guards

Frederick W. Adam 21ˢᵗ Foot

Thomas Aird Royal Waggon Train

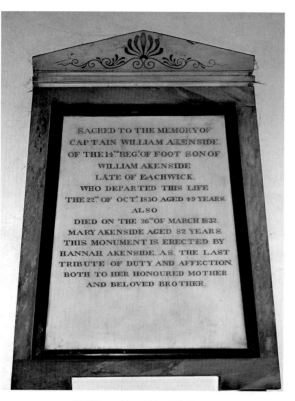

SACRED TO THE MEMORY OF
CAPTAIN WILLIAM AKENSIDE.
OF THE 14TH REG! OF FOOT SON OF
WILLIAM AKENSIDE
LATE OF EACHWICK.
WHO DEPARTED THIS LIFE
THE 22ND OF OCT! 1830 AGED 49 YEARS.
ALSO
DIED ON THE 26TH OF MARCH 1832.
MARY AKENSIDE AGED 82 YEARS.
THIS MONUMENT IS ERECTED BY
HANNAH AKENSIDE, AS THE LAST
TRIBUTE OF DUTY AND AFFECTION,
BOTH TO HER HONOURED MOTHER
AND BELOVED BROTHER

William Akenside 14th Foot

ERECTED
To the memory of
WILLIAM ALCORN who died
at Foco 1825 aged 71 years
Also
JAMES ALCORN his Son who died
in 1814 aged 28 years
And
WILLIAM ALCORN his Son who fell
at Waterloo aged 20 years
Also
EUPHEMIA his Daughter who died
at Sisterpath in 1831 aged 71 years
Also
NICOL ALCORN his Son who died
at Polwarth June 17th 1869 aged 71 years

William Alcorn 2nd Dragoons

SACRED TO THE MEMORY OF

LIEU! GENERAL SIR THOMAS ARBUTHNOT K.C.B.

WHO DIED AT MANCHESTER WHEN IN COMMAND OF THE

NORTHERN AND MIDLAND DISTRICTS

ON THE 26TH DAY OF JANUARY 1849,

AGED 72 YEARS.

REQUIESCAT IN PACE

Sir Thomas Arbuthnot 57th Foot

Donald Andrew 79th Foot

Francis H. Ansell 74th Foot

Samuel Auchmuty 7th Foot

William Austin 52nd Foot

Benjamin Baddeley 23rd Foot

Collet Barker 39th Foot

George Barney Royal Engineers

Charles L. Barnard 2nd Dragoons

Richard Bentinck 23rd Foot

William B. Bishop 1st Life Guards

Richard Bogue Royal Artillery

John I. Boswell Coldstream Guards

John H. Beaufoy 7th Foot

NEAR THIS PLACE IS INTERRED THE BODY
OF LIEUT. COLONEL HENRY BOOTH, K.H. OF
THE 43RD REGIMENT OF LIGHT INFANTRY:
FIFTH SON OF THE LATE WM BOOTH ESQRE OF BRUSH HOUSE,
IN THE PARISH OF ECCLESFIELD, IN THE COUNTY OF YORK.
HE DIED AT NORTHALLERTON, MAY 6TH 1841, AGED 51.

HIS MILITARY LIFE WAS PASSED IN THE 43RD REGIMENT. HE ENTERED IT AS ENSIGN
MARCH 6TH 1806, WAS PROMOTED TO BE LIEUTT COLONEL JUNE 29TH 1830,
AND RETAINED THE COMMAND OF IT UNTIL THE DAY OF HIS DEATH.
HE SERVED WITH THE ARMIES IN SPAIN AND PORTUGAL
UNDER SIR JOHN MOORE AND THE DUKE OF WELLINGTON, AND WAS PRESENT AT
VIMIERO, CORUNNA, THE PASSAGE OF THE COA, BUSACO, SALAMANCA, VITTORIA,
AND THE ATTACK ON THE HEIGHTS OF VERA.

THIS TABLET WAS ERECTED BY THE
OFFICERS, NON-COMMISSIONED OFFICERS, AND PRIVATES OF THE REGIMENT,
WHO HAD SERVED UNDER HIS COMMAND, TO RECORD THEIR RESPECT FOR HIS CHARACTER, AND THEIR
ESTEEM AND AFFECTION FOR HIS GALLANT, GENEROUS, AND AMIABLE QUALITIES, BY WHICH
HE WON THE HEARTS OF ALL WHO SERVED UNDER HIM, AND INFUSED THROUGH EVERY RANK
A HIGH AND HONOURABLE FEELING.

Henry Booth 43rd Foot

Barnard F. Bowes 6th Foot

Joseph Bradby 28th Foot

Sir Henry H. Bradford 1ˢᵗ Foot Guards

Orlando Bridgeman 1ˢᵗ Foot Guards

John F. Briggs 28ᵗʰ Foot

Francis Brooke 1st Dragoon Guards

John R. Bruce Royal Artillery

John Brumwell 43rd Foot

Henry R. Buck 33rd Foot

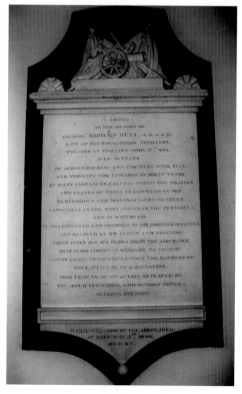

Robert Bull Royal Artillery

John F. Burgoyne Royal Engineers

Robert Burne 36ᵗʰ Foot

SACRED TO THE MEMORY
of
THE HONORABLE HENRY CADOGAN,
LIEUT-COLONEL OF THE 71ᴼʀ GLASGOW REG.
HONORARY BURGESS OF THIS CITY,
WHO GLORIOUSLY FELL AT THE HEAD OF HIS BATTALION,
IN THE EVER MEMORABLE BATTLE OF VITTORIA, JUNE 21ᵗ, 1813
AGED THIRTY-THREE YEARS.

THIS MONUMENT IS ERECTED
BY A FEW OF HIS FRIENDS IN THIS CITY AND NEIGHBOURHOOD
TO PERPETUATE THE REMEMBRANCE
OF HIS WORTH AS A MAN, AND HIS
GALLANTRY AS A SOLDIER.

Henry Cadogan 71ˢᵗ Foot

SACRED TO THE MEMORY OF
JOHN CHARLES BUCKERIDGE,
ENSIGN IN THE COLDSTREAM REGᵗ OF FOOT GUARDS.
HE SERVED IN *SPAIN*
UNDER THE COMMAND OF MARQUIS WELLINGTON,
WAS AT THE BATTLE OF SALAMANCA.
AND GALLANTLY FELL AT HIS POST
AT THE SIEGE OF THE CASTLE OF BURGOS,
OCTᴼʀ THE 9ᵀᴴ 1812, IN THE 18ᵀᴴ YEAR OF HIS AGE.

"THE LORD GAVE AND THE LORD HATH TAKEN AWAY,
BLESSED BE THE NAME OF THE LORD."

John C. Buckeridge Coldstream Guards

Daniel Cadoux 95th Foot

Robert M. Cairnes Royal Artillery

Archibald Campbell 6th Foot

Archibald Argyle Campbell 42ⁿᵈ Foot

Duncan Campbell 88ᵗʰ Foot

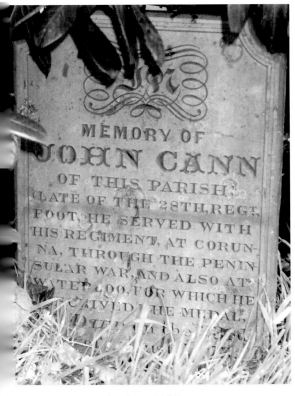

John Cann 28ᵗʰ Foot

Hon George Cathcart 6ᵗʰ Dragoon Guards

Alexander K. Clark 1st Dragoons

William Claus 54th Foot

George Cooke 1st Foot Guards

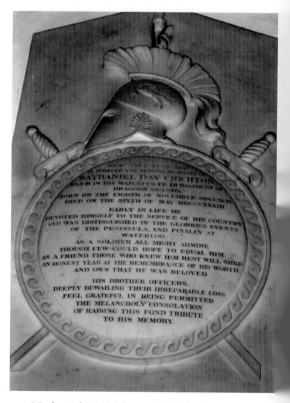

Nathaniel D. Crighton 16th Light Dragoons

William Coulter 66th Foot

Robert N. Crosse 36th Foot

Alexander Cruickshank 79th Foot

William Cumin 88th Foot

Hon William Curzon 69th Foot

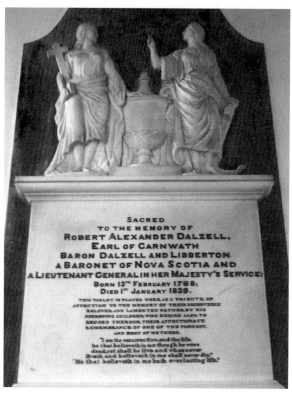

Robert A. Dalzell 60th Foot

Edward W. Drewe 27th Foot

ERECTED / BY / JAMES CAIRNS. / .... / ALSO OF THE ABOVE / JAMES CAIRNS, WHO DIED THE 4TH JULY 1856 AGED 70 YEARS. / ....

Served in the Peninsula with 1/95th Aug 1808 – Jan 1809 and with 2/95th 1810 – Apr 1814. Present at Vimeiro, Corunna, Fuentes d'Onoro, Ciudad Rodrigo (in the Forlorn Hope), Badajoz, Salamanca, Vittoria, Pyrenees, Nivelle, Nive, Orthes and Toulouse. MGS medal for Vimeiro, Corunna, Fuentes d'Onoro, Ciudad Rodrigo, Badajoz, Salamanca, Vittoria, Pyrenees, Nivelle, Nive, Orthes and Toulouse.

CALCRAFT, Sir Granby Thomas
Lieutenant Colonel. 3rd (Prince of Wales's) Dragoon Guards.
Memorial tablet: St Mary's Church, Wareham, Dorset. (Photograph)

SACRED / TO THE MEMORY OF / MAJOR GENERAL / SIR GRANBY THOMAS CALCRAFT KNIGHT, / (OF THE ORDERS / MARIA THERESA AND TOWER AND SWORD. / A DISTIN-GUISHED OFFICER IN THE / 15TH REGT. OF LIGHT DRAGOONS & THE 3RD REGT. OF DRAGOON GUARDS) / SON OF THE / LATE JOHN CALCRAFT ESQR. OF REMPSTONE, / HE DEPARTED THIS LIFE AT BATH, / AUGUST THE 20TH 1820, / AGED 53 YEARS.

Cornet 15th Lt Dragoons Mar 1788. Lt 20 Apr 1793. Capt Apr 1794. Major 25 Lt Dragoons 7 May 1799. Major 3rd Dragoon Guards 1800. Lt Colonel 25 Dec 1800. Bt Colonel 25 Jul 1810. Major General 4 Jun 1813.
    Served in the Peninsula Apr 1809 – Jun 1813 (Commanded Heavy Cavalry Brigade Dec 1811 – Jan 1812 and Dec 1812 – Apr 1813). Present at Talavera, Campo Mayor, Los Santos, Albuera, Usagre, Aldea da Ponte, Maguilla (Mentioned in Despatches) and Llera 11 Jun 1812 (Mentioned in Despatches). Returned home due to ill health 1813. Given staff appointment in Scotland but felt that he had been treated badly. Gold Medal for Talavera. KTS. Also served in Flanders 1793–1795 (present at Famars, Valenciennes, Villiers-en-Couche. All eight officers of the 15th Dragoons who were present were knighted on the order of Maria Theresa), Dunkirk, Boxtel and Nimwegen) and the Helder 1799 (present at Alkmaar where he was wounded. ADC to Lord Paget).
REFERENCE: *Dictionary of National Biography. Royal Military Calendar, Vol 3, p. 287.*

CALDECOT, Henry
Lieutenant. 39th (Dorsetshire) Regiment of Foot.
Low monument: Locksbrook Cemetery, Bath, Somerset. (Photograph)

IN MEMORY OF / HENRY CALDECOT ESQR OF HOLTON HALL LINCOLNSHIRE. / LATE BREVET MAJOR GRENADIER GUARDS, / DIED AT BATH AUGUST 12TH 1873, AGED 81. / (VERSE)

Ensign 20 Jul 1809. Lt 10 Jun 1813. Capt 2nd Dragoon Guards 12 Aug 1824. Bt Major 28 Jun 1838.
    Served in the Peninsula with 1/39th Oct – Dec 1811, 2/39th Jan 1812 and 1/39th Apr 1813 – Apr 1814. Present at Vittoria, Pyrenees, Nivelle, Nive, Garris, Orthes, Aire and Toulouse. Also served in Malta, Sicily and North America 1814–1815. MGS medal for Vittoria, Pyrenees, Nivelle, Nive, Orthes and Toulouse. Half pay 17 Mar 1825.

CALDER, Thomas
Sergeant. Royal Artillery Drivers.
Headstone: Holy Trinity Churchyard, Berwick-on-Tweed, Northumberland. (Photograph)

IN MEMORY / OF THOMAS CALDER, / LATE SERGEANT IN / THE ROYAL ARTILLERY, / WHO DEPARTED THIS / LIFE ON THE 7TH OF MARCH / 1836 AGED 57 YEARS. / ....

Pte 28 Apr 1800. Cpl 1804. Sgt 1814.

Served in the Peninsula. Served at Waterloo in Capt W. H. Humphrey's H. Troop. Discharged 31 May 1816 with a pension of one shilling and four pence per day, owing to ill health he was no longer fit for service.

CALLENDER, Alexander James
Captain. 91st Regiment of Foot.
Grave: Kensal Green Cemetery, London . (No longer extant: Grave number 5658/161)

Ensign 25th Foot 1798. Lt 62nd Foot 1799. Capt 25th Foot 1804. Capt 91st Foot 10 Oct 1811. Bt Major 4 Jun 1814

Served in the Peninsula Apr 1813 – Apr 1814. Present at Pyrenees, Orthes, Aire and Toulouse (wounded). Present in the Waterloo campaign in reserve at Hal, siege of Cambrai and the Capture of Paris. Half pay 1821. Buried in Kensal Green 25 Aug 1845 aged 62.

CAMAC, Burges
Captain. 1st Life Guards.
Table tomb: St Nicholas Churchyard, St Nicholas, Glamorgan, Wales. (Photograph)

SACRED / TO / THE MEMORY OF / MAJOR GENERAL / SIR BURGES CAMAC. / FORMERLY OF THE / FIRST REGIMENT OF / LIFE GUARDS, / WHO DIED WHILST ON A / VISIT TO DYFFRYN / IN THIS PARISH / ON THE 17TH NOV 1845 / AGED 69 YEARS.

Ensign 29 May 1803. Lt 25th Dragoons 4 Dec 1806. Capt 18th Foot 18 Aug 1808. Bt Major 11 Jun 1811. Bt Lt Colonel 29 Jul 1813. Capt 1st Life Guards 10 Jun 1815. Bt Colonel 22 Jul 1830. Major General 23 Nov 1841.

Served in the Peninsula 1811 – Apr 1814. Present at Massena's retreat from Torres Vedras (brought despatches back to England). Appointed Deputy Adjutant General to communicate between British and Spanish armies. In Spanish service as Lt Colonel of Cavalry. Present at Cadiz, Pancorbo, Pamplona, Sorauren, Vera, Sarre, Nivelle, Nive and Bayonne. Knight of Charles III of Spain. Retired on half pay 29 Jun 1828. REFERENCE: *Gentleman's Magazine Mar 1846, pp. 318–9. Annual Register, 1845, Appx, p. 316.*

CAMERON, Sir Alan (Erracht)
Colonel. 79th (Cameron Highlanders) Regiment of Foot.
Gravestone: Old Marylebone Churchyard, Paddington Street, London. Inscription not recorded.
Memorial stained glass window (Donated by the regiment in 1948): Marylebone Church, London. (Photograph)

Major (Commandant) 17 Aug 1793. Lt Colonel (Commandant) 30 Jan 1794. Lt Colonel 3 May 1795. Bt Colonel 26 Jan 1797. Colonel 79th Foot 1 Jan 1805. Major General 25 Jul 1810. Lt General 12 Aug 1819.

Served in the Peninsula Aug 1808 – Dec 1810 (Commanded 7 Brigade Apr – Jun 1809 and Commanded 2 Brigade 1st Division Jun 1809 – Nov 1810). In 1808 Cameron was in Portugal advancing to meet Sir John Moore when he found that Moore's Army was in retreat to Corunna. Cameron took his 79th Foot back to Lisbon collecting the sick and stragglers on the way. These men were able to assist Wellington in his attack on Soult in April 1809 and at Talavera. Present at Talavera and Busaco. Gold Medal for Talavera. KCB 2 Jan 1814.

Also served in Flanders 1794, West Indies 1796 (present at Martinique), the Helder 1799 (present at Egmont-op-Zee where he was wounded and lost the use of one arm for the rest of his life), Ferrol 1800, Egypt 1801 (Gold Medal from Sultan Selim III) and the Baltic 1807–1808.

Sir Alan raised the 79th Regiment and led it to victory in every campaign from 1794 until 1810 when he handed over command to his eldest son, Lt Colonel Phillips Cameron who was killed the following year at Fuentes d'Onoro. He was constantly looking after the welfare of the regiment and was indeed the father of the regiment and his men adored him. His regiment suffered badly at Waterloo, only nine officers out of 41 were not killed or wounded and 288 men survived out of 735. His nephew Lt Alexander Cameron commanded the regiment at the close of the battle, as the most senior unwounded officer. Cameron himself went to Brussels to see the wounded. Died in Fulham 9 Mar 1828. Uncle of Lt Ewen Cameron (Scamadale) 79th Foot who was killed at Toulouse and Lt Alexander Cameron 79th Foot who died in Tobago. Father of Capt Ewen Cameron 79th Foot who died in Lisbon 1810 and Lt Colonel Phillips Cameron 79th Foot who died at Fuentes d'Onoro.

REFERENCE: *Dictionary of National Biography. Gentleman's Magazine, Apr 1828, pp. 327–8. Annual Register, 1828, Appx, pp 225–6. Maclean, L, Indomitable Colonel, 1986.*

CAMERON, Alexander
Major. 95th Regiment of Foot.
Obelisk: Kilmallie Churchyard, Corpach, Invernesshire, Scotland. (Photograph)

SACRED / TO THE MEMORY OF / MAJOR GENERAL / SIR ALEXANDER CAMERON, KCB, / OF INVERAILART, / DIED 26TH JULY 1850, / AGED 71 YEARS.

Named on the Regimental Memorial: Winchester Cathedral, Winchester, Hampshire. (Photograph)

Ensign Breadalbane Fencibles Nov 1797. Volunteer 92nd Foot 1799. Ensign 92nd Foot 23 Oct 1799. Lt 95th Foot 6 Sep 1800. Capt 6 May 1805. Bt Major 30 May 1811. Bt Lt Colonel 27 Apr 1812. Major 95th Foot 14 May 1812. Bt Colonel 22 Jul 1830. Major General 28 Jun 1838.

Served in the Peninsula with 1/95th Aug 1808 – Jan 1809 and Jun 1809 – Aug 1813. Present at Vimeiro, Cacabellos, Corunna, Coa, Busaco, Pombal, Redinha, Casal Nova, Foz d'Arouce, Sabugal, Fuentes d'Onoro, (awarded Bt Majority), Ciudad Rodrigo, Badajoz (Mentioned in Despatches and awarded Bt Lt Colonelcy), Salamanca, San Millan and Vittoria (severely wounded and returned to England).

Present at Quatre Bras and Waterloo. Commanded the Light Companies of the Brigade on 16th and 17th June and the 1st Battalion of 95th Foot on 18th June after Colonel Barnard was injured. Towards the end of the day Cameron himself was severely wounded in the throat and it was thought he would die, but he recovered. Awarded two pensions of £200 and £300 per annum. Half pay 1817. CB for Waterloo. Gold Medal for Ciudad Rodrigo, Badajoz and Salamanca. MGS medal for Vimeiro, Corunna, Busaco, Fuentes d'Onoro and Vittoria. 2nd Class Order of St Anne of Russia.

Also served at the Helder 1799 (as a volunteer), Ferrol 1800, Egypt 1801 (severely wounded at Alexandria), Hanover 1805, Baltic 1807, Netherlands 1814–1815 (commanded a Provisional Battalion of 95th. Present at Merxem where he was Mentioned in Despatches). KCB 1838. Colonel 74th Foot 24 Apr 1846. Deputy Governor of St Mawes 1832.

REFERENCE: *Dictionary of National Biography. Gentleman's Magazine, Oct 1850, p. 437. United Service Magazine, Sep 1850, pp. 159–60. Annual Register, 1850, Appx, p. 264.*

CAMERON, Charles
Captain. 3rd (East Kent) Regiment of Foot.
Memorial: Burial Ground, Chinsurah, India. (M.I.)

"SACRED TO THE MEMORY OF / LIEUT – COL CHARLES CAMERON / MAJOR IN HIS MAJESTY'S 3RD REGT OF FOOT (OR BUFFS) / A BRAVE AND DISTINGUISHED OFFICER; / DIED ON THE 15TH MAY 1827, AGED 48 / YEARS. / THIS TABLET IS ERECTED BY HIS BROTHER – OFFICERS AS A / MARK OF THEIR ESTEEM."

Lt 92nd Foot 15 Jun 1799. Lt 3rd Foot 12 Apr 1800. Capt 1 Dec 1804. Bt Major 22 Nov 1813. Bt Lt Colonel 21 Jan 1819. Major 3rd Foot 23 May 1826.

Served in the Peninsula Sep 1808 – Apr 1814. Present at Douro (his company was the first to cross the Douro), Talavera, Busaco, Albuera (wounded and taken prisoner, but managed to escape and rejoin his battalion), Vittoria, Pyrenees, Nivelle (wounded), Nive (wounded and Mentioned in Despatches), St Pierre and Garris (wounded). Awarded pension of £100 per annum for all his wounds. Gold Medal for Nivelle and Nive. Regiment arrived too late for Waterloo but took part in the Army of Occupation. Also served at the Helder 1799 (present at Egmont-op-Zee where he was wounded), North America 1814–1815 and India 1826.

CAMERON, Donald
Lieutenant. 79th (Cameron Highlanders) Regiment of Foot.
Named on the Regimental Memorial: St Joseph's Church, Waterloo, Belgium. (Photograph)

Ensign 10 Apr 1806. Lt 13 May 1807.
   Served in the Peninsula 1808 – Jan 1809 and 1810 – Apr 1814. Present at Corunna, Cadiz (wounded), Busaco, Foz d'Arouce, Fuentes d'Onoro, Salamanca, Burgos, Nivelle, Nive and Toulouse (severely wounded). Present at Quatre Bras and Waterloo where he was severely wounded and died of his wounds 21 Jun 1815. Also served at Copenhagen 1807 and Walcheren 1809.

CAMERON, Dugald
1st Lieutenant. 95th Regiment of Foot.
Headstone: Kilmallie Churchyard, Corpach, Invernesshire, Invernesshire, Scotland. (Photograph)

TO THE MEMORY OF / LIEUT DUGᴰ CAMERON OF BARR. / FOR SOMETIME OF THE 92ᴰ AND LATTERLY / OF THE 89ᵀᴴ FOOT, WHO DIED AT BALACHUL – / ISH, ON THE 3ᴰ AUGUST 1846, AGED 77 YEARS / ....

Lt Royal East Middlesex Militia. 2nd Lt 95th Foot 19 Apr 1809. Lt 1 May 1811.
   Served in the Peninsula with 2/95th May 1812 – Sep 1813 and Jan – Apr 1814. Present at Salamanca, San Millan, Vittoria, Pyrenees, Vera, Orthes, Tarbes and Toulouse. Present at Waterloo where he was wounded. Exchanged to half pay of 89th Foot 13 Nov 1817. (Note: incorrectly shown as in the 92nd not 95th Regiment on headstone).

CAMERON, Duncan (Clunes)
Lieutenant. 79th (Cameron Highlanders) Regiment of Foot.
Named on the Memorial: St Andrew's Church, (now Musée Historique), Biarritz, France. (Photograph)

Volunteer 79th Foot. Ensign 79th Foot 19 Jul 1810. Lieutenant 2 Apr 1812.
   Served in the Peninsula Jan 1810 – May 1812 and Nov 1813 – Apr 1814. Present at Cadiz (served as a volunteer during the defence of Cadiz and was appointed Ensign during the operation), Busaco, Foz d'Arouce, Fuentes d'Onoro (wounded), Nivelle, Nive and Toulouse where he was killed. Buried in the same grave in the Citadel at Toulouse as Capt Patrick Purvis, Capt John Cameron and Lt Ewen Cameron, all of the 79th Foot. Brother of Lt Kenneth Cameron 79th Foot.

CAMERON, Ewen (1)
Lieutenant. 79th (Cameron Highlanders) Regiment of Foot.
Ledger stone: Templemore Parish, County Tipperary, Ireland. (Slab broken). (Photograph)

ERECTED / TO THE MEMORY / OF / LIEUT EWEN CAMERON / OF 79ᵀᴴ REGᵀ OF FOOT / WHO DEPARTED THIS LIFE / AT TEMPLEMORE / ON THE 27ᵀᴴ DAY OF FEBʸ 1822 / AGED 31 YEARS. / SINCERELY LAMENTED / BY HIS BROTHER OFFICERS

Volunteer 79th Foot 1808. Ensign 79th Foot 16 Mar 1809. Lt 29 May 1811.

Served in the Peninsula Jan – Dec 1811 and Sep 1813 – Apr 1814. Present at Corunna (as a Volunteer), Foz d'Arouce, Fuentes d'Onoro, Nivelle, Nive, and Toulouse (severely wounded and awarded pension of £70 per annum). Present at Quatre Bras and Waterloo (wounded). Also served in the Baltic 1808, Walcheren 1809 and Ireland 1820. He had been out shooting game while the regiment was in Ireland and was attacked by a crowd at a turnpike. He was so severely injured that he was unable to give evidence before a magistrate, and died from brain fever caused by a blow from a stone.

CAMERON, Ewen (Scamadale) (2)

Lieutenant. 79th (Cameron Highlanders) Regiment of Foot.
Named on the Memorial: St Andrew's Church, (now Musée Historique), Biarritz, France. (Photograph)

Ensign 26 Jul 1810. Lt 1 Oct 1812.

Served in the Peninsula Apr 1812 – Apr 1814. Present at Salamanca, Burgos, Pyrenees, Nivelle, Nive and Toulouse, where he was severely wounded, and died the next day of his wounds on 11 Apr 1814. Buried in the same grave in the Citadel at Toulouse as Capt Patrick Purvis, Capt John Cameron and Lt Duncan Cameron, all of the 79th Foot. Brother of Lt Alexander Cameron 79th Foot who died in Tobago in 1820. Nephew of Colonel Sir Alan Cameron of Erracht who raised the regiment.

CAMERON, Ewen

Lieutenant. 92nd Regiment of Foot.
Table stone: Glen Nevis Burial Ground, Invernesshire, Scotland. (Photograph)

SACRED / TO / THE MEMORY OF / LIEUTENANT EWEN CAMERON / LATE OF THE 92ND REGT OF FOOT / WHO DIED THE 2 JUNE 1831 / IN THE 58TH YEAR OF HIS AGE / GLORIOUSLY REGRETTED. / ERECTED / BY MARGARET McCORMACK / HIS SPOUSE IN TOKEN / OF THE REGARD SHE BEARS TO / HIS MEMORY.

Quartermaster Sgt promoted to Ensign 22 Oct 1812. Lt 16 Sep 1813.

Served in the Peninsula Nov 1812 – Apr 1814. Present at Alba de Tormes, Vittoria, Pyrenees, Nive, Orthes, Aire, Tarbes and Toulouse. Half pay 1814.

CAMERON, Hector

Captain. 9th (East Norfolk) Regiment of Foot.
Memorial tablet: Queen's Chapel of the Savoy, Savoy Hill, Covent Garden, London. (Eastern exterior wall of church). (Photograph)

IN MEMORY OF / LT COLONEL HECTOR CAMERON / 41ST AND 9TH REGIMENTS / SON OF HECTOR CAMERON / OF GLASGOW / AND HIS WIFE JANET MACLEAN OF DRIMMIN / SERVED IN THE PENINSULAR CAMPAIGN / (BREVET MAJORITY AND MENTIONED IN / DESPATCHES FOR THE ACTION AT SAN SEBASTIAN) / BORN GLASGOW 25TH NOV 1777 / DIED AT HOXTON 2ND JAN 1833. / ERECTED BY VERNEY LOVETT CAMERON / ARCHIBALD LOVETT CAMERON / AND OTHER DESCENDANTS

Ensign 41st Foot 11 Oct 1794. Lt 27 Feb 1796. Capt 9th Foot 25 Aug 1804. Bt Major 21 Sep 1813. Bt Lt Colonel 22 Jul 1830.

Served in the Peninsula with 1/9th Aug 1808 – Jan 1809, Mar 1810 – May 1812 and Apr 1813 – Apr 1814. Present at Rolica, Vimeiro, Corunna, Busaco, Fuentes d'Onoro, Osma, Vittoria, San Sebastian (severely wounded and Mentioned in Despatches for the capture of Santa Clara Island 27 Aug 1813 and awarded a Bt Majority), Bidassoa, Nivelle, Nive and Bayonne. Served in France with the Army of Occupation after returning from North America. Also served in the West Indies 1795, North America

1799–1804, Walcheren 1809 and North America 1814. Retired on half pay 14 Aug 1817.
REFERENCE: *Gentleman's Magazine, Apr 1834, p. 444.*

CAMERON, Sir John
Lieutenant Colonel. 9th (East Norfolk) Regiment of Foot.
Buried in Town Church Burial Ground, St Peter Port, Guernsey, Channel Islands. (Burial record)

Ensign 43rd Foot 25 Sep 1787. Lt 30 Sep 1790. Capt 11 Jul 1794. Major 9 Oct 1800. Lt Colonel 7th West India Regt 28 May 1807. Lt Colonel 9th Foot 3 Sep 1807. Bt Colonel 4 Jun 1814. Major General 19 Jul 1821. Lt General 10 Jan 1837.

Served in the Peninsula with 2/9th Aug- Sep 1808 and 1/9th Oct 1808 – Jan 1809, Mar- Dec 1810, Apr 1811 – Aug 1812 and Dec 1812 – Apr 1814. Present at Vimeiro, Corunna, Busaco (Mentioned in Despatches), Fuentes d'Onoro, Badajoz, Salamanca, Osma, Vittoria, San Sebastian (wounded), Bidassoa, Nivelle, Nive and Bayonne. Returned to France Aug 1815 and served with the Army of Occupation. Gold Cross for Vimeiro, Corunna, Busaco, Salamanca, Vittoria, San Sebastian and Nive. KCB 2 Jan 1815. Citation reads 'In consideration of his eminent service and we can honestly assert that there was not a better soldier in any army'. KTS. Also served at Martinique and Guadeloupe 1794 (wounded and taken prisoner for two years), West Indies 1799, Walcheren 1809 and North America 1814–1815. Lt Governor of Plymouth 1818. Colonel 93rd Foot Jul 1832. Colonel 9th Foot 31 May 1833. Died in Guernsey 23 Nov 1844 aged 71 years.
REFERENCE: *Dictionary of National Biography. Royal Military Calendar, Vol 4, pp. 176–80. Gentleman's Magazine, Jan 1845, pp. 97–8. Annual Register, 1844, Appx, pp. 284–5.*

CAMERON, John (Fassiefern)
Lieutenant Colonel. 92nd Regiment of Foot.
Obelisk: Kilmallie Churchyard, Corpach, Invernesshire, Scotland. (Photograph)

SACRED TO THE MEMORY / OF / COLONEL JOHN CAMERON / ELDEST SON OF EWEN CAMERON OF FASSFERN, BARONET. / WHOSE MORTAL REMAINS, / TRANSPORTED FROM THE FIELD OF GLORY WHERE HE DIED, / REST HERE WITH THOSE OF HIS FOREFATHERS. / DURING TWENTY YEARS OF ACTIVE MILITARY SERVICE, / WITH A SPIRIT WHICH KNEW NO FEAR AND SHUNNED NO DANGER, / HE ACCOMPANIED OR LED / IN MARCHES, IN SIEGES, IN BATTLES, / THE GALLANT NINETY SECOND REGIMENT OF / SCOTTISH HIGHLANDERS, / ALWAYS TO HONOUR; ALMOST ALWAYS TO VICTORY: / AND AT LENGTH, / IN THE 42ND YEAR OF HIS AGE, / UPON THE MEMORABLE 16TH DAY OF JUNE 1815, / WAS SLAIN IN COMMAND OF THAT CORPS, / WHILE ACTIVELY CONTRIBUTING TO ACHIEVE THE DECISIVE VICTORY / OF / WATERLOO, / WHICH GAVE PEACE IN EUROPE. / THUS CLOSING HIS MILITARY CAREER / WITH THE LONG AND EVENTFUL STRUGGLE, IN WHICH / HIS SERVICES HAD BEEN SO DISTINGUISHED: / HE DIED LAMENTED / BY THAT UNRIVALLED GENERAL, / TO WHOSE LONG TRAIN OF SUCCESS AND OF VICTORY / HE HAD SO OFTEN CONTRIBUTED; / BY THE COUNTRY / FROM WHICH HE HAD REPEATEDLY RECEIVED MARKS / OF THE HIGHEST CONSIDERATION, / AND / BY HIS SOVEREIGN / WHO GRACED HIS SURVIVING FAMILY / WITH THOSE MARKS OF HONOUR / WHICH COULD NOT FOLLOW, TO THIS PLACE, / HIM WHOSE MERIT / THEY WERE DESIGNED TO COMMEMORATE. / READER, / CALL NOT HIS FATE UNTIMELY, / WHO, THUS HONOURED & LAMENTED, / CLOSED A LIFE OF FAME BY A DEATH OF GLORY.

Ledger stone in walled enclosure: Kilmallie Churchyard, Corpach, Invernesshire, Scotland. (Photograph)

COLONEL / JOHN CAMERON / OF / THE 92ND REGT / WHO FELL / AT / QUATRE BRAS / 1815.

Memorial tablet in walled enclosure: Kilmallie Churchyard, Corpach, Invernesshire, Scotland. (Photograph)

COLONEL / JOHN CAMERON / OF / FASSIEFERN. KTS / 1815.

Memorial monument: Waterloo Cairn, Kinrara, Torr Alvie Hill, Morayshire, Scotland. (On private land). (Photograph)

TO / THE MEMORY OF / SIR ROBERT MACARA / OF /THE 42ND REGIMENT OR, ROYAL HIGH-LANDERS / COLONEL JOHN CAMERON / OF / THE 92ND REGIMENT OR, GORDON HIGHLANDERS / AND / THEIR BRAVE COUNTRYMEN / WHO GLORIOUSLY FELL AT THE BATTLE OF WATERLOO / IN JUNE 1815 / ERECTED BY / THE MOST NOBLE MARQUIS OF HUNTLY / AUGUST / 16TH 1815.

Ensign 26th Foot 12 Apr 1793. Lt in Captain Campbell's Independent Highland Company 1793. Capt 92nd Foot 13 Feb 1794. Major 5 Apr 1801. Bt Lt Colonel 25 Apr 1808. Lt Colonel 23 Jun 1808. Bt Colonel 4 Jun 1814.
    Served in the Peninsula Oct 1810 – Apr 1814 (Commanded 1 Brigade 2nd Division Jun – Jul 1813). Present at Fuentes d'Onoro, Arroyo dos Molinos (wounded and Mentioned in Despatches), Almarez (Mentioned in Despatches), Alba de Tormes (Mentioned in Despatches), Vittoria (took command of the Brigade when Cadogan fell), Pyrenees (wounded 25 Jul at Maya), Nivelle, Nive, Garris (Mentioned in Despatches), Orthes, Aire, Tarbes and Toulouse. Gold Medal for Vittoria, Nive and Orthes. KTS. Awarded CB the day before the battle of Quatre Bras, where he commanded the regiment and was killed 16 Jun. Also served in Gibraltar 1795–1797, Ireland 1798, the Helder 1799 (wounded), Egypt 1801 (present at Alexandria where he was wounded) and Walcheren 1809.
    Colonel Cameron, a born leader of men, used his influence to mould the character of the regiment. He was respected by his officers and revered by his men. He had served in every campaign with the Gordon Highlanders from its formation to Quatre Bras, except for Corunna, where he was in the second Battalion at Athlone. He took command Mar 1809 and soon had the regiment fit for service again after the disaster of Corunna. He was a strict disciplinarian, knowing the importance of discipline and drill to his men in battle. But he also ensured that his men were well looked after.
    Following his wounding at Quatre Bras he was taken back to Waterloo but died during the night. His body was later taken back to Scotland and buried at Kilmallie with thousands in attendance. The monument erected to him there, has an epitaph written by Sir Walter Scott.
    REFERENCE: *Dictionary of National Biography. Clerk, Revd. Archibald, Memoir of Colonel John Cameron, 1858. Mollo, J. and B, Waterloo officers – 2. Colonel John Cameron, Journal of the Society for Army Historical Research, Vol 39, No 158, Jun 1961, pp. 73–4.*

CAMERON, John (1)
Captain. 79th (Cameron Highlanders) Regiment of Foot.
Named on the Regimental Memorial: St Joseph's Church, Waterloo, Belgium. (Photograph)

Ensign 23 Apr 1805. Lt 29 May 1806. Capt 1 Apr 1812.
    Served in the Peninsula Aug 1808 – Jan 1809 and Jan 1810 – May 1812. Present at Corunna, Cadiz, Busaco, Foz d'Arouce and Fuentes d'Onoro. Present at Quatre Bras and Waterloo (severely wounded and died of his wounds). Also served in Sweden 1808 and Walcheren 1809. Son of Major Donald Cameron who also served in the regiment in the Peninsula, Baltic and Walcheren.

CAMERON, John (2)
Captain. 79th (Cameron Highlanders) Regiment of Foot.
Named on the Memorial: St Andrew's Church, (now Musée Historique), Biarritz, France. (Photograph)

Ensign 1805 (promoted from the ranks). Lt 8 Apr 1806. Capt 13 Jan 1814.

Served in the Peninsula Aug 1808 – Apr 1814 (unbroken service). Served with the 1st Battalion Detachments Feb – Sep 1809. Present at Douro, Talavera, Busaco, Fuentes d'Onoro, Salamanca, Burgos, Pyrenees, Nivelle, Nive and Toulouse where he was killed. Buried in the same grave in the Citadel at Toulouse as Capt Patrick Purvis, Lt Duncan Cameron and Lt Ewen Cameron, all of the 79th Foot. Also served at Copenhagen 1807 and Sweden 1808.

CAMERON, John
Lieutenant. 33rd (1st Yorkshire West Riding) Regiment of Foot.
Named on the Regimental Memorial: St Joseph's Church, Waterloo, Belgium. (Photograph)

Ensign 14 May 1812. Lt 9 Feb 1815.

Served at Quatre Bras and Waterloo where he was killed. Also served in the Netherlands 1814–1815.

CAMERON, Kenneth (Clunes)
Lieutenant and Adjutant. 79th (Cameron Highlanders) Regiment of Foot.
Obelisk: Beaverton-Thorah, Ontario, Canada. (Photograph)

IN MEMORY / OF / COLONEL KENNETH CAMERON / FORMERLY / MAJOR IN HER / MAJESTY'S 79TH OR / CAMERON HIGHLANDERS / WHO DIED / JUNE 20, 1872 / AGED 84 YEARS.

Ensign 22 Apr 1805. Lt 10 Apr 1806. Adjutant 21 Feb 1811. Capt 18 May 1814. Half pay 1814. Capt 79th Foot. 15 May 1817. Major 13 Mar 1835.

Served in the Peninsula Aug 1808 – Jan 1809 and Jan 1810 – Apr 1814. Present at Corunna, Cadiz, Busaco, Sobral, Foz d'Arouce, Fuentes d'Onoro, Salamanca, Burgos, Pyrenees, Nivelle, Nive and Toulouse (wounded in capturing the redoubt of Le Tour des Augustins where his brother Duncan was killed). Also served in the Baltic 1807–1808 and Walcheren 1809. MGS medal for Corunna, Busaco, Fuentes d'Onoro, Salamanca, Pyrenees, Nivelle, Nive and Toulouse. Emigrated to Thorah in Canada 1835. Played an important part in the area, setting up a Post Office and educational institutions. Brother of Lt Duncan Cameron (Clunes) 79th Foot who was killed at Toulouse. Retired 7 Aug 1835.
REFERENCE: *Canadian Post, Lindsay, Ontario. Friday 28 Mar 1884.*

CAMERON, Phillips
Lieutenant Colonel. 79th (Cameron Highlanders) Regiment of Foot.
Memorial tablet: Monument near a Church at Villa Formosa, Portugal. (M.I.)

"HERE LIE THE REMAINS / OF / LT COLONEL PHILLIPS CAMERON / OF THE 79TH REGT. OR / CAMERON HIGHLANDERS. / HE COMMANDED / UNDER THE IMMEDIATE EYE OF / LORD WELLINGTON / AT THE GALLANT / AND SUCCESSFUL DEFENCE / FUENTES D'ONORO / ON THE 3RD, 4TH & 5TH DAYS OF MAY 1811 / ON THE LATTER DAY HE FELL / GLORIOUSLY / WHILE CHARGING AT THE HEAD / OF HIS / FAITHFUL HIGHLANDERS. / AE 29."

Ensign 82nd Foot 1793. Lt 91st Foot 1793. Capt-Lieut 79th Foot 1 Jun 1794 aged 12. Capt 6 Jun 1794. Major 3 Sep 1801. Bt Lt Colonel 19 Apr 1804. Lt Colonel 79th Foot, 2nd battalion 25 Mar 1805. Lt Colonel 1st battalion 19 Apr 1806.

Served in the Peninsula Aug 1808 – Jan 1809, Jan – Dec 1810 and Mar – May 1811. Present at Corunna, Cadiz, Busaco, Foz d'Arouce and Fuentes d'Onoro (Mentioned in Despatches, severely wounded and died of his wounds 13 May 1811). Gold Medal for Corunna and Fuentes d'Onoro. Also served at the Helder 1799 (present at Egmont-op-Zee), Ferrol 1800, Egypt 1801 (present at Alexandria, awarded Sultan's Gold Medal), the Baltic 1807–1808 and Walcheren 1809. Eldest son of Major General Alan Cameron of Erracht who raised the regiment in 1794. Phillips Cameron took over command of the regiment in 1810. 'The 2nd

Battalion of the 79th Regiment is commanded by Lt Colonel Cameron, who is a very intelligent officer and is indefatigable in his exertions to promote the good discipline of his Battalion both in the field and in barracks.' (Inspection report 6 Sep 1806). Brother of Capt Ewen Cameron (Erracht) 79th Foot, who was ADC to Major General Cameron at Talavera. Ewen died of fever at Lisbon 15 Apr 1810 brought on by the hardship of the campaign. When Phillips Cameron was mortally wounded at Fuentes d'Onoro his last words were 'this will kill my father to lose two sons in this country'.

CAMERON, Robert
Captain. 35th (Sussex) Regiment of Foot.
Family Memorial: Callart, Fort William, Scotland. (M.I.)

" .... CAPT ROBERT CAMERON, LATE OF THE 35TH REGIMENT OF FOOT DIED AT CALLART 13 JUNE 1822 AGED 46 YEARS. ...."

Ensign Reay Fencibles 28 Oct 1800. Ensign 79th Foot 4 May 1805. Lt 35th Foot 26 Jun 1805. Capt 10 Jun 1813.
    Served at Waterloo in reserve at Hal, siege of Cambrai, Capture of Paris and with the Army of Occupation. Also served in Egypt 1807 (present at Marabout where he was wounded), capture of the Ionian Islands 1810 and the Netherlands 1814–1815. Half pay 1817.

CAMERON, William
Captain. 79th (Cameron Highlanders) Regiment of Foot.
Mural Memorial tablet: Kilmallie Churchyard, Corpach, Invernesshire, Scotland. (Photograph)

IN MEMORY OF / CAPT WILLIAM CAMERON / OF THE 79TH REGT OF FOOT / WHO DIED AT CAMISKY AUGUST 15TH 1836 / AGED 50 YEARS.

Ensign 18 Apr 1805 (promoted from the ranks) Lt 8 Apr 1806. Capt 17 Jun 1813.
    Served in the Peninsula Aug 1808 – Jan 1809 and Jan 1810 – Sep 1813. Present at Corunna, Cadiz, Busaco, Foz d'Arouce, Fuentes d'Onoro, Salamanca, Burgos and Pyrenees. Also served in the Baltic 1808 and Walcheren 1809. Half pay 25 Feb 1816.

CAMPBELL, Adam Gordon
Captain. 26th (Cameronian) Regiment of Foot.
Memorial tablet: St George's Chapel, Windsor, Berkshire. (Low wall on south side of Dean's Cloisters). (Photograph)

SACRED TO THE MEMORY OF LIEU^T COL: ADAM GORDON CAMPBELL / LATE COMMANDING THE XVI FOOT. HE DIED AT WINDSOR / THE XXI OF DECEMBER MDCC-CXLVIII AGED LXV YEARS / UNIVERSALLY BELOVED AND DEEPLY LAMENTED. AFTER XLVII / YEARS ZEALOUS SERVICE.

Ensign 22 Nov 1798. Lt 27 Jun 1800. Capt 13 Jun 1805. Bt Major 12 Aug 1819. Major 13 Jul 1826. Lt Colonel 16th Foot 8 Feb 1834.
    Served in the Peninsula Oct 1808 – Jan 1809 and Jul 1811 – Jun 1812. Present at Corunna. Also served in Egypt 1801 (present at Alexandria) and Walcheren 1809 (present at siege and capture of Flushing). MGS medal for Corunna. Military Knight of Windsor 1848. Died at Windsor 21 Dec 1848.

CAMPBELL, Sir Alexander (Gartsford)
Colonel. York Light Infantry Volunteers.
Floor Memorial tablet: St Mary's Church, Fort St George, Madras, India. (Photograph)

HERE / ARE DEPOSITED THE REMAINS / OF / GENERAL SIR ALEXANDER CAMPBELL / BART AND K.C.B. / COMMANDER-IN-CHIEF OF THE MADRAS ARMY / DIED 11 DECEMBER 1824 / AGED 64 YEARS.

Memorial tablet: St Mary's Church, Fort St George, Madras, India. (Photograph)

NEAR THIS SPOT / LIE THE REMAINS OF / SIR ALEXANDER CAMPBELL BAR^T K.C.B. / COMMANDER IN CHIEF OF THE FORCES / IN THIS PRESIDENCY, / WHO DIED ON THE 11TH OF DECEMBER 1824; / .... / THIS TABLET IS ERECTED BY THEIR GRANDSONS. / SIR ALEXANDER COCKBURN CAMPBELL BAR^T / AND / LIEUT GENERAL GEORGE ALEXANDER MALCOLM C.B.

Ensign 1st Foot 1 Nov 1776. Lt 25 Dec 1778. Capt 97th Foot 13 Apr 1780. Capt 74th Foot 25 Dec 1787. Lt Colonel 4 Dec 1795. Bt Colonel 25 Sep 1803. Colonel York Lt Infantry Volunteers 27 Dec 1809. Major General 25 Jul 1810. Lt General 4 Jun 1814.

Served in the Peninsula Apr 1809 – Nov 1811. (GOC 5th Division Apr – Jun 1809, GOC 4th Division Jun – Jul 1809, Commanded 1 Brigade 4th Division Feb – Oct 1810 and GOC 6th Division Oct 1810 – Nov 1811).

Present at Douro, Talavera (wounded and Mentioned in Despatches), Busaco, Massena's retreat (Mentioned in Despatches), Fuentes d'Onoro (Mentioned in Despatches) and Fuente Guinaldo. Gold Medal for Talavera. KCB 1812. Also served in the siege of Gibraltar 1781–1783, India 1793–1807 (present at Malavelly, Seringapatam, Mysore, Mahratta War 1803. Succeeded Sir Arthur Wellesley as governor of Seringapatam in 1803) and Mauritius and Bourbon 1813–1816. Colonel 80th Foot 28 Dec 1815. Commander in Chief of King's and East India Company's Troops in Madras Dec 1820. Both his two sons were killed with the 74th Foot, one at Assaye and one at Sorauren. Three nephews were also killed. REFERENCE: *Dictionary of National Biography. Gentleman's Magazine, Jun 1825, pp. 564–7.*

CAMPBELL, Alexander
2nd Lieutenant. 95th Regiment of Foot.
Named on the Memorial: St Andrew's Church, (now Musée Historique), Biarritz, France. (Photograph)

2nd Lt 13 May 1812.
Served in the Peninsula with 2/95th Oct 1813. Present at Bidassoa where he was killed 7 Oct 1813.

CAMPBELL, Sir Archibald (Duneavens)
Lieutenant Colonel. 71st (Highland Light Infantry) Regiment of Foot.
Mural Monument: St John the Evangelist Churchyard, Edinburgh, Scotland. (Second bay below the church near the Lothian Road). (Photograph)

THIS TRIED AND TRUE AFFECTION / IS CONSECRATED BY HIS FAMILY / TO THE BELOVED AND HONORABLE MEMORY OF / LIEUTENANT GENERAL SIR ARCHIBALD CAMPBELL, / BART., KCB, KTS, COLONEL 62ND REGIMENT / WHO DIED ON 6th OCTOBER 1843 AGED 74. / HIS SOVEREIGN AND HIS COUNTRY HAVE RECORDED / THEIR REGARD OF THESE SERVICES WHICH EXTENDED / OVER A PERIOD OF 56 YEARS, EMBRACING ALMOST / ALL THE VICTORIES OF THE PENINSULA, / IN WHICH HE BORE A CONSPICUOUS PART, / HIS EARLY SERVICES IN INDIA AND HIS ACHIEVEMENTS / IN THE BURMESE EMPIRE AND VARIOUS PORTIONS / OF THE GLOBE, WHERE THEY WERE EQUALLY DISTINGUISHED / BY MILITARY SKILL, GALLANTRY AND SUCCESS.

Ensign 77th Foot 28 Dec 1787. Lt and Adjutant 26 Apr 1791. Capt 88th 24 May 1799. Major 6th Battalion of Reserve 14 Sep 1804. Major 71st Foot 18 Apr 1805. Lt Colonel 16 Feb 1809. Bt Colonel 4 Jun 1814.

Lt Colonel 38th Foot 9 Aug 1821. Major General 27 May 1825. Lt General 28 Jun 1838. Portuguese Army: Lt Colonel 4th Line 25 Mar 1809. Colonel 24 May 1809. Brigadier 16 Dec 1811.

Served in the Peninsula with 71st Foot Aug 1808 – Jan 1809 and with Portuguese Army Mar 1809 – Jan 1814. Present at Rolica, Vimeiro, Corunna, Busaco, Albuera (Mentioned in Beresford's Despatches), Arroyo dos Molinos, first and second sieges of Badajoz, Vittoria, Pyrenees (Mentioned in Beresford's Despatches), Nivelle (Mentioned in Beresford's Despatches) and Nive (Mentioned in Beresford's Despatches). Gold Cross for Albuera, Vittoria, Pyrenees, Nivelle and Nive. Appointed to help Beresford in the organisation of the Portuguese Army Feb 1809. KCB and KTS. Also served in India (Cannamore 1790, Malavelly 1795 and the siege of Seringapatam 1799), Portugal 1816–1820 (in command of Lisbon Division of the Portuguese Army), Cape of Good Hope 1822, India 1824 (present in the Burmese War in command of the expedition to Rangoon, Kemmendine and Melloon). This was so successful that the East India Company granted him £1,000 per year for life and a Gold Medal. Returned to England 1829 through ill health. Lt Governor of New Brunswick 1831–1837. Colonel 95th Foot 21 Sep 1829, Colonel 77th Foot 23 Dec 1834. Colonel 62nd Foot 13 Feb 1840.
REFERENCE: *Dictionary of National Biography. Gentleman's Magazine, Dec 1843, pp. 653–4. Annual Register, 1843, Appx, pp. 300–1.*

CAMPBELL, Archibald (Inverneil)
Lieutenant Colonel. 6th (1st Warwickshire) Regiment of Foot.
Memorial tablet: Parish Church of St Helier, Jersey, Channel Islands. (Photograph)

IN MEMORY OF HIS EXCELLENCY / MAJOR GENERAL ARCHIBALD CAMPBELL, / OF INVERNEIL, N.B. / COMPANION OF / THE MOST HONOURABLE MILITARY ORDER OF THE BATH, / LIEUTENANT-GOVERNOR AND COMMANDER-IN-CHIEF / IN THIS ISLAND. / HIS ZEALOUS AND ABLE ADMINISTRATION OF THE / GOVERNMENT; HIS GALLANT BEARING AS A SOLDIER / THROUGH A LONG CAREER OF MOST ACTIVE SERVICE, / HIS BENEVOLENCE OF DISPOSITION, AND AMIABLE / MANNERS SECURED FOR HIM THE LOVE AND / ESTEEM OF ALL CLASSES OF SOCIETY. / HE DIED ON THE 12TH OF MAY, 1838, AGED 64 YEARS.

Capt 84th Foot 3 Dec 1794. Capt 94th Foot 16 Jun 1801. Bt Major 1 Jan 1805. Major 84th Foot 14 Feb 1807. Major Royal West India Rangers 29 Oct 1807. Lt Col 4 Ceylon Regt 8 Mar 1810. Lt Col 6th Foot 17 Sep 1812. Bt Colonel 12 Aug 1819. Major General 22 Jul 1830.

Served in the Peninsula with 6th Foot Nov 1812 – Oct 1813 and Feb – Apr 1814. Present at Vittoria, Pyrenees, Bidassoa, Nivelle, Orthes and Bordeaux. Present in France with the Army of Occupation until 1818. Gold Medal for Martinique and Vittoria. CB. Also served in the Cape of Good Hope 1795, India 1805–1806 (present at the siege of Bhurtpore where he was severely wounded in the first assault on the Fort), Martinique 1809, Canada 1814 (present at Fort Erie). Lt Governor and Commander in Chief in Jersey 1835–1838.
REFERENCE: *Gentleman's Magazine, Aug 1838, p. 230.*

CAMPBELL, Archibald
Lieutenant. 5th (Northumberland) Regiment of Foot.
Memorial: Greyfriars Burying Ground, Perth, Scotland. (Block G on west wall). (Photograph)

SACRED TO THE MEMORY / OF / COLONEL ARCHIBALD CAMPBELL / WHO SERVED FIVE CAMPAIGNS OF THE PENINSULAR WAR / IN THE 4TH PORTUGUESE REGT, / AND IN THE 5TH 13TH AND 99TH REGTS OF FOOT / AND DIED ON 18TH JANUARY 1879, IN HIS 89TH YEAR.

Ensign 5th Foot 26 Apr 1810. Lt 29 Jul 1813. Lt 99th Foot 19 Sep 1826. Capt 11 Jun 1829. Bt Major 9 Nov 1846. Bt Lt Colonel 20 Jun 1854. Bt Colonel 26 Oct 1858. Portuguese Army: Lt 4th Line 22 Jul 1810. Capt 28 Jul 1813.

Served in the Peninsula with Portuguese Army Jul 1810 – Apr 1814. Present at Busaco, Torres Vedras, Campo Mayor, Albuera, first and second sieges of Badajoz, Arroyo dos Molinos, Vittoria, Pyrenees (promoted Captain for his bravery on 28 Jul 1813), Pamplona (severely wounded), Nive, Bayonne, Adour, Orthes, Aire and Toulouse. Awarded Gold Cross from the King of Portugal for serving five campaigns with the Portuguese Army. Retired from Portuguese Army 10 Oct 1814. MGS medal for Busaco, Albuera, Vittoria, Pyrenees, Nive, Orthes and Toulouse. Staff Officer of Pensions 1842 for the Perth Division. Half pay 1858.

CAMPBELL, Archibald
Lieutenant. 77th (East Middlesex) Regiment of Foot.
Pedestal tomb: Locksbrook Cemetery, Bath, Somerset. (Top of tomb with inscription in disc laid flat on raised kerb base). (Grave number FK 430). (Photograph)

IN / REMEMBRANCE OF / COLONEL ARCHIBALD CAMPBELL / LATE OF THE 20TH REGT OF FOOT / WHO DIED 28 NOV 1874 / AGED 85 YEARS / ....

Ensign Londonderry Militia 1809. Ensign 77th Foot 7 Mar 1811. Lt 5 Mar 1812. Lt 47th Foot 30 Mar 1826. Lt 2nd Foot 2 Dec 1831. Lt 22nd Foot 23 Nov 1832. Capt 22nd Foot 27 Oct 1837. Capt 76th Foot 15 Feb 1846. Bt Major 11 Nov 1851. Capt 30th Foot 29 Apr 1853. Bt Lt Colonel 11 Mar 1858. Major 20th Foot 23 Apr 1858. Bt Colonel 16 Nov 1860.
Served in the Peninsula with 77th Foot Dec 1812 – Apr 1814. Present at the siege of Bayonne and Sortie from Bayonne. Also served in India, West Indies, Australia, the Mediterranean and with 30th Foot in the Crimea (present at Sebastopol 1855 where he was wounded at the Redan 8 Sep 1855). Awarded medal and clasp and 5th Class of Medjidie. Both his sons were with him in the Crimea in the same regiment. Retired 1861 on full pay with honorary rank of Colonel.
REFERENCE: *Annual Register, 1874, Appx, p. 173.*

CAMPBELL, Archibald Argyle
Major. 42nd (Royal Highland) Regiment of Foot.
Mural memorial tablet: Old Calton Cemetery, Edinburgh (In a mausoleum which backs onto the wall separating the Cemetery from Waverley Railway station. (Photograph)
Buried in Stoke Churchyard, Plymouth, Devon.

THIS / MONUMENT / WAS ERECTED / BY THE OFFICERS OF THE 42D. R. H. R. / TO THE MEMORY / OF / MAJOR ARCHD ARGYLE CAMPBELL / WHO DURING 24 YEARS SERVICE / WAS AN ORNAMENT TO HIS PROFESSION / AND TO THE 42D. REGT/ BY THE OFFICERS AND SOLDIERS / OF WHICH HE WAS REGARDED / AS A BROTHER AND A FATHER / IN HIM WERE UNITED / THE HEROICK VIRTUES OF THE MILITARY CHARACTER / WITH THOSE BENEVO- LENT / AND AMIABLE DISPOSITIONS / WHICH EXCITED / GENERAL ESTEEM AND ADMIRATION / THE HARDSHIPS OF WAR / UNDERMINED HIS / CONSTITUTION / BUT DID NOT SUBDUE HIS SPIRIT / HE FINISHED HIS MILITARY CAREER / IN THE SPANISH PENIN- SULAR / FIGHTING FOR THE OPPRESSED / AND HAVING DISTINGUISHED HIMSELF / AT THE BATTLE OF CORUNNA ON THE 16TH / DIED / AT PLYMOUTH / ON THE 27TH DAY OF / JANUARY 1809 / AGED 40 YEARS.

Ensign 10 Sep 1785. Lt 1791. Capt 1 Sep 1795. Major 9 Jul 1803.
Served in the Peninsula with 1/42nd Aug 1808 – Jan 1809. Present at Corunna (severely wounded). Returned home with regiment but on reaching Plymouth died from his wounds. Also served in Flanders 1794–1795, West Indies 1796–1797, Genoa, Cadiz, Malta 1799–1800 and Egypt 1801 (present at Alexandria where he was wounded).
REFERENCE: *Obit: Courant, (Edinburgh), 6 Feb 1809.*

CAMPBELL, Charles

Major 94th Regiment of Foot.
Low monument with hipped top: Abbey Cemetery, Bath, Somerset. (Photograph)

SACRED / TO THE MEMORY OF / LIEUT^T COLONEL CHARLES CAMPBELL, / FORMERLY OF THE 94TH REGT, OR SCOTCH BRIGADE, / WHO DIED APRIL 17TH 1852.

Ensign 80th Foot 27 Sep 1803. Lt 94th Foot 17 Mar 1804. Capt 14 Jul 1808. Bt Major 12 Apr 1814. Major 16 Feb 1815. Bt Lt Colonel 22 Jul 1830.

Served in the Peninsula Feb – Jul 1810 and Jan 1811 – Apr 1814. (Brigade Major 2 Brigade 3rd Division Jul 1812 – Apr 1814). Present at Cadiz, Redinha, Casal Nova, Foz d'Arouce, Sabugal, Fuentes d'Onoro, second siege of Badajoz, El Bodon, Ciudad Rodrigo, Badajoz, Salamanca, Vittoria, Pyrenees, Nivelle, Nive, Orthes, Vic Bigorre and Toulouse. Also served in India 1803 (present at Asseerghur, Argaum and Gawilghur. Awarded Army of India medal for all three battles). MGS medal for Fuentes d'Onoro, Ciudad Rodrigo, Badajoz, Salamanca, Vittoria, Pyrenees, Nivelle, Nive, Orthes and Toulouse. Retired on half pay 25 Dec 1818.

CAMPBELL, Sir Colin

Captain and Lieutenant Colonel. Coldstream Regiment of Foot Guards.
Memorial tablet: Saint James's Church, Piccadilly, London. (Photograph)

SACRED TO THE MEMORY OF / GENERAL SIR COLIN CAMPBELL / COLONEL OF THE 72ND HIGHLANDERS / KNIGHT COMMANDER / OF THE MOST HONOURABLE ORDER OF THE BATH / KNIGHT OF MARIA THERESA OF AUSTRIA / KNIGHT OF ST GEORGE OF RUSSIA / KNIGHT OF MAXIMILLIAN JOSEPH OF BAVARIA / KNIGHT COMMANDER / OF THE PORTUGUESE ORDER OF THE TOWER AND SWORD / HE WAS THE FIFTH SON OF JOHN CAMPBELL / MELFORT ESQUIRE IN THE COUNTY OF ARGYLE / BORN APRIL 18TH 1776 / DIED JUNE 13TH 1847 / HIS REMAINS ARE INTERRED / IN THE VESTRY VAULT OF THIS CHURCH / ....

Lt Breadalbane Fencibles Feb 1795. Ensign 1st West India Regt 3 Oct 1799. Lt 35th Foot 21 Aug 1801. Lt 78th Foot 23 Feb 1802. Capt 75th Foot 9 Jan 1805. Bt Major 2 Sep 1808. Major 70th Foot 15 Dec 1808. Bt Lt Colonel 3 May 1810. Bt Colonel 4 Jun 1814. Capt and Lt Colonel Coldstream Guards 25 Jul 1814. Lt Colonel 65th Foot 1818. Major General 27 May 1825. Lt General 28 Jun 1838.

Served in the Peninsula Aug – Sep 1808 (ADC to Wellington), Apr 1809 – Jan 1811 (AAG), Mar – Jun 1811 and Apr 1812 – Apr 1814 (AQMG). Present at Rolica, Vimeiro, Douro (Mentioned in Despatches), Talavera, Busaco (wounded), Fuentes d'Onoro, Badajoz, Salamanca, Burgos, Vittoria (Mentioned in Despatches), Pyrenees (Mentioned in Despatches), Nivelle (Mentioned in Despatches), Nive (Mentioned in Despatches) and Toulouse. After Rolica was sent home with the despatches, but hearing the guns at Vimeiro, disembarked in time for the battle and then took both despatches back to London. Gold Cross for Talavera, Busaco, Fuentes d'Onoro, Badajoz, Salamanca, Vittoria, Pyrenees, Nivelle, Nive and Toulouse. KCB. Knight of Maria Theresa, Fourth Class of St George, Knight of Maximilian Joseph, Commander of the Tower and Sword. Present at Waterloo (on Staff as Commandant at Head Quarters until 1818).

Also served in Ireland (Irish Rebellion 1798 with Breadalbane Fencibles), India 1801–1806 (present at Ahmednuggar, Assaye where he was severely wounded and Argaum), Hanover 1806 and Copenhagen 1807 (present at Kiöge). After the war held many overseas appointment, among them Lt Governor of Tobago 1828, Lt Governor of Nova Scotia 1833 and Governor of Ceylon 1840–1847. Colonel 99th Foot 1834. Colonel 72nd Foot 15 Aug 1836. Returned to England from Ceylon in Jun 1847 and died on 13 Jun the same year. He had a long association with Wellington. It began in India at the siege of Ahmednuggar where Wellington was impressed with his bravery. His friendship with Wellington continued to the end.

While Campbell was in Ceylon Wellington wrote to him 'We are both growing old; God knows if we shall ever meet again. Happen what may; I shall never forget our first meeting under the walls of Ahmednuggar'.
REFERENCE: *Dictionary of National Biography. Dictionary of Canadian Biography. Gentleman's Magazine, Aug 1847, p. 207.*

CAMPBELL, Colin (Later Lord Clyde)
Captain. 60th (Royal American) Regiment of Foot.
Floor slab: Westminster Abbey, London. [Photograph]

BENEATH THIS STONE / REST THE REMAINS OF / COLIN CAMPBELL LORD CLYDE / WHO BY HIS OWN DESERTS / THROUGH FIFTY YEARS OF ARDUOUS SERVICE / FROM THE EARLIEST BATTLES IN THE PENINSULA WAR / TO THE PACIFICATION OF INDIA IN 1858 / ROSE TO THE RANK OF FIELD MARSHAL AND THE PEERAGE / HE DIED LAMENTED / BY THE QUEEN THE ARMY AND THE PEOPLE / AUGUST 14TH 1863 / IN THE 71ST YEAR OF HIS AGE

Statue: Waterloo Place, London. (Photograph)

COLIN CAMPBELL / FIELD MARSHAL LORD CLYDE / BORN 1792 DIED 1863

Statue: George Square, Glasgow, Lanarkshire, Scotland. (Photograph)

FIELD MARSHAL LORD CLYDE / G.C.B: K.S.I. / BORN IN GLASGOW 20 OCTOBER 1792. / THIS MEMORIAL / OF HIS DISTINGUISHED MILITARY SERVICE / IS ERECTED BY / HIS FELLOW CITIZENS / 1867

Stained glass window: Church of the Ascension, Southam, Gloucestershire. (Photograph)

FIELD MARSHAL COLIN LORD CLYDE GCB DIED 1863

Ensign 9th Foot 26 May 1808. Lt 28 Jun 1809. Capt 60th Foot 9 Nov 1813. Major 26 Nov 1825. Lt Colonel 26 Oct 1832. Colonel 98th Foot 23 Dec 1842. Major General 20 Jun 1854. Lt General 4 Jun 1856. General 14 May 1858. Field Marshal 9 Nov 1862.
  Served in the Peninsula with 2/9th Aug – Sep 1808, 1/9th Oct 1808 – Jan 1809, 2/9th 1810 – Dec 1812 and 1/9th Jan – Dec 1813. Present at Vimeiro, Corunna, Tarifa, Barrosa, Tarragona, Osma, Vittoria, San Sebastian (present in the assault on 17 Jul 1813 where he was wounded, Mentioned in Despatches and led the storming party on 25 July) and Bidassoa (wounded 6 Oct 1813 and awarded pension of £100 per annum). MGS medal for Vimeiro, Corunna, Barrosa, Vittoria and San Sebastian.
  Also served at Walcheren 1809, North America 1814–1815 (present at Bladensburg and New Orleans with 60th Foot), China 1842 where he commanded the 98th Foot (present at Chinkiangfoo and Nankin) and India 1848–1849 In the second Sikh War commanded 3rd Division of Army of Punjab, present at Ramnuggar, Chillianwallah (Mentioned in Despatches), Gujerat (wounded and Mentioned in Despatches). KCB 1849. Served again in India 1851–1853 in commanded of Peshawar district (present in action against the Hill Tribes of the area culminating in the action at Isakote where 3,000 men defeated 8,000 of the enemy), Crimea 1854–1856 in command of the Highland Brigade and Highland Division (present at Alma, Balaclava and Sebastopol) and India 1857 as Commander in Chief, appointed 3 Jul 1857 to quell the Mutiny (present at the Relief of Lucknow where he was wounded, Cawnpore and Futteghur). Created Lord Clyde in recognition of his services in India. GCB, Grand Officer of Legion of Honour, Grand Cross of St Maurice and St Lazarus, 1st Class of the Medjidie, the Chinese medal and the Punjab medal. Colonel 93rd Foot 15 Jan 1858 and Colonel Coldstream Guards Jun 1860.
REFERENCE: *Shadwell, Laurence, The life of Colin Campbell, 2 vols, 1881. Roy, J. M., Old Take Care: the story of Field Marshal Sir Colin Campbell, Lord Clyde, 1985. Watson, B., The Great Indian Mutiny:*

Colin Campbell and the campaign at Lucknow, 1991. Dictionary of National Biography (Entered under Campbell). Gentleman's Magazine, Oct 1863, pp. 503–6. (Entered under Clyde). Household Brigade Journal, 1863, pp. 325–6. (Entered under Clyde). Annual Register, 1863, Appx, p. 194–7. (Entered under Clyde).

CAMPBELL, Donald
Major. 79th (Cameron Highlanders) Regiment of Foot.
Headstone: Golf Road Burial Ground, Dornoch, Sutherland, Scotland. (Photograph)

TO THE MEMORY OF / LIEUT. COLONEL DONALD CAMPBELL, / LATE OF THE 79TH OR CAMERON HIGHLANDERS / WITH WHICH DISTINGUISHED REGIMENT / HE SERVED / FROM EGYPT IN 1801 TO TOULOUSE IN 1814. / HE DIED AT CREICH HOUSE, / ON THE 6TH OF DECEMBER 1844, / AGED 69 YEARS. / THIS MONUMENT IS ERECTED TO / COMMEMORATE HIS WORTH AND VIRTUES / HIS GALLANTRY AS A SOLDIER / BY HIS AFFECTIONATE NEPHEW / CAPT WM. CAMPBELL / LATE OF THE 64TH REGT.

Sinclair's Fencibles. Ensign 79th Foot 24 Jul 1800. Lt 22 Oct 1803. Capt 19 Apr 1804. Major 13 Jan 1814. Bt Lt Colonel 22 Jul 1830.
Served in the Peninsula Aug 1808 – Jan 1809 and Jan 1810 – Apr 1814. Present at Corunna, Cadiz, Busaco, Foz d'Arouce, Fuentes d'Onoro, Salamanca, Burgos, Pyrenees, Nivelle, Nive and Toulouse. Also served in Ireland 1798 (present in the Irish Rebellion with Sir John Sinclair's Fencibles), Egypt 1801 (awarded Gold Medal from Sultan for Egyptian campaign), Baltic 1807–1808 and Walcheren 1809. Half pay 25 Feb 1816. Took part in 30 battles, sieges, engagements and minor affairs whilst serving with the Cameron Highlanders but was never wounded. 'A brave and undaunted officer, respected by all who served with him'.
REFERENCE: Gentleman's Magazine, Mar 1845, pp. 313–4. Annual Register, 1844, Appx, p. 289.

CAMPBELL, Dugald (Trishnish)
Captain. 91st Regiment of Foot.
Memorial tablet: St Catherine's Cathedral, Spanish Town, Jamaica. (In church floor). (Photograph)

CAPT D. CAMPBELL, / OF HIS MAJESTY'S. XCI OR / ARGYLLSHIRE, REGIMENT, / DIED, 29TH NOVR 1824. / AGED, 42 YEARS.

Ensign 22 Oct 1801. Lt 9 Aug 1804. Adjutant 14 Apr 1808 – 25 Apr 1810. Capt 23 Nov 1809.
Served in the Peninsula Aug 1808 – Jan 1809 and Jan 1813 – Apr 1814. Present at Rolica, Vimeiro, Cacabellos, Corunna, Pyrenees, Nivelle, Nive, Orthes, Aire and Toulouse. Present at Waterloo in reserve at Hal, the capture of Cambrai and with the Army of Occupation. Also served at Walcheren 1809 and the Netherlands 1813–1814 (present at Bergen-op-Zoom and Antwerp).

CAMPBELL, Dugald
Captain. 92nd Regiment of Foot.
Headstone: Auld Kirk, Ayr, Ayrshire, Scotland. Seriously eroded. (Photograph)

TO THE MEMORY OF / DUGALD CAMPBELL, / MAJOR, 92ND REGT, / WHO DIED IN 1821, AGED 53. / SERVED AT WATERLOO. / THIS WAS ERECTED BY / BARBARA CAMPBELL HIS WIDOW

Private North Fencibles 1788. Sgt Major 1796. Ensign North Fencibles 1796. Ensign 100th Foot 1796. (100th Foot became 92nd Foot Oct 16 1798). Adjutant 92nd Foot Dec 10 1798. Lt 92nd Foot 1800. Capt 13 Jun 1805. Bt Major 11 Jun 1816.
Served in the Peninsula Nov 1810 – Feb 1814. Present at Fuentes d'Onoro, Arroyo dos Molinos, Alba

de Tormes, Vittoria and Pyrenees (severely wounded and awarded pension of £200 per annum). Present at Waterloo where he was wounded. Retired 1816. A very handsome man described as a most superb specimen of the human race.

CAMPBELL, Duncan
Paymaster. 88th (Connaught Rangers) Regiment of Foot.
Memorial tablet: Fortingall Churchyard, Perthshire, Scotland. (In walled enclosure). (Photograph)

ERECTED / TO THE MEMORY OF / CAP. DUNCAN CAMPBELL / FORMERLY PAYMASTER OF THE 88TH REGT / WHO DIED AT PERTH 11 DEC. 1845 / IN THE 84 YEAR OF HIS AGE. / ESTEEMED AND RESPECTED / BY ALL WHO KNEW HIM, / HE ENTERED THE ARMY AS ENSIGN / IN THE 84TH REGT IN 1780, / AND SERVED WITH DISTINGUISHED ZEAL / AND ABILITY IN ALL QUARTERS OF / THE GLOBE, AND WAS ONE OF THE / OFFICERS WHO ACCOMPANIED THE / EXPEDITION UNDER / SIR DAVID BAIRD / FROM BOMBAY TO EGYPT IN 1801. / HE WAS THE ELDEST SON OF / CAP. ARCHIBALD CAMPBELL 12. REGT.

Ensign 84th Foot 1780. Paymaster 88th Foot 21 Mar 1805.
    Served in the Peninsula with 2/88th Jan – Dec 1810. Present at Cadiz. Also served in the Cape of Good Hope 1796, India 1798 and Egypt 1801. Retired in 1810.

CAMPBELL, Frederick
Captain. 94th Regiment of Foot.
Gravestone: Kilkerran Cemetery, Campbell Town, Argyllshire, Scotland. Inscription not recorded.

Ensign 86th Foot 27 Feb 1796. Lt 94th Foot 23 Feb 1800. Capt 85th Foot 21 Dec 1809. Capt 94th Foot 25 Jan 1813.
    Served in the Peninsula with 85th Foot Mar – Oct 1811. Present at Fuentes d' Onoro and second siege of Badajoz. Also served in India 1799 (present at Argaum Nov 1803 where he was wounded). Retired on half pay 25 Dec 1818. Died 31 Oct 1829.

CAMPBELL, Sir Guy
Major. 6th (1st Warwickshire) Regiment of Foot.
Low monument: Arbour Hill Cemetery, Dublin, Ireland. (Photograph)

MAJOR GENERAL / SIR GUY CAMPBELL BART. C.B. / COLONEL OF THE 3RD WEST INDIA REGIMENT / AND IN COMMAND OF THE / WESTERN DISTRICT / OF IRELAND. / DIED JAN 27TH 1849 / AGED 64 YEARS

Ensign 9 Dec 1794. Lt 4 Apr 1796. Capt 14 Sep 1804. Major 1 Apr 1813. Bt Lt Colonel 26 Aug 1813. Colonel 22 Jul 1830. Major General 23 Nov 1841.
    Served in the Peninsula Aug 1808 – Jan 1809 and Mar – Oct 1813. Present at Rolica, Vimeiro, Corunna, Vittoria and Pyrenees (wounded at Echalar 2 Aug 1813 and awarded Bt Lt Colonelcy). Gold Medal for the Pyrenees where he commanded the regiment. MGS medal for Rolica, Vimeiro and Vittoria. CB. Present at Quatre Bras and Waterloo (on Staff as AAG). Also served in Ireland (DQMG Jul 1830). Colonel 3rd West India Regt 24 Oct 1847. Educated at Eton. Eldest son of Sir Colin Campbell, Governor of Gibraltar, Colonel 6th Foot who died 1814.
REFERENCE: *Dictionary of National Biography. Gentleman's Magazine, Apr 1849, p. 426. Annual Register, 1849, Appx, pp. 218–9.*

CAMPBELL, Sir Henry Frederick
Third Major. 1st Regiment of Foot Guards.
Memorial: Royal Military Chapel, Wellington Barracks, London. (M.I.) (Destroyed by a Flying Bomb 1944)

"IN MEMORY OF LIEUT.-COLONEL ALEXANDER CAMPBELL AND GENERAL SIR HENRY FREDERICK CAMPBELL, K.C.B., G.C.H. LIEUT.-COLONEL CAMPBELL SERVED IN THE 3RD GUARDS, 1755–1773. SIR H. F. CAMPBELL, HIS SON JOINED THE 1ST GUARDS IN 1786, AND SERVED IN THE CAMPAIGNS IN HOLLAND IN 1793–94, AND THE EXPEDITION TO SICILY, 1806–7. HE COMMANDED THE 2ND BRIGADE OF GUARDS AT THE PASSAGE OF THE DOURO, AT THE BATTLE OF TALAVERA WHEN HE WAS SEVERELY WOUNDED IN THE FACE, AT THE BATTLE OF BUSACO, IN THE PURSUIT OF THE FRENCH FROM BEFORE THE LINES OF TORRES VEDRAS, AT THE BATTLE OF FUENTES D'ONOR, AND AT THE CAPTURE OF CUIDAD RODRIGO AND OF BADAJOS. HE COMMANDED A DIVISION AT THE BATTLE OF SALA-MANCA, AND AT THE SIEGE OF BURGOS. HE WAS REMOVED FROM THE REGIMENT IN JULY, 1814. PLACED BY HIS SON, COLONEL GEORGE H. F. CAMPBELL, WHO SERVED IN THE GRENADIER GUARDS FROM 1830 TO 1842".

Ensign 20 Sep 1786. Lt and Capt 25 Apr 1793. Capt and Lt Colonel 6 Apr 1796. Bt Colonel 23 Sep 1803. Major General 25 Jul 1810. 3rd Major 31 Oct 1813. Lt General 4 Jun 1814. General 10 Jan 1837.
    Served in the Peninsula Apr 1809 – Jul 1809, Jun 1811 – Jun 1812 (Commanded 1 Brigade 1st Division) and Jul – Oct 1812 (GOC 1st Division). Present at Douro, Talavera (severely wounded), Ciudad Rodrigo (Mentioned in Despatches), Salamanca and Burgos. Gold Medal for Talavera and Salamanca. KCB. GCH. Also served in Flanders 1793–1794 (present at Boxtel) and Sicily 1806–1807. Colonel 88th Foot 16 Jan 1824. Colonel 25th Foot 20 Oct 1831.
REFERENCE: *Royal Military Calendar, Vol 2, p. 410.*

CAMPBELL, Sir James (Craignish)
Captain. 79th (Cameron Highlanders) Regiment of Foot.
Interred in Catacomb B (v78 c9) Kensal Green Cemetery, London.

Ensign 91st Foot 17 Sep 1803. Lt 25 Aug 1804. Capt 31 Mar 1808. Capt 79th Foot 2 Jul 1812. Major 3 Jun 1819. Lt Colonel (unattached) 10 Jul 1824. Lt Colonel 95th Foot 27 Sep 1831. Bt Colonel 28 Jun 1838, Major General 11 Nov 1851.
    Served in the Peninsula Aug 1808 – Jan 1809. Present at Rolica and Vimeiro. MGS medal for Rolica and Vimeiro. KH. Also served in Ireland 1798 (present in the Irish Rebellion, where he was wounded at Wilson's Hospital), Hanover 1805, Walcheren 1809 and the Netherlands 1815. Commanded the 95th (Derbyshire) Foot for 20 years. Died in London 18 Nov 1853.

CAMPBELL, Sir John
Captain. 7th (Queen's Own) Regiment of Light Dragoons.
Ledger stone: Kensal Green Cemetery, London. (8178/23–24/RS). (Photograph)

.... / ALSO MAJOR GENERAL / SIR JOHN CAMPBELL / KB. KCTS. / BORN 9TH MAY 1780, / DIED 19TH DECEMBER 1863. / CAMPBELL.

Cornet 1800. Lt 1801. Capt 28 Jan 1806. Bt Major 16 Feb 1809. Bt Lt Colonel 3 Oct 1811. Lt Colonel 75th Foot 1820. Portuguese Army: Lt Colonel 4th Cavalry 1809. Colonel 5 Feb 1812. Major General 1825.
    Served in the Peninsula on Staff Aug 1808 – Jan 1809 (DAQMG) and with the Portuguese Army Mar 1809 – Apr 1814. Present at Rolica, Vimeiro, Sahagun, Benevente, Douro, Fuente del Maestre (Mentioned in Beresford's Despatches 3 Jan 1812) and Tarbes (Mentioned in Beresford's Despatches). Appointed by

Beresford to train the Portuguese Cavalry 1809. MGS medal for Rolica, Vimeiro, Sahagun and Benevente. Also served at Cape of Good Hope 1805 and South America 1807 (Brigade Major to General Craufurd's Division, present at Buenos Ayres where he was taken prisoner). At the end of the war in 1814 stayed in Portugal for next six years to organise the Portuguese forces. KB 1815. KTS. Colonel 75th Foot 9 Aug 1821. Retired 1824. Returned to Portugal to support Dom Miguel of the Absolute Party who failed to find support for his cause and so Campbell returned home. Educated at Harrow.
REFERENCE: *Dictionary of National Biography. Gentleman's Magazine, Mar 1864, pp. 389–90.*

CAMPBELL, John
Lieutenant. 44th (East Essex) Regiment of Foot.
Mural memorial: Ford Park Cemetery, Plymouth, Devon. (Photograph)

LIEUT. GEN. CAMPBELL'S / FAMILY VAULT / IN / LOVING MEMORY OF / LIEUT. GENERAL JOHN CAMPBELL, COLONEL / 92ND GORDON HIGHLANDERS, / BORN JULY 19TH 1798; DIED DECEMBER 28TH 1871. / ....

Ensign 44th Foot 23 Jan 1812. Lt 28 Mar 1814. Capt 49th Foot 2 Apr 1818. Major 22 Apr 1826. Bt Lt Colonel 29 Mar 1839. Bt Colonel 11 Nov 1851. Major General 6 Jul 1857. Lt General 4 Jul 1864.
   Present at Quatre Bras (wounded) and Waterloo in Capt T. A. Dudie's Company. Took command of the Light Company when senior officers were wounded. Also served in India 1824 (present in Burma where he served at the capture of Rangoon 11 May 1824 – awarded medal), Canada 1838 (commanded the Beauharnois district during the Canadian Rebellion – promoted to Lt Colonel). Colonel 92nd Foot Mar 1869.
REFERENCE: *The Times, 1 Jan 1872, p. 5.*

CAMPBELL, John
Lieutenant. 48th (Northamptonshire) Regiment of Foot.
Ledger stone shared with Capt George Mackay: Pioneer Memorial Park, Bunnerong Cemetery, Sydney, New South Wales, Australia. (Photograph)

IN THIS TOMB IS DEPOSITED / THE MORTAL PART OF / LIEUT JOHN CAMPBELL 48 REGT / IN RESPECT OF WHOM / THIS MONUMENT IS ERECTED / BY HIS BROTHER OFFICERS. / HE DIED THE 3RD FEBY 1821, / AGED 40 YEARS.

Ensign 8 Oct 1805. Lt 26 Nov 1807.
   Served in the Peninsula Jul 1809 – Apr 1814. Present at Talavera, Busaco, Aldea da Ponte, Ciudad Rodrigo, Badajoz, Salamanca, Vittoria, Pyrenees, Nivelle, Orthes and Toulouse (wounded). Also served in Australia 1817–1821 in the Garrison at Sydney where he died.

CAMPBELL, Neil (Ardnahow)
Captain. 79th (Cameron Highlanders) Regiment of Foot.
Named on the Regimental Memorial: St Joseph's Church, Waterloo, Belgium. (Photograph)

Ensign 78th Foot 17 Apr 1804. Lt 79th Foot 25 Mar 1805. Capt 8 Apr 1806.
   Served in the Peninsula Sep 1811 – Apr 1814. Present at Salamanca, Burgos, Pyrenees, Nivelle, Nive and Toulouse. Present at Quatre Bras (wounded) and Waterloo (severely wounded and died of his wounds in Brussels 17 Jul 1815). After his death his mother was granted a pension of £50 per annum in consideration of his services.

CAMPBELL, Norman
Lieutenant. 71st (Highland Light Infantry) Regiment of Foot.
Buried in Parish Churchyard, St Helier, Jersey, Channel Islands. (Burial register)

Ensign 27 Jun 1811. Lt 14 Apr 1814.
    Served in the Peninsula Dec 1812 – Apr 1814. Present at Vittoria where he was severely wounded. Present at Waterloo. Half pay 25 Dec 1818. Died in Jersey 13 Jul 1836 aged 49.

CAMPBELL, Patrick
Captain. 52nd (Oxfordshire) Light Infantry Regiment of Foot.
Memorial Tablet: St Andrew's Old Parish Church, Hove, Sussex. (Photograph)

TO THE MEMORY OF / A FATHER AND A BROTHER. / TO / Lt COLONEL PATRICK CAMPBELL C. B. / WHO SERVED THROUGHOUT / THE PENINSULAR WAR AND AT WATERLOO / WITH THE 52ND LIGHT INFANTRY, / AND DIED ON THE 31ST MAY 1850 AGED 73. / ………………..

Ensign 53rd Foot 31 Aug 1797. Lt 52nd 1 Mar 1800. Capt 16 Aug 1804. Bt Major 21 Jun 1813. Bt Lt Colonel 22 Jul 1830.
    Served in the Peninsula with 1/52nd Aug 1808 – Jan 1809, Feb 1810 – May 1811 and Aug 1812 – Apr 1814. Present at Corunna, Coa, Busaco, Pombal, Redinha, Casal Nova, Foz d'Arouce, Sabugal (severely wounded, lost sight in his right eye and sent home to England to recover), Vittoria, Pyrenees, Vera (wounded twice leading the regiment), Bidassoa (wounded), Nivelle, Nive, Orthes (wounded), Vic Bigorre, Tarbes and Toulouse. CB and Knight of Charles III (Spain). Gold Medal for Nivelle and Nive. MGS medal for Busaco, Vittoria, Pyrenees, Orthes and Toulouse (also entitled to a clasp for Corunna but he omitted to send in his claim, and so did not receive it). Present at Waterloo. Also served at Ferrol 1800, Sicily 1806–1807 and the Baltic 1808.
REFERENCE: *Gentleman's Magazine, Jul 1850, pp. 93–4. Annual Register, 1850, Appx, p. 232.*

CAMPBELL, Patrick
Captain. Royal Artillery.
Family box tomb: Old Common Cemetery, Southampton, Hampshire. Inscription seriously eroded and not recorded. (HO56 006). (Photograph)

2nd Lt 6 Mar 1795. 1st Lt 3 Oct 1795. Capt-Lieut 20 Mar 1803. Capt 1 Jun 1806. Bt Major 14 Oct 1813. Bt Lt Colonel 1 Jun 1815. Major 5 Jan 1825. Lt Colonel 29 Jul 1825. Bt Colonel 10 Jan 1837. Major General 9 Nov 1846. Lt General 20 Jun 1854. General 28 Nov 1854.
    Served in the Peninsula Jan 1809 – Apr 1814. Present at Talavera (mentioned in General Cuesta's despatches), East Coast of Spain (present at Castalla – mentioned in General Murray's Despatches). Employed on diplomatic missions as well as in command of a Spanish regiment Jan 1809 – Jun 1821. Also served in the West Indies 1796 (present at the capture of St Lucia and the Caribb War in St Vincent), Gibraltar 1803–1809 and Columbia 1823–1825 on diplomatic missions. Retired on full pay 11 Nov 1836. Died in Southampton 29 Aug 1857.

CAMPBELL, Thomas Dundas
Major. 50th (West Kent) Regiment of Foot.
Interred in Catacomb B (5947 v100 c3) Kensal Green Cemetery, London.

Ensign 82nd Foot 28 Nov 1794. Lt 31 Dec 1795. Lt 12th Foot 18 Aug 1796. Lt 36th Foot 8 Jan 1798. Capt 50th Foot 3 Aug 1804. Major 13 Jun 1811. Bt Lt Colonel 12 Aug 1819.
    Served in the Peninsula Sep 1810 – Dec 1813. Present at Fuentes d'Onoro, Arroyo dos Molinos,

Almarez, Alba de Tormes, Vittoria and Pyrenees. Also served in Sicily 1809 (ADC to Major General Campbell). Buried in Kensal Green 11 Feb 1846.

CAMPBELL, William
Captain. 23rd (Royal Welch Fusiliers) Regiment of Foot.
Ledger stone: Kensal Green Cemetery, London. (8178/23–24/RS). (Photograph)

ELISABETH UDEA / WIFE OF / WILLIAM CAMPBELL C B. / DIED MAY 1849 / ALSO THE SAID / MAJOR GENERAL / DIED 3RD JUNE 1852

Cornet 7th Lt Dragoons 4 May 1804. Lt 18 Apr 1805. Capt 23 Jun 1808. Capt 23rd Foot 15 Jun 1809. Bt Major 12 Apr 1814. Bt Lt Colonel 18 Jun 1815. Bt Colonel 10 Jan 1837. Major General 9 Nov 1846.
    Served in the Peninsula with 7th Lt Dragoons Nov 1808 – Jan 1809 and 23rd Foot Jul 1809 – Apr 1814 (on Staff as ADC to General Robert Craufurd. Later DAQMG). Present at Corunna, Busaco, Fuentes d'Onoro, Pyrenees, Vittoria, Nivelle, Nive, Orthes and Toulouse. Present at Waterloo as AQMG. Awarded CB and Bt Lt Colonelcy, Russian Order of St Anne 2nd Class. MGS medal for Busaco, Fuentes d'Onoro, Pyrenees, Vittoria, Nivelle, Nive, Orthes and Toulouse. Half pay 25 Oct 1821.

CAMPBELL, William M.
Lieutenant. 71st (Highland Light Infantry) Regiment of Foot.
Named on the Memorial: St Andrew's Church, (now Musée Historique), Biarritz, France. (Photograph)

Ensign 25 Oct 1807. Lt 22 Jun 1809.
    Served in the Peninsula Aug 1808 – Jan 1809 and May 1811 – Dec 1813. Present at Rolica, Vimeiro (wounded), Corunna, Arroyo dos Molinos, Almarez, Vittoria, Pyrenees and Nive where he was killed 13 Dec 1813.

CAMPION, William
Private. 3rd Regiment of Foot Guards.
Headstone: St Michael and All Angels Churchyard, Bassingham, Lincolnshire. Inscription seriously eroded and recorded from memorial inscription. (Photograph)

WILLIAM CAMPION / ALSO HIS WIFE / ANNA CAMPION

Served in the Peninsula Apr 1810 – Apr 1814. Present at Busaco, Fuentes d'Onoro, Ciudad Rodrigo, Salamanca, Vittoria, Nivelle and Nive. MGS for Busaco, Fuentes d'Onoro, Ciudad Rodrigo, Salamanca, Vittoria, Nivelle and Nive. Died at Bassingham 15 Dec 1864 aged 77.

CANCH, Thomas
Lieutenant. 5th (Northumberland) Regiment of Foot.
Monument: Dean Cemetery, Edinburgh, Scotland. (Grave number F – 695). (Photograph)

THIS MONUMENT HAS BEEN ERECTED / BY THE OFFICERS OF THE GARRISON AND OTHER FRIENDS / TO MARK THEIR RESPECT FOR THE MEMORY OF / MAJOR THOMAS CANCH, / FORT-MAJOR, EDINBURGH CASTLE, / OB. 19 FEB 1850. AET 69. / THE MILITARY ACTS OF THIS GALLANT OFFICER / ARE RECORDED IN THE HISTORY OF HIS COUNTRY. / IN HIS PRIVATE CHARACTER WERE UNITED THE ZEAL / OF THE SOLDIER AND THE PIETY OF THE CHRISTIAN. / ROLICIA. VIMEIRO. TALAVERA. BUSACO. FUENTES D'ONORO. CIUDAD RODRIGO. / BADAJOZ. SALAMANCA. NIVELLE. NIVE. ORTHES. TOULOUSE.

Volunteer Aug 1808. Ensign 28 Sep 1809. Adjutant 26 Mar 1812. Lt 13 May 1813. Capt 2 Nov 1830. Bt Major 30 Jul 1847.

Served in the Peninsula with 2/5th Aug 1808 – Dec 1812 and 1/5th Nov 1813 – Apr 1814. Present at Rolica, Vimeiro, Talavera, Busaco, Pombal, Redinha, Casal Nova, Foz d'Arouce, Sabugal (wounded), Fuentes d'Onoro, second siege of Badajoz, El Bodon, Aldea da Ponte, Ciudad Rodrigo (carried colours and was wounded), Badajoz (carried colours and led the attack on the castle. Major Ridge and Canch led their men up the ladders to the parapet of the castle. After the capture of the castle, Ridge was killed at the head of his men whilst attempting to take the town, but Canch survived), Salamanca, Nivelle, Nive, Adour, Orthes, Vic Bigorre and Toulouse. Served in France with the Army of Occupation until Nov 1818. Also served in North America 1814 (present at Plattsburg) and West Indies 1819–1826. Fort Major at Edinburgh Castle and Inspecting Field Officer of Recruiting Districts 21 Feb 1840. MGS medal for Rolica, Vimeiro, Talavera, Busaco, Fuentes d'Onoro, Ciudad Rodrigo, Badajoz, Salamanca, Nivelle, Nive, Orthes and Toulouse.

REFERENCE: *Gentleman's Magazine, Apr 1850, p. 455. Annual Register, 1850, Appx, p. 211.*

CANN, John
Private. 28th (North Gloucestershire) Regiment of Foot.
Headstone: St John the Baptist Churchyard, Bradworthy, Devon. (Photograph)

IN / MEMORY OF / JOHN CANN / OF THIS PARISH / LATE OF THE 28TH REGT / FOOT, HE SERVED WITH / HIS REGIMENT, AT CORUN – / NA, THROUGH THE PENIN – / SULAR WAR, AND ALSO AT / WATERLOO, FOR WHICH HE / RECEIVED THE MEDAL. / HE DIED ON THE 23RD / AUGUST 1873. / AGED 101 YEARS / HAVING FOUGHT THE / GOOD FIGHT OF FAITH / AS A GOOD SOLDIER.

Pte 4 Aug 1803.
Served in the Peninsula. Present at Vittoria where he was wounded. MGS medal for Vittoria. Discharged 3 Aug 1814 as unfit for service. Was 101 years old when he died in 1873.

CANNING, Charles Fox
Captain and Lieutenant Colonel. 3rd Regiment of Foot Guards.
Memorial tablet: St Joseph's Church, Waterloo, Belgium. (Photograph)

SACRED TO / LIEUTENANT COLONEL CHARLES FOX CANNING, / LATE CAPTAIN IN HIS BRITANNIC MAJESTY'S 3RD REGIMENT OF FOOT GUARDS, / AND AIDE DE CAMP TO HIS GRACE THE DUKE OF WELLINGTON, / WHO, AFTER HAVING SERVED BY THE SIDE OF THAT ILLUSTRIOUS COMMANDER / IN PORTUGAL, SPAIN AND FRANCE, / THROUGH SEVERAL SUCCESSFUL AND MOST MEMORABLE CAMPAIGNS, / WAS KILLED ON THE 18TH DAY OF JUNE 1815, AT THE BATTLE OF WATERLOO, / BY A SHOT FROM THE ENEMY'S LINE, WHILE ENGAGED IN THE ZEALOUS DISCHARGE OF HIS DUTY. / HE EXPIRED IN THE 33RD YEAR OF HIS AGE. / HIS BODY WAS BURIED ON THE SPOT WHERE HE FELL. / OF TEMPER MILD, WITH KIND AFFECTIONS WARM'D, / FOR LIFE'S MORE PEACEFUL WALK BY NATURE FORM'D, / RUDE WAS THE SHOCK HIS GENTLE HEART WITHSTOOD, / WHEN FIRST BY DUTY CALL'D TO FIELDS OF BLOOD: / BUT ONCE IN ARMS, ALL FONDER THOUGHTS REPRESS'D, / THE SOLDIER'S SPIRIT MOUNTED IN HIS BREAST: / NEAR HIS GREAT CHIEF, ON MANY A TRYING DAY, / HE BRAV'D EACH PERIL OF THE DEADLY FRAY, / AND WHEN ON WATERLOO'S ENSANGUIN'D PLAIN, / HE FELL IN GLORY MIDS'T THE GLORIOUS SLAIN, / UNMOV'D BY AUGHT TO SELFISH MINDS ALLIED. / "THANKS HEAVENS! MY LEADER LIVES", HE SAID AND DIED.

Named on Memorial Panel VIII for Waterloo: Royal Military Chapel, Wellington Barracks, London. (M.I.) (Destroyed by a Flying Bomb 1944)

Named on the Regimental Memorial: St Joseph's Church, Waterloo, Belgium. (Photograph)

Ensign 29 Dec 1803. Lt and Capt 25 Dec 1807. Bt Major 27 Apr 1812. Bt Lt Colonel 19 Aug 1813. Capt and Lt Colonel 21 Mar 1814.

Served in the Peninsula May 1809 – Apr 1814 (Acting Brigade Major 3rd Brigade of Guards Jan – Mar 1809 and ADC to Wellington Apr 1809 – Apr 1814). Present at Talavera, Busaco, Fuentes d'Onoro, second siege of Badajoz, Ciudad Rodrigo, Badajoz, Salamanca, Burgos, Vittoria, Pyrenees, Bidassoa, Nivelle, Nive, Orthes and Toulouse. Gold Cross for Nivelle, Nive, Orthes and Toulouse. Present at Waterloo as ADC to Wellington, where he was killed whilst carrying a message from the Duke to rally the Brunswick troops. Also served in Copenhagen 1807 and Netherlands Jul 1814.

CANNON, William
Lieutenant. 94th Regiment of Foot.
Monument: St Michael's Churchyard, Dumfries, Dumfriesshire, Scotland. (Photograph)

SACRED / TO THE MEMORY OF / MAJOR WILLIAM CANNON, WHO DIED AT / CORBERRY PLACE ON THE 15TH NOVEMBER / 1851, AGED 69 YEARS. / YOUNGEST SON OF THE LATE JOHN CANNON / ESQR. OF BALOCHAN, GALLOWAY. MAJOR CANNON / SERVED WITH DISTINCTION IN THE OLD 94TH / REGIMENT DURING THE PENINSULAR WAR / FROM 1808 TO 1818, FOR WHICH HE RECEIVED / THE WAR MEDAL AND 7 CLASPS. HE AGAIN / SERVED IN THE 97TH REGT. FROM 1824 – 1842 / WHEN HE RETIRED FROM THE SERVICE.

Ensign 26 Aug 1807. Lt 7 Jun 1810. Lt 97th Foot 25 Mar 1824. Capt 7 Apr 1825. Bt Major 28 Jun 1838. Major 97th Foot 26 Oct 1841.

Served in the Peninsula Feb 1810 – Apr 1814. Present at Cadiz (Mentioned in Despatches by Sir Thomas Graham for his conduct at the siege of Fort Matagorda), Redinha, Casal Nova, Foz d'Arouce, Sabugal, Fuentes d'Onoro, second siege of Badajoz, El Bodon, Ciudad Rodrigo (wounded), Salamanca, Vittoria, (wounded), Pyrenees, Orthes, Vic Bigorre and Toulouse. Also served in Ceylon 1825–1830. Retired on full pay 27 Sep 1842. MGS medal for Fuentes d'Onoro, Ciudad Rodrigo, Salamanca, Vittoria, Pyrenees, Orthes and Toulouse. Died at Maxwelltown, Dumfriesshire 15 Nov 1851.

CAPEL, Daniel
Captain. 14th (Duchess of York's Own) Regiment of Light Dragoons.
Ledger stone: St Mary's Churchyard, Prestbury, Cheltenham, Gloucestershire. (Photograph)

IN MEMORY OF / DANIEL CAPEL / LATE CAPTAIN / IN THE 14TH LIGHT DRAGOONS / FOURTH SON OF WILLIAM / AND SUSAN CAPEL / OF PRESTBURY / DIED MARCH 16TH 1834 / AGED 48 YEARS

Cornet 20 Oct 1803. Lt Jan 24 Jan 1805. Capt 8 Mar 1810.

Served in the Peninsula Dec 1808 – Apr 1813. Present at Douro, Talavera, Sexmiro, Coa, Busaco, Sobral, Pombal, Redinha, Casal Nova, Foz d'Arouce, Sabugal, Fuentes d'Onoro, El Bodon, Badajoz, Llerena, Castrejon and Salamanca. Retired on half pay 1820.

CAPEL, Thomas
Captain. 43rd (Monmouthshire) Light Infantry Regiment of Foot.
Named on the Memorial: St Andrew's Church, (now Musée Historique), Biarritz, France. (Photograph)

Ensign 20 Feb 1806. Lt 11 Dec 1806. Capt 1 Jul 1813.

Served in the Peninsula with 2/43rd Aug 1808 – Jan 1809 and 1/43rd Jul 1809 – Aug 1812 and Apr – Nov 1813. Present at Vimeiro, Corunna, Coa, Sabugal, Busaco, Fuentes d'Onoro, Ciudad Rodrigo and Badajoz (severely wounded), Vittoria, Pyrenees, Bidassoa and Nivelle where he was killed 10 Nov 1813.

CAPEL, Hon. Thomas Edward
Captain and Lieutenant Colonel. 1st Regiment of Foot Guards.
Low monument: Kensal Green Cemetery, London. (10750/77/IC). (Photograph)

SACRED TO THE MEMORY OF / GENL THE HONOURABLE THOMAS EDWARD CAPEL / SON OF WILLIAM ANNE HOLLES 4TH EARL OF ESSEX / BORN MARCH 24TH 1770 / DIED FEBRUARY 3RD 1855

Ensign 26 Apr 1793. Lt and Capt 4 Oct 1794. Capt and Lt Colonel 25 Jun 1803. Bt Colonel 1 Jan 1812. Major General 4 Jun 1814. Lt General 29 Jul 1830. General 9 Nov 1846.

Served in the Peninsula with 3rd Battalion Oct 1808 – Jan 1809 and Jul 1811 – Apr 1814. (Sep 1811 – Jun 1813 AAG, Jul 1813 – Apr 1814 GOC at Cadiz). Present at Corunna, Cadiz and Tarifa. MGS medal for Corunna. Also served in Flanders 1794.
REFERENCE: *Gentleman's Magazine, Mar 1855, p. 305.*

CARADOC, John Francis see CRADOCK, Lord John Francis

CAREY, Octavius
Major. 10th (Lincolnshire) Regiment of Foot.
Buried in Family vault: St Mary-Abchurch Church, London.
Memorial tablet: Town Church, St Peter Port, Guernsey, Channel Islands. (Photograph)

IN MEMORY OF / MAJOR GENERAL SIR OCTAVIUS CAREY, C.B. K.C.H. / (EIGHTH SON OF THE LATE JOHN CAREY ESQ. / A MUCH RESPECTED JURAT OF THE ROYAL COURT OF THIS ISLAND) / HE SERVED WITH DISTINCTION DURING THE LATE WAR ON THE / EASTERN COAST OF SPAIN, AND CLOSED AN HONOURABLE CAREER / OF 44 YEARS SERVICE WHILE IN COMMAND OF THE CORK DISTRICT / ON THE 13TH OF MARCH 1844, AGED 58. / HIS REMAINS ARE DEPOSITED IN THE SAME VAULT WITH / THOSE OF HIS MOTHER IN THE PARISH CHURCH OF SAINT / MARY-ABCHURCH IN THE CITY OF LONDON.

Lt 3rd Dragoons 26 Jun 1801. Capt 10th Foot 27 Aug 1804. Major 2 Nov 1809. Bt Lt Colonel 30 Sep 1811. Major 62nd Foot 13 Jun 1816. Major 57th Foot 2 Jul 1818. Lt Colonel 30 Sep 1819. Bt Colonel 27 May 1825. Major General 10 Jan 1837.

Served in the Peninsula Aug 1812 – Apr 1814 attached to the Calabrian Free Corps. Present at Alcoy, Biar, Castalla, Tarragona, Ordal, Mollina del Rey and Barcelona. Also served in Scylla 1809 and Ireland (in command of the Cork district). KCB and KCH. Knighted 4 Aug 1830.
REFERENCE: *Gentleman's Magazine, Jul 1844, p. 92. Annual Register, 1844, Appx, pp. 221–2. United Service Magazine, Apr 1844, pp. 639–40.*

CARGILL, William
Captain. 74th (Highland) Regiment of Foot.
Monument: South Cemetery, Dunedin, New Zealand. (Photograph)

IN MEMORY / OF / WILLIAM CARGILL ESQ / FORMERLY A CAPTAIN / IN THE 74TH HIGH-LANDERS, / FOUNDER OF THE SETTLEMENT / AND FIRST SUPERINTENDENT OF THE / PROVINCE OF OTAGO, / WHERE HE LANDED 23RD MARCH 1848 / AND DIED 6TH AUGUST 1860,

/ AETAT 76. / HERE ALSO BY HIS SIDE / LIE THE REMAINS OF / MARY ANN YATES / HIS WIFE FOR 45 YEARS / WHO SURVIVED HIM BY 11 YEARS, / AND DIED 25TH OCTOBER 1871 / AETAT 81 / ....

Ensign 84th Foot 1802. Lt 74th Foot 23 Sep 1803. Capt 31 Dec 1812.
    Served in the Peninsula Feb 1810 – Jun 1811 and Sep 1812 – Apr 1814. Present at Busaco (severely wounded), Vittoria, Pyrenees, Nivelle, Nive, Orthes, Vic Bigorre, Tarbes and Toulouse. Also served in India 1803–1805 (present in the Mahratta wars). MGS medal for Busaco, Vittoria, Pyrenees, Nivelle, Nive, Orthes and Toulouse. Retired by the sale of his commission in 1820 and became a wine merchant in Edinburgh until 1834. In 1841 joined a London bank and considered emigration owing to his financial difficulties. Sailed for New Zealand to establish a Scottish settlement at Otago 1847. By 1853 had been elected Foundation Superintendent of the Province but was autocratic and inflexible and inclined to nepotism (he had 11 children surviving out of the original 17). By the time he died in 1860 Otago had the makings of a successful settlement.
REFERENCE: *Dictionary of New Zealand Biography.*

CARLETON, Hon Dudley
Captain. 4th (Queen's Own) Regiment of Dragoons.
Family Memorial tablet: St Swithun's Church, Nateley Scures, Hampshire. (M.I.)

"DUDLEY CARLETON 1790 – 1820. CAPT 4TH DRAGOONS."

Cornet 16 Jun 1804. Lt 9 Jan 1806. Capt 10 Oct 1811.
    Served in the Peninsula Apr 1809 – Feb 1811 and Jul – Sep 1811. Present at Busaco. Retired Apr 1814. Son of General Sir Guy Carleton who fought in the American War of Independence and brother of the Hon. George Carleton Lt Colonel 44th Foot.

CARLETON, Hon George
Lieutenant Colonel. 44th (East Essex) Regiment of Foot.
Family Memorial tablet: St Swithun's Church, Nateley Scures, Hampshire. (M.I.)

"GEORGE CARLETON 1781 – 1814. WOUNDED AT BADAJOZ. SLAIN AT BERGEN-OP-ZOOM."

Ensign 9th Foot 14 Jul 1798. Lt 27 Nov 1798. Capt 22 Jul 1800. Capt 60th Foot 19 Mar 1803. Capt 9th Foot 19 Jul 1803. Major 40th Foot 22 Oct 1805. Major 27th Foot 29 Oct 1805. Bt Lt Colonel 28 Jan 1808. Lt Colonel 44th Foot 22 Aug 1811.
    Served in the Peninsula Dec 1811 – Apr 1812. Present at Badajoz (wounded in command of 44th Foot). Gold Medal for Badajoz. Also served in Canada 1808 (Inspecting Field Officer of Militia), Netherlands 1814 (present at Bergen-op-Zoom where he commanded 44th Foot and was killed 8 Mar 1814. 200 of his 350 men were killed or wounded). Son of General Sir Guy Carleton who fought in the American War of Independence and brother of Capt Hon. Dudley Carleton 4th Dragoons.

CARMICHAEL, Alexander
Lieutenant. 1st Line Battalion, King's German Legion.
Gravestone: Old Protestant Cemetery, Naples, Italy. (M.I.)

"ALEXANDER CARMICHAEL DIED 6TH JANUARY 1854, AGED 68 YEARS. CAPTAIN .... "

Ensign 1st Line King's German Legion 20 May 1813. Lt 6 May 1814. Lt 97th Foot 25 Mar 1824. Capt 30 Dec 1836

Served in the Peninsula Aug 1813 – Apr 1814. Present at Nive, St Etienne and Bayonne. Present at Waterloo with 1st Line K.G.L. Also served in the Netherlands 1814–1815. MGS medal for Nive.

CARMICHAEL, Lewis
Lieutenant. 59th (2nd Nottinghamshire) Regiment of Foot.
Monument: Cromdale Churchyard, Cromdale, Morayshire, Scotland. (Photograph)

LIEUT-COLONEL. LEWIS CARMICHAEL / BORN AT KINRARA, JUNE 26, 1792, / DIED AT FORRES, AUGUST 8, 1844. / ENTERING THE ARMY IN 1809, / AS AN ENSIGN IN THE 59TH REGT. OF FOOT, / HE SERVED HIS COUNTRY 34 YEARS / WITH DISTINGUISHED HONOUR. / AT VITTORIA, SAN SEBASTIAN, NIVELLE, NIVE AND WATERLOO, / HE EARNED THE REPUTA- TION / OF A ZEALOUS AND INTREPID OFFICER; / AND AT THE ASSAULT OF BHURTPORE, / FOR A FEAT OF EXTRAORDINARY VALOUR, / HE WAS OFFICIALLY THANKED / BY THE GENERAL IN COMMAND, / SIR JASPER NICOLLS. / HIS EFFORTS IN CONTRIBUTING TO RESTORE ORDER / IN CANADA DURING THE COMMOTIONS OF 1838, &C., / WERE DULY APPRECIATED AND ACKNOWLEDGED / BY THE LOCAL GOVERNMENT, / AND BY ALL THE WELL-AFFECTED IN THAT COLONY. / AS A MAN HE WAS KIND AND GENEROUS, / DEVOTED TO THE INTERESTS OF HIS COUNTRY, / BELOVED BY HIS COMPANIONS IN ARMS, / AND ESTEEMED BY ALL WHO KNEW HIM. / AFTER A SHORT BUT PAINFUL ILLNESS, / WHICH HE BORE WITH CHRISTIAN SUBMISSION TO THE DIVINE WILL, / HE DIED IN THE HOPE OF A BLESSED RESURRECTION. / THIS MONUMENT / HIS SORROWING SISTERS HAVE ERECTED / TO AN AFFECTIONATE AND LAMENTED BROTHER, / 1845.

Ensign 8 Jun 1809. Lt 7 Mar 1812. Capt 5 Dec 1826. Major 26 Nov 1830. Lt Colonel 29 Mar 1839.
Served in the Peninsula Sep 1812 – Jan 1814. Present at Cadiz, Vittoria, San Sebastian (severely wounded), Nivelle and Nive (severely wounded and awarded pension of £70 per annum). Present at Waterloo in reserve at Hal, siege of Cambrai and with the Army of Occupation. On his return from France with 59th Foot in the *Lord Melville* transport he was involved in the shipwreck at Kinsale where many men were lost from the three transport ships. Owing to his courage and coolness he was able to save nearly all of the regiment on board his ship. Also served in India 1817–1818 (present in the Pindari War), Ceylon (present in the Kandian Rebellion) and India 1824–1826 (ADC to Sir Jasper Nicolls, present at the assault of Bhurtpore with the 59th Foot and one of the first soldiers into the Citadel. Three days before the assault he managed to examine part of the interior defences of the Fort, for which he received official thanks). Became a Major in a Corps raised for a particular service – used during the Canadian Rebellion of 1838. Commanded the regular militia employed in recovering Beauharnais from the rebels 18 Nov 1838. It was at his suggestion that a cairn was erected to Lord Seaton, who was Governor General at the time, on an island in Lake St Francis, Ontario.

CARMICHAEL, Thomas
Ensign. 47th (Lancashire) Regiment of Foot.
Headstone: Glasgow Necropolis (Western Division), Glasgow, Lanarkshire, Scotland. (M.I.)

"ERECTED / TO THE MEMORY OF / THOMAS CARMICHAEL ESQ. LATE / LIEUT. 47TH REGT WHO SAW SERVICE / IN THE PENINSULAR WAR PARTICULARLY / THE NIVE NIVELLE / SIEGE OF CADIZ VITTORIA / BADAJOZ SALAMANCA / WHO DIED AT GLASGOW / AGED 87 YEARS."

Pte 1795. Cpl 1798. Sgt 1802. Sgt Major Oct 1811. Ensign and Acting Adjutant 23 Oct 1813.
Served in the Peninsula with 2/47th 1810–1814. Present at Cadiz, Tarifa, Vittoria, and San Sebastian. Promoted from the ranks and served at Bidassoa, Nivelle, Nive and Bayonne. Retired on half pay in 1814. MGS medal for Vittoria, San Sebastian, Nivelle and Nive. Died 19 Mar 1864.

CARNWATH, 10th Earl see DALZELL, Robert Alexander

CARONDEL, J. C.
1st Lieutenant. 7th Infantry Battalion, Duthc Infnatry.
Named on the Memorial to Dutch officers killed at Waterloo: St Joseph's Church, Waterloo, Belgium. (Photograph)

CARR, James
Major. 76th Regiment of Foot.
Headstone: Brompton Cemetery, London. (BR 1734). (Photograph)

TO THE MEMORY OF / JAMES CARR ESQ. / LATE MAJOR IN H. Mˢ. 76ᵀᴴ REGᵀ OF FOOT / WHO DEPARTED THIS LIFE / THE 11ᵀᴴ DAY OF DECEMBER 1846 / IN THE 68ᵀᴴ YEAR OF HIS AGE. / HE BEGAN HIS MILITARY CAREER / AT A VERY EARLY AGE / IN THE ABOVE REGᵀ AS ENSIGN / AND SERVED WITH MUCH DISTINCTION / IN THE EAST INDIES DURING THE WAR / UNDER LORD LAKE, / AND ON THE REGIMENT'S RETURN / TO EUROPE WAS PRESENT WITH IT / AT WALCHEREN CORUNNA AND BAYONNE.

Ensign 28 Feb 1797. Capt 14 Sep 1804. Major 26 Apr 1810.
　Served in the Peninsula Nov 1808 – Jan 1809 and Aug 1813 – Apr 1814. Present at Corunna, Bidassoa, Nivelle, Nive and Bayonne. Also served in India 1803–1805 and Walcheren 1809. Retired in 1814.

CARR, Stephen
Quartermaster. 87th (Prince of Wales's Own Irish) Regiment of Foot.
Memorial tablet: St Mary's Roman Catholic Church, Newport, Monmouthshire, Wales. (Photograph)

BARROSA / SACRED / TO THE MEMORY OF / STEPHEN CARR, ESQᴿ / QUARTER MASTER / 87ᵀᴴ ROYAL IRISH FUSILIERS, / WHO FOR 44 YEARS / SHARED IN ALL THE GLORIES OF THE REGI-MENT / AT TALAVERA, TARIFA AND AT BARROSA / THROUGHOUT THE CAMPAIGNS OF THE / ILLUSTRIOUS WELLINGTON, / IN SPAIN, PORTUGAL AND FRANCE, / SUBSEQUENTLY / IN THE EAST INDIES, AND IN BURMAH, / AND DIED AT THE AGE OF 62 YEARS / AT NEWPORT, MONMOUTHSHIRE / THE 22ᴺᴰ MAY 1847 / BELOVED AND ESTEEMED BY ALL WHO KNEW HIM, / IN THE HUMBLE HOPE / THAT ZEALOUS AND EVER READY IN ALL HIS DUTIES / WHILE ON EARTH / HE WILL BE FOUND NOT UNPREPARED / FOR THE LAST DREAD TRUMPET / THROUGH THE MERITS OF / A MERCIFUL REDEEMER. / THIS TABLET IS ERECTED TO HIS MEMORY / BY HIS AFFECTIONATE AND BEREAVED WIDOW / JANE CARR / WHO IS LEFT TO DEPLORE HIS LOSS / HIS MORTAL REMAINS INTERRED / IN STOW CHURCH-YARD / REQUI-ESCAT IN PACE / I.H.S.

Quartermaster 24 Jun 1824.
　Served in the Peninsula Mar 1809 – Apr 1814. Present at Douro, Talavera, Cadiz, Barrosa, Tarifa (wounded), Vittoria, Bidassoa, Nivelle, Orthes, Vic Bigorre and Toulouse. Fought with distinction in the Peninsula. Also served in India (present in the Pindari campaign 1817–1818 and the Ava campaign 1824–1826).

CARROL, Sir William Parker
Major. Staff Appointment in Spain and Portugal.
Obelisk: Kilkeary Churchyard, County Tipperary, Ireland. (Photograph)

ERECTED BY Wᴹ HUTCHINSON CARROL / IN MEMORY OF HIS FATHER / Lᵀ GENᴸ SIR Wᴹ PARKER CARROL, / CB. KCH. / WHO DIED AT TULLA HOUSE, / JULY 2ᴺᴰ 1842 / AGED 66 YRS.

/ TORMES ALBUERA PENAFLOR / NAVA DURANGO TAMAMES / BILBAO BAYONNE PAMPLONA / ST PAYO BADAJOZ ASTURIAS

Memorial tablet: Silvermines Church, Parish of Kilmore, County Tipperary, Ireland. (M.I.)

"SACRED TO THE MEMORY LIEUT GENERAL SIR WILLIAM PARKER CARROL, CB, KCH, WHO DEPARTED THIS MORTAL LIFE AT TULLA HOUSE, JULY 2ND 1842, AGED 66."

Ensign 88th Foot Oct 1794. Lt 29 Nov 1794. Capt 13th Regiment of Reserve 9 Jul 1803. Capt 88th Foot 1 Aug 1804. Major 13 Apr 1809. Lt Colonel 18th Foot 30 May 1811. Major General 22 Jul 1830. With Spanish Army: Lt Colonel 1808. Colonel Hibernian Regt 1809. Brigadier General 1810. Major General 1814. Lt General 23 Nov 1841.

Served in the Peninsula Mar 1809 – Apr 1814 with Spanish Army. Present at Bilbao, Durango (wounded), Colombres, Penaflor, St Payo, Tamames, Alba de Tormes (wounded), Carpio, Medina de Campo, first siege of Badajoz, Albuera, coast of Calabria, Pamplona and Adour. Also served in Flanders 1796 and South America 1807 (present at Buenos Ayres), where his knowledge of Spanish was invaluable. Taken prisoner and when Whitelocke was freed to leave the country with the rest of the troops, Capt Carrol offered to stay as a hostage. He was able to rescue other British troops imprisoned further in the mainland, who would have been lost for ever. His knowledge of the language and customs of Spain was again recognised in 1808 and was sent to Spain as a Military Commissioner and remained with the Spanish Army for the whole of the Peninsular War. Gold Medal for Albuera. CB and KCH. Awarded numerous crosses and medals from Spain and the French King.
REFERENCE: *Royal Military Calendar, Volume 4, pp. 346–51. Gentleman's Magazine, Mar 1843, pp. 319–20.*

CARROLL, John
Captain. 28th (North Gloucestershire) Regiment of Foot.
Named on the Memorial: St Andrew's Church, (now Musée Historique), Biarritz, France. (Photograph)

Lt 22 Oct 1803. Capt 17 Mar 1810.
Served in the Peninsula with 1/28th Jul 1808 – Jan 1809 and Mar – Jun 1810, 2/28th Sep 1810 – May 1811 and 1/28th Nov 1813 – Apr 1814. Present at Corunna, Tarifa, Busaco, first siege of Badajoz, Albuera (wounded), Nivelle, Nive, Garris, Orthes and Aire where he was severely wounded 18 Mar 1814 and died his of wounds 7 Apr 1814. Also served at Walcheren 1809.

CART, Richard
Corporal. Royal Regiment of Horse Guards.
Headstone: St David's Churchyard, Welshpool, Montgomeryshire, Wales. (In retaining wall in overgrown and inaccessible area). (M.I.)

"IN MEMORY OF / A BRAVE SOLDIER, AN AFFECTIONATE / HUSBAND AND A GOOD FATHER / RICHARD CART / DEPARTED THIS LIFE ON THE / 6TH NOVEMBER 1846 AGED 59 / HE WAS FORMERLY / QUARTER MASTER / IN THE ROYAL HORSE GUARDS / WITH WHICH REGIMENT HE SERVED / IN THE PENINSULAR AND AT / WATERLOO."

Cpl 1814. Quartermaster 7 Aug 1823.
Served in the Peninsula Nov 1812 – Apr 1814. Present at Vittoria and Toulouse. Served at Waterloo in Capt Thoyt's Troop. Retired on half pay 1 Jan 1831.

CARTWRIGHT, William

Lieutenant. 10th (Prince of Wales's Own) Regiment of Light Dragoons.
Box tomb: St Michael's Churchyard, Aynho, Northamptonshire. (Photograph)

SACRED TO THE MEMORY OF / GENERAL WILLIAM CARTWRIGHT. / HE WAS BORN 28TH FEBRUARY 1797 / AND DEPARTED THIS LIFE IN LONDON / ON THE 5TH JUNE 1873. / PYRE-NEES ORTHES / NIVELLE TOULOUSE / NIVE WATERLOO

Memorial tablet: All Saints Church, Flore, Northamptonshire. (M.I.)

"SACRED TO THE MEMORY OF GENERAL WILLIAM CARTWRIGHT / SECOND SON OF THE LATE WILLIAM RALPH CARTWRIGHT MP. / HE WAS BORN 28 FEB 1797 AND DIED IN LONDON / 5 JUNE 1873. / WHILE YET YOUNG HE SAW MUCH MILITARY SERVICE / IN THE PENINSULA, HOLDING COMMISSIONS IN THE 61ST FOOT / AND THE 3RD DRAGOONS AND 10TH HUSSARS BEING PRESENT AT THE / BATTLE OF THE PYRENEES, NIVELLE, NIVE AND ORTHES, / AND ALSO AT THE FINAL VICTORY OF WATERLOO. / THE COUNTY OF NORTHAMPTONSHIRE HAS LOST IN HIM A / MAGISTRATE DISTINGUISHED BY AN UNUSUAL CAPACITY FOR BUSINESS / AND THIS PARISH, THE PLACE OF HIS RESIDENCE FOR THIRTY YEARS / A MUNIFICENT BENEFACTOR TO THE POOR AND A CONSTANT / SUPPORTER OF THE CHURCH."

Ensign 61st Foot 2 Jul 1812. Lt 3rd Dragoons 6 Jan 1814. Lt 10th Lt Dragoons 12 Nov 1814. Capt 16 Nov 1820. Major 19 May 1825. Lt Colonel 28 Aug 1838. Major General 16 May 1857. Lt General 9 Oct 1863. General 19 Nov 1871.
    Served in the Peninsula with 61st Foot Jun 1813 – Feb 1814, and 3rd Dragoons Mar – Apr 1814. Present at Pyrenees, Nivelle, Nive, Orthes and Toulouse. Present at Waterloo with 10th Lt Dragoons. After the battle he acquired one of Napoleon's dinner services. MGS medal for Pyrenees, Nivelle, Nive, Orthes and Toulouse. Retired from the army 1822 and became a magistrate and interested in local politics. Appointed the first Inspector of Constabulary 1856 (one of the provisions of the County and Borough Police Act of 1856, the Inspectorate was set up to ensure that all police forces were of an efficient standard. Many of his ideas were adopted and are still in use today – pension schemes, detective departments and national pay structure). Retired 1869.

CASEY, Bartholomew

Lieutenant. 43rd (Monmouthshire) Light Infantry Regiment of Foot.
Box tomb: Sandpits Cemetery, Gibraltar. (Photograph)

IN MEMORY OF / LIEUTENANT B. CASEY 43RD LIGHT INFANTRY / WHO DIED AT GIBRALTAR / ON THE 9TH APRIL 1829 / AFTER A PERIOD OF NINETEEN YEARS / SERVICE IN THE REGI-MENT

Ensign 43rd Foot 23 Aug 1810. Lt 21 May 1812. Portuguese Army: Ensign 4th Line 17 Aug 1809. Lt 14th Line 3 Nov 1810. Capt 26 Feb 1814.
    Served in the Peninsula with the Portuguese Army, Apr 1809 – Dec 1813 and Mar – Apr 1814. Present at Busaco, second siege of Badajoz, Burgos and retreat from Burgos, Vittoria, Pyrenees, Nivelle and Nive. Retired from the Portuguese Army Oct 1814. Also served with the Army of Occupation until 1818 and Gibraltar 1823–1829.

CATER, Thomas Orlando

1st Lieutenant. Royal Artillery.
Box tomb: Kensal Green Cemetery, London. (W) (13211/131/PS). (Photograph)

TO THE MEMORY OF MAJOR-GENERAL THOMAS ORLANDO CATER / OF THE ROYAL ARTILLERY / WHO DIED MAY 29TH 1862. AGED 71. / HE SERVED IN THE PENINSULA CAMPAIGN FROM APRIL 1810 TO JANUARY 1813 / INCLUDING THE BATTLE OF BARROSA AND THE SIEGES OF CADIZ AND TARRAGONA / ALSO IN THE CAMPAIGN OF 1815, / THE BATTLE OF WATERLOO AND TAKING OF CAMBRAI AND PARIS.

2nd Lt 1 Apr 1809. 1st Lt 16 Apr 1812. 2nd Capt 22 Jul 1830. Capt 20 Jul 1840. Bt Major 9 Nov 1846. Lt Colonel 28 May 1847. Colonel 28 Nov 1854. Major General 26 May 1857.

Served in the Peninsula Apr 1810 – Jan 1814 (with Spanish Army Oct 1812 – Jan 1814). Present at Cadiz, Tarragona and Barrosa. Received Cross for his services from the Regency of Spain. Present at Waterloo, siege of Cambrai, Capture of Paris and with the Army of Occupation. Also served in the Ionian Islands 1834–1840, Canada 1841–1845 and Mauritius 1850–1854. MGS medal for Barrosa. Retired on full pay 1857.

CATHCART, Hon. Charles Murray see GREENOCK, Hon. Charles Murray, Lord

CATHCART, Hon. George
Lieutenant. 6th Dragoon Guards.
Grave: Cathcart's Hill Cemetery, Crimea, Ukraine. Severely damaged during the Second World War. (Photograph)

SACRED TO THE MEMORY / OF / THE HONBLE / SIR GEORGE CATHCART KCB / LIEUT GENL COMMANDING / THE 4TH DIVISION OF THE BRITISH ARMY IN THE / CRIMEA. / BORN 1794. KILLED 5TH NOV 1854 / AT THE BATTLE OF / INKERMAN. / HE SERVED WITH THE RUSSIAN ARMY IN / THE YEARS 1813 AND 1814 AND WAS AIDE DE CAMP / TO THE DUKE OF WELLINGTON AT WATERLOO. / HE WAS APPOINTED IN 1852 / GOVERNOR OF THE CAPE OF GOOD HOPE / FROM WHICH PLACE HE HAD JUST RETURNED. / THIS TOMB WAS PLACED HERE / BY THE OFFICERS AND MEN OF THE 4TH DIVISION.

Brass Memorial tablet: Royal Garrison Church, Portsmouth, Hampshire. (Back of a choir stall). (Photograph)

LIEUTENANT GENERAL / THE HON. SIR GEORGE / CATHCART K.C.B. / KILLED AT INKERMAN / NOVEMBER 5 1854 / AGED 60: DD / THE EARL CATHCART

Cornet 2nd Life Guards 10 May 1810. Lt 6th Dragoon Guards 1 Jul 1811. Capt 1st West India Regt 24 Dec 1818. Capt 7th Hussars 16 Dec 1819. Major 8 Apr 1826. Lt Colonel 7th Hussars 13 May 1826. Lt Colonel 57th Foot 24 Jan 1828. Lt Colonel 8th Hussars 20 Mar 1830. Lt Colonel 1st Dragoon Guards 11 May 1838. Bt Colonel 23 Nov 1841. Major General 11 Nov 1851.

Served in Europe 1813 (ADC to his father, Lord Cathcart, who was ambassador to the Czar and military commissioner to the Russian Army). Present at Lutzen, Bautzen, Dresden, Leipzig (1813), Brienne Bar-sur-Aube, Arcis (1814). Then entered Paris with the Allies in March 1814.

Present at Quatre Bras and Waterloo (ADC to the Duke of Wellington) and with the Army of Occupation until 1818. Also served in the Canadian Rebellion 1838 (Commander of all troops south of the River Lawrence to protect the frontier of Lower Canada). Deputy Lieutenant of the Tower of London 13 Feb 1846. Succeeded Sir Harry Smith as Governor and Commander in Chief at the Cape of Good Hope Jan 1852. He crushed the Rebellion and ended the Kaffir Wars Dec 1852. KCB Jul 1853. Adjutant General at Horse Guards 12 Dec 1853, and arrived back in London to find the Army on its way to the Crimea. Appointed to command the 4th Division. Did not play any part in the battle of the Alma and the rest of the generals rejected his advice to storm Sebastopol at once. Killed at the battle of Inkerman 5 Nov 1854. Author of *Commentaries on the War in Russia and Germany in 1813 and 1814*, 1850. Younger brother of Lt Colonel Charles Murray Cathcart, Lord Greenock AQMG.

REFERENCE: *Dictionary of National Biography. Gentleman's Magazine, Jan 1855, pp. 81–3. Annual Register, 1854, Appx, pp. 353–4.*

CAVE, James

Private. 7th (Queen's Own) Regiment of Light Dragoons.
Headstone: St Andrew's Churchyard, Newcastle on Tyne, Northumberland. (No longer extant). (M.I.)

"SACRED TO THE MEMORY / OF JAMES CAVE, WHO DIED FEBRUARY 6TH 1835 / AGED 45 YEARS. / HAVING FAITHFULLY SERVED HIS KING / AND COUNTRY FOR A PERIOD OF TWENTY FIVE YEARS / IN THE 7TH (QUEEN'S OWN) REGIMENT OF THE HUSSARS. / THIS STONE HAS BEEN ERECTED BY THE / OFFICERS, NON – COMMISSIONED OFFICERS, / TRUMPETERS, AND PRIVATES AS A TESTIMONY / OF THEIR RESPECT FOR A GOOD AND DESERVING / OLD SOLDIER

Pte 1810.
 Served in the Peninsula Nov 1808 – Jan 1809 and Sep 1813 – Apr 1814. Present at Benevente, Orthes and Toulouse. Present at Waterloo.

CAVENAGH, George Walter

Captain. 87th (Prince of Wales's Own Irish) Regiment of Foot.
Box tomb: St Patrick's Churchyard, Wexford, County Wexford, Ireland. (Photograph)

SACRED TO THE MEMORY OF / MATHEW CAVENAGH ESQ^R LATE OF WEXFORD / WHO DIED THE 27TH OF MAY 1819, / HIS WIFE CATHERINE HYDE GREGORY / WHO DIED THE 27TH OF MAY 1814. / THEY HAD NINE SONS, SIX OF WHICH SERVED / AS OFFICERS IN HER MAJESTY'S ARMY AND NAVY. / .... / CAPT GEORGE WALTER CAVENAGH / H. M. 87TH FOOT. / ....

Memorial: South Park Street Burial Ground, Calcutta, India. (No longer extant: Section 2 Grave number 1286). (M.I.)

"SACRED TO THE MEMORY OF / GEORGE WALTER CAVENAGH / LATE CAPT. IN H. M. 87TH REGT. DIED 28TH / MAY 1822, AGED 39 YEARS. / THIS STONE IS ERECTED AS A TOKEN OF REGARD BY HIS / BROTHER OFFICERS".

Ensign 7th Garrison Battalion. Lt 87th Foot 8 Oct 1807. Capt 22 Nov 1810.
 Served in the Peninsula Mar 1809 – Apr 1814. Present at Douro, Talavera (wounded), Cadiz, Barrosa, Tarifa, Vittoria, Pyrenees, Nivelle, Orthes, Vic Bigorre and Toulouse. Also served in India 1815 (present in the Nepaul War and Pindari War — present at Fort of Hattrass) where he died in 1822.

CHADWICK, Nicholas

Lieutenant. 59th (2nd Nottinghamshire) Regiment of Foot.
Interred in Kensal Green Cemetery, London. (No longer extant: 1484/40/RS)

Ensign 21 Sep 1808. Lt 5 Dec 1811. Capt 29 Apr 1824. Capt 13th Foot 3 Aug 1826.
 Served in the Peninsula Oct 1808 – Jan 1809. Present at Corunna (wounded). Present at Waterloo in reserve at Hal, siege of Cambrai and with the Army of Occupation. Also served at Walcheren 1809, Java 1812 and India 1824–1826 (present at Bhurtpore). Died 4 Jun 1838. Brother of Capt William Chadwick 34th Foot.

CHADWICK, William

Captain. 34th (Cumberland) Regiment of Foot.
Headstone: Brompton Cemetery, London. (Section A, Block F). (M.I.)

"SACRED TO THE MEMORY OF / CAPTAIN WILLIAM CHADWICK / OF THE ROYAL HOSPITAL CHELSEA / WHO DIED ON THE 31ST JANUARY 1868 / AGED 78 YEARS."

Ensign 59th Foot 9 Jul 1803. Lt 2 Feb 1805. Capt 34th Foot 20 Feb 1812.
   Served in the Peninsula Apr – Nov 1812 and Feb – Apr 1814. Present at Almarez, Orthes and Toulouse. MGS medal for Orthes and Toulouse. Half pay 25 Aug 1814. Brother of Lt Nicholas Chadwick 59th Foot.

CHALMERS, William

Captain. 52nd (Oxfordshire) Light Infantry Regiment of Foot.
Named on the Family Memorial: Howff Cemetery, Dundee, Angus, Scotland. (M.I.)

"LIEUTENANT GENERAL SIR WILLIAM CHALMERS, CB. KCH. DIED 2 JUNE 1860 AGED 75."

Ensign 9 Jul 1803. Lt 25 Oct 1803. Capt 24 Aug 1807. Bt Major 26 Aug 1813. Bt Lt Colonel 18 Jun 1815. Bt Colonel 10 Jan 1837. Major General 9 Nov 1846. Lt General 20 Jun 1854.
   Served in the Peninsula with 2/52nd Aug 1808 – Jan 1809, Aug 1810 – Jun 1811 (Brigade Major to Colonel Disney), Aug 1811 (Brigade Major 3 Brigade 2nd Division), Sep – Oct 1811 (Brigade Major 7th Division) and Nov 1811 – Feb 1814 (Brigade Major 2 Brigade 7th Division). Present at Vigo, Cadiz, Barrosa, Ciudad Rodrigo, Badajoz, Moriscos, Salamanca, San Munos, Vittoria, Maya, Pyrenees (present at Sarre where he was severely wounded and awarded Bt Majority), San Sebastian, San Marcial and Nivelle.
   Present at Waterloo. At the commencement of the Waterloo Campaign he was at Ostend (ADC to his cousin Sir Kenneth Mackenzie), but rode to the battlefield and requested a post on the front line. Wellington knew of his exploits in the Peninsula and gave him the left wing of the 52nd. He commanded these troops admirably, had three horses shot under him and was awarded a Bt Lt Colonelcy. Stayed with the 52nd and was present at the Capture of Paris and with the Army of Occupation.
   Retired in 1817 as his health had suffered through years of campaigning. Returned to his estates in Scotland and pursued his favourite hobbies of riding and walking. When he was quite elderly he thought nothing of walking 25 miles to his estate in Glenericht in Perthshire, having lunch and walking back the 25 miles. He had all the trees at Glenericht planted in the battle order of the Allied troops at Waterloo.
   Also served in Sicily 1806–1807 and Walcheren 1809 (present at Flushing). MGS medal for Barrosa, Ciudad Rodrigo, Badajoz, Salamanca, Vittoria, Pyrenees, San Sebastian and Nivelle. CB. KCH. Knighted 1848. Colonel 20th Foot 1850–1853. Colonel 78th Foot Sep 1853 to his death on 2 Jun 1860. On his death he was carried to his grave, reputedly at Glenericht, by the tenantry of his estate instead of being buried with full military honours.
REFERENCE: *Dictionary of National Biography. Gentleman's Magazine, Jul 1860 pp. 104–5. Annual Register, 1860, Appx, p 402. Oxfordshire and Buckinghamshire Light Infantry Chronicle, 1901, pp. 164–6.*

CHAMBERS, Courtney

Ensign. 1st Regiment of Foot Guards.
Memorial tablet: St James's Church, Piccadilly, London. (Photograph)

SACRED / TO THE MEMORY / OF / COLONEL COURTNEY CHAMBERS, / LIEUTENANT COLONEL OF THE 25TH REGIMENT, / THE KING'S OWN BORDERERS / WHO, WHEN PROCEEDING FROM MADRAS TO ENGLAND / ON MEDICAL CERTIFICATE, / DIED AT THE POINT DE GALLE, / CEYLON ON THE 18TH JUNE 1848 / AGED 50 YEARS. / HE COMMANDED

THE REGIMENT IN THE UNITED KINGDOM, / IN THE WEST INDIES, AT THE CAPE OF GOOD HOPE / AND INDIA FOR THE LONG PERIOD OF EIGHTEEN YEARS / AND WAS EVER UNIVERSALLY ESTEEMED AND RESPECTED BY ALL RANKS. / THIS TABLET IS ERECTED TO THE OFFICERS AND SOLDIERS / TO REVERE THEIR JOINT SENSE OF THE CHARACTER / AND WORTH OF THEIR LAMENTED COMMANDING OFFICER.

Ensign 10 Jun 1813. Lt and Capt 6 Jul 1815. Capt 25th Foot 26 Nov 1818. Capt 57th Foot 18 Jul 1822. Capt 99th Foot 25 Mar 1824. Capt 29th Foot 24 Jun 1824. Major 25th Foot 3 Nov 1825. Lt Colonel 31 Aug 1830. Bt Colonel 9 Nov 1846.

Present at Waterloo. Also served in the Netherlands 1814, West Indies, Cape of Good Hope and India. Commanded the 25th Foot from 1830 to his death in Ceylon on his way home to England in 1848. Brother of Lt and Capt Newton Chambers 1st Foot Guards.

CHAMBERS, Newton
Lieutenant and Captain. 1st Regiment of Foot Guards.
Memorial tablet: St James's Church, Piccadilly, London. (In tower). (Photograph)

CAPTAIN LIEUTENANT IN THE FIRST REGIMENT OF FOOT GUARDS / AND AIDE DE CAMP TO LIEUTENANT GENERAL SIR THOMAS PICTON / WITH WHOM HE FELL AT THE BATTLE OF WATERLOO / ON THE 18TH JUNE 1815, IN THE 24TH YEAR OF HIS AGE. / HE WAS THE PRIDE AND IDOL OF HIS FAMILY / BELOVED BY ALL WHO KNEW HIM / A TOKEN OF HIS WORTH AND IN FOND AND LASTING REMEMBRANCE / OF THE UNBOUNDED FILIAL AFFECTION, WHICH HAD MADE / THEIR APPRECIATION AND HAPPINESS THE DEAREST OBJECT OF HIS WORLDLY THOUGHTS. / THIS STONE IS ENSCRIBED TO HIS LOVED MEMORY BY HIS AFFLICTED MOTHER / THE HONBLE JANE CHAMBERS.

Named on the Regimental Memorial: St Joseph's Church, Waterloo, Belgium. (Photograph)
Named on Memorial Panel VIII for Waterloo: Royal Military Chapel, Wellington Barracks, London. (M.I.) (Destroyed by a Flying Bomb 1944)

Ensign 26 Jan 1809. Lt and Capt 7 Apr 1813.

Served in the Peninsula with 2nd Battalion, Mar – Nov 1810, 1st Battalion, Sep 1812 – May 1813 and Dec 1813 – Apr 1814 (ADC to Lt. General Picton). Present at Cadiz, Orthes, Vic Bigorre and Toulouse. Present at Waterloo where he was again ADC to Picton. Killed immediately after the death of Picton. Brother of Ensign Courtney Chambers 1st Foot Guards.

CHAMBERS, Thomas Walker
Major. 30th (Cambridgeshire) Regiment of Foot.
Memorial tablet: St Margaret's Church, Lowestoft, Suffolk. (Photograph)

SACRED / TO THE MEMORY OF / MAJOR THOMAS WALKER CHAMBERS OF / HIS MAJESTY'S 30TH REGIMENT OF FOOT, / WHO AFTER HIGHLY DISTINGUISHING HIMSELF IN / EUROPE AND INDIA FOR 13 YEARS FELL / GLORIOUSLY FIGHTING AT THE MEMORABLE BATTLE OF / WATERLOO / ON THE 18TH DAY OF JUNE, 1815 / IN THE 34TH YEAR OF HIS AGE. / TO COMMEMORATE THEIR SEVERE LOSS AND / PERPETUATE THE AFFECTIONATE REGARD OF HIS / FATHER, MR JOHN CHAMBERS, AND OTHER RELATIVES, / THE ABOVE INSCRIPTION IS TO BE PLACED IN THIS / HIS NATIVE PARISH CHURCH.

Named on the Regimental Memorial: St Joseph's Church, Waterloo, Belgium. (Photograph)

Ensign 7 Jul 1803. Lt 15 Dec 1804. Capt 2 Apr 1807. Major 16 Feb 1815.

Served with 2/30th in the Peninsula Sep 1810 – Jun 1813. Present at Cadiz, Sabugal, Fuentes d'Onoro, Barba del Puerco, Ciudad Rodrigo, Badajoz (severely wounded), Burgos and Villa Muriel. Present at Waterloo where he was killed by one of the last shots of the day. Also served in India with 1/30th 1807 and the Netherlands with 2/30th 1814 (present at Antwerp).

CHAMP, Thomas
Captain. 43rd (Monmouthshire) Light Infantry Regiment of Foot.
Pedestal tomb: St Nicholas Churchyard, Kenilworth, Warwickshire. (Photograph)

SACRED / TO THE MEMORY OF / MAJOR THOMAS CHAMP / FORMERLY OF THE 43RD LIGHT INFANTRY / WHO DIED AT LEAMINGTON / SEPT 22ND 1851 AGED 73 / (VERSE)

Ensign 5 Dec 1799. Lt 18 Nov 1803. Capt 15 Dec 1808. Bt Major 27 May 1825.
   Served in the Peninsula with 1/43rd Oct – Dec 1808 and Aug 1812 – Apr 1814. Present at San Munos, Bidassoa, Nivelle, Nive, Tarbes and Toulouse. Also served at Copenhagen 1807 and North America 1814–1815 (present at New Orleans). Half pay 19 Sep 1826. Retired 27 Sep 1831. MGS medal for Nivelle, Nive and Toulouse.
REFERENCE: *Oxfordshire Light Infantry Chronicle, 1901, pp. 187–8.*

CHANDOS-POLE, Edward Sacheverell see POLE, Edward Sacheverell Chandos

CHAPLIN, Thomas
Lieutenant and Captain. Coldstream Regiment of Foot Guards.
Memorial: Royal Military Chapel, Wellington Barracks, London. (M.I.) (Destroyed by a Flying Bomb 1944)

"PLACED BY HIS RELATIVES, 1880, IN MEMORY OF COLONEL THOMAS CHAPLIN, / COLD-STREAM GUARDS, 1811–51. WOUNDED AT SAN SEBASTIAN, 1813".

Ensign 18 Apr 1811. Lt and Capt 6 Oct 1814. Capt and Lt Colonel 15 Aug 1826. Bt Colonel 23 Nov 1841.
   Served in the Peninsula Apr – Sep 1813. Present at San Sebastian (severely wounded 31 Aug 1813 and awarded pension of £50 per annum). Also served in the Netherlands 1814–1815. MGS medal for San Sebastian. Joined the regiment from the Royal Military College. MP for Stamford 1826 and Deputy Lieutenant of Lincolnshire. Resigned his seat in 1838 and went with his regiment to Canada during the Rebellion. Retired from the army 25 Nov 1841. Died 10 May 1863.
REFERENCE: *Gentleman's Magazine, Jun 1863, p. 808.*

CHAPMAN, Stephen Remnent
Lieutenant Colonel. Royal Engineers.
Memorial tablet: St Mary's Church, Kingston St Mary, Somerset. (Photograph)

SIR STEPHEN REMNENT CHAPMAN, C.B. & K.C.H. / LIEUT GENL ROYAL ENGINEERS, / (THIRD SON OF THE ABOVE LIEUT GENL CHAPMAN, / AND CATHERINE HIS WIFE.) / DEPARTED THIS LIFE MARCH 6TH 1851, / AGED 75 YEARS.

Named on the Regimental Memorial: Rochester Cathedral, Rochester, Kent. (Photograph)

2nd Lt Royal Artillery. 18 Sep 1793. 2nd Lt Royal Engineers. 1 Jan 1794. Lt 20 Nov 1796. Capt-Lt 18 Apr 1801. 2nd Capt 19 Jul 1804. Capt 2 Mar 1805. Bt Major 30 Sep 1810. Bt Lt Colonel 26 Apr 1812. Lt Colonel 21 Jul 1813. Colonel 29 Jul 1825. Major General 10 Jan 1837. Lt General 9 Nov 1846. Colonel Commandant Royal Engineers. 9 Mar 1850.

Served in the Peninsula Apr 1809 – Feb 1811. Present at Talavera, Torres Vedras (Mentioned in Despatches) and Busaco (Mentioned in Despatches). Gold Medal for Busaco. CB. KCH. Knighted 1831. Also served in the West Indies 1796–1797, the Helder 1799, Cape of Good Hope 1800 and Copenhagen 1807. For several years was secretary to Earl Mulgrave, Master General of Ordnance. Governor, Vice Admiral and Commander in Chief at Bermuda 1831–1839.

REFERENCE: *Dictionary of National Biography. Gentleman's Magazine, May 1851, p 553. Annual Register, 1851, Appx, pp. 269–70.*

CHAPMAN, Thomas
Private. 7th (Royal Fusiliers) Regiment of Foot.
Family Headstone: Igtham Churchyard, Kent. (Photograph)

.... / ALSO / THOMAS CHAPMAN / WHO DIED 2 AUGUST 1883 / AGE 92 YEARS. / HE SERVED IN THE 7TH REGIMENT OF ROYAL / FUSILIERS UNDER THE GREAT DUKE OF / WELLINGTON / AT ALBUERA, WHERE HE WAS WOUNDED, / AND AT SALAMANCA, VITTORIA, AND / THE PYRENEES ALSO IN AMERICA. / A GOOD SOLDIER OF JESUS CHRIST.

Pte 12 May 1809. Pte 95th Foot 25 Apr 1826. Pte 7th Foot 25 May 1829.
    Served in the Peninsula with 1/7th Aug 1810 – Apr 1814. Present at Albuera (wounded and remained in hospital for a year), Salamanca, Vittoria and Pyrenees (wounded). Served in the Army of Occupation 1815–1818. Also served in North America 1814–1815 (present at New Orleans) and in the Mediterranean (present at Corfu and Malta). MGS medal for Albuera, Salamanca, Vittoria and Pyrenees. Received a Good Conduct Medal. Discharged 18 May 1838.

CHAPMAN, Thomas
Private. 95th Regiment of Foot.
Headstone: St Mary's Churchyard, Comberton, Cambridgeshire. (Photograph)

IN MEMORY OF / THOMAS CHAPMAN / WHO SERVED AT WATERLOO / 2/95th RIFLE BRIGADE BORN FEB 14 1790 / DIED 18 JUNE 1875. / TC 1875

Pte 1 Apr 1809.
    Served in the Peninsula Sep 1810 – Apr 1814. Present at Ciudad Rodrigo, Badajoz, Salamanca, Vittoria, Pyrenees and Bayonne (wounded). Served with 2/95th at Waterloo in Capt Francis Le Blanc's Company and with the Army of Occupation. MGS medal for Ciudad Rodrigo, Badajoz, Salamanca. Vittoria and Pyrenees. Discharged 15 Sep 1818 as a result of his wound at Bayonne.

CHARLETON, Andrew Robert
Lieutenant. 85th (Buckinghamshire Volunteers) Light Infantry Regiment of Foot.
Memorial tablet: Prison Chapel, Fort Augusta, Kingston, Jamaica. (The Fort is now a women's prison). (Photograph)

SACRED / TO THE MEMORY OF / ANDREW ROBERT CHARLETON / MAJOR IN THE 92ND HIGH-LANDERS / WHO DEPARTED THIS LIFE / MONDAY AUGUST THE 15TH 1825 / AGED 30 YEARS.

Ensign 8th Foot 7 Jun 1811. Lt 89th Foot 13 Aug 1812. Lt 85th Foot 25 Jan 1813. Capt 22 May 1817. Major 92nd Foot 25 Sep 1823.
    Served in the Peninsula Aug 1813 – Apr 1814. Present at Nivelle, Nive and Bayonne. Also served in North America (present at Bladensburg and New Orleans where he was severely wounded), and in the West Indies, where he died 15 Aug 1825. His gravestone was used to make part of the floor of the prison chapel and has been well preserved.

CHARRETIE, Thomas

Captain. 2nd Life Guards.
Monument: Kensal Green Cemetery, London. (9667/87/IC). (Photograph)

SACRED / TO THE MEMORY OF / GENERAL THOMAS CHARRETIE / LATE OF THE 2ND REGT LIFE GUARDS / A BRAVE AND ACCOMPLISHED OFFICER. / HE SERVED HIS MAJESTY GEORGE 3RD / IN THE BATTLES OF / VITTORIA, PAMPLONA AND TOULOUSE / AND DEPARTED THIS LIFE / JANUARY 12TH 1866 / IN THE 81ST YEAR OF HIS AGE.

Cornet 22nd Dragoons 9 Jun 1804. Lt 6 Feb 1805. Capt 46th Foot 25 Dec 1807. Capt 2nd Life Guards 23 Jan 1812. Major 7th West India Regt 27 Apr 1815. Bt Lt Colonel 21 May 1815. Bt Colonel 10 Jan 1837. Major General 9 Nov 1846. Lt General 11 Nov 1851.

Served in the Peninsula Nov 1812 – Apr 1814. Present at Vittoria, Pamplona and Toulouse. MGS medal for Vittoria and Toulouse. Also served in India 1804–1806 (present at the Vellore Mutiny where he had a narrow escape when nearly all the officers and men were massacred in the barracks) and West Indies 1807. Half pay 24 Jul 1816. CB.
REFERENCE: *Household Brigade Journal, 1866, pp. 308–9. Gentleman's Magazine, Mar 1866, p. 441.*

CHATTERTON, James Charles

Lieutenant. 12th (Prince of Wales's) Regiment of Light Dragoons
Low monument: Brookwood Cemetery, Brookwood, Surrey. (Plot 40). (Photograph)

IN MEMORY OF / SIR JAMES C. CHATTERTON BART. / KNIGHT GRAND CROSS OF THE MOST HONOURABLE ORDER OF THE BATH, GENERAL IN THE ARMY, / COLONEL OF THE 4TH ROYAL IRISH DRAGOON GUARDS, KNIGHT OF THE GUELPHIC HANOVERIAN ORDER / AND OF SAN FERNANDO OF SPAIN, GENTLEMAN OF THE PRIVY CHAMBER, SOMETIME MP FOR CORK, / DL OF THE COUNTY AND CITY OF CORK, LLD, PROVINCIAL GRAND MASTER OF THE FREEMASONS OF MUNSTER. / HAVING ENTERED THE ARMY AS CORNET IN 1809, HE SERVED IN THE PENINSULA, PORTUGAL, SPAIN, FLANDERS AND FRANCE. / FROM 1811 TO 1818, WAS PRESENT AT 37 BATTLES SIEGES AND ENGAGEMENTS BESIDES VARIOUS / SKIR- MISHES AND MINOR AFFAIRS / THE BATTLE OF QUATRE BRAS AND WATERLOO AND THE ADVANCE ON AND CAPTURE OF PARIS. / HE RECEIVED THE COMMANDS OF HIS SOVER- EIGN IN CONSIDERATION OF HIS LONG FAITHFUL AND DISTINGUISHED SERVICES / TO BEAR THE BANNER OF ENGLAND AT THE FUNERAL OF THE LATE ILLUSTRIOUS F. M. THE DUKE OF WELLINGTON / UNDER WHOM HE HAD SO LONG AND HONOURABLY SERVED. BORN 18 DECEMBER 1794 DIED 5 JANUARY 1874. / …………

Stained glass memorial window: St Fin Barre's Cathedral, Cork, Ireland. (Photograph)

THE ABOVE ROSE WINDOW, AND THE LANCET WINDOWS OVER IT, WERE ERECTED BY THE FREEMASONS OF THE PROVINCE OF MUNSTER, AND DEDICATED TO THE MEMORY OF GENERAL SIR JAMES CHARLES CHATTERTON, BARONET, GCB. KH. ETC FOR MANY YEARS THEIR PROVINCIAL GRAND MASTER. HE DEPARTED THIS LIFE V. DAY OF JANUARY MDCC- CLXXIV. THE FREEMASONS OF MUNSTER ERECTED THE SYMBOLS OF THE FOUR EVANGELISTS, SURROUNDING EXTERNALLY THE WESTERN WINDOW.

Cornet 23 Nov 1809. Lt 6 Jun 1811. Capt 4th (Royal Irish) Dragoon Guards 26 Mar 1818. Major 22 Jul 1824. Lt Colonel 18 Oct 1827. Bt Colonel 23 Nov 1841. Major General 20 Jun 1854. Lt General 13 Dec 1859. General 31 Mar 1866

Served in the Peninsula Jun 1811 – Apr 1814. Present at Aldea da Ponte, Usagre, Llerena, Castrejon, Salamanca, Venta del Poza, retreat from Burgos, Osma, Vittoria, Bidassoa, Nivelle, Nive, Adour, Bayonne, and Bordeaux. Present at Quatre Bras and Waterloo and in France with the Army of Occupation until 1818. MGS medal for Salamanca, Vittoria, Nivelle and Nive. KCB and KH. Colonel 4th Dragoon Guards 1837. Colonel 5th Royal Irish Dragoons 1858.

REFERENCE: *Journal of the Society for Army Historical Research, Vol 68, Summer 1990, No 274, pp. 71–4.*

CHEEK, Edward

Lieutenant. 20th (East Devonshire) Regiment of Foot.
Headstone: St Mary the Virgin Churchyard, Carisbrooke, Isle of Wight. (Grave number 311). Seriously eroded and inscription recorded from memorial inscription. (Photograph)

"LIEUT EDWARD CHEEK, 20TH REGT DIED 2 APR 1821. AGED 40 YEARS"

Ensign 5 Apr 1809. Lt 7 Nov 1811.
    Served in the Peninsula Nov 1812 – Apr 1814. Present at Vittoria, Pyrenees, Nivelle, Nive, Orthes and Toulouse. Also served at Walcheren 1809.

CHENEVIX, George see SMITH, George

CHENEY, Edward Hawkins

Captain. 2nd (Royal North British) Regiment of Dragoons.
Memorial tablet: St Luke's Church, Gaddesby, Leicestershire. (Photograph)

IN / AFFECTIONATE REMEMBRANCE OF / EDWARD HAWKINS CHENEY C.B. / COLONEL IN THE ARMY / SECOND SON OF ROBERT CHENEY ESQR / OF MEYNELL LANGLEY, DERBYSHIRE: HE WAS BORN 4TH NOV. 1778, / HE JOINED AS CORNET THE SCOTS GREYS IN HOLLAND; / UNDER THE DUKE OF YORK, 1794; WHERE HE WAS SEVERELY WOUNDED; / AND SERVED WITH HONOUR IN THE SAME REGIMENT AT WATERLOO / IN THE BATTLE OF THE 18TH JUNE. FOUR HORSES WERE KILLED / AND THE FIFTH WOUNDED UNDER HIM; AND THE COMMAND / OF THE REGIMENT DEVOLVED UPON HIM. / HE MARRIED IN 1811 ELIZA, YOUNGEST DAUGHTER OF / JOHN AYRE ESQR OF GADDESBY; / AND DIED THERE 3RD MARCH 1848.

Statue: St Luke's Church, Gaddesby, Leicestershire. (Photograph)

EDWARD H CHENEY. C.B. COLONEL IN THE ARMY. LATE SCOTS GUARDS.

The statue was originally in Gaddesby Hall (or Paske Hall as it was then), but when the contents were sold in 1917, the monument was moved into the church below the memorial tablet to Colonel Cheney.

Cornet 16 Sep 1794. Lt 22 Oct 1794. Capt/Lieut 3 May 1800. Capt 25 May 1803. Bt Major 1 Jan 1812. Bt Lt Colonel 18 Jun 1815. Major 2nd Dragoons 20 Jul 1815. Bt Colonel 10 Jan 1837.
    Present at Waterloo. During the cavalry charge Lt Col Hamilton was killed and Majors Clarke and Hankin were wounded. Cheney then commanded the regiment during the last three hours. He had four horses killed under him and one horse wounded. Awarded CB and a Bt Lt Colonelcy. Also served in Flanders 1794 where he was severely wounded. Retired on half pay 17 Sep 1818.
REFERENCE: *Gentleman's Magazine, May 1848, p. 548. Annual Register, 1848, Appx, p. 219.*

CHENEY, Robert

Captain and Lieutenant Colonel. 1st Regiment of Foot Guards.
Memorial tablet: St Mary's Church, Beverley, Yorkshire. (South west end of south transept). (Photograph)

SACRED TO THE MEMORY / OF / ROBERT CHENEY ESQ^R OF LANGLEY HALL IN THE COUNTY / OF DERBY A LIEU^T GENERAL IN THE ARMY / DESCENDED FROM AN ANCIENT AND HONORABLE FAMILY, / HE ENTERED AT THE AGE OF 17 INTO THE FIRST REG^T OF / FOOT GUARDS, / AND IN THAT REGIMENT, WHICH HE NEVER QUITTED, / HE SERVED HIS KING AND COUNTRY / IN MANY CAMPAIGNS IN DIFFERENT PARTS OF EUROPE, / WAS SUCCESSIVELY APPOINTED AIDE-DE-CAMP / TO H.R.H DUKE OF GLOUCESTER AND TO HIS LATE / MAJESTY GEORGE III, / AND SUBSEQUENTLY HELD A COMMAND IN THIS DISTRICT. / THE WHOLE OF HIS LONG MILITARY CAREER / WAS EQUALLY HONORABLE TO HIMSELF, USEFUL / TO THE SERVICE, / AND CONCILIATORY TO THOSE UNDER HIS ORDERS. / IN SOCIAL LIFE HIS CONDUCT WAS EXEMPLARY. / TO POLISHED MANNERS, HE ADDED A CULTIVATED MIND, / TO THE KINDEST AFFECTIONS, AND MOST INDULGENT / DISPOSITION, / FIRMNESS OF RESOLUTION, AND INVIOLABLE INTEGRITY. / HIS PIETY WAS SINCERE AND ENLIGHTENED, / HIS BENEVOLENCE UNBOUNDED, HIS CHARITY DIRECTED / A SOLDIER, A MAN, AND CHRISTIAN, BRAVE AND JUST. / NEED IT BE RECORDED THAT HE WAS ESTEEMED, / ADMIRED, BELOVED, AND REGRETTED! / HIS EARTHLY COURSE WAS TERMINATED BY / A TYPHUS FEVER ON THE 8TH MARCH 1820, / IN THE 54TH YEAR OF HIS AGE. / HIS REMAINS ARE INTERRED IN A VAULT IN THE CHANCEL. / HIS SORROWING WIDOW AND CHILDREN HAVE ERECTED / THIS TABLET AS A FEEBLE TESTIMONIAL / OF THEIR RESPECT FOR HIS MEMORY / AND OF THEIR GRIEF FOR HIS LOSS

Memorial tablet and Stained glass window: Royal Military Chapel, Wellington Barracks, London. (M.I.) (Destroyed by a Flying Bomb 1944). (Photograph of stained glass window in the Apse. The only original part of the Chapel)

"HIS SON EDWARD CHENEY, OF BADGER HALL, AND HIS GRANDSON, COLONEL / ALFRED CAPEL CURE, / LATE GRENADIER GUARDS, TO THE MEMORY OF / LIEUT.-GENERAL ROBERT CHENEY, / BORN, 1766; DIED, 1820. / 1ST GUARDS, 1784 TO 1814. HE SERVED WITH THE REGIMENT IN FLANDERS IN 1794–5, / IN SICILY, 1806–7, AND THROUGHOUT THE CORUNNA CAMPAIGN".

Cornet 6th Dragoons 9 Jan 1784. Ensign 1st Foot Guards 7 Apr 1784. Lt and Capt 15 Jun 1791. Capt and Lt Colonel 25 Oct 1797. Bt Colonel 1 Jan 1805. Major General 25 Jun 1810. Lt General 12 Aug 1819.

Served in the Peninsula with 1st Battalion Oct 1808 – Jan 1809. Present at Corunna in command of a brigade of infantry in the absence of Major General Leith. Gold Medal for Corunna. Also served in Flanders 1794–1795 and Sicily 1806–1807.

CHESTER, John
Captain. Royal Artillery.
Memorial tablet: St Lawrence's Church, Chicheley, Buckinghamshire. (M.I.)

"IN / MEMORY OF / JOHN / LIEUTENANT GENERAL R.A. 5TH SON OF / CHARLES CHESTER ESQ / BORN 3 AUG 1779, DIED 19 MAY 1857."

2nd Lt 28 Apr 1798. 1st Lt 6 Oct 1799. 2nd Capt 29 Dec 1805. Capt 7 Oct 1813. Bt Major 12 Aug 1819. Lt Colonel 3 Sep 1831. Bt Colonel 9 Nov 1846. Major General 20 Jun 1854. Lt General 4 Feb 1857.

Served in the Peninsula Sep 1808 – Jan 1809. Present at Benevente, Villa Franca, Lugo and the retreat to Corunna. Also served at the Helder 1799 (present at Bergen) and Canada 1824–1825. Half pay 26 Oct 1831. Retired on full pay 7 Apr 1847. MGS medal for Benevente.

CHETHAM, Isaac

Lieutenant. 40th (2nd Somersetshire) Regiment of Foot.
Headstone: General Cemetery, Nottingham, Nottinghamshire. (Photograph)

SACRED / TO THE MEMORY OF / ISAAC CHETHAM, / ADJUTANT OF H M. 40TH FOOT, / WHO FELL ASLEEP IN CHRIST, OCTR 19TH 1854, / AGED 73 YEARS. / HE WAS ACTIVELY ENGAGED IN NINETEEN GENERAL / BATTLES AND SIEGES DURING THE EXPEDITION TO / HOLLAND AND THE PENINSULAR WAR, AND WAS / THREE TIMES DANGEROUSLY WOUNDED. / HE LIVED AND DIED IN THE FAITH OF THE GOSPEL. / ....

Pte 29th Foot 1797. Cpl 1800. Sgt 1802. Sgt Major 1811. Ensign 79th Foot 6 Aug 1811. Lt 40th Foot 10 Dec 1812. Adjutant 17 Dec 1812.

Served in the Peninsula with 29th Foot Aug 1808 – Jul 1811, with 79th Foot Sep 1811 – Nov 1812 and with 40th Foot Feb 1813 – Apr 1814. Present at Rolica, Vimeiro, Douro, Talavera, Busaco, Albuera, Salamanca, Vittoria, Pyrenees, Nivelle (wounded), Orthes and Toulouse. Also served at the Helder 1799. Retired on half pay 25 Mar 1817. MGS medal for Rolica, Vimeiro, Talavera, Busaco, Albuera, Salamanca, Vittoria, Pyrenees, Orthes and Toulouse.

CHEYNE, Alexander

2nd Captain. Royal Engineers.
Headstone: St David's Anglican Cemetery, Hobart, Tasmania, Australia. The headstones were removed in the 1920's and placed around the wall. (No longer extant)
Named on the Regimental Memorial: Rochester Cathedral, Rochester, Kent. (Photograph)

2nd Lt 1 May 1806. Lt 1 Jul 1806. 2nd Capt 1 May 1811. Capt 1 Dec 1815.

Served in the Peninsula Oct 1808 – Jan 1809 and Apr 1812 – Apr 1814. Present at Corunna and Tarragona (Mentioned in Despatches). Half pay 8 Mar 1825. Sold commission 8 Feb 1833. Sailed for Australia and arrived in Tasmania in 1835. Became Director General of Roads and Bridges. Won the support of the Lt Governor but the Colonial Secretary disliked him and had him dismissed. He was accused of altering the plans of a church tower at St George's to a more elaborate style. Two years later documents were found clearing his name but for the rest of his life he had great difficulty in finding further employment and endured financial hardship. Died at Hobart, Tasmania, 6 Jul 1858.
REFERENCE: *Australian Dictionary of Biography.*

CHILDERS, Michael

Captain. 11th Regiment of Light Dragoons.
Ledger stone: St Mary's Churchyard, Sand Hutton, Yorkshire. (Photograph)

HERE LIE / THE REMAINS OF / COLONEL MICHAEL CHILDERS, C. B. / LATE OF THE 11TH LIGHT DRAGOONS / WHO DIED AT SAND HUTTON, / ON JANUARY 9TH 1854, / AGED 70 YEARS.

Memorial tablet: St Mary's Church, Sand Hutton, Yorkshire. (Photograph)

IN A VAULT IN THE CHURCH YARD / LIE THE REMAINS OF / MICHAEL CHILDERS, LATE OF THE 11TH LIGHT DRAGOONS, / A COLONEL IN THE ARMY AND COMPANION OF THE BATH, / WHO DIED AT SAND HUTTON JANUARY 9TH 1854, / AGED 70 YEARS: / HE WAS THE YOUNGEST SON OF THE LATE / CHILDERS WALBANKE CHILDERS ESQ. / OF CANTLEY NEAR DONCASTER. / COLONEL CHILDERS WAS WITH THE ARMY THROUGHOUT / THE PENINSULAR WAR, / WAS AT THE BATTLE OF WATERLOO, AND AFTERWARDS / SERVED 13 YEARS WITH HIS REGIMENT IN INDIA, / WHERE HE COMMANDED A BRIGADE OF CAVALRY / AT THE SIEGE OF BHURTPOOR.

Ensign 2nd West India Regt 25 Feb 1799. Cornet 11th Lt Dragoons 5 Aug 1799. Lt 25 Aug 1801. Capt 14 Jun 1805. Bt. Major 25 Aug 1814. Bt Lt Colonel 18 Jun 1815. Major 60th Foot 15 Apr 1819. Major 11th Lt Dragoons 24 Jun 1819. Lt Colonel 21 Sep 1820. Bt Colonel 10 Jan 1837.

Served in the Peninsula Jun 1811 – Apr 1814. Present at El Bodon, Morales, Castrejon, Salamanca, Venta del Poza, Vittoria, Tolosa (Mentioned in Despatches) and Bayonne. Present at Waterloo (Brigade Major to Major General Vandeleur). Also served at the Helder 1799 and India 1823–1836 (present at the siege and capture of Bhurtpore 1825–1826 where he commanded the cavalry). Awarded Army of India medal. MGS medal for Salamanca and Vittoria. CB. Retired on half pay 1836.

CHISHOLM, Harold
Private. 92nd Regiment of Foot.
Headstone: Old High Churchyard, Inverness, Invernesshire, Scotland. (South side of Church). (Photograph)

SACRED / TO THE MEMORY OF / HAROLD CHISHOLM, / LATE OF THE 92D HIGHLANDERS / WHO DIED 19 SEPT 1855, / AGED 63 YEARS. / ....

Served in the Peninsula Oct 1810 – Apr 1814. Present at Fuentes d'Onoro, Vittoria, Pyrenees, Orthes and Toulouse. Served at Waterloo in Capt Peter Wilkie's Company. MGS medal for Fuentes d'Onoro, Vittoria, Pyrenees, Orthes and Toulouse.

CHISHOLM, Stuart
2nd Assistant Surgeon. Ordnance Medical Department, Royal Artillery.
Cross: St Mary's Churchyard, Eskadale, Invernesshire, Scotland. (M.I.)

"THE CROSS OF / STUART CHISHOLM / LATE DEPT INSPECTOR GENERAL / OF ARMY HOSPI-TALS / DEPARTED THIS LIFE ON 30 SEPT 1862 / IN THE 69TH YEAR OF HIS LIFE / AND IN THE 50TH YEAR OF HIS MILITARY SERVICE."

Extra Asst Surgeon 30 Nov 1813. 2nd Asst Surgeon 20 Oct 1814. 1st Asst Surgeon 13 May 1827. Surgeon 11 Sep 1838. Senior Surgeon 18 Jun 1846. Surgeon Staff 1st Class 20 Jul 1855.

Present at Waterloo, the Capture of Paris and with the Army of Occupation. Also served in Canada (present in both Rebellions in Upper Canada 1838–1839). Accompanied several naval expeditions against the rebels on Lake Ontario, the only medical officer of the regular force in the field. Served as a volunteer at Prescott 13 Nov 1838 in the affair between the rebels and Americans against the regular forces where 80 men were killed or wounded including the two officers who led the expedition. (Mentioned in Despatches). Retired with the honorary rank of Deputy Inspector General 7 Dec 1858.
REFERENCE: *Gentleman's Magazine, Nov 1862, p. 652. Annual Register, 1862, Appx, p. 341.*

CHOWNE, Christopher Tilson
Colonel. 76th Regiment of Foot.
Chest tomb: Kensal Green Cemetery, London. (196/90/IC). (Photograph)

SACRED TO THE MEMORY OF / GENERAL CHRISTOPHER TILSON CHOWNE / COLONEL OF THE 76TH REGT OF FOOT / THIRD SON OF THE LATE / JOHN TILSON OF WALLINGTON PARK OXON ESQ / DIED 15TH JULY 1834 AGED 63 YEARS

2nd Lt 23rd Foot 16 Feb 1788. Lt 3 Apr 1790. Capt Independent Company 7 Aug 1793. Lt Colonel 99th Foot 15 Nov 1794. Lt Colonel 44th Foot 24 Jun 1799. Bt Col 1 Jan 1801. Major General 25 Apr 1808. Lt General 4 Jun 1813. Colonel 76th Foot 17 Feb 1814. General 22 Jul 1830.

Served in the Peninsula Apr 1809 – Mar 1810 and Mar 1812 – Jan 1813. (Commanded 3 Brigade Apr

– Jun 1809, Commanded 2 Brigade 3rd Division Jun 1809, Commanded 1 Brigade 2nd Division Jul – Dec 1809 and GOC 2nd Division under Lt General R. Hill Apr – Dec 1812). Present at Talavera (Mentioned in Despatches) and Almarez. Gold Medal for Talavera. Also served in Egypt 1801 (present at Alexandria where he was wounded). Changed his name from Christopher Tilson to Christopher Tilson Chowne in Jan 1812.

REFERENCE: *Gentleman's Magazine, Oct 1834, p. 432.*

CHÜDEN, Georg Wilhelm Cyriaeus
Major. 4th Line Battalion, King's German Legion.
Named on the Regimental Memorial: La Haye Sainte, Waterloo, Belgium. (Photograph)

Lt 9 Feb 1805. Major 4 Jun 1814.
   Present at Waterloo where he was severely wounded and died of his wounds 19 Jun. Also served at Hanover 1805, the Baltic 1807, North Germany 1813–1814 and Netherlands 1814.

CHÜDEN, Paul Gottlieb
Major. 2nd Line Battalion, King's German Legion.
Named on the Memorial: St Andrew's Church, (now Musée Historique), Biarritz, France. (Photograph)

Capt 5th Line King's German Legion 18 Oct 1803. Major 2nd Line 7 Feb 1809.
   Served in the Peninsula 1808 – Jan 1809 and Mar 1809 – Apr 1814. Present at Douro, Talavera, Busaco, Fuentes d'Onoro, Ciudad Rodrigo, Moriscos, Salamanca, Vittoria, Tolosa, San Sebastian, Bidassoa, Nivelle, Nive, St Etienne (severely wounded) and Bayonne where he was killed at the Sortie from Bayonne Apr 1814. Also served in the Baltic 1807–1808.

CHURCHILL, Chatham Horace
Lieutenant and Captain. 1st Regiment of Foot Guards.
Named on the Regimental Memorial Cenotaph: Government Park, Barrackpore, India. (M.I.)

"MAJOR GENERAL CHURCHILL, CB. HMS".

Memorial: Cemetery of Agra, Duolop and Bombay Road, Agra, India. (M.I.)

"TO THE MEMORY OF COLONEL CHURCHILL, C. B. OF H. M. 31ST REGT OF FOOT, WHO AFTER SERVING WITH DISTINGUISHED HONOUR DURING THE PENINSULA WAR AND SHARING THE DANGERS AND GLORY OF WATERLOO, FELL MORTALLY WOUNDED IN THE DISCHARGE OF HIS DUTIES AS QUARTERMASTER-GENERAL OF H. M. FORCES IN INDIA AT THE BATTLE OF MAHARAJPUR ON THE 29 DEC 1843. THIS HUMBLE MONUMENT IS ERECTED BY THE BROTHER OFFICERS OF HIS TROOP ON THE FIELD WHERE HE FELL AND IS BURIED AS A MARK OF THEIR ESTEEM AND ADMIRATION OF A GALLANT SOLDIER".

Ensign 1st Foot Guards 19 Jun 1806. Lt and Capt 27 Aug 1812. Bt Major 22 Nov 1813. Bt Lt Colonel 18 Jun 1815. Capt 18th Foot 26 Dec 1822. Capt 1st Ceylon Regt 22 May 1823. Major 27 Jul 1826 (unattached). Lt Colonel 31st Foot 20 Apr 1832. Bt Colonel 10 Jan 1837.
   Served in the Peninsula Nov 1808 – Jan 1809 (ADC to Major General Broderick), Jul 1809 – Sep 1810 (ADC to Major General C. Craufurd), Oct 1810 – Nov 1812 (ADC to Lord Hill) and Dec 1812 – Apr 1814 (Deputy AAG 2nd Division). Present at Corunna, Arroyo dos Molinos, Almarez, Vittoria, Pyrenees, Heights of Ainhoe, Nivelle, Nive, Garris, Orthes, Aire, Tarbes and Toulouse. Present at Waterloo (ADC to Lord Hill). CB. Half pay 16 Jul 1830. Later served in India 11 Aug 1837 (QMG with the rank of Major General). Present at Maharajpore where he was killed 27 Dec 1843.

CLARE, Charles
Private. 12th (Prince of Wales's) Regiment of Light Dragoons.
Named on the Regimental Memorial: St Joseph's Church, Waterloo, Belgium. (Photograph)
   Killed at Waterloo.

CLARK, Alexander Kennedy
Captain. 1st (Royal) Regiment of Dragoons.
Family Memorial: St Michael's Churchyard, Dumfries, Dumfriesshire, Scotland. (Photograph)

IN MEMORY OF / LIEUTENANT GENERAL / SIR ALEX KENNEDY CLARK KENNEDY KCB KH / OF KNOCKGRAY, WHO DIED IN LONDON / ON THE 30TH DAY OF JANUARY 1864 AGED 81 YEARS. / HIS REMAINS ARE INTERRED IN THIS SPOT. / ....

Cornet 8 Sep 1802. Lt 15 Dec 1804. Capt 13 Dec 1810. Major 7th Dragoon Guards 26 May 1825. Lt Colonel 11 Jun 1830. Bt Colonel 23 Nov 1841. Major General 20 Jun 1854. Lt General 19 Jun 1860.
   Served in the Peninsula Sep 1809 – Sep 1813. (Acting Brigade Major Dec 1810 and Oct 1811 – Jan 1812). Present covering the retreat to Torres Vedras, Quinta de Torre, Fuentes d'Onoro, Fuente Guinaldo, Aldea da Ponte (Brigade Major to General Slade), Maguilla, Vittoria and Pamplona. MGS medal for Fuentes d'Onoro and Vittoria. Present at Waterloo where he covered the retreat of infantry from Quatre Bras on 17 June. On 18 June was wounded twice and had two horses killed under him, but he captured the Eagle of the French 105th Foot which was taken to the rear by Cpl Stiles. KCB and KH. Colonel 6th Dragoon Guards 14 Jun 1858. Colonel 2nd Dragoons (Scots Greys) 1862 until his death 30 Jan 1864. Later assumed the name of Alexander Kennedy Clark Kennedy.
REFERENCE: *Gentleman's Magazine, Apr 1864, pp. 527–8. Annual Register, 1865, Appx, pp. 176–7.*

CLARK, John
Ensign. 54th (West Norfolk) Regiment of Foot.
Grave: St Andrew's Churchyard, Hove, Sussex. (No longer extant). (M.I.)

".................. ALSO TO THE BELOVED MEMORY OF MAJOR GENERAL CLARK, KH. COLONEL H M 59TH REG^T ENTERED INTO REST MARCH 22 1865."

Ensign 2 Jun 1814. Lt 27 Nov 1821. Capt 29 Aug 1826. Major 25 Dec 1829. Bt Lt Colonel 23 Nov 1841. Bt Colonel 29 Jun 1854. Major General 26 Oct 1858.
   Present at Waterloo in reserve at Hal, siege of Cambrai and with the Army of Occupation. Also served in India until 1840(present at Ava 1824–1826 – Rangoon, Kemmendine, Kamaroot and Mahattee. Led the attack at Aracan 1825 where he was severely wounded) and Gibraltar 1845–1854. KH. Colonel 59th Foot. Served in the army for 51 years.

CLARK, John
Staff Surgeon. Medical Department.
Grave: Protestant Cemetery, Naples, Italy. (M.I)

"DR JOHN CLARK, KH. / DEP. INSPECTOR GENERAL OF BRITISH ARMY HOSPITALS / OB 18 DEC 1845."

Memorial: St Luke's Churchyard, Charlton, Kent. (No longer extant: Grave number 55). (M.I)

"................... JOHN CLARK MD, WHO DIED AT NAPLES THE 18TH DEC 1845 AND IS INTERRED THERE. DR JOHN CLARK KH AND INSPECTOR GENERAL OF ARMY HOSPITALS................"

Asst Surgeon Jan 1804. Asst Surgeon South Ayrshire Militia 1806. Asst Surgeon Staff 12 Jul 1809. Staff Surgeon Portuguese Army 12 Oct 1809. Staff Surgeon 25 Sept 1814. Asst Inspector of Hospitals 3 Jul 1823. Deputy Inspector General 29 Jan 1836.

Served in the Peninsula Nov 1809 – Dec 1813 with the Portuguese Army. KH. MD St Andrew's 1806. FRCP Edinburgh 1813. MD Edinburgh 1821.

CLARK, Joseph
Sergeant. 3rd (Prince of Wales's) Dragoon Guards.
Headstone: St Mary's Churchyard, Bath, Somerset, (Photograph)

TO THE MEMORY OF / MARY CLARK. / RELICT OF / SERGEANT JOSEPH CLARK / 3RD DRAGOON GUARDS. / WHO ACCOMPANIED HER HUSBAND / THROUGHOUT THE PENIN-SULAR WAR. / AND DIED IN THIS PARISH. / OCTOBER 26TH 1863 / AGED 86 YEARS.

Served in the Peninsula 1809 – Apr 1814. Present at Talavera, Albuera, Usagre, Aldea da Ponte, Maguilla, Vittoria and Toulouse. His wife Mary accompanied her husband during his service the Peninsula. She died in Bath in 1863.

CLARK, Joseph Taylor
Lieutenant. 28th (North Gloucestershire) Regiment of Foot.
Headstone: St Bride's Churchyard, Kirkbride, Cumbria. (South side near entrance porch). (Photograph)

IN MEMORY OF / LIEUT JOSEPH TAYLOR CLARK, / OF THE 28TH REGT OF FOOT. SON OF / DANIEL & ISABELLA CLARK OF KIRKBRIDE / WHO FELL GLORIOUSLY FIGHTING FOR HIS KING / AND COUNTRY, AT THE BATTLE OF WATERLOO / ON THE 18TH DAY OF JUNE 1815 AGED 31 YEARS.

Ensign 22 Sep 1808. Lt 1 Mar 1810.
Served in the Peninsula with 1/28th Aug 1808 – Jan 1809, Sep 1810 – Aug 1811 and Sep 1813 – Apr 1814. Present at Corunna, Tarifa, Nivelle, Nive (wounded at St Pierre 13 Dec 1813), Garris, Orthes, Aire and Toulouse (wounded). Present at Waterloo where he was killed.

CLARK, Mary see Joseph Clark

CLARKE, Isaac Blake
Major. 2nd (Royal North British) Regiment of Dragoons.
Headstone: St Peter in Thanet Churchyard, Broadstairs, Kent. (No longer extant: Plot number 712). (M.I.)

"IN MEMORY OF ISAAC BLAKE CLARKE WHO DIED JAN VII MDCCCL AGED LXXVI YEARS ...."

Cornet 8th Lt Dragoons 21 Feb 1795. Cornet 2nd Dragoons 11 Jul 1795. Lt 1796. Capt 7 Sep 1797. Major 16 Jun 1807. Bt Lt Colonel 4 Jun 1814. Lt Colonel 20 Jul 1815.
Present at Waterloo where he was wounded. After Waterloo promoted Lt Colonel commanding the Scots Greys, after the death of Lt Colonel Inglis Hamilton during the battle. Also served in Flanders 1795 and Ireland Southern District 1797 (AAG). CB. Retired 11 Oct 1821.

CLARKE, John
Lieutenant. 66th (Berkshire) Regiment of Foot.
Headstone: Old Churchyard, Spital, Windsor, Berkshire. (Photograph)

IHS / LIEUTENANT COLONEL / JOHN CLARKE MKW. / LATE 66TH FOOT. / DIED 21ST MARCH 1859.

Ensign 14 Jul 1808. Lt 3 Oct 1809. Captain 13 Jan 1825. Bt Major 28 Jun 1836. Bt Lt Colonel 28 Nov 1854.
   Served in the Peninsula Apr 1809 – Apr 1814. Present at Douro, Talavera, Campo Mayor, Albuera (in command of a company of flankers when he was struck down by a Polish Lancer and taken prisoner, but escaped during a cavalry charge), Arroyo dos Molinos, Vittoria, Pyrenees, Nivelle, Nive, Garris, Orthes, Aire and Toulouse. Also served at St Helena 1816–1821 and Canada 1837–1838 (present in the Rebellion). Military Knight of Windsor 1846. MGS medal for Talavera, Albuera, Vittoria, Pyrenees, Nivelle, Nive, Orthes and Toulouse.

CLARKE, Joseph
Lieutenant. 48th (Northamptonshire) Regiment of Foot.
Memorial tablet: Scottish Church, St George's, Grenada, West Indies. (M.I.)

"SACRED / TO THE MEMORY OF / JOSEPH CLARKE / WHO AFTER SERVING AS A / LIEUTENANT IN THE 48TH REGIMENT / THROUGHOUT THE PENINSULA / CAMPAIGN, WAS APPOINTED OFFICER OF H M CUSTOMS AND / DIED WHILST ON THAT SERVICE / ON THE 15TH DAY OF AUGUST, 1838. / AGED 53 YEARS."

Ensign 15 Jun 1809. Lt 18 Jun 1811.
   Served in the Peninsula Oct 1809 – Jul 1812 and Dec 1812 – Apr 1814. Present at Busaco, Albuera, Vittoria, Pyrenees, Nivelle, Orthes and Toulouse. Half pay 1814. Later became Customs Officer at St George's, Grenada.

CLARKE, Thomas
Private. 12th (Prince of Wales's) Regiment of Light Dragoons.
Named on the Regimental Memorial: St Joseph's Church, Waterloo, Belgium. (Photograph)
   Killed at Waterloo.

CLAUS, William
Lieutenant. 54th (West Norfolk) Regiment of Foot.
Family Memorial: St Mark's Churchyard, Niagara, Canada. (Photograph)

.... TWO SONS OF COLONEL CLAUS / DIED IN THE SERVICE OF THE BRITISH ARMY. / LT WILLIAM 1791 - 1824 SERVED AT THE BATTLE OF WATERLOO AND / DIED IN INDIA AND / LT DANIEL DIED IN 1813 FROM WOUNDS RECEIVED AT / THE BATTLE OF CHRYSTLER'S FARM.

Ensign 15 Dec 1808. Lt 22 Feb 1810.
Served at Waterloo in reserve at Hal in Capt Leslie's Company, siege of Cambrai and with the Army of Occupation. Also served in the Netherlands1814 (present at Antwerp), Cape of Good Hope 1819 and India 1823 (present in the first Burmese War) where he died 1824. Brother of Lt Daniel Claus who died of wounds received at the battle of Chrystler's Farm in North America 11 Nov 1813.

CLAVERING, James
Lieutenant. 14th (Duchess of York's Own) Regiment of Light Dragoons.
Memorial tablet: St George's Chapel, Hyde Park Place, Cumberland Gate, London. (M.I.)

"SACRED TO THE MEMORY OF / JAMES CLAVERING ESQ., / ELDEST SON OF SIR THOMAS

JOHN CLAVERING / OF AXWELL PARK IN THE COUNTY OF DURHAM, BARONET / AND AN OFFICER IN THE 14ᵀᴴ LIGHT DRAGOON MILITARY. / DURING HIS ARDUOUS SERVICES / HE ENJOYED THE ESTEEM AND REGARD OF HIS BROTHER OFFICERS. / HIS GALLANTRY IN THE FIELD WAS EMINENTLY CONSPICUOUS. / IN PORTUGAL, SPAIN, AMERICA AND FRANCE. / HE WAS A DUTIFUL AND ATTACHED SON, AND AN AFFECTIONATE BROTHER, / WHILE IN HIS FRIENDSHIP HE WAS WARM, FIRM, AND SINCERE. / HE DIED ON THE 23ᴿᴰ OF JANUARY, 1824, / IN THE 31ˢᵀ YEAR OF HIS AGE / AND HIS REMAINS ARE DEPOSITED IN A VAULT UNDERNEATH THIS CHAPEL. / THIS MONUMENT HAS BEEN ERECTED BY HIS DISCONSO-LATE FATHER / AS A MEMORIAL OF HIS AFFECTION / AND OF HIS LAMENTED SON'S VIRTUES."

Cornet. 2 Aug 1810. Lt 28 Feb 1812.

Served in the Peninsula Jul 1811 – Apr 1814. Present at El Bodon, Badajoz, Llerena, Castrejon, Salamanca, Vittoria, Pyrenees, Nivelle, Nive, Orthes, Vic Bigorre, Tarbes and Toulouse. Also served in North America Dec 1814.

CLAY, Matthew
Private. 3ʳᵈ Regiment of Foot Guards.
Double sided Headstone: Foster Hill Cemetery, Bedford, Bedfordshire. (Plot H8 Grave number 243). (Photograph)

SERJEANT MAJOR MATTHEW CLAY / SERVED WITH HIGH CHARACTER / FROM 1813 TO 1833 IN / THE THIRD (SCOTS FUSILIERS) REGIMENT / OF / FOOT GUARDS / AND / FROM 1833 – 1852 / SERJEANT MAJOR OF / THE BEDFORDSHIRE MILITIA / BORN IN THE PARISH OF BLID-WORTH / IN THE COUNTY OF NOTTINGHAM / DIED AT BEDFORD / ON THE 5ᵀᴴ JUNE 1873 / IN HIS 78ᵀᴴ YEAR

Reverse side of headstone:

THIS / TRIBUTE OF RESPECT / TO / THE MEMORY OF / SERJEANT MAJOR MATTHEW CLAY / HAS BEEN ERECTED / BY MANY INHABITANTS / OF BEDFORD / WHERE DURING FORTY YEARS / HE SO LIVED AS / TO WIN AND RETAIN / THE ESTEEM OF HIS FELLOW TOWNSMEN. / HE WAS ONE OF / THE INVINCIBLE DEFENDERS / OF / HOUGOUMONT, / IN / THE BATTLE OF WATERLOO / A STATELY VETERAN / DIGNIFIED AND MODEST / NOT LESS CONSCIEN-TIOUS THAN BRAVE

Pte 6 Dec 1813. Cpl 21 Mar 1818. Sgt 14 Feb 1822.

Present at Waterloo where he served in the defence of Hougoumont. Wrote a vivid account of this enti-tled *Narrative of the Battles of Quatre Bras and Waterloo; with the defence of Hougoumont*, published in Bedford 1853. Also served in the Netherlands 1814–1815 (present at Bergen-op-Zoom) and Portugal 1826–1828. Discharged 8 May 1833. Sgt Major of the Bedford Militia 1833–1852.
REFERENCE: Clay, Matthew, *Narrative of the Battles of Quatre Bras and Waterloo with the defence of Hougoumont, 1853, reprint edited by Gareth Glover, 2006.*

CLAYHILLS, James Menzies
Captain. 1ˢᵗ (Royal Scots) Regiment of Foot.
Mural memorial: Invergowrie Churchyard, Dundee, Angus, Scotland. (M.I.) (Photograph of family memo-rials on which this memorial tablet is no longer extant)

"JAMES MENZIES CLAYHILLS, LATE CAPT OF THE ROYAL SCOTS, DIED 5 NOV 1817, AGED 31 YEARS, TEN OF WHICH WERE DEVOTED TO THE SERVICE OF HIS KING AND COUNTRY."

Ensign 26 May 1801. Lt 28 Jan 1804. Capt 16 Jun 1808.

Served in the Peninsula Apr 1810 – Sep 1811. Present at Busaco and Fuentes d'Onoro. Also served at Walcheren 1809. Retired 12 Dec 1811.

CLAYTON, William Robert

Captain. Royal Regiment of Horse Guards.
Memorial tablet: All Saints Church, Marlow, Buckinghamshire. (Photograph)

ALSO TO THE MEMORY OF / GENERAL SIR WILLIAM ROBERT CLAYTON, BART / BORN AUGUST 28TH 1786. DIED SEPTEMBER 19TH 1866 AGED 80 YEARS. / SERVED IN THE PENINSULA AND WATERLOO CAMPAIGNS / MAGISTRATE AND DEPUTY LIEUTENANT AND IN 1846 HIGH SHERIFF FOR BUCKS. / HIS AFFECTIONATE AND ATTACHED CHILDREN HAVE INSCRIBED THIS TABLET / IN GRATEFUL REMEMBRANCE OF THOSE VIRTUES WHICH DURING HIS LIFE / SECURED THEIR AFFECTIONS, SUPPORTED THEIR PRINCIPLES / AND CHERISHED THEIR HAPPINESS.

Memorial tablet: St Mary the Virgin Church, Bletchingley, Surrey. (Photograph)

SACRED TO THE MEMORY OF / GENERAL SIR WILLIAM ROBERT CLAYTON, BART. / BORN AUGUST 28TH 1786, DIED SEPTEMBER 18TH 1866, AGED 80 YEARS. / SERVED IN THE PENINSULA THE ARDUOUS CAMPAIGN OF 1812, 1813 & 1814, UNDER THE / DUKE OF WELLINGTON. PRESENT AT THE BATTLES OF VITTORIA, SEVEN ACTIONS IN / THE PYRENEES, CROSSING THE DOURO, BEFORE PAMPELUNA IN PURSUIT OF DIVISIONS OF / MARSHAL SUCHET. SERVED THE CAMPAIGN IN THE NETHERLANDS. PRESENT AT THE / BATTLES OF QUATRE BRAS, GENAPPE AND WATERLOO. IN THE ADVANCE ON PARIS / AND THE SUBSEQUENT CAPITULATION. FREQUENTLY IN COMMAND OF THE ROYAL HORSE / GUARDS IN THE PENINSULA AND WATERLOO CAMPAIGNS. ACTED AS FIELD OFFICER / DURING THE CAMPAIGN IN THE NETHERLANDS IN 1815. COMMANDED FOR TWO YEARS / TWO SQUADRONS OF CAVALRY, DURING THE SERIOUS DISTURBANCE CALLED THE LUDDITE / REBELLION IN THE MANUFACTURING DISTRICTS OF YORKSHIRE, LANCASHIRE, CHESHIRE &c. &c. / RECEIVED ESPECIAL THANKS FOR HAVING WELL FULFILLED A MOST ARDUOUS / RESPONSIBLE AND DIFFICULT COMMAND FROM THE GENERAL COMMANDING. RECEIVED THE / WAR MEDAL AND CLASPS AND WATERLOO MEDAL. / MAGISTRATE AND DEPUTY LIEUTENANT AND IN 1846, HIGH SHERIFF FOR BUCKS. / HUMBLE AND SINCERE IN CHRISTIAN FAITH, / COMPASSIONATE, BENEVOLENT AND JUST HE ENDEAVOURED TO PERFORM ALL THE DUTIES / AND WAS FERVENT IN ALL THE CHARITIES OF LIFE. / HIS EARLY LIFE WAS HONOURABLY AND ZEALOUSLY ENGAGED IN THE SERVICE OF HIS COUNTRY. / HIS AFFECTIONATE AND ATTACHED CHILDREN HAVE INSCRIBED THIS TABLET / IN GRATEFUL REMEMBRANCE OF THOSE VIRTUES, WHICH DURING HIS LIFE / SECURED THEIR AFFECTIONS, SUPPORTED THEIR PRINCIPLES, / AND CHERISHED THEIR HAPPINESS.

Ensign 10th Foot 28 Sep 1804. Cornet Royal Regiment of Horse Guards 18 May 1805. Lt 14 Nov 1805. Capt 27 Apr 1809. Major 40th Foot 21 Dec 1815. Bt Lt Colonel 8 Apr 1826. Bt Colonel 23 Nov 1841. Major General 11 Nov 1851. Lt General 26 Oct 1858. General 12 Jan 1865.

Served in the Peninsula Nov 1812 – Sep 1813. Present at Vittoria, Pyrenees and Pamplona. Present after Quatre Bras to cover the retreat of the infantry, and at Waterloo. MGS medal for Vittoria. Also served in the Netherlands 1814–1815 and afterwards in command of cavalry during the Luddite Riots in the north of England.
REFERENCE: Mollo, J. and B., Waterloo officers – 1. Captain William Robert Clayton. Journal of the Society for Army Historical Research, Vol 39, No 158, Jun 1964, pp. 71–2. Gentleman's Magazine, Nov 1866, pp. 691–2.

CLEAR, Philip
Private. 32nd (Cornwall) Regiment of Foot.
Headstone: St Symphorian Churchyard, Veryan, Cornwall. (Photograph)

A / CHRISTIAN SOLDIER / PHILIP CLEAR / FOUGHT AT THE BATTLES OF / SALAMANCA, BADAJOS, PAMPELUNA, VITTORIA, PYRENEES, / TOULOUSE, WATERLOO. / DIED IN THE PARISH OF DECLINE, 1829 / AGED 40 YEARS. / "IN FORMER YEARS I SHED MY BLOOD / BOTH FOR MY KING AND FOR MY COUNTRY. / IN LATER YEARS IT WAS MY PRIDE TO BE A SOLDIER TO HIS MAJESTY / WHO SHED HIS BLOOD FOR ME."

Pte 1809.
    Served in the Peninsula Jul 1811 – Apr 1814. Present at Badajoz, Salamanca, Vittoria, Pamplona, Pyrenees and Toulouse. Present at Waterloo in Capt W. H. Toole's Company. Also served in the West Indies 1815–1826. Discharged through ill health 1826.
REFERENCE: *Edwards, Christine, Veryan's Waterloo soldier, 2008. (Local publication)*

CLEARY, Richard Stanton
Lieutenant. 76th Regiment of Foot.
Cross on pedestal: Green Street, St Helier, Jersey, Channel Islands. (Plot K2). Memorial damaged, inscription illegible and recorded from memorial inscription. (Photograph)

"IN MEMORY OF RICHARD STANTON CLEARY LIEUT 76TH REGT CAPT 13TH PORTUGUESE WHO DIED NOV 24TH 1851, AGED 61 YEARS. NIVE NIVELLE CORUNNA."

Ensign 7 Jun 1808. Lt 23 Mar 1809. Portuguese Army: Capt 13th Line 9 Nov 1813.
    Served in the Peninsula Nov 1808 – Jan 1809, Aug – Oct 1813 and with Portuguese Army Nov 1813 – Apr 1814. Present at Corunna, Bidassoa, Nivelle, Nive and Bayonne. MGS medal for Corunna, Nivelle and Nive. Also served at Walcheren 1809. Half pay 30 Sep 1819.

CLEEVES, Andrew
2nd Captain. Artillery, King's German Legion.
Ledger stone: Selby Abbey Churchyard, Selby, Yorkshire. (Photograph)

SACRED / TO THE MEMORY OF / LIEUTENANT COLONEL / ANDREW CLEEVES KH / WHO DEPARTED THIS LIFE / 8TH OF JUNE 1830

2nd Capt 5 Jun 1807. Major 18 Jun 1815. Bt Lt Colonel Hanoverian Artillery.
    Served in the Peninsula May 1809 – Apr 1814. Present at Douro, Talavera, Busaco, Albuera (taken prisoner but escaped), second siege of Badajoz, Madrid (severely wounded), Salamanca, Vittoria and San Sebastian. At the retreat from Madrid 31 Oct 1812, the arsenal at the Retiro Fort had to be blown up. The mines used were so carelessly laid that two Commissariat officers were killed and Capt Cleeves in charge was severely burnt and nearly died. Present at Waterloo. Promoted to Major 18 Jun 1815. Gold Medal for Albuera. Also served at Hanover 1804–1805 and the Baltic 1807–1808. Died in Selby 8 Jun 1830 on his way back to Hanover.

CLERKE, William Henry
Lieutenant. 52nd (Oxfordshire) Light Infantry Regiment of Foot.
Low monument: St Mary Magdalene Churchyard, Leintwardine, Herefordshire. (Grave number E 15). (Photograph)

TO THE MEMORY OF LIEUT COLONEL SIR WILLIAM HENRY CLERKE BART / OF MERTYN IN

THE COUNTY OF FLINT / WHO DIED AT THE HEATH FEBRUARY 16TH 1861 AGED 67 YEARS / HE SERVED WITH THE 52 REGT IN THE PENINSULA AND AT WATERLOO / BY HIS FAMILY HE WAS BELOVED AND BY HIS FRIENDS ESTEEMED.

Cornet 3rd Dragoons 10 Jan 1811. Lt 25 Jul 1811. Lt 52nd Foot 19 Sep 1811. Capt 42nd Foot 25 Apr 1822.
   Served in the Peninsula with 1/52nd Nov 1813 – Apr 1814. Present at Nivelle, Nive, Orthes, Tarbes and Toulouse. Present at Waterloo and with the Army of Occupation. Retired on half pay 2 May 1823. MGS medal for Nivelle, Nive, Orthes and Toulouse. Succeeded his father as 9th Baronet 10 Apr 1818. Educated at Charterhouse.

CLIFFE, Stephen
Private. 1st Life Guards.
Buried in St John the Baptist Churchyard, Kirkheaton, Yorkshire. No Inscription recorded. (Burial record)

Pte 4 Nov 1812.
   Served in the Peninsula 1813 – Apr 1814. Present at Toulouse. Served at Waterloo (severely wounded by a musket ball breaking his arm and had two horses shot from under him). Discharged 4 Nov 1817 due to his wound at Waterloo. MGS medal for Toulouse. Died 17 Apr 1856 aged 60 years.

CLIFTON, George
Captain and Lieutenant Colonel. 1st Regiment of Foot Guards.
Named on Memorial Panel VIII for Bergen-Op-Zoom: Royal Military Chapel, Wellington Barracks, London. (M.I.) (Destroyed by a Flying Bomb 1944)

Ensign 30 Oct 1799. Lt and Capt 3 Jul 1801. Capt 69th Foot 9 Jul 1803. Lt and Capt 1st Foot Guards 3 Dec 1808. Capt and Lt Col 25 Dec 1812.
   Served in the Peninsula with 3rd Battalion Oct 1808 – Jan 1809 and Apr 1811 – May 1813. Present at Corunna and Cadiz (Brigade Major May 1811 – Aug 1812). Also served in the Netherlands (present at Bergen-op-Zoom where he was severely wounded and died of his wounds 9 Mar 1814).

CLINTON, Sir Henry
Colonel. 60th (Royal American) Regiment of Foot.
Family Memorial tablet: St Mary Magdalene Church, Barkway, Hertfordshire. (Photograph)

SACRED ALSO TO THE MEMORY OF / LIEUT, GENL SIR HENRY CLINTON G.C.B. / AS A SOLDIER HE WAS DISTINGUISHED / BY A LONG CAREER OF ACTIVE SERVICE / IN THE EST & WST INDIES, THE PENINSULAR, FLANDERS & FRANCE / AND BY THE CONSPICUOUS PART HE BORE / IN THE BATTLES OF LASWAREE, SALAMANCA, TOULOUSE / AND FINALLY AT THE GREAT DAY OF WATERLOO. / AS A MAN & A CHRISTIAN, / HE WAS NOT LESS DISTIN-GUISHED / BY THE EXEMPLARY PATIENCE & FORTITUDE / WITH WHICH HE SUBMITTED DURING THIRTEEN YEARS / TO AN AFFLICTING & DESTRUCTIVE MALADY / WHICH FINALLY TERMINATED HIS EXISTENCE. / HE DIED AT ASHLEY COURT IN THE COUNTY OF SOUTHAMPTON / ON THE 11TH DECEMBER 1829, / IN THE 58TH YEAR OF HIS AGE / AND WAS BURIED NEAR THIS SPOT.

Family Mausoleum: St Mary Magdalene Churchyard, Barkway, Hertfordshire. (Photograph)

.... / GENERAL / SIR HENRY CLINTON G.C.B. / BORN 9TH MARCH 1771 / DIED 11TH DECEMBER 1829 / ....

Brass plate: Floor of Choir stall: St Mary Magdalene Church, Barkway, Hertfordshire. (Photograph)

BENEATH / THE LADY SUSAN CLINTON / DIED 24ᵀᴴ AUGUST 1816. / AND / LIEUTᵀ GENERAL / SIR HENRY CLINTON G.C.B. / DIED 11ᵀᴴ DECEMBER 1829

Memorial: Royal Military Chapel, Wellington Barracks, London. (M.I.) (Destroyed by a Flying Bomb 1944)

"THE CREDENCE TABLE IS GIVEN BY LIEUT.-COL. HENRY R. CLINTON, LATE GRENADIER GUARDS WITH OTHER MEMBERS OF HIS FAMILY, IN MEMORY OF .... / HIS GREAT-UNCLE, / LIEUT.-GENERAL SIR HENRY CLINTON, G.C.B., G.C.H., COLONEL OF THE BUFFS. / BORN, 1772; DIED, 1829. / HE SERVED AT INTERVALS WITH THE 1ˢᵀ GUARDS, FROM 1789 TO 1813. HE WAS IN THE FIELD IN THE / EAST AND WEST INDIES, THE PENINSULA, FLANDERS AND FRANCE, BEING PRESENT AT THE BATTLES OF LASWAREE, SALAMANCA, THE NIVE, THE NIVELLE, ORTHEZ, TOULOUSE, AND WATERLOO".

Ensign 11ᵗʰ Foot 10 Oct 1787. Ensign 1ˢᵗ Foot Guards 12 Mar 1789. Capt 15ᵗʰ Foot 6 Apr 1791. Lt and Capt 1ˢᵗ Foot Guards 30 Nov 1792. Bt Major 22 Apr 1794. Lt Col 66ᵗʰ Foot 30 Sep 1795. Capt and Lt Col 1ˢᵗ Foot Guards 20 Oct 1796. Bt Colonel 25 Sep 1803. Major General 25 Jul 1810. Col 60ᵗʰ Foot 27 May 1813. Lt General 4 Jun 1814. Colonel 3ʳᵈ Foot 9 Aug 1815.

Served in the Peninsula Aug 1808 – Jan 1809 (Adjutant General), Feb 1812 – Jul 1813 and Nov 1813 – Apr 1814 (GOC 6 Division). Present at Vimeiro, Corunna, siege of Salamanca Forts, Salamanca, Burgos and retreat from Burgos, Nivelle, Nive, Orthes and Toulouse. Present at Waterloo in command of 2ⁿᵈ British Infantry Division. Also served in the Netherlands 1788–1799, Flanders 1793–1794 (present at St Amand, Famars, Valenciennes, Lidroghem, Wattignies, Mauberge, Vaux, Camphin – wounded 10 May 1794 and Nimwegen), West Indies 1795 (present at St Lucia where he commanded the 66ᵗʰ Foot), Irish Rebellion 1798 (ADC to Lord Cornwallis), India 1803–1804 (present at Laswaree as Adjutant General), Sicily 1806 and the Baltic 1808.

Employed on missions to the Austro-Russian Army 1799–1800 and to the Russian Army in Moravia 1805. Gave him the opportunity to view military tactics during the battles, especially at Austerlitz. After Corunna he was the author of *A few remarks explanatory of the motives which guided the operations of the British Army during the late short campaign in Spain* to justify the retreat to Corunna under Sir John Moore and clear his reputation. Inspector of Infantry June 1814.

Gold Cross for Salamanca, Nivelle, Nive, Orthes and Toulouse. GCB. GCH. KTS. Knight of Austrian Order of Maria Theresa. Knight of Third Class Russian Order of St George. Knight of Third Class of Wilhelm Order by King of the Low Countries. Son of General Sir Henry Clinton in command of forces during the American War of Independence. Brother of Sir William Henry Clinton Colonel 55ᵗʰ Foot. Uncle of Lt and Capt Francis Henry Dawkins 1ˢᵗ Foot Guards and of Capt and Lt Colonel Henry Dawkins Coldstream Guards.

REFERENCE: *Dictionary of National Biography. Gentleman's Magazine, Feb 1830, pp. 171–4. Royal Military Calendar, Vol 2, pp. 390–7.*

CLINTON, Sir William Henry
Colonel. 55ᵗʰ (Westmoreland) Regiment of Foot.
Memorial tablet: St Mary Magdalene Church, Barkway, Hertfordshire. (Photograph)

IN MEMORY OF / GENERAL SIR WILLIAM HENRY CLINTON, / GRAND ORDER OF THE BATH. / LIEUTENANT GOVERNOR OF CHELSEA HOSPITAL. / COLONEL OF THE 55ᵀᴴ REGIMENT OF FOOT. / ELDEST SON OF GENERAL SIR HENRY CLINTON GCB COMMANDER-IN-CHIEF IN AMERICA, / WHO WAS THE ONLY SON OF THE HON. GEORGE CLINTON, ADMIRAL OF THE WHITE AND CAPTAIN GENERAL OF THE AMERICAN COLONIES, / SECOND SON OF FRANCIS, 6ᵀᴴ EARL OF LINCOLN. / HE SERVED WITH THE 1ˢᵀ REGᵀ OF FOOT GUARDS IN FLANDERS AND FRANCE IN 1793, IN IRELAND DURING THE REBELLION OF 1798 / AND IN HOLLAND

IN 1799. HE WAS SENT AS MILITARY ENVOY TO MARSHAL SUVAROV IN ITALY 1799 AND GUSTAVUS IV KING OF SWEDEN 1807. / HE WAS AIDE DE CAMP AND AFTERWARDS MILITARY SECRETARY TO THE DUKE OF YORK AND QUARTERMASTER GENERAL IN IRELAND. / HE COMMANDED THE FORCE WHICH TOOK POSSESSION OF THE ISLAND OF MADEIRA 1801. HE COMMANDED A DIVISION OF / THE ARMY IN SICILY 1812 AND ON THE EAST COAST OF SPAIN 1813 AND HE WAS EVENTUALLY PROMOTED TO THE CHIEF COMMAND OF THAT ARMY IN WHICH HE EFFECTIVELY HELD IN CHECK A GREATLY SUPERIOR FORCE UNDER MARSHAL SUCHET. / IN 1826 BEING THEN LIEUTENANT GENERAL OF THE ORDNANCE HE WAS SELECTED BY THE DUKE OF WELLINGTON TO CONDUCT / THE EXPEDITION TO PORTUGAL WHERE BY HIS JUDICIOUS MEASURES HE MAINLY CONTRIBUTED TO PRESERVE THE BLESSINGS OF PEACE. / FOR MANY YEARS HE WAS MP FIRST FOR BOROUGHBRIDGE AND AFTERWARDS FOR NEWARK. / IN PUBLIC DUTIES GALLANT, ABLE AND ZEALOUS WITH GENEROUS KINDNESS OF HEART, SEEKING THE / GOOD OR ADVANCEMENT OF OTHERS, NOT HIS OWN, AND DEVOTING HIS MEANS, TIME AND INFLUENCE WITH UNERRING ENERGY / TO THE RELIEF OF THE DISTRESSED AND TO THE CAUSE OF NEGLECTED MERCY. / HE WAS BORN AT LYONS IN FRANCE ON THE 25TH DECEMBER 1769 / AND DIED AT COKENACH 16TH FEBRUARY 1846. HE CLOSED A CAREER OF 61 YEARS IN THE SERVICE OF HIS COUNTRY, / DYING AS HE HAD LIVED IN THE CHARITY, FAITH AND HUMBLE BUT EARNEST HOPE OF A CHRISTIAN. / HE IS BURIED IN A VAULT IN THIS CHURCHYARD. / ....

Family Mausoleum: St Mary Magdalene Churchyard, Barkway, Hertfordshire. (Photograph)

GENERAL / SIR WILLIAM HENRY CLINTON G.C.B. / BORN 25TH DECEMBER 1769, / DIED 16TH FEBRUARY 1846 / ....

Memorial: Royal Military Chapel, Wellington Barracks, London. (M.I.) (Destroyed by a Flying Bomb 1944)

"THE CREDENCE TABLE IS GIVEN BY LIEUT.-COL. HENRY R. CLINTON, LATE / GRENADIER GUARDS WITH OTHER MEMBERS OF HIS FAMILY, IN MEMORY OF / .... / HIS GRANDFATHER, / GENERAL SIR WILLIAM H. CLINTON, G.C.B., COLONEL 55TH REGIMENT OF FOOT. / BORN, 1769; DIED, 1846. / 1ST GUARDS, 1790–1814. HE SERVED WITH THE REGIMENT IN THE CAMPAIGNS OF 1793-94-99; WAS / MILITARY ENVOY TO MARSHAL SUWARROW IN ITALY IN 1799, AND TO GUSTAVUS IV OF SWEDEN, / IN 1807. COMMANDED THE FORCE WHICH TOOK POSSESSION OF MADEIRA, 1801. HE COMMANDED A / DIVISION OF THE ARMY IN SICILY IN 1812, AND HELD THE CHIEF COMMAND OF THE FORCES ON THE EAST / COAST OF SPAIN, 1813-14. HE CONDUCTED THE EXPEDITION TO PORTUGAL IN 1826. / HE WAS LIEUT.-GOVERNOR OF CHELSEA HOSPITAL, 1842-46."

Cornet 7th Lt Dragoons 22 Dec 1784. Lt 7 Mar 1787. Capt 45th Foot 9 Jun 1790. Lt and Capt 1st Foot Guards 14 Jul 1790. Capt and Lt Colonel 29 Dec 1794. Bt Colonel 1 Jan 1801. Major General 25 Apr 1808. 3rd Major 1st Foot Guards 30 Jul 1812. Lt General 4 Jun 1813. Colonel 55th Foot 25 Apr 1814. General 22 Jul 1830.

Served in the Peninsula Oct 1812 – Aug 1813 and Sep 1813 – Apr 1814. (GOC Eastern Spain). Present at Castalla (GOC 1st Division and Mentioned in Despatches), Tarragona and Barcelona. Also served in Flanders 1793–1794 (present at Famars, Valenciennes, Dunkirk, Lannoi, Le Cateau and Fleurus), the Irish Rebellion 1798, employed on various secret missions 1799–1806 (in Italy and Madeira 1801) and Sicily 1812. GCB. Surveyor General of the Ordnance 1825. In command of a small force sent to Portugal 1826. MP for Newark 1826–1829. Lt Governor of Chelsea Hospital 1842–1846. Son of General Sir Henry Clinton in command of forces in the American War of Independence. Elder brother of Sir Henry Clinton

Colonel 60th Foot. Uncle of Lt and Capt Francis Henry Dawkins 1st Foot Guards and of Lt Colonel Henry Dawkins Coldstream Guards.

REFERENCE: *Dictionary of National Biography. Royal Military Calendar, Vol 2, pp. 319–22. United Service Magazine, Mar 1846, pp. 479–80. Gentleman's Magazine, Apr 1846, pp. 424–5. Annual Register, 1846, Appx, pp. 241–3.*

CLITHEROW, John

Captain and Lieutenant Colonel. 3rd Regiment of Foot Guards.
Memorial: Royal Military Chapel, Wellington Barracks, London. (M.I.) (Destroyed by a Flying Bomb 1944)

"LIEUT.-GENERAL JOHN CLITHEROW, / 3RD GUARDS. COLONEL 67TH REGIMENT. PRESENT WITH THE ARMY LANDING IN EGYPT, 1801, AND IN THE PENINSULA. WOUNDED AT FUENTES D'ONOR, AND AT BUSACO. DIED 14TH OCTOBER, 1852. / AGED 70."

Ensign 19 Dec 1799. Lt and Capt 24 Feb 1803. Capt and Lt Colonel 8 Oct 1812. Bt Colonel 25 Jul 1821. Major General 22 Jul 1830. Lt General 23 Nov 1841.

Served in the Peninsula Jan 1810 – Oct 1811 and May – Nov 1812. Present at Busaco, Fuentes d'Onoro (wounded), Salamanca and Burgos (severely wounded). Served in France with the Army of Occupation 1815. Also served in Egypt 1801, Hanover 1805 and Walcheren 1809. MGS medal for Egypt, Busaco, Fuentes d'Onoro and Salamanca. Served in Canada 1838 (Commanded a military district of Montreal. Commanded the left wing of the Army (15th and 24th Foot) that crushed the Rebellion). Presided over the courts to try the men charged with treason and was just and lenient. Remained in Montreal until Jul 1841 when he took command of the forces of Upper Canada. Deputy Governor Sep 1841 – Jan 1842 when he returned to England. Colonel 67th Foot 15 Jan 1844. Elder brother of Lt and Capt William Henry Clitherow 3rd Foot Guards who died at Garris Feb 1814.

REFERENCE: *Dictionary of Canadian Biography. Gentleman's Magazine, Feb 1853, p. 200.*

CLITHEROW, Robert

Captain and Lieutenant Colonel. 1st Regiment of Foot Guards.
Memorial: Royal Military Chapel, Wellington Barracks, London. (M.I.) (Destroyed by a Flying Bomb 1944)

"LIEUT.-COLONEL ROBERT CLITHEROW, / 1ST GUARDS. SERVED IN SICILY, AT CORUNNA, AND IN THE WALCHEREN EXPEDITION, 1809. AND AFTERWARDS IN THE PENINSULA. DIED 17TH APRIL, 1859. AGED 79."

Ensign 15 Mar 1799. Lt and Capt 23 Apr 1800. Capt and Lt Colonel 29 Oct 1812.

Served in the Peninsula Oct 1808 – Jan 1809 and Sep 1812 – Jan 1813. Present at Corunna. Also served in Sicily 1806 and Walcheren 1809. Retired 10 Mar 1814.

CLITHEROW, William Henry

Lieutenant and Captain. 3rd Regiment of Foot Guards.
Memorial tablet: St Mary the Virgin Church, Essendon, Hertfordshire. (Photograph)

SACRED TO THE MEMORY OF / JAMES CLITHEROW, / THIRD SON OF CHRISTOPHER CLITHEROW, ESQRE OF BIRDS PLACE, IN THIS PARISH; / LIEUTENANT IN THE ROYAL NAVY; / WHO DIED AT SEA ON BOARD HMS ARGO, OFF THE ISLAND OF JAMAICA / ON THE 29TH DAY OF MARCH 1813, IN THE 27TH YEAR OF HIS AGE. / ALSO OF HIS YOUNGER BROTHER / WILLIAM HENRY CLITHEROW, / LIEUTENANT AND CAPTAIN IN THE 3RD REGT OF FOOT-GUARDS; / WHO FELL GLORIOUSLY, AT THE HEAD OF MAJOR-GENERAL BYNG'S BRIGADE,

/ WITH WHOM HE WAS SERVING AS AID-DE-CAMP, / IN A SUCCESSFUL ATTACK ON THE ENEMY'S STRONG POSITION NEAR ST PALAIS, IN FRANCE, / ON THE 15TH OF FEBRUARY, 1814, IN THE 26TH YEAR OF HIS AGE. / THEIR ZEAL, ACTIVITY AND PROFESSIONAL KNOWL-EDGE, / PROCURED THEM THE ESTEEM AND ADMIRATION OF THEIR SUPERIORS; / THEIR UNSULLIED CHARACTER, AND AMIABLE MANNERS, / ENDEARED THEM TO THEIR FRIENDS AND COMRADES, / BY WHOM THEIR LOSS IS DEEPLY FELT AND LAMENTED.

Named on the Memorial: St Andrew's Church, (now Musée Historique), Biarritz, France. (Photograph)

Memorial: Royal Military Chapel, Wellington Barracks, London. (M.I.) (Destroyed by a Flying Bomb 1944)

"CAPTAIN WILLIAM HENRY CLITHEROW, / 3RD GUARDS. AIDE-DE-CAMP TO GENERAL JOHN BYNG. KILLED AT BAYONNE, 1814. AGED 26."

Also named on Memorial Panel VII for St Palais: Royal Military Chapel, Wellington Barracks, London. (M.I.) (Destroyed by a Flying Bomb 1944)

Ensign 22 Dec 1803. Lt and Capt 11 Dec 1806.
    Served in the Peninsula Sep 1811- Feb 1814 (ADC to Major General Byng from Mar 1813). Present at Ciudad Rodrigo, Salamanca, Burgos, Vittoria, Pyrenees, Nivelle, Nive (wounded) and Garris where he was severely wounded 15 Feb 1814 and died of his wounds 17 Feb 1814. Younger brother of Capt and Lt Colonel John Clitherow 3rd Foot Guards.

CLIVE, Edward
Lieutenant and Captain. 1st Regiment of Foot Guards.
Memorial: Royal Military Chapel, Wellington Barracks, London. (M.I.) (Destroyed by a Flying Bomb 1944)

"THE MARBLE COLUMNS OF THE BALUSTRADES OF THE GALLERIES ARE GIVEN BY / HIS BROTHERS, THE REV. ARCHER CLIVE AND GEORGE CLIVE, IN MEMORY OF / COLONEL EDWARD CLIVE. / GRENADIER GUARDS 1811–1846. HE SERVED IN THE FIELD WITH THE 1ST BATTALION IN 1818, AND WITH THE 3RD BATTALION IN 1814 AND 1815, INCLUDING THE BATTLES OF QUATRE BRAS AND WATERLOO. HE WAS APPOINTED MAJOR OF THE 2ND BATTALION IN 1840, AND WAS LIEUT.-COLONEL OF THE REGIMENT IN 1844 TILL HIS DEATH IN APRIL 1845, AGED 51."

Ensign 4 Jul 1811. Lt and Capt 13 Jan 1814. Capt and Lt Colonel 25 Sep 1826. Major 15 May 1840. Lt Colonel 8 Nov 1844.
    Served in the Peninsula Apr 1813 – Apr 1814. Present at Bidassoa, Nivelle, Nive, Adour and Bayonne. Present at Quatre Bras, Waterloo, the siege of Peronne and with the Army of Occupation. Also served in Canada.

CLOSE, Edward Charles
Lieutenant. 48th (Northamptonshire) Regiment of Foot.
Grave: St James's Church of England Cemetery, Morpeth, near Maitland, South Australia, Australia. (No longer extant)
Memorial window: St James' Church, Morpeth, near Maitland, South Australia, Australia.

Ensign 8 Feb 1809. Lt 2 Jun 1809.
    Served in the Peninsula with 2/48th Jul 1809 – Jul 1811 and 1/48th Aug 1812 – Apr 1814. Present at

Douro, Talavera, Busaco, Albuera, Vittoria, Nivelle, Orthes and Toulouse. Also served in Australia 1817–1824, where he served as Acting Engineer and helped to improve the harbour at Newcastle. Resigned from the army 1824 and had a grant of land at Morpeth where he took an active part in local affairs. He had made a vow during the Peninsular War that if he survived he would build a church and so built the church of St James in Morpeth. MGS medal for Talavera, Busaco, Albuera, Vittoria, Nivelle, Orthes and Toulouse. Died 7 May 1866.
REFERENCE: *Australian Dictionary of Biography*.

CLUBB, Robert
Clerk of the Stores. Field Train Department of Ordnance.
Named on the Regimental Memorial: British Cemetery, Lisbon, Portugal. (Grave number D11). (M.I.)

"..................MR ROBERT CLUBB, CLERK OF STORES WHO WAS KILLED IN ACTION AT THE SIEGE OF ALMEIDA, 27 AUGUST 1810. ...."

Killed at the explosion at the fort of Almeida 27 Aug 1810.

CLÜDEN, Paul Gottlieb see CHÜDEN, Paul Gottlieb

CLUTTERBUCK, William
Lieutenant. 2nd (Queen's Royal) Regiment of Foot.
Named on the Regimental Memorial: St Michael's Cathedral, Bridgetown, Barbados, West Indies. (Photograph)

Ensign 12 Aug 1806. Lt 17 Mar 1808.
    Served in the Peninsula Aug 1808 – Jan 1809, Mar 1811 – Dec 1812, and with the 2nd Provisional Battalion Jan 1813 – Apr 1814. Present at Vimeiro, Corunna, Almeida, siege of Salamanca Forts and Salamanca. Also served at Walcheren 1809 (wounded at Flushing) and West Indies 1815. Died in Barbados 13 Dec 1816 during a yellow fever epidemic.

CLYDE, John
1st Lieutenant. 23rd (Royal Welch Fusiliers) Regiment of Foot.
Memorial: Inside Mausoleum, Evere Cemetery , Brussels, Belgium. (M.I.)

"LIEUTENANT JOHN CLYDE 23RD ROYAL WELCH FUSILIERS. AGED 22"

2nd Lt. 20 Jun 1811. 1st Lt 14 May 1812.
    Served in the Peninsula with 1/23rd May 1812 – Oct 1813 and Apr 1814. Present at Salamanca (wounded). Present at Waterloo where he was wounded and died of his wounds 3 Jul 1815. One of the select band of soldiers buried in the Mausoleum at Evere.

CLYDE, Lord see CAMPBELL, Colin (Lord Clyde)

COCHRANE, Andrew Coutts
Ensign. 3rd Regiment of Foot Guards.
Family mausoleum: Kensal Green Cemetery, London. (21777 Section 140RS). Inscription not recorded. (Photograph)

Ensign 13 Jan 1814. Lt and Capt 2 Jul 1815.
    Served at Waterloo. Half pay 14 Sep 1820. Died 22 Jun 1870.

COCHRANE, Charles
Private. 12th (Prince of Wales's) Regiment of Light Dragoons.
Named on the Regimental Memorial: St Joseph's Church, Waterloo, Belgium. (Photograph)
   Killed at Waterloo.

COCHRANE, Christopher Irwin
Lieutenant. 47th (Lancashire) Regiment of Foot.
Tombstone: Colaba Cemetery, Bombay, India. (M.I.)

"SACRED TO THE MEMORY OF A RESPECTED AND / AFFECTIONATE BROTHER CHRISTO-PHER I. COCHRANE, / LIEUTENANT OF HIS MAJESTY'S 47TH REGIMENT / WHO DEPARTED THIS LIFE ON THE 27TH DECEMBER / 1821, AGED 35 YEARS. THIS IS ERECTED BY / HIS BROTHER LIEUTENANT ROBERT COCHRANE OF / THE SAME CORPS, AS A SMALL TRIBUTE DUE TO / THE MEMORY OF A DESERVEDLY BELOVED, AND / EVER TO BE LAMENTED BROTHER."

Ensign 30 Jun 1808. Lt 6 Sep 1809.
   Served in the Peninsula Jan 1812 – Dec 1813. Present at Cadiz, Seville, Puente Largo, Vittoria and San Sebastian. Also served in India 1816 until his death in 1821. Brother of Capt Robert Cochrane 47th Foot.

COCHRANE, James Johnstone
Capt and Lieutenant Colonel. 3rd Regiment of Foot Guards.
Box tomb: St Swithin's Churchyard, Bathford, Somerset. Seriously eroded. Inscription recorded from memorial inscription. (Photograph)

"UNDERNEATH ARE DEPOSITED THE REMAINS OF JOHN SHAW ESQ .... SACRED TO THE MEMORY OF COLONEL JAMES JOHNSTONE COCHRANE LATE OF THE SCOTS FUSILIER GUARDS WHO DIED JANUARY 24TH 1852 AGED 70."

Ensign 26 Dec 1799. Lt and Capt 5 Jan 1804. Capt and Lt Colonel 10 Dec 1812. Bt Colonel 25 Jul 1821.
   Served in the Peninsula Oct 1810 – Apr 1812. Present at Fuentes d'Onoro and Ciudad Rodrigo. Also served in Egypt 1801. MGS medal for Egypt, Fuentes d'Onoro and Ciudad Rodrigo.

COCHRANE, Robert
Lieutenant. 47th (Lancashire) Regiment of Foot.
Headstone: Old Churchyard, Spital, Windsor, Berkshire. (Photograph)

SACRED TO THE BELOVED MEMORY OF / CAPTAIN ROBERT COCHRANE, / MILITARY KNIGHT OF WINDSOR, / WHO SERVED IN THE PENINSULAR CAMPAIGNS & IN THE / EAST INDIES WITH THE 47TH FOOT. WAS PRESENT AT THE / BATTLES OF VITTORIA, NIVELLE, NIVE, BAYONNE, TARIFA, / DEFENCE OF CADIZ AND STORMING OF SAN SEBASTIAN. / HIS THREE ONLY BROTHERS BEING ALSO OFFICERS AT THE / SAME TIME IN THE ABOVE REGIMENT. / DIED AT WINDSOR 25TH MARCH 1878 / AGED 89 / HIS END WAS PEACE / ....

Ensign 6 Jun 1809. Lt 26 Jun 1811. Capt 26 Oct 1830.
   Served in the Peninsula Jan 1812 – Jan 1814. Present at Cadiz, Seville, Puente Largo, Vittoria, San Sebastian, Bidassoa and Bayonne. Also served in India 1816–1822. MGS medal for Vittoria and San Sebastian. Military Knight of Windsor 14 Jan 1864. Brother of Lt Christopher Irwin Cochrane 47th Foot. Two other brothers, James Robert Cochrane and Thomas Noble Cochrane also served in the 47th Foot. All four brothers were Lieutenants in the same regiment at the same time.

COCHRANE, Robert

1st Lieutenant. 95th Regiment of Foot.
Named on the Memorial slab to his father: St John the Baptist Churchyard, Chester. (No longer extant: Grave number 1204). (M.I.)

"ROBERT COCHRANE, LATE OF THE ROYAL FLINTSHIRE MILITIA DIED 9 JAN 1829, AGED 79. ALSO IN MEMORY OF HIS SON MAJOR ROBERT COCHRANE, LATE 2ND BATTN PRINCE ALBERT'S OWN RIFLE BRIGADE AND MILITARY KNIGHT OF WINDSOR DIED AT WINDSOR CASTLE, 27 MAY 1864, AGED 69."

Buried in St George's Chapel, Windsor, Berkshire. (Burial record)

2nd Lt 9 Nov 1809. Lt 8 May 1812. Capt 22 May 1828.
    Served in the Peninsula with 2/95th Jul 1811 – Sep 1813. Present at Cadiz, San Munos, San Millan, Vittoria, Pyrenees and Vera (severely wounded in the action at the Bridge of Vera). MGS medal for Vittoria and Pyrenees. Present at Waterloo (wounded), Capture of Paris (first officer to enter the City) and with Army of Occupation. Retired on full pay 1841 and appointed Military Knight of Windsor. Honorary Major 28 Nov 1854. Brother of Lt Thomas Cochrane 95th Foot.
REFERENCE: *Gentleman's Magazine, Jul 1864, p. 122.*

COCHRANE, Thomas

1st Lieutenant. 95th Regiment of Foot.
Memorial tablet: St Multose Church, Kinsale, County Cork, Ireland. (Photograph)

SACRED TO THE MEMORY / OF LIEUTENANT THOMAS COCHRANE / OF THE RIFLE BRIGADE / WHO DIED II JULY MDCCCXXIII AGED XXXIV YEARS. / AS A SOLDIER, / HIS ZEAL, GALLANTRY, AND INTELLIGENCE, / RENDERED HIM VALUABLE TO HIS COUNTRY. / AS A MAN / HIS PRIVATE VIRTUES EMBRACING EVERY ENNOBLING / AND ENDEARING QUALIFICATION / SECURED TO HIM THE ESTEEM AND LASTING ATTACHMENT / OF HIS BROTHER OFFICERS / WHO HAVE RAISED THIS MONUMENT TO HIS MEMORY.

Lt Royal Flintshire Militia. 2nd Lt 95th Foot 25 Aug 1807. Lt 22 Feb 1809.
    Served in the Peninsula with 2/95th Aug 1808 – Jan 1809 and Mar 1810 – Apr 1814. Present at Obidos, Rolica (wounded), Vimeiro, Vigo, Cadiz, Barrosa (severely wounded), San Millan, Vittoria, Pyrenees, Vera, Bidassoa, Nivelle, Nive, Orthes, Tarbes and Toulouse. Present at Waterloo. Also served at Walcheren, 1809. Brother of Lt Robert Cochrane 95th Foot.

COCHRANE, William George

Captain. 73rd (Highland) Regiment of Foot.
Ledger stone: Kensal Green Cemetery, London. (14053/86/PS). (Photograph)

IN MEMORY OF / LIEUT GENL WILLIAM GEORGE COCHRANE, / BORN 19TH APRIL 1790, / DIED 4TH SEPTEMBER 1857.

Ensign 40th Foot 13 Feb 1805. Lt 29 May 1806. Capt 73rd Foot 11 Aug 1812. Bt Major 17 Mar 1814. Bt Lt Colonel 15 Jul 1824. Bt Colonel 28 Jun 1838. Major General 11 Nov 1851. Lt General 20 Jun 1854.
    Served in the Peninsula Aug 1808 – May 1812. Present at Rolica, Vimeiro, Talavera, Busaco, Redinha, Olivencia, first siege of Badajoz, Albuera and Ciudad Rodrigo. Also served in Canada 1813–1814 (ADC to Lt General Sir George Prevost, Governor General and Commander of the Forces) and 1824–1826 (Inspecting Field Officer of Militia of Nova Scotia). Half pay 10 Jul 1837 and joined Staff at Horse Guards

(AAG). MGS medal for Rolica, Vimeiro, Talavera, Busaco, Albuera and Ciudad Rodrigo. Also served in Ireland where he died as Lt General in command of the Dublin District.

COCKBURN, Francis
Lieutenant Colonel. New Brunswick Fencibles.
Box tomb: St Michael and All Angels Churchyard, Harbledown, Canterbury, Kent. (Photograph)

GENERAL SIR FRANCIS COCKBURN / DIED AT EAST CLIFF DOVER / ON THE 24TH AUGUST 1868 / AGED 88 YEARS / AND HIS REMAINS NOW REST / BESIDES THOSE OF HIS BELOVED WIFE

Memorial Tablet: St Michael and All Angels Church, Harbledown, Canterbury, Kent. (Photograph)

.... / ALSO TO THE MEMORY OF GENERAL SIR FRANCIS COCKBURN / COLONEL OF THE 95TH REGT AND LATE GOVERNOR OF / THE BAHAMAS WHO DEPARTED THIS LIFE DEEPLY / RESPECTED BY ALL WHO KNEW HIM / AUGUST 24TH 1868 AGED 88 YEARS

Cornet 7th Dragoon Guards 16 Oct 1800. Lt 60th Foot 6 Apr 1803. Capt 3rd Dragoons 3 Mar 1804. Capt 60th Foot 23 Apr 1807. Major Canadian Fencible Infantry 27 Jun 1811. Lt Colonel New Brunswick Fencibles 27 Oct 1814. Bt Colonel 10 Jan 1837. Major General 9 Nov 1846. Lt General 20 Jun 1854. General 12 Nov 1860.
    Served in the Peninsula on Staff as DAAG with 4th Division May – Dec 1809 and with 3rd Division Feb – Jun 1810. Deputy Judge Advocate in Spain and Portugal. Also served in South America 1807, Canada 1811–1814 (DQMG) and West Indies (Governor of Bahamas and Governor of Honduras). Colonel 95th (Derbyshire) Foot 26 Dec 1853.

COCKS, Edward Charles
Major, 79th (Cameron Highlanders) Regiment of Foot.
Obelisk: On the hill overlooking Eastnor, Herefordshire. (Photograph)

INSCRIBED TO THE MEMORY OF THE HONOURABLE EDWARD CHARLES COCKS, ELDEST SON OF JOHN SOMERS, LORD SOMERS AND MARGARET, LADY SOMERS, HIS WIFE. / WITH STRONG INDUCEMENTS TO APPLY HIMSELF TO THE SAFER DUTIES OF CIVIL LIFE THE ENERGY OF HIS MIND DETERMINED HIM ON A MILITARY CAREER. HAVING CHOSEN A PROFESSION HE DEVOTED HIMSELF TO IT WITH SUCCESSFUL ARDOUR AND PERSEVER-ANCE. AT THE AGE OF TWENTY SIX HE FELL, RESPECTED, BELOVED AND REGRETTED. HIS GREAT COMMANDER THE MARQUIS OF WELLINGTON THUS OFFICIALLY ANNOUNCED HIS DEATH TO THE SECRETARY OF STATE, LORD BATHURST, / AT 3 IN THE MORNING OF THE 8TH OCTOBER 1812, WE HAD THE MISFORTUNE TO LOSE THE HON MAJOR COCKS OF THE 79TH WHO WAS FIELD OFFICER OF THE TRENCHES AND WAS KILLED IN THE ACT OF RALLYING THE TROOPS WHO HAD BEEN DRIVEN IN. I HAVE FREQUENTLY HAD OCCASION TO DRAW YOUR LORDSHIP'S ATTENTION TO THE CONDUCT OF MAJOR COCKS AND IN ONE INSTANCE, VERY RECENTLY, IN THE ATTACK OF THE HORNWORK OF THE CASTLE OF BURGOS AND I CONSIDER HIS LOSS AS ONE OF THE GREATEST IMPORTANCE TO THE ARMY AND TO HIS MAJESTY'S SERVICE. / LORD WELLINGTON HAD SUCCESSFULLY RECOM-MENDED HIM TO THE BREVET RANK OF MAJOR AND LIEUTENANT COLONEL IN THE ARMY; THE FORMER IN ACKNOWLEDGEMENT OF PREVIOUS GOOD CONDUCT AND THE LATTER AS A REWARD FOR HIS GALLANT ACTS IN THE SIEGE WHICH PROVED FATAL TO HIM. BOTH RECOMMENDATIONS WERE CONFIRMED BY AUTHORITY BUT THAT TO BE LIEUTENANT COLONEL NOT TILL 5 DAYS AFTER HE HAD BRAVELY FALLEN BEFORE BURGOS. A FATHER WHO LOVED AND THOUGHT HIGHLY OF HIS SON FEELS JUSTIFIED IN

INSCRIBING THESE TRUTHS TO HIS MEMORY AND BOUND TO ADD THAT HE ACTED ON PUBLIC AND RELIGIOUS PRINCIPLES AND THAT HE WAS DUTIFUL TO HIS PARENTS, AN AFFECTIONATE BROTHER, A SINCERE FRIEND AND A BENEVOLENT MAN.

Family Memorial tablet: St John the Baptist Church, Eastnor, Herefordshire. (In Somers family vault). (Photograph)

.... / MARGARET COUNTESS COCKS / .... / THEIR ELDEST SON EDWARD CHARLES WHO FELL HONOURABLY / DURING THE PENINSULAR WAR IN 1812.

Cornet 16th Lt Dragoons 29 Apr 1803. Lt 1 Aug 1805. Capt 48th Foot 25 Dec 1806. Capt 16th Lt Dragoons 12 Mar 1807. Bt Major 30 May 1811. Major 79th Foot 20 Feb 1812.

Served in the Peninsula Apr 1809 – Mar 1811 (ADC to General Sir Stapleton Cotton Apr – Dec 1809) and May 1811 – Oct 1812. Present at Douro, Talavera, El Bodon (Mentioned in Despatches), Llerena (Mentioned in Despatches), Salamanca and Burgos (Mentioned in Despatches and killed during the siege 8 Oct 1812). Had been recommended for promotion to Bt Lt Colonel for his conduct in the assault on 19 Sep but did not survive to hold the rank. His body was brought back under a flag of truce and his funeral attended by Lord Wellington, the Staff and all officers of the 79th Foot and 16th Lt Dragoons. Buried at Villimar near Burgos.

His friend William Tomkinson of the 16th said 'He was regretted by the whole army'. Mainly employed on intelligence duties he was admirably suited for this task. One of the most intelligent officers in the war, Wellington thought highly of him. He studied all aspects of the art of war and left 11 volumes of a diary detailing all the actions and his thoughts on the tactics employed during the three years he fought in the Peninsula. Wellington said to D'Urban at the funeral 'that had Cocks outlived the campaigns, which from the way he exposed himself was morally impossible, he would have become one of the first Generals of England'.

REFERENCE: Page, Julia V., *Intelligence officer in the Peninsula: letters and diaries of Major the Hon. Edward Charles Cocks, 1786–1812*, 1986. McGrigor, Mary, *Wellington's spies*, 2005.

COCKS, Hon. Philip James
Captain and Lieutenant Colonel. 1st Regiment of Foot Guards.
Memorial: Royal Military Chapel, Wellington Barracks, London. (M.I.) (Destroyed by a Flying Bomb 1944)

"COLONEL THE HON. PHILIP JAMES COCKS. / BORN DECEMBER 2ND, 1774; DIED APRIL 1ST, 1857. / 1ST GUARDS, 1790–1809. COMMANDED THE 1ST BATTALION AT THE BATTLE OF CORUNNA. / D.D. HIS SURVIVING SONS, 1879."

Cross on stepped base: St Mary the Virgin Churchyard, Cleobury Mortimer, Shropshire. (Photograph)

HON MICHAEL PHILIP JAMES COCKS OF STEPPLE HALL. BORN 1774. DIED 1857; ALSO HIS ELDEST SON CHARLES RICHARD SOMERS COCKS, CLERK TO HOLY ORDERS, VICAR OF THIS PARISH FOR 32 YEARS. B 1814. D 1876.

Ensign 24 Nov 1790. Lt and Capt 9 Oct 1793. Capt-Lieut 9 May 1800. Capt and Lt Colonel 9 May 1800.

Served in the Peninsula Oct 1808 – Jan 1809. Present at Corunna. MGS medal for Corunna. Also served at Walcheren 1809. Retired 23 Nov 1809.

CODRINGTON, John Morgan see MORGAN, John

COENEGRACHT, L. P.
Lieutenant Colonel. 1st Carabineers Regiment, Dutch Cavalry.
Named on the Memorial to Dutch officers killed at Waterloo: St Joseph's Church, Waterloo, Belgium.
(Photograph)

COFFIN, Edward Pine
Deputy Commissary General. Commissariat Department.
Low monument: Walcot Cemetery, Lansdown, Bath, Somerset. (Photograph)

EDWARD PINE COFFIN KNIGHT C.B. / OBIT 31ST JULY 1862 AETAT 76. / FOR MANY YEARS COMMISSARY GENERAL IN H. M. SERVICE.

Commissary Clerk 25 Jul 1805. Acting Asst Comm Gen 1806. Asst Comm Gen 1 Aug 1809. Dep Comm Gen 4 Aug 1814. Comm Gen 1 Jul 1840.
    Served in the Peninsula Aug 1808 – Jan 1809, May 1809 – Jun 1810 and Aug 1812 – Apr 1814. (Attached to HQ from Oct 1812). Present at Corunna, Vittoria and Toulouse. Served in France with the Army of Occupation 1816. Also served at the Cape of Good Hope 1805–1808, Netherlands 1815, Brussels 1819, Canada 1819–1822, China 1822–1832, Canada 1833–1835, Mexico 1835–1841, China 1843–1845 and Ireland 1846–1848 (during the famine had charge of the relief operations at Limerick and on the west coast of Ireland). Served as one of the Commissioners of inquiry into the workings of the Royal Mint 1848. KCB. MGS medal for Corunna, Vittoria and Toulouse.
REFERENCE: *Dictionary of National Biography. Gentleman's Magazine, Sep 1862, pp. 372–3. Annual Register, 1862, Appx, p. 341.*

COGHLAN, Andrew
Lieutenant Colonel. York Chasseurs.
Memorial tablet: St Swithun's Church, Bath, Somerset. (Photograph)

THIS TABLET TO THE MEMORY OF / LIEUT COLONEL ANDREW COGHLAN / WHO DIED ON THE 31ST MARCH 1837 AND WHOSE / REMAINS REPOSE IN THE VAULT BENEATH THIS CHURCH, / HAS BEEN PLACED BY HIS WIDOW, AS A FEEBLE TOKEN / OF HER RESPECT AND AFFECTION, / AND TO SERVE AT THE SAME TIME AS A PLAIN AND SIMPLE RECORD / OF HER HUSBAND'S LONG, AND FAITHFUL SERVICES, TO HIS KING / AND COUNTRY. / THEY EXTENDED OVER A PERIOD ABOVE 40 YEARS, AND TO ALL PARTS / OF THE WORLD WHERE OUR ARMS HAVE BEEN BORNE, / COMMENCING IN INDIA WITH THE OVERTHROW OF THE TIPPOO SAIB, / AND FALL OF SERINGAPATAM, WHERE THE COLONEL WAS BADLY WOUNDED. / HE SERVED SUBSEQUENTLY IN THE WEST INDIES, SOUTH AMERICA, / FINALLY IN THE CAMPAIGNS OF PORTUGAL AND SPAIN, / WHICH TERMINATED IN THE EXPULSION OF THE ENEMY / FROM THE PENINSULAR.

Ensign H.E.I.C. Artillery. Ensign 72nd Foot Mar 1792. Lt 14 Sep 1792. Lt 1st West India Regt 24 Aug 1795. Capt 45th Foot 1 May 1796. Bt Major 25 Apr 1808. Lt Colonel York Chasseurs 11 Nov 1813. Lt Colonel 7th Royal Veteran Battalion 1 Nov 1819. Lt Colonel 3rd Royal Veteran Battalion 23 Oct 1822.
    Served in the Peninsula Aug 1808 – Sep 1809 with 45th Foot. Present at Rolica, Vimeiro and Talavera (commanded the 45th Foot). Also served in India 1790 (present in the First War against Tippoo Sultan under command of Marquis Cornwallis where he was severely wounded), West Indies (under Sir Ralph Abercromby where he was severely wounded) and South America 1807 (present at Buenos Ayres). Retired on full pay. His rank was held in abeyance otherwise he would have been one of the oldest Colonels in the Army. At his death, his only regret was that it had not taken place on the field of battle.

COGHLAN, Charles see COGHLAN, John Robert

COGHLAN, John Robert
Lieutenant Colonel. 61st (South Gloucestershire) Regiment of Foot.
Memorial tablet: St John's Church, Margate, Kent. (Photograph)

SACRED TO THE MEMORY / OF LIEUTENANT COLONEL / JOHN ROBERT COGHLAN K.T.S. 61ST INFANTRY, / WHO AFTER HAVING DISTINGUISHED HIMSELF / IN THE MEMORABLE BATTLES OF / TALAVERA, VITTORIA, THE PYRENEES, / NIVELLE, NIVE, AND ORTHES; / FELL GLORIOUSLY LEADING HIS REGIMENT / TO THE HEIGHTS OF TOULOUSE, / THE 10TH DAY OF APRIL 1814. / BORN JULY 29TH 1782. / THIS MONUMENT IS ERECTED BY HIS / BROTHER ROBERT, IN TESTIMONY / OF HIS LOVE AND ADMIRATION.

Named on the Memorial: St Andrew's Church, (now Musée Historique), Biarritz, France. (Named in error as Charles Coghlan). (Photograph)

Lt 1798. Capt 1 Jul 1803. Major 9 Jan 1806. Bt Lt Colonel 30 May 1811. Lt Colonel 13 Jun 1811.
    Served in the Peninsula Jun 1809 – Dec 1811 and Oct 1812 – Apr 1814. Present at Talavera (severely wounded and taken prisoner by the French. After his wound healed he was sent to a prison from where he escaped Nov 1809 and rejoined his regiment), Busaco, Pyrenees, Nivelle, Nive, Orthes, Tarbes and Toulouse where he was killed 10 Apr 1814. Gold Cross for Talavera, Pyrenees, Nivelle, Nive, Orthes and Toulouse.

COLBORNE, Sir John
Lieutenant Colonel. 52nd (Oxfordshire) Light Infantry Regiment of Foot.
Low monument: Holy Cross Church, Newton Ferrers, Devon. (Photograph)

THE RIGHT HONBLE JOHN COLBORNE FIELD MARSHAL LORD SEATON GCB. / GCH. GCMG. COLNL / 2ND LIFE GUARDS COLONEL-IN-CHIEF RIFLE BRIGADE BORN FEBRUARY 1778 / DIED 1863.

Statue: Peninsular Barracks, Winchester, Hampshire. (Photograph)
    The statue was originally erected at Mount Wise, moved to Seaton Barracks, Plymouth in 1939 and later relocated to the Peninsular Barracks, Winchester.

Front flank:

JOHN COLBORNE / BARON SEATON / BORN MDCCLXXVIII / DIED MDCCCLXIII

Rear flank:

IN MEMORY OF / THE DISTINGUISHED CAREER / AND STAINLESS CHARACTER OF / FIELD MARSHAL LORD SEATON / GCB GCMG GCH / THIS MONUMENT IS ERECTED / BY HIS FRIENDS AND COMRADES

Right flank:

PENINSULA / WATERLOO

Left flank:

Statue: Upper Canada College Quadrangle, Toronto, Canada. (Photograph)

JOHN COLBORNE / FIELD MARSHAL LORD SEATON / GCB, GCMG, GCH / 1778–1863 / FOUNDER OF THE COLLEGE. / HE WAS RENOWNED AND CHIVALROUS IN WAR / IN PEACE A GENEROUS AND ENLIGHTENED FRIEND OF LEARNING. / A MAN WHO PUT EVER FIRST HIS DUTY TO HIS GOD AND TO HIS / KING. / THIS MONUMENT, THE GIFT OF THE MASSEY FOUNDATION WAS / PLACED HERE ON MAY 2ND 1934 IN THE SEVENTEENTH YEAR OF / THE PRINCIPALSHIP OF WILLIAM LAWSON GRANT UNDER WHOSE / GUIDANCE THE COLLEGE FLOURISHED. / GUERNSEY – UPPER CANADA – IONIAN ISLANDS – PENINSULAR – / WATERLOO.

Cairn: On an island in Lake St Francis, Ontario, Canada. (M.I.)

"TO THE SAVIOUR OF CANADA"

Ensign 20th Foot 10 Jul 1794. Lt 4 Sep 1795. Capt 12 Jan 1800. Major 21 Jan 1808. Lt Colonel 5th Garrison Battalion 2 Feb 1809. Lt Colonel 66th Foot 2 Nov 1809. Lt Colonel 52nd Foot 18 Jul 1811. Bt Colonel 4 Jun 1814. Major General 27 May 1825. Lt General 28 Jun 1838. General 20 Jun 1854. Field Marshal 1 Apr 1860.

Served in the Peninsula Sep 1808 – Jan 1809 (Military Secretary to Sir John Moore), Aug – Dec 1809 (attached to the Spanish Army) Jan 1810 – Aug 1811 (Commanded 1 Brigade 2nd Division until May 1811), Dec 1811 – Apr 1812, Jul 1813 – Apr 1814 (Commanded 2 Brigade Lt Division from Sep 1813). Present at Benevente, Corunna, Ocana, Busaco, Campo Mayor, Albuera (Mentioned in Despatches), Ciudad Rodrigo (severely wounded in command of the Light Division and Mentioned in Despatches), Pyrenees, Vera, Bidassoa (Mentioned in Despatches), Nivelle, Nive, Orthes (Mentioned in Despatches), Tarbes and Toulouse. Appointed Lt Colonel by the dying wish of Sir John Moore. Present at Waterloo where he commanded the 52nd Lt Infantry with great skill. His final achievement was the decisive action he took on his own initiative, to contribute to the final retreat of the French.

Also served at the Helder 1799, Egypt 1801, Calabria 1806 (present at Maida) and the Baltic 1808. Gold Cross for Corunna, Albuera, Ciudad Rodrigo, Nivelle, Nive, Orthes and Toulouse. MGS medal for Egypt, Maida, Benevente, Busaco and Pyrenees. Knight of Maria Theresa of Austria and Fourth Class St George of Russia. GCB. GCMG. GCH.

Lieutenant Governor of Guernsey 1821–1827. Lieutenant Governor of Upper Canada 1828–1836. He encouraged immigration from Britain to counteract the American influence which he felt was too strong in the country. During his tenure of office the population increased by 70 per cent. Resigned in 1836 and was offered the post of first Commander in Chief of the Forces in Canada and remained in Canada until 1839, crushing the Canadian Rebellion of 1837–1838. Created Baron Seaton 14 Dec 1839. Lord High Commissioner of the Ionian Islands 1843–1849. Commander of the Forces in Ireland 1855–1860. Colonel 94th Foot 12 Dec 1834, Colonel 26th Foot 28 Mar 1838, Colonel 2nd Life Guards 25 Mar 1854 and Colonel Rifle Brigade Feb 1862.

REFERENCE: *Dictionary of National Biography. Dictionary of Canadian Biography. Moore, George Charles, Life of John Colborne, Field Marshal Lord Seaton, 1903. Leeke, William, The History of Lord Seaton's Regiment (the 52nd Light Infantry) at the Battle of Waterloo, 2 vols, 1866, Supplement 1871. Household Brigade Journal, 1863, p. 323. The Times, 18 Apr 1863. Gentleman's Magazine, Jun 1863, pp. 786–8 (Under Seaton). Annual Register, 1863, Appx, pp. 211–3 (Under Seaton).*

COLCROFT, John
Lieutenant. 36th (Herefordshire) Regiment of Foot.
Grave: Garrison Cemetery, Malta. (M.I.)

"IN MEMORY OF LIEUT JOHN COLCROFT / LATE GARRISON QUARTERMASTER IN HIS 84TH YEAR / DIED OCT 25TH 1849."

Pte 1 Aug 1786. (Promoted from the ranks). Ensign 36th Foot 28 Feb 1812. Lt 27 May 1813. Lt and Adjt 1817. Quartermaster Malta Garrison 16 Nov 1826.

Served in the Peninsula Aug 1808 – Jan 1809. Present at Rolica, Vimeiro, Corunna (rescued the regimental colours in the harbour at Corunna when their ship was set on fire). Also served in India 1788–1793 (present at Sittimimgalam, Shoar 1790, Bangalore, Nundydroog 1791, outworks of Seringapatam 1792 and capture of Pondicherry 1793 where he was wounded), Quiberon Bay 1801, Minorca 1802, Hanover 1805, South America 1806–1807 (present at Buenos Ayres) and Walcheren 1809. Garrison Quartermaster at Malta Nov 1826 and on his death the position was abolished. Served 54 years with the 36th Foot.

COLE, Sir Galbraith Lowry
Colonel. 70th (Glasgow Lowland) Regiment of Foot.
Statue: Enniskillen Parish Church, County Fermanagh, Northern Ireland. (North wall of chancel). Buried in the Family vault. (Photograph)

SACRED TO THE MEMORY / OF / GENERAL THE HON. SIR GALBRAITH LOWRY COLE G.C.B. / COMMANDER OF THE 4TH DIVISION / OF THE BRITISH ARMY DURING THE PENINSULAR WAR, / GOVERNOR OF GRAVESEND AND TILBURY FORT, / AND COLONEL OF THE 27TH OR ENNISKILLEN REGIMENT OF FOOT. / BORN MAY 1ST 1772, DIED OCTOBER 4TH, 1842. / HIS HISTORY MAY BE FOUND IN THAT OF HIS COUNTRY, / HIS CHARACTER IN THE DEVOTED ATTACHMENT OF HIS / FRIENDS, AND THE DEEP AFFECTION OF HIS / FAMILY BY WHOM THIS MONUMENT IS ERECTED.

Monumental column: Fort Hill, Enniskillen, County Fermanagh, Northern Ireland. (Photograph)

Over the Entrance Door to Column: (Photograph)

IN MEMORY OF / GENERAL THE HONBLE SIR GALBRAITH LOWRY COLE, G.C.B. / COLONEL OF THE 27TH REGIMENT. / ERECTED BY HIS FRIENDS, / 1843

Brass plaque inside door of Column: (Photograph)

THIS PILLAR IS ERECTED BY HIS FRIENDS AND / FELLOW-COUNTRYMEN IN MEMORY OF / GENERAL THE HONBLE SIR G. LOWRY COLE, / KNIGHT GRAND CROSS OF THE ORDER OF THE BATH. / KNIGHT OF THE PORTUGUESE ORDER OF THE TOWER / AND SWORD, AND OF THE TURKISH ORDER OF THE CRESCENT. / COLONEL, OF THE 27TH INNISKILLING REGIMENT OF FOOT. / GENERAL COMMANDING THE / 4TH DIVISION OF THE BRITISH ARMY, / THROUGHOUT THE PENINSULAR WAR. / GOVERNOR OF GRAVESEND, AND TILBURY FORT. / M.P. IN THE IRISH HOUSE OF COMMONS, FOR THE / BOROUGH OF ENNISKILLEN FROM 1798 TO 1800, / AND IN THE IMPERIAL PARLIAMENT FOR THE / COUNTY OF FERMANAGH FROM 1803 TO 1823. / HE TWICE RECEIVED THE THANKS OF BOTH HOUSES / OF PARLIAMENT FOR HIS DISTINGUISHED MILITARY SERVICES. / BORN MAY 1ST. 1772. DIED OCT 4TH 1842. / THE STATUE IS THE CONTRIBUTION OF THE TENANTRY / OF THE ENNISKILLEN ESTATES. SIDE 1: MARTINIQUE GUADELOUPE EGYPT MAIDA. SIDE 2: OLIVENCA ALBUERA SALAMANCA VITTORIA. SIDE 3: PYRENEES NIVELLE ORTHEZ TOULOUSE.

Cornet 12th Lt Dragoons 31 Mar 1787. Lt 5th Dragoon Guards 31 May 1791. Capt 70th Foot 30 Nov 1792. Major 86th Foot 31 Oct 1793. Lt Colonel Hon Robert Ward's Regiment of Foot 26 Nov 1794. Bt Colonel 1 Jan 1801. Capt and Lt Colonel 3rd Foot Guards 25 May 1803. Lt Colonel 27th Foot 4 Aug 1804.

Major General 25 Apr 1808. Colonel 103rd Foot 13 Jun 1812. Lt General 4 Jun 1813. Colonel 70th Foot 12 Jan 1814. General 22 Jul 1830.

Served in the Peninsula Oct 1809 – Dec 1811, Jul 1812 and Oct 1812 – Apr 1814 (GOC 4th Division). Present at Busaco, Olivencia, first siege of Badajoz, Albuera (wounded and Mentioned in Beresford's Despatches), Aldea da Ponte, Castrejon, Salamanca (severely wounded), Vittoria (Mentioned in Despatches), Pyrenees (Mentioned in Despatches), Nivelle (Mentioned in Despatches), Nive, Orthes and Toulouse. Gold Cross for Maida, Albuera, Salamanca, Vittoria, Pyrenees, Nivelle, Orthes and Toulouse. GCB. KTS. Not present at Waterloo owing to his marriage the day before Quatre Bras although Wellington had asked for him to be on his staff. Rejoined the Army 15 Aug and served in France with the Army of Occupation until Nov 1818.

Also served in the West Indies 1794 (present at Martinique, St Lucia and Guadeloupe), Egypt 1801 and Maida 1806. MP for County Fermanagh 1803–1823. Resigned his seat in the House of Commons to become Governor of Mauritius 1823–1828, where he improved the conditions of the slaves in the colony and Governor of Cape of Good Hope 1828–1833, where he became one of its most successful Governors. Governor Gravesend and Tilbury Fort 1818–1842. Colonel 34th Foot 21 May 1816. Colonel 27th Foot 16 Dec 1826. (the family was always associated with the regiment). Died at Highfield Park, near Hartford Bridge, Hampshire 4 Oct 1842.

REFERENCE: *Cole, Maud and Stephen Gwynn eds., Memoirs of Sir Lowry Cole, 1934, reprint 2011. Dictionary of National Biography. Gentleman's Magazine, Nov 1842, p. 544. Royal Military Calendar, Vol 2, pp. 305–14. Annual Register, 1842, Appx, p. 294. Cole, John William, Memoirs of British Generals, Vol 1, 1856, pp. 267–352.*

COLE, John
Captain. 45th (Nottinghamshire) Regiment of Foot.
Ledger stone: Kensal Green Cemetery, London. Inscription illegible. (4231/145/RS). (Photograph)

Ensign 14 Feb 1805. Lt 5 Jun 1805. Capt 28 Feb 1811. Major 26 Jun 1826.

Served in the Peninsula Aug 1808 – Sep 1811 and Apr 1814. Present at Rolica, Vimeiro, Talavera (wounded and taken prisoner from Aug – Oct 1809), Busaco, Redinha, Casal Nova, Foz d'Arouce, Sabugal, Fuentes d'Onoro, second siege of Badajoz, El Bodon and Toulouse. Half pay 2 Apr 1829. Buried in Kensal Green 28 Jun 1843.

COLE, John
Private. 1st Regiment of Foot Guards.
Headstone: All Saints Churchyard, North Benfleet, Essex. (Photograph)

SACRED TO THE MEMORY OF / JOHN COLE / A SOLDIER OF WATERLOO / OF THE 2ND BAT. GRENADIER GUARDS. / AT THE CELEBRATED COMMAND / "UP GUARDS AND AT EM" / HE WAS WOUNDED BY A MUSKET BALL / BUT HEROICALLY PERSEVERED / TILL THE VICTORY. / HE DIED IN THIS PARISH APRIL 10TH 1836. / AGED 51 / BEQUEATHING HIS MEDAL TO THE CURATE / WHOSE LAST ACT WAS / THE ERECTION OF THIS TABLET. THIS GRAVE STONE WAS RECUT BY THE GRENADIER GUARDS ASSOCIATION JULY 1981.

Served at Waterloo with the 2nd Battalion, in Lt Colonel Barclay's Company.

COLE, Pennel
Lieutenant. Royal Engineers.
Named on the Regimental Memorial: Rochester Cathedral, Rochester, Kent. (Photograph)

2nd Lt 1 Feb 1810. Lt 1 May 1811. 2nd Capt 7 Feb 1817. Capt 2 Dec 1830. Bt Major 10 Jan 1837. Lt Colonel 1 Apr 1846. Colonel 20 Jun 1854. Major General 11 Aug 1856.

Served in the Netherlands 1814–1815 and in France with the Army of Occupation. Also served in South Africa 1851–1853 (commanded the Royal Engineers, present in the Kaffir Wars). Retired on full pay 11 Aug 1856. Died at Boulogne 25 Mar 1862.

COLLIER, Charles
Staff Surgeon. Medical Department.
Memorial: Highgate Cemetery, London. (Photograph)

SACRED TO THE MEMORY OF / .... / CHARLES COLLIER, ESQ. MD, FRS, / WHO, FOR UPWARDS OF 31 YEARS, SERVED IN THE / CAPACITY OF ARMY SURGEON, AT BERMUDA, WEST INDIES, / THE PENINSULA, BELGIUM AND HANOVER, / CEYLON, THE MAURITIUS AND BOMBAY. / HE WAS APPOINTED, IN 1830, / DEPUTY INSPECTOR GENERAL OF HOSPITALS, / AND RETIRED IN THE YEAR 1838. / HE DIED MAY 6TH, 1870, IN THE 86TH YEAR OF HIS AGE.

Hospital Assistant 25 Sep 1805. Asst Surgeon 13th Foot 2 Oct 1806. Surgeon 60th Foot 10 Aug 1809. Surgeon 70th Foot 1 Feb 1810. Staff Surgeon 4 Jun1812. Deputy Inspector General of Hospitals 22 Jul 1830.
   Served in the Peninsula Sep 1812 – Apr 1814 (attached to 7th Division Mar – Jun 1813 and 6th Division Jul 1813 – Apr 1814) Present at Vittoria, Orthes and Toulouse. Assisted with the wounded after Waterloo. Also served in Martinique 1809, Ceylon 1825 and Mauritius 1829. MGS medal for Martinique, Vittoria, Orthes and Toulouse. MD St Andrew's1840.

COLLIER, William George
Captain and Lieutenant Colonel. Coldstream Regiment of Foot Guards.
Memorial tablet: St Mary's Church, Bury St Edmunds, Suffolk. (Photograph)

SACRED TO THE MEMORY OF / THE GALLANT / LIEUTENANT COLONEL COLLIER / OF THE COLDSTREAM GUARDS / WHO DIED THE 10TH OF MAY 1814 OF THE SEVERE WOUNDS HE RECEIVED / IN THE DREADFUL SORTIE OF THE FRENCH FROM BAYONNE. / HE WAS AN OFFICER UNIVERSALLY BELOVED BY THE SOLDIERS, / AND ESTEEMED BY HIS BROTHER OFFICERS FOR HIS UNREMITTING ATTENTION, ZEAL / AND COURAGE IN THE COURSE OF 14 YEARS DISTINGUISHED SERVICE WITH THE GUARDS / IN EGYPT, GERMANY, DENMARK, PORTUGAL, SPAIN AND FRANCE. / HE WAS THE ELDEST SON OF THE LATE ADMIRAL SIR G. COLLIER BY HIS WIFE ELIZTH FRYER / AND GODSON AND GREAT NEPHEW OF THE LATE BENJAMIN COLLIER ESQ. / OF GROTON PLACE IN THE COUNTY OF SUFFOLK. / THIS SMALL TRIBUTE TO HIS MEMORY SO INESTIMABLY DEAR AND VALUED / HIS EVER AFFECTIONATE AND AFFLICTED MOTHER DEDICATES TO HER DARLING SON, / TAKEN FROM HER IN THE PRIME OF LIFE AND GLORY. / AT THE AGE OF 31 YEARS.

Ledger stone: Coldstream Guards Cemetery, St Etienne, Bayonne, France. (Photograph)

LT COL G. C.

Named on the Memorial: St Andrew's Church, (now Musée Historique), Biarritz, France. (Photograph)

Named on Memorial Panel VII for the Sortie from Bayonne: Royal Military Chapel, Wellington Barracks, London. (M.I.) (Destroyed by a Flying Bomb 1944)

Cornet 14th Lt Dragoons. Ensign Coldstream Guards 10 Dec 1799. Lt and Capt 14 May 1801. Capt and Lt Colonel 3 Oct 1811.
   Served in the Peninsula Mar 1809 – Nov 1811 and Nov 1812 – Apr 1814. Present at Douro, Talavera

(wounded), Busaco, Fuentes d'Onoro, Vittoria, Bidassoa, Nivelle, Nive, Adour and Bayonne, (severely wounded in the Sortie from Bayonne 14 Apr 1814. Both legs had to be amputated, died of his wounds 10 May 1814 and is buried in the Guards Cemetery at St Etienne). Also served in Egypt 1801, Hanover 1805 and Copenhagen 1807.

COLLINS, Bassett
Captain. 74th (Highland) Regiment of Foot.
Named on the Regimental Memorial: St Giles's Cathedral, Edinburgh, Scotland. (Photograph)

Capt 20 Aug 1805.
    Served in the Peninsula Feb 1810 – Mar 1812. Present at Busaco, Casal Nova, Foz d'Arouce, Fuentes d'Onoro, second siege of Badajoz, El Bodon, Ciudad Rodrigo (wounded) and Badajoz where he was killed during the siege 26 Mar 1812.

COLLINS, George
Lieutenant: 58th (Rutlandshire) Regiment of Foot.
Ledger stone: St Mary's Churchyard, Enniscorthy, County Wexford, Ireland. (Photograph)

GEORGE COLLINS / LATE CAPTAIN 58TH REGIMENT / DIED 18TH DECEMBER 1839 / AGED 50 YEARS.

Ensign 19 Nov 1807. Lt 16 Nov 1809. Capt 22 Jul 1830.
    Served in the Peninsula Oct 1809 – Jan 1812. Present at Lisbon.

COLLINS, Richard
Lieutenant Colonel. 83rd Regiment of Foot.
Monument: Gouveia, Portugal. (M.I.)

"SACRED TO THE MEMORY OF COLONEL RICHARD COLLINS / OF HIS BRITANNIC MAJESTY'S 83RD REGIMENT, / DIED IN THE SERVICE OF HIS COUNTRY ON 13TH FEBRUARY 1813. / THIS INSCRIPTION IS ENTRUSTED TO BE ADDED TO THE TRIBUTE / OF ESTEEM OFFERED BY HIS BROTHER OFFICERS IN THE / RE-ERECTION OF THE MONUMENT, BY A FRIEND / WHO KNEW PERFECTLY HIS VIRTUES."

Major 3rd Garrison Battalion 20 Feb 1805. Major 83rd Foot 9 May 1805. Bt Lt Colonel 25 Apr 1808. Lt Colonel 17 Aug 1809. Portuguese Army: Colonel 11th Line 22 Oct 1810. Brigadier 7th and 19th Line 27 Feb 1812.
    Served in the Peninsula with 83rd Foot Oct 1809 – Sep 1810 and Portuguese Army Oct 1810 – Feb 1813. Present at Busaco, Albuera (severely wounded and Mentioned in Despatches) and Salamanca (wounded). Gold Medal for Albuera and Salamanca. His leg was amputated after being struck by a cannon ball at Albuera and he returned to England. Returned to Spain in 1812 with a cork leg and continued to lead his brigade. Also served in the West Indies 1795–1802 (present at St Lucia where he was wounded and Trinidad 1802) and Cape of Good Hope 1805. Was an expert linguist and military historian. Died 17 Feb 1813.
REFERENCE: *Gentleman's Magazine, Apr 1813, pp. 386–7.*

COLLIS, Charles
Captain. 24th (Warwickshire) Regiment of Foot.
Memorial tablet: St Peter and St Paul Church, Bishop's Hull, Taunton, Somerset. (Photograph)

THIS TABLET / IS ERECTED TO THE MEMORY OF / LIEUT COLL SIR CHARLES COLLIS, / AND

HIS ELDEST SON, / ENSIGN HECTOR C. B. COLLIS, BOTH OF H. M^S 24TH REG^T / LIEU^T COL^L COLLIS, / WAS SEVERELY WOUNDED, AND TAKEN PRISONER, / AT THE BATTLE OF TALAVERA IN 1809, / AND DIED AT WILTON ON 26 AUGUST 1849, / AGE 64 YEARS. / ....

Ensign 5th Foot 23 Jan 1800. Lt 12th Foot 24 Jun 1802. Lt 5th Foot 17 Sep 1803. Capt 24th Foot 31 Oct 1805. Bt Major 12 Aug 1819. Bt Lt Colonel 10 Jan 1837.

Served in the Peninsula 1809 – Apr 1814. Present at Talavera where he was severely wounded and taken prisoner 29 Jul 1809. Remained a prisoner until the end of the war in 1814. MGS medal for Talavera. Retired on half pay 8 Dec 1819 as a consequence of his wounds. His son Ensign Hector Collis died January 1849 at the Battle of Chillianwallah.

COLLYER, George
2nd Captain. Royal Engineers.
Memorial tablet: St Mary the Virgin Church, Wroxham, Norfolk. (Photograph)

SACRED TO THE MEMORY OF / CAPT^N GEORGE COLLYER / OF THE ROYAL ENGINEERS / WHO AT THE SIEGE OF SAN SEBASTIAN / AFTER HAVING, WITH COURAGE AND JUDGE-MENT, / LED ON A COLUMN TO THE ATTACK, / WAS KILLED IN THE BREACH / ON THE 31ST DAY OF AUGUST 1813 / IN THE 25TH YEAR OF HIS AGE. / WEEP NOT! HE DIED AS HEROES DIE, / THE DEATH PERMITTED TO THE BRAVE: / MOURN NOT! HE LIES WHERE SOLDIERS LIE, / AND VALOUR ENVIES SUCH A GRAVE. / YET, NE'ER HAS FAME ALONE, AFFECTION'S TEAR SUPPRESS'D, / GRIEF TURNS FROM GLORY'S FIELD, TO HIS CELESTIAL REST.

Monument to Fletcher, Rhodes, Collyer and Machell: San Sebastian, Spain. (Photograph)

TO FLETCHER, RHODES, COLLYER AND MACHELL.

Named on the Regimental Memorial: Rochester Cathedral, Rochester, Kent. (Photograph)

1st Lt 1 May 1807. 2nd Capt 5 Mar 1812.

Served in the Peninsula Aug 1813. Present at the siege of San Sebastian where he was killed 31 Aug 1813. Collyer landed at Passages 19 Aug 1813 and went straight to the siege. Twelve days later he was killed in the breach at the assault. Also served in the Baltic 1807.

COLQUHOUN, James Nesbit
1st Lieutenant. Royal Artillery.
Memorial: St Mary's Churchyard, Woolwich, Kent. (No longer extant. Church bombed in the Second World War). (M.I.)

"JAMES NESBIT COLQUHOUN, COLONEL IN THE ROYAL ARTILLERY AND INSPECTOR OF THE ROYAL CARRIAGE DEPARTMENT DIED 17 SEPTEMBER 1853 IN 65TH YEAR."

2nd Lt 1 Jun 1808. 1st Lt 8 Sep 1810. Bt 2nd Capt 6 Nov 1827. 2nd Capt 22 Mar 1829. Capt 11 Dec 1838. Bt Major 2 Dec 1836. Bt Lt Colonel 10 Nov 1840. Lt Colonel 9 Nov 1846. Colonel 11 Nov 1851.

Served in the Peninsula Sep 1812 – Apr 1814. Present at Cadiz and Tarifa. Served in France with the Army of Occupation until Nov 1818. Also served in the West Indies 1810 – Jun 1812, Netherlands 1814–1815, Spain 1836–1840 (in command of detachment of artillery in Spanish Civil War 1838–1839. Awarded Order of St Fernando, Cross of Bilbao and Order of Isabella), Syria 1840–1841 (NGS Medal and medal for Syria) and Malta 1841–1842.

Retired on half pay 19 Aug 1835 and rejoined 5 Nov 1836. Inspector of Royal Carriage Department

6 Apr 1852. Talented officer with exceptional scientific knowledge. He was able to make many improvements in the Royal Carriage Department and substituted machinery for manual labour making the department more efficient.

COLQUHOUN, Robert
Quartermaster. 1ˢᵗ Regiment of Foot Guards.
Headstone: St John's Westminster Burial Ground, London. (M.I.)

"IN MEMORY OF ROBERT COLQUHOUN ESQ, LATE OF THE GRENADIER GUARDS WHO DIED 1 AUG 1840."

Quartermaster 21 Aug 1806.
 Served in the Peninsula with 2ⁿᵈ Battalion Mar 1810 – May 1811 and 3ʳᵈ Battalion May 1811 – Mar 1814. Present at Cadiz, Bidassoa, Nivelle, Nive, Adour and Bayonne. Present at Waterloo.

COLQUITT, John Scrope
Captain and Lieutenant Colonel. 1ˢᵗ Regiment of Foot Guards.
Headstone: La Cruz del Inglés, Alcalá de Guadaira, near Seville, Spain. (In local museum). (Photograph)

SACRED / TO / THE MEMORY OF / JOHN SCROPE COLQUITT ESQᴿᴱ / LIEUT COLONEL IN HIS BRITTANIC / MAJESTY'S 1ˢᵀ REGᵀ OF FOOT GUARDS / WHO DIED IN SEVILLE THE 5 OF / SEPTEMBER 1812 AGED 37 YEARS / OF A FEVER BROUGHT ON IN / CONSEQUENCE OF EXCESSIVE / FATIGUE DURING THE MARCH TO / SEVILLE, AND OF THE GREAT / EXERTIONS WHICH HE MADE / WHILST GALLANTLY LEADING / ON HIS BATTALION TO THE / ATTACK ON THE BRIDGE / OF TRIANS, ON THE 27 OF AUGUST / 1812.

Note: A new memorial in the form of a Pedestal tomb with Cross erected in May 2012. (Inscription is identical to the headstone above). (Internet image).

Named on Memorial Panel VI: Royal Military Chapel, Wellington Barracks, London. (M.I.) (Destroyed by a Flying Bomb 1944)

Ensign 14 May 1794. Lt and Capt 25 Oct 1797. Capt and Lt Col 14 Sep 1809.
 Served in the Peninsula with 2ⁿᵈ Battalion Sep 1810 - Apr 1811 and 3ʳᵈ Battalion Apr 1811 - Sep 1812. Present at Cadiz, Barrosa (severely wounded) and Seville (led the attack on the capture of Seville, severely wounded, Mentioned in Despatches, and died of his wounds 5 Sep 1812). His brother Capt and Lt Colonel Goodwin Colquitt served with the regiment at Waterloo and was awarded the CB.

COLVILLE, Hon. Sir Charles
Colonel. 94ᵗʰ Regiment of Foot.
Interred in Catacomb B (v97 c1) Kensal Green Cemetery, London.

Ensign 28ᵗʰ Foot 26 Dec 1781 aged 11. Joined the regiment June 1787. Lt 30 Sep 1787, Capt 13ᵗʰ Foot 26 May 1791, Major 2 Sep 1795, Lt Colonel 26 Aug 1796, Bt Colonel 1 Jan 1805, Major General 25 Jun 1810, Colonel 5ᵗʰ Garrison Battalion 10 Oct 1812. Colonel 94ᵗʰ Foot 29 Apr 1815. Lt General 12 Aug 1819. General 10 Jan 1837.
 Served in the Peninsula Oct 1810 – Apr 1814 (Commanded 2 Brigade 4ᵗʰ Division Oct 1810 – Dec 1811), (Temporary GOC 4ᵗʰ Division Dec 1811 – Apr 1812), (GOC 3ʳᵈ Division Jan – May 1813), (Temporary GOC 6ᵗʰ Division May – Aug 1813), (GOC 3ʳᵈ Division Sep – Dec 1813) and (GOC 5ᵗʰ Division Dec 1813 – Apr 1814)
 Present during the pursuit of Massena, Fuentes d'Onoro, second siege of Badajoz, El Bodon (in

command of the small body of troops who were repeatedly attacked by a large force of enemy cavalry. The conduct and discipline of these troops in battle and their subsequent retreat before overwhelming numbers of infantry was an example to the rest of the Army), Ciudad Rodrigo, Badajoz (wounded and awarded pension of £350 per annum), Vittoria (wounded), Nivelle, Bidassoa, Nive and Bayonne (took command of siege operations after Sir John Hope was taken prisoner). Present at Waterloo in command of the reserves at Hal, siege of Cambrai and with the Army of Occupation. Gold Cross for Egypt, Martinique, Fuentes d'Onoro, Badajoz, Vittoria and Nivelle. GCB. GCH. KCTS. Also served in the West Indies 1793–1795 (present at Jamaica and San Domingo where he was wounded), Irish Rebellion 1798, Ferrol 1800, Egypt 1801 (present at Alexandria), Martinique 1808–1809 and India 1819–1825 (Commander in Chief at Bombay), Governor of Mauritius 1828–1832. Colonel 74th Foot 13 Jun 1823. Colonel 14th Foot 12 Dec 1834. Colonel 5th Foot 25 Mar 1837. Died 27 Mar 1843.
REFERENCE: Colville, John, Portrait of a general: a chronicle of the Napoleonic Wars, 1980. Dictionary of National Biography. Royal Military Calendar, Vol 3, pp. 16–9. Gentleman's Magazine, May 1843, p. 532.

COMBERMERE, Lord see COTTON, Sir Stapleton

COMMERELL, William Henry
Ensign. 1st Regiment of Foot Guards.
Named on Memorial Panel VI for Barrosa: Royal Military Chapel, Wellington Barracks, London. (M.I.) (Destroyed by a Flying Bomb 1944)

Ensign 27 Apr 1809.
    Served in the Peninsula with 2nd Battalion Mar 1810 – Mar 1811. Present at Cadiz and Barrosa where he was killed 5 Mar 1811.

CONNELL, John
Quartermaster. 26th (Cameronian) Regiment of Foot.
Headstone: Trafalgar Cemetery, Gibraltar. (Grave number 87). (Photograph)

AS A MARK OF RESPECT / THE OFFICERS OF THE 26TH REG / HAVE ERECTED THIS STONE / TO / THE MEMORY / OF / QUARTER MASTER JOHN CONNELL / WHO DEPARTED THIS LIFE THE 22 AUGT 1812 / IN THE 56TH YEAR OF HIS AGE / AFTER A SERVICE 40 YEARS.

Pte 1772. Quartermaster 14 May 1804.
    Served in the Peninsula Oct 1808 – Jan 1809 and Jul 1811 – Jun 1812. Present at Corunna.

CONNOLLY, James
Sergeant. 42nd (Royal Highland) Regiment of Foot.
Gravestone: Dumbarton Cemetery, Dumbartonshire, Scotland. (No longer extant. Cemetery destroyed for redevelopment). (M.I.)

"JAMES CONNOLLY DIED 16TH DEC 1853 AGED 63, FOUGHT IN PENINSULA IN ACTION MANY TIMES AND IN 9 GENERAL BATTLES."

Served in the Peninsula Apr 1812 – Apr 1814. Present at Pyrenees, Nivelle, Nive, Orthes and Toulouse. MGS medal for Pyrenees, Nivelle, Nive, Orthes and Toulouse.

CONNOR, Ogle Nesbit see O'CONNOR, Ogle Nesbit

CONSIDINE, James
Lieutenant. 43rd (Monmouthshire) Light Infantry Regiment of Foot.
Mural Memorial tablet: Meerut Cantonment Cemetery, Meerut, India. (Photograph)

SACRED / TO THE MEMORY OF / MAJOR GENERAL / JAMES CONSIDINE K.H. / WHO DIED AT MEERUT / IN COMMAND OF / H.M.'S 10 REGT OF FOOT / ON THE 4TH SEPT 1845 / AT THE AGE OF 50.

Ensign 20 Jul 1809. Lt 27 Dec 1810. Capt 29 Aug 1822. Major 11 Jul 1826. Lt Colonel 1 Jul 1828 (unattached). Lt Colonel 53rd Foot 2 Apr 1829. Major General (local rank) 25 May 1838 Bt Colonel 23 Nov 1841. Colonel 10th Foot 29 Mar 1842.

Served in the Peninsula with 1/43rd May 1810 – Feb 1814 Present at Coa, Busaco, Redinha, Casal Nova, Foz d'Arouce, Sabugal, Fuentes d'Onoro, Ciudad Rodrigo, Badajoz (severely wounded), Salamanca, San Munos, Pyrenees, Bidassoa and Nivelle (severely wounded). Awarded pension of £70 per annum for wounds at Badajoz and Nivelle. Served in France with the Army of Occupation 1815–1818. Also served in North America 1814–1815 (present at New Orleans), Portugal 1826–1827, Gibraltar 1827–1834 and Malta 1834–1836. Sent on a special mission to Constantinople 1836. KH. Went to Meerut in India in command of the 10th Foot, where he died Sep 1845 shortly before the 10th Foot left Meerut to join the Army of the Sutlej. 'General Considine was an excellent officer. His system of regimental discipline and the selection of field movements on parade proved to all military men that he was from the Peninsular school. All his manoeuvres were for the practical exhibition of what was most required on service and to be done in the shortest and most expeditious manner. He was fond of his profession, to which he was an ornament'.
REFERENCE: *Oxfordshire Light Infantry Chronicle, 1904, p. 147.*

COOKE, George
Captain and Lieutenant Colonel. 1st Regiment of Foot Guards.
Memorial tablet: St Mary's Church, Harefield, Middlesex, London. (Photograph)

SACRED TO THE MEMORY OF / LIEUTENANT GENERAL SIR GEORGE COOKE, KCB. KSG. KW. KS. / ELDEST SON OF GEORGE JOHN COOKE ESQR OF HAREFIELD PARK IN THIS COUNTY / AND PENELOPE DAUGHTER OF SIR WILLIAM BOWYER ESQR / HE DIED UNIVERSALLY LAMENTED THE 4TH FEBRUARY 1837 AGED 71 YEARS. / ....

Memorial: Royal Military Chapel, Wellington Barracks, London. (M.I.) (Destroyed by a Flying Bomb 1944)

"TO THE MEMORY OF / MAJOR-GENERAL SIR GEORGE COOKE, K.C.B., / 1ST GUARDS, 1784 – 1814. HE SERVED IN HOLLAND DURING THE CAMPAIGNS OF 1794 – 95, AND ALSO 1799, WHEN HE WAS SEVERELY WOUNDED. HE WAS PRESENT AT WALCHEREN. HE COMMANDED A DIVISION AT BERGEN-OP-ZOOM AND THE DIVISION OF THE GUARDS DURING THE CAMPAIGN OF 1815, / TILL HE WAS SEVERELY WOUNDED AT WATERLOO".

Ensign 20 Oct 1784. Lt and Capt 30 May 1792. Capt-Lieut 4 Jun 1798. Capt and Lt Colonel 4 Jun 1798. Bt Colonel 25 Apr 1808. Major General 4 Jun 1811. Lt General 19 Jul 1821.

Served in the Peninsula with 3rd Battalion Oct 1808 – Jan 1809 and Apr 1811 – Jul 1813 (Commanded Brigade May – Jun 1811 and GOC at Cadiz Jul 1811 – Jul 1813). Present at Cadiz and Tarifa. Present at Waterloo in commanded of the 1st Division of the Guards where he was severely wounded and lost his right arm. Awarded pension of £350 per annum. KCB 20 Jun 1815. Awarded Order of St George of Russia

3rd Class and Order of Wilhelm of the Netherlands 3rd Class. Also served in Flanders 1794–1795 (present at Boxtel. ADC to Major General Hulse), the Helder 1799 (severely wounded), Sicily 1806, Walcheren 1809 and the Netherlands 1813–1814 (commanded a Division at Bergen-op-Zoom). Lieutenant Governor of Portsmouth 1819. Colonel 77th Foot 23 Jun 1815. Colonel 40th Foot 23 Dec 1834. Elder brother of Lt Colonel Henry Frederick Cooke 12th Foot. Educated at Harrow.

REFERENCE: *Dictionary of National Biography. Gentleman's Magazine, Jun 1837, pp. 656–57. Royal Military Calendar, Vol 3, pp. 173–4.*

COOKE, Henry Frederick

Lieutenant Colonel. 12th (East Suffolk) Regiment of Foot.
Memorial tablet: St Mary's Church, Harefield, Middlesex, London. (Photograph)

..................../ MAJOR GENERAL SIR HENRY FREDERICK COOKE / KCH. CB. KSG. KMM. KTS. / YOUNGEST SON OF GEORGE JOHN COOKE ESQR AND MANY YEARS / AIDE DE CAMP TO HIS ROYAL HIGHNESS THE DUKE OF YORK. / HE DIED THE 10TH MARCH 1837 AGED 42 YEARS.

Ensign 40th Foot 20 Sep 1793. Lt 55th Foot 30 Sep 1793. Lt 43rd Foot 8 Aug 1798. Ensign 1st Foot Guards 25 Nov 1799. Lt and Capt 21 Aug 1801. Lt and Capt Coldstream Guards 5 Nov 1803. Capt and Lt Colonel 7 Nov 1811. Lt Colonel 12th Foot 4 Jun 1813. Lt Colonel 6th West India Regt 12 Oct 1815. Bt Colonel 27 May 1825. Major General 10 Jan 1837.

Served in the Peninsula Aug 1808 – Sep 1811 on the Staff (Aug – Oct 1808 DAAG), Apr 1809 (DAQMG), May 1809 – Apr 1810 (DAAG), May – Sep 1810 (DAAG 4th Division), and Oct 1810 – Sep 1811 (DAAG 1st Division) Present at Rolica, Vimeiro, Douro, Talavera, Busaco and Fuentes d'Onoro. Exchanged to Staff in North America Jul 1812. Inspecting Field Officer of Militia in Nova Scotia 1813. ADC to Duke of York 1814. CB. KCH. KTS. KSG. KMM. Younger brother of Capt and Lt Colonel George Cooke 1st Foot Guards.

REFERENCE: *Gentleman's Magazine, Jun 1837, p. 657.*

COOKE, John Henry

Lieutenant. 43rd (Monmouthshire) Light Infantry Regiment of Foot.
Memorial: Highgate Cemetery, (Grave number 37222), London. Inscription not recorded.

Ensign 1st West Yorkshire Militia 6 Jan 1805. Lt 21 Nov 1806. Ensign 43rd Foot 15 Mar 1809. Lt 19 Apr 1810. Capt 25th Foot 31 Dec 1823. Bt Major 28 Jun 1838. Capt 35th Foot 27 Jul 1838. Bt Lt Colonel 11 Nov 1851.

Served in the Peninsula with 1/43rd Jul 1811 – Apr 1814. Present at Ciudad Rodrigo, Badajoz (wounded), Castrejon, Salamanca, San Munos, San Millan, Vittoria (wounded), Pyrenees, San Sebastian, Heights of Vera, Bidassoa, Nivelle, Nive, Tarbes and Toulouse. Served in France with the Army of Occupation 1815–1818. Also served at Walcheren 1809 and North America 1814–1815 (present at New Orleans) Accompanied Lt Colonel Considine on a special mission to Constantinople 1836. Brigade Major at Newport 1839–1840. MGS medal for Ciudad Rodrigo, Badajoz, Salamanca, Vittoria, Pyrenees, Nivelle, Nive and Toulouse. Spanish Silver Cross for the storming of Ciudad Rodrigo. Appointed to the Corps of Gentleman at Arms 2 Oct 1844. Ensign Yeoman of the Guard 16 Sep 1862, Lt 2 Feb 1866. Knighted by Queen Victoria 11 Dec 1867. Honorary Secretary and Military Vice President for Army recipients of the MGS medals and clasps. Died 23 Jan 1870. Author of *Memoirs of the late war 1807–1814*, 2 vols, 1831.
REFERENCE: *Hathaway, E., A true soldier gentleman: the Memoirs of Lt John Cooke 1791–1813, 2000.*

COOKE, William

Private. 40th (2nd Somersetshire) Regiment of Foot.
Headstone: Whittingham Cemetery, near Singleton, New South Wales, Australia. (Photograph)

SACRED / TO / THE MEMORY OF / JANE COOKE / .... / .ALSO OF / WILLIAM COOKE. / DIED NOV 1852 / AGED 66 YEARS. / A WATERLOO VETERAN.

Pte Apr 1805. Cpl 1818.

Served in the Peninsula Aug 1808 – Apr 1814. Present at Vimeiro, Talavera, Busaco, Ciudad Rodrigo, Badajoz, Salamanca, Vittoria, Pyrenees (wounded), Nivelle (wounded), Orthes and Toulouse. Served at Waterloo in Capt J. H. Barnett's Company. Also served in South America 1807. After his discharge 29 Jan 1819 he went to Australia, eventually running a public house 'The Rose Inn' at Singleton. MGS medal for Vimeiro, Talavera, Busaco, Ciudad Rodrigo, Badajoz, Salamanca, Vittoria, Pyrenees, Nivelle, Orthes and Toulouse. Died 22 Nov 1852 at Singleton.

COOKSON, George
Colonel. Royal Artillery.
Family Memorial tablet: St George's Church, Esher, Surrey. (North wall). (Photograph)

SACRED TO THE MEMORY OF / LIEUTENANT GENERAL GEORGE COOKSON OF THE ROYAL ARTILLERY, / WHO DEPARTED THIS LIFE AT ESHER, THE 12TH OF AUGUST 1835, / IN THE 76TH YEAR OF HIS AGE. / HE WAS A KIND, TENDER AND AFFECTIONATE HUSBAND AND FATHER, / A TRUE FRIEND, A SINCERE CHRISTIAN, A GALLANT BRAVE AND ENERGETIC SOLDIER / HE SERVED IN EVERY QUARTER OF THE GLOBE / WITH DISTINGUISHED CREDIT TO HIMSELF, AND HONOR TO HIS SOVEREIGN AND HIS COUNTRY. / HIS LOSS IS LAMENTED AS HIS MEMORY WILL BE CHERISHED / BY HIS BEREAVED WIDOW AND CHILDREN, HIS FRIENDS, AND ALL WHO KNEW HIS WORTH, / FOR HE WAS A MAN OF THE FINEST FEELING, OF IRREPROACHABLE REPUTATION, / AND OF THE STRONGEST INTEGRITY. / ....

2nd Lt 19 Aug 1778. 1st Lt 12 Jul 1780. Capt-Lieut 16 Nov 1792. Capt 6 Mar 1795. Bt Major 1 Jan 1800. Major 12 Sep 1803. Lt Colonel 20 Jul 1804. Colonel 17 Mar 1812. Major General 4 Jun 1814. Lt General 22 Jul 1830.

Served in the Peninsula 1808 – Jan 1809. Present at Benevente, the Corunna campaign (in command of 48 guns and 1,200 men landed at Corunna under Sir David Baird). Also served in the West Indies 1773–1777 (in the Royal Navy), and 1781–1786 (in the Royal Artillery), Flanders 1793 (present at Valenciennes), Ferrol 1800, Egypt 1801 (present at Aboukir and Alexandria – appointed Commandant of Pharos Castle and all artillery forces in Egypt. Gold Medal from Grand Seigneur which he was allowed to wear even though he was only a Major), Hanover 1805, Copenhagen 1807 (in command of all artillery), Walcheren 1809 (commanded a division of artillery). Retired 25 Jun 1814 with a pension of £700 per annum. Father of Ensign George Parker Cookson 3rd Foot Guards who died at Fuentes d'Onoro.
REFERENCE: *Dictionary of National Biography. Gentleman's Magazine, Oct 1835, pp. 428–9.*

COOKSON, George Parker
Ensign. 3rd Regiment of Foot Guards.
Family Memorial tablet: St George's Church, Esher, Surrey. (North wall). (Photograph)

.... / ALSO TO THE MEMORY OF GEORGE P. COOKSON, ELDEST SON OF THE ABOVE, / AN ENSIGN IN THE 3RD REGT OF FOOT GUARDS, WHO FELL AT THE BATTLE OF VIMEIRO IN SPAIN / GALLANTLY LEADING ON HIS MEN AGAINST THE ENEMY ON THE 5TH OF MAY 1811 / IN THE 18TH YEAR OF HIS AGE. / ....

Note: He died at Fuentes D'Onoro which took place 5 May 1811, not Vimeiro as on tablet.

Named on Memorial Panel VI for Fuentes D'Onoro: Royal Military Chapel, Wellington Barracks, London. (M.I.) (Destroyed by a Flying Bomb 1944)

Ensign 29 Jun 1809.

Served in the Peninsula Jan – May 1811. Present at Fuentes d'Onoro where he was killed 5 May 1811. Son of Colonel George Cookson Royal Artillery.

COOPE, William Jesser
Deputy Commissary General. Commissariat Department.
Memorial tablet: Falmouth Parish Church, Falmouth, Cornwall. (Photograph)

BENEATH THE ALTAR OF THIS CHURCH ARE DEPOSITED THE REMAINS OF / WILLIAM JESSER COOPE ESQUIRE, / A DEPUTY COMMISSARY GENERAL IN HIS MAJESTY'S SERVICE. HE WAS BORN ON / THE 30TH DAY OF JANUARY 1763. HE DIED ON THE 15TH DAY OF APRIL 1838. / IN THE COURSE OF HIS PUBLIC DUTY EXTENDED OVER A PERIOD OF / FORTY FOUR YEARS, HE SERVED WITH THE TROOPS IN HOLLAND IN 1791 TO 1795: / WAS ATTACHED TO THE RUSSIAN FORCES WHO RETURNED FROM THE HELDER TO JERSEY IN / 1799, JOINED THE EXPEDITION TO FERROL, PROCEEDED TO RHODES, THENCE TO EGYPT IN WHICH / COUNTRY HE REMAINED UNTIL THE FINAL EVACUATION BY THE BRITISH: WAS IN CHARGE / OF HIS DEPARTMENT WITH GENERAL SIR DAVID BAIRD'S DIVISION IN THE EXPE- DITION / TO CORUNNA: WAS PRESENT DURING THE WHOLE OF SIR JOHN MOORE'S MEMORABLE / RETREAT: AND SUBSEQUENTLY PERFORMED AT VARIOUS INTERVALS GARRISON DUTY, / AT MALTA, GIBRALTAR, THE CHANNEL ISLANDS AND IN ENGLAND. / VERY GENERALLY KNOWN BY HIS CONTEMPORARIES OF ALL RANKS IN / THE ARMY, THOSE OF THEM WHO SURVIVE HIM AND READ THIS MEMORIAL / WILL BEAR TESTIMONY THAT TO AN EXACT AND HONOURABLE DISCHARGE OF PUBLIC DUTY, / WAS UNITED IN HIM AN URBANITY OF DISPOSITION AS BENEFICIAL TO THE REGULAR PERFORMANCE / OF THE PUBLIC SERVICE AS IT WAS IMPERATIVE OF THE RESPECT AND ESTEEM OF THOSE / WITH WHOM HE ACTED: ON OTHER TABLETS THAN THIS INADEQUATE MEMORIAL / IS INSCRIBED THE REMEMBRANCE OF HIS PRIVATE WORTH. / THE PATRON OF THIS BENEFICE, HE RECEIVED THE ACCOMPLISHMENT OF HIS AFFECTIONATE / DESIRES ONLY A FEW DAYS; HIS FREQUENT PRAYERS FULFILLED, RETURNING FROM / THIS CHURCH ON GOOD FRIDAY HE WAS THROWN FROM HIS CARRIAGE AND RECEIVED INJURIES / WHICH TERMINATED HIS LIFE ON EASTER SUNDAY IN THE 73RD YEAR OF HIS AGE.

Dep Comm Gen 2 Aug 1801. Comm Gen 1814.

Served in the Peninsula 1808 – Jan 1809. Present during the retreat to Corunna. Also served in Flanders 1794–1795, the Helder 1799, Ferrol 1800, Egypt 1801 and Egypt 1807, Malta and Gibraltar.

COOPER, Robert
Private. 16th (Queen's) Regiment of Light Dragoons.
Buried in Holy Trinity Churchyard, Hurdsfield, Cheshire. Inscription not recorded.

Pte 6 Sep 1813 aged 16.

Present at Quatre Bras and Waterloo in Capt Brown's Company where he was wounded in the right foot. Discharged 17 Jan 1816. Served for two years and 134 days. For 30 years he was a teacher in the Roe Street Sunday School. Buried 11 Mar 1879 aged 80.
REFERENCE: *Oldham Standard, 29 Mar 1879, p. 11, column 3.*

COOPER, Robert Henry Spencer
Lieutenant. Royal Engineers.
Named on the Regimental Memorial: Rochester Cathedral, Rochester, Kent. (Photograph)

2nd Lt 20 Mar 1813. Lt 21 Jul 1813. 2nd Capt 23 May 1829.

Served in France with the Army of Occupation 1815–1818. Also served in the Netherlands 1813–1815 and Portugal 1826–1827. Retired on half pay 15 Feb 1830. Died in London 17 Apr 1843.

COOPER, Samuel
Staff Surgeon. Medical Department
Pedestal tomb: Kensal Green Cemetery, London. (7870/75/IC). (Photograph)

TO THE MEMORY OF / SAMUEL COOPER ESQ^{RE} / LATE PRESIDENT OF THE / ROYAL COLLEGE OF SURGEONS / OF ENGLAND / SENIOR SURGEON TO THE / UNIVERSITY COLLEGE HOSPITAL / PROFESSOR OF SURGERY / IN THE SAME COLLEGE / SURGEON TO THE QUEEN'S BENCH / WHO DIED AT SHEPPERTON / IN THE COUNTY OF MIDDLESEX / IN THE 67TH YEAR OF HIS AGE / AUTHOR OF THE RENOWNED SURGICAL DICTIONARY

Hospital Mate 1801–1802 and Jan 1813. Asst Surgeon 14 Oct 1813. Staff Surgeon 26 May 1814.
     Served in the Peninsula 1812–1813. Present at Waterloo. Retired on half pay 25 Jul 1816. Author of *First lines of surgery* 1807 and *Surgical dictionary*, 1809. After Waterloo spent his time revising these two works which each ran into several editions. Became Surgeon and Professor of Surgery, University College, London. Died at Shepperton 2 Dec 1848.
REFERENCE: *Dictionary of National Biography.*

COOTE, Robert
Major. 32nd (Cornwall) Regiment of Foot.
Headstone: St Mary's Churchyard, Dublin, Ireland. (M.I.) (Church deconsecrated and is now a restaurant. Churchyard opened as a public space. Gravestones were removed and placed in three rows along a wall to the rear of the open space. Some slabs form part of the pavement, but this memorial not visible).

"SACRED TO THE MEMORY OF LIEUTENANT-COLONEL COOTE / LATE OF HIS MAJESTY'S 32ND REGIMENT OF FOOT / WHO DEPARTED THIS LIFE / ON THE 23RD DAY OF OCTOBER 1828 / IN THE 59TH YEAR OF HIS AGE. / THIS MONUMENT IS ERECTED BY HIS AFFECTIONATE SISTER MARIA COOTE."

Ensign Earl of Belvedere's Regiment 1794. Lt 118th Foot 30 Oct 1794. Lt 46th Foot 5 Sep 1795. Capt 32nd Foot 4 Oct 1797. Bt Major 25 Apr 1808. Major 27 Aug 1813. Bt Lt Colonel 4 Jun 1814.
     Served in the Peninsula Aug 1808 – Jan 1809 and Jul 1811 – Apr 1814. Present at Rolica, Vimeiro, Corunna, siege of Salamanca Forts, Salamanca, Burgos and retreat from Burgos, Pyrenees, Bidassoa, Nivelle, Nive and Orthes. Also served as a Marine in Lord Bridport's action 1795, with 32nd Foot in the Baltic 1807 and Walcheren 1809. Half pay 1814.

COPELAND, George
Corporal. 3rd Regiment of Foot Guards.
Headstone: Old Churchyard, Spital, Windsor, Berkshire. (Photograph)

IN AFFECTIONATE / REMEMBRANCE OF / CAPTAIN GEORGE COPELAND / MILITARY KNIGHT OF WINDSOR / AND LATE SCOTS FUSILIER GUARDS / DIED 18TH APRIL 1871 / AGED 78 / HIS END WAS PEACE.

Private 5 May 1812. Corporal 25 Jan 1813. Sgt 19 Feb 1817. Quartermaster 6 Apr 1837.
     Served in the Peninsula Mar 1813 – Apr 1814. Present at Vittoria, siege of San Sebastian, passage of Bidassoa, Nive, Nivelle, siege of Bayonne and repulse of the Sortie of Bayonne. MGS medal for Vittoria,

Nivelle, and Nive. Present at Quatre Bras and Waterloo. Half pay 2 Sep 1851. Honorary rank of Captain 1 Jul 1859. Military Knight of Windsor 1865.
REFERENCE: *Household Brigade Journal, 1871, p. 316.*

CORMICK, Edward
Captain. 20th Regiment of Light Dragoons.
Gravestone: Ambala Cemetery, India. (M.I.)

"SACRED TO THE MEMORY OF / CAPTAIN EDWARD CORMICK, / PAYMASTER 3RD K. O. LIGHT DRAGOONS / WHO DEPARTED THIS LIFE ON THE 19TH MAY 1848. / AGED 63 YEARS. / DEEPLY AND SINCERELY REGRETTED BY HIS FAMILY AND FRIENDS."

Cornet 4 Dec 1806. Lt 25 Sep 1807. Capt 23 Sep 1813. Paymaster 4th Lt Dragoons 24 Jan 1828. Paymaster 3rd Lt Dragoons 1833.
    Served in the Peninsula Aug 1808 – Sep 1809 and Sep 1812 – Sep 1813. Present at Rolica, Vimeiro, Douro, Sicily and East Coast of Spain (present at Castalla). MGS medal for Rolica and Vimeiro. After the war, the regiment was disbanded and he went on half pay 1818. Later served in India with both the 4th Lt Dragoons and the 3rd Lt Dragoons, with whom he served in Afghanistan 1842 (awarded medal for Kabul). Present throughout the Sutlej campaign of 1845–1846 (present at Ferozeshah and Sobraon, for which he received a medal with two clasps). Died two years later at Ambala 1848.

COSGROVE, John
Private. 39th (Dorsetshire) Regiment of Foot.
Buried in the Private Soldiers Burial Ground, Royal Hospital, Kilmainham, Dublin, Ireland.

Pte 9 Dec 1806.
    Served in the Peninsula 1809 – Apr 1814. Present at Albuera, Vittoria, Pyrenees, Nivelle, Nive, Orthes and Toulouse. MGS medal for Albuera, Vittoria, Pyrenees (wounded at Maya Jul 1813), Nivelle, Nive, Orthes and Toulouse. Discharged 25 May 1825.

COSTELLO, Edward
Private. 95th Regiment of Foot.
Grave: Nunhead Cemetery, London (Grave number 10536 Sq 123/107). Inscription not recorded.
Named on the Regimental Memorial: Winchester Cathedral, Winchester, Hampshire. (Photograph)

Enlisted from Dublin Militia. Private 95th Foot 1806.
    Served in the Peninsula 1810 – Apr 1814. Present at Busaco (wounded), Fuentes d'Onoro, Ciudad Rodrigo (took part in the Forlorn Hope), Badajoz, (wounded in the Forlorn Hope), Salamanca, Vittoria, Pyrenees, Nivelle, Nive, Orthes and Toulouse. Present at Waterloo in Captain Jonathan Leach's Company. MGS medal for Busaco, Fuentes d'Onoro, Ciudad Rodrigo, Badajoz, Salamanca, Vittoria, Pyrenees, Nivelle, Nive, Orthes and Toulouse. Awarded 1st Battalion Regimental Medal. Served with the British Legion in Spain 1835–1836 (severely wounded at San Sebastian). Awarded Order of Knight of San Ferdinand and Isabella II. Yeoman Warder of the Tower of London 1838. Author of *Adventures of a soldier*, 1852. Died 27 Jun 1869 aged 84.
REFERENCE: Hathaway, Eileen, Costello: *the true story of a Peninsular War rifleman: including Adventures of a soldier*, 1997.

COTTON, Edward
Private 7th (Queen's Own) Regiment of Light Dragoons.
Low monument: In the orchard at Hougoumont, Waterloo, Belgium. (Photograph)

SACRED TO THE MEMORY / OF / EDWARD COTTON / AUTHOR / A VOICE FROM WATERLOO / LATE SERGEANT / OF THE 7TH HUSSARS / DEPARTED THIS LIFE / MONT ST JEAN / 24 DAY OF JUNE 1849 / IN HIS 58 YEAR.

Memorial tablet: Inside Mausoleum, Evere, Cemetery, Brussels, Belgium. (Photograph)

SERGEANT-MAJOR / EDWARD COTTON / 7TH HUSSARS

Pte 13 Jan 1813. Cpl 1816. Sgt 1821. Sgt Major 1825.

Served in the Peninsula Aug 1813 – Apr 1814. Present at Orthes and Toulouse. Present at Waterloo where his horse was killed under him. MGS medal for Orthes and Toulouse.

After his discharge from the regiment 15 Feb 1828 he bought a property on the edge of the battlefield of Waterloo and turned it into a hotel for tourists who were flocking to see the famous site. He advertised his services as a guide and was in effect the first battlefield guide, incorporated a museum in the hotel filling it with artefacts found on the battlefield. Wrote a guide to the battlefield entitled *A voice from Waterloo*, published in 1846. One of the most popular histories of the campaign and by 1913 thirteen editions had been published. Died 24 Jun 1849 and was buried in the orchard at Hougoumont. Later when the Waterloo mausoleum was built at Evere his remains were removed there.

REFERENCE: *Cotton, Edward, A Voice from Waterloo, revised by S. Monick, reprint 2001. Gentleman's Magazine, Sep 1849, p. 335. Annual Register, 1849, Appx, p. 251.*

COTTON, Sir Stapleton, Lord Combermere
Colonel. 20th Regiment of Light Dragoons.
Memorial tablet: St Margaret's Church, Wrenbury, Cheshire. (Photograph)

SACRED TO THE MEMORY OF / STAPLETON COTTON VISCOUNT COMBERMERE, / FIELD MARSHAL G.C.B. K.S.I. K.T.S. G.C.H. P.C. / BORN NOVEMBER 14TH 1773. DIED FEBRUARY 21ST 1865. / HE WAS SUCCESSIVELY GOVERNOR OF BARBADOES, / COMMANDER IN CHIEF OF THE LEEWARD ISLANDS, / COMMANDER IN CHIEF IN IRELAND, AND ALSO IN THE EAST INDIES, / COLONEL OF THE FIRST LIFE GUARDS, / CONSTABLE OF THE TOWER OF LONDON. / THIS MONUMENT IS ERECTED BY HIS DEEPLY SORROWING WIDOW / MARY VISCOUNTESS COMBERMERE, / TO COMMEMORATE HIS DOMESTIC VIRTUES / WHILE HISTORY RECORDS THE PUBLIC SERVICES / THAT HIS COUNTRY ACKNOWLEDGED / BY THE HIGHEST MILITARY HONORS.

Statue: Outside Chester Castle, Chester, Cheshire. (Photograph)

ERECTED / IN HONOUR OF / STAPLETON COTTON / VISCOUNT COMBERMERE / FIELD MARSHAL

Left flank:

FLANDERS. LINCELLES / THE DOURO. TALAVERA. TORRES VEDRAS. BUSACO. VILLA GARCIA. LLERENA. CASTREJON. / FUENTES D'ONOR. SALAMANCA. / CIUDAD RODRIGO. EL BODON. / THE PYRENEES. ORTHES. / TOULOUSE.

Right flank:

CAPE OF GOOD HOPE. MALLAVELLY. SERINGAPATAM. / WEST INDIES. BHURTPORE.

Rear flank:

BORN 1773. DIED 1865.

Obelisk: Combermere Park, Cheshire (Photograph)

IN MEMORY OF FIELD MARSHAL VISCOUNT / COMBERMERE G.C.B K:S:I K:T:S G:C:H P:C / BORN 1773 AND DIED 1865. ERECTED IN 1890 / BY THE DIRECTION OF HIS WIDOW / MARY VISCOUNTESS COMBERMERE WHO DIED 1889

2nd Lt 23rd Foot 26 Feb 1790. 1st Lt 16 Mar 1791. Capt 6th Dragoon Guards 28 Feb 1793. Major 59th Foot Mar 1794. Lt Colonel 25th Lt Dragoons 9 Mar 1794. Bt Colonel 1 Jan 1800. Lt Colonel 16th Lt Dragoons 14 Feb 1800. Major General 30 Oct 1805. Lt General 1 Jan 1812. General 27 May 1825. Field Marshal 2 Oct 1855.

Served in the Peninsula Jan – Jun 1809 (GOC Cavalry), Jun – Dec 1809 (Commanded Cavalry 2 Brigade), May 1810 – Jan 1811 and Apr – Jun 1811 (GOC Cavalry), Jun 1811 – Dec 1812 (GOC Cavalry 1st Division) and Jun 1813 – Apr 1814 (GOC Cavalry). Present at Douro, Talavera (Mentioned in Despatches), Busaco, Fuentes d'Onoro (Mentioned in Despatches), El Bodon (Mentioned in Despatches), Ciudad Rodrigo (Mentioned in Despatches), Llerena (Mentioned in Despatches), Castrejon (Mentioned in Despatches), Salamanca (severely wounded and Mentioned in Despatches), Venta del Poza (Mentioned in Despatches), Pyrenees (Mentioned in Despatches), Orthes and Toulouse. Not present at Waterloo as the Duke of York insisted on Uxbridge being in command of the cavalry against Wellington's wishes. After the battle when Uxbridge had lost his leg, Stapleton Cotton was asked to go to Paris and command the cavalry during the Army of Occupation. Wellington always knew that he could trust Cotton to carry out his orders with discretion as well as zeal. While not having the flair of Paget, Cotton was very reliable.

Also served in Flanders 1793–1794 (present at Lincelles and Le Cateau), Cape of Good Hope 1796, India 1799 (present at Malavelly and Seringapatam), West Indies 1817–1820, Ireland 1822 – 1823 and India 1824 –1826 (in command at the siege of Bhurtpore 1825–1826). Gold Cross for Talavera, Fuentes d'Onoro, Salamanca, Orthes and Toulouse. MGS medal for Busaco, Ciudad Rodrigo and Pyrenees. GCB. GCH. Grand Cross of the Tower and Sword, Grand Cross of Charles III and Grand Cross of St Fernando. Army of India medal for Bhurtpore. Colonel 20th Lt Dragoons 27 Jan 1813. Colonel 3rd Lt Dragoons 25 Jan 1821. Colonel 1st Life Guards 16 Sep 1829. On his return from India in 1830 he spent the next 30 years mainly in Parliament having been raised to the peerage in 1814 as Baron Combermere of Combermere. On Wellington's death in 1852 appointed Constable of the Tower 11 Oct 1852. Educated at Westminster. Died 21 Feb 1865.

REFERENCE: *Dictionary National Biography. Household Brigade Journal 1865, pp. 320–2. Gentleman's Magazine, Apr 1865, pp. 511–4. (Under Combermere) Annual Register, 1865, Appx, pp. 190–2. (Under Combermere). Royal Military Calendar, Vol 2, pp. 210–7. Cotton, Mary W. S. and William W. Knollys, Memoirs and correspondence of Field Marshal Viscount Combermere, 2 vols, 1866.*

COULTER, William
Ensign. 66th (Berkshire) Regiment of Foot.
Tablestone: Greyfriars Churchyard, (Division 7), Edinburgh, Scotland. (Photograph)

IN MEMORY / OF / WILLIAM COULTER ESQ. / LORD PROVOST OF EDINBURGH / .... / THE WIDOWED MOTHER IS CALLED TO INSCRIBE / THIS STONE WITH A TRIBUTE TO HER ONLY SON, / ENSIGN WILLIAM COULTER, / WHO LATELY JOINED IN RAISING IT. HAVING / CHOSEN THE MILITARY PROFESSION, AND SERVED / TWO CAMPAIGNS IN PORTUGAL, DAILY GAINING / ON THE ESTEEM OF HIS EQUALS, AND CONFIDENCE / OF HIS SUPERIORS, HE FELL ON THE 16TH MAY, 1811, / AGED 21, AT THE BATTLE OF ALBUERA, BEARING THE /

COLOURS OF THE 66TH REGIMENT AND BEQUEATH / ING TO AN AFFLICTED PARENT THE SWEET CONSO: / LATION THAT HE WAS WORTHY OF HIS COUNTRY.

Ensign 29 May 1809.
    Served in the Peninsula Nov 1809 – May 1811. Present at Busaco and Albuera where he was killed 16 May 1811 carrying the regimental colours.

COUPER, George
Captain. 92nd Regiment of Foot.
Pedestal monument: Kensal Green Cemetery, London. (15304/102/PS). (Photograph)

SACRED / TO THE MEMORY OF / COL. SIR GEORGE COUPER, / BART CB – KH. / BORN JUNE 21ST 1788. / AFTER MANY YEARS OF DISTINGUISHED / MILITARY SERVICE / HE WAS APPOINTED PRINCIPAL EQUERRY / AND COMPTROLLER OF THE HOUSEHOLD / OF H.R.H. THE DUCHESS OF KENT / IN WHICH CAPACITY HE SERVED / FOR TWENTY TWO YEARS / WHEN HE DEPARTED HIS EARTHLY CAREER / FEBRUARY 28TH 1861. / IN HIS 73RD YEAR.

Ensign 69th Foot 2 Nov 1797. Lt 40th Foot 2 Nov 1799. Lt 92nd Foot 9 Jul 1803. Capt 14 Apr 1808. Bt Major 21 Jun 1813. Major 92nd Foot 30 Dec 1819. Bt Lt Colonel 23 Jul 1821. Bt Colonel 10 Jan 1837.
    Served in the Peninsula Jan – Sep 1812 (ADC to Lt General Clinton), Oct 1812 – Oct 1813 and Feb-Apr 1814 (ADC to Lord Dalhousie). Present at Badajoz, Salamanca, Vittoria. Pyrenees (wounded) and Bayonne. CB and KH. Also served in the Baltic 1807–1808, Walcheren 1809 (ADC to Lord Dalhousie), North America 1814–1815 (AQMG) and West Indies 1821 (DQMG in Jamaica). Secretary to General Sir James Kempt when he was Master General of Ordnance Nov 1830 – 1834. Served in the Governor General's office in Canada. Retired 10 Jan 1837. On the retirement of Sir John Conroy in 1839, became Principal Equerry and Controller of the Household of the Duchess of Kent, Queen Victoria's mother. MGS medal for Badajoz, Salamanca, Vittoria and Pyrenees.
REFERENCE: *Gentleman's Magazine, May 1861, p. 584. Annual Register, 1861, Appx, p. 424.*

COURCY, Hon Gerard see DE COURCY, Hon. Gerard

COVEY, Edward
Lieutenant. Royal Engineers.
Named on the Regimental Memorial: Rochester Cathedral, Rochester, Kent. (Photograph)

2nd Lt 20 Jul 1813. Lt 15 Dec 1813. 2nd Capt 2 Dec 1830.
    Served in the Netherlands 1814 and in France with the Army of Occupation 1815–1816. Died at Titchfield 23 Jun 1831.

COWELL, John Stepney
Lieutenant and Captain. Coldstream Regiment of Foot Guards.
Headstone: Kensal Green Cemetery, London. (15935/74/4). (Photograph)

.... / SIR JOHN COWELL STEPNEY BART. / **********

Memorial: Royal Military Chapel, Wellington Barracks, London. (M.I.) (Destroyed by a Flying Bomb 1944)

"LIEUT.-COL. SIR JOHN COWELL STEPNEY, BART., K.H. / SERVED WITH THE COLDSTREAM GUARDS IN THE CAMPAIGNS OF 1810–11–12–13 IN THE PENINSULA, BEING PRESENT DURING THE RETREAT FROM BUSACO, IN THE LINES OF TORRES VEDRAS, IN THE

ADVANCE AFTER MASSENA TO SANTAREM, AND HIS SUBSEQUENT RETREAT FROM PORTUGAL; AT THE AFFAIRS OF REDINHA AND FOZ D'AROUCE, THE BATTLE OF FUENTES D'ONOR, THE SIEGE OF CIUDAD RODRIGO, THE BATTLE OF SALAMANCA, THE AFFAIR OF LLERENA, THE SIEGE OF BURGOS, WHEN HE LED A STORMING PARTY, OCTOBER 18TH, 1812, AND THE SUCCEEDING OPERATIONS; AT THE AFFAIR OF OSMA, THE BATTLE OF VITTORIA, THE AFFAIR OF TOLOSA, THE SIEGE OF SAN SEBASTIAN, THE PASSAGE OF THE BIDASSOA; AFTER WHICH HE LEFT THE ARMY FOR ENGLAND, IN COMMAND OF A DETACHMENT IN CHARGE OF THE GARRISON OF SAN SEBASTIAN AS PRISONERS OF WAR. IN 1814 HE WAS AT THE BOMBARDMENT OF THE FRENCH FLEET AT ANTWERP; IN 1815, HE SERVED DURING THE WATERLOO CAMPAIGN AND AT THE CAPTURE OF PARIS, AND FROM 1816–18 WITH THE ARMY OF OCCUPATION IN FRANCE. HE RECEIVED THE WAR MEDAL WITH FOUR CLASPS, AND THE WATERLOO MEDAL. / PLACED TO HIS MEMORY BY HIS ONLY SURVIVING SON, SIR ARTHUR COWELL STEPNEY, BART."

Ensign 18 May 1809. Lt and Capt 9 Sep 1813. Bt Major 17 Feb 1820. Capt and Lt Colonel 15 Jun 1830.
    Served in the Peninsula Oct 1810 – Aug 1813. Present at Redinha, Foz d'Arouce, Fuentes d'Onoro, Ciudad Rodrigo, Salamanca, Llerena, Burgos (led a storming party), retreat from Burgos, Osma, Vittoria, Tolosa, San Sebastian and Bidassoa. Then left for England in charge of the French Garrison from San Sebastian as prisoners of war. Also served in the Netherlands 1814 (present at Antwerp). Went to Quatre Bras in 1815 but was taken ill and sent to Brussels so he missed Waterloo. Served in France with the Army of Occupation. MGS medal for Fuentes d'Onoro, Ciudad Rodrigo, Salamanca and Vittoria. KH. Later took the additional surname of Stepney. Retired 21 Jun 1832. Appointed Deputy Lieutenant of Carmarthenshire, High Sherriff 1862 and MP for Carmarthen 1868–1874. Died 15 May 1877.
REFERENCE: Cowell, John Stepney, Leaves from the diary of an officer of the Guards, 1854, reprint 1994. Household Brigade Journal, 1877, p. 308. (Entered under Stepney).

COWELL, William
Major. 42nd (Royal Highland) Regiment of Foot.
Headstone: St Nathy's Churchyard, Dundrum, County Dublin, Ireland. (Photograph)

SACRED TO THE MEMORY OF / LIEUT.-COLN. WM. COWELL, CB. / LATE OF THE 42ND ROYAL HIGHLANDERS / WHOSE PREMATURE DEATH WAS / OCCASIONED BY SEVERE CAMPAIGNS / AND WOUNDS RECEIVED ON THE PENINSULA / DURING THE WAR / DIED 24 SEPTEMBER 18** / AGED ** YEARS.

Ensign 89th Foot 1 Apr 1797. Lt 2nd Foot 1 Jun 1801. Lt 68 Foot 1803. Capt Royal Regt of Malta 8 Dec 1804. Bt Major 16 Mar 1809. Major 42 Foot 30 May 1811. Bt Lt Colonel 3 Mar 1814.
    Served in the Peninsula Apr 1812 – Apr 1814. Present at Salamanca, Burgos, Vittoria, Pyrenees, Nivelle, Nive and Orthes (severely wounded). Gold Medal for Nivelle and Orthes. CB. Also served in Ireland 1798 (present in the Rebellion), Malta 1800 (helped to form the Royal Regiment of Malta), Egypt 1801 (present at Alexandria) and Calabria 1804.
REFERENCE: Royal Military Calendar, Vol 5, p. 21.

COWSELL, John
Lieutenant. 71st (Highland Light Infantry) Regiment of Foot.
Memorial tablet: All Saints Church, Fornham All Saints, Suffolk. (South wall of West addition). (Photograph)

TO THE MEMORY OF / LIEUT JOHN COWSELL / OF HIS MAJESTY'S 71 REG. / WHO FELL ON THE 3. OF MAY 1811 / IN THE 28. YEAR OF HIS AGE WHILE GALLANTLY / LEADING ON HIS COMPANY / TO CHARGE THE ENEMY THROUGH THE VILLAGE / OF EL FUENTES D'HONOR

IN PORTUGAL. / HIS DEATH THO' GLORIOUS WAS GREATLY / REGRETTED BY HIS BROTHER OFFICERS, WHO / HAD THE HIGHEST ESTEEM FOR HIS BRAVERY / AS AN OFFICER, AND A WARM REGARD FOR / HIM AS A FRIEND. / HIS LOSS IS DESERVEDLY LAMENTED / BY HIS FAMILY / WHO HAVE PLACED THIS TABLET TO HIS MEMORY

Lt 25 Aug 1806.
 Served in the Peninsula Aug 1808 – Jan 1809 and Sep 1810 – May 1811. Present at Rolica, Vimeiro, Corunna, Sobral, Fuentes d'Onoro where he was killed 3 May 1811. Also present at Walcheren 1809.

COX, John
1st Lieutenant. 95th Regiment of Foot.
Tomb: St Mary's Cemetery, Cheltenham, Gloucestershire. (M.I.)

"TO THE BELOVED AND CHERISHED MEMORY OF MAJOR-GENERAL COX, K.H., COLONEL OF THE 88TH REGIMENT, WHO DIED IN CHELTENHAM, FEBRUARY 7TH, 1863, DEEPLY REGRETTED; A BRAVE AND DISTINGUISHED PENINSULAR AND WATERLOO SOLDIER, HAVING RECEIVED THE WAR MEDAL WITH TEN CLASPS; AND A SINCERE AND HUMBLE CHRISTIAN."

2nd Lt 16 Mar 1808. Lt 8 Jun 1809. Capt 23 Dec 1819. Major 19 Aug 1828. Lt Colonel 17 Feb 1837. Bt Colonel 11 Nov 1851. Major General 18 Dec 1855.
 Served in the Peninsula with 2/95th Aug 1808 – Jan1809 and 1/95th Jun 1809 – Apr 1814. Present at Obidos, Rolica, Vimeiro (wounded), Vigo, Coa, Barba del Puerco, Busaco, Pombal, Redinha (wounded), Casal Nova, Foz d'Arouce, Sabugal, Fuentes d'Onoro, Ciudad Rodrigo (wounded), San Millan, Vittoria, Pyrenees, Vera, Bidassoa, Nivelle, Nive, Orthes and Tarbes (severely wounded). Present at Quatre Bras, Waterloo, the capture of Paris and with the Army of Occupation until 1818. KH. MGS medal for Rolica, Vimeiro, Busaco, Fuentes d'Onoro, Ciudad Rodrigo, Vittoria, Pyrenees, Nivelle, Nive and Orthes. Colonel 88th Foot 18 Oct 1855.
REFERENCE: *Gentleman's Magazine, Apr 1863, pp. 527–8. Obit. Cheltenham Looker-On, 14 Feb 1863 and 19 Sep 1863 and Cheltenham Journal and Gloucestershire Gazette, Oct 1863.*

COX, Philip Zachariah
Captain. 23rd Regiment of Light Dragoons.
Memorial tablet: St Laurence Churchyard, Upminster, Essex. (Photograph)

TO THE MEMORY OF / PHILIP ZACHARIAH COX / OF HARWOOD HALL IN THIS PARISH ESQR. / WHO DIED ON THE 21ST MAY 1858 AGED 79. / CAPTAIN IN THE 23RD LIGHT DRAGOONS. / HE SERVED AT TALAVERA AND AT WATERLOO. / A JUST AND UPRIGHT MAN, KIND AND / GENEROUS, A ZEALOUS & TRUE / FRIEND, HE LIVED BELOVED & DIED / REGRETTED BY ALL.

Cornet 3rd Dragoon Guards 4 Sep 1804. Lt 23rd Lt Dragoons 17 Jan 1806. Capt 15 Mar 1810.
 Served in the Peninsula Jun 1809 – Dec 1809. Present at Talavera. MGS medal for Talavera. Present at Waterloo. Half pay 1817.

COX, Samuel Fortnam
Cornet. 1st Life Guards.
Box tomb: St Martin's Churchyard, Sandford St Martin, Oxfordshire. (Photograph)

SACRED / TO THE MEMORY OF / CAPT. SAMUEL FORTNAM COX, LIFE GUARDS / OF SAND-FORD PARK, / DEPARTED THIS LIFE THE 22ND OF NOVEMBER 1849 / IN THE 55TH YEAR OF HIS AGE. / WATERLOO

Cornet 1 Jun 1814. Lt 14 Dec 1815. Capt 21 Aug 1821.

Present at Waterloo where he was wounded. Retired on half pay 7 Aug 1829.

COX, William

Major. 61st (South Gloucestershire) Regiment of Foot.
Memorial tablet: Monkstown Church of Ireland, Monkstown, County Dublin, Ireland. (Photograph)

TO THE MEMORY OF A BELOVED HUSBAND / COLONEL SIR WILLIAM COX / LATE OF COOL-CLIFFE, Co. WEXFORD / WHO DIED 1st JULY 1864 / AGED 87 YEARS. / (VERSE)

Ledger stone: St Munna's Church of Ireland, Taghmon, County Wexford, Ireland. (Memorial inscription indicates that this was previously a box tomb, but top has apparently been removed and laid flat in the ground). (Photograph)

IN MEMORY OF / JOHN COX JNR ESQR OF COOLCLIFFE / .... / THEIR SON COLL SIR W. / COX BORN 1776. DIED 1st JULY 1864 WAS BURIED / AT MONKSTOWN, CO DUBLIN.

Ensign 68th Foot 1 Oct 1794. Lt 3 Sep 1795. Capt-Lieut and Capt 3 Aug 1800. Capt 16 Feb 1802. Capt 61st Foot 1803. Major 19 Jun 1806. Bt Lt Colonel 16 Feb 1809. Bt Colonel 12 Aug 1819. Portuguese Army: Colonel 24th Line 14 Jun 1809. Major General 12 Oct 1815.

Served in the Peninsula Sep 1808 – Jan 1809 and with Portuguese Army Apr 1809 – Apr 1814 (Governor of the Fort of Almeida). Present at Lugo, Corunna and Almeida. The magazine at Almeida exploded in an unfortunate accident while the fort was being besieged by the French on 27 Aug 1810. Cox was forced to surrender the garrison and was held in France as a prisoner until Apr 1814. After the war he was court-martialled, but only as a formality and was honourably acquitted. Awarded KTS and promoted Major General in the Portuguese Army.

Also served in Grenada 1795, Egypt 1801 (AQMG), Gibraltar and Spain 1807 (on intelligence service). MGS medal for Corunna.
REFERENCE: *Royal Military Calendar. Vol 4, pp. 248–9.*

COX, Wilson

Sergeant. 12th (Prince of Wales's) Regiment of Light Dragoons.
Named on the Regimental Memorial: St Joseph's Church, Waterloo, Belgium. (Photograph)

Killed at Waterloo.

COXEN, Edward

1st Lieutenant. 95th Regiment of Foot
Headstone and Low monument: St John's Churchyard, Meerut Cantonment, Meerut, India. (Photograph)

SACRED / TO THE MEMORY OF / CAPTAIN EDWARD COXEN / FOR 31 YEARS PAYMASTER / TO THE 1st BATTALION 60TH ROYAL RIFLES / WHO DIED AT MEERUT / ON THE 14TH OF FEBRUARY 1857 / AGED 77 YEARS. / HE SERVED AT FLUSHING, / THROUGHOUT THE PENIN-SULA WAR, / AT WATERLOO, / AND IN THE PUNJAB CAMPAIGN OF 1848 AND 1849 / AND RECEIVED THREE MEDALS AND TWELVE CLASPS. / ERECTED BY THE OFFICERS OF THE 1st BATTN 60TH ROYAL RIFLES.

2nd Lt 5 Apr 1809. Lt 28 Jun 1810. Capt 8 Apr 1825. Paymaster 60th Rifles 9 Feb 1826.

Served in the Peninsula with 2/95th Jul 1810 – Apr 1814. (from July 1813 attached to the Commissariat Department). Present at Cadiz, Pombal, Redinha, Casal Nova, Foz d' Arouce, Almeida, Sabugal, Fuentes d'Onoro, Ciudad Rodrigo, Badajoz, Salamanca, San Millan, Vittoria, Pyrenees, Vera, Bidassoa, Nivelle, Nive, Orthes, Tarbes and Toulouse. Present at Waterloo with 2/95th (severely wounded). Also served at

Walcheren 1809 (present at Flushing). Joined 60th Rifles 9 Feb 1826 and was Paymaster for 31 years. Went to India and served in the Sikh Wars of 1848–1849 for which he was awarded a medal. MGS medal for Fuentes d'Onoro, Ciudad Rodrigo, Badajoz, Salamanca, Vittoria, Pyrenees, Nivelle, Nive, Orthes and Toulouse. Died at Meerut 14 Feb 1857.

COZENS, Benjamin Howard
Private. 10th (Prince of Wales's Own) Regiment of Light Dragoons.
Headstone: St Dunstan's Churchyard, Cranford, Middlesex, London. (M.I.)

"SACRED TO THE MEMORY OF / BENJAMIN HOWARD COZENS / OF KENSINGTON WHO DIED DECEMBER 29TH 1868 / AGED 72. / AN AFFECTIONATE HUSBAND / KIND FATHER AND SINCERE FRIEND. / HE SERVED IN THE 10TH PRINCE OF WALES'S OWN ROYAL REGIMENT / HUSSARS AT THE BATTLE OF WATERLOO / WHERE HE WAS WOUNDED ON THE EVE OF THE 18TH."

Served at Waterloo in Capt Grey's Troop No 4 where he was wounded in one of the last actions of the day.

CRADOCK, Sir John Francis (Lord Howden) (Later Caradoc)
Colonel. 43rd (Monmouthshire) Light Infantry Regiment of Foot.
Interred in Catacomb B (v87 c7) Kensal Green Cemetery, London.

Cornet 7th Dragoon Guards 1777. Ensign Coldstream Guards 9 Jul 1779. Lt and Capt 12 Dec 1781. Major 12th Dragoons 25 Jun 1785. Major 13th Foot 1786. Lt Colonel Jun 1789. Colonel 127th Foot 1795. Major General 1 Jan 1798. Lt General 1 Jan 1805. Colonel 43rd Foot 7 Jun 1809.
    Served in the Peninsula Dec 1808 – Jul 1809 (in command of troops left behind in Portugal by Sir John Moore, mainly 10,000 sick and injured. Ordered to defend Lisbon against Soult but Wellington arrived in Portugal to supersede him). Appointed Governor of Gibraltar, but resigned and returned to England. Governor of Cape of Good Hope 1811–1814. Also served in Martinique 1793 (wounded), Irish Rebellion 1798 (QMG, present at Vinegar Hill and Ballynahinch where he was wounded), Egypt 1801 (present at Cairo and Alexandria), India 1803–1807 (present at Vellore mutiny). GCB. Colonel 54th Foot 1801. Colonel 71st Foot 1802. Created Baron Howden 1819. Changed his surname to Caradoc 1820. Died 26 Jul 1839.
    REFERENCE: *Dictionary of National Biography. Royal Military Calendar, Vol 2, p.12–4. Gentleman's Magazine, Sep 1839, pp. 310–2. United Service Journal, Sep 1839, pp. 94–8. Annual Register, 1839, Appx, p. 356.*

CRAIG, Phillip
Sergeant. 43rd (Monmouthshire) Light Infantry Regiment of Foot.
Headstone: St Issell's Churchyard, Saundersfoot, Pembrokeshire, Wales. (Against east wall of church). (Photograph)

IN / MEMORY OF / PHILLIP CRAIG. IN / THIS PARISH. WHO DEPARTED / THIS LIFE. JUNE 28TH 1854. / AGED 77 YEARS. / .... / (VERSE)

Pembrokeshire Militia. Pte 43rd Foot Jan 1808. Cpl 25 Mar 1811. Sgt 25 Jun 1813.
    Served in the Peninsula Aug 1808 – Jan 1809 and Jul 1810 – Apr 1814. Present at Vimeiro (wounded), Corunna, Busaco, Fuentes d'Onoro, Ciudad Rodrigo (in the Forlorn Hope), Badajoz (wounded in the Forlorn Hope), Salamanca, Vittoria, Pyrenees, Nivelle and Nive (wounded). Also served at Walcheren 1809.
    Returned to Pembrokeshire after his discharge 26 Oct 1814 and worked as a labourer. Later became

the local postman. MGS medal for Vimeiro, Corunna, Busaco, Fuentes d'Onoro, Ciudad Rodrigo, Badajoz, Salamanca, Vittoria, Pyrenees, San Sebastian, Nivelle and Nive.
REFERENCE: *Jackson, Janice, My ancestor – the forgotten hero, Pembrokeshire Life, Jan 2010, pp. 24–6.*

CRAMPTON, James
Private. 11th Regiment of Light Dragoons.
Headstone: Holy Trinity Churchyard, Barnard Castle, County Durham. (Photograph)

IN MEMORY OF / SARAH CRAMPTON, WIDOW OF / JAMES CRAMPTON / WHO DIED DEC^R 30TH 1850, / AGED 85 YEARS. / .... / ALSO JAMES, THEIR SON, / SG^T 11TH LIGHT DRAGOONS / WHO DIED AT CAWANPOORE EAST INDIA / SEPT 9TH 1831, AGED 36 YEARS. / ....

Served at Waterloo in Capt James Duberly's Troop and with the Army of Occupation. Also served in India 1819 (present at the siege of Bhurtpore). Died at Cawnpore 9 Sep 1831 aged 36.

CRANSTON, Thomas
Private. 1st Regiment of Foot Guards.
Ledger stone: Public Park between Aberystwyth Castle and St Michael's Church, Aberystwyth, Wales. (Photograph)

SACRED / TO THE MEMORY OF / THOMAS CRANSTON, / SERJEANT IN THE 1ST FOOT GUARDS, / AND AFTERWARDS SERJEANT-MAJOR / IN THE CARDIGANSHIRE MILITIA, / WHO AFTER 41 YEARS SERVITUDE / IN THE ARMY, / DIED ON THE 6TH NOVEMBER, / 1848, / AGED 74 YEARS.

Served in the Peninsula Oct 1808 – Jan 1809. MGS medal for Corunna.

CRAUFURD, Alexander Charles Gregon
Volunteer Captain. 12th (Prince of Wales's) Regiment of Light Dragoons.
Memorial tablet: St George and St Mary Church, Church Gresley, Derbyshire. (Photograph)

TO THE MEMORY OF COLONEL ALEXANDER CHARLES GREGON CRAUFURD, ELDEST SON OF SIR / JAMES CRAUFURD, BART. OF KILBIRNIE N. B. HE SERVED IN THE PENINSULAR WAR AND AT / WATERLOO, AND DIED AT DRAKELOW MARCH 12 1838 IN THE 42ND YEAR OF HIS AGE. / TO THE MEMORY OF LADY BARBARA CRAUFURD, WIFE OF COLONEL CRAUFURD / SHE DIED IN LONDON / SEPTEMBER 4TH 1838; / IN THE 37TH YEAR / OF HER AGE. / THEY WERE BOTH INTERRED IN THE GRESLEY VAULT IN THIS CHURCH.

Family Memorial tablet: Church of Reconciliation, Hengrave, St Edmundsbury, Suffolk. (M.I.)

" .... / THE ABOVE MENTIONED ALEXANDER CHARLES SECOND SON OF SIR JAMES CRAUFURD DIED MARCH 12TH 1838 AGED 43 YEARS; HIS WIFE LADY BARBARA, IN THE FOLLOWING SEPTEMBER, BOTH WERE BURIED IN THE SAME VAULT IN THE CHURCH AT DRAKELOW PARK, NEAR BURTON UPON TRENT."

Ensign 3rd Foot Guards 30 May 1811. Lt 10th Lt Dragoons 9 Dec 1813. Capt 2nd Ceylon Regt 9 Jun 1814. Volunteer Capt 12th Lt Dragoons May 1815. Capt 12th Lancers 26 Oct 1820. Bt Major 30 Aug 1821. Lt Colonel (unattached) 10 Jun 1826
  Served in the Peninsula with 10th Lt Dragoons Feb – Apr 1814. Present at Toulouse. Present at Waterloo with 12th Lt Dragoons as a volunteer from 2nd Ceylon Regiment. After the battle he was searching for his

commanding officer, Lt Col F. C. Ponsonby when he discovered the body of his brother Thomas in the orchard at Hougoumont. Brother of Lt and Capt Thomas Craufurd 3rd Foot Guards.

CRAUFURD, George Douglas
Lieutenant. 91st Regiment of Foot.
Buried at Sorauren, Spain.

Ensign 27 Dec 1806. Lt. 18 May 1808. Portuguese Army: Capt 23rd Line 18 Sep 1811.
    Served in the Peninsula with 91st Foot Aug 1808 – Jan 1809 and Portuguese Army Sep 1811 – Aug 1813. Present at Rolica, Vimeiro, Corunna, Ciudad Rodrigo, Badajoz, Castrejon, Salamanca (wounded), Vittoria and Pyrenees where he was killed at Sorauren 28 Jul 1813 aged 22 years. 'The affectionate gratitude of his men induced them to erect a little stone to mark the spot where the remains of this revered commander were deposited'
REFERENCE: *Gentleman's Magazine, Dec 1813, p. 621.*

CRAUFURD, Robert
Lieutenant Colonel 60th (Royal American) Regiment of Foot.
Memorial: St Paul's Cathedral, London. (North transept). (Photograph)

ERECTED BY THE NATION / TO MAJOR-GENERAL ROBERT CRAUFORD, / AND MAJOR GENERAL HENRY MACKINNON, / WHO FELL AT CIUDAD RODRIGO JANRY 19TH 1812.

Memorial plaque: Walls of Ciudad Rodrigo, Spain. (Above breach where he is buried). (Photograph)

MAJOR GENERAL ROBERT CRAUFURD / TO THE MEMORY OF MAJOR GENERAL ROBERT CRAUFORD AND THOSE OF THE 43RD AND 52ND LIGHT INFANTRY AND THE 95TH RIFLES OF THE LIGHT DIVISION, WHICH HE COMMANDED WITH SUCH DISTINCTION, AND THEIR COMRADES OF THE 60TH, ALL OF WHOM FELL IN THE STORMING OF THE BREACHES THROUGH WHICH CIUDAD RODRIGO WAS LIBERATED ON 19TH JANUARY 1812. / THIS PLAQUE IS ERECTED BY THEIR HEIRS THE ROYAL GREEN JACKETS MINDFUL OF THE HISTORIC EFFORTS OF THE SPANISH AND BRITISH TO FREE THE PENINSULA 1808 – 1813.

Memorial window: Sir John Moore Library, Shorncliffe, Kent. (Photograph)

ROBERT CRAUFURD

Ensign 65th Foot 6 May 1780. Ensign 26th Foot 6 May 1780. (Transferred in the same Gazette). Lt 98th Foot 24 Feb 1781. Lt 26th Foot 17 Mar 1781. Capt 92nd Foot 11 Dec 1782. Capt and Capt Lt 45th Foot 19 Mar 1783. Capt 33rd Foot 6 Oct 1787. Capt 75th Foot 1 Nov 1787. Lt Colonel Hompesch's Regiment 1795. Lt Colonel 60th Foot 23 Jan 1798. Bt Colonel 30 Oct 1805. Major General 4 Jun 1811.
    Served in the Peninsula Oct 1808 – Jan 1809 (Commanded Lt Brigade in Corunna campaign), Jul 1809 – Feb 1810 (Commanded 1 Brigade 3rd Division and GOC 3rd Division), Feb 1810 – Jan 1811 and Apr 1811 – Jan 1812 (GOC Lt Division) Present on retreat to Corunna in command of the rear guard, (Castro Gonzalo 28 Dec 1808), Vigo, Sexmiro (Mentioned in Despatches), Coa (Mentioned in Despatches), Busaco (Mentioned in Despatches), Fuentes d'Onoro (Mentioned in Despatches), Gallegos (Mentioned in Despatches 6 Jun 1811), Ciudad Rodrigo (severely wounded 19 Jan 1812, died of his wounds on 24 Jan and Mentioned in Despatches. Buried in the breach). Gold Medal for Busaco and Ciudad Rodrigo.
    Also served in India 1790–1792 (War against Tippoo Sultan), Austrian HQ 1793–1797, Ireland 1798 (DQMG during the Rebellion). Employed on a military mission to the Austrian armies in Switzerland 1799, the Helder 1799 and South America 1807 (present at Buenos Ayres where he took command of a light brigade).

He was able to form the light companies of various regiments with a battalion of the 95th Foot into a formidable fighting force known as the Light Brigade. By the time he returned to the Peninsula in 1809 he had the 43rd, 52nd and 95th Foot under his command. By Feb 1810 this became the Light Division which Wellington was able to use to great effect in the following years. Craufurd made enemies amongst those who thought him too severe with his men, but his men learned that this was Craufurd's way of looking after their welfare. Wellington writing to the Prime Minister in January 1812 reported that 'I cannot report his death to your Lordship without expressing my sorrow and regret, that His Majesty has been deprived of the services, and I of the assistance of an Officer of tried talents and experience, who was an ornament to his profession, and was calculated to render the most important services to his country.' MP for East Retford 1802–1806. Educated at Harrow.

REFERENCE: *Dictionary of National Biography. Gentleman's Magazine, Feb 1812, p. 191. Craufurd, A. H., General Craufurd and his light division, 1891, reprint 2004. Cole, John William, Memoirs of British Generals, Vol 1, 1856, pp. 219–66.*

CRAUFURD, Thomas Gage
Lieutenant and Captain. 3rd Regiment of Foot Guards.
Memorial tablet: On garden wall at Hougoumont. (Photograph)

IN MEMORY OF / CAPTAIN THOMAS CRAUFURD / OF THE 3RD GUARDS / ELDEST SON OF THE BARONET OF KILBIRNIE, / KILLED IN THE EXTREME SOUTH WEST ANGLE OF THIS WALL. / THIS STONE WAS PLACE BY HIS KINSMAN / SIR WILLIAM FRASER / OF MORAR / 1889

Memorial tablet: Regimental Memorial, St Joseph's Church, Waterloo, Belgium. (Photograph)

Named on Memorial Panel VIII for Quatre Bras: Royal Military Chapel, Wellington Barracks, London. (M.I.) (Destroyed by a Flying Bomb 1944)

Family Memorial tablet: Church of Reconciliation, Hengrave, St Edmundsbury, Suffolk. (M.I.)

"IN REMEMBRANCE OF / THOMAS GAGE CRAUFURD / LIEUTENANT 3RD GUARDS / ELDEST SON OF SIR JAMES CRAUFURD BART AND / MARIA THERESA, DAUGHTER OF THE HONBLE GENERAL / THOMAS GAGE, HIS WIFE. BORN FEBRUARY 23RD 1793. / HE FELL WHILE CHEERING ON HIS MEN IN THE ORCHARD / OF HOUGOUMONT DURING THE BATTLE OF WATERLOO, / THERE HE WAS FOUND BY HIS BROTHER LT A CRAUFURD / WHILE SEARCHING FOR HIS OWN COMMANDING OFFICER / (WHOSE LIFE HE HEREBY SAVED) AND THE BODY WAS / AT HIS FATHER'S REQUEST REMOVED TO ENGLAND) / UNDER THE KIND SYMPATHETIC CARE OF JOHN GAGE / ROOKWOOD ESQ. WHO WITH THE GENEROUS PERMISSION / OF SIR THOMAS GAGE DEPOSITED IT NEAR THIS SPOT."

Ensign 28 May 1811. Lt and Capt 1 Sep 1814.
Served in the Peninsula with 2nd battalion Dec 1812 – Apr 1814. Present at Nive, Adour and Bayonne. Present at Waterloo where he was killed at Hougoumont. Found on the battlefield by his brother Alexander of the 12th Lt Dragoons who was looking for his commanding officer, Lt Colonel F. C. Ponsonby. Thomas's body was returned to Suffolk. Brother of Capt Alexander Craufurd 12th Lt Dragoons. Educated at Eton.

CRAWFORD, Adam Fife
2nd Captain. Royal Artillery.
Buried in St Saviour's Churchyard, St Helier, Jersey, Channel Islands. (Burial register)

2nd Lt 17 Aug 1803. 1st Lt 12 Sep 1803. 2nd Capt 3 Aug 1810. Capt 29 Jul 1825. Bt Major 22 Jul 1830. Lt Colonel 10 Jan 1837. Colonel 20 Jul 1847. Major General 28 Nov 1854.

Served in the Peninsula Sep 1808 – Dec 1810. Present at Lisbon and Sobral. Also served in Bomb vessels off the coast of France 1805, Sicily 1811–1813, Genoa 1814 and North America 1814–1815 (present at Washington, New Orleans and Bladensburg). Retired on full pay 13 Dec 1854. Died at Jersey 10 Sep 1864. REFERENCE: *Gentleman's Magazine, Oct 1864, p. 534.*

CRAWFORD, William

Sergeant Major. 2nd (Royal North British) Regiment of Dragoons.
Memorial tablet: St Lawrence's Church, Warkworth, Northumberland. (Photograph)

TO THE GLORY OF GOD / AND IN MEMORY OF / CAPTAIN WILLIAM CRAWFORD, / LATE OF THE SECOND DRAGOONS OR / ROYAL SCOTS GREYS / WHO SERVED WITH HIS REGIMENT IN THE / CAMPAIGN AND BATTLE OF WATERLOO. / THIS TABLET IS ERECTED BY HIS NEPHEW. / HE DIED OCT 8 1865 AGED 81.

Promoted from the ranks. Cornet and Adjutant 17 Aug 1815. Lt and Adjutant 25 Jun 1819. Paymaster 24 Mar 1829.
    Present at Waterloo with the Scots Greys and was given a commission after the battle. Resigned the Adjutancy 25 Nov 1828 and in 1829 was appointed Paymaster. Half pay 1849.

CRAWFURD, Henry

Major. 9th (East Norfolk) Regiment of Foot.
Memorial tablet: Wellpark Mid Kirk, Greenock, Renfrewshire, Scotland. (Photograph)

ROLEIA / VIMEIRA / BUZACO / BADAJOZ / SALAMANCA / VITTORIA / TO THE MEMORY OF / LIEUTENANT-COLONEL HENRY CRAWFURD, / OF HIS MAJESTY'S XLV REGIMENT OF FOOT, / A NATIVE OF GREENOCK, WHO FELL GLORIOUSLY AUGᴛ 31sᴛ 1813 / IN THE BREACH, AT THE STORMING OF Sᴛ SEBASTIAN, / WHILE LEADING ON A DIVISION OF HIS MAJESTY'S IX REGᴛ OF FOOT / THIS MONUMENT IS ERECTED / BY HIS SCHOOL-FELLOWS, AND EARLY FRIENDS.

Capt 9th Foot 1 Sep 1794. Major 21 Nov 1801. Bt Lt Colonel 25 Apr 1808.
    Served in the Peninsula with 1/9th Aug 1808 – Jan 1809 and Mar 1810 – Aug 1813. Present at Rolica, Vimeiro, Corunna, Busaco, Fuentes d'Onoro, Castrejon, Salamanca, Villa Muriel, Osma, Vittoria and San Sebastian where he was killed in the final assault 31 Aug 1813. Gold Medal for Rolica, Vimeiro, Busaco and San Sebastian. Also served at Walcheren 1809.
Note: Regiment is incorrectly recorded on memorial tablet.

CREIGHTON, Thomas

Sergeant. 71st (Highland Light Infantry) Regiment of Foot.
Ledger stone: Malew Churchyard, Malew, Isle of Man. (Photograph)

SACRED / TO THE MEMORY OF / QUARTER MASTER / THOMAS CREIGHTON, / LATE OF THE 71sᴛ REGIMENT / OF HIGHLAND LIGHT INFANTRY. / A NATIVE OF ST ANDREWS FIFESHIRE / SCOTLAND. / HE DIED AT CASTLETOWN ON THE 30ᴛʜ / OF JULY 1853, AGED 67 YEARS. / HE WAS A HIGHLY DISTINGUISHED OFFICER / AND WAS PRESENT / IN THE FOLLOWING ENGAGEMENTS / ROLICA, VIMIERO, CORUNNA, / FUENTES D'ONORO, VITTORIA, PYRE-NEES, / ORTHES AND TOULOUSE. / AND ALSO AT WATERLOO.

Quartermaster 19 Sep 1827.
    Served in the Peninsula Aug 1808 – Jan 1809 and Sep 1810 – Apr 1814. Present at Rolica, Vimeiro, Corunna, Sobral, Fuentes d'Onoro, Arroyo dos Molinos, Almarez, Alba de Tormes, Vittoria, Pyrenees,

Orthes, Tarbes and Toulouse. Present at Waterloo in Capt Samuel Reed's Company. MGS medal for Rolica, Vimeiro, Corunna, Fuentes d'Onoro, Vittoria, Pyrenees, Orthes and Toulouse. Half pay 24 Jan 1840.

CRESPIGNY, George Champion
Major. 68th (Durham) Regiment of Foot.
Altar tomb: St Mary's Churchyard, Harefield, Middlesex, London. (Photograph)

.... / ALSO IN MEMORY OF HIS BROTHER, / GEORGE CHAMPION CRESPIGNY / A MAJOR OF THE 68TH LIGHT INFANTRY, / WHO FELL AT THE HEAD OF HIS REGIMENT / IN AN ENGAGEMENT WITH A BATTALION OF THE FRENCH ARMY / UNDER MARSHAL SOULT, IN THE PYRENEES / ON 30 JULY 1813, IN THE 26TH YEAR OF HIS LIFE / QUIS DESIDERIS SIT PUDOR AUT MODUS TUM CARI CAPITIS.

Ensign 13th Foot 13 May 1804. Lt 24 Nov 1804. Capt 1st Foot 14 May 1807. Captain 68th Foot 17 Nov 1808. Major 8 Oct 1812.
    Served in the Peninsula Jun 1811 – Jan 1812 and Dec 1812 – Jul 1813. Present at Vittoria and Pyrenees where he was killed 30 Jul 1813. Also served at Walcheren 1809 (present at Flushing where he was wounded).

CREWE, John Frederick
Captain. 27th (Inniskilling) Regiment of Foot.
Interred in Catacomb B (v98 c8) Kensal Green Cemetery, London.

Ensign 27 Jun 1805. Lt 13 Feb 1806. Capt 7 Jul 1814. Lt Colonel (unattached) 5 Jun 1817.
    Served in the Peninsula with 1/27th Nov 1812 – Apr 1814. Present at Castalla, Tarragona and Barcelona. Half pay 5 Jun 1827.

CRICHTON, Nathaniel Day
Lieutenant. 16th (Queen's) Regiment of Light Dragoons.
Memorial tablet: St Mary's Church, Hendon, London. (Photograph)

NEAR THIS SPOT ARE / DEPOSITED THE MORTAL REMAINS OF / NATHANIEL DAY CRICHTON, / MAJOR IN HIS MAJESTY'S FIFTH REGIMENT OF / DRAGOON GUARDS. / BORN ON THE EIGHTH OF NOVEMBER MDCCXCIV, / DIED ON THE SIXTH OF NOVEMBER MDCC-CXXXIII. / EARLY IN LIFE HE / DEVOTED HIMSELF TO THE SERVICE OF HIS COUNTRY / AND WAS DISTINGUISHED IN THE GLORIOUS EVENTS / OF THE PENINSULA, AND FINALLY AT / WATERLOO: / AS A SOLDIER ALL MIGHT ADMIRE, / THOUGH FEW COULD HOPE TO EQUAL HIM: / AS A FRIEND, THOSE WHO KNEW HIM BEST WILL SHED / AN HONEST TEAR AT THE REMEMBRANCE OF HIS WORTH / AND OWN THAT HE WAS BELOVED. / HIS BROTHER OFFI-CERS, / DEEPLY BEWAILING THEIR IRREPARABLE LOSS / FEEL GRATEFUL, IN BEING PERMITTED / THE MELANCHOLY CONSOLATION / OF RAISING THIS FOND TRIBUTE / TO HIS MEMORY.

Cornet 29 May 1811. Lt 20 Feb 1812. Capt 5th Dragoon Guards 5 Jul 1821. Major 6 Apr 1826.
    Served in the Peninsula Jun 1812 – May 1813. Present at Salamanca and Venta del Pozo. Present at Waterloo where he was wounded.

CROALL, James

Sergeant. 24th (Warwickshire) Regiment of Foot.
Family Headstone: Friockheim Cemetery, Friockheim, Angus, Scotland. (Inscription on reverse of family headstone). (Photograph)

HIS FATHER IN LAW / JAMES CROALL / DIED 4TH JUNE 1857 / AGED 71 YEARS

Pte 6th Garrison Battalion 25 Dec 1806. Pte 24th Foot 30 Jun 1809.
    Served in the Peninsula 1809 – Dec 1812. Present at Busaco, Fuentes d'Onoro. Ciudad Rodrigo, Salamanca and siege of Burgos (severely wounded and right arm amputated 4 Oct 1812). Discharged to a Chelsea out pension 30 Apr 1813 – 'an excellent soldier'. Returned to Scotland and became a merchant. MGS medal for Busaco, Fuentes d'Onoro, Ciudad Rodrigo and Salamanca.

CROFT, Sir Thomas Elmsley

Ensign. 1st Regiment of Foot Guards.
Memorial: Royal Military Chapel, Wellington Barracks, London. (M.I.) (Destroyed by a Flying Bomb 1944)

"IN MEMORY OF / SIR THOMAS ELMSLEY CROFT, BART. / ENSIGN AND LIEUTENANT 2ND / BATTALION GRENADIER GUARDS. / WOUNDED SEVERELY AT QUATRE BRAS, JUNE 16TH, 1815. / BORN SEPTEMBER 2ND, 1798; DIED OCTOBER 29TH, 1835."

Ensign 28 Apr 1814.
    Present at Quatre Bras where he was severely wounded. Succeeded as 2nd Baronet 1818. Retired on half pay 2 Mar 1820. Educated at Westminster.

CROFTON, Hon. William George

Lieutenant and Captain. Coldstream Regiment of Foot Guards.
Ledger stone: Coldstream Guards Cemetery, St Etienne, Bayonne France. (Photograph)

W.G.C.

Named on the Memorial: St Andrew's Church, (now Musée Historique), Biarritz, France. (Photograph)
Memorial: Royal Military Chapel, Wellington Barracks, London. (M.I.) (Destroyed by a Flying Bomb 1944)

"IN MEMORY OF / LIEUTENANT AND CAPTAIN THE HON. WILLIAM CROFTON. / COLD-STREAM GUARDS, 1803–14. HE SERVED AT COPENHAGEN AND WALCHEREN. HE COMMANDED THE / GRENADIER COMPANY, 1ST BATTALION, IN THE PENINSULAR WAR DURING THE CAMPAIGNS / 1811-12-13-14, AND WAS WOUNDED AT BURGOS. OVERPOW-ERED ON PICQUET BY THE FRENCH SORTIE / FROM BAYONNE, HE REFUSED TO SURRENDER, AND DIED AT HIS POST 14TH APRIL, 1814. / PLACED BY HIS GREAT-NEPHEWS, EDWARD HENRY CHURCHILL, THIRD LORD CROFTON, AND / LIEUT.-COLONEL. J. A. CAULFIELD, COLDSTREAM GUARDS, 1880."

Also named on Memorial Panel VII for the Sortie from Bayonne: Royal Military Chapel, Wellington Barracks, London. (M.I.) (Destroyed by a Flying Bomb 1944)

Ensign 7 Dec 1803. Lt and Capt 10 Mar 1808.
    Served in the Peninsula Dec 1810 – Apr 1814. Present at Fuentes d'Onoro, Salamanca, Burgos (wounded), Vittoria, Bidassoa, Nivelle, Nive, Adour and Bayonne, where he was killed at the Sortie from Bayonne 14 Apr 1814. Also served at Copenhagen 1807 and Walcheren 1809. Educated at Eton.

CROKAT, William
Captain. 20th (East Devonshire) Regiment of Foot.
Low monument: Warriston Cemetery, Edinburgh, Scotland. (Section C2 Grave number 233). (Photograph)

IN MEMORY OF GENERAL WILLIAM CROKAT. BORN 25 JULY 1789. DIED 6 NOVEMBER 1879

Ensign 9 Apr 1807. Lt 30 Jun 1808. Capt 31 Mar 1814. Major 5 Jul 1821. Bt Lt Colonel 10 Jan 1837. Bt Colonel 11 Nov 1851. Major General 31 Aug 1855. Lt General 21 Dec 1862. General 25 Oct 1871.
   Served in the Peninsula Aug 1808 – Jan 1809 and Nov 1812 – Sep 1813. Present at Vimeiro, Corunna, Vittoria and Pyrenees (wounded at Roncesvalles 25 Jul 1813). Also served in Sicily 1807, Walcheren 1809, St Helena 1820–1821 (in charge of St Helena when Napoleon died and brought home the despatches of his death) and India 1822–1838. MGS medal for Vimeiro, Corunna, Vittoria and Pyrenees.

CROMIE, James
Ensign. 36th (Herefordshire) Regiment of Foot.
Named on the Memorial: St Andrew's Church, (now Musée Historique), Biarritz, France. (Photograph)

Ensign 3 Sep1812.
   Served in the Peninsula May 1813 – Apr 1814. Present at Pyrenees, Bidassoa, Nive, Orthes, Vic Bigorre, Tarbes, and Toulouse where he was killed Apr 1814.

CROMIE, Michael Thomas
1st Lieutenant. Royal Artillery.
Named on the Regimental Memorial: St Joseph's Church, Waterloo, Belgium. (Photograph)
Memorial tablet: Mausoleum, Evere Cemetery, Brussels, Belgium. (Photograph)

LIEUTENANT / MICHAEL THOMAS / CROMIE / ROYAL HORSE / ARTILLERY / AGED 25

2nd Lt 17 Dec 1807. 1st Lt 25 Jan 1809.
   Served in the Peninsula Jun 1813 – Apr 1814 (with 'D' troop Royal Horse Artillery). Present at Bidassoa, Orthes, Tarbes and Toulouse. Present at Waterloo in Major Bean's Troop. Had both legs injured by one shot at Waterloo and died later while undergoing amputation. One of the select band of soldiers buried in the Mausoleum at Evere.

CROMPTON, Richard
Captain. York Light Infantry Volunteers.
Grave: British Cemetery, Lisbon, Portugal. (Grave number A.459). (M.I.)

"TO THE MEMORY OF CAPT R. CROMPTON LATE 9TH FOOT WHO DIED UNIVERSALLY REGRETTED 23 NOV 1823."

Ensign Royal Lancs Militia 29 Jun 1803. Lt 9th Foot 28 Oct 1807. Capt York Lt Infantry Volunteers 6 Jun 1811.
   Served in the Peninsula with 2/9th Oct 1808 – Jun 1811. (on staff as Town Adjutant of Lisbon from Jan 1809).

CRONHELM, Theodor von
Ensign. 4th Line Battalion, King's German Legion.
Named on the Regimental Memorial: La Haye Sainte, Waterloo, Belgium. (Photograph)

Ensign 9 Jul 1814.
   Present at Waterloo where he was killed.

CROOKSHANK, Arthur Chichester William
Major. 38th (1st Staffordshire) Regiment of Foot.
Brass memorial tablet: St James the Great Church, South Stoke, Somerset. (Photograph)

IN MEMORY OF LT-COLONEL / CHICHESTER W. CROOKSHANK / KNIGHT OF HANOVER. BORN / 24 MAY 1783. ENSIGN 68TH FOOT / 12 JAN 1799. WAR SERVICES / WEST INDIES. SOUTH AFRICA. / SOUTH / AMERICA. WALCHEREN. 1ST AND 2ND / PENINSULAR WARS. BREVET LT-COLONEL / 4 JUNE 1814. DIED 1 SEPT 1838

Box tomb: St James the Great Churchyard, South Stoke, Somerset. (Photograph)

LT COL CHICHESTER WILLIAM CROOKSHANK / DIED SEPTR 1ST 1838 / AGED 56 YEARS. / HE NEEDS NO PILLAR TO DECLARE HIS FAME / NO SCULPTURED TOMB TO IMMORTALIZE HIS NAME / EACH OF US ALONE HAS POWER TO RAISE / HIS MONUMENT, A GRATEFUL PEOPLE'S PRAISE

Ensign 68th Foot 12 Jan 1799. Lt 26 Mar 1800. Capt 38th Foot 18 Sep 1802. Major 29 Oct 1809. Bt Lt Colonel 4 Jun 1814. Portuguese Army: Lt Colonel 15th Line 16 May 1810. Lt Colonel 12th Caçadores 6 Jun 1811.
   Served in the Peninsula with 1/38th Aug 1808 – Jan 1809 and 1st Battalion detachments Feb-Mar 1809. With Portuguese Army: May 1810 – Apr 1813. Present at Rolica, Vimeiro, Busaco, Fuentes d'Onoro, Salamanca (wounded) and retreat from Burgos. Commanded the 12th Caçadores at Salamanca taking the eagle of the 22nd Regiment of French Infantry and presented it to Major General Pakenham. On the retreat from Burgos he was taken ill with a fever and had to return to England Jun 1813, resigning his Portuguese command. Rejoined his former regiment but on its reduction placed on half pay. Gold Medal for Salamanca. Portuguese Medal for Salamanca and medals for three campaigns in the Peninsula. KH. Also served in the West Indies 1800 (present at Martinique), Cape of Good Hope 1806, South America (present at Montevideo where he was wounded four times and Buenos Ayres where he was taken prisoner) and Walcheren 1809.
REFERENCE: *Royal Military Calendar, Vol 5, pp. 65–6. United Service Journal, Oct 1838, pp. 287–8.*

CROSS, Richard
Lieutenant. 38th (1st Staffordshire) Regiment of Foot.
Ledger stone: St John's Churchyard, Preston, Lancashire. (South side of church). (Photograph)

SACRED / TO THE MEMORY OF LIEUTENANT / RICHARD CROSS, OF HIS MAJESTY'S / 38TH REGT OF FOOT DEPARTED / THIS LIFE ON THE 27TH DAY OF MAY 1815 / IN THE 38TH YEAR OF HIS AGE. / THIS VETERAN OFFICER HAVING SERVED / UNDER THE DUKE OF WELLINGTON THREE / CAMPAIGNS IN THE PENINSULA DIS / – TINGUISHED HIMSELF IN SEVERAL BATTLES / PARTICULARLY AT THE STORMING OF ST / SEBASTIAN, WHEN HE WAS SEVERELY / WOUNDED. HE WAS REWARDED WITH A / PENSION FOR LIFE BY THE PRINCE REGENT. / ....

Ensign 9th Garrison Battalion. Lt 38th Foot 4 Nov 1807.
   Served in the Peninsula Mar – Dec 1813. Present at Osma, Vittoria and San Sebastian where he was severely wounded at the storming 31 Aug 1813.

CROSSE, Robert Noble

Captain. 36th (Herefordshire) Regiment of Foot.
Memorial tablet: Bath Abbey, Bath, Somerset. (Photograph)

.... / SACRED ALSO TO THE MEMORY / OF MAJOR ROBERT NOBLE CROSSE K.H. / LATE OF THE 36TH REGIMENT OF INFANTRY / SON OF THE ABOVE / WHO DIED OF YELLOW FEVER ON BOARD HER MAJESTY'S SHIP HERCULES / NOVR 13TH 1838 IN CARLISLE BAY, BARBADOES / WHEN ON THE EVE OF DEPARTING FOR CANADA. / HIS REMAINS ARE ENTOMBED / WITHIN THE PRECINCTS OF ST JOHN'S CHURCH IN THE ABOVE NAMED ISLAND / WHERE A TABLET HAS ALSO BEEN ERECTED IN THE CATHEDRAL / BY HIS BROTHER COMPANIONS IN ARMS IN TESTIMONY OF THEIR REGARD / FOR ONE SO GREATLY BELOVED AND REGRETTED. / ....

Memorial tablet: St Paul's Chapel, Bridgetown, Barbados. West Indies. (North wall of Nave). (Photograph)

SACRED TO THE MEMORY OF / MAJOR ROBERT NOBLE CROSSE. K. H. / 36TH REGIMENT, WHO DIED OF YELLOW FEVER / IN THE 50TH YEAR OF HIS AGE, ON THE / 13TH NOVEMBER 1838, ON BOARD H. M. SHIP HERCULES: / IN CARLISLE BAY BARBADOES: HAVING EMBARKED / WITH THE REGIMENT FOR NORTH AMERICA ON THE 10TH. / THIS TABLET IS ERECTED BY HIS BROTHER / OFFICERS AS A TRIBUTE OF RESPECT AND ESTEEM / FOR HIS CHARACTER AND AS A MARK OF REGRET / FOR HIS LOSS. / HE SERVED IN THE 36TH REGIMENT FOR AN / UNINTERRUPTED PERIOD OF 33 YEARS, AND / WAS PRESENT WITH IT IN THE FOLLOWING / ACTIONS VIZ. BUENOS AYRES, ROLEIA, VIMIERA / CORUNNA, ALMEIDA, FLUSHING, FUENTES D'ONOR / BOTH STORMINGS OF THE FORT OF SALAMANCA / THE ACTION OF SALAMANCA (WHERE HE WAS WOUNDED) / AND THE OPERATION BEFORE BURGOS.

Ensign 19 Nov 1805. Lt 26 Feb 1807. Capt 10 Sep 1812. Bt Major 22 Jul 1830. Major 31 Aug 1830.
   Served in the Peninsula Aug 1808 – Jan 1809 and Mar 1811 – Jan 1813. Present at Rolica, Vimeiro, Corunna, Barba del Puerco, Fuentes d'Onoro, siege of Salamanca Forts, Salamanca (wounded) and Burgos. KH. Also served in South America 1807 (present at Buenos Ayres), Walcheren 1809 and West Indies (caught yellow fever and died before embarking with the regiment for North America on board HMS *Hercules* in Carlisle Bay, Barbados 13 Nov 1838). Served with the regiment for 33 years.

CROWDER, John

Major. 7th (Royal Fusiliers) Regiment of Foot.
Memorial tablet: Holy Trinity Church, Cheltenham, Gloucestershire. (Photograph)

TO THE BELOVED AND LAMENTED MEMORY / OF COLONEL JOHN CROWDER, K.H / LATE OF THE 7TH OR ROYAL FUSILIERS, / AND OF / BROTHERTON IN THE COUNTY OF YORK, / WHO DIED / AUGUST 27TH 1838 , / AGED 57 YEARS / ....

Lt West Riding Yeomanry. Lt 7th Foot 16 Jun 1803. Capt 5 Nov 1806. Bt Major 17 Aug 1812. Major 9 Sep 1813. Bt Lt Colonel 27 May 1825. Bt Colonel 28 Jun 1838.
   Served in the Peninsula with 2/7th Apr 1809 – Jul 1810, 1/7th Aug 1810 – Dec 1811 and May 1812 – Jan 1814. Present at Douro, Talavera, Busaco, Pombal, Condeixa, Olivencia, first siege of Badajoz, Albuera (wounded), Aldea da Ponte, Castrejon, Salamanca (severely wounded, Mentioned in Despatches for gallantry while commanding a detachment of two companies of the 7th Foot in support of the Guards in the village of Arapiles and awarded a Bt Majority), Vittoria, Pyrenees (wounded) and Nivelle. KH. Also served at Copenhagen 1807. Half pay 25 May 1815.
REFERENCE: *Gentleman's Magazine, Dec 1838, pp. 659–60.*

CROWE, George William
Paymaster. 27th (Inniskilling) Regiment of Foot.
Memorial tablet: St Mary's Church, Alton Barnes, Wiltshire. (Photograph)

SACRED TO THE MEMORY OF / GEORGE WILLIAM CROWE ESQUIRE, / LATE DIPLOMATIC AGENT AND CONSUL GENERAL / IN THE REGENCY OF TRIPOLI, STATES OF BARBARY. / FORMERLY IN THE 27TH ENNISKILLENS, / WITH WHICH REGIMENT HE SERVED FROM 1811 TO 1824, / IN SICILY, THE PENINSULA, THE WATERLOO CAMPAIGN, / AT THE CAPITULATION OF PARIS AND IN THE WEST INDIES. / WAS CONSUL FOR THE MOREA, GREECE, FROM 1829 T0 1846. / ON ALL OCCASIONS HIS CONDUCT WAS / ACKNOWLEDGED WITH DISTINGUISHED PRAISE / BY THE BRITISH GOVERNMENT. / HE DIED FULL OF YEARS AND HONOR / AT DEVIZES 24TH MAY 1867, AGED 87, / MUCH MOURNED AND BELOVED / BY HIS SORROWING WIFE, CHILDREN / AND NUMEROUS FRIENDS.

Paymaster 7 Mar 1811.
Served in the Peninsula with 1/27th Nov 1812 – Nov 1813. Present at Castalla and Tarragona. Served in France at the Capture of Paris and with the Army of Occupation, Also served in Sicily 1807, West Indies and Greece 1829–1846 (Consul in Morea). Half pay 25 Dec 1824.

CROWE, John
Captain. 32nd (Cornwall) Regiment of Foot.
Low monument: Old Town Cemetery, Bideford, Devon. (Photograph)

SACRED TO THE MEMORY OF / LT COLONEL JOHN CROWE K.H. LATE H. M. 32ND REGT / WHO DIED MARCH 7TH 1860 AGED 70. / HE SERVED IN THE PENINSULA FROM 1811 TO 1814 BEING ENGAGED IN THE / BATTLES OF ORTHES AND SALAMANCA. / AND THE SIEGES OF CUIDAD RODRIGO, / BADJOS, / BURGOS AND SALAMANCA: / HE WAS ALSO SEVERELY WOUNDED ON THE 16TH JUNE 1815, / WHILST IN COMMAND OF THE LIGHT COMPANY / OF H. M. 32ND REGT AT QUATRE BRAS.

Ensign 30 May 1800. Lt 2 Apr 1803. Capt 30 May 1805. Bt Major 12 Aug 1819. Bt Lt Colonel 10 Jan 1837.
Served in the Peninsula Jul 1811 – Oct 1812 and Oct 1813 – Apr 1814. Present at the siege of Ciudad Rodrigo (but did not take part in the attack), Usagre, Badajoz (but did not take part in the attack), siege of Salamanca Forts, Salamanca, Burgos, action before Bayonne and Orthes. Present at Quatre Bras (severely wounded) and Waterloo. MGS medal for Salamanca and Orthes. KH.

CRUIKSHANK, Alexander
Private 79th (Cameron Highlanders) Regiment of Foot.
Family Obelisk: Glasgow Necropolis, Glasgow, Lanarkshire, Scotland. (Photograph)

COPENHAGEN / CORUNNA / FLUSHING / BUSACO / FUENTES D'ONORO / BADAJOS / NIVELLE / NIVE / TOULOUSE / QUATRE BRAS / WATERLOO / .... / ALSO TO THE MEMORY OF HIS UNCLE / ALEXANDER CRUIKSHANK / 79TH HIGHLANDERS / LATE FORT MAJOR EDIN-BURGH CASTLE, / WHO FOUGHT IN THE ABOVE ENGAGEMENTS. / DIED 22ND AUGUST, 1857, AGED 69 YEARS. / ....

Obelisk: Warriston Cemetery, Edinburgh, Scotland. (Photograph)

COPENHAGEN / CORUNNA / FLUSHING / BUSACO / FUENTES D'ONOR / BADAJOS / NIVELLE / NIVE / TOULOUSE / QUATRE BRAS / WATERLOO / ERECTED BY / JAMES CRUIKSHANK /

BUILDER, GLASGOW. / IN MEMORY OF HIS UNCLE / QUARTER-MASTER A. CRUIKSHANK. / BORN 1789. DIED 1857. / HE SERVED HIS COUNTRY / FOR THE LONG PERIOD OF 50 YEARS, / 44 OF WHICH WAS IN THE 79TH REGIMENT, / AND 6 YEARS AS FORT MAJOR IN EDINBURGH CASTLE, / AND WAS PRESENT AT THE ABOVE ENGAGEMENTS. / HE WAS GREATLY BELOVED / BY HIS BROTHER OFFICERS, MEN, AND ALL WHO KNEW HIM.

Pte 18 May 1805. Cpl 1819. Sgt 1824. Quartermaster Sgt 1833. Quartermaster 12 Oct 1838.

Served in the Peninsula Aug 1808 – Jan 1809 and Mar 1810 – Apr 1814. Present at Corunna, Busaco, Fuentes d'Onoro (taken prisoner but escaped), Badajoz (did not take part in the attack), Nivelle, Nive and Toulouse. Present at Quatre Bras and Waterloo in Capt William Marshall's Light Company and with the Army of Occupation. (named as Carrickshank). Also served at Copenhagen 1807 and Walcheren 1809 (present at Flushing). Half pay 11 May 1849. MGS medal for Busaco, Fuentes d'Onoro, Nivelle, Nive and Toulouse. Fort Major Edinburgh Castle 7 Feb 1851.

CRUIKSHANK, James
Private. 92nd Regiment of Foot.
Family Obelisk: Glasgow Necropolis, Glasgow, Lanarkshire, Scotland. (Photograph)

.... / JAMES CRUIKSHANK / 92ND HIGHLANDERS / WHO FOUGHT AT QUATRE BRAS / AND WATERLOO, / DIED 18TH APRIL 1880, AGED 86 YEARS.

Served at Quatre Bras and Waterloo in Captain John Warren's Company.

CRUIKSHANK, William
Private. 92nd Regiment of Foot.
Headstone: Kirriemuir Parish Churchyard, Angus, Scotland. (Photograph)

IN MEMORY OF / WILLIAM CRUIKSHANK / FOR 21 YEARS A PRIVATE IN 92ND REGT / AND LATTERLY OUT PENSIONER / OF CHELSEA HOSPITAL / WHO DIED 21ST NOVR 1850. / AGED 71 YEARS / .... / ERECTED / BY HIS WIDOW AND THE REVD / FREDERICK CRUIKSHANK / MINISTER NOVAR AND LETLNOCK / THE ONLY SURVIVOR OF HIS CHILDREN

Served in the Peninsula 1809 – Apr 1814. Present at Talavera (probably left behind sick in Lisbon after the regiment left for Corunna and so served at Talavera in the Battalion of Detachments 1809), Fuentes d'Onoro, Vittoria, Pyrenees and Toulouse. Present at Waterloo in Capt Claud Alexander's Company. MGS medal for Talavera, Fuentes d'Onoro, Vittoria, Pyrenees and Toulouse. Chelsea Out Pensioner.

CRUMMER, James Henry
Lieutenant. 28th (North Gloucestershire) Regiment of Foot.
Headstone: Cemetery, Port Macquarie, New South Wales, Australia. (Photograph)

M. S. / MAJOR JAMES HENRY / CRUMMER, / LATE OF H. M. 28TH REGIMENT OF FOOT, / WITH WHICH CORPS / HE FOUGHT, / DURING THE EVENTFUL YEARS / FROM 1807 TO 1815. / IN THIS COLONY. / HE SERVED AS POLICE MAGISTRATE / AT NEWCASTLE, MAITLAND, / AND PORT- MACQUARIE, / FROM 1836 TO 1864. / DIED 29 DECEMBER 1867, / AGED 76 YEARS. / COPENHAGEN, BUSACO, BADAJOS (FIRST SIEGE), CAMPO MAYOR / ALBUERA, VITTORIA, PUERTO-DE-MAYA, / PYRENEES, NIVELLE, NIVE, BAYONNE, / ST PALAIS, ORTHES, LAMEGO, TOULOUSE, / QUATRE-BRAS, WATERLOO.

Ensign Jul 1805. Lt 2 Jul 1807. Capt 20 Jul 1815. Bt Major 1 Mar 1839.

Served in the Peninsula with 2/28th Jul 1809 – Aug 1811, and 1/28th Sep 1812 – Apr 1814. Present at

Busaco, Campo Mayor, first siege of Badajoz, Albuera, (wounded), Vittoria, Pyrenees, (present at Maya where he was wounded), Nivelle, Nive, Garris, Orthes, Aire and Toulouse. Present at Quatre Bras and Waterloo and with the Army of Occupation. Returned to England 1818 and entered the Royal Military College Sandhurst, passing out in 1821. MGS medal for Busaco, Albuera, Vittoria, Pyrenees, Nivelle, Nive, Orthes and Toulouse. Also served at Copenhagen 1807, Ionian Islands 1821–1828 (Commandant of Calamos in the Greek War of Independence) and Ireland 1829. In 1832 applied for a pension as his wounded leg was still painful, but it was refused owing to the length of time since he was wounded. Went to Sydney, Australia 1835. Appointed JP and Police Magistrate at Newcastle and later at Maitland. Sold his commission in 1840 and stayed in New South Wales, where he was buried with full military honours in 1867.

REFERENCE: *Australian Dictionary of Biography. Crummer papers, Mitchell Library, Sydney, Australia.*

CRUMP, Ely
Staff Surgeon. Medical Department.
Memorial tablet: All Saints Church, Maidstone, Kent. (Photograph)

SACRED / TO THE MEMORY OF / ELY CRUMP ESQ. / WHO DEPARTED THIS LIFE ON THE 28TH OCTOBER 1829 / AGED 57 YEARS. / THIRTY SIX OF WHICH WERE PASSED AS A / MEDICAL OFFICER IN HIS MAJESTY'S SERVICE. / HE WAS ACTIVELY EMPLOYED IN / EUROPE, AFRICA AND AMERICA / AND WAS INDEFATIGABLE IN HIS DUTIES AND UNREMITTING / IN HIS ATTENTIONS TO THOSE / WHO REQUIRED HIS CARE. / HE DIED BELOVED AND LAMENTED. / ....

Hospital Mate 4 Mar 1794. Apothecary (Mediterranean) 19 Oct 1798. Staff Surgeon 4 Apr 1800. Staff Surgeon 9 Jun 1804. Deputy Inspector of Hospitals 18 Jan 1816.

Served in the Peninsula Aug 1808 – Jan 1809. Present at Corunna. Also served in Egypt 1801, Hanover 1806, South America 1807 and Walcheren 1809. Retired 18 Jan 1816.

CUBITT, Edward George
Lieutenant. 4th (Queen's Own) Regiment of Dragoons.
Memorial tablet: St Peter and St Paul Church, Honing, Norfolk. (M.I.)

"SACRED TO THE MEMORY OF EDWARD GEORGE CUBITT OF THIS PARISH ESQRE. HE SERVED IN HER MAJESTY'S 4TH DRAGOONS DURING A GREAT PART OF THE PENINSULAR WAR; WAS IN THE RETREAT FROM BURGOS; WAS ALSO PRESENT AT THE BATTLE OF VITTORIA, PAMPELUNA AND TOULOUSE; CAPTURE OF PARIS WITH THE ALLIED ARMIES OF OCCUPATION IN 1815. THIS MONUMENT WAS ERECTED BY HIS SORROWING WIDOW AND CHILDREN. HE DIED DECR 20TH 1865, AGED 70 YEARS."

Cornet 31 Oct 1811. Lt 23 Jan 1812.

Served in the Peninsula Sep 1812 – Apr 1814. Present at the retreat from Burgos, Vittoria, Pamplona and Toulouse. Served in France at the Capture of Paris with the Army of Occupation 1815. MGS medal for Vittoria and Toulouse. Half pay 8 Jan 1824.

CUBITT, Thomas
2nd Captain. Royal Artillery.
Memorial tablet: All Saints Church, Catfield, Norfolk. (M.I.)

"TO THE MEMORY OF / THOMAS CUBITT OF THIS PARISH ESQ., / LIEUT COLONEL IN THE ROYAL ARTILLERY / WHO DIED AT KINGSTON IN UPPER CANADA / ON THE 15TH OF MARCH 1840 IN THE 56TH YEAR OF HIS AGE / WHILE IN COMMAND OF HIS CORPS / IN THAT

PROVINCE / LEAVING A WIDOW AND TEN CHILDREN / TO LAMENT THEIR IRREPARABLE LOSS."

2nd Lt 20 Dec 1800. 1st Lt 11 Jun 1802. 2nd Capt 1 Feb 1808. Capt 20 Jan 1817. Bt Major 27 May 1825. Lt Colonel 25 May 1836.

   Served in Gibraltar and Malta 1804, Sicily 1806 (present at Maida), Walcheren 1809 and Upper Canada 1836–1840.

CUMBERLAND, Richard Francis George
Lieutenant and Captain. 3rd Regiment of Foot Guards.
Memorial tablet: St Mary the Virgin Church, Hampton-on-Thames, London. (Photograph)

.................../ RICHARD FRANCIS GEORGE CUMBERLAND, CAPT/ ONLY SON OF THE ABOVE, FORMERLY OF THE THIRD GUARDS, / WHO DIED 9TH MARCH 1870, IN HIS 77TH YEAR, / WAS ALSO BURIED NEAR THIS PLACE. / HE WAS A.D.C. TO THE DUKE OF WELLINGTON

Ensign 27 Aug 1809. Lt and Capt 13 Jan 1814.
   Served in the Peninsula Jul 1811 – Apr 1812 (extra ADC to Wellington), Apr – Aug 1812 and Oct 1813 – Apr 1814. Present at Badajoz, Nivelle, Nive, Adour and Bayonne where he was wounded at the Sortie from Bayonne. MGS medal for Badajoz, Nivelle and Nive. Retired 24 Feb 1825. One of the last survivors of Wellington's personal staff.

CUMIN, William
Surgeon. 88th (Connaught Rangers) Regiment of Foot.
Pedestal tomb: Walcot Cemetery, Bath, Somerset. (Area 1 Row C). (Photograph)

SACRED / TO THE MEMORY OF / WILLIAM CUMIN M.D. / SOMETIME PROFESSOR IN THE / UNIVERSITY OF GLASGOW / WHO DIED AT BATH / 17TH JANUARY 1854 / AGED 69

Hospital Mate 6 Apr 1806. Asst Surgeon 43rd Foot 7 May 1807. Surgeon 88th Foot 15 Oct 1812.
   Served in the Peninsula with 2/43rd Aug 1808 – Dec 1808, 1/43rd Jan 1809 and Jul 1809 – Nov 1812 and with 88th Foot Dec 1812 – Sep 1813. Present at Vimeiro, Vigo, Coa, Busaco, Redinha, Casal Nova, Foz d'Arouce, Sabugal, Fuentes d'Onoro, Badajoz, Salamanca, Vittoria and Pyrenees. Tried by Court Martial and dismissed the service 10 Jan 1816. Re-admitted as Asst Surgeon 3rd Royal Veteran Battalion 21 Mar 1816. Retired on half pay 4 Sep 1816. MGS medal for Vimeiro, Busaco, Fuentes d'Onoro, Badajoz, Salamanca, Vittoria, and Pyrenees. MA Glasgow 1805. MD 1813. Professor of Midwifery in University of Glasgow 1834–1840.

CUMMING, Henry John
Lieutenant Colonel. 11th Regiment of Light Dragoons.
Low monument in railed enclosure: Kensal Green Cemetery, London. (6285/27/IR). (Photograph)

IN MEMORY OF / GENERAL / HENRY JOHN CUMMING KCH / COLONEL OF THE 12TH ROYAL LANCERS. / BORN AT CALCUTTA ** DECEMBER 1771, / DIED 28 NOVEMBER 1856. / THE ELDEST SON OF / SIR JOHN CUMMING KT / COLONEL IN THE SERVICE / OF THE EAST INDIA COMPANY / WHO DIED AT ST HELENA 26 AUG 1786, AGED 46.

Cornet 12 May 1790. Lt 9 Feb 1793. Capt 21 Feb 1794. Major 25 Oct 1798. Lt Colonel 17 Feb 1803. Bt Colonel 1 Jan 1812. Major General 4 Jun 1814. Lt General 22 Jul 1830. General 9 Nov 1846.
   Served in the Peninsula Jun 1811 – Jan 1812 and May 1812 – Apr 1813. Present at El Bodon (wounded and Mentioned in Despatches), Morales, Castrejon, Salamanca and Venta del Poza. Gold Medal for

Salamanca where he commanded the 11ᵗʰ Lt Dragoons. Also served in Flanders 1793–1795 (present at Valenciennes, Dunkirk, Famars and Le Cateau) and the Helder 1799. Colonel 12ᵗʰ Lancers 20 Jan 1837. KCH. Retired Jul 1842.

REFERENCE: *Royal Military Calendar, Vol 3, pp. 365–6.*

CUMMING, William

Assistant Commissary General. Commissariat Department.
Memorial: Arbroath Abbey, Angus, Scotland. (M.I.)

"WILLIAM CUMMING ESQᴿᴱ OF KIRKWALL, N. B., DEPUTY COMMISSARY GENERAL TO H. M. FORCES, WHO DIED 10ᵀʰ MAY 1833 AGED 72 YEARS."

Dep Asst Comm Gen 6 Dec 1810. Asst Comm Gen 25 Dec 1814. Dep Comm Gen 10 Sep 1830.

Served in the Peninsula May 1809 – Feb 1814 (attached to 2ⁿᵈ Division Oct 1812 – Feb 1814). Present at Talavera, Cadiz, Barrosa, Vittoria, Pyrenees, Nivelle, Nive, Garris and Orthes. MGS medal for Talavera, Barrosa, Vittoria, Pyrenees, Nivelle, Nive and Orthes.

CUMMING, William G.

Lieutenant. 83ʳᵈ Regiment of Foot.
Memorial tablet: St Giles Church, Matlock, Derbyshire. (North aisle). (Photograph)

TO THE MEMORY / OF / CAPTAIN WILLIAM CUMMING, / OF THE 83ᴿᴰ BRITISH REGIMENT, / AND 9ᵀʰ PORTUGUESE CAÇADORES, / WHO / HAVING FOUGHT IN THE BATTLES / OF / OPORTO, TALAVERA, BUZACO, / AND FUENTES DE ONORO, / FELL IN AN ATTACK ON THE FRENCH OUTPOST / NEAR BAYONNE, / OCTOBER 9ᵀʰ, 1813, / IN THE 30ᵀʰ YEAR OF HIS AGE. / THIS TABLET WAS ERECTED BY HIS BROTHERS, / IN WHOSE AFFECTION AND ESTEEM HE HAD / THAT PLACE, TO WHICH FIRMNESS / OF MIND AND URBANITY OF / MANNERS, JUSTLY ENTITLED / THEIR POSSESSOR.

Ensign 28 Jan 1808. Lt Mar 1809. Portuguese Army: Capt 9ᵗʰ Caçadores 1 Jul 1811.

Served in the Peninsula with 83ʳᵈ Foot Apr 1809 – Jun 1811 and Portuguese Army Jul 1811 – Oct 1813. Present at Douro, Talavera, Redinha, Casal Nova, Foz d'Arouce, Sabugal, Salamanca, Burgos, Pyrenees and Bidassoa where he was killed 7 Oct 1813.

Note: Discrepancy in date of death with date recorded on memorial tablet.

CUPPAGE, Stephen

Captain. 39ᵗʰ (Dorsetshire) Regiment of Foot.
Gravestone: St Mary's Churchyard, Cheltenham, Gloucestershire. (No longer extant). (M.I.)

"SACRED TO THE MEMORY OF COL STEPHEN CUPPAGE. BORN 27ᵀʰ NOVR 1786. DIED 29ᵀʰ JANY 1855."

Ensign 5 Nov 1803. Lt 30 Jun 1804. Capt 15 Oct 1807. Bt Major 19 Jul 1821. Major 25 May 1826. Bt Lt Colonel 10 Jan 1837. Bt Colonel 11 Nov 1851.

Served in the Peninsula with 2/39ᵗʰ Jul 1809 – Jan 1812 and 1/39ᵗʰ Aug 1813 – Apr 1814. Present at Busaco, first siege of Badajoz, Albuera, Arroyo dos Molinos, Pyrenees, Nivelle, Nive, Garris, Orthes, Aire and Toulouse. Also served in North America 1814–1815. MGS medal for Busaco, Albuera, Pyrenees, Nivelle Nive, Orthes and Toulouse.

CURBY, Edward
Assistant Surgeon. Medical Department.
Headstone: British Cemetery, Lisbon, Portugal. (Grave number E 17). (Photograph)

SACRED TO THE MEMORY / OF / EDWARD CURBY ESQ^R. / ASSISTANT STAFF SURGEON / WHO DEPARTED THIS LIFE / JANUARY 10TH 1813 / IN THE 23RD YEAR OF HIS AGE.

Asst Surgeon 29th Foot 20 Mar 1806. Assist Surgeon Staff 12 Nov 1812.
  Served in the Peninsula Jul 1808 – Aug 1811 and Jan 1813. Present at Rolica, Vimeiro, Douro, Talavera and Albuera. Taken prisoner after Talavera but rejoined his regiment Oct 1810.

CURETON, Charles Robert
Cornet 20th Regiment of Light Dragoons.
Grave: Barahdari Garden, Ramnagar, India. (M.I.)

"SACRED TO THE MEMORY OF BRIGADIER GENERAL CHARLES ROBERT CURETON, CB. / ADJUTANT GENERAL, 16TH LIGHT DRAGOONS, QUEEN'S TROOPS, WHO FELL IN THE / ENGAGEMENT WITH THE SIKH TROOPS NEAR THIS SPOT, ON THE 22ND NOVEMBER 1848, / WHEN IN COMMAND OF THE CAVALRY OF THE ARMY UNDER GENERAL LORD GOUGH, AGED 60 YEARS."

Named on the Regimental Memorial: Barahdari, Ramnagar, India. (Recently restored). (Photograph)

IN MEMORY / OF THOSE WHO FELL IN THE CAVALRY ACTION NEAR THIS PLACE / ON THE / 2ND NOVEMBER 1848. 16 KILLED 64 WOUNDED & 10 MISSING / OFFICERS KILLED / BRIGADIER GENERAL C. R. CURETON CB. COMMANDING THE CAVALRY DIVISION / LT. COL W. HAVELOCK KH. 14TH LIGHT DRAGOONS / SUBADAR MAJOR MIR SHER ALI SIRDAR BAHADAR / 88TH LIGHT CAVALRY (AGED 78) / DIED OF WOUNDS / CAPT. J. F. FITZGERALD, 14TH LIGHT DRAGOONS / DIED 26TH NOVEMBER 1848 / THIS SITE WAS RESTORED WITH SUPPORT FROM BACSA, THE KING'S ROYAL HUSSARS, / AND EX-MEMBERS OF 14TH / 20TH KING'S HUSSARS, 2000.

Memorial Sarcophagus: St Mary's Church, Shrewsbury, Shropshire. (Entrance Porch). (Photograph)

SACRED TO THE MEMORY OF / COLONEL C. R. CURETON CB. AND ADC TO THE QUEEN / ADJUTANT GENERAL OF H. M. FORCES IN INDIA / AND LATE LIEUT. COLONEL COMMANDING THE 16TH LANCERS / WHO FELL IN AN ENGAGEMENT WITH THE SIKH TROOPS AT RAMNAGGUR / ON THE 22ND NOVEMBER 1848 / WHEN COMMANDING THE CAVALRY OF THE BRITISH ARMY / UNDER GENERAL LORD GOUGH GCB. / THIS MONUMENT IS ERECTED BY HIS COMRADES AND BROTHER OFFICERS IN INDIA / BY WHOM HE WAS HELD IN UNIVERSAL ADMIRATION AND RESPECT, / AND IN LOVE AND ESTEEM AS A FRIEND.

Ensign Shropshire Militia 21 Apr 1806. Lt 20 Jan 1806. Pte 14th Lt Dragoons 1808 (under the name of Charles Roberts). Ensign 40th Foot 24 Feb 1814 (as Charles Robert Cureton). Cornet 20th Lt Dragoons 20 Oct 1814. Lt and Adjt 16th Lt Dragoons 7 Jan 1819. Capt 12 Nov 1825. Major 6 Dec 1833. Bt Lt Colonel 23 Jul 1839. Lt Colonel 21 Aug 1839. Bt Colonel 3 Aug 1846.
  Served in the Peninsula with 14th Lt Dragoons as Private Charles Roberts 1809 – Jan 1814. With 40th Foot as Ensign Charles Robert Cureton Feb – Apr 1814. Present at Talavera, Villa de Puerco, Coa, Busaco, Retreat to the Lines of Torres Vedras (severely wounded near Coimbra), Redinha, Casal Nova, Foz d'Arouce, Sabugal, Fuentes d'Onoro, (severely wounded), Badajoz, Salamanca, Vittoria, Pyrenees, Nivelle, Nive, Orthes, Tarbes and Toulouse.

Also served in Ireland and India with 16th Lt Dragoons 1822 (present at the siege and capture of Bhurtpore 1825–1826). Assistant Adjutant General of Cavalry 1838. Served in Afghanistan 1839–1840 (present at Kandahar and Ghuznee – awarded medal and appointed to Bt Lt Colonelcy). Brigadier commanding the Third Brigade of Cavalry of the Army of Gwalior 1843 (present at Maharajpore – awarded Bronze Star and CB). Brigadier commanding the Third Brigade of Cavalry in first Sikh War 1846, he served throughout the Sutlej campaign (present at Buddiwal, Aliwal and Sobraon). Appointed Colonel in the Army and Adjutant General of Her Majesty's forces in India. Commanded the Cavalry Division of the Army of Punjab in the second Sikh War 1848. Killed at Ramnagar 22 Nov 1848, in an attempt to stop a fatal charge by the 14th Lt Dragoons under Colonel Havelock. He died at the front of the regiment that he had joined forty years previously as a private. His youngest son Augustus was killed two months later at the battle of Chillianwala. MGS medal for Talavera, Fuentes d'Onoro, Badajoz, Salamanca, Vittoria, Pyrenees, Nivelle, Nive, Orthes and Toulouse

The reason for his change of name was that while in the militia he got into financial difficulties and could not pay his debts. He decided to disappear by leaving his clothes on a beach to give the impression that he had drowned. He enlisted as a private and remained in the ranks until early 1814, when he was seen by Lord Fitzroy Somerset who knew him from his days in the Militia. A commission was obtained for him as Ensign of 40th Foot 24 Feb 1814.

REFERENCE: *Dictionary of National Biography. Journal of the Society for Army Historical Research, Vol 47, 1969, pp. 157–60. United Service Magazine, Mar 1849, pp. 477–8. Gentleman's Magazine, Mar 1849, pp. 317–8. Annual Register, 1848, Appx, pp. 264–5.*

CURRIE, Edward

Major. 90th (Perthshire Volunteers) Regiment of Foot.
Memorial tablet: Troutbeck Chapel, St Mary's on the Hill, Chester, Cheshire. Seriously eroded. (Photograph) The church is now redundant and used as an education centre.

IN THE VAULT BENEATH LIE THE REMAINS OF / ANNA MARIA CURRIE / WHO DIED AUG. THE 30TH 1845 AGED 57, / RELICT OF LIEUT COLONEL EDWARD CURRIE, / WHO SERVED WITH MUCH DISTINCTION ON THE PERSONAL / STAFF OF THE LATE GENERAL LORD HILL, G.C.B. THROUGHOUT THE / PENINSULAR CAMPAIGNS AND FELL ON THE FIELD OF WATERLOO / WHERE HE WAS EMPLOYED AS AN ASSISTANT ADJUTANT GENERAL / IN THE ARMY UNDER THE COMMAND OF FIELD MARSHAL / HIS GRACE THE DUKE OF WELLINGTON K.G. &C. / THIS HUMBLE TRIBUTE TO THE MEMORY OF THEIR LAMENTED / PARENTS IS INSCRIBED BY THEIR SURVIVING CHILDREN.

Ensign 58th Foot 6 Dec 1794. Capt-Lt and Capt 1801. Capt 7 Nov 1801. Capt 90th Foot 25 Dec 1802. Bt Major 5 Dec 1811. Bt Lt Colonel 19 Jun 1812. Major 13 Oct 1814.

Served in the Peninsula Jun 1809 – Jan 1811 and Jun 1811 – Apr 1814 (ADC to Lord Hill). Present at Douro, Talavera (Mentioned in Despatches), Busaco, Arroyo dos Molinos (Mentioned in Despatches), Almarez (Mentioned in Despatches), Vittoria, Pyrenees, Nivelle, Nive, Garris, Orthes, Aire, Tarbes and Toulouse.

Present at Waterloo (AAG), where he was killed in the evening. He was with Major Egerton of 34th Foot when he died, who marked the spot where he fell. Next morning Egerton found his body, stripped and barely recognisable. Received his first commission at the age of 13 in recognition of the military services of his father. Also served in Egypt 1801 (present at Mandora and Alexandria – severely wounded) and the West Indies 1805.

CURRIE, Lachlan

Sergeant. 68th (Durham) Regiment of Foot.
Pedestal monument: St Andrew's Cemetery, Niagara, Ontario, Canada. (Photograph)

IN / MEMORY OF / LACHLAN / CURRIE / DIED / MAY 25, 1872 / AGED 84 YRS.

Cpl 10 Apr 1809. Sgt 17 Sep 1810. Quartermaster Sgt 25 Sep 1825.
　　Served in the Peninsula Jun 1811 - Apr 1814. Present at Salamanca, Vittoria, Pyrenees and San Sebastian. Also served at Walcheren 1809 (present at the siege of Flushing) and Canada 1817-1829.. Discharged 27 May 1834. MGS medal for Salamanca, Vittoria, Pyrenees and San Sebastian.

CURSON, Andrew
Sergeant. 51st (2nd Yorkshire West Riding) Light Infantry.
Named on the Regimental Memorial: KOYLI Chapel, York Minster, Yorkshire. (Photograph)
　　Killed in the Peninsula.

CURZON, Hon. William
Captain. 69th (South Lincolnshire) Regiment of Foot.
Memorial tablet: All Saints Church, Kedleston, Derbyshire. (Photograph)

SACRED TO THE MEMORY OF WILLIAM CURZON, / 4TH SON OF LORD SCARSDALE, LATE CAPT IN THE 69TH FT. & D.A.A.G. / A YOUTH OF FAIREST PROMISE! / WHOSE PROFESSIONAL MERIT, AMIABLE QUALITIES, & PRIVATE WORTH, / HAD DISTINGUISHED HIM AS A SOLDIER, ENDEAR'D HIM TO HIS FAMILY, FRIENDS, & COMRADES. / HE ENTERED THE ARMY AT THE AGE OF 16, / APPOINTED TO AN ENSIGNCY IN THE 9TH FROM THE R. M. COLLEGE, / AND HAVING HONORABLY SERVED THROUGHOUT THE WAR IN THE PENINSULA, / AND ALREADY BLED IN THE CAUSE OF NATIONS, / FELL ALAS! FIGHTING WITH DEVOTED GALLANTRY, / ON THAT DAY OF TRIUMPH & TEARS, WHICH SEAL'D THEIR DELIVERANCE: / BEING SLAIN IN THE BATTLE OF WATERLOO JUNE 18TH 1815, IN HIS 24 YEAR. / HIS COUNTRY WILL RECORD HIS NAME IN THE FIRST OF THE BRAVE: / TO PRESERVE IT ON THE SPOT WHERE ITS REMEMBRANCE WILL BE MOST PRECIOUS. / THIS TABLET IS RAISED BY AFFECTIONATE PARENTS, / WHO DEPLORING HIS LOSS, WITH THEIR SURVIVING CHILDREN, / BOW TO THE DIVINE WILL & REPOSE IN THE BLESSED BELIEF, / THAT HE HAS EXCHANG'D HIS LAURELS, FOR A CROWN OF GLORY, / THE MEED OF HIS VIRTUES.

Ensign 9th Foot 15 Dec 1807. Lt 8 Aug 1808. Capt 69th Foot 17 Dec 1812.
　　Served in the Peninsula with 1/9th Aug – Oct 1808, 2/9th Nov 1808 – Jun 1809, 1/9th Nov 1810 – Feb 1813 and with 69th Foot Aug 1813 – Apr 1814 (ADC to Lord Aylmer). Present at Rolica, Vimeiro, Douro, Tarifa, Fuentes d'Onoro, Castrejon, Salamanca, retreat from Burgos, Villa Muriel (wounded 25 Oct 1812), Bidassoa, Nivelle, Nive and Bayonne. Present at Waterloo on Staff (DAAG) where he was killed when galloping by the side of his friend Lord March. As he fell from his horse he called out 'Goodbye dear March' and died aged 24.

CUST, Hon. Edward
Captain. 60th (Royal American) Regiment of Foot.
Low monument: St Peter and St Paul Churchyard, Belton, Lincolnshire. (Photograph)

IN LOVING MEMORY OF / GENERAL THE HONBLE SIR EDWARD CUST BARONET / SIXTH SON OF BROWNLOW FIRST LORD BROWNLOW. / BORN 17TH OF MARCH 1794. DIED 14TH OF FEBRUARY 1878.

Cornet 16th Lt Dragoons 15 Mar 1810. Lt 57th Foot 27 Dec 1810. Lt 14th Lt Dragoons 7 Mar 1811. Capt 60th Foot 9 Dec 1813. Major 24 Oct 1821. Lt Colonel 26 Dec 1826. Bt Colonel 23 Nov 1841. Major General 11 Nov 1851. Lt General 14 May 1859. General 12 Jan 1866

Served in the Peninsula Feb 1811 – Dec 1813. Present at Redinha, Casal Nova, Foz d'Arouce, Sabugal, Fuentes d'Onoro, El Bodon, Badajoz, Llerena, Castrejon, Salamanca, Vittoria, Pyrenees, Nivelle and Nive. KCH. Half pay 9 Dec 1813, after which he did not see active service again. Member of Parliament for Grantham 1818–1826 and Lostwithiel 1826–1832. Master of Ceremonies to the Queen 1847. Colonel 16th Lancers 9 Apr 1859. Author of *Annals of the Wars of the Eighteenth Century*, 5 vols, 1857–1860 and *Lives of the Warriors of the Thirty Years War*, 2 vols, 1865–1867. Younger brother of Capt Peregrine Francis Cust 3rd Dragoon Guards. MGS medal for Fuentes d'Onoro, Badajoz, Salamanca, Vittoria, Pyrenees, Nivelle and Nive.
REFERENCE: *Dictionary of National Biography. Annual Register, 1878, Appx, p. 130.*

CUST, Hon. Peregrine Francis
Captain. 3rd (Prince of Wales's) Dragoon Guards.
Table tomb: St Peter and St Paul Churchyard, Belton, Lincolnshire. Inscription illegible and recorded from memorial inscription. (Photograph)

"COLONEL THE HONORABLE PEREGRINE FRANCIS CUST BORN AT BELTON 13 AUGUST 1791 DIED 15 SEPTEMBER 1873 LEAVING TWO SURVIVING CHILDREN JOHN FRANCIS CUST AND CHARLOTTE ISABELLA CLARK KENNEDY."

Cornet 3rd Dragoon Guards 31 Mar 1808. Lt 3 May 1810. Capt 60th Foot 17 Oct 1811. Capt 3rd Dragoon Guards 4 Jun1812.
    Served in the Peninsula May 1809 – Nov 1811 and Oct 1813 – Apr 1814. Present at Talavera, Busaco and Toulouse. Retired 9 Nov 1846. MGS medal for Talavera, Busaco and Toulouse. Elder brother of Capt Edward Cust 60th Foot.

CUSTANCE, Holman
Captain. 50th (West Kent) Regiment of Foot.
Monument: St John the Evangelist Churchyard, Lothian Road, Edinburgh, Scotland. (Second bay below church). (Photograph)

SACRED TO THE MEMORY OF / COLONEL HOLMAN CUSTANCE, / LATE COMMANDANT IN THE ISLE OF WIGHT, / WHO SERVED MANY YEARS IN THE PENINSULA / IN THE 50TH REGI-MENT AND AFTERWARDS COMMANDED / THE 9TH AND 10TH REGIMENTS OF FOOT. / HE DIED AT / EDINBURGH THE 4TH OF OCTOBER 1850 / AGED 61 YEARS.

Ensign 20 Oct 1808. Lt 22 Feb 1810. Capt 26 May 1814. Major 2 Sep 1824. Lt Colonel 10th Foot 12 Dec 1826. Bt Colonel 23 Nov 1841.
    Served in the Peninsula Feb 1813 – Apr 1814. Present at Nivelle, Nive (severely wounded at St Pierre and awarded pension of £100 per annum), Garris, Orthes, Aire (wounded), Tarbes and Toulouse. Also served at Walcheren 1809. Half pay 1814. Colonel 9th Foot 1831–1837. MGS medal for Nivelle, Nive, Orthes and Toulouse.
REFERENCE: *Gentleman's Magazine, Jan 1851, p. 96.*

CUYLER, Augustus
Ensign. Coldstream Regiment of Foot Guards.
Memorial tablet: St Paul's Church, North King Street, Dublin, Ireland. (M.I.) (Church deconsecrated in about 1990 and converted into an Enterprise Centre. Intact memorials were removed to St Michan's Church but many memorials are illegible or inaccessible around the perimeter wall).

"SACRED TO THE MEMORY OF / LIEUT. COLONEL AUGUSTUS CUYLER / CHIEF COM-MISSIONER OF THE METROPOLITAN POLICE OF THE CITY OF DUBLIN / AND FORMERLY IN

THE COLDSTREAM REGIMENT OF FOOT GUARDS. / DIED JUNE 14TH 1837 AGED 40 YEARS. / RESPECTED, BELOVED AND LAMENTED / BY ALL WHO KNEW HIM. / HE WAS THE THIRD SON OF THE LATE GENERAL SIR C. CUYLER, BART. / FAREWELL TO HIM WHOM YOUTHFUL VALOUR DREW / TO SEEK A SOLDIERS FAME AT WATERLOO. / FAREWELL TO HIM SO PROMPT WITH FRIENDSHIP'S BALM / THE ANGUISH OF THE SORROWING HEART TO CALM / OF PINING WANT TO CHEER THE LOW ABODE / THE HAND CONCEALING WHENCE THE BOUNTY FLOWED. / TO HIM FAREWELL BENEVOLENT AND KIND / SPIRIT JOYOUS AND OF ARDENT MIND. / FAREWELL TO HIM WHOSE EARLY GRAVE CONTAINS / ALL THAT WAS EARTHLY OF HIS DEAR REMAINS / BUT CHRISTIAN HOPE IS NOT BESTOWED IN VAIN / THAT THOSE WE LOVED ON EARTH MAY MEET AGAIN / WHERE GRIEF NO MORE SHALL PAIN OR DEATH DESTROY / BUT FAITH IN CHRIST BE CROWNED WITH HEAVENLY JOY."

Ensign 69th Foot. Ensign Coldstream Guards 15 Oct 1812. Lt and Capt 27 Feb 1817. Capt and Lt Colonel 10 Jun 1826.

Present at Waterloo (on staff as extra ADC to Major General George Cooke). Retired on half pay 1826. Chief Commissioner of the Metropolitan Police in Dublin. Son of General Cornelius Cuyler.

CUYLER, Henry
Lieutenant Colonel. 46th (South Devonshire) Regiment of Foot.
Memorial: St Nicholas Church, Rochester, Kent. (M.I.)

"COLONEL HENRY CUYLER OBIT 22 NOV 1841, AGED 72."

Ensign 30th Foot 1 Dec 1782. Lt 3 Sep 1788. Capt 18 Dec 1793. Bt Major 9 Sep 1797. Major 27th Foot 3 Nov 1797. Lt Colonel 16 May 1800. Lt Colonel 3rd Foot 5 Feb 1805. Lt Colonel 85th Foot 13 Nov 1806. Bt Colonel 25 Jul 1810. Lt Colonel 46th Foot 25 Jan 1813.

Served in the Peninsula with 85th Foot Mar – Oct 1811. Present at Fuentes d'Onoro and second siege of Badajoz. Retired 4 Feb 1813.

DACRE, Lord see Otway, Hon Henry

DAEY, H. A.
2nd Lieutenant. 4th Dragoons, Dutch Cavalry.
Named on the Memorial to Dutch officers killed at Waterloo: St Joseph's Church, Waterloo, Belgium. (Photograph)

D'AGUILAR, George Charles
Major. 1st (Duke of York's) Greek Light Infantry Regiment.
Brass Memorial tablet: Royal Garrison Church, Portsmouth, Hampshire. (Back of a choir stall). (Photograph)

LIEUT. GEN. SIR GEORGE / CHARLES D'AGUILAR / K.C.B. COL. OF THE / 23RD ROYAL WELSH / FUSILIERS DIED MAR / 21 1855 AGE 71.

Ensign 86th Foot 24 Sep 1799. Lt 1 Dec 1802. Capt 81st Foot 30 Mar 1808. Major Greek Lt Infantry 1 Apr 1813. Bt Lt Colonel 20 May 1813. Major Rifle Brigade 6 Mar 1817. Bt Colonel 22 Jul 1830. Major General 23 Nov 1841. Lt General 11 Nov 1851.

Served in the Peninsula Jul 1812 – Apr 1813 (AAG and Military Secretary to Sir John Murray). Present on the east coast of Spain (present at Biar and Castalla. Mentioned in Despatches and carried despatches to England). Awarded Bt Lt Colonelcy. Present at the Capture of Paris and with the Army of Occupation, but not at Waterloo as he did not arrive in time from the Greek Islands. Also served in India 1799 – 1806

(present at the siege of forts in Gujerat and Maleva and assault on fort of Bhurtpore under Lord Lake 1806 where he was wounded), Walcheren 1809, Ireland 1832–1842 (DAG), China 1847 (commanded the expedition which seized the forts of Bocca Tigris and Canton.). CB 1838. Colonel 58th Foot 1848. Colonel 23rd Foot 31 Jan 1851. KCB 1852. While in Ireland wrote *Practice and Forms of District and Regimental Courts Martial* and *Officers Manual – a translation of Military Maxims of Napoleon*, 1831.
REFERENCE: *Dictionary of National Biography. Royal Military Calendar, Vol 4, pp. 444–5. Gentleman's Magazine, Jul 1855, p. 94. Annual Register, 1855, Appx, pp. 274–5.*

DALBIAC, James Charles
Lieutenant Colonel. 4th (Queen's Own) Regiment of Dragoons.
Memorial tablet: St Michael's Church, Kirklington, Yorkshire. (Photograph)

IN THE SAME VAULT WITH THOSE OF HIS WIFE, / ARE DEPOSITED THE REMAINS OF / LIEUTENANT GENERAL, / SIR JAMES CHARLES DALBIAC, K.C.H. / COLONEL OF THE 4TH REGIMENT OF DRAGOONS, / WHO DEPARTED THIS LIFE / ON THE 8TH DAY OF DECEMBER 1847, / AGED 71 YEARS. / THIS TABLET TO THE MEMORY OF / HER ADMIRABLE FATHER, IS ERECTED BY HIS / MOST AFFECTIONATE AND ONLY CHILD, / SUSAN, DUCHESS OF ROXBURGHE.

Cornet 4 Jul 1793. Lt 24 Feb 1794. Capt 3 May 1800. Major 15 Oct 1801. Lt Colonel 25 Nov 1808. Bt Colonel 4 Jun 1814. Major General 27 May 1825. Lt General 28 Jun 1838.
   Served in the Peninsula Apr – Oct 1809, Sep 1810 – Sep 1811 and Mar 1812 – May 1813. Present at Talavera, Torres Vedras, Campo Mayor, Los Santos, Llerena and Salamanca. Accompanied by his wife on all his Peninsular campaigns especially at the battle of Salamanca. Also served in India 1822–1824 (in command of the Gujerat district of the Bombay Army). Prosecutor at Court Martial of Colonel Brereton after the Bristol riots 1831. Knighted 1831. MP for Ripon 1835–1837. Wrote *A military catechism for the use and instruction of young officers and non commissioned officers of cavalry*, 1806. MGS medal for Talavera and Salamanca. KCH. His entire military service was spent in the 4th Dragoons. Colonel 3rd Dragoon Guards 1 Jan 1839. Colonel 4th Lt Dragoons 24 Sep 1842.
REFERENCE: *Dictionary of National Biography. Royal Military Calendar, Vol 4, pp. 211–2. Gentleman's Magazine, Mar 1848, p. 308. Annual Register, 1848, Appx pp. 271–2.*

DALBIAC, Susanna Isabella
Memorial tablet: St Michael's Church, Kirklington, Yorkshire. (Photograph)

ENTOMBED ON THE WEST SIDE OF THE CHURCH YARD, LIE THE REMAINS OF / SUSANNA ISABELLA, THE WIFE OF MAJOR GENERAL DALBIAC, / ELDEST DAUGHTER OF / JOHN AND SUSANNA DALTON OF SLENINGFORD HALL, NEAR THIS PLACE. / SHE FULFILLED IN A PRE-EMINENT DEGREE ALL THE DUTIES WHICH BELONG / TO THE WIFE, THE MOTHER, THE DAUGHTER, AND THE FRIEND, / UNITING TO A MOST AFFECTIONATE DISPOSITION AND TO A FORTITUDE OF / MIND ALMOST WITHOUT PARALLEL, AN UNCOMPROMISING RECTITUDE OF / PURPOSE IN EVERY IMPORTANT ACT OF HER LIFE. / AMONGST NUMEROUS PROOFS OF SELF-DEVOTION SHE DISPLAYED THE / SINGULAR FIRMNESS OF ACCOMPANYING HER HUSBAND THROUGH SEVERAL / CAMPAIGNS, UNDER THE DUKE OF WELLINGTON, AND WAS PRESENT IN THE / BATTLE OF SALAMANCA ON THE 22D JULY 1812. / TO PERPETUATE THE MEMORY OF SO BELOVED AN OBJECT, A MOURNING / HUSBAND ERECTS THIS MONUMENT, A FAINT MEMORIAL OF HIS / VENERATION FOR HER VIRTUES, A FEEBLE TESTIMONY OF HIS GRIEF / FOR HER IRREPARABLE LOSS. / SHE DEPARTED THIS LIFE ON THE 25TH DAY OF JANRY 1829, / AGED 45 YEARS.

Accompanied her husband on all his Peninsular campaigns especially at the battle of Salamanca where she is reported to have scoured the battlefield searching for her husband amongst the dead and wounded. William Tomkinson mentions her in his diary and Sir William Napier in the *History of the War in the Peninsula* calls her 'an English lady of gentle disposition and possessing a very delicate frame – she had braved the dangers and endured the privation of two campaigns, with the patient fortitude which belongs only to her sex: and in the battle, forgetful of everything but that strong affection which had so long supported her, she rode deep amidst the enemy's fire, trembling yet irresistibly impelled forward by feelings more imperious than horror, more piercing than the fear of death.'

DALGAIRNES, William

Lieutenant. 55th (Westmoreland) Regiment of Foot.
Grave: Candie Cemetery, St Peter Port, Guernsey, Channel Islands. (No longer extant: Grave number B118Z)

Ensign 17th Foot 7 Sep 1809. Lt 7th Foot 5 Jul 1810. Lt and Adjt 55th Foot 8 Dec 1813.
    Served in the Peninsula with 1/7th Aug – Oct 1810, 2/7th Nov 1810 – Jul 1811 and 1/7th Dec 1812 – Nov 1813. Present at Busaco, Pombal, Condeixa, Olivencia, first siege of Badajoz, Albuera, Vittoria and Pyrenees. Also served in Holland 1814 as Adjutant of 55th Foot (present at Bergen-op-Zoom where he was wounded and taken prisoner). MGS medal for Busaco, Albuera, Vittoria and Pyrenees. Half pay 24 Jul 1817. Died in Guernsey 26 Feb 1869.

DALLAS, Alexander Robert Charles

Assistant Commissary General, Commissariat Department.
Low monument: Holy Trinity Churchyard, Wonston, Hampshire. (Photograph)

SACRED TO THE MEMORY OF / THE REVᴰ ALEXANDER ROBERT CHARLES DALLAS M.A. / FORTY ONE YEARS RECTOR OF THIS PARISH / WHO DIED DECEMBER 12TH 1869 AGED 78 YEARS.

Memorial tablet: St Patrick's Cathedral, Dublin, Ireland. (Photograph)

SACRED / TO THE MEMORY OF / ALEXANDER ROBERT CHARLES DALLAS, / ONE OF IRELAND'S BEST FRIENDS; / WHO DIED DECEMBER 12TH 1869, AGED 78 YEARS. / IN EARLY LIFE A BRAVE PENINSULAR OFFICER, / IN LATER YEARS RECTOR OF WONSTON, / AND CHAPLAIN TO THE BISHOP OF WINCHESTER, / SERVED WITH EQUAL FIDELITY, HIS COUNTRY, / HIS CHURCH, AND HIS GOD. / LIKE HIM WHOSE NAME THE CATHEDRAL BEARS, / HAVING VISITED IRELAND'S SHORES, / EVER AFTER PRAYED AND WORKED FOR IRELAND'S SPIRI-TUAL WELFARE, / AND NOT IN VAIN; / FOR THROUGH GOD'S BLESSING ON HIS LABOURS, / MANY WERE LED TO RENOUNCE THE INNOVATIONS OF ERROR, / AND TO HOLD FAST IN ALL ITS SCRIPTURAL PURITY, / THAT ANCIENT FAITH WHICH, NEAR THIS VERY SPOT / Sᵀ PATRICK PREACHED OF OLD. / READER, WOULD YOU HONOUR THE MEMORY OF THIS GOOD MAN? / LET THEN PRAYER OF HIS LIFE BE YOURS: – / "O GOD, FOR CHRIST'S SAKE, GIVE ME THE HOLY SPIRIT!"

Memorial: Christ Church, Clifden, Connemara, County Galway, Ireland. Inscription not recorded.

Dep Asst Comm Gen 5 Jun 1810. Asst Comm Gen 1 Jul 1814.
    Served in the Peninsula Sep 1810 – Apr 1814. Present at Cadiz, Barrosa and Vittoria. Present at Waterloo. MGS medal for Barrosa and Vittoria. Retired in 1815 and studied to become a lawyer, but decided to enter the Church. Became Vicar of Wonston in 1828 where he remained for forty one years. Founded the Society for Irish Church Missions in 1843. By the time of his death 21 churches, 49 schools, 12 parsonages and 4 orphanages had been built in Ireland. Wrote extensively on church and religious

matters. Cousin of Ensign Charles Robert King Dallas 32nd Foot and of Lord Byron. Edited *Correspondence of Lord Byron with a friend, including letters to his mother, written from Portugal, Spain, Greece and the shores of the Mediterranean, in 1809, 1810, 1811, 3 volumes, 1825.*
REFERENCE: *Dictionary of National Biography. Dallas, Anne Briscoe, Incidents in the life and ministry of the Rev. Alex. R. C. Dallas, Rector of Wonston, 3rd edition 1873. (Includes his experiences in Spain and at Waterloo).*

DALLAS, Charles Robert King
Ensign. 32nd (Cornwall) Regiment of Foot.
Brass memorial tablet: St John the Evangelist Church, Farncombe, Surrey. (Photograph)

TO THE LOVED MEMORY OF / CHARLES ROBERT KING DALLAS / FOR TWENTY ONE YEARS RECTOR OF THIS PARISH / BORN IN JAMAICA JUNE 8TH 1794. DIED AT SHACKLEFORD JAN^Y 1ST 1881 / FORMERLY AN ENSIGN IN THE 32ND REG^T AND WOUNDED AT QUATRE BRAS / RECTOR OF STRATTON HANTS FROM 1834 – 1859 / THIS TABLET IS PLACED OVER HIS GRAVE BY HIS NEPHEWS AND NIECES

Ensign 23 Mar 1815.
  Present at Quatre Bras where he was severely wounded. Half pay by 1820. On leaving the service, he entered the church and became Curate at Micheldever, Hampshire, Vicar of Stratton, Hampshire 1834–1859 and of Farncombe, Surrey 1859–1878. Cousin of Asst Commissary General Alexander R. C. Dallas and of Lord Byron.

DALLAS, Robert William
Captain. York Chasseurs.
Memorial tablet: Holy Trinity Church, Tunbridge Wells, Kent. (M.I)

"ROBERT WILLIAM DALLAS, ONLY SON OF THE LATE RIGHT HONOURABLE LORD CHIEF JUSTICE DALLAS, MAJOR IN THE 9TH REGIMENT OF FOOT, SERVED WALCHEREN AND PENINSULAR, DIED 11TH SEPTEMBER 1849 IN HIS 60TH YEAR, AT TUNBRIDGE WELLS, ERECTED BY HIS WIDOW."

Ensign 1 Sep 1808. Lt 13 Oct 1811. Capt York Chasseurs 15 Mar 1815. Capt 9th Foot 15 May 1817. Bt Major 10 Jan 1837.
  Served in the Peninsula with 1/9th Mar 1810 – Feb 1814. Present at Busaco, Fuentes d'Onoro, Castrejon, Salamanca, Villa Muriel, Osma, Vittoria, San Sebastian, Bidassoa, Nivelle and Nive where he was severely wounded 10 Dec 1813. Also served at Walcheren 1809. Half pay 1818. MGS medal for Busaco, Fuentes d'Onoro, Salamanca, Vittoria, San Sebastian, Nivelle and Nive.

DALLING, Edward
Lieutenant and Captain. Coldstream Regiment of Foot Guards.
Named on Memorial Panel VI for Fuentes D'Onoro: Royal Military Chapel, Wellington Barracks, London. (M.I.) (Destroyed by a Flying Bomb 1944)

Ensign 37th Foot 16 Apr 1793. Lt 30 Aug 1794. Capt-Lieut 31 Jan 1797. Lt and Capt Coldstream Guards 6 Dec 1799. Bt Major 25 Oct 1809.
  Served in the Peninsula Dec 1809 – Jul 1811. Present at Busaco and Fuentes d'Onoro. Died of fever 31 Jul 1811.

DALRYMPLE, Sir Adolphus John
Lieutenant Colonel. 60th (Royal American) Regiment of Foot.
Family Memorial tablet: St John the Baptist Church, Aldenham, Hertfordshire. (Photograph)

IN THE FAMILY VAULT / TO THE EAST OF THIS CHURCH / .... / ALSO OF / GEN: SIR ADOLPHUS JOHN DALRYMPLE, / SECOND AND LAST BARONET OF HIGH MARK, CO: WIGTON, / WHO WAS BORN 3RD OF FEBRUARY, 1784, / AND DIED AT DELROW HOUSE, 3RD OF MARCH, 1866.

Altar tomb: St John the Baptist Churchyard, Aldenham, Hertfordshire. (Photograph)

.... IN THE VAULT BENEATH LIE THE REMAINS OF / .... / ALSO OF / GEN SIR ADOLPHUS JOHN DALRYMPLE BART / OF DELROW HOUSE / WHO DIED 3RD OF MARCH 1866 / AGED 82 YEARS

Ensign 55th Foot 25 Oct 1799. Lt 37th Foot 12 Jun 1800. Lt 1st Dragoon Guards 5 Feb 1801. Capt 18th Dragoons 7 Jan 1803. Bt Major 15 Sep 1808. Major 19th Lt Dragoons 17 Nov 1808. Lt Colonel 60th Foot 1 Jun 1814. Bt Colonel 22 Jul 1830. Major General 23 Nov 1841. Lt General 11 Nov 1851. General 11 Apr 1860.
    Served in the Peninsula Aug – Oct 1808 (DAQMG and Military Secretary to his father Lt General Sir Hew Dalrymple) Also served in Malta, Naples and Sicily Jul 1803 – May 1806 (ADC to Sir James Craig). MP for Weymouth, Appleby, Haddington and Brighton 1817–1841. Edited the memoirs of his father *'Memoirs written by General Sir Hew Dalrymple'*, 1830.
REFERENCE: *Gentleman's Magazine, May 1866, p. 745.*

DALRYMPLE, Sir Hew Whiteford
Colonel. 57th (West Middlesex) Regiment of Foot.
Family Memorial tablet: St John the Baptist Church, Aldenham, Hertfordshire. (Photograph)

EAST OF THIS CHURCH IN A VAULT ARE DEPOSITED / THE MORTAL REMAINS OF / .... / ALSO OF / GENERAL SIR HEW WHITEFORD DALRYMPLE BART. / OF DELROW HOUSE, / WHO DIED APRIL 9TH 1830 IN THE 80TH YEAR OF HIS AGE. / ....

Ensign 31st Foot 3 Apr 1763. Lt 1766. Capt 1st Foot 14 Jul 1768. Major 77th Foot Dec 1777. Lt Colonel 68th Foot 21 Sep 1781. Bt Colonel 18 Nov 1790. Capt and Lt Colonel 1st Foot Guards 23 May 1783. Major General 3 Oct 1794. Lt Colonel 65th Foot 20 Oct 1796. Lt General 1 Jan 1801. General 1 Jan 1812.
    Served in the Peninsula Aug – Oct 1808 (in command of the Army in Portugal). Took part in the Convention of Cintra, the treaty by which the French would leave Portugal after the battles of Rolica and Vimeiro. Also served in Flanders 1793–1794 (present at Famars, Valenciennes and Dunkirk), Guernsey and Gibraltar. Father of Lt Colonel Adolphus Dalrymple 60th Foot and Lt Colonel Leighton Dalrymple 15th Lt Dragoons.
REFERENCE: *Dictionary of National Biography. Gentleman's Magazine, Jun 1830, p. 558. Dalrymple, Sir Hew Whiteford, Memoir written by General Sir Hew Dalrymple, of his proceedings as connected with the affairs of Spain, and the commencement of the Peninsular War, edited by Sir Adolphus J. Dalrymple, 1830.*

DALRYMPLE, Leighton Cathcart
Lieutenant Colonel. 15th (King's) Regiment of Light Dragoons.
Family Memorial tablet: St John the Baptist Church, Aldenham, Hertfordshire. (Photograph)

EAST OF THIS CHURCH IN A VAULT ARE DEPOSITED / THE MORTAL REMAINS OF / LT COL: LEIGHTON CATHCART DALRYMPLE, / COMPANION OF THE BATH, / AND SECOND SON OF

SIR HEW WHITEFOORD DALRYMPLE, BART / AND FRANCES HIS WIFE. / HE DIED ON THE 6TH OF JUNE 1820. / ....

Altar tomb: St John the Baptist Churchyard, Aldenham, Hertfordshire. (Photograph)

.... / AND LEIGHTON CATHCART DALRYMPLE SECOND SON OF SIR HEW WHITE-FOORD DALRYMPLE / LIEUTENANT COLONEL OF / THE 15TH KING'S HUSSARS / AT THE HEAD OF WHICH GALLANT REGIMENT / HE HIGHLY DISTINGUISHED HIMSELF AT THE BATTLE OF WATERLOO / WHERE HE HAD THREE HORSES KILL'D UNDER HIM / AND AFTER RECEIVING TWO CONTUSIONS / TOWARD THE CLOSE OF THAT MEMORABLE DAY / HIS LEFT LEG WAS CARRIED OFF BY A CANNON BALL. / HE DEPARTED THIS LIFE AT DELROW HOUSE / THE 6TH OF JUNE 1820 AGED THIRTY FIVE YEARS. / DEEPLY DEPLORED BY HIS PARENTS, HIS FAMILY / AND ALL WHO WERE ACQUAINTED WITH HIS VIRTUES..................

Ensign 55th Foot 10 Jul 1800. Cornet 3rd Dragoon Guards 1 May 1801. Lt 25 Nov 1802. Lt 15th Lt Dragoons 17 Dec 1802. Capt 29 Dec 1804. Major 14 Mar 1812. Lt Colonel 16 Dec 1813.
    Served in the Peninsula Nov 1808 – Jan 1809 and Mar – Apr 1814. Present at Sahagun, Caçabellos, Corunna, Tarbes and Toulouse. Gold Medal for Toulouse. Present at Waterloo in command of his regiment, where he was severely wounded (three horses were killed under him, his left leg blown off and awarded pension of £300 per annum). CB. Brother of Lt Colonel Adolphus Dalrymple 60th Foot and second son of Colonel Sir Hew Dalrymple 57th Foot.

DALRYMPLE, Robert
Lieutenant and Captain. 3rd Regiment of Foot Guards.
Named on Memorial Panel VI for Talavera: Royal Military Chapel, Wellington Barracks, London. (M.I.) (Destroyed by a Flying Bomb 1944)

Ensign 1801. Lt and Capt 24 Mar 1803.
    Served in the Peninsula Mar – Jul 1809. Present at Douro and Talavera where he was killed 28 Jul 1809. Also served in Egypt 1801 and the Baltic 1807.

DALTON, George
Lieutenant. Royal Engineers.
Grave: St John the Baptist Church, Hillingdon, Middlesex, London. (M.I.)

"CAPT GEORGE DALTON OF THE ROYAL ENGINEERS, DIED 10 JUNE 1854 IN THE 60TH YEAR OF HIS AGE."

Named on the Regimental Memorial: Rochester Cathedral, Rochester, Kent. (Photograph)

2nd Lt 1 Jan 1814. Lt 1 Aug 1814. 2nd Capt 19 Aug 1835.
    Served in the Netherlands and in France with the Army of Occupation 1815–1816. Retired on full pay 30 Feb 1841. Died at Uxbridge 10 Jun 1854.

DALZELL, Robert Alexander
Captain. 60th (Royal American) Regiment of Foot.
Memorial tablet: St Mary's Church, Storrington, Sussex. (Photograph)

SACRED / TO THE MEMORY OF / ROBERT ALEXANDER DALZELL, / EARL OF CARNWATH / BARON DALZELL AND LIBBERTON / A BARONET OF NOVA SCOTIA AND / A LIEUTENANT GENERAL IN HER MAJESTY'S SERVICE: / BORN 13TH FEBRUARY 1768, / DIED 1ST JANUARY

1839. / THIS TABLET IS PLACED HERE AS A TRIBUTE , OF / AFFECTION TO THE MEMORY OF THEIR DESERVEDLY / BELOVED AND LAMENTED FATHER, BY HIS / SORROWING CHILDREN, WHO DESIRE ALSO TO / RECORD THEREON, THEIR AFFECTIONATE / REMEMBRANCE OF ONE OF THE FONDEST, / AND BEST OF MOTHERS. / (VERSE)

Memorial: Royal Military Chapel, Wellington Barracks, London. (M.I.) (Destroyed by a Flying Bomb 1944)

"LIEUT.-GENERAL ROBERT ALEXANDER DALZELL, TENTH EARL OF CARNWATH. / BORN 18TH FEBRUARY, 1768; DIED 7TH JANUARY, 1839. / SOME YEARS MAJOR OF BRIGADE; ASSISTANT ADJUTANT-GENERAL; PRESENT AT THE BATTLE OF CORUNNA; / PLACED TO HIS MEMORY BY HIS SON, FOURTEENTH EARL OF CARNWATH, LATE BENGAL ARTILLERY".

Note discrepancy in date of death on Royal Military Chapel memorial. (Should be 1st January 1839).

Bt Major 1 Jan 1798. Lt and Capt 1st Foot Guards 2 May 1800. Bt Lt Colonel 25 Sep 1803. Bt Colonel 1 Jan 1812. Capt 60th Foot 24 Sep 1812. Major General 4 Jun 1814. Lt General 22 Jul 1830.
    Served in the Peninsula Oct 1808 – Jan 1809. Present at Corunna. Also served at Walcheren 1809 (Judge Advocate General) and Ireland (DAG).
REFERENCE: *Gentleman's Magazine, Feb 1839, pp. 208–9.*

DAMER, Hon George Lionel Dawson see DAWSON, Hon George Lionel

DAMPIER, Lud Westley
Captain. 40th (2nd Somersetshire) Regiment of Foot.
Low monument with hipped top: Abbey Cemetery, Bath, Somerset. (Photograph)

SACRED TO THE MEMORY OF / LUD WESTLEY DAMPIER / LATE CAPT. IN HER MAJESTY'S 40TH REGIMENT / AND MAJOR IN THE 1ST SOMERSET MILITIA. / DIED AT BATH APRIL 25TH 1850 AGED 68 YEARS.

Ensign 8 Aug 1801. Lt 1 Feb 1803. Capt 22 Dec 1803.
    Served in the Peninsula Aug 1808 – Jun 1811. Present at Rolica, Vimeiro, Redinha and first siege of Badajoz. Resigned Jul 1811. Later served in the militia becoming a Major in the 1st Somerset Militia. MGS medal for Rolica and Vimeiro.

DANCE, Sir Charles Webb
Captain. 23rd Regiment of Light Dragoons.
Memorial tablet: St Peter and St Paul Church, Bishop's Hull, Taunton, Somerset. (Photograph)

IN MEMORY OF / COL. SIR CHARLES WEBB DANCE, K.H. / LATE OF THE 2ND REGIMENT OF LIFE GUARDS / WHO DIED AT BARR HOUSE IN THIS PARISH / 13 NOVEMBER 1844, AGED 58 YEARS. / IN EARLY LIFE HE SERVED IN THE 23RD LIGHT DRAGOONS / AT THE BATTLE OF TALAVERA, AND WATERLOO WHERE / HE WAS WOUNDED AND DURING SEVERAL CAMPAIGNS / OF THE ARMY UNDER THE DUKE OF WELLINGTON / IN SPAIN, PORTUGAL, FRANCE AND THE NETHERLANDS.

Cornet 10th Lt Dragoons 7 Sep 1804. Lt 23rd Dragoons 5 Sep 1805. Capt 9 Apr 1807. Bt Major 20 Jun 1816. Major and Lt Colonel 2nd Life Guards 24 Jul 1816. Bt Lt Colonel 27 Mar 1817. Bt Colonel 10 Jan 1837. Portuguese Army: Major 6th Cavalry.
    Served in the Peninsula with 23rd Lt Dragoons Jun – Nov 1809, with Staff Nov 1809 – Jun 1810 (ADC

to General Slade) and with Portuguese Army Jul 1810 – Nov 1811. Present at Talavera (his horse shot from under him, and nearly killed when a musket ball went through his helmet). The regiment returned to England after Talavera, but Dance remained in Portugal and commanded two squadrons of Portuguese Cavalry under Beresford. Recalled to England in 1811 to rejoin 23rd Lt Dragoons. Present at Waterloo where he was wounded. Knighted by George IV 1821. Retired in 1822. KH 1836.

REFERENCE: *Gentleman's Magazine, Jan 1845, p. 99. Annual Register, 1844, Appx p. 282.*

DANIEL, Robert

Lieutenant. 30th (Cambridgeshire) Regiment of Foot.
Ledger stone: Kensal Green Cemetery, London. (10373/41/2). (Photograph)

SACRED / TO THE MEMORY OF / ROBERT DANIEL ESQUIRE / WHO AFTER LONG AND DISTIN-GUISHED / SERVICES TO HIS COUNTRY / IN THE CAMPAIGN IN EGYPT / THE PENINSULA AND AT WATERLOO / AS AN OFFICER OF / H. M. 30TH REGIMENT / DEPARTED THIS LIFE / ON THE 7TH DAY OF AUGUST 1852 / IN / THE 82ND YEAR OF HIS AGE / ....

Ensign 21 Sep 1809. Lt 15 Jul 1811. Lt 59th Foot Aug 1820.

Served in the Peninsula Jun 1810 – Dec 1813. Present at Cadiz (promoted Ensign from Quartermaster Sergeant), Torres Vedras and Sabugal. Present at Quatre Bras and Waterloo where he was wounded. Also served in Egypt 1801, Netherlands 1814 (present at Antwerp) and India 1817–1818 (present in the Pindari War).

In 1814 sailed from the Peninsula on the transport ship *Queen* with 466 men, women and children, among them his wife and five children. On 14 Jan 1814 arrived in Falmouth but was caught in a gale and the ship wrecked on the rocks. 363 people were drowned including Daniel's wife and all his children.

DANIEL, Catherine

Headstone: Mylor Churchyard, Cornwall. (M.I.)

"IN MEMORY OF CATHERINE, WIFE OF LIEUT. ROBERT DANIEL, 30TH REGT. ALSO THEIR CHILDREN VIZ. MARGARET, ELEANOR, WILLIAM, ROBERT AND EDWARD ALEXANDER, WHO UNHAPPILY PERISHED IN THE WRECK OF THE 'QUEEN' TRANSPORT ON THE AWFUL MORNING OF THE 14TH JAN 1814. LEAVING AN UNFORTUNATE HUSBAND AND FATHER TO LAMENT THEIR LOSS TO THE END OF HIS EXISTENCE."

DANSEY, Charles Cornwallis

2nd Captain. Royal Artillery.
Interred in Catacomb B (v200 c11) Kensal Green Cemetery, London.

2nd Lt 19 Jul 1803. 1st Lt 12 Sep 1803. 2nd Capt 1 Oct 1809. Capt 29 Jul 1825. Bt Major 22 Jul 1830. Lt Col 10 Jan 1837. Col 9 Nov 1846.

Served in the Peninsula Jan 1812 – Apr 1814. Present at Badajoz, Salamanca, Madrid, Burgos (wounded), Osma, Vittoria, Tolosa, San Sebastian, Bidassoa, Nivelle, Nive, Adour and Bayonne. Present at Waterloo where he was severely wounded serving with the 2nd Rocket Troop. CB. MGS medal for Badajoz, Salamanca, Vittoria, San Sebastian, Nivelle and Nive.

Also served at the siege of Ischia 1809 and the Ionian Islands 1810. Chief Fire Master, Royal Laboratory Woolwich Aug 1839 – Dec 1846. Died 21 Jul 1853 aged 66 years.

REFERENCE: *Glover, Gareth, ed., The letters of 2nd Captain Charles Dansey, Royal Artillery, 1806–1813, 2006.*

D'ARCEY, Edward
Lieutenant. 43rd (Monmouthshire) Light Infantry Regiment of Foot.
Box tomb: Officers' Graveyard, Royal Hospital, Kilmainham, Dublin, Ireland. (Photograph)

"THIS TABLET IS ERECTED BY THE YOUNGEST SURVIVING CHILD, CHARLOTTE DARCEY, TO THE MEMORY OF HER BELOVED PARENTS ELLEN DARCEY, WHO DIED THE 18TH MARCH 1834, AND CAPTAIN EDWARD DARCEY, LATE THE 43RD LIGHT INFANTRY, WHO DEPARTED THIS LIFE 25TH DECEMBER 1848."

From East Suffolk Militia. Ensign 43rd Foot 18 Apr 1809. Lt 22 Aug 1810. Capt 6th Royal Veteran Battalion 3 Aug 1815.

Served in the Peninsula with 1/43rd Apr 1813 – Apr 1814. Present at Vittoria, Pyrenees, Bidassoa, Nivelle (wounded), Nive and Tarbes. Also served in North America 1814–1815 (present at New Orleans (severely wounded, had both legs amputated and awarded pension of £200 per annum). Later Captain of Invalids at Kilmainham Hospital, Dublin. MGS medal for Vittoria, Pyrenees, Nivelle and Nive.

D'ARCY, George Pitt
Captain. 39th (Dorsetshire) Regiment of Foot.
Buried at Parramatta, New South Wales, Australia. (Burial record)

Lt 1798. Capt 9 Jul 1803. Bt Major 22 Nov 1813.

Served in the Peninsula with 1/39th Oct 1811 – Apr 1814. Present at Vittoria, Pyrenees, Nivelle, Nive, Garris, Orthes, Aire and Toulouse. Also served in North America 1814–1815 and Australia 1826. Retired from the army the same year and settled in Australia. Magistrate for Paramatta 1829. Buried at Parramatta 23 Jul 1849.

DARLEY, Edward
Major. 62nd (Wiltshire) Regiment of Foot.
Chest tomb: Kensal Green Cemetery, London. Inscription illegible. (5222/131/5). (Photograph)

Ensign 49th Foot 21 Nov 1792. Lt 30 Apr 1794. Capt Royal Dublin Regt 13 Dec 1794. Capt 62nd Foot 1797. Major 2 May 1811. Bt Lt Colonel 1 Jan 1812 Major 58th Foot 18 Sep 1817. Bt Colonel 22 Jul 1830. Major General 28 Jun 1838. Lt General 11 Nov 1851.

Served in the Peninsula Oct 1813 – Apr 1814. Present at Nivelle, Nive and Bayonne. Returned with the regiment to Ireland 1814, but in July 1815 they returned to France to assist the Army of Occupation until Jan 1816. Also served in the West Indies 1805 (present at St Lucia), Egypt 1807 and West Indies 1818. MGS medal for Nivelle and Nive. Died 1854 aged 79.
REFERENCE: *Royal Military Calendar, Vol 4, pp. 384–5.*

DARLING, Ralph
Lieutenant Colonel. 51st (2nd Yorkshire West Riding) Light Infantry.
Low monument: St Andrew's Old Churchyard, Hove, Sussex. (Photograph)

GENERAL SIR RALPH DARLING KNIGHT GRAND CROSS OF THE ROYAL HANOVERIAN GUELPHIC ORDER CONFERRED ON HIM BY HIS MAJESTY KING WILLIAM THE FOURTH AND COLONEL OF THE 41ST REGIMENT WHO DEPARTED THIS LIFE OF LONG COURSE OF PUBLIC SERVICE HAVING FOR A SERIES OF YEARS ADMINISTERED THE CIVIL GOVERNMENT AND ALSO HELD THE COMMAND OF THE TROOPS OF TWO OF HER MAJESTIES COLONIES AND THEIR DEPENDENTS DIED ON THE 2ND DAY OF APRIL 1858 AGED 83 YEARS. (REMAINDER OF INSCRIPTION ILLEGIBLE)

Ensign 45th Foot 15 May 1793. Lt 2 Sep 1795. Lt and Adjt 15th Foot 6 Jan 1796. Capt 27th Foot 6 Sep 1796. Major 4th West India Regt 2 Feb 1800. Lt Colonel 69th Foot 17 Jul 1801. Lt Colonel 51st Foot 8 May 1806. Colonel 25 Jul 1810. Major General 4 Jun 1813. Lt General 27 May 1825. General 23 Nov 1841.

Served in the Peninsula Oct 1808 – Jan 1809. He resigned his staff appointment as Principal AAG and took command of 51st Foot in the Peninsula. Present at Lugo and Corunna. Gold Medal for Corunna. Also served in the West Indies 1793–1801 (present in Grenada with 45th Foot in expedition to capture Trinidad and Surinam and Saints Islands), Walcheren 1809 (DAG. Present at Flushing) and Mauritius (Head of Staff to command the troops 1816–1823 where he dealt actively in trying to suppress the slave trade). Governor in Chief of New South Wales and Van Diemen's Land 1825–1831 where he encouraged expeditions into the interior. The Darling River was named after him. GCH. Colonel 90th Foot 9 Oct 1823. Colonel 41st Foot 26 Sep 1837. Colonel 69th Foot 5 Feb 1848. Brother in law of Capt Henry Dumaresq 9th Foot and Lt William Dumaresq Royal Staff Corps.
REFERENCE: *Dictionary of National Biography. Australian Dictionary of Biography. Gentleman's Magazine, May 1858, p. 568. Annual Register, 1858, Appx, p. 398.*

DASHWOOD, Charles
Captain and Lieutenant Colonel. 3rd Regiment of Foot Guards.
Family vault: St Mary the Virgin Church, Kidlington, Oxfordshire. (Burial register)

CHARLES DASHWOOD ESQ. LATE LIEUT COL: 3RD GUARDS / 30 APRIL 1832, AGED 44.

Ensign 8 Dec 1803. Lt and Capt 17 Apr 1806. Bt Major 26 Aug 1813. Capt and Lt Colonel 25 Dec 1813.
Served in the Peninsula Aug 1808 – Jan 1809 (ADC to General C. Stewart), Mar 1809 – Apr 1812 (Feb – May 1810 DAAG 4th Divison), Nov 1812 – Apr 1814 (May – Sep 1813 DAAG Cavalry Division) and Oct 1813 – Apr 1814 (DAAG 1st Division). Present at Sahagun, Benevente, Douro, Talavera, Busaco, Fuentes d'Onoro, Ciudad Rodrigo, Badajoz, Vittoria, Pyrenees, Nivelle, Nive, Adour and Bayonne. Gold Medal for Nive. CB. Present at Waterloo where he was wounded. Also served at Hanover 1805.

DAUBENEY, Henry
Lieutenant Colonel. 84th (York and Lancaster) Regiment of Foot.
Memorial tablet: Christ Church, Bath, Somerset. (Photograph)

IN MEMORY OF / HENRY DAUBENEY ESQUIRE, / A LIEUTENANT GENERAL IN THE ARMY, / COLONEL OF THE 80TH REGIMENT OF FOOT, / AND KNIGHT OF THE HANOVERIAN GUELPHIC ORDER. / A BRAVE SOLDIER. / A GOOD CITIZEN. / AND A STEADY SUPPORTER OF THE CHARITIES / OF THIS CITY. / HE DIED AT ROME ON THE 10TH APRIL 1855 / AGED 71 YEARS. / ALSO ELIZABETH HIS WIFE / .... / THEIR REMAINS ARE DEPOSITED IN THE / PROTESTANT CEMETERIES OF ROME AND FLORENCE. / (VERSE)

Column: Protestant Cemetery, Rome, Italy. Inscription illegible. (Old Zone Grave number 415). (Photograph)

Ensign 8 Jul 1795. Lt 21 Oct 1795. Capt 7 Sep 1797. Major 26 May 1808. Lt Colonel 11 Dec 1813. Bt Colonel 22 Jul 1830. Major General 23 Nov 1841. Lt General 11 Nov 1851.
Served at Walcheren 1809 (present at the siege of Flushing). Also served in the Cape of Good Hope 1795–1798 and India 1798–1805 (present in the Mahratta Wars – assault and capture of Kurree and the Gujerat campaigns 1802–1804). Returned to India in 1811 with 1st battalion. After he was promoted Lt Colonel, he obtained leave to join the 2nd battalion in France but did not arrive in time to be present at Waterloo. Half pay 21 Nov 1822. Colonel 80th Foot 31 Jan 1850.
REFERENCE: *Gentleman's Magazine, Jul 1853, p. 655. Royal Military Calendar, Vol 5, p. 11.*

DAVENPORT, Edmund
Lieutenant. 82nd (Prince of Wales's Volunteers) Regiment of Foot.
Named on the Regimental Memorial: St Multose Church, Kinsale, Ireland. (Photograph)

SACRED / TO THE MEMORY OF LIEUTS / EDMUND DAVENPORT, EDWIN HARDING / ASST SURGEON HENRY RANDOLPH SCOTT / AND HIS WIFE / EIGHT SERJEANTS, NINE CORPORALS, / ONE HUNDRED AND FORTY PRIVATES, / THIRTEEN WOMEN AND SIXTEEN CHILDREN / OF THE 82D REGT, WHO PERISHED / ON BOARD THE BOADICEA TRANSPORT, / WRECKED ON GARRETSTOWN STRAND / ON THE NIGHT OF THE 30TH JANY 1816 / THIS TRIBUTE IS ERECTED / BY THE OFFICERS OF THE REGT.

Buried in Old Court Burial Ground, Kinsale, Ireland.

Ensign 87th Foot 6 Oct 1807. Lt 17 Mar 1808. Portuguese Army: Capt 18th Line Apr – Oct 1814. Served in the Peninsula with 82nd Foot Feb 1811 – Mar 1814 and with Portuguese Army from Apr 1814. Present at Barrosa, Tarifa, Burgos and Nivelle. Served in France with the Army of Occupation. On 8 Dec 1815 the regiment marched from Paris en route to Calais to embark for England. Landed in Dover on 3 Jan 1816 and were immediately re-shipped for Ireland on 30 Jan on the transport ship *Boadicea*. The ship was wrecked at Kinsale off the coast of Ireland and of 289 people on board only 102 were saved.

DAVIDSON, Benjamin
Private. 79th (Cameron Highlanders) Regiment of Foot.
Ledger stone: Old St Peter's Churchyard, Thurso, Caithness, Scotland. (Photograph)

IN LOVING MEMORY / OF / BENJAMIN DAVIDSON / BORN JUNE 16TH 1793 / FOUGHT AT WATERLOO JUNE 18TH 1815 / DIED OCTOBER 16TH 1875.

Pte 4 Jan 1812.
   Served at Quatre Bras and Waterloo in Captain William Marshall's Light Company where he was wounded and with the Army of Occupation until 1818. Discharged at Thurso 1821 aged 29 years.

DAVIDSON, James
Lieutenant and Adjutant. 27th (Inniskilling) Regiment of Foot.
Memorial in walled enclosure: St Peter's Churchyard, Thurso, Scotland. (M.I.)

"JOHN DAVIDSON, BUCKIE, 20 MARCH 1820 .... HIS SON JAMES LT AND ADJUTANT 27TH REGT FELL AT SALAMANCA, JULY 1812 AGED 27."

Ensign 36th Foot 31 Dec 1805. Lt 27th Foot 15 Jan 1807.
   Served in the Peninsula with 3/27th Nov 1808 – Jul 1812. Present at Busaco, Redinha, Olivencia, first siege of Badajoz, Badajoz (wounded) and Castrejon where he was killed in the Salamanca campaign 18 Jul 1812. Brother of Capt Sinclair Davidson 79th Foot who was killed at Fuentes D'Onoro May 1811.

DAVIDSON, James
Private. 29th (Worcestershire) Regiment of Foot.
Headstone: Migvie Churchyard, near Huntly, Aberdeenshire, Scotland. (Photograph)

ERECTED / BY / JAMES DAVIDSON / PARKNOOK / TO THE MEMORY OF / HIS AFFECTIONATE WIFE / DOROTHEA TAYLOR / WHO DIED 23D JUNE, 1836 IN THE / 51ST YEAR OF HER AGE. / JAMES DAVIDSON SERVED 21 YEARS / IN 29TH FOOT. STOOD IN THE CHIEF / BATTLES OF THE PENINSULA / AND DIED 22ND MARCH 1863 / AGED 82.

Served in the Peninsula Aug 1808 – Nov 1811. Present at Rolica, Vimeiro, Talavera (wounded) and Albuera. MGS medal for Rolica, Vimeiro, Talavera and Albuera.

DAVIDSON, Sinclair
Captain. 79th (Cameron Highlanders) Regiment of Foot.
Memorial in walled enclosure: St Peter's Churchyard, Thurso, Caithness, Scotland. (M.I.)

"JOHN DAVIDSON, BUCKIE, 20TH MARCH 1820. .... ELDEST SON SINCLAIR 79TH HIGHLANDERS MORTALLY WOUNDED FUENTES D'ONORO MAY 1811."

Caithness Highlanders. Ensign 79th Foot 22 Jul 1800. Lt 31 Mar 1804. Adjutant 13 Aug 1807. Capt 14 Feb 1811.
    Served in the Peninsula Aug 1808 – Jan 1809 and Jan 1810 – May 1811. Present at Corunna, Cadiz, Busaco, Foz d'Arouce and Fuentes d'Onoro (severely wounded and died of his wounds 7 May 1811). Also served in Egypt 1801, the Baltic 1807–1808 and Walcheren 1809. Brother of Lt James Davidson 27th Foot who was killed at Castrejon 1812.

DAVIES, David
Lieutenant and Adjutant. 32nd (Cornwall) Regiment of Foot.
Buried in Nunhead Cemetery, London. (No longer extant: Grave number 3140 Sq 81)

Ensign 16 Apr 1807. Lt 18 Jun 1807. Adjutant 16 Mar 1809. Capt 19 Jul 1815.
    Served in the Peninsula Oct 1808 – Jan 1809 and Dec 1812 – Apr 1814. Present at Corunna, Pyrenees, Bidassoa, Nivelle and Nive. Present at Quatre Bras (wounded) and Waterloo (severely wounded). MGS medal for Corunna, Pyrenees, Nivelle and Nive. Half pay 24 Jul 1828. Died 6 Oct 1854 aged 69.

DAVIES, Edward
Private. 1st Regiment of Foot Guards.
Ledger stone: St David's Churchyard, Newton, Montgomeryshire, Wales. (Photograph)

SACRED / TO THE MEMORY OF / EDWARD DAVIES / LATE OF THE GRENADIER GUARDS / DIED 10TH SEPT 1858 / AGED 72. / THE WARRIOR IS AT REST.

Pte 18 Mar 1807.
    Served in the Peninsula Oct 1808 – Jan 1809 and Oct 1812 – Apr 1814. Present at Corunna, Bidassoa, Nivelle, Nive and Bayonne. MGS medal for Corunna, Nivelle and Nive.

DAVIES, Francis John
Lieutenant and Captain. 1st Regiment of Foot Guards.
Memorial: Royal Military Chapel, Wellington Barracks, London. (M.I.) (Destroyed by a Flying Bomb 1944)

"IN MEMORY OF COLONEL THOMAS HENRY HASTINGS DAVIES; GENERAL FRANCIS JOHN DAVIES, COLONEL OF THE 67TH REGIMENT; .... / GENERAL F. J. DAVIES, BORN MAY 1ST, 1791; DIED DEC. 4, 1874; SERVED IN THE 52ND REGIMENT DURING THE RETREAT ON CORUNNA, AT FUENTES D'ONOR, BADAJOS (WHERE HE WAS WOUNDED), SALAMANCA, VITTORIA, IN THE PYRENEES, AND IN THE GRENADIER GUARDS 1815 TO 1841. .... / PLACED BY THE LADY HAMPTON AND COLONEL H. F. DAVIES, GRENADIER GUARDS."

Ensign 52nd Foot 3 Feb 1808. Lt 26 Jan 1809. Capt 3rd Ceylon Regt 12 Aug 1813. Capt 69th Foot 17 Feb 1814. Lt and Capt 1st Foot Guards 13 Apr 1815. Capt and Lt Colonel 30 Apr 1827. Colonel 23 Nov 1841. Major General 20 Jun 1854. Lt General 14 Aug 1859. General 14 Jan 1866.

Served in the Peninsula with 1/52nd Aug – Dec 1808, 2/52nd Jan 1809 and Mar – Jul 1811, Aug 1811 – Mar 1812 (on Staff as extra ADC to Major General Dunlop) and 1/52nd Mar 1812 – Sep 1813. Present at Vigo, Sabugal, Fuentes d'Onoro, Badajoz (wounded), Salamanca, San Millan, Vittoria and Pyrenees. Retired on half pay 18 May 1841. Colonel 67th Foot 15 Jan 1858. MGS medal for Fuentes d'Onoro, Badajoz, Salamanca, Vittoria and Pyrenees. Brother of Lt and Capt Thomas Henry Hastings Davies 1st Foot Guards.

REFERENCE: *Household Brigade Journal, 1874, p. 316.*

DAVIES, John

Private. 52nd (Oxfordshire) Light Infantry Regiment of Foot.
Headstone: St Mary's Churchyard, Llanllwch, Carmarthenshire, Wales. (Photograph)

IN MEMORY OF / JOHN DAVIES OF LLANLLWCH. / PENSIONER, / DIED AUGUST 15TH 1858 AGED 82. / FOUGHT AT / CORRUNNA, CUIDAD RODRIGO, / BADAJOS, SALAMANCA, &C &C / TRADEL INE VILAE.

Served in the Peninsula 1808 – Jan 1809 and 1811–1814.
  Present at Corunna, Ciudad Rodrigo, Badajoz and Salamanca. Served at Waterloo. MGS medal for Corunna, Ciudad Rodrigo, Badajoz and Salamanca.

DAVIES, Thomas

Colour Sergeant. 23rd (Royal Welch Fusiliers) Regiment of Foot.
Grave: Abbey Churchyard, Shrewsbury, Shropshire. (No longer extant). (M.I.)

"HERE LIES THE BODY OF THOMAS DAVIES, FIFTEEN YEARS SERJEANT IN THE ROYAL WELSH FUSILIERS, AND FIRST COLOUR SERJEANT OF THE SAME REGIMENT. AFTER TWENTY YEARS SERVICE IN VARIOUS COUNTRIES, AND BEING PRESENT AT ELEVEN GENERAL ACTIONS, HE RETIRED, ON THE PEACE, TO HIS NATIVE COUNTY, AND WAS APPOINTED BY HIS GENERAL, LORD HILL, WHOSE ORDERLY HE WAS AT THE FAMOUS BATTLE OF WATERLOO, FIRST KEEPER OF THE COLUMN IN THIS PARISH, AS A REWARD FOR HIS UNIFORM GOOD CONDUCT. HE DIED 15TH AUGUST 1820, AGED 41 YEARS, UNIVERSALLY ESTEEMED BY HIS NEIGHBOURS, FOR HIS RESPECTABLE AND QUIET DEMEANOUR. / DEATH DWELLS NOT ON THE TENTED FIELD ALONE: / ALL STATES THAT UNIVERSAL EMPIRE OWN: / DAVIES RETURNED FROM WAR WITH SCARCE A WOUND, / IN PEACE, AT HOME, AN EARLY GRAVE HE FOUND. / CHRISTIAN! LEARN HENCE THE END: PREPARE TO DIE, / AND SEEK BY FAITH THROUGH GRACE, A LIFE ON HIGH."

Pte 1795. Cpl 1798. Sgt 1800. Colour Sgt 1813.
  Served in the Peninsula with 1/23rd Dec 1810 – Apr 1814. Present at Albuera, Ciudad Rodrigo, Badajoz (wounded), Salamanca, Vittoria, Pyrenees, Orthes and Toulouse. Present at Waterloo in Capt Farmer's Company No 7 as Lord Hill's Orderly Sergeant. Also served at Hanover 1805, West Indies, Copenhagen 1807 and Walcheren 1809. After twenty years in the army he retired to Shropshire and on Lord Hill's recommendation became the Lodge Keeper to Lord Hill's column in Shrewsbury, which opened in 1816.

DAVIES, Thomas Henry Hastings

Lieutenant and Captain. 1st Regiment of Foot Guards.
Memorial tablet: St Mary the Virgin Church, Elmley Castle, Worcestershire. (Photograph)

TO THE MEMORY OF / COLONEL THOMAS HENRY HASTINGS DAVIES / OF ELMLEY PARK, IN THIS PARISH, / ELDEST SON OF THOMAS DAVIES ESQUIRE / AND GRANDSON OF THOMAS DAVIES ESQR OF NEWHOUSE, IN THE / COUNTY OF HEREFORD / DIED DECEMBER 11TH 1846,

AGED, 57. / HE SERVED UNDER THE DUKE OF WELLINGTON IN 52ND REG. & IN THE / 1ST FOOT GUARDS & WAS PRESENT AT THE BATTLES OF VIMEIRA, SABUGAL, / FUENTES D'ONOR, PYRENEES, NIVELLE, NIVE AND / WATERLOO, AND / LASTLY AT THE TAKING OF PERONNE WHERE HE COMMANDED THE STORMING PARTY. / HE REPRESENTED THE CITY OF WORCESTER IN PARLIAMENT FOR NEARLY 20 YEARS / AS A LIBERAL AND HONEST POLITICIAN. / HE WAS A BRAVE SOLDIER, A KIND FRIEND, AN AFFECTIONATE HUSBAND, AND / A PATIENT & RESIGNED SUFFERER DURING A SEVERE AND LINGERING AFFLICTION. / ………………..

Low monument: St Mary the Virgin Churchyard, Elmley Castle, Worcestershire. (Photograph)

IN THIS VAULT / ARE DEPOSITED THE REMAINS / OF / COLONEL T. H. H. DAVIES / OF ELMLEY PARK IN THIS PARISH / BORN JAN 27TH 1789 / DIED DEC 11TH 1846. / ………………..

Memorial: Royal Military Chapel, Wellington Barracks, London. (M.I.) (Destroyed by a Flying Bomb 1944)

"IN MEMORY OF COLONEL THOMAS HENRY HASTINGS DAVIES; GENERAL FRANCIS JOHN DAVIES, COLONEL OF THE 67TH REGIMENT; ……………….. / COLONEL T. H. H. DAVIES, BORN JAN. 27, 1789; DIED DEC.11, 1846; WAS IN THE 52ND REGIMENT AT VIMIERA; ON THE STAFF AT SABUGAL AND FUENTES D'ONOR; AND WITH THE 1ST GUARDS IN THE PYRENEES, AT NIVELLE, NIVE, PASSAGE OF THE ADOUR, BAYONNE, QUATRE BRAS, AND WATERLOO. / ……………….. / PLACED BY THE LADY HAMPTON AND COLONEL H. F. DAVIES, GRENADIER GUARDS."

Ensign 52nd Foot 2 Jun 1804. Lt 31 Jan 1805. Capt 4 Feb 1808. Lt and Capt 1st Foot Guards 7 Dec 1809. Capt and Lt Colonel 3 Jul 1815. Bt Colonel 10 Jan 1837.
    Served in the Peninsula with 2/52nd Aug 1808 – Jan 1809, with 1st Foot Guards Nov 1810 – Jul 1811 and Jul 1812 – Apr 1814 (ADC to Major General Dunlop Nov 1810 – Jul 1811). Present at Vimeiro, Vigo, Cadiz, Sabugal, Fuentes D'Onoro, Bidassoa, Nivelle, Nive, Adour and Bayonne. Present at Waterloo, the siege of Peronne (commanded the storming party) and with the Army of Occupation. Also served at Walcheren 1809. Half pay March 1818. MP for Worcester between the years 1818–1841. Brother of Lt and Capt Francis John Davies 1st Foot Guards.
REFERENCE: *Gentleman's Magazine*, Mar 1847, pp. 310–1. *Annual Register*, 1846, Appx, pp. 304–5. *Oxfordshire Light Infantry Chronicle*, 1900, pp. 263–7.

DAVIS, George Lenox
Lieutenant. 9th (East Norfolk) Regiment of Foot.
Memorial tablet: St Nicholas Church, Galway, Ireland. (Photograph)

TO THE MEMORY OF / LIEUT COLL. GEO. LENOX DAVIS CB / INSPECTING FIELD OFFICER OF THE / LIVERPOOL RECRUITING DISTRICT, / WHO SERVED FOR 44 YEARS / IN THE 9TH REGT AND DIED, / A FEW DAYS AFTER RESIGNING ITS COMMAND / ON THE 14TH APRIL 1852, / AGED 61 YEARS. / THIS TABLET WAS ERECTED / BY THE OFFICERS OF THAT CORPS / AS A MARK OF THEIR ESTEEM. / TO THE SERVICES OF HIS COUNTRY / IN THE PENINSULA / (WHERE HE WAS TAKEN PRISONER), / ON THE MOUNTAINS OF AFFGHANISTAN, / AND ON THE HARD-FOUGHT FIELD / OF SUBRAON, / HE STROVE TO ADD THE BETTER SERVICE / OF A FAITHFUL SOLDIER / OF THE LORD JESUS.

Ensign 15 Sep 1808. Lt 15 Oct 1811. Capt 7 Apr 1825. Major 17 Oct 1837. Lt Colonel 19 Dec 1845.
    Served in the Peninsula Sep 1808 – Apr 1814. Present in the Corunna campaign (on the retreat to

Corunna he was left seriously ill in Lugo and was captured by the French. Remained in prison until Apr 1814). Also served in the West Indies 1819–1826, Mauritius 1832–1835 and India1835–1848 (Afghanistan 1842 in the Expedition under General Pollock – present at the Passes of Khyber, Jagduluk, Tezeen, Hoft Kotel, assault and capture of Istaliff) and the First Sikh War 1846–1848 (present at Sobraon 1846 where he commanded the 9th Foot). Awarded medals for Afghanistan and the Sikh Wars. CB. Served with the 9th Foot for 44 years. Later Inspecting Field Officer for Liverpool Recruiting District.
REFERENCE: *Gentleman's Magazine, Jul 1852, p. 106. Annual Register, 1852, Appx, p. 274.*

DAVIS, William
Private. 14th (Buckinghamshire) Regiment of Foot.
Memorial Cross: West Terrace Cemetery, Adelaide, South Australia, Australia. (Photograph)

IN LOVING MEMORY / OF / .... / WILLIAM DAVIS / FATHER OF THE ABOVE / DIED APRIL 1887 / AGED 90 YEARS / WATERLOO VETERAN

Served at Waterloo in Captain C. Wilson's Company where he was wounded. In 1848 he took his family to Australia where he was employed as a gardener.

DAVY, Charles William
Captain. 29th (Worcestershire) Regiment of Foot.
Low monument on a base (formerly a railed enclosure): Abbey Churchyard, Malvern, Worcestershire. (Photograph)

SACRED TO THE MEMORY OF THE REVD. CHARLES WILLIAM DAVY M.A. / OF HEATHFIELD HAMPSHIRE / FORMERLY CAPTAIN IN HM XXIXTH REGIMENT / HE DIED AT MALVERN FEBRUARY 5TH 1855, AGED 74 / YEARS.

Ensign 44th Foot Nov 1800. Lt 27 Mar 1801. Lt 3rd Foot 3 Feb 1803. Capt 9 May 1805. Capt 29th Foot 19 Dec 1805.
    Served in the Peninsula Jul 1808 – Feb 1810. Present at Rolica and Vimeiro. Retired in 1811 and entered the church. MGS medal for Rolica and Vimeiro.

DAVY, Henry
Lieutenant. Royal Engineers.
Named on the Regimental Memorial: Rochester Cathedral, Rochester, Kent. (Photograph)

2nd Lt 1 Nov 1807. Lt 2 May 1808.
    Served in the Peninsula Oct 1808 – Jan 1809. Present in the Corunna campaign where he was killed 10 Jan 1809, when blowing up the bridge at Betanzos.

DAVY, William Gabriel
Lieutenant Colonel. 7th Garrison Battalion.
Buried in the Family vault at Gloucester Cathedral.
Family Memorial tablet: Gloucester Cathedral, Gloucester, Gloucestershire. (Above entrance door). (Photograph).

...............THE ABOVE MENTIONED AFTERWARDS / GENERAL SIR WILLIAM GABRIEL DAVY, CB & KCH / AND COL: OF THE 1ST BATTN 60TH REGT / DIED AT TRACY PARK, GLOUCESTER-SHIRE / JANUARY 25TH 1856, / AGED 76.

Ledger stone in floor (South aisle). Inscription not recorded.

Funeral hatchment: Holy Trinity Church, Doynton, Gloucestershire. (Photograph)

The hatchment was made in 1856 for his funeral. The shield is encircled with the Order of Guelph. It also depicts the Order of Guelph, Order of the Bath and an MGS medal with a clasp for Talavera and reference to Rolica and Vimeiro.

Ensign 61ˢᵗ Foot Mar 1797. Lt 22 May 1797. Capt 60ᵗʰ Foot 1 Jan 1802. Major 5 Feb 1807. Lt Colonel 7ᵗʰ Garrison Battalion 28 Dec 1809. Bt Colonel 12 Aug 1819. Major General 22 Jul 1830. Lt General 23 Nov 1841. General 20 Jun 1854.
    Served in the Peninsula Aug 1808 – Dec 1809. Present at Rolica, Vimeiro (Mentioned in Despatches), Douro and Talavera (commanded the 5ᵗʰ battalion of the 60ᵗʰ Foot). Gold Medal for Rolica, Vimeiro, and Talavera. CB and KCH. Also served in the West Indies. Knighted 1836. Colonel 60ᵗʰ Foot 2 Nov 1842.
REFERENCE: *Gentleman's Magazine, Apr 1856, p. 423. Annual Register, 1856, Appx, p. 235.*

DAWKINS, Francis Henry
Lieutenant and Captain. 1ˢᵗ Regiment of Foot Guards.
Memorial: Royal Military Chapel, Wellington Barracks, London. (M.I.) (Destroyed by a Flying Bomb 1944)

"COLONEL FRANCIS HENRY DAWKINS. / SERVED IN THE 1ˢᵗ GUARDS, 1812–1826. / HE WAS PRESENT WITH THE REGIMENT AT THE PASSAGE OF THE BIDASSOA, AND WAS AIDE-DE-CAMP TO MAJOR-GENERAL SIR HENRY CLINTON AT WATERLOO REMAINING ON THE STAFF WITH THE ARMY OF OCCUPATION. HE WAS ALSO AIDE-DE-CAMP TO LIEUT.-GENERAL VISCOUNT COMBERMERE AT THE SIEGE OF BHURTPORE, AND HELD VARIOUS APPOINTMENTS ON THE STAFF UNTIL HIS DEATH, ON APRIL 16, 1847 / PLACED BY HIS WIDOW AND DAUGHTERS."

Ensign 25 Jun 1812. Lt and Capt 28 Apr 1814. Bt Lt Colonel 8 Apr 1826. Bt Colonel 23 Nov 1841.
    Served in the Peninsula with 3ʳᵈ Battalion Aug – Nov 1813. Present at Bidassoa. Present at Waterloo and with the Army of Occupation (ADC to his uncle Sir Henry Clinton). Also served in India (present at siege of Bhurtpore 1825–1826 as ADC to Lt General Combermere for which he was awarded a Bt Lt Colonelcy). Brother of Capt and Lt Colonel Henry Dawkins, Coldstream Guards. Nephew of Colonel Sir Henry Clinton 60ᵗʰ Foot and Colonel Sir William Henry Clinton 55ᵗʰ Foot.

DAWKINS, George Augustus Frederick
Lieutenant. 15ᵗʰ (King's) Regiment of Light Dragoons.
Family Memorial tablet: St Mary's Parish Church, Chipping Norton, Oxfordshire. (Photograph)

.... / GEORGE AUGUSTUS FREDERICK DAWKINS ESQ / ONLY SURVIVING SON OF JAMES DAWKINS ESQ / OF OVER NORTON AND HIS WIFE HANNAH THE DAUGHTER / OF THOMAS PHIBBS, ESQ / DIED NOVᴿ XIV MDCCCXXI AGED XXX YEARS / AND IV DAYS / ....

Ensign 3ʳᵈ Foot Guards 1 Feb 1812. Lt 15ᵗʰ Lt Dragoons 3 Jun 1813.
    Present at Waterloo where he was wounded. Died 14 Nov 1821 aged 30.

DAWKINS, Henry
Captain and Lieutenant Colonel. Coldstream Regiment of Foot Guards.
Family Memorial tablet: St Mary's Church, Chipping Norton, Oxfordshire. (Photograph)

.... / COLONEL HENRY DAWKINS / OF OVER NORTON / LATE OF THE

COLDSTREAM GUARDS / ELDEST SON OF HENRY DAWKINS ESQ / AND AUGUSTA HIS WIFE / DAUGHTER OF GENERAL SIR HENRY CLINTON K.B. / DIED NOVEMBER XIII, MDCCCLXIV, / AGED LXXV YEARS.

Ensign 10 Mar 1804. Lt and Capt 25 Aug 1808. Capt and Lt Colonel 25 Jul 1814. Bt Colonel 10 Jan 1837.

Served in the Peninsula Dec 1809 – Apr 1814. (Brigade Major 1 Brigade, 1st Division Jun 1810 – Oct 1812 and Brigade Major 2 Brigade, 1st Division Nov 1812 – Apr 1814). Present at Fuentes d'Onoro, Ciudad Rodrigo, Salamanca, Burgos, Vittoria, Nivelle, Nive, Adour and Bayonne (severely wounded in the Sortie from Bayonne). Present at Waterloo and with the Army of Occupation. MGS medal for Fuentes d'Onoro, Ciudad Rodrigo, Salamanca, Vittoria, Nivelle and Nive. Half pay 31 Aug 1826. MP for Boroughbridge 1820–1830. Deputy Lieutenant for Oxfordshire. Died 13 Nov 1864. Brother of Lt and Capt Francis Henry Dawkins 1st Foot Guards and nephew of Colonel Sir Henry Clinton 60th Foot and Colonel Sir William Henry Clinton 55th Foot.
REFERENCE: *Gentleman's Magazine, Dec 1864, pp. 809–10.*

DAWSON, Hon. George Lionel
Captain. 1st (King's) Dragoon Guards.
Memorial tablet: St Peter's Church, Winterbourne Came, Dorchester, Dorset. (East wall of Chancel). (Photograph)

SACRED TO THE MEMORY OF / THE RIGHT HON^{BLE} COL. G. L. DAWSON DAMER CB: PC. / 3RD SON OF JOHN 1ST EARL OF PORTARLINGTON: / IN 1812, ON THE STAFF OF SIR R. WILSON, WAS PRESENT / WITH THE RUSSIAN ARMY AT THE RETREAT OF THE / FRENCH CAVALRY FROM MOSCOW: / IN 1813, WITH THE ALLIES AT THE BATTLES OF / DRESDEN, LUTZEN, BAUTZEN, WURTZEN, AND CULM: / ALSO AT THE OPERATIONS BEFORE HAMBURG AND HOLSTEIN: / IN 1814, ENTERED FRANCE WITH THE ALLIES; WAS THEN / EMPLOYED IN THE LOW COUNTRIES, THEN APPOINTED / QUARTER MASTER GENERAL TO THE / PRINCE OF ORANGE, / UNDER WHOM HE WAS PRESENT AT QUATRE BRAS / AND WATERLOO, WHERE HE WAS WOUNDED AND HAD / TWO HORSES SHOT UNDER HIM. / HE REPRESENTED THE BOROUGHS OF / PORTARLINGTON AND DORCHESTER FOR MANY YEARS, / DURING WHICH PERIOD HE WAS APPOINTED COMPTROLLER / OF HER MAJESTY'S HOUSEHOLD. / HE MARRIED MARY GEORGINA EMMA / 2ND DAUGHTER OF ADMIRAL LORD HUGH SEYMOUR. / BORN 28th OCTOBER, 1788. / DIED 14th APRIL, 1856. / AND IS BURIED NEAR THIS PLACE.

Cornet 4 Dec 1806. Lt 31 Dec 1807. Capt 31 Dec 1812. Bt Major 10 Mar 1814. Bt Lt Colonel 4 Dec 1815. Capt 22nd Lt Dragoons 29 Jan 1818. Capt 65th Foot 8 Jun 1826. Major 65th Foot 19 Sep 1826. Major 89th Foot 13 Dec 1833.

Present at Quatre Bras and Waterloo where he was wounded (AQMG to Prince of Orange). Also served in Russia 1812 (on Lord Cathcart's staff as ADC to Sir Robert Wilson). Present with the Russian Army at the retreat of French Army from Moscow. Also served with the Allied Army at Dresden, Lutzen, Bautzen, Wurtzen, Culm 1813 (present at the sieges of Hamburg and Holstein). Entered France in 1814 with the Allied Army. CB. Retired 24 Dec 1833. MP for Portarlington 1835–1841 and Dorchester 1847–1852. Assumed the surname of Damer 14 Mar 1829.
REFERENCE: *Gentleman's Magazine, Jun 1856, pp. 644–5. Annual Register, 1856, Appx, pp. 250–1.*

DAWSON, William Francis
2nd Captain. Royal Engineers.
Obelisk: Summit of Kadugannawa Pass, Kandy, Ceylon. (M.I.)

"CAPTAIN W. F. DAWSON, DURING THE GOVERNMENT OF GENERAL SIR E. BARNES, G.C.B.,

COMMANDING ROYAL ENGINEER, CEYLON, WHOSE SCIENCE AND SKILL PLANNED AND EXECUTED THIS ROAD AND OTHER WORKS OF PUBLIC UTILITY. DIED AT COLOMBO, 28TH MARCH, 1829. BY A SUBSCRIPTION AMONG HIS FRIENDS AND ADMIRERS IN CEYLON THIS MONUMENT WAS RAISED TO HIS MEMORY. 1832."

Buried in a vault in St Peter's Church, Colombo, Ceylon (M.I.)
Named on the Regimental Memorial: Rochester Cathedral, Rochester, Kent. (Photograph)

2nd Lt 1 Apr 1807. Lt 14 Jul 1807. 2nd Capt 25 Sep 1812. Capt 23 Mar 1825.
    Served in France with the Army of Occupation 1815–1818. Also served in the Netherlands 1814–1815 and Ceylon 1819–1829. Appointed Commanding Royal Engineer in Ceylon by the Governor Sir Edward Barnes. While in Ceylon Dawson built many roads to open up the mountainous regions, only accessible before on foot. One of the roads was up the Kadugannawa pass, which is now the site of his obelisk which stands 125 feet high. This was built in 1832 at the same time and with the same dimensions as the Duke of York's monument in Waterloo Place, London. Dawson died in Colombo 28 Mar 1829, much regretted 'In Captain Dawson H.M. Service and his country have been deprived of a highly talented and most truly valuable officer, and its Corps of one of its brightest ornaments.'
REFERENCE: *Lewis, J. Penry, List of inscriptions on tombstones and monuments in Ceylon, 1913, reprint 1994, pp. 339–40.*

DAXTER, William
Private. 12th (Prince of Wales's) Regiment of Light Dragoons.
Named on the Regimental Memorial: St Joseph's Church, Waterloo, Belgium. (Photograph)
    Killed at Waterloo.

DAY, James
1st Lieutenant. Royal Artillery.
Buried in St Saviour's Churchyard, St Helier, Jersey, Channel Islands. (Burial register)

2nd Lt 10 Jun 1807. 1st Lt 1 Feb 1808. 2nd Capt 6 Nov 1827.
    Served in the Peninsula Mar 1813 – Apr 1814 with 'A' Troop RHA. Present at Vittoria, Bidassoa, Nivelle (severely wounded), Nive and Orthes. Present at Waterloo (wounded) in Lt Col Sir Hew D. Ross's Troop. Half pay 3 Feb 1820. Died in Jersey 1 Aug 1843.

DAY, Richard
Private. 23rd (Royal Welch Fusiliers) Regiment of Foot.
Headstone: St Andrew's Churchyard, Banwell, Somerset. (Photograph)

IN AFFECTIONATE REMEMBRANCE / OF / RICHARD DAY, / WHO DIED MAY 13TH 1868, / AGED 73 YEARS. / ....

Somerset Volunteers. Pte 23rd Foot 1 Apr 1813 .
    Served at Waterloo in Capt Joliffe's Company. Discharged 7 Apr 1820.

DAY, Thomas
Sergeant. 82nd (Prince of Wales's Volunteers) Regiment of Foot.
Buried in St Alkmund's Churchyard, Whitchurch, Shropshire. (No longer extant). (Burial register)

Pte 15 Oct 1799. Cpl Dec 1802. Sgt 1804.
    Served in the Peninsula Aug 1808 – Jan 1809 and Jun 1812 – Apr 1814. Present at Vimeiro, Corunna, Vittoria, Pyrenees, Nivelle and Orthes. Also served in Ireland 1802–1808. Returned home to Shropshire

to work as a plasterer. Chelsea Out Pensioner. Award MGS medal for Vimeiro, Corunna, Vittoria, Pyrenees, Nivelle and Orthes. Died Apr 1859 aged 79.

DAYMAN, Charles
Chaplain to the Forces. Chaplains Department.
Memorial tablet: St John the Evangelist Church, Great Tew, Oxfordshire. (Photograph)

IN THE / ADJOINING CHURCHYARD / REST IN HOPE / OF THE RESURRECTION TO ETERNAL LIFE / THROUGH JESUS CHRIST / THE REMAINS OF / THE REV^D CHARLES DAYMAN MA / THIRTEEN YEARS VICAR OF THIS PARISH / AND SOME TIME / FELLOW OF EXETER HALL, OXFORD. / HE WAS BORN IN POUGHILL / IN THE COUNTY OF CORNWALL / AND BURIED AT GREAT TEW / AUGUST 19TH 1844 / IN THE 57TH YEAR OF HIS AGE. / (VERSE)

Chaplain to the Forces 18 Oct 1811.
   Served in the Peninsula Jan 1812 – Apr 1814 (attached to 1st Divison from Feb – Nov 1812). Captured on retreat from Burgos 24 Oct 1812 and imprisoned in Givey and Verdun until the end of the war. Rural Dean and Vicar of Great Tew 1830–1844. MA 1814.
REFERENCE: Gentleman's Magazine, Oct 1844, p. 438.

DEAN, George
Captain. Royal West India Rangers.
Cross on a stepped base: Symonds Street Cemetery, Auckland, New Zealand. (Block F). (Photograph)

IN / MEMORY / OF HIS EXCELLENCY MAJOR GENERAL / GEORGE DEAN PITT KH / LIEUT GOVERNOR OF THE NORTHERN PROVINCE / OF NEW ZEALAND / AND COMMANDER OF HM FORCES / IN THE COLONY / HE DIED JANUARY 8TH 1851 / AGED 79 YEARS

Ensign Royal African Corps 4 Jun 1805. Lt West India Rangers 5 Dec 1805. Capt 10 Aug 1809. Major 80th Foot 19 Aug 1819. Lt Colonel 18 Apr 1822. Bt Colonel 10 Jan 1837. Major General 9 Nov 1841.
   Served in the Peninsula Jan 1811 – Jan 1814. Present at Albuera, Usagre, Almarez, Badajoz, Vittoria, Pamplona and Pyrenees. Also served at Martinique 1809. KH and MGS medal for Martinique, Albuera, Badajoz and Vittoria. Inspecting Field Officer for Leeds Recruiting District Mar 1837. Superintendent of Recruiting Department 1840. Appointed to command the forces in New Zealand 1847. Lt Governor of the Northern Province. Assumed surname of Pitt in 1819. Died 8 Jan 1851.
REFERENCE: Gentleman's Magazine, Sep 1851, p. 328 (Under Pitt). Annual Register, 1851, Appx, p. 249 (Under Pitt). United Service Magazine, Jul 1851, p. 475 (Under Pitt).

DE BATHE, William Plunkett
Captain. 85th (Buckinghamshire Volunteers) Light Infantry Regiment of Foot.
Monument: Kensal Green Cemetery, London. (11837/77/IC). (Photograph)

IN MEMORY OF / SIR WILLIAM DE BATHE / BAR^T / ....

Ensign 4th Garrison Battalion 17 Dec 1807. Ensign 27th Foot 3 Mar 1808. Lt 21 Sep 1809. Capt 3rd West Indian Regt 5 Mar 1812. Capt 94th Foot 30 Jul 1812. Capt 85th Foot 25 Jan 1813. Bt Major 27 Oct 1814. Major 85th Foot 26 Jun 1819. Lt Colonel 9 Apr 1825. Lt Colonel 53rd Foot 28 Feb 1828. Lt Colonel 8th Foot 25 Sep 1835.
   Served in the Peninsula with 94th Foot Nov 1812 – Feb 1813 and 85th Foot Oct 1813 – Apr 1814. Present at the retreat from Burgos, Nivelle, Nive and Bayonne. MGS medal for Nivelle and Nive. Also served in Sicily 1808 and North America 1814–1815 (present at Baltimore, Bladensburg, Washington and New Orleans). Retired 2 Oct 1835. Died 1870.

DE BERLAERE, A. J. L. Ponthieure

1st Lieutenant. 7th Infantry Battalion, Dutch Infantry.
Named on the Memorial to Dutch officers killed at Waterloo: St Joseph's Church, Waterloo, Belgium. (Photograph)

DE BOURGH, Anthony Philip

Lieutenant. 60th (Royal American) Regiment of Foot.
Mural memorial: Abbey Churchyard, Kelso, Roxburghshire, Scotland. Seriously eroded. (Photograph)

SACRED / TO THE MEMORY OF / ……………….. BARON A. DE BOURGH OF THE 60TH / RIFLES WHO DIED OCTOBER 22ND 1852 / AGED 81. / HE WAS A NATIVE OF METZ / ………………..

Ensign 60th Foot 7 Mar 1810. Lt 18 Apr 1811. Portuguese Army: Capt 11th Caçadores 18 Sep 1811.
    Served in the Peninsula with Portuguese Army Sep 1811 – Apr 1814. Half pay 25 Dec 1816.

DE BRAXION, Ernst

Captain. Duke of Brunswick Oels' Corps (Infantry).
Named on the Memorial: St Andrew's Church, (now Musée Historique), Biarritz, France. (Photograph)

Lt 25 Sep 1809. Capt 16 Aug 1810.
    Served in the Peninsula Sep 1810 – Feb 1814. (from Aug 1813 attached to the 4th Division). Present at Moriscos, Salamanca, Burgos, San Millan, Vittoria, Pyrenees (wounded), Nivelle and Orthes where he was killed Feb 1814.

DE COLLAERT, Baron J. A.

Lieutenant General. Staff, Dutch Cavalry.
Named on the Memorial to Dutch officers killed at Waterloo: St Joseph's Church, Waterloo, Belgium. (Photograph)

Commanded the Netherlands Cavalry Division at Waterloo where he was severely wounded and died from his wounds in 1816. Had fought for the French before 1814.

DE COURCY, Hon. Gerard

Major. 70th (Glasgow Lowland) Regiment of Foot.
Low monument: English Cemetery, Florence, Italy. (Grave number B12H). (Photograph)

SACRED / TO THE MEMORY OF THE HONOURABLE / LIEUT. COL. GERARD COURCY / SON OF THE RIGHT HONOURABLE JOHN COURCY / 19TH BARON KINGSALE AND SUSANNA HIS WIFE / DIED AT FLORENCE OCTOBER 20 / 1848.

Capt 24 Jul 1804. Major 4 Jun 1813. Bt Lt Colonel 25 Nov 1814.
    Served in the Peninsula Jul – Oct 1812 (Military Secretary in Eastern Spain). Brother of Lt and Capt Hon. John De Courcy 1st Foot Guards.

DE COURCY, Hon. John

Lieutenant and Captain. 1st Regiment of Foot Guards.
Named on Memorial Panel VII: Royal Military Chapel, Wellington Barracks, London. (M.I.) (Destroyed by a Flying Bomb 1944)

Ensign 64th Foot. Lt 86th Foot Jul 1793. Lt in Hunt's Regt of Foot 30 Oct 1794. Lt 9th Foot 27 Aug 1799. Lt and Capt 1st Foot Guards 8 May 1800. Bt Major 1 Jan 1805. Bt Lt Col 1 Jan 1812.

Served in the Peninsula with 3rd Battalion Oct 1808 – Jan 1809 and Oct 1811 – Nov 1812. Present at Corunna, Cadiz and Seville. Died 4 Jun 1813 a few days after his return from Spain. Brother of Major Hon. Gerard De Courcy 70th Foot.

DE GILLERN, William
Captain. Duke of Brunswick's Oels' Corps (Infantry).
Memorial tablet: St David's Burial Ground, Hobart, Tasmania, Australia. (Burial ground is now converted into a park). (Photograph)

SACRED / TO THE / MEMORY OF / WILLIAM DE GILLERN ESQ. / FORMERLY MAJOR / IN THE BRUNSWICK OELS / SERGEANT AT ARMS TO THE / HONOURABLE / THE HOUSE OF ASSEMBLY. / BORN 15TH NOVEMBER 1788 / DIED 2ND NOVEMBER 1857. / ....

Lt 27 Sep 1809. Capt 4 Jun 1812. Bt Major Jul 1815.
Present at Waterloo (ADC to the Duke of Brunswick who was killed at Quatre Bras). Retired on half pay 1816. Decided to settle in Australia and arrived there in 1823. Bought land and built a distillery. This became a disaster when the Governor Sir Thomas Brisbane raised taxes on locally distilled spirits and reduced duties on imports. So he turned to farming and was supplying the local barracks in Hobart with produce until 1840 when his barns burnt down. He then tried public service and was responsible for bridge building on the coastal road. Justice of the Peace 1856. First Sergeant at Arms at Tasmania House of Assembly but died soon after the appointment 2 Nov 1857.
REFERENCE: *Australian Dictionary of Biography.*

DE HAAN, J.
1st Lieutenant. 5th National Militia Battalion, Dutch Infantry.
Named on the Memorial to Dutch officers killed at Quatre Bras: St Joseph's Church, Waterloo, Belgium. (Photograph)

DEICHMANN, Wilhelm
Cornet. 3rd Regiment of Hussars, King's German Legion.
Named on the Regimental Memorial: La Haye Sainte, Waterloo, Belgium. (Photograph)

Present at Waterloo where he was killed. Also served in North Germany 1813–1814 and Netherlands 1814.

DEIGHTON, William
Private. 69th (South Lincolnshire) Regiment of Foot.
Headstone: St Mary's Churchyard, Elloughton, Beverley, Yorkshire. (Photograph)

WILLIAM DEIGHTON / A WATERLOO VETERAN. / D 27TH NOVEMBER 1871 / AGED 82 YEARS / OF ELLOUGHTON / ....

Pte 11 Aug 1811.
Served at Waterloo in Captain Charles Lowne's Company (wounded in the head and body). Also served in the Netherlands 1814 (present with the 2/69th at Bergen-op-Zoom where he was again wounded in the head). Owing to these wounds and on the reduction of the battalion after the war he was discharged Oct 1816, having served 5 years and 157 days.

DE LA CHEROIS, Nicholas

Ensign. 47th (Lancashire) Regiment of Foot.
Memorial tablet: Donaghadee Parish Church, Donaghadee, County Down, Northern Ireland. (North transept). (Photograph)

SACRED TO THE MEMORY OF / NICHOLAS DE LA CHEROIS ESQ^R. / ENSIGN IN THE 47TH REGI-MENT OF THE LINE, / WHOSE VIRTUOUS MIND AND GENEROUS DISPOSITION / ENDEARED HIM TO THE AFFECTIONS AND FORMED A CHIEF SOURCE / OF THE HAPPINESS OF HIS FAMILY. / HONOURABLY ENGAGED IN THE SERVICE OF HIS COUNTRY / AND EMPLOYED IN THE CAUSE OF SPAIN / AGAINST THE USURPATION OF FRANCE, / HE WAS KILLED AT THE BATTLE OF BARROSA IN ANDALUSIA / ON THE 5TH OF MARCH 1811, / AGED 22 YEARS

Ensign 30 Mar 1809.
   Served in the Peninsula Oct 1810 – Mar 1811. Present at Cadiz and Barrosa where he was killed 5 Mar 1811 aged 22.

DE LA HOWARDERIE, Graaf Duchastel

Captain. 8th Hussars, Dutch Cavalry.
Named on the Memorial to Dutch officers killed at Quatre Bras: St Joseph's Church, Waterloo, Belgium. (Photograph)

DE LANCEY, Sir William Howe

Deputy Quartermaster General.
Memorial tablet: Collegiate Church, Dunglass, East Lothian, Scotland. (Photograph)

SACRED / TO THE MEMORY OF / COLONEL SIR W^M DE LANCEY / KNIGHT COMMANDER OF THE BATH, / AND / ACTING QUARTER-MASTER-GENERAL / AT THE / BATTLE OF WATERLOO, / IN WHICH HE WAS MORTALLY WOUNDED / ON 18TH OF JUNE 1815. / HE DIED THERE ON THE 26TH OF JUNE, / ATTENDED BY HIS WIFE MAGDALENE, / DAUGHTER OF SIR JAMES HALL, BART. / HIS BODY WAS LAID TO REST IN THE / GROUND ALLOTTED TO PROTESTANTS / NEAR BRUSSELS.

Low monument: Evere Cemetery, Brussels, Belgium. (In front of British memorial). (Photograph)

HERE LIE THE REMAINS / OF / COLONEL SIR WILLIAM HOWE / DE LANCEY / QUARTER-MASTER GENERAL / OF THE BRITISH ARMY / WHO WAS WOUNDED AT THE / BATTLE OF WATERLOO / JUNE 18 / AND WHO DIED JUNE 26 1815

Memorial tablet: Inside Mausoleum, Evere, Brussels, Belgium. (Photograph)

COLONEL / SIR WILLIAM / HOWE DE LANCEY / QUARTER MASTER / GEN^L OF THE / BRITISH ARMY

Cornet 16th Lt Dragoons 17 Jul 1792. Lt 26 Feb 1793. Capt Independent Company 25 Mar 1794. Capt 80th Foot 1 Oct 1794. Capt 17th Lt Dragoons 20 Oct 1796. Major 45th Foot 17 Oct 1799. Bt Lt Colonel QMG's Dept 1 Jan 1805. Bt Colonel 4 Jun 1813.
   Served in the Peninsula Aug 1808 – Jan 1809 and May 1809 – Apr 1814 (on Staff as AQMG and DQMG). Present at Lugo, Corunna, Douro (Mentioned in Despatches), Talavera, Busaco, Fuentes d'Onoro, El Bodon, Ciudad Rodrigo, Badajoz, Salamanca (Mentioned in Despatches), Burgos, Vittoria (Mentioned in Despatches), Villa Formosa, Tolosa, San Sebastian (Mentioned in Despatches). Bidassoa,

Nivelle, Nive, (Mentioned in Despatches), Adour and Bayonne. Gold Cross for Corunna, Talavera, Busaco, Fuentes d'Onoro, Badajoz, Salamanca, Vittoria, San Sebastian and Nive. KCB.

Present at Waterloo as DQMG. Organised the retreat from Quatre Bras. Wellington wanted Colonel George Murray for the post but he was still in America, so De Lancey was sent out even though he had just married. Severely wounded by a cannon ball and died ten days later.

Also served in Flanders 1794 and India 1796 (where he met Wellington for the first time). Entered the Royal Military College at High Wycombe 1800–1802. He was so successful he was promoted to the permanent staff of the Quartermaster General. Went to Spain in 1808 with Sir John Moore and returned in 1809 as DQMG under Colonel George Murray. On the occasions that Murray was absent from the Peninsula De Lancey was in charge of the department. One of the select band of soldiers buried in the Mausoleum at Evere. Brother in law of Colonel Sir Hudson Lowe Corsican Rangers.

REFERENCE: *Dictionary of National Biography. Miller, D. M. O., Lady de Lancey at Waterloo, 2000. De Lancey, Magdalene, A week at Waterloo in 1815 – Lady de Lancey's narrative. Being an account of how she nursed her husband, Colonel Sir William Howe De Lancey, mortally wounded in the great battle, 1906.*

DELMAR, John

Ensign. 28th (North Gloucestershire) Regiment of Foot.
Memorial tablet: St Margaret's Church, (now The Canterbury Tales – a tourist attraction), Canterbury, Kent. (Photograph)

SACRED TO THE MEMORY / OF / ENSIGN JOHN DELMAR LATE OF H. M. 28TH REG[T]. / OF INFANTRY, FOURTH SON OF MR. DELMAR OF THIS CITY. / HE FELL BY A SHOT WHICH INSTANTLY DEPRIV'D HIM OF / HIS LIFE IN THE 19TH YEAR OF HIS AGE WHILST DISPLAYING / THE BRITISH COLOUR AT THE PUERTO DE MAYA IN / THE FIRST BATTLE OF THE PYRENEES ON THE 25TH JULY 1813. / HE WAS NOT LESS RESPECTED BY HIS BROTHER OFFICERS / THAN BELOVED BY HIS FAMILY, WHO HAVE ERECTED / THIS SINCERE THO' SMALL MEMORIAL AS A PLEDGE / OF THEIR AFFECTION AND ESTEEM.

Ensign 23 Jul 1812.
Served in the Peninsula with 1/28th Apr – Jul 1813. Present at Vittoria and Pyrenees where he was killed carrying the colours at Maya 25 Jul 1813 aged 19.

DE NAVE, B. D. J.

Captain. 27th Jager Battalion, Durch Infantry.
Named on the Memorial to Dutch officers killed at Quatre Bras: St Joseph's Church, Waterloo, Belgium. (Photograph)

DENECKE, George

Physician. Medical Department.
Memorial tablet: St Thomas's Church, Newport, Isle of Wight. (Photograph)

SACRED / TO THE MEMORY OF / GEORGE DENECKE, ESQ[RE] M.D. / WHO DEPARTED THIS LIFE / AUGUST 19TH 1838 / IN THE 63RD YEAR OF HIS AGE. / HIS AFFLICTED WIDOW, SUMS UP HIS CHARACTER / IN THE FOLLOWING COMPREHENSIVE SENTENCE, / HE LIVED AND DIED A CHRISTIAN.

Asst Surgeon King's German Legion 12 Jan 1805. Surgeon 2nd Battalion of Line 25 May 1805. Staff Surgeon 6 Jul 1809. Physician 17 Jun 1813. Bt Deputy Inspector of Hospitals (on Continent) 22 Feb 1816. Deputy Inspector General 26 Oct 1826.

Served in the Peninsula Aug 1808 – Jan 1809 and Jun 1811 – Apr 1814 (Oct 1811 – Mar 1813 attached to 7th Division and Apr – Jun 1813 attached to 1st Division) Present at Vigo and the Corunna campaign. Present at Quatre Bras (wounded) and Waterloo. Also served at Hanover 1805, Copenhagen 1807, Walcheren 1809 and the Netherlands 1814–1815. MD 1801.

DENT, Abraham
Lieutenant and Adjutant. 59th (2nd Nottinghamshire) Regiment of Foot.
Named on the Regimental Memorial monument: Christ Church Churchyard, Tramore, County Waterford, Ireland. (Photograph)

Ensign 15 Mar 1808. Lt 4 Jun 1809.
Served in the Peninsula Sep 1808 – Jan 1809 and Sep 1812 – Apr 1814. Present at Corunna and Cadiz (Town Adjutant at Cadiz Jan – Apr 1813). Military Secretary to Major General Cooke May 1813 – Apr 1814. Present at Waterloo in reserve at Hal, siege of Cambrai and with the Army of Occupation. Also served at Walcheren 1809. Lost in the *Sea Horse* shipwreck off the coast of Ireland 30 Jan 1816.

DENT, Thomas
Captain. 10th (North Lincolnshire) Regiment of Foot.
Ledger stone: Kensal Green Cemetery, London. Inscription illegible. (3617/106/3). (Photograph)

Ensign 17 Feb 1798. Lt 27 Feb 1798. Capt 26 Sep 1805. Bt Major 12 Aug 1819.
Served in the Peninsula Aug 1812 – Apr 1814. Present at Alicante, Castalla, Ordal and Barcelona. Also served in Egypt 1801. Buried in Kensal Green 8 Jul 1842.

DE RENZY, George Webb
Captain. 82nd (Prince of Wales's Volunteers) Regiment of Foot.
Headstone: Kensal Green Cemetery, London. Inscription illegible. (23119/73/5). (Photograph)

Ensign 6th Garrison Battalion 27 Nov 1806. Lt 82nd Foot 25 Dec 1807. Capt 20 Apr 1815. Bt Major 10 Jan 1837.
Served in the Peninsula Jun 1812 – Oct 1813. Present at Vittoria (severely wounded, his right arm amputated and awarded pension of £100 per annum). MGS medal for Vittoria. Also served at Walcheren 1809 (present at the siege and capture of Flushing). Half pay 25 Feb 1816. Barrack Master at Exeter with rank of Major. Retired Jan 1837. Died 30 Dec 1871.

DE SALABERRY, Edward A.
Lieutenant. Royal Engineers.
Named on the Regimental Memorial: Rochester Cathedral, Rochester, Kent. (Photograph)

2nd Lt 21 Jul 1810. 1st Lt 1 Mar 1811.
Served in the Peninsula Jul 1811 – Apr 1812. Present at the Lines of Torres Vedras, Ciudad Rodrigo and siege of Badajoz where he was killed when he and Capt John Williams of the Engineers were directing the Light Division in the assault on the breach in the Maria Flank.
REFERENCE: Grodzinski, John R, 'Universally esteemed by his brothers in arms,' Lieutenant Edward De Salaberry, Royal Engineers. at the storming of Badajoz, 6 Apr 1812, Journal of the Society for Army Historical Research, Vol 88, No 353, Spring 2010, pp. 29–37.

DE SCHULZEN, Detlef
Lieutenant. Artillery, King's German Legion.
Named on the Royal Artillery Regimental Memorial: St Joseph's Church, Waterloo, Belgium. (Photograph)

Lt 1 May 1807.
 Served in the Peninsula 1808–1809 and 1810–1814. Present at Waterloo where he was killed. Also served in the Baltic 1807–1808 and Netherlands 1814.

DES VOEUX, Benfield
Lieutenant. 11th Regiment of Light Dragoons.
Altar tomb: Kensal Green Cemetery, London. Inscription illegible. (3117/102/IC). (Photograph)

Cornet 10 Oct 1811. Lt 23 Dec 1813. Lt 30 Mar 1815. Lt and Capt 3rd Foot Guards 29 Mar 1821. Bt Lt Colonel (unattached) 3 Jul 1829.
 Served in the Peninsula Dec 1812 – Jun 1813. Rejoined the regiment Mar 1815 after leaving at the reduction of the 11th Dragoons in 1814. Present at Quatre Bras and Waterloo. Retired 18 Apr 1834. Died 30 Nov 1864 aged 73.
REFERENCE: *Household Brigade Journal, 1864, p. 336.*

DEUCHAR, DAVID
Captain. 1st (Royal Scots) Regiment of Foot.
Headstone: Warriston Cemetery, Edinburgh, Scotland. (Section O Grave number 92). (Photograph)

IN MEMORY OF CHRISTIAN ROBERTSON / WIDOW OF DAVID DEUCHAR OF MORNINGSIDE, / ALSO OF THEIR SONS / .... / DAVID DEUCHAR / MAJOR 1ST THE ROYAL SCOTS REGIMENT. / DIED 7TH MAY 1847 / AGED 66. / ....

Lt 2 Jan 1808. Capt 12 Dec 1811. Major 6 Apr 1826.
 Served in the Peninsula Apr 1810 – Jun 1811. Present at Busaco and Fuentes d'Onoro. Also served at Walcheren 1809.

DEVEY, Henry Fryer
Captain. 7th (Royal Fusiliers) Regiment of Foot.
Grave: St Mary's Churchyard, Handsworth, Staffordshire. (Grave number 161). (M.I.)

"TO THE MEMORY OF / HENRY FRYER DEVEY / LATE CAPTAIN OF THE ROYAL FUSILIERS / MAGISTRATE FOR THE COUNTY OF STAFFORD / AND CHURCHWARDEN OF THIS PARISH / WHO DIED JUNE 13TH 1840 / AGED 57 YEARS."

Lt Worcestershire Militia. Lt 7th Foot 30 Aug 1807. Capt 28 Oct 1813.
 Served in the Peninsula with 1/7th Apr 1811 – May 1812 and Nov 1813 – Apr 1814. Present at Albuera, Aldea da Ponte, Ciudad Rodrigo, Badajoz (severely wounded 6 Apr 1812 and awarded pension of £100 per annum), Orthes and Toulouse. Retired on half pay 25 Aug 1814 owing to his wounds from Badajoz.

DE VILLERS, C. N. J. F. M.
Major. 8th Hussars, Dutch Cavalry.
Named on the Memorial to Dutch officers killed at Waterloo: St Joseph's Church, Waterloo, Belgium. (Photograph)

DEVITT, Guy
Private. 12th Prince of Wales's Regiment of Light Dragoons.
Named on the Regimental Memorial: St Joseph's Church, Waterloo, Belgium. (Photograph)
 Killed at Waterloo.

DE WENDT, Edward Michael
Captain. 60th (Royal American) Regiment of Foot.
Memorial tablet: St Michael's Cathedral Churchyard, Bridgetown, Barbados, West Indies. (Photograph)

TO THE MEMORY OF / BREVET MAJOR / EDWARD MICHAEL DE WENDT / 4TH BATTALION 60TH REGIMENT / WHO DIED AT / GARRISON OF SAINT ANN'S BARBADOS, / THE 9TH DAY OF MAY, / AD 1816.

Capt 9 Dec 1804. Bt Major 4 Jun 1814.
   Served in the Peninsula Aug 1808 – Mar 1811. (from Jun 1810 attached to the 2nd Division). Present at Rolica, Vimeiro, Douro, Talavera and Busaco. Also served in the West Indies.

DICK, Robert Henry
Major. 42nd (Royal Highland) Regiment of Foot.
Memorial tablet: St Giles's Cathedral, Edinburgh, Scotland. (Above organ loft). (Photograph)

IN MEMORY OF / MAJOR GENERAL / SIR ROBERT HENRY DICK / K. C. B. & K. C. H. / OF TULLYMET / WHO WAS KILLED AT SOBRAON ON THE BANKS / OF THE SUTLEDGE ON THE 10TH OF FEBRUARY 1846 / WHILE GALLANTLY LEADING HIS DIVISION WITHIN / THE ENEMY'S TRENCHES. / THIS LAMENTED OFFICER WAS / LT COL. COMMANDING THE 42ND ROYAL HIGHLANDERS / FOR 14 YEARS, & SERVED WITH IT IN THE PENINSULA / AND AT WATERLOO. / THIS TABLET IS ERECTED BY / THE OFFICERS & RETIRED OFFICERS IN THE 42ND / AS A TRIBUTE OF THE HIGH ESTEEM & REGARD / THEY ENTERTAINED FOR HIM / AS A KIND FRIEND AND A / GALLANT SOLDIER.

Memorial tablet: St George's Cathedral, Madras, India. (Photograph)

MAIDA / EGYPT / ALEXANDRIA / ROSETTA / BUSACO / TORRES VEDRAS / FUENTES D'ONORO / BADAJOZ / SALAMANCA / FORT ST MICHAEL / PORTUGAL / QUATRE BRAS / WATERLOO / SOBRAON / SACRED TO THE MEMORY OF / MAJOR GENL SIR ROBERT HENRY DICK K. C. B. K.C.H. / OF TULLYMET, N. B. / ONE OF THE HEROES OF THE PENINSULAR WAR. / WHO, AFTER A BRILLIANT MILITARY CAREER IN H. M. 42ND ROYAL HIGHLANDERS / WHICH REGIMENT HE BROUGHT OUT OF ACTION AT QUATRE BRAS / CLOSED A LONG AND BRILLIANT MILITARY CAREER / ON THE MEMORABLE FIELD OF / SOBRAON, / FEBRUARY 10TH 1846. / RAISED IN GRATEFUL ADMIRATION BY THE PUBLIC / OF THE PRESIDENCY OF MADRAS. / WHERE FOR SOME TIME HE HELD THE CHIEF MILITARY COMMAND.

Memorial tablet: Dunkeld Cathedral, Perthshire, Scotland. (Photograph)

MAIDA EGYPT BUSACO FUENTES D'ONOR SALAMANCA WATERLOO / SACRED TO THE MEMORY OF / MAJOR-GENERAL SIR ROBERT HENRY DICK K.C.B K.C.H / WHO AFTER DISTINGUISHED SERVICE IN THE PENINSULA / IN THE COMMAND OF A LIGHT BATTALION, / AND AT WATERLOO WITH THE 42ND ROYAL HIGHLAND REGIMENT, / FELL MORTALLY WOUNDED WHILST LEADING THE 3RD DIVISION / OF THE ARMY OF THE SUTLEDGE / TO THE ATTACK ON THE SEIKH ENTRENCHED CAMP AT SOBRAON / ON THE 10TH FEBRUARY 1846, / THE OFFICERS WHO HAD THE HONOUR OF SERVING / UNDER HIM IN HIS LAST BATTLE AND OTHERS, HIS FRIENDS IN HER MAJESTY'S / AND THE HONOURABLE EAST INDIA COMPANY'S SERVICE IN BENGAL, / HAVE CAUSED THIS MONUMENT TO BE PLACED IN HIS PARISH CHURCH, / IN TESTIMONY OF THEIR RESPECT AND AFFECTION / FOR A GENEROUS COURTEOUS AND CONSIDERATE COMMANDER / A GALLANT AND DEVOTED SOLDIER.

Memorial: Ferozepore Civil Cemetery, Ferozepore, India. (M.I.)

"HERE LIES IN THE HOPE OF A JOYFUL RESURRECTION SIR ROBERT HENRY DICK OF TULLYMET PERTHSHIRE N.B. MAJOR-GENERAL KNIGHT COMMANDER OF THE ORDERS OF THE BATH AND OF HANOVER. KNIGHT OF THE AUSTRIAN MILITARY ORDER OF MARIA THERESA AND OF THE RUSSIAN ORDER OF VLADIMIR COLONEL OF H.M. 73RD REGT. / FOR HIS COUNTRY HE FOUGHT & BLED: IN EGYPT AT MAIDA THRO'OUT THE PENINSULA AND WATERLOO & IN INDIA. FOR HIS VALOUR AND SKILL AT FUENTES D'ONOR BUSACO SALA-MANCA AND WATERLOO HE RECEIVED TWO MEDALS AND TWO HONORARY CLASPS. BORN ON THE 29TH JULY 1787 A.D. HE FELL IN THE MOMENT OF VICTORY ON THE 10TH FEBY 1846 A.D. WHILE CHEERING ON H.M.'S 80TH REGT HAVING LED HIS DIVISION IN THE ASSAULT ON THE ENTRENCHED CAMP OF THE SEIKH AT SOBRAON. HONOURED AND BELOVED HE LIVED HONOURED AND LAMENTED HE DIED."

Named on the brass tablet to Officers and Men who fell at Sobraon: St Andrew's Church, Ferozepore, India, (M.I.)

"MAJOR GENL SIR R. H. DICK, KCB & KCH COMDG: 3RD INFY: DIVISON".

Ensign 75th Foot 22 Nov 1800. Lt 62nd Foot 27 Jun 1802. Lt 9th Battalion of Reserve 20 Dec 1803. Capt 78th 17 Apr 1804. Major 42nd 14 Jul 1808. Bt Lt Colonel 8 Oct 1812. Lt Colonel 42nd Foot 18 Jun 1815. Bt Colonel 27 May 1825. Major General 10 Jan 1837.

Served in the Peninsula Jul 1809 – Dec 1812. Present at Busaco (in command of the battalion and on the retreat to Torres Vedras), Foz d'Arouce (wounded), Fuentes d'Onoro (Mentioned in Despatches), Ciudad Rodrigo, Badajoz, Salamanca, Burgos (Mentioned in Despatches) and retreat from Burgos. Returned to England Dec 1812.

Present at Waterloo (commanded the regiment at Quatre Bras on the death of Lt Colonel Robert Macara. Shortly afterwards Dick was also wounded and Bt Major John Campbell took command). Served in France with the Army of Occupation until Spring 1816 when the regiment returned to Edinburgh. CB for Waterloo. Appointed Lt Colonel and took command of the regiment. Also served at Maida 1805 with 78th Foot (wounded), Egypt 1807 (present at Rosetta where he was wounded), Ireland 1817–1825, Gibraltar 1825–1827. Retired on half pay 1828 and returned to his estate at Tulliemet in Scotland.

Rejoined the Army 1838 and was sent to India where he was appointed to command a division of the Madras Army. Commander in Chief Jan 1841. Served in the First Sikh War 1845 (present at Sobraon 10 Feb 1846 where he successfully led his troops to victory but was killed by one of the last shots of the day). Buried in Ferozepore. Gold Medal for Busaco, Fuentes d'Onoro and Salamanca. KCH 1831. KCB 1838. Knight of the Austrian Military Order of Maria Theresa. Fourth Class of Russian Order of St Wladimar. Colonel 73rd Foot 1843. Educated at Winchester.
REFERENCE: *Dictionary of National Biography. United Service Magazine, 1846, Vol 2, pp. 298–300. Gentleman's Magazine, May 1846, pp. 539–40.*

DICKENS, James
Deputy Commissary General. Commissariat Department.
Memorial: St Mary's Churchyard, Hadley, London. (M.I.)

"SACRED / TO THE MEMORY OF / COMMY GENL JAMES DICKENS, / OF THIS PARISH / WHO DEPARTED THIS LIFE 31ST MARCH 1854 / IN THE 76TH YEAR OF HIS AGE / AFTER A PERIOD OF 60 YEARS / IN THE PUBLIC SERVICE."

Deputy Comm Gen 17 Mar 1807. Comm Gen 19 Jul 1821.

Served in the Peninsula Sep 1808 – Jan 1809, Jun 1809 – Dec 1811 and Dec 1812 – Apr 1814. (from

Jun 1813 – Apr 1814 at Lisbon). Present at Corunna, Talavera and Busaco. MGS medal for Corunna, Talavera and Busaco.

DICKENS, Thomas Mark
Captain. Royal Engineers.
Named on the Regimental Memorial: Rochester Cathedral, Rochester, Kent. (Photograph)

2nd Lt 15 Mar 1803. Lt 27 Jul 1803. 2nd Capt 3 Jan 1808. Capt 21 Jul 1813. Major 27 May 1825. Lt Colonel 29 Jul 1825.
    Served in the Peninsula Oct 1813 – Apr 1814. Present at Bidassoa, Adour and Bayonne (severely wounded). Also served in Sicily 1807 and 1809–1810. Retired by sale of his commission 22 May 1829.

DICKENSON, Sebastian
2nd Captain. Royal Engineers.
Named on the Regimental Memorial: Rochester Cathedral, Rochester, Kent. (Photograph)

2nd Lt 1 Oct 1804. 1st Lt 1 Mar 1805. 2nd Capt 29 May 1810.
    Served in the Peninsula Mar 1810 – May 1811. Present at the Lines of Torres Vedras. Went to Elvas Apr 1811 to prepare for the first siege of Badajoz on 11 May 1811 and was killed by a cannon ball whilst standing on a parapet urging the men on to the work against Fort St Cristobal. Also served in South America 1807 (present at Buenos Ayres) and Walcheren 1809.

DICKSON, Sir Alexander
Captain. Royal Artillery.
Buried in St Nicholas's Churchyard, Plumstead, Kent. (No longer extant. Destroyed by a flying bomb in the Second World War)
Monument: Royal Military Repository, Woolwich, Kent. (Photograph)

THE / ROYAL REGIMENT OF ARTILLERY / TO / MAJOR GENERAL / SIR ALEXANDER DICKSON GCB KCH / BUENOS AYRES / GRIZO / OPORTO / BUSACO / TORRES VEDRAS / CAMPO MAYOR / ALBUERA / ALMAREZ / SALAMANCA / VITTORIA / BIDASSOA / NIVELLE / NIVE / ADOUR / TOULOUSE / QUATRE BRAS / WATERLOO / ERECTED BY OFFICERS OF THE CORPS TO HIS MEMORY

Brass Memorial tablet: Royal Garrison Church, Portsmouth, Hampshire. (Back of a choir stall)

GENERAL SIR ALEXAN- / DER DICKSON G.C.B. / ROYAL ARTILLERY / DIED APRIL 22 1840 / AGE 63. / DD: OFFICERS / 12TH BRIGADE R.A.

Named on the Regimental Memorial: St Nicholas Church, Plumstead, Kent. (No longer extant. Destroyed by a flying bomb in the Second World War).
Named on the Memorial tablet to Master Gunners: Royal Artillery Barracks, Woolwich, Kent. (Photograph)

2nd Lt 6 Nov 1794. 1st Lt 6 Mar 1795. Capt-Lieut 14 Oct 1801. Capt 10 Apr 1805. Bt Major 6 Feb 1812. Bt Lt Colonel 27 Apr 1812. Major 26 Jun 1823. Lt Colonel 2 Apr 1825. Colonel 1 Jul 1836. Major General 10 Jan 1837. Portuguese Army: Lt Colonel 1809 – 1814.
    Served in the Peninsula Apr 1809 – Apr 1814 (Brigade Major Royal Artillery Apr – Jun 1809 and OC Portuguese Artillery from Jun 1809). Present at Grijon, Douro, Oporto, Busaco, Torres Vedras, Campo Mayor, Olivencia, Albuera (Mentioned in Despatches), first and second sieges of Badajoz (Mentioned in Despatches), Ciudad Rodrigo, (Mentioned in Despatches), Badajoz, Almarez (wounded), siege of

Salamanca Forts (Mentioned in Despatches), Salamanca, Burgos, Vittoria (Mentioned in Despatches), San Sebastian (Mentioned in Despatches), Bidassoa, Nivelle (Mentioned in Despatches), Nive, Adour and Toulouse. Gold Cross for Albuera, Busaco, Ciudad Rodrigo, Badajoz, Salamanca, Vittoria, San Sebastian Bidassoa, Nivelle Nive and Toulouse.

Present at Quatre Bras and Waterloo. Commanded the battering train with the Prussian Army at the siege of Mauberge, Landrecy, and Philippville Jul – Aug 1815. Also served in Minorca 1798, Malta 1800, South America 1807 (present at Montevideo and Buenos Ayres), North America 1814–1815 (present at Fort Bowyer and New Orleans). KCB 1815, GCB 1838, KCH, Prussian Order of Merit, KTS, Portuguese medal for the Peninsular War, and Spanish Gold Cross for Albuera. Inspector of Artillery Sep 1822. Deputy Adjutant General Royal Artillery Apr 1827. Master Gunner, St James' Park 1833 – 1840. Director General of Artillery (Field Train Department) 1838. Died 22 Apr 1840.

Sir Alexander Dickson was one of the finest artillery men of his day. This was acknowledged by Wellington who appointed him to the command of the Portuguese Artillery with the rank of Lt Colonel Jun 1809 which gave him seniority over other artillery officers enabling Wellington to treat him as his chief of Artillery. When Colonel Robe, the commander of Artillery was severely wounded at Burgos in 1812, and had to return to England, Wellington gave Dickson the command of the Allied Artillery owing to this seniority.

REFERENCE: *Dictionary of National Biography. Gentleman's Magazine, Jun 1840, p. 650–1. Leslie, John H. editor, The Dickson manuscripts: being diaries, letters, maps, account books and various other papers of the late Major General Sir Alexander Dickson, Royal Artillery, Vol 1 For the year 1809, Vol 2 For the year 1810, 1908, reprint 1987 – 1991.*

DICKSON, John

Corporal. 2nd (Royal North British) Regiment of Dragoons.
Grave: Nunhead Cemetery, London. Inscription not recorded. (Grave number 2571 sq 124)

Pte 24 Mar 1807. Cpl 25 Apr 1815. Sgt 19 Oct 1915

Served at Waterloo in Captain Vernor's Troop. On his way back to the Allied lines after the charge of the Scots Greys was reputed to have found the bodies of General William Ponsonby and his ADC Major Thomas Reignolds. It is possible that he also found Ponsonby's watch and miniature of his wife which Ponsonby had given to Reignolds for safe keeping. Reignolds had the better horse and could probably escape from the French Lancers. Discharged 10 Jul 1834. Died 16 Jul 1880 aged 90.

DIEDEL, Friedrich

Captain. 3rd Line Battalion, King's German Legion.
Named on the Regimental Memorial: La Haye Sainte, Waterloo, Belgium. (Photograph)

Capt 17 Dec 1804.

Present at Waterloo where he was killed. Also served at Hanover 1805, Baltic 1807, Mediterranean 1808–1814 and Netherlands 1814.

DIGGLE, Charles

Captain. 52nd (Oxfordshire) Light Infantry Regiment of Foot.
Memorial tablet: St Philip and St James Church, Leckhampton, Gloucestershire. (North transept). (Photograph)

TO THE MEMORY OF / MAJOR GENERAL CHARLES DIGGLE K.H. / LATE OF H. M. 52ND REGT / THIS FAITHFUL SOLDIER / TOOK AN ACTIVE PART IN THE / GALLANT SERVICES OF THAT CORPS, / FROM 1806 TO 1815 INCLUDING THE / RETREAT AND BATTLE OF CORUNNA, / AND WAS SEVERELY WOUNDED AT / WATERLOO. / HE DIED SEPTR 18TH 1862, AGED 74. / BLESSED ARE THE DEAD WHICH DIE IN THE LORD, / THIS TABLET WAS ERECTED / BY HIS AFFEC-TIONATE / NIECE.

Ensign 31 Aug 1804. Lt 14 Feb 1805. Capt 24 May 1810. Bt Major 18 Jun 1815. Bt Lt Col 10 Jan 1837. Bt Colonel 11 Nov 1851. Major General 3 Aug 1855.

Served in the Peninsula with 1/52nd Aug 1808 – Jan 1809 and Jul 1809 – Nov 1810 and 2/52nd Feb – Mar 1812. Present at Corunna, Coa, Busaco and the Lines of Torres Vedras. Present at Waterloo (severely wounded during the repulse of the Imperial Guard. Awarded Bt Majority and pension of £200 per annum). Also served in Sicily 1806–1807, Sweden 1808 and the Netherlands 1813–1814 (present at Merxem and commanded the 2nd Battalion in the advance on Antwerp). KH and MGS medal for Corunna and Busaco. Appointed Captain of a Company of Gentleman Cadets at the Royal Military College 10 Aug 1820. Half pay 23 Jun 1843. Became Gentleman Usher to the Queen.
REFERENCE: *Gentleman's Magazine, Nov 1862, p. 650. Annual Register, 1862, Appx, pp. 345–6.*

DILKES, William Thomas
Captain and Lieutenant Colonel. 3rd Regiment of Foot Guards.
Memorial: Royal Military Chapel, Wellington Barracks, London. (M.I.) (Destroyed by a Flying Bomb in 1944)

"TO THE MEMORY OF / GENERAL WILLIAM THOMAS DILKES, / WHO ENTERED THE ARMY IN 1780, AND SERVED IN THE 3RD GUARDS FROM 1783 TO 1811, WHEN HE BECAME MAJOR-GENERAL. HE WAS PRESENT DURING THE CAMPAIGNS OF 1793, '94, '95, INCLUDING THE CAPTURE OF VALENCIENNES AND VAUX; THE BATTLE OF LINCELLES, AND THE ACTIONS AT ROUBAIX, AND AT RHENEN. HE SERVED IN THE EXPEDITION TO THE HELDER, INCLUDING THE ACTIONS AT HELDER POINT AND ST MARTIN, AND THE BATTLES OF BERGEN AND ALKMAAR. HE WAS BRIGADIER OF THE GUARDS IN 1811, AND WAS SECOND IN COMMAND AT THE VICTORY OF BARROSA. / HE DIED DECEMBER 27TH, 1841. / PLACED BY HIS DAUGHTERS ANNA ELIZABETH DILKES AND WILHELMINA HAMILTON, 1879".

Ensign 49th Foot 4 Dec 1779. Lt 103rd Foot 1781. Ensign 3rd Foot Guards Mar 1783. Adjt 30 Oct 1790. Lt and Capt 28 Apr 1792. Capt and Lt Colonel 4 Feb 1797. Bt Colonel 30 Oct 1805. Major General 4 Jun 1811. Lt General 12 Aug 1819. General 10 Jan 1837.

Served in the Peninsula Apr 1810 – Apr 1811 (Commanded Brigade of Guards). Present at Cadiz and Barrosa (Mentioned in Despatches – second in command to Lt General Graham). Returned to England for family reasons 1811. Gold Medal for Barrosa. Also served in Gibraltar 1788–1789 (ADC to General O'Hara), Flanders 1793–1795 (present at Valenciennes, Vaux, Lincelles, Roubaix and Rhenen), Irish Rebellion 1798 and the Helder 1799 (present at Bergen and Alkmaar). Educated at Winchester.
REFERENCE: *Gentleman's Magazine, Oct 1842, p. 427.*

DIROM, John Pasley
Ensign. 1st Regiment of Foot Guards.
Family Mausoleum and Memorial tablet: Annan Old Parish Churchyard, Annan, Dumfriesshire, Scotland. (Photograph)

ENTOMBED HERE / ARE THE MORTAL REMAINS OF / .... / ALSO THEIR ELDEST SON LT. COLONEL DIROM, / WHO DIED ON THE 2ND JUNE, 1857 AGED 62 / ....

Ensign 62nd Foot 1 Aug 1811. Lt 44th Foot 2 Sep 1813. Ensign 1st Foot Guards 18 Nov 1813. Lt and Capt 6 Jan 1820. Capt and Lt Col 27 Mar 1828.

Served in the Peninsula with the 3rd Battalion Mar – Apr 1814. Present at Bayonne. Present at Waterloo. Retired 1 Jul 1836.
Note: The Mausoleum which had been vandalised was restored in 2004 by the Friends of the Annan Museum.

DISBROWE, George
Lieutenant and Captain. 1st Regiment of Foot Guards.
Memorial: Royal Military Chapel, Wellington Barracks, London. (M.I.) (Destroyed by a Flying Bomb 1944)

"IN MEMORY OF / COLONEL GEORGE DISBROWE, K.H. / 1ST GUARDS, 1809–34. SERVED IN PENINSULAR CAMPAIGNS, 1810–11–12–13, AND WAS AIDE – DE – CAMP TO / MAJOR-GENERAL COOKE IN HOLLAND, 1813–15. HE WAS WOUNDED AT BERGEN-OP-ZOOM AND ALSO AT WATERLOO. DIED 22ND JULY, 1876. / PLACED BY HIS DAUGHTER, L. E. A. PEPYS, 1880."

Ensign 2 Mar 1809. Lt and Capt 8 Apr 1813. Bt Major 21 Jun 1817. Bt Lt Colonel 17 Aug 1821. Capt and Lt Colonel 3 Jul 1828.
   Served in the Peninsula with 2nd Battalion Mar 1810 – May 1811 (ADC to Major General Stewart Sep 1810 – Feb 1811) and with 3rd Battalion May 1811 – Jun 1813. Present at Cadiz and Seville. Present at Waterloo (ADC to Major General Cooke). Also served in the Netherlands 1814–1815 (present at Bergen-op-Zoom where he was wounded).

DISNEY, Sir Moore
Colonel. 15th (Yorkshire East Riding) Regiment of Foot.
Interred in Catacomb B (v120 c8) Kensal Green Cemetery, London.

Ensign 1st Foot Guards 17 Apr 1783. Lt and Capt 3 Jun 1791. Capt and Lt Colonel 12 Jun 1795. Bt Colonel 29 Apr 1802. Major General 25 Oct 1809. Third Major 21 Jan 1813. Second Major 21 Oct 1813. First Major 28 Apr 1814. Lt General 4 Jun 1814. General 10 Jan 1837.
   Served in the Peninsula Oct 1808 – Jan 1809 (Commanded Brigade of Guards) and Oct 1810 – Jul 1811 (Commanded a Brigade). Present at Corunna and Cadiz. Gold Medal for Corunna (commanded the reserve force that covered the retreat). Also served in the American War of Independence 1784, Flanders 1793–1795, the Helder 1799, Sicily 1806 and Walcheren 1809. Colonel 15th Foot 23 Jul 1814. KCB 7 Apr 1815. Died 19 Apr 1846 aged 80 years.
REFERENCE: *Dictionary of National Biography. Gentleman's Magazine, Jul 1846, p. 94. Annual Register, 1846, Appx, p. 251.*

DITMAS, John
Ensign   27th (Inniskilling) Regiment of Foot.
Memorial tablet: Beverley Minster, Beverley, Yorkshire. (Near font). (Photograph)

SACRED TO THE MEMORY OF / JOHN DITMAS ESQRE / SON OF LT. COL. DITMAS OF THIS PARISH / BORN ON THE 20TH DAY OF FEBRUARY 1798. / HE OBTAINED AN ENSIGNCY / IN THE 27TH REGIMENT JUNE 3RD 1813, / AND BORE THE COLOURS OF THAT REGIMENT / AT THE BATTLE OF WATERLOO JUNE 18TH 1815, / IN WHICH BATTLE HE WAS WOUNDED. / HE RETIRED ON HALF-PAY FROM THE 68TH FOOT / ON THE 12TH DECEMBER 1821. / A SOLDIER, GENTLEMAN AND CHRISTIAN / HE ENTERED ON HIS REST ON THE 29TH DAY AUGUST 1823 / AFTER A PAINFUL AND LINGERING ILLNESS, / BORNE WITH FORTITUDE AND RESIGNA-TION, / WHICH NOTHING BUT A FIRM & RELIGIOUS PRINCIPLE / COULD HAVE INSPIRED.

Ensign 3 Jun 1813. Lt 9 Nov 1815. Lt 25th Foot 21 May 1818.
   Present at Waterloo where he carried the colours and was wounded. Retired on half pay 1821.

DIXON, Francis
1st Lieutenant. 95th Regiment of Foot.
Buried in St Saviour's Churchyard, St Helier, Jersey, Channel Islands. (Burial register)

Ensign Cambridgeshire Militia. 2nd Lt 95th Foot 12 Apr 1809. 1st Lt 11 Jan 1810.
    Served in the Peninsula with 2/95th May 1812 – Apr 1814. Present at Salamanca, San Millan, Vittoria, Pyrenees, Vera, Bidassoa, Nivelle, Nive, Orthes and Tarbes (severely wounded). Present at Waterloo. Also served at Walcheren 1809. Half pay 11 Dec 1817. Died in Jersey 30 Oct 1832.

DIXON, Robert
Private. 1st (Royal Scots) Regiment of Foot.
Headstone: Preston Cemetery, Preston, Lancashire. (Grave B43 Non conformist section). (Photograph)

IN MEMORY OF ROBERT DIXON / WHO DIED OCTOBER 20TH 1867 AGED 76 YEARS /
………………..

Served in the Peninsula with 3/1st Oct 1808 – Jan 1809 and Apr 1810 – Apr 1814. Present at Corunna, Busaco, Fuentes d'Onoro, Badajoz, Salamanca, Vittoria, San Sebastian, Nivelle and Nive. Present at Waterloo. MGS medal for Corunna, Busaco, Fuentes d'Onoro, Badajoz, Salamanca, Vittoria, San Sebastian, Nivelle and Nive.

DOBBIN, Robert Brown
Lieutenant. 66th (Berkshire) Regiment of Foot.
Named on the Memorial: St Andrew's Church, (now Musée Historique), Biarritz, France. (Photograph)

Lt 22 Sep 1808.
    Served in the Peninsula Apr 1809 – Dec 1813. Present at Douro, Talavera, Busaco, Albuera, Arroyo dos Molinos, Vittoria, Pyrenees (wounded) and Nivelle where he was severely wounded and died of his wounds 10 Dec 1813.

DOBBS, John
Lieutenant. 52nd (Oxfordshire) Light Infantry Regiment of Foot.
Headstone in railed enclosure: McGarrel Cemetery, Larne, Ireland. (Photograph)

JOHN DOBBS / LATE / CAPTAIN 52ND LIGHT INFANTRY / BORN 24TH MARCH 1791, / DIED 23RD AUGUST 1880.

Ensign 4 Feb 1808. Lt 14 Feb 1809. Capt 25 Oct 1814. Portuguese Army: Capt 5th Caçadores. 14 Sep 1813.
    Served in the Peninsula with 1/52nd Aug 1808 – Jan 1809, 2/52nd Mar – Jul 1811, 1/52nd Aug 1811 – Apr 1813 and Portuguese Army Sep 1813 – Apr 1814. Present at Corunna, Sabugal, Fuentes d'Onoro, Ciudad Rodrigo, Badajoz, Salamanca, San Munos, Vittoria, Pyrenees, San Sebastian, Bidassoa, Nivelle, Nive and Bayonne (wounded). Had the doubtful distinction of being the last officer to be wounded in the Peninsular War. Retired from Portuguese Army 13 Oct 1814. Also served in Sweden 1808 and Walcheren 1809. Half pay 25 Feb 1816. Barrack Master at Nenagh 1823. MGS medal for Corunna, Fuentes d'Onoro, Ciudad Rodrigo, Badajoz, Salamanca, Vittoria, Pyrenees, San Sebastian, Nivelle, and Nive. Governor of Waterford District Lunatic Asylum 1841–1863.
REFERENCE: *Dobbs, John, Recollections of an old 52nd man, 1859, 2nd edition, 2000.*

DOBBYN, Alexander
Ensign. 40th (2nd Somersetshire) Regiment of Foot.
Named on the Memorial: St Andrew's Church, (now Musée Historique), Biarritz, France. (Photograph)

Ensign 24 Aug 1813.
    Served in the Peninsula Sep – Nov 1813. Present at Bidassoa and Nivelle where he was killed 10 Nov 1813.

DODD, Robert
Lieutenant. 51st (2nd Yorkshire West Riding) Light Infantry.
Named on the Regimental Memorial: KOYLI Chapel, York Minster, Yorkshire. (Photograph)

Ensign 17 Aug 1809. Lt 9 May 1811.
    Served in the Peninsula Feb – Aug 1811 and Aug – Sep 1813. Present at Fuentes d'Onoro and second siege of Badajoz. Returned to England 1811 and came back to the Peninsula in time for the battle at San Marcial where he was severely wounded and died of his wounds 13 Sep 1813.

DOHERTY, George
Lieutenant. 13th Regiment of Light Dragoons.
Memorial tablet: St Paul's Church, Dublin, Ireland. (M.I.) (Church deconsecrated in about 1990 and converted into an Enterprise Centre. Intact memorials were removed to St Michan's Church but many memorials are illegible or inaccessible around the perimeter wall).

"SACRED TO THE MEMORY OF / MAJOR GEORGE DOHERTY KH / OF THE 27TH ENNISKILLINERS / WHO LIVED BELOVED / AND WHO DIED MOST DEEPLY LAMENTED / ON THE 26TH DAY OF DECEMBER 1834 / AFTER AN ILLNESS OF ONLY 4 DAYS / AGED 44 YEARS."

Family Chest tomb: Old Common Cemetery, Southampton, Hampshire. (H056 031). (Photograph)

.... / MAJOR GEORGE DOHERTY / DIED DECEMBER 26TH 1834 AGED 44, AND WAS BURIED IN DUBLIN.

Cornet 13th Lt Dragoons Jan 1805. Lt 18 Sep 1806. Capt 31 Jul 1817. Major 27th Foot 14 Sep 1832.
    Served in the Peninsula Apr 1810 – Jan 1813 and Sep 1813 – Apr 1814. Present at Campo Mayor, Albuera, Usagre, Arroyo dos Molinos, Alba de Tormes, Nivelle, Nive, Garris, Orthes, St Gaudens and Toulouse. Present at Waterloo where his father Lt Colonel Patrick Doherty commanded the regiment and his brother Joseph, Captain in 13th Foot fought alongside him. George was severely wounded but his life was saved by his watch. He had taken it out of his pocket to see the time when the regiment was ordered to advance. Having no time to put it away he slipped it into his jacket and the musket ball struck the watch. KH. Retired on half pay 29 Aug 1826.

DOHERTY, Joseph
Captain. 13th Regiment of Light Dragoons.
Obelisk: Agram Cemetery, Bangalore, Mysore State, India. (Photograph)

TO COMMEMORATE THE DEATH OF MAJOR JOSEPH DOHERTY 13TH DRAGOONS 12TH JUNE 1820 / LT JOHN POTTS 31ST JANUARY 1822 / LT W. A. BROWN 4TH NOVEMBER 1822 / CAPTAIN F. GROVE 6TH MAY 1827 / D. MACGREGOR ASST SURGEON 13TH DRAGOONS 16TH SEPTEMBER 1822 / AND MAJOR EDWARD TAYLOR GILLESPIE 26TH NOVEMBER 1836.

Cornet Feb 1803. Lt 20 Mar 1804. Capt 19 Mar 1807. Bt Major 4 Jun 1813.
    Served in the Peninsula Apr 1810 – Jul 1811 and Sep 1812 – Apr 1814. Present at Campo Mayor, Alba de Tormes, Vittoria, Pyrenees, Nivelle, Garris, Orthes, Aire, St Gaudens and Toulouse. Present at Waterloo (wounded). His father Lt Colonel Patrick Doherty was commanding the regiment and his brother George, also wounded, was a Lieutenant in the same regiment. Also served in India and died there 12 Jun 1820, aged 32.

DOHERTY, Patrick
Lieutenant Colonel. 13ᵗʰ Regiment of Light Dragoons.
Memorial tablet: St Saviour's Church, Larkhall, Bath, Somerset. (Photograph)

IN THE VAULT BENEATH ARE DEPOSITED THE MORTAL / REMAINS OF COLᴸ SIR PATRICK DOHERTY, C.B. K.C.H. / WHO DEPARTED THIS LIFE 20ᵀᴴ JANᴿʸ 1837. / HE SERVED IN THE 13ᵀᴴ Lᵀ DRAGⁿˢ UPWARDS OF 33 YEARS / BELOVED AND RESPECTED, AND COMMANDED THAT / REGIMENT DURING THE MOST ARDUOUS PART OF THE / PENINSULAR WAR. HIS HIGH CHARACTER AS A SOLDIER / WAS ACKNOWLEDGED BY THE MANY MARKS OF FAVOR, AND / DISTINCTION CONFERRED UPON HIM BY HIS SOVEREIGN; / AND HIS PRIVATE WORTH AND SOCIAL VIRTUES, / WERE FELT AND APPRECIATED BY A LARGE CIRCLE / OF FRIENDS. / THIS TABLET IS ERECTED / BY HIS WIDOW AND DAUGHTER, / AS A TESTIMONY OF THE LOVE THEY BORE HIM, / AND THEIR DEEP AFFLICTION FOR HIS / IRREPARABLE LOSS. /
………………..

Cornet 15 Apr 1794. Lt Sep 1794. Capt 30 Apr 1795. Major 6 Apr 1800. Bt Lt Col 25 Apr 1808. Lt Col 11 Jun 1813. Bt Colonel 4 Jun 1814.

Served in the Peninsula Apr 1810 – Jul 1811 and Apr 1812 – Apr 1814 (Commanded D Cavalry Brigade Mar – Apr 1814). Present at Campo Mayor, Alba de Tormes, Vittoria, Nivelle, Nive, Garris, Orthes, Aire, Tarbes, St Gaudens and Toulouse. In command of the regiment in all these battles. Present in the Waterloo campaign until 18 June when he had a severe attack of yellow fever, a legacy of his campaigning in the West Indies. Commanded the regiment in the Army of Occupation. Both his sons, Capt Joseph and Lt George, also in the 13ᵗʰ Lt Dragoons were wounded at Waterloo.

Also served in the West Indies 1796 (present at the storming of St Domingo), where he became ill with yellow fever and was sent home to recover. 22 officers died of the fever and so rapid promotion ensued for Doherty and he was soon in command of the regiment. Gold Medal for Vittoria and Orthes. CB. KCH.

DON, George
Colonel. 96ᵗʰ Regiment of Foot.
Memorial tablet: Holy Trinity Cathedral, Gibraltar. (Photograph)

SACRED / TO THE MEMORY OF / GENERAL SIR GEORGE DON, / G.C.B. G.C.H. & G.C.M.M. / COLONEL OF THE THIRD REGIMENT OF FOOT / AND / GOVERNOR OF SCARBOROUGH CASTLE / WHO AFTER SIXTY YEARS OF UNINTERRUPTED AND ACTIVE SERVICE / DIED AT GIBRALTAR ON THE 17 OF JANUARY 1832 / AGED 76 YEARS. / HAVING BEEN ENTRUSTED BY HIS SOVEREIGN / THRO' A SERIES OF 39 YEARS / WITH MANY HIGH COMMANDS / HE CLOSED HIS LIFE / FULL OF YEARS AND HONOURS / IN THAT IMPORTANT FORTRESS WHERE HE HAD COMMANDED / AS LIEUTENANT GOVERNOR / WITH DEVOTED ZEAL AND CONSUMMATE ABILITY / DURING THE LONG PERIOD OF 17 YEARS.

Bust: Main Street, Gibraltar. (Photograph)

BY VOLUNTARY SUBSCRIPTION OF THE INHABITANTS, / AND IN GRATEFUL REMEM-BRANCE OF / HIS PATERNAL GOVERNMENT, / UNDER WHICH THIS BUILDING WAS ERECTED, / ANNO DOMINI 1818, / IS PLACED THIS BUST OF / GEORGE DON / KNIGHT GRAND CROSS OF THE ROYAL GUELPHIC ORDER, / AND KNIGHT GRAND CROSS OF THE ROYAL ORDER OF / MILITARY MERIT OF FRANCE, / GENERAL OF HIS MAJESTY'S FORCES, / COLONEL OF THE THIRTY SIXTH REGIMENT OF FOOT. / LIEUTENANT GOVERNOR / AND COMMANDER IN CHIEF OF THE GARRISON / AND TERRITORY OF GIBRALTAR, / &C, &C, &C.

Statue: St Helier, Jersey, Channel Islands. (Photograph)

DON / 1806 / & / 1814 / GENERAL SIR GEORGE DON (1756 – 1832) / SERVED IN JERSEY 1792–1793, 1806–1809 AND 1810–1814. / ON 21ST MAY 1810 PRESENTED BY THE MILITIA WITH / GOLD-HILTED SWORD. NOW IN EDINBURGH WAR MUSEUM. / LEFT JERSEY IN 1814 TO BECOME GOVERNOR OF GIBRALTAR. / DIED 1ST JANUARY 1832. AND BURIED ON SITE OF / GIBRALTAR CATHEDRAL. / MONUMENT UNVEILED 29TH OCTOBER 1885.

Ensign 51st Foot 26 Dec 1770. Lt 3 Jun 1774. Bt Major 25 Nov 1783. Major 59th Foot 21 Apr 1784. Lt Colonel 9 Apr 1788. Colonel 26 Feb 1795. Major General 1 Jan 1798. Lt General 1 Jan 1803. Colonel 96th Foot 10 Oct 1805. General 4 Jun 1814.

Present at Walcheren 1809 (appointed to command the island until it was evacuated). Also served in Minorca 1781, Flanders 1794 (DAG. Remained in Germany until 1798 on military missions to the Prussian Army), Helder 1799 (when sent out with a flag of truce at the end of the campaign was taken prisoner and not released until Jun 1800), Hanover 1805 (in command of the King's German Legion in Cathcart's expedition), Jersey 1806–1814 (Lt Governor. Absent 1809–1810 while serving at Walcheren), Governor General in Gibraltar 1814–1831, where he improved sanitation and water supply and built hospitals. He was fortunate to have John Hennen as Principal Medical Officer and between them they did much to avert the epidemic of yellow fever which plagued Gibraltar. Don built a court house and his Sanitary Police evolved in 1830 into the first British police force outside the United Kingdom. GCH. GCB. Colonel 9th West India Regt 22 Nov 1799. Colonel 36th Foot 4 Apr 1818. Colonel 3rd Foot 1829. Died 1 Jan 1832.
REFERENCE: *Dictionary of National Biography. Gentleman's Magazine, Mar 1832, pp. 272–3. Royal Military Calendar Vol 2, p. 11–2.*

DONALDSON, Gordon Graham
Captain and Lieutenant Colonel. 1st Regiment of Foot Guards.
Memorial tablet: St Nicholas's Church, Harwich, Essex. (South side of Chancel). (M.I)

"TO THE MEMORY OF / GORDON GRAHAM DONALDSON / OF THE FIRST REGIMENT OF FOOT GUARDS / THIS MONUMENT IS ERECTED / BY THE DIRECTION OF HIS BROTHER OFFICERS / AS A TESTIMONY OF THEIR ESTEEM. / HE DIED MOST SINCERELY REGRETTED / ON THE 7TH OF SEPTEMBER 1809 / ON HIS RETURN FROM THE SCHELDT / IN THE 34TH YEAR OF HIS AGE."

Headstone: St Nicholas's Churchyard, Harwich, Essex. (M.I.)

"THE REMAINS OF THE LATE / LIEUT COLN DONALDSON / OF THE FIRST FOOT GUARDS / WERE DEPOSITED HERE WITH MILITARY / HONOURS ON THE 9TH SEPT 1809 / AND A MONU-MENT ERECTED IN / CHANCEL ON THE SOUTH SIDE / BY HIS BROTHER OFFICERS / AS A TESTIMONY OF THEIR ESTEEM / AND RESPECT."

Named on Memorial Panel VI for the Expedition to the Scheldt: Royal Military Chapel, Wellington Barracks, London. (M.I.) (Destroyed by a Flying Bomb 1944)

Ensign 57th Foot 24 Feb 1791. Ensign 1st Foot Guards 23 Oct 1793. Lt and Capt 23 Sep 1795. Capt and Lt Colonel 8 Nov 1804.
Served in the Peninsula with 1st Battalion Oct 1808 – Jan 1809. Present at Corunna. Also served at Walcheren 1809. Died from fever on return from the Walcheren expedition.

DONNEGAN, Hugh
Private. 12th (Prince of Wales's) Regiment of Light Dragoons.
Named on the Regimental Memorial: St Joseph's Church, Waterloo, Belgium. (Photograph)
Killed at Waterloo.

DONOVAN, Henry Douglas
Ensign. 48th (Northamptonshire) Regiment of Foot.
Ledger stone: St Nicholas Churchyard, Cardiff, Glamorgan, Wales. (Photograph)

IN MEMORY OF / LIEUTENANT HENRY DOUGLAS DONOVAN / LATE OF HER MAJESTY'S 9TH
REGT OF FOOT / BURIED IN THIS CHURCHYARD ON THE 28TH DAY OF MAY 1863 / AGED 68
YEARS

Ensign Tower Hamlets Militia 1811. Ensign 48th Foot 25 Aug 1813. Lt 9th Foot Feb 1817.
Volunteered for service in Spain 1811 to drill the troops. Served in the Peninsula Jul 1813 – Mar 1814.
Present at Pyrenees, San Sebastian, Nivelle and Orthes. Retired on half pay 13 Feb 1817. MGS medal for
Pyrenees, San Sebastian, Nivelle and Orthes. After he retired became agent for the first steamer between
Cardiff and Bristol which became very successful. One of his sons became Lt Colonel in the Confederate
Army in the American Civil War.

DORNFORD, Joseph
Volunteer. 95th Regiment of Foot.
Headstone: St John the Baptist Churchyard, Plymtree, Devon. (Photograph)

JOSEPH DORNFORD, M. A. / BORN JANUARY 9, 1794. / ASLEEP IN JESUS JANUARY 18, 1868.

Volunteer.
Served in the Peninsula Jun – Aug 1813. Present at Vittoria and Pyrenees. MGS medal for Vittoria and
Pyrenees. Later entered the church.

DOUGLAS, Archibald Murray
Captain. 52nd (Oxfordshire) Light Infantry Regiment of Foot.
Headstone with Cross: St Brynach's Church, Llanfrynach, Brecon, Wales. (Against boundary wall).
(Photograph)

TO / THE / MEMORY / OF / ARCHIBALD / MURRAY DOUGLAS / CAPTAIN / H.M. 52ND REGT /
YOUNGEST SON OF / WILLIAM DOUGLAS ESQRE / OF BRIGTON / IN THE COUNTY OF /
FORFAR, N.B. / WHO DIED AT TY MAWR / IN THIS PARISH / THE 6TH FEBRY 1872 / AGED 82.

Ensign 30 Jan 1808. Lt 13 Feb 1809. Capt 28 Apr 1814.
Served in the Peninsula with 1/52nd Aug 1808 – Jan 1809, 2/52nd Mar – Jun 1811, 1/52nd Jul 1811- Mar
1812 and Nov 1813 – Apr 1814. Present at Corunna, Sabugal, Fuentes d'Onoro, Ciudad Rodrigo, Nivelle,
Nive, Orthes, Tarbes and Toulouse. Also served at Walcheren 1809. Half pay 25 Feb 1817. MGS medal
for Corunna, Fuentes d'Onoro, Ciudad Rodrigo, Nivelle, Nive, Orthes and Toulouse.
REFERENCE: *Oxfordshire Light Infantry Chronicle, 1906, pp. 187–9.*

DOUGLAS, Charles
Major. 59th (2nd Nottinghamshire) Regiment of Foot.
Named on the Regimental Memorial monument: Christ Church Churchyard, Tramore, County
Waterford, Ireland. (Photograph)

Ensign 9 Aug 1803. Lt 6 Sep 1805. Capt 19 May 1808. Major 20 Apr 1815.

Served in the Peninsula Dec 1813 – Apr 1814. Present at Bayonne. Present at Waterloo in reserve at Hal, siege of Cambrai and with the Army of Occupation. Lost in the *Sea Horse* shipwreck off the coast of Ireland 30 Jan 1816.

DOUGLAS, Charles Aytoyne W.

Captain. 51st (2nd Yorkshire West Riding) Light Infantry.
Named on the Regimental Memorial: KOYLI Chapel, York Minster, Yorkshire. (Photograph)

Ensign 10th Foot 11 Jun 1794. Lt 7 Jul 1795. Capt 2nd Ceylon Regt 3 Dec 1803. Capt 51st Foot 25 Apr 1806.

Served in the Peninsula Oct 1808 – Jan 1809 and Feb 1811 – Aug 1813. Present at Corunna, Fuentes d'Onoro, second siege of Badajoz, Burgos, San Millan, Vittoria, Pyrenees and San Marcial where he was killed while helping to carry off a wounded man. 'Captain Douglas died in the very act of displaying one of the noblest qualities of our nature. The brigade was ordered to retire, having suffered much from bravely maintaining its ground against a very superior body of the enemy. Captain Douglas who was everywhere he could be most useful, and where most was going on was in the very act of encouraging some of the skirmishers to return for the purpose of carrying off a wounded man, when he was shot through the heart. So much was he beloved by his men, that although under heavy fire, four soldiers of the 51st endeavoured to remove his body; persisting in this attempt, two of them were killed and one wounded: when the other being pressed by the enemy, was obliged to relinquish his precious charge which was plundered of everything valuable'. (*Gentleman's Magazine*). Also served in India, Egypt 1801 and Walcheren 1809. Nephew of Major Sir Howard Douglas Royal York Rangers.
REFERENCE: *Gentleman's Magazine, Nov 1813, p. 499.*

DOUGLAS, Sir Howard

Major. Royal York Rangers.
Low monument: St John the Baptist Churchyard, Boldre, Hampshire. (Grave number 221 on north side of church). (Photograph)

HOWARD DOUGLAS BARONET. GENERAL C.B. / DIED NOV 9TH 1861 AGED 85 YEARS.

2nd Lt Royal Artillery 1 Jan 1794. 1st Lt 30 May 1794. Capt- Lieut 2 Oct 1799. Capt 12 Sep 1803. Major Royal York Rangers 12 Oct 1804. Bt Lt Colonel 31 Dec 1806. Bt Colonel 4 Jun 1814. Major General 19 Jul 1821. Lt General 10 Jan 1837. General 11 Nov 1851.

Served in the Peninsula 1808 – Jan 1809 (AQMG) and 1811 – Oct 1812 (Intelligence Officer with the Spanish Army). Present at Corunna, Astorga and Burgos. Also served in Flanders 1794–1795, and Walcheren 1809 (present at the siege of Flushing).

Served in the Royal Artillery until 1804, employed by Colonel Congreve to explore the use of field batteries of eight inch mortars mounted on travelling carriages. In 1804 he transferred to the Royal Military College to organise a department for the education of Staff Officers. Went to Spain and Portugal 1805. During his time with the Spanish Army he closely observed the guerrilla defence of Spain and wrote about it in *Observations of a modern systems of fortification*, 1859. He was always, at heart, an artillery man and his knowledge of the science and practice of gunnery made him one of the foremost authorities on the subject. CB. GCMG. MGS medal for Corunna. Order of Charles III from King of Spain. Lt Governor of New Brunswick 1823–1831. Lord High Commissioner of the Ionian Islands 1835 (included command of the troops). MP for Liverpool 1842–1847. Colonel 99th Foot 1841. Colonel 15th Foot 1851. Uncle of Capt Charles Aytoyne Douglas 51st Foot.
REFERENCE: *Fullom, S. W., The life of General Sir Howard Douglas, 1863. Dictionary of National Biography. Royal Military Calendar, Vol 4, pp. 165–6.*

DOUGLAS, John Graham
Captain. 52nd (Oxfordshire) Light Infantry Regiment of Foot.
Named on the Memorial: St Andrew's Church, (now Musée Historique), Biarritz, France. (Photograph)

Ensign 90th Foot 5 Apr 1801. Ensign 8th Foot 5 Aug 1802. Lt 52nd Foot 26 May 1803. Captain 27 Aug 1804. Bt Major 1813.
    Served in the Peninsula with 2/52nd Aug 1808 – Jan 1809 and 1/52nd Jul 1809 – Dec 1813. Present in the Corunna campaign, Coa, Busaco, Pombal, Redinha, Casal Nova, Foz d'Arouce, Sabugal, Fuentes d'Onoro, Ciudad Rodrigo, Badajoz, Salamanca, San Marcial, Vittoria, Pyrenees, Vera (severely wounded), Bidassoa (wounded), and Nive where he was severely wounded 10 Dec and died of his wounds 24 Dec 1813. The bullet which killed him is in the Regimental Museum.
REFERENCE: *Oxfordshire Light Infantry Chronicle, 1906, pp. 187–9.*

DOUGLAS, Joseph
Lieutenant. 45th (Nottinghamshire) Regiment of Foot.
Buried in St George's Chapel, Windsor, Berkshire. (Burial record)

2nd Lt Royal Marines 1804. Ensign 32nd Foot 14 Jul 1808. Lt 47th Foot 20 Dec 1810. Lt 45th Foot 10 Apr 1811.
    Served in the Peninsula Dec 1812 – Apr 1814. Present at Nivelle, Nive, Orthes, Vic Bigorre and Toulouse (wounded whilst carrying the King's Colours). Also served in the Royal Marines 1804–1808 (watching Dutch fleet in 1804, employed in cutting out the boats of enemy ships and storming batteries. Awarded medal) and Walcheren 1809 (present at the siege or Flushing). MGS medal for Nivelle, Nive, Orthes and Toulouse. Half pay 14 Aug 1828. Military Knight of Windsor 13 Feb 1856. Died at Windsor 11 May 1866.

DOUGLAS, Kenneth see MACKENZIE, Kenneth

DOUGLAS, Robert
Captain. Royal Artillery.
Low monument: Holy Trinity Churchyard, Claygate, Surrey. (North side of church). Inscription illegible. (Photograph)

2nd Lt 1 Nov 1796. 1st Lt 1 Sep 1798. 2nd Capt 20 Jul 1804. Capt 1 May 1809. Bt Major 4 Jun 1814. Lt Colonel 31 Dec 1827. Bt Colonel 23 Nov 1841. Major General 20 Jun 1854. Lt General 28 Nov 1854. General 25 Sep 1859.
    Served in the Peninsula Mar 1812 – Mar 1814 (Commanded 10th Company, 9th Battalion). Present at Salamanca, Vittoria, Pyrenees, second siege of San Sebastian and Nivelle. Bt Majority for his service in the Peninsula. Gold Cross for Salamanca, Vittoria, Pyrenees and Nivelle. MGS medal for San Sebastian. CB. Also served in the West Indies 1801–1805, Hanover 1805–1806 and Malta 1819–1820. Retired on full pay 6 May 1835. Died at Claygate 10 Feb 1871 aged 93.
REFERENCE: *Annual Register, 1871, Appx, p. 144.*

DOUGLAS, Robert
Surgeon. 91st Regiment of Foot.
Headstone: St Mary's Churchyard, Hawick, Roxburghshire, Scotland. (Photograph)

IN MEMORY OF / ROBERT DOUGLAS, SURGEON, HAWICK, / WHO DIED 28TH APRIL 1829, AGED 78 YEARS / ………………..

Hospital Mate 13 Aug 1801. Asst Surgeon 91st Foot 25 Jun 1802. Surgeon 5 Jun 1805.

Served in the Peninsula Aug 1808 – Jan 1809 and Oct 1812 – Apr 1814. Present at Rolica, Vimeiro, Cacabellos, Corunna, Pyrenees, Nivelle, Nive, Orthes, Aire and Toulouse. Present at Waterloo in reserve at Hal, siege of Cambrai, Capture of Paris and with the Army of Occupation. Also served at Hanover 1805, Cape of Good Hope 1806 and Walcheren 1809. Retired from the army 1821 and returned to Hawick to help his father who was a surgeon. Robert's health had suffered in the Peninsula and his brother John took over most of the work of the practice. John had also been an army surgeon, serving in North America with the 8th Foot.
REFERENCE: *Kelso Mail, 1845.*

DOUGLAS, Sholto
Lieutenant. 50th (West Kent) Regiment of Foot.
Memorial tablet in walled enclosure: Parish Church, Cummertrees, Dumfriesshire, Scotland. (Photograph)

MAJOR SHOLTO DOUGLAS. / SON OF JAMES SHOLTO. / DIED 1838. / EDWARD SHOLTO DOUGLAS R.N. / HIS ONLY SON. / DIED 1855. / AGED 22. / BROTHER AND NEPHEW OF SARAH. / MARCHIONESS OF / QUEENSBURY.

Ensign 19 Dec 1811. Lt 15 Jul 1813. Capt 63rd Foot 18 Jul 1823. Major 23 Aug 1827.
Served in the Peninsula Jan 1813 – Apr 1814. Present at Vittoria, Pyrenees, Nivelle, Nive, Garris, Orthes, Aire, Tarbes and Toulouse. Also served in Portugal 1826–1828 (with expedition under Sir William Clinton), Tasmania 1828 (in command of 63rd Foot guarding convicts and in 1830 commanded the troops and armed civilians in the Black Line sweep of the Colony to remove the warlike tribes of Aborigines down to the Tasmanian Peninsula).
After leaving the army he had various administrative posts in Tasmania, but did not like the country and often had disputes with the Lieutenant Governor George Arthur. Returned to England 1838 and died 24 Dec 1838. Younger brother of Lt General Sir James Douglas and of the Marchioness of Queensberry, both of whom helped him in his early military career.
REFERENCE: *Australian Dictionary of Biography.*

DOUGLAS, Sir William
Lieutenant Colonel. 91st Regiment of Foot.
Table tomb in railed enclosure: Valenciennes, France. (Photograph)

ERECTED / BY THE / OFFICERS, NON – COMS AND PRIVATES / XCI BRITISH REGIMENT / TO THE MEMORY / OF / COLONEL SIR WILLIAM DOUGLAS / K.C.B. / THEIR COMMANDING OFFICER / AS A FEEBLE TESTIMONY OF REGARD / AND THEIR REGRET / FOR / ONE OF THE BRAVEST AND THE BEST OF MEN / DIED XXIII AUG MDCCCXVIII AGED XLII

Memorial tablet: St John's Episcopal Church, Forfar, Angus, Scotland. (Photograph)

IN MEMORY OF / COLL SIR WILLIAM DOUGLAS KCB. / THIS MONUMENT IS ERECTED / BY HIS BROTHER OFFICERS OF THE 91ST OR ARGYLLSHIRE REGIMENT / AS A TRIBUTE OF THEIR RESPECT AND ESTEEM / FOR HIS DISTINGUISHED SERVICES IN THE FIELD / AND AMIABLE QUALITIES IN PRIVATE LIFE. / HE FELL AN EARLY VICTIM TO THE DUTIES OF HIS PROFES-SION / AT VALENCIENNES, IN FRANCE, / UNIVERSALLY REGRETTED BY THE ARMY, AND ALL WHO KNEW HIM.

Ensign 28th Foot 1793. Lt 78th Foot 1793. Capt 108th Foot 1794. Capt 84th Foot 1795, Capt 91st Foot 27 Jun 1798. Major 2 Aug 1804. Lt Colonel 25 Nov 1808. Bt Colonel 4 Jun 1814.
Served in the Peninsula in command of 91st Foot Aug 1808 – Jan 1809 and Jan 1813 – Apr 1814.
Present at Rolica, Vimeiro, Cacabellos, Corunna, Pyrenees, Nivelle, Nive, Orthes (wounded), Aire,

Tarbes and Toulouse (wounded). Gold Cross for Corunna, Pyrenees, Nivelle, Nive, Orthes and Toulouse. KCB. Present at Waterloo in reserve at Hal, siege of Cambrai (Mentioned in Despatches), Capture of Paris and with the Army of Occupation. Also served in the Cape of Good Hope 1795, Hanover 1805 and Walcheren 1809, where he caught the fever, never fully recovered and died from it in Valenciennes in 1818, where his remains are buried and where a memorial was erected to his memory. Commanded the regiment from 1808 until his death in 1818.

DOW, Edward
Surgeon. 37th (North Hampshire) Regiment of Foot.
Monument: Burial Ground, The Savannah, Roseau, Barbados, West Indies. (M.I.)

"TO THE MEMORY OF / EDWARD DOW ESQUIRE / DEPUTY INSPECTOR GENERAL OF HOSPITALS / AIDE-DE-CAMP TO THE GOVERNOR / AND / LIEUTENANT COLONEL OF MILITIA / WHO WAS KILLED BY FALLING WITH HIS HORSE / OVER A PRECIPICE IN THIS ISLAND / ON THE 8TH OF APRIL 1832. / THIS MEMORIAL IS RAISED / BY / SIR EUAN JOHN MURRAY MACGREGOR, BART."

Hospital Mate 17 May 1804. Asst Surgeon Royal Corsican Rangers 28 Jan 1808. Asst Surgeon 20th Dragoons 7 Dec 1809. Asst Surgeon 33rd Foot 19 Dec 1811. Staff Surgeon 12 Nov 1812. Surgeon 37th Foot 25 Dec 1812. Staff Surgeon 17 Mar 1814. Deputy Inspector General of Hospitals 5 Nov 1829.
    Served in the Peninsula Mar – Apr 1814. Present at Bayonne. Accompanied Sir Euan MacGregor to the West Indies as his Secretary 1831.

DOWDALL, Patrick
Major. 31st (Huntingdonshire) Regiment of Foot.
Ledger stone: St Patrick's Church of Ireland, Newry, Northern Ireland. Seriously eroded and inscription recorded from memorial inscription. (Photograph)

"SACRED TO THE MEMORY OF / MAJOR PATRICK DOWDALL OF / H M 31ST REGT OF FOOT, / DEPARTED THIS LIFE NOV 1822 AGED 42 YEARS. / IN GRATEFUL REMEMBRANCE OF HIS MANIFOLD VIRTUES / AND UNDER A DEEP SENSE OF HER OWN IRREPLACEABLE LOSS / AN AFFECTIONATE WIDOW CONSECRATES THIS HUMBLE TRIBUTE / TO THE BEST OF HUSBANDS, THE KINDEST OF FATHERS, / AND ONE OF THE MOST EXEMPLARY OF MEN."

Ensign 30 Aug 1800. Lt 5 Nov 1800. Capt 4 Dec 1806. Bt Major 26 Dec 1813.
    Served in the Peninsula Jan 1812 – Apr 1814 (on Staff from Feb 1814 as Brigade Major). Present at Vittoria, Pyrenees and Nive.

DOWLING, Joseph
Lieutenant. 73rd (Highland) Regiment of Foot.
Monument: Kensal Green Cemetery, London. Inscription illegible. (5681/108/4). (Photograph)

Ensign 66th Foot 18 Jan 1810. Lt 73rd Foot 13 Aug 1812. Lt 1st Royal Veteran Battalion 27 Nov 1823.
    Served in the Peninsula with 66th Foot Jan 1810 – Aug 1812. Present at Albuera and Arroyo dos Molinos. Present at Waterloo with 73rd Foot where he was wounded. Also served in Hanover 1813 (present at Ghorde). Barrack Master at Coventry 1830 and later at Wellington Barracks in London. Buried in Kensal Green 30 Aug 1845.
REFERENCE: *Lagden, Alan and John Sly, The 2/73rd at Waterloo, 2nd edition, 1998, pp. 58–9.*

DOWNING, Adam Gifford
Captain. 81st Regiment of Foot.
Memorial tablet on Family mausoleum: Bellaghy Parish Church, Bellaghy, County Londonderry. (Photograph)

.... / ADAM GIFFORD DOWNING ESQ^RE / LIEUT. COLONEL ON THE HALF PAY OF / HER MAJESTY'S 81ST REGIMENT, IN WHICH / HE HAD SERVED WITH DISTINCTION. YOUNGEST SON / OF THE ABOVE NAMED REV^D ALEXANDER CLOTWORTHY DOWNING / DIED ON 21ST FEB 1847 AGED 63 YEARS AND WAS / INTERRED HERE ON 23RD FEBRUARY 1847. / ....

Ensign 34th Foot 26 Jun 1799. Lt 7 Mar 1800. Capt 81st Foot 26 Dec 1805. Bt Major 21 Dec 1815. Bt Lt Colonel 10 Jan 1837.
    Served in the Peninsula Nov 1808 – Jan 1809 and Aug 1812 – Oct 1813. Present at Corunna where he was wounded and Eastern Spain. Also served at Walcheren 1809.

DOWNMAN, Thomas
Lieutenant Colonel. Royal Artillery.
Tomb: St Mary's Churchyard, West Malling, Kent. (M.I.)

"LIEUTENANT GENERAL SIR THOMAS DOWNMAN KCB, KCH, MAR 3 1773 – AUG 10 1862, HAVING SERVED HIS COUNTRY FAITHFULLY FOR 60 YEARS. BELOVED BY HIS FAMILY AND RESPECTED BY ALL WHO KNEW HIM. ...."

2nd Lt 24 Apr 1793. 1st Lt 11 Sep 1793. Capt-Lieut 1 Nov 1797. Capt 25 Jul 1802. Major 22 Jan 1810. Bt Lt Colonel 17 Dec 1812. Lt Colonel 20 Dec 1814. Bt Colonel 27 May 1825. Colonel 29 Jul 1825. Major General 10 Jan 1837. Colonel Commandant 26 Sep 1843. Lt General 9 Nov 1846.
    Served in the Peninsula Nov 1808 – Jan 1809 (Commanded 'B' Troop RHA, attached to the cavalry) and Apr 1811 – Nov 1813 (GOC RHA). Present at Sahagun, Benevente, Corunna, Aldea da Ponte, Ciudad Rodrigo, siege of Salamanca Forts, Castrejon, Salamanca, Madrid, siege of Burgos and retreat from Burgos (Mentioned in Despatches and awarded Bt Lt Colonelcy) and Fuente Guinaldo. Gold Medal for Salamanca. MGS medal for Sahagun and Benevente, Corunna and Ciudad Rodrigo. Also served in Flanders 1793–1794 (present at Lannoy, Rauxhain, Mourveaux, Tournai, Roubaix (taken prisoner from May 1794 – Jul 1795), West Indies 1798 (present at San Domingo). Director General of Artillery 1843–1844. Commandant at Woolwich Apr 1846–1852.
REFERENCE: *Dictionary of National Biography. Royal Military Calendar, Vol 4, p. 437. Gentleman's Magazine, Sep 1852, pp. 313–4. Annual Register, 1852, Appx, p. 299.*

DOWNS, James
Sergeant. 51st (2nd Yorkshire West Riding) Light Infantry.
Named on the Regimental Memorial: KOYLI Chapel, York Minster, Yorkshire. (Photograph)
    Killed in the Peninsula.

DOYLE, Carlo Joseph
Major. 4th Garrison Battalion.
Monument: Kensal Green Cemetery, London. (7357/75/IC). (Photograph)

SACRED / TO THE MEMORY OF / MAJOR-GENERAL / CARLO J. DOYLE / WHO DEPARTED THIS LIFE / ON THE 3RD DAY OF FEB^Y 1848 / IN HIS 61ST YEAR / ....

Ensign Coldstream Guards 28 Jul 1803. Capt 87th Foot 13 Mar 1806. Major 4th Garrison Battalion 23

Jan 1812. Bt Lt Colonel 8 Mar 1815. Bt Colonel 10 Jan 1837. Major General 9 Nov 1846.

Served in the Peninsula 1808–1809 (attached to the Spanish Army and appointed a Military Commissioner to the Guerrillas in the north of Spain) and Mar 1809 – Jul 1811, (DAQMG Jun 1809 – Jul 1811). Present at Espinosa 1808 (wounded), Corunna, Douro, Talavera, Campo Mayor and Fuentes d'Onoro. Also served in Hanover 1805, Ireland 1806 (ADC to the Duke of Bedford), Guernsey 1812 (commanded 4th Garrison Battalion), India 1813–1818 (Military Secretary to Governor General, present in Pindari and Mahratta Wars). CB. Lieutenant Governor of Grenada.
REFERENCE: *Gentleman's Magazine, May 1848, p. 547. Royal Military Calendar, Vol 5, p. 87.*

DOYLE, Charles Simon
Surgeon. 35th (Sussex) Regiment of Foot.
Gravestone: Officer's Cemetery, Military Burial Ground, Eve Leary, Demerara, British Guiana, West Indies. (M.I.)

"CHARLES SIMON DOYLE, M.D. SURGEON TO THE FORCES, DIED 30TH OCTOBER 1836, AGED 48."

Hospital Mate 7 Feb 1801. Asst Surgeon 55th Foot 12 Oct 1802. Asst Surgeon 85th Foot 8 Jan 1807. Surgeon 35th Foot 31 Mar 1808. Staff Surgeon 7 Sep 1815.

Present at Waterloo in reserve at Hal. Also served at Walcheren 1809 and the Netherlands 1814. MD St Andrew's 1816.

DOYLE, James
Drummer. 40th (2nd Somersetshire) Regiment of Foot.
Headstone: St Michael's Churchyard, Alnwick, Northumberland. (M.I.)

"IN MEMORY OF / MARGARET / WIFE OF SERGT JAMES DOYLE WHO / DIED JULY 8 1856 AGED 61 YEARS. / ALSO IN MEMORY OF THE ABOVE NAMED / SRGT JAMES DOYLE / WHO DIED AUG 5 1856 AGED 61 YEARS / 28½ OF WHICH WERE PASSED IN SERVICE / OF HIS COUNTRY / WITH THE 40 REGIMENT IN / EUROPE, ASIA AND AMERICA. / HE WAS ENGAGED DURING THE PENINSULAR WAR / IN THE FOLLOWING BATTLES / CUIDAD RODRIGO BADAJOS SALA- MANCA / VITTORIA PYRENESE NIVELLE / ORTHES AND TOULOUSE. / HE WAS ALSO PRESENT AT THE EVER MEMORABLE / ENGAGEMENT / THE BATTLE OF WATERLOO. / HE WAS A GOOD SOLDIER, A LOVING HUSBAND, / KIND FRIEND AND AN UPRIGHT MAN. / REQUI- ESCAT IN PACE."

Drummer 40th Foot 25 Aug 1809. Pte 26 Sep 1817. Cpl 25 Nov 1827. Sgt 1 Aug 1832.

Served in the Peninsula. Present at Ciudad Rodrigo, Badajoz, Salamanca, Vittoria, Pyrenees, Orthes and Toulouse. Present at Waterloo. MGS medal for Ciudad Rodrigo, Badajoz, Salamanca, Vittoria, Pyrenees, Orthes and Toulouse. Also served in India 21 Jan 1829 – 31 Oct 1834. Discharged 1836 aged 40 after 27 years service.

DOYLE, John
1st Lieutenant. 95th Regiment of Foot.
Named on the Memorial: St Andrew's Church, (now Musée Historique), Biarritz, France. (Photograph)

Volunteer 5th Foot. 2nd Lt 95th Regiment 10 Oct 1811. Lt 25 Nov 1813.

Served in the Peninsula Jan 1812 – Nov 1813. Present at Ciudad Rodrigo, Badajoz, Salamanca, San Millan, Vittoria, Pyrenees and Nivelle where he was severely wounded 10 Nov 1813 and died the same day.

DOYLE, Sir John Milley
Captain. 87th (Prince of Wales's Own Irish) Regiment of Foot.
Buried in St George's Chapel, Windsor, Berkshire. (On Green south of the Chapel). (Burial record).

Ensign 107th Foot 31 May 1794. Lt 108th Foot 21 Jun 1795. Lt 92nd Foot 1800. Capt 81st Foot 9 Jul 1803. Capt 5th Foot 3 Sep 1804. Capt 87th Foot 7 Dec 1804. Bt Major 16 Feb 1809. Bt Lt Colonel 26 Sep 1811. Portuguese Army: Lt Colonel 16th Line 2 Apr 1809. Lt Colonel 8th Line 11 Aug 1810. Lt Colonel 19 Line 5 Apr 1811. Colonel 5 Feb 1812.

Served in the Peninsula with Portuguese Army Apr 1809 – Apr 1814. Present at Grijon (Mentioned in Beresford's Despatches), Douro, Fuentes d'Onoro, first siege of Badajoz, Ciudad Rodrigo, Vittoria, Pyrenees, Nivelle (Commanded 6 Portuguese Brigade. Mentioned in Beresford's Despatches), Nive and Orthes. Gold Cross for Fuentes d'Onoro, Ciudad Rodrigo, Vittoria, Pyrenees and Orthes. MGS medal for Nivelle, Nive and Egypt. KCB. KTS. Knighted on his return to England 1814. Also served in Ireland, Mediterranean, Egypt 1801 (present at Aboukir, Grand Cairo and Alexandria – awarded Gold Medal) and Guernsey 1814 (Inspector of Military) Returned to Portugal 1823 on service of the King of Portugal.

MP for Carlow 1831. Returned to Portugal 1832 to fight with liberating Army of Don Pedro. The war ended in 1834 but Doyle and his fellow officers were not paid for this service. A commission was set up to obtain the money and the officers all received payment except Doyle, allegedly because he had instigated the complaint against the Portuguese. Military Knight of Windsor Jul 1853. Died in Windsor 9 Aug 1856.

REFERENCE: *Royal Military Calendar, Vol 4, pp. 370–2. Gentleman's Magazine, Sep 1856, pp. 382–4. Annual Register, 1856, Appx p. 264.*

DOYLE, Thomas
Sergeant. 51st (2nd Yorkshire West Riding) Light Infantry.
Named on the Regimental Memorial: KOYLI Chapel, York Minster, Yorkshire. (Photograph)
    Killed in the Peninsula.

D'OYLY, Sir Francis
Captain and Lieutenant Colonel. 1st Regiment of Foot Guards.
Memorial tablet: St Margaret the Queen Church, Buxted Park, Buxted, Sussex. (Photograph)

SACRED / TO THE MEMORY OF / LT COLL SIR FRANCIS D'OYLY, K.C.B. / OF THE FIRST REGIMENT OF FOOT GUARDS. / HE ENTERED THE MILITARY PROFESSION AT AN EARLY AGE, / AND HAVING SERVED IN THE EXPEDITION / AGAINST HOLLAND, IN THE YEAR 1799, / AND AGAIN IN 1809, IN THE ATTACK / OF THE BRITISH FORCES UPON WALCHEREN, / HE WAS AFTERWARDS ACTIVELY EMPLOYED AS FIELD-OFFICER, / DURING THE GREATER PROPORTION OF THE CAMPAIGNS IN SPAIN, / UNDER THE COMMAND OF / FIELD MARSHAL THE DUKE OF WELLINGTON, / AND BORE A SHARE IN THE VICTORY OF SALAMANCA, OF VITTORIA, / OF THE PYRENEES, OF THE NIVELLE, AND OF ORTHES. / IN THE GREAT BATTLE OF WATERLOO, JUNE 18TH 1815, / HE COMMANDED A BATTALION OF THE GUARDS, / AND WAS KILLED AT THE CLOSE OF THAT DECISIVE ACTION, / AT THE MOMENT WHEN HIS MEN WERE ADVANCING / AGAINST THE FRENCH LINE, / AND WHEN THE VICTORY WAS NO LONGER DOUBTFUL. / HE WAS THE 3RD SON OF MATTHIAS AND MARY D'OYLY; / AND DIED IN THE 39TH YEAR OF HIS AGE. / A TABLET INSCRIBED TO HIS MEMORY AS WELL AS TO THE MEMORY / OF OTHER BRITISH OFFICERS, / IS PLACED IN THE CHURCH AT WATERLOO. /
....

Memorial: Royal Military Chapel, Wellington Barracks, London. (M.I.) (Destroyed by a Flying Bomb in 1944)

"IN MEMORY OF LIEUT.-COLONEL SIR FRANCIS D'OYLY, COLONEL 67TH REGIMENT................... SIR F. D'OYLY WAS WITH THE 1ST GUARDS ON THE HELDER, IN SICILY, DURING THE CORUNNA CAMPAIGN, AND AT THE DEFENCE OF CADIZ; HE WAS ASSISTANT ADJUTANT-GENERAL TO A DIVISION AT SALAMANCA, VITTORIA, ORTHES, TOULOUSE; HE WAS AT QUATRE BRAS, AND WAS KILLED BY A MUSKET BALL WHEN IN COMMAND OF THE 2ND BATTALION AT WATERLOO...................... / PLACED BY THE WIDOW OF GENERAL HENRY D'OYLY, AND OTHER MEMBERS OF THE FAMILY."

Also named on Memorial Panel VIII for Waterloo: Royal Military Chapel, Wellington Barracks, London. (M.I.) (Destroyed by a Flying Bomb 1944)

Named on the Regimental Memorial: St Joseph's Church, Waterloo, Belgium. (Photograph)

Ensign 10 Mar 1795. Lt and Capt 19 Apr 1799. Bt Major 4 Jun 1811. Capt and Lt Colonel 23 Sep 1812.
     Served in the Peninsula Nov 1808 – Jan 1809 and Apr 1811 – Apr 1814. (ADC to Major General Disney Nov 1808 – Jan 1809 and May – Jun 1811, AAG 7th Division Dec 1811 – Apr 1814). Present at Corunna, Cadiz, Salamanca, Vittoria, Pyrenees, Nivelle and Orthes. Gold Cross for Salamanca, Vittoria, Pyrenees, Nivelle and Orthes. KCB. Present at Quatre Bras and Waterloo where he was killed in command of the 2nd Battalion during the last moments of the battle. Also served at the Helder 1799 and Sicily 1806. Brother of Capt and Lt Colonel Henry D'Oyly 1st Foot Guards.

D'OYLY, Henry
Captain and Lieutenant Colonel. 1st Regiment of Foot Guards.
Headstone with Cross: St Paul's Churchyard, Tunbridge Wells, Kent. (Photograph)

IN MEMORY OF / GENERAL HENRY D'OYLY / COLONEL OF H. M. 33RD FOOT / BORN APRIL 1ST 1780 / DIED SEPTEMBER 26TH 1855 / LATE COMMANDING GRENADIER GUARDS IN / WHICH HE SERVED 41 YEARS DURING THE / PENINSULA CAMPAIGN AND AT THE BATTLE / WATERLOO WHERE HE WAS WOUNDED.

Stained glass window: Church of St Paul, Rusthall, Tunbridge Wells, Kent. (West wall). (Photograph)

TO THE GLORY OF GOD AND IN MEMORY OF HER HUSBAND / GENERAL HENRY D'OYLY DIED 26 SEP 1855 / ....

Memorial: Royal Military Chapel, Wellington Barracks, London. (M.I.) (Destroyed by a Flying Bomb in 1944)

"IN MEMORY OF .... GENERAL HENRY D'OYLY, COLONEL 33RD REGIMENT.................. / GENERAL D'OYLY ENTERED THE 1ST GUARDS 1797, AND SERVED ON THE HELDER, IN SICILY DURING THE CORUNNA CAMPAIGN, AT WALCHEREN; AIDE-DE-CAMP AT THE DEFENCE OF CADIZ; PRESENT AT BERGEN-OP-ZOOM, AND SEVERELY WOUNDED AT WATERLOO. LIEUT-COLONEL OF THE REGIMENT 1837. DIED 1855. / PLACED BY THE WIDOW OF GENERAL HENRY D'OYLY, AND OTHER MEMBERS OF THE FAMILY."

Ensign 2 Aug 1797. Lt and Capt 25 Nov 1799. Capt and Lt Colonel 27 May 1813. Bt Major 4 Jun 1811. Major 12 Feb 1830. Major General 28 Jun 1838. Lt General 11 Nov 1851. General 30 Jan 1855.
     Served in the Peninsula with 3rd Battalion Oct 1808 – Jan 1809, Apr 1811 – May 1813 (ADC to Major General Cooke) and May – Jul 1813 (Brigade Major). Present at Corunna, Cadiz (Mentioned in Despatches on raising of siege and went home with despatches). Present at Waterloo (severely wounded). MGS medal for Corunna. Also served at the Helder 1799 (taken prisoner), Sicily 1805, Walcheren 1809, Netherlands

1814 (present at Bergen-op-Zoom). Colonel 33rd Foot 28 Sep 1847. Brother of Capt and Lt Colonel Sir Francis D'Oyly 1st Guards who was killed at Waterloo.
REFERENCE: *Gentleman's Magazine, Dec. 1855, pp. 650–1. Annual Register, 1855, Appx, pp. 308–39.*

DRAKE, Thomas
Captain. 95th Regiment of Foot.
Interred in Catacomb B (v171 c4) Kensal Green Cemetery, London.

2nd Lt 23 May 1805. Lt 15 May 1806. Capt Canadian Fencibles 28 May 1807. Capt 95th Foot 25 Mar 1808. Bt Major 22 Apr 1813. Bt Lt Col 16 Nov 1826. Bt Colonel 23 Nov 1841.
  Served in the Peninsula with 2/95th Aug 1808 – Jan 1809, Jun 1810 – Apr 1811 (ADC to Lt General Brent Spencer May – Jul 1811) and on Staff Mar – Nov 1813 (DAQMG). Present at Vigo, Busaco, Fuentes d'Onoro and Nivelle. CMG. Also served in Hanover 1805, Walcheren 1809 and Ionian Islands 16 Nov 1826 (DQMG). MGS medal for Busaco, Fuentes d'Onoro and Nivelle. Retired 14 Jul 1843. Died 22 Dec 1851 aged 69 years.
REFERENCE: *Gentleman's Magazine, Feb 1852, p. 212. Annual Register, 1851, Appx, p. 369.*

DRAKE, William Tyrwhitt
Captain. Royal Regiment of Horse Guards.
Memorial tablet: St Mary's Church, Amersham, Buckinghamshire. (Photograph)

SACRED / TO THE MEMORY OF / WILLIAM TYRWHITT-DRAKE, ESQRE / LATE LIEUTENANT COLONEL / OF THE ROYAL HORSE GUARDS / SECOND SON OF THOMAS DRAKE TYRWHITT-DRAKE, / OF SHARDLOES, ESQRE / BORN ON OCTOBER 21ST 1785, DIED DECEMBER 21ST 1848. / HE REPRESENTED THIS BOROUGH IN PARLIAMENT / FOR 22 YEARS / AND SERVED WITH HIS REGIMENT IN THE PENINSULAR WAR, / AND ON THE FIELD OF WATERLOO. / HIS DEEP ROOTED PRINCIPLES OF RELIGION, / HIS TRULY CHRISTIAN CHARITY, / HIS UNSULLIED HONOUR AND UNASSUMING MANNERS, / GAINED FOR HIM IN LIFE THE ESTEEM AND LOVE OF ALL / AND AS A HUSBAND AND FATHER, / FRIEND AND BROTHER, / HIS DEATH WAS SINCERELY AND DESERVEDLY LAMENTED. / ....

Cornet 10 Sep 1805. Lt 6 Aug 1807. Capt 29 Aug 1811. Lt Colonel 22 Jun 1820.
  Served in the Peninsula Sep 1813 – Apr 1814. Present at Toulouse. MGS medal for Toulouse. Present at Waterloo. Afterwards MP for Amersham for 22 years.
REFERENCE: *Gentleman's Magazine, Mar 1849, p. 318.*

DRANGMEISTER, Heinrich
Cornet. 2nd Regiment of Dragoons, King's German Legion.
Named on the Regimental Memorial: La Haye Sainte, Waterloo, Belgium. (Photograph)

Cornet 2 Oct 1812.
  Served in the Peninsula Nov 1812 – Apr 1814. Present at Vittoria, Vic Bigorre and Toulouse. Present at Waterloo where he was killed. Also served in the Netherlands 1814.

DRAWATER, Augustus Charles
Captain. 62nd (Wiltshire) Regiment of Foot.
Buried in St Mary's Churchyard, Bathwick, Bath. (Burial register). (No longer extant).

Ensign 45th Foot 1 May 1805. Lt 7th Foot 20 Mar 1806. Capt 15 Aug 1811. Capt 70th Foot 2 Jul 1812. Capt 62nd Foot 16 Mar 1815. Capt 26th Foot 23 Jul 1818. Paymaster 64th Foot 11 Nov 1819. Paymaster 4th Dragoon Guards 29 Dec 1825.

Served in the Peninsula with 1/7th Aug – Dec 1810 and Jun 1811 – Feb 1812. Present at Busaco and Aldea da Ponte. Also served at Copenhagen 1807 and Martinique 1809. MGS medal for Busaco and Martinique. Retired on half pay 9 Apr 1847. Died in Bath 12 Sep 1857.

DRAWBRIDGE, Charles
1st Lieutenant. Royal Artillery.
Monument: St Mary's Churchyard, Honley, Yorkshire. (Photograph)

IN MEMORY OF / THE REV^D CHARLES DRAWBRIDGE / WHO WAS BORN / AT BROMPTON, KENT / NOV 5TH 1790. / IN THE YEAR 1809 / HE WAS GAZETTED AS ENSIGN / IN THE ROYAL ARTILLERY / AND WAS PROMOTED / TO BE 1ST LIEUTENANT IN 1811. / HE SERVED WITH HIS CORPS / IN THE PENINSULAR WAR / AND AT WATERLOO. HAVING / RETIRED ON HALF PAY IN 1820 / HE WAS ORDAINED IN 1823 / AND FOR MORE THAN 38 YEARS / HE FULFILLED THE DUTIES FIRST OF CURATE, / THEN OF INCUMBENT OF THIS CHAPELRY / WITH UNTIRING ZEAL, FIDELITY AND LOVE. / HE FELL ASLEEP IN JESUS, / FEBRUARY 1ST 1862 AGED 71 YEARS

Memorial tablet: St Mary's Church, Honley, Yorkshire. (Photograph)

IN MEMORY OF / THE / REVD CHARLES DRAWBRIDGE / WHO WAS THIRTY EIGHT YEARS / CURATE AND INCUMBENT / IN THIS CHAPELRY / AS THE MINISTER OF CHRIST / HE DIED / ON THE 1ST DAY OF FEBRUARY 1862 / IN THE 71ST YEAR OF HIS AGE / THIS TABLET IS ERECTED BY / AN AFFECTIONATE AND ********** FRIEND / ********** / ********** MINISTRY 38 YEARS. ....

Grave: St Mary's Churchyard, Honley, Yorkshire. (M.I.)

"BENEATH THIS STONE REPOSE THE REMAINS OF .... ALSO THE ABOVE NAMED REV^D CHARLES DRAWBRIDGE FOR UPWARDS OF 38 YEARS A FAITHFUL MINISTER OF CHRIST AT THIS CHAPELRY, WHO DIED FEBRUARY 1ST 1862 AGED 71".

2nd Lt 21 Dec 1808. 1st Lt 3 Dec 1811.
    Present at Waterloo in reserve with the unattached artillery. Also served at Walcheren (present at the siege of Flushing). Retired 24 Aug 1820 and entered the Church. Died 1 Feb 1862.

DRECHSELL, Baron Frederick von
Captain and Brigade Major. Staff Corps, King's German Legion.
Named on the Memorial: St Andrew's Church, (now Musée Historique), Biarritz, France. (Photograph)

Lt King's German Legion Artillery 20 Apr 1807. Lt 5th Line 1810. Capt and Brigade Major 18 Jul 1810.
    Served in the Peninsula Oct 1810 – Apr 1814 (Brigade Major 3 Brigade 1st Division). Present at Fuentes d'Onoro, Ciudad Rodrigo, Salamanca, Burgos, Vittoria, Tolosa, Bidassoa, Nivelle, Nive, St Etienne, Bayonne (wounded) and the Sortie from Bayonne where he was killed 14 Apr 1814. Also served in the Baltic 1807.

DREW, J. H.
Lieutenant. 51st (2nd Yorkshire West Riding) Light Infantry.
Named on the Regimental Memorial: KOYLI Chapel, York Minster, Yorkshire. (Photograph)

Ensign 5 Apr 1806. Lt 21 Aug 1806.
    Served in the Peninsula Oct 1808 – Jan 1809. Present in the retreat to Corunna. Was reported absent in Jan 1809, and to have been sent to Lugo 'very ill' and is assumed to have died on the road to Corunna.

DREWE, Edward Ward

Lieutenant. 27th (Inniskilling) Regiment of Foot.
Memorial: Monkstown Church of Ireland, Monkstown, County Dublin, Ireland. (Photograph)

SACRED / TO THE LOVED MEMORY / OF A BRAVE PENINSULAR / AND WATERLOO SOLDIER / EDWD WARD DREWE / LATE MAJOR UNATTACHED / WHOSE REMAINS REPOSE / IN A VAULT / BENEATH THIS CHURCH, / OBIIT FEB 20TH 1862. / (VERSE)

Ensign South Downshire Militia 4 Apr 1803. Ensign 27th Foot 5 Oct 1806. Lt 9 Feb 1808. Capt 7 Jan 1824. Capt 95th Foot 19 May 1825. Bt Major 9 Jun 1837.

Served in the Peninsula on Staff Dec 1812 – Jul 1813 and with 2/27th Aug 1813 – Apr 1814. Present at Castalla, Tarragona, Ordal (wounded) and Barcelona. Present at Waterloo with 27th Foot where he was wounded. Only three out of 19 officers in the Regiment were not killed or wounded. Also served in North America 1814. Retired 9 Jul 1837.

DRUMMOND, George Duncan

1st Lieutenant. 95th Regiment of Foot.
Grave: Abbey Cemetery, Bath, Somerset. Seriously eroded and inscription recorded from burial register. (Headstone 30). (Photograph)

"GEORGE DUNCAN DRUMMOND AGED 69, MAJOR LATE OF 95TH REGT OR RIFLE BRIGADE OF 18 CHARLES STREET, DIED ON 20 JULY 1863."

2nd Lt 30 May 1811. Lt 28 Jan 1813. Lt 82nd Foot 30 Nov 1820. Lt 3rd Royal Veteran Battalion 1 Apr 1824 (Battalion disbanded 1825). Capt with local rank at Chatham 22 Dec 1825.

Served in the Peninsula with 3/95th Jul 1811 – Dec 1812 and Jul 1813 – Apr 1814. Present at Ciudad Rodrigo Badajoz, Salamanca, Pyrenees, Vera, Bidassoa, Nivelle, Nive, Orthes, Tarbes and Toulouse. Present at Waterloo. Later became Barrack Master at Manchester with rank of Major. MGS medal for Ciudad Rodrigo, Badajoz, Salamanca, Pyrenees, Nivelle, Nive, Orthes and Toulouse.

DRUMMOND, John

Private. 71st (Highland Light Infantry) Regiment of Foot.
Headstone: Beechworth Cemetery, Victoria, Australia. (Photograph)

TO THE MEMORY OF / JOHN / DRUMMOND / 1791–1865 / SGT. 71ST FOOT / A VETERAN OF / WATERLOO / PIONEER OF / BEECHWORTH

Pte 71st Foot 25 Mar 1807. Cpl 1817. Sgt 1819.

Enlisted in the 71st Foot at Glasgow in 1807 aged 16. Served in the Peninsula Aug 1808 – Jan 1809 and Sep 1810 – Apr 1814. Present at Rolica, Vimeiro, Corunna, Fuentes d'Onoro (wounded), Vittoria, Pyrenees, Nivelle, Nive, Orthes and Toulouse. Present at Waterloo in Capt Samuel Reed's Company. Discharged from the army 1828. MGS medal for Rolica, Vimeiro, Corunna, Fuentes d'Onoro, Vittoria, Pyrenees, Nivelle, Nive, Orthes and Toulouse. Discharged 29 May 1828. Emigrated with his wife and children to Australia 1830, where he died 1865 and was buried in an unmarked grave. A memorial stone was unveiled in 1995.

DRUMMOND, Percy

Major. Royal Artillery.
Grave: St Nicholas Churchyard, Plumstead, Kent and named on the Regimental Memorial: St Nicholas Church, Plumstead, Kent. (No longer extant. Destroyed by a flying bomb in the Second World War)

2nd Lt 1 Jan 1794. 1st Lt 14 Aug 1794. Capt-Lieut 7 Oct 1799. Capt 22 Sep 1803. Major 4 Jun 1811. Bt Lt Colonel 12 Aug 1819. Lt Colonel 6 Nov 1820. Colonel 13 Oct 1827. Major General 10 Jan 1837.

Served in the Peninsula Aug 1808 – Jan 1809. Present in the Corunna campaign. Present at Waterloo as Field officer commanding the Reserve Artillery. CB. Also served in the Baltic 1807–1808 and Walcheren 1809 (present at the siege of Flushing). Lt Governor Royal Military Academy 9 Apr 1829. Director General of Royal Artillery 23 Apr 1840 on the death of Sir Alexander Dickson. Died at Woolwich 1 Jan 1843. REFERENCE: *Gentleman's Magazine, March 1843, p. 320. Annual Register, 1843, Appx, pp. 223–4.*

DRUMMOND, Peter
Private. 3rd Regiment of Foot Guards.
Headstone: Logie Kirk, Bridge of Allan, Stirlingshire, Scotland. (South side of Church). (Photograph)

ERECTED BY / ARCHIBALD BORLAND STIRLING / IN MEMORY OF HIS FATHER IN LAW / PETER DRUMMOND / BAKER AND CONFECTIONER, STIRLING / BORN IN THE PARISH OF LOGIE, 21ST SEPTEMBER 1789 / ENLISTED IN THE THIRD FOOT GUARDS 25TH JULY 1809 / WAS ENGAGED IN THE FOLLOWING ACTIONS / BARROSA 5TH MAR 1811 / RODRIGO 19TH JAN 1812 / SALAMANCA 22ND JULY 1812 / VITTORIA 21ST JUNE 1813 / NIVELLE 10TH NOV 1813 / NIVE 9TH DEC 1813 / BAYONNE 11TH APRIL 1814. / DIED AT STIRLING 17TH JANUARY 1855 / AGED 66 YEARS

Served in the Peninsula 1810–1814. Present at Barrosa, Ciudad Rodrigo, Salamanca, Vittoria, Nivelle, Nive and Bayonne. On his discharge from the army he returned to Stirling in Scotland and took up the trade of baker and confectioner. MGS medal for Barrosa, Ciudad Rodrigo, Salamanca, Vittoria, Nivelle and Nive.

DRYDEN, James
Captain. Staff Corps of Cavalry.
Memorial: All Saints Churchyard, Hurworth on Tees, County Durham. (Photograph)

TO THE / MEMORY OF / CAPTAIN JAMES DRYDEN / WHO DIED OCTOBER 5TH 1836 / AGED 68 YEARS. FROM A VERY HUMBLE STATION IN THIS VILLAGE, HE ROSE SOLELY / BY HIS OWN MERIT TO BE AN / OFFICER IN HIS MAJESTY'S / SECOND REGIMENT OF / LIFE GUARDS. / ERECTED BY THE INHABITANTS OF HURWORTH / VERSE (ILLEGIBLE)

Promoted from the ranks. Lt and Adjt 2nd Life Guards 28 Aug 1806. Capt Staff Corps of Cavalry 22 Apr 1813.
Served in the Peninsula Aug 1813 - Apr 1814 (Oct 1813 - Mar 1814 attached to 1st Divison) and Apr 1814 (attached to 5th Division). Present at Bayonne. Retired 1814 on reduction of the regiment.

DRYSDALE, Alexander
Captain. 27th (Inniskilling) Regiment of Foot.
Mural monument: Dean Cemetery, Edinburgh, Scotland. (Photograph)

SACRED TO THE MEMORY OF / CAPT ALEXANDER DRYSDALE / LATE OF H. M. 27TH REGT OF FOOT / WHO DIED ON THE 27TH OF AUGUST 1864 / AGED 80. / DEEPLY REGRETTED BY ALL WHO KNEW HIM.

Ensign 1 Jul 1804. Lt 10 Oct 1805. Capt 10 Feb 1814.
Served in the Peninsula Nov 1812 – Apr 1814 attached to Calabrian Free Corps. Present at Alcoy, Biar, Castalla, Tarragona, Ordal and Barcelona. Also served in Ischia and Procida 1809. Half pay 26 Mar 1816.

DUCKWORTH, George Henry
Lieutenant Colonel. 48th (Northamptonshire) Regiment of Foot.
Memorial tablet: St Margaret's Church, Topsham, Devon. (South transept). (Photograph)

SACRED / TO THE MEMORY OF / GEORGE HENRY DUCKWORTH / LATE LIEUTENANT COLONEL OF / THE 48TH REGT OF FOOT, / WHO FELL AT THE BATTLE OF ALBUERA / ON THE 16TH OF MAY 1811, / AT THE HEAD OF THE FIRST BATTALION / WHILE ENCOURAGING HIS MEN TO / CHARGE THE ENEMY. / HE HAD NOT COMPLETED THE 29TH YEAR / OF HIS AGE. / ON THE FIELD WHERE HE NOBLY FELL / HIS REMAINS LIE BURIED.

Ensign 39th Foot 25 Apr 1801. Lt 68th Foot 25 Jun 1801. Lt 11th Foot 25 Aug 1801. Capt 60th Foot 17 Aug 1803. Capt 55th Foot 6 Jul 1804. Capt 7th Foot 23 Feb 1805. Capt 59th Foot 14 Nov 1805. Major Yorkshire Lt Infantry Volunteers 25 Jul 1806. Major 67th Foot 2 Oct 1806. Lt Colonel 1st West India Regt 14 Jan 1808. Lt Colonel 48th Foot 16 Jun 1808.
     Served in the Peninsula Apr – Sep 1809 and Apr 1810 – May 1811. (Temporary Commander 1 Brigade 2nd Division Dec 1809 – Jul 1810). Present at Douro (Mentioned in Despatches), Talavera, Busaco and Albuera where he was severely wounded but refused to leave the field and was killed shortly afterwards. Mentioned in Despatches. The news of his death reached his home in Plymouth on the day when his only son, a four year old had died. Gold Medal for Talavera and Albuera.
REFERENCE: *Gentleman's Magazine, 1811, Part 1, Supplement, p. 679.*

DUDGEON, Peter
Captain. 58th (Rutlandshire) Regiment of Foot.
Named on the Family Mural memorial tablet: Dean Cemetery (Number 2136), Edinburgh, Scotland. (Photograph)

.... / MAJOR GENERAL PETER DUDGEON / BORN ** NOV 1780. DIED 2ND AUG 1866.

Ensign 4 Apr 1800. Lt 3 Sep 1801. Capt 19 Mar 1807. Bt Major 19 Jul 1821. Bt Lt Colonel 10 Jan 1837. Bt Colonel 11 Nov 1851. Major General 31 Aug 1854.
     Served in the Peninsula Oct 1809 – Dec 1812. Present at Torres Vedras, Salamanca, capture of Madrid, and the siege of Burgos (wounded 19 Sep 1812 and severely wounded 4 Oct 1812). Also served in Egypt 1801 (present at Grand Cairo and Alexandria) and Sicily 1805–1806. MGS medal for Egypt and Salamanca. Half pay 4 May 1826.

DUDLEY, Samuel
Captain. 3rd (Prince of Wales's) Dragoon Guards.
Buried in St Mary the Virgin Churchyard, Iffley, Oxfordshire. (Burial register).

Lt 16th Lt Dragoons 17 Mar 1804. Capt 3rd Dragoons Guards 22 Nov 1810.
     Served in the Peninsula Jan – Dec 1809 and Apr 1810 – Jul 1811 (ADC to Lt General Stapleton Cotton) and Aug – Sep 1811 (OC Cavalry Detachments at Belem, Lisbon). Present at Douro, Talavera and Fuentes d'Onoro. MGS medal for Talavera and Fuentes d'Onoro. Half pay 17 Nov 1814. Died 7 Jan 1848 aged 77.

DUFFY, John
Major. 43rd (Monmouthshire) Light Infantry Regiment of Foot.
Interred in Catacomb B (v51 c9) Kensal Green Cemetery, London.

Ensign 10th Foot 21 Oct 1795. Lt 6 Jan 1796. Capt 43rd Foot 12 Aug 1804. Bt Major 6 Feb 1812. Major 43rd Foot 17 Jun 1813. Bt Lt Colonel 22 Nov 1813. Lt Colonel 95th Foot 21 Sep 1815. Lt Colonel 8th Foot

9 Sep 1819. Colonel 22 Jul 1830. Major General 23 Nov 1841. Lt General 11 Nov 1851.

Served in the Peninsula with 1/43rd Oct 1808 – Jan 1809, Jul – Dec 1809, Mar – Jul 1810, Dec 1810 – May 1812 and Feb 1813 – Jan 1814. Present at Vigo, Redinha, Casal Nova, Foz d'Arouce, Sabugal, Fuentes d'Onoro, Ciudad Rodrigo (Mentioned in Despatches, commanded a storming party – awarded Bt Majority), Badajoz, Vittoria (wounded), Pyrenees, Bidassoa, Nivelle (awarded Bt Lt Colonelcy) and Nive. Gold Medal for Badajoz where he commanded the regiment at the siege after the death of Lt Colonel Charles Macleod. MGS medal for Egypt, Fuentes d'Onoro, Ciudad Rodrigo, Vittoria, Pyrenees, Nivelle and Nive. CB. Also served in the West Indies 1796, India 1799, Egypt 1801 and the Baltic 1807. Colonel 28th Foot 18 May 1849 and Colonel 8th Foot 10 Oct 1854. Died in London 17 Mar 1855 aged 77 years. REFERENCE: *Gentleman's Magazine, Jul 1855, pp. 94–5.*

DUKINFIELD, Samuel George
Captain. 7th (Queen's Own) Regiment of Light Dragoons.
Memorial tablet: St James the Great Church, Ruscombe, Wokingham, Berkshire. (Photograph)

TO THE MEMORY OF / CAPTAIN SAMUEL GEORGE DUKINFIELD OF THE 7TH LIGHT DRAGOONS / (ELDEST SON OF SIR NATHL DUKINFIELD BARONET OF STANLAKE), WHO / WAS WRECKED ON THE COAST OF CORNWALL ON THE 22ND OF JANUARY 1809 / IN THE 25TH YEAR OF HIS AGE, RETURNING FROM SPAIN WHERE HE / HAD SERVED A CAMPAIGN WITH MUCH CREDIT. THIS TABLET IS / PLACED BY HIS AFFLICTED PARENTS, WHO SHARE, WITH THEIR / SURVIVING CHILDREN, AN AGGRAVATION OF GRIEF (YET THE BEST / SOURCE OF CONSOLATION) IN THE DISTINGUISHED CHARACTER AND / EXEMPLARY VIRTUE OF A SON AND A BROTHER.

Cornet 13 Oct 1801. Lt May 1804. Capt 20 Nov 1806.

Served in the Peninsula Nov 1808 – Jan 1809. Present at Benevente. Drowned in the shipwreck of the transport ship *Dispatch* on the return from Corunna. The ship struck the rocks near Coverack and everyone on board drowned except for seven privates in the Dragoons. Three officers – Major Cavendish, Capt Dukinfield and Lt Waldegrave, 70 men and 30 horses all returning from Corunna were drowned. The ship's captain was drunk and Capt Dukinfield went on deck to take command. The mast broke and swept him overboard.

DUMARESQ, Henry
Captain. 9th (East Norfolk) Regiment of Foot.
Chest tomb in railed enclosure: Muswellbrook Cemetery, New South Wales, Australia. (Tablets have been removed due to decay and vandalism). Inscription recorded from memorial record. (Photograph)

"BENEATH THIS TOMB ARE DEPOSITED THE MORTAL REMAINS OF LT COL. DUMARESQ WHO DEPARTED THIS LIFE AT PT. STEPHENS ON THE 5TH MARCH MDCCCXXXVIII AGED 46 YEARS. HE ENTERED THE ARMY AT AN EARLY AGE AND GIFTED WITH SUPERIOR TALENTS DISTINGUISHED HIMSELF IN THE PENINSULAR WAR AND ON THE FIELD AT WATERLOO WHERE HE RECEIVED A WOUND WHICH EVENTUALLY OCCASIONED HIS DEATH. IN N.S.W. HE FILLED IMPORTANT CIVIL OFFICES UNDER THE ADMINISTRATION OF HIS BROTHER-IN-LAW SIR RALPH DARLING AND DURING THE LAST FOUR YEARS OF HIS LIFE HELD THE APPOINTMENT OF COMMISSIONER TO THE A. A CO. WHOSE AFFAIRS FLOURISHED UNDER HIS JUDICIAL AND CAREFUL MANAGEMENT. IN THE RELATIVE DUTIES OF LIFE HE WAS MOST EXEMPLARY AND HIS LOSS IS DEEPLY MOURNED AS A HUSBAND, FATHER AND FRIEND. STRICT IN THE OBSERVANCES OF ALL RELIGIOUS DUTIES HE YET RELIED NOT UPON HIS OWN VIRTUES BUT TRUSTED TO SALVATION ONLY THROUGH THE MERITS OF THE DIVINE REDEEMER. THE FASHION OF THIS WORLD PASSETH AWAY, BUT HE THAT DOETH THE WILL OF GOD ABIDETH FOR EVER."

Lt 9 Aug 1808. Capt 3rd Garrison Battalion 4 Feb 1813. Bt Major 4 Feb 1813. Capt 9th Foot 21 Oct 1813. Bt Lt Colonel 21 Jun 1817.

Served in the Peninsula with 2/9th Aug 1808 – Jun 1809, 1/9th Nov 1810 – Jan 1813 and on Staff Dec 1813 – Apr 1814 (DAQMG). Present at Vimeiro, Douro, Fuentes d'Onoro, Badajoz, Castrejon, siege of Salamanca Forts, Salamanca, Burgos, Villa Muriel (wounded 25 Oct 1812 during the retreat from Burgos) and Vittoria. At Badajoz and Burgos he volunteered to serve as Acting Engineer to lead the troops in the assault. At Salamanca Forts he again volunteered to lead the assault.

Present at Waterloo (ADC to Major General Sir John Byng). Severely wounded at Hougoumont whilst delivering a message from Wellington. He rode back with the answer to the Duke and fell from his horse, shot through the lungs. Awarded pension of £100 per annum. This wound subsequently caused his death at the early age of 46. Retired in 1834. Died 5 Mar 1838 in Australia as manager of the Australian Agricultural Company. Regarded as one of the heroes of Waterloo. Brother of Lt William Dumaresq Royal Staff Corps and brother on law of Lt Colonel Ralph Darling 51st Foot.
REFERENCE: *Australian Dictionary of Biography. United Service Magazine, Aug 1838, p. 591. Gentleman's Magazine, Aug 1838, p. 330 and Oct 1838, pp. 443–4.*

DUMARESQ, William John
Lieutenant. Royal Staff Corps.
Chest tomb in railed enclosure: St Stephen's Anglican Church Cemetery, Camperdown, Sydney, New South Wales, Australia. Inscription illegible. (Photograph)
Memorial tablet: St James's Church, Sydney, Australia. (Photograph)

WILLIAM JOHN DUMARESQ / CAPT ROYAL STAFF CORPS / SERVED IN THE PENINSULA CANADA AND NEW SOUTH WALES / BORN XXV FEBRUARY A.D. MDCCXCIII DIED IX NOVEMBER MDCCCLXVIII

Ensign 17 Jun 1809. Lt 13 Aug 1811. Capt 7 Mar 1816.

Served in the Peninsula Jul 1811 – Apr 1814. Present at Ciudad Rodrigo, Badajoz, Pyrenees, Nivelle and Bayonne. MGS medal for Ciudad Rodrigo, Badajoz, Pyrenees and Nivelle. Also served in Canada and then went to Australia as Acting Chief Engineer to the colony of New South Wales. Brother of Capt Henry Dumaresq 9th Foot and brother-in-law of Lt Colonel Ralph Darling 51 Foot. Died 9 Nov 1868.
REFERENCE: *Australian Dictionary of Biography.*

DUNBAR, George
Private. 1st Regiment of Foot Guards.
Buried in Essil Churchyard, Garmouth, Morayshire, Scotland. (Unmarked grave).

Pte 1813.

Served in the Netherlands 1814 (present at Bergen-op-Zoom, taken prisoner but later released in exchange of prisoners). Present at Quatre Bras and at Waterloo in Lt Colonel Sir Noel Hill's Company (wounded three times). Discharged 1820. Returned to his pre-war occupation as a gardener in Morayshire. Granted a military pension in 1868. Died 30 Dec 1883 aged 90.

DUNCAN, John
Captain. 95th Regiment of Foot.
Named on the Memorial: St Andrew's Church, (now Musée Historique), Biarritz, France. (Photograph)

Ensign 71st Foot 7 Jul 1800. Lt 19 Sep 1800. Lt 92nd Foot 9 Jul 1803. Lt 95th 15 Jun 1804. Capt 27 Apr 1809.

Served in the Peninsula with 1/95th Aug 1808 – Jan 1809 and 2/95th Feb 1812 – Mar 1814. Present at Cacabellos, Corunna, Cadiz, San Millan, Vittoria, Pyrenees, Vera, Bidassoa, Nivelle. Nive, Orthes and Tarbes where he was killed Mar 1814. Also served at Walcheren 1809.

DUNCOMBE, Slingsby

Ensign. 1st Regiment of Foot Guards.
Memorial tablet: St Michael and All Angels Church, Copgrove, Yorkshire. (Photograph)

SLINGSBY DUNCOMBE ESQRE / FORMERLY OF LANGFORD, NOTTS. / YOUNGEST SON OF
CHARLES SLINGSBY DUNCOMBE ESQRE / OF DUNCOMBE PARK IN THE COUNTY, WHO WAS
BORN NOVR 21ST 1779. / HE ENTERED THE ARMY IN 1806 AS ENSIGN IN THE FIRST REGI-
MENT OF FOOT GUARDS, / IN WHICH CORPS HE SERVED DURING THE CAMPAIGN IN SPAIN,
/ UNDER SIR JOHN MOORE, / AND WAS PRESENT AT THE BATTLE OF CORUNNA, FOUGHT
JANUARY 16TH 1809. / HE DIED IN LONDON OCTR 12TH 1851, LEAVING A WIDOW AND NINE
CHILDREN, / AND WAS BURIED IN THIS CHURCHYARD.

Chest tomb with carved cross within railings: St Michael and All Angels Churchyard, Copgrove, Yorkshire.
Inscription illegible. (Photograph)

Ensign 10 Jul 1806.
    Served in the Peninsula with 3rd Battalion Oct 1808 – Jan 1809. Present at Corunna. MGS medal for
Corunna. Retired 27 Apr 1809.

DUNDAS, Hon. Sir Robert Lawrence

Major. Royal Staff Corps.
Memorial: St Germain Church, Marske by the Sea, Yorkshire. (M.I.)

"CHARLOTTE, LADY DUNDAS .... HER SON SIR ROBERT DUNDAS, 22 NOV 1844,
AGED 64."

2nd Lt Royal Artillery 1 Dec 1797. 2nd Lt Royal Engineers 1 Apr 1798. 1st Lt 2 May 1800. Capt Royal Staff
Corps attached to QMG's Dept 6 Aug 1802. Major 14 Jul 1804. Bt Lt Colonel 11 Apr 1811. Bt Colonel
19 Jul 1821. Major General 22 Jul 1830. Lt General 23 Nov 1841.
    Served in the Peninsula Apr 1809 – Jul 1811 and Jul 1812 – Apr 1814. Present at Talavera, Salamanca
(Mentioned in Despatches), Vittoria, Pyrenees, Nivelle, Nive (wounded) and Toulouse. Also served at the
Helder 1799, Egypt 1801 (present at Alexandria) and Hanover 1805. Gold Cross for Talavera, Salamanca,
Vittoria, Pyrenees, Nivelle, Nive and Toulouse. KCB and KTS. Colonel 59th Foot 15 Jun 1840. Died at
Loftus, near Guisborough 22 Nov 1844.
REFERENCE: *Gentleman's Magazine, Jan 1845, p. 97.*

DUNDAS, Thomas

Captain. 15th (King's) Regiment of Light Dragoons.
Memorial tablet: Larbert Churchyard, Larbert, Stirlingshire, Scotland. (In walled enclosure). (Photograph)

IN LOVING MEMORY OF / LT COLONEL THOMAS DUNDAS / OF CARRON HALL, / LATE OF THE
52ND LT INFANTRY / 1ST ROYAL DRAGOONS / AND 15TH HUSSARS. / SON OF MAJOR GENERAL
THOMAS DUNDAS / AND LADY ELEANOR DUNDAS / BORN 13TH FEB 1792 / DIED 24TH MAY 1860

Ensign 52nd Foot 17 Feb 1808. Lt 16 Feb 1809. Lt 1st Dragoons 12 Oct 1809. Capt 60th Foot 26 Dec 1811.
Capt 15th Lt Dragoons 13 Aug 1812.
    Served in the Peninsula with 2/52nd Aug – Sep 1808, 1/52nd Oct 1808 – Jan 1809, 1st Dragoons Feb 1811
– Feb 1812 and 15th Lt Dragoons Jan 1813 – Apr 1814. Present at Vimeiro, Corunna, Fuentes d'Onoro,
Aldea da Ponte, Morales, Vittoria, Orthes and Toulouse. Also served at Walcheren 1809. MGS medal for
Vimeiro, Corunna, Fuentes d'Onoro, Vittoria, Orthes and Toulouse. Retired 24 Sep 1839.
REFERENCE: *Annual Register, 1860, Appx, p. 613.*

DUNDAS, William Bolden
2nd Captain. Royal Artillery.
Mural Memorial tablet: Dean Cemetery, Edinburgh, Scotland. (Section M. No 1765). (Photograph)

IN MEMORY OF / MAJOR GEN. W. B. DUNDAS, C.B. / BORN 28TH MAY 1787, / DIED 8TH AUG[T] 1858.

2nd Lt 8 Sep 1803. 1st Lt 12 Sep 1803. 2nd Capt 11 Jul 1811. Bt Major 21 Jan 1819. Capt 29 Jul 1825. Lt Colonel 23 Jun 1837. Major General 28 Nov 1854.

 Served in the Peninsula Mar – Aug 1810 and Apr 1811 – Jun 1812 (in Capt Holcombe's 3rd Company, 6th Battalion). Present at Cadiz, Tarragona, Ciudad Rodrigo (wounded and Mentioned in Despatches), Badajoz (severely wounded – his left arm amputated, hip bone shattered and left thigh dislocated – sent home from the Peninsula). Assistant Inspector of Small Arms 1 Feb 1813. Inspector of Artillery at the Royal Gun Factory Oct 1839–1852. MGS medal for Ciudad Rodrigo and Badajoz. CB 1837. Also served in Jamaica 1803–1805 and Walcheren 1809 (present at the siege of Flushing).
Reference: Gentleman's Magazine, Oct 1858, p. 424. Annual Register, 1858, Appx, pp. 423–4.

DUNK, Jesse
Private. 39th (Dorsetshire) Regiment of Foot.
Headstone: St Paul's Churchyard, Cobbity, New South Wales, Australia. (Photograph)

IN MEMORY OF / JESSIE DUNK / BORN 22ND APRIL 1787 / SUSSEX ENGLAND / DIED 15TH JUNE 1860 / CAMDEN AUSTRALIA / WITHOUT YOUR JOURNEY / WE WOULD NOT BE HERE / OUR THANKS / THE DUNK FAMILY / SHIRLEY 2009 CAMDEN

Pte 1809.
 Served in the Peninsula Oct 1811 – Apr 1814. Present at Busaco, Albuera, Vittoria, Pyrenees and Toulouse. Also served in North America 1814. Discharged Jun 1816. Emigrated to Australia in 1839 with his seven children, his wife having died. MGS medal for Busaco, Albuera, Vittoria, Pyrenees and Toulouse.
Reference: Camden (Queensland, Australia) District Reporter, 4 May 2009, p 16.

DUNKLEY, William
Lieutenant. 11th (North Devonshire) Regiment of Foot.
Named on the Memorial: St Andrew's Church, (now Musée Historique), Biarritz, France. (Photograph)

Ensign 7 Jun 1810. Lt 17 Nov 1812.
 Served in the Peninsula Aug 1813 – Apr 1814. Present at Bidassoa, Nivelle, Nive, Bayonne, Orthes and Toulouse where he was killed 10 Apr 1814.

DUPERIER, Henry
Lieutenant. 18th Regiment of Light Dragoons.
Box tomb: St Mylor Churchyard, Falmouth, Cornwall. (Photograph)

SACRED / TO / THE / MEMORY / OF / LIEU[T] HENRY DUPERIER, / LATE 18TH HUSSARS, / WHO DEPARTED THIS LIFE / 15TH OF DECEMBER / 1846, AGED 74 YEARS.

Commissioned from the ranks. Cornet and Adjutant 10th Lt Dragoons 15 Jan 1807. Lt 29 Sep 1808. Cornet and Adjutant 18th Lt Dragoons 7 Oct 1813. Lt 23 Feb 1814.
 Served in the Peninsula with 10th Lt Dragoons Nov 1808 – Jan 1809 and 18th Lt Dragoons Aug 1813 – Apr 1814. Present at Sahagun, Benevente, the Corunna campaign, Nivelle, Nive, Orthes, Croix d'Orade and Toulouse. Present at Waterloo where he was the only officer in the regiment to be wounded. Half pay

1821. Duperier rose through the ranks and was an excellent adjutant for the 10th Lt Dragoons. Appointed to the 18th Lt Dragoons after Vittoria when Colonel Murray of the 18th thought that there was a need for a strong adjutant to restore the regiment to a fighting unit, after criticisms from Wellington about their conduct at Vittoria.

DU PLAT, Georg Carl August
Lieutenant Colonel. 4th Line Battalion, King's German Legion.
Named on the Regimental Memorial: La Haye Sainte, Waterloo, Belgium. (Photograph)

Lt Colonel 30 Jun 1805. Bt Colonel 4 Jun 1813.

   Served in the Peninsula Aug 1812 – Apr 1814 (Command Brigade from Oct 1813). Present in Eastern Spain, Castalla and Tarragona. Present at Waterloo where he was severely wounded and died of his wounds 21 Jun. Also served in Hanover 1805, Copenhagen 1807, Mediterranean 1808–1812 and Netherlands 1814.

D'URBAN, Sir Benjamin
Lieutenant Colonel. 2nd West India Regiment of Foot.
Obelisk: Field of Honour, Pointe Claire, Montreal, Canada. (Photograph)

THIS PLAQUE WAS ERECTED BY THE CITY COUNCIL / OF DURBAN, IN THE PROVINCE OF NATAL, REPUBLIC / OF SOUTH AFRICA, TO HONOUR THE MEMORY OF / SIR BENJAMIN D'URBAN, AFTER WHOM THE CITY / WAS NAMED, IN 1835, WHILE HE WAS GOVERNOR OF / THE CAPE OF GOOD HOPE. DURBAN IS THE PREMIER / HARBOUR ON THE AFRICAN CONTINENT, AND THE GATE – / WAY TO THE FASTEST DEVELOPING AREA IN AFRICA.

Cornet 2nd Dragoon Guards Apr 1794. Lt 1 Jul 1794. Capt 2 Jul 1794. Capt 29th Dragoons Dec 1795. Major 20th Dragoons Dec 1797. Major Warwickshire Fencible Cavalry 21 Nov 1799. Major 25th Lt Dragoons Jan 1801. Bt Lt Colonel 1 Jan 1805. Major 89th Foot Jan 1805. Lt Colonel 9th Garrison Battalion Dec 1806. Lt Colonel 1st West India Regt Oct 1807. Lt Colonel 2nd West India Regt 7 Jan 1808. Bt Colonel 4 Jun 1813. Major General 12 Aug 1819. Lt General 10 Jan 1837.

   Served in the Peninsula Oct 1808 – Mar 1809 (AQMG on Staff) and Apr 1809 – Apr 1814 (QMG to Portuguese Army with rank of Major General). Present at Douro, Busaco, Albuera, Ciudad Rodrigo, Badajoz, Salamanca (Mentioned in Beresford's Despatches), Burgos, Vittoria, Pyrenees, Nivelle, Nive (Mentioned in Beresford's Despatches), Adour and Toulouse (Mentioned in Beresford's Despatches). Gold Cross for Busaco, Albuera, Badajoz, Salamanca, Vittoria, Pyrenees, Nivelle, Nive and Toulouse. GCB 1840. KCH. KTS.

   Appointed to the Royal Military College 1800. Became a very efficient staff officer, and Beresford, when reorganising the Portuguese Army, selected him as QMG. Also served in the Netherlands 1795, West Indies 1795–1796, Hanover 1805 and Ireland 1806–1807. Governor of Antigua 1820. Colonel 51st Foot 1829. Governor and Commander in Chief of Cape of Good Hope 1833 – Jan 1838. Retired and lived in the Cape until 1846. Recalled to command forces in Canada Jan 1847. Died at Montreal 25 May 1849 aged 72 years. Originally buried in the old Military Cemetery, Papineau Avenue, Montreal. Moved Jul 1944 to the Field of Honour, Pointe Claire, Montreal.

REFERENCE: *Dictionary of National Biography. Rousseau, I. J., The Peninsular journal of Major-General Sir Benjamin D'Urban 1808–1817, 1930, reprint 1988. Gentleman's Magazine, Dec 1849, pp. 647–8. Annual Register, 1849, Appx, pp. 242–3.*

DUTHIE, William
Bombardier. Royal Artillery.
Gravestone: Fetteresso Parish Churchyard, Kincardineshire, Scotland. (M.I.)

"CANNON ERECTED BY WILLIAM FINDLEY FROM BISHOPTON, PORTLETHEN IN MEMORY OF HIS UNCLE WILLIAM DUTHIE LATE SERGEANT IN ROYAL ARTILLERY, DIED STONE-HAVEN 1 SEPT 1859."

Gunner 16 Jan 1806. Bombardier 1 Jul 1811. Sgt 1 Feb 1823. Colour Sgt 1 Feb 1825.

Served in the Peninsula. Present at Cadiz (wounded), Busaco (severely wounded), Vittoria, Pyrenees and Bayonne. Also served in Canada and Halifax. Served for 25 years and discharged with chronic rheumatism and impaired vision 6 Sep 1837 aged 44 years. MGS medal for Busaco, Vittoria and Pyrenees.

DYAS, Joseph

Lieutenant. 51st (2nd Yorkshire West Riding) Light Infantry.
Low monument: Ballymena Old Graveyard, Ballymena, County Antrim, Northern Ireland. (Photograph)

CAPTAIN JOSEPH DYAS 51ST LIGHT INFANTRY / BORN KILBEG CO. MEATH 17TH MARCH 1791 / DIED 26TH APRIL 1850 / SERVED IN THE PENINSULAR WAR AND AT WATERLOO / AS AN ENSIGN HE TWICE LED THE STORMERS / IN THE ASSAULT AT BADAJOZ IN 1811 / ONE OF THE COOLEST AND BRAVEST OFFICERS IN THE ARMY.

Louth Militia. Ensign 31 Aug 1809. Lt 11 Jul 1811. Capt 2nd Ceylon Regt Dec 1820.

Served in the Peninsula Feb 1811 – Sep 1813. Present at Fuentes d'Onoro, second siege of Badajoz (Mentioned in Despatches for leading the Forlorn Hope on first and second assaults), Salamanca, Burgos, San Munos, Vittoria and Pyrenees. Present at Waterloo. MGS medal for Fuentes d'Onoro, Salamanca, Vittoria and Pyrenees.

Famous for his exploits at the assault of Fort San Cristobal at Badajoz on 6 and 9 Jun 1811. The failure of the first assault in which he led the Forlorn Hope, was caused by the supporting body of men going the wrong way to the breach and the discovery that the ladders were too short. Dyas insisted on leading the Forlorn Hope on the next assault on the 9th but again it proved a failure. Only 25 out of the original 200 men remained. Dyas himself was wounded in the second attempt. Wellington mentioned his bravery in his *Dispatch* and recommended him for further promotion, but Dyas refused to serve in any other regiment other than the 51st. Promotion to Lieutenant came to him because Lt Ralph Westropp of the 51st was killed trying to rescue a wounded soldier in the breach. Dyas would have received this rank even if he had not been in the Forlorn Hope. However he accepted a Captaincy in the Ceylon Regiment in 1820 but never served with the regiment as he went on half pay 9 Aug 1821 owing to ill health due to his exertions in the Peninsula and at Waterloo. Retired from the army 1826. 'He was during his military career considered to be one of the coolest and at the same time one of the bravest officers of any grade in the British Army. He frequently volunteered his services for the most arduous and hazardous duties and 'Dyas and the Stormers' was a standing toast of the most distinguished campaigners of the day.' (*Naval and Military Gazette*, 1850, p 274).

DYER, Sir John

Lieutenant Colonel. Royal Artillery.
Grave: St Nicholas Churchyard, Plumstead and named on the Regimental Memorial: St Nicholas Church, Plumstead, Kent. (No longer extant. Destroyed by a flying bomb in the Second World War)

2nd Lt 24 Apr 1793. 1st Lt 1 Jan 1794. Capt- Lieut 1 Jun 1798. Capt 9 Apr 1803. Major 17 Mar 1812. Lt Colonel 12 Apr 1814.

Served in the Peninsula Dec 1812 – Apr 1814. Present at Pamplona, Pyrenees, second siege of San Sebastian, Bidassoa, Nivelle, Nive, Orthes and Toulouse. Gold medal for Pyrenees, San Sebastian, Nive, Orthes and Toulouse. KCB. Also served in Flanders 1795. Killed 3 Jul 1816 when he was accidentally run over as he tried to stop Colonel Fyer's runaway carriage at Woolwich.
REFERENCE: *Gentleman's Magazine*, 1816, Jul p. 92.

DYKE, William
Private. 1st Regiment of Foot Guards.
Headstone: St Michael's and All Angels Churchyard, Clifton Hampden, Oxfordshire. (Photograph)

IN MEMORY OF / WILLIAM DYKE / OF THE GRENADIER GUARDS / WITH WHICH REGIMENT HE SERVED / AT THE BATTLE OF WATERLOO / HE WAS FOR MANY YEARS / A CONSTANT AND DEVOUT / WORSHIPPER / AT THIS CHURCH / DIED FEB 28 1866 / AGED 71 YEARS

Volunteer from Oxford Militia. Pte 1st Foot Guards 7 Apr 1814.

Served at Waterloo. Reputed to have accidentally fired the first shot at the Battle of Waterloo, siege of Peronne and with the Army of Occupation 1816–1818. Also served in the Netherlands 1814 (present at Bergen-op-Zoom). Discharged 4 Aug 1837. Awarded Long Service Good Conduct medal. Became a Chelsea Out Pensioner.

DYOTT, William
Lieutenant Colonel. 25th (King's Own Borderer's) Regiment of Foot.
Memorial tablet: Dyott Chapel, St Mary's Church, Lichfield, Staffordshire. (Photograph)

SACRED TO THE MEMORY OF / GENERAL WILLIAM DYOTT, COLONEL OF THE 63RD REGIMENT, / A MAGISTRATE & A DEPUTY LIEUTENANT COLONEL FOR THE COUNTY OF STAFFORD. / THE FIDELITY AND ZEAL WITH WHICH HE DISCHARGED ALL HIS / DUTIES, THE HIGH HONOUR AND INTEGRITY OF CHARACTER WHICH / MARKED EVERY ACTION OF HIS LIFE, SECURED TO HIM / THE DISTINGUISHED APPROVAL OF HIS SOVEREIGN, / THE AFFECTION OF HIS FAMILY, THE ESTEEM OF HIS FRIENDS / THE CONFIDENCE AND RESPECT OF ALL WHO KNEW HIM. / HE DIED AT FREEFORD, MAY 7 1847, IN THE 87TH YEAR OF HIS AGE, / LEAVING TWO SONS AND A DAUGHTER, TO MOURN THE LOSS / OF A MOST KIND, MOST INDULGENT FATHER. / HIS REMAINS REST IN THE VAULT BENEATH.

Ensign 4th Foot 14 Mar 1781. Lt 3 Apr 1785. Capt 25 Apr 1793. Major 103rd Foot 19 May 1794. Lt Colonel 18 Sep 1794. Lt Colonel 25th Foot Nov 1795. Bt Colonel 1 Jan 1800. Major General 25 Apr 1808. Lt General 4 Jun 1813. General 22 Jul 1830.

Appointed to staff of Sir John Moore, Dec 1808 and sailed for Corunna, but on the way met ships bringing the Army home. Served at Walcheren 1809 (when part of the Army returned to England was ordered to garrison the island of Walcheren. Of the 14,000 men left there, 8,000 were sick with fever. Returned home with the despatches 31 Oct 1809). Also served in the West Indies 1796, Egypt 1801 (present at Alexandria) and Ireland 1803–1806. Colonel 63rd Foot 7 Apr 1825. Dyott had the reputation of being a very good staff officer. Deputy Lieutenant of the County of Stafford and an active magistrate. REFERENCE: *Gentleman's Magazine, Jul 1847, pp. 89–92. Annual Register, 1847, Appx, pp. 227–8.*

EADIE, Edward
Private. 12th (Prince of Wales's) Regiment of Light Dragoons.
Named on the Regimental Memorial: St Joseph's Church, Waterloo, Belgium. (Photograph)
Killed at Waterloo.

EAGER, Francis Russell
Captain. 31st (Huntingdonshire) Regiment of Foot.
Grave: Karnal Cemetery, Karnal, India. Inscription illegible. (M.I.)

Ensign Feb 1804. Lt 19 Sep 1804. Capt 15 Jan 1807. Bt Major 19 Jul 1821. Major 2 Jun 1825.

Served in the Peninsula with 2/31st Nov 1808 – Apr 1814. Present at Talavera, Olivencia, Badajoz, Albuera, Arroyo dos Molinos, Almarez, Vittoria, Pyrenees, Orthes, Garris and Toulouse. The 2nd battalion was disbanded after the war and he transferred to the 1st. Also served in Ireland 1806–1808, Sicily and Naples 1815, Malta 1816 and India 1825 – 1832. Succeeded to the command of the regiment Apr 1832, until his death at Karnal 21 Dec 1832.

EARLY, John
Private. 12th (Prince of Wales's) Regiment of Light Dragoons.
Named on the Regimental Memorial: St Joseph's Church, Waterloo, Belgium. (Photograph)
   Killed at Waterloo.

ECCLES, Thomas
Lieutenant. 60th (Royal American) Regiment of Foot.
Named on the Memorial: St Andrew's Church, (now Musée Historique), Biarritz, France. (Photograph)

Ensign 34th Foot 2 Nov 1809. Lt 5 Mar 1812. Lt 60th Foot 8 Apr 1813.
   Served in the Peninsula with 34th Foot Mar 1810 – May 1813 and 60th Foot May 1813 – Nov 1813. Present at Busaco, Olivencia, first siege of Badajoz, Albuera, Arroyo dos Molinos, Almarez, retreat from Burgos, Vittoria, Pyrenees and Nivelle where he was killed 10 Nov 1813.

ECKERSLEY, Nathaniel
Captain. 1st (Royal) Regiment of Dragoons.
Memorial tablet: All Saints Church, Hindley, Lancashire. (Photograph)

TO THE MEMORY OF / LIEUNT COLNL NATHANIEL ECKERSLEY, K.H. / SON OF JAMES AND MARY ECKERSLEY OF HINDLEY, / WHO DIED AT HIS RESIDENCE IN THIS TOWNSHIP / ON THE 12TH OF NOVEMBER 1837, / AGED 58 YEARS, / AND WAS INTERRED IN THE CEMETERY OF THIS CHAPEL. / HE ENLISTED INTO THE 10TH REGIMENT OF LIGHT DRAGOONS / AS A PRIVATE IN THE YEAR 1795, AND WAS IN ACTIVE SERVICE / UNDER THE COMMAND OF THE DUKE OF WELLINGTON / DURING THE PENINSULAR WAR. / HE WAS STATIONED IN MANCHESTER 8 YEARS / FROM 1819 TO 1827, / AS BRIGADE MAJOR OF THE DISTRICT, / AND WAS AFTERWARDS 6 YEARS AT BARBADOS / AS DEPUTY QUARTER MASTER GENERAL OF THE FORCES / IN THE WINDWARD AND LEEWARD ISLANDS, WEST INDIES.

Low monument in Family railed enclosure: All Saints Churchyard, Hindley, Lancashire. (Photograph)

Pte 10th Lt Dragoons 1795. Adjutant 1st Dragoons 9 Aug 1800. Cornet 25 Jun 1802. Lt 8 Sep 1804. Capt 16 Oct 1811. Bt Major 21 Jun 1817. Bt Lt Colonel 8 Nov 1827.
   Served in the Peninsula Sep 1809 – Apr 1814 (ADC to Major General Slade Jan 1810 – Jul 1812), on Staff (DAAG 2nd Division Oct 1812 – Apr 1813 and DAAG at HQ May 1813 – Apr 1814). Present at Fuentes d'Onoro, Aldea da Ponte, Maguilla, Vittoria, Pyrenees, Nivelle, Nive, Orthes and Toulouse. KH. Brigade Major in Manchester 1819–1827. Also served in the West Indies 1827–1833 (DQMG in the Windward and Leeward Islands).

EDGELL, Charles James
Captain. 4th (King's Own) Regiment of Foot.
Gravestone: St Michael's Cathedral Churchyard, Bridgetown, Barbados, West Indies. (M.I.)

"HERE LIE THE REMAINS / OF / CAPT CHAS JAMES EDGELL / OF THE 4TH (KING'S OWN) REG. / WHO DIED AT SEA / ON THE 4TH DAY OF JUNE 1819 / AGED 39."

Named on the Regimental Memorial: St Michael's Cathedral, Bridgetown, Barbados, West Indies. (Photograph)

Ensign 1801. Lt 1803. Capt 5 Sep 1805.

Served in the Peninsula with 1/4th Jun 1812 – Oct 1813. Present at Salamanca, retreat from Burgos, Villa Muriel and Vittoria (wounded and awarded pension of £100 per annum). Present at Waterloo (wounded). Went to the West Indies with his regiment, but died at sea on his way to Barbados, 1819.

EDWARDES, David John
1st Lieutenant. Royal Artillery.
Family Memorial tablet: St Mary's Church, Llanllwch, Carmarthen, Wales. (Photograph)

……………….. / LIKEWISE TO THE MEMORY OF / CAPTAIN DAVID JOHN EDWARDES, / OF RHYD-Y-GORS, A CAPTAIN IN THE / ROYAL HORSE ARTILLERY, WHO DIED / APRIL 14TH 1866, AGED 79 YEARS. / ………………..

2nd Lt 1 Nov 1805. 1st Lt 1 Jun 1806. 2nd Capt 1 Jun 1822.

Served in the Peninsula Feb 1813 – Apr 1814 with 'F' Troop Royal Horse Artillery. Present at Vittoria, second siege of San Sebastian, Bidassoa, Nivelle, Nive, Adour and Bayonne. Present at Waterloo in Lt Colonel Webber-Smith's Troop. MGS medal for Vittoria, San Sebastian, Nivelle and Nive. Retired on half pay 1825.

EDWARDS, Benjamin Hutchins
Lieutenant. 43rd (Monmouthshire) Light Infantry Regiment of Foot.
Memorial tablet: St Peter's Church, Freshford, Somerset. (Photograph)

TO THE MEMORY OF / BENJAMIN HUTCHINS EDWARDS. / MAJOR FORMERLY OF THE 43D / LIGHT INFANTRY, / WHO DIED IN THIS PARISH / ON 23D FEBY 1873 / AGED 79 YEARS.

Low monument: St Peter's Churchyard, Freshford, Somerset. (North east of tower). (Photograph)

BENJAMIN HUTCHINS EDWARDS / DIED 23RD FEBRUARY 1873

Portuguese Army: Ensign 9th Line 19 Dec 1811. Ensign 43rd Foot 14 May 1812. Lt 21 Oct 1813. Lt 98th Foot 12 Mar 1829.

Served in the Peninsula with Portuguese Army as volunteer Ensign. With 1/43rd Jul 1812 – Apr 1814. Present at Badajoz (wounded), Salamanca, Vera, Pyrenees, Bidassoa Nivelle, Nive (wounded), Tarbes and Toulouse. Half pay 1 Jul 1836. Adjutant Glasgow Recruiting Staff 7 May 1847 and Liverpool District 10 Mar 1848. Appointed Captain of Recruiting Staff 20 Dec 1864 and Major 20 Feb 1866. MGS medal for Badajoz, Salamanca, Pyrenees, Nivelle, Nive and Toulouse.

EELES, Charles
Captain. 95th Regiment of Foot.
Family Memorial tablet: St Mary's Church, Amersham, Buckinghamshire. (Photograph)

SACRED / TO THE MEMORY OF / CHARLES EELES ESQR / LATE CAPTAIN IN HIS MAJESTY'S / 95TH RIFLE REGIMENT, / WHO AFTER SERVING WITH THE BRITISH ARMY / THRO' THE VARIOUS CAMPAIGNS IN / THE SPANISH PENINSULA; / TERMINATED HIS GLORIOUS CAREER / ON THE 18TH JUNE 1815, / IN THE 30TH YEAR OF HIS AGE. / HE NOBLY FELL IN THE COUNTRY'S CAUSE, / ON THE EVER MEMORABLE FIELD OF / WATERLOO. / ESTEEMED, LAMENTED AND BELOVED. / ……………..

Ensign 89th Foot 31 Jul 1806. Lt 95th Foot 9 Jun 1808. Adjutant 30 May 1811. Capt 20 Jul 1814.

Served in the Peninsula with 1/95th Aug 1808 – Jan 1809, 3/95th 1810 – Jan 1811 and 1/95th Feb 1811

– Apr 1814. (Brigade Major 1st Brigade Light Division Aug 1812 – Apr 1814). Present at Cacabellos (wounded), Cadiz, Sobral (severely wounded), Pombal, Redinha, Casal Nova, Marialva (affair at bridge over river Azava 23 Apr 1811 – Mentioned in Despatches), Foz D'Arouce, Sabugal, Fuentes d'Onoro, Ciudad Rodrigo, Badajoz, Salamanca, Vittoria, Pyrenees, Vera, Bidassoa, Nivelle, Nive, Orthes, Tarbes and Toulouse. Present at Waterloo (Brigade Major under Sir James Kempt). After surviving 22 battles in the Peninsula, he was killed in the final battle at Waterloo. Brother of Capt William Eeles 95th Foot.

EELES, William
Captain. 95th Regiment of Foot.
Family Memorial tablet: St Mary's Church, Amersham, Buckinghamshire. (On tablet for his brother Charles Eeles). (Photograph)

.... / HIS BROTHER WILLIAM EELES, K. H. COLONEL IN THE RIFLE BRIGADE (OLD 95TH) / DIED AT WOOLWICH IN 1838. WAS AT BUENOS AYRES (UNDER WHITELOCK) / PENINSULAR CAMPAIGN AND WATERLOO.

Headstone: St Luke's Churchyard, Charlton, Kent. (Grave number 146). (Photograph)

BY HIS BROTHER OFFICERS / OF THE 1ST BATTALION RIFLE BRIGADE / THIS STONE IS RAISED / TO THE MEMORY OF THE LATE / LIEUT – COLONEL WILLIAM EELES, KH, / ONE WHOM THEY LOVED AND ESTEEMED / AS A TRUE FRIEND AND COMRADE, / AS MUCH AS THEY REGARDED AND APPRECIATED / HIS HIGH QUALITIES AS A SOLDIER. / BORN OCT 12, 1783. / DIED AT WOOLWICH OCT 12, 1838.

Ensign 12 Dec 1805. Lt 17 Dec 1807. Capt 7 Dec 1813. Bt Major 18 Jun 1815. Major 8 Jan 1824. Lt Colonel 22 Jul 1830.
   Served in the Peninsula with 1/95th Aug 1808 – Jan 1809 and Jul 1809 – Sep 1809. Present at Cacabellos and Corunna (wounded). Returned to England after Sep 1809 due to ill health from the retreat to Corunna. Present at Waterloo with 3/95th. Also served in South America 1807 (present at Buenos Ayres), Sweden 1808 and the Netherlands 1814–1815 (present at Merxem where he was wounded). KH. Became Lt Colonel commanding 1st Battalion 1830–1837. Brother of Capt Charles Eeles 95th Foot.

EFFINGHAM 1ST Earl see HOWARD, Kenneth Alexander

EGERTON, Richard
Captain. 34th (Cumberland) Regiment of Foot.
Memorial brass tablet: St Helen's Church, Tarporley, Cheshire. (Arden Chapel). (Photograph)

IN THIS CHURCHYARD LIETH THE BODY / OF RICHARD EGERTON OF EATON BANKS, / LIEUT: GENERAL CB. EIGHTH SON OF / PHILIP EGERTON OF EGERTON AND / OULTON ESQRE. HE WAS BORN ON THE 7TH DAY / OF OCTOBER A.D. 1783. AND DEPARTED THIS / LIFE ON THE 18TH DAY OF NOVEMBER, AD. 1854. / ....

Ensign 89th Foot 1 Dec 1798. Lt 29th Foot 29 Mar 1800. Capt 28 Sep 1804. Capt 89th Foot 8 Nov 1805. Capt 34th Foot 14 Apr 1808. Bt Major 26 Aug 1813. Bt Lt Colonel 18 Jun 1815. Bt Colonel 10 Jan 1837. Major General 9 Nov 1846. Lt General 20 Jun1854.
   Served in the Peninsula with 34th Foot Jul 1809 – Jun 1810, Mar 1812 – Oct 1812 on Staff (DAAG 2nd Division Jul 1810 – Feb 1811, DAAG 4th Division Mar 1811 – Feb 1812 and ADC to General Lord Hill Nov 1812 – Apr 1814). Present at Busaco, Torres Vedras, Olivencia, first siege of Badajoz, Albuera (wounded), Aldea da Ponte, Vittoria, Pyrenees (awarded Bt Majority), Nivelle, Nive, Orthes and Toulouse. Present at Waterloo (again ADC to Lord Hill) and with the Army of Occupation. Awarded Bt Lt Colonelcy.

CB and MGS medal for Busaco, Albuera, Vittoria, Pyrenees, Nivelle, Nive, Orthes and Toulouse. Also served in North America 1800 with 29th Foot and South America 1807 with 89th Foot. Lord Hill's private secretary and first ADC 1828. Colonel 46th Foot 24 Jan 1853. Brother of Major Thomas Egerton 29th Foot and brother in law of Capt William Tomkinson 16th Lt Dragoons.
REFERENCE: *Gentleman's Magazine, Apr 1855, p. 421. Annual Register, 1854, Appx, p. 366.*

EGERTON, Thomas
Major. 29th (Worcestershire) Regiment of Foot.
Memorial: St Mary Magdalene Church, South Bersted, Sussex. (M.I.)

"HERE REST THE REMAINS OF THOS EGERTON ESQ / LATE MAJOR OF THE 29TH REG. OF FOOT WHO / DEPARTED THIS LIFE JANY 29TH ANNO DOMINI / 1812. AGED 34 YEARS"

Cornet 25th Lt Dragoons 27 Sep 1794. Lt 29 Nov 1794. Capt 106th Foot 6 Mar 1795. Capt 56th Foot 31 Dec 1795. Capt 29th Foot 20 Oct 1796. Bt Major 25 Apr 1808. Major 8 Sep 1808.
　　Served in the Peninsula Jul 1808 – Jun 1809 and Aug 1810 – Jun 1811. Present at Rolica (severely wounded). Retired 29 Aug 1811 and died in 1812 from the effects of his wounds from the assault on the ridge above Columbeira. Also served at the Helder 1799. Educated at Charterhouse. Brother of Capt Richard Egerton 34th Foot.

EKINS, Clement
Assistant Surgeon. 38th (1st Staffordshire) Regiment of Foot.
Grave: Barbados Military Cemetery, Barbados, West Indies. (M.I.)

"IN MEMORY OF SURGEON CLEMENT EKINS DIED 16 JULY 1832."

Family tombstone: St John the Evangelist Churchyard, Brecon, Breconshire, Wales. (Underneath yew tree). (M.I.)

"BELOW REST THE REMAINS OF TWO CHILDREN OF CLEMENT AND MARY ANNE EKINS WHO DIED IN 1821 AND 1833. THE BELOVED FATHER OF THE ABOVE NAMED CHILDREN WAS FORMERLY CORONER FOR THE COUNTY. HE DIED AT BARBADOS, IN THE WEST INDIES JULY 16, 1832, AGED 42, TO WHICH PLACE HE ACCOMPANIED HIS REGIMENT, THE 93RD HIGHLANDERS AS SURGEON ...."

Hospital Assistant 13 Apr 1813. Asst Surgeon 38th Foot 9 Sep 1813. Asst Surgeon 9th Foot 24 Nov 1814. Asst Surgeon 38th Foot 24 Aug 1815. Surgeon 93rd Foot 2 Nov 1830.
　　Served in the Peninsula Jul – Oct 1813 as Hospital Assistant and Nov 1813 – Apr 1814 with 1/38th. Present at Nive and Bayonne. Also served in the West Indies 1830 where he died in Barbados 1832.

ELDER, Sir George
Major. Staff Appointment in Spain and Portugal.
Low monument: St George's Cathedral Cemetery, Madras, India. (Photograph)

UNDERNEATH / ARE DEPOSITED THE REMAINS / OF / MAJOR GENERAL / SIR GEORGE ELDER, K.C.B. / WHO / AFTER A LONG CAREER OF / DISTINGUISHED SERVICE AS A SOLDIER / IN VARIOUS PARTS OF THE WORLD, / LOST HIS LIFE / BY ACCIDENT AT MADRAS, / ON THE 3RD DECEMBER, 1836, / AGED 57 YEARS.

Ensign Cambridgeshire Militia. Ensign 46th Foot 29 Nov 1799. 2nd Lt 95th Foot 5 Nov 1800. 1st Lt 24 Mar 1803. Capt 23 May 1805. Major 13 Apr 1809. Bt Lt Colonel 30 May 1811. Bt Colonel 19 Jun 1821.

Major General 22 Jul 1830. Portuguese Army: Major 13 Apr 1809. Lt Colonel 3rd Caçadores 14 Jun 1809. Colonel 6th Line 10 Jul 1813. Colonel 7th Line 26 Feb 1814.

Served in the Peninsula with 95th Foot Aug 1808 – Jan 1809, and with the Portuguese Army Jun 1808 – Jun 1812. Present at Corunna, Almeida, Coa (Mentioned in Despatches), Busaco, Foz d'Arouce, Sabugal (Mentioned in Despatches), Fuentes d'Onoro, Ciudad Rodrigo (Mentioned in Despatches) and Badajoz (wounded, Mentioned in Despatches and awarded pension of £300 per annum). Gold Cross for Busaco, Fuentes d'Onoro, Ciudad Rodrigo and Badajoz. KCB, KTS. Lieutenant Governor of St John's Newfoundland 4 Oct 1826. Also served in India Jun 1836 in command of the Mysore division of the Army. He was killed by his horse running him violently against a tree Dec 1836.
REFERENCE: *Gentleman's Magazine, Aug 1837, p. 207.*

ELGEE, William
1st Lieutenant. Royal Artillery.
Box tomb: Rathaspeck Churchyard, Rathaspeck, County Wexford, Ireland. (Photograph)

SACRED TO THE MEMORY OF / MAJOR WILLIAM ELGEE, / ROYAL ARTILLERY, WHO DEPARTED THIS LIFE / ON THE 20TH OF DECEMBER 1849. / AGED 59 YEARS. / HIS END WAS PEACE.

2nd Lt 1 Jul 1807. 1st Lt 20 May 1808. 2nd Capt 6 Nov 1827. Capt 10 Jan 1837. Bt Major 23 Nov 1841.
Served in the Peninsula Apr 1809 – Apr 1814. Present at Douro, Talavera, Fuentes d'Onoro, siege of Burgos (wounded) and Bayonne. Also served in North America May 1829 – Dec 1830 and West Indies Dec 1838 – Apr 1840 and Feb 1842 – Jun 1844. MGS medal for Talavera and Fuentes d'Onoro. Retired on full pay 1 Apr 1846.

ELIGÉ, John Peter
Captain. Royal Artillery.
Memorial tablet: St Peter and St Paul Church, Nutfield, Surrey. (M.I.)

"TO THE MEMORY / OF JOHN PETER ELIGÉ ESQRE. / .... / ALSO OF JOHN PETER ELIGÉ, SON OF THE ABOVE / CAPTAIN IN THE ROYAL ARTILLERY WHO WAS KILLED / AT THE COMMENCEMENT OF STORMING THE FORTS AT SALAMANCA IN SPAIN / ON THE 19TH OF JUNE 1812, AGED 32 YEARS / AND WAS INTERRED WITH MILITARY HONOURS IN THE GROUND OF A CONVENT. / TO A MOST AMIABLE DISPOSITION WERE UNITED ALL THOSE QUALITIES / WHICH NEVER FAIL TO GAIN ESTEEM. / HIS MERITS MAY BE APPRECIATED FROM THE FOLLOWING EXTRACT OF A LETTER / ADDRESSED TO HIS AFFLICTED MOTHER BY A SUPERIOR OFFICER / "CAPT ELIGÉ'S UNBLEMISHED CHARACTER AS A GENTLEMEN, AND UNSULLIED HONOR / AS A SOLDIER WILL EVER BE REMEMBERED BY ALL WHO KNEW HIM. THIS TRIBUTE / I BEG TO OFFER AS COMING FROM HIS COMRADES IN ARMS WHO DESIRE TO DO JUSTICE / TO HIS MEMORY: AND I AM DEPUTED BY THEM TO OFFER THIS GRATEFUL COMMUNICATION."

2nd Lt 18 Mar 1797. 1st Lt 16 Jul 1799. 2nd Capt 11 Oct 1804. Capt 5 Sep 1811.
Served in the Peninsula Jan – Jul 1812 (OC 10th Company 8th Battalion). Present at the siege of Salamanca Forts where he was killed 19 Jun 1812. Also served at the Helder 1799 where he was wounded and taken prisoner.

ELKINGTON, James Goodall
Surgeon. 30th (Cambridgeshire) Regiment of Foot.
Low monument: Arbour Hill Cemetery, Dublin, Ireland. (Photograph)

WITHIN THIS VAULT LIE THE REMAINS / OF / JAMES GOODALL ELKINGTON ESQ.ᴿ / STAFF SURGEON FORMERLY OF THE 17ᵀᴴ LANCERS / AND LATE OF THE / ROYAL HIBERNIAN MILITARY SCHOOL PHOENIX PARK. / HE DEPARTED THIS LIFE DEEPLY REGRETTED / ON THE 3ᴿᴰ OF OCTOBER 1853 / AGED 69 YEARS / AFTER A LENGTHY SERVICE OF 47 YEARS / HAVING SERVED THROUGH / THE PENINSULA AND WATERLOO.

Hospital Mate 8 Aug 1807. Asst Surgeon 24ᵗʰ Foot 7 Jul 1808. Surgeon 30ᵗʰ Foot 11 Mar 1813. Surgeon 1ˢᵗ Foot 12 Jul 1821. Surgeon 17ᵗʰ Lancers 11 Sep 1828. Surgeon Hibernian School 5 Mar 1841.

Served in the Peninsula with 24ᵗʰ Foot Apr 1809 – Jan 1813. Present at Talavera (taken prisoner whilst tending the wounded and sent to Verdun, France. Exchanged and rejoined the regiment Jul 1810), Fuentes d'Onoro, Ciudad Rodrigo, Badajoz, Salamanca, capture of Madrid and retreat from Burgos (taken prisoner again when he was in charge of the wounded, but managed to escape). MGS medal for Talavera, Fuentes d'Onoro, Ciudad Rodrigo, Badajoz and Salamanca. Present at Quatre Bras and Waterloo with the 30ᵗʰ Foot. Also served in Madeira 1807, the Netherlands 1814–1815, Barbados 1823 and Ireland 1828. Half pay 1817. Staff Surgeon Royal Hibernian Medical School 1841 where he remained until his death. REFERENCE: Elkington, H. P., *Some episodes in the life of James Goodall Elkington, an Army surgeon in the Peninsula days, together with extracts from his journal, Royal Army Medical Corps Journal, Vol 16, Jan 1911, pp. 79–104.*

ELLEY, Sir John

Lieutenant Colonel. Royal Regiment of Horse Guards.
Memorial tablet: St George's Chapel, Windsor, Berkshire. (North Choir aisle). (Photograph)

ERECTED TO THE MEMORY OF / LIEUᵀ. GENERAL SIR JOHN ELLEY, K.C.B. K.C.H. / COLONEL OF HER MAJESTY'S 17ᵀᴴ REGIMENT OF LANCERS, / GOVERNOR OF THE GARRISON AT GALWAY; / WHO WAS BORN A.D. 1764, DIED JANUARY 23ᴿᴰ 1839, AND IS BURIED IN THIS CHAPEL. / SIR JOHN ELLEY ENTERED THE ARMY IN 1790, / AS A PRIVATE IN THE ROYAL REGIMENT OF HORSE GUARDS; / UNAIDED BY DIGNITY OF BIRTH, OR THE INFLUENCE OF FORTUNE, HE RAISED HIMSELF / TO THE HIGHEST RANK IN THE BRITISH ARMY BY DISTINGUISHED CONDUCT IN THE FIELD. / IN THE YEAR 1793 HE WAS PRESENT AT THE / SIEGE OF VALENCIENNES: / HE SERVED WITH DISTINCTION UNDER SIR JOHN MOORE / IN THE CAMPAIGN OF 1808, AND AT THE SUBSEQUENT / BATTLE OF CORUNNA. / THROUGHOUT THE PENINSULA WAR HE WAS THE COMPANION IN ARMS OF THE / DUKE OF WELLINGTON. / TO ENUMERATE THE VARIOUS OCCASIONS ON WHICH HE DISPLAYED / CONSPICUOUS SKILL AND BRAVERY, WOULD BE TO ENUMERATE THE SEVERAL BATTLES / WHICH HAVE THROWN AN IMPERISHABLE GLORY AROUND THAT TREMENDOUS CONTEST. / IN 1815 HE FOUGHT AND WAS SEVERELY WOUNDED AT / WATERLOO. / IN THAT CROWNING AND MAGNIFICENT TRIUMPH OF BRITISH VALOUR / HE ADDED LUSTRE TO HIS FORMER ACHIEVEMENTS; / AND HIS NAME IS LASTINGLY WRITTEN ON THE RECORDS OF THAT FAMOUS DAY / WHICH GAVE PEACE TO THE NATIONS OF THE CIVILISED WORLD. / IN THE YEAR 1835 SIR JOHN ELLEY WAS RETURNED TO PARLIAMENT / AS REPRESENTATIVE OF THE BOROUGH OF NEW WINDSOR. / THE CAUSE HE HAD SO NOBLY DEFENDED WITH HIS SWORD / HE CONSCIENTIOUSLY BELIEVED TO BE THE CAUSE OF FREEDOM, RELIGION AND LAW. / IN THE SENATE, NO LESS THAN IN THE FIELD, / HE FOUGHT FOR THE ANCIENT INSTITUTIONS OF EUROPE, / FOR THE HAPPINESS, THE VIRTUE, AND DIGNITY OF THE HUMAN RACE: / HE WAS A TRUE BRITISH SOLDIER; A SINCERE CHRISTIAN; / A ZEALOUS AND AFFECTIONATE FRIEND.

Private 5 Nov 1789. Troop Quartermaster 4 Jun 1790. Cornet 6 Jun 1794. Lt 28 Jan 1796. Capt 24 Oct 1799. Major 29 Nov 1804. Lt Colonel 5 Mar 1806. Bt Colonel 7 May 1813. Major General 12 Aug 1819. Lt General 10 Jan 1837.

Served in the Peninsula Nov 1808 – Jan 1809 and Jun 1809 – Apr 1814 (AAG of Cavalry). Present at

Sahagun, Benevente, Lugo, Corunna, Talavera (commanded the rear guard of the cavalry), Sabugal, Fuentes d'Onoro, Llerena (Mentioned in Despatches), Salamanca (wounded and Mentioned in Despatches), Vittoria, Orthes and Toulouse. Present at Waterloo as DAG (wounded). Also served in Flanders 1793–1795 (present at Valenciennes). Gold Cross for Sahagun and Benevente, Talavera, Fuentes d'Onoro, Salamanca, Vittoria, Orthes and Toulouse. KCB. KCH. Governor of Galway 1826. Colonel 7th Hussars. Colonel 17th Lancers 23 Nov 1829. Knight of the Austrian Order of Maria Theresa and Knight 4th Class of the Russian Order of St George. Entered the regiment as a private and rose through the ranks to command the regiment. MP for Windsor 1835. Died 23 Jan 1839.
REFERENCE: *Dictionary of National Biography. Gentleman's Magazine, Apr 1839, pp. 430–1. Annual Register, 1839, Appx, pp. 318–9.*

ELLICOMBE, Charles Grene
Captain. Royal Engineers.
Named on the Regimental Memorial: Rochester Cathedral, Rochester, Kent. (Photograph)

Lt 1 Jul 1801. 2nd Capt 1 Jul 1806. Capt 1 May 1811. Bt Major 27 Apr 1812. Bt Lt Colonel 21 Sep 1813. Lt Colonel 23 Mar 1825. Bt Colonel 22 Jul 1830. Colonel 10 Jan 1837. Major General 23 Nov 1841. Lt General 11 Nov 1851. General 20 Apr 1861.
    Served in the Peninsula Nov 1811 – Apr 1814 (Brigade Major from Oct 1812). Present at Ciudad Rodrigo, Badajoz (Mentioned in Despatches and awarded Bt Majority), Vittoria, San Sebastian (Mentioned in Despatches and awarded Bt Lt Colonelcy), Bidassoa, Nivelle, Nive, Adour, siege and Sortie from Bayonne. Gold Medal for San Sebastian. CB. MGS medal for Ciudad Rodrigo, Badajoz, Vittoria, Nivelle and Nive. KCB 1862. Also served in India and Ceylon 1801–1809. Inspector General of Fortifications 1821–1842. Colonel Commandant Royal Engineers. 1856. Noted for his administrative ability and scientific knowledge. Died at Worthing 7 Jun 1871.
REFERENCE: *Dictionary of National Biography. Royal Military Calendar, Vol 4, p. 495. Annual Register 1871, Appx, p. 153.*

ELLIOT, Gilbert
Captain. 83rd Regiment of Foot.
Ledger stone: St John's Cathedral Churchyard, Sligo, Ireland. (Photograph)

HERE LIETH THE REMAINS OF LIEUT / COL GILBERT ELLIOT OF THE 47TH REGT / WHO DEPARTED THIS LIFE SEPT 6, 1836, / AGED 45 YEARS. / ....

Ensign 6th Garrison Battalion 29 Nov 1806. Lt 83rd Foot 12 Feb 1807. Capt 14 Jun 1810. Bt Major 1 Apr 1814. Capt 32nd Foot 23 Jul 1818. Bt Lt Colonel 22 Jul 1830. Capt 47th Foot 1 Jun 1832.
    Served in the Peninsula Apr 1809 – Nov 1810 and Sep 1812 – Apr 1814. Present at Douro, Talavera, Vittoria, Nivelle, Nive and Orthes (severely wounded). Gold Medal for Orthes. Retired on half pay 19 Dec 1822.

ELLIOT, William Rowley
Captain. 29th (Worcestershire) Regiment of Foot.
Memorial tablet: St Mary's Church, Cheltenham, Gloucestershire. (Photograph)

IN PIOUS MEMORY OF / LIEUT COL WILLIAM ROWLEY ELLIOT K.H. / SON OF THE LATE REV WILLIAM ELLIOT, / MANY YEARS RECTOR OF TRIM, IRELAND, / AND ELIZABETH HIS WIFE. / UPWARDS OF 38 YEARS OF HIS LIFE HAD BEEN SPENT IN THE ACTIVE / SERVICE OF HIS COUNTRY ENTERING THE ARMY IN EARLY YOUTH / HE ACCOMPANIED H. M. 29TH REGT THROUGHOUT THE GREATER PORTION OF / THE PENINSULAR & SECOND AMERICAN WARS, AND AFTERWARDS TO THE / MAURITIUS. HE LIKEWISE SERVED FOR SOME YEARS

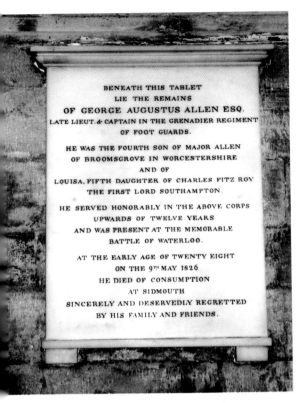

BENEATH THIS TABLET
LIE THE REMAINS
OF GEORGE AUGUSTUS ALLEN ESQ.
LATE LIEUT. & CAPTAIN IN THE GRENADIER REGIMENT
OF FOOT GUARDS.

HE WAS THE FOURTH SON OF MAJOR ALLEN
OF BROOMSGROVE IN WORCESTERSHIRE
AND OF
LOUISA, FIFTH DAUGHTER OF CHARLES FITZ ROY
THE FIRST LORD SOUTHAMPTON.

HE SERVED HONORABLY IN THE ABOVE CORPS
UPWARDS OF TWELVE YEARS
AND WAS PRESENT AT THE MEMORABLE
BATTLE OF WATERLOO.

AT THE EARLY AGE OF TWENTY EIGHT
ON THE 9TH MAY 1826
HE DIED OF CONSUMPTION
AT SIDMOUTH
SINCERELY AND DESERVEDLY REGRETTED
BY HIS FAMILY AND FRIENDS.

George A. Allen 1st Foot Guards

Charles von Alten King's German Legion

Georg Freiherr von Baring
geboren zu Hannover den 8ten März 1773
seit 1786 in der Hannöverischen Armee
später in der Königl. Deutschen Legion
Vertheidiger von La Haye sainte
in der Schlacht von Waterloo
gestorben zu Wiesbaden als Königl. Hannover.
Generallieutenant den 27ten Februar 1848

George von Baring Kings German Legion

Robert Barker 95th Foot

Henry Beere 30th Foot and Hercules Beere 61st Foot

William Bell Royal Artillery

Lord William C. Bentinck 11th Lt Dragoons

Henry Bird 5th Foot

Augustus Blythman 95th Foot

Charles Boothby Royal Engineers

John P. Buchanan 16th Lt Dragoons

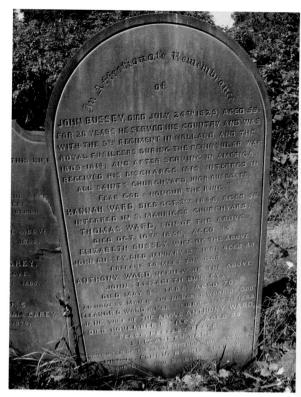

John Bussey 7th Foot

Thomas Calder Royal Artillery Drivers

John Scrope Colquitt 1st Regiment of Foot Guards

Alexander Cameron 95th Foot

John Cameron (Fassiefern) 92nd Foot

Thomas Canch 5th Foot

William Cargill 74th Foot

Thomas Champ 43rd Foot

Edward H. Cheney 2nd Dragoons

Sir John Colborne 52nd Foot

Stapleton Cotton 20th Lt Dragoons

William G. Collier Coldstream Guards

Edward Coxen 95th Foot

Henry Crawfurd 9th Foot

Henry Daubeney 84th Foot

Sir Robert H. Dick 42nd Foot

Sir Alexander Dickson Royal Artillery

Nathaniel Eckersley 1st Light Dragoons

Sir Henry W. Ellis 23rd Foot

Mildmay Fane 44th Foot

Richard Fletcher Royal Engineers

Thomas Forbes 45th Foot

Edward Gibbs 52nd Foot

Dugald L. Gilmour 95th Foot

Henry Gomm 6th Foot

Alexander Gordon 3rd Foot Guards

John Gordon 2nd Foot

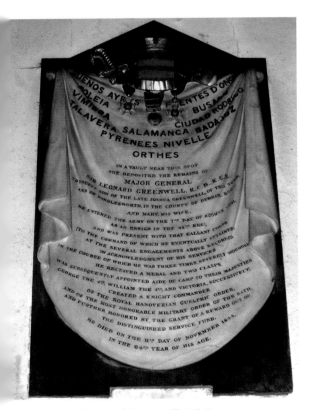

Leonard Greenwell 45th Foot

Alexander Hair 43rd Foot

Colin Halkett King's German Legion

William F. Hamilton 3rd Foot Guards

Richard Hardinge Royal Artillery

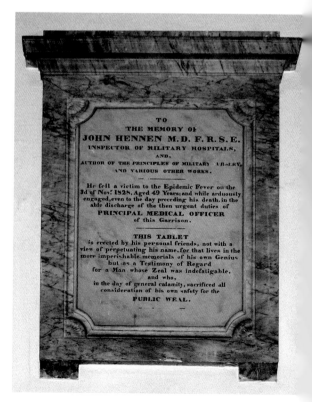

John Hennen Medical Department

William Hildreth 1st Foot

Clement Hill Royal Regiment of Horse Guards

John Hill (Sgt) 40th Foot

Francis R. T. Holburne 3rd Foot Guards

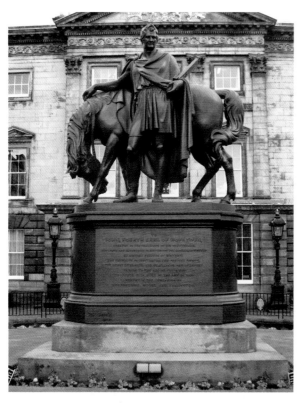

Sir John Hope 92nd Foot

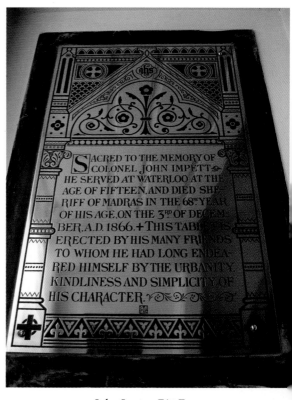

John Impett 71st Foot

James Johnston 40th Foot

Harry D. Jones Royal Engineers

Thomas Kibble 1st Dragoon Guards

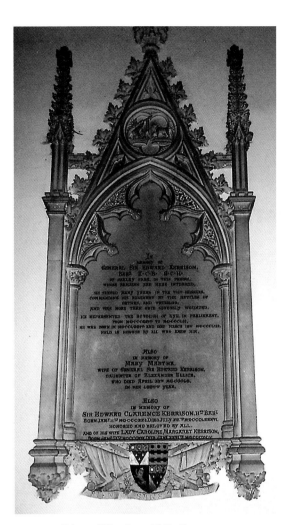

Edward Kerrison 7th Lt Dragoons

Robert Knowles 7th Foot

George A. F. Lake 29th Foot

Matthew Latham 3rd Foot

William Light 3rd Foot

Richard Lloyd 84th Foot

William J. Lyon 14th Lt Dragoons

ON THE STAFF / OF H. M. FORCES IN THE WEST INDIES AND SUBSEQUENTLY WAS / APPOINTED TO RAISE AND ORGANISE THE ROYAL CANADIAN RIFLE REG^T / IN COMMAND OF WHICH HE DIED DEC^R 17TH 1845. / HIS EARTHLY REMAINS REST IN THE CHURCHYARD / AT NIAGARA, CANADA WEST WHERE A MONUMENT HAS BEEN ERECTED / OVER THEM BY HIS BROTHER OFFICERS. / THIS TABLET HAS BEEN PLACED NEAR THE VAULT WHERE HIS PARENTS / ARE INTERRED, AS A TRIBUTE OF AFFECTIONATE REMEMBRANCE / BY HIS WIDOW AND CHILDREN. (VERSE)

Memorial tablet: St Mark's Church, Niagara, Ontario, Canada. (Photograph)

SACRED TO THE MEMORY OF / LIEU^T. COL. WILLIAM ELLIOT K.H. OF THE R. C. RIFLE REG^T, / COLONEL COM. NIAGARA FRONTIER, / WHO DIED AT NIAGARA DEC. 17, 1845. AGED 55 YEARS. / 39 YEARS OF HIS LIFE WERE DEVOTED TO HIS COUNTRY, / HE HAVING SERVED IN MOST OF THE GLORIOUS ACTIONS / OF THE PENINSULAR WAR. / THIS TABLET IS ERECTED BY THE OFFICERS / OF THE ROYAL C. RIFLE REG^T / AS A MEMORIAL OF AFFECTION AND OF SINCERE / REGRET FOR HIS LAMENTED DEATH.

Low monument: St Mark's Churchyard, Niagara, Ontario, Canada. (Rear of Cemetery). (Photograph)

SACRED TO THE MEMORY OF / L^T COL. WILLIAM ELLIOT K. H. / OF THE R. C. R. REGIMENT. / DIED DEC. 17, 1845. / AGED 55 YEARS.

Ensign 96th Foot 26 Nov 1807. Lt 29th Foot 28 Jan 1808. Capt 9 Oct 1811. Major 2 May 1822. Lt Colonel 13 Jul 1832.

   Served in the Peninsula Aug 1808 – Nov 1811 and Apr 1813 – Apr 1814. Present at Vimeiro, Douro, Talavera, Busaco, first siege of Badajoz, Albuera and Eastern Spain (present at Cadiz). Returned from America too late for Waterloo, he served in France with the Army of Occupation as Brigade Major 1815–1818. Also served in North America 1814–1815, Mauritius, West Indies (DQMG in Jamaica Jul 1832), and Canada where he was appointed to raise the Royal Canadian Rifle Regiment. Appointed Colonel commanding the Niagara frontier until his death in 1845. KH.
REFERENCE: *Gentleman's Magazine, Apr 1846, p. 432.*

ELLIOTT, Robert Thomas
Ensign. 82nd (Prince of Wales's Volunteers) Regiment of Foot.
Cross on stepped base: Kingston Cemetery, Portsmouth, Hampshire. (Photograph)

SACRED TO THE MEMORY OF / CAPT^N ROBERT THOMAS ELLIOTT / LATE OF THE 82ND AND FORMERLY OF THE 45TH REG^T / WHO DIED AUGUST 19TH 1865 AGED 78 YEARS. / HE SERVED DURING THE WHOLE OF THE PENINSULAR CAMPAIGN / AND WAS PRESENT AT THE BATTLE OF ROLEIA, / TALAVERA, BUSACO, CIUDAD RODRIGO, FORT PICERENO, / NIVELLE, PYRE-NEES, SALAMANCA, VITTORIA, / PAMPELUNA, AND OTHERS, / AND AT THE STORMING OF BADAJOZ. / FOR THESE SERVICES / HE RECEIVED A MEDAL WITH ELEVEN BARS. / "NEC ASPERA TERRENT"

Sgt Major 45th Foot. Ensign 82nd Foot 7 Jan 1814. Lt and Adjt 23 Jul 1818. Capt 20 Nov 1827.
   Served in the Peninsula with 45th Foot Aug 1808 – Apr 1814. Present at Rolica, Vimeiro, Talavera, Busaco, Ciudad Rodrigo, Badajoz, Salamanca, Vittoria, Pyrenees, Nivelle and Orthes. Awarded an Ensigncy for his bravery in the Peninsula after the battle of Nivelle. MGS medal for Rolica, Vimeiro, Talavera, Busaco, Ciudad Rodrigo, Badajoz, Salamanca, Vittoria, Pyrenees, Nivelle and Orthes.

ELLIOTT, Theodore Henry
Lieutenant. Royal Engineers.
Interred in Catacomb A (v14 c14) Kensal Green Cemetery, London.

2nd Lt 7 May 1810. 1st Lt 1 May 1811. Capt 18 Nov 1820. Major 20 Mar 1827.
    Served in the Peninsula Jun 1811 – Aug 1813. Present at Ciudad Rodrigo, Badajoz and Tarragona. Also served in India in the Pindari War 1817–1818 (present at Mehidpur where he was wounded). Died 2 Apr 1842.

ELLIOTT, William Henry
Lieutenant. 51st (2nd Yorkshire West Riding) Regiment of Foot.
Interred in the South East Catacomb, Vault Number 3, Brompton Cemetery, London. (BR 74965). (Photograph)

GENERAL SIR WILLIAM / HENRY ELLIOTT. G.C.B. K.H. / (WATERLOO) / DIED 27TH MARCH 1874, / AGED 81 YEARS.

Ensign 6 Dec 1809. Lt 13 Aug 1812. Capt 9 Nov 1820. Major 12 Jul 1831. Lt Colonel 27 Jun 1838. Bt Colonel 11 Nov 1851. Major General 29 Jan 1857. Lt General 27 Jul 1863. General 25 Oct 1871.
    Served in the Peninsula Feb 1811 – Apr 1814. Present at Fuentes d'Onoro, second siege of Badajoz, Moriscos, Salamanca, capture of Madrid, siege of Burgos and retreat (wounded – ADC to Col Mitchell), Pyrenees (wounded – ADC to Major General Inglis), Lesaca, Adour, Nivelle, St Pé and Orthes. (Brigade Major 1 Brigade, 7th Division 1813 – Apr 1814). MGS medal for Fuentes d'Onoro, Salamanca, Pyrenees, Nivelle and Orthes. GCB. KH. Present at Waterloo, the siege of Cambrai, Capture of Paris and with the Army of Occupation. Also served in the Ionian Islands 1821–1834, Australia, New Zealand and India 1838–1852, Burmese War 1852–1853 in command of the Madras Brigade (present at the storming and capture of Rangoon). Colonel 55th Foot 15 Nov 1861. Colonel 51st Foot 1 Jun 1862.
REFERENCE: *Dictionary of National Biography. United Service Magazine, May 1874, p. 115.*

ELLIS, Charles Parker
Lieutenant and Captain. 1st Regiment of Foot Guards.
Memorial: St Andrews Church, Clevedon, Somerset. (Photograph)

IN MEMORY OF / COLONEL CHARLES PARKER ELLIS, / FORMERLY OF THE GRENADIER GUARDS; / THIS TABLET IS PLACED BY / JULIANA MARIA, HIS WIDOW. / HE SERVED WITH HIS REGIMENT / IN THE CAMPAIGNS OF 1812, 1813, 1814 AND 1815, / WAS SEVERELY WOUNDED AT QUATRE BRAS / AND WOUNDED AT WATERLOO, / AND RECEIVED THE WAR MEDAL WITH CLASPS / FOR NIVELLE AND NIVE. / SKILLED AND DISTINGUISHED IN HIS PROFESSION, / HIS LITERARY TALENTS ENABLED HIM TO RECORD / SOME INTERESTING PARTICULARS / ON THE MILITARY HISTORY OF HIS TIME, / IN A STYLE REFLECTING / THE MANLINESS AND MODESTY OF HIS CHARACTER, / HE ENJOYED THE ESTEEM / OF HIS BROTHER OFFICERS OF EVERY RANK / AND IN PRIVATE LIFE WAS AN EXAMPLE OF / PURITY OF HEART, SINCERITY AND KINDNESS, / AN ATTACHED MEMBER OF THE CHURCH OF ENGLAND / AND TRUSTING IN THE REMISSION OF HIS SINS BY JESUS CHRIST, / HE DIED HERE ON THE 6TH OF AUGUST 1850, / AGED 56.

Ensign 28 Feb 1811. Lt and Capt 10 Jan 1814. Bt Lt Colonel 16 Feb 1826. Capt and Lt Colonel 18 May 1826. Bt Colonel 23 Nov 1841.
    Served in the Peninsula with 3rd Battalion Jul 1812 – Mar 1814. Present at Cadiz, San Munos, Bidassoa, Nivelle, Nive, Adour and Bayonne. Present at Quatre Bras (severely wounded) and Waterloo (wounded). MGS medal for Nivelle and Nive. Retired on half pay 10 May 1831. Educated at Eton.

ELLIS, Sir Henry Walton

Lieutenant Colonel. 23rd (Royal Welch Fusiliers) Regiment of Foot.
Monument: Worcester Cathedral, Worcestershire. (Photograph)

IN MEMORY OF / COLONEL SIR HENRY WALTON ELLIS, K.C.B. / A NATIVE OF THIS CITY / WHO, AT AN EARLY AGE, ENTERED THE 23RD REGIMENT OR ROYAL WELCH FUSILIERS, / THEN COMMANDED BY HIS FATHER, MAJOR – GENERAL JOHN JOYNER ELLIS, / AND AFTERWARDS LED ON TO HONOURABLE DISTINCTION BY HIMSELF, DURING SEVEN YEARS OF UNEXAMPLED MILITARY RENOWN, / HAVING RECEIVED EIGHT WOUNDS, AND RENDERED SERVICES AS IMPORTANT AS THEY WERE BRILLIANT, / IN HOLLAND, EGYPT, THE WEST-INDIES, AMERICA, SPAIN, PORTUGAL, AND FRANCE. / HE FELL BY A MUSKET-SHOT, AT THE HEAD OF HIS REGIMENT, ALMOST IN THE GLORIOUS MOMENT / WHICH ANNOUNCED VICTORY TO GREAT-BRITAIN, AND PEACE IN EUROPE, ON THE MEMORABLE PLAINS OF / WATERLOO. / HE DIED OF HIS WOUND, ON THE 20TH OF JUNE 1815, AGED 32 YEARS. / HIS LOSS WAS LAMENTED, AND HIS WORTH RECORDED, BY HIS ILLUSTRIOUS COMMANDER / WELLINGTON, / IN WORDS THAT WILL PERISH ONLY WITH HISTORY ITSELF ! / THIS MONUMENT WAS ERECTED / BY THE OFFICERS, NON-COMMISSIONED OFFICERS, AND PRIVATES OF THE ROYAL WELCH FUSILIERS, / AS A TRIBUTE OF THEIR RESPECT AND AFFECTION TO THE MEMORY OF A LEADER, / NOT MORE DISTINGUISHED FOR HIS VALOUR AND CONDUCT IN THE FIELD, / THAN BELOVED FOR EVERY GENEROUS AND SOCIAL VIRTUE.

Memorial tablet: St Joseph's Church, Waterloo, Belgium. (Photograph)

SACRED / TO THE MEMORY OF / COLONEL SIR HENRY WALTON ELLIS K.C.B. / LATE OF THE 23RD ROYAL WELCH FUSILIERS, / WHO AFTER SERVING WITH DISTINCTION / IN EGYPT, AMERICA, THE WEST INDIES, / AND THROUGHOUT THE PENINSULAR WAR, / FELL GALLANTLY AT THE HEAD OF HIS REGIMENT / ON THE PLAINS OF WATERLOO, / IN THE 32ND YEAR OF HIS AGE. / THIS TABLET IS ERECTED / BY LIEUT: COLONEL ROSS, AND THE OFFICERS / OF THE 23RD FUSILIERS.

Low monument: Garden of the Waterloo Museum, Waterloo, Belgium. (Photograph)

TO THE MEMORY OF / COLONEL SIR H. W. ELLIS KCB. / 23RD REGT. R. WELSH FUSILIERS / KILLED IN ACTION AT WATERLOO / 18 JUNE 1815.

Inscription on Silver gilt cup presented to Ellis from the citizens of Worcester, 26 Dec 1814, now preserved in the Regimental Museum, Carmarthen, Wales.

TO / COL HENRY WALTON ELLIS / OF THE 23RD ROYAL FUSILIERS. / THIS TRIBUTE TO HIS MERITOUS AND DISTINGUISHED / CONDUCT, DURING THE FIFTEEN YEARS OF ACTIVE SERVICE / IN HOLLAND, EGYPT, AMERICA, THE WEST INDIES / SPAIN, PORTUGAL AND FRANCE / IS RESPECTFULLY OFFERED BY THE COUNTY, / AND HIS NATIVE CITY OF WORCESTER, / AND PRESENTED AT THEIR DESIRE, / BY THE EARL OF COVENTRY / LORD LIEUTENANT AND RECORDER.

Ensign 41st Foot 1788 (aged 5). Lt 1792. Capt 23rd Foot 20 Jun 1794. Major 23 Oct 1804. Lt Colonel 23 Apr 1807. Colonel 4 Jun 1814.

Served in the Peninsula with 1/23rd Dec 1810 – Apr 1814 (Temporary Commander 2 Brigade 4th Division May – Oct 1812). Present at Redinha, Olivencia, first siege of Badajoz, Albuera (wounded), Aldea da Ponte, Ciudad Rodrigo, Badajoz (wounded), Salamanca (wounded), Vittoria, Pyrenees (wounded at Sorauren),

Bidassoa, Nivelle, Nive, Orthes and Toulouse. KCB. Gold Cross for Martinique, Albuera, Badajoz, Salamanca, Vittoria, Pyrenees, Orthes and Toulouse.

Present at Waterloo where he was severely wounded in command of the Regiment, thrown from his horse whilst riding to the rear for medical help. He was carried to an outhouse and his wounds were dressed, but that night the building caught fire. Ellis was rescued by Assistant Surgeon Munro but was so severely burnt that he died the following day. Also served at the Helder 1799 (wounded), Egypt 1801 (wounded), Hanover 1805, Copenhagen 1807 and West Indies 1809 (present at Martinique).

Ellis succeeded to the command of the regiment at the early age of 25 years. This was owing to the fact that his father secured an Ensigncy for him at the age of five in a line regiment, by 13 he was a Captain, and a Major aged 19 years. His youth did not detract from his abilities and he led the regiment with great success in all his campaigns.

REFERENCE: *Dictionary of National Biography*.

ELLIS, Richard Rogers
Captain. 18th Regiment of Light Dragoons.
Memorial tablet: St James's Church, Cheltenham, Gloucestershire. (Photograph)

IN MEMORY OF / MAJOR RICHARD ROGERS ELLIS, / FORMERLY OF THE 18TH HUSSARS. / HE DIED AT HIS RESIDENCE AT CHELTENHAM / FEBRUARY 3RD 1859, / IN THE 71ST YEAR OF HIS AGE.

Cornet 28 Jul 1807. Lt 25 Sep 1807. Capt 24 Sep 1812. Bt Major 22 Jul 1830.

Served in the Peninsula Sep 1808 – Jan 1809. Present at Benevente and the Corunna campaign. Half pay 25 May 1816.

ELLISON, John Montagu
Lieutenant. 61st (South Gloucestershire) Regiment of Foot.
Grave: St Andrew's Churchyard, Holborn Burial Ground, London. (M.I.)

"SACRED / TO THE MEMORY / OF LIEUT JOHN MONTAGU / ELLISON / WHO DIED AUGUST 13TH 1822 / AGED 31 YEARS."

Ensign 28 Feb 1812. Lt 19 Jan 1814.

Served in the Peninsula Apr 1813 – Apr 1814. Present at Pyrenees, Nivelle, Nive, Orthes, Tarbes and Toulouse where he was wounded.

ELLISON, Robert
Lieutenant and Captain. 1st Regiment of Foot Guards.
Chest tomb: Kensal Green Cemetery, London. (4257/90/PS). (Photograph)

TO THE MEMORY OF / COLONEL ROBERT ELLISON / WHO DIED ON THE THIRD DAY OF JULY 1843 / IN THE ACTUAL ENACTION OF HIS DUTY / THIS MONUMENT IS ERECTED / BY THOSE WHO COULD BEST APPRECIATE HIS MERITS / FIELD MARSHAL THE DUKE OF WELLINGTON / AND THE OFFICERS OF HIS REGIMENT OF GRENADIER GUARDS.

Memorial: Royal Military Chapel, Wellington Barracks, London. (M.I.) (Destroyed by a Flying Bomb in 1944)

"THE PULPIT IS GIVEN BY GENERAL HENRY LORD ROKEBY, G.C.B., COLONEL OF THE SCOTS GUARDS, AND GENERAL SIR WILLIAM CODRINGTON, G.C.B., COLONEL OF THE COLD-STREAM GUARDS, AND THE REMAINDER OF THE SCREEN IS A MEMORIAL TO THE

FOLLOWING OFFICERS: – / COLONEL ROBERT ELLISON, / .... COLONEL ELLISON, BORN 1790, DIED 1843, WAS FOR 36 YEARS IN THE GRENADIER GUARDS. JOINING THE REGIMENT IN 1807, HE FOLLOWED THE EXPEDITION TO WALCHEREN IN 1809, AND TOOK PART IN THE CAMPAIGNS OF THE PENINSULA DURING 1811 AND 1812. HE WAS PRESENT AT THE INVESTMENT OF BAYONNE; THE STORMING AND CAPTURE OF PERONNE, JUNE 27, 1815, AND THROUGH THE CANADIAN DIFFICULTIES 1838–40. HE FOUGHT BOTH AT QUATRE BRAS AND AT WATERLOO, WHERE, FOR COMMANDING A COMPANY DURING THE HEROIC DEFENCE OF THE CHATEAU OF HOUGOUMONT, HE GAINED A BREVET MAJORITY, 1815. GIVEN BY HIS NIECE, LADY JAMES."

Ensign 17 Dec 1807. Lt and Capt 20 Dec 1812. Bt Major 18 Jun 1815. Lt Colonel 15 Apr 1824. Major and Colonel 9 Jan 1838.

Served in the Peninsula with 1st Battalion Oct 1808 – Jan 1809 and 3rd Battalion Jul 1811 – May 1813 and Mar – Apr 1814. Present at Corunna, Cadiz, Seville and Bayonne. Present at Quatre Bras and Waterloo, the siege of Peronne and with the Army of Occupation. Awarded Bt Majority for his part in the defence of Hougoumont. Also served at Walcheren 1809 and Canada 1838–1840 (present in the Canadian Rebellion). Died in Hyde Park while taking part in a review.
REFERENCE: *Gentleman's Magazine, October 1843, p. 435.*

ELPHINSTONE, Howard
Lieutenant Colonel. Royal Engineers.
Named on the Regimental Memorial: Rochester Cathedral, Rochester, Kent. (Photograph)

2nd Lt Royal Artillery 24 Apr 1793. 2nd Lt Royal Engineers 17 Oct 1793. Lt 5 Feb 1796. Capt-Lt 1 Jul 1800. 2nd Capt 19 Jul 1804. Capt 1 Mar 1805. Bt Major 1 Jan 1812. Lt Colonel 21 Jul 1813. Colonel 2 Dec 1824. Colonel Commandant 7 Jul 1834. Major General 10 Jan 1837.

Served in the Peninsula Aug – Sep 1808 and Feb 1813 – Apr 1814. Present at Rolica (severely wounded), San Sebastian, Nivelle, Nive, Adour and the siege and Sortie from Bayonne. Gold Medal for Rolica, Nivelle and Nive. CB. Also served at the Cape of Good Hope 1795–1796, Egypt 1801, South America 1807 (present at Buenos Ayres and Montevideo as Commanding Engineer). Died at Hastings 28 Apr 1846.
REFERENCE: *United Service Magazine Jun 1846, p. 319. Gentleman's Magazine Jul 1846, p. 93. Annual Register 1846, Appx, pp. 252–3.*

ELPHINSTONE, James Drummond Fullerton
Captain. 7th (Queen's Own) Regiment of Light Dragoons.
Family Mural memorial: St Michael's Churchyard, Inveresk, Scotland. (East wall of main churchyard). (Photograph)

.... / LIEU. COL JAMES FULLERTON ELPHINSTONE / 4TH SON OF THE HONBLE W. F. E. ELPHINSTONE / BORN 4TH MAY 1788 / DIED AT CARBERRY 8TH MARCH 1857.

Cornet 23 May 1810. Lt 19 Dec 1811. Capt 23 Dec 1813. Bt Lt Colonel 12 Nov 1813. Capt and Lt Colonel 3rd Foot Guards 8 May 1823.

Served in the Peninsula Nov 1808 – Jan 1809 and Aug 1813 – Apr 1814. Present at Benevente, Orthes and Toulouse. Present at Quatre Bras covering the retreat of the infantry and Waterloo. MGS medal for Orthes and Toulouse. Half pay 1 Jan 1828. Brother of Lt Colonel William Keith Elphinstone 33rd Foot.

ELPHINSTONE, William Keith
Lieutenant Colonel. 33rd (1st Yorkshire West Riding) Regiment of Foot.
Family Memorial: St Michael's Churchyard, Inveresk, Scotland. (East wall of main churchyard). (Photograph)

.... / TO MAJOR GEN. WILLIAM KEITH ELPHINSTONE / DIED IN INDIA APRIL 1842. / ....

Memorial tablet: Afghan Memorial Church, St John the Evangelist, Colaba, Bombay, India. (Photograph)

COMMANDER / IN / AFGHANISTAN / MAJOR GENERAL / W. K. ELPHINSTONE

Ensign 29th Foot 24 Mar 1804. Lt 60th Foot 4 Aug 1804. Lt 41st Foot 12 Oct 1804. Capt 93rd Foot 7 Aug 1806. Lt and Capt 1st Foot Guards 6 Aug 1807. Capt 52nd Foot 7 Dec 1809. Capt 15th Lt Dragoons 18 Jan 1810. Major 8th West India Regt 2 May 1811. Major 6th Dragoon Guards 30 Jan 1812. Major 15th Lt Dragoons 28 Apr 1812. Lt Colonel 33rd Foot 30 Sep 1813. Lt Colonel 16th Lt Dragoons 12 Apr 1821. Bt Colonel 27 May 1825. Major General 10 Jan 1837.

Present at Waterloo in command of 33rd Foot. CB and Knight of St Gertrude of Russia and St Wilhelm of Holland. Also served in the Netherlands 1814–1815 (present at Bergen-op-Zoom where he was severely wounded), India 1839 (appointed to command Benares division of the Bengal Army and sent to Kabul to command the troops there although he was in poor health). He was unable to cope with the insurrection at Kabul Nov 1841. The garrison was destroyed in the retreat through the Afghan passes. Elphinstone was amongst those captured and taken hostage on 12 Jan 1842. Imprisoned for months he lost the will to live and died 23 Apr 1842 at Zanduk. Akbar Khan sent his body to Jalalabad where he was buried in an unmarked grave. He should never have been given the command in Afghanistan, always a risky venture, owing to his ill health and lack of battle experience since Waterloo. Brother of Capt James Drummond Fullerton Elphinstone 7th Lt Dragoons.

REFERENCE: *Dictionary of National Biography. Gentleman's Magazine, Sep 1842, p. 332. Annual Register, 1842, Appx, p. 264.*

ELRINGTON, John Hamilton
Lieutenant and Captain. 3rd Regiment of Foot Guards.
Interred in Catacomb A (v57 c2, 5&6) Kensal Green Cemetery, London.
Memorial: Royal Military Chapel, Wellington Barracks, London. (M.I.) (Destroyed by a Flying Bomb in 1944)

"IN MEMORY OF / JOHN HAMILTON ELRINGTON, GEORGE DOUGLAS STANDEN, AND SIR / HUGH SEYMOUR BLANE, BART, / OF THE LIGHT COMPANY 3RD GUARDS, DURING THE DEFENCE OF HOUGOUMONT AT / THE BATTLE OF WATERLOO. / PLACED BY THE REVEREND WILLIAM FREDERICK ELRINGTON, B.A., / LATE LIEUT.-COLONEL SCOTS FUSILIER GUARDS."

Ensign 71st Foot 15 Oct 1809. Ensign 3rd Foot Guards 27 Mar 1811. Lt and Capt 19 May 1814. Capt and Lt Colonel 16 Nov 1826.

Served in the Peninsula with 71st Foot Sep 1810 – Jun 1811 and 3rd Foot Guards Aug 1812 – Apr 1814. Present at Sobral, Fuentes d'Onoro, Burgos, Bidassoa, Nivelle, Nive, Adour and Bayonne. Present at Waterloo. Died Nov 1843.

ELTON, Isaac Marmaduke
Lieutenant. Royal Engineers.
Named on the Regimental Memorial: Rochester Cathedral, Rochester, Kent. (Photograph)

2nd Lt 14 Dec 1811. Lt 1 Jul 1812.

Served in the Peninsula Jul 1813 – Apr 1814. Also served in North America 1814–1815 (present at New Orleans) and in France with the Army of Occupation 1815–1818. Died in Switzerland 24 May 1823.

ELWIN, Fountain

Major. 44th (East Essex) Regiment of Foot.
Family Memorial: All Saint's Churchyard, Edmonton, London. (M.I.)

".................... / ALSO THE REMAINS OF / LT COL. FOUNTAIN ELWIN, K. C., / 44TH REGT, SON OF THE ABOVE, / WHO DIED SUDDENLY / DECEMBER 8TH 1846, AGED 67 YEARS."

Ensign 44th Foot Apr 1798. Lt 10 May 1798. Capt 44th Foot 14 Jan 1802. Bt Major 4 Jun 1813. Major 31 Mar 1814. Bt Lt Colonel 22 Jul 1830.

Served in the Peninsula Sep 1813 – Apr 1814. (AAG on the east coast of Spain). Present at Tarragona and Tudela (wounded). Present at the Capture of Paris (commanded 44th Foot) and with the Army of Occupation. Also served in Egypt 1801 (awarded medal and became Knight of the Crescent – the Turkish Order), Naples 1806 and Sicily 1813. Half pay 1816.
REFERENCE: *Gentleman's Magazine, Mar 1847, p. 311. Annual Register, 1846, Appx, p. 304.*

EMERY, Henry Gresley

Staff Surgeon. Medical Department.
Memorial tablet: St Andrew's Church, Banwell, Somerset. (Photograph)

SACRED TO THE MEMORY OF HENRY GRESLEY EMERY / OF THIS PARISH M. D. MEMBER OF THE ROYAL COLLEGE OF SURGEONS / INSPECTOR OF MILITARY HOSPITALS &C &C &C OBT 14 SEPR 1826 Æ 49 YEARS. / HE ENTERED THE MEDICAL DEPARTMENT OF THE ARMY AT AN / EARLY PERIOD OF LIFE, SERVING IN THE FRENCH, SPANISH AND / PORTUGUESE CAMPAIGNS (IN WHICH HE WAS SEVERELY WOUNDED) / AND WAS PRESENT AT NEARLY ALL THE BATTLES AND SIEGES / OF THAT EVENTFUL PERIOD CONTINUING IN THE MOST ACTIVE / DEPARTMENTS OF HIS PROFESSION UNTIL THE MEMORABLE / VICTORY OF WATERLOO, AND SURRENDER OF PARIS IN 1815. / THIS TABLET HAS BEEN ERECTED BY HIS NEAREST / AND DEAREST RELATIVES, TO COMMEMORATE / THE CHARACTER OF A SINCERE KIND AND / TRULY HONOURABLE MAN.

Asst Surgeon 32nd Foot 30 Dec 1800. Surgeon 3rd Battalion Lt Infantry of the Line 28 Apr 1804. Surgeon 53rd Foot 30 May 1805. Staff Surgeon 11 Aug 1808. Deputy Inspector of Hospitals. 7 Sep 1815.

Served in the Peninsula Nov 1808 – Jan 1809, Apr 1810 and Jan 1813 (from Aug 1810 – Apr 1811 and Dec 1811 – Jul 1812 attached to 5th Division). Present in the Corunna campaign (remained at Lugo with the wounded and eventually treated both French and English wounded. Ney was most impressed and allowed him to return home in 1809), Busaco, Torres Vedras, Ciudad Rodrigo, Badajoz, Salamanca and the siege and retreat from Burgos. Returned home because of ill health. Present at Waterloo and with the Army of Occupation until Mar 1816. Also served in Ireland 1798 (present in the Irish Rebellion) and Walcheren 1809. MD 1811. Retired on half pay 28 Mar 1816.
REFERENCE: *Milner, David L., A military surgeon in the early nineteenth century: a broad portrait of Henry Gresley Emery MD, Waterloo Journal, Aug 2002, pp. 21–7. Gentleman's Magazine, Sep 1826, p. 285.*

EMES, Thomas

Major. 5th (Northumberland) Regiment of Foot.
Memorial tablet: St George's Church, Roseau, Dominica, West Indies. (M.I.)

"TO PERPETUATE THE MEMORY OF / THEIR BELOVED AND GALLANT COMRADE, / LIEU-TENANT-COLONEL THOMAS EMES / OF THE 5TH REGIMENT / WHO DIED ON THIS ISLAND / ON THE 2ND DAY OF NOVEMBER 1824 / IN THE 55TH YEAR OF HIS AGE. / THIS TABLET OF RESPECT AND ATTACHMENT / IS INSCRIBED BY HIS BROTHER OFFICERS."

Cornet 1st Dragoons Guards 10 Aug 1794. Lt 10th Foot 16 Sep 1795. Capt 5th Foot 8 Oct 1803. Major 8 May 1806. Bt Lt Colonel 4 Jun 1813.

Served in the Peninsula with 1/5th Jul 1808 – Jan 1809 and Jun 1812 – Apr 1814. Present at Rolica (wounded), Vimeiro, Corunna, Salamanca, retreat from Burgos, Vittoria, Pyrenees, Nivelle, Nive, Adour, Orthes, Vic Bigorre and Toulouse. Gold Medal for Corunna. Also served in Guernsey 1804–1805 (Brigade Major), Hanover 1805, Walcheren 1809 and West Indies 1819–1824 (in command of 5th Foot at St Lucia, St Vincent and St Dominica). He was well respected in the Islands. Fever broke out in Dominica Nov 1824 and Emes died with nearly half of the regiment of the 5th Foot.

EMMETT, Anthony
2nd Captain. Royal Engineers.
Named on the Regimental Memorial: Rochester Cathedral, Rochester, Kent. (Photograph)

2nd Lt 16 Feb 1808. Lt 24 Jun 1809. 2nd Capt 21 Jul 1813. Bt Major 5 Jul 1821. Capt 23 Mar 1825. Lt Colonel 10 Jan 1837. Colonel 11 Nov 1851. Major General 21 May 1855.

Served in the Peninsula Apr 1809 – Jun 1812 and Nov 1813 – Apr 1814. Present at first and second sieges of Badajoz, El Bodon, Badajoz (severely wounded), Nive, Garris, Orthes, Tarbes and Toulouse. Also served in North America 1814–1815 (present at New Orleans and Fort Bowyer). MGS medal for Badajoz, Nive, Orthes and Toulouse. Retired on full pay 21 May 1855. Died at Brighton 23 Jul 1872.

EMSLIE, John
Lieutenant. 83rd Regiment of Foot.
Table stone: St Nicholas Kirk, Aberdeen, Aberdeenshire, Scotland. (Photograph)

TO THE MEMORY OF / HELEN LONGMORE, / WIFE OF / LIEUTENANT JOHN EMSLIE, / 83RD REGIMENT / WHO DIED 30 APRIL 1812, AGED 29 YEARS. / .... / JOHN EMSLIE / LATE CAPTAIN 83RD / REGIMENT OF FOOT / DIED AT ABERDEEN, / 24TH JULY 1844, AGED 68 YEARS / AND WAS INTERRED HERE. / ....

Ensign 26 Mar 1808. Lt 8 Nov 1809. Capt 22 May 1829.

Served in the Peninsula Sep 1813 – Apr 1814. Present at Nivelle, Nive, Orthes, Vic Bigorre and Toulouse. Also served in Ceylon (present in the Kandian Rebellion 1817–1818).

ENGEL
1st Lieutenant. 28th Orange-Nassau Regiment, Dutch Infantry.
Named on the Memorial to Dutch officers killed at Quatre Bras: St Joseph's Church, Waterloo, Belgium. (Photograph)

ENGLISH, Frederick
Captain. Royal Engineers.
Grave: St Luke's Churchyard, Charlton, Kent. (No longer extant: Grave number 228). (M.I.)

"IN MEMORY OF FREDERICK ENGLISH, COLONEL OF THE ROYAL ENGINEERS, WHO DIED IN COMMAND OF THE ABOVE CORPS AT WOOLWICH, ON THE 30 JUL, 1849, AGED 59 YEARS."

2nd Lt 8 Sep 1807. 1st Lt 1 Apr 1808. 2nd Capt 21 Jul 1813. Lt Colonel 10 Jan 1837.

Served in the Peninsula Aug 1808 – Jan 1809 and Dec 1813 – Apr 1814. Present at Rolica, Vimeiro, Corunna, Orthes and Toulouse. Also served with the Army of Occupation until Aug 1817. MGS medal for Rolica, Vimeiro, Corunna, Orthes and Toulouse.
REFERENCE: *Gentleman's Magazine, Aug 1849, p. 220. Annual Register, 1849, Appx, p. 250.*

ENOCH, John
1st Lieutenant. 23rd (Royal Welch Fusiliers) Regiment of Foot.
Headstone: West Norwood Cemetery, London. Inscription illegible. (Photograph)

2nd Lt 30 Mar 1809. 1st Lt 15 Aug 1811. Adjt 16 Sep 1813. Capt 22 Jul 1830. Major 14 Apr 1846. Lt Colonel (unattached) 1 Feb 1851. Bt Colonel 28 Nov 1854.
    Served in the Peninsula with 1/23rd Apr 1811 – Dec 1812. Present at Olivencia, first siege of Badajoz, Albuera, Aldea a Ponte, Ciudad Rodrigo, Badajoz and Salamanca (severely wounded). Present at Waterloo, siege of Cambrai, the Capture of Paris and with the Army of Occupation. MGS medal for Albuera, Ciudad Rodrigo, Badajoz and Salamanca. Also served at Walcheren 1809 (present at the siege of Flushing). Died in London 13 Jul 1855.

EPPES, William Randolph
Treasury Clerk. Commissariat Department.
Low monument: Old Army Base Graveyard, Newcastle, Jamaica, West Indies. (Photograph)

SACRED / TO THE MEMORY OF / WILLIAM RANDOLPH EPPES / DEPUTY COMMISSARY GENERAL / DIED / OF YELLOW FEVER / AUGUST 14TH 1849 / AGED 55 YEARS. / ....

Treasury Clerk 24 Dec 1811. Dep Asst Com Gen 19 Jul 1821. Asst Com Gen 7 Jul 1827.
    Served in the Peninsula. Present at Merida, Alter do Chao and Pamplona (Headquarters). Also served in Malta, Cape Colony 1821 (DACG), Canada 1827 (ACG) and West Indies where he died in a yellow fever epidemic 14 Aug 1849.

ERSKINE, Robert
Captain. 4th (King's Own) Regiment of Foot.
Headstone: Sandpits Cemetery, Gibraltar. (M.I.)

"MAJOR ROBERT ERSKINE, A NATIVE OF CAVAN, / IRELAND, SERVED IN THE 4TH REGT 28 YEARS / AND FOUGHT IN 23 ENGAGEMENTS. HE DIED / 30 DEC., 1827, A. 42."

Lt 25 Jun 1803. Capt 8 Sep 1808. Bt Major 11 May 1826.
    Served in the Peninsula Aug 1808 – Jan 1809. Present at Corunna. With part of the 2/4th Foot shipwrecked off Cadiz 1810 and taken prisoner until Apr 1814. Also served in North America, 1814 (present at New Orleans where he was wounded).

ERSKINE, William Howe Knight
Major. 27th (Inniskilling) Regiment.
Ledger stone: Kensal Green Cemetery, London. Inscription largely illegible. (4433/50/3). (Photograph)

IN MEMORY OF / WILLIAM HOWE KNIGHT ERSKINE / ....

Lt 3 Sep 1795. Capt 19 Dec 1799. Major 12 Sep 1805. Bt Lt Colonel 1 Jan 1812. Bt Colonel 12 Feb 1830.
    Served in the Peninsula with 3/27th Nov 1808 – Jun 1809 and Apr 1810 – Jun 1812. Present at Busaco, Redinha, Olivencia, first siege of Badajoz and Badajoz 6 Apr 1812 where he led the 27th Foot at the siege and was wounded. Gold Medal for Badajoz and CB. Half pay 1813. In 1813 he added Erskine to his name from William Howe Knight. Died 1843.

ESTE, Michael Lambton
Surgeon. 1st Life Guards.
Monument: Brompton Cemetery, London. (BR 36387). (Photograph)

MICHAEL LAMBTON ESTE / MD / LATE OF THE 1ST LIFE GUARDS / OBIT / AD 1864 / 26TH JANUARY / AETATIS 85. / EGYPT, MEDITERRANEAN 1808. PENINSULA. FRANCE.

Asst Surgeon 3rd Foot Guards 4 Sep 1800. Surgeon 1st Life Guards 3 Oct 1812.
 Served in the Peninsula Nov 1812 – Apr 1814. Present at Vittoria, Pamplona, Orthes and Toulouse. Present at Waterloo. Also served in Egypt 1801 (present at the siege of Alexandria where he was wounded) and with Nelson off Toulon 1804. MGS medal for Egypt, Vittoria and Toulouse. Half pay 6 Nov 1835. MD 1798.

EVANS, George
Lieutenant. 3rd Garrison Battalion.
Headstone: Stradbally Parish Churchyard, Stradbally, County Waterford, Ireland. (Photograph)

TO THE MEMORY OF / GEORGE EVANS / LATE LIEUTENANT 50TH REGT / WHO SERVED / THROUGHOUT THE PENINSULAR WAR / DIED APRIL 1849 / AGED 72 YEARS. / ....

Ensign 50th Foot 30 Aug 1807. Lt 25 Dec 1807. Lt 3rd Garrison Battalion 3 Jul 1812.
 Served in the Peninsula Dec 1808 – Jan 1809 and Sep 1810 – Sep 1812. Present at Corunna. Also served at Walcheren 1809. Half pay 25 Sep 1817.

EVANS, Sir George de Lacy
Captain. 5th West India Regiment of Foot.
Altar tomb: Kensal Green Cemetery, London, (7355/100 – 113/PS). (Photograph)

....................HERE TOO, LIE THE REMAINS OF GENERAL SIR DE LACY EVANS G.C.B. / COLONEL OF THE 21st ROYAL NORTH BRITISH FUSILIERS / B.1787 D.1870 / HE COMMENCED HIS CAREER IN INDIA. / FOUGHT UNDER WELLINGTON IN THE PENINSULA AND SOUTH OF FRANCE. / SERVED WITH DISTINCTION IN AMERICA. / WAS ENGAGED AT QUATRE BRAS AND WATERLOO. / COMMANDED WITH MARKED ABILITY THE BRITISH LEGION IN THE SERVICE OF SPAIN. / AND IN OLD AGE NOBLY LED THE SECOND BRITISH DIVISION IN THE CRIMEA. / DURING 30 YEARS HE WAS MP FOR THE CITY OF WESTMINSTER. / AN ENTER-PRISING AND SKILFUL COMMANDER. AN ACCOMPLISHED POLITICIAN. / HIS COMRADES MOURN THE CHIVALROUS SOLDIER, / AND MANY FRIENDS AFFECTIONATELY CHERISH HIS MEMORY. /....................

Ensign 22nd Foot 1 Feb 1807. Lt 1 Dec 1808. Lt 3rd Dragoons 26 Mar 1812. Capt 5th West India Regiment. 12 Jan 1815. Bt Major 11 May 1815. Bt Lt Colonel 18 Jun 1815. Bt Colonel 10 Jan 1837. Major General 9 Nov 1846. Lt General 20 Jun 1854. General 10 Mar 1861.
 Served in the Peninsula Sep 1812 – Apr 1814 (on Staff Sep 1813 – Feb 1814, DAQMG Mar – Apr 1814). Present at the retreat from Burgos, Vittoria, Pyrenees, Vic Bigorre, Tarbes (wounded) and Toulouse. Present at Quatre Bras, Waterloo (extra ADC to Major General Sir William Ponsonby), the Capture of Paris and with the Army of Occupation.
 Also served in India1807–1810 (present at the capture of Mauritius), North America 1814–1815 (present at Bladensburg, Washington – captured the Congress House with a very small force of infantry, Baltimore and New Orleans where he was severely wounded). Returned from America in time for Waterloo. MGS medal for Vittoria, Pyrenees and Toulouse. After the war he entered Parliament, advo-cating radical reforms. MP for the City of Westminster for 30 years. In his last ten years as an MP pressed for Army reform especially the abolition of the purchase system.
 GOC British Legion in Spain 1835 until the Legion returned to England in 1837. Colonel 21st Royal North British Fusiliers 29 Aug 1853. Given command of the 2nd Division in the Crimea 1854. Present at the Alma (wounded), Balaklava, Inkerman and the siege of Sebastopol. GCB Jul 1855, Grand Officer of

the Legion of Honour and 1ˢᵗ Class of the Medjidie. Died in 1870 aged 82.
REFERENCE: *Dictionary of National Biography. Annual Register, 1870, Appx, pp. 154–1. Spiers, E. M., Radical general: Sir George de Lacy Evans, 1787 – 1870, 1983.*

EVANS, John

Assistant Surgeon. 30ᵗʰ (Cambridgeshire) Regiment of Foot.
Gravestone: Old Lancers Lines Cemetery, Secunderabad, India. (M.I.)

"SACRED TO THE MEMORY OF / JOHN EVANS ESQUIRE, / ASSISTANT SURGEON 30ᵀᴴ FOOT, / WALCHEREN, PENINSULA, WATERLOO".

Hospital Mate 1 Mar 1810. Asst Surgeon 30ᵗʰ Foot 22 Aug 1811.
    Served in the Peninsula Nov 1811 – Jun 1813. Present at Ciudad Rodrigo and Badajoz. Present at Waterloo. Also served in the Netherlands 1814 and India (present in the Pindari War 1818). Died at Secunderabad 16 Jul 1821.

EVANS, Joseph Blewitt

Lieutenant and Captain. 1ˢᵗ Regiment of Foot Guards.
Family Memorial tablet: All Saints Church, Weston, near Bath, Somerset. (Photograph)

.... / LIKEWISE OF JOSEPH BLEWITT EVANS, CAPᵀ IN THE 1ˢᵀ REGᵀ OF FOOT GUARDS / YOUNGEST SON OF THE ABOVE MENTIONED KINGSMILL AND KATHERINE EVANS / WHO DIED ON THE 19ᵀᴴ OF MAY 1814, AT BAYONNE IN FRANCE. / ....

Ensign 5 Nov 1805. Lt and Capt 28 Feb1811.
    Served in the Peninsula with 1ˢᵗ Battalion Oct 1808 – Jan 1809 and Dec 1813 – Apr 1814. Present at Corunna and Bayonne where he was wounded in the Sortie from Bayonne Apr 1814 and died of his wounds 19 May 1814.

EVANS, Kingsmill

Lieutenant and Captain. 1ˢᵗ Regiment of Foot Guards.
Memorial tablet: St Michael and All Angels Church, Walford, Herefordshire. (Photograph)

SACRED TO THE MEMORY OF / KINGSMILL EVANS ESQUIRE, / OF THE HILL COURT, / LORD OF THE MANORS OF ROSS & WALFORD, / A DEPUTY LIEUᵀ AND FOR 40 YEARS MAGISTRATE / OF THE COUNTY OF HEREFORD. / BORN JULY 1ˢᵀ 1781, DIED JULY 16ᵀᴴ 1851. / DEEPLY LAMENTED. / HE WAS THE LAST SURVIVOR OF THE MALE LINE OF THE / FAMILY OF EVANS OF LLANGATTOCK, COUNTY OF MONMOUTH, / & ELDEST SON OF Lᵀ. COLᴸ KINGSMILL EVANS LATE OF / LYDART HOUSE NEAR MONMOUTH, BY KATHERINE, HIS WIFE. / (VERSE)
....

Ensign 19 Jul 1799. Lt and Capt 1 May 1801.
    Served in the Peninsula with 1ˢᵗ battalion Oct 1808 – Jan 1809. Present at Corunna. Retired 20 Feb 1811. MGS medal for Corunna. Magistrate and Deputy Lieutenant for County of Hereford.

EVELEGH, Henry

Lieutenant Colonel. Royal Artillery.
Low monument: St John the Baptist Churchyard, Northwood, Newport, Isle of Wight. Seriously eroded and inscription recorded from memorial inscription. (Photograph)

"HENRY EVELEGH, DIED SEPT 24ᵀᴴ 1859 IN HIS 87ᵀᴴ YEAR."

2nd Lt 24 Apr 1793. 1st Lt 1 Jan 1794. Capt-Lieut 3 Nov 1797. Capt 1 Nov 1802. Bt Major 25 Jul 1810. Major 8 May 1811. Lt Colonel 20 Dec 1814. Colonel 29 Jul 1825. Colonel Commandant 6 Feb 1845. Major General 10 Jan 1837. Lt General 9 Nov 1846. General 20 Jun 1854.

Served in the Peninsula Nov 1808 – Jan 1809 (Commanded 'C' Troop R.H.A.) Present at Benevente, Cacabellos, Corunna (in rear guard on retreat to Corunna. Lost most of their horses and equipment, so on reaching Corunna their guns were placed on board ship). Also served in the West Indies 1794–1796 and 1814–1816. MGS medal for Benevente.

EVELYN, George
Lieutenant and Captain. 3rd Regiment of Foot Guards.
Memorial tablet: St John's Church, Wooton, Surrey. Inscription illegible and recorded from memorial inscription. (Photograph)

"TO THE MEMORY OF GEORGE EVELYN ESQRE ONLY SURVIVING SON OF JOHN AND ANNE EVELYN OF WOOTON HOUSE IN THIS PARISH. HE ENTERED THE ARMY IN 1810 WAS PROMOTED TO THE RANK OF LIEUTENANT AND CAPTAIN IN THE 3RD REGIMENT OF FOOT GUARDS IN 1814. HE SERVED IN THE PENINSULAR WAR, AND RECEIVED AT WATERLOO, WHILE EMPLOYED IN THE DEFENCE OF HOUGOUMONT A SEVERE WOUND IN THE ARM WHICH DISABLED HIM FROM ACTIVE SERVICE. HIS CONSTITUTION NEVER FULLY RECOV-ERED FROM EFFECT OF FATIGUES AND SUFFERINGS AND AN ILLNESS BROUGHT ON BY A FALL FROM HIS HORSE TERMINATED HIS LIFE ON THE 15TH FEBRUARY 1829. / HIS PUBLIC SERVICES WERE ACKNOWLEDGED BY A MEDAL, HIS PRIVATE WORTH IS COMMEMORATED IN THE FOLLOWING LINES FROM THE PEN OF HIS EARLY FRIEND THE REV'D DOCTOR ARNOLD, HEADMASTER OF RUGBY SCHOOL. / "HIS EARLY YEARS GAVE A BEAUTIFUL PROMISE OF VIGOUR OF UNDERSTANDING, KINDNESS OF HEART AND CHRISTIAN NOBLE-NESS OF PRINCIPLE: HIS MANHOOD ABUNDANTLY FULFILLED IT. LIVING AND DYING IN THE FAITH OF CHRIST, HE HAS LEFT TO HIS FAMILY A HUMBLE BUT LIVELY HOPE THAT, AS HE WAS RESPECTED AND LOVED BY MEN HE HAS BEEN FORGIVEN AND ACCEPTED BY GOD".

Ensign 30 Dec 1810. Lt and Capt 31 Mar 1814.
Served in the Peninsula May 1812 – Mar 1814. Present at Salamanca, Burgos, Vittoria, Bidassoa, Nivelle, Nive, Adour and Bayonne. Present at Waterloo where he was severely wounded and awarded pension of £100 per annum.

EVEREST, Henry Bennett
Lieutenant. 6th (1st Warwickshire) Regiment of Foot.
Buried in Holy Trinity Churchyard, Cheltenham, Gloucestershire. (Burial register)

"EVEREST, HY. BENNETT. LT COL OF 6TH FOOT SEPTEMBER 17TH 1848 AGED 61."

Ensign 22 Dec 1804. Lt 1 Mar 1807. Capt 22 Jun 1820. Major 23 Dec 1831. Lt Colonel Apr 1840.
Served in the Peninsula Aug 1808 – Jan 1809 and Nov 1812 – Apr 1814. Present at Rolica, Vimeiro, Corunna, Vittoria, Pyrenees, Echellar (wounded), Nivelle, Nive, Orthes and Bordeaux. Also served at Walcheren 1809 and North America 1814 (present at Fort Erie). MGS medal for Rolica, Vimeiro, Corunna, Vittoria, Pyrenees, Nivelle and Orthes. Retired in 1842. Died at Cheltenham 17 Sept 1848.

EVES, John
Gunner. Royal Artillery.
Headstone: St Mary the Virgin Churchyard, Hayton, near Brampton, Cumbria. (Photograph)

IN MEMORY OF / JOHN EVES / OF HAYTON WHO DIED JULY / 27TH 1842 AGED 56 / YEARS. / HE WAS A NATIVE OF ESSEX / AND SERVED IN THE ROYAL HORSE / ARTILLERY DURING A PERIOD / OF 12 YEARS AND WAS / PRESENT AT THE MEMORABLE / BATTLE OF WATERLOO. / HE WAS FOR MANY YEARS A CONFI- / DENTIAL COACHMAN TO COL. WHINYATES / OF STONE-HOUSE IN WHOSE SERVICE HE / BREATHED HIS LAST / HE WAS MUCH ESTEEMED AND / HIS DEATH WAS GREATLY / LAMENTED.

Pte 11 Jul 1803
Served at Waterloo as a Gunner in Major Whinyates Rocket Troop. Discharged on reduction of Artillery on a pension of five pence per day. After the war became coachman to Colonel Whinyates.

EWART, Charles
Sergeant. 2nd (Royal North British) Regiment of Dragoons.
Monument: Edinburgh Castle Forecourt, Edinburgh, Scotland. (Photograph)

HERE LIES / ENSIGN EWART / ROYAL NORTH BRITISH DRAGOONS / AT WATERLOO AS SERGEANT IN THE ROYAL NORTH BRITISH DRAGOONS / HE CAPTURED THE STANDARD OF THE FRENCH 45TH REGIMENT FROM WHICH / THE EAGLE BADGE NOW WORN BY THE ROYAL SCOTS GREYS IS DERIVED / ERECTED TO HIS MEMORY IN APRIL 1938 BY THE OFFI- CERS WARRANT OFFICERS / NON COMMISSIONED OFFICERS AND MEN PAST AND PRESENT OF THE ROYAL SCOTS GREYS

Original gravestone set in ground behind modern monument, Edinburgh Castle forecourt, Edinburgh, Scotland. (Photograph)

IN MEMORY OF / ENSIGN CHARLES EWART / WHO DIED MARCH 23RD /1846, AGED 77 YEARS.

Pte 1789. Sgt 1814. Ensign 5th Royal Veteran Battalion 22 Feb 1816.
Served at Waterloo. Born in 1769 at Kilmarnock he was 45 years old at Waterloo. He was an expert swordsman and with his height of over 6 ½ feet had an added advantage. During the cavalry charge Ewart captured the Eagle of the 45th French Regiment after a fierce fight. Commissioned from the ranks. Also served in Flanders 1793–1795 (taken prisoner).
On the reduction of his regiment in 1821 retired to Salford on an army pension of five shillings and ten pence per day. He made a living teaching swordsmanship. Died in 1846 and was buried in a Salford churchyard. In 1938 his remains were reburied beneath a granite memorial in the esplanade of Edinburgh Castle.

EWART, John Fredrick
Lieutenant Colonel. Royal York Chasseurs.
Monument: Kensal Green Cemetery, London. (11939/87/IC). (Photograph)

IN / GRATEFUL REMEMBRANCE OF / A BELOVED HUSBAND AND FATHER / THIS MONUMENT IS ERECTED TO THE MEMORY OF / LIEUTENANT GENERAL / JOHN FREDERICK EWART, / OF BEECHGROVE, SUNNINGHILL, BERKSHIRE. / COMPANION OF THE MOST HONOURABLE ORDER OF THE BATH, / COLONEL OF THE 67TH (SOUTH HANTS) REGIMENT, / AND AFTER A PERIOD OF FIFTY ONE YEARS / SPENT IN THE SERVICE OF HIS COUNTRY, / IN THE PENIN- SULAR WAR, IN DENMARK AND HOLLAND, / AND IN THE EAST AND WEST INDIES, / DEPARTED THIS LIFE / WITH HUMBLE AND EARNEST FAITH / IN THE MERITS OF THE REDEEMER, / AND / IN PERFECT CHARITY WITH ALL MEN, / ON THE 23RD DAY OF OCTOBER 1854, / IN THE SIXTY-NINTH YEAR OF HIS AGE.

Ensign 52nd Foot 1 Nov 1803. Lt 10 Mar 1804. Capt 3rd Garrison Battalion 17 Apr 1806. Capt 52nd Regt 8 May 1807. Major Royal York Rangers 29 Oct 1812. Lt Colonel York Chasseurs 15 Sep 1814. Lt Colonel 67th Foot 5 Feb 1818. Bt Colonel 10 Jan 1837. Major General 9 Nov 1846. Lt General 20 Jun 1854.

Served in the Peninsula with 2/52nd Aug 1808 – Jan 1809, Mar – Jul 1811 and 1/52nd Aug 1811 – Dec 1812. Present at Vimeiro (severely wounded), Vigo, Sabugal, Fuentes d'Onoro, Ciudad Rodrigo, Badajoz (wounded when commanding a detachment of the Light Division carrying ladders to the assault), Salamanca and San Munos. CB. MGS medal for Vimeiro, Fuentes d'Onoro, Ciudad Rodrigo, Badajoz and Salamanca. Also served in Copenhagen 1807, Walcheren 1809, West Indies 1813–1816 (present at the capture of Guadeloupe) and India with 67th Foot Mar 1819 – Feb 1823 (present at the siege of Asseerghur 1819). Later appointed to the Recruiting Staff as an Inspecting Field Officer. Colonel 67th Foot 30 Oct 1852.

REFERENCE: *Ewart, John Frederick, The Peninsular diary of Captain John F. Ewart, 52nd Light Infantry, 1811–12, edited by Gareth Glover, reprint, 2010. Gentleman's Magazine, Jan 1855, p. 84. Annual Register, 1854, Appx, pp. 349–50.*

EWING, Daniel
Lieutenant. 74th (Highland) Regiment of Foot.
Named on the Memorial: St Andrew's Church, (now Musée Historique), Biarritz, France. (Photograph)
Named on the Regimental Memorial. St Giles's Cathedral, Edinburgh, Scotland. (Photograph)

Ensign 1 Oct 1807. Lt 7 Jun 1810.
Served in the Peninsula Feb 1810 – Mar 1814. Present at Busaco, Casal Nova, Foz d'Arouce, Fuentes d'Onoro, second siege of Badajoz, El Bodon, Ciudad Rodrigo, Badajoz, Salamanca (severely wounded), Vittoria, Pyrenees, Nivelle, Nive and Orthes where he was severely wounded 27 Feb and died of his wounds 2 Mar 1814.

EYRE, Gervase Anthony
Ensign. 1st Regiment of Foot Guards.
Named on Memorial Panel VI for Barrosa: Royal Military Chapel, Wellington Barracks, London. (M.I.) (Destroyed by a Flying Bomb 1944)

Ensign 9 Feb 1809.
Served in the Peninsula with 2nd Battalion Mar 1810 – Mar 1811 (from Aug 1810 acting ADC to Colonel Wheatley). Present at Cadiz and Barrosa where he was killed 5 Mar 1811 Educated at Eton.

EYRE, James William
Lieutenant. Royal Engineers.
Named on the Regimental Memorial: Rochester Cathedral, Rochester, Kent. (Photograph)

2nd Lt 1 Jul 1812. Lt 21 Jul 1813.
Served in France with the Army of Occupation 1815–1818. Also served in the Netherlands 1813–1815 and West Indies where he died in Tobago 21 Aug 1825.

FACEY, Peter
Sergeant. 28th (North Gloucestershire) Regiment of Foot.
Headstone: St Hieritha's Churchyard, Chittlehampton, Devon. (Photograph)

SACRED / TO THE MEMORY OF / PETER FACEY / OF THIS PARISH WHO DIED / ON THE 20TH DAY OF JUNE 1844 / AGED 63 YEARS

Pte 16th Foot 26 Jul 1799. Pte Regt of Reserve Aug 1803. Pte 28rth Foot 14 Jul 1804. Cpl 1809. Sgt 1814.

Served in the Peninsula with 1/28th Aug 1808 – Jan 1809 and March 1810 – Apr 1814. Present at Corunna, Barrosa, Arroyo dos Molinos, Almarez, Vittoria, Nive and Toulouse. Served at Waterloo in Captain Charles Cadell's Company. Also served at Copenhagen 1807 and Walcheren 1809. Discharged 1820.

REFERENCE: Glover, Gareth, ed., *The diary of a veteran: the diary of Sergeant Peter Facey, 28th Foot (North Gloucestershire) Regiment of Foot, 1803–1819*, 2007.

FADDY, Peter
2nd Captain. Royal Artillery.
Named on the Shelton Family vault: Ballingarry Churchyard, County Limerick, Ireland. (Photograph)

………………. / PETER FADDY, GENERAL R.A. DIED JULY 17 1879.

Midshipman in Royal Navy 1795–1798. 2nd Lt Royal Artillery 8 Sep 1803. 1st Lt 1 Nov 1803. 2nd Capt 5 Sep 1811. Capt 22 Apr 1826. Bt Major 22 Jul 1830. Lt Colonel 10 Aug 1839. Major General 14 Jun 1856. Lt General 20 Sep 1865. General 7 Feb 1870.

Served in the Peninsula Jul 1810 – Mar 1812 and Aug 1813 – Apr 1814. Present at Arroyo dos Molinos, San Sebastian (on board HMS *Freeza*), Adour and Bayonne. Naval GSM for San Sebastian. Also served as Midshipman on HMS *Asia* 1795–1798 (present at the capture of the Dutch fleet off Cape of Good Hope), West Indies 1807–1810 (present in Jamaica and capture of St Domingo 1809 where he commanded the R.A. acting with Spanish troops – in command of 2,000 Spanish troops with rank of Lt Colonel on Spanish service. Gold Cross for St Domingo), Newfoundland 1816–1820, Canada 1827–1830 and Gibraltar 1839–1842. Married widow of Capt John Willington Shelton of the 28th Foot.

FAIR, David
Lieutenant. 81st Regiment of Foot.
Headstone: Coldingham Graveyard, Coldingham Priory, Berwickshire, Scotland. (Photograph)

…..……... / ALSO / DAVID FAIR THEIR ELDEST SON LATE LIEUT / IN HIS MAJESTIES 81ST REG[T] OF FOOT / WHO DIED IN LONDON 31ST MARCH 1819 / AGED 36 YEARS.

Ensign 20 Mar 1806. Lt 7 Jan 1808.

Served in the Peninsula Nov 1808 – Jan 1809 and Aug 1812 – Apr 1814. Present at Corunna (wounded) and Eastern Spain (Mentioned in Despatches at Denia 6 Oct 1812). Also served at Walcheren 1809.

FAIRFAX, Henry
Captain. 85th (Buckinghamshire Volunteers) Light Infantry Regiment of Foot.
Mural Memorial tablet: St Boswell's Churchyard, St Boswell, Roxburghshire, Scotland. (Photograph)

IN MEMORY OF / COL. SIR HENRY FAIRFAX BAR[T] / LATE OF THE 85TH REGIMENT, / ONLY SURVIVING SON OF VICE ADMIRAL / SIR WILLIAM GEORGE FAIRFAX. / BORN 3[D] FEB[Y] 1790, DIED IN EDINBURGH / 3[D] FEB[Y] 1860. / THIS TABLET IS ERECTED / AS A SMALL TRIBUTE OF RESPECT / AND AFFECTION, BY HIS DEEPLY ATTACHED / AND SORROWING WIDOW, SARAH; / DAUGHTER OF THE LATE WILLIAM ASTELL ESQ. / (VERSE)

Ensign Canadian Fencibles 21 Apr 1808. Ensign 49th Foot 8 Jun 1809. Lt 41st Foot 23 Nov 1809. Lt 95th Foot 21 Jun 1810. Lt 85th Foot 2 Feb 1813. Capt 22 Jul 1813. Major 17 Jul 1823. Lt Colonel (unattached) 6 Nov 1827. Bt Colonel 23 Nov 1841.

Served in the Peninsula Jul 1812 – Feb 1813. Present in the retreat from Madrid and at San Munos. Exchanged to 2nd Life Guards 30 Dec 1845 and retired the same day.

FAIRFOOT, Robert
Colour Sergeant. 95th Regiment of Foot.
Memorial tablet: St Mary's Cathedral, Tuam, County Galway, Ireland. (North wall to left of altar). (Photograph)

TO / THE MEMORY / OF / ROBERT FAIRFOOT / LATE / QUARTER MASTER IN THE RIFLE BRIGADE / THIS TABLET IS INSCRIBED / BY HIS BROTHER OFFICERS / TO RECORD / HIS GOOD AND GALLANT SERVICES / AS A RIFLEMAN / IN THE / PENINSULA / FRANCE / AND THE / NETHERLANDS / HE DIED AT TUAM IN SEPTR 1838 / AGED 55

Private Royal Surrey Militia. Private 95th Foot Apr 1809. Cpl Oct 1810. Colour Sgt Sep 1813. Quartermaster 28 Apr 1825.
    Served in the Peninsula May 1809 – Apr 1814. Present at Barba del Puerco, Coa, Busaco, Ciudad Rodrigo, Badajoz (severely wounded), Salamanca and Pyrenees. Present at Quatre Bras and Waterloo in Capt H. Lee's Company. Retired on half pay 2 Jun 1837.
REFERENCE: Urban, Mark, Rifles, 2003.

FALCK, Neil
Lieutenant. 1st (Royal Scots) Regiment of Foot.
Memorial window: St Budock Church, Falmouth, Cornwall. (Photograph)

NEIL FALCK LIEUTENANT 1ST REGT OF FOOT / FELL MORTALLY / WOUNDED AT THE BATTLE OF SALAMANCA / WHILST IN PURSUIT OF THE ENEMY / 22ND JULY 1812

Ensign 1 Sep 1807. Lt 21 Jul 1809.
    Served in the Peninsula Sep 1808 – Jan 1809 and Apr 1810 – Jul 1812. Present at Corunna, Busaco, Fuentes d'Onoro, Badajoz, Castrejon and Salamanca where he was killed.

FALCONER, Chesborough Grant
Captain. 78th (Highland) Regiment of Foot.
Mural monument: Dean Cemetery, Edinburgh, Scotland. (Section M–763). (Photograph)

SACRED TO THE MEMORY OF / CHESBOROUGH GRANT FALCONER / KNIGHT OF THE GUELPHIC ORDER / LIEUTENANT GENERAL OF H. M. FORCES / AND / COLONEL OF THE 73RD REGIMENT. / BORN 4TH OCTOBER 1781, DIED 10TH JANUARY 1860. / HAVING RECEIVED HIS FIRST COMMISSION AT THE AGE OF THIRTEEN / HE SERVED WITH REPUTATION AND HONOUR FOR SIXTY THREE YEARS / IN THE CAMPAIGNS / FIRST AND SECOND IN EGYPT – CALABRIA – THE NETHERLANDS – / AT MAIDA – ROSELLA – EL HAMET – MERXEM AND / THE SIEGE OF ANTWERP. / HIS GALLANTRY WAS CONSPICUOUS. / BY THE PRAYERFUL STUDY OF GOD'S WORK AND THE TEACHING / OF THE HOLY SPIRIT, HE WAS LED TO REST UPON THE / FINISHED WORK OF CHRIST, AND THUS HIS END WAS PEACE. / ISAIAH XII. 2. / THIS MONUMENT IS A TRIBUTE OF LOVE TO THE MEMORY / OF A DEVOTED HUSBAND BY THE WIFE OF FIFTY YEARS, / AND HIS DEEPLY ATTACHED AND SORROWING WIDOW, / MARY RANDOLL JANE FALCONER.

Ensign 1 Sep 1795. Lt 61st Foot 1 Nov 1799. Capt 26 Dec 1805. Capt 78th Foot 7 Aug 1806. Bt Major 12 Aug 1819. Major 26 Jun 1823. Bt Lt Colonel 22 Oct 1825. Lt Colonel 22nd Foot 24 Nov 1828. Bt Colonel 28 Jun 1838. Major General 11 Nov 1851. Lt General 20 Jul 1858.
    Served in the Netherlands 1814 (in command of 78th Foot present at Merxem and Antwerp) Also served in the Cape of Good Hope 1801, Egypt 1801–1803 and 1807 (present at Alexandria, Rosetta and El Hamet), Italy 1804–1805 and Maida 1806 (ADC to General Acland). KH. MGS medal for Egypt and

Maida. Sultan's Gold Medal for Egypt. Commanded 22nd Foot from 1828–1839. Colonel 73rd Foot 11 Feb 1857. Inspecting Field Officer with Recruiting Staff 1840.

FALLS, Thomas
Captain. 20th (East Devonshire) Regiment of Foot.
Ledger stone: St Patrick's Churchyard, Newry, Northern Ireland. (Photograph)

IN MEMORY / OF / MAJOR GENERAL THOMAS FALLS / DIED / 26TH OF MAY 1858 AGED 72 YEARS.

Ensign 21 Mar 1805. Lt 4 Dec 1806. Capt 23 Sep 1813. Major 29 Sep 1814. Lt Colonel 23 Dec 1836. Bt Colonel 9 Nov 1846. Major General 20 Jun 1854
   Served in the Peninsula with 20th Foot Aug 1808 – Jan 1809 and Nov 1812 – Jun 1813 and on Staff Jul 1813 – Apr 1814 (ADC to Major General Ross). Present at Vimeiro, Corunna, Pyrenees (wounded), Nivelle and Orthes. Also served in Sicily 1805–1806 (present at Maida), Walcheren 1809, North America 1814–1815 (present at Washington), the riots in South Wales 1831 (wounded at Merthyr Tydfil) and West Indies (present in the Windward and Leeward Islands – DAG 1836). MGS medal for Maida, Vimeiro, Corunna, Pyrenees, Nivelle and Orthes. Half pay 25 Dec 1836.

FANE, Charles
Lieutenant Colonel. 59th (2nd Nottinghamshire) Regiment of Foot.
Memorial tablet: St Nicholas Church, Fulbeck, Lincolnshire. (Photograph)

THIS MARBLE / IS DEDICATED TO THE MEMORY OF / COLONEL CHARLES FANE / SECOND SON OF THE HON. HENRY FANE / AND OF ANNE HIS WIFE / HE FELL / AT THE BATTLE OF VITTORIA / IN THE THIRTY THIRD YEAR OF HIS AGE / WHAT WAS MORTAL IN HIM / REPOSES NEAR THE LAST SCENE / OF HIS VALUABLE LIFE / WHAT IS IMMORTAL / IS WITH THOSE PATRIOTS / WHO LIKE HIM HAVE DIED / FIGHTING FOR A VIRTUOUS CAUSE / 1813

Ensign Lord Mountnorris's Regiment. Lt Lord Landaff's Regiment 20 Jul 1794. Capt 9th Foot 22 Aug 1794. Lt and Capt Coldstream Guards 11 Dec 1799. Adjt 26 May 1803. Bt Major 1 Jan 1805. Major 8th Foot 18 Apr 1805. Lt Colonel 59th Foot 20 Jun 1805.
   Served in the Peninsula Sep 1808 – Jan 1809 and Feb – Jun 1813. Present at Corunna (severely wounded and part of his skull blown off), Vittoria (severely wounded, lost a leg, died from his wounds 27 Jun 1813 and was buried in the garden of the convent in Vittoria). Gold Medal for Corunna and Vittoria. Also served in Egypt 1801 and Walcheren 1809. Before he joined the army he went to Germany to study military science and from there joined Abercrombie's expedition to Egypt. Educated at Eton. Brother of Colonel Sir Henry Fane 4th Dragoon Guards and Capt Mildmay Fane 44th Foot.
REFERENCE: *Gentleman's Magazine, Jul 1813, p. 94.*

FANE, Sir Henry
Colonel. 4th (Royal Irish) Dragoon Guards.
Memorial tablet: St Nicholas Church, Fulbeck, Lincolnshire. (Photograph)

TO THE MEMORY OF / GENERAL SIR HENRY FANE, / KNIGHT GRAND CROSS OF THE MOST HON^{BLE} ORDER OF THE BATH, / COLONEL OF THE 1ST OR KING'S REGIMENT OF DRAGOON GUARDS, / COMMANDER IN CHIEF OF THE ARMIES IN INDIA, / DOCTOR OF CIVIL LAW IN THE UNIVERSITY OF OXFORD, / SON OF THE HON^{BLE} HENRY FANE, BY ANNE BATSON, HIS WIFE: / THIS DISTINGUISHED AND GALLANT SOLDIER DEPARTED THIS LIFE / IN THE 61ST YEAR OF HIS AGE, ON BOARD THE EAST INDIA SHIP MALABAR, / ON HIS PASSAGE FROM BOMBAY ON THE 25TH OF MARCH 1840: / HE COMMANDED BRIGADES / IN THE BATTLES OF ROLEIA, VIMIERA,

BUSACO, IN PORTUGAL: / CORUNNA, TALAVERA, AND VITTORIA, IN SPAIN: / ORTHES, AIRE, AND TOULOUSE IN FRANCE: / UNDER THE COMMAND OF / THE DUKE OF WELLINGTON AND SIR JOHN MOORE: / HE RECEIVED THE PUBLIC THANKS OF HIS COUNTRY, THREE TIMES, / IN HIS PLACE IN THE HOUSE OF COMMONS, / FOR HIS DISTINGUISHED CONDUCT / IN THE ABOVE MEMORABLE ACTIONS: / HIS SERVICES WERE LOST TO HIS COUNTRY, / BY A DISEASE CONTRACTED IN INDIA / WHERE HE HAD COMMANDED FOUR YEARS AND SIX MONTHS.

Cornet 6th Dragoon Guards 31 May 1792. Lt 55th Foot 29 Sep 1792. Captain-Lieut 4th Dragoon Guards 1794. Major 24 Aug 1795. Lt Colonel 1 Jan 1797. Lt Colonel 1st Dragoon Guards 25 Dec 1804. Bt Colonel 1 Jan 1805. Major General 25 Jul 1810. Colonel 4th Dragoon Guards 3 Aug 1814. Lt General 12 Aug 1819. General 10 Jan 1837.

Served in the Peninsula Aug – Oct 1808 (Commanded 6th Brigade), Oct 1808 – Jan 1809 (Commanded 2 Brigade 3rd Division), Apr 1809 – Nov 1809, Jan – May 1810 (Commanded 'A' Cavalry Brigade), May – Dec 1810 (GOC Cavalry 2nd Division) and May 1813 – Apr 1814 (GOC 'B and C' Cavalry Brigade). Present at Rolica, Vimeiro, Corunna, Talavera (Mentioned in Despatches), Busaco, Vittoria, Orthes, Aire and Toulouse. Returned home after Busaco owing to ill health and returned to the Peninsula 1813. Commanded the cavalry and artillery in the withdrawal from the south of France to Calais at end of the Peninsular War. Gold Cross for Rolica, Vimeiro, Corunna, Talavera, Vittoria and Orthes.

Not at Waterloo but later commanded Cavalry and Horse Artillery in France with the Army of Occupation. KCB 5 Jun 1815. GCB 24 Jan 1826. Colonel 1st Dragoon Guards 24 Feb 1827. Surveyor General of Ordnance 1829. Also served in the Irish Rebellion 1798, commanded troops quelling the riots in the Midlands 1816 and India 1835–1840. Commander in Chief India 1835, which was peaceful at first but by 1838 there was trouble on the North West Frontier and Fane organised the Army of the Indus which later took part in the first Afghan War. By Jan 1839 he was not well and handed over command to Sir John Keane. He left for England but died at sea off the Azores. At his request he was buried in Fulbeck. Educated at Eton. MP for Lyme Regis 1802–1818 and MP for Sandwich 1831–1832. Brother of Lt Colonel Charles Fane 59th Foot and Capt Mildmay Fane 44th Foot.
REFERENCE: *Dictionary of National Biography. Gentleman's Magazine, Oct 1840, pp. 426–7. Annual Register, 1840, Appx, p. 157.*

FANE, Mildmay
Captain. 44th (East Essex) Regiment of Foot.
Memorial tablet: St Nicholas Church, Fulbeck, Lincolnshire. (Photograph)

IN MEMORY OF / GENERAL MILDMAY FANE, / 7TH SON OF THE HONBLE H. FANE, OF FULBECK, / WHO SERVED IN THE PENINSULA AT / THE BATTLE OF VITTORIA, / ASSAULT & CAPTURE OF SAN SEBASTIAN, / AND THE BATTLE OF THE NIVE, / ALSO IN THE CAMPAIGN OF 1815, / INCLUDING THE BATTLE OF / QUATRE BRAS IN WHICH HE WAS WOUNDED. / DIED MARCH 12TH 1868, AGED 73. / THIS TABLET IS ERECTED BY OFFICERS OF THE 54TH REGIMENT, / WHO SERVED UNDER HIM AS THEIR COMMANDING OFFICER / BETWEEN 1828 AND 1851, IN TOKEN OF THEIR GREAT / ESTEEM FOR HIS MEMORY, AND OF THE HONOR, RESPECT, / AND LOVE WITH WHICH THEY REGARDED HIM.

Ensign 59th Foot 11 Jun 1812. Lt 25 Sep 1813. Capt 28 Jul 1814. Capt 44th Foot 30 Mar 1815. Capt 36th Foot 22 Feb 1816. Major 1st West India Regt 2 Mar 1820. Lt Colonel 54th Foot 12 Jun 1823. Colonel 28 Jun 1838. Major General 11 Nov 1851. Lt General 30 Jan 1855. General 27 Mar 1863.

Served in the Peninsula Feb 1813 – Feb 1814. Present at Cadiz, Vittoria, San Sebastian and Nive. Present at Quatre Bras (severely wounded) and Waterloo. MGS medal for Vittoria, San Sebastian and Nive. Colonel 96th Foot 11 Aug 1855. Colonel 54th Foot 1860. Brother of Lt Colonel Charles Fane 59th Foot and Colonel Sir Henry Fane 4th Dragoon Guards. Died in a hunting accident.
REFERENCE: *Gentleman's Magazine, Apr 1868, p. 550.*

FANSHAWE, Edward
Captain. Royal Engineers.
Family Memorial tablet: St John the Baptist Church, Aldenham, Hertfordshire. (Photograph)

IN THE VAULT ABOVE NAMED / REST THE REMAINS OF / LIEUT: GENERAL EDWARD FANSHAWE C. B. / COLONEL COMMANDANT ROYAL ENGINEERS / DIED 22ND NOVEMBER 1858 AGED 73 YEARS. / ....

1st Lt 1 Jul 1801. 2nd Capt 1 Jul 1806. Capt 1 May 1811. Bt Major 12 Aug 1819. Lt Colonel 23 Mar 1825. Colonel 10 Jan 1837. Major General 9 Nov 1846. Lt General 20 Jun 1854.

Served in the Peninsula Aug – Oct 1808 (ADC to Lt General Sir Hew Dalrymple). Also served at the Cape of Good Hope 1806, South America 1807 (present at Montevideo), and Walcheren 1809 (present at the siege of Flushing). CB. Son-in-law of Colonel Sir Hew Dalrymple 57th Foot.

FARIS, James Fleming
Lieutenant. 88th (Connaught Rangers) Regiment of Foot.
Pedestal tomb: Templemore Parish Churchyard, County Tipperary, Ireland. (In front of church). (Photograph)

CAPTN, JAMES F. FARIS / 88TH REGT OR CONNAUGHT RANGERS / DIED AT / TEMPLEMORE 1ST AUGST 1825 / AGED 37 YEARS. / THIS MONUMENT IS ERECTED TO HIS / MEMORY AS A TRIBUTE TO HIS WORTH / BY HIS BROTHER OFFICERS WHO / SINCERELY DEPLORE HIS DEATH.

Ensign 27 Oct 1807. Lt 11 Jul 1809. Capt 28 Nov 1822.

Served in the Peninsula with 1/88th Jul 1809 – Apr 1814. Present at Busaco, Redinha, Casal Nova, Foz d'Arouce, Sabugal, Fuentes d'Onoro, second siege of Badajoz, El Bodon, Ciudad Rodrigo (wounded), Badajoz (severely wounded), Salamanca, Vittoria (wounded), Pyrenees, Nivelle, Nive, Orthes (wounded) and Toulouse. Named as George F. Faris in Army Lists.

FARIS, William
Lieutenant. Royal Engineers.
Named on the Regimental Memorial: Rochester Cathedral, Rochester, Kent. (Photograph)

2nd Lt 1 Jan 1814. Lt 1 Aug 1814. 2nd Capt 1 Mar 1835. Capt 23 Nov 1841. Bt Major 9 Nov 1846. Lt Colonel 6 Aug 1849. Bt Colonel 28 Nov 1854. Major General 2 Aug 1860. Lt General 7 Sep 1867. General 8 Jun 1871.

Served in the Netherlands 1815 and in France with the Army of Occupation 1815–1816. Retired on full pay 24 Nov 1851. Died in London 4 Dec 1874.

FARQUHARSON, Donald
Lieutenant. 42nd (Royal Highland) Regiment of Foot.
Named on the Memorial: St Andrew's Church, (now Musée Historique), Biarritz, France. (Photograph)

Ensign 25 Oct 1810. Lt 17 Mar 1813.

Served in the Peninsula Apr 1812 – Apr 1814. Present at the Pyrenees, Nivelle, Nive, Orthes and Toulouse where he was severely wounded and died of his wounds 12 Apr 1814.

FARQUHARSON, John
Lieutenant Colonel. 42nd (Royal Highland) Regiment of Foot.
Pedestal Monument: Greyfriars Churchyard, Edinburgh, Scotland. (Photograph)

IN MEMORY OF / LIEUTENANT COLONEL / JOHN FARQUHARSON, / LATE OF THE 42ND REGI-MENT / AND / LIEUTENANT GOVERNOR OF CARLISLE. / HE WAS IN ACTIVE SERVICE FOR THIRTY-SIX YEARS. / HE SERVED UNDER THE DUKE OF YORK / IN FRANCE AND HOLLAND / UNDER SIR RALPH ABERCROMBY / IN THE WEST INDIES AND EGYPT, / AND UNDER GENERAL MOORE / IN PORTUGAL AND SPAIN. / HIS LAST SERVICE IN THE FIELD / WAS AGAIN IN HOLLAND, / AS ASSISTANT ADJUTANT GENERAL / TO THE MARQUIS OF HUNTLY, / ON THE EXPEDITION TO WALCHEREN. / HE DIED AT NEWINGTON, / ON THE 3RD NOVEMBER 1835 / AGED 82 YEARS. / IN GRATEFUL REMEMBRANCE OF HIS VIRTUES, / THIS MONUMENT IS ERECTED BY HIS WIDOW / ANN FARQUHARSON. / MRS ANN FARQUHARSON / DIED 17TH JANUARY 1839.

Lt 77th Foot 12 Jan 1778. Lt 42nd Foot Jan 1786. Adjutant 1791. Capt Jan 1795. Major 8th Garrison Battalion Jul 1803. Major 42nd Foot Sep 1804. Lt Colonel 3 Mar 1808.

Served in the Peninsula Aug 1808 – Jan 1809. Present at Corunna. Also served in Flanders 1793–1795 (present at Nimwegen, Boxtel and Geldermalsen), West Indies 1796 (present at St Lucia and the Charib War in St Vincent), Irish Rebellion 1798, Egypt 1801 (AAG. Present at Alexandria), Gibraltar 1805–1808 and Walcheren 1809 (AAG). Retired due to ill health 1812. Lieutenant Governor of Carlisle.
REFERENCE: *Gentleman's Magazine, May 1836, pp. 549–50. Royal Military Calendar, Vol 4, pp. 321–2.*

FAULKNER, Sir Arthur Brooke
Physician. Medical Department.
Memorial tablet: St Catherine's Church, Leigh, Gloucestershire. (Photograph)

.... / IN MEMORY OF / SIR ARTHUR BROOKE FAULKNER WHO DIED 23RD OF MAY 1845.

Floor slab: St Catherine's Church, Leigh, Gloucestershire. (M.I.)

"SIR ARTHUR BROOKE FAULKNER, DIED MAY 23RD 1845."

Memorial tablet: Castletown Parish Church, County Carlow, Ireland. (West wall). (Photograph)

SACRED TO THE MEMORY OF / SIR ARTHUR BROOKE FAULKNER, / WHO DIED AT EVINGTON, GLOUCESTERSHIRE, THE 23RD OF MAY 1845, / YOUNGEST SON OF HUGH FAULKNER ESQR OF CASTLETOWN, IN THIS PARISH, / BY FLORENCE COLE, DAUGHTER OF THE REVD HENRY COLE, / BROTHER OF THE FIRST EARL OF ENNISKILLEN, / MARRIED ANN, DAUGHTER OF DONALD MCLEOD ESQR OF LEWIS. / SOUND LEARNING, REFINED WIT, CLASSIC ELEGANCE, LOVE OF FREEDOM, AND BENEVOLENCE OF SPIRIT, / CHARACTERISED HIS PUBLISHED SENTIMENTS AND PUBLIC CONDUCT. / THAT GENTLE SIMPLICITY AND AMIABLE MODESTY, WHICH ACCOMPANIED HIS VIRTUES / AND ACCOMPLISHMENTS ENDEARED HIM TO ALL IN PRIVATE LIFE / AND ADORNED THOSE FINE ARTS IN WHICH HE EXCELLED. / HE LOVED HIS FATHERLAND WITH FILIAL AFFECTION, / AND WAS THE ELOQUENT AND POWERFUL ADVOCATE OF ITS RIGHTS AND LIBERTIES. / THE CHARM OF HIS FRANK AND POLISHED MANNERS BROUGHT / HIM INTO INTIMATE CONNEXION WITH THE PRINCES / AND EMINENT MEN OF HIS TIME. / THE PURITY, PIETY, AND HUMILITY OF THE CHRISTIAN / ADORNED HIS LIFE AND CONSECRATES HIS MEMORY. / THIS MONUMENT IS ERECTED BY HER TO WHOM HIS MEMORY IS HALLOWED / BY BOUNDLESS AND UNCEASING DEVOTION, AND WHOSE UNION OF 35 YEARS / APPEARED AS THE HAPPY VISION OF A LENGTHENED BRIDAL DAY.

Physician to the Forces 28 Jul 1808.

Served in the Peninsula Nov 1808 – Jan 1809. Also served at Walcheren 1809, Sicily 1811 and Malta 1813. Retired on half pay 25 Sep 1814. MD Edinburgh 1803.

Author of *Considerations on the Expediency of Establishing an Hospital for Officers on Foreign Service*, 1810. After witnessing an outbreak of plague in Malta in 1813 he was able to trace the spread of the disease and contained it by directing a strict quarantine procedure. He was helped by the support of General Paul Anderson in command of the Garrison, so much so that not one soldier caught the disease. His conclusions were published in *A Treatise on the Plague*, 1820.

REFERENCE: *Dictionary of National Biography. Gentleman's Magazine, Oct 1845, pp. 427–8.*

FAUNCE, Alured Dodsworth

Major. 4th (King's Own) Regiment of Foot.
Buried in the Family vault in Crypt: Clifton Church, Bristol, Somerset. (Recorded from Will)

Ensign 4th Foot 2 Dec 1795. Lt 13 Dec 1796. Capt 6 Aug 1803. Major 14 Feb 1811. Bt Lt Colonel 27 Sep 1814. Lt Colonel 24 Jan 1822. Bt Colonel 6 May 1831. Major General 23 Nov 1841.

Served in the Peninsula Aug 1808 – Jan 1809, with 1/4th Nov 1810 – Jun 1812, 2/4th Jul 1812 – Jan 1813 and 1/4th Mar – Apr 1814. Present at Corunna (in command of the Grenadier Company during the retreat), Fuentes d'Onoro, Barba del Puerco, Badajoz (wounded by a musket ball in his leg that was never taken out), Salamanca (commanded Lt Infantry Companies of the Brigade) and Bayonne.

Also served in Canada 1797, the Helder 1799, Hanover 1805, Copenhagen 1807, Sweden 1808, Walcheren 1809, North America 1814–1815 (commanded the regiment at Bladensburg, capture of Washington and present at New Orleans where he was severely wounded) and West Indies 1822–1826. Inspecting Field Officer of the Bristol District 1832–1841. When he was promoted Major General in 1841 he had been in military service for 46 years. CB. Gold Medal for Salamanca. MGS medal for Corunna, Fuentes d'Onoro and Badajoz. Died 1 Mar 1850 aged 74.

REFERENCE: *United Service Magazine, Apr 1850, p. 640. Gentleman's Magazine, May 1850, pp. 535–6. Annual Review, 1850, Appx, p. 211.*

FAVELL, William Anthony

Ensign. 61st (South Gloucestershire) Regiment of Foot.
Named on the Memorial: St Andrew's Church, (now Musée Historique), Biarritz, France. (Photograph)

Ensign 18 Nov 1812.

Served in the Peninsula Sep 1813 – Apr 1814. Present at Nivelle, Nive, Orthes, Tarbes and Toulouse where he was severely wounded and died of his wounds 11 Apr 1814.

FAWCETT, John James

Assistant Surgeon. 62nd (Wiltshire) Regiment of Foot.
Ledger stone: St Macartin's Cathedral, Enniskillen, County Fermanagh, Northern Ireland. (Photograph)

JOHN JAMES FAWCETT / ASSISTANT SURGEON, 62ND REGIMENT, / DEPARTED THIS LIFE / 29TH MAY, 1827, / AGED 34 YEARS. / THIS STONE IS ERECTED TO HIS MEMORY / BY HIS BROTHER OFFICERS, / IN TESTIMONY OF THEIR ESTEEM / AND REGARD.

Hospital Mate 12 Mar 1812. Asst Surgeon 62nd Foot 4 Feb 1813.

Served in the Peninsula Oct 1813 – Feb 1814. (from Nov 1813 Acting Staff Asst Surgeon). In Eastern Spain where he was present at Tarragona.

FEAD, George
Captain and Lieutenant Colonel. 1st Regiment of Foot Guards.
Grave: St Nicholas Churchyard, Plumstead, Kent. (No longer extant. Destroyed by a flying bomb in the Second World War). (M.I.)

"GEORGE FEAD DIED 13 SEPT 1847."

Ensign 19 Dec 1799. Lt and Capt 3 Dec 1803. Capt and Lt Colonel 13 Dec 1813.
    Served in the Peninsula Oct 1808 – Jan 1809, with 2nd Battalion Mar – Aug 1810 and Apr – May 1811. Present at Corunna and Cadiz. Present at Waterloo where he was wounded. CB for Waterloo. MGS medal for Corunna. Retired 27 Mar 1828.

FEARON, Peter
Captain. 31st (Huntingdonshire) Regiment of Foot.
Named on the Memorial: St Andrew's Church, (now Musée Historique), Biarritz, France. (Photograph)

Ensign 21 Apr 1804. Lt 29 Dec 1804. Capt 17 Aug 1809. Bt Major 26 Dec 1813. Portuguese Army: Major 7th Caçadores 22 Jul 1810. Major 1st Line 8 Feb 1812. Bt Lt Colonel 3 Aug 1813. Lt Colonel 6th Caçadores 27 Aug 1813.
    Served in the Peninsula with 31st Foot Jan 1810 – Jun 1810 and with the Portuguese Army Jul 1810 – Feb 1814. Present at Albuera, Ciudad Rodrigo, Salamanca, Burgos, Vittoria, Pyrenees, Nivelle, Nive (wounded and Mentioned in Despatches) and Garris where he was Mentioned in Despatches and killed Feb 1814. Gold Medal for Albuera, Nivelle and Nive.

FEHRSZEN, Oliver George
Major. 53rd (Shropshire) Regiment of Foot.
Memorial: Salem Cemetery, Madras, India. (M.I.)

"UNDERNEATH / REPOSE THE REMAINS / OF / LIEUTT COLL FEHRSZEN, H.M. 53RD REGT / A MAN / CELEBRATED FOR HIS LEARNING, / DISTINGUISHED FOR HIS VALOR, / ESTEEMED FOR HIS PIETY, / WHO WAS / A SOLDIER BY NATURE; A GENTLEMAN BY BIRTH; / A FRIEND TO ALL ; AN ENEMY OF NONE. / HE DIED AT NAMCUL / OF / CHOLERA MORBUS, / AFTER AN INEFFECTUAL STRUGGLE OF ONLY 12 HOURS, / ON THE 19TH JANUARY, / 1820, / AT THE EARLY AGE OF 34. / PRAY FOR HIS SOUL."

Ensign 39th Foot 17 Mar 1803. Lt 31 Mar 1804. Capt 53rd Foot 31 Oct 1805. Bt Major 26 Aug 1813. Major 24 Dec 1813. Bt Lt Colonel 21 Jun 1817.
    Served in the Peninsula Apr 1809 – Apr 1814. Present at Douro, Talavera, Busaco, Fuentes d'Onoro, siege of Salamanca Forts, Salamanca (severely wounded and taken prisoner, but was able to rejoin shortly afterwards), Vittoria, Pyrenees (awarded Bt Majority), Nivelle (wounded when capturing a gun from the enemy) and Toulouse. Also served in India 1817 where he died of cholera 1820.

FELIX, Orlando
1st Lieutenant. 95th Regiment of Foot
Memorial tablet: Holy Trinity Church, Geneva, Switzerland. (East wall of south transept). (Photograph)

TO THE MEMORY / OF / THEIR BELOVED AND VALUED FRIEND / MAJOR GENERAL FELIX, / WHO DIED AT GENEVA / APRIL 5TH 1860. / THIS TABLET IS ERECTED BY / FELIX AND MORAY BROWN.

2nd Lt Royal Marines 14 Aug 1810. Ensign 27th Foot 26 Aug 1813. Lt 14th Foot 10 Nov 1814. 1st Lt 95th

Foot 4 May 1815. Capt 20 May 1824. Major 31 Oct 1826 (unattached). Bt Lt Colonel 18 Jun 1841. Bt Colonel 11 Nov 1851. Lt Colonel (unattached) 23 Oct 1855. Major General 26 Oct 1858.

Served in the Peninsula with 2/27th Oct 1813 – Mar 1814. Present at Ordal and Barcelona. Present at Quatre Bras (wounded) and Waterloo with 95th Foot.

Travelled extensively in the East 1826–1829 (Egypt, Nubia and Levant). His companion was Lord Prudhoe, second son of the Duke of Northumberland. They journeyed up the Nile recording inscriptions on the tombs of the Pharaohs and noting evidence of the tomb robbers. He was one of the first people to decipher the names and titles of the Pharaohs and his *Notes on hieroglyphics* was published in 1828 and later translated into French and Italian. Also served in India Jun 1841 – Oct 1855 (DQMG at Madras).

FELL, William
Private. 52nd (Oxfordshire) Light Infantry Regiment of Foot.
Headstone: St Anne's Churchyard, Haverthwaite, Cumbria. (Photograph)

REQUIESCAT IN PACE / WILLIAM FELL / A SOLDIER OF THE 52ND LIGHT INFANTRY / WHO FOUGHT IN THAT GALLANT REGIMENT, AT / POMBAL / ALMEIDA / ON THE PLAINS OF CONDILLIA / AT SABUGAL / BUSACO / FUENTES D'ONOR / AT THE SIEGE AND STORMING OF / CIUDAD RODRIGO / (A VOLUNTEER) / BADAJOZ / (SEVERELY WOUNDED) / SALAMANCA / VITTORIA / AND / ORTHES / (DANGEROUSLY / WOUNDED.) / WAS BORN AT BROW-EDGE AND BURIED / HERE ON THE 27TH JUNE 1852 / IN / HAVERTHWAITE CHURCH YARD. / B. G. TO WHOM HE LEFT HIS MEDAL OF SIX CLASPS / DEDICATED TO BRITISH VALOUR THIS HUMBLE STONE.

Royal Cheshire Militia 1804. Pte 52nd Foot 4 Apr 1809.

Served in the Peninsula with 1/52nd 1809–1814. Present at Pombal, Almeida, Sabugal, Busaco, Fuentes d'Onoro, Ciudad Rodrigo (storming party), Badajoz (severely wounded), Salamanca, Vittoria and Orthes (severely wounded). Also served with 2/52nd in the Netherlands 1815. Not at Waterloo but transferred back to 1/52nd Jul 1815 and served in France with the Army of Occupation until 1818. Discharged Aug 1821 and returned to Cumbria to his former trade of papermaker. Later worked in a cotton factory where one of his duties was being the armed messenger to collect the wages each week for the factory. MGS medal for Busaco, Ciudad Rodrigo, Badajoz, Salamanca, Vittoria and Orthes.
REFERENCE: *Martin, Janet D., A Furness soldier in the Peninsular War, Cumberland and Westmorland Antiquarian and Archaeological Society Transactions, 2004, pp. 221–8.*

FELTOM, Thomas
Paymaster. 7th (Queen's Own) Regiment of Light Dragoons.
Memorial tablet: St Ann's Parish Church, Dublin, Ireland. (Photograph)

THOMAS FELTOM ESQ^{RE} / LATE PAYMASTER 7TH HUSSARS / DIED 4TH SEPTEMBER 1830, / AGED 43 YEARS. / THIS TABLET IS ERECTED BY / HIS BROTHER OFFICERS / AS A MARK OF RESPECT / TO HIS MEMORY.

Paymaster 23rd Foot 8 Aug 1811. Half pay on reduction of the regiment 1814. Paymaster 7th Lt Dragoons 16 Apr 1815.

Present at Waterloo.

FENSHAM, George
1st Lieutenant. 23rd (Royal Welch Fusiliers) Regiment of Foot.
Family Altar tomb with rails: St Mary's Churchyard, Woolwich, Kent. (South side of church). No longer extant. Church bombed in the Second World War). (M.I.)

"LIEUTENANT GEORGE FENSHAM OF THE ROYAL WELSH FUSILIERS WHO FELL IN THE EVER MEMORABLE BATTLE OF WATERLOO 18 JUNE 1815. ...."

2nd Lt 20 Apr 1808. 1st Lt 4 Jan 1810.
    Served in the Peninsula with 1/23rd Sep 1812 – Jan 1814. Present at Vittoria, Pyrenees, Nivelle and Nive. Present at Waterloo where he was killed. Also served at Walcheren 1809.

FENTON, John James
Lieutenant. 44th (East Essex) Regiment of Foot.
Memorial tablet: St Michael's Church, Bath, Somerset. (Photograph)

IN MEMORY OF / SARAH FENTON, / .... / JOHN JAMES FENTON, ESQR / / FORMERLY A LIEUTENANT OF H. M. 44TH REGT, / HUSBAND AND FATHER OF THE ABOVE. / DIED AT BATH JULY 2ND 1864, AGED 75, / AND WAS BURIED IN THE WALCOT CEMETERY, AT LOCKSBROOK, / A BRAVE MAN AND A SINCERE FRIEND.

Ensign 22 Feb 1810. Lt 12 May 1812.
    Served in the Peninsula Jul 1810 – Sep 1811. Present at Cadiz and Fuentes d'Onoro. MGS medal for Fuentes D'Onoro.

FENTON, Thomas Charles
Captain. 2nd (Royal North British) Regiment of Dragoons.
Headstone: St Mary with St Peter Churchyard, Tidenham, Gloucestershire. Seriously eroded and inscription recorded from memorial inscription. (Photograph)

"IN MEMORY OF / THOMAS CHARLES FENTON / CAPT 4TH DRAGOONS (PENINSULAR 1808 – 1814) / 2ND RNB DRAGOONS SCOTS GREYS / (WATERLOO 18TH JUNE 1815) / DIED FEBRUARY 5TH 1841 AGED 52 YEARS."

Cornet 4th Dragoons 8 Nov 1804. Lt 17 Jul 1806. Capt 2 Jan 1812. Capt 2nd Dragoons 6 Feb 1815.
    Served in the Peninsula Apr 1809 – Apr 1814. Present at Talavera, Busaco, Albuera, Usagre, Aldea da Ponte, Llerena, Salamanca, Vittoria and Toulouse. On reduction of the Army at the end of the Peninsular war placed on half pay. Joined the Scots Greys Feb 1815. Served with them at Waterloo. Retired 1819. One of the few officers in the Scots Greys at Waterloo who had seen recent active service in the Peninsula.
REFERENCE: Fenton, C, Campaigning in Spain and Belgium: the letters of Captain Thomas Charles Fenton, 4th Dragoons and the Scots Grey's 1809–1815, edited by Gareth Glover, 2010. Journal of the Society for Army Historical Research, 1975, Vol 53, No 216, pp. 210-3.

FENWICK, William
Lieutenant Colonel. 34th (Cumberland) Regiment of Foot.
Chest tomb: St Budock Churchyard, Falmouth, Cornwall. (Photograph)

SACRED / TO THE MEMORY OF / LIEUT COL. W. FENWICK CB / LATE GOVERNOR OF PENDENNIS CASTLE / DIED 7TH JULY 1832 / AGED 77. / ....

Ensign Jun 1792. Lt Jul 1793. Capt 22 Aug 1794. Bt Major Jan 1803. Major 15 May 1805. Lt Col 15 Dec 1808.
    Served in the Peninsula Jul 1809 – Oct 1813 in command of 2/34th. Present at Busaco, Olivencia, first siege of Badajoz, Albuera, Arroyo dos Molinos (Mentioned in Despatches), Almarez, retreat from Burgos, Vittoria and Pyrenees (severely wounded at Maya Pass 25 Jul 1813, his right leg amputated, taken prisoner, remained in prison until Sep 1813 and awarded pension of £300 per annum). On his return to

England appointed Lieutenant Governor of Pendennis Castle in Cornwall. Gold Medal for Albuera and Vittoria. CB and KTS. Also served in Ireland and West Indies 1795–1796. Cape of Good Hope 1799–1802 and India 1802–1807.
REFERENCE: *Royal Military Calendar, Vol 4, pp. 322–3. Gentleman's Magazine, Aug 1832, p. 181.*

FERGUSON, Adam
Captain. 58th (Rutlandshire) Regiment of Foot.
Memorial tablet: Greyfriars Churchyard, Edinburgh, Scotland. (Located in the Covenanters' Prison which is an inaccessible section of the churchyard). (M.I.)

"DR ADAM FERGUSON PROF MORAL PHILOSOPHY EDR UNIV, 1 SON CAPT SIR ADAM FERGUSON, FIRST DEPUTY KEEPER OF THE REGALIA, 21.12.1770, 23.12. 1854. ...."

Ensign 21st Foot 1 Dec 1805. Lt 34th Foot 23 Oct 1806. Lt 87th Foot 16 Apr 1807. Capt 58th Foot 4 Feb 1808.
Served in the Peninsula Jul 1809 – Apr 1814. Present at Salamanca and Burgos (taken prisoner and remained a prisoner of war until Apr 1814). MGS medal for Salamanca. Half pay 8 Oct 1816. Friend of Sir Walter Scott. Became Keeper of Scottish Regalia. Knighted by George IV 1820. CB Sep 1831. Died 23 Dec 1854.
REFERENCE: *Annual Register, 1855, Appx, p. 238.*

FERGUSON, Sir Ronald Crauford
Colonel. Sicilian Regiment of Foot.
Monument: Kensal Green Cemetery, London. (2989/91/RS). (Photograph)

GENERAL / SIR RONALD CRAUFORD FERGUSON / G.C.B. / COLONEL OF THE 79TH HIGH-LANDERS / AND / M. P. NOTTINGHAM / OBIIT 10TH APRIL 1841 / AETAT 66

Ensign 53rd Foot 3 Apr 1790. Lt 24 Jan 1791. Capt 19 Feb 1793. Major 84th Foot 31 May 1794. Lt Colonel 18 Sep 1794. Bt Colonel 1 Jan 1800. Major General 25 Apr 1808. Colonel Sicilian Regt 25 Jan 1809. Lt General 4 Jun 1813. General 22 Jul 1830.
Served in the Peninsula Aug – Dec 1808 (Commanded 2 Brigade). Present at Rolica (Mentioned in Despatches), Vimeiro (Mentioned in Despatches) and Cadiz. Appointed second in command at Cadiz 1810, but returned home after a few months owing to ill health. Gold Medal for Rolica and Vimeiro. GCB. Also served in Flanders 1793–1794 (present at Valenciennes and Dunkirk where he was wounded), Cape of Good Hope 1796, Ferrol 1800, Cape of Good Hope 1806 (appointed to command Highland Brigade to recapture the Cape) and Netherlands 1814 (appointed second in command). Colonel 79th Foot 24 Mar 1828. MP for Kirkcaldy 1806–1826 and Nottingham 1830–1837.
REFERENCE: *Dictionary of National Biography. Gentleman's Magazine, Oct 1841, pp. 427–8. Annual Register, 1841, Appx, pp. 195–6.*

FERGUSSON, James
Lieutenant Colonel. 3rd (East Kent) Regiment of Foot.
Pedestal tomb: Locksbrook Road Cemetery, Bath, Somerset. (Grave number F 18). (Photograph)

FERGUSSON. / TO THE MEMORY OF / GENERAL SIR JAMES FERGUSON GCB / COLONEL 43RD REGT/ OF THE FAMILY OF THE FERGUSSONS / OF CRAIGDARROCH / IN THE COUNTY OF DUMFRIESSHIRE NB. / HE SERVED DURING THE PENINSULAR / CAMPAIGNS FROM 1808 – 1814 / IN THE LIGHT DIVISION AND / WAS THREE TIMES A VOLUNTEER IN / THE STORMING PARTIES OF THE 43RD REGT / HE TERMINATED HIS LONG AND / DISTINGUISHED SERVICES AS / GOVERNOR AND COMMANDER-IN-CHIEF / OF THE FORTRESS OF GIBRALTAR. / BORN MARCH 17 1787. DIED SEPT 4 1865.

Ensign 18th Foot 20 Aug 1801. Lt 90th Foot 27 Aug 1803. Lt 43rd Foot 7 Aug 1804. Capt 1 Dec 1806. Major 79th Foot 3 Dec 1812. Major 85th Foot 25 Jan 1813. Lt Colonel 3rd Foot 16 May 1814. Lt Colonel 88th Foot 12 Aug 1819. Lt Colonel 52nd 2 Jun 1825. Bt Colonel 22 Jul 1830. Major General 23 Nov 1841. Lt General 11 Nov 1851. General 21 Feb 1860.

Served in the Peninsula with 2/43rd Aug 1808 – Jan 1809, 1/43rd Jul 1809 – Jan 1813 and with 85th Foot Aug 1813 – Apr 1814. Present at Vimeiro (wounded), Corunna, Coa, Busaco, Pombal, Redinha, Foz d'Arouce, Sabugal, Fuentes d'Onoro, Ciudad Rodrigo (severely wounded), Badajoz (severely wounded), Salamanca, San Munos, Bidassoa, Nivelle, Nive and Bayonne. Gold Medal for Badajoz (led the storming party even though he was wounded). Also served at Walcheren 1809, Malta and Gibraltar (Governor and Commander in Chief 1850–1859).

He wanted to go to the Crimea but was unfit due to his Peninsular wounds. Never left his regiment for one day except when he was wounded. MGS medal for Vimeiro, Corunna, Busaco, Fuentes d'Onoro, Ciudad Rodrigo, Salamanca, Nivelle and Nive. GCB. Colonel 43rd Foot 26 Mar 1850. When Fergusson retired in 1839, General Lord Hill remarked 'that after commanding regiments for more than a quarter of a century he was at liberty to do what he thought proper.'
REFERENCE: *United Service Magazine, Oct 1865, p. 287. Gentleman's Magazine, Dec 1865, pp. 783–4. Oxfordshire Light Infantry Chronicle, 1895, pp. 122–7.*

FERGUSSON, William
Inspector of Military Hospitals.
Memorial: Highgate Cemetery, London. (Photograph)

BENEATH THIS STONE / ARE LAID / THE MORTAL REMAINS OF / WILLIAM FERGUSSON, MD. / INSPECTOR GENERAL OF MILITARY HOSPITALS. / BORN AT AYR, 19TH JUNE 1773 / DIED IN LONDON, 2ND JAN 1847.

Surgeon 90th Foot 19 May 1794. Surgeon 67th Foot 23 Mar 1796. Surgeon 5th Foot 27 Feb 1799. Staff Surgeon 4 Apr 1800. Deputy Inspector of Hospitals 5 Sep 1805. Inspector of Hospitals in the Peninsula (Portugal only) 23 Nov 1809. Inspector of Military Hospitals 18 Feb 1813.

Served on the Staff in the Peninsula Aug 1808 – Jan 1809 and Jun 1809 – Nov 1809. With Portuguese Army Nov 1809 – Nov 1813. Present at Corunna, Douro, Talavera, Busaco. Also served in Flanders 1794, West Indies 1796–1798 (present at St Domingo), the Helder 1799, Copenhagen 1801 and Guadeloupe 1815. MD St Andrew's 1812. He wrote *'The nature and history of marsh poison'*, 1820 in Transactions of the Royal Society of Edinburgh. He had studied the effect of malaria on troops in the Netherlands, Portugal and West Indies. This became an important step to understanding the disease.
REFERENCE: *Dictionary of National Biography. Fergusson, J., Notes and recollections of a professional life, 1846.*

FERRIAR, Thomas Ilderton
Lieutenant. 43rd (Monmouthshire) Light Infantry Regiment of Foot
Memorial tablet: St Ann's Church, St Ann's Square, Manchester, Lancashire. (Photograph)

SACRED TO THE MEMORY OF / JOHN FERRIAR MD / .... / ALSO THEIR ELDEST SON, / THOMAS ILDERTON FERRIAR, / A COLONEL IN THE COLUMBIAN ARMY, WHO WAS / MORTALLY WOUNDED IN THE BATTLE OF CARABOBO, / ON THE 24TH OF JUNE 1821, / AND DIED AT VALENCIA ON THE 17TH OF JULY FOLLOWING / .... / AND / OF THEIR YOUNGEST SON, / JOHN FERRIAR, / LIEUTENANT COLONEL OF THE BATTALION OF CARABOBO, / WHO DIED AT PASTO, COLUMBIA / ON THE 18TH OF MARCH 1839.

Bust on pedestal: Carabobo, Venezuela. (Photograph)

Lt Durham Militia 21 Sep 1812. Ensign 28th Foot 3 Jun 1813. Lt 19 May 1814. Half pay 1814. Lt 43rd Foot 20 Apr 1815. Half pay 25 Mar 1817.

Served in the Peninsula with 1/28th Nov 1813 – Apr 1814. Present at Nivelle, Nive, Garris, Orthes, Aire and Toulouse. At the end of the Peninsular War, some battalions were reduced and many officers not retained. In 1817 Farriar joined the many veterans who were recruited to fight for the independence of Columbia in South America. Simon Bolívar was determined to rid his country of Spanish invaders and these Peninsular veterans were important in his fight for freedom. Ferrier sailed to South America in 1818 and at first commanded a unit of artillery. His previous battle experience was soon evident and by 1821 he was appointed Colonel in command of the British Legion. At the battle of Carabobo 24 Jun 1821, he was able to stem the retreat of the native troops against the Spanish and turn the battle to Bolivar's favour. He was wounded twice and died of his wounds on 17 July. Acknowledged to be one of the heroes in Bolivar's fight for independence. His younger brother John followed him to South America, became Lt Colonel in the Battalion of Carabobo and died there eight years later.
REFERENCE: *Hughes, Ben, Conquer of Die: Wellington's veterans and the liberation of the new world, 2010.*

FERRIOR, Samuel
Major and Lieutenant Colonel. 1st Life Guards.
Memorial tablet: St Mary's Church, Tenby, Wales. (Photograph)

IN MEMORY OF COL CHARLES FERRIOR / .... / HE WAS THE YOUNGEST BROTHER OF / COLONEL SAMUEL FERRIOR / WHO GALLANTLY FELL AT WATERLOO / WHILST CHARGING AT THE HEAD / OF HIS REGIMENT THE 1ST LIFE GUARDS.

Lt 1800. Capt 1 Aug 1802. Major and Lt Colonel 22 Jun 1809.

Commanded his regiment at Waterloo where he was killed. Is reputed to have led his regiment in eleven charges, in some of them when wounded.
REFERENCE: *Dyfed Family History Journal, Vol 8, No 1, Dec 2002, pp. 22–5.*

FILTON, John
Private. 51st (2nd Yorkshire West Riding) Light Infantry.
Buried in St John the Baptist Churchyard, Kirkheaton, Yorkshire. (Burial record)

Served in the Peninsula Oct 1808 – Jan 1809 and Feb 1811 – Apr 1814. Present at Corunna, Fuentes d'Onoro, Salamanca, Vittoria, Pyrenees, Nivelle and Orthes. Died at Rowley Lipton 10 Jun 1852 aged 66 years. MGS medal for Corunna, Fuentes d'Onoro, Salamanca, Vittoria, Pyrenees, Nivelle and Orthes.

FINDLAY, Alexander
Ensign. 2nd West India Regiment of Foot.
Mural memorial in walled enclosure: Kirkton of Ardersier, near Fort George, Invernesshire, Scotland. Seriously eroded. (Photograph)

SACRED / TO / THE MEMORY / OF / COLL ALEXR FINDLAY KH / OF MILLBANK / WHO DIED AT FORT GEORGE ON THE / 9TH MAY 1851, AGED 66 YEARS. / MUCH ESTEEMED AND DEEPLY REGRETTED / BY ALL WHO KNEW HIM. / COLONEL FINDLAY COMMENCED HIS / MILITARY CAREER IN THE 78TH REGT OF FOOT / AND SERVED WITH IT IN EGYPT AND THROUGH THE / CAMPAIGN IN CALABRIA UNDER SIR JOHN STEWART, / WAS PRESENT AT THE BATTLE OF MERXEM FOR WHICH / HE WAS PROMOTED TO ENSIGN IN / THE WEST INDIES AND WAS SUBSEQUENTLY APPOINTED / GOVERNOR OF THE GAMBIA AND SIERRA

LEONE / IN AFRICA, WHERE HE LIVED MANY YEARS AND FOR HIS SERVICES / ON THE COAST IN THE SUPPRESSION OF THE SLAVE TRADE, / RECEIVED FROM THE HANDS OF HIS / SOVEREIGN THE BADGE OF KNIGHTHOOD OF THE 3RD CLASS / OF THE R. H. G. ORDER, IN ADDITION TO A / MAGNIFICENT PIECE OF PLATE PRESENTED TO HIM / BY THE MERCHANTS AND INHABITANTS OVER WHOM HE / PRESIDED, IN TESTIMONY OF THEIR REGARD AND APPROBATION OF HIS MERITS. ON HIS / RETIREMENT FROM THE GOVERN-MENT ON THE 12TH FEBY 1845, / HE RECEIVED THE APPOINTMENT ON THE STAFF AT / FORT GEORGE, INVERNESS AS ACTG GOVERNOR / AND FORT MAJOR, WHICH HE HELD TILL THE DAY OF HIS DEATH. / THIS MONUMENT IS ERECTED BY HIS SON / LIEUT COLL ALEXR FINDLAY OF MILLBANK, NAIRN / AS A TRIBUTE OF FILIAL GRATITUDE AND RESPECT.

Sgt 78th Foot 1813. Ensign 2nd West India Regt 27 Jul 1814. Lt 1 Feb 1816. Capt 24 Oct 1821. Capt Royal African Corps 24 Oct 1824. Major 28 Dec 1826. Lt Colonel 19 Mar 1829. Colonel 26 Oct 1830.

Served in the Netherlands 1813–1814 (present at Merxem where he was awarded a commission as Ensign in 2nd West India Regt for his bravery). Later Governor of Sierra Leone with local rank of Colonel where he was active in suppressing the slave trade. Acting Governor and Fort Major at Fort George 1847–1851. Also served in Egypt 1801 and Maida 1806. Half pay 19 Mar 1829. MGS medal for Maida. KH. REFERENCE: *Annual Register, 1851, Appx, p. 287. United Service Magazine, Jun 1851, p. 320.*

FINDLAY, William
Colour Sergeant. 66th (Berkshire) Regiment of Foot.
Headstone: St Andrew's Churchyard, Kilmarnock, Ayrshire, Scotland. (M.I.)

"WILLIAM FINDLAY, LATE COLOUR SERGEANT 66TH REGT AND BURGH OFFICER WHO DIED IN U. P. CHURCH SUNDAY 23 JUNE 1850, AGED 69."

Served in the Peninsula from Apr 1809. Present at Talavera. MGS medal for Talavera.

FINLEY, Thomas
Sergeant. 12th (Prince of Wales's) Regiment of Light Dragoons.
Named on the Regimental Memorial: St Joseph's Church, Waterloo, Belgium. (Photograph).
    Killed at Waterloo.

FISHER, George Bulteel
Lieutenant Colonel. Royal Artillery.
Memorial tablet: St Luke's Church, Charlton, Kent. (Photograph)

IN MEMORY OF / MAJOR GENERAL SIR GEORGE BULTEEL FISHER K. C. H. / LATE COMMAN-DANT OF THE GARRISON OF WOOLWICH, / WHO DEPARTED THIS LIFE / ON THE 8TH OF MARCH 1834, / IN THE 70TH YEAR OF HIS AGE. / THIS TABLET IS ERECTED BY HIS AFFEC-TIONATE / DAUGHTER.

Altar tomb: St Luke's Churchyard, Charlton, Kent. (No longer extant: Grave number 305). (M.I)

"SACRED TO THE MEMORY OF MAJOR – GENERAL SIR GEORGE BULTEEL FISHER, KCH., COMMANDANT OF WOOLWICH GARRISON, WHO DEPARTED THIS LIFE THE 8TH MARCH, 1834, AGED 70 YEARS."

2nd Lt 1 Jul 1782. 1st Lt 28 May 1790. Capt-Lieut Lt 6 Mar 1795. Capt 18 Apr 1801. Major 3 Dec 1806. Lt Colonel 28 Jun 1808. Colonel 6 Nov 1820. Major General 27 May 1825,

Served in the Peninsula Apr 1809 – May 1813. (GOC Royal Artillery in Lisbon until Nov 1812, Commandant Royal Artillery Nov 1812 – May 1813). KCH. Also served in Gibraltar 1790–1791, Canada 1791–1794 and West Indies 1794–1795 (present at Martinique, St Lucia and Guadeloupe). Commandant of Woolwich Garrison Feb 1827. He was a talented artist who used the scenery in his various postings to great advantage, especially in Canada.

REFERENCE: *Dictionary of Canadian Biography. Gentleman's Magazine, Jun 1834, p. 656.*

FISHER, Henry
Assistant Surgeon. 7th (Royal Fusiliers) Regiment of Foot.
Low monument: Dunkeld Cathedral Churchyard, Perthshire, Scotland. (Grave number 126/72). (Photograph)

IN MEMORY OF HENRY FISHER, ESQ, M. D., / LATE OF THE SEVENTH ROYAL FUSILIERS AND SIXTY THIRD REGIMENTS, / BORN AT DUNKELD 22ND MAY 1790. DIED AT HILLHEAD 21ST SEPTR 1865

Asst Surgeon 7th Foot 3 Jun 1813. Asst Surgeon 63rd Foot 18 Jan 1816.
Served in the Peninsula with 1/7th Jun 1813 – Apr 1814. Present at Vittoria, Pyrenees, Bidassoa, Nivelle, Nive, Orthes and Toulouse. Also served in North America 1814. MGS medal for Vittoria, Pyrenees, Nivelle, Nive, Orthes and Toulouse. MD Edinburgh 1811. Retired on half pay 19 Jan 1821.

FISHER, James
Private. 12th (Prince of Wales's) Regiment of Light Dragoons.
Named on the Regimental Memorial: St Joseph's Church, Waterloo, Belgium. (Photograph)
Killed at Waterloo.

FISHER, William
Captain. 40th (2nd Somersetshire) Regiment of Foot.
Memorial tablet: St Mary's Church, Wavendon, Buckinghamshire. (Photograph)

TO THE MEMORY OF / CAPTAIN WILLIAM FISHER, / OF THE 40TH REGT OF FOOT, / WHO, / AFTER SERVING HIS COUNTRY / THROUGH THE WHOLE OF THE / WAR IN THE PENINSULA, / AS WELL AS IN / NORTH AND SOUTH AMERICA, / FELL AT WATERLOO, / JUNE 18TH 1815 / AGED 28. / HAY, PICTON, PONSONBY! A GRATEFUL LAND / IN HER PROUD ANNALS NOW INSCRIBES HER GRIEF / ON ARCH, URN, OBELISK, WITH TREMBLING HAND / YOUR NAMES INDENTING; THINE NO HIGH RELIEF / SHALL TELL, MY BROTHER, BUT INSCRIPTION BRIEF, THE SIMPLE / TRIBUTE TO AFFECTION DUE: / WHILST ENGLAND HOLDS THE DUST OF EACH LOVED CHIEF, / MINE IS THE REMINISCENCE EVER NEW, / THAT ONE SMALL SPECK IS THINE IN GRAVE STREW'D / WATERLOO.

Lt 9 May 1805. Capt 19 Sep 1811. Portuguese Army: Capt 24th Line 29 Dec 1810
Served in the Peninsula with 40th Foot Aug 1808 – Dec 1810 and Sep 1813 – Apr 1814, and Portuguese Army Dec 1810 – May 1813. Retired from the Portuguese Army Nov 1813.
Present at Rolica, Vimeiro, Busaco, Salamanca, Burgos, Nivelle, Nive, Orthes and Toulouse. Present at Waterloo where he was killed in a square by a cannon ball. Also served in South America 1807 and North America 1814–1815.

FITTON, John
Sergeant. 51st (2nd Yorkshire West Riding) Light Infantry.
Named on the Regimental Memorial: KOYLI Chapel, York Minster, Yorkshire. (Photograph)
Killed in the Peninsula.

FITZCLARENCE, George

Captain. 24th Regiment of Light Dragoons.
Memorial slab: St Mary the Virgin Church, Hampton-on-Thames, London. (In floor of the centre aisle, covered with a carpet). (M.I.)

"THE RIGHT HONOURABLE GEORGE EARL OF MUNSTER / VISCOUNT FITZCLARENCE & BARON TEWKESBURY. ELDEST / SON OF HIS LATE MAJESTY KING WILLIAM THE FOURTH / PRIVY COUNSELLOR. MAJOR GENERAL IN THE ARMY. / GOVERNOR & CAPTAIN ALSO CONSTABLE & LIEUTENANT / OF WINDSOR CASTLE. KNIGHT GRAND CROSS OF THE / ORDER OF FERDINAND OF WURTEMBURG. / BORN 29 JANUARY 1794 / DIED 20 MARCH 1842 / ...."

Cornet 10th Lt Dragoons 3 Feb 1807. Lt 9 Mar 1809. Capt 2 Aug 1811. Capt 24th Lt Dragoons Nov 1814. Bt Major 16 Jun 1818. Bt Lt Colonel 21 Jan 1819. Capt 14th Lt Dragoons 21 Mar 1822. Major 1st West India Regt 12 Dec 1822. Major 6th Dragoon Guards 29 Dec 1822. Capt and Lt Colonel Coldstream Guards 6 Jul 1825. Bt Colonel 22 Jul 1830. Major General 23 Nov 1841.

Served in the Peninsula Nov 1808 – Oct 1809, May 1810 – Oct 1811 and Feb 1813 – Apr 1814. (ADC to Major General Slade Nov – Dec 1808, ADC to Major General Charles Stewart May 1810 – Oct 1811 and Feb – Apr 1813. DAAG at Headquarters May – Aug 1813). Present at Busaco, Fuentes d'Onoro (wounded), Vittoria, Pyrenees, Orthes and Toulouse (severely wounded). Also served in India 1815–1818. Brought home despatches from India, but broke his leg on arrival. While he was incapacitated wrote *Journal of the Tour in India*, 1819. Half pay 24 Dec 1828. DAG 21 Aug 1830, but only held the post for a few months.

Founding member of the Royal Asiatic Society and Oriental Translation Fund. This introduced Oriental literature to a wider audience. He was about to produce a book on eastern military art and weapons of war when he died. Later became Earl of Munster. Illegitimate son of William IV.
REFERENCE: *Gentleman's Magazine, May 1842, pp. 548–50 (under Munster). Annual Register, 1842, Appx, pp. 258–9 (under Munster).*

FITZGERALD, Edward Thomas

Captain. 25th (King's Own Borderer's) Regiment of Foot.
Box tomb: Turlough Church, County Mayo, Ireland. (In chapel of roofless church). (Photograph)

TO THE MEMORY OF / LT COLONEL EDWARD THOMAS FITZGERALD K.H. / SECOND SON OF / COL CHARLES AND DOROTHEA FITZGERALD / OF TURLO CO. MAYO. / HE SERVED FAITHFULLY / AT THE BATTLES OF / MERXEM, BERGEN OP ZOOM AND WATERLOO / AND DEPARTED THIS LIFE / VERY DEEPLY LAMENTED / SEPTEMBER 19TH 1845 / AGED 60 YEARS.

Ensign 13 Jun 1804. Lt 16 May 1806. Capt 28 Aug 1806. Bt Major 17 Mar 1814. Bt Lt Colonel 22 Jul 1830.

Present at Waterloo on Staff as DQMG (wounded). Also served in the Netherlands 1814–1815 (present at Merxem and Bergen-op-Zoom). KH. Half pay 25 Jan 1818.

FITZGERALD, James

Lieutenant. 87th (Prince of Wales's Own Irish) Regiment of Foot.
Named on the Memorial: St Andrew's Church, (now Musée Historique), Biarritz, France. (Photograph)

Ensign 29 Dec 1809. Lt 24 Jun 1812.

Served in the Peninsula Apr 1810 – Feb 1814. Present at Cadiz, Barrosa, Tarifa, Vittoria, Pyrenees, Nivelle and Orthes where he was killed 27 Feb 1814.

FITZGERALD, Richard
Captain. 2ⁿᵈ Life Guards.
Memorial tablet: Wellington Museum, Waterloo, Belgium. Seriously eroded. (Photograph)

D.O.M. / SACRED TO THE MEMORY OF LIEUTENANT-COLONEL RICHARD FITZGERALD OF THE 2 REGIMENT OF LIFE GUARDS OF HIS BRITANNIC MAJESTY'S WHO FELL GLORIOUS AT THE BATTLE OF BELLE ALLIANCE, NEAR THE TOWN ON THE 18ᵀᴴ JUNE 1815 IN THE 41ˢᵀ YEAR OF HIS LIFE DEEPLY AND DESERVEDLY REGRETTED BY HIS FAMILY AND FRIENDS. TO A MANLY LOFTINESS OF SOUL HE UNITED ALL THE VIRTUES THAT COULD RENDER HIM AN ORNAMENT TO HIS PROFESSION AND TO PRIVATE AND SOCIAL LIFE.

Memorial tablet: Wellington Museum, Waterloo, Belgium. (Photograph)

"A ... / ... DU PLUS VERTUEUX DES HOMES GÉNÉRALEMENT ESTIMÉ / ET REGRETTÉ DE SA FAMILLE ET DE SES AMIS LE LIEUTENANT COLONEL / RICHARD FITZGERALD DE LA GARDE DU CORPS DE SA MAJESTÉ / BRITANNIQUE TUÉ GLORIEUSEMENT A LA BATAILLE DE LA BELLE ALLIANCE, / LE 18 JUIN 1815. RIP."

Memorial tablet: St Joseph's Church, Waterloo, Belgium. (Photograph)

SACRED / TO THE MEMORY / OF / LIEUᵀ COLᴺ RICHᴿᴰ FITZGERALD. / OF HIS B. Mˢ. 2ᴺᴰ LIFE GUARDS / WHO FELL IN THE FIELD OF WATERLOO / JUNE 18ᵀᴴ 1815, / IN THE 41ˢᵀ YEAR OF HIS AGE. / HIS REMAINS ARE DEPOSITED IN THE CHURCH YARD. / THIS TABLET IS ERECTED AS A TRIBUTE OF GRATITUDE / TO HIS WORTH BY HIS AFFLICTED FATHER.

Memorial tablet: St Marylebone Church, Marylebone, London. (Photograph)

IN MEMORY OF / LIEUT-COL RICHARD FITZGERALD, OF THE IIᴰ LIFE GUARDS, / WHO FELL IN THE XLIII YEAR OF HIS AGE, IN THE FIELD OF / WATERLOO; / ....

Capt 18 May 1812. Bt Lt Colonel 4 Jun 1814.
   Served in the Peninsula Mar – Apr 1814. Present at Toulouse. Present at Waterloo where he was killed leading a charge. He had been detained in France with his family for ten years from 1802–1812. On his return to England, he purchased a troop in the 2ⁿᵈ Life Guards and went to southern France to fight at Toulouse at the end of the war.
Note discrepancy in age between St Marylebone memorial and Waterloo.

FITZGIBBON, James
Captain. Glengarry Light Infantry Fencibles.
Buried in St. George's Chapel, Windsor, Berkshire.

Ensign and Adjt 49ᵗʰ Foot 6 Feb 1806. Lt 7 Jun 1809. Capt Glengarry Lt Infantry Fencibles 14 Oct 1813.
   Served with the 49ᵗʰ Foot as a marine on board HMS *Monarch* at Copenhagen 1807. Also served in North America 1812–1814. (present at Stoney Creek, Fort St George, siege of Fort Erie and Weaver Dams). Military Knight of Windsor 12 Jun 1850. Died at Windsor 13 Dec 1863.

FITZROY, Lord Charles
Lieutenant and Captain. 1ˢᵗ Regiment of Foot Guards.
Family Memorial tablet: St John the Evangelist Church, Wicken, Northamptonshire. (South wall of Nave). (Photograph)

................./ AND IN MEMORY OF / LORD CHARLES FITZROY / WHO DIED JUNE XVII MDCC-CLXV / IN THE LXXIVTH YEAR OF HIS AGE / HE WAS SECOND SON OF AUGUSTUS HENRY DUKE OF GRAFTON / BOTH FATHER AND DAUGHTER ARE BURIED IN THE CHANCEL / (VERSE)

Stone Cross: St Mary the Virgin Churchyard, Hampton-on-Thames, London. (No longer extant). (The cross was dismantled in the early 1970's and the inscription was illegible at that time)

Ensign 82nd Foot 27 May 1807. Ensign 1st Foot Guards 25 Jun 1807. Lt and Capt 23 Sep 1812. Bt Major 18 Jun 1815. Bt Lt Colonel 21 Jan 1819. Major 55th Foot 27 Jan 1820. Major 64th Foot 18 May 1826. Lt Colonel 10 Jun 1826. Lt Colonel 87th 27 Sep 1833.

Served in the Peninsula with 3rd Battalion Oct 1808 – Jan 1809 and Jul 1811 – Apr 1814. Present at Corunna, Cadiz, Badajoz, Almarez, Alba de Tormes, Vittoria, Pyrenees, Nivelle, Nive, Garris, Orthes, Aire, Tarbes and Toulouse. Present at Waterloo (DAG) and with the Army of Occupation 1815–1817. Also served in the Ionian Islands (Inspecting Field Officer of Militia 3 Apr 1828) and Ireland 1832 (AAG). Retired 4 Oct 1833. MP for Thetford 1818–1832 and Bury St Edmunds. MGS medal for Corunna, Badajoz, Vittoria, Pyrenees, Nivelle, Nive, Orthes and Toulouse. Died 17 Jun 1865.
REFERENCE: *Gentleman's Magazine, Jul 1865, p. 126.*

FLEMING, Edward

Major. 2nd West India Regiment of Foot.
Monument: Kensal Green Cemetery, London. Inscription largely illegible (15911/87/RS). (Photograph)

SACRED / TO THE MEMORY OF / LIEUT GENERAL / EDWARD FLEMING / ....

Ensign 66th Foot 9 Jul 1803. Lt 31st Foot 6 Jul 1804. Capt 30 May 1807. Major 2nd West India Regt 1 Apr 1813. Lt Colonel 18 Jul 1816. Lt Colonel 2nd Ceylon Regt 12 Aug 1819. Lt Colonel 53rd Foot 24 Feb 1826. Bt Colonel 10 Jan 1837. Major General 9 Nov 1846. Lt General 20 Jun 1854.

Served in the Peninsula Nov 1808 – Jun 1811 with 31st Foot. Present in the Corunna campaign, Talavera, Busaco, first siege of Badajoz and Albuera where he was severely wounded. Also served in Sicily 1805, Egypt 1807 (present at Alexandria and Rosetta), West Indies 1813–1819 (went to Southern States of America 1814), India 1820–1823 and Canada 1829–1833. CB. Inspecting Field Officer with the Recruiting staff 1840. MGS medal for Talavera, Busaco and Albuera. Colonel 27th Foot 19 Sep 1853. Died 23 Apr 1860.

FLEMING, Hugh

Lieutenant. 24th (Warwickshire) Regiment of Foot.
Buried in St George's Chapel, Windsor, Berkshire. (Burial record)

Ensign 11 Jan 1810. Adjutant 11 Jun 1810. Lt 26 Mar 1813.

Served in the Peninsula Jan 1810 – Apr 1814 (from Dec 1812 in 3rd Provisional Battalion). Present at Douro (taken prisoner at Plascencia 2 Aug 1809, but escaped ten days later and rejoined regiment), Busaco, Foz d'Arouce, Fuentes d'Onoro, Ciudad Rodrigo, Salamanca, Burgos and retreat from Burgos, Vittoria, Pyrenees (wounded at Echellar 2 Aug 1813), Bidassoa, Nivelle, Orthes and Bordeaux.

Also served in the ranks in Flanders 1793–1795 (present at Lincelles and Tournai), the Helder 1799, Hanover 1805 and Copenhagen 1807. MGS medal for Busaco, Fuentes d'Onoro, Ciudad Rodrigo, Salamanca, Vittoria, Pyrenees, Nivelle and Orthes. Military Knight of Windsor 28 Jan 1835. Died at Windsor 30 Aug 1856.

FLEMING, Pierre Edward

Captain. 3rd (East Kent) Regiment of Foot.
Gravestone: Protestant Cemetery, Naples, Italy. (M.I.)

"CAPT. PIER. EDWD. FLEMING, 3ᴿᴰ FOOT, OB. A. PORTICI, 21 JULY 1835, A. 64."

Ensign 88ᵗʰ Foot 2 Jun 1804. Lt 3ʳᵈ Garrison Battalion 25 Feb 1805. Lt 48ᵗʰ Foot 18 Feb 1808. Capt 57ᵗʰ Foot 23 Mar 1809. Capt 3ʳᵈ Foot 4 Jun 1812.
    Served in the Peninsula May – Jul 1809. Half pay 3 Oct 1816.

FLETCHER, John Wynne
Captain. 4ᵗʰ (King's Own) Regiment of Foot.
Memorial tablet: St Michael's Cathedral, Bridgetown, Barbados, West Indies. (Photograph)

SACRED TO THE MEMORY / OF A GOOD CHRISTIAN, A GALLANT SOLDIER, AND AN HONEST MAN / IN LIFE BELOVED AND IN DEATH LAMENTED. / NEAR THIS SPOT REST THE MORTAL REMAINS OF BREVET MAJOR / JOHN WYNNE FLETCHER. / (CAPTAIN IN THE 4ᵀᴴ KING'S OWN REGIMENT OF FOOT / AND AIDE-DE-CAMP TO Lᵀ GENᴸ SIR HENRY WARDE.) / WHO DEPARTED THIS LIFE / ON THE 24ᵀᴴ OF OCTOBER 1824. / AGED 39 YEARS.

Named on the Regimental Memorial: St Michael's Cathedral, Bridgetown, Barbados, West Indies. (Photograph)

Ensign 12 Nov 1799. Lt 6 Jan 1801. Capt 4 Jun 1807. Bt Major 19 Jul 1821
    Served in the Peninsula with 1/4ᵗʰ Jun 1812 – Apr 1814. Present at Salamanca, retreat from Burgos, Villa Muriel, Vittoria, San Sebastian (wounded), Bidassoa, Nive and Bayonne. Also served in North America 1814 (wounded at New Orleans) and West Indies (ADC to Lt General Sir Henry Warde, Governor of Barbados).

FLETCHER, Sir Richard
Lieutenant Colonel. Royal Engineers.
Column: Alhandra, Lisbon, Portugal. (Photograph)

TO THE MEMORY OF J. (SIC) FLETCHER LIEUTENANT / COLONEL OF ENGINEERS IN THE ENGLISH ARMY / TO WHOSE SKILL AND TIRELESS ENERGY IS DUE / THE RAPID CONSTRUC-TION OF THE LINES / OF TORRES VEDRAS. / THE OFFICERS OF THE ENGINEERS OF THE / PORTUGUESE ARMY. / ERECTED 1883

A' MEMORIA / DE / J. (SIC) FLETCHER / TENENTE-CORONEL DE ENGENHARIA DO EXERCITO INGLEZ / A CUJA COMETENCIA E INCANSARD ACTIVIDADE / SE DEVE A RAPIDA CONSTRUCCAS DAS / LINHAS DE TORRES VEDRAS / OF OFFICIAES / DA ARMA DE ENGEN-HARIA / DO / EXERCITO PORTUGUEZ / 5-III–1911

(The statue is also dedicated to J. M. das Neves Costa.)

Memorial: Westminster Abbey. (Inscription recorded from memorial inscription. (Detail of Photograph only)

"ERECTED BY THE CORPS OF ENGINEERS TO THE MEMORY OF LIEU. COLONEL SIR RICHARD FLETCHER KNT. AND BARONET WHO AFTER HIGHLY DISTINGUISHED SERVICES AS COMMANDING ROYAL ENGINEER WITH THE ARMY UNDER THE DUKE OF WELLINGTON IN THE PENINSULAR WAR WAS KILLED AT THE STORMING OF SAN SEBAS-TIAN IN THE 45ᵀᴴ YEAR OF HIS AGE".

Monument to Fletcher, Rhodes, Collyer and Machell: San Sebastian, Spain. (Photograph)

TO FLETCHER, RHODES, COLLYER AND MACHELL.

Named on the Regimental Memorial: Rochester Cathedral, Rochester, Kent. (Photograph)

Named on the headstone to his son: St John the Baptist Churchyard, Pitchcombe, Gloucestershire. (Photograph)

IN REMEMBRANCE / OF / SIR RICHARD JOHN FLETCHER / WHO DIED AT PITCHCOMBE HOUSE / 25TH DEC^R 1870 / AGED 70 YEARS. / HE WAS SON OF THE LATE / SIR RICHARD FLETCHER / OF THE ROYAL ENGINEERS / WHO FELL AT THE STORMING OF / ST SEBASTIAN 31ST AUGUST 1813.

2nd Lt Royal Artillery 9 Jul 1788. 2nd Lt Royal Engineers 29 Jun 1790. 1st Lt 16 Jan 1793. Capt–Lt 18 Jun 1797. Capt 18 Apr 1801. Bt Major 2 Apr 1807. Bt Lt Colonel 4 Mar 1809. Lt Colonel 24 Jun 1809.
    Served in the Peninsula Aug 1808 – Jan 1809 and May 1809 – Aug 1813. Present at Corunna, Talavera (Mentioned in Despatches), Busaco (Mentioned in Despatches), Torres Vedras (reconnaissance for route of lines made with Wellington, and QMG Oct 1809. Mentioned in Despatches), first siege of Badajoz (Mentioned in Despatches), second siege of Badajoz (Mentioned in Despatches), Ciudad Rodrigo (Mentioned in Despatches), Badajoz (Mentioned in Despatches and wounded 19 Mar 1812), Vittoria (Mentioned in Despatches), San Sebastian (wounded 25 Jul 1813 and later killed at San Sebastian 31 Aug 1813. Mentioned in Despatches). Gold Cross for Talavera, Busaco, Ciudad Rodrigo, Badajoz, Vittoria and San Sebastian. KB May 1812. Baronet Dec 1812. KTS. Also served in the West Indies 1794–1796 (present at Martinique, St Lucia where he was wounded and Guadeloupe), Egypt 1801 and the Baltic 1807. Took command of the Royal Engineers in the Peninsula after the battle of Vimeiro, and then joined Wellington's staff as Commanding Royal Engineer. He was a brilliant engineer and the Lines of Torres Vedras were an example of his work. Augustus Frazer said at his death 'no loss will be more deeply felt, no place more difficult to be filled up'.
REFERENCE: *Dictionary of National Biography.*

FLETCHER, Simon
Private. 1st (Royal) Regiment of Dragoons.
Headstone: Old Churchyard, Langholm, Dumfriesshire, Scotland. (Reverse of stone to Simon Fletcher, late Gamekeeper). (Photograph)

IN MEMORY OF / SIMON FLETCHER, PENSIONER FROM / 1ST ROYAL DRAGOONS IN WHICH HE / SERVED 21 YEARS IN GREAT BRITAIN, / IRELAND, HOLLAND, PORTUGAL, SPAIN / & FRANCE, WHERE HE FOUGHT IN 32 / BATTLES INCLUDING WATERLOO. / HE DIED FEB 4TH 1824 AGED 45 YEARS.

Pte 1803.
    Served in the Peninsula Sep 1809 – Apr 1814. Present at Fuentes d'Onoro, Aldea da Ponte, Maguilla, Vittoria and Toulouse. Present at Waterloo in Captain C. E. Radclyffe's No 1 or 'E' Troop. Also served in Ireland and the Netherlands.

FLETCHER, Thomas
Captain. 4th Ceylon Regiment.
Memorial tablet: St Paul's Church, Kandy, Ceylon. (Photograph)

TO THE MEMORY OF / LIEU^T COLONEL THOMAS FLETCHER / WHO FOR ELEVEN YEARS HELD THE COMMAND OF THE CEYLON RIFLE REGIMENT, / CONJOINED LATTERLY WITH THAT OF THE TROOPS IN THESE PROVINCES. / THIS TABLET IS ERECTED BY HIS BROTHER OFFICERS / TO COMMEMORATE THEIR DEEP SORROW FOR HIS LOSS / AND TO BEAR RECORD OF THE MILITARY WORTH FOR WHICH HE WAS / SO HIGHLY APPRECIATED AS A SOLDIER. / THE ZEAL AND RECTITUDE THAT MARKED HIS PUBLIC SERVICES, / AND THE AMIABLE, SINCERE, AND SOCIAL VIRTUES THAT ENDEARED HIM TO ALL / AND ADORNED HIS CHARACTER AS A MAN. / HAVING SERVED IN EARLY LIFE IN THE PENINSULA AND AT WALCHEREN IN THE 6TH FOOT / AND BEEN PRESENT AT ROLEIA, VIMIERA, AND CORUNNA, / HE WAS APPOINTED TO THE CEYLON REGIMENT IN 1810, / WAS ACTIVELY EMPLOYED IN THE KANDIAN OPERATIONS IN 1815, AND 1818, / AND AFTER THIRTY FIVE YEARS OF CIVIL AND MILITARY DUTIES IN CEYLON, HE RETIRED / AND DIED AT MALTA ON THE 8TH MARCH 1846, AGED 60, / WHEN RETURNING TO HIS NATIVE LAND.

Ensign 6th Foot 28 Jul 1803. Lt 13 Mar 1805. Capt 12 Mar 1810. Capt 4th Ceylon Regt 6 Oct 1810. Major 6 Dec 1827. Lt Colonel 27 Feb 1835.

Served in the Peninsula Aug 1808 – Jan 1809. Present at Rolica, Vimeiro and Corunna. Also served at Walcheren 1809 and Ceylon (present in the Kandian Rebellion 1815–1818). Remained in Ceylon for 35 years undertaking military and civil duties. Retired in 1846, but died in Malta on his way back to England. REFERENCE: *Lewis, J. Penry, List of inscriptions on tombstones and monuments in Ceylon, 1913, reprint 1994, p. 324.*

FLOYD, Henry
Captain. 10th (Prince of Wales's Own) Regiment of Light Dragoons.
Pedestal tomb: Kensal Green Cemetery, London. (20822/102/IC). (Photograph)

TO THE MEMORY OF / MAJOR GENERAL / SIR HENRY FLOYD, BART. / BORN 2ND SEPTEMBER 1793 / DIED 4TH MARCH 1868. / SERVED IN THE PENINSULA, / AND AT WATERLOO.

Memorial window: St Giles and St Nicholas Church, Sidmouth, Devon. (Photograph)

IN MEMORY OF GENERAL SIR HENRY FLOYD BART. 1868.

Cornet 8th Lt Dragoons 7 Jul 1808. Cornet 19th Lt Dragoons 20 Apr 1809. Lt 15 Mar 1810 Capt York Chasseurs 2 Dec 1813. Capt 10th Lt Dragoons 12 Nov 1814. Major 16 Nov 1820. Major 8th Lt Dragoons 28 Jun 1821. Lt Colonel 6 May 1824. Bt Colonel 28 Jun 1838. Major General 11 Nov 1851.

Served in the Peninsula Oct 1812 – Apr 1814 (ADC to Major General W. H. Clinton). Present at Biar, Castalla, Tarragona, Ordal and blockade of Barcelona. Present at Quatre Bras, Waterloo, the Capture of Paris and with the Army of Occupation. Also served in Sicily 1811 (ADC to Major General W. H. Clinton). Succeeded to baronetcy 1818. Half pay 6 May 1824.

FLOYD, Thomas
Sergeant. 16th (Queen's) Regiment of Light Dragoons.
Headstone: St Mary the Virgin Churchyard, Eccles. Lancashire. (No longer extant)

HERE / RESTETH THE BODY OF / THOMAS FLOYD OF ECCLES WHO / DEPARTED THIS LIFE MAY 7TH / 1859 AGED 74. / ....

Funeral memoriam card: (Photograph)

IN MEMORIAM / THOMAS FLOYD / LATE SERGEANT IN THE 16TH LIGHT DRAGOONS. / MR

FLOYD JOINED THE 16TH LIGHT DRAGOONS IN 1805, / AND WAS AT THE BATTLES OF TALAVERA, BENACO, FUENTOS / DE ONORE, CIUDAD RODRIGO, BADAJOS, SALAMANCA, VITTORIA, / ST SEBASTIAN AND WATERLOO. AT THE INDUCEMENT OF THE / ARMY IN 1817, HE WAS DISCHARGED AT DUBLIN, AND PASSED / THE ROYAL HOSPITAL KILMAINHAM. HE WAS WOUNDED AT / THE BATTLE OF FUENTES DE ONORE ON THE RIGHT SHOULDER BY A / SWORD CUT, AND TAKEN PRISONER, BUT WAS IMMEDIATELY / RESCUED BY ONE OF THE FIRST ROYALS, WHO FOUGHT THE CAPTURER / SINGLE- HANDED AND KILLED HIM. MR FLOYD WAS ALSO / WOUNDED IN THE HEAD BY A SWORD CUT AT THE BATTLE OF / TALAVERA, AND HIS HORSE WAS SHOT UNDER HIM. HE DIED AT / HIS RESIDENCE IN ECCLES ON THE 7TH MAY, 1859, AND WAS / INTERRED AT ECCLES CHURCH, ON THE 12TH. HE WAS IN THE / 75TH YEAR OF HIS AGE. THE PENINSULAR AND OTHER MEDALS / WHICH HE GAINED WERE LEFT AS MEMENTOS TO HIS DESCENDANTS.

Pte 1805.

Served in the Peninsula Apr 1809 – Apr 1814. Present at Talavera (wounded), Busaco, Fuentes d'Onoro (wounded, taken prisoner but immediately rescued by a soldier in the 1st Royal Dragoons), Ciudad Rodrigo, Badajoz, Salamanca, Vittoria and Nive. Present at Waterloo. MGS medal for Talavera, Fuentes d'Onoro, Salamanca, Vittoria and Nive. Retired on half pay 1817.
REFERENCE: Obit. Eccles and Patricroft Journal, 5 Nov 1886.

FLUDYER, George
Ensign. 1st Regiment of Foot Guards.
Memorial: Royal Military Chapel, Wellington Barracks, London. (M.I.) (Destroyed by a Flying Bomb in 1944)

"CHANCEL STALLS ARE GIVEN BY................. /THE REVEREND SIR J. HENRY FLUDYER, / BART, IN MEMORY OF HIS BROTHER, / LIEUT.-COLONEL GEORGE FLUDYER, GRENADIER GUARDS, 1814–34, WOUNDED AT WATERLOO."

Ensign 13 Jan 1814. Lt and Capt 15 Mar 1821. Capt and Lt Colonel 19 Nov 1830.
Present at Quatre Bras (severely wounded) and Waterloo. Retired 9 May 1834. Died Feb 1856.

FOGO, James
2nd Captain. Royal Artillery.
Headstone: Wauchope Old Cemetery, near Langholm, Dumfriesshire, Scotland. (Photograph)

JAMES FOGO / LIEUTENANT GENERAL R. A. / DIED AT KIRTLETON, 7TH AUGUST 1866, / AGED 78 YEARS.

2nd Lt 18 Jun 1804. 1st Lt 21 Dec 1804. 2nd Capt 14 Oct 1814. Capt 25 Nov 1828. Bt Major 10 Jan 1837. Lt Colonel 23 Nov 1841. Major General 29 Aug 1857.
Served in Belgium and the Netherlands 1815–1817. Also served in North America 1805–1815 (present at Plattsburgh), West Indies 1822–1827, 1829–1830 and 1831–1833. Retired on full pay 12 Apr 1842.

FOLLETT, George
Lieutenant. 43rd (Monmouthshire) Light Infantry Regiment of Foot.
Family Memorial tablet: St Margaret's Church, Topsham, Devon. (Photograph)

.... / ALSO TO THE MEMORY OF / GEORGE FOLLETT THEIR ELDEST SON / LIEUT. IN THE 43RD REGT OF LIGHT INFANTRY WHO WAS / KILLED IN ACTION NEAR ST SEBASTIAN IN SPAIN / AUGUST 31ST 1813, AGED 18 YEARS. / ....

Ensign 22 Aug 1810. Lt 14 May 1812.
    Served in the Peninsula Aug 1813. Present at San Sebastian where he was killed 31 Aug 1813.

FORBES, Alexander
Lieutenant. 79th (Cameron Highlanders) Regiment of Foot.
Family Memorial monument: Holy Rood Churchyard (Auld Kirk), Stirling, Stirlingshire, Scotland. (Photograph)

………… / ALEXANDER FORBES / MAJOR 79TH HIGHLANDERS. DIED AT KINGSTON / UPPER CANADA, 30TH MARCH 1851. AGED 58 YEARS. / ………………..

Ensign 28 Sep 1809. Lt 8 Aug 1811. Capt 17 Mar 1825. Major 7 Aug 1835.
    Served in the Peninsula Aug 1811 – Jul 1812, and Sep 1813 – Apr 1814. Present in a covering capacity at two sieges of Badajoz, Nivelle and Nive. MGS medal for Nivelle and Nive. Served at Quatre Bras and Waterloo (wounded). Also served in Canada 1829–1836 (especially mentioned in regimental orders for his care of the sick during the cholera epidemic 1832). Retired 3 Apr 1846.

FORBES, Charles Ferguson
Deputy Inspector General of Hospitals. Medical Department.
Interred in Catacomb B (Pub v Ave 10 – 12 1/160) Kensal Green Cemetery, London.

Hospital Mate 1798. Asst Surgeon 1st Foot 9 Jan 1799. Surgeon 1st Foot 22 Dec 1804. Staff Surgeon 21 Jul 1808. Asst Inspector of Physicians 31 Jan 1811. Deputy Inspector General 18 Feb 1813.
    Served in the Peninsula Nov 1808 – Jan 1809, Aug 1809 – Jun 1811 and Dec 1811 – Apr 1814. Present at Corunna, Busaco, Badajoz and San Sebastian. KCH. KC. Also served at the Helder 1799, Ferrol 1800, Egypt 1801 and West Indies 1803 (present at St Lucia and Tobago). MGS medal for Egypt, Corunna, Busaco, Badajoz and San Sebastian.
    After the war practised as a physician in London having gained his MD in Edinburgh 1808. Appointed to the newly opened Royal Westminster Infirmary for Diseases of the Eye along with George James Guthrie 1816. In 1827 they disagreed over some treatment and it almost became a libel case. Forbes, after a duel between himself and one of Guthrie's supporters, resigned and set up in private practice. Died 22 Mar 1852.
    REFERENCE: *Dictionary of National Biography. Gentleman's Magazine, Apr 1852, p. 422. Annual Register, 1852, Appx, pp. 267–8.*

FORBES, Duncan
Captain. 36th (Herefordshire) Regiment of Foot.
Family Memorial tablet: Canongate Cemetery, Edinburgh, Scotland. (M.I.)

"GEORGE STUART FORBES ESQ REPRESENTATIVE OF THE ANCIENT FAMILY OF BRUX ………………… ONLY SON CAPT DUNCAN BARBAROUSLY MURDERED BY THE PORTUGUESE NEAR ABRANTES 28 JULY 1812."

Lt 6 Feb 1806. Capt 28 Feb 1812.
    Served in the Peninsula Aug 1808 – Jan 1809 and Mar 1811 – Jul 1812. Present at Rolica, Vimeiro, Corunna and Barba del Puerco. Murdered near Abrantes 28 Jul 1812.

FORBES, Duncan
Private. 2nd (Royal North British) Regiment of Dragoons.
Memorial tablet: Irvine Churchyard, Irvine, Ayrshire, Scotland. (Photograph)

TO THE MEMORY OF / DUNCAN FORBES / PRIVATE IN THE 2ND OR ROYAL / SCOTS GREYS / WHO FELL GLORIOUSLY AT / WATERLOO / 18TH JUNE 1815 / ERECTED BY HIS TOWNSMEN

Served at Waterloo where he was killed in the cavalry charge.

FORBES, Hon. Hastings Brudenel
Lieutenant and Captain. 3rd Regiment of Foot Guards.
Memorial tablet: Inside Mausoleum, Evere Cemetery, Brussels, Belgium. (Photograph)

CAPTAIN / THE HON^{BLE} / HASTINGS BRUDENEL / FORBES / 3RD ROYAL / FOOT GUARDS / AGED 22

Ledger stone: Evere Cemetery, Brussels, Belgium. Seriously eroded and largely illegible. (M.I.)

"CAPTAIN H. B. FORBES, 18 JUNE 1815"

Named on the Regimental Memorial: St Joseph's Church, Waterloo, Belgium. (Photograph)
Named on Memorial Panel VIII for Waterloo: Royal Military Chapel, Wellington Barracks, London. (M.I.) (Destroyed by a Flying Bomb 1944)

Ensign 17 Jan 1811. Lt and Capt 5 May 1814.
   Served in the Peninsula Jul 1812 – Apr 1814. Present at Burgos and Bayonne. Present at Waterloo where he was killed. One of the select band of soldiers buried in the Mausoleum at Evere.

FORBES, Hon. James
Ensign. Coldstream Regiment of Foot Guards.
Tombstone: Old British Cemetery, Leghorn, Italy. (M.I.)

"SACRED TO THE MEMORY / OF LIEUTENANT COLONEL / THE HONOURABLE JAMES FORBES / OF H. B. M. COLDSTREAM REG^{T} OF GUARDS / (ELDEST SON OF GENERAL LORD FORBES OF SCOTLAND) / WHO IN THE PRIME OF LIFE, AND AT A MOMENT / OF PARTICI-PATION IN THE SPLENDOUR, / AND FESTIVITIES OF A BALL IN THE PITTI PALACE / AT FLORENCE ON THE 25TH OF FEBRUARY 1835 / WAS SUDDENLY REMOVED FROM THE WORLD / BY AN ATTACK OF APOPLEXY / IN THE 38TH YEAR OF HIS AGE / THUS AFFORDING / AN AWEFULLY STRIKING INSTANCE / OF THE INSTABILITY OF HUMAN ENJOYMENT / AND OF THE UNCERTAINTY OF HUMAN LIFE / HIS AFFLICTED FAMILY HAVE CAUSED / THIS STONE WITH THIS SIMPLE RECORD / OF HIS UNTIMELY FATE WHICH IT BEARS / TO BE PLACED OVER HIS GRAVE."

Memorial: Royal Military Chapel, Wellington Barracks, London. (M.I.) (Destroyed by a Flying Bomb in 1944)

"LIEUTENANT-COLONEL THE HON. JAMES FORBES. / COLDSTREAM GUARDS, 1812–35. DIED, 1835. / "BAYONNE," "WATERLOO.""

Ensign 13 Feb 1812. Lt and Capt 14 Dec 1815. Capt and Lt Colonel 22 Jul 1830.
   Served in the Peninsula Mar – Apr 1814. Present at Bayonne. Present at Waterloo. Elder brother of Ensign Walter Forbes Coldstream Guards.

FORBES, James

Physician. Medical Department.

Memorial tablet: Rochester Cathedral, Rochester, Kent. (Photograph)

SACRED TO THE MEMORY / OF JAMES FORBES, ESQ. M. D. / INSPECTOR GENERAL OF ARMY HOSPITALS. / AFTER A SERVICE OF NEARLY THIRTY FIVE YEARS / IN ALMOST EVERY QUARTER OF THE GLOBE / THIS ABLE AND DISTINGUISHED OFFICER RETURNED FROM CEYLON IN 1836 / EXHAUSTED BY HIS ABLE AND ZEALOUS DISCHARGE OF DUTY / TO HIS KING AND COUNTRY, / AND DIED THE FOLLOWING YEAR, LAMENTED / AS HE HAD LIVED RESPECTED, THROUGHOUT THE BRITISH ARMY. / HIS REMAINS ARE DEPOSITED WITHIN THE WALLS OF THIS CATHEDRAL, / AND IN THE VICINITY OF THE MILITARY HOSPITAL / WHICH HE HAD SUPERINTENDED FOR SEVERAL YEARS.

Hospital Mate 8 Oct 1803. Asst Surgeon 30th Foot 9 Feb 1804. Asst Surgeon 15th Lt Dragoons 26 Oct 1804. Surgeon 95th Foot 15 Jun 1809. Staff Surgeon 13 Jul 1809. Physician 5 Nov 1812.

Served in the Peninsula Nov 1808 – Jan 1809 and Oct 1810 – Apr 1814. From Nov 1812 attached to HQ (staff officer to Sir James McGrigor). Present at Sahagun and the Corunna campaign. Half pay 1814. In charge of the large General Hospital at Colchester for the sick and wounded from Waterloo 1815. Later Superintendent of Chelsea Hospital and Medical Director of Fort Pitt, Chatham. MD Edinburgh 1803. Deputy Inspector of Hospitals 1828. Inspector General of Army Hospitals 1837. Also served at Walcheren 1809, West Indies 1822, Nova Scotia Canada (Principal Medical Officer) and Ceylon 1829. Died 7 Nov 1837.

REFERENCE: *United Service Journal, Jan 1838, pp. 98–9.*

FORBES, James Staats

Gunner. Royal Artillery.

Headstone: St Mary's Churchyard, Woolwich, Kent. (No longer extant. Church bombed in the Second World War). (M.I.)

"QUARTER MASTER JAMES STAATS FORBES, DIED 1 JULY 1846, AGED 51."

Served at Waterloo in Capt Ilbert's Company and with the Army of Occupation until 6 Mar 1816. Quartermaster 4th Battalion 24 Mar 1841.

FORBES, Thomas

Lieutenant Colonel. 45th (Nottinghamshire) Regiment of Foot.

Sepulchre: Terre Cabade Cemetery, Toulouse, France. (Section 3 Division 15). Tablet on sepulchre to John Hunter. (Photograph)

TOMBEAU / DE / FORBES COLONEL / ANGLAIS / ICI TUÉ LE 10 AVRIL / 1814

Named on the Memorial: St Andrew's Church, (now Musée Historique), Biarritz, France. (Photograph)

Ensign 80th Foot 22 Jul 1794. Lt 100th Foot 16 Aug 1794. Capt 37th Foot 25 Oct 1796. Major Macdonald's Levy 6 Dec 1800. Bt Lt Colonel 25 Apr 1808. Major 6 West India Regt 28 Jun 1808. Major 45th Foot 20 Oct 1808. Lt Colonel 7 Oct 1813.

Served in the Peninsula Jan 1812 – Jan 1813 and Jul 1813 – Apr 1814. Present at Badajoz, Salamanca (wounded), Nivelle, Nive, Orthes (wounded), Vic Bigorre and Toulouse where he was killed Apr 1814. Gold Cross for Badajoz, Nivelle, Orthes and Toulouse.

FORBES, Walter
Ensign. Coldstream Regiment of Foot Guards.
Memorial window: St Ninian's Cathedral, Perth, Scotland. (Photograph)

IN PIOUS MEMORY OF THE FOUNDERS, WALTER LORD FORBES, & GEORGE FREDERICK, EARL OF GLASGOW THIS WINDOW IS ERECTED 1891.

Memorial tablet and window: Royal Military Chapel, Wellington Barracks, London. (M.I.) (Destroyed by a Flying Bomb 1944)

" .... WALTER, EIGHTEENTH LORD FORBES. / COLDSTREAM GUARDS, 1814–25. DIED, 1868. / "WATERLOO." / HORACE COURTNEY, NINETEENTH LORD FORBES, SON OF THE LAST-NAMED, PLACED THIS TABLET A.D. 1880."

"THIS WINDOW IS GIVEN BY HIS WIDOW, IN MEMORY OF WALTER, EIGHTEENTH LORD FORBES, AND PREMIER BARON OF SCOTLAND. BORN 1798; DIED 1868. COLDSTREAM GUARDS, 1814–25. HE COMMANDED A COMPANY IN THE DEFENCE OF HOUGOUMONT, AT THE BATTLE OF WATERLOO."

Ensign 2 Jun 1814. Lt and Capt 20 Feb 1823.
    Present at Waterloo where he took part in the defence of Hougoumont. He had previously served in the navy before joining the regiment in 1814. Retired 20 Apr 1825. After leaving the army he became interested in church affairs. One of the founders of St Ninian's Cathedral in Perth. Magistrate and Deputy Lieutenant of Aberdeenshire. Died 2 May 1868. Younger brother of Ensign James Forbes Coldstream Guards.
REFERENCE: *Dictionary of National Biography. Gentleman's Magazine, May 1868, p. 777.*

FORD, William Henry
Lieutenant Colonel. Royal Engineers.
Named on the Regimental Memorial: Rochester Cathedral, Rochester, Kent. (Photograph)

2nd Lt Royal Artillery. 5 Jul 1791. 2nd Lt Royal Engineers. 16 Jan 1793. Lt 1 Nov 1793. Capt-Lt 29 Aug 1798. Capt 13 Jul 1802. Bt Major 25 Jul 1810. Lt Colonel 1 May 1811. Colonel 26 Nov 1816. Major General 27 May 1825.
    Served in the Netherlands and France with the Army of Occupation 1815–1816. Also served in Flanders 1793–1795 and Egypt 1801. Died at Woolwich 7 Apr 1829.

FORESTER, Francis
Major. 15th (King's) Regiment of Light Dragoons.
Low Monument: Brompton Cemetery, London. (BR 28395 Compartment AH:87.6x134). (Photograph)

BENEATH ARE DEPOSITED THE REMAINS OF / MAJOR FRANCIS FORESTER / LATE OF (THE KING'S) REGIMENT OF HUSSARS / BROTHER OF CECIL WELD 1ST LORD FORESTER / HE ENTERED THE ARMY EARLY IN LIFE AND SAW MUCH FOREIGN SERVICE / IN 1813 HE MARRIED THE LADY LOUISA KATHERINE BARBARA VANE / ELDEST DAUGHTER OF WILLIAM HARRY DUKE OF CLEVELAND KG. / WHOM HE SURVIVED MANY YEARS AND DIED AT AN ADVANCED AGE 22ND OCT 1861

Ensign 47th Foot 12 Feb 1793. Lt Independent Co 4 May 1793. Capt 15th Lt Dragoons 6 Aug 1799. Major 9 Aug 1804.
    Served in the Peninsula Nov 1808 – Jan 1809. Present at Sahagun and the Corunna campaign. Retired by sale of his commission 31 Aug 1809. MGS medal for Sahagun. Died in London 22 Oct 1861.

FORREST, George William
Captain. 59th (2nd Nottinghamshire) Regiment of Foot.
Family Headstone: Old Parish Burial Ground, Annan, Dumfriesshire, Scotland. (Photograph)

GEORGE WILLIAM FORREST, / CAPTAIN IN THE 59TH REGT. OF FOOT, / WHO DIED AT PISA IN ITALY / ON THE 19TH DAY OF DECEMBER, 1818: AGED 31 YEARS. / ....

Memorial: Old British Cemetery, Leghorn, Italy. (M I.)

"SACRED TO THE MEMORY / OF / CAP G. WM FORREST, LATE HS BC MS / 59TH REGT / A NATIVE / OF ANNAN, DUMFRIESSHIRE / SCOTLAND. / DIED THE 19TH DECEMBER 1818 / AGED 31 YEARS."

Ensign 23 Nov 1805. Lt 1 Oct 1807. Capt 1 Jul 1813.
    Served in the Peninsula Sep 1808 – Jan 1809. Present at Corunna. Also served at Walcheren 1809.

FORRESTER, Richard
Sergeant. 51st (2nd Yorkshire West Riding) Light Infantry.
Named on the Regimental Memorial: KOYLI Chapel, York Minster, Yorkshire. (Photograph)
    Killed in the Peninsula.

FORSTER, Henry
Sergeant. 28th (North Gloucestershire) Regiment of Foot.
Headstone: Mortis Street Cemetery, Goulburn, New South Wales, Australia. (Photograph)

SACRED / TO THE / MEMORY / OF / HENRY FORSTER / WHO DIED 14 OF MAY / 1861 / AGED 77 / YEARS / OF HM 28 REGIMENT / ....

Pte 24 May 1805. Cpl 25 Sep 1806. Pte 9 Jan 1807. Cpl 25 Mar 1810. Sgt 25 Sep 1810. Quartermaster Sgt 20 Aug 1833.
    Served in the Peninsula 1808 – Jan 1809 and Mar 1810 – Apr 1814. Present at Corunna, Barrosa, Vittoria, Pyrenees, Nivelle, Nive, Orthes and Toulouse. Present at Waterloo. Also served at Hanover 1805, Copenhagen 1807, Sweden 1808, Walcheren 1809, Netherlands 1814–1815, Ionian Islands 1820, and Australia 1835. Discharged 28 Feb 1839 after 35 years service and awarded a pension. MGS medal for Corunna, Barrosa, Vittoria, Pyrenees, Nivelle, Nive, Orthes and Toulouse. His medals are in the Paddington Barracks Museum, Sydney.

FORSTER, William Frederick
Lieutenant. Royal Engineers.
Named on the Regimental Memorial: Rochester Cathedral, Rochester, Kent. (Photograph)

1st Lt 1 Mar 1808.
    Served in the Peninsula 1808 – Jan 1809 and Jun 1809 – Jun 1811. Present at Corunna, Talavera, Torres Vedras, first siege of Badajoz, Olivencia and second siege of Badajoz where he reached the breach during the assault but was severely wounded and died of his wounds 8 June 1811. Also served in the Baltic 1808.

FOSTER, Augustus
Captain. 14th (Duchess of York's Own) Regiment of Light Dragoons.
Memorial tablet: Holy Trinity Church, Warmwell, Dorset. (Photograph)

IN MEMORY OF / AUGUSTUS FOSTER / OF WARMWELL HOUSE / FORMERLY CAPT 14 LIGHT DRAGOONS / SERVED ALL THROUGH THE PENINSULAR WAR / DEPUTY LIEUT AND J.P. FOR THE COUNTY OF DORSET / DIED JANUARY 25TH 1879 / IN HIS 93RD YEAR.

Low monument: Holy Trinity Church, Warmwell, Dorset. (Photograph)

IN MEMORY OF / AUGUSTUS FOSTER ESQ / OF WARMINSTER HOUSE / WHO DIED JAN XXV MDCCCLXXIX

Cornet 16 Apr 1807. Lt 24 Dec 1808. Capt 18 Mar 1813.
    Served in the Peninsula Dec 1808 – Feb 1811 and Jul 1811 – Sep 1813. Present at Douro, Talavera, Sexmiro, Coa, Busaco, Sobral, El Bodon, Llerena, Castrejon, Salamanca, Vittoria, and Pyrenees. Half pay 25 Mar 1816. Magistrate and Deputy Lieutenant for Dorset. MGS medal for Talavera, Busaco, Salamanca, Vittoria and Pyrenees.

FOSTER, Charles Edward
Lieutenant. 1st (Royal) Regiment of Dragoons.
Memorial tablet: St Andrew's Cathedral, Wells, Somerset. (Cloister wall). (Photograph)

SACRED / TO THE MEMORY OF / CHARLES EDWARD FOSTER, / LIEUTENANT IN THE 1ST OR ROYAL DRAGOONS, / AND SON OF REVD EDWARD FOSTER, / PREBENDARY AND PRIEST VICAR / OF WELLS CATHEDRAL. / DURING THE WAR WITH SPAIN, HE WAS ENGAGED IN / VARIOUS ACTIONS WITH THE FRENCH, AND HIS / GALLANTRY IS RECORDED IN THE "DISPATCHES" OF THE / GREAT GENERAL UNDER WHOM HE SERVED. / SUBSEQUENTLY HE ACCOMPANIED HIS REGIMENT / TO BELGIUM, AND FELL, MORTALLY WOUNDED / ON THE FIELD OF WATERLOO, JUNE 18TH 1815, / IN THE 26TH YEAR OF HIS AGE.

Cornet 8 Mar 1806. Lt 18 Nov 1807.
    Served in the Peninsula Aug 1810 – Sep 1811 and Mar 1812 – Jul 1813. Present at Fuentes d' Onoro (wounded) and Maguilla. Mentioned in Despatches for a cavalry patrol action at Alverca 26 Mar 1811. Present at Waterloo where he was killed.

FOSTER, Francis
Private. 12th (Prince of Wales's) Regiment of Light Dragoons.
Named on the Regimental Memorial: St Joseph's Church, Waterloo, Belgium. (Photograph)
    Killed at Waterloo.

FOTHERGILL, John
Captain 59th (2nd Nottinghamshire) Regiment of Foot.
Named on the Family Memorial tablet: St Peter and St Paul Church, Pickering, Yorkshire. (Photograph)

.... / THEIR DEAR SON, JOHN, LATE CAPTAIN IN THE 59TH FOOT DIED ON THE 7TH SEPTEMBER, / 1813, AGED 22 YEARS, AT THE SIEGE OF ST SEBASTIAN IN SPAIN: NEAR UNTO / WHICH PLACE HE WAS BURIED: HE WAS EVERYTHING THAT FOND PARENTS / COULD WISH, AND WAS PARTICULARLY SOLICITOUS THAT THIS MONUMENT / MIGHT BE ERECTED TO PERPETUATE THE MEMORY OF HIS DEAR / DEPARTED MOTHER, WHOM I PRAY TO BLESS AMEN. / (VERSE)

Ensign 18 Dec 1806. Lt 28 Apr 1808. Capt 15 Oct 1812.
    Served in the Peninsula Sep 1808 – Jan 1809 and Sep 1812 – Aug 1813. Present at Corunna (wounded),

Cadiz, Vittoria and San Sebastian (severely wounded 31 Aug and died of his wounds 7 Sep 1813). Also served at Walcheren 1809.
REFERENCE: *Gentleman's Magazine, Dec 1813, p. 621.*

FOTHERGILL, Joshua
Lieutenant. 98th Regiment of Foot.
Memorial: St Mary's Parish Church, Fishponds, Bristol, Somerset. (Photograph)

TO THE MEMORY OF / LIEUT JOSHUA FOTHERGILL / LATE OF THE 1ST ROYAL VETERAN BATTALION / WHO DEPARTED THIS LIFE FEBRUARY 5TH 1840 / AGED 55 YEARS. / HE WAS PATRIOTIC AND USEFUL: / HAVING PASSED MANY YEARS IN THE SERVICE / OF HIS COUNTRY IN THE FOLLOWING PLACES: / GERMANY COPENHAGEN SPAIN PORTUGAL / AND AMERICA. / HIS HONORABLE CONDUCT, STRICT INTEGRITY, KIND / MANNERS AND EXEM-PLARY MORALITY GAINED HIM / MUCH ESTEEM AND AFFECTION FROM / ALL WHO KNEW HIM. / THIS TABLET IS ERECTED BY HIS WIDOW / BUT NOT AS ONE WITHOUT HOPE / FOR BLESSED ARE THE REDEEMED OF THE LORD.

Commissioned from the ranks. Ensign 39th Foot 19 Apr 1810. Lt 98th Foot 10 Jun 1813.
　　Served in the Peninsula with 2/39th Jun 1810 – Mar 1812. Present at Busaco, first siege of Badajoz, Albuera and Arroyo dos Molinos. Also served in Hanover 1805, Copenhagen 1807, North America 1814–1815. Retired on full pay from 1st Veteran Battalion 1828.

FOULKES, Thomas
Private. 23rd (Royal Welch Fusiliers) Regiment of Foot.
Ledger stone: St Mary and All Saints Churchyard, Conway, Wales. (Close to main door). (Photograph)

IN HOPES OF A JOYFUL RESURRECTION, / HERE LIETH THE BODY OF / THOMAS FOULKES, / WHO SERVED HIS KING AND COUNTRY / THROUGHOUT THE PENINSULAR WAR AND AT / WATERLOO, IN THE 23RD REGIMENT OF FOOT, / (WELSH FUSILIERS) : / HE DIED ON THE 17TH DAY OF NOVR. 1847, / AGED 65 YEARS.

Pte 25 Aug 1807
　　Served in the Peninsula with 2/23rd Oct 1808 – Jan 1809 and with 1/23rd Dec 1810 – Apr 1814. Present at Corunna, Albuera, Ciudad Rodrigo, Badajoz, Salamanca, Vittoria and Nive. Present at Waterloo. MGS Medal for Corunna, Albuera, Ciudad Rodrigo, Badajoz, Salamanca, Vittoria and Nive.

FOURACRES, Thomas
Private. 69th (South Lincolnshire) Regiment of Foot.
Headstone: Christ Church Churchyard, Heaton Norris, Stockport, Cheshire. (Photograph)

IN MEMORY OF / THOMAS FOURACRES / WHO DIED SEPT 29TH 1859 AGED 62 YEARS.

Pte 25 Aug 1807.
　　Served at Waterloo in Captain W. H. West's Company where he was wounded. Listed in the muster roll as Thomas Forakiss.

FOWLER, Richard
2nd Lieutenant. 95th Regiment of Foot.
Low monument: St James's Churchyard, Barton-under-Needwood, Staffordshire. (Photograph)

THE FAMILY VAULT OF THE / FOWLER-BUTLERS, NOW CLOSED, / ERECTED IN MEMORY OF
.................../ RICHARD FOWLER BUTLER / DIED 13 MARCH 1864 / AGED 70 YEARS. / ....

Ensign 43rd Foot 22 Feb 1813. 2nd Lt 95th Foot 22 Oct 1813. Lt 8th May 1817.
   Served in the Peninsula with 2/95th Apr 1814. Present at Toulouse. Present at Waterloo. MGS medal for Toulouse. Half pay 25 Dec 1818 on reduction of the 3rd battalion. Assumed surname of Butler on inheriting the Barton estate in Staffordshire 1824. Retired 2 Aug 1833.

FOX, William Augustus Lane
Lieutenant and Captain. 1st Regiment of Foot Guards.
Memorial: Royal Military Chapel, Wellington Barracks, London. (M.I.) (Destroyed by a Flying Bomb in 1944)

"DEDICATED BY MAJ.-GEN. AUGUSTUS LANE FOX PITT RIVERS, GRENADIER GUARDS, 1845–67, / IN MEMORY OF / WILLIAM AUGUSTUS LANE FOX, / HIS FATHER, WHO SERVED WITH THE 1ST GUARDS IN SPAIN AND THE SOUTH OF FRANCE, FROM / 11TH NOVEMBER, 1812, TO 14TH FEBRUARY, 1814, AND RETIRED 1818."

Ensign 24 Jan 1811. Lt and Capt 13 Dec 1813. Capt 98th Foot 3 Sep 1818.
   Served in the Peninsula with 3rd Battalion Jan 1812 – Mar 1814. Present at Cadiz, Seville, San Sebastian, Bidassoa, Nivelle, Nive and Adour. Half pay 25 Sep 1818. On disbandment of 98th Foot joined the Yorkshire Hussars, becoming a Cornet 14 Jul 1823, Lt 18 Nov 1823 and Capt 26 Jul 1824. Died 11 Feb 1832.

FRAMINGHAM, Sir Haylett
Colonel. Royal Artillery.
Memorial tablet: St Mary's Church, Cheltenham, Gloucestershire. (High in the nave). (Photograph)

TO THE MEMORY OF / MAJOR GENERAL / SIR HAYLETT FRAMINGHAM, / KNIGHT COMMANDER OF THE / ORDER OF THE BATH / AND OF THE / HANOVERIAN ORDER OF GUELPH, / COLONEL IN THE ROYAL HORSE / ARTILLERY / HE DIED IN THIS TOWN / MAY 10TH 1820 / AGED 54 YEARS.

2nd Lt 29 Apr 1780. 1st Lt 8 Mar 1784. Capt-Lieut 14 Aug 1794. Capt 28 Sep 1797. Major 20 Jul 1804. Lt Col 29 Dec 1805. Colonel 20 Dec 1814. Major General 12 Aug 1819.
   Served in the Peninsula Apr 1809 – Sep 1812. Second in command Royal Artillery 1809 – Jul 1811. In command Aug 1811 – Aug 1812. Present at Douro, Talavera (wounded), Busaco, Fuentes d'Onoro, second siege of Badajoz (Mentioned in Despatches), Badajoz, siege of Salamanca Forts and Salamanca (Mentioned in Despatches). Gold Cross for Talavera, Busaco, Fuentes d'Onoro, Badajoz and Salamanca. KCB. Returned to England Aug 1812. Also served in North America 1781, West Indies 1795 (present at Martinique, St Lucia, Guadeloupe) and Minorca 1798.
REFERENCE: Royal Military Calendar, Vol 4, pp. 129–30.

FRANCE, Harold
Assistant Commissary General. Commissariat Department.
Headstone: St Anthony's Churchyard, Montserrat, West Indies. (M.I.)

"IN MEMORY OF / HAROLD FRANCE ESQR / ASSISTANT COMMISSARY GENERAL / WHO DIED / AT THE ISLAND OF MONTSERRAT / IN THE WEST INDIES / JUNE THE 20, 1820, / AGED 48 YEARS."

Dep Asst Comm Gen 8 Sep 1810. Asst Comm Gen 1 Nov 1814.
   Served in the Peninsula Jul 1810 – Apr 1814. Attached to 1st Royal Dragoons Oct 1811 – Apr 1813.

FRANKLAND, Frederick William
Lieutenant. 2nd (Queen's Royal) Regiment of Foot.
Family Memorial tablet: Holy Trinity Cathedral, Gibraltar. (North wall). (M.I.)

"FREDERICK ROGER FRANKLAND, MIDSHIPMAN, HMS WINCHESTER, DIED OF A FEVER AT SIERRA LEONE, 21 JAN 1844, AGED 20. THOMAS FRANKLAND, LIEUTENANT MADRAS NATIVE INFANTRY, AND SECOND IN COMMAND OF THE 2ND PUNJAB REGT, KILLED IN ACTION WITH THE SEPOY REBELS WHILST LEADING AN ASSAULT AT THE RELIEF OF LUCKNOW, 17 NOV 1857, AGED 29. HARRY ALBERT FRANKLAND, MIDSHIPMAN, HMS ALARM, DIED OF FEVER OFF VERA CRUZ, 9 MAY 1847, AGED 17. ALL SONS OF SIR FREDERICK WILLIAM FRANKLAND, BART., OF THIRKLEBY, YORK, LATE CAPT 20TH REGT, AND 14 YEARS BARRACK MASTER IN THIS FORTRESS."

Buried in the Family vault: All Saints Church, Thirkleby, Yorkshire. (Photograph)

Ensign 7 Oct 1812. Lt 12 Jan 1815. Capt 3 Jan 1822, Capt 20th Foot 6 Jun 1822, Capt 34th Foot 12 Jun 1826.
  Served in the Peninsula Nov 1812 – Apr 1814. Present at Pamplona, Pyrenees, Bidassoa, Nivelle, Nive, Bayonne and Toulouse (ADC to General Sir William Anson). Present at Waterloo and the siege of Cambrai (ADC to Lt General Sir Charles Colville). MGS medal for Pyrenees, Nivelle, Nive and Toulouse. Barrack Master at Gibraltar 1852. Became Sir Frederick William Frankland Bart. Died 1878.

FRASER, Alexander George see SALTOUN , Alexander George Fraser Lord

FRASER, Alexander John
Ensign. 52nd (Oxfordshire) Light Infantry Regiment of Foot.
Named on the Memorial: St Andrew's Church, (now Musée Historique), Biarritz, France. (Photograph)

Ensign 12 May 1812. Lt 23 Sep 1813.
  Served in the Peninsula Apr 1813 – Oct 1813. Present at Vittoria, Pyrenees, Vera and Bidassoa where he was severely wounded and died of his wounds a few days later on 19 Oct 1813 aged 18.

FRASER, Alexander Mackenzie
Colonel. 78th (Highland) Regiment of Foot.
Box tomb: St Mary the Virgin Churchyard, Hayes, Bromley, Kent. (Photograph)
(Inscription is largely illegible. Details of the inscription are recorded from 'Hayes Parish Church: record of graves in the old and new graveyards'. N. W. Kent Family History Society, 1994).

"SACRED TO THE MEMORY OF / ALEXANDER MACKENZIE FRASER / LIEUTENANT GENERAL OF HIS MAJESTY'S FORCES / COLONEL OF THE 78TH REGT / WHO DIED SEPTEMBER 1809. / 52 YEARS / A CHRISTIAN UPON CONVICTION / HE MANIFESTLY ***** OF ***** / IN THE UNIFORMITY OF ***** AND VIRTUOUS LIFE / THROUGH HIS MARTIAL CAREER / HE WAS IN ZEAL AND STEAD NOR PASSED BY NONE / IN LENGTH AND ***** OF SERVICE EQUAL ***** BY FEW / WARM IN HIS AFFECTIONS / COOL IN HIS JUDGEMENT / MILD IN HIS MANNERS / FIRM IN HIS *****"

Ensign 74th Foot 1778. Lt 73rd Foot 1778. Capt 1781. Major 78th Foot 1793. Lt Colonel 1793. Bt Colonel 3 May 1796. Major General 1803. Lt General 25 Apr 1808.
  Served in the Peninsula Sep 1808 – Jan 1809 (GOC 3rd Division). Present at Benevente and Corunna. Gold Medal for Corunna. A personal friend of Moore, he was aged 52 at Corunna, the oldest of Moore's divisional commanders, but had seen more active service than Moore. Also served in Gibraltar 1778–1783,

North America (wounded), Flanders 1793–1795, Cape of Good Hope 1796, India 1796–1800, Hanover 1805, Sicily 1806–1807, Egypt 1807, Sweden 1808 and Walcheren 1809 where he caught the fever which caused his death on 13 Sep 1809. MP for Cromarty 1802 and Ross-shire until 1809.

REFERENCE: *Dictionary of National Biography. Gentleman's Magazine, Sep 1809, p. 894.*

FRASER, Charles Mackenzie

Lieutenant and Captain. Coldstream Regiment of Foot Guards.
Memorial: Royal Military Chapel, Wellington Barracks, London. (M.I.) (Destroyed by a Flying Bomb in 1944)

"IN MEMORY OF / CAPTAIN CHAS. MACKENZIE FRASER, / BORN 9TH JUNE. 1792. / ENSIGN 78TH HIGHLANDERS, 18TH DECEMBER, 1806. SERVED IN THE 52ND REGIMENT IN SPAIN, AND AT WALCHEREN, FROM 4TH FEBRUARY, 1808, TO 16TH AUGUST, 1810. TRANSFERRED TO COLDSTREAM GUARDS. WAS PRESENT AT SALAMANCA AND BURGOS. SEVERELY WOUNDED IN THE HEAD AND LEG. HE RETIRED WITH THE ARMY TO SALAMANCA, WHERE HIS LEG WAS AMPUTATED, AND WITHIN A FEW HOURS OF THE OPERATION HE MOVED WITH THE ARMY TO CASTEL BRANCO. / DIED 7TH MARCH, 1871."

Ensign 78th Foot 18 Dec 1806. Lt 52nd Foot 4 Feb 1808. Capt 72nd Foot 22 Mar 1810. Capt 50th Foot Jul 1810. Lt and Capt Coldstream Guards 16 Aug 1810.
Served in the Peninsula with 2/52nd Aug 1808 – Jan 1809 and Coldstream Guards May – Oct 1812. Present at Vigo, Salamanca and Burgos (severely wounded, his leg amputated Sep 1812 and awarded pension of £100 per annum). Also served at Walcheren 1809. MGS medal for Salamanca.
REFERENCE: *Oxfordshire Light Infantry Chronicle, 1904, pp. 146–7.*

FRASER, Erskine Alexander

Lieutenant 9th (East Norfolk) Regiment of Foot. (Photograph)
Memorial tablet: Canterbury Cathedral, Kent. On the same memorial as his father, George Fraser, see below. (Photograph)

Ensign 82nd Foot 4 Feb 1808. Lt 2 Nov 1809. Lt 9th Foot 28 Dec 1809.
Served in the Peninsula with the 1st Battalion Apr – Aug 1813. Present at Osma, Vittoria and San Sebastian where he was killed in the action of the final assault 31 Aug 1813 aged 18 years. Son of Paymaster George Fraser 9th Foot.

FRASER, George

Paymaster. 9th (East Norfolk) Regiment of Foot.
Memorial tablet: Canterbury Cathedral, Kent. (Photograph.)

SACRED TO THE MEMORY / OF GEORGE FRASER, ESQR / MANY YEARS PAYMASTER OF THE 2ND BATTALION, 9TH REGT OF FOOT. / THE LOSS OF HIS MUCH BELOVED SON ERSKINE ALEXANDER FRASER, / LIEUTENANT OF THE SAME REGIMENT, / WHOSE EARLY DISTIN-GUISHED TALENTS / PROMISED A BRIGHT ORNAMENT TO THE PROFESSION, / AND WHO GALLANTLY FELL, AT THE STORMING OF SAN SEBASTIAN, IN SPAIN, / ON THE 31ST OF AUGUST, 1813, BEFORE HE HAD COMPLETED HIS 18TH YEAR. / THE SEVERE DISPENSATION SO PREYED ON THE MIND OF THE AFFLICTED FATHER, / THAT HE BECAME THE VICTIM OF INCREASING GRIEF, / AND EXPIRED ON THE 4TH DECEMBER IN THE FOLLOWING YEAR, / IN THE 54TH YEAR OF HIS AGE. / ....

Paymaster 9th Foot 24 Jan 1805.
Served in the Peninsula with 2nd Battalion Aug 1808 – Dec 1808. Present at Vimeiro. Died of grief in 1814 for the death of his son Lt Erskine Alexander Fraser 9th Foot.

FRASER, James

Lieutenant. 79th (Cameron Highlanders) Regiment of Foot.
Memorial tablet in walled enclosure: Glen Convinth Churchyard, Invernesshire, Scotland. (Near head of Glen Convinth). (Photograph)

SACRED TO THE MEMORY OF / JAMES FRASER, ESQUIRE. / OF BALLINDOWN, / LATE CAPT^N 79TH HIGHLANDERS. / BORN 18 SEPT 1788, / DIED 29 MAY 1849. / ……………..

Ensign 30 Apr 1807. Lt 16 Mar 1809. Capt 3 Jun 1819.
    Served in the Peninsula Nov 1811 – Apr 1814. Present at Salamanca, Burgos, Pyrenees, Nivelle, Nive and Toulouse (severely wounded and saved by his breastplate). Present at Quatre Bras (wounded) and Waterloo. Also served at Copenhagen 1807–1808. Retired 2 Feb 1830. MGS medal for Salamanca, Pyrenees, Nivelle, Nive and Toulouse, but did not claim it.

FRASER, James John

Captain. 7th (Queen's Own) Regiment of Light Dragoons.
Memorial tablet: Wimborne Minster, Dorset. (North east pillar of Western Tower). (Photograph)

IN / MEMORY / OF / SIR JAMES / JOHN FRASER / 3RD BARONET OF / LEDECLUNE / AND MORAR / IN THE COUNTY OF / INVERNESS / DESCENDED FROM / THE LORDS FRASER / OF LOVAT / LIEUTENANT COLONEL / 7TH HUSSARS / WHO FOUGHT AT ORTHEZ / TOULOUSE & WATERLOO / DIED AT UDDENS HOUSE / JUNE 5 1834 / A BRAVE AND SAGACIOUS / SOLDIER AND A GENTLEMAN / IN THE HIGHEST SENSE / OF THAT NOBLE TERM / THIS TABLET WAS PLACED / BY HIS ELDEST SON

Memorial tablet: All Saint's Church, Langton Long, Dorset. (Photograph)

IN MEMORY OF / SIR JAMES JOHN FRASER BAR^T / COLONEL OF THE 7TH HUSSARS / A REGI-MENT IN WHICH HE SERVED 20 YEARS / AND WHICH HE ULTIMATELY COMMANDED / HE ACTED AS AIDE-DE-CAMP / TO THE MARQUIS OF ANGLESEY / AT THE MEMORABLE BATTLE OF WATERLOO / AND AFTER RETIRING FROM THE ARMY / IN WHICH HE HAD SERVED / ZEALOUSLY AND HONORABLY / DIED JUNE 5TH 1834 / IN THE 45TH YEAR OF HIS AGE. / HIS KIND AND GALLANT SPIRIT THUS AT AN EARLY PERIOD / OF LIFE SNATCHED FROM OBJECTS OF HIS FERVENT AFFECTION / MET THE CALL AND SUBMITTED TO THE WILL OF HIS CREATOR / WITH ENTIRE HUMILITY WITH A FIRM HOPE IN THE MERCY / OF GOD AND THE MERITS OF HIS SAVIOUR / IN TENDER AND GRATEFUL REMEMBRANCE OF HIS / AFFEC-TION AND WORTH HIS WIDOW INSCRIBES THIS / BRIEF RECORD TO HIS MEMORY.

Named on the Family Memorial tablet: Boleskine Old Churchyard, Drumtemple, Invernesshire, Scotland. (Photograph)

……………. / SIR JAMES JOHN FRASER / OF LEDECLUNE AND MORAR BARONET. / LIEU-TENANT COLONEL 7TH QUEEN'S OWN REGIMENT OF HUSSARS, / WHO FOUGHT AT ORTHEZ, TOULOUSE AND WATERLOO: / AND WAS WOUNDED AT THAT LAST BATTLE.

Lt 6 Jun 1811. Capt 17 Jun 1813. Major 27 Feb 1823. Lt Colonel 28 Sep 1826.
    Served in the Peninsula Aug 1813 – Apr 1814. Present at Orthes and Toulouse. Present at Waterloo (ADC to the Earl of Uxbridge), where he was wounded. Succeeded to the Baronetcy 1827. Retired on half pay 15 Jun 1830.

FRASER, John
Captain. 1st Ceylon Regiment.
Chest tomb: British Garrison Cemetery, Kandy, Ceylon. (Photograph)

IN MEMORY / OF / LIEUT GENERAL JOHN FRASER / COLONEL OF THE 37TH REGIMENT / AND FOR MANY YEARS / DEPUTY QUARTER MASTER GENERAL / TO THE TROOPS SERVING IN CEYLON / WHO DIED AT KANDY / THE 24TH MAY 1862 / AGED 72 YEARS. / A BRAVE AND ACCOMPLISHED SOLDIER / A DEVOTED AFFECTIONATE FATHER. / THIS TOMB IS DEDI-CATED / BY HIS SURVIVING CHILDREN.

Ensign 24th Foot 19 Apr 1809. Lt 12 Sep 1811. Capt 1st Ceylon Regt 28 Jan 1813. Bt Major 31 Oct 1818. Major 21 Jun 1821. Bt Lt Colonel 24 May 1827. Bt Colonel 23 Nov 1841. Major General 20 Jun 1854. Lt General 17 Oct 1859.
   Served in the Peninsula with 24th Foot Jul 1809 – Mar 1813. Present at Busaco, Foz d'Arouce, Fuentes d'Onoro, Ciudad Rodrigo, Salamanca, Burgos (present at the capture of the Horn Work 19 Sep 1812 and led the storming party to the breach 4 Oct. Mentioned in Despatches) and retreat from Burgos. MGS medal for Busaco, Fuentes d'Onoro, Ciudad Rodrigo and Salamanca. Also served in Ceylon (present in the Kandian War 1815–1818 and awarded a Bt Majority). DQMG to troops in Ceylon. Had the whole island surveyed, roads built and produced maps. Also had built the Peradenia Bridge, spanning the Mahaweli-ganga which became one of the famous sights of Ceylon. It was built in six months in 1832 with a single span of 205 feet, made in satinwood without a nail or bolt. This bridge lasted until 1905 and was then replaced with an iron bridge. Colonel 37th Foot 11 Jan 1858. Remained in Ceylon and became a coffee planter on his extensive estates.
   REFERENCE: *Lewis, J. Penry, List of inscriptions on tombstones and monuments in Ceylon, 1913, reprint 1994, pp. 313–4.*

FRASER, John
Lieutenant. 4th (King's Own) Regiment of Foot.
Memorial tablet: St Andrew's Church, (now Musée Historique), Biarritz, France. (Photograph)

Ensign 9 Sep 1808. Lt 21 Nov 1809.
   Served in the Peninsula with the 2/4th May 1812 – Jan 1813 and 1/4th Sep 1813 – Feb 1814. Present at Salamanca, retreat from Burgos, Bidassoa, Nivelle and Nive where he was severely wounded 10 Dec 1813, and died of his wounds at St Jean de Luz, 11 Feb 1814. Also served at Walcheren 1809.

FRASER, Thomas
Lieutenant Colonel. 1st (Royal Scots) Regiment of Foot.
Obelisk: Neembolah, India. (Photocopy of book illustration)

TO THE MEMORY OF / COLONEL FRASER, / 2ND BATTN, THE ROYAL SCOTS, / WHO COMMANDED THE COLUMN OF ATTACK / ON ASIRGHAR FORT MARCH 1819 / AND WAS KILLED DURING A SORTIE OF THE ENEMY ON THE NIGHT OF THE 19TH / THIS TABLET WAS ADDED / TO THE OBELISK WHICH MARKS COLONEL FRASER'S GRAVE / BY THE OFFICERS OF HIS OLD BATTALION IN 1907. R. I. P.

Memorial monument: Boleskine Old Churchyard, Drumtemple, Invernesshire, Scotland. (Photograph)

SACRED / TO THE MEMORY OF / LIEUTENANT COLONEL THOMAS FRASER / OF THE ROYAL SCOTS REGIMENT OF INFANTRY, WHO AFTER / A COURSE OF DISTINGUISHED SERVICE IN EVERY QUARTER / OF THE GLOBE, FELL BY A RANDOM SHOT AFTER LEADING AND / COMMANDING WITH COMPLETE SUCCESS THE STORMING OF THE / PETTAH OR OUTER

WORKS OF THE STRONG FORT OF ASSEER GHUR / IN THE EAST INDIES IN THE MONTH OF APRIL 1819. / HE WAS HIGHLY ESTEEMED IN HIS REGIMENT AND BY ITS / ILLUSTRIOUS COLONEL THE LATE DUKE OF KENT AND STRATHKERNE, / AND BY THE WHOLE ARMY, WITH WHICH HE SERVED / DURING THE LATE WAR; AND HIS DEATH WAS EQUALLY LAMENTED / BY ALL WHO WERE EVER ASSOCIATED WITH HIM AS A SOLDIER, / OR HAD THE HAPPINESS TO KNOW HIM IN PRIVATE LIFE. / .... / COLONEL FRASER BY HIS WILL DIRECTED THAT A MONUMENT / SHOULD BE ERECTED BY HIS EXECUTORS, / TO THE MEMORY OF HIS FATHER AND MOTHER, AND / THE EXECUTORS ANXIOUS TO DISCHARGE THE TRUST / REPOSED IN THEM BY THE GALLANT RELATIVE AND COMPANION / AND FRIEND; AND AT THE SAME TIME TO PERPETUATE / HIS OWN MEMORY IN A SPOT, CONCENTRATING THE / REPOSITORY OF THE ASHES OF HIS FOREFATHERS HAVE DIRECTED / THIS MONUMENT TO BE PLACED HERE IN THE / YEAR OF OUR LORD 1822. / ....

Ensign 97th Foot 8 Jul 1794. Lt 18 Jul 1795. Lt 1st Foot 12 Dec 1795. Capt 24 Sep 1803. Major 8 Jun 1809. Bt Lt Colonel 4 Jun 1814.

Served in the Peninsula Jan 1811 – Mar 1812. Present at Fuentes d'Onoro. Also served in Portugal 1798, Ireland 1799, Egypt 1801, West Indies 1803–1809 and India 1816 with the 2nd battalion where he was killed at the siege of Fort Asseerghur 1819.

REFERENCE: *Thistle – (Quarterly Journal of the Royal Scots), Vol 2, No 8, 1908, Photograph of Memorial obelisk and tablet at Neembolah, India).*

FRASER, William
Lieutenant. 93rd Regiment of Foot.
Memorial tablet: St Machar's Cathedral, Aberdeen, Aberdeenshire, Scotland. (Behind organ). (Photograph)

IN MEMORY OF / COLONEL WILLIAM FRASER / LATE OF / THE 43RD REGT: LIGHT INFANTRY; / ONLY SON OF / COL: ERSKINE FRASER, / AND HIS WIFE ELIZABETH FORBES; / BORN NOVR 21ST 1796, / DIED JULY 13TH 1872. / ....

Ensign 92nd Foot 8 Apr 1813. Lt 19 Jan 1814. Lt 93rd Foot 1 Jun 1815. Lt Rifle Brigade 21 May 1818. Lt 43rd Foot 6 Jul 1820. Capt 9 Dec 1824. Bt Major 28 Jun 1838. Major 7 May 1841. Bt Lt Colonel 11 Nov 1851. Bt Colonel 29 Aug 1857.

Served in the Peninsula with 92nd Regiment Oct 1813 – Mar 1814. Present at Nive (severely wounded 13 Dec 1814). MGS medal for Nive. Half pay 1814. Also served in Gibraltar 1822–1826, 1829 and Canada 1838–1839 (present at the suppression of the Canadian Rebellion. One of those who crossed the Portage of the Medawska. Awarded Bt Majority). Retired 21 May 1858.

FRASER, William
Ensign. 42nd (Royal Highland) Regiment of Foot.
Buried in Kensal Green Cemetery, London. Inscription not recorded. (No longer extant: 9807/94–95/2)

Ensign 10 Jun 1813. Lt 19 Jul 1815. Capt 23 Sep 1824. Major 3 Jul 1826. Lt Colonel 8 Feb 1831.

Present at Quatre Bras (wounded) and Waterloo (wounded). Buried in Kensal Green 6 Oct 1851.

FRAZER, Sir Augustus Simon
Lieutenant Colonel. Royal Artillery.
Memorial tablet: St Luke's Church, Charlton, Kent. (Photograph)

IN MEMORY OF / SIR AUGUSTUS SIMON FRAZER, K.C.B. F.R.S. / COLONEL OF THE ROYAL

HORSE ARTILLERY, / DIRECTOR OF THE ROYAL LABORATORY, / WHO DIED 11TH JUNE 1835, AGED 59 YEARS. / WITH ZEAL RARELY EXCEEDED HE TOOK A DISTINGUISHED PART / IN THE CAMPAIGNS IN HOLLAND AND FLANDERS IN 1794, / IN SOUTH AMERICA IN 1807, / AND OF THOSE OF 1812 – 15, IN PORTUGAL, SPAIN AND FRANCE. / HE OBTAINED HONORABLE DISTINCTIONS FOR SERVICES / AT VITTORIA, NIVELLE, NIVE, TOULOUSE, AND WATERLOO. / IN TIMES OF PEACE, EQUALLY READY TO PROMOTE THE PUBLIC SERVICE, / HIS ATTENTIONS TO OFFICIAL DUTIES WERE UNWEARIED. / FEW HAVE DIED MORE EXTENSIVELY AND DEEPLY LAMENTED. / THIS TABLET IS ERECTED BY THOSE WHO WERE NEAREST AND DEAREST TO HIM, / IN TESTIMONY OF THEIR IRREPLACEABLE LOSS.

Gravestone: St Luke's Church, Charlton, Kent. (No longer extant; Grave number 307). (M.I.)

"SACRED TO THE MEMORY OF COLONEL SIR AUGUSTUS SIMON FRAZER, K.C.B. R.H.A. WHO DEPARTED THIS LIFE THE 11 JUNE 1835, IN HIS 59TH YEAR."

1st Lt 1 Jan 1794. Capt-Lieut 16 Jul 1799. Capt 12 Sep 1803. Major 4 Jun 1811. Lt Colonel 20 Dec 1814. Colonel 29 Jul 1825.

Served in the Peninsula Nov 1812 – Apr 1814 (Commanded Royal Horse Artillery Apr 1813 – Apr 1814). Present at Osma, Vittoria, first and second sieges of San Sebastian, Bidassoa, Nivelle, Nive, Adour, Bayonne (wounded) and Toulouse. KCB Jan 1815. Present at Waterloo in command of the Horse Artillery. Also served in Flanders 1793 (present at Mouveaux, Le Cateau, Tournai and Boxtel) the Helder 1799 and South America 1807 (present at Buenos Ayres). Gold Cross for Vittoria, San Sebastian, Nivelle, Nive and Toulouse.

REFERENCE: *Dictionary of National Biography. Sabine, Edward ed., Letters of Colonel Sir Augustus Simon Frazer, KCB, 1859, reprint 2001.*

FRAZER, John Whitley
2nd Assistant Surgeon. Ordnance Medical Department, Royal Artillery.
Ledger stone: Clonmacnoise Churchyard, County Offaly, Ireland. (Photograph)

JOHN WHITLEY FRAZER, / LATE SURGEON OF THE ROYAL ARTILLERY / DIED ON THE 2ND OF MARCH 1827, / AGED 36 YEARS.

2nd Asst Surgeon 28 Dec 1810. 1st Asst Surgeon 5 Apr 1820.
Served in the Peninsula Jan 1812 – Apr 1814. Retired on half pay 1 Feb 1822.

FREDERICK, Edward Henry
Captain. 51st (2nd Yorkshire West Riding) Light Infantry.
Slab on plinth from which railings have been removed: St Peter's Old Churchyard (Section A), Hersham, Surrey. (M.I.)

"EDWARD HENRY FREDERICK ESQR / LATE CAPTN 51ST LIGHT INFANTRY. / DIED 15TH MARCH 1846, / IN HIS 58TH YEAR / ...."

Ensign 21 Aug 1806. Lt 7 May 1807. Capt 28 Apr 1814.
Served in the Peninsula Oct 1808 – Jan 1809 and Feb 1811 – Oct 1813. Present at Corunna, Fuentes d'Onoro, second siege of Badajoz, Moriscos, Salamanca, Burgos, San Munos, Vittoria, Pyrenees and San Marcial (severely wounded). Present at Waterloo. Half pay 7 Apr 1826. Younger brother of Capt Roger Frederick 7th Royal Veteran Battalion.

FREDERICK, Roger
Captain. 7th Royal Veteran Battalion.
Slab on plinth from which railings have been removed: St Peter's Old Churchyard, (Section A), Hersham, Surrey. (M.I.)

".............. / ROGER FREDERICK / BORN NOVEMBER 23RD 1791, / DIED JUNE 21ST 1854, / AGED 63."

Ensign 43rd Foot 4 Oct 1808. Lt 18 Oct 1809. Capt 7th Royal Veteran Battalion 2 Jul 1812.
    Served in the Peninsula with 2/43rd Oct 1808 – Jan 1809 and 1/43rd Jul 1809 – Oct 1810. Present at Corunna and Coa (severely wounded, his left leg amputated and awarded pension of £100 per annum). Joined the 7th Royal Veteran Battalion and when it was disbanded in 1814, retired on full pay. Educated at Eton. Elder brother of Capt Edward Henry Frederick 51st Foot.

FREEMAN, Robert
Corporal. 52nd (Oxfordshire) Light Infantry Regiment of Foot.
Buried in the Private Soldiers Burial Ground, Royal Hospital, Kilmainham, Dublin, Ireland.

Pte 11 Sep 1806. Cpl 1809. Sgt 1815.
    Served in the Peninsula Jul 1809 - Sep 1814. Present at Busaco, Fuentes d'Onoro, Ciudad Rodrigo, Badajoz, Salamanca, Vittoria, Pyrenees, Nivelle, Nive, Orthes and Toulouse. Awarded MGS medal for Busaco, Fuentes d'Onoro, Ciudad Rodrigo, Badajoz, Salamanca, Vittoria, Pyrenees, Nivelle, Nive, Orthes and Toulouse. Served at Waterloo in Capt George Young's Company. Promoted to Sergeant after the battle. Discharged 1817 on reduction of the regiment. Brother of Pte Thomas Freeman 52nd Foot.

FREEMAN, Thomas
Corporal. 52nd (Oxfordshire) Light Infantry Regiment of Foot.
Buried in the Private Soldiers Burial Ground, Royal Hospital, Kilmainham, Dublin, Ireland.

Pte 11 Sep 1806. Cpl 1813. Sgt 1816.
    Served in the Peninsula Jul 1809 - Apr 1814. Present at Busaco, Fuentes d'Onoro, Ciudad Rodrigo, Badajoz, Salamanca, Vittoria, Pyrenees, Nivelle, Nive, Orthes and Toulouse. Awarded MGS medal for Busaco, Fuentes d'Onoro, Ciudad Rodrigo, Badajoz, Salamanca, Vittoria, Pyrenees, Nivelle, Nive, Orthes and Toulouse. Present at Waterloo in Capt John Shedden's Company. Discharged 1817 on reduction of the regiment. Brother of Pte Robert Freeman 52nd Foot.

FREEMAN, William
Private. Coldstream Regiment of Foot Guards.
Headstone: St John the Baptist Churchyard, Pampisford, Cambridgeshire. (Photograph)

IN MEMORY OF / WILLIAM FREEMAN / FORMERLY OF THE COLDSTREAM GUARDS / HAVING SERVED HIS KING AND COUNTRY / WITH FIDELITY AND VALOUR THROUGHOUT THE / GREAT PENINSULAR WAR AND AT THE FINAL / STRUGGLE ON THE PLAINS OF WATERLOO WHERE HE / WAS SEVERELY WOUNDED. THIS AGED SOLDIER / HERE RESTS IN PEACE. / HE DEPARTED THIS LIFE / MAY 11TH 1866 / AGED 81 YEARS.

Private 5 May 1812.
    Served in the Peninsula. Present at Vittoria. Present at Waterloo where he was severely wounded. Discharged 13 Apr 1817. MGS medal for Vittoria. Chelsea Out Pensioner.

FREER, Edward Gardner
Lieutenant. 43rd (Monmouthshire) Light Infantry Regiment of Foot.
Memorial tablet: All Saints Church, Oakham, Rutland. (Photograph)

SACRED TO THE MEMORY OF / .... / ALSO EDWARD GARDNER FREER. / LIEUT. 43RD LIGHT INFANTRY (THIRD SON OF THE ABOVE) / WHO FELL IN THE PYRENNEES, / NOVEMBER 10TH 1813. AGED 20. / ....

Named on the Memorial: St Andrew's Church, (now Musée Historique), Biarritz, France. (Photograph)

Ensign 6 Apr 1809. Lt 12 Jul 1810.
    Served in the Peninsula with 1/43rd Jul 1810 – Nov 1813. Present at Coa, Busaco, Redinha, Casal Nova, Foz d'Arouce, Sabugal, Fuentes d'Onoro, Ciudad Rodrigo, Badajoz (severely wounded), Salamanca, San Munos, Vittoria, Bidassoa and Nivelle where he was killed 10 Nov 1813 aged 20. Took part in the storming party at Ciudad Rodrigo and at Badajoz. At Badajoz he reached a high wall, found himself alone, all his companions killed or wounded. Rather than retreat he threw stones at the French. He was shot and severely wounded. He recovered to take part in further battles but was killed the following year at Nivelle. Napier commented: 'Edward Freer had seen more combats and sieges than he could count years'. Also served at Walcheren. Brother of Capt William Gardner Freer 43rd Foot.
REFERENCE: *Scarfe, Norman, Letters from the Peninsular: the Freer Family Correspondence, 1807- 14, 1953. Gentleman's Magazine, Dec 1813, p. 623.*

FREER, William Gardner
Captain. 43rd (Monmouthshire) Light Infantry Regiment of Foot.
Memorial tablet: All Saints Church, Oakham, Rutland. (Photograph)

SACRED TO THE MEMORY OF / LT. COLONEL WILLIAM GARDNER FREER K.H. / WHO DIED AT CORFU COMMANDING H B. M. TENTH REGIMENT OF INFANTRY / ON THE 2ND AUGUST 1836, AGED 45 YEARS. / HE SERVED IN THE 43RD (OR MONMOUTHSHIRE) LIGHT INFANTRY / (ONE OF THE REGIMENTS OF THE LIGHT DIVISIONS OF THE ARMY) / IN ALL THE CAMPAIGNS OF THE PENINSULAR WAR / FROM 1808 TO 1814. / HE WAS PRESENT DURING THE EVENTFUL PERIOD / IN THE BATTLES AND SIEGES OF / VIMIERA – CORUNNA – BUSACO – / FUENTES D'ONOR – CUIDAD RODRIGO – BADAJOS – VITTORIA – NIVELLE – / NIVE – TOULOUSE – / AND LOST HIS RIGHT ARM AT THE STORMING OF BADAJOS. / THIS TRIBUTE TO THE MEMORY OF A DISTINGUISHED SOLDIER / AND SINCERE FRIEND / IS ERECTED BY HIS BROTHER OFFICERS, / BY WHOM A MONUMENT HAS BEEN PLACED OVER HIS REMAINS / WHICH WERE INTERRED AT CORFU.

Obelisk: British Cemetery, Corfu Town, Corfu, Greece. (Photograph)

SACRED / TO THE MEMORY OF / LIEUTENANT COLONEL / WILLIAM GARDNER FREER / WHO DIED AT CORFU / COMMANDING HBM XTH REGIMENT / INFANTRY ON THE 2ND AUGUST 1836 / AGED 45 YEARS / HE SERVED IN THE 43RD OR MONMOUTHSHIRE / LIGHT INFANTRY ONE OF THE REGIMENTS OF / THE LIGHT DIVISION OF THE ARMY IN ALL / THE CAMPAIGNS OF THE PENINSULAR WAR FROM / 1808 – 1814 / HE WAS PRESENT DURING THAT EVENTFUL PERIOD / IN THE BATTLES AND SIEGES OF / VIMIERA / CORUNNA BUSACO / FUENTES D' ONOR CIUDAD RODRIGO / BADAJOS VICTORIA / NIVELLE NIVE / TOULOUSE / AND LOST HIS RIGHT ARM AT THE / STORMING OF BADAJOS

Ensign 12 Dec 1805. Lt 5 Feb 1807. Capt 1 Dec 1813. Major 10th Foot 8 Jun 1826. Lt Colonel 24 May 1833.

Served in the Peninsula with 2/43rd Aug 1808 – Jan 1809, 1/43rd Jul 1809 – May 1812 and Feb 1813 – Apr 1814. Present at Vimeiro (wounded), Corunna, Coa (wounded), Busaco, Redinha, Casal Nova, Foz d'Arouce, Sabugal (wounded), Fuentes d'Onoro, Ciudad Rodrigo, Badajoz (severely wounded, his right arm amputated and awarded pension of £100 per annum), Vittoria, Pyrenees, Bidassoa, Nivelle (wounded), Tarbes and Toulouse. Present in France with the Army of Occupation. Also served in Gibraltar 1826 with 10th Foot and the Ionian Islands 1829 where he died of a heart attack 1836. KH. Died aged 45 having served in the Army for 30 years. Brother of Lt Edward Gardner Freer 43rd Foot.
REFERENCE: *Scarfe, Norman, Letters from the Peninsula: the Freer Family Correspondence, 1807 – 1814, 1953. Gentleman's Magazine, Jan 1838, pp. 99–101.*

FREESTONE, Anthony
Private. 43rd (Monmouthshire) Light Infantry Regiment of Foot.
Headstone: St Andrew's Churchyard, Wissett, Suffolk. (Photograph)

IN MEMORY OF ANTHONY FREESTONE / WHO DIED JUNE 21ST 1866. AGED 76 YEARS. / (VERSE)

Pte 1809.
　　Born at Halesworth Suffolk 1789. Enlisted 1809. Served for 16 years and 61 days. Served in every action in the Peninsula from the Coa (wounded) to Toulouse. MGS medal for Ciudad Rodrigo, Badajoz (one of the Forlorn Hope), Salamanca, Vittoria, Pyrenees, Nivelle and Nive. Also served in North America (present at New Orleans). Returned to Europe and was present in France at the Capture of Paris. Chelsea out-pensioner 1825.

FREETH, James
Lieutenant. Royal Staff Corps.
Low monument: Brompton Cemetery, London. (BR 47492. Compartment AJ:30.9x28.5). (Photograph)

.... / GENERAL SIR JAMES FREETH, / K.C.B. – K.H. / BORN 5TH MARCH 1786, / DIED 19TH JANUARY 1867. / ....

Ensign 25 Dec 1806. Lt 30 May 1809. Capt 21 Apr 1814. Bt Major 21 Jan 1819. Lt Colonel 11 Jul 1826. Bt Colonel 23 Nov 1841. Major General 11 Nov 1851. Lt General 26 Oct 1858. General 9 Mar 1865.
　　Served in the Peninsula May 1809 – Jan 1814. Present at Fuentes d'Onoro, Ciudad Rodrigo, Badajoz, Salamanca, Burgos, Vittoria, Pyrenees, Nivelle and Nive. Later became AQMG 1840. MGS medal for Fuentes d'Onoro, Ciudad Rodrigo, Badajoz, Salamanca, Vittoria, Pyrenees, Nivelle and Nive. KCB and KH. Colonel 64th Foot 13 Aug 1855.

FREMANTLE, John
Lieutenant and Captain. Coldstream Regiment of Foot Guards.
Memorial: Royal Military Chapel, Wellington Barracks, London. (M.I.) (Destroyed by a Flying Bomb in 1944)

"IN MEMORY OF MAJOR-GENERAL JOHN FREMANTLE, C.B., WHO ENTERED THE COLD-STREAM GUARDS ON 17TH OCTOBER, 1805, AND TOOK PART IN THE EXPEDITION TO GERMANY UNDER LORD CATHCART; THE EXPEDITION TO AND STORMING OF BUENOS AYRES UNDER GENERAL WHITELOCKE; THE PENINSULAR WAR AND THE CAMPAIGN OF WATERLOO, INCLUDING THE PASSAGE OF THE DOURO, BATTLE OF TALAVERA, BATTLE OF BUSACO, RETREAT ON TORRES VEDRAS, BATTLE OF FUENTES D'ONOR, SIEGE OF CIUDAD RODRIGO, BATTLE OF SALAMANCA, SIEGE OF BURGOS, BATTLE OF VITTORIA, BATTLE OF ST MARCIAL, PASSAGES OF THE BIDASSOA, THE NIVE, AND THE NIVELLE, BATTLE OF

ORTHES, BATTLES OF QUATRE BRAS AND WATERLOO. HE SERVED BOTH AS ADJUTANT AND COMMANDING OFFICER OF THE COLDSTREAM, AND WAS AIDE-DE-CAMP TO THE DUKE OF WELLINGTON FROM 1812 TO 1817. HE DIED IN LONDON ON 6TH APRIL, 1845, AGED 55 YEARS. PLACED BY HIS SON, COLONEL ARTHUR LYON FREMANTLE, COMMANDING COLDSTREAM GUARDS."

Ensign 17 Oct 1805. Lt and Capt 2 Aug 1810. Bt Major 21 Jun 1813. Bt Lt Colonel 21 Mar 1814. Capt and Lt Colonel 1 Aug 1822. Bt Colonel 22 Jul 1830. Major General 23 Nov 1841.

Served in the Peninsula Jan 1809 – Feb 1810, Oct 1810 – Jun 1813 and Aug 1813 – Feb 1814. (ADC to Lt General Craddock Jan 1809 – Apr 1809, ADC to the Duke of Wellington Nov 1809 – Feb 1810, Oct 1810 – Jun 1813 and Aug 1813 – Feb 1814. Adjutant 16 Nov 1809 – 2 Dec 1812). Present at Douro, Talavera, Busaco, Fuentes d'Onoro, Ciudad Rodrigo, Salamanca, Burgos, Vittoria (Mentioned in Despatches), San Marcial, Nivelle, Nive and Orthes. After Vittoria carried Wellington's despatches, the captured French colours and Marshal Jourdain's baton to England. Also carried the despatch from Orthes. CB and Gold medal for Orthes. Present at Waterloo (ADC to Wellington). Also served at Hanover 1806 and South America 1807.

One of the earliest scholars in the junior department of the Military College at Marlow. Studied in Germany 1805. From there he joined Cathcart's expedition to Hanover. Served in South America 1807 (ADC to General Whitelocke at Buenos Ayres where he volunteered to serve with the Rifle Corps and was taken prisoner while under the command of Major General Robert Craufurd). Accompanied Lord Howden to Lisbon in 1808 as his private secretary then rejoined his regiment in the Peninsula. Also served in Jamaica (DAG).
REFERENCE: Glover, Gareth ed., The Candid letters of Lt Colonel Freemantle Coldstream Guards, 2012. Gentleman's Magazine, Jun 1845, p. 650. Annual Register, 1845, Appx, p. 268.

FRENCH, Henry John
Lieutenant. 85th (Buckinghamshire Volunteers) Light Infantry Regiment of Foot.
Headstone with Cross: St Mary's Catholic Cemetery, Kensal Green, London. (3293RS). (Photograph)

LIEUT GENERAL / HENRY JOHN FRENCH / LATE COLONEL OF THE 80TH FOOT. / DIED 25TH OF JANUARY 1874 / IN HIS 78TH YEAR. / ....

Ensign 90th Foot 27 Aug 1812. Lt 85th Foot 21 Jul 1813. Capt 25 Sep 1823. Major 23 May 1836. Lt Colonel 31 Jul 1846. Bt Colonel 20 Jun 1854. Major General 18 Jan 1861. Lt General 9 Aug 1870.

Served in the Peninsula Aug 1813 – Apr 1814. Present at San Sebastian, Bidassoa, Nivelle, Nive and Bayonne. Also served in North America 1814 –1815 (present at Bladensburg, Baltimore, New Orleans and Fort Bowyer), Canada 1837–1838 (during the Rebellion), West Indies 1846 (present in the Leeward and Windward Islands as DQMG). MGS medal for Nivelle and Nive. Colonel 80th Foot Sep 3 1867.
REFERENCE: Annual Register, 1874, Appx, p. 139.

FROST, George
Bombardier. Royal Artillery.
Grave: Nottingham Road Cemetery, Derby, Derbyshire. Inscription not recorded. (Grave number 18066). (Burial record)

Bombardier 26 Jan 1807.
Served in the Peninsula. Present at Badajoz where he was knocked off the scaling ladder in the Forlorn Hope and wounded. Discharged 3 May 1815. MGS medal for Badajoz. Died 28 Apr 1871.

FRY, John
1st Lieutenant. 95th Regiment of Foot.
Memorial tablet: St Peter and St Paul's Church, Weedon Beck, Northamptonshire. (Photograph)

SACRED TO THE MEMORY OF / CAPTAIN JOHN FRY, / RIFLE BRIGADE. / WHO DIED ON THE 19TH JULY 1840, AGED 48 YEARS. / HE SERVED IN THE RIFLE BRIGADE, / DURING THE PENINSULAR WAR AND AT WATERLOO. / THIS TABLET IS ERECTED BY HIS BROTHER OFFICERS / AS A TESTIMONY OF THEIR RESPECT AND ESTEEM.

2nd Lt 21 Jun 1810. Lt 10 May 1812. Capt 22 Jul 1830.
    Served in the Peninsula with 2/95th May 1812 – Nov 1813. Present at Salamanca, San Millan, Vittoria, Pyrenees, Heights of Vera (wounded) and Bidassoa (severely wounded). Served at Waterloo where he was wounded. Died at Northampton 19 Jul 1840.

FRY, William Dowell
Assistant Surgeon. 33rd (1st Yorkshire West Riding) Regiment of Foot.
Ledger stone: Kensal Green Cemetery, London. (1100/59/RS). (Photograph)

SACRED / TO THE MEMORY OF / WILLIAM DOWELL FRY / SURGEON / IN HM 33RD REGIMENT OF FOOT / WHO DEPARTED THIS LIFE / THE 21ST AUGUST 1837 / AGED 53 YEARS

Asst Surgeon 30th Foot 25 Oct 1803. Superseded (absent without leave 19 Dec 1805). Re-appointed as Hospital Mate General Services 29 Oct 1812. Asst Surgeon 33rd Foot 12 Nov 1812.
    Present at Waterloo. Also served in the Netherlands 1814. Half pay 24 Jul 1817.

FUGION, Edward
Lieutenant. 58th (Rutlandshire) Regiment of Foot.
Low monument: Kensal Green Cemetery, London. Inscription illegible. (391/80–81/RS). (Photograph)

Ensign 4 May 1809. Lt 25 Jul 1811. Paymaster 23 Dec 1819.
    Served in the Peninsula Jul 1809 – Apr 1814. Present at Salamanca, Burgos and Orthes. MGS medal for Salamanca and Orthes. Half pay 1 Apr 1851. Buried in Kensal Green 15 Jan 1878.

FULLER, Francis
Captain. 59th (2nd Nottinghamshire) Regiment of Foot.
Grave: Nunhead Cemetery, London. (Grave number 2462 Sq 107)

Ensign 9 Jul 1803. Lt 5 Sep 1804. Capt 5 Oct 1809. Major 17 Jul 1817. Bt Lt Colonel 19 Jan 1826. Lt Colonel 25 Nov 1828.
    Served in the Peninsula Dec 1812 – Jan 1814. Present at Vittoria, San Sebastian Nivelle, Nive (wounded 9 Dec and severely wounded 11 Dec 1813). Present at Waterloo in reserve at Hal, siege of Cambrai, Capture of Paris and with the Army of Occupation. Also served at the Cape of Good Hope 1806, Canada 1809 (ADC to Lt General Fuller) and India 1818–1827 (present at the siege of Bhurtpore 1825–1826 where he was wounded and awarded Army of India medal). Gold Medal for San Sebastian. MGS medal for Vittoria, Nivelle and Nive. CB. Died in Greenwich 27 Jul 1853 aged 62. Son of Lt General Francis Fuller.
REFERENCE: *Gentleman's Magazine, Jul 1853, p. 100.*

FULLER, Sir Joseph
Captain and Lieutenant Colonel. Coldstream Regiment of Foot Guards.
Chest tomb: Kensal Green Cemetery, London. (3236/102/IC). (Photograph)

SACRED TO THE MEMORY OF / LIEUT-GEN.^L SIR JOSEPH FULLER GCH. / WHO DIED 16TH OCTOBER 1841 / AGED 70 YEARS.

Ensign Coldstream Guards 1 Aug 1792. Lt and Capt 22 Jan 1794. Capt-Lieut 18 Jun 1801. Capt and Lt Colonel 25 May 1803. Bt Colonel 25 Jul 1810. Major General 4 Jun 1813. Lt General 27 May 1825.

Served in the Peninsula Mar 1809 – Mar 1810 and Apr 1811 – May 1812. Present at Douro, Talavera (commanded the Coldstream Guards), Fuentes d'Onoro and Ciudad Rodrigo. Gold Medal for Talavera. GCH. Also served in Flanders 1793–1794 (present at Valenciennes and Dunkirk), Ireland 1798 (present in the Rebellion) and the Helder 1799. Colonel 75th Foot 9 Apr 1832. Brother of Lt Colonel William Fuller 1st Dragoon Guards who was killed at Waterloo.
REFERENCE: *Dictionary of National Biography. Royal Military Calendar, Vol 3, p. 311. Gentleman's Magazine, Jan 1842, p. 98. Annual Register, 1841, Appx, p. 227.*

FULLER, William
Lieutenant Colonel. 1st (King's) Dragoon Guards.
Memorial tablet: St Joseph's Church, Waterloo, Belgium. (Photograph)

SACRED TO THE MEMORY / OF COLONEL W^M FULLER OF THE 1ST / (OR KING'S OWN) REG^T. OF D^{GN}. G^{DS}. / IN THE ROYAL HORSE G^D. BRIGADE, / WHO GLORIOUSLY FELL, / ON THE 18TH OF JUNE 1815, / AT THE MEMORABLE BATTLE / OF WATERLOO, WHILST LEADING / HIS GALLANT REG^T. / TO THE CHARGE OF THE / ENEMY'S CAVALRY. / THIS STONE WAS ERECTED / BY HIS AFFECTIONATE BROTHER / M. GENERAL FULLER, / LATE OF THE COLDS^{TM} GUARDS.

Cornet 10th Lt Dragoons 1793. Lt 30 Apr 1793. Capt-Lieut 7 Oct 1794. Capt 16 May 1795. Major 19 Oct 1799. Lt Colonel 1st Dragoon Guards 22 Aug 1805. Bt Colonel 4 Jun 1813.

Present at Waterloo where he was killed leading the cavalry charge of the King's Dragoon Guards. Brother of Capt and Lt Colonel Sir Joseph Fuller Coldstream Guards.

FULLERTON, Alexander
Conductor of Stores. Field Train Department of Ordnance.
Memorial tablet: Kingston Church of Christ, Jamaica, West Indies. (Photograph)

SACRED / TO THE MEMORY OF / ALEXANDER FULLERTON ESQ^{RE}. / LATE AND FOR MANY YEARS / ORDNANCE STOREKEEPER / IN THIS ISLAND. / HE DEPARTED THIS LIFE / THE 4TH DAY OF JANUARY 1850 / AGED 62 YEARS. / HE SERVED IN THE PENINSULAR CAMPAIGN / AND HAD A MEDAL WITH / THREE CLASPS AWARDED HIM FOR / VIMIERA, CORUNNA AND NIVELLE. / HE DIED BELOVED AND RESPECTED / BY ALL WHO KNEW HIM. / ....

Served in the Peninsula 1808–1814. Present at Vimeiro, Corunna and Nivelle. Also served in the West Indies as Ordnance storekeeper. MGS medal for Vimeiro, Corunna and Nivelle.

FULLERTON, James
Captain. 95th Regiment of Foot.
Chest tomb: Old Burying Ground, Halifax, Nova Scotia, Canada. (Photograph)

SACRED TO THE MEMORY OF / LIEUT COLONEL JAMES FULLERTON C.B. & K.H. / LATE COMMANDING 96TH REGIMENT, / WHO DIED AT GOVERNMENT HOUSE, HALIFAX 8TH MARCH 1834. / HE SERVED WITH DISTINCTION IN DIFFERENT PARTS OF THE WORLD, / AND DIED ESTEEMED AND LAMENTED / BY THE OFFICERS OF THE REGIMENT, / AND NUMEROUS ACQUAINTANCES IN THE TOWN OF HALIFAX.

Ensign 51ˢᵗ Foot 24 Dec 1802. Lt 2 Jul 1803. Capt 95ᵗʰ Foot 7 May 1809. Bt Major 7 Apr 1814. Bt Lt Colonel 18 Jun 1815. Major 24 Oct 1821. Lt Colonel (unattached) 10 Oct 1821. Lt Colonel 96ᵗʰ Foot 13 Sep 1827.

Served in the Peninsula Oct 1808 – Jan 1809 and Aug 1810 – Jan 1812. Present at Corunna, Cadiz and Barrosa. Present at Waterloo (wounded and awarded Bt Lt Colonelcy. Commanded 3ʳᵈ Battalion 95ᵗʰ Foot after Major Ross was wounded). Also served in Ceylon 1803–1805 (present in the Kandian War), Netherlands1814 (present at Merxem and Antwerp) and Canada. CB and KH.
REFERENCE: *Gentleman's Magazine, Aug 1834, p. 212.*

FULTON, Robert
Lieutenant Colonel. 79ᵗʰ (Cameron Highlanders) Regiment of Foot.
Gravestone: Paisley Abbey Churchyard, Renfrewshire, Scotland. (M.I.)

".....................ROBERT FULTON OF HARTFIELD AND CRAIGMUIR 1776–1851, LIEUT COL 79ᵀᴴ REGT FOUGHT AT ABOUKIR 1801, COPENHAGEN 1807, SALAMANCA 1812, THE LAIRD COLONEL OF A SCOTTISH REGIMENT ...."

Ensign 20ᵗʰ Foot 31 Jan 1798. Lt 21ˢᵗ Fusiliers 19 May 1798. Capt 79ᵗʰ Foot 10 Jul 1800. Major 25 Mar 1805. Lt Colonel 2/79ᵗʰ 28 May 1807. Lt Colonel 1/79ᵗʰ 13 May 1811.

Served in the Peninsula Sep 1811 – Feb 1813. Present at Salamanca and Burgos. Gold Medal for Salamanca. Also served in Egypt 1801 (Gold Medal from Sultan Selim III) and Copenhagen 1807. Retired 3 Dec 1812.

FURNACE, William H.
Captain. 61ˢᵗ (South Gloucestershire) Regiment of Foot.
Named on the Memorial: St Andrew's Church, (now Musée Historique), Biarritz, France. (Photograph)

Volunteer. Ensign 28 Nov 1795. Lt 12 Jul 1796. Capt 28 Apr 1804.

Served in the Peninsula Jun 1809 – Aug 1812 and Sep – Nov 1813. Present at Talavera (wounded), Busaco and Nivelle where he was killed 10 Nov 1813. His two brothers Edward and Norbury were also in the Peninsula. Ensign Edward was killed at Albuera, one of the colour party of the 29ᵗʰ and Lt Norbury in the 61ˢᵗ survived the war.

FYERS, Edward
2ⁿᵈ Captain. Royal Engineers.
Named on the Regimental Memorial: Rochester Cathedral, Rochester, Kent. (Photograph)

2ⁿᵈ Lt 23 Apr 1808. Lt 24 Jun 1809. 2ⁿᵈ Capt Royal Engineers 21 Jul 1813. Capt Royal Invalid Engineers 19 Dec 1819.

Served in the Peninsula 1809. Retired 23 Dec 1831. Died at Inverness 12 Dec 1854.

FYERS, Peter
Lieutenant Colonel. Royal Artillery.
Chest tomb: St Luke's Churchyard, Charlton, Kent. (Grave number 281). (Photograph)

SACRED TO THE MEMORY OF MAJOR PETER FYERS CB, COLONEL COMMANDING 7ᵀᴴ BATTALION R.A.

2ⁿᵈ Lt 24 Apr 1793. 1ˢᵗ Lt 1 Jan 1794. Capt-Lieut 16 Jul 1799. Capt 12 Sep 1803. Bt Major 4 Jun 1811. Major 14 Feb 1814. Lt Colonel 20 Dec 1814. Colonel 29 Jul 1825. Major General 10 Jan 1837. Colonel Commandant 14 Jun 1845.

Served in the Netherlands 1814–1815 (present at Merxem where he was highly commended for his use of artillery and awarded CB and at Bergen-op-Zoom). Also served in Flanders 1794–1795, Copenhagen 1801 (served with Nelson's fleet where he was highly commended in Nelson's Dispatch), Copenhagen 1807 and Walcheren 1809 (present at the siege of Flushing). Died 17 May 1846.

FYERS, Thomas
Captain. Royal Engineers.
Named on the Regimental Memorial: Rochester Cathedral, Rochester, Kent. (Photograph)

2nd Lt 2 May 1800. Lt 18 Apr 1801. 2nd Capt 21 Sep 1805. Capt 23 Apr 1810. Bt Major 12 Aug 1819. Lt Colonel 23 Mar 1825. Colonel 10 Jan 1837. Major General 9 Nov 1846.
    Served in the Peninsula 1808 – Jan 1809. Present at Corunna. Served in the Royal Engineers for 47 years. Died at Woolwich 11 May 1847.

FYERS, William
Colonel. Royal Engineers.
Memorial tablet: Christ Church Cathedral, Dublin, Ireland. (M.I.) (The tablet has been removed from the original location and is stored in the crypt awaiting restoration)

"LIEUT. GENERAL FYERS, / OB. A.D. 1829. / TO THE MEMORY / OF / LIEUT-GENERAL WILLIAM FYERS / COLONEL COMMANDANT / AND COMMANDING ROYAL ENGINEERS IN IRELAND, / WHO DIED OCTOBER, 27TH, 1829, AGED 77 YEARS, / AND WAS HERE BURIED. / THIS TABLET IS ERECTED BY THE OFFICERS / OF THE CORPS OF ROYAL ENGINEERS / WHO SERVED UNDER THE LIEUTENANT GENERAL / IN TESTIMONY OF THEIR SINCERE RESPECT AND ESTEEM."

Ensign 8 Nov 1773. 2nd Lt 11 Nov 1773. 1st Lt 7 May 1779. Capt-Lieut 20 Apr 1787. Capt 27 Nov 1793. Bt Major 6 May 1795. Bt Lt Colonel 1 Jan 1800. Lt Colonel 1 Jul 1800. Colonel 1 Jul 1806. Major General 4 Jun 1811. Lt General 12 Aug 1819.
    Served at Walcheren 1809 (Commanding Engineer). Also served in North America 1775 (present at Brooklyn, Brandywine, Philadelphia and Charlestown), Halifax, Gibraltar 1795–1807 (Commanding Engineer and Deputy Inspector General of Fortifications) and Ireland 1811–1829 (Commanding Engineer).
REFERENCE: *Royal Military Calendar, Vol 3, pp. 62–63. United Service Journal, Nov 1829, p. 783. Gentleman's Magazine, Dec 1829, p. 560.*

FYFE, William
Captain. 92nd Regiment of Foot.
Headstone: Speymouth Essil, Morayshire, Scotland. (M.I.)

"CAPT WILLIAM FYFE, LATE OF 92ND REGT. DIED 18 OCT 1858, AGED 83."

Ensign 2 Jun 1804. Lt 29 Aug 1805. Capt 16 Sep 1813.
    Served in the Peninsula Aug 1808 – Jan 1809 and Oct 1810 – Apr 1814. Present at Corunna, Fuentes d'Onoro, Arroyo dos Molinos, Almarez, Alba de Tormes, Vittoria, Pyrenees (wounded 25 Jul 1813), Nivelle, Nive, Garris, Orthes and Aire (severely wounded). Also served in the Baltic 1808 and Walcheren 1809. Retired on half pay 1814. MGS medal for Corunna, Fuentes d'Onoro, Vittoria, Pyrenees, Nivelle, Nive and Orthes.

GALE, Arthur
Captain. 28th (North Gloucestershire) Regiment of Foot.
Named on the Memorial: St Andrew's Church, (now Musée Historique), Biarritz, France. (Photograph)

Ensign 29 Aug 1795. Lt 1798. Capt 19 Oct 1804.

Served in the Peninsula with 2/28th Jul 1809 – Jul 1811 and 1/28th Apr 1813 – Feb 1814. Present at Busaco, first siege of Badajoz, Albuera (wounded), Vittoria, Pyrenees, Nivelle, Nive and Garris where he was killed 15 Feb 1814.

GAMMELL, James
Lieutenant. 61st (South Gloucestershire) Regiment of Foot.
Grave: Locksbrook Cemetery, Bath, Somerset. (No longer extant). (Photograph of site)

Ensign 59th Foot 29 Sep 1813. Lt Sicilian Regiment 23 Feb 1815. Lt 61st Foot 1 Jun 1815. Lt 64th Foot 21 Aug 1823. Capt 92nd Foot 14 Apr 1825.

Served in the Peninsula Dec 1813 – Apr 1814. Present at Nive, Bayonne and the Sortie from Bayonne Also served in the West Indies. Retired 6 Oct 1825.

Capt James Gammell was the last surviving officer of the Peninsular War. He did not receive his MGS medal, awarded for Nive, until 1889 due to an oversight. In a ceremony later the MGS medal was presented to him at his home in Bath and Queen Victoria also awarded him a Jubilee medal. Died in Bath 23 Sep 1893 aged 96. Brother of 1st Lt William Gammell 95th Foot.
REFERENCE: *Orders and Medals Research Society Journal, Mar 2009, pp. 41–2.*

GAMMELL, William
1st Lieutenant. 95th Regiment of Foot.
Pedestal tomb: Ford Park Cemetery, Plymouth, Devon. (Section CHB 6 3). (Photograph)

SACRED TO THE MEMORY OF / MAJOR WILLIAM GAMMELL / (ELDEST SON OF GENERAL ANDREW GAMMELL, FIRST FOOT GUARDS) / WHO DIED AT HIS RESIDENCE AT STONE-HOUSE / IN THE COUNTY OF DEVON / ON THE 21ST FEBRUARY 1853 AGED 61 / DEEPLY LAMENTED BY HIS WIDOW / AND CHILDREN. / HE SERVED IN THE 85TH REGIMENT OF LIGHT INFANTRY / IN THE PENINSULAR / IN WHICH HE DISTINGUISHED HIMSELF / BY HIS GALLANTRY / DURING THE FIRST SIEGE OF BADAJOS IN 1811 / ON WHICH OCCASION HE WAS SEVERELY WOUNDED. / HE WAS SUBSEQUENTLY APPOINTED TO THE / 95TH RIFLE CORPS / WITH WHICH HE SERVED IN THE PENINSULA / AND WAS ESTEEMED AS / A MOST ZEALOUS AND EFFICIENT OFFICER. / BOTH IN THE 85TH AND 95TH REGIMENTS / HE WAS BELOVED BY HIS COMPANIONS IN ARMS / AND HE RECEIVED A PENINSULAR MEDAL / FROM HER MAJESTY QUEEN VICTORIA FOR HIS SERVICES.

Ensign 25th Foot 16 Jan 1808. Lt 85th Foot 25 Jan 1809. Lt 95th Foot 25 Jan 1813. Capt 104th Foot 18 Apr 1816. Capt 86th Foot 11 Dec 1817. Major (unattached) 29 Aug 1826. Major 87th Foot 11 Oct 1833.

Served in the Peninsula with 85th Foot Mar – Oct 1811 and 95th Foot Dec 1813 – Apr 1814. Present at second siege of Badajoz (wounded), Orthes, Tarbes and Toulouse. MGS medal for Orthes and Toulouse. Also served at Walcheren 1809. Retired 18 Oct 1833. Brother of Lt James Gammell 61st Foot.

GARDINER, David
Lieutenant. 88th (Connaught Rangers) Regiment of Foot.
Family Headstone: Abernyte Churchyard, Abernyte, Perthshire, Scotland. (Photograph)

IN MEMORY OF / ALEXANDER GARDINER / FARMER / THEIR SONS .... / DAVID, CAPTAIN IN THE 8 (KING'S) REGIMENT, / BORN 14 MARCH 1786, DIED 5 APRIL 1862.

Ensign Royal Perth Militia 24 May 1811. Ensign 88th Foot 27 Jul 1811. Lt 24th Nov 1814. Lt 8th Foot 5 May 1825. Captain 22 Nov 1837.

Served in the Peninsula Oct 1812 – Apr 1814. Present at Vittoria. Retired 12 Dec 1848. Brother of 1st Lt John Gardiner 95th Foot.

GARDINER, James Ballard

Captain. 50th (West Kent) Regiment of Foot.
Chest tomb: St Andrew's Churchyard, Hove, Sussex. (Photograph)

SACRED TO THE MEMORY OF / LIEUTENANT COLONEL JAMES BALLARD GARDINER / LATE OF THE 1ST REGIMENT OF LIFE GUARDS / WHO DIED AUGUST THE 8TH 1851 AGED 73. / THIS GALLANT AND LAMENTED OFFICER WAS ENGAGED / IN THE EXPEDITION AGAINST COPENHAGEN IN 1807, / SERVED THROUGHOUT THE CAMPAIGN / IN THE PENINSULAR IN 1808 AND 1809, / IN WALCHEREN IN 1809, / AND AGAIN IN THE PENINSULAR FROM 1810 TO 1813. / THROUGH THE WHOLE OF THESE SERVICES / DURING WHICH HE WAS PRESENT AT THE BATTLES OF / ROLICA, VIMIERO, CORUNNA AND VITTORIA, / AT THE LATTER OF WHICH HE WAS SEVERELY WOUNDED / HIS LEFT THIGH BEING FRACTURED BY A MUSKET SHOT. / HE EMINENTLY DISTINGUISHED HIMSELF / BY EVERY ATTRIBUTE OF A BRITISH OFFICER. / THIS HUMBLE TRIBUTE / TO THE DEPARTED WORTHS OF HER BELOVED HUSBAND / IS ERECTED BY HIS SORROWING WIDOW.

Ensign 3 Aug 1803. Lt 50th Foot 4 Jan 1805. Capt 20 Jul 1809. Bt Major 17 Feb 1820. Capt 1st Life Guards 1820. Bt Lt Col 10 Jan 1837.

Served in the Peninsula Aug 1808 – Jan 1809 and Apr – Sep 1813. Present at Rolica, Vimiero, Corunna and Vittoria (severely wounded). Also served at Copenhagen 1807 and Walcheren 1809. MGS medal for Rolica, Vimiero, Corunna and Vittoria. Half pay 20 Jun 1822.

REFERENCE: *Gentleman's Magazine, Sep 1851, p. 335. Annual Register, 1851, Appx, p. 318.*

GARDINER, John

Major. 6th (1st Warwickshire) Regiment of Foot.
Family Pedestal tomb: Kensal Green Cemetery, London. (3328/102/IC). (Photograph)

SACRED / .... / AND OF LIEUT GENL / SIR JOHN GARDINER / KCB. / BORN JULY 6TH 1777. / DIED JUNE 6TH 1851.

Ensign 3rd Foot 23 Nov 1791. Lt 12 Jul 1793. Capt 17 May 1796. Major 9th Garrison Battalion 18 Dec 1806. Major 6th Foot 28th May 1807. Bt Lt Colonel 29 Oct 1809. Bt Colonel 12 Aug 1819. Lt Col 6th Foot 18 Dec 1824. Major General 22 Jul 1830. Lt Gen 23 Nov 1841.

Served in the Peninsula Oct 1813 – Apr 1814 (Commanded 1 Brigade 7th Division). Present at Nivelle, Orthes and Bordeaux. Gold Medal for Nivelle and Orthes. KCB. Also served in Flanders 1794–1795, West Indies 1795–1802 (AQMG), Walcheren 1809 (AAG). Remained on the Staff as AAG at Horse Guards 1814 when his regiment went to North America. Also served in Ireland 1822–1830 (DAG 1822). Colonel 6th Foot 28 Mar 1849. Was well liked by his men – he took great pleasure in finding employment for them on their discharge if they deserved it. Married sister of Capt Thomas Wildman 7th Lt Dragoons. Brother of Major General Sir R. W. Gardiner, R.A.

REFERENCE: *United Service Magazine, Jul 1851, pp. 477–8. Gentleman's Magazine, Oct 1851, p. 432. Annual Register, 1851, Appx, p. 294.*

GARDINER, John

Lieutenant and Adjutant. 3rd (East Kent) Regiment of Foot.
Headstone: Errol Churchyard, Errol, Perthshire, Scotland. (Photograph)

SACRED / TO THE MEMORY OF / JOHN GARDINER, ESQ. / OF CARSEYGRANGE. BORN 14TH

OCT. 1779, WHO, / AFTER HAVING SERVED AS AN OFFICER / IN THE ARMY TILL THE END OF / THE PENINSULAR WAR, / RETIRED AND SPENT THE REST OF / HIS LIFE IN HIS NATIVE PLACE, / WHERE, AFTER SOME YEARS OF FEEBLE / HEALTH, HE DIED 3RD DEC. 1843 / AGED 64. / HE WAS MUCH AND JUSTLY LAMENTED / BY AN AFFECTIONATE FAMILY / AND A LARGE CIRCLE OF FRIENDS.

Lt 1 May 1806. Adjt 13 Jul 1809.
Served in the Peninsula Sep 1808 – Jul 1809 and May 1812 – Apr 1814. Present at Douro, Vittoria, Pyrenees, Nivelle, Nive, Garris, Orthes, Aire and Toulouse. Also served in North America 1814.

GARDINER, John
1st Lieutenant. 95th Regiment of Foot.
Family Headstone: Abernyte Churchyard, Abernyte, Perthshire, Scotland. (Photograph)

IN MEMORY OF / ALEXANDER GARDINER / FARMER / THEIR SONS .... / JOHN MAJOR IN THE 82 REGIMENT, / BORN 11 NOVEMBER 1782. DIED 18TH JUNE 1852. / THE ANNIVERSARY OF THE BATTLE OF WATERLOO SO / GLORIOUS TO THE BRITISH ARMS, IN WHICH HE WAS / SEVERELY WOUNDED.

Ensign Royal Perthshire Militia. 2nd Lt 95th Foot 9 Apr 1809. 1st Lt 30 Aug 1810. Capt 71 Foot 16 Jun 1825. Bt Major 28 Jun 1838. Capt 82nd Regiment 16 Jul 1841.
Served in the Peninsula Jan 1813 – Apr 1814. Present at San Millan, Vittoria, Pyrenees, Vera, Bidassoa, Nivelle, Nive, Orthes, Tarbes and Toulouse. Present at Waterloo (severely wounded). Also served at Walcheren 1809. MGS medal for Vittoria, Pyrenees, Nivelle, Nive, Orthes and Toulouse. Retired 27 May 1842. Died on the anniversary and at the same hour, on which he was carried severely wounded from the field of Waterloo). Brother of Lt David Gardiner 88th Foot.

GARDNER, Daniel
Captain. 43rd (Monmouthshire) Light Infantry Regiment of Foot.
Memorial tablet: St Michael's Old Cathedral, Coventry, Warwickshire. (No longer extant. Cathedral bombed in the Second World War). (M.I.)

" .... ALSO DAVID, YOUNGEST SON OF THE ABOVE ELIZABETH, LATE CAPTAIN IN THE 43RD REGIMENT AND MAJOR OF BRIGADE, DISTINGUISHED BY HIS BRAVERY, HE FELL (SINCERELY REGRETTED) IN THE BATTLE OF TALAVERA DE LA REYNA ON THE 28TH JULY 1809, AGED 26. HIS REMAINS LIE INTERRED IN THE BANKS OF THE TAGUS NEAR THE PLACE WHERE HE FELL."

Ensign 12 Dec 1800. Lt 4 Mar 1802. Capt 27 Aug 1804.
Served in the Peninsula Aug 1808 – Jan 1809 (Brigade Major to Colonel R. Stewart). Present at Douro and Talavera where he was killed 28 Jul 1809.

GARDNER, Thomas
Private. 1st Life Guards.
Memorial tablet: St Mary and St Michael Churchyard, Great Urswick, Cumbria. (Photograph)

THE / NON-COMMISSIONED / OFFICERS / AND PRIVATES / OF THE / FURNESS CUIRASSIERS / ERECTED THIS MONUMENT / TO THE MEMORY OF / THOMAS GARDNER / THEIR DRILL SERGEANT, / FORMERLY OF THE FIRST REGIMENT / OF LIFE GUARDS / WHO WAS KILLED BY A FALL / FROM HIS HORSE / ON THE 21ST DAY OF APRIL 1821 / IN THE 32ND YEAR OF HIS AGE.

Pte Oct 1809.

Served in the Peninsula and at Waterloo. At Waterloo his horse fell on him and damaged his lungs. As a result of this fall and poor health which he encountered in the Peninsula he was discharged 23 Dec 1818. Served for 11 years and 60 days.

GARLICK, Moses Bendle
Private. 9th (East Norfolk) Regiment of Foot.
Obelisk: Uley Baptist Cemetery, Uley Road, One Tree Hill, South Australia, Australia. (Photograph)

Southern Face:

IN / MEMORY OF / MOSES BENDLE GARLICK / BORN SEPTEMBER 1* 1784 / DIED OCTOBER 1ST 1859 / HE RESTS FROM HIS LABOURS / AND HIS WORKS DO / FOLLOW HIM

Eastern Face:

HE / SERVED DURING THE / WHOLE OF THE / PENINSULAR CAMPAIGN / WAS PRESENT / IN SIX GENERAL ACTIONS / VIMIERA / CORUNNA / BUSACO / SALAMANCA / VITTORIA / ST SEBASTIAN

Western Face:

HE WAS A / GOOD SOLDIER OF / JESUS CHRIST / ONE OF THE TWELVE WHO / FOUNDED THE / BAPTIST CHURCH / IN SOUTH AUSTRALIA / IN THE YEAR 1838 / HE WAS SUBSEQUENTLY DEACON OF THE BAPTIST CHURCHES / IN KERMODE STREET / AND LEFEVRE TERRACE / NORTH ADELAIDE / AND FOUNDER / OF THE PLACE OF WORSHIP / NEAR WHICH / HIS DUST REPOSES / SOLDIER OF CHRIST WELL DONE! / PRAISE BE THY BE IT EMPLOY (sic) / THE BATTLE FOUGHT THE VICTORY WON / REST IN THY SAVIOURS JOY

Served in the Peninsula Aug 1808 – Jan 1809 and Mar 1810 – Apr 1814. Present at Vimeiro, Corunna, Busaco, Salamanca, Vittoria and San Sebastian. After the war emigrated to Australia and became a successful timber merchant. Founded the local school and the Baptist Church in South Australia 1838. MGS medal for Vimeiro, Corunna, Busaco, Salamanca, Vittoria and San Sebastian.

GARRETT, Robert
Captain. 97th (Queen's Own) Regiment of Foot.
Memorial window and memorial tablet: St Laurence's Church, Ramsgate, Kent. (South aisle). (Photograph)

IN MEMORY OF LIEUT. GENERAL SIR ROBERT GARRETT WHO SERVED HIS COUNTRY WITH DISTINCTION IN THE PENINSULAR AND CRIMEAN WARS, KNIGHT COMMANDER OF THE BATH, KNIGHT OF HANOVER, OFFICE OF THE LEGION OF HONOUR, KNIGHT OF THE MEDJIDIE, KNIGHT OF THE SARDINIAN MILITARY ORDER, COLONEL OF THE XLIII REGIMENT OF FOOT; ELDEST SON OF JOHN AND ELIZABETH GARRETT OF ELLINGTON. HE WAS BORN SEPTEMBER XVIII, MDCCXCI, DIED JUNE XIII, MDCCCLXIX. THIS WINDOW IS ERECTED AS A TRIBUTE OF RESPECT AND AFFECTION BY HIS SON LIEUTENANT COLONEL ALGERNON ROBERT GARRETT, LATE LXVI REGIMENT.

Family Mural Memorial tablet: St Laurence's Churchyard, Ramsgate, Kent. (Photograph)

SACRED TO THE MEMORY OF / LIEUTENANT GENERAL SIR ROBERT GARRETT / COLONEL

OF THE XLIII REGIMENT OF FOOT / SON OF JOHN AND ELIZABETH GARRETT OF ELLINGTON.

Ensign 2nd Foot 6 Mar 1811. Lt 2nd Garrison Battalion 3 Sep 1812. Lt 7th Foot 2 Oct 1812. Capt 97th Foot 7 Jul 1814. Major (unattached) 19 Sep 1826. Major 46th Foot 7 Feb 1834. Bt Lt Colonel 23 Nov 1841. Lt Colonel 46th Foot 16 May 1845. Bt Colonel 20 Jun 1854. Major General 20 Oct 1858. Lt General 10 Mar 1866.

Served in the Peninsula with 2nd Foot Apr 1811 – Nov 1812 and 7th Foot Jan – Oct 1813. Present at Fuentes d'Onoro, siege of Salamanca Forts (wounded but took command of the light company and artillery of 2nd Foot as he was the only officer left in his attack column), Salamanca, Vittoria, Pyrenees (severely wounded at Sorauren 27 Jul 1813 – sent back to England to recover from his wound). MGS medal for Fuentes d'Onoro, Salamanca, Vittoria and Pyrenees. KH. Also served in the Crimea with 46th Foot (present at the siege of Sebastopol – awarded medal. KCB, Officer of the Legion of Honor, Sardinian Medal and 3rd Class of Medjidie) and in India (on staff in Bengal Division 1860). Colonel 4th West India Regt 1 Apr 1862 and Colonel 43rd Regt 14 Jan 1866. Educated at Harrow.
REFERENCE: *Dictionary of National Biography*.

GASCOIGNE, Ernest Frederick
Lieutenant. 85th (Buckinghamshire Volunteers) Light Infantry Regiment of Foot.
Family mausoleum: Kensal Green Cemetery, London. (23982/141/PS). (Photograph)

BENEATH THE MAUSOLEUM REST ALL THAT WAS MORTAL OF / ERNEST FREDERICK GASCOIGNE, / GENERAL IN HER MAJESTY'S ARMY. COLONEL OF THE 69TH REGIMENT. / BORN SEPTEMBER 26TH, 1796. DIED JULY 18TH, 1876. / HE ENTERED THE ARMY AT THE AGE OF 15; WAS PRESENT AT THE PASSAGE OF THE BIDASSOA, THE BATTLES OF THE NIVELLE AND NIVE, AND THE INVESTMENT OF BAYONNE. HE SERVED IN THE AMERICAN WAR, WAS PRESENT AT THE BATTLE OF BLADENSBURG (WHERE HE WAS SEVERELY WOUNDED), AND AT THE CAPTURE OF WASHINGTON. HE ALSO SERVED DURING THE CANADIAN REBELLION OF 1838–1839, AND AS GENERAL OFFICER HELD APPOINTMENTS ON THE STAFF. HIS SERVICE IN THE ARMY COMPRISED A PERIOD OF 65 YEARS.

Memorial: Royal Military Chapel, Wellington Barracks, London. (M.I.) (Destroyed by a Flying Bomb in 1944)

"TO THE BELOVED MEMORY OF ERNEST FREDERICK GASCOIGNE, GENERAL IN HER MAJESTY'S ARMY; COLONEL OF THE 69TH REGIMENT. BORN SEPTEMBER 26TH, A.D. 1796. DIED JULY 18TH, A.D. 1876. HE ENTERED THE ARMY AT THE AGE OF 15; AND WAS PRESENT AT THE PASSAGE OF THE BIDASSOA, THE BATTLES OF THE NIVELLE AND NIVE, AND THE INVESTMENT OF BAYONNE. HE SERVED IN THE AMERICAN WAR, AND WAS PRESENT AT THE BATTLE OF BLADENSBURG (WHERE HE WAS VERY SEVERELY WOUNDED), AND AT THE CAPTURE OF WASHINGTON. HE ALSO SERVED DURING THE CANADIAN REBELLION IN 1838–39; AFTERWARDS, FOR 10 YEARS, IN THE GRENADIER GUARDS; AND, AS A GENERAL OFFICER, HELD APPOINTMENTS ON THE STAFF. HIS SERVICES IN THE ARMY COMPRISED A PERIOD OF 65 YEARS. PLACED BY HIS WIDOW."

Ensign 39th Foot 2 May 1811. Lt 85th Foot 13 May 1813. Capt 3rd Garrison Battalion 6 Jul 1815. Capt 54th Foot 24 Dec 1818. Major (unattached) 19 May 1825. Major 32nd Foot 11 May 1826. Lt Colonel 3 Jun 1828. Lt Colonel (appointed to a particular service) 1 Jan 1838. Capt and Lt Colonel 1st Foot Guards 7 Aug 1840. Bt Colonel 23 Nov 1841. Major General 20 Jun 1854. Lt General 13 Feb 1860. General 20 Jan 1867.

Served in the Peninsula Aug 1813 – Apr 1814. Present at San Sebastian, Bidassoa, Nivelle, Nive and

Bayonne. Also served in North America 1814–1815 (present at Bladensburg, capture of Washington and New Orleans). He was severely wounded at Washington and awarded pension of £70 per annum. Also present in Canada 1838–1839 during the Rebellion. MGS medal for San Sebastian, Nivelle and Nive. Colonel 69th Foot 3 Apr 1858. Served in the army for a total of 65 years.

REFERENCE: *Annual Register, 1876, Appx, p. 147. Household Brigade Journal, 1876, p. 309.*

GAWLER, George

Lieutenant. 52nd (Oxfordshire) Light Infantry Regiment of Foot.
Memorial tablet: St Simon's Church, Portsmouth, Hampshire. (West facing wall behind pulpit). (Photograph)

IN MEMORY OF / COLONEL GEORGE GAWLER KH / LATE 52ND LIGHT INFANTRY WHO DIED AT SOUTHSEA MAY 7TH 1869. / HE WAS THE ONLY SON OF THE LATE CAPTN SAMUEL GAWLER 73RD REGT. / COLONEL GAWLER WAS A FAITHFUL SOLDIER OF HIS GOD AND OF HIS / COUNTRY. HE ENTERED THE 52ND REGT IN OCTOBER 1810 AND WAS PRESENT / AT THE STORMING OF BADAJOZ, THE BATTLES OF VITTORIA, VERA, THE / NIVELLE, THE NIVE, ORTHES, TOULOUSE AND WATERLOO. HE RETIRED / ON HALF-PAY IN 1834 WAS APPOINTED GOVERNOR OF SOUTH AUSTRALIA / IN 1838 AND RETURNED TO ENGLAND IN 1842. FOR UPWARDS OF / 50 YEARS HE "FOLLOWED THE LORD FULLY" AND BY GOD'S GRACE / MAINTAINED A STEADY CHRISTIAN WALK UNTIL AFTER A SHORT ILL / NESS HE WAS CALLED TO ENTER INTO THE JOY OF HIS LORD. IN HIS / DYING MOMENTS HE FERVENTLY SAID "NEVER A CLOUD ON MY / ONENESS WITH JESUS IN THE FULNESS OF THE SPIRIT" / HIS REMAINS ARE INTERRED IN THE PORTSMOUTH CEMETERY.

Headstone: Highland Road Cemetery, Portsmouth, Hampshire. (Re-erected by the Royal Green Jackets Regiment in 2002). (Photograph)

LT. COL. / GEORGE GAWLER K.H. / 52ND LIGHT INFANTRY / SERVED WITH DISTINCTION / IN THE PENINSULA / AND AT WATERLOO. / GOVERNOR OF / SOUTH AUSTRALIA, / BORN 21 – 7 – 1795 / DIED 7 – 5 – 1869

Ensign 4 Oct 1810. Lt 12 May 1812. Capt 9 Jun 1825. Major 8 Feb 1831. Lt Colonel 12 Aug 1834. Bt Colonel 9 Nov 1846.

Served in the Peninsula with 1/52nd Feb 1812 – Apr 1814. Present at Badajoz (wounded), San Munos (wounded), Vittoria, Pyrenees, Vera, Bidassoa, Nivelle, Nive, Orthes, Tarbes and Toulouse. At Badajoz he was shot in the leg and fell into the water filled ditch. He would have drowned if he had not been pulled out by another soldier. This unknown man was then shot and killed, his generous action costing him his life. Gawler managed to crawl down the glacis and escape. Present at Waterloo. Also served in Ireland 1820–1823 and Canada 1823–1826. Half pay 1834. MGS medal for Badajoz, Pyrenees, Nivelle, Nive, Orthes and Toulouse.

While on half pay, Gawler helped Siborne with his model of Waterloo and also wrote several books and pamphlets including *Close and crisis of Waterloo* and *The essentials of good skirmishing*, both very well received. KH 1837. Appointed second Governor of South Australia 1838. He served there until 1841 when he was recalled. Although he had done good work in the Colony, he had overspent his budget, which was not surprising when he had settled 6,000 colonists, created a police force and established many public works, putting South Australia on its feet. The government of the day did not like spending too much money on the colonies and he was recalled.

He took no further part in public life, retiring from the Army in 1850. *The Historical record* of the 52nd states: 'Colonel Gawler was essentially a 52nd officer. He served in the Regiment only, and was a type of that steady, cool and gallant set of campaigning officers, whose attention to Regimental duty and experience in the field so materially helped to place the 52nd among the most distinguished on the service of Britain'.

REFERENCE: *Dictionary of National Biography. Australian Dictionary of Biography. Cox Gawler, Jane, George Gawler, KH, 52nd Lt Infantry – a life sketch, 1900. Oxfordshire and Buckinghamshire Light Infantry Chronicle, 1901, pp. 159–63.*

GEARY, Henry

Captain. Royal Artillery.
Brass memorial tablet: St Olave's Church, Gatcombe, Isle of Wight. (Photograph)

IN MEMORY OF CAPT[N] HENRY GEARY, SON / OF COMMANDER THOMAS GEARY, R. N. OF / NEWPORT, ISLE OF WIGHT. BORN NOVEMBER XXVII / MDCCLXXIII, KILLED IN ACTION AT ROLICA AUG[T] XVII MDCCCVIII / ……………….

Headstone: Old Cemetery, Mortlake, Surrey. (M.I.)

"FRANCES GEARY, WIDOW OF CAPT HENRY GEARY OF THE ROYAL ARTILLERY, WHO WAS KILLED IN ACTION AT THE BATTLE OF ROLICA IN PORTUGAL UNDER SIR ARTHUR WELLESLEY 17 AUGUST 1808 ………………."

2nd Lt 23 Jan 1793. 1st Lt 15 Aug 1793. Capt-Lt 4 Mar 1797. Capt 12 Apr 1802.
    Served in the Peninsula Aug 1808. Present at Rolica where he was killed. Also served in Flanders 1793, the Irish Rebellion 1798 and the Helder 1799. Cashiered 1 Sep 1803, but reinstated 15 Sep 1803, taking rank below a more junior Captain.
REFERENCE: *Gentleman's Magazine, Sep 1808, p. 854.*

GEDDES, John

Captain. 27th (Inniskilling) Regiment of Foot.
Family Memorial: Canongate Burial Ground, Edinburgh, Scotland. (East side). (Photograph)

BURIAL PLACE / BELONGING TO / JOHN GEDDES / LATE ADJUTANT GENERAL'S OFFICE / EDINBURGH. / ……………….. / L[T] GENERAL JOHN GEDDES, / COLONEL 27TH INNISKILLING REG[T], / DIED 26TH APRIL 1864, AGED 73 YEARS.

Ensign 22 Dec 1804. Lt 25 Oct 1805. Capt 1 Dec 1808. Major 24 Feb 1825. Lt Colonel 11 Nov 1831. Colonel 9 Nov 1846. Major General 20 Jun 1854. Lt General 23 Mar 1861.
    Served in the Peninsula with 3/27th Aug 1813 – Apr 1814. Present at Nivelle, Nive, Orthes and Toulouse (wounded and awarded pension of £100 per annum). Served in France with the Army of Occupation. Also served in Calabria 1806, Ischia and Procida 1809 and Sicily 1810. MGS medal for Nivelle, Nive, Orthes and Toulouse. Half pay Nov 1831. KH 1838. Served in the army for 60 years. Colonel 27th Foot 24 Apr 1860.
REFERENCE: *United Service Magazine, Jun 1864, p. 284. Gentleman's Magazine, Jun 1864, p. 810.*

GEE, Francis

Private. 39th (Dorsetshire) Regiment of Foot.
Headstone: Old Churchyard, Spital, Windsor, Berkshire. (Photograph)

SACRED / TO THE MEMORY OF / ELIZA GEE, THE BELOVED WIFE OF CAPTAIN GEE, M. K. W. / (LATE 39TH REG[T]) / WHO DEPARTED THIS LIFE 19TH MAY 1871 / IN THE 68TH YEAR OF HER AGE / ALSO / HER HUSBAND FRANCIS GEE, / (MAJOR LATE 39TH REG[T] & M. K.W.) / WHO DIED 11TH APRIL 1883, AGED 84.

Enlisted as Boy Private at the age of 7 in 1806. Drummer 1812. Promoted Ensign from Sgt Major 39th Foot 18 Sep 1840. Lt 5 Jun 1843. Capt 13 Sep 1853. Major 21 Feb 1882.

Served in the Peninsula 1811 – Apr 1814. Present at Vittoria, Maya, Pyrenees, Pamplona, Nivelle, Nive, Bayonne, Garris, Orthes and Toulouse. Also served in Australia 1825–1832 and India (present at the battle of Maharajpore Dec 1843 – awarded Maharajpore Star). Military Knight of Windsor 1860. By the age of 15 he had won the six clasps of his MGS medal for Vittoria, Pyrenees, Nivelle, Nive, Orthes and Toulouse. Retired 1854 after 48 years service with the same regiment. When he died in 1883 he was the last Peninsular War veteran left in the Military Knights of Windsor.

GELL, Thomas
Captain. 29th (Worcestershire) Regiment of Foot.
Headstone: Chapel Street Cemetery, Spondon, Derbyshire. Seriously eroded. (Photograph)

IN MEMORY OF / ANNE THE WIFE OF / MAJOR THOMAS GELL / OF SPONDON / .... / ALSO OF / THOMAS GELL / MAJOR H. M. 29TH REGIMENT, / W**********

Ensign 5 Oct 1804. Lt 12 Dec 1805. Capt 17 Nov 1808. Bt Major 26 Jun 1815. Major 28 Dec 1820.
    Served in the Peninsula 1808 – Nov 1811 and Apr 1813 – Feb 1814. Present at Rolica, Vimeiro, Douro, Talavera, Busaco, first siege of Badajoz, Albuera and Cadiz. Gold Medal for Albuera where he took command of the regiment when all the senior officers had been killed or wounded. MGS medal for Rolica, Vimeiro, Talavera and Busaco. Also served in North America 1814 in expedition up the Penobscot where he was severely wounded at Hampden 3 Sep 1814. Retired 2 May 1822. Died 14 Nov 1865.

GIBBONS, Frederick
Captain. 56th (West Essex) Regiment of Foot.
Grave: St John's Wood Churchyard, London. (M.I.)

"SACRED TO THE MEMORY OF CAPTAIN FREDERICK GIBBONS, 95TH REGT WHO DIED 24 MAR 1829 AGED 40."

Ensign 37th Foot 4 Mar 1806. Lt 16th Foot 21 Aug 1806. Lt 7th Foot 1 Sep 1808. Capt 56th Foot 7 Nov 1813. Capt 91st Foot 21 Jan 1819. Capt 95th Foot 1 Dec 1823.
    Served in the Peninsula with 2/7th Apr 1809 – Mar 1811 and 1/7th Apr – Jul 1811. Present at Busaco, Pombal, Condeixa, Olivencia, first siege of Badajoz and Albuera where he was severely wounded and awarded pension of £70 per annum. Sent home to recover from his wounds. Retired 18 Dec 1828.

GIBBONS, George
Captain. 95th Regiment of Foot.
Named on the Memorial: St Andrew's Church, (now Musée Historique), Biarritz, France. (Photograph)

Ensign 25th Foot 25 Jun 1803. Lt 26 Jun 1803. Capt 12 Jan 1809. Capt 95th Foot 26 Jul 1810.
    Served in the Peninsula with 2/95th Jan – Oct 1813. Present at San Millan, Vittoria, Pyrenees, Bidassoa and Vera where he was wounded and died 7 Oct 1813 of the wounds received at the heights above Vera while leading his company through the French entrenchments. Also served in Martinique 1809 with 25th Foot. Educated at Eton.

GIBBS, Edward
Lieutenant Colonel. 52nd (Oxfordshire) Light Infantry Regiment of Foot.
Memorial tablet: St Saviour's Church, St Helier, Jersey, Channel Islands. (Photograph)

SACRED TO THE MEMORY OF / GENERAL SIR EDWARD GIBBS, K.C.B. / SON OF THE LATE SAMUEL GIBBS ESQRE / OF HAWKSLEY PARK IN THE COUNTY OF ESSEX / AND ARABELLA DAUGHTER OF / GENERAL SIR WILLIAM ROWLEY G.C.B. / HE SHARED THE LAURELS GAINED

BY THE / 52ND LIGHT INFANTRY IN THE PENINSULA WAR / LOST AN EYE AT BADAJOS WHEN HE LED ONE OF / ITS BATTALIONS TO VICTORY AND WAS FINALLY / APPOINTED COLONEL OF THAT DISTINGUISHED / CORPS. SUCCESSIVELY A.D.C. TO GEORGE 4TH / AND WILLIAM THE 4TH HE WAS AT LENGTH / REWARDED WITH THE GOVERNMENT OF THIS / ISLAND WHICH HE HELD FOR UPWARDS OF 8 YEARS. / HE DIED AT GRAINVILLE HOUSE IN THIS PARISH / ON THE 24TH OF JAN^{Y} 1847, TEN DAYS AFTER HE / HAD GIVEN UP THE COMMAND, AGED 68 AND / HIS MORTAL REMAINS WERE DEPOSITED IN THE / FAMILY VAULT OF JOHN POINGESTRE, ESQ^{RE}.

Table tomb: St Saviour's Church, St Helier, Jersey, Channel Islands. (Photograph)

UNDER THIS VAULT ARE DEPOSITED / THE REMAINS OF / LIEUT GENERAL SIR EDWARD GIBBS KCB WHO DIED 24TH OF JUNE 1847. / A MONUMENT TO HIS MEMORY IS ERECTED / IN THE CHURCH.

Ensign 59th Foot 14 Nov 1798. Lt 52nd Foot 28 Nov 1799. Capt 24 Feb 1803. Major 4 Feb 1808. Bt Lt Colonel 6 Feb 1812. Lt Colonel 8 Apr 1813. Bt Colonel 27 May 1825. Major General 10 Jan 1837. Lt General 9 Nov 1846.
    Served in the Peninsula with 2/52nd Aug 1808 – Jan 1809 and 1/52nd Mar 1811 – May 1812 and May – Aug 1813 (Commanded 2 Brigade Lt Division Jan – 6 Apr 1812). Present at Vimeiro, Vigo, Sabugal, Fuentes d'Onoro, Ciudad Rodrigo (Mentioned in Despatches and awarded a Bt Lt Colonelcy), Badajoz (severely wounded losing an eye and awarded pension of £300 per annum) and Vittoria. CB. Gold Medal for Ciudad Rodrigo, Badajoz and Vittoria. KCB 1838. Also served at Ferrol 1800, Sicily 1806–1807, Netherlands 1814 (present at Merxem and Antwerp). Later Lieutenant Governor of Jersey 1839–1847. Colonel 68th Foot 1844. Colonel 52nd Foot 7 Dec 1844.
REFERENCE: *Gentleman's Magazine, Aug 1847, pp. 207–8. Annual Register, 1847, Appx, p. 239. Oxfordshire Light Infantry Chronicle, 1895, pp. 116–7.*

GIBBS, John
Paymaster. 51st (2nd Yorkshire West Riding) Light Infantry.
Interred in Catacomb B (Pub v24 2/3) Kensal Green Cemetery, London.

Paymaster 15 Feb 1810. Capt 15 Mar 1846.
    Served in the Peninsula Feb 1811 – Apr 1814. Present at Fuentes d'Onoro, Llerena (severely wounded). The 51st Foot had just reached Llerena and Sir Thomas Graham and his staff had been out to explore forward positions, when they came galloping back. The rest of the regiment thought that French cavalry were upon them and opened fire causing great confusion. Paymaster Gibbs was severely wounded and Surgeon Hamilton was killed. Also present at Moriscos, Salamanca, Burgos, San Munos, Vittoria, Pyrenees, San Marcial, Nivelle and Orthes. Present at Waterloo. Also served in Australia 1838–1846. Returned home due to ill health and died the same year. Half pay 1846 after 36 years service in the regiment. Died 21 Nov 1846.

GIBBS, Sir Samuel
Lieutenant Colonel. 59th (2nd Nottinghamshire) Regiment of Foot.
Memorial statue: St Paul's Cathedral, London. (Joint statue with Sir Edward Pakenham). (Photograph)

ERECTED AT THE PUBLIC EXPENSE / TO THE MEMORY OF / MAJOR GENERAL THE HONB^{LE}. SIR EDWARD PAKENHAM, K.B. / AND OF / MAJOR GENERAL SAMUEL GIBBS / WHO FELL GLORIOUSLY ON THE 18TH JANUARY 1815, / WHILE LEADING THE TROOPS TO AN ATTACK / OF THE ENEMIES WORKS IN THE FRONT OF NEW ORLEANS.

Ensign East Suffolk Militia. Ensign 102nd Foot Oct 1783. Ensign 60th Foot 14 Mar 1788. Lt 11th Foot 11 Feb 1792. Capt-Lt 25 Sep 1795. Capt 19 Dec 1795. Major 25 Aug 1799. Lt Colonel 10th West India Regt 1802. Lt Colonel 12th Battalion of Reserve 9 Jul 1803. Lt Colonel 59th Foot Aug 1804. Bt Colonel 28 Jul 1810. Major General 4 Jun 1813.

Served in Sweden 1813 (present at Stralsund where he commanded the British garrison), the Netherlands 1814 (in Lt General Graham's expedition) and North America (appointed second in command to Sir Edward Pakenham 1814, present at New Orleans where he was killed 8 Jan 1815). KCB 2 Jan 1815. Also served in Canada 1783–1792, Gibraltar 1792, Corsica 1794, Ostend 1798 (taken prisoner), Cape of Good Hope 1805–1806, India 1806, capture of Mauritius 1810 and capture of Java 1811 (present at Fort Cornelis).
REFERENCE: *Dictionary of National Biography*.

GIBSON, John
Sergeant. 33rd (1st Yorkshire West Riding) Regiment of Foot.
Headstone: Old Cemetery, Kendal, Cumbria. (Grave number 15. Peg No 3). (Photograph)

IN MEMORY OF / JOHN GIBSON / LATE COLOUR SERGEANT 33RD REGT. / BORN MAY 25TH 1788 / DIED JULY 13TH 1878. / "HIS END WAS PEACE"

Private 26 Dec 1812. Cpl 25 Mar 1813. Sgt 10 Mar 1814.

Present at Waterloo (wounded). Also served in the Netherlands 1814 (present at Bergen-op-Zoom where he was wounded) and West Indies 1822–1826. Promoted Colour Sergeant. After serving for over 21 years with the regiment, was discharged 11 Apr 1832 with a pension of 1 shilling and eight pence per day. Settled in Kendal, his birthplace, and served for 18 years as an officer in the Kendal House of Correction. Died 13 Jul 1878 aged 90.

GIFFORD, George St John
Captain. 43rd (Monmouthshire) Light Infantry Regiment of Foot.
Headstone: St Michael's Churchyard, Minehead, Somerset. Seriously eroded. (Photograph)

IN / MEMORY OF / MAJOR GEORGE / ST JOHN GIFFORD / DIED MAY 17TH 1869 / AGED 88

Ensign 26th Foot 20 Feb 1796. Lt 25 Apr 1797. Capt 1st Foot 3 Sep 1804. Capt 43rd Foot 8 Dec 1804. Capt 11th Royal Veteran Battalion 11 Mar 1809. Bt Major 28 Nov 1854.

Served in the Peninsula with 2/43rd Aug – Oct 1808. Present at Vimeiro. Retired on full pay 1814 when the 11th Royal Veteran Battalion was disbanded.

GILBERT, Francis Yarde
Lieutenant. Royal Engineers.
Named on the Regimental Memorial: Rochester Cathedral, Rochester, Kent. (Photograph)

2nd Lt 1 May 1811. Lt 10 Jun 1811. 2nd Capt 23 Mar 1825.

Served in the Peninsula Dec 1812 – Apr 1814. Present at Vittoria, Pyrenees, Nivelle, Nive and Bayonne where he was severely wounded. Present at Waterloo. Half pay 7 Jun 1825. MGS medal for Vittoria, Pyrenees, Nivelle and Nive. Died at Killaloe, Co Clare, 30 Nov 1871.

GILES, John
Captain. 53rd (Shropshire) Regiment of Foot.
Tombstone: Cantonment Cemetery, Cannamore, India. (M.I.)

"MAJOR JOHN GILES, H. M. 53RD REGT., AGED 41, DIED 2 MAY 1821."

Ensign 27th Foot 27 Sep 1798. Lt 14 Feb 1799. Capt 30 Oct 1801. Capt 53rd Foot 9 Jul 1803. Bt Major 4 Jun 1813.

Served in the Peninsula Oct 1810 – Apr 1814. Present at siege of Salamanca Forts, Salamanca, Vittoria, Pyrenees, Nivelle and Toulouse. Also served in India where he died 1821.

GILLAN, Martin
Private. 88th (Connaught Rangers) Regiment of Foot.
Headstone: St John's Churchyard, Cork, County Cork, Ireland. (No longer extant). Church is closed and is part of St John's College. Churchyard redeveloped. (M.I.)

"HERE LIES THE BODY OF MARTIN GILLAN LATE PRIVATE SOLDIER IN THE 88TH CONNAUGHT RANGERS, WHO DIED ON THE 5TH NOV^R 1825 AGED 38 YEARS. HE WAS A BRAVE SOLDIER, AND FOUGHT WITH HIS REGIMENT IN THE FOLLOWING ACTIONS, BUSACO, FUENTES D'ONOR, CIUDAD RODRIGO, BADAJOZ, SALAMANCA, VITTORIA, PYRE-NEES, NIVELLE, ORTHES AND TOULOUSE. THIS STONE IS ERECTED BY HIS COMRADES, NON-COMMISSIONED OFFICERS, DRUMMERS AND PRIVATES OF CAPTAIN BULLOCK'S COMPANY AS A TESTIMONY OF THEIR REGARD."

Served in the Peninsula 1810 – Apr 1814. Present at Busaco, Fuentes d'Onoro, Ciudad Rodrigo, Badajoz, Salamanca, Vittoria, Pyrenees, Nivelle, Orthes and Toulouse.

GILLESPIE, William
Quartermaster. 29th (Worcestershire) Regiment of Foot.
Buried in St George's Chapel, Windsor, Berkshire. (Burial record)

Quartermaster 13 Jul 1805.
Served in the Peninsula June 1808 – Oct 1811 and Apr 1813 – Feb 1814. Present at Rolica, Vimeiro, Douro, Talavera and Cadiz. Also served at the Helder 1799, North America 1814 (present in Nova Scotia in the expedition up the Penobscot). Retired on full pay 23 May 1822. Military Knight of Windsor 1822. Died 17 Feb 1824 aged 50.

GILLIES, John
Sergeant. 2nd (Royal North British) Regiment of Dragoons.
Headstone: Duns Parish Churchyard, Duns, Berwickshire, Scotland. (Photograph)

TO THE MEMORY OF / SERGEANT MAJOR JOHN GILLIES OF THE / ROYAL NORTH BRITISH DRAGOONS OR SCOTS GREYS. / BORN IN 1771, DIED 14 JULY 1860. / HE SERVED IN THE DISAS-TROUS RETREAT IN / HOLLAND AND WAS ENGAGED AT / THE BATTLE OF WATERLOO.

Pte 26 Feb 1793. Cpl 1805. Sgt 1810. Sgt Major 1816.
Present at Waterloo in Capt Barnard's troop. Also served in Flanders 1793–1795 (wounded). Discharged 21 Mar 1817.

GILLKREST, James
Surgeon. 43rd (Monmouthshire) Light Infantry Regiment of Foot.
Interred in Catacomb B (Pub v Ave 10 – 12 1/164) Kensal Green Cemetery, London.

Hospital Assistant 10 Oct 1800. Asst Surgeon 53rd Foot 19 Aug 1801. Surgeon 43rd Foot 15 Dec 1804. Deputy Inspector General 5 Nov 1829. Inspector General 16 Dec 1845.
Served in the Peninsula with 2/43rd Aug 1808 – Jan 1809 and 1/43rd Jul 1809 – Apr 1814. Present at Vimeiro, Corunna, Coa, Busaco, Redinha, Casal Nova, Foz d'Arouce, Sabugal, Fuentes d'Onoro, Ciudad

Rodrigo, Salamanca, San Munos, Vittoria, Pyrenees, San Sebastian (member of the storming party), Nivelle, Nive, Tarbes and Toulouse. Also served in the West Indies 1801 and North America 1814–1815 (present at New Orleans), Portugal 1827 (with Sir William Clinton's expedition), Gibraltar 1828 and 1833 (to help with cholera outbreaks). MGS medal for Vimeiro, Corunna, Busaco, Fuentes d'Onoro, Ciudad Rodrigo, Salamanca, Vittoria, Pyrenees, San Sebastian, Nivelle, Nive and Toulouse. MD Glasgow 1820. Died 25 Dec 1853. Also known as Gilchrist or Gillcrest.
REFERENCE: *Annual Register, 1853, Appx, p. 277.*

GILMOUR, Dugald Little
Lieutenant Colonel. 95th Regiment of Foot.
Memorial tablet: Greyfriar's Churchyard, Edinburgh, Scotland. (In walled enclosure). (Photograph)

SACRED TO THE MEMORY / OF / LIEUT. GENERAL SIR DUGALD LITTLE GILMOUR K.C.B. / COLONEL OF THE 2ND BATTALION 95TH THE RIFLE BRIGADE / WHO DIED AT ROME / ON THE 25TH DAY OF MARCH / 1847, / IN THE 73RD YEAR OF HIS AGE. / HE WAS THE SEVENTH SON OF / WILLIAM CHARLES LITTLE GILMOUR, / OF CRAIGMILLAR, / AND EARLY IN LIFE ENTERED THE ARMY / WHERE HIS CAREER WAS MARKED / BY A LONG SERIES OF DISTIN-GUISHED SERVICES. / THE ARDOUR AND GALLANTRY WHICH HE DISPLAYED / IN VARIOUS QUARTERS OF THE GLOBE / ARE RECORDED IN THE MILITARY ANNALS OF HIS COUNTRY / AND ARE ATTESTED BY THE HIGHEST RANK / AND HONOURS WHICH WERE AWARDED HIM. / IN PRIVATE LIFE HE WAS ENDEARED TO ALL WHO KNEW HIM / BY HIS MANY VIRTUES, / AND ALTHOUGH HIS REMAINS / REST FAR FROM THE TOMB OF HIS FATHERS, / YET HIS SURVIVING RELATIVES HAVE THE CONSOLATION / TO KNOW THAT HIS LAST LONG ILLNESS / WAS WATCHED OVER WITH UNREMITTING CARE, / AND SOOTHED BY THE MOST AFFECTIONATE FRIENDSHIP.

Buried in the Protestant Cemetery, Rome.

Ensign Independent Company 10 Jul 1794. Lt 20 Aug 1794. Lt 57th Foot 7 Nov 1794. Capt 93rd Foot 31 May 1795. Capt 4th Foot 11 Aug 1799. Major 95th Foot 23 May 1805. Bt Lt Colonel 30 May 1811. Lt Colonel 16 Jun 1814. Colonel 19 Jul 1821. Major General 22 Jul 1830. Lt General 23 Nov 1841.
　　Served in the Peninsula with 1/95th Aug 1808 – Jan 1809, Jun 1809 – Dec 1811 and Aug 1813 – Apr 1814 (commanded the regiment from 1810). Present at Vimeiro, Cacabellos, Corunna, Talavera, Barba del Puerco, Coa, Busaco, Pombal, Redinha (Mentioned in Despatches), Casal Nova, Foz d'Arouce, Sabugal (Mentioned in Despatches), Fuentes d'Onoro, Bidassoa, Nivelle, Nive, Tarbes and Toulouse. Gold Cross for Busaco, Fuentes d'Onoro, Nive and Toulouse. KCB 1831. Also served at Quiberon 1795, Demerara 1796, the Helder 1799 (wounded and taken prisoner) and the Baltic 1807–1808. Colonel Commandant 2nd Battalion Rifle Brigade 25 Apr 1842.
REFERENCE: *Gentleman's Magazine, September 1847, p. 315. Annual Register, 1847, Appx, p. 220.*

GIPPS, George
2nd Captain. Royal Engineers.
Memorial tablet: Canterbury Cathedral, Kent (South aisle of Nave). (Photograph)

IN THE ADJOINING CLOISTERS / ARE INTERRED THE REMAINS OF / LT COLONEL SIR GEORGE GIPPS, / OF THE ROYAL ENGINEERS; / LATE GOVERNOR IN CHIEF OF NEW SOUTH WALES, / AND ITS DEPENDENCIES, / WHO DIED THE 28TH FEBRUARY 1847, / AGED 56 YEARS. / AFTER AN HONOURABLE AND USEFUL CAREER OF 39 YEARS / IN THE MILITARY AND CIVIL SERVICE OF HIS COUNTRY, / HE RETURNED TO ENGLAND FROM THE ABOVE COLONY IN IMPAIRED HEALTH, / AND SHORTLY AFTERWARDS EXPIRED IN THIS CITY, / BELOVED, HONOURED, AND REGRETTED BY ALL WHO KNEW HIM. / "THE MEMORY OF THE JUST IS BLESSED."

Memorial tablet: Canterbury Cathedral, Kent. (Cloister Garth). (M.I.)

"AT THIS PLACE / ARE INTERRED THE REMAINS OF / L^T COL^{NL} SIR GEORGE GIPPS / OF THE ROYAL ENGINEERS. / LATE GOVERNOR IN CHIEF / OF NEW SOUTH WALES / AND ITS DEPENDENCIES / WHO DIED THE 28TH FEB^Y 1847 / AGED 56 YEARS."

2nd Lt 11 Jan 1809. 1st Lt 21 Dec 1809. 2nd Capt 30 Sep 1814. 1st Capt 8 Apr 1826. Bt Major 10 Jan 1837. Lt Col 23 Oct 1841.

Served in the Peninsula May 1811 – Apr 1814. Present at the second and third sieges of Badajoz (Mentioned in Despatches. In the third siege he led one of the assault columns on Fort Picurina where he was wounded), Biar, Castalla, Tarragona (Mentioned in Despatches) and Barcelona. Not present at Waterloo as he was engaged in fortifying the fortress at Ostend. Also served in the Netherlands 1814–1815 and in France with the Army of Occupation 1815–1817, West Indies and Mexico 1824–1827. Knighted and appointed Commissioner to Canada 1835 (to investigate the grievances affecting H. M's subjects in that Colony). This was achieved successfully and on his return he was immediately appointed Governor of New South Wales. His health was affected and after eight years he returned to England and died of a heart attack. Governor of New South Wales 1837–1845.
REFERENCE: *Dictionary of National Biography. Australian Dictionary of Biography. Gentleman's Magazine, Apr 1847, p. 425. United Service Magazine, Apr 1847, p. 639. Annual Register, 1847, Appx, p. 214.*

GIRARDOT, Charles Andrew
Lieutenant and Captain. Coldstream Regiment of Foot Guards.
Cross on stepped base: St Andrew's Churchyard, Buckland, near Dover, Kent. (Photograph)

LIEUT COLONEL / CHARLES GIRARDOT. / LATE COLDSTREAM GUARDS. / DIED NOV^R 16TH 1864 / AGED 70 YEARS.

Ensign 4 Apr 1811. Lt and Capt 1 Sep 1814. Capt and Lt Colonel 27 Jul 1826.

Served in the Peninsula Feb 1813 – Apr 1814. Present at Vittoria, Bidassoa, Nivelle, Nive, Adour and Bayonne. Also served in France with the Army of Occupation. MGS medal for Vittoria, Nivelle and Nive. Retired from the army 11 Jul 1826.
REFERENCE: *Household Brigade Journal, 1864, p. 335.*

GIRDLESTONE, Charles
Lieutenant. 2nd (Queen's Royal) Regiment of Foot.
Tombstone: Colaba Cemetery, Bombay, India. (M.I.)

"SACRED TO THE MEMORY OF CAPTAIN CHAS. GIRDLESTONE OF HIS MAJESTY'S QUEEN'S ROYALS, DIED 19TH AUGUST 1831, AGED 39 YEARS."

Ensign 2 Foot 10 May 1810. Lt 9 Jun 1813. Capt 24 Jun 1825.

Served in the Peninsula with 2nd Foot Mar 1811 – Dec 1812 and with 2nd Provisional Battalion Jan – Mar 1813. Present at Almeida, siege of Salamanca Forts, Salamanca, Burgos and the retreat from Burgos. Also served in India 1829.

GIRLING, Thomas Andrews
Captain. 5th (Northumberland) Regiment of Foot.
Marble Cross: St Andrew's Churchyard, Holt, Norfolk. (M.I.)

"MAJOR THOS ANDREWS GIRLING DIED MARCH 25TH 1849 IN HIS 63RD YEAR."

Ensign 28 Aug 1804. Lt 21 Sep 1805. Capt 13 Oct 1814. Bt Major 10 Jan 1837. Capt 91st Foot 29 Apr 1842.

Served in the Peninsula with 1/5th Sep 1808 – Jan 1809 and Jun 1812 – Apr 1813. Present at Corunna and Salamanca. Also served at Walcheren 1809 and North America 1814–1815. MGS medal for Corunna and Salamanca. Retired on half pay 24 May 1829. Later Deputy Lieutenant for the County of Norfolk and Capt and Adjutant of the Norfolk Yeomanry Cavalry.

GLASS, John
Private. 12th (Prince of Wales's) Regiment of Light Dragoons.
Named on the Regimental Memorial: St Joseph's Church, Waterloo, Belgium. (Photograph)
   Killed at Waterloo.

GLEIG, George Robert
Lieutenant. 85th (Buckinghamshire Volunteers) Light Infantry Regiment of Foot.
Memorial tablet: Royal Hospital, Chelsea, London. (Photograph)

IN MEMORY OF THE REVᴰ. G .R. GLEIG, M.A. / CHAPLAIN GENERAL OF THE FORCES. / MR GLEIG SERVED IN THE PENINSULAR CAMPAIGNS OF 1813–1814 / AS A SUBALTERN IN THE 85ᵀᴴ L .I. WAS PRESENT AT / THE SIEGE OF SAN SEBASTIAN, PASSAGE OF THE BIDASSOA, / BATTLE OF THE NIVELLE, BATTLE OF THE NIVE AND / INVESTMENT OF BAYONNE. / RECEIVED THE PENINSULAR MEDAL WITH THREE CLASPS. / SERVED IN THE AMERICAN WAR AT BLADENSBURG, / BALTIMORE, NEW ORLEANS, AND FORT BOWYER. / ON THE CONCLUSION OF THE PEACE / MR. GLEIG ENTERED HOLY ORDERS, WAS APPOINTED / CHAPLAIN OF CHELSEA HOSPITAL IN 1834, / AND CHAPLAIN TO THE FORCES 1ˢᵀ APRIL 1846, / WAS INSPECTOR GENERAL OF MILITARY SCHOOLS / FROM 1846 TO 1858. RETIRED 1875. / BECAME A PREBENDARY OF ST PAUL'S 1848, AND / WAS DISTINGUISHED AS AN AUTHOR. / DIED 9ᵀᴴ JULY 1888. AET 92.

Ensign 3rd Garrison Battalion 13 Aug 1812. Ensign 85th Foot 25 Jan 1813. Lt 20 Jul 1813.
Served in the Peninsula Aug 1813 – Apr 1814. Present at San Sebastian, Bidassoa, Nivelle, Nive and Bayonne. Also served with the 85th in North America 1814–1815 (present at Baltimore, Bladensburg where he was wounded, New Orleans and Fort Bowyer). MGS medal for San Sebastian, Nivelle and Nive. Half pay 25 Jan 1816. At the end of the war returned to Oxford to take his degree 1819, entered the church 1820 and became Chaplain to Chelsea Hospital 1834. Principal Chaplain to the Forces 1 Apr 1844 and Chaplain General 2 Jul 1846. Inspector General of Military Schools 1846–1858, due to his devising a scheme for education of soldiers. Retired 1875.
He was a prolific author writing extensively on military history. His books included *The Subaltern* (about life in the 85th Regiment), *Life of Arthur, First Duke of Wellington*, 1862, *Personal recollections of the First Duke of Wellington*, edited by M. Gleig, 1904 and *The Light Dragoon*, (Private George Farmer), 1850, and other subjects. He died at Bylands, a cottage in the grounds of Stratfield Saye, which had been set aside for his use by the second Duke of Wellington.
REFERENCE: *Dictionary of National Biography. Annual Register, 1888, Appx, p. 159. Gleig, George Robert, The Subaltern, 1845, (reprint with introduction by Ian Robertson, 2001). Jarvis, A. C. E., My predecessors in office, the Rev. G. R. Gleig, Royal Army Chaplains' Department Quarterly Journal, Vol 4, 1931, pp. 14–77 and pp. 230–358.*

GLEN, James
Driver. Royal Artillery Drivers.
Headstone: Holy Trinity Cathedral Churchyard, Brechin, Angus, Scotland. (Photograph)

SACRED / TO THE MEMORY OF / JAMES GLEN, PENSIONER. / WHO DIED 23ᴿᴰ OCTOBER 1876

/ IN HIS 86TH YEAR. / ………………... / JAMES GLEN FIRST NAMED SERVED IN / THE R H A AT WATERLOO IN 1815. /………………..

Private 7 Jul 1809. Driver 2nd Class 1816.

Stationed at Woolwich until 1814. Served at Waterloo as a Driver in Major Bull's 'I' Troop of Royal Horse Artillery. Also served with the Army of Occupation. Major Bull's Troop returned to Woolwich Oct 1818. Discharged and returned to Scotland 30 Nov 1818. Out Pensioner at Chelsea Hospital and received a pension of 15 pence per day.

GLOSTER, Thomas
Lieutenant. 61st (South Gloucestershire) Regiment of Foot.
Monument: Kensal Green Cemetery, London. (9173/31/PS). (Photograph)

SACRED / TO THE MEMORY OF / COLONEL THOMAS GLOSTER / LATE OF THE / SIXTY FIRST REGIMENT / WHO DIED / JULY 19TH 1861 / AGED 74 YEARS

Ensign 1 Apr 1807. Lt 17 Mar 1808. Capt 7 Apr 1823. Major 8 Oct 1830. Bt Lt Colonel 9 Nov 1846. Bt Colonel 20 Jun 1854.

Served in the Peninsula Nov 1809 – Apr 1814. Present at Busaco, Fuentes d'Onoro, siege of Salamanca Forts, Salamanca (wounded), Pyrenees, Nivelle, Nive, Orthes, Tarbes and Toulouse where he was severely wounded. Also served in Gibraltar 1808 and West Indies 1816–1821. Half pay 8 Oct 1830. MGS medal for Busaco, Salamanca, Pyrenees, Nivelle, Nive, Orthes and Toulouse.
REFERENCE: *Gentleman's Magazine, Sep 1861, p. 334. Annual Register, 1861, Appx, p. 441.*

GLUBB, Frederick
Captain. Royal Artillery.
Grave: St Nicholas Churchyard, Plumstead and named on the Regimental Memorial: St Nicholas Church, Plumstead, Kent. (No longer extant. Destroyed by a flying bomb in the Second World War)

Joined the Royal Artillery from the Royal Irish Artillery. 2nd Lt Royal Artillery 25 Jul 1795. 1st Lt 21 Feb 1799. Capt/Lieut 14 Sep 1803. Capt 1 Feb 1808.

Served in the Peninsula Mar 1809 – Jul 1810 and 1812–1813. Present at Ciudad Rodrigo, Badajoz, Almarez, Salamanca, Burgos and San Sebastian (wounded). Joined the Invalid Battalion of the Royal Artillery 23 Jul 1813. Retired on full pay 1 March 1819. Died at Woolwich 23 Jan 1833.

GODLEY, Samuel
Private. 2nd Life Guards.
Headstone: St John's Wood Churchyard, London. (Photograph)

IN MEMORY OF / SAMUEL GODLEY / LATE PRIVATE IN THE SECOND / REGIMENT OF LIFE GUARDS / WHOSE DARING AND / HEROIC COURAGE / DISPLAYED WHEN CHARGING THE / FRENCH CUIRASSIERS AT THE / BATTLE OF WATERLOO / CAUSED HIS ACHIEVEMENT TO BE / RECORDED IN THE / ANNALS OF WAR / AND PRODUCED THIS TRIBUTE TO / HIS MEMORY FROM HIS COMRADES. / HE DIED 16 JANUARY 1832 / AGED 51 YEARS. / THIS STONE WAS ESTABLISHED / BY THE NON COMMISSIONED OFFICERS / OF HIS REGIMENT

Private 2 Jan 1804.

Served at Waterloo. Took part in one of the cavalry charges, had his horse shot under him and was thrown to the ground losing his helmet. A French Cuirassier attempted to cut him down but Godley although shaken from the fall, and with a head wound, managed to kill him and rode back to his regiment on the Frenchman's horse. He was known as the Marquis of Granby as he was completely bald like the former Marquis of Granby who led the British cavalry in the Seven Years War.

Discharged in 1824, he found a job in the Baker Street Bazaar not far from his old barracks. Died in a London street 16 Jan 1832 from the effects of the head wound he received at Waterloo. His gravestone was erected by the regiment in honour of his bravery at Waterloo.

REFERENCE: *Godley, Jocelyn, Samuel Godley: the story of a Waterlooman, Family Tree Magazine, Mar 2009, pp. 46–9. Derbyshire Times, 12 Jul 1930. Derby Evening Telegraph, 6 Jun 2005, pp. 4–5. Whitwell Local History Group web page: http://www.wlhg.freeuk.com/samgodly.htm*

GODWIN, Henry Thomas
Major. 5th West India Regiment.
Memorial tablet: St Mary the Virgin Church, Shalford, Surrey. (M.I.)

"TO THE MEMORY OF / MAJOR GENERAL HENRY THOMAS GODWIN, K.C.B. / WHO JOINED THE IXTH REGIMENT IN 1800, / SERVED ON THE EXPEDITION TO FERROL 1800, IN HANOVER 1805, / IN THE PENINSULA, / IN THE CAMPAIGN ON THE DOURO, AT TARIFA, MALAGA, FUENGEROLA, BARROSA / WAS SEVERELY WOUNDED. / IN INDIA, AS LIEUTENANT COLONEL OF THE 41ST REGIMENT, / IN BURMAH FROM 1824 TO 1827, / COMMANDED THE FIRST BRIGADE OF THE MADRAS DIVISION, / IN EVERY ACTION AND SIX SEPARATE COMMANDS, CAPTURED MARTABAN, TANTABAIN, AND SEMBIKE. / IN INDIA IN 1851, COMMANDING THE SIRHIND DIVISION. / WAS COMMANDER IN CHIEF OF THE COMBINED FORCES IN BURMAH, ARRACAN, AND TENASSERIM, / WHICH ACHIEVED THE CONQUEST OF PEGU IN 1853, / AND WHO DIED AT SIMLA, OCTOBER XXVI, MDCCCLIII. / FORTUNATE IN THOSE HE COMMANDED, / UNFORTUNATE IN THOSE HE SERVED. / THIS RECORD OF FIFTY THREE YEARS SERVICE / IS HERE PLACED / BY HIS ONLY DAUGHTER MARIA ELIZABETH AUSTEN."

Gravestone: New Cemetery, Simla, India. (M.I.)

"TO THE MEMORY OF / MAJOR GENERAL SIR HENRY THOMAS GODWIN KCB / COLONEL OF H. M. 20TH REGT. / WHO DIED AT SIMLAH, OCT 26TH 1853. / AGED 69 YEARS."

Memorial tablet: Christ Church, Simla, India. (M.I.)

"TO COMMEMORATE A FRIENDSHIP OF FIFTY THREE YEARS DURATION, AND / TO RECORD THE DEPARTURE OF GENUINE WORTH FROM THIS LIFE IN THE / HUMBLE BUT FIRM HOPE OF SHARING IN THAT OF A BLESSED HEREAFTER, / THIS TABLET IS DEDICATED TO THE MEMORY OF MAJOR GENERAL HENRY / GODWIN BY WILLIAM MAYNARD GOMM COMMANDER IN CHIEF IN INDIA. THE / MORTAL REMAINS WERE DEPOSITED WITH HONOUR AND BY / THE HANDS OF MANY MOURNERS IN THE GRAVEYARD OF SIMLA OCTOBER / 27TH 1853."

Ensign 9th Foot 30 Oct 1799. Lt 19 Aug 1803. Adjutant 7 Sep 1804. Capt 28 Mar 1808. Major 5th West India Regt 26 May 1814. Major 41st Foot 30 Nov 1815. Lt Colonel 26 Jul 1821. Lt Colonel 87th Foot Jan 1827. Bt Colonel 10 Jan 1837. Major General 9 Nov 1846.

Served in the Peninsula with 2/9th Nov 1808 – Jun 1809 and Gibraltar Jul 1809 – Sep 1813. During his time in Gibraltar the 2nd battalion supplied companies for Barrosa and Tarifa. Present at Douro, Barrosa (wounded and awarded pension of £200 per annum), Tarifa, Fuengirola and Cadiz. MGS medal for Barrosa. Also served at Ferrol 1800, Hanover 1805, India 1822–1828 (in command of the 41st Foot). From there he served in Burma 1824–1826 (present at Martaban, Tantabain and Sembike). CB and Army of India medal with clasp for Ava. Then unemployed for 24 years. In 1852 he was again in Burma in the

second Burmese War (present at the capture of Rangoon). Returned to India in 1853 and died 26 Oct 1853. Colonel 20th Foot. KCB. These last two honours did not arrive in India until after he had died.
REFERENCE: *Gentleman's Magazine, May 1854, pp. 529–30. Annual Register, 1853, Appx, p. 264. United Service Magazine, Feb 1854, pp. 310–6.*

GOEBEN, August Alexander von
Captain, 1st Battalion Light Infantry, King's German Legion.
Named on the Regimental Memorial: La Haye Sainte, Waterloo, Belgium. (Photograph)

Ensign 25 Jan 1806. Lt 25 Nov 1809. Captain May 1815.
    Served in the Peninsula Aug 1808 – Jan 1809 and Mar 1811 – Apr 1814. Present at Vigo, Albuera, second siege of Badajoz, siege of Salamanca Forts, Moriscos, Salamanca, Venta del Poza, San Millan, Vittoria, Tolosa, Bidassoa, Nivelle, Nive, Bayonne and St Etienne. Present at Waterloo where he was killed. Also served in the Baltic 1808–1809 and the Netherlands 1814.

GOLDFINCH, Henry
Lieutenant Colonel. Royal Engineers.
Headstone: Brookwood Cemetery, Brookwood, Surrey. (Plot No 27). (Photograph)

SACRED / TO THE MEMORY OF / LIEUT-GENL SIR HENRY GOLDFINCH KCB / WHO SERVED WITH DISTINCTION IN THE / PENINSULAR WAR / AND WAS PRESENT AT THE BATTLES OF / TALAVERA, BUSACO, VITTORIA, PYRENEES, / NIVE, ORTHES AND THOLOUSE. / DIED THE 21ST NOVEMBER 1854 / IN THE 73RD YEAR OF HIS AGE / BEING AT THE TIME ONE OF THE / COLONELS COMMANDANT OF THE CORPS OF / ROYAL ENGINEERS.

2nd Lt Royal Artillery 1 Mar 1798. 2nd Lt Royal Engineers 24 Jun 1798. 1st Lt 11 Jun 1800. 2nd Capt 1 Mar 1805. Capt 18 Nov 1807. Bt Major 17 Dec 1812. Bt Lt Colonel 21 Sep 1813. Lt Colonel 20 Dec 1814. Bt Colonel 22 Jul 1830. Colonel 10 Jan 1837. Major General 23 Nov 1841. Lt General 11 Nov 1851.
    Served in the Peninsula May 1809 – Feb 1812 and Jul 1812 – Apr 1814. Present at Douro (taken prisoner but escaped), Talavera, Busaco, Alba de Tormes (Mentioned in Despatches), Vittoria, Pyrenees, Nive (Mentioned in Despatches), Orthes and Toulouse. Gold Cross for Vittoria, Nive, Orthes and Toulouse. MGS medal for Talavera, Busaco and Pyrenees. Also served at Hanover 1805 and Copenhagen 1807. KCB 1852. Colonel Commandant Royal Engineers 2 Feb 1854.
REFERENCE: *Gentleman's Magazine, Feb 1855, p. 190. Annual Register, 1854, Appx, p. 336.*

GOLDIE, George Leigh
Captain. 66th (Berkshire) Regiment of Foot.
Grave: Millbrook and Freemantle Cemetery, Southampton, Hampshire. (M.I.)

"SIR GEORGE LEIGH GOLDIE, SON OF LIEUT GEN THOMAS GOLDIE OF GOLDIE LEIGH, DUMFRIESSHIRE, SCOTLAND, WHO DIED 26 MARCH 1863 AGED 78."

Cornet 6th Dragoon Guards 3 Sep 1803. Lt 14 Mar 1805. Capt 5th Garrison Battalion 4 Dec 1806. Capt 66th Foot 21 Jan 1808. Bt Major 20 Jun 1811. Bt Lt Colonel 12 Aug 1819. Major 50th Foot 4 May 1826. Lt Colonel 11th Foot 13 Aug 1830. Lt Colonel 87th Foot 25 Feb 1831. Bt Colonel 10 Jan 1837. Major General 9 Nov 1846. Lt General 20 Jun 1854. General 9 Nov 1862.
    Served in the Peninsula Apr 1809 – Oct 1813. Present at Douro, Talavera, Busaco, Albuera (awarded Bt Majority), Arroyo dos Molinos, Campo Major, Vittoria, Pyrenees (severely wounded 30 Jul 1813 by a musket ball which remained lodged in his lungs until he died and awarded pension of £250 per annum). Gold Medal for Albuera. MGS medal for Talavera, Busaco, Vittoria and Pyrenees. Also served in Ireland

1809 (Brigade Major), Canada 1838–1839 (held an important command in disputed territories action). Colonel 77th Foot 22 Dec 1854. Colonel 35th Foot 13 Feb 1861. KCB.
REFERENCE: *Gentleman's Magazine, May 1863, pp. 668–9.*

GOLDSMID, Albert

Lieutenant. 12th (Prince of Wales's) Regiment of Light Dragoons.
Memorial tablet: All Saints Church, Isleworth, Middlesex. (No longer extant. Church has been burnt down)

"................... ALSO TO MAJOR GENERAL ALBERT GOLDSMID, FORMERLY OF 12TH ROYAL LANCERS, WHO DIED JAN 6 1861 AGED 67 YEARS."

Cornet 30 May 1811. Lt 20 Feb 1812. Capt 22 Feb 1816. Major 10 Jun 1826. Bt Lt Colonel 23 Nov 1841. Bt Colonel 20 Jun 1854. Major General 26 Oct 1858
   Served in the Peninsula May 1812 – Apr 1814. Present at Castrejon, Monasterio, Salamanca, Venta del Poza, Vittoria, Nivelle, Nive, Adour and Bordeaux. Present at Waterloo. MGS medal for Salamanca, Nivelle and Nive. Half pay 10 Jun 1826.

GOMERSALL, John

Captain. 58th (Rutlandshire) Regiment of Foot.
Memorial tablet: St James the Great Church, Birstall, Leicestershire. (M.I.) (No longer extant). (Interred in Lambeth church)

"IN MEMORY OF / JOHN GOMERSALL ESQUIRE / COMPANION OF THE / HONORABLE ORDER OF THE BATH / MAJOR IN THE BRITISH ARMY/ AND / LIEUTENANT COLONEL IN THE / PORTUGUESE SERVICE / IN EGYPT AND SPAIN / UNDER THE COMMAND OF / SIR RALPH ABERCROMBIE / AND / THE DUKE OF WELLINGTON. / HE SHARED IN THE LABOURS / AND IN THE TRIUMPHS OF THOSE / MEMORABLE CAMPAIGNS. / BORN AT GOMERSALL JUNE 11TH 1769 / HE DEPARTED THIS LIFE IN LONDON / FEBRUARY 8TH 1820. / HIS REMAINS WERE INTERRED / IN LAMBETH CHURCH."

Ensign 31 Jan 1800. Lt 8 Mar 1801. Capt 25 Dec 1804. Bt Major 26 Dec 1813. Portuguese Army: Major 16th Line 7 May 1810. Lt Colonel 14 Apr 1812. Lt Colonel 2nd Line 10 Jul 1813.
   Served in the Peninsula with 58th Foot Jul 1809 – May 1810 and Portuguese Army May 1810 – Jan 1814. Present at Busaco, Pombal, Redinha, Ciudad Rodrigo (wounded), Salamanca, Burgos and the retreat, Vittoria, Pyrenees, Nivelle and Nive (wounded at St Pierre 13 Dec 1813). Retired on half pay 26 Dec 1813. Gold Medal for Salamanca, Vittoria and Nivelle. CB. Also served in Minorca, Malta 1800 and Egypt 1801 (wounded). Died 1821.

GOMM, Henry

Major. 6th (1st Warwickshire) Regiment of Foot.
Low monument on a base: Plainpalais Cemetery, Geneva, Switzerland. (Photograph)

IN MEMORY / OF LIEUTENANT COLONEL HENRY GOMM / OF THE 6TH REGIMENT OF INFANTRY / OF H. B. MAJESTY. / WOUNDED AT THE HEAD OF HIS REGIMENT / AT THE BATTLE OF THE PYRENEES. / VALIANT UNDER THE DUKE OF WELLINGTON / IN 1813. / AFTER THREE LONG YEARS / OF CONSIDERABLE SUFFERING / HE SOUGHT RELIEF IN ITALY. / HE DIED ON HIS WAY THITHER / AT PONT DE BEAUVOISIN / THE 5TH DEC 1816 AGED 30 / REMOVED TO GENEVA / BY THE COMPANION OF HIS JOURNEY / HIS BROTHER.

Ensign 6 Dec 1794. Lt 1798. Capt 25 Jun 1803. Major 18 May 1809. Bt Lt Colonel 26 Aug 1813.

Served in the Peninsula Aug 1808 – Jan 1809 and Nov 1812 – Feb 1814. Present at Vittoria and Pyrenees (severely wounded at Roncesvalles 25 Jul 1813 and awarded Bt Lt Colonelcy for his bravery). Brother of Capt and Lt Colonel William Maynard Gomm Coldstream Guards.

GOMM, Richard Stonier

Assistant Commissary General. Commissariat Department.
Mural Memorial tablet: St Jude and St Simon Churchyard, Bramdean, Hampshire. (On exterior wall of church). (Photograph)

IN MEMORY OF / RICHARD STONIER GOMM, ESQUIRE, / WHO DIED ON / THE XXIST OF MAY MDCCCXLIII: / HIS REMAINS ARE BURIED IN THE / CHURCHYARD. / HE SERVED HIS COUNTRY WITH ZEAL / AND FIDELITY IN THE COMMISSARIAT / DEPARTMENT OF THE ARMY, THROUGHOUT / THE WAR IN PORTUGAL, SPAIN, AND AT / WATERLOO: / HE WAS THE ELDEST SURVIVING SON OF / THE REVEREND WILLIAM GOMM, / FOR 38 YEARS RECTOR OF THIS / PARISH. / RESPECTED FOR HIS TALENTS / AND BELOVED FOR HIS WORTH, / THIS TABLET WAS ERECTED BY / HIS WIDOW.

Dep Asst Comm Gen 29 May 1810. Asst Comm Gen 1 Nov 1814.
Served in the Peninsula Sep 1810 – Mar 1811 and Nov 1811 – Mar 1814. Present at Cadiz. Half pay 1 Nov 1814.

GOMM, Sir William Maynard

Captain and Lieutenant Colonel. Coldstream Regiment of Foot Guards.
Headstone: Nunhead Cemetery, London. (Grave 44795 sq 32). Removed from Christ Church, Rotherhithe in 1979. (Photograph)

FIELD MARSHAL / SIR WILLIAM GOMM GCB / LORD OF THE MANOR / OF ROTHERHITHE / .... / BROUGHT HERE FROM / ROTHERHITHE 1979

Memorial window and brass memorial tablet: Bath Abbey, Bath, Somerset. (South aisle of choir). (Photograph)

THE ABOVE WINDOW ERECTED BY FIELD MARSHAL SIR WILLIAM GOMM, GCB. CONSTABLE OF THE TOWER OF LONDON / DECEASED 15TH MARCH 1875 IN HIS 91ST YEAR AND BURIED IN THE VAULT OF CHRIST CHURCH ROTHERHITHE, LONDON

Memorial: Royal Military Chapel, Wellington Barracks, London. (M.I.) (Destroyed by a Flying Bomb in 1944).

"IN MEMORY OF FIELD-MARSHAL SIR WILLIAM MAYNARD GOMM, G.C.B., CONSTABLE OF THE TOWER, WHO ENTERED THE ARMY MAY 24, 1794, AND FOR 16 YEARS KEPT THE FIELD DURING THE CAMPAIGNS AGAINST FRANCE. HE WAS TRANSFERRED TO THE GUARDS IN 1814, AND DIED, COLONEL OF THE COLDSTREAM, MARCH 15, 1875, IN THE 91ST YEAR OF HIS AGE, AFTER 80 YEARS PASSED IN THE SERVICE OF HIS COUNTRY. "PER COSTANZA E SPERANZA." PLACED BY MRS. CARR GOMM."

Memorial Brass: Chapel Royal of St Peter ad Vincula, Tower of London, London. (Photograph)

PER COSTANZA E SPERANZA / FIELD MARSHAL / WILLIAM MAYNARD GOMM / G.C.B. / CONSTABLE 1872 – 1875 / B. 1784 D. 1875

Ensign 9ᵗʰ Foot 24 May 1794. Lt 16 Nov 1794. Capt 25 Jun 1803. Major 10 Oct 1811. Bt Lt Colonel 17 Aug 1812. Capt & Lt Colonel Coldstream Guards 25 Jul 1814. Colonel 16 May 1829. Major General 10 Jan 1837. Lt General 9 Nov 1846. General 20 Jun 1854. Field Marshal 1 Jan 1868.

Served in the Peninsula with 1/9ᵗʰ Aug 1808 – Jan 1809, Feb – Jul 1810 and with Staff Sep 1810 – Apr 1814 (DAQMG and later AQMG). Present at Rolica, Vimeiro, Corunna, Busaco (Mentioned in Despatches), Fuentes d'Onoro, Badajoz, Salamanca, Burgos, Villa Muriel, Vittoria (Mentioned in Despatches), San Sebastian, Bidassoa, Nivelle, Nive (wounded and awarded pension of £300 per annum) and Bayonne. Present at Quatre Bras and Waterloo (AQMG).

Also served at the Helder 1799, Ferrol 1800, Hanover 1805, Copenhagen 1807, Walcheren 1809, West Indies 1839–1842 and India 1850–1855 (Commander-in-Chief in India). Colonel 13ᵗʰ Foot 10 Mar 1846. Colonel Coldstream Guards 15 Aug 1863. Constable of the Tower Oct 1872. Gold Cross for Badajoz, Salamanca, Vittoria, San Sebastian and Nive. MGS medal for Rolica, Vimeiro, Corunna, Busaco, Fuentes d'Onoro and Nivelle. KCB. GCB. Order of St Vladimir, Knight of 2ⁿᵈ Class of St Anne of Russia. Brother of Major Henry Gomm 6ᵗʰ Foot.

REFERENCE: *Dictionary of National Biography. Gomm, Sir William Maynard, Letters and Journals of Field Marshal Sir W. M. Gomm, edited by F. C. Carr-Gomm, 1881, reprint 2003. Household Brigade Journal, 1875, pp. 297–301. Annual Register, 1875, Appx, p. 135.*

GOOCH, Henry Edward
Ensign. Coldstream Regiment of Foot Guards.
Headstone: St Michael's Churchyard, Melbourne, Derbyshire. (Photograph)

HERE LIETH / THE BODY OF / HENRY / EDWARD GOOCH, / LATE LIEUTENANT COLONEL / OF THE COLDSTREAM GUARDS, / WHO DIED AT MELBOURNE HALL, / JANUARY 18ᵀᴴ 1867, AGED 73 YEARS. / ....

Ensign 23 Jul 1812. Lt & Capt 28 Oct 1819. Capt and Lt. Col 26 Nov 1832.

Present at Quatre Bras and Waterloo where he fought at Hougoumont. Also served in Holland in 1814 (present at Bergen-op-Zoom). Retired in 1841.

REFERENCE: *Household Brigade Journal, 1867, p. 323.*

GOODALL, George
Ensign. 55ᵗʰ (Westmoreland) Regiment of Foot.
Headstone: Aberelliot Cemetery, Angus, Scotland. (M.I.)

"MAJOR GEORGE GOODALL, 1ˢᵀ OR ROYAL REGT OF FOOT, BORN PEASIEHALL 3 APRIL 1794, DIED FOLKESTONE 19 AUG 1859".

Ensign 9 Sep 1813. Lt 1 Aug 1822. Capt 1ˢᵗ Foot 18 May 1832. Major 17 Dec 1841.

Served in the Netherlands 1814–1815 (present at Merxem, Antwerp and Bergen-op-Zoom where he was severely wounded).

GOODMAN, Stephen Arthur
Major. 48ᵗʰ (Northamptonshire) Regiment of Foot.
Memorial tablet: St George's Cathedral, George Town, Demerara, British Guiana, West Indies. (Above west door). (M.I.)

"SACRED TO THE MEMORY OF / MAJOR-GENERAL / STEPHEN ARTHUR GOODMAN, C.B AND K.H., / BORN 19ᵀᴴ JANUARY, 1780, DIED 2ⁿᵈ JANUARY, 1844. / HE SERVED THROUGHOUT THE WAR IN THE PENINSULA AND / THE NETHERLANDS / UP TO ITS TERMINATION BY THE GLORIOUS VICTORY OF / WATERLOO. / IN 1821, HE RECEIVED FROM HIS SOVEREIGN, THE

OFFICE (PATENT) / OF VENDUE MASTER OF DEMERARA AND ESSEQUIBO, / WHICH HE HELD TO HIS DECEASE. / IN 1823 / HE WAS APPOINTED TO THE COMMAND OF THE MILITIA, / AND DURING THE MANY YEARS HE HELD IT / RENDERED ESSENTIAL SERVICE TO THE COLONY, / IN THE PRESERVATION OF ITS INTERNAL TRANQUILLITY. / THIS TABLET IS ERECTED BY THE SURVIVING OFFICERS OF THE MILITIA / WHO SERVED UNDER HIM, AND BY FRIENDS / WHO SYMPATHISE WITH HIS SORROWING FAMILY / FOR THE IRREPARABLE LOSS THEY HAVE SUSTAINED. / HE WAS BELOVED IN LIFE AND HIS DEATH / WAS LAMENTED BY THE WHOLE COMMUNITY. / HIS REMAINS WERE INTERRED / WITH THE HONOURS DUE TO HIS RANK, / IN THE MILITARY BURIAL GROUND / AT EVE LEARY."

Grave: Military Burial Ground, Eve Leary, George Town, Demerara, British Guiana, West Indies. (M.I.)

"MAJOR GENERAL STEPHEN ARTHUR GOODMAN, C.B., K.H., BORN 19TH JANUARY, 1780, DIED 2ND JANUARY, 1844."

Ensign 48th Foot Oct 1794. Lt 5 Sep 1795. Capt 9 Jul 1803. Major 4 Jun 1813. Bt Lt Colonel 26 Dec 1813. Bt Colonel 22 Jul 1830. Major General 1842.

Served in the Peninsula May 1809 – Apr 1814. Present at Talavera, Badajoz, Salamanca and Burgos. Deputy Judge Advocate 1810. From Jul 1812 – Oct 1813 he was also DAAG. At Burgos took charge of the Adjutant General's Department as the Adjutant General was ill. Appointed to be Judge Advocate of the Forces ordered from the Peninsular Army to America, but at the last moment was ordered to Holland and to the troops left there under the Prince of Orange 1814. Present at Waterloo and with the Army of Occupation (Deputy Judge Advocate). Also served in Minorca and Malta 1800. CB and KH. Colonial Secretary of Berbice 1819. Vendue Master of Demerara and Essequibo 1821–1844.

REFERENCE: *Dictionary of National Biography. United Service Magazine, Mar 1844, p. 478. Gentleman's Magazine, May 1844, pp. 539–40. Annual Register, 1844, Appx, pp. 191–2.*

GORDON, Hon. Sir Alexander
Captain and Lieutenant Colonel. 3rd Regiment of Foot Guards.
Obelisk: Grounds of Haddo House, Ellon, Aberdeenshire, Scotland. (Photograph)

NEMO ME IMPUNE ACESSII / TO THE MEMORY OF / SIR ALEXANDER GORDON K.C.B. / COLONEL SCOTS GUARDS AND AIDE CAMP / TO THE DUKE OF WELLINGTON / AFTER SERVING HIS COUNTRY WITH DISTINCTION / HE WAS KILLED AT THE BATTLE OF WATERLOO / JUNE 18 1815 / THIS MONUMENT WAS ERECTED BY HIS BROTHER / GEORGE 4TH EARL OF ABERDEEN

Memorial Column: La Haye Sainte, Waterloo, Belgium. (Photograph)

Face 1:

SACRED TO THE MEMORY / OF / LIEUT-COL THE HON. SIR ALEXANDER GORDON / KNIGHT COMMANDER OF THE MOST HONOURABLE ORDER OF THE BATH / AIDE-DE-CAMP TO FIELD-MARSHAL THE DUKE OF WELLINGTON / AND ALSO BROTHER TO GEORGE EARL OF ABERDEEN / WHO IN THE TWENTY-NINTH YEAR OF HIS AGE / TERMINATED A SHORT BUT GLORIOUS CAREER / ON THE 18TH OF JUNE 1815 / WHILST EXECUTING THE ORDERS OF HIS GREAT COMMANDER / IN THE BATTLE OF WATERLOO / DISTINGUISHED FOR GALLANTRY AND GOOD CONDUCT IN THE FIELD / HE WAS HONOURED WITH REPEATED MARKS OF APPROBATION / BY THE ILLUSTRIOUS HERO / WITH WHOM HE SHARED THE DANGERS OF EVERY BATTLE / IN SPAIN PORTUGAL AND FRANCE / AND RECEIVED THE MOST FLAT- TERING PROOF OF HIS CONFIDENCE / ON MANY TRYING OCCASIONS / HIS ZEAL AND

ACTIVITY IN THE SERVICE OBTAINED THE REWARD / OF TEN MEDALS / AND THE HONOURABLE DISTINCTION OF THE ORDER OF THE BATH / HE WAS JUSTLY LAMENTED BY THE DUKE OF WELLINGTON / IN HIS PUBLIC DESPATCH / AS AN OFFICER OF HIGH PROMISE / AND A SERIOUS LOSS TO THE COUNTRY / NOT LESS WORTHY OF RECORD FOR HIS VIRTUES IN PRIVATE LIFE / HIS UNAFFECTED RESPECT FOR RELIGION / HIS HIGH SENSE OF HONOUR / HIS SCRUPULOUS INTEGRITY / AND THE MOST AMIABLE QUALITIES / WHICH SECURED THE ATTACHMENT OF HIS FRIENDS / AND THE LOVE OF HIS OWN FAMILY / IN TESTIMONY OF FEELINGS WHICH NO LANGUAGE CAN EXPRESS / A DISCONSOLATE SISTER AND FIVE SURVIVING BROTHERS / HAVE ERECTED THIS SIMPLE MEMORIAL / TO THE OBJECT OF THEIR TENDEREST AFFECTION. / REPAIRED IN 1863 BY HIS BROTHER / ADMIRAL THE HON^{BLE} J. GORDON. / REPAIRED IN 1871 AND 1888 BY HIS GREAT NEPHEW / JOHN, 7TH EARL OF ABERDEEN. / REPAIRED IN 1857 BY HIS FAMILY.

Face 2: The same inscription is reproduced in French on the opposite side of the column.

Face 3:
   TO THE MEMORY OF / THE HON. SIR ALEXANDER GORDON. K.C.B. / LT. COL. SCOTS GUARDS AND AIDE DE CAMP / TO THE DUKE OF WELLINGTON. / AFTER SERVING HIS COUNTRY WITH DISTINCTION / HE WAS KILLED AT THE BATTLE OF WATERLOO / 18TH JUNE 1815. / REPAIRED IN 1931 BY SUBSCRIPTION / OF THE GORDON FAMILY AND CLAN.

Named on the Regimental Memorial: St Joseph's Church, Waterloo, Belgium. (Photograph)

Memorial tablet: Inside Mausoleum, Evere Cemetery, Brussels, Belgium. (Photograph)

LIEUTENANT COLONEL / SIR ALEXANDER / GORDON / 3RD ROYAL / FOOT GUARDS / AGED 29

Ledger stone: Evere Cemetery, Brussels, Belgium. (Photograph)

HERE LIE THE ASHES / OF THE HONOURABLE SIR ALEXANDER GORDON, / LIEUTENANT-COLONEL, / KNIGHT COMMANDER / OF THE VERY HONOURABLE ORDER OF THE BATH, / AIDE-DE-CAMP TO THE DUKE OF WELLINGTON / AND 3RD BROTHER OF GEORGE, COUNT OF ABERDEEN. / HE DIED GLORIOUSLY / AT THE BATTLE OF WATERLOO, / ON 18 JUNE 1815 / AT THE AGE OF 29. / RESTORED BY ADMIRAL THE HONOURABLE JOHN GORDON / HIS LAST SURVIVING BROTHER IN 1865.

Named on Memorial Panel VIII for Waterloo: Royal Military Chapel, Wellington Barracks, London. (M.I.) (Destroyed by a Flying Bomb 1944)

Cornet 10th Lt Dragoons 13 Oct 1801. Ensign 3rd Foot Guards 26 May 1803. Lt and Capt 3 Apr 1806. Capt and Lt Col 25 Dec 1813.
   Served in the Peninsula Nov 1808 – Jan 1809 (ADC to Lt General Baird), Sep 1809 – Jan 1810, Oct 1810 – Jan 1812 and Sep 1812 – Apr 1814 (ADC to Lord Wellington). Present at Corunna (Mentioned in Despatches and returned with despatches), Busaco, Fuentes d'Onoro, Ciudad Rodrigo (Mentioned in Despatches and returned with despatches), El Bodon, Salamanca, Burgos, Vittoria, Pyrenees (severely wounded), Bidassoa, Nivelle, Nive, Orthes and Toulouse. Gold Cross for Salamanca, Vittoria, Pyrenees, Nivelle, Nive, Orthes and Toulouse. KCB 2 Jan 1815.
   Present at Waterloo (ADC to Wellington). Severely wounded near La Haye Sainte trying to rally a battalion of Brunswickers, and died later in Wellington's headquarters at Waterloo. Wellington in his Waterloo *Dispatch* writes of him as 'an officer of great promise whose death was a serious loss to the Army'. One of the select band of soldiers buried in the Mausoleum at Evere.

Also served at the Cape of Good Hope 1806 (ADC to his uncle Sir David Baird), South America 1807 (ADC to General Beresford) and the Baltic 1807 (ADC to Sir David Baird). Educated at Eton. Nephew of Colonel Sir David Baird 24th Foot.

REFERENCE: *Dictionary of National Biography. Gordon, Alexander, At Wellington's right hand: the letters of Lieutenant-Colonel Sir Alexander Gordon, edited by Rory Muir, 1808–1815, 2003.*

GORDON, Alexander

Ensign. Coldstream Regiment of Foot Guards.
Memorial tablet: Kirkyard of Aberdour, Aberdeenshire, Scotland. (Photograph)

TO THE MEMORY OF / WILLIAM GORDON, OF ABERDOUR, / WHO DIED 11TH NOVEMBER 1839, AGED 67. / AND OF HIS WIFE MARY ROSE, / ELDEST DAUGHTER OF WILLIAM ROSE OF BALLIVAT, / WHO DIED 18TH JANUARY 1828, AGED 49. / AND OF THEIR CHILDREN / ……………….. / ALEXANDER, LIEUTENANT OF THE COLDSTREAM GUARDS, / WHO DIED 1ST APRIL 1818, AGED 20. / ………………..

Ensign 19 May 1814. Lt 18 Jun 1815.
　　Present at Waterloo in Lt Col Hon. E. Acheson's Company. Served with the Army of Occupation. Killed at Cambrai in a duel with a French officer.

GORDON, Arthur Helsham

Major. 5th (Princess Charlotte of Wales's) Dragoon Guards.
Low monument: English Cemetery, Florence, Italy. (Grave number B16E). (Photograph)

SACRED TO THE MEMORY OF / COLONEL ARTHUR HELSHAM GORDON OF H. B. M.'S SERVICE / HE DIED AT ORVIETO ON THE WAY HOME 12 MAY 1865 AGED 84 YEARS / HE SERVED UNDER WELLINGTON IN THE PENINSULAR CAMPAIGNS / COMMANDED THE 5TH OR PRINCESS CHARLOTTE OF WALES'S DRAGOON GUARDS 8 YEARS / AND RETIRED FROM THE ARMY AS / COLONEL IN THE GRENADIER GUARDS

Cornet 5th Dragoon Guards 25 Apr 1796. Lt 6 Jul 1798. Capt 8 Apr 1799. Bt Major 4 Jun 1811. Major 8 Apr 1813. Lt Col 8 Feb 1816. Bt Colonel 10 Jan 1837.
　　Served in the Peninsula Sep 1811 – Jun 1813 (ADC to Major General W. Ponsonby Nov 1812 – May 1813). Present at Llerena and Salamanca. MGS medal for Salamanca. Colonel 5th Dragoon Guards 1816–1824. Half pay 6 May 1824.

GORDON, Charles John

Captain. 10th (Prince of Wales's Own) Regiment of Light Dragoons.
Family Memorial tablet: St Phillip and St Jacob Church, Bristol, Somerset. (Photograph)

SACRED / TO THE MEMORY OF JOHN GORDON ESQRE / ……………….. / ALSO OF / CHARLES JOHN GORDON, / ELDEST SON OF THE ABOVE, / A CAPTAIN IN THE 10TH ROYAL HUSSARS, / WHO WAS KILLED AT THE BATTLE OF TOULOUSE IN FRANCE, / COMMANDING A SQUADRON ON THE 10TH APRIL 1814, / AGED 26 YEARS. / ………………..

Named on the Memorial: St Andrew's Church, (now Musée Historique), Biarritz, France. (Photograph)

Memorial tablet: Chapel in Churchyard at Toulouse, France. (M.I.)

"CAROLI JOHANNIS GORDON ARMIGERI IN X MA LEGIONE / EQUITUM REGALIUM CAPITANI QUI DUM TURMAN SUAM / INEPROELIO PROPE THOLOSAM DUCEBAT HONESTAE

MORTI / OCCUBUIT. OMNIBUS SUIS CHARUS ET DEFLETUS. AETATIS / SUAE XXVII. FILIUS ERAT, NATU MAXIMUS JOHANNIS ET / CATHARINAE GORDON À CLIFTONIÂ GLOCESTE-RIENSI IN / ANGLIÂ QUI HOC MONUMENTUM FIERI FECERUNT."

Lt 2 Jan 1806. Capt 29 Jun 1809.
    Served in the Peninsula Oct 1808 – Jan 1809 and Feb 1813 – Apr 1814. Present at Sahagun, Benevente, Morales, Vittoria, Orthes and Toulouse where he was killed 10 Apr 1814. Educated at Eton.

GORDON, George (5th Duke of) see HUNTLY, George, Marquess of

GORDON, James
Paymaster. 92nd Regiment of Foot.
Family Memorial in form of a Cross: St Michael Archangel Churchyard, Kirkmichael, Morayshire, Scotland. (Photograph)

ANIMO NON ASTUTIA / CAPTAIN JAMES GORDON / DIED AT IVYBANK NAIRN, 9TH APRIL 1867 / AGED 90 YEARS. HE SERVED IN THE PENINSULA / WITH THE 92ND HIGHLANDERS, AND RECEIVED / THE WAR MEDAL WITH 7 CLASPS. HE WAS ALSO / PRESENT AT WATERLOO AND RECEIVED THE MEDAL. / "HE NEVER MADE AN ENEMY / OR LOST A FRIEND".

Ensign 20 Jun 1805. Lt 25 Dec 1806. Paymaster 16 Apr 1807.
    Served in the Peninsula Aug 1808 – Jan 1809 and Nov 1810 – Apr 1814. Present at Corunna, Fuentes d'Onoro, Almarez, Alba de Tormes, Vittoria, Pyrenees, Nive, Garris, Orthes, Aire, Tarbes and Toulouse. Present at Waterloo. Was a close friend of Colonel Cameron of Fassiefern whose funeral he attended on 17 Jun 1815, after Cameron's death at Quatre Bras. Also served at Walcheren 1809. Half pay 2 Mar 1820. Deputy Lieutenant for Elginshire and Nairnshire. 'One of the most popular men in the north'. MGS medal for Corunna, Fuentes d'Onoro, Vittoria, Pyrenees, Nive, Orthes and Toulouse.
REFERENCE: *Gentleman's Magazine, Jun 1867, pp. 816–7.*

GORDON, John
Major. 1st (Royal Scots) Regiment of Foot.
Headstone: Drummond Hill Presbyterian Churchyard, Lundy's Lane, Niagara, Canada. (Photograph)

IN MEMORY OF / LT. COL. GORDON / AND / CAPT. TORRENS / OF / FIRST ROYAL SCOTS, / KILLED AT FORT ERIE / DURING THE CAMPAIGN / OF 1814. / ERECTED BY MAJOR BARRY FOX, / LATE OF SAID REGIMENT / THEIR FRIEND AND COMPANION / JUNE 20 1851.

Memorial tablet: Church in Montreal, Canada. (M.I.)

"IN MEMORY OF LIEUT COLONEL JOHN GORDON COMMANDING THE 1ST BATTALION ROYAL SCOTS REGIMENT OF FOOT WHO DEPARTED THIS LIFE ON THE 25TH SEPTEMBER 1814 IN CONSEQUENCE OF A WOUND RECEIVED IN ACTION WITH THE ENEMY IN FRONT OF FORT ERIE ON THE 17TH OF THE SAME MONTH. THIS SLAB IS PLACED BY THE OFFICERS OF THE BATTALION TO COMMEMORATE THEIR HIGH ESTEEM OF HIM AS A MAN, AND THEIR RESPECT FOR HIS CHARACTER AS A SOLDIER."

Lt 30 Aug 1800. Capt 4 Sep 1804. Major 13 Aug 1807. Bt Lt Colonel 4 Jun 1813.
    Served in the Peninsula Oct 1808 – Jan 1809 and Aug 1810 – Feb 1811. Present at Corunna and Busaco. Gold Medal for Busaco. Also served at Walcheren 1809 and Canada 1812 where he was killed at Fort Erie Sep 1814.

GORDON, John (1)
Captain. 2ⁿᵈ (Queen's Royal) Regiment of Foot.
Named on the Regimental Memorial, St Michael's Cathedral, Bridgetown, Barbados, West Indies. (Photograph)

Ensign 1ˢᵗ West India Regt 4 Sep 1802. Lt 67ᵗʰ Foot 25 Jan 1803. Capt 13 Apr 1805. Capt 2ⁿᵈ Foot 19 Aug 1806.
    Served in the Peninsula with 2ⁿᵈ Foot Aug 1808 – Jan 1809, 2ⁿᵈ Battalion Detachments Feb – Sep 1809 and 2ⁿᵈ Foot Mar 1811 – Jan 1812 and Dec 1812 – Jan 1813. Present at Vimeiro, Douro, Talavera and Almeida. Also served in the West Indies where he died in Barbados 22 Dec 1816 during a yellow fever epidemic.

GORDON, John (2)
Captain. 2ⁿᵈ (Queen's Royal) Regiment of Foot.
Pedestal monument: New Calton Burial Ground, Edinburgh, Scotland. (Photograph)

……………….. / AND TO THE MEMORY OF / MAJOR JOHN GORDON / LATE OF THE 2ⁿᵈ OR QUEEN'S REGIMENT / WHO SERVED IN PORTUGAL, SPAIN / AND OTHER COUNTRIES. / HE DIED AT SOUTHAMPTON / ON THE 5ᵀᴴ SEPTᴿ 1850 AGED 68 YEARS, / AND HIS REMAINS ARE INTERRED HERE / …………….

Memorial tablet: Kildonan Church, Kildonan, Sutherland, Scotland. (M.I.)

"ADAM GORDON OF GRIAMACHARY, KILDONAN, ………. SON JOHN, MAJOR 2ⁿᵈ QUEEN'S REGT, SON WILLIAM, CAPTAIN 1ˢᵀ ROYAL SCOTS, SON ADAM, LT CAPE REGT, SERVED IN WARS WITH FRANCE".

Ensign 13 Nov 1804. Lt 16 Jan 1806. Capt 26 Apr 1810. Major 22 Mar 1821.
    Served in the Peninsula Aug 1808 – Jan 1809. Present at Vimeiro and Corunna. Also served at Walcheren 1809, West Indies 1816 – 1819 (present at Trinidad DQMG and Brigade Major). Retired 31 Jul 1823. MGS medal for Vimeiro and Corunna. Died 5 Sep 1850. Brother of Capt William Gordon 1ˢᵗ Foot and Lt Adam Gordon Cape Regt.

GORDON, Stephen
Lieutenant. 28ᵗʰ (North Gloucestershire) Regiment of Foot.
Named on the Memorial: St Andrew's Church, (now Musée Historique), Biarritz, France. (Photograph)

Ensign 10 Mar 1808. Lt 18 May 1809.
    Served in the Peninsula with 2/28ᵗʰ Aug 1809 – Jul 1811 and 1/28ᵗʰ Aug 1811 – Mar 1814. Present at Busaco, first siege of Badajoz, Albuera, Arroyo dos Molinos, Almarez, retreat from Burgos, Vittoria (wounded), Pyrenees (severely wounded), Nivelle, Nive, Garris, Orthes and Aire where he was killed 18 Mar 1814.

GORDON, Thomas
Lieutenant. 1ˢᵗ (Royal Scots) Regiment of Foot.
Pedestal monument: New Calton Burial Ground, Edinburgh, Scotland. (Photograph)

IN MEMORY OF / CAPTAIN THOMAS GORDON / LATE OF THE ROYAL REGIMENT, / WHO AFTER SERVING / IN EVERY PART OF THE GLOBE / HAVING BEEN ENGAGED AT WATERLOO, / IN MANY BRILLIANT ACTIONS IN SPAIN / AND THE EAST INDIES / DIED HERE ON THE 22ⁿᵈ FEBʸ 1844 / IN THE 49ᵀᴴ YEAR OF HIS AGE / UNIVERSALLY REGRETTED. / ……………….

Ensign 7 Mar 1811. Lt Bourbon Regt 2 Jul 1812. Lt 1st Foot 18 Feb 1813. Capt 26 Mar 1831.

Served in the Peninsula Mar – Apr 1814. Present at Bayonne. Present at Waterloo. Also served in India in Mahratta and Pindari War 1817 (present at Mehidpur). Half pay 7 Mar 1834.

GORDON, Thomas William
Captain and Lieutenant. 3rd Regiment of Foot Guards.
Pedestal tomb: Cemetery at Lyons, France. (Allée 52 No 364). (Photograph)

ICI REPOSE / THOMAS WILLIAM GORDON / LIEUTENANT COLONEL / 3RD REGIMENT OF GUARDS / DU ROI D'ANGLETERRE / PRISONIER DE GUERRE / A LA BATAILLE DE TALAVERA MORI / 11 NOVEMBRE / MDCCCXIII. /LYONS. / ********** / ********** / **********

Ensign 23 Jan 1796. Lt and Capt 5 Aug 1799. Capt and Lt Colonel 22 May 1806.

Served in the Peninsula Aug 1808 – Jan 1809 (DAAG) and Mar 1809 – Nov 1813. Present at Corunna, Douro and Talavera where he was wounded and taken prisoner until his death 11 Nov 1813 in Lyons.

GORDON, William
Captain. 1st (Royal Scots) Regiment of Foot.
Memorial tablet: Kildonan Church, Kildonan, Sutherland, Scotland. (M.I.)

"ADAM GORDON OF GRIAMACHARY, KILDONAN, ... SON JOHN, MAJOR 2ND QUEEN'S REGT, SON WILLIAM, CAPTAIN 1ST ROYAL SCOTS, SON ADAM, LT CAPE REGT, SERVED IN WARS WITH FRANCE".

Lt 18 Oct 1804. Capt 16 Jan 1812. Portuguese Army: Capt 24th Line 11 Aug 1812. Capt 3rd Caçadores 27 Apr 1814. Capt 12th Caçadores 15 Dec 1814.

Served in the Peninsula with 3/1st Jan – Jun 1812, and Portuguese Army Jul 1812 – Apr 1814. Present at Badajoz, Burgos, Osma, Vittoria, second siege of San Sebastian (Awarded Gold Medal), Nivelle and Nive. Present at Waterloo. Half pay Dec 1816. Died in 1834. Brother of Major John Gordon 2nd Foot and Lt Adam Gordon Cape Regt.

GORDON, William
Lieutenant. 42nd (Royal Highland) Regiment of Foot.
Named on the Memorial: St Andrew's Church, (now Musée Historique), Biarritz, France. (Photograph)

Ensign 24 Oct 1810. Lt 29 Oct 1812.

Served in the Peninsula Apr 1812 – Apr 1814. Present at Salamanca, Burgos, Nivelle, Nive, Orthes and Toulouse where he was killed 10 Apr 1814.

GORDON, William Alexander
Captain. 50th (West Kent) Regiment of Foot.
Family pedestal monument: Kirkmichael Churchyard, Kirkmichael, Banffshire, Scotland. (Photograph)

UNDERNEATH / LIE THE MORTAL REMAINS / OF / WILLIAM ALEXANDER GORDON / LIEU-TENANT GENERAL / IN HER MAJESTY'S SERVICE / COLONEL OF THE 54TH REGIMENT OF FOOT / COMPANION OF THE MOST HONOURABLE / MILITARY ORDER OF THE BATH. / HE WAS BORN AT CROUGHLY / ON THE 21ST DAY OF MARCH 1769 / AND DEPARTED THIS LIFE IN NAIRN / ON THE 10TH DAY OF AUGUST 1856 / AGED 87 YEARS. / BRAVE AND ZEALOUS IN HIS PROFESSION / INDULGENT AND SOCIAL IN DOMESTIC LIFE. / HE DIED REGRETTED BY ALL WHO KNEW HIM. / THIS TRIBUTE OF AFFECTION AND RESPECT / IS DEDICATED TO HIS MEMORY / BY / HIS WIDOW AND HER SONS.

Ensign 112th Foot 2 Oct 1794. Lt 11 Dec 1794. Lt 26th Foot 12 Jan 1796. Lt 92nd Foot 12 Apr 1799. Capt 85th Foot 2 Oct 1801. Capt 50th Foot 23 Oct 1806. Bt Major 4 Jun 1813. Bt Lt Colonel 25 Dec 1813. Bt Colonel 22 Jul 1830. Major General 23 Nov 1841. Lt General 11 Nov 1851.

Served in the Peninsula Sep 1810 – Apr 1814. Present at Fuentes d'Onoro, Arroyo dos Molinos, Vittoria (severely wounded), Nive and Garris (wounded). Gold medal for Nive and MGS medal for Fuentes d'Onoro and Vittoria. CB. Also served at the Helder 1799 and Walcheren 1809. Half pay Nov 1818. Colonel 54th Foot 15 Aug 1850.

GORE, Arthur
Lieutenant Colonel. 33rd (1st Yorkshire West Riding) Regiment of Foot.
Monument: St Paul's Cathedral, London. (To Major Generals Arthur Gore and John Byne Skerrett). (Photograph)

ERECTED AT THE PUBLIC EXPENSE / TO THE MEMORY OF / MAJOR GENERALS / ARTHUR GORE, AND JOHN BYNE SKERRETT, / WHO FELL GLORIOUSLY / WHILE LEADING THE TROOPS TO THE ASSAULT / ON THE FORTRESS OF BERGEN-OP-ZOOM, / ON THE NIGHT OF THE 8TH AND 9TH OF MARCH 1814.

Memorial tablet: Grange Silva Church, Goresbridge, County Kilkenny, Ireland. (Removed from Powerstown Parish Church). (Photograph)

SACRED TO THE MEMORY OF BRIGADIER GENERAL / ARTHUR GORE, LIEUTENANT COLONEL OF THE 33RD / REGIMENT WHO FELL ON THE 8TH OF MARCH / 1814 AT BERGEN-OP-ZOOM, WHILE GALLANTLY / LEADING HIS MEN TO THE ATTACK ON THE / RAMPARTS OF THAT PLACE. / THIS MERITORIOUS OFFICER IN THE / COURSE OF 26 YEARS SERVICE (20 OF WHICH WERE / PASSED IN INDIA AND IN THE COMMAND OF / THE 33RD REGT) DISTIN-GUISHED HIMSELF ON / VARIOUS AND TRYING OCCASIONS BY HIS GALLANTRY / AND ZEAL. / IN TESTIMONY OF THE HIGH ESTEEM / WHICH HIS PUBLIC CHARACTER EXCITED, AND / THE GRATEFUL FEELINGS OF REGARD WHICH / HIS MILD AND CONCILIATORY CONDUCT IN THE / COMMAND OF THE 33RD REGT, NEVER FAILED / TO CALL FORTH, THE OFFICERS OF THAT / CORPS HAVE ERECTED THIS / MONUMENT. / BORN AT KILKENNY 30 JUNE 1773.

Ensign 73rd Foot 1788. Lt 74th Foot 10 Nov 1792. Lt 73rd Foot 9 Aug 1794. Capt-Lieut 27 May 1800. Lt Col 33rd Foot 29 Oct 1802. Bt Colonel 4 Jun 1811. Major General 1813.

Served in the Netherlands 1814 (present at Bergen-op-Zoom where he led one of the columns to attack the fortress, but was killed in the attempt 8 Mar 1814). Also served in India 1799 (present at Seringapatam). While he served in India Arthur Gore took command of the 33rd Foot from Arthur Wellesley, remaining in command for eleven years from 1799–1810. During this time he revised the standing orders for the regiment which had first been drawn up by Wellesley. Twenty years of his 26 years in the service were spent in India.

GORE, Arthur
Lieutenant. 33rd (1st Yorkshire West Riding) Regiment of Foot.
Named on the Regimental Memorial: St Joseph's Church, Waterloo, Belgium. (Photograph)

Ensign 8 Oct 1811. Lt 11 Mar 1813.
Present at Quatre Bras where he was killed. Eldest son of Lt Colonel Ralph Gore 33rd Foot.

GORE, Hon. Sir Charles Stephen

Captain. 85th (Buckinghamshire Volunteers) Light Infantry Regiment of Foot.
Monument: Brompton Cemetery, London. (BR 57329). (Photograph)

GENERAL THE HON^BLE SIR CHARLES GORE / G.C.B. K.H. / LIEUTENANT GOVERNOR ROYAL HOSPITAL / CHELSEA: / DIED 4TH SEPTEMBER 1869, AGED 76. / PRESENT AT / TOULOUSE. VITTORIA. / ORTHES. SALAMANCA. / NIVE. BADAJOZ. / NIVELLE. CIUDAD RODRIGO. / PYRENEES. WATERLOO.

Memorial tablet: Royal Hospital, Chelsea, London. (Photograph)

IN MEMORY OF / GENERAL THE HON^BL. SIR CHARLES GORE / G.C.B. – K.H. / LIEUTENANT GOVERNOR ROYAL HOSPITAL / CHELSEA / DIED 4TH SEPTEMBER 1869, AGED 76. / PRESENT AT / CIUDAD RODRIGO. NIVELLE. / BADAJOZ. NIVE. / SALAMANCA. ORTHES. / VITTORIA. TOULOUSE. / PYRENEES. WATERLOO. / ERECTED BY HIS SURVIVING DAUGHTER THE DOWAGER / COUNTESS OF ERROLL, AND YOUNGEST SURVIVING SON / LIEUT. COL. FRED AUG GORE.

Cornet 16th Dragoons 21 Oct 1808. Ensign 6th Foot 7 Jun 1809. Lt 43rd Foot 4 Jan 1810. Capt York Chasseurs 13 Mar 1815. Capt 85th Foot 15 Jun 1815. Bt Major 21 Jan 1819. Bt Lt Colonel 19 Sep 1822. Major (unattached) 20 Aug 1825. Bt Colonel 10 Jan 1837. Major General 9 Nov 1846. Lt General 20 Jun 1854. General 12 Feb 1868.
　　Served in the Peninsula with 1/43rd Jul 1811 – Oct 1812, with Staff Nov 1812 – Feb 1813 (ADC to General Sir Andrew Barnard) and Mar 1813 – Apr 1814 (ADC to General Sir James Kempt). Present at Ciudad Rodrigo, Badajoz, Salamanca, San Munos, San Millan, Vittoria, Pyrenees, Vera, Bidassoa, Nivelle, Nive, Orthes, Tarbes and Toulouse. KCB and KH. Present at Quatre Bras (one horse shot under him), Waterloo (three horses shot under him), the Capture of Paris (ADC to Sir James Kempt) and with the Army of Occupation. MGS medal for Ciudad Rodrigo, Badajoz, Salamanca, Vittoria, Pyrenees, Nivelle, Nive, Orthes and Toulouse. Also served in Canada Apr 1814 (ADC to Sir James Kempt but returned in time for Waterloo). QMG in Canada 20 Apr 1826. Colonel 91st Foot 8 Aug 1855. Colonel 6th Foot 8 Mar 1864. Lieutenant Governor of Chelsea Hospital 11 Dec 1868.
REFERENCE: *Dictionary of National Biography.*

GORE, George

Major. 9th Regiment of Light Dragoons.
Pedestal tomb: St Andrew's Churchyard, Clifton, Bristol. (Grave number 0135). (Photograph)

SACRED / TO THE MEMORY OF / LT COLONEL GEORGE GORE / LATE OF H. M. 9TH LANCERS / WHO DIED AT CLIFTON / THE 25TH OF JULY 1862 / AGED 82 YEARS. / (VERSE)

Lt 11th Foot 28 May 1794. Lt 27th Dragoons 8 Jun 1796. Capt 15th Foot 14 Feb 1805. Capt 9th Dragoons 25 Sep 1806. Major 7 May 1812. Bt Lt Colonel 4 Dec 1817.
　　Served in the Peninsula 1809 (ADC to General Beresford) and Aug 1811 – Apr 1813. Present at Arroyo dos Molinos (Mentioned in Despatches), and Alba de Tormes. Also served in India 1802–1803 (present at Allyghur, Delhi and Laswaree. Brigade Major of Cavalry at Laswaree where he was severely wounded twice and awarded pension of £100 per annum), and Walcheren 1809. Awarded War Medal in 1851 for the 1803 Indian campaigns under Lord Lake (Allyghur, Delhi and Laswaree, one of the few recipients of this medal as most of the officers who took part in the campaign had already died). Retired on half pay 4 Dec 1817. KH.

GORNALL, John
Private. 1st (Royal) Regiment of Dragoons.
Tablestone: St Michael's Churchyard, Dumfries, Dumfriesshire, Scotland. (Photograph)

IN MEMORY OF / JOHN GORNALL / FORMERLY OF / THE 1ST ROYAL DRAGOON REGIMENT / WHO DIED IN DUMFRIES 9TH SEPTEMBER 1864. / AGED 77 YEARS.

Pte 13 Aug 1805.
    Served in the Peninsula. Present at Fuentes d'Onoro, Vittoria and Toulouse. Present at Waterloo in Capt Ralph Heathcote's No 4 Troop. MGS medal for Fuentes d' Onoro, Vittoria and Toulouse. Discharged 11 Jun 1828.

GOSSETT, John Noah
1st Lieutenant. 95th Regiment of Foot.
Headstone: St Saviour's Churchyard, St Helier, Jersey, Channel Islands. (Photograph)

TO / THE MEMORY OF / JOHN NOAH GOSSETT / FORMERLY MAJOR IN HER MAJESTY'S / RIFLE BRIGADE / SON OF MATTHEW GOSSETT OF BAGOT / IN THIS ISLAND / AND OF MARGARET HIS WIFE / DIED AUGUST 30TH 1870 / AGED 77.

2nd Lt 6 Jun 1811. Lt 17 Jun 1813. Capt 8 Jan 1824. Major 22 May 1835.
    Served in the Peninsula with 3/95th Dec 1813 – Apr 1814. Present at Nive, Orthes, Tarbes and Toulouse. Also served in North America 1814 (present at New Orleans where he was wounded Jan 1815). Retired May 1839. Barrack Master at Youghal and Dungarvon Jul 1839, at Derry, Lifford and Omagh Apr 1841 and Cork Jul 1846. MGS medal for Nive, Orthes and Toulouse. Resigned 1869.

GOUGH, Hugh
Lieutenant Colonel. 87th (Prince of Wales's Own Irish) Regiment of Foot.
Low monument in Family railed enclosure: St Brigid's Churchyard, Stillorgan, Dublin, Ireland. (Photograph)

HERE LIETH THE RIGHT HONOURABLE HUGH VISCOUNT GOUGH, KP GCB GCSI PC. / BORN 3RD NOV 1779 DIED 2 MARCH 1869

Statue: Chillingham Castle, Northumberland. (Photograph). Originally standing in Phoenix Park Dublin, Eire. (Photograph) Destroyed by IRA action in the 1950's. Now restored in the grounds of Chillingham Castle, Northumberland.

GOUGH

Limerick City Militia 1793. Ensign Robert Ward's Regt of Foot 7 Aug 1794. Ensign 119th Foot 11 Oct 1794. Lt 78th Foot 6 Jun 1795. Lt 87th Foot 1799. Capt 25 Jun 1803. Major 8 Aug 1805. Bt Lt Colonel 29 Jul 1809. Lt Colonel 25 May 1815. Colonel 12 Aug 1819. Major General 22 Jul 1830. Lt General 23 Nov 1841. General 20 Jun 1854. Field Marshal 9 Nov 1862.
    Served in the Peninsula Mar 1809 – Nov 1810 and Feb 1811 – Mar 1814. Present at Douro, Talavera (severely wounded and awarded pension of £300 per annum), Cadiz, Barrosa (Mentioned in Despatches), Tarifa (wounded and Mentioned in Despatches), Vittoria and Nivelle (severely wounded). For his conduct at Talavera he was awarded a Bt Lt Colonelcy and Wellington ante-dated it to the date of his *Dispatch*, making Gough the first officer to receive brevet promotion in action at the head of a regiment. Gold Cross for Talavera, Barrosa, Vittoria and Nivelle. KCB 1831.
    Also served at the Cape of Good Hope 1795, West Indies (Trinidad and Surinam), Ireland 1814–1826

(commanded 22nd Foot), India 1837–1843 (in command of Mysore division of the Madras Army 1837), China 1841–1842 (present in the first Opium War), India 1843–1849 (defeated Maratha Army at Maharajpore where he captured 56 guns) and First Sikh War 1845 (present at Moodkee, Ferozeshah, Sobraon – actions supported by Henry Hardinge the new Governor General). Second Sikh War 1845 (present at Ramnuggar, Chillianwala – where Gough's failure to reconnoitre the Sikh position led to a great loss of life, resulting in a public outcry in Great Britain). Finally defeated the Sikhs at Gujerat 1849. Returned to England 7 May 1849. GCB. Knight of the Order of St Patrick (the first non Irish peer to have this honour). Was in command of more general actions than any other British officer in the nineteenth century except for Wellington. Colonel Regiment of Royal Horse Guards 29 Jun 1855. Died 2 Mar 1869. His brother Capt William Gough served with 68th Foot in the Peninsula and lost his life in a shipwreck off the coast of Ireland 1822.

REFERENCE: *Dictionary of National Biography. Royal Military Calendar, Vol 4, pp. 254–60. Rait, R. S., The life of Hugh, first Viscount Gough, 2 vols, 1903. Gentleman's Magazine, May 1869, p. 745. Annual Register, 1869, Appx, pp. 164–6. Household Brigade Journal, 1869, pp. 317–9.*

GOUGH, Hugh

Lieutenant. 27th (Inniskilling) Regiment of Foot.
Named on the Memorial: St Andrew's Church, (now Musée Historique), Biarritz, France. (Photograph)

Ensign 10 Mar 1808. Lt 18 Jul 1811.
   Served in the Peninsula with 3/27th Nov 1808 – Apr 1814 (unbroken service). Present at Busaco, Redinha, Olivencia, first siege of Badajoz, Badajoz, Castrejon, Salamanca, Vittoria, Pyrenees, Nivelle, Nive, Orthes and Toulouse where he was killed 10 Apr 1814.

GOULBURN, Frederick

Captain. 13th Regiment of Light Dragoons.
Memorial: Christ Church Churchyard, Southgate, London. (M.I.)

"FREDERICK GOULBURN, / A LIEUTENANT COLONEL / IN HIS MAJESTY'S SERVICE; / BORN 7TH MAY 1788. / DIED 10TH FEBRUARY 1837."

Cornet 23rd Lt Dragoons 25 May 1805. Lt 11 Sep 1806. Capt 12 Jul 1810. Capt 13th Lt Dragoons 24 Jun 1813. Major 104th Regt 15 Feb 1816. Bt Lt Colonel 10 Jan 1837.
   Served in the Peninsula with 23rd Lt Dragoons May – Dec 1809 and 13th Lt Dragoons Apr 1814. Present at Talavera and Toulouse. Present at Waterloo with 13th Lt Dragoons. Half pay 1817. First official Colonial Secretary to New South Wales 1820–1826. His brother Henry was Under Secretary for the Colonies. Returned to England in 1827 and became Under Secretary in Dublin while his brother was Chief Secretary in Ireland.
REFERENCE: *Australian Dictionary of Biography.*

GOULD, Thomas

Private. 52nd (Oxfordshire) Light Infantry Regiment of Foot.
Low monument: Formerly in St Bridget's Churchyard, Chester, Cheshire. (Grave number 136). Now located on a roundabout opposite Chester Police station. (Photograph)

IN MEMORY OF THOMAS GOULD LATE OF THE 52ND REGT. OF FOOT WHO / DIED 1ST NOVEMBER 1865 AGED 72 YEARS, / 46 OF WHICH WERE SPENT IN THE SERVICE OF HIS COUNTRY. HE WAS / PRESENT IN THE FOLLOWING ENGAGEMENTS – VIMIERO, CORUNNA, CROSSING / THE COA NEAR ALMEIDA, BUSACO, POMBAL, REDINHA, CONDEIXA, FOZ D'ARONCE, / SABUGAL, FUENTES D' ONORO, STORMING OF CIUDAD RODRIGO, BADAJOS, SALAMANCA, / SAN MUNOS (TAKEN PRISONER), ST MILLAN, VITTORIA, PYRENEES, STORMING OF / FRENCH ENTRENCHMENTS AT VERA (WOUNDED), NIVELLE, PASSAGE OF

THE NIVE, ORTHEZ, TARBES, / TOULOUSE AND WATERLOO. HE RECEIVED THE PENIN-SULAR MEDAL WITH 13 CLASPS AND / THE WATERLOO MEDAL. THIS STONE IS PLACED OVER HIM BY A FEW FRIENDS.

Pte 16 Jun 1806
Served in the Peninsula with 1/52nd Aug 1808 – Jan 1809 and Jul 1809 – Apr 1814. Present at Vimeiro, Corunna, Coa, Busaco, Pombal, Redinha, Condeixa, Foz d'Arouce, Sabugal, Fuentes d'Onoro, Ciudad Rodrigo, Badajoz, Salamanca, San Munos (taken prisoner), St Millan, Vittoria, Pyrenees, Vera (wounded), Nivelle, Nive, Orthes, Tarbes and Toulouse. Also served at Waterloo in Capt Robert Campbell's Company. MGS medal for Vimeiro, Corunna, Busaco, Fuentes d'Onoro, Ciudad Rodrigo, Badajoz, Salamanca, Vittoria, Pyrenees, Nivelle, Nive, Orthes and Toulouse. Discharged 5 May 1823. Died 1 Nov 1865, aged 72 years.

GOURLAY, Alexander
Captain. 13th Royal Veteran Battalion.
Headstone: St Cuthbert's Churchyard, Norham, Northumberland. (Photograph)

SACRED / TO THE MEMORY OF / CAPT / ALEXANDER GOURLAY / LATE / 7 ROYAL VETERAN BATTALION / WHO DIED 24TH APRIL A.D. 1836 / IN THE 64TH YEAR OF HIS AGE

1st Lt 23rd Foot 12 Jan 1805. Capt 9 Oct 1811. Capt 13th Royal Veteran Battalion 25 Jan 1813.
Served in the Peninsula with 1/23rd Dec 1810 – Feb 1813 and 13th Royal Veteran Battalion Feb 1813 – Apr 1814. Present at Redinha, Olivencia, first siege of Badajoz, Albuera, Aldea da Ponte, Ciudad Rodrigo, Badajoz and Salamanca. Also served in Martinique 1809. Retired on full pay 1832.

GRACIE, James
1st Lieutenant. 21st (Royal North British Fusiliers) Regiment of Foot.
Family Memorial: St Michael's Churchyard, Dumfries, Dumfriesshire, Scotland. (Photograph)

.... / JAMES, LIEU^{T} 21ST FOOT, WHO WAS AT GENOA / AND BLADENSBURG: WITH 20 PICKED MEN / LED THE FORLORN HOPE, AT WASHINGTON, / AND FELL, LEADING ON THE LIGHT INFANTRY / AT BALTIMORE, 13TH SEP^{TR} 1813. ETA 37. / ....

2nd Lt 6 Nov 1808. 1st Lt 13 Jul 1809.
Served in the Peninsula 1812–1814. Present on the East Coast of Spain. With Sir William Bentinck's expedition to Italy Feb 1814 to try and recapture Italian towns from the French (present at the capture of Genoa Apr 1814). Also served in North America 1814–1815. Present at Bladensburg Aug 1814, Capture of Washington and Baltimore where he was killed Sep 13 1814. Of the 300 British casualties one third were from the 21st Foot and one third from 44th Foot. An indecisive action as the Royal Navy were not able to fulfil their part of the plan.
Note: Date of death on memorial is incorrect and should be 1814 not 1813.

GRAHAM, Henry
Captain.1st (King's) Dragoon Guards.
Memorial tablet: St Mary's Church, Harrow on the Hill, Middlesex, London. (Photograph)

.... / ALSO OF HIS SON MAJOR HENRY GRAHAM / OF THE 1ST REG^{T} OF DRAGOON GUARDS, / WHO FELL, IN THE 37TH YEAR OF HIS AGE, / AT THE BATTLE OF WATERLOO.

Lt 13 Jun 1795. Capt-Lieut 12 Jun 1799. Capt 10 May 1800. Bt Major 4 Jun 1811.
Served at Waterloo where he was killed. Also served in Ireland.

GRAHAM, James Reginald Torin

Lieutenant. 2nd (Royal North British) Regiment of Dragoons.
Low monument: Brompton Cemetery, London. (BR 47492. Compartment Q:164.6x116.3). (Photograph)

IN HOPE OF THE RESURRECTION OF LIFE / IS HERE LAID THE BODY OF / MAJOR JAMES REGINALD TORIN GRAHAM / 2ND R. N. B. DRAGOONS (SCOTS GREYS) / LATE OF RICHARDBY, COUNTY OF CUMBERLAND. / BORN FEB 23 1798. / DIED JAN 20 1865. / WATERLOO / (VERSE)

Brass memorial tablet: St Michael's Church, Stanwix, Carlisle, Cumbria. (Photograph)

TO THE GLORY OF GOD / AND THE HONOURED MEMORY OF / MAJOR JAMES REGINALD TORIN GRAHAM, / LATE OF RICHARDBY, SON OF JAMES GRAHAM / OF BARROCK LODGE AND RICHARDBY, ESQUIRE. / HE SERVED IN THE 2ND R.N.B. DRAGOONS (SCOTS GREYS) / AND WAS IN THE CHARGE OF THE HEAVY BRIGADE / AT WATERLOO. / BORN AT BARROCK LODGE 23RD FEBRUARY 1798, / DIED AT KENSINGTON 20TH JANUARY 1865.

Cornet 20 Jan 1814. Lt 8 Jun 1815. Capt 16 Mar 1820. Bt Major 10 Jan 1837.
   Served at Waterloo aged 16. After being on the battlefield all day, he was sent out after the battle finished, in command of the men looking for the wounded of the regiment and to bury their dead. Half pay 1821. Retired 5 Apr 1844.
REFERENCE: *Gentleman's Magazine, Mar 1865, p. 392.*

GRAHAM, Sir Thomas (Lord Lynedoch)

Colonel. 90th (Perthshire Volunteers) Regiment of Foot.
Obelisk: North Inches, Perthshire, Scotland. (Photograph)

IN HONOUR OF / THE 90TH LIGHT INFANTRY / (PERTHSHIRE VOLUNTEERS) / RAISED MAY 1794 BY / THOMAS GRAHAM OF BALGOWAN / WHO WAS PROMOTED FOR HIS / SERVICES IN ITALY SPAIN / AND HOLLAND / TO THE RANK OF GENERAL 1809 / MADE A KNIGHT OF THE BATH 1812 / AND CREATED BARON LYNEDOCH / 1814.

Mausoleum: Methven Churchyard, Methven, Perthshire, Scotland. (Photograph)

THIS MAUSOLEUM WAS ERECTED BY / THOMAS GRAHAM OF BALGOWAN / FOLLOWING THE DEATH OF HIS WIFE / MARY, IN 1792. BORN 19TH OCTOBER / 1748, HE HAD A DISTINGUISHED / MILITARY CAREER, PARTICULARLY BETWEEN / 1793 AND 1815, AND FROM 1810 ONWARDS / WAS NEXT IN SENIORITY TO THE DUKE / OF WELLINGTON. CREATED SIR THOMAS / GRAHAM IN MARCH 1812, AND BARON / LYNEDOCH OF BALGOWAN IN MAY 1814, / HE DIED 18TH DECEMBER 1843, AND / WAS INTERRED IN THIS MAUSOLEUM.

Memorial: United Service Club, now Institute of Directors, Waterloo Place, London. (Photograph)

TO LIEUTENANT-GENERAL / THOMAS LORD LYNEDOCK, KG. CB. / THE UNITED SERVICE CLUB, / AS A MEMORIAL OF THE HIGH SENSE WE ENTERTAIN / OF HIS JUDICIOUS EXERTIONS WHICH LED / TO ITS ESTABLISHMENT, / AND OF THE ZEAL WITH WHICH HE SO BENEFICIALLY / DEVOTED HIS UNCEASING ATTENTION TO ITS INTEREST, / HAS CAUSED / THIS PLATE TO BE INSCRIBED, / AND TO BE DEPOSITED / WITH THE FOUNDATION STONE OF THEIR HOUSE, / ON THE 1ST DAY OF MARCH, / AND THE 55TH YEAR OF THE REIGN OF / GEORGE III. / MDCCCXVII.

Bust on Pedestal Monument: Chiclana de la Frontera, Barrosa, Spain. (Photograph)

SIR THOMAS GRAHAM / (GLASGOW 1848 - LONDON 1843) / GENERAL AL MANDO DE LAS TOISPAS / ANGLOPORTUGUESAS DURANTE LA / BATTALLA DE CHICLANA DEL / 5 DE MAUE DE 1811

Lt Colonel 90th Foot 10 Feb 1794. Bt Colonel 22 Jul 1795. Colonel 25 Sep 1803. Major General 25 Sep 1803. Lt General 25 Jul 1810. General 19 Jul 1821.

Served in the Peninsula Nov 1808 – Jan 1809 (ADC to Sir John Moore), Apr 1810 – Jul 1811 (GOC Cadiz), Aug 1811 – Jun 1812 and Apr – Oct 1813 (GOC 1st Division). Present at Corunna, Cadiz, Barrosa, Ciudad Rodrigo (Mentioned in Despatches), siege of Salamanca Forts, Osma (Mentioned in Despatches), Vittoria (Mentioned in Despatches), Tolosa (wounded and Mentioned in Despatches), San Sebastian (Mentioned in Despatches four times) and Bidassoa (Mentioned in Despatches). Gold Cross for Barrosa, Ciudad Rodrigo, Vittoria and San Sebastian. GCB. GCMG. KTS. Also served at Toulon 1793, Quiberon 1794, Gibraltar 1795, Minorca 1798, Malta 1800, Baltic 1808, Walcheren 1809 and the Netherlands 1813–1814 (GOC at Merxem and Bergen-op-Zoom).

Served as a volunteer at Toulon, having decided on a military career after the death of his wife and desecration of her coffin by the Revolutionary Guards in France. Raised the 1st Battalion of 90th Foot 1794 and became its commanding officer. Owing to inactivity on the Gibraltar station he obtained permission to join the Austrian Army where he used his time to send intelligence reports back to London. Returned to Gibraltar 1798 and conducted the successful siege of Malta. Returned to England in 1801. Served in the Baltic with Sir John Moore 1808 and then followed him to Spain in the same year. Served in the Peninsula until autumn 1813 when he had to return home due to ill health. Was in action again in 1814 at the age of 66 in the Netherlands in command of the troops at Merxem and Bergen-op-Zoom.

Founded the United Service Club in Waterloo Place 1817, as a club for officers who had fought in the Napoleonic Wars, as a place to stay when they visited London and to meet colleagues. Colonel 14th Foot 1826. Governor of Dumbarton Castle 1829. Colonel 1st (Royal) Foot 1834. MP for the County of Perth. Played in the first recorded cricket match in Scotland 1785. Died 18 Dec 1843 aged 95 years.

REFERENCE: *Dictionary of National Biography. Gentleman's Magazine, Feb 1844, pp. 197–9. Annual Register, 1843, Appx, pp. 322–4. Royal Military Calendar, Vol 2, p. 147. Aspinall-Oglander, C., Freshly remembered: the story of Thomas Graham, Lord Lynedoch, 1956. Brett-James, Anthony, General Graham – Lord Lynedoch, 1959. Graham, J., Memoir of General Lord Lynedoch, 2006. Delavoye, Alexander Marin, Life of Thomas Graham, Lord Lynedoch, 1880. Cole, John William, Memoirs of British Generals, Vol 2, 1856, pp. 87–146.*

GRAHAME, Duncan
Captain. 6th (1st Warwickshire) Regiment of Foot.
Family Memorial tablet: Ruins of Inchmahome Priory, Island of Inchmahome, Lake of Monteith, Stirlingshire, Scotland. (Photograph)

SACRED / TO THE MEMORY OF / THE GRAHAMES OF GLENNY / WHO ARE HERE INTERRED / AS ALSO / MAJOR DUNCAN GRAHAME / 6TH REGIMENT / WHO FOUGHT THROUGH THE PENINSULAR WAR. / BORN 26TH MARCH 1776, DIED 22ND SEPTEMBER 1861

Lt 6th Foot 1 May 1805. Capt Nov 18 1813. Portuguese Army: Capt 6th Line 26 Aug 1809.

Served in the Peninsula with 6th Foot Aug 1808 – Jan 1809 and Portuguese Army Aug 1809 – Oct 1813. Present at Rolica, Vimeiro, Corunna, Busaco, Fuentes d'Onoro and Badajoz. MGS medal for Rolica, Vimeiro, Corunna, Busaco, Fuentes d'Onoro and Badajoz. Retired Dec 1813.

GRANGER, Early
Private. 54th (West Norfolk) Regiment of Foot.
Headstone: Greenwood Cemetery, Brooklyn, New York, United States of America. (Photograph)

MARY GRANGER, / DIED / DEC 8 1862 / AGED 56 YEARS / EARLY GRANGER, / DIED / 19 AUG 1853

Served at Waterloo with 54th Foot in reserve at Hal, siege of Cambrai and with the Army of Occupation. Emigrated to New York in 1830. Died at Jamaica, New York 19 Aug 1853. Founder of the Brooklyn Brass Band in 1835, which became the band of the 14th Regiment in the American Civil War. Also known as Eady Granger.

GRANT, Alexander
Lieutenant. 74th (Highland) Regiment of Foot.
Named on the Regimental Memorial: St Giles's Cathedral, Edinburgh, Scotland. (Photograph)

Ensign 8 Oct 1807. Lt 20 Sep 1810.
   Served in the Peninsula Feb 1810 – Apr 1812. Present at Busaco, Fuentes d'Onoro, second siege of Badajoz, Ciudad Rodrigo and Badajoz where he was severely wounded 6 Apr and died of his wounds 10 Apr 1812.

GRANT, Charles
Lieutenant. 2nd (Queen's Royal) Regiment of Foot.
Named on the Regimental Memorial: St Michael's Cathedral, Bridgetown, Barbados, West Indies. (Photograph)

Ensign Dorset Militia. Ensign 2nd Foot 8 Jun 1809. Lt 7 Oct 1812.
   Served in the Peninsula Mar 1811 – Dec 1812. Present at Almeida, siege of Salamanca Forts, Salamanca, Burgos and the retreat from Burgos. Also served at Walcheren 1809 and West Indies. Died in Barbados 1816 during a yellow fever epidemic.

GRANT, Colquhoun
Major. 11th (North Devonshire) Regiment of Foot.
Memorial tablet: St Lawrence's Church, Forres, Morayshire, Scotland. (Photograph)

SACRED TO THE MEMORY OF / LIEUTENANT COLONEL COLQUHOUN GRANT C.B. / OF THE 54TH REGIMENT. EIGHTH SON OF DUNCAN GRANT ESQRE OF LINGISTON / THE SELECTION OF THIS OFFICER BY THE DUKE OF WELLINGTON FOR THE IMPORTANT DUTY / OF ESTABLISHING AND CONDUCTING THE INTELLIGENCE DEPARTMENT OF THE ARMY / AND HIS HAVING FILLED THAT HIGHLY IMPORTANT AND CONFIDENTIAL SITUATION / DURING THE WHOLE OF THE CAMPAIGNS OF THE ARMY / IN THE PENINSULA FRANCE AND THE NETHERLANDS / BEST ATTEST THE SERVICES AND MERITS OF THIS DISTINGUISHED OFFICER / WHILE HIS DARING ENTERPRISE, AND RARE PRESENCE OF MIND, / SO EMINENTLY QUALIFIED HIM FOR HIS PUBLIC DUTIES; / NO LESS ENDEARED HIM TO HIS RELATIVES AND FRIENDS; / HE DIED AT AIX-LA-CHAPELLE ON THE 30TH DAY OF SEPTEMBER 1829, IN THE 48TH YEAR OF HIS AGE, / IN CONSEQUENCE OF HIS HEALTH HAVING BEEN IMPAIRED WHILE IN THE COMMAND / OF A BRIGADE OF THE ARMY, IN THE WAR AGAINST THE BURMESE IN INDIA, / WHERE HE RECEIVED THE THANKS OF THE COMMANDER IN CHIEF. / ....

Gravestone: Evangelical Cemetery, Aix-la-Chapelle, France. (Destroyed during the Second World War)

Ensign 11th Foot 9 Sep 1795 (age 14). Lt 5 Apr 1796. Capt 19 Nov 1801. Bt Major 30 May 1811. Bt Lt Colonel 19 May 1814. Major 11th Foot 13 Oct 1814. Lt Colonel 54th Foot 25 Nov 1821.
   Served in the Peninsula with 11th Foot Aug 1809 – Apr 1811 and with Staff May 1811 – Apr 1814

(AQMG and Intelligence Officer and DAAG). Present at Busaco. Captured on the banks of the Coa. Prisoner of war Jul – Dec 1812. His adventures before he escaped are related in *Life of Surgeon General Sir James McGrigor*, his brother in law. Present at Waterloo (AQMG). Also served in Flanders 1798 (present at Ostend and taken prisoner until 1799), India 1821 (served in Aracan during the first Burmese War, but caught malaria which later brought about his death). McGrigor and his brother Sir James Grant sent him to Aix-La-Chapelle for a cure but he died there 30 Oct 1829 aged 49. CB. One of the best intelligence officers who served Wellington who said 'No Army in the world ever produced the like of these exploring officers.' Brother of James Robert Grant, Inspector General of Hospitals and brother in law of Sir James McGrigor, Inspector General of Hospitals.

REFERENCE: *Dictionary of National Biography. Gentleman's Magazine, Nov 1829, p. 477. McGrigor, J., Autobiography and services of Sir. J. McGrigor, 1861. Haswell, Chetwynd, The first respectable spy, 1969. McGrigor, Mary, Wellington's spies, 2005.*

GRANT, Sir Colquhoun
Lieutenant Colonel. 15th (King's) Regiment of Light Dragoons.
Memorial tablet: St Mary's Church, Frampton, Dorset. (Photograph)

TO / THE MEMORY OF / SIR COLQUHOUN GRANT K.C.B. AND K.C.H. / WHO DEPARTED THIS LIFE ON THE 20TH DAY OF DECEMBER 1835 / AGED 63. / THIS BRAVE AND GALLANT OFFICER / AT AN EARLY AGE ENTERED THE MILITARY SERVICE, / IN WHICH HE ROSE TO THE RANK OF LIEUTENANT GENERAL. / DURING THE MYSORE CAMPAIGN OF 1798 / HE GREATLY DISTINGUISHED HIMSELF, / AND WAS PRESENT AT THE TAKING OF SERINGAPATAM. / HE COMMANDED THE 72D FOOT / AT THE CAPTURE OF THE CAPE OF GOOD HOPE; / AND THE 15TH HUSSARS / DURING SIR JOHN MOORE'S CAMPAIGN IN SPAIN. / HE WAS WOUNDED AT THE BATTLE OF SAHAGUN: / AND FOUGHT / AT THE ACTION OF MORALES AND THE BATTLE OF VITTORIA: / ON THE EVER MEMORABLE FIELD OF WATERLOO / (WHERE HE COMMANDED A BRIGADE) / HE HAD NO LESS THAN FIVE HORSES KILLED UNDER HIM. / HE WAS HONORED / BY THE PERSONAL FRIENDSHIP OF THE SOVEREIGN / AND THE ESTEEM OF HIS CONTEMPORARIES, / AND HAS LEFT A NAME RECORDED IN THE ANNALS OF HIS COUNTRY.

Ensign 36th Foot Sep 1793. Lt 1795. Lt 25th Lt Dragoons 1797. Capt 9th Dragoons 29 Sep 1800. Major 28th Lt Dragoons 21 Feb 1801. Lt Colonel 72nd Foot 1 May 1802. Lt Colonel 15th Lt Dragoons 25 Aug 1808. Bt Colonel 4 Jun 1811. Major General 4 Jun 1814. Lt General 22 Jul 1830.

Served in the Peninsula Nov 1808 – Jan 1809 and Feb 1813 – Apr 1814. Present at Sahagun (wounded), Corunna, Morales (wounded and Mentioned in Despatches), Vittoria and Nivelle (Mentioned in Despatches). Gold Medal for Sahagun and Vittoria. KCB. Between Jan 1809 and Feb 1813 the regiment was in England, quelling civilian unrest such as the Luddite riots and other disturbances. Present at Waterloo (commanded a brigade of the 7th and 15th Lt Dragoons and the 2nd Hussars K.G.L. Apart from having five horses killed under him he was also wounded). Colonel 15th Hussars 1827. Also served in India in the Mysore campaign (present at Malavelly and Seringapatam) 1799 with 25th Lt Dragoons and Cape of Good Hope with 72nd Foot 1806 (wounded). His only daughter eloped with Richard Brinsley Sheridan.

REFERENCE: *Dictionary of National Biography. Gentleman's Magazine, May 1836, p. 545. Annual Register, 1836, Appx, pp. 183–4.*

GRANT, James
Lieutenant. 97th (Queens Own) Regiment of Foot.
Headstone: Kilcruttin Churchyard, Tullamore, County Offaly, Ireland. (No longer extant). (M.I.)

"SACRED TO THE MEMORY OF LIEUT / JAMES GRANT OF THE 97TH REGT / WHO DIED ON THE 19TH JULY 1816 / IN THE 27TH YEAR OF HIS AGE."

Ensign 30 May 1811. Lt 14 Oct 1813.
    Served in the Peninsula Jun – Dec 1811. Present at the second siege of Badajoz.

GRANT, James Robert

Inspector General of Hospitals. Medical Department.
Low monument on a base: St Mary's Churchyard, Carlisle, Cumbria. (Now incorporated into the Cathedral grounds. (Photograph)

.... / ALSO THE ABOVE / SIR JAMES ROBERT GRANT C.B. K.H. / WHO DIED ON THE 10TH / OF JANUARY 1864 / AGED 90 YEARS

Asst Surgeon 11th Foot 22 Jan 1792. Surgeon 21st Lt Dragoons 12 Sep 1794. Staff Surgeon 18 May 1795. Deputy Inspector of Hospitals 16 Apr 1807. Inspector General 14 Jul 1814.
    Served at Waterloo (Principal Medical Officer) and with the Army of Occupation. Also served in Flanders 1793, Cape of Good Hope 1795 and Walcheren 1809. KH, CB and Order of St Anne of Russia (for services to the Russian army in France). Knighted 1819. Retired 1847. MD King's College, Aberdeen 1814. Brother of Lt Colonel Colquhoun Grant 11th Foot and brother in law of Sir James McGrigor, Inspector General of Hospitals.
REFERENCE: *Gentleman's Magazine, Feb 1864, p. 268.*

GRANT, John

Major. 89th Regiment of Foot.
Headstone: Trafalgar Cemetery, Gibraltar. (Tomb number 76). (Photograph)

TO THE MEMORY OF / MAJOR JOHN GRANT 2ND BATTN 89TH REGT / WHO AFTER HAVING EMINENTLY DISTINGUISHED HIMSELF / IN A COURSE OF LONG AND MERITORIOUS SERVICE / WAS MORTALLY WOUNDED / AT THE HEAD OF HIS BATTALION / IN AN ATTACK UPON FORT FUENGEROLA, / NEAR MALAGA 14th OCTOBER 1810 / AND DIED THE 20TH OF THE SAME MONTH / AGED 48 YEARS / SINCERELY REGRETTED BY HIS / BROTHER OFFICERS

Family Memorial tablet: Cromdale Church, Morayshire, Scotland. (Photograph)

.... / AND HIS SON / MAJOR JOHN GRANT 89TH REGT, / KILLED IN BATTLE AT MALAGA 1810.

Major 30 Nov 1809.
    Served in the Peninsula Oct 1810. Present at Fuengirola 14 Oct 1810 where he was severely wounded and died of his wounds 20 Oct 1810.

GRANT, Lewis

Captain. 71st (Highland Light Infantry) Regiment of Foot.
Ledger stone: Inveraven Churchyard, Morayshire, Scotland. (M.I.)

"CAPT ALLEN GRANT, TACKSMAN ADVIE AND MULDERIE................YOUNGEST SON, CAPT LEWIS, 71ST REGT DIED OF WOUNDS AT ASSAULT ON FORT NAPOLEON ON THE TAGUS MAY 1812."

Lt 13 Jun 1805. Capt 6 Jul 1809.
    Served in the Peninsula Aug 1808 – Jan 1809 and Sep 1810 – May 1812. Present at Rolica, Vimeiro, Corunna, Sobral, Fuentes d'Onoro, Arroyo dos Molinos and Almarez (severely wounded at the assault on Fort Napoleon, one of the four officers of the 71st Foot who were either killed or wounded and died of his

wounds 20 May 1812). Also served at Walcheren 1809.

GRANT, Sir Maxwell
Major. 42nd (Royal Highland) Regiment of Foot.
Family Memorial tablet: Duthil Churchyard, Duthil, Invernesshire. (Photograph)

HERE LIES INTERRED / JOHN GRANT / AND / ELIZABETH LUMSDEN / HIS SPOUSE / .... / AND / COL. SIR MAXWELL GRANT K.C.B. / THEIR SON / WHO DIED 22ND OCTOBER 1823.

Lt 42nd Foot 4 Sep 1795. Capt 9 Jul 1803. Major 10 Oct 1811. Bt Lt Colonel 26 Aug 1813. Portuguese Army: Major 6th Line 26 Aug 1809. Lt Colonel 6th Line 3 Jun 1810.
   Served in the Peninsula with 42nd Foot Aug 1808 – Jan 1809 and Portuguese Army Aug 1809 – Apr 1814. Present at Corunna (wounded), Busaco, Fuentes d'Onoro Arroyo dos Molinos, Almarez, Vittoria, Pyrenees (wounded and Mentioned in Beresford's Despatches 30 Jul 1813), Nivelle, Nive (severely wounded and Mentioned in Beresford's Despatches 13 Dec 1813), Garris, Orthes and Aire. Gold Cross for Vittoria, Pyrenees, Nivelle, Nive and Orthes. KCB. KTS. Also served in Minorca 1798 and Egypt 1801 (present at Alexandria).

GRANT, Turner
Lieutenant and Captain. 1st Regiment of Foot Guards.
Memorial tablet: St Thomas's Church, Neath, Glamorgan, Wales. (Photograph)

THIS MONUMENTAL TABLET / IS ERECTED TO THE MEMORY OF / COLONEL TURNER GRANT, / IN TESTIMONY OF THE SINCERE AFFECTION / OF HIS ONLY SURVIVING BROTHER HENRY JOHN GRANT, ESQUIRE, / OF THE GNOLL, IN THIS PARISH. / COL. GRANT SERVED ABOVE FORTY YEARS / IN THE GRENADIER GUARDS, / DURING WHICH PERIOD HIS CONSTITUTION WAS GRADUALLY EXHAUSTED / BY THE EFFECTS OF THE BANEFUL CLIMATE OF WALCHEREN, / AND OF THE VARIOUS CAMPAIGNS OF THE / PENINSULAR WAR. / HE DIED, LAMENTED IN PUBLIC, AND REGRETTED IN PRIVATE LIFE, / AT HIS HOUSE, IN PORTMAN SQUARE, MARCH 28TH 1845, / IN HIS 59TH YEAR. / AS AN OFFICER / AND IN THE COMMAND OF HIS REGIMENT, / HIS CHARACTER WAS MARKED BY JUSTICE, DISCRETION, AND FIRMNESS. AS A CHRISTIAN / HE FELT WITH THE HUMBLE PUBLICAN: / "GOD BE MERCIFUL TO ME A SINNER."

Ensign 13 Jun 1805. Lt and Capt 20 Feb 1811. Capt and Lt Colonel 26 Dec 1816. Bt Colonel 10 Jan 1837. Major with rank of Colonel 17 Feb 1837.
   Served in the Peninsula with 1st Battalion Oct 1808 – Jan 1809 and Sep 1812 – Apr 1814. Present at Corunna, Bidassoa, Nivelle, Nive, Adour and Bayonne. Also served at Walcheren 1809.

GRATTON, Charles
Sub Lieutenant. Royal Sappers and Miners.
Memorial tablet: St Mary's Church, Wirksworth, Derbyshire. (Photograph)

TO / THE MEMORY OF / CHARLES GRATTON. / COMMISSIONED SUB-LIEUTENANT / FROM 3RD FOOT GUARDS IN THE / ROYAL SAPPERS AND MINERS 1ST / DECEMBER 1812. BORN AT WIRKSWORTH / MARCH 23RD 1780 AND DIED / AT DEPTFORD 1848. / "CHARLES GRATTON COMMISSIONED / FOR HIS BRAVERY AT BURGOS, / SERVED IN THE ACTIONS OF THE / 8TH AND 19TH SEPTEMBER AND 2ND / AND 6TH OCTBR 1799 IN HOLLAND. / AT THE LAST HE WAS WOUNDED, / ALSO IN HANOVER, AT THE PASSAGE / OF THE DOURO, TALAVERA, BUSACO, / FUENTES D'ONOR, CUIDAD RODRIGO, / SALAMANCA AND BURGOS. IN THE / SAPPERS HE WAS AT SAN SEBASTIAN, / PAMPELUNA, PASSAGE OF THE ADOUR, / AND SIEGE OF BAYONNE,

AND ALSO / IN THE NETHERLANDS AND FRANCE." / EXTRACT FROM THE HISTORY OF THE ROYAL SAPPERS AND MINERS.

Sgt 3rd Foot Guards. Commissioned from the ranks. Sub Lt Royal Sappers and Miners 1 Dec 1812.
    Served in the Peninsula with 3rd Foot Guards Mar 1809 – Oct 1812 and with Royal Sappers and Miners Nov 1812 – Apr 1814. Present at Douro, Talavera, Busaco, Fuentes d'Onoro, Ciudad Rodrigo, Salamanca, Burgos, (after Burgos commissioned from the ranks to be Sub Lieutenant in Royal Sappers and Miners – later incorporated into the Royal Engineers), San Sebastian, Pamplona, Adour and Bayonne. Served in France with the Army of Occupation 1815. Also served at the Helder 1799, Hanover 1805 and the Netherlands 1814. MGS medal for Talavera, Busaco, Fuentes d'Onoro, Ciudad Rodrigo, Salamanca and San Sebastian. Died 4 Jul 1848.

GRAVES, Anthony
Captain. 32nd (Cornwall) Regiment of Foot.
Headstone: York Cemetery, York, Yorkshire. Headstone fallen on its face. Cemetery records indicate the inscription is totally illegible. (Grave number Y/02/20A). (Photograph)

Ensign 31st Foot 3 Feb 1803. Lt 32nd Foot 7 Aug 1804. Capt 14 Apr 1813.
    Served in the Peninsula with 32nd Foot Aug 1808 – Jan 1809 and Jul 1811 – Aug 1812 and on Staff Sep 1812 – Mar 1814 (Brigade Major 6th Division). Present at Rolica, Vimeiro, Corunna, siege of Salamanca Forts, Salamanca (severely wounded and awarded pension of £100 per annum), Burgos and Pyrenees. Also served at Copenhagen 1807 and Walcheren 1809. Retired 1814, joined the 2nd West York Militia and was their Adjutant for 27 years. MGS medal for Rolica, Vimeiro, Corunna, Salamanca and Pyrenees.
REFERENCE: Gentleman's Magazine, Jul 1853, p. 101.

GRAY, Charles George
Captain. 95th Regiment of Foot.
Memorial tablet: St Paul's Church, Ipswich, Queensland, Australia. (Photograph)

IN MEMORY OF / LIEUTENANT COLONEL / CHARLES GEORGE GRAY, / LATE OF THE / RIFLE BRIGADE (95TH REGIMENT.) / WHO DEPARTED THIS LIFE / ON THE 7TH DAY OF SEPTEMBER 1873, / AGED 86 YEARS. / THIS TABLET IS ERECTED AS A TOKEN / OF REMEMBRANCE AND ESTEEM / BY MANY OF HIS OLD FRIENDS.

Headstone: Ipswich Cemetery, Queensland, Australia. (M.I.)

COLONEL CHARLES GEORGE GRAY / DIED SEPTEMBER 1873 / FOUGHT NAPOLEON AT WATERLOO IN 1815. / BECAME POLICE MAGISTRATE OF IPSWICH.

Relocated Headstone: Ipswich Cemetery, Queensland, Australia. (Photograph)

SACRED / TO THE MEMORY OF / JANE / THE BELOVED WIFE OF / LIEUTENANT COLONEL / CHARLES GEORGE GRAY / .... / ALSO OF / LIEUTENANT COLONEL / CHARLES GEORGE GRAY / 7TH SEPTEMBER 1873.

Ensign 77th Foot 1 Sep 1796. Lt 5 Nov 1800. Lt 78th Foot 29 Jan 1801. Lt Sir Vere Hunt's Recruiting Corps 25 Jun 1801. Lt 75th Foot 25 Jun 1803. Capt 95th Foot 6 May 1809. Bt Major 21 Jan 1819. Major (unattached) 19 Dec 1826. Major 44th Foot 31 Aug 1830. Bt Lt Colonel 27 May 1836.
    Served in the Peninsula with 3/95th Feb 1810 – Apr 1814. Present at Cadiz, Barrosa, Badajoz (wounded), San Sebastian, Bidassoa, Nivelle, Nive, Orthes, Tarbes and Toulouse. Present at Waterloo on the Staff (ADC to Major General George Johnstone who served for several years in New South Wales from

1786–1809). MGS medal for Barrosa, Badajoz, San Sebastian, Nivelle, Nive, Orthes and Toulouse. Retired 10 Mar 1837, went to Australia and settled in Port Macquarie as a farmer from 1837–1851. Then moved to Ipswich where he became a magistrate from 1853–1866. First Usher of the Black Rod in the Queensland parliament. Died in New South Wales 1873 aged 86.

Gray kept a diary of his experiences as a settler, Australian colonial life and European military matters, containing an unusual picture of what an officer would have learned at a British military academy in the early nineteenth century, based on his attendance at the college for army officers at High Wycombe, founded by General Francois Jarry, later to become the Royal Military Academy at Sandhurst. The diary also contains manuscript records in Jarry's handwriting on forts and battle plans.

REFERENCE: Dutton, Kenneth, *A French general and a Scots colonel: a most unusual volume and the search for its authorship,* University of Newcastle, New South Wales, 2007.

GRAY, Frederick
Private. 2nd Life Guards.
Headstone laid flat: St Bartholomew with St Mary Churchyard, Armley, Leeds, Yorkshire. (Photograph).

SACRED / TO THE MEMORY OF / FREDERICK, SON OF / JAMES AND MARTHA GRAY, OF HOLBECK, / WHO BELONGED TO THE 2ND REGT L. G. / AND WAS SLAIN AT THE BATTLE OF WATERLOO / IN THE DEFENCE OF HIS COUNTRY / JUNE 18TH 1815, AGED 20 YEARS. / ....

Served at Waterloo aged 20 years. Killed in the Cavalry charge.

GRAY, John Walker
Lieutenant. 3rd (Prince of Wales's) Dragoon Guards.
Headstone: Christ Church, Harrogate, Yorkshire. (East end of Church). (Photograph)

SACRED / TO THE MEMORY OF / JOHN WALKER GRAY ESQR / LATE LIEUT / OF H. M. 3RD DRAGOON GUARDS, / WHO DIED MARCH 8TH 1828 / AGED 53 YEARS.

Lt 6 Aug 1807.
Served in the Peninsula May 1809 – Apr 1811 and Jun – Oct 1812. Present at Talavera.

GRAY, Loftus
Captain. 95th Regiment of Foot
Buried in St Giles and St Nicholas Churchyard, Sidmouth. (No longer extant: Grave number 30 Plot 11). (Photograph of site)

Cambridgeshire Militia. Ensign 46th Foot 25 Nov 1799. 2nd Lt 95th Foot 4 Nov 1800. Lt 25 Jun 1803. Capt 16 Apr 1807. Bt Major 12 Apr 1814. Bt Lt Colonel 22 Jul 1830.
Served in the Peninsula with 2/95th Aug 1808 – Jan 1809 and 1/95th Jul 1809 – Mar 1810 and Jan 1812 – Apr 1814. Present at Vigo, Ciudad Rodrigo, Badajoz (wounded), Salamanca, San Millan, Vittoria, Pyrenees, Vera, Bidassoa, Nivelle, Nive and Tarbes where he was severely wounded and awarded pension of £100 per annum. Lt Governor of Pendennis Castle 25 Jul 1832. Died 20 Aug 1835.

GRAY, William
Lieutenant. 2nd (Queen's Royal) Regiment of Foot.
Named on the Regimental Memorial: St Michael's Cathedral, Bridgetown, Barbados, West Indies. (Photograph)

Ensign Dorset Militia. Ensign 2nd Foot 10 Mar 1808. Lt 13 Sep 1809.

Served in the Peninsula with 2nd Foot Aug 1808 – Jan 1809, Apr 1811 – Dec 1812 and 2nd Provisional Battalion Jan – Mar 1813. Present at Vimeiro, Corunna, Almeida, siege of Salamanca Forts, Salamanca, Burgos and the retreat from Burgos. Also served at Walcheren 1809 and West Indies. Died in Barbados 7 Nov 1816 during a yellow fever epidemic.

GREEN, William
Private. 4th (King's Own) Regiment of Foot.
Headstone: St Helen's Churchyard, Selston, Nottinghamshire. (Photograph)

AFFECTIONATE / REMEMBRANCE OF / WILLIAM GREEN, / A WATERLOO VETERAN, / WHO DIED MARCH 15TH 1877, / AGED 80 YEARS. / I HAVE FOUGHT A GOOD FIGHT I HAVE FINISHED / MY COURSE I HAVE KEPT THE FAITH / ....

Served in the Peninsula 1808 – 1810 and May 1812 – Jan 1813. Remained behind sick in Lisbon so did not go to Corunna with 4th Foot. Joined the battalions of detachments at Talavera and also served at Salamanca. Present at Waterloo in Capt Wood's Light Infantry Company. MGS medal for Talavera and Salamanca.

GREEN, William
Private. 95th Regiment of Foot.
Headstone: Welford Road Cemetery, Leicester. (Grave number UL 23). New headstone erected April 2002. (Photograph)

95TH (RIFLE) REGIMENT / TO THE MEMORY OF / WILLIAM GREEN / DIED 27TH JANUARY 1881 / AGED 96 YEARS. / A VETERAN OF THE PENINSULAR WAR / PRESENT AT THE BATTLES OF CORUNNA, / BUSACO, CIUDAD RODRIGO AND BADAJOZ. / .... / "I SHALL GO WHERE MY DUTY CALLS"

Named on the Regimental Memorial: Winchester Cathedral, Winchester, Hampshire. (Photograph)

Leicestershire Militia Jun 1803. Pte 95th Foot 18 Apr 1805.
    Served in the Peninsula Aug 1808 – Jan 1809 and May 1809 – Jul 1812. Present at Corunna, Busaco, Ciudad Rodrigo and Badajoz (severely wounded and sent back to England). Discharged 9 Dec 1812 with a pension of 9 pence a day. Also served at Hanover 1805 and Copenhagen 1807. MGS medal for Corunna, Busaco, Ciudad Rodrigo and Badajoz. Wrote *Travels and adventures of William Green (late Rifle Brigade).* REFERENCE: *Green, William, Where duty calls me: Napoleonic war experiences of Rifleman William Green, edited by, John and Dorothea Teague, 2nd edition, 2007. Mileham, S, William Green 1784–1881: Peninsula War Veteran, Waterloo Journal, Winter 2004, pp. 10–8.*

GREENOCK, Hon Charles Murray, Lord
Lieutenant Colonel. Permanent Assistant Quartermaster General.
Low monument in railed enclosure: Church in the Woods, Hollington, Sussex. (Photograph)

GENERAL CHARLES MURRAY EARL / CATHCART / G.C.B. / BORN 1783. / DIED 1859. / ....

Cornet 2nd Life Guards 2 May 1799. Lt 10 Aug 1799. Capt 3 Feb 1803. Major 14 May 1807. Lt Colonel 30 Aug 1810. Lt Colonel Royal Staff Corps 26 Jun 1823. Major General 22 Jul 1830. Lt General 23 Nov 1841. General 20 Jun 1854.
    Served in the Peninsula Apr 1810 – Jul 1811 and Mar 1812 – Feb 1814 (AQMG). Present at Cadiz, Barrosa (Mentioned in Despatches), Salamanca and Vittoria. Gold Medal for Barrosa, Salamanca and

Vittoria. Present at Waterloo (AQMG. Had three horses shot under him). CB. Russian Order of St Vladimir and Order of St Wilhelm of Netherlands. Also served at the Helder 1799, Sicily 1805–1806 (AQMG), Walcheren 1809 (present at Flushing where he became ill with fever) and the Netherlands 1814–1815.

After leaving the Royal Staff Corps in 1830, lived in Edinburgh, devoting himself to scientific study. Discovered a new mineral, sulphate of cadmium which was named after him (Greenockite). Governor of Edinburgh Castle 1837–1842. Became second Earl Cathcart on death of his father in 1843. Took command of forces in British North America Jun 1845 at a time of possibility of war with America over the boundary with Oregon. The Governor had to resign due to ill health and Cathcart, as he was now called, combined both civil and military roles. By 1846 the Oregon dispute was settled and Lord Elgin replaced him as Governor. Cathcart returned to England in 1848.

Colonel 11th Hussars 1842. Colonel 3rd Dragoon Guards 1847. Colonel 1st Dragoon Guards 1851. KCB 1838 and GCB 1859. Elder brother of Lt Hon George Cathcart 6th Dragoon Guards. Died 15 Jul 1859 at his home at St Leonards-on-the-Sea aged 75.

REFERENCE: *Dictionary of National Biography. Dictionary of Canadian Biography. Gentleman's Magazine, Sep 1859, pp. 306–7. Annual Register, 1859, Appx, p. 416. (All references under Cathcart).*

GREENWELL, Leonard

Lieutenant Colonel. 45th (Nottinghamshire) Regiment of Foot.
Memorial tablet: St Nicholas Church, Newcastle upon Tyne, Northumberland. (Photograph)

BUENOS AYRES FUENTES D'ONORO / ROLEIA BUSACO / VIMIERA CUIDAD RODRIGO / TALAVERA SALAMANCA BADAJOZ / PYRENEES NIVELLE / ORTHES / IN A VAULT NEAR THIS SPOT / ARE DEPOSITED THE REMAINS OF / MAJOR GENERAL / SIR LEONARD GREENWELL, K.C.B. K.C.H. / YOUNGEST SON OF THE LATE JOSHUA GREENWELL OF THIS TOWN / AND OF KNIBBLESWORTH, IN THE COUNTY OF DURHAM, ESQ / AND MARY HIS WIFE. / HE ENTERED THE ARMY ON THE 7TH DAY OF / AUGUST 1801 / AS AN ENSIGN IN THE 45TH REGT. / AND WAS PRESENT WITH THAT GALLANT CORPS / (TO THE COMMAND OF WHICH HE EVEN-TUALLY ATTAINED) / AT THE SEVERAL ENGAGEMENTS ABOVE RECORDED. / IN ACKNOWLEDGEMENT OF HIS SERVICES / IN THE COURSE OF WHICH HE WAS THREE TIMES SEVERELY WOUNDED / HE RECEIVED A MEDAL AND TWO CLASPS, / WAS SUBSEQUENTLY APPOINTED AIDE-DE-CAMP TO THEIR MAJESTIES / GEORGE THE 4TH, WILLIAM THE 4TH, AND VICTORIA, SUCCESSIVELY; / CREATED A KNIGHT COMMANDER / OF THE ROYAL HANOVERIAN GUELPHIC ORDER, / AND OF THE MOST HONOURABLE MILITARY ORDER OF THE BATH, / AND FURTHER HONOURED BY THE GRANT OF A REWARD OF / THE DISTIN-GUISHED SERVICE FUND. / HE DIED ON THE 11TH DAY OF NOVEMBER 1844 / IN THE 64TH YEAR OF HIS AGE.

Ensign 7 Aug 1801. Lt 16 Sep 1802. Capt 31 Jul 1804. Major 20 Oct 1810. Bt Lt Colonel 17 Aug 1812. Lt Colonel 12 Apr 1814. Colonel 27 May 1825. Major General 10 Jan 1837.

Served in the Peninsula Aug 1808 – Jul 1811, Mar 1812 – Sep 1812 and Nov 1813 – Apr 1814. Present at Rolica, Vimeiro, Talavera, Busaco, Pombal, Redinha, Casal Nova, Foz d'Arouce, Sabugal, Fuentes d'Onoro, second siege of Badajoz, Ciudad Rodrigo, Badajoz, Salamanca (severely wounded and awarded pension of £200 per annum), Pyrenees, Nivelle, Orthes (wounded in command of the Light Infantry of the 3rd Division, under Picton) and Bayonne. Gold Medal for Badajoz, Fuentes d'Onoro and Orthes.

Also served in South America 1807 (present at Buenos Ayres where he was severely wounded), Ceylon and Burma 1819–1825. Retired on half pay 1827. Commandant at Chatham 1831, where he reformed the Garrison. KCB and KCH. Served for 43 years in the army.

REFERENCE: *Dictionary of National Biography. Royal Military Calendar, Vol 4, pp. 429–430. Gentleman's Magazine, Jan 1845, pp. 98–9. Annual Register, 1844, Appx, pp. 281–2.*

GREGORIE, Charles

Captain. 13th Regiment of Light Dragoons.

Low monument: English Cemetery, Florence, Italy. (Grave number B18E). Seriously damaged. (Photograph)

BREVET MAJOR CHARLES GREGORIE / LATE CAPTAIN 13TH LIGHT DRAGOONS. / OBIT 16 OCT 1858 AGED 67.

Ensign Coldstream Guards 1 May 1806. Lt 4 Aug 1808. Capt 2nd Ceylon Regt 4 Aug 1808. Capt 72nd Highland Regt 15 Sep 1808. Capt 6th Dragoon Guards 10 May 1810. Capt 13th Lt Dragoons 20 Jun 1811.

Served in the Peninsula with 13th Lt Dragoons Sep 1811 – Jan 1814. Present at Arroyo dos Molinos, Vittoria, Nivelle, Nive and Garris. MGS medal for Vittoria, Nivelle and Nive. Present at Waterloo. Retired 1818.

GREGORSON, Donald

Major. 91st Regiment of Foot.

Table tomb: Parish of Lismore, Lismore, Argyllshire, Scotland. (M.I.)

"LIEUT COL DONALD GREGORSON, LATE OF NINETY FIRST REGIMENT OF INFANTRY, DIED 12TH AUG 1829 AGED 51 YEARS."

Ensign 98th Foot 19 Nov 1794. Lt 91st Foot 18 Mar 1795. Capt 3 Aug 1804. Major 30 Apr 1812. Bt Lt Colonel 27 May 1825.

Served in the Peninsula Aug 1808 – Jan 1809. Present at Rolica, Vimeiro, Cacabellos and Corunna. Also served at Walcheren 1809 and the Netherlands 1814. Retired 1826.

GREGORY, Adam

Captain. 29th (Worcestershire) Regiment of Foot.

Low monument: Parish Churchyard, Llanfair, Wales. (Photograph)

HERE / LIETH IN PEACE / A GALLANT SOLDIER, / A TRUE GENTLEMAN, / A MOST CHARI-TABLE MAN / ADAM GREGORY / CAPTAIN IN THE 29TH REGIMENT. / AFTER SERVING THROUGH THE / WAR IN SPAIN / HE ENTERED PARIS IN 1815 / WITH WELLINGTON. / HE HAD CLASPS OF HONOUR / FOR / ROLICA, VIMIERA, TALAVERA, / BUSACO, ALBUHERA / HE DIED AT LLANFAIR MAY 11, 1868 / AGED 85 YEARS. / BELOVED AND RESPECTED / BY ALL.

Ensign 12 Jun 1806. Lt 8 Feb 1808. Capt 24 Nov 1814. Portuguese Army: Capt 16th Line 21 Apr 1810.

Served in the Peninsula with 29th Foot Jul 1808 – Apr 1810, Apr 1813 – Feb 1814 and Portuguese Army Apr 1810 – Nov 1811. Present at Rolica, Vimeiro, Douro, Talavera, Busaco, Albuera and Cadiz. Also served in France with the Army of Occupation. MGS medal for Rolica, Vimeiro, Talavera, Busaco and Albuera. Retired from Portuguese Army Nov 1811.

GREGORY, Arthur Francis

Lieutenant. 4th (Queen's Own) Regiment of Dragoons.

Memorial tablet: St James's Church, Styvechale, Coventry, Warwickshire. (Photograph)

IN MEMORY OF / ARTHUR FRANCIS GREGORY OF STYVECHALE / Cᵒ WARWICK ESQUIRE LATE CAPTAIN IN THE 4TH / QUEENS OWN DRAGOONS BORN OCTOBER 29TH 1792 / DIED AT STYVECHALE FEBRUARY 27TH 1853 AGED 61 YEARS / HE SERVED WITH HIS REGIMENT THROUGHOUT / THE PENINSULAR CAMPAIGN FROM 1809 TO 1814 / AND RECEIVED THE PENINSULAR MEDAL / WITH SIX CLASPS.

Cornet 26 Mar 1807. Lt 19 Mar 1808. Capt 53rd Foot 10 Jul 1817. Capt Rifle Brigade 11 Sep 1817. Capt 62nd Foot 9 Oct 1825.

Served in the Peninsula May 1809 – Nov 1812 and May 1813 – Apr 1814. Present at Talavera, Busaco, Albuera, Usagre, Aldea da Ponte, Llerena, Salamanca, Vittoria and Toulouse. MGS medal for Talavera, Busaco, Albuera, Salamanca, Vittoria and Toulouse. Retired 30 Oct 1835.

GREVILLE, Hon. Sir Charles James
Lieutenant Colonel. 38th (1st Staffordshire) Regiment of Foot.
Family vault: St Mary's Church, Warwick, Warwickshire. No inscription recorded. (Photograph of vault)

Ensign 1796. Lt 10th Foot 12 Jul 1796. Capt 26 Dec 1799. Major 38th Foot 13 Apr 1803. Lt Colonel 21 Mar 1805. Bt Colonel 4 Jun 1813. Major General 12 Aug 1819.

Served in the Peninsula with 1/38th Aug 1808 – Jan 1809 and Jun 1812 – Apr 1814 (from Jul 1812 – Oct 1813 temporary Commander 1 Brigade 5th Division). Present at Rolica, Vimeiro, Corunna, Castrejon, Salamanca, Burgos, Villa Muriel, Osma, Vittoria, San Sebastian (Mentioned in Despatches), Bidassoa, Nivelle, Nive and Bayonne. Served in France with the Army of Occupation. Also served in India 1799, Egypt 1801 and Walcheren 1809. Colonel 98th Foot 1832. Colonel 38th Foot 1835. Gold Cross for Rolica, Vimeiro, Corunna, Salamanca, Vittoria, San Sebastian and Nive. KCB. MP for Warwick 1812–1831. Died 2 Dec 1836.
REFERENCE: *Gentleman's Magazine, Feb 1837, p. 203. Spink's Medal Catalogue, 21 Sep 2001, pp. 138–40.*

GREY, George
Major. 30th (Cambridgeshire) Regiment of Foot.
Memorial tablet: Christ Church, Newton-Fertullagh Parish, County Westmeath, Ireland. (Photograph)

SACRED TO THE MEMORY OF / LIEUT COLL GEORGE GREY, / OF THE 30TH FOOT, / WHO FELL AT THE STORMING OF BADAJOZ, / ON THE NIGHT OF THE 6TH OF APRIL 1812, / IN THE 33D YEAR OF HIS AGE. / THIS MEMORIAL OF / THE ESTEEM, AFFECTION & SORROW OF HIS AFFLICTED WIDOW / (WHO NOW UNCEASINGLY LAMENTS HIM) / IS THE HUMBLE RECORD OF THOSE VIRTUES / IN WHICH THOUGH DEAD HE LIVETH. / THOUGH ABSENT, HE IS YET PRESENT, / IN THE REMEMBRANCE OF ALL WHO VALUED HIM / AS A CHRISTIAN, A HUSBAND, AND A FRIEND.

Capt -Lieut 12 Mar 1799. Major 1 Dec 1804. Bt Lt Colonel 4 Jun 1811.

Served in the Peninsula Apr – May 1809 and Jun 1810 – Apr 1812. Present at Cadiz, Sabugal, Fuentes d'Onoro, Barba del Puerco, Badajoz where he was severely wounded at the moment of victory 6th April and died of his wounds on 7th April. Also served in Malta 1800, Egypt 1801 (mentioned in Brigade Orders for his gallantry and awarded Sultan's Gold Medal for Egypt). Gold Medal for Badajoz where his gallantry was noted by Wellington.

GREY, John
Major. 5th (Northumberland) Regiment of Foot.
Stained glass window: St Lawrence Church, Warkworth, Northumberland. (Photograph)

TO THE HONOUR AND GLORY OF GOD AND IN MEMORY OF GENERAL SIR JOHN GREY, K.C.B. OF MORWICK, WHO DIED FEBRUARY 19, 1856, AGED 75 YEARS. THIS WINDOW WAS ERECTED BY HIS NEPHEW CAPTAIN GEORGE BYRRELL.

Ensign 75th Foot 28 May 1795. Lt 8 May 1799. Capt 15th Battalion of Reserve 31 Oct 1803. Capt 82nd Foot 23 Aug 1804. Major 9th Garrison Battalion 27 Nov 1806. Major 5th Foot 13 Jun 1811. Bt Lt Colonel

6 Feb 1812. Bt Colonel 22 Jul 1830. Major General 28 Jun 1838, Lt General 11 Nov 1851. General 20 Feb 1855.

Served in the Peninsula with 2/5th Sep 1811 – Apr 1812. Present at El Bodon and Ciudad Rodrigo (severely wounded and Mentioned in Despatches). MGS medal for Ciudad Rodrigo. Also served in India 1799 (present at Malavelly and Seringapatam), and in the Gwalior campaign 1843 (present at the battle of Punniar), the Sikh Wars 1845–1846 (commanded a division in the battles of the Sutlej). Governor General of Bombay. Colonel 5th Foot 1849. KCB. His elder brother Capt Charles Grey 85th Foot was killed at New Orleans in 1815.
REFERENCE: *Gentleman's Magazine, Apr 1856, p. 424.*

GREY, John
Captain. 10th (Prince of Wales's Own) Regiment of Light Dragoons.
Memorial tablet: St Mary and St Peter Church, Salcombe Regis, Devon. (Photograph)

SACRED / TO THE MEMORY OF / COLONEL JOHN GREY / LATE OF THE ROYAL SCOT'S GREYS, / FONDLY BELOVED, AND DEEPLY DEPLORED, / AS HUSBAND, FATHER AND FRIEND. / HE DIED AT SIDMOUTH, DECR 21ST 1842, AGED 55 YEARS. / HE WAS A DISTINGUISHED OFFICER / AND RECEIVED A WOUND AT / WATERLOO. / (VERSE)

Cornet 3rd Lt Dragoons 16 Mar 1805. Lt 21 Sep 1805. Capt 21st Lt Dragoons 6 Apr 1809. Capt 10th Lt Dragoons 12 Nov 1814. Major 2nd Lt Dragoons 11 Oct 1821. Lt Colonel 25 Oct 1825.

Present at Quatre Bras employed on outpost duties and was the first to discover the retreat of the Prussians after Ligny. Present at Waterloo where he was wounded and with the Army of Occupation. Took command of the Scots Greys 1825. Retired 1839.

GRIERSON, Crighton
Lieutenant. Royal Engineers.
Named on the Regimental Memorial: Rochester Cathedral, Rochester, Kent. (Photograph)

2nd Lt 1 Jun 1810. Lt 1 May 1811. 2nd Capt 1 Jul 1821. Capt 6 Nov 1834. Bt Major 10 Jan 1837. Lt Colonel 1 Apr 1846. Bt Colonel 20 Jun 1854. Major General 10 May 1859. Lt General 3 Aug 1863. General 8 Jun 1871.

Served in the Peninsula May 1812 – Apr 1814. Present at Cadiz, Tarifa and Tarragona. Also served at Genoa 1814. Retired on full pay 1 Sep 1847. Died in London 7 Nov 1871.

GRIEVE, Patrick
Captain. 10th (North Lincolnshire) Regiment of Foot.
Chest tomb: Lansdown Cemetery, Bath, Somerset. (Area 4, Row H, Plot number 11). (Photograph)

SACRED TO THE MEMORY OF / PATRICK GRIEVE / LATE LIEUT. COLONEL OF H M 75TH REGIMENT / WHO DEPARTED THIS LIFE / THE 11TH DAY OF JANUARY 1853 AGED 64. / (VERSE)

Ensign 8th Battery of Reserve 9 Jul 1803. Lt 10th Foot 1 Aug 1804. Capt 16 May 1809. Major 25 Nov 1819. Bt Lt Colonel 9 Nov 1830. Lt Colonel 75th Foot 7 Jul 1837.

Served in the Peninsula Aug 1812 – Apr 1814. Present at Alicante, Castalla, Ordal, Barcelona and Tarragona.

GRIFFITH, Edwin
Major. 15th (King's) Regiment of Light Dragoons.
Memorial tablet: St Mary's Church, Mold, Flintshire, Wales. (Rear of church). (Photograph)

SACRED TO THE MEMORY / OF THOMAS GRIFFITH ESQ^{RE} OF RHUAL / .... / AND OF EDWIN THEIR YOUNGEST SON, / MAJOR, IN THE 15TH LIGHT DRAGOONS / WHO, ON A DAY SO FATAL TO HIS FAMILY / JUNE 18TH 1815 / FELL, IN THE THIRTIETH YEAR OF HIS AGE / PIERCED IN THE BREAST BY FIVE HONOURABLE WOUNDS, WHILE GALLANTLY LEADING HIS REGIMENT, WHICH HE COMMANDED / TO A CHARGE OF A BODY OF FRENCH, IN THE SANGUINARY / AND EVER MEMORABLE BATTLE OF WATERLOO. / HIS REMAINS WERE INTER'D BY HIS AFFLICTED COMPANIONS / IN ARMS ON THE FIELD OF ARDUOUS CONFLICT. / PEACE TO THE GOOD AND BRAVE!

Named on the Regimental Memorial: St Joseph's Church, Waterloo, Belgium. (Photograph)

Cornet 25th Lt Dragoons 31 May 1800. Cornet 15th Lt Dragoons 20 Jan 1801. Lt 19 Mar 1803. Capt 27 Jun 1805. Major 5 Nov 1812.
    Served in the Peninsula Nov 1808 – Jan 1809 and Feb 1813 – Apr 1814. Present at Sahagun, Corunna campaign, Morales, Vittoria (Mentioned in Despatches), Orthes (Mentioned in Despatches) and Toulouse. Gold medal for Vittoria and Orthes. Present at Waterloo where he was killed leading the regiment.
REFERENCE: *Wylie, H. C., XVth (The King's Hussars), 1914. Rhual papers D/HE/439–55 – military letters and journals of Major Edwin Griffith and Capt Frederick Phillips, County Record Office, Hawarden, Flintshire, Wales.*

GRIFFITH, Joseph
Lieutenant. 15th (King's) Regiment of Light Dragoons.
Buried in St George' Chapel, Windsor, Berkshire. (Burial record)

Cornet 4 Aug 1814. Lt 24 May 1815. Adjutant 1816.
    Present at Waterloo. Retired on half pay 12 Mar 1829 and adopted the name of Henry Griffiths. Military Knight of Windsor 1848. Died 3 Oct 1852.

GRIFFITHS, Richard
Private. 1st Regiment of Foot Guards.
Headstone: St Beuno's Churchyard, Bettws Cedewain, Montgomeryshire, Wales. (Photograph)

IN / MEMORY OF / RICHARD GRIFFITHS / LATE OF THE GRENADIER GUARDS / DIED 31 JAN 1855 / AGED 72. / RESURGAM

Pte 21 May 1806.
    Served in the Peninsula Oct 1808 – Jan 1809. Present at Corunna. Present at Waterloo in Lt Colonel Sir Henry Hardinge's Company. MGS medal for Corunna. The headstone shows a Waterloo medal with clasps for Corunna, Talavera and Vittoria.

GRIFFITHS, Thomas
Drum Major. 23rd (Royal Welch Fusiliers) Regiment of Foot.
Ledger stone: St Elli's Churchyard, Llanelly, Breconshire, Wales. (Photograph)

TO THE MEMORY OF / THOMAS GRIFFITHS, / LATE DRUM MAJOR OF THE 23RD REG^T ROYAL WELSH FUSILEERS / WHO DIED 3RD SEP^{BR} 1864 AGED 88. / HE SERVED IN THE PENINSULAR WAR AND BATTLE OF WATERLOO, / AND RECEIVED THE WAR MEDAL AND CLASP, / WATERLOO MEDAL, / AND MEDAL FOR LONG SERVICE AND GOOD CONDUCT.

Sgt 1814. Drum Major 1815.
    Served in the Peninsula with 2/23rd Oct 1808 – Jan 1809. Present at Corunna. Served at Waterloo in

Capt Hawtyn's Grenadier Company. MGS medal for Corunna and Long Service and Good Conduct medal.

GRIMSHAW, John
Private. Coldstream Regiment of Foot Guards.
Memorial script: Immanuel Church, Oswaldtwistle, Lancashire. (Photograph)

JOHN GRIMSHAW / WEAVER AND SOLDIER / BORN CHURCH KIRK 13 APRIL 1789. / A WEAVER BY TRADE, HE ENLISTED IN THE / COLDSTREAM REGIMENT OF FOOT GUARDS IN 1806, SAW / ACTION IN THE LOW COUNTRIES IN SPAIN AND PORTUGAL / DURING THE PENINSULAR WAR UNDER THE COMMAND OF / THE DUKE OF WELLINGTON AND WAS AWARDED THE / MILITARY GENERAL SERVICE MEDAL WITH FOUR BARS FOR / HIS PART IN THE BATTLES OF BUSACO, FUENTES D'ONORO, / CIUDAD RODRIGO AND SALAMANCA. / HE ALSO FOUGHT AT THE BATTLE OF WATERLOO FOR WHICH / HE WAS AWARDED THE WATERLOO MEDAL. / HE WAS WOUNDED FOUR TIMES AND DISCHARGED FROM / THE ARMY IN 1818. / HE RETURNED TO HIS FORMER TRADE OF WEAVER AND / MARRIED PHOEBE TOMLINSON OF COCKER BROOK / 26 MAY 1828. PHOEBE WAS SENTENCED TO A YEAR IN / PRESTON GAOL FOR TAKING PART IN THE EAST LANCASHIRE / LOOM-BREAKING RIOTS IN 1826. / HE DIED AT WHITE CROFT, RED SHELL LANE, / OSWALDTWISTLE 17 AUGUST 1851 AND IS BURIED IN / IMMANUEL CHURCHYARD IN AN UNMARKED GRAVE.

Pte 24 Oct 1806.
    Served in the Peninsula. Present at Busaco, Fuentes d'Onoro, Ciudad Rodrigo and Salamanca. Present at Waterloo and with the Army of Occupation. Discharged 1818. MGS medal for Busaco, Fuentes d'Onoro, Ciudad Rodrigo and Salamanca. Died 17 Aug 1851.
Reference: Web site: http://www.grimshaworigin.org/WebPages/JohnGard.htm

GRINDROD, Timothy
Cornet and Adjutant. 11th Regiment of Light Dragoons.
Buried in the New Burial Ground, St Chad's Churchyard, Rochdale, Lancashire. (Burial record)

Sgt Major 16th Lt Dragoons. Cornet and Adjutant 11th Lt Dragoons 3 Jun 1813.
    Served in the Peninsula with 16th Lt Dragoons. Promoted from the ranks due to his bravery. Present at Waterloo. Half pay 1817. Died 13 Jun 1820 aged 41.

GRISEDALE, Levi
Sergeant. 10th (Prince of Wales's Own) Regiment of Light Dragoons.
Headstone, Beacon Edge Cemetery, Penrith, Cumbria. (Grave number 83TT). Adjacent to path near central circle. (Photograph)

IN / MEMORY / OF / LEVI GRISEDALE OF PENRITH / WHO DIED NOV^R 17TH 1855 / AGED 72 YEARS / HE SERVED WITH DISTINCTION / THROUGH THE PENINSULAR WAR / AND AT WATERLOO TAKING / PRISONER GENERAL LEFEVRE / OF THE FRENCH IMPERIAL GUARD / AT BENEVENTE IN SPAIN, / ON THE 29TH OF DEC^R 1808 / ....

Pte 26 May 1803. Cpl 1809. Sgt 1810. Sgt Major 1816.
    Served in the Peninsula Oct 1808 – Jan 1809 and Feb 1813 – Apr 1814. Present at Sahagun, Benevente, Morales, Vittoria, Orthes and Toulouse. Promoted to Corporal, by order of the Prince of Wales, on the capture of General Lefevre-Desnoëttes at Benevente. MGS medal for Sahagun and Benevente, Vittoria, Orthes and Toulouse. Present at Waterloo (wounded). Awarded Regimental medal. Discharged 17 Jul

1825 as a Chelsea Out Pensioner with a pension of 1 shilling and 10 pence a day. Later became an inn keeper in Penrith.

GROSE, Edward
Lieutenant and Captain. 1st Regiment of Foot Guards.
Memorial tablet: Inside Mausoleum, Evere Cemetery, Brussels, Belgium. (Photograph)

CAPTAIN / E. GROSE / .... / 3RD BATT. 1ST FOOT GUARDS.

Named on Memorial Panel VIII for Quatre Bras: Royal Military Chapel, Wellington Barracks, London. (M.I.) (Destroyed by a Flying Bomb 1944)

Named on the Regimental Memorial: St Joseph's Church, Waterloo, Belgium. (Photograph)

Ensign 25 Dec 1805. Lt and Capt 26 Sep 1811.
   Served in the Peninsula with 3rd Battalion Oct 1808 – Jan 1809 and Apr 1811 – Apr 1814 (Jul 1811 – May 1813. Military Secretary to Major General Cooke). Present at Corunna, Cadiz, San Sebastian, Bidassoa, Nivelle, Nive, Adour and Bayonne. Present at Quatre Bras where he was killed on 16 Jun 1815. One of the select band of soldiers buried in the Mausoleum at Evere. Educated at Eton.

GROVE, Henry
Captain. 23rd Regiment of Light Dragoons.
Headstone: Smallcombe Cemetery, Bathwick, Bath, Somerset. (Photograph)

BLESSED ARE THE DEAD WHICH DIE IN THE LORD / HERE RESTETH THE BODY OF / HENRY GROVE LT COLONEL / LATE OF THE 23RD LIGHT DRAGOONS / SON OF SILVANUS GROVE OF WOODFORD / IN THE COUNTY OF ESSEX ESQRE / WHO DEPARTED THIS LIFE / JULY 28TH 1858 AGED 79

Lt 29th Foot 9 Aug 1797. Capt 57th Foot 21 Feb 1800. Capt 4th Dragoon Guards 12 Jun 1800. Capt 18th Hussars 17 May 1803. Bt Major 1 Jan 1812. Capt 23rd Lt Dragoons 19 Apr 1815. Bt Lt Colonel 19 Jul 1821.
   Present at Waterloo. Also served in the Irish Rebellion 1798, the Helder 1799 (wounded) and on Staff in Ireland and England 1804–1814 as Brigade Major. After Waterloo became AAG in Ireland. Retired on half pay 1818.

GROWCOCK, Edward
Private. 12th (Prince of Wales's) Regiment of Light Dragoons.
Named on the Regimental Memorial: St Joseph's Church, Waterloo, Belgium. (Photograph)
   Killed at Waterloo.

GRUBBE, William Hunt
Lieutenant. Royal Regiment of Horse Guards.
Memorial tablet: St Mary's Church, Potterne, Wiltshire. (Photograph)

IN MEMORY OF / .... / WILLIAM HUNT GRUBBE, LIEUTENANT IN THE / R. H. G. (BLUE) WHO DIED WHILST ON SERVICE / WITH THE BRITISH ARMY IN SPAIN A. D. / 1813, AGED 23 YEARS.

Cornet 30 Sep 1812. Lt 13 May 1813.
   Served in the Peninsula from Nov 1812 – Sep 1813. Present at Vittoria. Died Sep 1813. Educated at Eton.

GRUEBER, Daniel

Lieutenant. 39ᵗʰ (Dorsetshire) Regiment of Foot.
Grave: St Nicholas Churchyard, Plumstead, Kent. (No longer extant. Destroyed by a flying bomb in the Second World War). (M.I.)

"DANIEL GRUEBER DIED 1860."

Ensign 24 Dec 1812. Lt 21 Apr 1814.
    Served in the Peninsula with 1/39ᵗʰ Mar – Apr 1814. Present at Aire and Toulouse. MGS medal for Toulouse. Also served in North America 1814. Retired on half pay 25 Mar 1817.

GUARD, William

Lieutenant Colonel. 45ᵗʰ (Nottinghamshire) Regiment of Foot.
Memorial tablet: Exeter Cathedral, Devon. (South transept end wall). (Photograph)

NEAR THIS SPOT / ARE INTERRED THE REMAINS OF / LIEUᵀ GENERAL WILLIAM GUARD, / MANY YEARS IN COMMAND OF THE 45ᵀᴴ REGIMENT. / HIS CONDUCT AS A SOLDIER / DURING A LONG PERIOD OF ACTIVE EMPLOYMENT / WAS MARKED BY A STRICT SENSE OF HONOR, / AND THE MOST ARDENT ZEAL FOR HIS PROFESSION. / IN ACKNOWLEDGMENT OF HIS EMINENT SERVICES / HE WAS MADE GOVERNOR OF KINSALE AND CHARLES FORT. / ALL WHO KNEW HIS WORTH LAMENTED HIM, / AND THE REMEMBRANCE OF HIS UNIFORM KINDNESS / IN THE SEVERAL RELATIONS OF PRIVATE LIFE / WILL EVER BE CHERISHED BY HIS AFFLICTED FAMILY / WITH FEELINGS OF AFFECTION AND GRATITUDE. / HE DIED AT EXETER 13ᵀᴴ JULY 1830. AGED 57. / THIS TABLET WAS ERECTED BY HIS CHILDREN.

Memorial slab: Exeter Cathedral, Devon. (Photograph)

UNDERNEATH / ARE DEPOSITED THE REMAINS OF / WILLIAM GUARD / LIEUTENANT GENERAL / GOVERNOR OF KINSALE AND / CHARLESFORT IN IRELAND / OBIIT JULY 13ᵀᴴ 1830, / AETAT 57.

Ensign 45ᵗʰ Foot 13 Jun 1789. Lt 27 Nov 1790. Capt 22 Sep 1795. Major 24 Nov 1797. Lt Colonel 3 Oct 1799. Bt Colonel 25 Oct 1809. Major General 1 Jan 1812. Lt General 27 May 1825.
    Served in the Peninsula Aug 1808 – Jan 1809 and Aug 1809 – Apr 1814. Present at Rolica, Vimeiro, Talavera (severely wounded, taken prisoner and remained in prison until Apr 1814). Gold Medal for Rolica, Vimeiro and Talavera. Also served in the West Indies 1791–1794 (present at Martinique), Ireland 1802–1805 and South America 1806–1807 (present at Buenos Ayres where he was Mentioned in Despatches). Governor of Kinsale and Charles Fort.
REFERENCE: *Royal Military Calendar, Vol 3, pp. 202–4. Gentleman's Magazine, Sep1830, pp. 275–6.*

GUBBINS, Richard

Major. 21ˢᵗ (Royal North British Fusiliers) Regiment of Foot
Mural monument: Kensal Green Cemetery, London. (482/Cat A. v. 29.c9). (Photograph)

TO THE MEMORY OF / LIEUT. COLONEL GUBBINS, C.B. / OF BELMONT, HAVANT / AND LATE OF THE 24. 85. 21. & 75 REGIMENTS / WHO DIED ON THE 2ᴺᴰ OF JAN 1836 AGED 54 YEARS.

Ensign 37ᵗʰ Foot 3 Feb 1803. Lt 24ᵗʰ Foot 26 May 1803 Capt 22 Dec 1804. Capt 85ᵗʰ Foot 25 Jan 1813. Bt Major 4 Jun 1814. Bt Lt Colonel 29 Sep 1814. Major 21ˢᵗ Foot 15 Jun 1815. Major 75ᵗʰ Foot 1 Apr 1818. Lt Colonel 67ᵗʰ Foot 8 Jul 1824.
    Served in the Peninsula with 85ᵗʰ Foot Aug 1813 – Apr 1814. Present at Nivelle, Nive and Bayonne.

Also served in North America 1814–1815 (present at Bladensburg and commanded the 85th at New Orleans where he was Mentioned in Despatches). CB.

GUDGIN, George
Private. 14th (Buckinghamshire) Regiment of Foot.
Memorial brass tablet: St James' Church, Pulloxhill, Bedfordshire. (Photograph)

IN MEMORY OF GEORGE GUDGIN, / DIED 25 APRIL 1841, AGED 47 AND / WILLIAM NEAL, DIED 25TH JAN^{RY} 1858, / AGED 63 WHO FOUGHT AT WATERLOO WHERE / THE LATTER WAS SEVERELY WOUNDED. / THEIR BODIES LIE IN THIS CHURCHYARD.

Pte 5 Apr 1814.
    Served at Waterloo. Also served in India for 14½ years. Discharged 13 Mar 1832.

GUISE, John Wright
First Major. 3rd Regiment of Foot Guards.
Buried in the Mausoleum: St John the Baptist Churchyard, Elmore, Gloucestershire. (Photograph)

Ensign 70th Foot 4 Nov 1794. Ensign 3rd Foot Guards 4 Mar 1795. Lt and Capt 25 Oct 1798. Capt and Lt Colonel 25 Jul 1805. Bt Colonel 4 Jun 1813. First Major 25 Jul 1814. Major General 12 Aug 1819. Lt General 10 Jan 1837. General 11 Nov 1851.
    Served in the Peninsula Nov 1809 – Apr 1814 (Commanded 2 Brigade 1st Division Apr 1814). Present at Busaco, Torres Vedras, Fuentes d'Onoro (commanded the regiment and Mentioned in Despatches), Ciudad Rodrigo, Salamanca, Burgos and retreat from Burgos, Vittoria, Bidassoa, Nive, Adour, siege of Bayonne and Sortie from Bayonne (Mentioned in Despatches and took command of the regiment when Major General Stopford was wounded).
    Also served at Ferrol, Vigo and Cadiz 1800, Egypt 1801 (present at Marabout and Alexandria), and Hanover 1805–1806. Gold Cross for Fuentes d'Onoro, Salamanca, Vittoria and Nive. MGS medal for Egypt and Busaco. KCB 13 Sep 1831. GCB 10 Nov 1862. Colonel 85th Foot 1 Jun 1847. Died at Elmore Court, Gloucestershire 1 Apr 1865.
    REFERENCE: *Dictionary of National Biography. Gentleman's Magazine, May 1865, p. 666.*

GUN, William
Captain. 91st Regiment of Foot.
Obelisk: Abbey Cemetery, Bath, Somerset. (Photograph)

.... / ALSO / IN MEMORY OF / MAJOR GUN. / FORMERLY OF THE 56TH REG^T / WHO DIED JULY 28TH 1859 / AGED 71.

Ensign 56th Foot 1800. Lt 29 Jan 1807. Capt 30 Nov 1809. Capt 91st Foot 7 Jun 1810. Capt 56th Foot 3 May 1821. Major 28 Aug 1827.
    Served in the Peninsula Jan 1813 – Apr 1814. Present at Pyrenees, Nivelle, Nive and Orthes where he was severely wounded and awarded pension of £100 per annum.

GUNNING, George Orlando
Lieutenant. 10th (Prince of Wales's Own) Regiment of Light Dragoons.
Family Memorial tablet: St Mary Magdalene Church, Horton, Northamptonshire. (Photograph)

THIS TABLET WAS PUT UP BY GEORGE GUNNING ESQ. / .... / ALSO TO THE MEMORY OF / A BELOVED SON GEORGE ORLANDO / WHOSE AMIABLE AND GENEROUS TEMPER / ENDEARED HIM TO ALL WHO KNEW HIM. / HE WAS EARLY BRED TO ARMS / AND

SERVED HIS FIRST CAMPAIGN IN FRANCE / WHERE HE WAS PRESENT AT THE BATTLE OF TOULOUSE. / THE FOLLOWING YEAR HE JOINED THE ARMY IN FLANDERS / UNDER THE IMMORTAL WELLINGTON / AS A LIEUTENANT IN THE 10TH HUSSARS / WHEN IN THE MOMENT OF VICTORY / WHILE CHARGING THE ENEMY / HE FELL IN THE PLAINS OF WATERLOO. / ENROLLED AMONG THE NAMES OF THOSE / HEROES WHOSE VALOUR AND INTREPIDITY / HAVE RAISED / THE NAME AND GLORY OF THEIR COUNTRY / TO A DEGREE UNEXAMPLED IN THE ANNALS OF THE WORLD. / HE WAS BORN DEC 18TH 1796. / DIED JUNE 18TH 1815 AGED 18 YEARS AND SIX MONTHS.

Memorial tablet: St Joseph's Church, Waterloo, Belgium. (Photograph)

SACRED TO THE MEMORY / OF LIEUTENANT GEORGE WILLIAM GUNNING / OF THE 10TH HUSSARS / KILLED AT THE BATTLE OF WATERLOO ON / THE 18TH OF JUNE 1815.

Lt 3rd Dragoons 8 Apr 1813. Lt 10th Lt Dragoon 26 Dec 1814.
    Served in the Peninsula Mar – Apr 1814. Present at Toulouse. Present at Waterloo where he was killed aged 18. Educated at Charterhouse, then entered the Royal Military Academy as a Cadet.
Note: Named as George William Gunning on memorial tablet in St Joseph's Church.

GUNNING, John
Deputy Inspector General of Hospitals. Medical Department.
Memorial plaque: Mont St Jean Farm, Waterloo, Belgium. (Photograph)

IN MEMORY OF / DEPUTY INSPECTOR GUNNING / PRINCIPAL MEDICAL OFFICER OF THE 1ST CORPS / THE SURGEONS AND OTHER MEMBERS / OF THE FIELD HOSPITAL / WHICH WAS ESTABLISHED IN THIS FARM / TO CARE FOR THE WOUNDED OF THE BATTLEFIELD / 18TH JUNE 1815. / THIS TABLET WAS ERECTED IN 1981 / BY THE ROYAL ARMY MEDICAL CORPS.

Staff Surgeon 20 Nov 1793. Deputy Inspector of Hospitals 17 Sep 1812. Inspector General of Hospitals 1 Feb 1816.
    Served in the Peninsula Aug 1808 – Apr 1814 (attached to Headquarters Jul – Dec 1812). Present at Rolica, Vimeiro, Talavera, Busaco, Fuentes d'Onoro, Ciudad Rodrigo, Badajoz, Salamanca, Vittoria, San Sebastian and Orthes. Present at Waterloo (where he amputated Fitzroy Somerset's arm) and with the Army of Occupation. Also served in Flanders 1793 – 1795. MGS medal for Rolica, Vimeiro, Talavera, Busaco, Fuentes d'Onoro, Ciudad Rodrigo, Badajoz, Salamanca, Vittoria, San Sebastian and Orthes. CB. Remained in Paris after the war and lived there until his death 11 Jan 1863 aged 89.
REFERENCE: *Gentleman's Magazine, Feb 1863, pp. 260–1. Annual Register, 1862, Appx, p. 354.*

GUNTHORPE, James
Lieutenant and Captain. 1st Regiment of Foot Guards.
Interred in Catacomb B (v207 c16) Kensal Green Cemetery, London.
Memorial: Royal Military Chapel, Wellington Barracks, London. (M.I.) (Destroyed by a Flying Bomb in 1944)

"LIEUT.-COLONEL JAMES GUNTHORPE. / 1ST GUARDS, 1805–33; SERVED IN SICILY, AT CORUNNA, AT WALCHEREN AND CADIZ. WAS ADJUTANT OF THE 3RD BATTALION, 1812–21, AND BRIGADE MAJOR DURING THE WATERLOO CAMPAIGN."

Ensign 24th Foot 26 Sep 1805. Ensign 1st Foot Guards 26 Dec 1805. Lt and Capt 7 Nov 1811. Adjutant 19 Nov 1811. Bt Major 18 Jun 1815. Capt and Lt Colonel 26 Dec 1821.
    Served in the Peninsula with 3rd Battalion Oct 1808 – Jan 1809 and Apr 1811 – Apr 1814. Present at

Corunna, Cadiz, Seville, Bidassoa, Nivelle, Nive, Adour and Bayonne. MGS medal for Corunna, Nivelle and Nive. Present at Waterloo (Brigade Major). Retired 27 Dec 1833. Died 28 Jul 1853. His elder brother Lewis Gunthorpe was killed at the Helder 1799.

GURWOOD, John
Captain. 10th (Prince of Wales's Own) Regiment of Light Dragoons.
Memorial tablet: St Paul's Cathedral, London. (Crypt south). (Photograph)

TO THE MEMORY OF COL. JOHN GURWOOD C.B. K.T.S. / DEPUTY LIEUTENANT OF THE TOWER OF LONDON. / HE SERVED WITH DISTINCTION IN THE PENINSULA / FRANCE AND WATERLOO. HE LED THE FORLORN / HOPE AT CIUDAD RODRIGO. HE WAS HONOURED / BY THE DUKE OF WELLINGTON WITH THE / TASK OF COMPILING HIS DESPATCHES / HE DIED ON THE 27TH DECR. 1845 AGED 57.

Memorial tablet: Chapel Royal of St Peter ad Vincula, Tower of London. (Photograph)

TO THE MEMORY / OF / COLONEL JOHN GURWOOD, / C.B. – K.T.S. / DEPUTY LIEUTENANT OF THE TOWER OF LONDON / WHOSE REMAINS ARE DEPOSITED / IN A VAULT OF THIS CHAPEL. / HAVING SERVED WITH DISTINCTION / AND BEEN REPEATEDLY WOUNDED / IN THE GLORIOUS FIELDS / OF THE PENINSULA, FRANCE AND WATERLOO. / HE WAS HONOURED / WITH THE TASK OF COMPILING / THE DESPATCHES AND OTHER RECORDS / OF HIS ILLUSTRIOUS COMMANDER / THE DUKE OF WELLINGTON. / KIND AS HE WAS BRAVE, / HE DIED ON THE 27TH DECEMBER 1846 / AGED 57. / DEEPLY DEPLORED BY HIS FAMILY / AND DESERVEDLY LAMENTED BY / A WIDE CIRCLE OF FRIENDS. / HE LED THE FORLORN HOPE AT C. RODRIGO / AND RECEIVED THE SWORD OF THE / GOVERNOR GEN. BARRIE / FROM THE COMMANDER IN CHIEF / ON THE FIELD OF BATTLE.

Ensign 52nd Foot 30 Mar 1808. Lt 3 Aug 1809. Capt Royal African Corps 6 Feb 1812. Capt 9th Lt Dragoons 30 Jul 1812. Capt 10th Lt Dragoons 12 Nov 1814. Bt Major 6 Mar 1817. Bt Lt Colonel 15 Mar 1827. Bt Colonel 23 Nov 1841.

Served in the Peninsula with 2/52nd Aug 1808 – Jan 1809, 1/52nd Jul 1809 – Aug 1811, 2/52nd Sep 1811 – Feb 1812 and 9th Lt Dragoons 1813 – Apr 1814 (Brigade Major Household Cavalry Brigade Dec 1812 – Oct 1813 and Brigade Major 2 Brigade 6th Division Nov 1813 – Apr 1814). Present at Vimeiro, Vigo, Coa, Busaco, Pombal, Redinha, Casal Nova, Foz d'Arouce, Sabugal (severely wounded), Ciudad Rodrigo (wounded and Mentioned in Despatches), Vittoria, Nivelle, Nive, Orthes and Toulouse. At Ciudad Rodrigo he led the Forlorn Hope and took the Governor, General Barrié prisoner. The Duke of Wellington presented Gurwood with Barrié's sword.

Present at Waterloo (ADC to Lt General Henry Clinton and severely wounded). CB. Private secretary to the Duke of Wellington and edited Wellington's *Dispatches*. Deputy Lieutenant of the Tower of London. Pressure of work and the effects of the head wound he received in the Peninsula, which had troubled him for years became too much and he committed suicide on 25 Dec 1845.
REFERENCE: *Dictionary of National Biography. Royal Military Calendar, Vol 5, p. 336. Gentleman's Magazine, Feb 1846, pp. 208–9. Annual Register, 1845, Appx, p. 323.*

GUTHRIE, George James
Deputy Inspector General of Hospitals. Medical Department.
Interred in Catacomb B (v124 c10 –12) Kensal Green Cemetery, London.

Hospital Assistant 23 Jun 1800. Asst Surgeon 29th Foot 5 Mar 1801. Surgeon 29th Foot 20 Mar 1806. Staff Surgeon 4 Jan 1810. Deputy Inspector General 16 Sep 1813.
Served in the Peninsula with 29th Foot Jul 1808 – Jan 1810 and as Staff Surgeon Jan 1811 – Apr 1814.

Present at Rolica, Vimeiro, Douro, Talavera, Albuera, Ciudad Rodrigo, Badajoz, Salamanca and Toulouse. After Waterloo, Guthrie, with other surgeons went to Brussels to tend the wounded. MD 1824. MGS medal for Rolica, Vimeiro, Talavera, Albuera, Ciudad Rodrigo, Badajoz, Salamanca and Toulouse.

After the war he became an eminent surgeon and lecturer. His military experience enabled him to make improvements in practical surgery and he lectured on surgery for 30 years. These lectures were free to all medical officers in the Army, Navy and East India Company. He did more to raise the standards of military surgery than anyone else. Founded an infirmary for treatment of diseases of the eye in 1811. Elected Assistant Surgeon to Westminster Hospital 1823 and Surgeon 1829. President of the Royal College of Surgeons 1833, 1842 and 1855. He was the first person to fill that office three times. He was a prolific writer. In 1855 his works were collected together and entitled *Commentaries on the surgery of war, 1808–1815*. In 1855 a sixth edition of this work was published including commentaries on surgery in the Crimean War. Died 1 May 1856.

REFERENCE: *Dictionary of National Biography. Gentleman's Magazine, Jun 1856, pp. 649–50. Annual Register, 1856, Appx, pp. 253–4. Crumplin, Michael, Guthrie's War; a Surgeon of the Peninsula and Waterloo, 2010.*

GUTHRIE, John Cleland
Captain. 44th (East Essex) Regiment of Foot.
Monument: South Park Street Burial Ground, Calcutta, India. (Photograph)

SACRED / TO THE MEMORY OF / JOHN CLELAND GUTHRIE / MAJOR OF H. M. 44TH REGIMENT. / BORN 21ST OF JULY 1783 / WHO DEPARTED THIS LIFE / ON THE 4TH OF JUNE 1823 / AGED 39 YEARS, 10 MTHS AND 14 DAYS.

Ensign 44th Foot 13 Nov 1801. Lt 26 Dec 1802. Capt 21 Mar 1805. Bt Major 12 Aug 1819. Major 31 May 1821.

Served in the Peninsula with 2/44th Nov 1810 – Jun 1813. Present at Fuentes d' Onoro, Badajoz, Salamanca, Burgos and Villa Muriel. Returned to England in June 1813 with the reduced ranks of the 2/44th where they merged with the remains of the 2/30th into a provisional battalion. Guthrie was second in command and for a time commanded this battalion. Also served in the Netherlands Dec 1814 (present at Merxem, Antwerp and Bergen-op-Zoom where he was wounded). Went with the 44th Foot to Belgium but was ordered to take part in a court martial in Ostend. As soon as he heard that his regiment was fighting the French he set off to join it as he had never been absent from it before. He arrived too late for Waterloo, but served in France with the Army of Occupation. Also served in India and died there 1823.

REFERENCE: *Gentleman's Magazine, May 1824, pp. 178–9.*

GWYN, William
Lieutenant Colonel. 89th Regiment of Foot.
Headstone: Old Govan Kirkyard, Govan, Lanarkshire, Glasgow, Scotland. (Photograph)

IN MEMORY / OF / LIEUT. COLONEL WILLIAM GWYN / LATE INSPECTING FIELD OFFICER / OF THIS DISTRICT WHO DIED / ON 30TH AUGUST 1815 AGED 41 YEARS / IN CONSEQUENCE OF / THE WOUNDS / HE RECEIVED / IN THE BATTLES / OF / TALAVERA / & / BUSACO.

Ensign 45th Foot 26 Aug 1788. Lt 6 Nov 1790. Capt 3 Sep 1795. Major 3 Aug 1804. Lt Colonel 89th Foot 11 Feb 1811.

Served in the Peninsula Aug 1808 – Dec 1810. Present at Rolica, Vimeiro, Talavera (wounded) and Busaco (severely wounded). Gold Medal for Talavera. Died from his wounds 1815. Also served in South America 1807 (present at Buenos Ayres).

GWYNNE, Henry Lewis Edwardes
Captain. 62nd (Wiltshire) Regiment of Foot.
Memorial tablet: St Mary's Church, Llanllwch, Carmarthen, Wales. (Photograph)

.... / ALSO TO THE MEMORY OF / HENRY LEWIS EDWARDES GWYNNE, / A CAPTAIN IN
H. M 62nd REGIMENT OF FOOT, / WHO DIED AUGUST 5TH 1866, / AGED 78 YEARS.

Ensign 25 Apr 1805. Lt 26 Jun 1806. Capt 23 Aug 1810.
    Served in the Peninsula Oct 1813 – Apr 1814. Present at Nivelle, Nive and Bayonne. MGS medal for
Nivelle and Nive. Half pay 25 Feb 1817.

HACKET, William
Staff Surgeon. Medical Department.
Grave: Sandpits Cemetery, Gibraltar. (M.I.)

"WILLIAM HACKET, M. D. INSP – GEN OF MILITARY HOSPITALS DIED 29 MAY 1854. AGED
74".

Asst Surgeon 15th Foot 12 Jun 1801. Surgeon North Downshire Militia 1802. Surgeon 8th Foot 25 Nov
1808. Staff Surgeon 6 Jan 1814. Retired on half pay 25 Feb 1816. Deputy Inspector General of Hospitals
6 Jan 1843. Inspector General 7 Jun 1854. This promotion did not reach him before he died.
    Also present at Walcheren 1809, North America 1813 (wounded at Stoney Creek), and the Netherlands
1814. MD St Andrews 1817.

HACKETT, John
Ensign. 88th (Connaught Rangers) Regiment of Foot.
Headstone: St Mary's Churchyard, Brixham, Devon. (No longer extant). (M.I.)

"IN MEMORY OF ENSIGN JOHN HACKETT, WHO DEPARTED THIS LIFE 19TH DECEMBER 1811
AGED 35 YEARS, BURIED 21 DECEMBER 1811. ADJUTANT 88TH "

Ensign Waterford Militia. Ensign 88th Foot 20 Dec 1809.
    Served in the Peninsula with 2/88th Jan 1810 – Jun 1811. Present at Cadiz, Sabugal and Fuentes d'Onoro
(wounded). Returned to England with 2nd Battalion Jun 1811, but died 19 Dec 1811.

HACKETT, Richard
Captain. 7th (Royal Fusiliers) Regiment of Foot.
Buried in the British Cemetery, Corfu, Greece. (No longer extant). (Photograph of site)

Lt North Down Militia. Lt 7th Foot 26 Oct 1807. Capt 17 Dec 1813. Capt 9th Foot 14 Aug 1817.
    Served in the Peninsula with 2/7th Apr 1809 – Nov 1810 and 1/7th Dec 1810 – Apr 1814. Present at
Talavera, Busaco, Pombal, Condeixa, Olivencia, first siege of Badajoz, Albuera, Aldea da Ponte, Vittoria,
Pyrenees, Bidassoa, Nivelle and Nive. Also served in North America 1814–1815 (present at New Orleans).
MGS medal for Talavera, Busaco, Albuera, Vittoria, Pyrenees, Nivelle and Nive. Half pay 6 Aug 1818.
Captain of Invalids at Kilmainham Hospital, Dublin. Died in Corfu 13 Jul 1848 aged 63 at his brother's
residence where he had gone due to ill health.

HADDEN, James
Lieutenant. 3rd (Prince of Wales's) Dragoon Guards.
Family Memorial tablet: St Nicholas Church, Harpenden, Hertfordshire. (Photograph)

..................../ AND ALSO TO THE MEMORY OF / JAMES HADDEN / THE SECOND SON OF / JAMES MURRAY HADDEN AND HARRIET FARRER / LATE A MAJOR IN HER MAJESTY'S 3ᴿᴰ REGIMENT OF / DRAGOON GUARDS / WHO DIED ON THE 12ᵀᴴ DAY OF FEBRUARY 1846 / AGED 56 YEARS

Cornet 4 Dec 1806. Lt 22 Apr 1813. Capt 23 May 1822. Major 8 Feb 1831.
    Served in the Peninsula Mar – Apr 1814. Present at Toulouse. Second son of Major General James Hadden, Royal Artillery. Brother of Capt William Frederick Hadden 6ᵗʰ Dragoons.

HADDEN, William Frederick
Captain. 6ᵗʰ (Inniskilling) Regiment of Dragoons.
Family Memorial tablet: St Nicholas Church, Harpenden, Hertfordshire. (Photograph)

..................../ LIKEWISE OF / WILLIAM FREDERICK HADDEN / ELDEST SON OF / JAMES MURRAY HADDEN AND HARRIET FARRER HIS WIFE / A CAPTAIN IN THE 6ᵀᴴ REGIMENT OF ENNISKILLEN / DRAGOONS / WHO DEPARTED THIS LIFE ON THE 1ˢᵀ DAY OF JUNE 1821 / AGED 32 YEARS

Cornet 6 Jul 1804. Lt 14 Nov 1805. Capt 28 Jan 1808.
    Present at Waterloo where he had his horse killed under him and with the Army of Occupation until Jan 1816. Half pay 11 Jan 1821. Eldest son of Major General James Hadden, Royal Artillery. Brother of Lt James Hadden 3ʳᵈ Dragoon Guards.

HADDOCK, Robert
Lieutenant. 87ᵗʰ (Prince of Wales's Own Irish) Regiment of Foot.
Headstone: Galle Face Burial Ground, Colombo, Ceylon. (Burial ground is no longer extant). (M.I.)

"SACRED TO THE MEMORY OF BT MAJOR ROBT. HADDOCK, LATE OF H.M. 97ᵀᴴ REGT. OF FOOT, WHO WAS UNFORTUNATELY KILLED BY AN ELEPHANT WHILST SPORTING IN THE NEIGHBOURHOOD OF RUWANWELLE, ON THE 26ᵀᴴ JUNE, 1828, AGED 41 YEARS. ERECTED BY HIS WIDOW."

Lt 87ᵗʰ Foot 25 Sep 1807. Capt 97ᵗʰ Foot 25 Mar 1824. Bt Major 12 Jun 1820. Portuguese Army: Capt 3ʳᵈ Caçadores 26 Sep 1810. Capt 12ᵗʰ Caçadores 6 Jun 1811. Major 22 May 1813.
    Served in the Peninsula with 87ᵗʰ Foot Mar 1809 – Sep 1810 and Portuguese Army Sep 1810 – Apr 1814. Present at Oporto, Talavera, Cadiz, Fuentes d'Onoro, Salamanca, Burgos and retreat from Burgos. Gold Medal for Salamanca. Half pay 25 Oct 1814 on reduction of British officers in the Portuguese Army. Also served in Ceylon with 97ᵗʰ Foot 1824–1828. Killed whilst trying to kill a rogue elephant in the jungle.
Rᴇꜰᴇʀᴇɴᴄᴇ: Lewis, J. Penry, List of inscriptions on tombstones and monuments in Ceylon, 1913, reprint 1994, p. 39.

HADEN, Francis Wastie
Assistant Commissary General. Commissariat Department.
Memorial tablet: King's Chapel, Gibraltar. (North Wall). (Photograph)

SACRED TO THE MEMORY OF / FRANCIS WASTIE HADEN, ESQᴿ / DEPUTY COMMISSARY GENERAL IN THE SERVICE OF HIS BRITANNIC MAJESTY, / WHO DIED IN THIS GARRISON ON THE 13ᵀᴴ DAY OF MARCH A. D. 1828. / HE WAS THE SECOND SON OF THE REVᴰ. ALEX DUNN HADEN, / VICAR OF WEDNESBURY, AND ONE OF THE MAGISTRATES FOR THE COUNTY OF WORCESTER. / HIS UNWEARIED ZEAL IN THE DISCHARGE OF HIS PROFESSIONAL DUTIES, / WITH THE ARMY UNDER THE COMMAND OF HIS GRACE THE DUKE OF WELLINGTON, /

DURING THE WHOLE OF THE PENINSULAR WAR, / SECURED HIM THE APPROBATION OF HIS SUPERIORS, / AND THE CONFIDENCE OF THE OFFICERS UNDER WHOM HE MORE IMMEDIATELY SERVED. / HE WAS NEXT EMPLOYED AS CHIEF OF THE COMMISSARIAT AT HALIFAX IN NOVA SCOTIA, / AND LATELY IN THIS PLACE. / HIS PRIVATE VIRTUES OBTAINING THEIR APPROPRIATE REWARD / IN THE AFFECTIONATE REGARD OF ALL, WHO KNEW HIM. / AN AFFLICTED WIDOW WHOM HE LEFT WITH THREE INFANT DAUGHTERS / THUS RECORDS HER SORROW AND THE PUBLIC LOSS. / HE DIED IN THE 42 YEAR OF HIS AGE.

Grave: Sandpits Cemetery, Gibraltar. Inscription not recorded. (Grave number 173)

Dep Asst Comm Gen 2 Jun 1810. Asst Comm Gen 10 Aug 1811.
    Served in the Peninsula May 1809 – Apr 1814. (Attached to 6th Division Oct 1810 – Oct 1811 and Headquarters Oct 1812 – Apr 1814). Also served in Halifax, Nova Scotia (Chief of Commissariat) and Gibraltar (Chief Commissary at the Garrison).

HAGAN, James
Surgeon. 59th (2nd Nottinghamshire) Regiment of Foot.
Named on the Regimental Memorial monument: Christ Church Churchyard, Tramore, County Waterford, Ireland. (Photograph)

Asst Surgeon 59th Foot 26 Nov 1807. Surgeon 53rd Foot 9 Sep 1813. Surgeon 59th Foot 25 Nov 1813.
    Present at Waterloo in reserve at Hal, siege of Cambrai and the Capture of Paris. Lost in the ship wreck of the *Sea Horse* 30 Jan 1816 off the coast of Ireland.

HAGGER, John
Lieutenant. 13th Royal Veteran Battalion.
Headstone: All Saints Churchyard, Cockermouth, Cumbria. Inscription illegible. (Photograph)

Quartermaster 47th Foot 20 Feb 1806. Lt 13th Royal Veteran Battalion 25 Jan 1813.
    Served in the Peninsula with 47th Foot Oct 1810 – Feb 1813, and 13th Royal Veteran Battalion Apr 1813 – Apr 1814. Present at Cadiz, Seville and Puente Largo. Served in Portugal with 13th Royal Veteran Battalion on garrison duty from Apr 1813 until end of the war.

HAIGH, John
Captain: 33rd (1st Yorkshire West Riding) Regiment of Foot.
Named on the Regimental Memorial: St Joseph's Church, Waterloo, Belgium. (Photograph)

Ensign 1800. Lt 16 Apr 1806. Capt 6 Aug 1812.
    Served at Quatre Bras where he was killed. Also served in the Netherlands 1814–1815 (present at Merxem). Brother of Lt Thomas Haigh 33rd Foot.

HAIGH, Thomas D.
Lieutenant. 33rd (1st Yorkshire West Riding) Regiment of Foot.
Named on the Regimental Memorial: St Joseph's Church, Waterloo, Belgium. (Photograph)

Ensign 15th Foot 19 Dec 1811. Lt 33rd Foot 29 Jul 1813.
    Present at Quatre Bras and Waterloo where he was killed. Also served in the Netherlands 1814–1815. Brother of Capt John Haigh 33rd Foot.

HAINES, Gregory
Deputy Commissary General. Commissariat Department.
Pedestal tomb: Mount Jerome Cemetery, Dublin, Ireland. (Grave number C80–2532). (Photograph)

SACRED / TO THE MEMORY OF / COMMISSARY GENERAL / GREGORY HAINES CB / DIED 6 AUGUST 1853 / IN THE 76TH YEAR OF HIS AGE / ………………..

Asst Comm Gen 7 Nov 1809. Dep Comm Gen 25 Dec 1814. Comm Gen 30 Aug 1833.
   Served in the Peninsula Aug 1808 – Jan 1809 and May 1809 – Apr 1814 (from Aug 1812 attached to HQ). Present at Corunna, Talavera, Busaco, Fuentes d'Onoro, Salamanca, Burgos, Vittoria, Pyrenees, Bidassoa, Nivelle, Nive, Orthes and Toulouse. Present at Waterloo. CB. Retired 30 Aug 1833. MGS medal for Corunna, Talavera, Busaco, Fuentes d'Onoro, Salamanca, Vittoria, Pyrenees, Nivelle, Nive, Orthes and Toulouse.

HAIR, Archibald
Assistant Surgeon. 43rd (Monmouthshire) Light Infantry Regiment of Foot.
Obelisk: St Bride's Churchyard, Sanquhar, Dumfriesshire, Scotland. (Photograph)

IN MEMORY OF / ARCHIBALD HAIR, M. D. / LATE SURGEON TO THE ROYAL HORSE GUARDS, / BORN / 31ST OCTOBER, 1785; / DIED 14TH DECEMBER, 1869.

Asst Surgeon 43rd Foot 12 Nov 1812. Surgeon Royal Horse Guards 12 Jan 1826.
   Served in the Peninsula with 1/43rd Feb 1813 – Apr 1814. Present at Vittoria, Pyrenees, Bidassoa, Nivelle, Nive and Orthes (attended to the serious wounds of the Earl of March, later 5th Duke of Richmond and also the Duke of Wellington who had a slight wound). Present at the Capture of Paris and with the Army of Occupation 1815. Also served in North America 1814–1815 (present at New Orleans). After his retirement from the Royal Horse Guards on 23 Jun 1843 became medical adviser to the Duke of Richmond and his family. MGS medal for Vittoria, Pyrenees, Nivelle, Nive and Orthes. MD Edinburgh 1824.
REFERENCE: *Household Brigade Journal, 1869, p. 323.*

HALFORD, Thomas
Private. 12th (Prince of Wales's) Regiment of Light Dragoons.
Named on the Regimental Memorial: St Joseph's Church, Waterloo Belgium. (Photograph)
   Killed at Waterloo.

HALKETT, Sir Colin
Colonel. 2nd Battalion Light Infantry, King's German Legion.
Chest tomb: Royal Hospital Cemetery, Chelsea, London. (Photograph)

SACRED TO THE MEMORY OF / GENERAL SIR COLIN HALKETT GCB GCH / AND KNIGHT OF SEVERAL FOREIGN ORDERS / COLONEL OF THE 45TH NOTTINGHAMSHIRE REGIMENT OF FOOT / AND GOVERNOR OF CHELSEA HOSPITAL. / HE RAISED THE 2ND LIGHT BATTALION OF THE KINGS GERMAN LEGION. / IN THE CAMPAIGN OF 1813 HE COMMANDED A BRITISH BRIGADE / AND SERVED THROUGHOUT THE WHOLE OF THE PENINSULAR WAR WITH GREAT DISTINCTION / AND AT WATERLOO THE COMMAND OF THE 3RD DIVISION. / THEN AT WATERLOO HE / HIMSELF WAS SEVERELY WOUNDED. / HE DEPARTED THIS LIFE ON THE 24TH SEPTEMBER 1856 / IN THE 83RD YEAR OF HIS AGE. / BELOVED RESPECTED AND HONOURED BY ALL WHO HAD THE HAPPINESS OF KNOWING HIM.

Lt Colonel 2nd Lt Battalion King's German Legion 9 Feb1805. Bt Colonel 1 Jan 1812. Major General 4 Jun 1814. Lt General 22 Jul 1830. General 9 Nov 1846.

Served in the Peninsula Aug 1808 – Jan 1809 and Mar 1811 – Dec 1813. (Commanded 1 Brigade 7th Division Oct 1811 – Dec 1812 and Commanded 3 Brigade 1st Division Dec 1812 – Dec 1813). Raised the 2nd Battalion of the Light Infantry King's German Legion to serve in the Peninsula. Present at Vigo, first siege of Badajoz, Albuera, second siege of Badajoz, siege of Salamanca Forts, Moriscos, Salamanca, San Munos, Venta del Pozo (Mentioned in Despatches), Vittoria (Mentioned in Despatches), Tolosa, (Mentioned in Despatches), Bidassoa, Nivelle and Nive. Present at Waterloo where he commanded the 5th British Brigade (30th, 33rd, 69th and 73rd) was severely wounded and awarded pension of £350 per annum. Gold Cross for Albuera, Salamanca, Vittoria and Nive. GCB. GCH. KTS. Knight 3rd Class of Wilhelm of the Netherlands, Commander of Bavarian Order of Maximilian Joseph. Also served at Hanover 1805, Baltic 1808, Walcheren 1809 and Netherlands 1814. Lt Governor of Jersey 1830. Colonel 31st Foot 28 Mar 1838. Colonel 45th Foot 1847. Governor of Chelsea Hospital 1849 until his death in 1856. Brother of Sir Hugh Halkett Commander in Chief of Hanoverian Army who died in Hanover 1863.
REFERENCE: *Gentleman's Magazine, Nov 1856, p. 649. Annual Register, 1856, Appx, p. 274. Royal Military Calendar, Vol 3, pp. 380–2.*

HALL, Charles
Ensign. 38th (1st Staffordshire) Regiment of Foot.
Memorial tablet: St Mary's Church, Nantwich, Cheshire. (Photograph)

SACRED TO THE MEMORY OF / ENSIGN CHARLES HALL, OF THE 38TH REGIMENT OF FOOT / (ONLY SON OF THE LATE DR CHARLES HALL, OF THIS TOWN,) / WHOSE AMIABLE DISPO-SITION ENDEAR'D HIM / TO HIS NUMEROUS FRIENDS. / HE DIED OF A FEVER BROUGHT ON BY EXCESSIVE / FATIGUE SOON AFTER HIS RETURN FROM SPAIN / AT PLYMOUTH, / ON THE TWENTY FIRST DAY OF JANUARY / 1809, / AGED 28. / HIS SORROWING SISTERS, SUSANNAH & ANN / HAVE CAUS'D THIS TABLET TO BE ERECTED / IN TOKEN OF THEIR AFFECTIONATE REGARD.

Ensign 28 Aug 1807.
Served in the Peninsula with 1/38th Aug 1808 – Jan 1809. Present at Rolica, Vimeiro and Corunna (wounded). Died on his return to Plymouth 21 Jan 1809.

HALL, Charles
Private. 32nd (Cornwall Regiment of Foot.
Buried in the Private Soldiers Burial Ground, Royal Hospital, Kilmainham, Dublin, Ireland.

Pte 17 Jul 1812. Cpl 1825.
Served at Waterloo in Captain Stopford Cane's Company and with the Army of Occupation. Also served in the Ionian Islands 1816–1824.

HALL, Edward S.
2nd Lieutenant. Royal Artillery.
Memorial: St Nicholas Churchyard, Plumstead, Kent. (No longer extant. Destroyed by a flying bomb in the Second World War). (M.I.)

"EDWARD S. HALL, LIEUT R. A. DIED AT VALENCIENNES 30 NOV 1817 AGED 18."

2nd Lt 11 Dec 1815. Served in France with the Army of Occupation. Died at Valenciennes 30 Nov 1817.

HALL, Henry Gallopine
Captain: 71st (Highland Light Infantry) Regiment of Foot.
Memorial tablet: St Margaret's Church, Harpsden, Oxfordshire. (M.I.)

"IN MEMORY OF CAPTAIN HENRY GALLOPINE HALL, 71ST REGT LT INFANTRY, ELDEST SON OF THOMAS HALL ESQ. KILLED BATTLE OF VITTORIA, 21 JUN 1813. AGED 23."

Cornet 13th Lt Dragoons 29 Jan 1805. Lt 1806. Capt 71st 26 Feb 1807.
    Served in the Peninsula Sep 1810 – Jul 1811 and Dec 1811 – Jun 1813. Present at Sobral, Fuentes d'Onoro, Almarez, Alba de Tormes and Vittoria where he was killed. Also served at Walcheren 1809.

HALL, Lewis Alexander
Lieutenant. Royal Engineers.
Headstone: Old Common Cemetery, Southampton, Hampshire. (E027 004). (Photograph)

ANNA SENHOUSE DAUGHTER OF / LT. COL. LEWIS ALEXANDER HALL R.E. / .... / ALSO LEWIS ALEXANDER HALL / LT. GEN. COL. COMMANDANT R.E. / BORN 8TH APRIL 1792 / DIED 15TH MARCH 1868 / ....

Reverse of headstone:

L. A. H. / 1868

Named on the Regimental Memorial: Rochester Cathedral, Rochester, Kent. (Photograph)

2nd Lt 21 Jul 1810. Lt 1 May 1811. 2nd Capt 12 Jan 1825. Bt Major 28 Jun 1838. Capt 19 Aug 1838. Lt Colonel 1 Apr 1846. Bt Colonel 20 Jun 1854. Colonel 23 Sep 1854. Major General 10 May 1859. Colonel Commandant 3 Aug 1863. Lt General 3 Aug 1863.
    Served in the Netherlands 1814–1815 and in France with the Army of Occupation 1815–1816.

HALL, Richard
Lieutenant. 47th (Lancashire) Regiment of Foot.
Memorial tablet: King's Chapel, Gibraltar. (M.I.)

"RICHARD HALL, LIEUTENANT OF 47TH FOOT, KILLED AT TARIFA 31 DECEMBER 1811".

Ensign 8th Garrison Battalion 31 Mar 1808. Lt 47th Foot 9 Nov 1809.
    Served in the Peninsula Oct 1810 – Dec 1811. Present at Cadiz and Tarifa where he was killed 31 Dec 1811.

HALL, William
Sergeant. 95th Regiment of Foot.
Buried in Nottingham Road Cemetery, Derby, Derbyshire. (No longer extant: Grave number 10012). (Burial record)

Leicester Militia. Pte 95th Foot 17 Apr 1805.
    Served in the Peninsula. Present at Corunna (wounded). Served at Waterloo in Capt William Eeles's Company. MGS medal for Corunna. Discharged 16 Feb 1819. Died 28 Jun 1876 aged 92.

HALL, William
Corporal. 23rd Regiment of Light Dragoons.
Memorial: Oakhampton Wesleyan Cemetery, near Maitland, New South Wales, Australia. (Photograph)

SACRED / TO THE MEMORY OF / WILLIAM HALL DIED 7 JUNE 1850 / ....

Pte 23rd Lt Dragoons 1812. Cpl Jun 1815.

Served at Waterloo in Capt Thomas Gerrard's Troop and with the Army of Occupation. Regiment disbanded in 1817. Went to Australia 1826 as a member of the Royal New South Wales Veterans Company. Employed at Newcastle as a convict overseer. Former cavalry men were preferred as mounted policemen. The company was disbanded in 1829 and he was granted land of 43 acres at Maitland where he died in 1850.

HALLIDAY, Andrew
Staff Surgeon. Medical Department.
Mural monument: St Michael's Churchyard, Dumfries, Dumfriesshire, Scotland. (Photograph)

VIRTUTE PARTA / SACRED / TO THE MEMORY OF / SIR ANDREW HALLIDAY K.H. / DEPUTY INSPECTOR GENERAL OF HOSPITALS / WHO DIED AT DUMFRIES, / ON THE 6TH SEPT 1839, / IN THE 58TH YEAR OF HIS AGE. / HE WAS A MAN OF GREAT INFORMATION AND / UNBOUNDED BENEVOLENCE, WAS INCESSANTLY / EMPLOYED IN DEVISING NEW MEANS FOR AMELIORATING / THE CONDITION OF HIS FELLOW-CREATURES AND / ALTOGETHER HIS LIFE WAS OF THE MOST / EXTENSIVE USEFULNESS. / THIS MONUMENT IS ERECTED TO HIS / MEMORY BY A FEW SINCERE FRIENDS.

Hospital Mate 30 Jul 1807. Asst Surgeon 13th Dragoons 17 Sep 1807. Asst Surgeon 4th Dragoon Guards 17 Mar 1808. Staff Surgeon Portuguese Army 17 Aug 1809. Staff Surgeon 29 Apr 1813. Deputy Inspector General 22 Jul 1830.

Served in the Peninsula with Portuguese Army Aug 1809 – Aug 1812. Transferred to British Army Aug 1812. Present at Waterloo. Also served in the Netherlands 1814 (present at Bergen-op-Zoom) and West Indies 1833. Halliday was educated for the church, but changed to medicine. MD Edinburgh 1806. Domestic physician to the Duke of Clarence (later William IV). Knighted 1821. Inspector of Hospitals in the West Indies 1833, but his health deteriorated and he returned to Scotland. KH. Prolific writer – *Observations on the present state of the Portuguese Army*, 1811, *Annals of the House of Hanover*, 2 vols, 1826. *General view of the present state of lunatics and lunatic asylums in Great Britain* ...., 1828. *Memoir of the campaign of 1815*, 1816.
REFERENCE: *Dictionary of National Biography. Gentleman's Magazine, Jan 1840, pp. 93–4. Annual Register, 1839, Appx, p. 363.*

HALPIN, William
Paymaster. 1st Regiment of Dragoons, King's German Legion.
Low monument: Kensal Green Cemetery, London. (17459/125/8). (Photograph)
Half buried uninscribed stone. The photograph shows the stone of his son General George Halpin which lies next to his own, because it records the name of William Halpin and his regiment.

COLONEL GEORGE HALPIN, MADRAS ARMY, / SECOND SON OF CAPTN WILLIAM HALPIN, 1ST HEAVY DRAGOONS,. K. G. L.

Paymaster 6 Jan 1807.
Served in the Peninsula Jan 1812 – Apr 1814. Present at Salamanca, Garcia Hernandez, Majalahonda, Venta del Pozo, Vittoria, Orthes, Tarbes and Toulouse. Present in the Waterloo campaign. Half pay 25 Jun 1816. MGS medal for Salamanca, Vittoria, Orthes and Toulouse. Also served in the Netherlands 1814. Died 1862.

HALY, William A.
Captain. 53rd (Shropshire) Regiment of Foot.
Memorial: Highgate Cemetery, London. (M.I.)

"CAPTAIN W. A. HALY / LATE 53ʳᴰ REGIMENT / DIED 27ᵀᴴ APRIL 1847 / ERECTED / TO HIS MEMORY / BY SOME OF HIS OLD FRIENDS AND COMPANIONS IN ARMS / A NOBLE SPIRIT SOARS ABOVE THE SKIES / BENEATH A NARROW CELL HIS BODY LIES".

Lt 4 Jun 1806. Capt 12 Jan 1809.
    Served in the Peninsula Jan 1810 – Mar 1813. Present at Busaco and siege of the Salamanca Forts. Taken prisoner near Salamanca 2 Jul 1812 – rejoined his regiment 30 Jul 1812. MGS medal for Busaco.

HAMERTON, John Millett
Lieutenant Colonel. 44ᵗʰ (East Essex) Regiment of Foot.
Pedestal Monument: Orchardstown Graveyard, near Clonmel, County Tipperary, Ireland. (Photograph)

SACRED TO THE MEMORY OF THE LATE / GENERAL JOHN MILLETT HAMERTON, C.B. / WHO DEPARTED THIS LIFE AT HIS RESIDENCE / ORCHARDSTOWN, ON THE 27 JANʸ 1855 / IN THE 79ᵀᴴ YEAR OF HIS AGE. / HE WAS COLONEL OF THE 55ᵀᴴ REGᵀ OF FOOT / & LATE LIEUᵀ COLONEL OF THE 44ᵀᴴ EAST ESSEX, / WHICH REGᵀ HE WAS APPOINTED ENSIGN / AT THE AGE OF 15. HE SERVED ALL THROUGH / THE PENINSULA CAMPAIGN & GALLANTLY COMMANDED / HIS REGᵀ AT THE MEMORABLE WATERLOO. SERVED UNDER / THE DUKE OF YORK IN 1794. UNDER SIR RALPH ABERCROMBIE HE / ASSISTED AT THE CAPTURE OF ST LUCIA IN 1796. HE WAS / MADE A COMPANION OF THE BATH & OBTAINED ALL HIS HONOURS. / HAD MEDALS FOR WATERLOO & EGYPT. HIS RESPECTED / MEMORY WILL BE LONG AND DEEPLY MOURNED BY HIS WIDOW / AND CHILDREN TO WHOM HE WAS FONDLY ATTACHED. / HE WAS AN INDULGENT LANDLORD AND GENEROUS / TO THE POOR. THIS MONUMENT HAS BEEN ERECTED / BY HIS WIFE AS A LASTING TRIBUTE OF HER AFFECTION.

Ensign 44ᵗʰ Foot 31 Oct 1792. Lt 31 Jan 1794. Capt 28 Oct 1796. Major 15 Jun 1804. Bt Lt Colonel 4 Jun 1811. Lt Colonel 31 Mar 1814. Bt Colonel 27 May 1825. Major General 10 Jan 1837.
    Served in the Peninsula Aug 1813 – Apr 1814. Served in Eastern Spain (present at Tarragona). Present at Waterloo (severely wounded in command of the 2ⁿᵈ battalion 44ᵗʰ Foot). He was left for dead on the battlefield, was found by one of his NCOs – Sgt Ryan who took him to the Medical staff. On his recovery he returned to England with Sgt Ryan who probably stayed with him to the end of his life. CB for Waterloo. Also served in Flanders 1794, West Indies 1795 (present at St Lucia), Gibraltar 1798 and Egypt 1801. Later served in Guernsey, Malta, Sicily and the Netherlands 1814. Half pay 24 Jun 1816. Colonel 55ᵗʰ Foot 17 Dec 1848.
REFERENCE: *Gentleman's Magazine, Mar 1855, p. 310.*

HAMILTON, Alexander
Lieutenant Colonel. 30ᵗʰ (Cambridgeshire) Regiment of Foot.
Grave: St Luke's Churchyard, Charlton, Kent. (No longer extant: Grave number 227). (M.I.)

"COLONEL ALEXANDER HAMILTON, LATE OF THE 30ᵀᴴ REGᵀ / DIED AT WOOLWICH THE 4 JUNE 1838, AGED 73 YEARS."

Ensign 84ᵗʰ Foot 1 Apr 1784. Ensign 30ᵗʰ Foot 2 Apr 1787. Lt 22 Mar 1791. Capt 2 Sep 1795. Major 1 Apr 1804. Lt Colonel 25 Jul 1811. Bt Colonel 27 May 1825.
    Served in the Peninsula Apr – May 1809, Jun 1810 – Aug 1811 and May 1812 – Jun 1813. Present at Cadiz, Fuentes d'Onoro (wounded), Barba del Puerco, Salamanca (commanded the battalion), Burgos and Villa Muriel. Gold Medal for Salamanca. Present at Waterloo where he commanded the battalion at Quatre Bras (severely wounded). Received the thanks of Sir Thomas Picton. Three times the surgeons were going to amputate his leg but each time they were diverted elsewhere, so Hamilton kept his leg and recov-

ered. CB for Waterloo. Also served at Toulon 1793 and Cape Brune 14 Oct 1793 (severely wounded), Corsica 1794, commanded a detachment of the 30th Foot acting as marines on board HMS *Terrible* 1795, the capture of Malta 1800 (Brigade Major to Lord Lynedoch), Egypt 1801 (awarded the Sultan's Gold Medal), Netherlands 1814 (present at Antwerp and Bergen-op-Zoom) and India 1818–1828. Retired in 1828.
REFERENCE: *Royal Military Calendar, Vol 4, pp. 354–5.*

HAMILTON, Digby

Colonel. Royal Waggon Train.
Memorial tablet: St James's Church, Piccadilly, London. (Photograph)

SACRED / TO THE MEMORY OF / MAJOR-GENERAL DIGBY HAMILTON / COLONEL OF THE ROYAL WAGGON TRAIN / WHO DEPARTED THIS LIFE / THE 18TH OF MARCH 1820, / IN THE 62ND YEAR OF HIS AGE.

Lt and Adjt 12th Lt Dragoons 1782. Lt 2nd Dragoons Apr 1785. Capt-Lt 27 Jun 1795. Lt Colonel Commandant Royal Waggon Train 20 Aug 1799. Colonel Commandant Royal Waggon Train, 5 Nov 1803. Major General 12 Aug 1813.
Served in the Peninsula 1808 – Jan 1809. Present in the Corunna campaign (Commander of the garrison and general hospital at Zamora). Also served in North America 1782, Flanders 1793 – 1795 (present at all battles from Valenciennes to the retreat to Westphalia), the Helder 1799, Baltic 1807 and Walcheren 1809.
REFERENCE: *Royal Military Calendar, Vol 3, p. 332.*

HAMILTON, George Augustus

2nd Captain. Royal Engineers.
Grave: St George's Cemetery, Lisbon, Portugal. Inscription not recorded. (Grave number C.1.19). (M.I.)
Named on the Regimental Memorial, Rochester Cathedral, Rochester, Kent. (Photograph)

1st Lt 2 Jan 1804. 2nd Capt 21 Jun 1809.
Served in the Peninsula May 1809 – May 1810. Present at Douro (severely wounded 12 May 1809). Had only just arrived in Lisbon with Burgoyne, Boothby and Mulcaster of the Royal Engineers to join Wellington in April 1809. Moved to Lisbon to treat his wounds. Although wounded he was drawing up plans for the Lines of Torres Vedras. Died of wounds at Lisbon 20 May 1810, aged 21 years.

HAMILTON, Henry Stewart

Lieutenant. 74th (Highland) Regiment of Foot.
Named on the Memorial: St Andrew's Church, (now Musée Historique), Biarritz, France. (Photograph)
Named on the Regimental Memorial: St Giles's Cathedral, Edinburgh, Scotland. (Photograph)

Ensign 21 Nov 1811. Lt 11 Nov 1813.
Served in the Peninsula May 1812 – Apr 1814. Present at Salamanca, Vittoria (severely wounded), Nivelle, Nive, Orthes, Vic Bigorre, Tarbes and Toulouse where he was severely wounded and died of his wounds 16 Apr 1814.

HAMILTON, James Inglis

Lieutenant Colonel. 2nd (Royal North British) Regiment of Dragoons.
Memorial tablet: Kirk of Shotts Church, Lanarkshire, Scotland. (Photograph)

SACRED TO THE MEMORY OF / COLONEL JAMES INGLIS HAMILTON, / OF MURDIESTON, / WHO DIED IN HIS 38TH YEAR, AT THE HEAD OF HIS REGIMENT, / THE SCOTS GREYS, / WHICH

HE COMMANDED AT THE BATTLE OF WATERLOO. / MARY INGLIS HAMILTON, HIS WIDOW, / CONSECRATES THIS HUMBLE TRIBUTE OF DUTY AND AFFECTION, / TO THE WORTH OF A HUSBAND WHOSE LOSS SHE MUST EVER DEPLORE. / RENEWED AND RE-ERECTED / BY / THE PRESENT & FORMER OFFICERS OF THE ROYAL SCOTS GREYS. / 1880.

Cornet 18 May 1793. Lt 15 Oct 1793. Capt 25 Apr 1794. Major 17 Feb 1803. Lt Colonel 16 Jun 1807. Bt Colonel 4 Jun 1814.

Present at Waterloo where he commanded the regiment. Escorted the infantry retreating from Quatre Bras. Took part in the charge of the Scots Greys on the 18th (severely wounded in both arms). He then held his reins in his teeth but was shot and killed. His real name was James Anderson, son of a Sergeant Major of the 21st Fusiliers, who after leaving the army settled in Glasgow. He met his former commanding officer, General James Inglis Hamilton, who paid for the education of the Sgt Major's children. James Anderson was appointed Cornet in the Scots Greys, thanks to the General's influence, under the name of James Inglis Hamilton, the name he kept until his death. His brother Lt John Anderson 38th Foot was severely wounded at Salamanca 1812 and died of his wounds 1816.

HAMILTON, Sir John
Colonel. 2nd Ceylon Regiment.
Interred in Catacomb A (v19 c2) Kensal Green Cemetery, London.

Ensign Bengal Native Infantry 2 Mar 1773. Lt 1775. Capt 15 Oct 1781. Capt 76th Foot 1 Nov 1788. Bt Major 1 Mar 1794. Lt Col 81st Foot 23 Dec 1795. Bt Colonel 29 Apr 1802. Major General 25 Oct 1809. Colonel 2nd Ceylon Regt 18 Jan 1812. Lt General 5 Feb 1812.

Served in the Peninsula with Portuguese Army Aug 1809 – Apr 1814. (Inspector General of Portuguese Infantry 27 Nov 1809). Present at Albuera, Alba de Tormes and Nivelle (Mentioned in Beresford's Despatches). Gold Medal for Albuera and Nivelle. KCB. KCH. KTS. Also served in India 1778–1791 (present in 1st Mahratta War), West Indies 1796–1797 (present at San Domingo) and Cape of Good Hope (present in the Kaffir War 1800). Governor of Duncannon Fort 10 May 1814. Created a Baronet 6 May 1815. Colonel 69th Foot 15 Mar 1823. Died 24 Dec 1835.
REFERENCE: *Dictionary of National Biography. Gentleman's Magazine, Mar 1836, p. 315.*

HAMILTON, John
Lieutenant. 60th (Royal American) Regiment of Foot.
Ledger stone: Coldstream Guards Cemetery, St Etienne, Bayonne, France. (Photograph)

J. H. LIEUT 60TH REGT.

Named on the Memorial: St Andrew's Church, (now Musée Historique), Biarritz, France. (Photograph)

Ensign 7 Oct 1811. Lt 31 Dec 1812.

Served in the Peninsula Apr 1812 – Apr 1814 (attached to 3rd Division Jun – Sep 1812 and 1st Division Apr 1813 – Apr 1814). Present at Salamanca, Vittoria, Bidassoa, San Sebastian, Nivelle, Nive, Adour (first man across the Adour 23 Feb 1814) and Bayonne where he died from wounds received at the Sortie from Bayonne 14 Apr 1814.

HAMILTON, John Potter
Captain and Lieutenant Colonel. 3rd Regiment of Foot Guards.
Cross on stepped base: Locksbrook Cemetery, Bath, Somerset. (Grave number JA 105). (Photograph)

.... / ALSO / IN MEMORY OF THE AFORESAID / COL. JOHN P. HAMILTON, K.H. / LATE SCOTS FUSILIER GUARDS / WHO DEPARTED THIS LIFE / JAN 26TH 1873 / AGED 92 YEARS.

Cornet 2nd Dragoons 1794. Lt 13 Aug 1794. Capt 16 Aug 1799. Major 27 Feb 1802. Major 4th Garrison Battalion 19 May 1808. Major 10th Foot 14 Dec 1809. Lt Colonel 83rd Foot 3 Jun 1813. Capt and Lt Colonel 3rd Foot 25 Jul 1814. Bt Colonel 12 Aug 1819.

Served in the Peninsula 1812 – Jul 1813. Served on the east coast of Spain (present at Castalla where he commanded a battalion and at the capture of Balaguer in Catalonia). Also served in Flanders 1794–1795 (present at Le Cateau and Nimwegen). Promoted to his lieutenancy by the Duke of York for carrying despatches from the Duke to the Prince of Orange under very difficult conditions. KH.

HAMILTON, Nicholas
Major. Inspecting Field Officer, Recruiting Staff.
Pedestal tomb: Mount Jerome Cemetery, Dublin, Ireland. (Photograph)

TO THE MEMORY OF / LT GEN^L N. HAMILTON K.H. / COLONEL OF 82ND REG^T / HE ENTERED THE FIFTH REG^T / AT AN EARLY AGE AND SAW / SEVERE AND VARIED SERVICE / IN THE PENINSULA & AMERICA / AND ON THE / WALCHEREN EXPEDITION / WHERE HE LOST A LEG / HE WAS FOR A LONG PERIOD / INSPECTING FIELD OFFICER AT NEWRY / AND AFTER A TOTAL SERVICE / OF SIXTY THREE YEARS / DIED AT DUBLIN / DEEPLY REGRETTED / ON THE 12TH DEC 1856 / IN THE 78TH YEAR OF HIS AGE.

Ensign 5th Foot 15 Jun 1796. Lt 9 Dec 1796. Capt 25 Jun 1803. Major Recruiting Staff 18 Jun 1812. Bt Lt Colonel 27 May 1825. Colonel 28 Jun 1838. Major General 11 Nov 1851. Lt General 20 Jun 1854.

Served in the Peninsula with 1/5th Aug 1808 – Jan 1809. Present at Rolica, Vimeiro and Corunna. Also served at the Helder 1799, Hanover 1805 (shipwrecked off coast of Holland and taken prisoner), South America 1806–1807 (present at Buenos Ayres – one of the hostages taken by the Spaniards) and Walcheren 1809 (present at the siege of Flushing where he was severely wounded and his leg amputated. Awarded pension of £200 per annum). On return to England became Inspecting Field Officer on Recruiting Staff, a position he held for many years. MGS medal for Rolica, Vimeiro and Corunna. KH. Colonel 82nd Regt 1856. His brother John was also Captain in 5th Foot, served in South America and Walcheren and died in Dover Nov 1809 from fever caught in the Walcheren expedition.

HAMILTON, Robert
Assistant Surgeon. 51st (2nd Yorkshire West Riding) Light Infantry.
Named on the Regimental Memorial: KOYLI Chapel, York Minster, Yorkshire. (Photograph)

Asst Surgeon 74th Foot 13 Ju1 1809. Asst Surgeon 51st Foot 22 Aug 1811.

Served in the Peninsula Feb 1810 – Mar 1812. Present at Busaco, Casal Nova, Foz d'Arouce, Fuentes d'Onoro and second siege of Badajoz. Accidentally shot and killed at Llerena 26 Mar 1812. When Sir Thomas Graham and staff came galloping back into camp after checking forward positions, the 51st Foot thought they were the French attacking them and opened fire. In the general confusion Hamilton was shot dead.

HAMILTON, William Frederick
Ensign. 3rd Regiment of Foot Guards.
Headstone with Cross: St Boniface Old Churchyard, Bonchurch, Isle of Wight. (Photograph)

THE REV W^M FREDERICK HAMILTON. MA. / BORN THE 22ND OCT^R 1798. / FOUGHT AT THE BATTLE OF WATERLOO / AS AN ENSIGN IN THE 3RD FOOT GUARDS / AND DIED THE 24TH OF JUNE 1871. / A MOST FAITHFUL PREACHER OF THE / GOSPEL OF PEACE.

Ensign 1 Apr 1813. Lt and Capt 17 Apr 1817.

Present at Waterloo in Lt Col C. Dashwood's Company. Retired on half pay 1 Feb 1821. Later entered the church.

HAMMERSLEY, Frederick

Lieutenant. 5th (Princess Charlotte of Wales's) Dragoon Guards.
Low monument: Kensal Green Cemetery, London. Inscription illegible. (16063/111/3). (Photograph)

Militia 1806. Cornet 5th Dragoon Guards 23 Jan 1812. Lt 9 Apr 1812. Capt 8 May 1840.
   Served in the Peninsula Dec 1812 – Apr 1814. Present at Vittoria and Toulouse. MGS medal for Vittoria and Toulouse. Half pay 1814. Later Paymaster 1st Dragoon Guards 26 Sep 1848. Half pay 1855. Also served in Ireland 1806 (wounded in Dublin). Died 1860.

HANDLEY, Benjamin

Lieutenant. 9th Regiment of Light Dragoons.
Memorial tablet: St Denys Church, Sleaford, Lincolnshire. (Photograph)

.........................../ THIS TABLET ALSO RECORDS THE MEMORY OF / BENJAMIN, A YOUNGER SON OF THE ABOVE, / BENJN, AND FRANCES HANDLEY, LIEUTT, IN / HIS MAJESTY'S 9TH REGT LT DRAGOONS WHO / PERISHED IN THE TAGUS, IN THE 22ND YEAR / OF HIS AGE, BY THE LOSS OF THE BOAT IN / WHICH HE WAS EMBARKED ON THE CONFIDENTIAL / DUTY OF CONVEYING THE STANDARDS OF THE / REGT FROM THE ADMIRAL'S SHIP TO THE / COMMANDING OFFICER'S TRANSPORTATION ON THE / REGTS RETURN FROM THE PENINSULAR WAR; / MAY 22ND 1813. / HIS REMAINS WERE RECOVERED AND INTERRED / IN THE BRITISH BURIAL GROUND AT LISBON.

Buried in the British Burial Ground, Lisbon, Portugal.

Cornet 13 May 1809. Lt 10 May 1810.
   Served in the Peninsula Jul 1811 – Apr 1813. Present at Arroyo dos Molinos, Alba de Tormes and Ribera (Mentioned in Despatches 1 Aug 1812). Drowned in the Tagus 17 Apr 1813 when the regiment was embarking for England. Also served at Walcheren 1809.
   The date of death on the monument (22 May 1813) must be erroneous, as an obituary appeared in the *Lincoln, Rutland and Stamford Mercury* the previous week on 14 May 1813 as having died on 17 April 1813: 'Lieutenant Handley, of the 9th Light Dragoons, eldest son of Benjamin Handley Esq. of Sleaford, after having served two campaigns in the Peninsula with distinguished reputation, met a premature and melancholy death on the 17th of last month, in the harbour of Lisbon, by the upsetting of the boat in which his cousin, Captain Handley, and himself, were conveying the standards of the regiment from the Admiral's ship to the Commanding Officer's Transport. Captain Handley's life was with extreme difficulty preserved, but the Sergeant Major met the same untimely fate as Lieutenant Handley. The regiment was on its return in consequence of the loss of the greater part of its horses in the service of the last campaign.'
REFERENCE: *Gentleman's Magazine, May 1813, p. 493. Lincoln, Rutland and Stamford Mercury, 14 May 1813, p. 3, col. 1.*

HANGER, John

Sergeant. 51st (2nd Yorkshire West Riding) Light Infantry.
Named on the Regimental Memorial: KOYLI Chapel, York Minster, Yorkshire. (Photograph)
   Killed in the Peninsula.

HANKIN, Thomas Pate

Major. 2nd (Royal North British) Regiment of Dragoons.
Memorial tablet: Norwich Cathedral, Norwich, Norfolk. (Choir triforium north, first floor over aisle adjacent to north transept). (Photograph)

"TO THE MEMORY OF / LIEUTENANT-COLONEL SIR THOMAS PATE HANKIN, KT., / WHO

DIED AT NORWICH / OCTOBER 26TH 1825, / IN THE 60TH YEAR OF HIS AGE. / THIS TABLET IS PLACED HERE AS A TRIBUTE OF RESPECT / BY THE / OFFICERS OF THE ROYAL SCOTS GREYS, / IN WHICH REGIMENT HE HAD PASSED THE GREATER PART OF HIS LIFE, AND COMMANDED IT / AT THE TIME OF HIS DEATH."

Cornet 22 Jul 1795. Lt 3 Aug 1796. Capt 18 Oct 1798. Major 4 Apr 1808. Bt Lt Colonel 4 Jun 1814.

Present at Waterloo where he was wounded. Having served in the regiment all his military days, he succeeded to the command of the Scots Greys 11 Oct 1821 until his death in 1825. Knighted by George IV 1822. Died at the Cavalry barracks in Norwich.
REFERENCE: *Gentleman's Magazine, Nov 1825, pp. 466–7.*

HANKS, William
Sergeant. 51st (2nd Yorkshire West Riding) Light Infantry.
Named on the Regimental Memorial: KOYLI Chapel, York Minster, Yorkshire. (Photograph)
    Killed in the Peninsula.

HANMER, Henry
Captain. Royal Regiment of Horse Guards.
Cross on stepped base: All Saints Churchyard, Soulbury, Buckinghamshire. (Plot number A 24). (Photograph)

IN MEMORY OF / LIEUTENANT COLONEL / HENRY HANMER / OF STOCKGROVE. / BORN JANUARY 23RD 1789. / DIED / FEBRUARY 2ND 1868.

Cornet 6 Oct 1808. Lt 5 Apr 1810. Capt 18 Nov 1813. Major 18 May 1826. Bt Lt Colonel 18 May 1826.

Served in the Peninsula Oct 1812 – Feb 1814. Present at Vittoria and Pamplona. MP for Westbury 1831 and Aylesbury 1832–1836. Retired from the army 4 Dec 1832. MGS medal for Vittoria. KH 1833. Magistrate for Bedfordshire, Buckinghamshire and Berkshire. High Sheriff of Buckinghamshire 1854.
REFERENCE: *Gentleman's Magazine, Mar 1868, p. 403.*

HANSON, William
Captain. 20th Regiment of Light Dragoons.
Memorial tablet: St George's Church, Great Bromley, Essex. (Photograph)

SACRED / TO THE MEMORY OF CAPTAIN WILLIAM HANSON OF THE 20TH LIGHT DRAGOONS, / ELDEST SON OF JOHN & MARY ISABELLA HANSON OF GREAT BROMLEY HALL, / WHO VALIANTLY FIGHTING FOR HIS KING & COUNTRY / WAS KILLED IN A SEVERE ACTION WITH THE FRENCH CAVALRY ON THE 13TH SEPTEMBER 1813, / NEAR VILLA FRANCA IN CATALONIA, WHERE HIS REMAINS ARE INTERRED, / AND A MONUMENT ERECTED BY THE OFFICERS OF HIS OWN REGIMENT, / IN TOKEN OF THEIR HEART FELT REGRET. / "HE FELL AT THE HEAD OF HIS TROOP AT THE MOMENT OF BRILLIANT SUCCESS / WHICH HIS GALLANT EXAMPLE HAD MUCH CONTRIBUTED TO OBTAIN". / ADMIRED EVEN BY THE ENEMY / AND DESIGNATED BY NAME IN THE PUBLIC DISPATCH OF MARSHAL SUCHET / "THE CAPTAIN OF DRAGOONS, HANSON, A MAN OF THE GREATEST DISTINC-TION FOR VALOUR" / AND IN THE WORDS OF HIS OWN COMMANDER / "AN OFFICER OF THE FIRST PROMISE, POSSESSING EVERY VIRTUE THAT COULD ADORN THE MAN OR GRACE THE SOLDIER" / HE WAS BORN SEPTEMBER THE 7TH 1788, / AND GLORIOUSLY TO HIMSELF, BUT PREMATURELY FOR HIS COUNTRY AND FRIENDS, / CLOSED HIS HONOURABLE CAREER AT THE EARLY AGE OF 25. / SOLA VIRTU INVICTA.

Monument: Church of Villa Franca, Catalonia, Spain. (*Gentleman's Magazine* reference)

"LET THOSE JOURNEYING HITHER BEHOLD THIS STONE – THE MEMORIAL ALIKE OF TENDERNESS AND OF MILITARY GLORY – ERECTED BY PERMISSION OF THE MOST REVEREND BISHOP OF BARCELONA. / ON THE 13TH SEPTEMBER, 1813, CAPTAIN WILLIAM HANSON, OF HIS BRITANNIC MAJESTY'S TWENTIETH REGIMENT OF LIGHT DRAGOONS, FELL IN A SEVERE ACTION WITH THE ENEMY'S CAVALRY ON THE FIELDS OF MONJOS, CONTIGUOUS TO THIS TOWN, WHILST GLORIOUSLY FIGHTING UNDER THE COMMAND OF COLONEL LORD FREDERICK BENTINCK FOR THE COMBINED CAUSE OF GREAT BRITAIN AND SPAIN. THAT THIS DISTINGUISHED OFFICER, THEREFORE, MAY LIVE BEYOND THE GRAVE, THE OFFICERS OF HIS OWN REGIMENT, DEEPLY LAMENTING HIS LOSS, HAVE CAUSED THIS INSCRIPTION TO BE DEDICATED TO HIS RESPECTED NAME."

Ensign 91st Foot 26 Dec 1806. Lt 17 May 1808. Capt 6th Dragoon Guards 14 Jul 1808. Capt 20th Lt Dragoons 31 May 1810.

Served in the Peninsula with 91st Foot Aug 1808 – Jan 1809 and 20th Lt Dragoons May – Sep 1813. Present at Rolica, Vimeiro, Cacabellos, Corunna and Ordal near Villa Franca on the east coast of Spain where he was killed in the cavalry action, and his bravery even mentioned in Marshal Suchet's despatch. Brother in law of Capt Richard Bogue Royal Artillery killed at Leipzig. Educated at Eton.
REFERENCE: *Gentleman's Magazine, Nov 1813, pp. 499–500 and Supplement to 1814 Part 1, p. 703.*

HARCOURT, George Simon see AINSLIE, George Simon Harcourt

HARCOURT, John
Assistant Surgeon. 27th (Inniskilling) Regiment of Foot.
Named on the Afghanistan War Memorial, Regimental Chapel of the Essex Regiment and the Royal Anglian Regiment, Warley, Essex. (Photograph)
The memorial was originally erected in St Mary's Church, Alverstoke, Hampshire, and moved to Warley in 1926 together with the regimental flag.

SACRED TO THE MEMORY OF ……………… SURGEON J. HARCOURT ………………..

Hospital Mate 10 May 1813. Hospital Assistant 10 Jan 1814. Asst Surgeon 27th Foot 26 May 1814. Asst Surgeon 11th Dragoons 23 May 1816. Surgeon 2nd Foot 7 Mar 1834. Surgeon 44th Foot 13 Jul 1838.

Served in the Peninsula Jun 1813 – Apr 1814. Also served in Afghanistan 1839 – 1842 (present in the retreat from Kabul. Died at Jagdalak 12 Jan 1842, where he was one of the last to be killed in the massacre)

HARDCASTLE, William Augustus
Ensign. 31st (Huntingdonshire) Regiment of Foot.
Family Memorial tablet: Clifton Street Cemetery, Belfast, Northern Ireland. (South wall in a railed enclosure). (Photograph)

ERECTED / BY / JAMES B. FERGUSON / IN MEMORY OF HIS BELOVED MOTHER, BELL FERGUSON / WHO DEPARTED THIS LIFE 11TH FEBY 1855 / ……………………… / CAPTAIN W. A. HARDCASTLE, HIS BROTHER-IN-LAW / WHO DIED 2ND FEBY 1858.

Ensign 7 Mar 1811. Lt 29 Apr 1819. Portuguese Army: Ensign 23rd Line 25 Aug 1810. Lt 10th Caçadores 6 Jun 1811. Capt 9 Nov 1813.

Served in the Peninsula with Portuguese Army Aug 1810 – Apr 1814 (ADC to Sir John Buck). Present at Busaco, Redinha, Albuera, Vittoria, Pyrenees, Nivelle, Nive, Orthes and Aire (wounded and awarded pension of £100 per annum). Retired from Portuguese Army 13 Oct 1814. MGS medal for Busaco, Albuera, Vittoria, Pyrenees, Nivelle, Nive and Orthes. Retired on half pay 14 Mar 1822.

HARDING, Edwin
Lieutenant. 82nd (Prince of Wales's Volunteers) Regiment of Foot.
Named on the Regimental Memorial: St Multose Church, Kinsale, Ireland. (Photograph)

SACRED / TO THE MEMORY OF LIEU^{TS} / EDMUND DAVENPORT, EDWIN HARDING / ASS^T SURGEON HENRY RANDOLPH SCOTT / AND HIS WIFE / EIGHT SERJEANTS, NINE CORPO-RALS, / ONE HUNDRED AND FORTY PRIVATES, / THIRTEEN WOMEN AND SIXTEEN CHILDREN / OF THE 82^D REG^T, WHO PERISHED / ON BOARD THE BOADICEA TRANSPORT, / WRECKED ON GARRETSTOWN STRAND / ON THE NIGHT OF THE 30TH JAN^Y 1816 / THIS TRIBUTE IS ERECTED / BY THE OFFICERS OF THE REG^T.

Buried in Old Court Burial Ground, Kinsale, Ireland.

Ensign 7 Jun 1810. Lt 14 Sep 1813.
   Served in the Peninsula Oct 1812 – Oct 1813. Present at Vittoria, Pyrenees, and San Marcial. Also served in France with the Army of Occupation. On 8 Dec 1815 the regiment marched from Paris en route to Calais to embark for England. Landed in Dover on 3 Jan 1816 and were immediately re-shipped for Ireland on 30 Jan on the transport ship *Boadicea*. The ship was wrecked at Kinsale off the coast of Ireland and of 289 people on board only 102 were saved.

HARDING, George Judd
1st Captain. Royal Engineers.
Chest tomb: Candie Cemetery, St Peter Port, Guernsey, Channel Islands. (Photograph)

SACRED / TO THE MEMORY OF / SIR GEORGE J. HARDING. K.C.B. / LT GENERAL ROYAL ENGI-NEERS / WHO DEPARTED THIS LIFE / MOST DEEPLY MOURNED / JULY 5 1860. AGED 73.

2nd Lt 1 Oct 1802. 1st Lt 1 Dec 1802. Capt 18 Nov 1807. Bt Major 19 Jul 1821. Lt Colonel 29 Jul 1825. Bt Colonel 28 Jun 1838. Colonel 23 Nov 1841. Major General 11 Nov 1851. Lt General 23 Nov 1858.
   Served in the Peninsula Oct 1810 and Aug 1812 – Apr 1814. Present at Fuengirola, Castalla, Denia and Tarragona. Commanding Engineer with the Prussian Army under Prince Augustus of Prussia 1815 (present at the sieges of Maubeuge, Landrecy, Marienberg, Philippeville and Rocroy). Served with the Army of Occupation until 1818. Also served in Sicily 1812. Colonel Commanding Royal Engineers 10 May 1859. KCB. Lt Governor of Guernsey.
REFERENCE: *Annual Register, 1860, Appx, p. 445.*

HARDING, John
Colonel. Royal Artillery.
Grave: St Luke's Churchyard, Charlton, Kent. (No longer extant: Grave number 219). (M.I.)

"SACRED TO THE MEMORY OF COLONEL JOHN HARDING, OF THE R. A. WHO AFTER HAVING DISTINGUISHED HIMSELF IN SEVERAL ENGAGEMENTS DIED 10 JUNE 1809 IN HIS 49TH YEAR. AN HONOR TO HIS HONORABLE PROFESSION."

2nd Lt 21 Feb 1776. 1st Lt 7 Jul 1779. Capt-Lieut 22 May 1790. Capt 14 Aug 1794. Major 12 Apr 1802. Lt Colonel 29 Apr 1802. Colonel 28 Jun 1808.
   Served in the Peninsula Aug 1808 – Jan 1809 (OC Royal Artillery). Present at Corunna. Gold Medal for Corunna. Also served at Copenhagen 1807.

HARDING, William

Lieutenant. 5th (Northumberland) Regiment of Foot.
Buried in St John the Baptist Churchyard, Pilton, near Barnstaple, Devon. (Burial register)

Ensign 11 Jul 1811. Lt 18 Nov 1813. Capt 13 Mar 1823. Bt Major 14 Nov 1826. Bt Lt Colonel 23 Nov 1841.

    Served in the Peninsula with 1/5th Oct 1812 – Apr 1814. Present in the retreat from Burgos, Vittoria, Pyrenees, Nivelle, Nive, Adour, Orthes, Vic Bigorre, Tarbes and Toulouse. Half pay 14 Nov 1826. When he died at Pilton aged 93 on 13 Jan 1886 he was the tenth of the last remaining Peninsular officers. Magistrate in Devon and author of *History of Tiverton*, 2 vols, 1845–1847. MGS medal for Vittoria, Pyrenees, Nivelle, Nive, Orthes and Toulouse.
REFERENCE: *Annual Register, 1886, Appx, p. 125.*

HARDINGE, Sir Henry

Captain and Lieutenant Colonel. 1st Regiment of Foot Guards.
Memorial tablet: St John the Baptist Church, Penshurst, Kent. (Photograph)

TO THE MEMORY OF / HENRY 1ST VISCOUNT HARDINGE. / THIS TABLET IS ERECTED BY HIS MOURNING / WIDOW AND CHILDREN. HIS PUBLIC SERVICES / ARE THUS RECORDED IN A GENERAL ORDER / ISSUED TO THE ARMY 2 OCT 1856. / THE QUEEN HAS A HIGH AND GRATEFUL SENSE / OF LORD HARDINGE'S VALUABLE AND UNREMITTING / SERVICES AND IN HIS DEATH DEPLORES THE LOSS / OF A TRUE AND DEVOTED FRIEND. / NO SOVEREIGN EVER POSSESSED A MORE HONEST / AND FAITHFUL COUNSELLOR OR A MORE LOYAL / FEARLESS AND DEVOTED SERVANT. / HE RESIGNED THE COMMAND OF THE ARMY / 9 JULY 1856 AND HIS FEW REMAINING / DAYS WERE SPENT AT SOUTH PARK WHERE / SURROUNDED BY HIS FAMILY, HE CLOSED / HIS EARTHLY CAREER IN HUMBLE CONFIDENCE / IN THE ATONING MERITS OF HIS REDEEMER. / HE DREW HIS LAST BREATH SEPTEMBER 23 1856 / IN THE 73RD YEAR OF HIS AGE. / (VERSE)

Low monument on a stepped base: St Peter's Churchyard, Fordcombe, Kent. (Photograph)

HERE RESTS THE BODY OF / FIELD MARSHAL / HENRY FIRST VISCOUNT HARDINGE / WHO LEFT THIS LIFE SEP 24 1856.

Stained glass window: Church of the Ascension, Southam, Gloucestershire. (Bottom centre). (Photograph)

FIELD MARSHAL HENRY HARDINGE GCB DIED 1856

Memorial: Royal Military Chapel, Wellington Barracks, London. (M.I.) (Destroyed by a Flying Bomb in 1944)

"IN MEMORY OF/ FIELD-MARSHAL HENRY VISCOUNT HARDINGE, G.C.B. / DISTINGUISHED IN THE FIELD, FROM 1808 TO 1815, UNDER THE GREAT DUKE OF WELLINGTON. EMINENT FOR / HIS CONDUCT AT THE BATTLE OF ALBUHERA; 1ST OR GRENADIER GUARDS, 1814–27; GOVERNOR- / GENERAL AND COMMANDER-IN-CHIEF IN INDIA, 1844 TO 1848; / COMMANDER-IN-CHIEF OF THE ARMY, 1852 TO 1856. / "MENS AEQUA REBUS IN ARDUIS." / PLACED BY HIS SONS, 1879."

Equestrian statue: Calcutta, India. Inscription not recorded. (Illustration from Art Journal 1859 p 36)

Ensign Queen's Rangers (Upper Canada) 23 Jul 1799. Lt 4th Foot 25 Mar 1802. Capt 57th Foot 7 Apr

1804. Lt Colonel 40th Foot Apr 1814. Capt and Lt Colonel 1st Foot Guards 25 Jul 1814. Colonel 19 Jul 1821. Major General 22 Jul 1830. Lt General 25 Nov 1841. General 28 Sep 1852. Field Marshal 2 Oct 1855. Portuguese Army: Major 13 Apr 1809. Lt Colonel 30 May 1811.

Served in the Peninsula Aug 1808 – Jan 1809 (on Staff as DAQMG) and Portuguese Army Apr 1809 – Apr 1814 (Commanded 5 Portuguese Brigade 22 Dec 1813). Present at Rolica, Vimeiro (wounded), Corunna, Douro, Busaco, first and second sieges of Badajoz, Albuera (Mentioned in Despatches), Ciudad Rodrigo, Badajoz, Salamanca, Vittoria (severely wounded), Pyrenees, Nivelle, Nive (Mentioned in Beresford's Despatches), Orthes (Mentioned in Beresford's Despatches) and Toulouse (Mentioned in Beresford's Despatches). Gold Cross for Busaco, Albuera, Badajoz, Salamanca, Vittoria, Pyrenees, Nivelle, Nive and Orthes. MGS medal for Rolica, Vimeiro, Corunna, Ciudad Rodrigo and Toulouse. KCB. KTS. Present at Waterloo (appointed to liaise with the Prussians). Present at Ligny (wounded, his hand amputated and so did not serve at Waterloo). Wellington presented him with Napoleon's sword. Prussians appointed him Knight of the Third Class of the Red Eagle of Prussia. Also served at Copenhagen 1807.

After the war he entered politics, serving as MP for Durham 1820 and 1826, Newport in Cornwall 1830 and 1831 and for Launceston 1834. Retired from the Army on half pay 27 Apr 1827. Secretary at War in Wellington's premiership 1828 – July 1830. Irish Secretary Jul – Nov 1830 and Dec 1834 – Apr 1835 until his departure for India. Reformed military pensions to reward longer service. Colonel 57th Foot 1843. GCB 1844. Governor General in India 1844 (at first peaceful but the first Anglo Sikh War started in Dec 1845. Served as second in command to Hugh Lord Gough at Moodki, Ferozeshah and Sobraon). Raised to the peerage as Viscount Hardinge of Lahore. Awarded medal and two clasps for the Sutlej campaign. Left India Jan 1848.

After the death of Wellington in 1852 became Commander in Chief of the Army. Started a series of reforms but there was no time left for these to take effect before the Crimean War started. After the war ended in 1856 Hardinge was partly blamed for the failure of the campaign, and when preparing the report for the Queen suffered a stroke and died 24 Sep 1856. Brother of 1st Lt Richard Hardinge Royal Artillery. REFERENCE: *Dictionary of National Biography. United Service Magazine, Oct 1856 pp. 271–8. Gentleman's Magazine, Nov 1856, pp. 646–9. Annual Register, 1856, Appx, pp. 271–4. Hardinge, Charles Stewart, Viscount Hardinge, 1891.*

HARDINGE, Richard
1st Lieutenant. Royal Artillery.
Family Memorial tablet: St Lawrence Church, Bidborough, Kent. (Photograph)

.................../ ALSO OF / MAJOR GENERAL RICHARD HARDINGE, K. H. / ROYAL ARTILLERY, (FATHER OF THE ABOVE) / WHO SERVED IN THE THREE LAST WELLINGTON CAMPAIGNS, / AND WAS ENGAGED AT VITTORIA, ST SEBASTIAN, / ORTHES, TOULOUSE, QUATRE BRAS, AND LIGNY; / DISTINGUISHED ALIKE FOR BRAVERY AND GENTLENESS, / HE DIED JULY 20TH 1864, AGED 74.

2nd Lt 23 May 1806. 1st Lt 19 Dec 1806. 2nd Capt 17 Jul 1823. Capt 6 May 1835. Bt Major 28 Jun 1838. Lt Colonel 5 Apr 1845. Colonel 20 Jun 1854. Major General 26 Oct 1858.

Served in the Peninsula Aug 1812 – Jan 1814 (with Raynsford's 9th Company 8th Battalion) and Jan – Apr 1814 (with R.H.A. 'A' Troop). Present at Osma, Vittoria, Tolosa, first siege of San Sebastian, Bidassoa, Orthes, Tarbes and Toulouse. Present at Waterloo (on staff at Ligny and Quatre Bras). MGS medal for Vittoria, San Sebastian, Orthes and Toulouse. KH. Also served in Canada May 1807 – Jun 1809 (present at Quebec) and West Indies 1822–1825. First Assistant Inspector Royal Carriage Dept May 1828 – Mar 1845. Director of Royal Laboratory 1 Jan 1847 – 31 Mar 1852. Superintendent of the Royal Military Repository 1 Apr 1852 – 31 Mar 1857. Brother of Capt and Lt Colonel Viscount Henry Hardinge 1st Foot Guards.
REFERENCE: *Gentleman's Magazine, Oct 1864, p. 526.*

HARDMAN, Job
Private. 1ˢᵗ (Royal Scots) Regiment of Foot.
Headstone: Preston Cemetery, Lancashire. (Section E, number 48). (Photograph)

SACRED / TO / THE MEMORY OF / JOB HARDMAN / WHO DEPARTED THIS LIFE / JULY 4ᵀᴴ 1858 AGED 75 YEARS / LATE OF THE 1ˢᵀ ROYAL SCOTCH *(SIC)* REGᵀ / HE WAS SEVERELY WOUNDED AT THE / BATTLE OF FLUSHING, AND WAS PRESENT / AT THE DEATH OF SIR JOHN MOORE / AT CORUNNA, JANUARY 16ᵀᴴ 1809.

Pte 5 Oct 1807.
   Served in the Peninsula 1808 – 1809. Present at the retreat and battle of Corunna. MGS medal for Corunna. Also served in the Walcheren expedition 1809 (present at Flushing where he was severely wounded). Discharged 24 Jun 1810.

HARDT, A.
1st Lieutenant. 2ⁿᵈ Nassau Regiment, Dutch Infantry.
Named on the Memorial to Dutch officers killed at Waterloo: St Joseph's Church, Waterloo Belgium. (Photograph)

HARDWICK, William
Captain. 45ᵗʰ (Nottinghamshire) Regiment of Foot.
Ledger stone on base: Abbey Churchyard, Malvern, Worcestershire. (Photograph)

WILLIAM HARDWICK / CAPTAIN LATE 45 REGIMENT / DIED / FEBRUARY 7ᵀᴴ 1859

Ensign 4ᵗʰ Foot 27 Aug 1804. Lt 12 Feb 1805. Capt 45ᵗʰ Foot 1 Mar 1810.
   Served in the Peninsula with 1/4ᵗʰ Aug 1808 – Sep 1809 and 45ᵗʰ Foot Mar 1813 – Apr 1814. Present in the Corunna campaign, Vittoria, Pyrenees, Nivelle, Nive, Orthes, Vic Bigorre and Toulouse. Half pay 26 Nov 1818. MGS medal for Vittoria, Pyrenees, Nivelle, Nive, Orthes and Toulouse.

HARDY, James
Ensign. 31ˢᵗ (Huntingdonshire) Regiment of Foot.
Named on the Memorial: St Andrew's Church, (now Musée Historique), Biarritz, France. (Photograph)

Ensign 20 Feb 1812.
   Served in the Peninsula Jun 1812 – Jan 1814. Present at Nive where he was severely wounded Dec 1813 and died of his wounds 5 Jan 1814.

HARE, John
Captain. 27ᵗʰ (Inniskilling) Regiment of Foot.
Memorial tablet: St James' Church, James Town, St Helena. (Photograph)

SACRED TO THE MEMORY OF / MAJOR GENERAL JOHN HARE, C.B. & K.H. / THIS DISTIN-GUISHED OFFICER / SERVED THROUGHOUT THE WHOLE OF THE / PENINSULAR CAMPAIGN; / HE COMMANDED THE GALLANT CORPS, / THE 27ᵀᴴ INNISKILLING REGIMENT AT THE / BATTLE OF WATERLOO. / IN THE COMMAND OF THAT REGIMENT / HE CONTINUED UNTIL THE YEAR 1837, / WHEN HE WAS APPOINTED LIEUT. GOVERNOR / AND COMMANDER OF THE FORCES / IN THE EASTERN PROVINCE AT THE CAPE OF GOOD HOPE. / AFTER 49 YEARS HONORABLY AND ACTIVELY PASSED / IN THE SERVICE OF HIS COUNTRY, / HE DIED ON THE 10ᵀᴴ OF DECEMBER 1846, / AT THE AGE OF 64 YEARS, / ON HIS PASSAGE TO ENGLAND, / HAVING BEEN COMPELLED TO RESIGN HIS COMMAND / FROM ILLNESS / BROUGHT ON

BY EXTREME FATIGUE AND EXPOSURE / DURING THE KAFIR WAR, / AND WHICH SHORTLY AFTER RESULTED IN HIS DEATH. / HIS REMAINS WERE DEPOSITED IN THIS ISLAND. / THIS TABLET IS ERECTED BY HIS WIDOW, / WHO DEEPLY DEPLORES HIS LOSS.

Ensign Tarbert Fencible Infantry 1799. Ensign 69th Foot 3 Aug 1799. Ensign 27th Foot 29 Oct 1799. Lt 17 May 1800. Capt 9 Sep 1805. Bt Major 17 Jun 1813. Bt Lt Colonel 18 Jun 1815. Bt Colonel 10 Jan 1837.

Served in the Peninsula with 2/27th Dec 1812 – Apr 1814. Present at Biar, Alcoy, Castalla (awarded Bt Majority), Tarragona, Ordal and Barcelona. Present at Waterloo in command of 1/27th (wounded and awarded Bt Lt Colonelcy) and with the Army of Occupation (in command of the regiment until the surrender of Paris when he was appointed one of the Military Commandants in Paris). For many years Governor of the eastern district of Cape of Good Hope (present in the Kaffir Wars). CB and KH. Also served at the Helder 1799 with 69th Foot, Ferrol 1800, Egypt 1801, Maida 1806 and Ischia and Procida 1809. Died on his way home from the Cape and was buried at St Helena.
REFERENCE: *Gentleman's Magazine, Jun 1847, pp. 659–60. Annual Register, 1847, Appx, pp. 216–7.*

HAREN, Baron C. F. S. van
1st Lieutenant and Adjutant. Staff, Dutch Infantry.
Memorial tablet: St Joseph's Church, Waterloo, Belgium. (Photograph)

DEN 18DE JUNY 1815 / SNEUVELDE DE INDE SLAG VAN WATERLOO / CL FC SD BARON VAN HAREN / KAMER JONKER VAN Z: M: / DEN KONING DER NEDERLANDEN / 1TE LEUT: BY DE GENLE STAF & / ADJT VAN DEN GENERAL MAJOR / GRAVE W: VAN BYLANDT. / GEBOOREN DEN 21 JUNY 1793. / ZYN VADER / CL WM BARON VAN HAREN / LEUT: COL: EN CAPT IN DE GARDES / DRAGONDERS DER NEDERLANDEN, / HADINSGELYKS ZYN LEVEN / VOOR ZYN VADERLAND GELATEN / DEN 18DE SEPT 1793 / BY WERWICK OPGERICHT DOOR ZYN GENERAAL

Named on the Memorial to Dutch officers killed at Waterloo: St Joseph's Church, Waterloo Belgium. (Photograph)

Present at Waterloo. Served on the Staff of Major General Count W. van Bijlandt. Son of Baron Willem van Haren, Lt Colonel Commanding the Dutch Dragoons who was killed in Flanders 18 Sep 1793 at Werwick.

HARKNESS, Agnes see RESTON, James

HARMAN, George
Lieutenant. 82nd (Prince of Wales's Volunteers) Regiment of Foot.
Family Memorial tablet: St Mary's Church, Hadley, London. (Photograph)

.... / ALSO IN MEMORY OF / GEORGE, / THIRD SON OF THE ABOVE S. AND ANN HARMAN, / LATE LIEUT IN THE 82ND FOOT; / WHO DIED IN PARIS THE 18TH OF NOVEMBER 1826, / IN HIS 34TH YEAR. / ....

Ensign 9 May 1811. Lt 18 Nov 1813.
Served in the Peninsula Sep 1813 – Apr 1814. Present at Nivelle and Orthes. Also served in North America 1814–1815.

HARRIS, Hon. Charles
Captain. 85th (Buckinghamshire Volunteers) Light Infantry Regiment of Foot.
Memorial tablet: St Michael and All Angels Church, Throwley, Faversham, Kent. (Photograph)

SACRED TO THE MEMORY OF / THE HONOURABLE CHARLES HARRIS THIRD SON OF THE
LORD HARRIS / AND CAPTAIN IN H. M. 85TH REGT OF LIGHT INFANTRY. / AFTER SERVING
TWO TRIUMPHANT CAMPAIGNS IN SPAIN / UNDER THE DUKE OF WELLINGTON, / HE FELL
IN THE MIDST OF THE ENEMY WHEN THE AMERICANS / ATTACKED THE BRITISH LINES
NEAR NEW ORLEANS / ON THE 23RD OF DECEMBER 1814, / AT THE EARLY AGE OF 21 YEARS.
/ AS SOON FAIR FLOWER WHEN EARLY SPRING APPEARS / IT'S BLOSSOM TO THE PARENT /
SUNBEAM REARS / AND GLITTERING LIGHT, AND STRENGTH, DIFFUSES FAR / ITS BALMY
SWEETNESS O'ER THE DESERT AIR, / AROUND THE RUDE STORM ARISE WITH FURIOUS
DUST / AND PROSTRATE ALL ITS BEAUTIES IN THE DUST / DESPITE OF CHILLING PLANTS
AND BEATING RAINS, / THE MEMORY OF ITS FRAGRANCE STILL REMAINS, / SO GALLANT
HARRIS TO HIS LINEAGE TRUE / FROM THE SAME FOUNT HIS LIFE AND VIRTUE DREW, / HIS
GREAT EXAMPLE WAS A FATHER'S NAME, / HIS PROUDEST WISH TO EMULATE HIS FAME. /
FIRED WITH THE HOPE HE CROSS'D THE ATLANTIC WAVE / BUT FOUND AMIDST THE FOG
A SOLDIER'S GRAVE. / HIS GRAVE THOUGH DISTANT ON NEW ORLEANS PLAINS / THE
MEMORY OF HIS VIRTUES THERE REMAINS / THAT GRAVE OF GLORY THERE BRITANNIA
KNEELS, / AND WEEPING POURS THE TENDER GRIEF SHE FEELS. / YES FEELS EXULTING, FOR
HER SOLDIERS BIER / IS STILL THE SHIELD OF EVERY BLESSING HERE. / POINT WHERE HIS
SOUL BY GRAVE DIVINE IS GIVEN / TO MEET HIS SAVIOUR IN THE REALMS OF HEAVEN /
CHECK THEN THAT SIGH, AND DRY THAT PIOUS TEAR, / YE SORROWING PARENTS OF A
CHILD SO DEAR / IN BRITAIN'S CAUSE HE LED THE HEROIC BAND, / AND GRASP'D HER
LAUREL WITH HIS DYING HAND.

Ensign 73rd Foot 11 Jan 1809. Lt 16th Aug 1810. Lt 3rd Dragoons 28 Aug 1811. Capt York Chasseurs 10
Oct 1813. Capt 85th Lt Infantry 23 Jun 1814.
    Served in the Peninsula Jul 1812 – Nov 1813. Present at Vittoria. Also served in North America 1814
(present at New Orleans where he was killed 23 Dec 1814 in a night action on the banks of the Mississippi
aged 21 years). Educated at Eton. Younger brother of Lt Colonel William George Harris 73rd Foot.

HARRIS, John Brenchley
2nd Captain. Royal Engineers.
Named on the Regimental Memorial: Rochester Cathedral, Rochester, Kent. (Photograph)

2nd Lt 7 Oct 1806. Lt 1 Feb 1807. 2nd Capt 10 Jan 1812. Capt 7 Feb 1817. Bt Major 22 Jul 1830.
    Served in the Netherlands and in France with the Army of Occupation 1814–1816. Also served in Sicily
1811–1812. Retired on full pay 5 Nov 1834. Died in London 26 Oct 1835.

HARRIS, Thomas Noel
Captain. 36th (Herefordshire) Regiment of Foot.
Memorial tablet and memorial window: St Laurence's Church, Ramsgate, Kent. (In nave under great west
window). (Photograph)

TO THE GLORY OF GOD / AND IN / MEMORY OF THOMAS NOEL HARRIS, / KNIGHT, K.C.H.,
ETC. / WHO SERVED AND BLED FOR HIS COUNTRY / IN THE GLORIOUS CAMPAIGNS OF THE
PENINSULA, / GERMANY AND FRANCE FROM 1811 TO 1814, / AND AT THE FAMOUS BATTLE
OF WATERLOO, 18TH JUNE 1815.

Low monument: St George's Churchyard, Ham, Kent. (Photograph)

LT COLONEL THOMAS NOEL HARRIS, K. C. H. DIED 23 MAY 1860.

Ensign 87th Foot 5 Feb 1801. Lt 96th Foot 24 Dec1802. Lt 18th Lt Dragoons 4 Apr 1805. Capt 27 Aug 1807. Capt 7th Foot 26 May 1808. Capt 1st Dragoons 15 Dec 1808. Retired 5 Jan 1808 (probably in deference to his father's wishes as his brother had been murdered in Burma). Rejoined Army: Cornet 13th Lt Dragoons 14 Mar 1811. Lt 18th Lt Dragons 15 Aug 1811. Capt York Chasseurs 9 Jun 1814. Capt 36th Foot 2 Jan 1815. Capt 1st Dragoon Guards 8 Sep 1815. Bt Major 14 May 1817. Bt Lt Colonel 13 Feb 1823. Major (unattached) 16 Jul 1830.

Served in the Peninsula May – Aug 1811 and Sep 1811 – Apr 1812 (DAAG May – Jul 1811 and ADC to Major General Charles Stewart Dec 1811 – Apr 1812). Present at Fuentes d'Onoro, Ciudad Rodrigo and Badajoz (wounded). Served in Germany with the Prussian Army 1813 until the surrender of Paris in 1814 (present at Grossbergen, Dennewitz and Leipzig Oct 1813). Sent to London with despatches announcing the Allies entering Paris March 1814. Present at Waterloo (Brigade Major to Major General Sir Hussey Vivian. Severely wounded by a musket ball in his spine, his right arm was amputated and awarded pension of £200 per annum).

MGS medal for Fuentes d'Onoro, Ciudad Rodrigo and Badajoz. KCH. Royal Prussian Order of Military Merit, Imperial Order of St Anne and St Wladimir of Russia. Also served in Canada 1830 (DAG) but had to return as his wounds from Waterloo were aggravated by the climate. The musket ball remained near his spine until he died. Retired on half pay 16 Jul 1830. Chief Magistrate at Gibraltar. Died 23 Mar 1860 at Updown, Eastry, Kent. Cousin of Lt John Clement Wallington 10th Hussars.
REFERENCE: *Annual Register, 1860, Appx, p. 445.*

HARRIS, William George (2nd Lord Harris)
Lieutenant Colonel. 73rd (Highland) Regiment of Foot.
Family Memorial tablet: St Michael and All Angels Church, Throwley, Faversham, Kent. (Photograph)

SACRED / TO THE / MEMORY / OF WILLIAM GEORGE / SECOND / LORD HARRIS, / K.C.H. AND C.B. / LIEUTENANT GENERAL / AND COLONEL OF THE / 73RD REGT ; / BORN 17TH JANUARY 1782, / DIED AT BELMONT / 30TH MAY 1845. / HE SERVED HIS COUNTRY / IN EVERY QUARTER / OF THE GLOBE / FOR 47 YEARS / AND WAS ENGAGED / AMONGST OTHERS / IN THE ACTIONS / OF / SERINGAPATAM, / COPENHAGEN, / CAPE OF GOOD HOPE, / AND / WATERLOO. / ....

Stained glass window: St Michael and All Angels Church, Throwley, Faversham, Kent. (Photograph)

MY PRINCE AND MY COUNTRY / GENERAL / THE LORD / HARRIS

Ensign 76th Ft 24 May 1795. Lt 36th Ft 3 Jan 1796. Lt 74th Ft 4 Sep 1796. Capt 49th Ft 16 Oct 1800. Major 73rd Ft 15 Jun 1804. Lt Colonel 29 Dec 1806. Bt Colonel 4 Jun 1814. Major General 19 Jul 1821. Lt General 10 Jan 1837.

Present at Quatre Bras and Waterloo in command of the 73rd Regiment (only 50 left unwounded out of 600 men). Harris led by example and encouraged his men when he himself was severely wounded. CB for Waterloo. Also served in India 1797–1799 under the command of his father George 1st Lord Harris. Present at Malavelly and Seringapatam (one of the first to enter the breach and sent home with the captured standards of Tippoo Sultan), Copenhagen 1801 (on board in Lord Nelson's fleet), Canada 1802, Cape of Good Hope 1806, Sweden 1813 (present at Stralsund), Hanover 1813 (present at Ghorde) and Netherlands 1814 (Under Lord Lynedoch. Took command of operations at Merxem and Antwerp). Retired 1817. Colonel 73rd Foot 4 Dec 1835. KCH. Elder brother of Capt Hon. Charles Harris 85th Foot.
REFERENCE: *Dictionary of National Biography. Royal Military Calendar, Vol 4, p. 162. Gentleman's Magazine, Jul 1845, pp. 76–8. Annual Register, 1845, Appx, pp. 279–80. Lagden, Alan and John Sly, The 2/73rd at Waterloo, 2nd edition 1998, pp. 87–92.*

HARRISON, Charles
Captain. 53rd (Shropshire) Regiment of Foot.
Memorial tablet: St Luke's Church, Holmes Chapel, Cheshire. (Photograph)

HARRISON / .... / ALSO CHARLES / FORMERLY MAJOR 53rd REGT DIED / AT GRES-
FORD NORTH WALES 2ND JULY 1856 / AGED 64 YEARS.

Lt 3 Apr 1805. Capt 20 Jan 1814. Major 5 Jul 1821.
    Served in the Peninsula Apr 1809 – Aug 1811 and Mar – Apr 1814. Present at Busaco. Half pay 11
May 1826. MGS medal for Busaco.

HARRISON, John
Assistant Surgeon. 1st Regiment of Foot Guards.
Memorial: Royal Military Chapel, Wellington Barracks, London. (M.I.) (Destroyed by a Flying Bomb in
1944)

"SURGEON-MAJOR JOHN HARRISON, / GRENADIER GUARDS, 1809–40. "WALCHEREN,"
"PENINSULA," "HOLLAND," "NETHERLANDS," / "FRANCE," "WATERLOO." / D.D. SURGEON
C. E. HARRISON, GRENADIER GUARDS."

Hospital Mate Dec 1808. Asst Surgeon 1st Foot Guards 29 Jun 1809. Surgeon 29 Apr 1824. Surgeon Major
17 Mar 1837.
    Served in the Peninsula with 3rd Battalion 1st Foot Guards Apr – Aug 1811 and Feb 1812 – Jul 1813.
Present at Cadiz and Seville. Present at Quatre Bras, Waterloo and siege of Peronne. Also served at
Walcheren 1809 and Netherlands 1814–1815 (present at Antwerp and Bergen-op-Zoom). Retired on half
pay 17 Apr 1840. Died in London 21 Mar 1873.
REFERENCE: *Household Brigade Journal, 1873, pp. 322–3.*

HARRISON, John
Sergeant Major. 18th Regiment of Light Dragoons.
Low monument: Dean Cemetery, Edinburgh, Scotland. (Section F. No 643). (Photograph)

TO THE MEMORY OF / JOHN HARRISON MAJOR IN HER MAJESTY'S SERVICE / BORN AT
LEICESTER 22ND JUNE 1790, DIED AT EDINBURGH 5TH DECEMBER 1875. / HE SERVED WITH
DISTINGUISHED GALLANTRY IN THE PENINSULAR AND INDIA / WITH THE 18TH HUSSARS
AND 4TH LIGHT DRAGOONS, / AND IN 1845 WAS APPOINTED / ADJUTANT / OF THE ROYAL
MIDLOTHIAN REGIMENT OF YEOMANRY CAVALRY. / THE OFFICERS OF WHICH HAVE
WITH CONSENT / OF THE SURVIVORS OF HIS FAMILY PLACED THIS MEMORIAL OVER HIS
REMAINS / IN TESTIMONY OF HIS EFFICIENT PERFORMANCE OF HIS DUTIES, / & OF THE
ESTEEM AND REGARD IN WHICH HE WAS HELD / BY ALL CONNECTED WITH THE REGI-
MENT DURING HIS / 25 YEARS OF SERVICE IN IT.

Pte 18th Lt Dragoons 1800. Promoted from the ranks: Cornet and Adjt 4th Lt. Dragoons 25 Jun 1824. Lt
82nd Foot 13 Aug 1825. Capt 27 Oct 1835.
    Served in the Peninsula with 18th Lt Dragoons Jan 1813 – Apr 1814. Present at Morales, Vittoria,
Pyrenees, Nivelle, Nive, Orthes and Toulouse. Also served in India. Half pay 25 Oct 1842. Adjutant Royal
Midlothian Yeomanry Cavalry 1845. On retirement was given the honorary rank of Major. MGS medal
for Vittoria, Nivelle, Nive, Orthes and Toulouse.
REFERENCE: *Annual Register, 1875, Appx, p. 154.*

HART, Henry
Assistant Surgeon. 5th Garrison Battalion.
Headstone: Kensal Green Cemetery, London. Inscription illegible. (12077/41/3). (Photograph)

Hospital Assistant 4 Dec 1809. Asst Surgeon 16th Foot 31 Jan 1811. Asst Surgeon 5th Garrison Battalion 14 Oct 1813. Asst Surgeon 13th Lt Dragoons 30 Oct 1816. Surgeon 31st Foot 21 Sep 1830. Staff Surgeon 1st Class 16 Mar 1849.
    Served in the Peninsula 1810–1811. Present at Coa, Busaco, Pombal, Redinha and Casal Nova. MGS medal for Busaco. Also served in the Afghan War of 1842 with the Army sent to avenge the massacre of Jan 1842 (present at Kabul). MD Aberdeen 1822. Died 1854.

HART, James
Lieutenant. 33rd (1st Yorkshire West Riding) Regiment of Foot.
Headstone: St Mary the Virgin Churchyard, Dover, Kent. (Photograph)

IN / MEMORY OF / LIEUTᵀ. CHARLES HART / 5TH ROYAL VETERANS, / WHO DIED ON THE 6TH OF JANY 1836, / AGED 86 YEARS. / AND OF / LIEUTᵀ JAMES HART / 33RD REGIMENT / WHO WAS KILLED AT THE / BATTLE OF WATERLOO, / AGED 23 YEARS. / ....

Named on the Regimental Memorial: St Joseph's Church, Waterloo Belgium. (Photograph)

Ensign 10 Aug 1809. Lt 25 Apr 1811.
    Present at Waterloo where he was killed. Also served in the Netherlands 1814–1815.

HARTLEY, William
Captain. 62nd (Wiltshire) Regiment of Foot.
Ledger stone: West Hill Cemetery, Winchester, Hampshire. (Photograph)

IN MEMORY OF / MAJOR HARTLEY, / WHO DEPARTED THIS LIFE ON / THE 18TH MAY OF JULY 1854.

2nd Lt 23rd Foot 15 Feb 1800. 1st Lt 5th Apr 1801. Lt 71st Foot 26 Aug 1804. Capt 62nd Foot 22 Dec 1808.
    Served in the Peninsula Aug – Dec 1808 and Oct 1813 – Apr 1814. Present at Rolica, Vimeiro, (wounded), Nivelle, Nive and Bayonne. Served in France with the Army of Occupation 1815. Also served in Egypt 1801. MGS medal for Egypt, Rolica, Vimeiro, Nivelle and Nive. Barrack Master at Waterford Oct 1836 and later at Winchester with honorary rank of Major.

HARVEY, Edward
Lieutenant and Captain. Coldstream Regiment of Foot Guards.
Memorial tablet: St Andrew's Church, Hempstead, Essex. (Photograph)

SACRED TO THE MEMORY OF / CAPTAIN EDWARD HARVEY / OF THE COLDSTREAM GUARDS, / ELDEST SON OF ADMIRAL HARVEY, / WHO FELL HONOURABLY IN THE LINES OF BURGOS / OCTOBER 18th 1812 AGED 22 YEARS. / LAMENTED BY HIS FRIENDS / AND RESPECTED BY ALL WHO KNEW HIM.

Named on Memorial Panel VII for Burgos: Royal Military Chapel, Wellington Barracks, London. (M.I.) (Destroyed by a Flying Bomb 1944)

Ensign 24 May 1804. Lt and Capt 17 Aug 1809.
    Served in the Peninsula Jun 1809 – Oct 1812. Present at Talavera, Busaco, Fuentes d'Onoro (wounded),

Ciudad Rodrigo, Salamanca and Burgos where he was killed at the siege of Burgos 18 Oct 1812. Son of Admiral Harvey who commanded the *Temeraire* at Trafalgar.

HARVEY, Robert John
Major. Staff Appointment in Spain and Portugal.
Memorial tablet: St Mary's Church, Tharston, Norfolk. (Photograph)

TO THE MEMORY OF / GENERAL SIR ROBERT JOHN HARVEY, / KNIGHT COMMANDER OF SAINT BENTO D' AVES, / KNIGHT COMPANION OF THE BATH, / KNIGHT COMPANION OF THE TOWER AND SWORD. / GENERAL HARVEY WAS PRESENT AT NINE BATTLES / OPORTO, BUSACO, SALAMANCA, VITTORIA, THE PYRENEES, / THE NIVE, THE NIVELLE, ORTHES, AND TOULOUSE, / AND AT THE FOUR SIEGES / OF CIUDAD RODRIGO, BADAJOS, BURGOS, AND ST SEBASTIAN, / AND ENGAGED IN SEVERAL MINOR ACTIONS WITH THE ENEMY / IN PORTUGAL, SPAIN, AND FRANCE, DURING SIX CAMPAIGNS. / WHILST ON THE STAFF OF THE ARMY / AS ASSISTANT QUARTER MASTER GENERAL / HE WAS EMPLOYED IN VARIOUS IMPORTANT SERVICES, / AND DURING THE LAST THREE YEARS OF THE WAR, / WAS THE ORGAN OF COMMUNICATION BETWEEN / FIELD MARSHAL THE DUKE OF WELLINGTON, / AS COMMANDER IN CHIEF OF THE ARMY / AND THE PORTUGUESE TROOPS IN THE FIELD, / RECEIVING ORDERS DAILY AND DIRECTLY FROM HIM, / BEING NEAR HIS GRACE'S PERSON IN ALL THE OPERATIONS / AND ENGAGEMENTS WITH THE ENEMY, / IN THE YEARS 1811, 1812, 1813, 1814. / HE DIED 18 JUNE 1860 AGED 73 YEARS. / AND AT THE TIME OF HIS DEATH WAS COLONEL OF / THE 2ND WEST INDIA REGIMENT / TO WHICH HE WAS APPOINTED BY HER MAJESTY IN 1849. / THIS MONUMENT IS ERECTED BY HIS WIDOW / CHARLOTTE MARY HARVEY / IN GRATEFUL AND AFFECTIONATE REMEMBRANCE.

Ensign 53rd Foot 8 Oct 1803. Lt 60th Foot 24 Mar 1804. Lt 4th Dragoons 14 Sep 1804. Capt 53rd Foot 2 Jan 1806. Bt Major 23 Jan 1810. Bt Lt Colonel 14 Apr 1812. Bt Colonel 22 Jul 1830. Major General 23 Nov 1841. Lt General 11 Nov 1851. General 17 Jul 1859. Portuguese Army: Bt Major 25 Jul 1811. Bt Lt Colonel 21 Jun 1813.

Served in the Peninsula Apr – Jun 1809 (AQMG) and with Portuguese Army Jun 1809 – Apr 1814 (AQMG). Present at Douro, Busaco, second siege of Badajoz, Ciudad Rodrigo, Badajoz (wounded and Mentioned in Beresford's Despatches), Salamanca, Burgos, Vittoria, Pyrenees (wounded), Nivelle, Nive, Orthes (Mentioned in Beresford's Despatches) and Toulouse (Mentioned in Beresford's Despatches). Gold Medal for Orthes. MGS medal for Busaco, Ciudad Rodrigo, Badajoz, Salamanca, Vittoria, Pyrenees, Nivelle, Nive and Toulouse. Employed in obtaining intelligence of the enemy for the advancing troops and organised nine Portuguese guerrilla bands 1809 – 1811. Was the link between the Portuguese troops and the Duke of Wellington 1811–1814. KTS and Knight Commander of St Bento d'Avis. Knighted 1817. CB 1831. Retired on half pay 25 Oct 1815.

Returned to his estates at Tharston in Norfolk and began to reorganise the land and property on military lines. His properties in Tharston, Forncett and Stoke Holy Cross were renamed after the battles that he had taken part in. Also introduced gas lighting to the area. Norwich became one of the first cities in England to benefit from this. Member of the Royal Society and Society of Antiquaries. Founding member of the United Service Club in London. Colonel 2nd West India Regt 15 Jun 1848.
REFERENCE: *Gentleman's Magazine, Aug 1860, pp. 190–3. Annual Register, 1860, Appx, p. 446. Obit. Norfolk News and Norfolk Mercury, 23 Jun 1860. Christie Medal Catalogue, Apr 1992, pp. 37–8.*

HARVEY, William Maundy
Lieutenant Colonel. 79th (Cameron Highlanders) Regiment of Foot
Family Memorial tablet: St Peter's Church, Sandwich, Kent. (Photograph)

.... / ALSO TO THE MEMORY OF THE ABOVE WILL^{M} MAUNDY HARVEY ESQ / LIEU^{T}

COLONEL OF THE 79TH REGIMENT OF FOOT. COLONEL IN THE / BRITISH ARMY. BRIGADIER GENERAL IN THE PORTUGUESE SERVICE / AND A KNIGHT COMMANDER OF THE PORTUGUESE ORDER OF THE / TOWER AND SWORD. HE DIED AT SEA ON HIS PASSAGE HOME FROM / LISBON ON THE 10TH JUNE 1813 AGED 38 YEARS, AND WAS / BURIED IN THE ATLANTIC OCEAN LAT 44:37. LONG 9:42.

Ensign Royal Marines 4 Feb 1794. Lt 24 Apr 1795. Capt 1st West India Regt 22 Jul 1797. Major 6 Jun 1805. Major 79th Foot 27 Feb 1806. Lt Colonel 2/79th Foot 30 May 1811. Bt Colonel 1 Jan 1812. Lt Colonel 1/79th 3 Dec 1812. Portuguese Army: Colonel 6th Line 26 Aug 1809. Brigadier 12 Jan 1810.

Served in the Peninsula with 79th Foot Aug 1808 – Jan 1809 and with Portuguese Army Aug 1809 – Jun 1813 (Commanded Portuguese Brigade Jun 1810 – Apr 1812). Present at Corunna, Sobral (wounded), Albuera (Mentioned in Beresford's Despatches) and Badajoz (severely wounded and Mentioned in Beresford's Despatches). Gold Medal for Albuera and Badajoz. KTS. Also served at Copenhagen 1807 and Sweden 1808. Died 10 Jul 1813 on board ship returning to England to recover from his wounds.

HASELFOOT, William Henry
Captain. 3rd (East Kent) Regiment of Foot.
Memorial tablet: St Andrews Church, Boreham, Essex. (Photograph)

SACRED TO THE MEMORY OF / CAPT. WILLIAM HENRY HASELFOOT / WHO DEPARTED THIS LIFE THE 15TH JULY 1850 / IN THE 73RD YEAR OF HIS AGE / IMPRISONED IN PARIS IN 1802 / HE WAS UNDER / THE ARBITRARY RULE OF NAPOLEON AGAINST / BRITISH SUBJECTS DETAINED AS A PRISONER OF / WAR. AFTER NINE YEARS CAPTIVITY HAVING / SUCCEEDED IN ESCAPING TO ENGLAND HE JOINED / THE WEST ESSEX MILITIA FROM WHICH HE / VOLUNTEERED INTO THE 3RD FOOT THEN ON / SERVICE IN FRANCE. AT THE CONCLUSION OF / HOSTILITIES IN THAT COUNTRY HE WAS SENT / TO CANADA AND AFTER SOME SEVERE SERVICE / IN NORTH AMERICA TOOK PART IN THE BATTLE / OF PLATTSBURGH. THE REMAINING PART OF HIS / LIFE WAS SPENT IN THIS HIS NATIVE PARISH. / HIS INTEGRITY AND SIMPLICITY OF CHARACTER / NEED NO LABOURED EPITAPH. HIS VIRTUES / ARE WRITTEN IN THE HEARTS OF THEM WHO / ENJOYED HIS FRIENDSHIP OR EXPERIENCED / HIS BENEVOLENCE.

West Essex Militia 1811. Volunteer 3rd Foot 1811. Capt 3rd Foot 25 Dec 1813.

Served in the Peninsula 1813 – Apr 1814. Present at Vittoria, Pyrenees, Nivelle, Nive, Garris, Orthes, Aire and Toulouse. Also served in North America 1814 (present at Plattsburgh). Imprisoned in Paris in 1802 at the age of 25. He escaped in 1811 and joined the West Essex Militia. He then volunteered for a line regiment and joined the 3rd Foot and went to the Peninsula. Half pay 25 Aug 1814.

HATTRELL, Daniel
Private. 3rd Regiment of Foot Guards.
Headstone: St Mary and St Andrew Churchyard, Fletching, Sussex. (Photograph)

DANIEL HATTRELL / HE SERVED AT WATERLOO / 1815. / HE DIED IN / FLETCHING / DEC 16TH 1874, / AGED 81 YEARS.

New ledger stone: St Mary and St Andrew Churchyard, Fletching, Sussex. (Photograph)

DANIEL HATTRELL / DIED IN FLETCHING / 16 DECEMBER 1874 / AGED 81 YEARS / HE SERVED AT WATERLOO / 18 JUNE 1815. / DUE TO THE SEVERE / DETERIORATION OF THE / ORIGINAL GRAVESTONE / IT WAS MOVED INTO / THE SAFETY OF THE CHURCH / ON 15 JUNE 2007

Pte 25 Sep 1813.
Present at Waterloo and with the Army of Occupation. Discharged 31 May 1826. Subsequently followed the trade of shoemaker.

HAVELOCK, William
Lieutenant. 43rd (Monmouthshire) Light Infantry Regiment of Foot.
Memorial tablet: All Saints Church, Maidstone, Kent. (Photograph)

SACRED / TO THE MEMORY OF / LT COLONEL WILLIAM HAVELOCK, KH. / HE SERVED IN PORTUGAL, SPAIN, AND FRANCE / AT QUATRE BRAS (WHERE HE WAS WOUNDED), / AND AT WATERLOO. / HE FELL AT THE HEAD OF HIS REGIMENT / CHARGING THE SIKHS, / AT RAMNUGGAR ON THE CHENAB, / ON THE 22ND OF NOVEMBER 1848, / AGED 56 YEARS. / .... / THE OFFICERS OF THE 14TH (KING'S) LIGHT DRAGOONS / ERECTED THIS MONUMENT / TO THEIR COMRADES / WHO FELL IN THE CAMPAIGN OF THE PUNJAB. / (VERSE)

Tombstone: Summer residence, Barahdari Garden, Ramnagar, India. (M.I.)

"SACRED / TO THE MEMORY OF / WILLIAM HAVELOCK LT. COL. H.M. 14TH LT DRAGOONS / WHO FELL NOBLY ON THE FIELD OF RAMNUGGAR / NEAR THIS SPOT AT THE HEAD OF HIS GALLANT / REGT ON THE 22ND NOV 1848. BORN 1793 / ENTERED THE ARMY 1808 AND JOINED THE / PENINSULAR ARMY, CAME TO INDIA IN 1824 / AND SERVED TILL HIS DEATH. REGARDED / THROUGHOUT INDIA FOR ALL THAT IS MANLY, / GALLANT AND BECOMING IN THE GENTLEMAN / AND SOLDIER AND IN THE WORDS OF HIS / BROTHER 'THE BEST AND BRAVEST OF / ENGLAND'S CHIVALRY NEED NOT DISDAIN TO / MAKE A PILGRIMAGE TO THIS SPOT' "

Named on the Regimental Memorial: Barahdari, Ramnagar, India. (Recently restored). (Photograph)

IN MEMORY / OF THOSE WHO FELL IN THE CAVALRY ACTION NEAR THIS PLACE / ON THE / 2ND NOVEMBER 1848. 16 KILLED 64 WOUNDED & 10 MISSING / OFFICERS KILLED / BRIGADIER GENERAL C. R. CURETON CB. COMMANDING THE CAVALRY DIVISION / LT. COL W. HAVELOCK KH. 14TH LIGHT DRAGOONS / SUBADAR MAJOR MIR SHER ALI SIRDAR BAHADAR / 88TH LIGHT CAVALRY (AGED 78) / DIED OF WOUNDS / CAPT. J. F. FITZGERALD, 14TH LIGHT DRAGOONS / DIED 26TH NOVEMBER 1848 / THIS SITE WAS RESTORED WITH SUPPORT FROM BACSA, THE KING'S ROYAL HUSSARS, / AND EX-MEMBERS OF 14TH / 20TH KING'S HUSSARS, 2000.

Memorial tablet: Charterhouse, London. (M.I.)

LIEUTENANT COLONEL / WILLIAM HAVELOCK KH / FELL AT THE HEAD OF HIS REGIMENT / THE 14TH LIGHT DRAGOONS IN / CHARGING THE SIKHS AT / RAMNUGGAR NOV 22ND 1848 / FROM 1810 TO 1814 HE / SERVED IN THE PENINSULA / AND IN 1815 IN THE NETHERLANDS / AND WAS WOUNDED AT QUATRE BRAS / HE WAS SIR HENRY HAVELOCK'S / ELDER BROTHER / BORN JANY 21ST 1793

Ensign 12 Jul 1810. Lt May 12 1812. Capt 32nd Foot 19 Feb 1818. Capt 4th Lt Dragoons 19 Jul 1821. Major 31 Dec 1830. Lt Colonel 14th Lt Dragoons 30 Apr 1841.
    Served in the Peninsula with 1/43rd Jul 1810 – Dec 1811 and Apr 1812 – Apr 1814 (on staff as ADC to Major General Charles Alten). Present at Coa (carried the colours for the 43rd Foot at the age of 15), Busaco, Pombal, Redinha, Casal Nova, Foz d'Arouce, Sabugal, Salamanca, San Munos, Vittoria, Bidassoa, Heights of Vera (where he earned the name of 'El Chico Blanco' from the Spaniards by his daring exploits), Nivelle, Nive, Tarbes and Toulouse. Present at Quatre Bras (wounded) and Waterloo (ADC to Lt General

Charles Alten). Served with the Army of Occupation 1815–1817. MGS medal for Busaco, Salamanca, Vittoria, Nivelle, Nive and Toulouse

Also served in India with 4th Lt Dragoons 1822. ADC to Sir Charles Colville, Commander in Chief Bombay 1824. KH. Later appointed Military Secretary to Lord Elphinstone, Governor of Madras. Lt Colonel commanding 14th Lt Dragoons 1845–1848. At the outbreak of the second Sikh War in 1848 commanded the 14th Lt Dragoons at the Battle of Ramnuggar 22 Nov 1848. He charged at the head of his 450 men against the Sikh Army of 15,000, although General Cureton tried to stop him and was killed by the heavy cannon fire. Elder brother of Sir Henry Havelock.

REFERENCE: *Dictionary of National Biography. Gentleman's Magazine, Mar 1849, pp. 318–9. Annual Register, 1848, Appx, pp. 265–6. Oxfordshire Light Infantry Chronicle, 1895, pp. 156–8.*

HAVERFIELD, John

Lieutenant Colonel. Staff – Assistant Quartermaster General to the Forces.
Memorial tablet: St Anne's Church, Kew Green, London. (North aisle). (M.I.)

"SACRED TO THE MEMORY OF / JOHN HAVERFIELD ESQR / OF HIS MAJESTY'S JUSTICES OF THE PEACE / FOR THE COUNTY OF SURREY / LATE LIEUTENANT COLONEL IN THE ARMY / AND ASSISTANT QUARTERMASTER GENL TO THE FORCES / WHO AFTER A LIFE PASSED IN THE ACTIVE DISCHARGE / OF HIS PUBLIC DUTIES / AND THE EXERCISE OF EVERY CHRISTIAN / AND DOMESTIC VIRTUE / DIED / WITH A PERFECT BUT HUMBLE CONFIDENCE / IN THE MERITS Of HIS REDEEMER / ON WEDNESDAY SEPTEMBER THE 1ST 1830 / AGED 50 YEARS / ...."

Ensign 32nd Foot 27 Feb 1799. Lt 10 Jul 1800. Adjutant 27 Jun 1801. Capt 43rd Foot 15 Aug 1804. Capt 48th Foot 6 Aug 1807. Bt Major and Permanent AQMG 6 Sep 1810. Bt Lt Colonel 7 Jan 1814.

Served in the Peninsula May – Dec 1809 (on Staff as AQMG). Present at Douro and Talavera. Later continued with the same Staff appointment in England. Retired 1826.

HAVERFIELD, William

Major. 43rd (Monmouthshire) Light Infantry Regiment of Foot.
Chest tomb: St Thomas à Becket Churchyard, Widcombe, Bath, Somerset. (Photograph)

SACRED TO THE MEMORY OF / WILLIAM HAVERFIELD / LATE LIEU. COLL OF HIS MAJESTY'S 43RD REG / OF LIGHT INFANTRY / ELDEST SON OF / THE REVD WILLIAM HAVERFIELD / AND ELIZABETH HIS WIFE / WHO DEPARTED THIS LIFE 1ST JUNE 1830 / AGED 42.

Ensign 25 Jul 1805. Lt 3 Apr 1806. Capt 31 Mar 1808. Major 11 Aug 1814. Lt Col 29 Aug 1822.

Served in the Peninsula with 2/43rd Aug 1808 – Jan 1809 and 1/43rd Dec 1810 – Dec 1811, Jun – Nov 1812 and Apr 1813 – Apr 1814. Present at Vimeiro (wounded), Corunna, Casal Nova, Sabugal, Salamanca (wounded), Vittoria, Pyrenees, Bidassoa, Nivelle, Nive, Tarbes and Toulouse. Also served at Copenhagen 1807 and Walcheren 1809.

HAWES, Thomas

Private. 32nd (Cornwall) Regiment of Foot.
Headstone: St Mary's Churchyard, West Winch, King's Lynn, Norfolk. Seriously eroded. Inscription largely illegible. (Photograph)

AFFECTIONATE / REMEMBRANCE. / THOMAS HAWES. / .... / DIED AT WEST WINCH. 4 APR 1869 AGED 83 YEARS. FOUGHT AT WATERLOO.

Served at Waterloo in Capt Charles Hames's Company.

HAWKER, James
Lieutenant Colonel. Royal Artillery.
Gravestone: St Nicholas Churchyard and named on the Regimental Memorial: St Nicholas Church, Plumstead, Kent. (No longer extant. Destroyed by a flying bomb in the Second World War)

2nd Lt 18 Sep 1793. 1st Lt 1 Jan 1794. Capt/Lieut 16 Jul 1799. Capt 12 Sep 1803. Bt Major 4 Jun 1811. Major 20 Dec 1814. Lt Colonel 16 May 1815. Colonel 29 Jul 1825.
    Served in the Peninsula Oct 1810 – Mar 1812. Present at the first siege of Badajoz, Albuera (wounded) and second siege of Badajoz. Gold Medal for Albuera. CB. Present at Waterloo. Also served in South America 1807 (present at Buenos Ayres). Lt Governor of Tilbury Fort. Retired 26 Jun 1823. Died at Woolwich 12 Oct 1827.

HAWKER, Peter
Captain. 14th (Duchess of York's Own) Regiment of Light Dragoons.
Interred in Catacomb B (v200 c15&16) Kensal Green Cemetery, London. Originally buried at Marylebone Church, London.

Cornet 1st Dragoons 29 Jan 1801. Lt 21 Jan 1802. Lt 14th Lt Dragoons 5 May 1803. Capt 4 Aug 1804. Major North Hampshire Militia 1815. Lt Colonel 1821.
    Served in the Peninsula Dec 1808 – Apr 1810. Present at Douro (wounded) and Talavera (severely wounded). Retired from active service in 1813 owing to his wounds from Talavera. An accomplished musician and sportsman. Publications include *Instructions to Young Sportsmen in all that relates to Guns and Shooting*, 1814. (By 1859 it had run into 11 editions), *Abridgement of the New Game Laws, with Observations and Suggestions for their Improvement*. Deputy Lieutenant for Hampshire 1830. Died 7 Aug 1853.
    REFERENCE: *Dictionary of National Biography. Hawker, Peter, Journal of a Regimental officer during the recent campaign in Portugal and Spain under Lord Viscount Wellington, 1810, reprint, 1981. Sumner, Percy, Captain Peter Hawker, 14th Lt Dragoons, 1812, Journal of the Society for Army Historical Research, Vol 25, No 101, Spring 1947, pp. 1–2. (Portrait and uniform). Gentleman's Magazine, Sep 1853, pp. 313–4. Annual Register, 1853, Appx, p. 240.*

HAWKER, Samuel
Lieutenant Colonel. 14th (Duchess of York's Own) Regiment of Light Dragoons.
Interred in Catacomb A (v52 c15) Kensal Green Cemetery, London.

Cornet 16th Lt Dragoons May 1779. Lt 1781. Capt-Lt 6 Jul 1792. Capt 26 May 1795. Major 6 Apr 1797. Lt Colonel 14th Lt Dragoons 12 Jun 1801. Bt Colonel 25 Apr 1808. Major General 4 Jun 1811. Lt General 19 Jul 1821.
    Served in the Peninsula Dec 1808 – Jun 1811. Present at Grijon, Oporto, Salamonde, Douro, Talavera (wounded), Busaco, Sobral, Pombal, Redinha, Casal Nova and Foz d'Arouce. After Talavera appointed second in command of Cavalry (head of a Brigade of 1st Royal Dragoons, 14th Lt Dragoons, Troop of Horse Artillery and 16th Lt Dragoons). Gold Medal for Talavera. GCB. Also served in Flanders 1793 – 1796 (present at Valenciennes, Tournai, Famars, Dunkirk and Boxtel). Colonel 3rd Dragoon Guards 22 Apr 1831. Died 27 Dec 1838.
    REFERENCE: *Royal Military Calendar, Vol 3, pp. 187–90. Gentleman's Magazine, Mar 1839, pp. 315–6.*

HAWKINS, Henry
Lieutenant and Captain. 3rd Regiment of Foot Guards.
Interred in Catacomb B (v162 c13) Kensal Green Cemetery, London.

Ensign 25 Jul 1806. Lt and Capt 12 Dec 1811. Capt and Lt Colonel 22 Jul 1830.

Served in the Peninsula Nov 1809 – Mar 1812. Present at Busaco and Ciudad Rodrigo. Present at Waterloo. MGS medal for Busaco and Ciudad Rodrigo. Half pay 1830. Died 1861.

HAWKINS, John Pauncefoot
Major. 68th (Durham) Regiment of Foot.
Chest tomb in railed enclosure and Family Memorial window: St Peter's Churchyard, Minsterworth, Gloucestershire. Inscriptions not recorded. (Photographs)

Lt 70th Foot 21 Apr 1802. Capt 24 Aug 1804. Capt 68th Foot 5 Jul 1806. Major 17 Sep 1812. Bt Lt Colonel 21 Jun 1813.
    Served in the Peninsula Jun 1811 – Dec 1813. Present at the siege of Salamanca Forts, Moriscos (wounded), Vittoria, Pyrenees, San Marcial (Mentioned in Despatches) and Nivelle (Mentioned in Despatches). Gold Medal for Vittoria, Pyrenees and Nivelle (in command of the 68th Foot). CB. Also served at Walcheren 1809. Died 5 Feb 1858 aged 74.

HAY, Alexander
Cornet. 16th (Queen's) Regiment of Light Dragoons.
Memorial tablet: St Joseph's Church, Waterloo, Belgium. (Photograph)

SACRED / TO THE MEMORY OF / ALEXANDER HAY ESQUIRE OF NUNRAW, / CORNET IN THE 16TH LIGHT DRAGOONS, AGED 18 YEARS, / WHO FELL GLORIOUSLY IN THE MEMORABLE BATTLE OF / WATERLOO JUNE 18TH 1815. / O DOLOR, ATQUE DECUS MAGNUM! / HAEC LE PRIMA DIES BELLO DEDIT, HAEC EADEM AUFERT! / THIS TABLET WAS PLACED HERE BY HIS / BROTHERS AND SISTERS.

Cornet 11 Nov 1813.
    Present at Waterloo where he was killed in the pursuit of the French on the evening of 18 June.

HAY, Andrew
Lieutenant Colonel. 1st (Royal Scots) Regiment of Foot.
Statue: St Paul's Cathedral, London. (North transept). (Photograph)

ERECTED AT THE PUBLIC EXPENSE TO THE MEMORY OF / MAJOR GENERAL ANDREW HAY, / HE WAS BORN IN THE COUNTY OF BANFF IN SCOTLAND, / AND FELL ON THE 14th APRIL 1814, / BEFORE THE FORTRESS OF BAYONNE IN FRANCE, / IN THE 52nd YEAR OF HIS AGE AND THE 34th OF HIS SERVICES, / CLOSING A MILITARY LIFE MARKED BY / ZEAL, PROMPT DECISION, AND SIGNAL INTREPIDITY.

Memorial tablet: St Mary's Church, Fordingbridge, Hampshire. (Photograph)

SACRED / TO THE MEMORY OF / MAJOR GENERAL ANDREW HAY, / OF MOUNTBLAIRIE, IN SCOTLAND, / WHO FELL AT BAYONNE, / ON THE NIGHT OF THE 14TH OF APRIL, 1814, / WHILE REPELLING GALLANTLY A SORTIE OF THE ENEMY. / THE LINEAL REPRESENTATIVE OF AN ANCIENT SCOTTISH FAMILY, / HE WAS EVER IN PRIVATE LIFE / RESPECTED AND BELOVED. / BUT THE RESPECT AND LOVE OF FRIENDS / THE ENJOYMENT AND THE HONOURS OF PRIVATE LIFE, / AND EVERY ORDINARY OBJECT OF AMBITION, / DISAPPEARED BEFORE HIS PASSION FOR / MILITARY FAME. / FITTED FOR CAMPS AS WELL BY TEMPER, AS BY SPIRIT, / CHEERFUL, ARDENT, VIGILANT AND BRAVE, / HE DISTINGUISHED THE WHOLE OF HIS MILI-TARY CAREER / BY AN ELEVATED SENSE OF THE DUTIES OF A SOLDIER, / SIGNAL INTREPIDITY, PROMPTITUDE AND ZEAL. / HE LIVED TO SEE HIS COUNTRY UNIVERSALLY TRIUMPHANT, / BUT BEING HIMSELF AMONG THE LATEST VICTIMS OF THE WAR, / HE HAS

LEFT A MEMORY DEAR TO HIS ASSOCIATES IN ARMS, / WHILE AS A COMPANION OF WELLINGTON, AND A PARTNER IN HIS VICTORIES, / HE HAS BEQUEATHED HIS RENOWN AMONG THE HEROES OF HIS TIME, / AS A GRATEFUL SOLACE TO HIS FRIENDS, / AND A SACRED / INHERITANCE TO HIS CHILDREN.

Ledger stone: Coldstream Guards Cemetery, St Etienne, Bayonne, France. (Photograph)

THIS TOMB IS PLACED / BY THE OFFICERS OF THE 5TH / BRIGADE 1ST OR ROYAL SCOTS / AS A TESTAMENT OF RESPECT / TO THE MEMORY OF THE / LATE MAJOR GENERAL A. / HAY COMMANDING THE / 5TH BRIGADE – 8TH DIVISION / OF THE BRITISH ARMY WHO / GALLANTLY FELL IN / DEFENCE OF THE GROUND / IN WHICH HIS BODY IS / DEPOSITED ON THE MORNING / OF THE 14TH APRIL 1814 / AGED 52 YEARS / ....

Named on the Memorial: St Andrew's Church, (now Musée Historique), Biarritz, France. (Photograph)

Ensign 1st Foot 6 Dec 1779. Lt 14 Aug 1781. Capt 88th Foot 8 Feb 1783. Capt 1st Foot 17 Apr 1784. Major 93rd Foot Sep 1794. Lt Colonel 16th Reserve Battalion 13 Sep 1803. Lt Colonel 72nd Foot 8 Dec 1804. Lt Colonel 1st Foot 19 Mar 1807. Bt Colonel 25 Apr 1808. Major General 4 Jun 1811.

Served in the Peninsula with 1st Foot Oct 1808 – Jan 1809 and with Staff Dec 1811 – Apr 1814 (Commanded 1 Brigade 5th Division Sep 1810 – Jun 1812 and Dec 1812 – Apr 1814. Temporary GOC 5th Division Jan – Apr 1813 and Oct 1813). Present at Corunna, Vittoria, San Sebastian, Bidassoa, Nive and Bayonne where he was killed at the Sortie from Bayonne 14 Apr 1814. He refused to believe French deserters that the garrison was about to break out and so when attacked they were ill prepared. The Allies lost over 800 men, killed, wounded or captured by the end of the battle, the French even more, a terrible tragedy as Napoleon had already abdicated and the War was over. Gold Cross for Corunna, Vittoria, San Sebastian and Nive. Also served at Walcheren 1809. Father of Capt George Hay 1st Foot who was killed at Vittoria.
REFERENCE: *Dictionary of National Biography.*

HAY, Andrew Leith
Captain. 11th (North Devonshire) Regiment.
Memorial tablet: Formerly in Kennethmont Church Aberdeenshire, Scotland, now converted into a dwelling house. The tablet has been removed for safe keeping and is now in the care of a family member). (M.I.)

"SACRED TO THE MEMORY OF SIR ANDREW LEITH-HAY OF RANNES, KNIGHT OF THE GUELPHIC ORDER OF HANOVER, KNIGHT OF THE ORDER OF CHARLES III OF SPAIN, AND KNIGHT OF THE LEGION OF HONOR OF FRANCE. HE SERVED WITH DISTINCTION THROUGH THE PENINSULAR WAR, FOR WHICH HE RECEIVED A MEDAL AND SIX CLASPS FOR GENERAL ACTIONS. HE WAS A MEMBER OF LORD MELBOURNE'S ADMINISTRATION, AND REPRESENTED THE ELGIN BURGHS IN PARLIAMENT FOR MANY YEARS. BORN FEBRUARY 17TH 1783, DIED AT LEITH-HALL, OCTOBER 13TH 1862."

Ensign 72nd Foot 8 Jan 1806. Lt 29th Foot 15 Apr 1808. Capt 11th Foot 15 Apr 1813. Bt Major 21 Sep 1815. Capt 4th West India Regt 27 Jun 1816. Capt 2nd Foot 21 Feb 1817. Lt Colonel 1st West India Regiment.

Served in the Peninsula with 29th Foot Jul 1809 – Mar 1810 and on Staff Apr 1810 – Apr 1814. Present at Corunna, Talavera, Busaco, Salamanca, Vittoria and San Sebastian. Also served in Spain 1808 (ADC to Major General Leith on a mission to the Spanish Armies), West Indies 1815–1830, (present at the capture of Guadeloupe 1815 and Grenada 1820. AQMG and Military Secretary and ADC to General Leith). Entered Parliament 1832. MP for Elgin Burghs and Clerk of the Ordnance. Resigned his seat 1838

to become Governor of Bermuda but unable to take up this appointment and re-entered Parliament 1841–1848. MGS medal for Corunna, Talavera, Busaco, Salamanca, Vittoria and San Sebastian. KH. Author of *A narrative of the Peninsular War*, 2nd edition, 2 volumes, 1834, reprint, 2008. (with his own illustrations) and *Memoirs of the late Lt General Sir James Leith*, 1818. Nephew of Colonel Sir James Leith 4th West India Regt.
REFERENCE: *Annual Register, 1862, Appx, pp. 358–9.*

HAY, Charles Peter
Captain. 18th Regiment of Light Dragoons.
Memorial: Mullye Cemetery, Bengal, India. (M.I.)

HERE LIES / THE BODY OF / MAJOR C. P. HAY, / WHO DIED THE 27TH DAY OF JULY 1820 / AGED 38 YEARS. HE RAISED AND COMMANDED THE CHUMPARUN LIGHT INFANTRY / WAS AN EXCELLENT OFFICER, A GOOD AND UPRIGHT MAN / AND DESERVEDLY REGRETTED BY ALL WHO KNEW HIM; / HE HAS LEFT A DISCONSOLATE WIDOW AND INFANT CHILD TO MOURN HIS IRREPARABLE LOSS. / THIS MONUMENT IS ERECTED / AS A SMALL TRIBUTE OF TENDER REGARD FOR THE REVERED MEMORY OF THE BEST OF HUSBANDS / BY HIS AFFEC-TIONATE WIFE.

Cornet 2nd Dragoons 17 Apr 1798. Lt 26th Lt Dragoons 25 Aug 1801. Capt 18th Lt Dragoons 9 Jul 1802.
    Served in the Peninsula Sep 1808 – Jan 1809. Present at Benevente and retreat to Corunna. Retired 1810. Went to India and joined the Bengal Native Infantry.

HAY, George
Captain. 1st (Royal Scots) Regiment of Foot.
Memorial tablet: St Mary's Church, Fordingbridge, Hampshire. (Photograph)

.... / THIS STONE ALSO RECORDS / THE PREMATURE FATE, AND EARLY FAME, / OF / MAJOR GEORGE HAY, / WHO FELL IN THE DECISIVE BATTLE OF VITTORIA, / IN THE HEROIC DISCHARGE OF DUTY / AS AIDE-DE-CAMP TO HIS FATHER. / IT IS ERECTED BY MRS ELIZABETH HAY, AS THE ONLY MEMORIAL / WHICH THE AFFECTIONATE DISTRESS OF A WIFE AND A MOTHER, / CAN CONSECRATE TO THE VALOUR / OF A HUSBAND AND A SON.

Ensign 92nd Foot 17 Mar 1804. Ensign 1st Foot Guards 26 Jul 1804. Capt 1st Foot 7 May 1807. Bt Major 21 Jun 1813.
    Served in the Peninsula Apr 1810 – Jun 1813 (ADC to Major General Hay). Present at Busaco and Vittoria (severely wounded 21 Jun and died of his wounds 24 Jun 1813). Also served at Walcheren 1809. Educated at Charterhouse. Eldest son of Lt Colonel Andrew Hay 1st Foot.

HAY, James
Lieutenant. 7th (Royal Fusiliers) Regiment of Foot.
Headstone: Officers' Graveyard, Royal Hospital, Kilmainham, Dublin, Ireland. (Photograph)

SACRED / TO THE MEMORY OF / CAPTAIN JAMES HAY, / PROVIDORE, ROYAL HOSPITAL, KILMAINHAM / DIED 2ND JULY 1854 AGED 79 YEARS. / HE SERVED IN THE WEST INDIES UNDER / ABERCROMBIE, AND IN THE PENINSULA / UNDER WELLINGTON AS ADJUTANT / OF THE 7TH ROYAL FUSILIERS / WITH WHICH CORPS HE WAS ENGAGED / IN SEVERAL SIEGES AND BATTLES FOR WHICH / HE BORE A MEDAL WITH ELEVEN CLASPS. / ERECTED BY HIS WIDOW / IN TESTIMONY OF HIS GREAT WORTH AS A / HUSBAND FATHER FRIEND.

Commissioned from the ranks. Lt 3 May 1810. Adjutant 22 Nov 1810. Capt 52nd Foot 31 Aug 1839.

Served in the Peninsula with 2/7th Aug 1809 – Dec 1810 and 1/7th Jan 1811 – Apr 1814. Present at Talavera, Busaco, Pombal, Condeixa, Olivencia, first siege of Badajoz, Albuera, Aldea da Ponte, Ciudad Rodrigo, Badajoz, Castrejon, Salamanca (wounded), Vittoria, Pyrenees, Bidassoa, Nivelle, Nive and Toulouse. Served as Adjutant throughout the Peninsular War and was not absent from his regiment except to recover from his wounds. Retired 8 Oct 1839. Appointed Providore at Royal Kilmainham Hospital. MGS medal for Talavera, Busaco, Albuera, Ciudad Rodrigo, Badajoz, Salamanca, Vittoria, Pyrenees, Nivelle, Nive and Toulouse.

HAY, James Lord
Ensign. 1st Regiment of Foot Guards.
Named on the Regimental Memorial: St Joseph's Church, Waterloo, Belgium. (Photograph)
Memorial tablet: Inside Mausoleum, Evere Cemetery, Brussels, Belgium. (Photograph)

JAMES LORD HAY A.D.C. / 3RD BATT / 1ST FOOT GUARDS

Named on Memorial Panel VIII for Quatre Bras: Royal Military Chapel, Wellington Barracks, London. (M.I.) (Destroyed by a Flying Bomb 1944)

Ensign 21 Oct 1813.
   Present at Quatre Bras (ADC to Major General Maitland) where he was killed. One of the select band of soldiers buried in the Mausoleum at Evere.

HAY, Lord James
Lieutenant and Captain. 1st Regiment of Foot Guards.
Family Memorial tablet: Old Machar Cathedral, Aberdeen, Aberdeenshire, Scotland. (On Wall of Churchyard). (Photograph)

SACRED / TO / THE MEMORY OF / .... / AND OF / GENERAL THE LORD JAMES HAY / SECOND SON OF GEORGE, 7TH MARQUIS OF TWEEDDALE AND HANNAH CHARLOTTE MAITLAND / HIS WIFE WHO WAS BORN 1788 AND DIED AT SPA ON THE 18TH AUGUST 1862. / LORD JAMES HAY WAS PRESENT AT THE BATTLES OF COPENHAGEN, VIMIERA, / BUSACO, FUENTOS D'ONOR, VITTORIA, PYRENEES, NIVELLE, NIVE AND WATERLOO, / WAS COLONEL OF THE 86TH REGIMENT OF FOOT AND RECEIVED THE WAR MEDAL WITH EIGHT CLASPS. / ....

Ensign 52nd Foot. Lt 6 Aug 1807. Capt 4th West India Regt 8 Feb 1810. Lt and Capt 1st Foot Guards 27 Jun 1811. Capt and Lt Colonel 26 Mar 1818. Bt Colonel 10 Jan 1837. Major General 9 Nov 1846. Lt General 20 Jun 1854.
   Served in the Peninsula with 2/52nd Aug 1808 – Jan 1809, Jul 1809 – Apr 1810 (ADC to Major General Sherbrooke) and May 1810 – Apr 1812 (ADC to Lt General S. Cotton). With 1st Battalion Foot Guards Nov 1813 – Feb 1814 and 3rd Battalion Mar – Apr 1814. Present at Vimeiro, Vigo, Douro, Talavera, Busaco, Fuentes d'Onoro, El Bodon, Llerena, Vittoria, Pyrenees, Nivelle, Nive, Adour and Bayonne. Present at Waterloo (ADC to Lt General Colville). Also served at Copenhagen 1807. Colonel 86th Foot 8 May 1854. MGS medal for Vimeiro, Talavera, Busaco, Fuentes d'Onoro, Vittoria, Pyrenees, Nivelle and Nive.
REFERENCE: *Gentleman's Magazine*, Oct 1862, p. 505.

HAY, Patrick
Ensign and Adjutant. 73rd (Highland) Regiment of Foot.
Memorial: St Mary's Cemetery, Madras, India. (M.I.)

"CAPTAIN PATRICK HAY, 73ʳᴰ REGT. ADC TO RIGHT HONOURABLE J R LUSHINGTON, GOVERNOR FORT ST GEORGE, DIED 18 NOV 1827."

Hospital Asst 10 May 1813. Asst Surgeon 73ʳᵈ Foot 10 Jun 1813. Ensign and Adjutant 73ʳᵈ Foot 19 Jan 1815. Lt 13 Feb 1816. Capt 7 Feb 1822.

Present at Quatre Bras and Waterloo where he was severely wounded. An unusual appointment from the medical staff to that of fighting soldier but Hay requested the transfer. His gallant actions at Quatre Bras and Waterloo were noted by Sir Colin Halkett, commander of the brigade thus proving that he had made the right decision. Also served in India (ADC to Governor of Fort St George at Madras).
REFERENCE: *Lagden, Alan and John Sly, The 2/73ʳᵈ at Waterloo, 2ⁿᵈ ed 1998, pp. 93–7.*

HEAD, Francis Bond
Lieutenant. Royal Engineers.
Named on the Regimental Memorial: Rochester Cathedral, Rochester, Kent. (Photograph)

2ⁿᵈ Lt 1 May 1811. Lt 13 May 1811. 2ⁿᵈ Capt 23 Mar 1825. Major Royal Waggon Train 23 Dec 1828.

Present at Waterloo and with the Army of Occupation 1815–1818. Also served in the Netherlands 1815. Retired on half pay 1828 and wrote several travel books on his experiences in South America. Lt Governor of Upper Canada 1836. KCH. He was a surprising choice to succeed Sir John Colborne as he had hardly any political experience. At first he was popular, but eventually disagreed with the reformers in the Province and this led to the uprising of 1837–1838. Head was not completely to blame for this as the tensions in the Province were there before he arrived. These were political as well as religious and also caused by the immigrants from Britain. A vast influx of people caused economic disaster which contributed to the Canadian uprising. Head was replaced as Lt Governor and returned to England. He never held any more government posts and instead concentrated on his writing which varied from more travel books to the life of Field Marshal Sir John Burgoyne (1872). Died 20 Jul 1885 in Croydon. Brother of George Head DACG.
REFERENCE: *Dictionary of Canadian Biography. Jackman, S.W., Galloping Head; the life of the Right Honourable Sir Francis Bond Head, Bart., PC., 1793–1875, late lieutenant governor of Upper Canada, 1958.*

HEAD, George
Deputy Assistant Commissary General. Commissariat Department.
Ledger stone: Kensal Green Cemetery, London. (12439/156/3). Inscription illegible. (Photograph)

Capt West Kent Militia 1808. Clerk Commissariat 1809. Deputy Asst Comm Gen 15 Jun 1811. Asst Comm Gen Dec 1814.

Served in the Peninsula May 1810 – Apr 1814 (from May 1813 attached to the 3ʳᵈ Division). Present at Busaco, Fuentes d'Onoro, Vittoria, Pyrenees, Nivelle, Nive, Orthes and Toulouse. Also served in Canada 1815–1820 and Ireland. Half pay 1823. Knighted for his services at the coronation of William IV 1831. MGS medal for Busaco, Fuentes d'Onoro, Vittoria, Pyrenees, Nivelle, Nive, Orthes and Toulouse. A prolific author his works include *Memoirs of an Assistant Commissary General – life in the 3ʳᵈ Division under Sir Thomas Picton* which was included as the second part of *A home tour through the manufacturing districts of England in the summer of 1835.* Died 2 May 1855. Brother of Lt Francis Bond Head Royal Engineers.
REFERENCE: *Dictionary of National Biography. United Service Magazine, May 1855, pp. 271–2. Gentleman's Magazine, Jul 1855, pp. 97–8.*

HEALEY, John
Lieutenant. 7ᵗʰ (Royal Fusiliers) Regiment of Foot.
Low monument: St Michael and All Angels, Middleton Tyas Churchyard, Yorkshire. (Photograph)

SACRED / TO THE MEMORY OF / JOHN HEALEY / LATE OF THE / 7TH ROYAL FUSILIERS, / WHO DIED ON THE 15TH DECR 1868 / AGED 83 YEARS.

Ensign 99th Foot 4 Jun 1808. Lt 7th Foot 8 Sep 1808. Capt 26 Jun 1823.
    Served in the Peninsula with 2/7th Apr 1809 – Aug 1811 and 1/7th Sep 1813 – Apr 1814. Present at Douro, Talavera, Busaco, Pombal, Condeixa, Olivencia, first siege of Badajoz, Albuera (severely wounded, his arm amputated and awarded pension of £70 per annum), Orthes, Bordeaux and Toulouse. Served in France with the Army of Occupation until Nov 1818. Also served in North America 1814–1815 (present at New Orleans). MGS medal for Talavera, Busaco, Albuera, Orthes and Toulouse. Half pay 25 Jan 1824 when he retired to his home at Morris Grange near Richmond, Yorkshire.

HEATHCOTE, Joseph
Sergeant. 1st (Royal) Regiment of Dragoons.
Headstone: St Giles Churchyard, Great Longstone, Derbyshire. Seriously eroded. (Photograph)

.... / SACRED / TO THE MEMORY OF / SERJT. JOSEPH HEATHCOTE / OF THE FIRST DRAGOONS / WHO WAS KILLED IN THE BATTLE OF / WATERLOO. / 18TH JUNE 1815 / AGED 31 YEARS / ********** / (REMAINDER OF STONE ILLEGIBLE)

Served at Waterloo where he was killed 18 Jun1815.

HECHMANN, G.
Major. 2nd Nassau Regiment, Dutch Infantry.
Named on the Memorial to Dutch officers killed at Waterloo: St Joseph's Church, Waterloo, Belgium. (Photograph)

HEDDERWICK, David
Corporal. 52nd (Oxfordshire) Light Infantry Regiment of Foot.
Family Headstone: Longforgan Churchyard, Perthshire, Scotland. (Opposite main door of church on reverse of headstone). (Photograph)

REVISED BY / JOHN HEDDERWICK / IN MEMORY OF HIS MOTHER / JANET WEBSTER / WHO DIED 21ST FEB 1840 / AGED 45 / ALSO HIS FATHER / DAVID HEDDERWICK / WHO DIED 22ND OF APRIL 1860 / AGED 70 YEARS / HE WAS ENGAGED IN FOURTEEN ENGAGEMENTS / DURING THE PENINSULAR WAR

Served in the Peninsula 1808 – 1814.
    Present at Vimeiro, Talavera, Busaco, Fuentes d'Onoro, Ciudad Rodrigo, Badajoz, Salamanca, Vittoria, Pyrenees, Nivelle, Nive, Orthes and Toulouse. Present at Waterloo in Capt W. Rowan's Company. MGS medal for Vimeiro, Talavera, Busaco, Fuentes d'Onoro, Ciudad Rodrigo, Badajoz, Salamanca, Vittoria, Pyrenees, Nivelle, Nive, Orthes and Toulouse.

HEDDING, William Levitt
Ensign. 35th (Sussex) Regiment of Foot.
Memorial tablet: St Mary with St Alban Church, Teddington, Middlesex, London. (Photograph)

IN A VAULT UNDERNEATH THIS CHURCH / ARE LAID THE REMAINS OF / WILLIAM LEVITT HEDDING / LATE LIEUT IN HER MAJESTY'S 35TH REGT OF FOOT / WHO WAS AN INHABITANT OF THIS VILLAGE / FOR 18 YEARS / AND BY HIS WILL BEQUEATHED A LEGACY TO FORM / AN ENDOWMENT FOR THE EDUCATION OF THE POOR OF THIS PARISH. / HE DIED AT TEDDINGTON JULY 2ND AD 1846 / AGED 56 YEARS.

Ensign 7 Jan 1813. Lt 25 Sep 1815.

Served at Waterloo in reserve at Hal, siege of Cambrai and with the Army of Occupation until 1817. Retired on half pay 1817. Left funds to endow his village school.

HEIDEN, F. M. van

Captain. 6th Hussars, Dutch Cavalry.
Named on the Memorial to Dutch officers killed at Waterloo: St Joseph's Church, Waterloo, Belgium. (Photograph)
Named on the Regimental Memorial to officers of the Dutch 6th Regiment of Hussars killed at Waterloo, St Joseph's Church, Waterloo. (Photograph)

HEIL, P.

2nd Lieutenant. 7th National Militia Battalion, Dutch Infantry.
Named on the Memorial to the Dutch officers killed at Waterloo: St Joseph's Church, Waterloo, Belgium. (Photograph)

HEINEMANN, Rudolf von

Quartermaster General. Duke of Brunswick's Oels' Corps.
Grave marker: Sold in Dix, Noon and Webb Auction, 27 Jun 2007. (Photograph)

ZUM / GEDÄCHTNIS / AN UNSUREN / GROSSVATER / RUDOLF VON HEINEMANN, / HERZOGL BRAUNSCHWEIG / OBERSTLEUTNANT, / GEB 8 MAI / 1769 / GEBLIEBEN / BEI BELLE – / ALLIANCE / 18 JUNI / 1815

English translation: To the memory of our Grandfather Rudolf von Heinemann, Lieutenant Colonel of the Duchy of Brunswick. Born 8 May 1769 fell at Belle-Alliance 18 June 1815.

Present at Waterloo as Quartermaster General where he was killed.

HEISE, Gabriel Wilhelm

Captain. 3rd Regiment of Hussars, King's German Legion.
Gravestone: St Mathew's Churchyard, Ipswich, Suffolk. (No longer extant). (M.I.)

"IN / MEMORY OF / .... GABRIEL HEISE / LATE CAPTAIN IN THE 3RD REGIMENT / KING'S GERMAN HUSSARS / WHO DIED JANUARY 2, 1810 IN THE / 46TH YEAR OF HIS AGE / OF WHICH HE SPENT 26 YEARS / IN THE HANOVERIAN AND 5 YEARS / IN THE ENGLISH SERVICE. / THIS STONE / IS ERECTED BY HIS BROTHER OFFICERS / AS A MARK OF THEIR ESTEEM / FOR HIS HIGH CHARACTER / AS AN OFFICER / AND A MAN."

Capt 7 Nov 1803.

Served in the Peninsula Aug 1808 – Jan 1809. Present at Benevente. Also served at Hanover 1805 and the Baltic 1807–1808.

HEISE, Georg

Captain. 4th Line Battalion, King's German Legion.
Named on the Regimental Memorial: La Haye Sainte, Waterloo Belgium. (Named as Friedrich on memorial). (Photograph)

Lt 18 Dec 1804. Capt 10 Mar 1812.

Served in the Peninsula Aug 1812 – Apr 1814. Present in Eastern Spain, Castalla and Tarragona. Present at Waterloo where he was severely wounded and died of his wounds 27 Jun 1815. Also served in Hanover 1805, the Baltic 1807, Mediterranean 1808–1812 and the Netherlands 1814.

HEMPHILL, William
Lieutenant. 1st (Royal Scots) Regiment of Foot.
Headstone: Drummond Hill Presbyterian Churchyard, Lundy's Lane, Niagara, Canada. (Photograph)

SACRED / TO / THE MEMORY / OF / LIEUTENANT / WILLIAM HEMPHILL / OF THE ROYALS, / WHO FELL AT THE BATTLE OF / LUNDY'S LANE / ON THE 25TH JULY 1814. / THIS STONE WAS PLACED BY HIS / SON, LIEUT-COL HEMPHILL / OF THE 26TH CAMERONIANS, / 17TH JULY 1854.

Named on the Memorial to the Battle of Lundy's Lane: Niagara, Canada. (Photograph)

Ensign 46th Foot 18 Nov 1806. Lt 1st Foot 10 Oct 1807.
    Served in the Peninsula Oct 1808 – Jan 1809. Present at Corunna. Afterwards served in Canada where he died at the battle of Lundy's Lane 25 Jul 1814.

HENDERSON, Alexander
Lieutenant. Royal Engineers.
Named on the Regimental Memorial: Rochester Cathedral, Rochester, Kent. (Photograph)

2nd Lt 20 Mar 1813. Lt 21 Jul 1813. 2nd Capt 24 Feb 1829. Capt 28 Mar 1837.
    Served in the Netherlands 1814–1815 and in France with the Army of Occupation 1815–1818. Died at the Cape of Good Hope 25 Dec 1844.

HENDERSON, Charles
Lieutenant. 71st (Highland Light Infantry) Regiment of Foot.
Named on the Memorial: St Andrew's Church, (now Musée Historique), Biarritz, France. (Photograph)

Ensign 7 Dec 1809. Lt 28 May 1812.
    Served in the Peninsula Nov – Dec 1813. Present at the Nive where he was killed 13 Dec 1813.
(Named as George Henderson on the Biarritz memorial)

HENDERSON, David
Captain. 10th (North Lincolnshire) Regiment of Foot.
Memorial: Bower Church, Caithness, Scotland. (M.I.)

"DAVID HENDERSON OF STEMPSTER, CAPT. HALF PAY, H. M. 10 FOOT. 31.10.1859 AGED 71."

Ensign 28 Nov 1806. Lt 23 Jan 1808. Capt 5 Jan 1815.
    Served in the Peninsula Aug 1812 – Apr 1814. Present at Alicante, Castalla, Ordal and Barcelona. Half pay 25 Feb 1816.

HENDERSON, Douglas Mercer see MERCER, Douglas

HENDERSON, George
Captain. Royal Engineers.
Named on the Regimental Memorial: Rochester Cathedral, Rochester, Kent. (Photograph)
Interred at All Saints Church, Southampton, Hampshire. (No longer extant. Church was bombed in the Second World War)

2nd Lt Royal Artillery 1 Aug 1799. 2nd Lt Royal Engineers 20 Dec 1799. Lt 18 Apr 1801. 2nd Capt 13 Jul 1805. Capt 2 Dec 1809. Bt Major 21 Sep 1813. Lt Colonel 30 Dec 1824.

Served in the Peninsula Sep 1813 – Apr 1814. Present at San Sebastian (Mentioned in Despatches for the capture of Santa Clara Island 26 August and Mentioned in Despatches at the siege of San Sebastian 31 Aug 1813. Awarded Bt Majority), Nivelle and Nive. Gold Medal for San Sebastian. MGS medal for Nivelle and Nive. Also served in Ceylon 1803–1812, Ireland 1815 and Canada 1816–1819. Retired 9 Apr 1825. Formed the London and South Western Railway Company in 1830, became General Superintendent and later a Director until 1855. Chairman London Equitable Gas Company and Southampton Gas Company. Died at Southampton 21 Apr 1855.
REFERENCE: *Dictionary of National Biography. Gentleman's Magazine, Jul 1855, p. 97.*

HENDERSON, John
Captain. 42nd (Royal Highland) Regiment of Foot.
Named on the Memorial: St Andrew's Church, (now Musée Historique), Biarritz, France. (Photograph)

Ensign 1801. Lt 9 Jul 1803. Capt 21 Feb 1811.
Served in the Peninsula Mar 1809, Jun 1811 – May 1812 and Sep 1813 – Apr 1814. Present at Ciudad Rodrigo, Nivelle, Nive, Orthes and Toulouse where he was severely wounded and died of his wounds Apr 1814.

HENEGAN, Richard Drake
Commissary. Field Train Department of Ordnance.
Headstone: St Brelade's Churchyard, Jersey, Channel Islands. (Photograph)

SACRED / TO THE / BELOVED MEMORY OF / SIR RICHARD D HENEGAN, KNT. / WHO SERVED IN THE / PENINSULAR WAR AND AT WATERLOO. / HE SLEPT IN JESUS, / ON HIS 89TH BIRTHDAY / 28TH DEC 1872. / (VERSE)

Conductor of Stores 6 Jul 1803. Clerk of Stores 17 Nov 1803. Asst Comm Gen 1 Nov 1808. Comm General 1 Jun 1814.
Served in the Peninsula Aug 1808 – Jan 1809, Apr 1809 – Mar 1810, May 1810 – May 1812 and Oct 1812 – Apr 1814. Present at Corunna, Cadiz, Barrosa, Tarifa, Vittoria, San Sebastian, Nivelle and Nive. Present at Waterloo. Also served at Walcheren 1809. MGS medal for Corunna, Barrosa, Vittoria, San Sebastian, Nivelle and Nive. Retired on half pay 1 Mar 1816.
REFERENCE: *Henegan, Sir Richard D., Narrative of the services of Sir R. D. Henegan, 1832. Henegan, Sir Richard D., Seven years campaigning in the Peninsula and the Netherlands 1808–1815, 2 vols, 1846, reprint 2005.*

HENNEN, John
Staff Surgeon. Medical Department.
Memorial tablet: King's Chapel, Gibraltar. (North wall). (Photograph)

TO / THE MEMORY OF / JOHN HENNEN, M. D., F. R. S. E., / INSPECTOR OF MILITARY HOSPI-TALS, / AND / AUTHOR OF THE PRINCIPLES OF MILITARY SURGERY, / AND VARIOUS OTHER WORKS. / HE FELL A VICTIM TO THE EPIDEMIC FEVER, ON THE / 3RD OF NOVR, 1828, AGED 49 YEARS, AND WHILE ARDUOUSLY / ENGAGED, EVEN TO THE DAY PRECEDING HIS DEATH, IN THE / ABLE DISCHARGE OF THE URGENT DUTIES OF / PRINCIPAL MEDICAL OFFICER / OF THIS GARRISON. / THIS TABLET / IS ERECTED BY HIS PERSONAL FRIENDS, NOT WITH A / VIEW OF PERPETUATING HIS NAME, FOR THIS LIES IN THE / MORE IMPERISHABLE MEMO-RIALS OF HIS OWN GENIUS / BUT AS A TESTIMONY OF REGARD / FOR A MAN WHOSE ZEAL

WAS INDEFATIGABLE, / AND WHO, / IN THE DAY OF GENERAL CALAMITY, SACRIFICED ALL / CONSIDERATION OF HIS OWN SAFETY FOR THE / PUBLIC WEAL.

Hospital Mate 24 Mar 1800. Asst Surgeon 40th Foot 4 Apr 1800. Asst Surgeon 3rd Dragoons 15 Oct 1801. Surgeon 3rd Division Irish Lt Infantry 12 Nov 1803. Surgeon 30th Foot 31 Dec 1807. Staff Surgeon 24 Oct 1811. Deputy Inspector of Hospitals 7 Sep 1815. Bt Inspector of Hospitals 11 Dec 1823.

Served in the Peninsula Apr – May 1809 and Jun 1810 – Oct 1811. Present at Cadiz, Sabugal, Fuentes d'Onoro and Barba del Puerco. Retired on half pay 1814. After Waterloo he was recalled to help with the casualties and promoted Deputy Inspector of Hospitals. His experiences during this time prompted him to write *Observation on some important points in the practice of military surgery and in the arrangement and police of hospitals* published in 1818 which ran to three editions. MD Edinburgh 1819. Also served in Egypt 1801. Principal Medical Officer for Gibraltar 1826, where he died 1828 dealing with an epidemic of yellow fever.
REFERENCE: *Dictionary of National Biography.*

HENNIS, William Howe
2nd Lieutenant. Royal Artillery.
Pedestal tomb: Brompton Cemetery, London. (BR 69877). (Photograph)

IN MOST AFFECTIONATE / AND SACRED MEMORY / OF / LIEUTENANT GENERAL / WILLIAM HOWE HENNIS / R. A. / WHO DIED 14TH DECEMBER 1871 / AGED 76 YEARS. / HE SERVED IN THE CAMPAIGN OF 1815 / AND WAS PRESENT AT / WATERLOO / ....

2nd Lt 13 Dec 1813. 1st Lt 1 Aug 1816. 2nd Capt 5 Jun 1835. Capt 20 Dec 1841. Bt Major 20 Oct 1846. Lt Colonel 23 May 1850. Major General 21 Jul 1864. Lt General 10 Nov 1868.

Present at Waterloo and with the Army of Occupation until Aug 1816. Temporarily on half pay at the reduction of the 10th Battalion 1817. Also served in the West Indies 1822–1826, Barbados 1842 –1844, and Canada 1849–1850. Retired on full pay 4 Apr 1851. Died at Boulogne 14 Dec 1872.

HENRY, J. J.
2nd Lieutenant. 2nd Carabineers Regiment, Dutch Cavalry.
Named on the Memorial to the Dutch officers killed at Waterloo: St Joseph's Church, Waterloo, Belgium. (Photograph)

HEPBURN, Francis Ker
Second Major. 3rd Regiment of Foot Guards.
Box tomb: St Peter's Churchyard, Chailey, Sussex. Seriously eroded. (Photograph)

HERE LIES THE BODY OF / MAJOR GENERAL FRANCIS HEPBURN C.B. / LATE OF THE THIRD GUARDS / IN WHICH REGIMENT HE SERVED FOR 26 YEARS / IN THE GREATEST PART ON ACTIVE SERVICE. / HE RETIRED FROM THE COMMAND OF IT IN 1821 ON PROMOTION / AND PASSED THE REMAINDER OF HIS LIFE AT HOOKE IN THIS PARISH. / HE DIED ON THE 7TH JUNE 1835 / IN THE 56TH YEAR OF HIS AGE.

Memorial tablet and Stained glass window: Royal Military Chapel, Wellington Barracks, London. (M.I.) (Destroyed by a Flying Bomb 1944) (Photograph of Stained glass window in the Apse. The only original part of the Chapel)

"MAJOR-GENERAL H. P. HEPBURN, C.B., LATE SCOTS FUSILIER GUARDS, AND THE REV. F. R / HEPBURN, HIS SONS, AND CHARLOTTE HEPBURN, HIS DAUGHTER, TO THE MEMORY OF / MAJOR-GENERAL FRANCIS KER HEPBURN, C.B. / BORN 19TH AUGUST, 1779; DIED 7TH JUNE

1835. / APPOINTED TO 3ʳᴰ GUARDS, 1794; LEFT, 1821, ON PROMOTION TO MAJOR-GENERAL. SERVED IN IRELAND, 1798; IN THE EXPEDITION TO THE HELDER; IN MALTA AND SICILY; ALSO DURING THE WAR IN THE PENINSULA; DISTINGUISHED AT BARROSA, WHERE HE WAS SEVERELY WOUNDED; AT VITTORIA, NIVELLE AND THE PASSAGE OF THE NIVE. COMMANDED 2ᴺᴰ BATTALION 3ᴿᴰ GUARDS AT QUATRE BRAS, AND THE TROOPS ENGAGED IN THE DEFENCE OF THE GARDEN AND ORCHARD OF HOUGOUMONT AT THE BATTLE OF WATERLOO."

Ensign 17 Dec 1794. Lt and Capt 28 May 1798. Capt and Lt Colonel 23 Jul 1807. Bt Colonel 4 Jun 1814. Second Major 25 Jul 1814. Major General 19 Jul 1821.

Served in the Peninsula Apr 1810 – May 1811 and Sep 1812 – Feb 1814. Present at Cadiz, Barrosa (severely wounded), Osma, Vittoria, San Sebastian, Bidassoa, Nivelle and Nive. He was so severely wounded at Barrosa that the surgeons wanted to amputate his leg but he refused as it would restrict his future military career. He had to return home until the autumn of 1812 to try to heal his leg but for the rest of his life he was troubled by the wound and his health suffered. On his return to the Peninsula he was given command of a corps of light troops from the Guards and 60ᵗʰ Foot. Gold Medal for Vittoria and Nive.

Present at Quatre Bras and Waterloo in command of the 2ⁿᵈ Battalion 3ʳᵈ Foot Guards and several battalions of foreign troops in the orchard and wood at Hougoumont. Owing to an unfortunate mistake his name was not mentioned in the official account of the action but that of Colonel Home who served under him. This was never publicly explained and Hepburn was not rewarded sufficiently for his actions on the 18ᵗʰ June. CB. Order of St Vladimir 4ᵗʰ Class and Order of Wilhelm of the Netherlands 4ᵗʰ Class. Also served in Ireland 1798, the Helder 1799, Malta 1805, Sicily 1805–1807 and Netherlands Feb 1814–1815.

REFERENCE: *Dictionary of National Biography. United Service Journal, Nov 1835, pp. 383–4. Royal Military Calendar, Vol 3, pp. 181–2. Gentleman's Magazine, Dec 1835, pp. 650–1.*

HERON, Basil Robinson

1ˢᵗ Lieutenant. Royal Artillery.
Box tomb: Sandpits Cemetery, Gibraltar. (Photograph)

SACRED TO THE MEMORY OF / BASIL ROBINSON HERON / CAPTAIN IN THE ROYAL ARTILLERY AND BREVET MAJOR / BORN ON THE 28ᵀᴴ NOVEMBER IN THE YEAR OF OUR LORD 1789. / AND DIED AT ROSIA IN THIS GARRISON ON THE 4ᵀᴴ DAY / OF JUNE 1841. / HE ENTERED THE ARTILLERY IN THE YEAR 1805, SERVED AT SCYLLA / ON CALABRIA AND IN THE EXPEDITION FROM SICILY IN 1807 / WAS AT THE CAPTURE OF MARTINIQUE AT THE SIEGE OF PIGEON / ISLAND AND FORT BOURBON 1810. SERVED WITH THE BRITISH ARMY / IN THE PENINSULA AND FRANCE UNDER THE DUKE OF WELLINGTON / FROM MAY 1812 TO AUGUST 1814 HAVING BEEN AT THE BATTLE OF / AND THE STORMING OF THE TOWN, AT VITTORIA WHERE HE WAS WOUNDED, / BOTH SIEGES OF SAN SEBASTIAN / AND THE STORMING OF THE TOWN AT THE PASSAGE OF BIDASSOA / NIVELLE AND NIVE. AT THE ACTIONS OF THE 10ᵀᴴ, 11ᵀᴴ, AND 12ᵀᴴ / OF DECEMBER 1813 IN FRONT OF BAYONNE AND THE SORTIE IN / APRIL 1814. / THIS MONUMENT IS ERECTED BY HIS WIDOW / AND THREE DAUGHTERS WHO SURVIVED HIM / WAS RESTORED BY HIS / GRANDCHILDREN

2ⁿᵈ Lt 13 Sep 1805. 1ˢᵗ Lt 1 Jun 1806. 2ⁿᵈ Capt 6 Nov 1820. Capt 1 Aug 1833. Bt Major 10 Jan 1837.

Served in the Peninsula May 1812 – Apr 1814. Present at Osma, Vittoria (wounded), first and second sieges of San Sebastian, Bidassoa, Nivelle, Nive, Bayonne and Sortie from Bayonne. Also served in Calabria and Sicily 1807, Martinique 1810 (present at sieges of Pigeon Island and Fort Bourbon), Portugal 1826 –1828 and Gibraltar 1834–1841.

REFERENCE: *Annual Register, 1841, Appx, pp. 211–2.*

HERON, John
Private. 6th (Inniskilling) Regiment of Dragoons.
Low monument: St Augustine's Churchyard, Hedon, Yorkshire. (Photograph)

JOHN HERON OF THE 6TH DRAGOON GUARDS / WHO DIED AT / WATERLOO / 18TH JUNE 1815 / AGED 29 YEARS / ....

Served at Waterloo where he was killed.
Note: With 6th Inniskilling Regiment of Dragoons, not 6th Dragoon Guards as on monument.

HERRIES, William Lewis
Major. Permanent Assistant Quartermaster General.
Memorial tablet: St Mary the Virgin Church, Lynton, Devon. (Photograph)

SACRED TO THE MEMORY / OF LT GENL SIR WILLIAM LEWIS HERRIES KCH AND CB. / COLONEL, OF H. M. 68TH REGT. HE WAS A RESIDENT IN THIS / PARISH FOR MANY YEARS AND DIED IN LONDON JUNE 3RD 1857 / AGED 71; HE WAS BURIED IN THE CEMETERY AT BROMPTON. / HIS MILITARY SERVICES WERE IN SOUTH AMERICA, / AT WALCHEREN, AND ALL THROUGH THE PENINSULAR WAR / WITH THE DUKE OF WELLINGTON'S ARMY; HE LOST A LEG / BEFORE BAYONNE IN 1814. / HE MARRIED IN 1828 MARY FRANCIS, DAUGHTER OF / JOSHUA CROMPTON ESQR OF ESHOLT HALL, YORKSHIRE, / BY WHOM HE LEFT TWO SONS, HERBERT CROMPTON HERRIES, / AND FREDERIC STANSFIELD HERRIES. THIS TABLET IS PLACED / BY HIS WIDOW AND SONS IN REMEMBRANCE OF HIM WHOM THEY / DEEPLY LOVED AND WHOSE DEATH IS GENERALLY LAMENTED.

Low Monument: Brompton Cemetery, London. (BR 15841. Compartment U:59.6x111). (Photograph)

IN THIS VAULT ARE DEPOSITED THE REMAINS OF / LIEUTT GENERAL SIR WILLIAM LEWIS HERRIES. KCH AND CB. / COLONEL OF THE 68TH REGIMENT / WHO DIED JUNE 3RD 1857, AGED 71 / AFTER A LONG ILLNESS BORNE WITH GREAT PATIENCE / AND RESIGNATION.

Cornet 19th Dragoons 23 Jan 1801 (as he was only 14 years old given two years leave of absence). Lt 17 May 1803. Lt 9th Dragoons 14 Apr 1804. Capt 1st Dragoon Guards 19 Oct 1809. Capt Meuron's Regt 18 Jun 1812. Major 2 Jun 1814. Lt Colonel 31 Jul 1817. Bt Colonel 10 Jan 1837. Major General 9 Nov 1846. Lt Gen 20 Jun 1854.
   Served in the Peninsula Oct 1812 – Apr 1814. (ADC to Lt General Sir E. Paget Oct – Nov 1812. When Paget was taken prisoner on the retreat from Burgos, Herries was appointed DAQMG Dec 1812 – Apr 1814). Present at San Munos, Vittoria, San Sebastian, Bidassoa, Nivelle, Nive and Bayonne (severely wounded, taken prisoner, leg amputated and awarded pension of £300 per annum). MGS medal for Vittoria, San Sebastian, Nivelle and Nive. CB and KCH. Also served in South America 1807 (Brigade Major at Buenos Ayres), Walcheren 1809 (present at the siege of Flushing), Ireland 1815–1817 and Mediterranean 1817 (DAQMG). Colonel 68th Foot 17 May 1854.
REFERENCE: *Royal Military Calendar, Vol 5, pp. 143–4. Gentleman's Magazine, Aug 1857, p. 226. Annual Register, 1857, Appx, p. 312.*

HERRING, Robert
Captain. 48th (Northamptonshire) Regiment of Foot.
Memorial tablet: St Mary's Church, Snettisham, Norfolk. (Photograph)

TO THE MEMORY OF / ROBERT, / THIRD SON OF THE LATE / REVD THOMAS HERRING, / VICAR OF NORTH ELMHAM / IN THIS COUNTY, / HE WAS A CAPTAIN IN THE 48TH REGIMENT

/ AND WAS SEVERELY WOUNDED / AT THE BATTLE OF ALBUERA IN SPAIN, / HE DIED 12 DEC^R 1831, / AGED 46 YEARS.

Ensign Nov 1804. Lt 29 May 1806. Capt 26 Aug 1813.

Served in the Peninsula Jul 1809 – Jul 1811. Present at Talavera, Busaco and Albuera where he was severely wounded and took no further part in the Peninsular campaign. Half pay 1814.

HERVEY, Felton Elwill Bathurst

Lieutenant Colonel. 14th (Duchess of York's Own) Regiment of Light Dragoons.
Memorial tablet: St John the Baptist Church, Egham, Surrey. (South wall of nave). (Photograph)

NEAR THIS PLACE ARE DEPOSITED THE REMAINS OF / SIR FELTON ELWILL BATHURST HERVEY BAR^T CB. &c &c &c. / LIEUT^T COLONEL OF THE 14TH REG^T OF DRAGOONS, COLONEL IN THE ARMY, / AND AID-DE-CAMP TO HIS ROYAL HIGHNESS THE PRINCE REGENT; / HE SERVED THE OFFICE OF MILITARY SECRETARY TO / FIELD MARSHAL THE DUKE OF WELLINGTON, / UNDER WHOM HE WAS ACTIVELY EMPLOYED DURING THE CAMPAIGN / IN THE PENINSULA, / AND LOST HIS RIGHT ARM AT THE PASSAGE OF THE DOURO. / HE WAS AT HIS SIDE IN THE MEMORABLE BATTLE OF WATERLOO, / AND BY HIS GRACE'S AUTHORITY SIGNED THE CONVENTION / OF PARIS ON THE 3RD JULY 1815. / HE MARRIED ON THE 24TH JULY 1817 / LOUISA CATON, OF BALTIMORE IN AMERICA / AND DIED ON THE 24TH SEP^T 1819, IN THE 37TH YEAR OF HIS AGE / IN PRIVATE LIFE HE WAS A TENDER HUSBAND, / AN AFFECTIONATE AND DUTIFUL SON, / AND JUSTLY BELOVED BY ALL WHO KNEW HIM. / THIS TESTIMONY OF RESPECT TO HIS MEMORY / IS ERECTED / BY THE COLONEL AND OFFICERS OF HIS REGIMENT.

Cornet 3rd Dragoon Guards 6 May 1800. Capt 14th Light Dragoons 28 Jul 1803. Major 8 May 1806. Lt Colonel 12 Jul 1810. Bt Colonel 4 Jun 1814.

Served in the Peninsula Dec 1808 – Apr 1814. Present at Douro (Mentioned in Despatches, severely wounded, his right arm amputated and awarded pension of £300 per annum), Sexmiro, Coa, Pombal, Redinha, Casal Nova, Foz d'Arouce, Sabugal, Fuentes d'Onoro (wounded), El Bodon (Mentioned in Despatches), Badajoz, Llerena, Castrejon, Salamanca, Vittoria, Pyrenees, Nivelle, Nive, Orthes, Vic Bigorre, Tarbes and Toulouse. Gold Cross for Fuentes d'Onoro, Salamanca, Vittoria and Orthes. CB and KH. Present at Waterloo (on Staff as AQMG). Russian Order of St George of Wladimir, Austrian Order of Maria Theresa, Portuguese Order of the Tower and Sword, Bavarian Order of Joseph Maximilian, Prussian Order of Merit and Knight of St Henry of Saxony.

Took command of 14th Lt Dragoons in 1810 on the death of Lt Colonel Talbot at Sexmiro and during the next four years under his leadership the 14th Lt Dragoons became famous as a light cavalry regiment and performed well on outpost duties. Served on the personal staff of the Duke of Wellington at Waterloo and afterwards Secretary to the Master General of the Ordnance. Educated at Eton. Became Sir Felton Elwill Hervey-Bathurst (Bart) in 1818.

HESKETH, Robert H. Bamford

Lieutenant and Captain. 3rd Regiment of Foot Guards.
Memorial tablet: St Michael's Church, Abergele, Wales. (Photograph)

SACRED / TO THE MEMORY OF / ROBERT H. BAMFORD HESKETH / BORN JULY 26TH 1789 / DIED SEPT 15TH 1828. / HE WAS LIEUTENANT IN HIS / MAJESTY'S 3RD FOOT GUARDS, / AND MAJOR IN THE ARMY. FROM / A WOUND RECEIVED AT THE / MEMORABLE BATTLE OF WATERLOO, / HE NEVER RECOVERED, AND FROM / THAT TIME TO THE DAY OF HIS DEATH / HIS SUFFERINGS WERE SEVERE AND / HEART RENDING TO HIS NUMEROUS / RELATIONS

WHO DEPLORE THE LOSS / OF AN AMIABLE KIND HEARTED / FRIEND AND RELIGIOUS / GOOD CHRISTIAN.

Ensign 10 Apr 1806. Lt and Capt 31 Oct 1811. Bt Major 4 Dec 1815.
   Served in the Peninsula Apr 1809 – Dec 1811. Present at Douro, Talavera, Busaco and Fuentes d'Onoro. Present at Waterloo where he was severely wounded through the neck in the orchard at Hougoumont. Also served at Copenhagen 1807, Netherlands 1814 (present at Merxem and Bergen-op-Zoom). Died 1820 from the wound received at Waterloo. Educated at Eton. (Date of death on memorial given incorrectly as 1828).
REFERENCE: *Royal Military Calendar, Vol 5, pp. 330–1.*

HEWAT, Richard
Assistant Surgeon. 21st Foot.
Headstone: Earlston Churchyard, Earlston, Berwickshire, Scotland. (Photograph)

SACRED TO THE MEMORY / OF / RICHARD HEWAT, / REGIMENTAL SURGEON R.C.S. ENGLAND, / WHO DIED THE 16TH DAY OF DECEMBER 1861, / AGED 71. / ....

Hospital Assistant 10 Jan 1811. Asst Surgeon 21st Foot 15 Jun 1815. Asst Surgeon 94th Foot 27 Nov 1817. Asst Surgeon 46th Foot 10 Jan 1824.
   Served in the Peninsula 1811–1814. Also served in North America 1815. Retired 22 Nov 1827.

HEWETT, William
Captain. 14th (Buckinghamshire) Regiment of Foot.
Headstone: Old Common Cemetery, Southampton, Hampshire. (Grave number FO 35 152). (Photograph.)

IN MEMORIAM / SARAH WIFE OF WILLIAM HEWETT / BORN 16TH JANUARY 1806 / DIED 28TH DECEMBER 1883. / .... / ALSO LT. COL. WILLIAM HEWETT / LAST SURVIVOR OF THE ENGLISH OFFICERS / WHO TOOK PART IN THE / GREAT BATTLE OF WATERLOO 1815. / BORN 2ND JULY 1795 / DIED 26TH OCTOBER 1891 AGED 96.

Ensign 22nd Foot 19 Dec 1811. Lt Bourbon Regt 16 Jul 1812. Lt 33rd Foot 23 Jul 1812. Capt 92nd Foot 24 Nov 1814. Capt 14th Foot 13 Apr 1815. Capt 33rd Foot 24 Oct 1816. Capt Rifle Brigade 14 Aug 1823. Major 8 Jun 1826. Lt Colonel (unattached) 19 Aug 1828. Lt Colonel 53rd Foot 13 May 1836.
   Present at Waterloo (served as Captain in Capt Henry Hill's Company aged 19 years) and with the Army of Occupation. Retired 13 May 1836. When he died in 1891 he was the last surviving officer present at Waterloo.

HEYLAND, Arthur Rowley
Major. 40th (2nd Somersetshire) Regiment of Foot.
Pedestal tomb: Garden of Waterloo Museum, Waterloo, Belgium. (Originally buried in the garden of the old Auberge du Cheval Blanc, the grave was removed to make way for a road and relocated in 1889). (Photograph)

SACRED / TO THE MEMORY OF / MAJOR ARTHUR ROWLEY HEYLAND / OF HIS BRITANNIC MAJESTY'S / FORTIETH REGIMENT OF FOOT / WHO WAS BURIED ON THIS SPOT. / HE FELL GLORIOUSLY IN THE BATTLE OF / WATERLOO / ON THE 18TH JUNE 1815. / AT THE MOMENT OF VICTORY / AND IN COMMAND OF HIS REGIMENT / AGED 34 YEARS.

Memorial tablet: St Deiniol Cathedral, Bangor, Gwynedd, Wales. (Photograph)

SACRED / TO THE MEMORY OF / ARTHUR ROWLEY HEYLAND / OF BALLIN TEMPLE IN THE COUNTY OF LONDON-DERRY, ESQUIRE / MAJOR OF THE 40TH REGIMENT, / WHO CLOSED A LIFE OF PRIVATE EXCELLENCE AND PROFESSIONAL HONOR / IN THE GLORIOUS VICTORY OF WATERLOO. JUNE 18TH 1815, IN THE 34TH YEAR OF HIS AGE. / HE WAS THE SECOND SON OF / ROWLEY HEYLAND ESQUIRE OF GLEN OAK CO. ANTRIM, IRELAND. / DEVOTING HIMSELF TO THE SERVICE OF HIS COUNTRY, / HE SECURED BY HIS ZEAL, GALLANTRY AND JUDGEMENT / ON THE MANY TRYING OCCASIONS OF THE SIX CAMPAIGNS IN / PORTUGAL, SPAIN AND FRANCE, / THE LOVE OF HIS ASSOCIATES, AND NOTICE AND CONFIDENCE OF / THE DUKE OF WELLINGTON, / BY WHOM HIS VALUE WAS FREQUENTLY AND SIGNALLY DISTINGUISHED. / HE COMMANDED THE 40TH REGT IN TWO GENERAL ACTIONS, / AND AGAIN AT THE HEAD OF HIS BELOVED AND ADMIRING FOLLOWERS, / WHILE IN THE ACT OF CONTRIBUTING BY HIS HEROIC EXAMPLE / TO THE TOTAL DEFEAT OF THE ENEMY, / HE EXCHANGED THE GLORIES OF EARTHLY TRIUMPH AND HUMAN APPLAUSE / FOR A BLESSED IMMORTALITY; / LEAVING TO HIS WIDOW AND SEVEN CHILDREN / THOSE DEEP AND PERMANENT REGRETS WHICH NO MEMORIAL CAN RECORD, / AND WHICH ARE THE BEST OFFERINGS TO THE MEMORY OF / A HUSBAND AND FATHER / WHO BLENDED THE MANLY QUALITIES OF THE SOLDIER / WITH THE TENDERNESS OF EVERY DOMESTIC VIRTUE / AND CHRISTIAN GRACE. / THIS TABLET WAS ERECTED BY HIS WIDOW, / MARY, ELDEST DAUGHTER OF THE REVD. JOHN KYFFYN OF THIS CITY. / ....

Ensign 49th Foot 26 Apr 1802. Lt 14th Foot 2 Apr 1803. Capt 40th Foot 7 Aug 1804. Bt Major 26 Aug 1813. Major 10 Nov 1814.

Served in the Peninsula Aug 1808 – Apr 1814. Present at Rolica, Vimeiro, Talavera, Busaco, Redinha, first siege of Badajoz (severely wounded), Vittoria, Pyrenees (severely wounded), Bidassoa, Nivelle, Nive, Orthes and Toulouse (Commandant of Toulouse Apr 1814 and supervised the embarkation of troops at Bordeaux). Retired on half pay but returned to the regiment for Waterloo, where he was killed on 18 June in command of the 40th Foot. Gold Medal for Vittoria. Educated at Eton.

HIBBERT, John Gray
Assistant Surgeon. Royal Waggon Train.
Headstone: St Saviour's Churchyard, St Helier, Jersey, Channel Islands. (Photograph)

JOHN GRAY HIBBERT M. D. / LATE SURGEON / OF / HER MAJESTY'S 59TH REGT FOOT / WHO / DEPARTED THIS LIFE / IN THE PARISH OF ST SAVIOUR'S / ON THE 18TH OF JUNE 1841 / IN THE 56TH YEAR OF HIS AGE.

Hospital Mate 6 May 1805. Asst Surgeon 60th Foot 12 Oct 1809. Asst Surgeon 4th Garrison Battalion 28 Jan 1811. Asst Surgeon 93rd Foot 5 Sep 1811. Asst Surgeon Royal Waggon Train 5 Dec 1811. Surgeon 31st Foot 26 May 1816. Surgeon 60th Foot 8 Dec 1816. Surgeon York Lt Infantry Volunteers 20 Nov 1817. Surgeon 99th Foot 17 Jun 1824. Surgeon 7th Hussars 21 Sep 1830. Surgeon 59th Foot 12 Aug1834.

Served in the Peninsula Nov 1812 – Apr 1814. Present at Vittoria. Retired on half pay 1841. MD St Andrews 1825.

HIBBERT, John Nembhard
Lieutenant. 1st (King's) Dragoon Guards.
Brass memorial tablet: St Peter's Church, Chalfont St Peter, Buckinghamshire. (Photograph)

IN MEMORY OF JOHN NEMBHARD HIBBERT ESQ OF CHALFONT PARK THIRD SON OF / ROBERT HIBBERT ESQ OF CHALFONT PARK AND OF BIRTLES HALL CHESHIRE / BY LETITIA DAUGHTER OF JOHN FREDERICK NEMBHARD ESQ OF ST MARY'S IN / THE ISLAND OF JAMAICA MAJOR IN THE ARMY AND FORMERLY CAPTAIN IN THE / KING'S DRAGOON

443

GUARDS IN WHICH REGIMENT HE WAS A CORNET AT WATERLOO / A DEPUTY LIEUTENANT AND JUSTICE OF THE PEACE FOR THIS COUNTY OF WHICH / HE WAS HIGH SHERIFF IN THE YEAR 1838 BORN 11TH MARCH 1796 DIED 3RD / JANUARY 1886 HAVING MARRIED 6TH AUGUST 1833, JANE ANNE DAUGHTER / OF SIR ROBERT ALEXANDER BART

Cornet 13 Jan 1814. Lt 30 Mar 1815. Capt 7 Sep 1820. Bt Major 10 Jan 1837.

Present at Waterloo where he took part in the cavalry charge. From his letters he reported that 'Our Brigade, never having been on service before, hardly knew how to act. They knew they were to charge but never thought about stopping at the proper time.' The regiment lost 12 officers killed or wounded but Hibbert was uninjured. Present at the Capture of Paris and with the Army of Occupation. Returned to England in 1816. Retired on half pay 25 Oct 1821.

REFERENCE: Glover, Gareth, ed., The 1815 letters of Lieutenant John Hibbert, 1st King's Dragoon Guards, 2007.

HICKEY, Jeremiah
Private. 12th (Prince of Wales's) Regiment of Light Dragoons.
Named on the Regimental Memorial: St Joseph's Church, Waterloo, Belgium. (Photograph)
Killed at Waterloo.

HICKMAN, Charles
Regimental Sergeant Major. 15th (King's) Regiment of Light Dragoons.
Memorial tablet: Cahir Church, Cahir, County Tipperary, Ireland. (M.I.)

"SACRED TO THE MEMORY OF LIEUT AND ADJUTANT CHARLES HICKMAN, LATE OF THE 7TH OR PRINCESS ROYAL'S REGIMENT OF DRAGOON GUARDS, AND FORMERLY THE 15TH OR KING'S HUSSARS, IN WHICH DISTINGUISHED CORPS HE SERVED DURING THE LONG PERIOD OF 24 YEARS. HE WAS PRESENT AT THE AFFAIR OF SAHAGUN, AND ALL THE ACTIONS IN WHICH THIS REGIMENT WAS ENGAGED DURING THE PENINSULAR WAR, AS ALSO AT WATERLOO. HE WAS APPOINTED ADJUTANT OF THE 7TH DRAGOON GUARDS IN 1826, WHICH SITUATION HE FILLED FOR 10 YEARS WITH ADVANTAGE TO THE REGIMENT AND CREDIT AND HONOUR TO HIMSELF. HE DIED AT CAHIR BARRACKS 7 MAY 1834, AETAT 55 HAVING DEVOTED 38 TO HIS COUNTRY'S SERVICE. THIS TABLET IS ERECTED BY HIS BROTHER OFFICERS OF THE 7TH DRAGOON GUARDS IN TESTIMONY OF THE HIGH OPINION THEY ENTERTAINED OF HIS MERITS AS A GALLANT SOLDIER AND A ZEALOUS OFFICER."

Pte 15th Lt Dragoons 1800. Promoted from the ranks: Lt and Adjt 7th Dragoon Guards 12 Jan 1826.
Served in the Peninsula with 15th Lt Dragoons Nov 1808 – Jan 1809 and Feb 1813 – Apr 1814. Present at Sahagun, Cacabellos, Morales, Vittoria, Orthes and Toulouse. Present at Waterloo. Served for 24 years with the 15th Lt Dragoons. Promoted from the ranks and became Adjutant of the 7th Dragoon Guards 1826.

HIGGINS, Thomas
Lieutenant. 5th (Northumberland) Regiment of Foot.
Grave: St George's Churchyard, Doncaster, Yorkshire. (Grave number 245). (M.I.)

"SACRED TO THE MEMORY OF / SARAH HIGGINS, WIFE / OF LIEUT THOMAS HIGGINS / LATE OF THE 5TH REGT OF FOOT / WHO LOST HIS LIFE IN THE / SERVICE OF HIS COUNTRY / AT THE BATTLE OF VITTORIA IN 1813."

Lt 26 Sep 1805.
Served in the Peninsula with 1/5th Jul 1808 – Jan 1809 and Jul 1812 – Jul 1813. Present at Rolica,

Vimeiro, Corunna, Salamanca, retreat from Burgos and Vittoria where he was severely wounded 21 Jun and died of his wounds 5 Jul 1813.

HIGGINSON, Alexander

Lieutenant and Captain. 1st Regiment of Foot Guards.
Memorial: Royal Military Chapel, Wellington Barracks, London. (M.I.) (Destroyed by a Flying Bomb in 1944)

"IN MEMORY OF COLONEL ALEXANDER HIGGINSON, AND HIS BROTHER, GENERAL GEORGE P. HIGGINSON, BOTH OF THE 1st OR GRENADIER REGIMENT OF FOOT GUARDS. THE FORMER SERVED CONTINUOUSLY FROM 1804 TO 1841, WHEN HE RETIRED FROM THE ARMY, DYING IN 1855. HE WAS PRESENT AT CORUNNA, WALCHEREN, AND IN THE CAMPAIGNS OF 1812–13–14...................."

Ensign 26 Jan 1804. Lt and Capt 14 Sep 1809. Capt and Lt Colonel 1 Jul 1815. Bt Colonel 10 Jan 1837. Major with rank of Colonel 28 Jun 1838.

Served in the Peninsula with 1st Battalion Oct 1808 – Jan 1809 and Sep 1812 – Apr 1814. Present at Corunna, Bidassoa, Nivelle, Nive, Adour and Bayonne. Also served at Walcheren 1809. MGS medal for Corunna, Nivelle and Nive. Brother of Lt and Capt George Powell Higginson 1st Foot Guards.

HIGGINSON, George Powell

Lieutenant and Captain. 1st Regiment of Foot Guards.
Memorial: Royal Military Chapel, Wellington Barracks, London. (M.I.) (Destroyed by a Flying Bomb in 1944)

"IN MEMORY OF COLONEL ALEXANDER HIGGINSON, AND HIS BROTHER, GENERAL GEORGE P. HIGGINSON, BOTH OF THE 1st OR GRENADIER REGIMENT OF FOOT GUARDS. / .... / THE LATTER SERVED ALSO CONTINUOUSLY FROM 1805 TO 1830, WHEN HE WAS APPOINTED AIDE-DE-CAMP TO THE COMMANDER IN-CHIEF, AND RETIRED FROM THE REGIMENT. HE SERVED IN SICILY, AT CORUNNA, WHEN HE CARRIED THE KING'S COLOUR, AT WALCHEREN; AT ST SEBASTIAN HE LED THE STORMING PARTY OF THE REGIMENT, AND WAS ALSO PRESENT AT NIVE, NIVELLE, AND THE ACTIONS IN THE PYRENEES. COLONEL 94TH REGIMENT IN 1856. HE DIED HONOURED AND LAMENTED IN 1866, AGED 80. / THIS MONUMENT IS DEDICATED BY HIS SON, MAJOR-GENERAL GEORGE WENTWORTH HIGGINSON, C.B., LATE LIEUT. COLONEL OF THE GRENADIER GUARDS, 1879".

Ensign 6 Nov 1805. Lt and Capt 3 Apr 1811. Capt and Lt Colonel 26 Oct 1820. Bt Colonel 10 Jan 1837. Major General 9 Nov 1846. Lt General 20 Jun 1854. General 9 Nov 1862.

Served in the Peninsula with 1st Battalion Oct 1808 – Jan 1809 and Jan 1813 – Apr 1814. Present at Corunna (carried the colours), San Sebastian (led one of the storming parties), Nivelle, Nive, Adour and Bayonne. Present in France with the Army of Occupation until 1818. Also served in Sicily 1807 and Walcheren 1809. MGS medal for Corunna, San Sebastian, Nivelle and Nive. ADC to Lord Hill, the Commander in Chief 1830 and served him for 12 years. Colonel 94th Foot 29 Jan 1855. Educated at Winchester. Died at Cannes 19 Apr 1866. Brother of Lt and Capt Alexander Higginson 1st Foot Guards.
REFERENCE: *Gentleman's Magazine, Jun 1866, p. 916.*

HIGGINSON, Philip Talbot

Lieutenant. 87th (Prince of Wales's Own Irish) Regiment of Foot.
Gravestone: Kacheri Cemetery, Cawnpore, India. (M.I.)

"SACRED TO THE MEMORY OF LIEUT PHILIP / TALBOT HIGGINSON, LATE OF HIS MAJESTY'S

/ 87TH REGT. WHO DEPARTED THIS LIFE ON THE / 9TH DAY OF AUGUST 1818. AGED 27 YEARS. / THIS STONE IS ERECTED BY HIS BROTHER OFFICERS / IN TESTIMONY OF THEIR RESPECT."

Ensign 22 Jul 1806. Lt 23 Sep 1807.
    Served in the Peninsula May 1810 – Sep 1813. Present at Cadiz, Barrosa, Tarifa and Vittoria where he was severely wounded. Also served in India where he died in 1818.

HILDITCH, Neil
Apothecary. Medical Department.
Grave: St Pancras Old Churchyard, London. (M.I.)

"NEIL HILDITCH / LATE APOTHECARY TO HIS MAJESTY'S FORCES, / DIED DECEMBER 25TH 1824. / AGED 43. / REQUIESCAT IN PACE"

Hospital Assistant 2 Feb 1811. Apothecary 9 Sep 1813.
    Served in the Peninsula Jun 1813 – Apr 1814. Half pay 1814.

HILDRETH, William
Private. 1st (Royal Scots) Regiment of Foot.
Headstone: St Agatha's Churchyard, Gilling West, Yorkshire. (Photograph)

SACRED / TO THE MEMORY OF / WILLIAM HILDRETH PRIVATE / SOLDIER IN THE 3RD BATTN 1ST FOOT / WHO DIED IN PORTUGAL JUNE 1ST 1812 / AGED 38 YEARS. / ....

Served in the Peninsula with 3/1st Apr 1810 – May 1812. Present at Busaco, Fuentes d'Onoro, and Badajoz.

HILL, Lord Arthur Moyse William
Captain. 10th (Prince of Wales's Own) Regiment of Light Dragoons.
Memorial tablet: St Andrew's Church, Ombersley, Worcestershire. (Photograph)

THIS STONE / IS SACRED TO THE MEMORY OF / HER SECOND SON / THE LORD ARTHUR MOYSE WILLIAM HILL, / FIRST LORD SANDYS OF THE SECOND CREATION. / HE BECAME A LIEUTENANT GENERAL IN 1854, / HAVING SERVED IN THE PENINSULAR WAR, / AND AT WATERLOO, / WHERE HE WAS A.D.C. TO THE ILLUSTRIOUS / DUKE OF WELLINGTON, / AND WAS, AT THE TIME OF HIS DEATH, / COLONEL OF THE ROYAL REGIMENT OF SCOTS GREYS. / HE REPRESENTED / THE PATERNAL COUNTY OF DOWN IN IRELAND / FOR TWENTY YEARS, / AND SUCCEEDED TO HIS MOTHER'S BARONY AND PROPERTY / ON HER DEATH IN 1836. / HE DIED AT OMBERSLEY COURT ON THE 16TH OF JULY 1860, / JUSTLY BELOVED AND RESPECTED, / IN THE 69TH YEAR OF HIS AGE, / AND IS BURIED IN THE OLD CHANCEL / NEAR THIS SPOT.

Cornet 10th Lt Dragoons 27 Jul 1809. Lt 19 Jul 1810. Capt 25 Aug 1813. Bt Major 27 Jul 1815. Capt 2nd Dragoons 19 Sep 1816. Bt Lt Colonel 21 Jan 1819. Major 25 Oct 1825. Lt Colonel 2nd Dragoons 23 Mar 1832. Bt Colonel 16 Jan 1837. Major General 9 Nov 1841. Lt General 20 Jun 1854.
    Served in the Peninsula Feb – Sep 1813. Present at Morales, Vittoria and Pamplona. Present at Waterloo (on Staff as ADC to Wellington). MP for County Down for 20 years 1817–1836. Colonel 7th Dragoon Guards 15 Mar 1853. Colonel 2nd Regt of Dragoons 26 Aug 1858.
REFERENCE: *Annual Register, 1860, Appx, p. 486.*

HILL, Charles
Lieutenant Colonel. 50th (West Kent) Regiment of Foot.
Memorial tablet: Cathedral Church, Kingston, Jamaica, West Indies. (Photograph)

IN THE CEMETERY OF THIS PARISH LIE INTERRED THE MORTAL REMAINS OF / COLONEL CHARLES HILL, LIEUT. COLONEL OF THE 50TH REGIMENT OF FOOT / COMPANION OF THE MOST HONOURABLE MILITARY ORDER OF THE BATH. / AS MAJOR, AND AFTERWARDS AS LIEUT. COLONEL COMMANDING THIS BRAVE AND DISTINGUISHED / REGIMENT, HE WAS HIMSELF EMINENTLY CONSPICUOUS IN THE NUMEROUS ACTIONS OF THE WAR, / IN WHICH IT WAS ENGAGED, AND ASSISTED, IN PLACING IN ITS COLOURS THE GLORIOUS DISTINCTIONS / OF VIMIERA, VITTORIA, PYRENEES, AND PENINSULA, COVERED WITH WOUNDS AND WITH HONOR, / HE MIGHT, AT THE PEACE, HAVE RETIRED TO THE ENJOY-MENT OF HIS COUNTRY'S BLESSINGS AND / APPLAUSE, BUT ANXIOUS TO SEE HIS OLD REGIMENT RESTORED TO ITS WONTED FORCE, AND DISCIPLINE / AND THEN UNWILLING TO QUIT IT WHEN AGAIN ORDERED ON DISTANT DUTY AND AN UNFAVOURABLE / CHANGE OF CLIMATE. HE ULTIMATELY FELL A VICTIM TO HIS EVER ANXIOUS SOLICITUDE FOR / THOSE WITH WHOM HIS BLOOD HAD BEEN SO OFTEN SHED AND, TOGETHER WITH A NUMEROUS / BAND OF HIS GALLANT OFFICERS AND SOLDIERS, PERISHED BY A DESO-LATING FEVER ON THE / 31ST OF AUGUST 1819; IN THE 57 YEAR OF HIS AGE, AND THE 41ST OF HIS MILITARY SERVICE. / THIS STONE IS ERECTED TO HIS MEMORY BY HIS AFFEC-TIONATE WIFE ANNE HILL.

Grave: Fort Augusta, Jamaica. (M.I.)

BENEATH THIS STONE / LIE THE REMAINS OF / COL^L CHARLES HILL / WHO DIED 31ST OF AUGUST 1819 / AGED 57 YEARS. / IN THE COMMAND OF / THE 50TH REGIMENT OF FOOT.

Ensign 27 Dec 1778. Lt 13 Sep 1780. Capt 17 Feb 1794. Bt Major 25 Sep 1803. Major 1 Aug 1804. Bt Lt Colonel 25 Jul 1810. Lt Colonel 13 Jun 1811. Bt Colonel 12 Aug 1819.

Served in the Peninsula Aug 1808 – Jan 1809 and May 1813 – Apr 1814. Present at Rolica (wounded), Vimeiro, Vittoria, Pyrenees (severely wounded and awarded pension of £300 per annum) and Toulouse. Gold Medal for Vittoria. CB. Also served in Gibraltar 1782, Copenhagen 1807, Walcheren 1809 and West Indies 1816 until his death in a yellow fever epidemic in August 1819.

HILL, Clement Delves
Captain. Royal Regiment of Horse Guards.
Memorial tablet: St Chad's Church, Prees, Shropshire. (Photograph)

TO THE MEMORY OF / CLEMENT HILL / MAJOR GENERAL H. M. SERVICE / THIS MONUMENT WAS ERECTED BY THE SUBSCRIPTION / OF HIS FRIENDS AND COMRADES IN THE MADRAS PRESIDENCY, / AND BY THE OFFICERS OF THE ROYAL HORSE GUARDS, / IN TESTIMONY OF THEIR LOVE FOR HIS / PERSON AND CHARACTER. / MODEST AND UNASSUMING IN MIND AND DEPORTMENT, / AND UTTERLY CARELESS TO ADVANCE HIMSELF; / IN SERVING HIS COUNTRY, HIS FRIENDS AND EVERY GOOD CAUSE / HE WAS FULL OF ZEAL AND PERSE-VERANCE. / IN THE CAMPAIGNS OF THE PENINSULA / WHILST FIGHTING UNDER THE COMMAND OF HIS BROTHER / GEN^L. LORD HILL G.C.B. / HE WAS AMPLY SATISFIED WITH CONTRIBUTING TO HIS GLORY / WITHOUT SEEKING, ALTHOUGH DESERVING, TO SHARE IN HIS HONOURS. / DURING HIS COMMAND OF THE MYSORE DIVISION / OF THE MADRAS ARMY / BY A RARE UNION OF FIRMNESS WITH SUAVITY / HE UPHELD AND SECURED / THE DIGNITY OF HIS OFFICE, THE DISCIPLINE OF THE TROOPS, / AND THE AFFECTION OF ALL WHO SERVED / UNDER HIM. / HE WAS BORN AT PREES, SHROPSHIRE / ON 6TH DECEMBER

1781. / DIED AT THE FALLS OF GUERSOPPA ON 20TH JANUARY / AND WAS BURIED AT HONOWUR 22ND JANUARY 1845, / HAVING BEEN IN COMMAND IN MYSORE / FROM 24TH NOVEMBER 1841.

Statue: Trinity Church, Bangalore, India. (Photograph)

TO THE MEMORY OF / CLEMENT DELVES HILL ESQRE / MAJOR GENERAL H. M. SERVICE / THIS MONUMENT WAS ERECTED BY THE SUBSCRIPTION / OF HIS FRIENDS AND COMRADES IN THE MADRAS PRESIDENCY / AND BY THE OFFICERS OF THE ROYAL HORSE GUARDS / IN TESTIMONY OF THEIR LOVE FOR HIS / PERSONAL CHARACTER. / MODEST AND UNAS-SUMING IN MIND AND DEPORTMENT / AND UTTERLY CARELESS TO ADVANCE HIMSELF, / IN SERVING HIS COUNTRY, HIS FRIENDS, AND EVERY GOOD CAUSE / HE WAS FULL OF ZEAL AND PERSEVERANCE, / IN THE CAMPAIGNS OF THE PENINSULA / WHILST FIGHTING UNDER THE COMMAND OF HIS BROTHER / LORD HILL / HE WAS AMPLY SATISFIED WITH CONTRIBUTING TO HIS GLORY / WITHOUT SEEKING, ALTHOUGH DESERVING, TO SHARE IN HIS HONORS. / DURING HIS COMMAND OF THE MYSORE DIVISION / OF THE MADRAS ARMY / BY A RARE UNION OF FIRMNESS AND SUAVITY / HE UPHELD AND SECURED / THE DIGNITY OF HIS OFFICE, THE DISCIPLINE OF THE TROOPS / AND THE AFFECTION OF ALL WHO SERVED / UNDER HIM. / HE WAS BORN AT PREES, SHROPSHIRE ON THE 6TH OF DECEMBER 1781, DIED AT THE FALLS OF GUERSOPPA ON 20TH JANUARY / AND WAS BURIED AT HONAWAR 22ND JANUARY 1845 / HAVING BEEN IN COMMAND IN MYSORE / FROM 20TH NOVEMBER 1841.

Ensign 22 Aug 1805. Lt 6 Mar 1806. Capt 4 Apr 1811. Bt Major 26 Dec 1811. Bt Lt Colonel 30 Dec 1813. Major 21 May 1820. Lt Colonel 24 Jul 1823. Bt Colonel 21 Jun 1827. Major General 10 Jan 1837.
    Served in the Peninsula Aug 1808 – Jan 1809, May 1809 – Nov 1810 and May 1811 – Apr 1814 (ADC to his brother Lord Hill). Present at Rolica, Vimeiro, Corunna, Douro (wounded and Mentioned in Despatches), Talavera, Busaco, Arroyo dos Molinos (Mentioned in Despatches, sent home with despatches and awarded Bt Majority), Almarez (Mentioned in Despatches), Vittoria, Pyrenees, Nivelle, Nive (Mentioned in Despatches, sent home with despatches and awarded Bt Lt Colonelcy), Orthes, Aire, Tarbes and Toulouse. Present at Waterloo (ADC to Lord Hill, but preferred to serve with his regiment – severely wounded). Also served in India (commanded the Mysore division of the Madras Army 1841). Died in India 20 Jan 1845. Brother of Colonel Lord Hill 72nd Foot, Capt and Lt Colonel Thomas Noel Hill 1st Foot Guards and Lt Colonel Robert Chambré Hill Royal Horse Guards.
REFERENCE: *Gentleman's Magazine, May 1845, p. 548.*

HILL, Dudley St Leger
Captain. Royal West India Rangers.
Gravestone: Ambala Cemetery, Bengal, India. (M.I.)

"SACRED TO THE MEMORY OF / MAJOR GENERAL SIR DUDLEY ST LEGER HILL, KCB. / COLONEL OF H. M. 50TH REGT. / WHO DIED AT UMBALLAH WHILE IN COMMAND / OF THE SIRHIND DIVISION ON 21ST FEBRUARY 1851."

Ensign 9th Foot 27 Aug 1804. Lt 95th Foot 10 Oct 1805. Capt Royal West India Rangers 16 Aug 1810. Bt Major 27 Apr 1812. Bt Lt Colonel 21 Jun 1813. Major 95th Foot 1 Dec 1823. Bt Colonel 22 Jul 1830. Major General 23 Nov 1841. Portuguese Army: Major 2nd Lusitanian Legion and 8th Caçadores 26 Sep 1810. Lt Colonel 28 Jan 1813. Major Spanish and Portuguese Staff 25 Oct 1814.
    Served in the Peninsula with 2/95th Aug 1808 – Jan 1809, 1/95th Jun 1809 – Aug 1810 and Portuguese Army Sep 1810 – Apr 1814. Present at Obidos, Rolica (wounded), Vimeiro (wounded), Corunna campaign, Talavera, Coa, Busaco, Fuentes d'Onoro, Ciudad Rodrigo, Badajoz (Mentioned in Despatches

and awarded Bt Majority), Salamanca (severely wounded), Burgos, Villa Muriel (wounded, Mentioned in Despatches and taken prisoner but escaped), Vittoria (awarded Bt Colonelcy), San Sebastian (severely wounded and Mentioned in Despatches) and Bayonne. CB 1815. Knighted 1816. Gold Cross for Fuentes d'Onoro, Badajoz, Salamanca, Vittoria, and San Sebastian. MGS medal for Rolica, Vimeiro, Busaco and Ciudad Rodrigo. Also served in South America 1807 (with the Forlorn Hope at the storming of Montevideo and at Buenos Ayres where he was wounded and taken prisoner), Portugal 1814–1824 (in command of a Portuguese corps. KTS and four medals). Ionian Islands 1824–1826, West Indies 1834 (Governor of St Lucia) and India 1848 (General on Staff in Bengal). KCB 1848. Colonel 50th Foot 28 Mar 1849. Died in India 21 Feb 1851.

REFERENCE: *Dictionary of National Biography. Royal Military Calendar, Vol 4, pp. 475–6. United Service Magazine, May 1851, pp. 155–6. Gentleman's Magazine, May 1851, p. 552. Annual Register, 1851, Appx, p. 264.*

HILL, Henry
Lieutenant and Adjutant. 23rd Regiment of Light Dragoons.
Cross on three stepped base: St Cross Churchyard, Knutsford, Cheshire. (South east corner of churchyard). (Photograph)

IN MEMORY OF / CAPTAIN HILL / BORN OCT 18TH 1786. / DIED MARCH 4TH 1875. / PENINSULA & WATERLOO. / ………………..

Pte 11th Lt Dragoons Jul 1800. Sgt 1814. Commissioned from the ranks: Cornet 23rd Lt Dragoons 19 Jan 1815. Lt and Adjt 5 May 1815. Lt and Adjt 1st Dragoon Guards 16 Apr 1818. Adjutant Cheshire Yeomanry 1836. Retired 1868.

Served in the ranks with the 11th Lt Dragoons in the Peninsula May 1811 – Jun 1813. Present at El Bodon, Salamanca, advance on Burgos and retreat from Burgos, where the regiment formed the rear guard. Promoted from the ranks Jan 1815 in the 23rd Lt Dragoons and served with them at Waterloo. On reduction of the regiment in 1818 joined the 1st Dragoon Guards as Lt and Adjutant. MGS medal for Salamanca. After retiring on half pay in 1836, he was Adjutant to the Cheshire Yeomanry for thirty years. Captain Hill was the inspiration for Elizabeth Gaskell's portrayal of Capt Brown in *Cranford*.

HILL, John
2nd Lieutenant. 95th Regiment of Foot.
Named on the Memorial: St Andrew's Church, (now Musée Historique), Biarritz, France. (Photograph)
Memorial stone: Base of Church Tower, Vera, Spain. (Photograph)

NEAR HERE REPOSE THE / MORTAL REMAINS OF / JOHN HILL 2D LT 95TH ENGH / REGT WHO FELL 7TH OCTR / 1813 AGED 24 YEARS. 1850.

2nd Lt 10 May 1812.
Served in the Peninsula with 2/95th Oct 1813. Present at Bidassoa. Killed at the assault on La Bayonette redoubt north of Vera, led by John Colborne, 7 Oct 1813.
REFERENCE: *Gentleman's Magazine, Nov 1813, p. 505.*

HILL, John
Sergeant. 40th (2nd Somersetshire) Regiment of Foot.
Headstone: St George's Churchyard, Georgeham, Devon. (Photograph)

IN / MEMORY OF / SERGT. JOHN HILL / OF THE 40TH REGT OF INFANTRY. / A WATERLOO MAN, AND THROUGH / THE PENINSULAR WAR, WITH THE / DUKE OF WELLINGTON. / DIED 28TH OF FEBRY 1861, AGED 77. / NOR CANNONS ROAR, NOR RIFLE SHOT, / CAN WAKE HIM

IN THIS PEACEFUL SPOT: / WITH FAITH IN CHRIST AND TRUST IN GOD, / THE SERGEANT SLEEPS BENEATH THIS CLOD. / ....

Pte 3rd Dragoon Guards 25 Mar 1800. Pte 40th Foot 20 Apr 1805. Cpl 1808. Sgt 1810.
    Served in the Peninsula and Waterloo. Awarded MGS medal for Badajoz and Salamanca. Discharged 12 Jan 1824.

HILL, John Montgomery
Lieutenant. 43rd (Monmouthshire) Light Infantry Regiment of Foot.
Buried in Kensal Green Cemetery, London. (No longer extant: 22208/124/9)

Ensign 16 Mar 1809. Lt 28 Jun 1810. Capt 31 Dec 1822.
    Served in the Peninsula with 1/43rd Apr – Aug 1813. Present at Vittoria and Pyrenees. MGS medal for Vittoria and Pyrenees. Retired 1 Sep 1825. Buried in Kensal Green 9 Jun 1870.

HILL, Robert
Private. 14th (Buckinghamshire) Regiment of Foot.
Headstone: General Cemetery, Nottingham, Nottinghamshire. (Photograph)

IN / AFFECTIONATE / REMEMBRANCE OF / ROBERT HILL, / 3RD BATTN 10TH REGM. WATERLOO 1815, / WHO DEPARTED THIS LIFE, / MAY 24TH 1860, AGED 64 YEARS.

Served at Waterloo in 3rd Battalion 14th Foot in Capt J. L. White's Company, not as headstone states 3rd Battalion 10th Foot who were not at Waterloo.

HILL, Sir Robert Chambré
Lieutenant Colonel. Royal Regiment of Horse Guards.
Ledger stone: St Chad's Churchyard, Prees, Shropshire. (North east section). (Photograph)

.... / COL. SIR ROBERT CHAMBRÉ HILL C.B. / LAST SURVIVING SON OF SIR JOHN HILL OF HAWKSTONE BART. M.P. / BORN AT PREES HALL, MARCH 25 1778 – ENGAGED IN THE PENINSULAR WAR. / WOUNDED IN COMMAND OF THE BLUES, AT WATERLOO. / DIED IN THE HOUSE OF HIS BIRTH MARCH 5 1860. / ....

Memorial tablet: St Chad's Church, Prees, Shropshire. (Photograph)

IN A VAULT / ON THE NORTH SIDE OF THE CHURCH / REST THE REMAINS OF / COLONEL SIR ROBERT HILL. C.B. / BROTHER AND COMPANION IN ARMS / OF ROWLAND, FIRST VISCOUNT HILL, / BORN AT PREES HALL, / WHERE HE DIED MARCH 5TH 1860 / AGED 82. / ....

Cornet 29 Jul 1795. Lt 11 Nov 1797. Capt 11 Apr 1800. Major 14 Nov 1805. Bt Lt Colonel 1 Jan 1812. Lt Colonel 13 May 1813. Bt Colonel 1 Jan 1819.
    Served in the Peninsula Nov 1812 – Apr 1814. (Commanded Household Cavalry Brigade Feb – Jun 1813). Present at Vittoria and Toulouse. Gold Medal for Vittoria and MGS medal for Toulouse. Present at Waterloo (severely wounded and awarded pension of £300 per annum). CB. Also served in Flanders 1794–1795. Brother of Colonel Lord Rowland Hill 72nd Foot, Capt and Lt Colonel Thomas Noel Hill 1st Foot Guards and Capt Clement Hill Royal Horse Guards.

Sacred to the Memory
of
Enfign JOHN DELMAR late of H.M. 28th Regt
of Infantry, fourth Son of Mr DELMAR of this City:
He fell by a Shot which inftantly depriv'd him of
life in the 19th Year of his age, whilft difplaying
the Britifh Colour at the Puerto de Maya, in
the firft battle of the Pyrenees, on the 25th July 1813.
He was not lefs refpected by his brother Officers,
than belov'd by his Family, who have erected
this fincere tho' fmall Memorial as a pledge
of their affection and efteem

John Delmar 28th Foot

TO THE MEMORY OF
71
JOHN
DRUMMOND
1791-1865
SGT. 71ST FOOT
A VETERAN OF
WATERLOO
PIONEER OF
BEECHWORTH

John Drummond 71st Foot

TO THE
MEMORY OF
CAPTAIN JAMES DRYDEN

James Dryden Staff Corps of Cavalry

George H. Duckworth 48th Foot

Benjamin D'Urban 2nd West India Regiment

Charles Diggle 52nd Foot

Joseph Dyas 51st Light Infantry

Charles and William Eeles 95th Foot

Michael L. Este 1st Life Guards

Sir Henry Fairfax 85th Foot

Chesborough G. Falconer 78th Foot

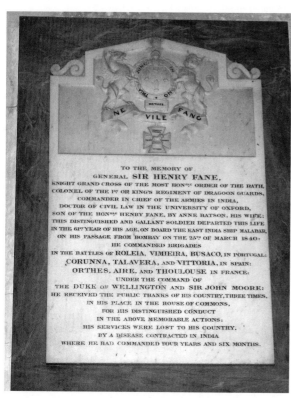

Sir Henry Fane 4th Dragoon Guards

John Farquharson 42nd Foot

Orlando Felix 95th Foot

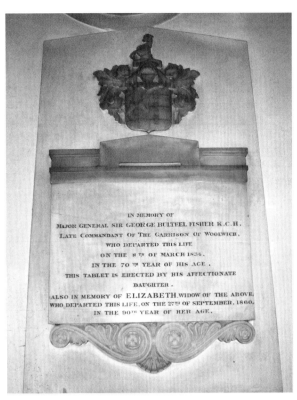

George B. Fisher Royal Artillery

Thomas Fletcher 4th Ceylon Regiment

James J. Fraser 7th Light Dragoons

Thomas Fraser 1st Foot

David Gardiner 88th Foot and John Gardiner 95h Foot

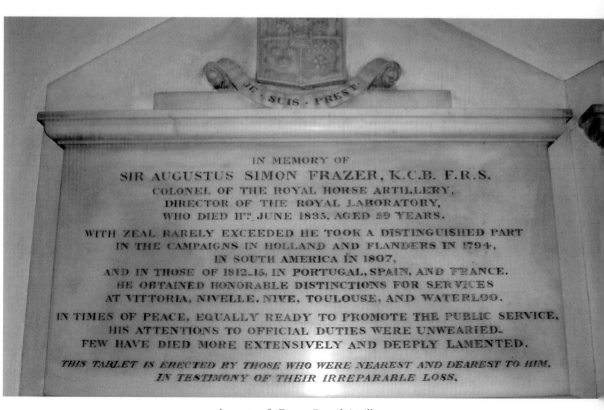

Augustus S. Frazer Royal Artillery

James Gordon 92nd Foot

Hugh Gough 87th Foot

Alexander Gourlay 13th R. Veteran Battalion

Sir Thomas Graham 90th Foot

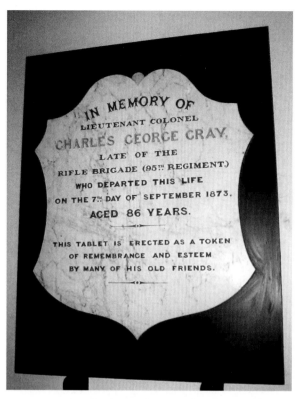

Charles G. Gray 95th Foot

William Green 95th Foot

Levi Grisedale 10th Light Dragoons

William Guard 45th Foot

William Gun 91st Foot

Charles Hall 38th Foot

Henry Hanmer Royal Regiment of Horse Guards

John Hare 27th Foot

John Harrison 18th Light Dragoons

William Havelock 43rd Foot

William Haverfield 43rd Foot

James Hay 7th Foot

William Hewett 14th Foot

Felton E. B. Hervey 14th Light Dragoons

Lord Rowland Hill 72nd Foot
Commander II Corps at Waterloo

TO THE MEMORY OF
JOHN HOPWOOD LIEUT! IN THE
95TH OR RIFLE REGIMENT,
WHO FELL AT ARCANGUES, BEFORE BAYONNE,
DECEMBER THE 10TH 1813.
Æ. 22.

HE DISTINGUISHED HIMSELF, AT THE BATTLES OF
BUSACO, SALAMANCA, AND VITTORIA, AND
AT THE SIEGES OF CUIDAD RODRIGO, AND BADAJOS
WHERE HE RECEIVED SEVERE WOUNDS; AND FELL
COMMANDING A COMPANY OF THE REGIMENT
TO WHICH HE BELONGED, BELOVED AND LAMENTED.

TO PERPETUATE HIS REMEMBRANCE,
HIS TOWNSMEN HAVE CAUSED THIS MONUMENT
TO BE ERECTED.

John Hopwood 95th Foot

James Hughes 18th Light Dragoons

TO THE
MEMORY OF
GEORGE THOMSON JACOB ESQ?
OF SHILLINGSTONE IN THE
COUNTY OF DORSET,
LIEU COLONEL OF THE DORSET
REGIMENT OF MILITIA,
HE DIED AT RAY RIGG IN THIS
PARISH ON THE 1? OF MAY 1855
AGED 61.

George T. Jacob 1st Foot Guards

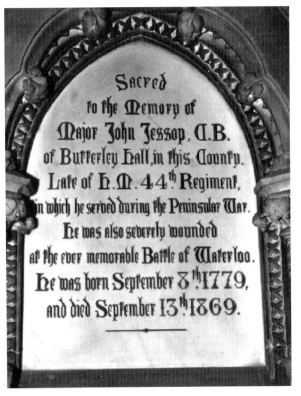

Sacred
to the Memory of
Major John Jessop, C.B.
of Butterley Hall, in this County,
Late of H.M. 44th Regiment,
in which he served during the Peninsular War.
He was also severely wounded
at the ever memorable Battle of Waterloo.
He was born September 8th 1779,
and died September 13th 1869.

John Jessop 44th Foot

SACRED TO THE MEMORY OF
COLONEL WILLIAM KELLY C.B.
LIEUT COL: OF HIS MAJESTY'S 24TH REGT OF FOOT,
WHO DEPARTED THIS LIFE AT LITTLECOTT,
THE 21ST OF AUGUST 1818.
COLONEL KELLY'S SERVICES WERE EXTENDED TO THE
FOUR QUARTERS OF THE GLOBE:
HE WAS SEVERELY WOUNDED AT THE BATTLE OF THE PYRENEES,
AND EXHAUSTED AFTERWARDS BY HIS SUCCESSFUL EXERTIONS
IN THE NEPAUL WAR IN INDIA.
HE RETURNED ONLY TO BREATHE HIS LAST WITH HIS FRIENDS.
ADMIRED IN HIS PROFESSION AS A SOLDIER,
AND ESTEEMED BY ALL AS A MAN.

William Kelly 24th Foot

William J. King Royal Staff Corps

Joseph A. De Lautour 1st Foot Guards

William Lawrence 40th Foot

Sir Alexander Leith 31st Foot

Francis Livingstone 90th Foot

John Locke 84th Foot

Patrick Logan 57th Foot

Thomas G. Logan 13th Light Dragoons

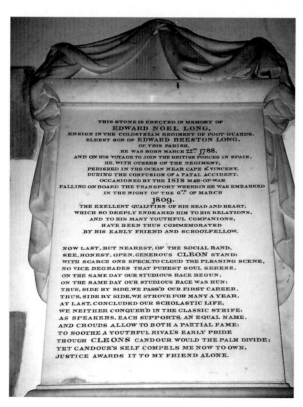

Edward N. Long Coldstream Guards

Henry Blois Lynch Royal York Rangers

HILL, Lord Rowland

Colonel. 72nd (Highland) Regiment of Foot
Memorial tablet: St Mary Magdalene Church, Hadnall, Shropshire. (Photograph)

BENEATH THE TOWER OF THIS CHURCH, THE SPOT SELECTED BY HIMSELF, / ARE INTERRED THE REMAINS OF / ROWLAND FIRST VISCOUNT HILL, / WHO DIED DECEMBER 10TH 1842 IN THE 71ST YEAR OF HIS AGE. / IN HIM WERE COMBINED, IN AN UNUSUAL DEGREE, / GENTLENESS AND FIRMNESS, HUMANITY AND HEROISM, CALMNESS AND ARDOUR GAINING FOR HIM NOT ONLY PUBLIC APPLAUSE BUT CORDIAL ESTEEM AND AFFECTION. / HIS WELL KNOWN SERVICES ARE RECORDED IN THE HISTORY OF THE TIMES. / THEY RAISED HIM TO THE DISTINCTION OF THE PEERAGE, / AND OF GENERAL IN CHIEF COMMANDING THE BRITISH FORCES, / THE DUTIES OF WHICH HIGH OFFICE HE DISCHARGED FOR MORE THAN FOURTEEN YEARS / WITH REMARKABLE IMPARTIALITY AND EFFICIENCY. / IN THE AUTUMN OF 1842 DECLINING HEALTH OBLIGED HIM TO RETIRE TO HIS NATIVE COUNTY / WHERE HE HAD BEFORE SPENT MOST OF HIS HOURS OF RELAXATION IN THE CULTIVATION / OF THE ARTS OF PEACE, AND PROVED HIMSELF THE FRIEND OF ALL CLASSES AND THE SPECIAL / BENEFACTOR OF THE POOR. THE EARTHLY HONOURS CONFERRED UPON HIM / DID NOT BLIND HIM TO HIS SPIRITUAL WANTS AND NECESSITIES, / NOR RENDER HIM INSENSIBLE TO HIS DEEP NEED OF A SAVIOUR. / HE PASSED THE BRIEF EVENING OF HIS REPOSE IN SINCERE PENITENCE AND PRAYER, / AND DIED IN PEACE LOOKING UNTO HIM ALONE WHO IS / THE WAY, THE TRUTH AND THE LIFE.

Memorial column: Shrewsbury, Shropshire. (Photograph)

North side:

TO LIEUTENANT-GENERAL ROWLAND / LORD HILL BARON HILL OF ALMAREZ AND / HAWKSTONE. G.C.B. / NOT MORE DISTINGUISHED FOR HIS / SKILL AND COURAGE IN THE FIELD, / DURING THE ARDUOUS CAMPAIGNS IN / SPAIN AND PORTUGAL, THE SOUTH OF / FRANCE, AND THE MEMORABLE PLAINS OF / WATERLOO, / THAN FOR HIS BENEVOLENT AND / PATERNAL CARE IN PROVIDING FOR THE / COMFORTS AND SUPPLYING THE / NECESSITIES OF HIS VICTORIOUS / COUNTRYMEN / AND FOR THAT HUMANITY AND / GENEROSITY WHICH THEIR VANQUISHED / FOES EXPERIENCED AND / ACKNOWLEDGED / THE INHABITANTS OF THE TOWN AND / COUNTY OF SALOP HAVE ERECTED THIS / COLUMN AND STATUE, AS A MEMORIAL / OF THEIR RESPECT AND GRATITUDE TO AN / ILLUSTRIOUS CONTEMPORARY / AND AN INCITEMENT TO EMULATION / IN THE HEROES AND PATRIOTS OF FUTURE / AGES. / A. D. MDCCCXVI.

South Side:

CIVI. SVO. ROLANDO / DOMINO BARONI HILL. AB. ALMAREZ / ET HAWKSTONE POPVLARES, EIVS EX. / AGRO. ATQVE. MVNICIPIO. SALOPIENSI. / COLVMNAM, HANCCE. CVM. STATUA. P.C. / A.S. MDCCCXVI / IS IN RE. MILITARI. QVEMADMODVM. / SE. GESSERIT TESTES. SINT. LVSITANIA / HISPANIA. GALLIAE NARNONENSIS. AC / BELCICA ARTVRIS. ET: QVIDEM. / HOSTIVM. EXERCITVS.

East Side:

ROLICA PYRENEES / VIMIERA NIVELLE / CORUNNA NIVE / DOURO HILLETTE / TALAVERA ORTHEZ / BUSACO AIRE / ARROYO DEL MOLINO TARBES / ALMAREZ TOULOUSE / VITTORIA WATERLOO

Brass Memorial tablet: Royal Garrison Church, Portsmouth, Hampshire. (Back of a choir stall).

GENERAL VISCOUNT HILL / G: C: B: COMMANDING IN / CHIEF 1828–1842. / DIED DEC 10: 1842. AGED 70. / D: D: HIS NEPHEW VIS- / COUNT HILL.

Ensign 38th Foot 31 Jul 1790. Lt Independent Co 24 Jan 1791. Lt 53rd Foot 16 Mar 1791. Capt Independent Co 23 Mar 1793. Capt 86th Foot 30 Oct 1793. Major 90th Foot 10 Feb 1794. Lt Colonel 13 May 1794. Bt Colonel 1 Jan 1800. Major General 30 Oct 1805. Lt General 1 Jan 1812. General 27 May 1825.

Served in the Peninsula Aug 1808 – Jan 1809 and Apr – Jun 1809 (GOC 1st Brigade), Jun 1809 – Jan 1811 and Jun 1811 – Apr 1814 (GOC 2nd Division). Present at Rolica (Mentioned in Despatches), Vimeiro (Mentioned in Despatches), Corunna (Mentioned in Despatches), Douro (Mentioned in Despatches), Talavera (wounded and Mentioned in Despatches), Busaco (Mentioned in Despatches), Arroyo dos Molinos (Mentioned in Despatches), Almarez (wounded and Mentioned in Despatches), Vittoria, Pyrenees (Mentioned in Despatches), Nivelle, (Mentioned in Despatches), Nive (Mentioned in Despatches), Garris, Aire (Mentioned in Despatches), Orthes, Tarbes and Toulouse. Took part in the whole of the Peninsular War except for six months in 1811 when he caught malaria and had to return home. Gold Cross for Rolica, Vimeiro, Corunna, Talavera, Vittoria, Pyrenees, Nivelle, Nive and Orthes.

Present at Waterloo in command of the Second Corps which was split between the reserves at Hal and reserves at Mont St Jean. In the evening of the battle he led Major General Frederick Adam's brigade to repulse the Imperial Guard. His horse was shot and rolled over him bruising him severely. Second in Command of the Army of Occupation. Also served at Toulon 1793 (wounded – ADC to Gen O'Hara), Egypt 1801 (wounded) and Hanover 1805. Colonel 3rd Garrison Battalion 7 Jun 1809, Colonel 94th Foot 18 Sep 1809, Colonel 72nd Foot 29 Apr 1815, Colonel 53rd Foot 24 Feb 1817 and Colonel Royal Horse Guards 19 Nov 1830. GCB, GCH, Grand Cross of Tower and Sword, Commander of Maria Theresa of Austria, Second Class St George of Russia, Third Class Wilhelm of Netherlands and Second Class of Crescent of Turkey.

Appointed Commander in Chief of the Army in 1828 when the Duke of Wellington became Prime Minister, and held the post until Hill's death in 1842. Hill was the only General who was trusted by Wellington to have independent command. He was respected by his men as he always treated them well and looked after their welfare, especially after the Corunna retreat. Brother of Lt Colonel Robert Chambré Hill Royal Horse Guards, Capt Clement Hill Royal Horse Guards and Capt and Lt Colonel Thomas Noel Hill 1st Foot Guards who all fought with him in the Peninsula.

REFERENCE: *Dictionary of National Biography. Royal Military Calendar, Vol 2, pp. 218–26. Gentleman's Magazine, May 1843, pp. 529–32. Annual Register, 1842, Appx, pp. 306–9. Sidney, Edwin, The life of Lord Hill, 1845. Teffeteller, Gordon L., The Surpriser: the life of Rowland, Lord Hill, 1983. Hill, Joanna, Wellington's right hand man: Rowland Viscount Hill, 2011. Ridgley, Paul, A monument to Lord Hill, First Empire, No 43, Nov 1998, pp. 18–9. Ridgeley, Paul, Lord Hill's column, Shrewsbury, Waterloo Journal, Summer, 2002, pp. 29–31. Cole, John William, Memoirs of British Generals, Vol 2, 1856, pp. 175–223.*

HILL, Rowland F.
Ensign. 59th (2nd Nottinghamshire) Regiment of Foot.
Named on the Regimental Memorial monument: Christ Church Churchyard, Tramore, County Waterford, Ireland. (Photograph)

Ensign 25 May 1814.

Present at Waterloo with 2nd Battalion in reserve at Hal, siege of Cambrai and with the Army of Occupation. Drowned when the *Sea Horse* transport was wrecked in a storm in Tramore Bay, 30 Jan 1816.

HILL, Sir Thomas Noel
Captain and Lieutenant Colonel. 1st Regiment of Foot Guards.
Memorial tablet: All Saints Church, Maidstone, Kent. (Photograph)

THIS MONUMENT WAS ERECTED BY HIS AFFLICTED WIDOW TO THE MEMORY OF / COLONEL SIR THOMAS NOEL HILL KCB KTS &C / LATE COMMANDER OF THE CAVALRY DEPOT AT MAIDSTONE. / SEVENTH SON OF SIR JOHN HILL OF HAWKSTONE IN THE COUNTY OF SALOP. BAR^T. / WHO DIED IN THIS TOWN ON JANUARY 8TH 1832 AGED 47 YEARS.

Cornet 10th Dragoons 25 Sep 1801. Lt 2 Feb 1803. Capt 28 Feb 1805. Capt 53rd Foot 25 Apr 1806. Bt Lt Colonel 3 Oct 1811. Capt and Lt Colonel 1st Foot Guards 25 Jul 1814. Bt Colonel 27 May 1825. Portuguese Army: Major Portuguese and Spanish Staff 16 Feb 1809. Colonel 1st Line 5 Feb 1812.
   Served in the Peninsula with the Portuguese Army Apr 1809 – Sep 1813. Present at Rolica, Vimeiro, Corunna, Busaco (Mentioned in Despatches), Ciudad Rodrigo (Mentioned in Despatches), Salamanca (Mentioned in Despatches), retreat from Burgos (Mentioned in Despatches), Vittoria and San Sebastian. Gold Cross for Busaco, Ciudad Rodrigo, Salamanca, Vittoria, and San Sebastian. Retired from the Portuguese Army Oct 1814. Knighted 1814. Present at Waterloo (AAG). Also served in Canada 1827 (DAG). KCB and KTS. Later commanded the Cavalry depot at Maidstone. Brother of Colonel Lord Hill 72nd Foot, Capt Clement Hill Royal Horse Guards and Lt Colonel Robert Chambré Hill Royal Horse Guards.
REFERENCE: *Dictionary of National Biography. Royal Military Calendar, Vol 4, pp. 72–3. Gentleman's Magazine, Jan 1832, p. 84.*

HILLIARD, Morgan
Ensign. 87th (Prince of Wales's Own Irish) Regiment of Foot.
Named on the Memorial: St Andrew's Church, (now Musée Historique), Biarritz, France. (Photograph)

Volunteer 5th Foot. Ensign 87th Foot 15 Apr 1813.
   Served in the Peninsula with 5th Foot Sep 1812 – Mar 1813 and 87th Foot Apr – Nov 1813. Present at the retreat from Burgos, Vittoria, Pyrenees and Nivelle where he was killed 10 Nov 1813.

HILLIER, George
Captain. 74th (Highland) Regiment of Foot.
Gravestone: New Burial Ground, Circular Road, Calcutta, India. (M.I.)

"TO THE MEMORY OF / COLONEL GEORGE HILLIER, H. M. 62ND REGT. / WHO DEPARTED THIS LIFE ON THE 21ST DEC. 1840. / AGED 52 YEARS."

Ensign 29th Foot 23 Mar 1809. Lt 10 May 1810. Capt Royal African Corps 12 Apr 1812. Capt 74th Foot 9 Jul 1812. Major 62nd Foot 17 Oct 1826. Bt Lt Colonel 24 Jul 1828. Lt Colonel 62nd Foot 27 Sep 1835.
   Served in the Peninsula with 29th Foot Jul 1809 – Mar 1811, Portuguese Army Apr 1811 – Jul 1812 and 74th Foot Dec 1813 – Apr 1814. Present at Talavera. Present at Waterloo (DAQMG). Also served in Canada 1818–1828 (ADC to Sir Peregrine Maitland and very influential as Maitland's secretary), Jamaica 1828–1832 (DQMG) and India 1832–1840 (present in Burma 1832–1835). Commandant of Moulmien. Returned to Calcutta due to ill health in 1840 where he died.
REFERENCE: *Dictionary of Canadian Biography. United Service Journal, 1841, Part 1, p. 575. Gentleman's Magazine, Aug 1841, p. 222. Annual Register, 1841, Appx, p. 210.*

HILTON, Thomas
Captain. 45th (Nottinghamshire) Regiment of Foot.
Memorial tablet: Chester Cathedral, Chester, Cheshire. (Great western entrance). (Photograph)

DIED IN THE CANTONMENT / AT MOULMIEN IN THE BURMAN EMPIRE / ON THE 2ND OF FEBRUARY 1829. / MAJOR THOMAS HILTON LATE IN / COMMAND OF THE 45TH REGT OF FOOT, AGED 40 / AFTER A SERVICE OF 24 YEARS IN HIS MAJESTY'S / ARMY AND 20 OF THAT PERIOD IN THE 45TH / IN WHICH HE SERVED WITH THE HIGHEST HONOUR / TO HIMSELF AND CREDIT TO HIS CORPS, SHARING / WITH IT THE GREATER NUMBER OF THE MANY / DISTINGUISHED LAURELS ACQUIRED BY THAT / REGIMENT DURING THE PENINSULAR WAR. / AS THE LAST TRIBUTE OF RESPECT AND ESTEEM / FOR THE SOLDIERLIKE AND MANY AMIABLE QUALITIES / THAT DISTINGUISHED HIM AS A COMMANDING / OFFICER AND FRIEND, THIS MONUMENT IS ERECTED / BY LIEUT. COL. VIGOUREUX, C. B., / AND THE OFFICERS OF THE 45TH REGIMENT.

Lt 6th Dragoons 25 Jul 1805. Capt 45th Foot 23 Aug 1810. Major 25 Jun 1825.
    Served in the Peninsula Sep 1813 – Apr 1814. Present at Nivelle, Nive, Orthes, Vic Bigorre and Toulouse (severely wounded). Gold Medal for Orthes. Also served in Ceylon 1819, India and Burma (first Burmese War 1824–1826, present at Moulmien).

HIMBURY, John
Private. 95th Regiment of Foot.
Named on the Regimental Memorial: Winchester Cathedral, Winchester, Hampshire. (Photograph)

Militia 5 Aug 1807. Pte 25 Mar 1809. Cpl 1818. Sgt 1825.
    Served in the Peninsula 1810 – Apr 1814. Present at Cadiz, Seville, Barrosa, Almarez, retreat from Burgos, San Munos (taken prisoner but escaped), San Millan, Vittoria, Pyrenees, San Sebastian (took part in the Forlorn Hope and received medal), Nivelle, Nive, Orthes, Tarbes and Toulouse. Present at Waterloo in Capt G. Miller's Company and with the Army of Occupation. Also served at Walcheren 1809, Ireland 1819, Spain 1835 (Sgt Major in expedition to the Carlist Wars under Col De Lacey Evans). Promoted from the ranks to 2nd Lt and in 1836 1st Lt Rifle Regt. Retired at end of war in 1836. MGS medal for Barrosa, Vittoria, Pyrenees, San Sebastian, Nivelle, Nive, Orthes and Toulouse. Died 28 Jun 1872.
REFERENCE: *Shankland, Anne, John Himbury: Sergeant of the 95th Regiment of Foot, Waterloo Journal, Winter 2007, p. 15 and Spring 2008, p. 8.*

HINCKS, John
1st Lieutenant. Royal Artillery.
Memorial tablet: St Gregory's Church, Bedale, Yorkshire. (Side chapel to south nave). (Photograph)

TO THE MEMORY OF / JOHN HINCKS, ESQR / CAPTAIN ROYAL ARTILLERY, / WHO DIED AT COWLING HALL, / IN THE COUNTY OF YORK, / OCTOBER 17 1842, / AGED 55 YEARS.

Small stone plaque on east side of Church wall:

J. H. / 1842

2nd Lt 8 Nov1806. 1st Lt 1 Feb 1808. 2nd Capt 29 Jul 1825.
    Present at Waterloo in Captain Mercer's G. Troop where he was wounded. Also served at Copenhagen 1807. Retired on half pay 1826.

HINDE, Samuel Venables
Lieutenant Colonel. 32nd (Cornwall) Regiment of Foot.
Memorial slab: St Mary's Church, Hitchin, Hertfordshire (In floor of aisle). (Photograph)

.... / SAMUEL VENABLES HINDE ESQ., / SON OF THE ABOVE ROBERT HINDE. / LIEUT GEN. IN HIS MAJESTY'S FORCES.

Ensign 25th Foot 24 Jan 1788. Lt 28 Mar 1792. Capt 3 Apr 1795. Bt Major 6 Jul 1797. Major 32nd Foot 5 Nov 1800. Bt Lt Colonel 29 Apr 1802. Lt Colonel 32nd Foot 1 Aug 1804. Bt Colonel 4th Jun 1811. Major General 4th Jun 1814. Lt General 22 Jul 1830.

Served in the Peninsula Aug 1808 – Jan 1809, Jul 1811 – Jun 1812 and Jul 1812 – Dec 1813. (Commanded 1 Brigade 6th Division on the death of Major General Bowes at Salamanca Forts). Present at Rolica, Vimeiro, Corunna, siege of Salamanca Forts, Salamanca, Burgos, retreat from Burgos, Pyrenees and Bidassoa (severely wounded and unfit for further active service). Also served on marine duty under Hood at Toulon 1793 (Hinde was the last man on shore covering the embarkation) and the attack on Cadiz under Nelson 1797, the Helder 1799 (wounded at Alkmaar), Copenhagen 1807 and Walcheren 1809 (present at Flushing). Awarded Gold Medal for Rolica, Vimeiro, Corunna, Salamanca and Pyrenees. KCB. KTS. Colonel 32nd Foot 28 Feb 1832. Died in Hitchin 20 Sep 1837.

REFERENCE: *Gentleman's Magazine, Nov 1837, pp. 531–2.*

HINDE, William
Sergeant. 95th Regiment of Foot.
Headstone: St Mary's Churchyard, Dumfries, Dumfriesshire, Scotland. (Photograph)

IN / MEMORY OF / WILLIAM HINDE / WHO DIED / AT CARLISLE 24TH FEBRUARY / 1875, IN HIS 91ST YEAR. / ………………

Private 91st Foot 1803. Private 95th Foot 1808. Sgt 1814.

Served in the Peninsula 1809 – Apr 1814. Present at Corunna, Fuentes d'Onoro, Ciudad Rodrigo, Badajoz, Salamanca, Vittoria, Pyrenees, Nivelle, Nive, Orthes and Toulouse. Retired in 1821 on a pension. MGS medal for Corunna, Fuentes d'Onoro, Ciudad Rodrigo, Badajoz, Salamanca, Vittoria, Pyrenees, Nivelle, Nive, Orthes and Toulouse.

HIRD, John
Private: 2nd Life Guards.
Headstone: St John's Churchyard, Chapeltown, Sheffield, Yorkshire. (Photograph)

IN LOVING / MEMORY OF / JOHN HIRD / WHO DIED JUNE 30TH 1873, / AGED 83 YEARS. / HE SERVED HIS KING AND COUNTRY / ON THE FIELD OF WATERLOO / ………………

Pte 9 Jun 1813.

Served at Waterloo where he was wounded five times and lost the use of his left hand. Discharged 4 Mar 1816.

HISCOTT, Richard
Private. 76th Regiment of Foot.
Obelisk: St Mark's Cemetery, Niagara, Ontario, Canada. (Photograph)

IN MEMORY OF / RICHARD HISCOTT / BORN IN WILTSHIRE IN 1790. / DIED AT NIAGARA, CANADA 1874. / DESERVEDLY ESTEEMED BOTH AS A CITIZEN AND AS A SOLDIER. / IN EARLY LIFE HE SERVED WITH HONOUR / IN HER MAJESTY'S 76TH REGIMENT OF FOOT / AND WAS IN MANY BATTLES OF THE PENINSULAR WAR AND IN CANADA. / HE SETTLED IN NIAGARA WHERE A LARGE FAMILY OF DESCENDANTS / AND NUMEROUS FRIENDS / LAMENT HIS DEATH.

Pte 1 Apr 1804. Cpl 17 Sep 1815. Sgt 25 Aug 1816.

Served in the Peninsula Aug 1813 – Apr 1814. Present at Bidassoa, Nivelle, Nive and Bayonne. MGS medal for Nivelle and Nive. Also served in Canada. Discharged 16 Jan 1830.

HOARE, Henry
Private. 15th (King's) Regiment of Light Dragoons.
Ledger stone: York Cemetery, York, Yorkshire. (Grave number 15633). (Photograph)

HENRY HOARE / LATE OF THE 15TH HUSSARS / WHO DIED 15TH SEPTEMBER 1872 / AGED 82 YEARS

Pte 1810.
    Served in the Peninsula Feb 1813 – Apr 1814. Present at Vittoria, Orthes (wounded) and Toulouse. Present at Waterloo. MGS medal for Toulouse. Believed to be the last Waterloo veteran in York when he died in 1872.
REFERENCE: *Obit. York Herald, 21 Sep 1872, p. 9.*

HODGE, Edward
Major. 7th (Queen's Own) Regiment of Light Dragoons.
Memorial tablet: St Joseph's Church, Waterloo, Belgium. (Photograph)

SACRED / TO THE MEMORY / OF / MAJOR EDWARD HODGE / AND / LIEUT. ARTHUR MYERS / OF THE / 7TH REGIMENT OF HUSSARS / WHO / WERE KILLED ON THE 17TH OF JUNE 1815. / THIS MONUMENT IS ERECTED / BY THEIR BROTHER OFFICERS / AS A TOKEN OF THEIR RESPECT / AND ESTEEM.

Low monument: St George's Churchyard, Beckenham, Kent. (Photograph)

IN MEMORY OF MARIA WIDOW OF MAJOR HODGE 7TH HUSSARS KILLED AT GENAPPE

Cornet 2nd Dragoon Guards 15 Sep 1798. Lt 12 Jun 1800. Bt Capt 19 Dec 1804. Capt 7th Lt Dragoons 16 May 1805. Major 7 May 1812.
    Served in the Peninsula Nov 1808 – Jan 1809. Present at Benevente. Present in the Waterloo campaign where he was killed in the cavalry action at Genappe 17 Jun 1815.

HODGE, Peter
Major. 29th (Worcestershire) Regiment of Foot.
Ledger stone: St Budock Churchyard, Falmouth, Cornwall. (Inside main gate). (Photograph)

PETER HODGE, / LATE LIEUT: COL / COMG 29 REGT FOOT. / DIED 25TH FEB, 1839 / AGED 57 YEARS.

Ensign 3 Mar 1798. Lt 31 May 1798. Capt 2 May 1800. Bt Major 20 Jun 1811. Major 29 Aug 1811. Bt Lt Colonel 21 Jun 1817. Lt Colonel 28 Dec 1820.
    Served in the Peninsula Jul – Dec 1808, Aug 1809 – Nov 1811 and Jan-Feb 1814. Present at Rolica (wounded and awarded pension of £100 per annum). Busaco, first siege of Badajoz, Albuera (wounded and awarded Bt Majority) and Cadiz. Also served at the Helder 1799, North America 1814 (present with Sherbrooke's expedition up the Penobscot and Mentioned in Despatches). On return from America, present at the Capture of Paris and with the Army of Occupation. Served with 29th Foot for nearly 30 years. Retired 28 Feb 1822.

HODGES, William Arthur
Captain. 47th (Lancashire) Regiment of Foot.
Memorial tablet: St Luke's Church, Holmes Chapel, Cheshire. (Photograph)

WILL^M ARTHUR HODGES ESQ^R. / CAPTAIN IN THE 47TH REG^T. / HAVING BEEN TWICE WOUNDED IN / THE BATTLE OF VITTORIA: FELL AT / THE STORMING OF ST SEBASTIAN / IN SPAIN, AUGST 31ST / ANNO DOMINI 1813, / AETATIS 26.

Ensign 14th Foot 21 Apr 1804. Lt 29 Dec 1804. Capt 14th Foot 22 Dec 1808. Capt 47th Foot 18 Oct 1810.
 Served in the Peninsula with 2/47th Foot May 1812 – Aug 1813. Present at Cadiz, Seville, Puente Larga, Vittoria (wounded) and San Sebastian where he was killed 31 Aug 1813.

HODGSON, Ellis
Lieutenant. 10th (Prince of Wales's Own) Regiment of Light Dragoons.
Headstone: St Giles's Churchyard, Skelton, Yorkshire. (Photograph)

TO / THE MEMORY OF / CAPTAIN ELLIS HODGSON / LATE OF THIS PLACE, AND / FORMERLY OF THE 10TH HUSSARS, / WHO DIED 23RD APRIL 1868, / AGED 74 YEARS.

Lt 10th Lt Dragoons 28 Dec 1814. Capt 3rd Dragoons 23 Nov 1820.
 Present at Quatre Bras to cover the retreat of the infantry on 17th June and at Waterloo. Also served in Scotland after the war where he was stationed in Glasgow to quell the riots there. During one disturbance he was wounded and his horse killed. Appointed to a troop in the 3rd Dragoons for his conduct. Half pay Oct 1821.

HOEY, William
Captain. 99th (Prince of Wales's Tipperary) Regiment of Foot.
Memorial tablet: Dunganstown Church of Ireland, County Wicklow, Ireland. (Photograph)

SACRED / TO THE MEMORY OF / CAPTAIN / WILLIAM HOEY / OF THE XVIII / LIGHT DRAGOONS / AIDE DE CAMP / TO THE / RIGHT HONOURABLE / LORD STEWART K.B. / KILLED / BY A CANNON SHOT / ON THE / HEIGHTS OF BUSACO / 20TH OF OCTOBER 1810 / AGED 21

Family Pedestal tomb: Dunganstown Churchyard, County Wicklow, Ireland. (Photograph)

HOEY / OF / DUNGANSTOWN

Lt 18th Lt Dragoons 26 Aug 1806. Capt 99th Foot 30 Aug 1810.
 Served in the Peninsula Sep 1808 – Jan 1809 and Aug 1809 – Sep 1810 (ADC to Major General Charles Stewart Aug 1809 – Sep 1810 and DAAG May – Sep 1810). Present at Benevente and Busaco where he was severely wounded 27 Sep 1810 and died of his wounds 20 Oct 1810.

HOGGE, Fountain
Lieutenant Colonel. 26th (Cameronian) Regiment of Foot.
Memorial tablet: St Michael's Church, Lyndhurst, Hampshire. (Photograph)

SACRED / TO THE MEMORY OF / LIEU^T COL^L FOUNTAIN HOGGE, / LATE OF / THE 26TH REGT OF FOOT, / OR CAMERONIANS; / WHO DIED AT LYNDHURST, / THE 20TH OF JAN^Y 1843, / AGED 69 YEARS. / ....

Ensign 19 Dec 1795. Lt 9 Apr 1796. Capt 20 Jan 1801. Major 20 Jun 1805. Bt Lt Colonel 1 Jan 1812. Lt Colonel 2 Jan 1812.
 Served in the Peninsula Oct 1808 – Jan 1809 and Aug 1811 – Feb 1812. Present in the Corunna campaign. Also served at Walcheren 1809. Retired 1812.

HOGHTON, Daniel
Lieutenant Colonel. 8th (King's) Regiment of Foot.
Ledger stone: British Cemetery, Elvas, Portugal. (Photograph)

UNDERNEATH IS DEPOSITED THE BODY / OF / MAJOR GENERAL HOGHTON / OF HIS BRIT-
TANIC MAJESTY'S SERVICE / WHO FELL IN THE BATTLE OF / ALBUHERA / ON THE 16 OF MAY
1811 / AT THE HEAD OF HIS BRIGADE / ....

Memorial tablet: St Leonard's Church, Walton-le-Dale, Lancashire. (Photograph)

MAJOR GENERAL DANIEL HOGHTON, / DIED IN BATTLE AT ALBUERA IN SPAIN / MAY 16TH
1811, AGED 41.

Memorial tablet: St Paul's, London. (North west transept). (Photograph)

ERECTED AT THE PUBLIC EXPENSE TO THE MEMORY OF / MAJOR GENERAL DANIEL
HOGHTON, / WHO FELL GLORIOUSLY THE 16TH MAY 1811, IN THE BATTLE OF ALBUERA.

Cornet 11th Lt Dragoons 5 Apr 1793. Lt 8 Jun 1793. Capt 82nd Foot 29 Sep 1793. Major 97th Foot 9 Feb
1794. Major 67th Foot 12 Aug 1795. Bt Lt Colonel 3 May 1796. Major 88th Foot 31 Jan 1799. Lt Colonel
8th Foot 22 Nov 1804. Bt Colonel 1 Jan 1805. Major General 25 Jul 1810.
    Served in the Peninsula Sep 1810 – May 1811. (Commanded 2 Brigade 2nd Division). Present at Cadiz,
first siege of Badajoz and Albuera where he was killed and Mentioned in Despatches. Gold Medal for
Martinique and Albuera. Also served in the West Indies 1796–1798, India 1799–1804, Egypt 1801, Ireland
1806, Copenhagen 1807 and Martinique 1809.
REFERENCE: *Dictionary of National Biography. Panikkar, M., A short biography of Major-General Daniel
Hoghton, hero of Albuera, 1993. Gentleman's Magazine, 1811, Part 1, Supplement, p. 679.*

HOLBURNE, Francis Ralph Thomas
Lieutenant and Captain 3rd Regiment of Foot Guards.
Obelisk: Third Guards Cemetery, St Etienne, Bayonne, France. (Photograph)

SACRED TO THE MEMORY OF / FRANCIS R. T. HOLBURNE / CAPT AND ADJT OF 3RD REG.
GUARDS / ELDEST SON OF / SIR FRANCIS HOLBURNE BART. / WHO WAS SEVERELY WOUNDED
/ WHILE GALLANTLY LEADING HIS MEN / AGAINST THE SORTIE MADE / BY THE FRENCH
FROM BAYONNE / APRIL 14TH 1814 / AND DIED OF THE WOUNDS / APRIL 23RD 1814. HE LIES
BURIED / IN THIS CEMETERY. / HIS LOSS GREATLY DEPLORED / BY HIS AFFLICTED FAMILY
AND / ALL WHO KNEW HIM / THIS MONUMENT IS ERECTED / AS A TRIBUTE OF AFFECTION
/ BY HIS LAST SURVIVING SISTER.

Headstone: Third Guards Cemetery, St Etienne, Bayonne, France. (Photograph)

IN MEMORY / OF / CAPTAIN HOLBURNE / THIRD GUARDS / WHO DIED OF WOUNDS
RECEIVED IN / ACTION BEFORE BAYONNE ON THE / 14 APRIL / 1814

Pedestal tomb: Lansdowne Cemetery, Bath, Somerset. (Photograph)

IN MEMORY OF / FRANCIS R. T. HOLBURNE / CAPT AND ADJT 3 REGT GUARDS / ELDEST SON
OF / SIR FRANCIS HOLBURNE BART / WHO WAS SEVERELY WOUNDED / WHILE GALLANTLY
LEADING HIS MEN / AGAINST THE SORTIE MADE BY THE / ENEMY FROM BAYONNE AND
DIED / OF HIS WOUND APRIL 23RD 1814. HE / LIES BURIED IN THE SMALL CEMETERY / WITH

OTHER OFFICERS JUST OUTSIDE THE / TOWN. HIS LOSS WAS GREATLY DEPLORED / BY HIS AFFLICTED FAMILY AND ALL / WHO KNEW HIM.

Named on the Memorial: St Andrew's Church, (now Musée Historique), Biarritz, France. (Photograph)

Memorial: Royal Military Chapel, Wellington Barracks, London. (M.I.) (Destroyed by a Flying Bomb in 1944)

"CAPTAIN AND ADJUTANT FRANCIS RALPH THOMAS HOLBURNE, / 3ᴿᴰ GUARDS, WHO WAS SEVERELY WOUNDED WHILST GALLANTLY LEADING HIS MEN AGAINST THE SORTIE MADE BY / THE FRENCH FROM BAYONNE, APRIL 14ᵀᴴ, 1814, AND DIED OF HIS WOUND, APRIL 23ᴿᴰ 1814. / GIVEN BY HIS LAST-SURVIVING SISTER, 1879".

Also named on Memorial Panel VII for the Sortie from Bayonne: Royal Military Chapel, Wellington Barracks, London. (M.I.) (Destroyed by a Flying Bomb 1944)

Memorial tablet: St Nicholas Church, Tuxford, Nottinghamshire. (Photograph) (Named on the memorial tablet to Captain Charles Lawrence White)

THE DESIGN ABOVE REPRESENTS THE BURIAL PLACE OF CAPTᴺ WHITE AND THREE OF / HIS BROTHER OFFICERS, I. B. SHIFFNER FRANCIS R. HOLBURNE AND LUKE MAHON. / CAPTS WHITE AND SHIFFNER WERE BURIED TOGETHER IN THE GRAVE MARKED WITH THEIR / INITIALS, THE CROSS WAS FORMED OF A LARGE TREE AS IT GREW THE TOP BEING CUT OFF / AND PLACED ACROSS, ABOVE WHICH IT HAD BEEN PENETRATED BY A 24ᴸᴮ SHOT WHICH / REMAINED IN THE TREE AS REPRESENTED, WITH THE DRUMS AND COLOURS AS PLACED / AT THE FUNERALS IN A VALLEY ABOUT A MILE FROM BAYONNE. / THERE WERE AFTER-WARDS STONES PLACED AT THE HEAD OF EACH GRAVE BY THE / SURVIVING OFFICERS OF THE REGIMENT. / ....

(Remainder of this memorial refers exclusively to Lt and Capt Charles Lawrence White)

Lt 7ᵗʰ Foot 7 Apr 1808. Ensign 3ʳᵈ Foot Guards 22 Jun 1809. Lt and Capt and Adjt 25 Dec 1813.
    Served in the Peninsula with 7ᵗʰ Foot Apr – Jul 1809 and 3ʳᵈ Foot Guards Oct 1810 – Apr 1814. Present at Douro, Fuentes d'Onoro, Ciudad Rodrigo, Salamanca, Burgos (severely wounded), Vittoria, Bidassoa, Nivelle, Nive (wounded), Adour and Bayonne where he was severely wounded at the Sortie from Bayonne 14 Apr and died of his wounds 23 Apr 1814.

HOLCOMBE, Harcourt Forde
Captain. Royal Artillery.
Mural monument: Dunkeld Cathedral, Perthshire, Scotland. (Old ruined nave). (Grave number 3/9). (Photograph)

TO THE MEMORY OF / HARCOURT F. HOLCOMBE, C. B., / LT. COL. ROYAL ARTILLERY, / BORN 6ᵀᴴ JANUARY 1778. / DIED 6ᵀᴴ MARCH 1847. / HE WAS IN HIS EARLIER YEARS / A DISTIN-GUISHED OFFICER / AND / BECAME IN HIS LATTER DAYS, / BY THE GRACE OF GOD, / AN EMINENT CHRISTIAN.

Ledger stone: In front of Mural monument, Dunkeld Cathedral, Perthshire, Scotland. (Old ruined nave). (Grave number 3/11). (Photograph)

Lᵀ COLONEL HOLCOMBE.

2nd Lt 6 Mar 1795. 1st Lt Jul 1795. Capt-Lieut 12 Sep 1803. Capt 3 Dec 1806. Bt Major 6 Feb 1812. Bt Lt Colonel 27 Apr 1812. Major 29 Jul 1825. Lt Colonel 29 Aug 1825.

Served in the Peninsula Oct 1808 – Jan 1809 and Apr 1811 – Apr 1814. Present in the Corunna campaign, Ciudad Rodrigo (Mentioned in Despatches), Badajoz, Castalla (Mentioned in Despatches) and Tarragona. Gold Medal for Badajoz. CB. After Badajoz he was in command of several companies of British and Portuguese Artillery and went to the Mediterranean where he joined the Army from Sicily and took part in actions on the east coast of Spain. C/O Artillery at Lisbon 1813 and remained there until 1815 to supervise the dismantling of all the ordnance depots in Spain and Portugal. Also served in North America 1795.

HOLLAND, Thomas Edward
Ensign. 4th (King's Own) Regiment of Foot.
Interred in Catacomb B (v103 c4) Kensal Green Cemetery, London.

Ensign 9 Dec 1813.
Present at Waterloo. Half pay 14 Jan 1819. Died 1865.

HOLLE, Carl von
Captain. 1st Line Battalion, King's German Legion.
Named on the Regimental Memorial: La Haye Sainte, Waterloo, Belgium. (Photograph)

Lt 27 Jan 1806. Capt 19 Feb 1813.
Served in the Peninsula Dec 1808 – Apr 1814. Present at Douro, Talavera (severely wounded), Busaco, Fuentes d'Onoro, Ciudad Rodrigo, Moriscos, Salamanca, Burgos, Vittoria, Tolosa, San Sebastian, Bidassoa, Nivelle, Nive, St Etienne and Bayonne. Present at Waterloo where he was killed. Also served in Hanover 1805, Sicily 1806–1807, the Baltic 1807–1808 and the Netherlands 1814.

HOLLINGSWORTH, Henry
Sergeant Major. 20th (East Devonshire) Regiment of Foot.
Buried in St George's Chapel, Windsor, Berkshire. (Burial record)

Pte 1798. Promoted from the ranks. Ensign and Adjutant 5 Dec 1823. Lt 56th Foot 29 May 1828. Bt Capt 28 Jun 1850.
Served in the Peninsula 1808 – Jan 1809 and Oct 1812 – Apr 1814. Present at Vimeiro, Corunna, Vittoria, Roncesvalles, Pyrenees, Nivelle, Nive and Orthes (severely wounded). Also served at the Helder 1799, Egypt 1801, Sicily 1805–1806 (present at Maida), Walcheren 1809 and St Helena (with 20th Foot guarding Napoleon). Awarded MGS medal for Egypt, Maida, Vimeiro, Corunna, Vittoria, Pyrenees, Nivelle, Nive and Orthes. Half pay 28 Jun 1850 after 52 years service. Military Knight of Windsor 10 Feb 1852. Joined the 20th Foot at a very early age and rose through the ranks to be commissioned in 1823. Died at Windsor 14 Sep 1865.

HOLLOWAY, William Cuthbert Elphinstone
Captain. Royal Engineers.
Headstone: Ford Park Cemetery, Plymouth, Devon. (CʟB 3 10). (Photograph)

IN THIS VAULT LIE THE REMAINS OF / COL. WILLIAM CUTHBERT ELPHINSTONE HOLLOWAY / LATE COMMANDER OF THE ROYAL ENGINEERS / IN THE WESTERN DISTRICT / WHO DIED IN THE CITADEL PLYMOUTH / SEPTEMBER 9TH 1850 / ....

2nd Lt 1 Jan 1804. 1st Lt 1 Mar 1805. 2nd Capt 24 Jun 1809. Capt 21 Jul 1813. Bt Major 21 Jun 1817. Lt Colonel 26 Feb 1828. Colonel 23 Nov 1841.

Served in the Peninsula Mar 1810 – May 1812. Present at Torres Vedras (engaged in strengthening the fortress of Peniche at Lisbon, from where he helped to make several successful attacks on the enemy. Constructed jetties at the mouth of the Tagus in case the Army had to embark) and siege of Badajoz (wounded 26 Mar 1812 in command of the 5th Brigade of Engineers. At the final assault on 6 April he led one of the detachments attacking Fort Picurina, where he was severely wounded, shot through the lungs and had to return to England. Mentioned in Despatches). CB and MGS medal for Badajoz. Also served in Madeira 1807.
REFERENCE: *Royal Military Calendar, Vol 5, pp. 340–1.*

HOLMES, Adam

Private. 52nd (Oxfordshire) Light Infantry Regiment of Foot.
Obelisk: St Lawrence's Churchyard, Eyam, Derbyshire. (Photograph)

ALSO IN / MEMORY OF / ADAM HOLMES, / A PENINSULAR & WATERLOO VETERAN, / A BRAVE SOLDIER & GOOD CHRISTIAN, / BORN APRIL 1ST 1793, / DIED OCTOBER 20TH 1878, / HE WAS ENGAGED IN / HIS MAJESTY'S 52ND FOOT / UNDER WELLINGTON / AND FOUGHT AT THE BATTLES OF / VITTORIA, PYRENEES, ORTHES, / NIVELLE, NIVE, TOULOUSE, / AND LOST HIS LEFT LEG AT / WATERLOO.

Private 12 Apr 1810.
   Served in the Peninsula 1812 – Apr 1814. Present at Vittoria, Pyrenees (wounded), Nivelle, Orthes and Toulouse. Served at Waterloo in Captain Love's Company (wounded and lost his left leg). MGS Medal for Vittoria, Pyrenees, Nivelle, Orthes and Toulouse. Discharged 16 Apr 1816.

HOLMES, Samuel

Captain. 13th Regiment of Light Dragoons.
Buried in St George's Chapel, Windsor, Berkshire. (Burial record)

Cornet and Adjutant 17 Sep 1802. Lt 24 Feb 1804. Capt 10 Sep 1812.
   Served in the Peninsula Apr 1810 – Jan 1813. Present at Campo Mayor (wounded) and Alba De Tormes. Military Knight of Windsor 1830. Died 27 Dec 1840.

HOLMES, Stephen

Captain. 78th (Highland) Regiment of Foot.
Memorial: Mount Jerome Cemetery, Dublin, Ireland. Inscription not recorded. (Grave number C58–238).

Ensign 6th Garrison Battalion 1806. Lt and Adjt 1808. Lt 24th Foot 30 Nov 1809. Capt 8th West India Regt 28 Jan 1813. Capt 78th Foot 4 Feb 1814. Capt 90th Foot Feb 1820. Major (unattached) 24 Dec 1825. Bt Lt Colonel 28 Jun 1838.
   Served in the Peninsula Apr 1810 – Feb 1813. Present at Busaco, Fuentes d'Onoro, Ciudad Rodrigo, Salamanca, Burgos and retreat from Burgos (Mentioned in Despatches in the assault on Burgos 4 Oct 1812 when he led the storming party, for which he was appointed Captain in 8th West India Regt). Present at Waterloo (Brigade Major to Major General Johnston of 6th Division at Hal – but the Division was not in the action and so he lost the chance of promotion), siege of Cambrai and with the Army of Occupation. Returned to England Jan 1816 and went on half pay until Feb 1820 when he joined the 90th Foot. Also served in the Netherlands 1814 (present at Antwerp), Malta and the Ionian Islands 1820 (Brigade Major at Corfu). KH. Half pay 24 Dec 1825. Joined Irish Constabulary 1837 (Provisional Inspector of Leinster and Deputy Inspector of Constabulary in Ireland 1838. Died suddenly in Dublin 19 Dec 1839 at the same time as his younger son and both were buried in the same grave at Mount Jerome.
REFERENCE : *Gentleman's Magazine, Apr 1840, pp. 434–5.*

HOLT, Richard
Private. 40th (2nd Somersetshire) Regiment of Foot.
Headstone: St Mary and All Saints Churchyard, Bingham, Nottinghamshire. (Photograph)

IN / LOVING MEMORY / OF / RICHARD HOLT, / WHO DIED AUGST 1ST 1872 / AGED 77 YEARS / HE SERVED AT THE BATTLE / OF WATERLOO JUNE 18TH 1815. / ....

Pte 11 Feb 1811. Cpl 12 May 1821. Sgt 25 Nov 1827.
   Served in the Peninsula 1813-1814. Present at Waterloo in Capt G. Morrow's Company. Also served in North America 1814-1815 (arrived too late for New Orleans so the regiment returned home in time for Waterloo), New South Wales 1823-1829 and India 1829-1831. Discharged 14 Sep 1831.

HOLZERMAN, Philipp
Captain. 1st Line Battalion, King's German Legion.
Named on the Regimental Memorial: La Haye Sainte, Waterloo, Belgium. (Photograph)

Ensign 23 Jan 1804. Lt 25 Jun 1806. Capt 20 Mar 1812.
   Served in the Peninsula Aug 1808 – Jan 1809. Present at Vigo. Present at Waterloo where he was killed. Also served at Hanover 1805, Baltic 1807–1808, Walcheren 1809 and North Germany 1813–1814.

HOME, John
Paymaster. 42nd (Royal Highland) Regiment of Foot.
Memorial: Reverse side of the monument to Sir James Stirling, St Michael's Churchyard, Inveresk, Scotland. (Photograph)

JOHN HOME. L^T AND PAYMASTER 42ND R H / 1795 – 1820 / DIED 13TH APRIL 1849 AGED 72.

Ensign 6 Aug 1796. Lt 1798. Paymaster 21 Mar 1800.
   Served in the Peninsula Aug 1808 – Jan 1809 and May 1812 – Apr 1814. Present at Corunna, Salamanca, Burgos, Pyrenees, Nivelle, Nive, Orthes and Toulouse. Also served at Walcheren 1809. MGS Medal for Corunna, Salamanca, Pyrenees, Nivelle, Nive, Orthes and Toulouse. Son-in-law of Lt Colonel Sir James Stirling 42nd Foot.

HONEY, Henry
Lieutenant. 51st (2nd Yorkshire West Riding) Light Infantry.
Named on the Regimental Memorial: KOYLI Chapel, York Minster, Yorkshire. (Photograph)

Ensign Apr 1804. Lt 1 Sep 1804.
   Served in the Peninsula Oct 1808 – Jan 1809. Present in the Corunna campaign. Missing during the retreat on Lugo and reported to have died 4 Jan 1809.

HOOD, Hon. Francis Wheler
Captain and Lieutenant Colonel. 3rd Regiment of Foot Guards
Memorial: Ruins of St Michael's Old Cathedral, Coventry, Warwickshire. Severely damaged in Air raid in the Second World War. (Photograph)

"SACRED TO THE MEMORY OF / THE HONOURABLE FRANCIS WHELER HOOD, / LIEU-TENANT-COLONEL IN THE 3RD REGIMENT OF FOOT GUARDS, / ASSISTANT-ADJUTANT GENERAL TO THE 2ND DIVISION OF THE FORCES / UNDER THE MARQUIS OF WELLINGTON, / WHO WAS KILLED IN ACTION WITH THE ENEMY, AT AIRE, IN GASCONY, / IN THE 33RD YEAR OF HIS AGE, ON THE 2ND OF MARCH 1814, / AND WAS INTERRED IN THE CEMETERY

OF THAT PLACE WITH MILITARY HONOURS. / THIS SIMPLE MONUMENT IS ERECTED BY CAROLINE, HIS WIDOW, / IN AFFECTIONATE REMEMBRANCE OF HIS PUBLIC AND PRIVATE WORTH."

Memorial: Royal Military Chapel, Wellington Barracks, London. (M.I.) (Destroyed by a Flying Bomb in 1944)

"PLACED BY LIEUT.-COLONEL FRANCIS WHELER VISCOUNT HOOD, LATE GRENADIER GUARDS, / IN MEMORY OF HIS GRANDFATHER, / LIEUT.-COLONEL HON. FRANCIS WHELER HOOD, 3ᴿᴰ GUARDS, / ASST ADJT.-GENERAL TO THE 2ᴺᴰ DIVISION OF LORD WELLINGTON'S ARMY; KILLED IN ACTION AT / AIRE, IN THE SOUTH OF FRANCE, 2ᴺᴰ MARCH, 1814."

Also named on Memorial Panel VII for Aire: Royal Military Chapel, Wellington Barracks, London. (M.I.) (Destroyed by a Flying Bomb 1944)

Named on the Memorial: St Andrew's Church, (now Musée Historique), Biarritz, France. (Photograph)

Memorial: Toulouse Churchyard, France. (M.I.)

"SACRED TO THE MEMORY OF THE HON FRANCIS WHEELER HOOD, COLONEL IN THE BRITISH ARMY AND A. A. GEN. OF THE 2ᴺᴰ DIVISION OF THE FORCES UNDER THE COMMAND OF THE DUKE OF WELLINGTON. BORN 4 OCT 1781. FELL IN ACTION AT AIRE 2 MARCH 1814. HIS BODY IS INTERRED IN THE CEMETERY OF THIS PLACE WITH THE HONOUR DUE TO HIS RANK AND HIGH MILITARY CHARACTER."

Ensign 44th Foot 28 Apr 1798. Ensign 3rd Foot Guards 9 Jun 1798. Lt and Capt 25 Nov 1799. Capt and Lt Colonel 16 May 1811.
    Served in the Peninsula Mar 1809 – 1811 and Sep 1812 – Mar 1814. (AAG 2nd Division Dec 1813 – Mar 1814). Present at Douro, Talavera, Busaco, Vittoria, Bidassoa, Nivelle, Nive, Garris, Orthes and Aire where he was killed 2 Mar 1814 and Mentioned in Despatches. Gold Medal for Nive and Orthes. Grandson of Admiral Samuel Viscount Hood. Educated at Eton.

HOOD, George
Lieutenant. 43rd (Monmouthshire) Light Infantry Regiment of Foot.
Ledger stone: St Andrew's Churchyard, Clifton, Bristol. (Grave number 0562). (Photograph)

SACRED TO THE MEMORY OF / CAPTAIN GEORGE HOOD / PAYMASTER OF THE / BRISTOL RECRUITING DISTRICT / AND FOR 37 YEARS ATTACHED / TO THE 43ᴿᴰ REGIMENT OF / LIGHT INFANTRY. / HE DIED AT CLIFTON / ON THE 2ᴺᴰ DAY OF MAY 1853, / IN THE 58ᵀᴴ YEAR OF HIS AGE.

Ensign 11 Feb 1811. Lt 28 Mar 1812. Capt and Paymaster 43rd Foot 25 Oct 1828.
    Served in the Peninsula Apr 1814. Present at Toulouse. Also served in North America 1814–1815 (present at New Orleans). MGS medal for Toulouse. Later Paymaster of the Bristol Recruiting District.

HOPE, James
Lieutenant. 92nd Regiment of Foot.
Headstone: Kensal Green Cemetery, London. Inscription illegible. (15825/15/2). (Photograph)

Volunteer 26 Jul 1809. Ensign 92nd Foot 1 Nov 1809. Lt 7 Jan 1813. Lt 75th Foot 3 Feb 1832. Lt 29th Foot. 6 Apr 1832.

Served in the Peninsula Oct 1811 – Dec 1813. Present at Arroyo dos Molinos, Alba de Tormes, Vittoria, Pyrenees (severely wounded at Maya) and Nivelle. Present at Quatre Bras and Waterloo (wounded). Half pay 30 Dec 1842. Also served at Walcheren 1809. MGS medal for Vittoria, Pyrenees and Nivelle Died at Kensington 18 May 1860.

REFERENCE: *Monick, S. ed., The Iberian and Waterloo campaigns: the letters of Lt James Hope (92nd Highland Regiment), 1811–1815, revised edition 2000. (Originally published anonymously in 1819 under the pseudonym of 'A British Officer').*

HOPE, John

Lieutenant Colonel. 60th (Royal American) Regiment of Foot.
Vault: St John's Episcopalian Churchyard, Edinburgh. Scotland. (Lothian Road end). (Photograph of vault area). (M.I.)

"LT GEN SIR JOHN HOPE GCH. COL 72ND HIGHLANDERS SERVED IN FLANDERS, CAPE OF GOOD HOPE, WEST INDIES. DAG TO THE FORCES IN SCOTLAND. AG TO THE ARMY UNDER LORD CATHCART AT EXPEDITION AGAINST COPENHAGEN. COMMANDED A DIVISION AT SALAMANCA UNDER THE DUKE OF WELLINGTON. HEALTH FAILING RETURNED TO GREAT BRITAIN. COMMANDED THE FORCES IN SCOTLAND. DIED AT ROTHESAY 1ST AUGUST 1836 AGED 71."

Ensign Scots Brigade Dec 1779. Capt 26 Apr 1782. Capt 60th Foot 29 Sep 1787. Capt 13th Lt Dragoons Jun 1788. Major 28th Lt Dragoons 25 Mar 1795. Lt Colonel 20 Feb 1796. Lt Colonel 37th Foot 19 Apr 1799. Lt Colonel 60th Foot 30 Jun 1804. Bt Colonel 1 Jan 1805. Major General 25 Jul 1810.

Served in the Peninsula May – Oct 1812 (Commanded 7th Division). Present at Salamanca. Gold Medal for Salamanca. GCH. Also served in Flanders 1779–1781 and 1793–1795 (ADC to Lt General Sir William Erskine). Cape of Good Hope 1797–1799, West Indies 1800–1804 and Copenhagen 1807 (AG). Colonel 92nd Foot 1820. Colonel 72nd Foot 6 Sep 1823. Ill health forced him to retire from the Peninsular War and Wellington recorded in his *Dispatches* that 'he was very sorry to lose Major General Hope as he is very attentive to his duties'.

REFERENCE: *Dictionary of National Biography. Royal Military Calendar, Vol 3, pp. 1–2. Gentleman's Magazine, Dec 1836, pp. 653–4.*

HOPE, Sir John (Baron Niddry, then Earl of Hopetoun)

Colonel. 92nd Regiment of Foot.
Statue: Forecourt of Royal Bank of Scotland, St Andrew's Square, Edinburgh, Scotland. (Photograph)

Inscription on the front of the Plinth:

TO / JOHN, FOURTH EARL OF HOPETOUN, / ERECTED BY THE GRATITUDE OF HIS COUN-TRYMEN, / WHO LOVED AND REVERENCED IN HIS PERSON THE ASSEMBLED VIRTUES / OF DISTANT PERIODS OF HISTORY; / THE UNSHAKEN PATRIOTISM OF THE ANCIENT ROMAN; / THE SPIRIT OF HONOUR, AND GENTLENESS, AND COURTESY / PROPER TO THE AGE OF CHIVALRY; / TOGETHER WITH SKILL IN THE ART OF WAR, / WORTHY OF THE COMPANION OF / ABERCROMBIE, MOORE AND WELLINGTON.

Inscription on the back of the Plinth:

MEMORIAE SACRUM / JOANNIS COMITIS DE HOPETOUN QUARTI / IN QUO UNO ENITUERUNT DIVERSISSIMORUM TEMPORUM VIRTUTES / MIRABILITER CONJUNCTAE / UT NEQUE PRISCUM CIVEM ROMANUM AMOR PATRIAE ET CONSTANTIA / NEQUE NOBILEM INFERIORIS AEVI EVIMILITEM / MORUM COMITAS ET GRATIA ET INTEMBRATA FIDES /

MAGIS DISTINGUERENT / NEQUE DEESSET POMO EGREGIA BELLICAE ARTIS NOSTRAE PERITIA / WELLINGTON COMMILITONE AC SOCIO HAUD IN DIGNA / VIRUM TOT NOMINIBUS CARUM SCOTI SUI / DESIDERIO AC REVERENTIA PROSEQUENTES / M.P.C.

Buried in the Hopetoun Mausoleum, Hopetoun House, Abercorn, Midlothian, Scotland (South east of church.) (Photograph)

Column: Mount Hill, Cupar, Fife, Scotland.

"THIS MONUMENT WAS ERECTED TO THE MEMORY OF THE GREAT AND GOOD JOHN FOURTH EARL OF HOPETOUN BY HIS AFFECTIONATE AND GRATEFUL TENANTRY IN EAST LOTHIAN. MDCCCXXIV."

Column: Byres Hill, near Haddington, East Lothian, Scotland.

"THIS MONUMENT WAS ERECTED TO THE MEMORY OF THE GREAT AND GOOD JOHN FOURTH EARL OF HOPETOUN BY HIS AFFECTIONATE AND GRATEFUL TENANTRY IN EAST LOTHIAN, MDCCCXXIV."

(The monuments at Cupar and Haddington are of similar construction).

Cornet 10th Lt Dragoons 28 May 1784. Lt 100th Foot 24 Dec 1785. Lt 27th Foot 26 Apr 1786. Capt 17th Dragoons 31 Oct 1789. Major 2nd Foot 25 Apr 1792. Major 25th Foot 24 Apr 1793. Lt Colonel 26 Apr 1793. Bt Colonel 3 May 1796. Colonel North Lowland Fencible 27 Aug 1799. Major General 29 Apr 1802. Colonel 6th Battalion 60th Foot 3 Oct 1805. Colonel 92nd Foot 3 Jan 1806. Lt General 25 Apr 1808. General 1819.

Served in the Peninsula Sep 1808 – Jan 1809 (GOC 2nd Division Oct 1808 – Jan 1809) and Oct 1813 – Apr 1814 (GOC 1st Division). Present at Corunna (took command of the British Army on the death of Sir John Moore), Bidassoa (Mentioned in Despatches), Nivelle (Mentioned in Despatches), Nive (Mentioned in Despatches), Adour (Mentioned in Despatches), Bayonne (in command of troops at the siege where he was wounded and taken prisoner). Gold Medal for Corunna and Nive. GCB. Also served in the West Indies 1795–1797, the Helder 1799, Egypt 1801, Baltic 1808 and Walcheren 1809. Colonel 42nd Foot 1820. Governor Royal Bank of Scotland. He was praised by Abercrombie, Moore and Wellington who called him the ablest man in the Peninsular Army. Died 23 Aug 1823.
REFERENCE: *Dictionary National Biography. Gentleman's Magazine, Sep 1823, pp. 369–72. Royal Military Calendar, Vol II, pp. 96–7. Cole, John William, Memoirs of British Generals, Vol 2, 1856, pp. 147–74.*

HOPE, John Charles
1st Lieutenant. 95th Regiment of Foot.
Interred in Catacomb B (v90 c5) Kensal Green Cemetery, London.

Ensign 26th Foot 8 Jan 1807. 2nd Lt 95th Foot 21 May 1807. 1st Lt 2 Feb 1809. Capt 9 Nov 1820. Major 22 Jun 1830. Lt Colonel 21st Foot 4 Dec 1835. Lt Colonel Rifle Brigade 10 Nov 1837.

Served in the Peninsula with the 2/95th 1808 – 1809 and Mar 1810 – Sep 1811. Present in the Corunna campaign, siege of Cadiz and Barrosa where he was severely wounded and awarded pension of £70 per annum. Present at Waterloo where he took command of the 3/95th and was recommended for promotion by General Sir Henry Clinton for gallantry, the Capture of Paris and with the Army of Occupation. Also served at Copenhagen 1807, Sweden 1808, Walcheren 1809 and the Netherlands 1814. KH. Succeeded to the command of the 1st Battalion Rifle Brigade 1837. Half Pay 1841. Died in London 12 Oct 1842.

HOPKINS, Henry Lewis
Lieutenant. 5th (Northumberland) Regiment of Foot.
Named on the Memorial: St Andrew's Church, (now Musée Historique), Biarritz, France. (Photograph)

Ensign 1805. Lt 21 May 1807.
    Served in the Peninsula with 2/5th Jul 1809 – Aug 1812, and 1/5th Sep 1812 – Feb 1814. Present at Busaco, Redinha, Casal Nova, Foz d'Arouce, Ciudad Rodrigo, Badajoz (wounded), Salamanca, Nivelle, Nive, Adour and Orthes where he was killed 17 Feb 1814. Also served in Hanover 1805 and South America 1806–1807.

HOPKINS, John Paul
Captain. 43rd (Monmouthshire) Light Infantry Regiment of Foot.
Brass Memorial tablet: St George's Chapel, Windsor, Berkshire. (Photograph)

IN MEMORY OF / MAJOR SIR JOHN PAUL HOPKINS, KT. / GOVERNOR OF THE MILITARY KNIGHTS / WHO DIED ON THE 7TH OF MARCH 1875 / AGED 90 YEARS. / HE SERVED IN THE 43RD REGT. IN THE / PENINSULAR AND RECEIVED A / MEDAL AND SEVEN CLASPS FOR BUSACO, / FUENTES D'ONORO, CIUDAD RODRIGO, / BADAJOZ, SALAMANCA, VITTORIA AND / PYRENEES. / THIS PLATE WAS ERECTED BY HIS BROTHER OFFICER MAJOR / GENERAL TYRON, IN TOKEN OF HIS REGARD AND ESTEEM.

Ensign 61st Foot 12 Oct 1804. Ensign 43rd Foot 17 Nov 1804. Lt 19 Jun 1805. Capt 29 Aug 1811. Major 5 Nov 1825 (unattached). Major 98th Foot 25 Jun 1826.
    Served in the Peninsula Sep 1808 – Jan 1809 and Jul 1809 – Sep 1813. Present at Vigo, Coa (severely wounded), Busaco, Pombal, Redinha, Casal Nova, Foz d'Arouce, Sabugal, Fuentes d'Onoro, Almarez, Ciudad Rodrigo, Badajoz, Castrejon, Salamanca, San Millan, Vittoria and Pyrenees. Also served at Copenhagen 1807. MGS medal for Busaco, Fuentes d'Onoro, Ciudad Rodrigo, Badajoz, Salamanca, Vittoria and Pyrenees. KH. Knighted for his military service 11 Dec 1867. Military Knight of Windsor 1856 and became Governor of the Military Knights.
REFERENCE: *Oxfordshire Light Infantry Chronicle, 1901, pp. 242–5.*

HOPWOOD, John
1st Lieutenant. 95th Regiment of Foot.
Memorial tablet: St Chad's Parish Church, Rochdale, Lancashire. (Photograph)

TO THE MEMORY OF / JOHN HOPWOOD, LIEUT IN THE / 95TH OR RIFLE REGIMENT; / WHO FELL AT ARCANGUES BEFORE BAYONNE, / DECEMBER 10TH 1813, / AE 22. / HE DISTIN-GUISHED HIMSELF, AT THE BATTLES OF / BUSACO, SALAMANCA, AND VITTORIA; AND / AT THE SIEGES OF CUIDAD RODRIGO AND BADAJOS / WHERE HE RECEIVED SEVERE WOUNDS; AND FELL / COMMANDING A COMPANY OF THE REGIMENT / TO WHICH HE BELONGED, BELOVED AND LAMENTED. / TO PERPETUATE HIS REMEMBRANCE, / HIS TOWNSMEN HAVE CAUSED THIS MONUMENT / TO BE ERECTED.

Named on the Memorial: St Andrew's Church, (now Musée Historique), Biarritz, France. (Photograph)

Ensign 1st Lancashire Militia. 2nd Lt 95th Foot 13 Apr 1809. 1st Lt 6 Feb 1811.
    Served in the Peninsula with 1/95th Sep 1810 – Dec 1813. Present at Busaco, Pombal (wounded), Ciudad Rodrigo, Badajoz, Salamanca, San Millan, Vittoria (severely wounded), Pyrenees, Vera, Bidassoa, Nivelle and Nive where he was killed at Arcangues near Bayonne 10 Dec 1813. Lt Hopwood and Sgt Brotherton were both killed by the same cannon ball as they were standing behind each other. They were buried

together in the same grave. To receive his commission from the militia to the 95th Foot, he recruited 50 men in two days from the Rochdale area.

HORNBY, Charles
Lieutenant and Captain. 3rd Regiment of Foot Guards.
Memorial: Royal Military Chapel, Wellington Barracks, London. (M.I.) (Destroyed by a Flying Bomb in 1944)

"A CHANCEL STALL IS GIVEN BY SURVIVING RELATIVES AND FRIENDS, 1881, IN MEMORY OF / LIEUT.-COLONEL CHARLES HORNBY, / BORN, 1790. 3RD GUARDS, 1808. / "CADIZ," "CIUDAD RODRIGO," "BADAJOS," "VITTORIA," "SAN SEBASTIAN." / RETIRED, 1840; DIED, 1867."

Ensign 9 Jun 1808. Lt and Capt 26 Aug 1813. Capt and Lt Colonel 31 Aug 1832.
   Served in the Peninsula Apr 1810 – Mar 1811 and Nov 1811 – Sep 1813. Present at Cadiz, Ciudad Rodrigo, Vittoria. MGS medal for Ciudad Rodrigo and Vittoria. Retired 1840.

HORNE, James
Private. 32nd (Cornwall) Regiment of Foot.
Buried in St Mary the Virgin Churchyard, Carlton, Bedfordshire. (Burial register)

Pte Essex Fencibles Nov 1796. Pte 32nd Foot 15 Mar 1801.
   Served in the Peninsula 1808 – Jan 1809 and Jul 1811 – Apr 1814. Present at Corunna, Salamanca, Burgos and retreat from Burgos and Bidassoa. Present at Quatre Bras (wounded in both legs). Also served at Copenhagen 1807 and Walcheren 1809 (present at Flushing). Discharged 5 Jan 1816 due to his wounds from Quatre Bras. MGS medal for Corunna and Salamanca. Buried in Carlton 17 Jul 1849.

HORSTON, William
Corporal. 12th (Prince of Wales's) Regiment of Light Dragoons.
Named on the Regimental Memorial: St Joseph's Church, Waterloo, Belgium. (Photograph)
   Killed at Waterloo.

HORTON, Pickwick Baxter Posthumus
Captain. 61st (South Gloucestershire) Regiment of Foot.
Memorial tablet: St Nicholas Church, Fulbeck, Lincolnshire. (Photograph)

SACRED TO THE MEMORY OF / PICKWICK BAXTER POSTHUMUS HORTON ESQ. / SON OF PICKWICK HORTON / LATE CAPTAIN IN THE 61ST REGIMENT OF FOOT / WHO AT THE AGE OF 28 YEARS / FELL IN THE ARMS OF VICTORY / AT THE BATTLE OF SALAMANCA / ON JULY 22ND 1812 / AS HE LIVED HONOURABLE AND BELOVED / SO HE DIED GLORIOUS. / (VERSE)

Ensign 49th Foot. Lt 27 Mar 1802. Capt 61st Foot 21 Aug 1806.
   Served in the Peninsula Nov 1809 – Jul 1812. Present at Busaco, siege of Forts of Salamanca, and Salamanca where he was killed 22 Jul 1812.

HOSTE, Sir George Charles
Captain. Royal Engineers.
Grave: St Luke's Churchyard, Charlton, Kent. (No longer extant: Grave number 225). (M.I.)

"BENEATH RESTS THE BODY OF COL. SIR GEORGE CHARLES HOSTE, C.B. K.S.F. LATE COMMANDING ROYAL ENGINEERS WOOLWICH DISTRICT. HE ENTERED THE ARMY

MDCCCII AT THE AGE OF 16 AND AFTER A DISTINGUISHED AND VARIED CAREER OF 43 YEARS DEPARTED THIS LIFE THE 21 APRIL MDCCCXLV."

2nd Lt 20 Dec 1802. 1st Lt 21 Dec 1802. Capt 18 Nov 1807. Bt Major 17 Mar 1814. Lt Colonel 29 Jul 1825. Bt Colonel 28 Jun 1838. Colonel 23 Nov 1841.

Present at Waterloo (senior officer of the Engineers attached to the Prince of Orange), the siege of Peronne, Capture of Paris and with the Army of Occupation. Also served in Sicily 1805–1807 (present at Maida and siege of Scylla Castle 1806), Egypt 1807 (present at Alexandria and Rosetta), Sicily 1807–1811, Netherlands 1813 – 1815, (present at Antwerp and Bergen-op-Zoom where he led the Guards in the attack). CB and Knight of St Ferdinand (Naples).
REFERENCE: *Dictionary of National Biography. Royal Military Calendar, Vol 5, p. 247. Gentleman's Magazine, Jul 1845, pp. 650–1. Annual Register, 1845, Appx, p. 270.*

HOTHAM, Beaumont Lord
Lieutenant and Captain. Coldstream Regiment of Foot Guards.
Memorial tablet: St Mary's Church, South Dalton, Yorkshire. (Photograph)

IN THE VAULT BENEATH IS LAID / THE BODY OF / BEAUMONT LORD HOTHAM / A GENERAL IN THE ARMY / ONE OF THE KNIGHTS OF THE SHIRE FOR THIS RIDING / IN SUCCESSIVE PARLIAMENTS / FOUNDER OF THIS CHURCH / BORN 9TH AUGUST, 1794. DIED 12TH DECEMBER 1870.

Ensign 27 Jun 1810. Lt and Capt 25 Dec 1813. Bt Major 21 Jan 1819. Lt Colonel 24 Dec 1825. Bt Colonel 28 Jun 1838. Major General 11 Nov 1851. Lt General 26 Aug 1858. General 12 Jan 1865.

Served in the Peninsula Mar 1812 – Mar 1814. Present at Salamanca (wounded), Vittoria, Bidassoa, Nivelle, Nive, Adour and Bayonne. Present at Waterloo. Also served in the Netherlands 1814. MGS medal for Salamanca, Vittoria, Nivelle and Nive. Half pay 1827. Member of Parliament 1820 –1868 and always supported measures to improve efficiency in the Army. Educated at Westminster.
REFERENCE: *Dictionary of National Biography. Household Brigade Journal 1870, p. 310.*

HOUGHTON, Henry
Private. 73rd (Highland) Regiment of Foot.
Headstone: St Peter's Churchyard, Wootton-Wawen, Warwickshire. (Photograph)

IN MEMORY OF / HENRY HOUGHTON / LATE OF / H.M. 73RD FOOT / WHO WAS / WOUNDED AT WATERLOO / ....

Warwickshire Militia. Pte 73rd Foot 4 May 1812.
Served at Waterloo (wounded). Also served in the Netherlands 1814. Discharged 3 May 1816 owing to his wound. Died 1 Mar 1880 aged 87.
REFERENCE: *Lagden, Alan and John Sly, The 2/73rd at Waterloo, 2nd edition, 1998, pp. 108–9.*

HOUGHTON, Richard Rollo
Captain. 3rd (East Kent) Regiment of Foot.
Headstone: New Cemetery, Cheltenham, Gloucestershire. (M.I.)

"SACRED TO THE MEMORY OF MAJOR RICHARD ROLLO HOUGHTON, LATE OF THE 73RD REGIMENT, FORMERLY OF SPRINGFIELD, CO. ANTRIM, IRELAND WHO DIED AT CHELTENHAM MARCH 10TH 1868 AGED 77."

Ensign 11 Apr 1807. Lt 14 Apr 1808. Capt 7 Jul 1814. Capt 73rd 24 Oct 1822. Bt Major 10 Jan 1837.

Served in the Peninsula Sep 1808, Feb – Sep 1811, Mar – Nov 1812 and Sep 1813 – Mar 1814. Present at Albuera (severely wounded), Nivelle and Nive (wounded). MGS medal for Albuera, Nivelle and Nive. Retired on half pay 11 Jun 1830.

HOULTON, Sir George
Lieutenant. 43rd (Monmouthshire) Light Infantry Regiment of Foot.
Memorial tablet: St Leonard's Church, Farleigh-Hungerford, Somerset. (Photograph)

SACRED / TO THE MEMORY OF / SIR GEORGE HOULTON, / CAPTAIN 43RD LT INFANTRY, 27 YEARS / ENSIGN / OF THE QUEEN'S ROYAL BODY GUARD. / BORN DECR 22ND 1788. / FROM 1806 TO 1816, DURING THE WAR WITH FRANCE / HE SERVED IN THE RETREAT OF CORUNNA UNDER / SIR JOHN MOORE, AND AT THE SIEGES OF FLUSHING, / AND AT WALCHEREN. AGAIN IN THE PENINSULA, IN / THE RETREAT OF THE LINES OF TORRES VEDRAS, IN THE / PURSUIT OF MASSENA. ACTIONS OF POMBAL, REDINHA, / CASAL NOVA, MIRANDA DE CORVO. FOZ D'AROUCE, / CONDEIXA, SABUGAL, CASTREJON, SAN CHRIS-TOVAL, / SAN MUNOS, SAN MILAN, BATTLES OF BUSACO, / FUENTES D'ONOR, SALAMANCA, VITTORIA, / (SEVERELY WOUNDED), PYRENEES, NIVELLE, NIVE, AND / TOULOUSE, SIEGE AND STORMING OF CUIDAD / RODRIGO, SIEGE AND STORMING OF BADAJOS. / ALSO IN THE STORMING AND THE LINES OF / NEW ORLEANS, THE TAKING OF PARIS, AND / WITH THE ARMY OF OCCUPATION IN FRANCE / IN 1817. HE RECEIVED THE WAR MEDAL, WITH / TEN CLASPS. / BEARING A SPOTLESS REPUTATION, / UNIVERSALLY BELOVED AND MOST DEEPLY LAMENTED, / HE DIED SEPT. 16TH 1862. / THAT DEATH MIGHT NOT DISUNITE THEIR NAMES / AFTER 42 YEARS OF MARRIED LIFE, / HERE BY THEIR MUTUAL WISH IS ALSO PLACED THAT OF / ANNA, / HIS TENDERLY LOVED AND DEVOTED WIFE, / WHO SURVIVED HIS LOSS.

Ensign 26 Nov 1806. Lt 6 Oct 1808. Capt. 2 Nov 1815.
   Served in the Peninsula with 1/43rd Sep 1808 – Jan 1809 and Sep 1810 – Apr 1814. Present at Vigo, Busaco, Pombal, Redinha, Casal Nova, Foz d'Arouce, Sabugal, Fuentes d'Onoro, Ciudad Rodrigo (member of storming party), Badajoz (also member of storming party), Castrejon, Salamanca, San Millan, Vittoria (severely wounded), Pyrenees, Bidassoa, Nivelle, Nive and Toulouse (severely wounded). Served in France with the Army of Occupation 1815–1817. Also served at Walcheren 1809 (present at Flushing), North America 1814–1815 (present at New Orleans). MGS medal for Busaco, Fuentes d'Onoro, Ciudad Rodrigo, Badajoz, Salamanca, Vittoria, Pyrenees, Nivelle, Nive and Toulouse. Retired on half pay 1817. Ensign in Yeoman of the Guard 25 Dec 1835. Knighted 1835.
REFERENCE: Gentleman's Magazine, Oct 1862, pp. 509–10. Annual Register, 1862, Appx, p. 364.

HOUSTOUN, Sir William
Colonel. 20th (East Devonshire) Regiment of Foot.
Memorial tablet: Edrom Church, Edrom, Berwickshire, Scotland. (Inside former family area, now partitioned from the main church, and used as a store, accessed from the rear of the church). (Photograph)

IN MEMORY OF / GENERAL / SIR WILLIAM HOUSTOUN, / BARONET, / G.C.B. – G.C.H., / COLONEL OF THE 20TH REGT. / BORN 1764, / DIED 1842.

Low monument in railed enclosure: All Saints Church, Carshalton, Surrey. Inscription illegible. (Photograph)

Ensign 31st Foot 18 Jul 1781. Lt 2 Apr 1782. Capt 77th Foot 13 Mar 1783. Capt 19th Foot 1784. Major 1 Mar 1794. Lt Colonel 84th Foot 18 Mar 1795. Lt Colonel 58th Foot 10 Jun 1795. Colonel 29 Apr 1802. Major General 25 Oct 1809. Lt General 4 Jun 1814. General 10 Jan 1837.
   Served in the Peninsula Jan – Aug 1811 (Commanded 7th Division Mar – Aug 1811). Present at Fuentes

d'Onoro (Mentioned in Despatches) and second siege of Badajoz (Mentioned in Despatches). By autumn 1811 he was so ill with Walcheren fever that he was ordered home. Gold Medal for Fuentes d'Onoro. GCB. GCH. Lieutenant Governor of Portsmouth. Colonel 20th Foot Apr 1815. Also served in Flanders 1794, Minorca, 1798, Egypt 1801 (present at Alexandria) and Walcheren 1809. Died 8 Apr 1842.
REFERENCE: *Dictionary of National Biography. Gentleman's Magazine, Jul 1842, p. 93. Annual Register, 1842, Appx, pp. 262–3.*

HOVENDEN, Nicholas

Lieutenant. 59th (2nd Nottinghamshire) Regiment of Foot.
Memorial tablet: Royal Garrison Church, Portsmouth, Hampshire. (North wall of transept above Vestry door). (Photograph).

SACRED TO THE MEMORY OF / MAJOR NICHOLAS HOVENDEN, 59TH REGIMENT / WHO DIED AT / LEEDS, ON THE 30TH SEPTEMBER 1845 / AGED 52 YEARS / 36 OF WHICH HE PASSED IN THE 59TH REGIMENT / HAVING SERVED WITH IT IN THE PENINSULAR / AT WATERLOO AND BHURTPORE / THIS TABLET IS ERECTED BY HIS BROTHER OFFICERS / AS A TOKEN OF THEIR ESTEEM

Ensign 6 Apr 1809. Lt 12 Dec 1811. Capt 19 Jan 1826. Major 22 Aug 1834.
    Served in the Peninsula Sep 1812 – Feb 1814. Present at Cadiz, Vittoria and San Sebastian (severely wounded). Present at Waterloo in reserve at Hal, siege of Cambrai, Capture of Paris and with the Army of Occupation. Also served in India present in Mahratta Wars 1817–1818 and at the siege and storming of Bhurtpore 1825–1826.

HOWARD, Hon. Frederick

Major. 10th (Prince of Wales's Own) Regiment of Light Dragoons.
Memorial tablet: St Joseph's Church, Waterloo, Belgium. (Photograph)

TO THE MEMORY OF / THE HONBLE FREDERICK HOWARD / MAJOR THE 10TH HUSSARS KILLED AT THE BATTLE OF / WATERLOO. / HIS MUTILATED REMAINS WERE REMOVED FROM THE FIELD / OF BATTLE BY ORDER OF HIS AFFECTIONATE FATHER FREDERICK / EARL OF CARLISLE TO BE DEPOSITED IN THE FAMILY MAUSOLEUM / AT / CASTLE HOWARD. / THIS TABLET WAS DIRECTED TO BE PLACED IN THE CHAPEL OF / WATERLOO BY HIS BROTHER OFFICERS.

Memorial tablet: Mausoleum, Castle Howard, Yorkshire. (Not open to the public). (Photograph)

THE HONOURABLE FREDERICK HOWARD / 3RD SON OF FREDERICK 5TH EARL OF CARLISLE, / MAJOR OF 10TH HUSSARS, / BORN IN DECEMBER 1785, / KILLED AT THE BATTLE OF WATERLOO, 1815 / BURIED IN THE PARISH CHURCH / OF STREATHAM SURREY, / IN THE MONTH OF JULY 1815 / REMOVED TO THIS MAUSOLEUM / ON THE 23RD DAY OF MAY 1879.

Ensign 85th Foot 26 May 1801. Lt 10th Lt Dragoons 14 Dec 1802. Capt 60th Foot 5 Jan 1805. Capt 10th Lt Dragoons 26 Jan 1805. Major 9 May 1811.
    Served in the Peninsula Nov 1808 – Jan 1809 and Dec 1813 – Apr 1814. Present at Sahagun, Benevente, Orthes and Toulouse. Present at Waterloo where he was killed leading the last charge. His body was brought home from Waterloo and buried at Streatham Aug 1815. In 1879 he was re-interred in the Mausoleum at Castle Howard. His death was immortalised in the poem *Childe Harold* by Lord Byron his kinsman. Educated at Eton.

HOWARD, Sir Kenneth Alexander

2nd Major. Coldstream Regiment of Foot Guards.
Monument and family vault: All Saints Church, Rotherham, Yorkshire.
Memorial: Royal Military Chapel, Wellington Barracks, London. (M.I.) (Destroyed by a Flying Bomb in 1944)

"A CHANCEL STALL IS GIVEN IN MEMORY OF / GENERAL KENNETH ALEXANDER HOWARD, EARL OF EFFINGHAM, / G.C.B., K.T.S. / COLONEL OF THE 3RD REGIMENT OF FOOT, THE BUFFS. BORN, 1767; DIED, 1845. PAGE OF HONOUR TO GEORGE III; COLDSTREAM GUARDS, 1786–1814; ADJUTANT 1ST BATTALION, 1793–1797; MAJOR 2ND BATTALION, 1808; SERVED IN FLANDERS, 1793–1795; WAS PRESENT AT ST AMAND, WHERE HE CARRIED A COLOUR AND WAS WOUNDED, THE SIEGE OF VALENCIENNES, THE ACTION AT LINCELLES, THE SIEGE OF DUNKIRK, ALSO DURING THE CAMPAIGN IN HOLLAND, 1799. HE JOINED THE ARMY IN THE PENINSULA IN 1811 AS A MAJOR-GENERAL, AND TOOK COMMAND OF THE 1ST BRIGADE OF GUARDS, NOVEMBER, 1812, AND OF THE 1ST DIVISION, JUNE, 1813, AND SERVED TO THE END OF THE WAR, BEING PRESENT AT THE ACTIONS OF FUENTES D'ONOR, ARROYO DE MOLINOS, AND ALMAREZ, THE BATTLE OF VITTORIA, THE ATTACK ON TOLOSA, THE PASSAGE OF THE BIDASSOA, AND OF THE NIVELLE, THE NIVE, AND THE ADOUR, THE INVESTMENT OF BAYONNE, AND THE REPULSE OF THE SORTIE. / GIVEN BY HIS SON HENRY, SECOND EARL OF EFFINGHAM".

Ensign 21 Apr 1786. Lt and Capt 25 Apr 1793. Capt and Lt Colonel 30 Dec 1797. Bt Colonel 1 Jan 1805. 2nd Major 4 Aug 1808. Major General 25 Jul 1810. Lt General 12 Aug 1819. General 10 Jan 1837.

Served in the Peninsula Jan 1811 – Apr 1814. (Commanded 4 Brigade 1st Division Feb – Jun 1811, Commanded 1 Brigade 2nd Division Jun 1811 – Oct 1812, Commanded 1 Brigade 1st Division Oct 1812 – Oct 1813 and GOC 1st Division Oct 1813 – Apr 1814). Present at Fuentes d'Onoro (Mentioned in Despatches), Arroyo dos Molinos (Mentioned in Despatches), Almarez (Mentioned in Despatches), Alba de Tormes (Mentioned in Despatches), Burgos, Vittoria, Tolosa, Bidassoa (Mentioned in Despatches), Nivelle, Nive (Mentioned in Despatches), Adour, Bayonne and the Sortie from Bayonne.

Served in France with the Army of Occupation (Commanded 1st Division in Paris). Gold Medal for Vittoria and Nive. GCB. KTS. Lt Governor of Portsmouth 1814. Colonel 70th Foot 24 Oct 1816. Colonel 3rd Foot 30 Jan 1832. Also served in Flanders 1793–1795 (present at St Amand where he was wounded, Valenciennes, Lincelles and Dunkirk), the Irish Rebellion 1798 and the Helder 1799. Created 1st Lord Effingham 27 Jan 1837. Died 13 Feb 1845.

REFERENCE: *Dictionary of National Biography. Royal Military Calendar, Vol 3, pp. 32–3. Gentleman's Magazine, Apr 1845, pp. 429–30. Annual Register, 1845, Appx, pp. 243–4. Obit. The Times, 17 Feb 1845.*

HOWARD, Thomas Phipps

Captain. 23rd Regiment of Light Dragoons.
Memorial tablet: St Mary's Church, Weymouth, Dorset. (Photograph)

SACRED / TO THE MEMORY OF / MAJOR GENERAL THOMAS PHIPPS HOWARD / K.H., & K.C.S. OF THE LATE 23RD LANCERS, / WHO DEPARTED THIS LIFE ON 11 OCTOBER 1847, / IN THE 80TH YEAR OF HIS AGE: / HIS REMAINS ARE DEPOSITED IN THE CATACOMBS / OF TRINITY CHURCH WEYMOUTH. / ....

Cornet 1793. Lt Royal York Hussars 25 Nov 1795. Capt 4 Jun 1798. Capt 23rd Lt Dragoons 25 May 1803. Bt Major 15 Mar 1810. Bt Lt Colonel 12 Aug 1819. Bt Colonel 10 Jan 1837. Major General 9 Nov 1846.

Served in the Peninsula Jun 1809 – Apr 1814. Present at Talavera (severely wounded in the charge made by the 23rd Lt Dragoons, taken prisoner until Apr 1814 and awarded pension of £200 per annum). Also served in the West Indies 1795–1799 (present at St Domingo). Retired on half pay 1818. MGS medal for Talavera. KH 1837.

REFERENCE: *Gentleman's Magazine, Dec 1847, p. 640. Annual Register, 1847, Appx, p. 257.*

HOWDEN, Lord John Caradoc see CRADOCK, John Francis

HOWE, John
Private. 23rd Regiment of Light Dragoons.
Memorial tablet: St Mary's Old Parish Church, Newtown, Montgomeryshire, Wales, (Seriously eroded). (Photograph)

SACRED TO THE MEMORY OF / JOHN HOWE / (SERGEANT MAJOR IN THE 10TH ROYAL HUSSARS / AND WHO SHARED THE LAURELS OF WATERLOO). / HE DIED NOV 22ND 1844 AGED 52.

Pte 23rd Light Dragoons.
Served at Waterloo in Capt Thomas Gerrard's Troop No 1. After disbandment of the regiment in 1817, transferred to 10th Hussars and by the time of his death in 1844 had become Sgt Major in that regiment.

HOYSTED, Frederick William
Major. 59th (2nd Nottinghamshire) Regiment of Foot.
Ledger stone: Graveyard inside Kildangan Stud, Kildangan, County Kildare, Ireland. (Photograph)

TO THE MEMORY / OF / FREDERICK WILLIAM HOYSTED, ESQ / LATE / LIEUTENANT COLONEL 59TH REGIMENT OF FOOT. / HE DIED AT KILBOGGIN / ON THE 26TH OF FEBRUARY 1818 / AGED 59 YEARS.

1st Lt Monasterevan Cavalry 20 Nov 1796. Capt 59th Foot 5 Jan 1805. Major 17 Jun 1813. Bt Lt Colonel 26 Dec 1813.
Served in the Peninsula Aug 1813 – Jan 1814. Present at San Sebastian, Nivelle, Nive (severely wounded 10 Dec 1813, awarded Bt Lt Colonelcy and awarded pension of £250 per annum). Gold Medal for Nive. Present at Waterloo in reserve at Hal, siege of Cambrai, Capture of Paris and with the Army of Occupation.

HUGHES, James
Major. 18th Regiment of Light Dragoons.
Chest tomb: English Cemetery, Florence, Italy. (Grave number C21H). (Photograph)

SACRED TO THE MEMORY OF / COLONEL JAMES HUGHES C.B. / THIRD SON OF THE REVEREND EDWARD HUGHES KINMEL / PARK IN THE COUNTY OF DENBIGH AND OF LLIS-DULAS IN THE COUNTY / OF ANGLESEA HE DIED ON THE 29TH DECEMBER 1845. / THIS MEMORIAL IN TOKEN OF HIS GREAT AFFECTION WAS ERECTED / BY HIS ONLY SURVIVING BROTHER WILLIAM LEWIS LORD DINORBEN. / COLONEL HUGHES ENTERED THE ARMY AT AN EARLY AGE AS CORNET IN THE 16TH LANCERS. / HAVING BEEN PROMOTED INTO THE 18TH HE ENTERED IN THE REGIMENT IN PORTUGAL AND SPAIN / UNDER THE COMMAND OF LT GEN MOORE HE WAS WITH / THE ADVANCED GUARD AT THE / ESCURIAL AND PRESENT AT THE DIFFERENT AFFAIRS / WHICH WERE HAD DURING THE / RETREAT AND AT THE MEMORABLE ACTION OF / CORUNNA WHERE THE BRAVE SIR JOHN / MOORE FELL EARLY IN 1809. THE COLONEL / JOINED THE ARMY IN SPAIN COMMANDED / BY THE DUKE OF WELLINGTON HE / WAS PRESENT AT THE BATTLE OF MORALES AND HAD / THE GOOD FORTUNE / TO COMMAND THE 18TH AT THOSE OF VITTORIA, / NIVELLE, NIVE / AND

ORTHES / ON THE 28TH OF MARCH 1814 AT THE HEAD OF ONE SQUADRON OF THIS / DISTIN-GUISHED REGIMENT HE CHARGED AND DROVE A FRENCH REGIMENT / OF DRAGOONS UNDER THE GUNS OF ST CYPRIAN AND ON THE 18TH APRIL / FOLLOWING HE ATTACKED / AND CARRIED THE BRIDGE OF CROIX D'ORADE / DEFENDED BY VIAL'S DRAGOONS WHILST / THE OPPOSITE BANKS WERE / LINED WITH DISMOUNTED CARBINIERS. THIS SUCCESS SECURED THE / COMMUNICATION OF THE ALLIED COLUMNS AND OPENED THE ROAD TO / TOULOUSE / THE COLONEL WAS SEVERELY WOUNDED IN AN AFFAIR AT ELLITE / FOR HIS SEVERAL SERVICES HE WAS REWARDED WITH DISTINGUISHING CROSSES

Cornet 16th Lt Dragoons 4 Apr 1800. Lt 16 Sep 1802. Capt 48th Foot 22 Sep 1802. Capt 18th Lt Dragoons 10 Sep 1803. Major 24 Sep 1812. Bt Lt Colonel 21 Jun 1817. Bt Colonel 10 Jun 1837.
    Served in the Peninsula Sep 1808 – Jan 1809 and Feb 1813 – Apr 1814. Present at Mayorga (wounded), Benevente, retreat to and battle of Corunna (commanded the last of the British cavalry which remained to cover the embarkation). Morales, Vittoria, Bidassoa, Nivelle, Nive, Orthes, Croix d'Orade and Toulouse. Severely wounded at Mendionde, near Ellite in the south of France 18 Dec 1813. Gold Medal for Vittoria, Orthes and Toulouse. CB. Half pay 1821. M.P. for Grantham 1831–1832. Died in Florence 26 November 1845, not December as on inscription.
REFERENCE: *Gentleman's Magazine, Feb 1846, pp. 209–10. Annual Register, 1845, Appx, p. 318. Royal Military Calendar, Vol 5, p. 134.*

HUGHES, Richard
Private. 1st (Royal Scots) Regiment of Foot.
Buried in the Private Soldiers Burial Ground, Royal Hospital, Kilmainham, Dublin, Ireland. (Burial register)

Pte 2 Jul 1811.
    Served in the Peninsula 1812 – Apr 1814. Present at Vittoria and San Sebastian. Served at Waterloo in Capt Robert Dudgeon's Company No 8 (wounded). Discharged 24 Feb 1816 as a result of his wound at Waterloo. Awarded MGS medal for Vittoria and San Sebastian.

HUGONIN, James
Major. 4th (Queen's Own) Regiment of Dragoons.
Buried in the Family vault: St Mary's Church, Buriton, Hampshire.

Cornet 4 Apr 1795. Lt 30 Sep 1795. Capt 25 Jun 1803. Major 19 Dec 1811. Br Lt Colonel 21 Jan 1819.
    Served in the Peninsula Apr 1809 – Jan 1811 and Jul 1811 – Apr 1814. Present at Talavera, Busaco, Aldea da Ponte, Llerena, Salamanca, Vittoria and Toulouse. Gold Medal for Toulouse. Retired 1819. Died 30 Mar 1854 aged 72.

HULME, John Lyon
2nd Captain. Royal Engineers.
Named on the Regimental Memorial: Rochester Cathedral, Rochester, Kent. (Photograph)

2nd Lt 24 Jun 1809. Lt 10 Jul 1810. 2nd Capt 20 Dec 1814. Capt 23 Mar 1829. Bt Major 28 Nov 1854.
    Served in the Peninsula Mar 1810 – Apr 1814. Present at Torres Vedras, second siege of Badajoz, Nivelle, Nive, Adour and Bayonne. Also served in the Netherlands and in France with the Army of Occupation 1815–1817. MGS medal for Nivelle and Nive. Retired on full pay 5 Dec 1835. Died at Exeter 26 Feb 1870.

HULSE, Richard

Captain and Lieutenant Colonel. Coldstream Regiment of Foot Guards.
Named on Memorial Panel VII: Royal Military Chapel, Wellington Barracks, London. (M.I.) (Destroyed by a Flying Bomb 1944)

Ensign 24 Mar 1790. Lt and Capt 25 Apr 1793. Capt-Lieut 23 Sep 1799. Capt and Lt Colonel 9 May 1800. Bt Colonel 25 Oct 1809. Major General 1 Jan 1812.

Served in the Peninsula Mar 1809 – Sep 1812. (Commanded 1 Brigade 1ˢᵗ Division Nov – Dec 1809, Commanded 1 Brigade 6th Division Nov 1810 – Jul 1812 and Commanded 1 Brigade 5th Division Aug – Sep 1812). Present at Douro, Talavera, Busaco and Salamanca (Mentioned in Despatches). Gold Medal for Talavera and Salamanca. Died in Spain 7 Sep 1812.

HUMBLEY, Philip

Lieutenant. 66th (Berkshire) Regiment of Foot.
Family Memorial floor tablet: St Mary's Church, Eynesbury, Huntingdonshire. (Photograph)

.... / PHILIP HUMBLEY / LIEUTENANT IN HIS MAJESTY'S 66 REGIMENT / OF FOOT, THIRD SON OF THE ABOVE, DIED AT SALAMANCA / IN SPAIN, AUGUST 1ˢᵀ 1809, AGED 21 YEARS, IN CONSEQUENCE / OF A WOUND RECEIVED IN THE MEMORABLE BATTLE / FOUGHT AT THAT PLACE ON THE / 28ᵀᴴ JULY PRECEDING WHEN THE COMBINED / BRITISH AND SPANISH FORCES UNDER THE COM – / MAND OF GENERAL SIR ARTHUR WELLESLEY, BEAT / A DIVISION OF THE FRENCH ARMY OF VERY SUPERIOR / NUMBERS COMMANDED BY JOSEPH BONAPARTE, / BROTHER OF NAPOLEON, EMPEROR OF THE FRENCH.

Ensign 15th Foot 9 Apr 1808. Lt 66th Foot 1 Dec 1808.

Served in the Peninsula Apr – Aug 1809. Present at Douro and Talavera where he was severely wounded Jul 1809. He was taken to Salamanca and died from his wounds 4 Aug 1809. Brother of 1ˢᵗ Lt William Humbley 95th Foot.
Note: The inscription incorrectly implies that he was wounded at Salamanca, rather than Talavera.

HUMBLEY, William

1ˢᵗ Lieutenant. 95th Regiment of Foot
Memorial tablet: St Mary's Church, Eynesbury, Huntingdonshire. (In Porch). (Photograph)

IN MEMORY OF LT COL WILLIAM HUMBLEY LATE OF THE RIFLE BRIGADE WHOSE REMAINS ARE DEPOSITED IN A VAULT NEAR THIS PLACE

Brass Memorial tablet: St Mary's Church, Eynesbury, Huntingdonshire. (In Porch). (Photograph)

Upper plaque: (Photograph)

BENEATH THIS PORCH / IS DEPOSITED ALL THAT / IS MORTAL OF / LIEUT. COL. WILLIAM HUMBLEY / A GALLANT & DISTINGUISHED OFFICER / OF THE RIFLE BRIGADE (OLD 95ᵀᴴ) / WHO AFTER SERVING FAITHFULLY / HIS KING AND COUNTRY / ON MANY HARD FOUGHT FIELDS / IN DENMARK, SPAIN, PORTUGAL, FRANCE, / & HOLLAND WHEREIN THE BRITISH WERE / ALWAYS VICTORIOUS / WAS HIMSELF OVERCOME & CONQUERED BY / THE LAST GREAT ENEMY IN THE QUIET / RETIREMENT OF THIS VILLAGE. / HE WAS BORN NOVEMBER 23 1783 & DIED OCTOBER 26 1857. / (VERSE)

Lower plaque: (Photograph)

AS A / THANK OFFERING / TO / ALMIGHTY GOD / FOR PRESERVATION IN THE FOLLOWING BATTLES / FOUGHT IN FIVE DIFFERENT KINGDOMS / IN WHICH HE WAS PRESENT AND ACTIVELY ENGAGED / THIS PORCH WAS ERECTED BY / LIEUT. COL. HUMBLEY RIFLE BRIGADE / SEPTEMBER 1856.

1. KIOGH IN DENMARK & SURRENDER OF COPENHAGEN AUG 29 1807. / 2 ROLIA IN PORTUGAL SEPT 7 1807. / 3 VIMIERO IN PORTUGAL AUG 17 1808. / 4 SAHAGUN & BENEVENTE SPAIN DEC 21 1808 & JAN 3 1809. 5 CORUNNA IN SPAIN JAN 16 1809. / 6 FLUSHING IN NETHERLANDS AUG 1 1809 (SEVERELY WOUNDED IN HEAD, BALL EXTRACTED & TREPANNED). 7 BUSACO IN SPAIN SEP 27 SEP 1810. 8 BARROSA IN SPAIN MAR 5 1811. 9 SALA-MANCA IN SPAIN JULY 22 1812. 10 ST MILLAN IN SPAIN JUNE 21 1813. 11 LA PUEBLA IN SPAIN JUNE 21 1813. 12 VITTORIA IN SPAIN JUNE 21 1813. 13 PAMPLONA IN SPAIN 21 JULY 28, 29 & 30 1813. 14 BARA IN SPAIN AUG 1 1813 15 PYRENEES IN SPAIN AUG 2 1813. 16 NIVELLE IN FRANCE NOV 10 1813. 17 BAYONNE IN FRANCE NOV 23 1813. 18 NIVE IN FRANCE DEC 9, 10, 11, 12, 13 1814. 19 ORTHES IN FRANCE (WOUNDED IN RT THIGH) 27 FEB 1814. 20 TARBES IN FRANCE MAR 20 1814. 21 TOULOUSE IN FRANCE APR 10 1814. 22 WATERLOO IN NETHER-LAND JUNE 18 1815 (SEVERELY WOUNDED IN BOTH SHOULDERS, TWO BALLS LODGED).

Inscription on Font in Church: (Photograph)

"IN MEMORY OF LIEU COL. HUMBLEY 1858". (SIC)

Brass Memorial tablet under west window: (M.I.)

"IN MEMORY OF LT-COL WILLIAM HUMBLEY LATE OF THE RIFLE BRIGADE WHOSE REMAINS ARE DEPOSITED IN A VAULT NEAR THIS PLACE."

2nd Lt 15 Apr 1807. Lt 13 Oct 1808. Capt 20 Jul 1815. Bt Major 10 Jan 1837. Bt Lt Colonel 11 Nov 1854.
     Served in the Peninsula with 1/95th Aug 1808 – Jan 1809, 2/95th Mar 1810 – Aug 1812 and Mar 1813 – Apr 1814. Present at Rolica, Vimeiro, Cacabellos, Corunna, Busaco, Cadiz, Matagorda, Barrosa, Tarifa, Salamanca, Vittoria (severely wounded), Pyrenees (wounded), Vera, Bidassoa, Nivelle, Nive, Orthes (severely wounded), Tarbes (wounded) and Toulouse. Present at Waterloo where he was severely wounded and awarded pension of £70 per annum. Also served in the Baltic 1807, Walcheren 1809 (present at Flushing where he was wounded). Half pay 1818. MGS medal for Rolica, Vimeiro, Corunna, Busaco, Barrosa, Salamanca, Vittoria, Pyrenees, Nivelle, Nive, Orthes and Toulouse.
     His son was born 18th June 1815 and was christened William Wellington Waterloo Humbley – later becoming Lieutenant Colonel 9th Royal Lancers. Brother of Lt Philip Humbley 66th Foot.
     REFERENCE: *Gentleman's Magazine*, Dec 1857, p. 687. *Annual Register*, 1857, Appx, p. 342.

HUME, John Robert
Deputy Inspector General of Hospitals. Medical Department.
Ledger stone: Kensal Green Cemetery, London. (13725/77/2). (Photograph)

SACRED / TO THE MEMORY OF / DR JOHN ROBERT HUME CB. / WHO DIED IN LONDON / AT HIS RESIDENCE / 9 CURZON STREET MAYFAIR / ON 1ST MARCH 1857

Hospital Mate 28 Oct 1798. Asst Surgeon 92nd Foot 9 May 1800. Surgeon 14th Battalion of Reserve 9 Jul 1803. Surgeon 79th Foot 25 May 1805. Staff Surgeon 17 Aug 1809. Deputy Inspector of Hospitals 26 May 1814.
     Served in the Peninsula Aug 1808 – Jan 1809 and Apr 1810 – Apr 1814. (attached to 1st Division Oct 1811 – Aug 1812 and HQ Nov 1812 – Apr 1814). Present at Corunna, Cadiz, Barrosa, siege of Salamanca

Forts, Salamanca, Burgos, Vittoria, Pyrenees, Bidassoa, Nivelle, Nive, Orthes and Toulouse. Present at Waterloo. CB. Also served at the Helder 1799, Egypt 1801, Baltic 1808 and Walcheren 1809. MGS medal for Egypt, Corunna, Barrosa, Salamanca, Vittoria, Pyrenees, Nivelle, Nive, Orthes and Toulouse. MD St Andrew's 1816. Duke of Wellington's friend and his physician for many years.

REFERENCE: *Dictionary of National Biography. Balham, Life of J. D. Hume, 1859.*

HUMFREY, Robert Blake see BLAKE, Robert

HUMPHREYS, Charles Gardiner
Lieutenant. 14th (Duchess of York's) Regiment of Light Dragoons.
Pedestal tomb in railed enclosure: St Nicholas Churchyard, Montgomery, Montgomeryshire, Wales. (Side C). (Photograph)

TO THE MEMORY OF / CHARLES GARDINER HUMPHREYS, ESQ. / ELDEST SON OF / CHARLES GARDINER HUMPHREYS / AND ELIZABETH HIS WIFE, WHO DIED / ON THE 15TH DAY OF JANUARY 1862, / IN THE 70TH YEAR OF HIS AGE AND / WHOSE REMAINS ARE INTERRED ON / THE EAST SIDE OF THIS MONUMENT. / HE HELD A CAPTAIN'S COMMISSION / IN THE ROYAL MONTGOMERYSHIRE / MILITIA REGIMENT, AND WAS / FORMERLY A LIEUTENANT IN THE / 14TH LIGHT DRAGOONS, HAVING / SERVED WITH THAT CORPS IN THE / PENINSULAR WAR AND OBTAINED / THE MEDAL WITH SEVEN CLASPS FOR / SALAMANCA, VITTORIA, PYRENEES, / NIVELLE, NIVE, ORTHES AND TOULOUSE.

Cornet 20 Jun 1811. Lt 11 Mar 1813.
    Served in the Peninsula Jun 1812 – Apr 1814. Present at Castrejon, Salamanca, Vittoria, Pyrenees, Nivelle, Nive, Orthes, Vic Bigorre, Tarbes and Toulouse. Half pay 4 Sep 1817. Later Capt in Royal Montgomeryshire Militia. MGS medal for Salamanca, Vittoria, Pyrenees, Nivelle, Nive, Orthes and Toulouse.

HUNT, Arthur
Captain. Royal Artillery.
Gravestone: St Nicholas Churchyard, Plumstead, Kent and named on the Regimental Memorial: St Nicholas Church, Plumstead, Kent. (No longer extant. Destroyed by a flying bomb in the Second World War).

Royal Irish Artillery. 2nd Lt Royal Artillery 11 Nov 1798. 1st Lt 18 Apr 1801. 2nd Capt 1 Jun 1806. Capt 17 Feb 1814. Bt Major 12 Aug 1819. Lt Colonel 26 Oct 1831. Colonel 23 Nov 1841.
    Served in the Peninsula Apr 1810 – Apr 1814. Present at Cadiz, Carthagena and Tarragona. Present at Waterloo (at Rocroi) and with the Army of Occupation 1815–1818. Also served in the Irish Rebellion 1798, West Indies 1800–1806, Gibraltar 1807–1810, Newfoundland 1827–1831 and Gibraltar 1832–1835. Died 8 Mar 1853.

HUNT, John Philip
Lieutenant Colonel. 60th (Royal American) Regiment of Foot.
Box tomb: Blessed St Mary Churchyard, Upper Walmer, Kent. (Photograph)

IN MEMORY OF / JOHN PHILIP HUNT COMPANION OF THE BATH LATE LIEUT-COLONEL COMMANDING / THE 11TH REGIMENT OF FOOT, AND FORMERLY OF THE 52ND REGIMENT OF / LIGHT INFANTRY, WITH WHICH GALLANT REGIMENT, DURING THE PENINSULAR WAR, / HE FOUGHT FOR HIS COUNTRY IN MANY BATTLES. DIED 26TH NOVEMBER 1858; AGED 77.

Ensign 52nd Foot 8 Mar 1799. Lt 29 Nov 1799. Capt 10 Feb 1803. Major 8 Sep 1808. Bt Lt Colonel 27 Apr 1812. Lt Colonel 60th Foot 11 Nov 1813. Lt Colonel 11th Foot 19 Nov 1818.

Served in the Peninsula Aug 1808 – Oct 1808 (ADC to Sir John Moore), with 2/52nd Oct 1808 – Jan 1809 and Mar – Oct 1811 and 1/52nd Mar 1812 – Sep 1813. Present at Vigo, Sabugal, Fuentes d'Onoro, Badajoz (awarded Bt Lt Colonelcy in command of 2nd Brigade Lt Division), Salamanca, San Munos, Pyrenees, San Sebastian (severely wounded 31 Aug 1813 and Mentioned in Despatches. Awarded Lt Colonelcy in 60th Foot). Gold Medal for Badajoz, Salamanca and San Sebastian. MGS medal for Fuentes d'Onoro and Pyrenees. CB. Also served at Ferrol 1800, Baltic 1808 and Walcheren 1809. After his serious wounds at San Sebastian was appointed Inspecting Field Officer of Enniskillen, Athlone and Chelmsford recruiting districts.
REFERENCE: *Royal Military Calendar, Vol 4, pp. 412–3. Annual Register, 1858, Appx, p. 450.*

HUNT, Richard
Lieutenant. Royal Engineers.
Named on the Regimental Memorial: Rochester Cathedral, Rochester, Kent. (Photograph)

2nd Lt 1 Jul 1808. 1st Lt 1 Aug 1809.
Served in the Peninsula Mar – Jun 1811. Present at the first and second sieges of Badajoz, where he was killed 9 Jun 1811 as officer in charge of the ladder party, following the storming party in the attack on Fort Cristobal.

HUNTER, John
Captain. 3rd (King's Own) Regiment of Dragoons.
Sepulchre: Terre Cabade Cemetery, Toulouse, France. (Section 3 Division 15). Also contains a memorial tablet to Lt Colonel Thomas Forbes of the 45th Foot. (Photograph)

ERIGÉ / PAR LA RECONNAISSANCE / ET L'ANNE / A LA MÉMOIRE / DE / JOHN HUNTER / ESQUIRE A MAJOR / DANS / LES ARMEES BRITTANNIQUES / .... / LE 2ND NOVBR 1838 / AGE DE 68 ANS

Lt 31 Mar 1808. Capt 31 Dec 1812.
Served in the Peninsula Mar – Apr 1814. Present at Toulouse. MGS medal for Toulouse.

HUNTER, William
Assistant Surgeon. Coldstream Regiment of Foot Guards.
Family Obelisk: Haylie Brae Cemetery, Largs, Ayrshire, Scotland. (Photograph)

SACRED / TO THE MEMORY OF / HELEN WILKIE, / WIFE OF / WILLIAM HUNTER, M. D. / OF WOODBANK. / .... / THE ABOVE WILLIAM HUNTER M. D. / BORN 21ST MARCH 1794, / DIED AT WOODBANK, LARGS, 28TH JUNE 1871, / WAS LATE SURGEON MAJOR OF THE / COLDSTREAM GUARDS. / HE JOINED HIS REGIMENT ON THE 10TH FEB. 1814, / AND RETIRED FROM THE SERVICE 2ND SEP. 1843. / HE WAS PRESENT AT THE SORTIE FROM / BAYONNE AND THE BATTLE OF WATERLOO. / IN BOTH ENGAGEMENTS THE GUARDS / SUFFERED SEVERELY IN MEN AND OFFICERS. / HE WAS ALSO AT THE CAPTURE OF PARIS / 1815.

Asst Surgeon 10 Feb 1814. Surgeon 4 Sep 1836. Surgeon Major 16 Mar 1838.
Served in the Peninsula Apr 1814. Present at the Sortie from Bayonne. Present at Waterloo and with the Army of Occupation. Retired on half pay 2 Sep 1845.

HUNTLY, George, Marquess of
Colonel. 42nd (Royal Highland) Regiment of Foot..

Statue: Golden Square, Aberdeen, Aberdeenshire, Scotland. (Photograph)

GEORGE / FIFTH AND LAST / DUKE OF GORDON / BORN 1770 / DIED 1836 / FIRST COLONEL / 92ND GORDON HIGHLANDERS

Memorial column: Lady Hill, Elgin, Morayshire. (Photograph)

THIS COLUMN / IS / DEDICATED TO THE MEMORY OF GEORGE THE LAST / DUKE OF GORDON / THE PATRON AND GENEROUS PROMOTER OF AGRICULTURE / A GALLANT AND DISTINGUISHED SOLDIER A WARM AND / ZEALOUS FRIEND AND A NOBLEMAN DESERVEDLY POPULAR / WITH ALL RANKS OF SOCIETY. / THIS COLUMN WAS BUILT BY PUBLIC SUBSCRIPTION / IN 1839 AND EMBELLISHED BY THE ERECTION OF THE STATUE / IN 1855 IN TERMS OF A BEQUEST BY ALEXANDER CRAIG / ESQUIRE OF CRAIGTON / ASSISTED CHIEFLY BY MEMBERS / OF THE MORAYSHIRE FARMER CLUB.

Ensign 35th Foot 1790. Lt 67th Foot 14 Oct 1790. Capt 42nd Foot 27 Jan 1791. Lt and Capt 3rd Foot Guards 20 Jul 1792. Lt Colonel 100th Foot 1794. Colonel 92nd Foot 3 May 1796. Major General 1 Jan 1801. Colonel 42nd Foot 3 Jan 1806. Lt General 25 Apr 1808. General 12 Aug 1819.

Served at Walcheren 1809 (GOC 2nd Division). Also served in Flanders 1793 (present at St Amand, Famars, Lannoy, Dunkirk and Valenciennes), Gibraltar 1794, Corsica 1795, Irish Rebellion 1798, the Helder 1799 (wounded at Egmont-op-Zee where he led the 100th Foot, now the 92nd Foot Gordon Highlanders). Unveiled the Waterloo Cairn at Kinrara on Tor Alvie Hill to Macara (42nd Foot) and Cameron (92nd Foot). Became 5th Duke of Gordon 1827. KCB. Colonel 1st Foot 1820–1834. Colonel 3rd Foot Guards 1834. MP for Eye 1806–1807. Lord Lieutenant of the County of Aberdeen 1808. Governor of Edinburgh Castle and Keeper of the Great Seal of Scotland. Died 10 Jun 1836 and is buried in the family vault in Elgin Cathedral.

REFERENCE: *Dictionary of National Biography. Annual Register, 1836, Appx, p. 204.*

HURST, George
Private. 12th (Prince of Wales's) Regiment of Light Dragoons.

Named on the Regimental Memorial: St Joseph's Church, Waterloo, Belgium. (Photograph)
Killed at Waterloo.

HUSON, Charles
Captain. 45th (Nottinghamshire) Regiment of Foot.

Box tomb: Ardolm Church of Ireland Churchyard, Castlebridge, County Wexford, Ireland. (Photograph)

HERE LIE / THE REMAINS OF NARCISSUS HUSON ESQ., / LATE MAJOR IN THE 45TH REGIMENT / .... / ALSO CHARLES HUSON, LATE CAPTAIN 45TH / REGIMENT DIED APRIL 21ST 1861 AGED 78 YEARS.

Ensign 9 Nov 1802. Lt 14 Jul 1804. Capt 14 Nov 1805.
Served in the Peninsula Jun – Dec 1809. Present at Talavera. Retired 1810. MGS medal for Talavera.

HUSTLER, Robert Samuel
Captain. Royal Engineers.

Named on the Regimental Memorial: Rochester Cathedral, Rochester, Kent. (Photograph)

2nd Lt 1 Mar 1806. Lt 1 Jul 1806. 2nd Capt 1 May 1811. Capt 20 Dec 1814. Lt Colonel 9 Jun 1830.

Served in the Peninsula Aug 1812 – Apr 1814. Present at Tarragona. Also served in Sicily 1810–1812 and Genoa 1814. Died at Armagh, Ireland 23 Jan 1835.

HUTCHESSON, Thomas
Captain. Royal Artillery.
Low monument: St James' Cemetery, Dover, Kent. (Photograph)

IN MEMORY OF / LIEUT. GENERAL THOMAS HUTCHESSON, / COLONEL COMMANDANT OF THE 13TH BATTALION ROYAL ARTILLERY / WHO DIED AT DOVER ON THE 28TH AUGUST 1857. AGED 76.

2nd Lt 1 Dec 1797. 1st Lt 2 Oct 1799. 2nd Capt 10 Apr 1805. Capt 24 Oct 1812. Bt Major 12 Aug 1819. Lt Col 22 Jul 1830. Colonel 23 Nov 1841. Major General 20 Jun 1854. Lt General 14 Jun 1856.
  Served in the Peninsula Mar 1813 – Apr 1814. Present at Garris. Present in the Waterloo campaign (commanding at Ostend and in France with the Army of Occupation until Nov 1818). Also served at the Helder 1799, Gibraltar 1828–1830 and the Ionian Islands 1835–1840. Colonel Commandant Royal Artillery 30 Aug 1854.

HUTCHINS, Thomas
Major. 3rd (King's Own) Regiment of Dragoons.
Memorial tablet: St Mary Abbots Church, Kensington, London. (Resurrection Chapel). (Photograph)

PENINSULA / SALAMANCA / VITTORIA / TOULOUSE / SACRED TO THE MEMORY OF / LIEUT, COLONEL THOMAS HUTCHINS, / MAJOR OF THE THIRD OR KING'S OWN LIGHT DRAGOONS, / WHO DEPARTED THIS LIFE IN CHRISTIAN HUMILITY AND HOPE / ON THE 2ND OF JULY 1823, AGED 44. / THE COLONEL, OFFICERS, NON COMMISSIONED OFFICERS AND PRIVATES / OF THE REGIMENT IN WHICH HE SERVED BOTH AT HOME AND ABROAD / FOR UPWARD OF 23 YEARS / HAVE CAUSED THIS TABLET TO BE ERECTED / IN GRATEFUL REMEM-BRANCE OF HIS MILITARY AND SOCIAL WORTH, / AND AS A LASTING TRIBUTE OF THEIR AFFECTIONATE REGARD.

Cornet 5 Sep 1799. Lt 8 May 1801. Capt 27 Jun 1805. Major 10 Dec 1812. Bt Lt Colonel 21 Jan 1819.
  Served in the Peninsula Oct 1811 – Apr 1814. (Oct 1811 – May 1812 Brigade Major 5 Cavalry Brigade, Sep 1812 – Jan 1813 DAQMG and Feb – Mar 1813 AQMG). Present at Llerena, Castrejon, Salamanca, Vittoria and Toulouse. Gold Medal for Toulouse.

HUTCHINSON, John
Captain. 94th Regiment of Foot.
Family Box tomb: Kirkmichael Churchyard, Kirkmichael, Ayrshire, Scotland. (Photograph)

ERECTED / BY / MRS. MARION HUTCHINSON / IN MEMORY OF / ALEXANDER HUTCHINSON / HER HUSBAND, / .... / AND OF HIS SECOND SON, / CAPT JOHN HUTCHINSON, / OF THE 82ND REGT OF FOOT, / WHO DIED AT DEVONPORT, ENGLAND, / ON THE 8TH OF JAN 1824. / AGED 40 YEARS.

Ensign 94th Foot 12 Apr 1809. Lt 27 Dec 1810. Capt 16 Feb 1815. Capt 83rd Foot 20 Aug 1818. Capt 82nd Foot 12 Nov 1818.
  Served in the Peninsula Feb – Oct 1810 and Mar – Apr 1814. Present at Cadiz, Vic Bigorre and Toulouse. Retired 4 Dec 1823.

HUTCHINSON, John Hely, Third Earl of Donoughmore

Lieutenant and Captain. 1st Regiment of Foot Guards.

Memorial tablet: St Lawrence's Church, Chapelizod, Dublin, Ireland. (West wall of nave). (Photograph)

SACRED TO THE MEMORY OF / JOHN HELY HUTCHINSON / THIRD EARL OF DONOUGH-MORE, KNIGHT OF St PATRICK, / LORD LIEUTENANT OF THE COUNTY OF TIPPERARY, / AND A PRIVY COUNCILLOR. / HAVING SERVED HIS COUNTRY IN THE PENINSULAR WAR, / AND THE SENATE; AND HIS COUNTRY IN TROUBLED TIMES, / HE DIED ON THE 12TH SEPTEMBER 1851, / IN THE 64TH YEAR OF HIS AGE. / LOVED, RESPECTED, AND REGRETTED, BY ALL WHO KNEW HIM. / THIS TABLET / HAS BEEN ERECTED IN THE CHURCH WHERE / HE USUALLY WORSHIPPED, TO RECORD HIS MANY VIRTUES / BY HIS WIDOW.

Memorial: Royal Military Chapel, Wellington Barracks, London. (M.I.) (Destroyed by a Flying Bomb in 1944)

"IN MEMORY OF / JOHN HELY-HUTCHINSON, THIRD EARL OF DONOUGHMORE, K.B. / 1ST GUARDS, 1807–19. / "CORUNNA," "WALCHEREN," "CADIZ," "PENINSULA," "QUATRE BRAS." / PLACED BY HIS GRAND-DAUGHTER, LADY MARY LOYD."

Ensign 25 Sep 1807. Lt and Capt 19 Nov 1812.

Served in the Peninsula with 3rd Battalion Oct 1808 – Jan 1809 and Jul 1811 – Apr 1814. Present at Corunna, Cadiz and Bayonne. MGS medal for Corunna. Present at Quatre Bras, Waterloo and with the Army of Occupation. Also served at Walcheren 1809.

While in Paris in 1815 he helped General Lavalette to escape the guillotine. With Sir Robert Wilson and Lt Michael Bruce they hid the general after he escaped from prison in his wife's clothes. They then disguised him as a British general and escorted him to the frontier. The three officers were arrested and charged with treason, the penalty for which was death. However Wellington intervened and had the case tried in an ordinary assize court. The jury were sympathetic to them and only gave them three months in prison. On his return to England he lost his commission but was later reinstated. Half pay 27 May 1819. MP for Tipperary and Lord Lieutenant for the County.

REFERENCE: *Dictionary of National Biography. Gentleman's Magazine, Nov 1851, pp. 539–40. Annual Register, 1851, Appx, pp. 329–30. United Service Magazine, Oct 1851, p. 320.*

HUTCHINSON, Scroop

Surgeon. 52nd (Oxfordshire) Light Infantry Regiment of Foot.

Obelisk: Kensal Green Cemetery, London. Inscription not recorded. (7156/103/RS). (Photograph)

Hospital Mate 10 Feb 1801. Asst Surgeon 52nd Foot 12 Feb 1801. Surgeon 20 Jun 1805.

Served in the Peninsula with 1/52nd Aug 1808 – Jan 1809 and Jul – Oct 1809. Present at Corunna. MGS medal for Corunna. Resigned 20 Dec 1810. Buried in Kensal Green 29 Nov 1847.

HUTCHINSON, Thomas Kitchingman

2nd Captain. Royal Engineers.

Memorial tablet: St Mary's Church, North Stainley, Yorkshire. (Photograph)

SACRED / TO THE MEMORY OF / THOMAS KITCHINGMAN STAVELEY ESQRE J.P. / OF OLD SLENINGFORD HALL, IN THIS COUNTY, / WHO DEPARTED THIS LIFE ON THE 20TH FEBY 1860, / AGED 69 YEARS. / FORMERLY CAPTAIN ROYAL ENGINEERS / AND MEMBER OF PARLIA-MENT FOR THE CITY OF RIPON, / HE WAS ORIGINATOR / AND PRINCIPAL FOUNDER OF THE CHURCH, / SCHOOL HOUSE AND PARSONAGE / OF NORTH STAINLEY. / THIS TABLET IS ERECTED BY HIS / AFFLICTED WIDOW.

Chest tomb: St Mary's Church, North Stainley, Yorkshire. Inscription illegible. (Photograph)

2nd Lt 15 Jan 1808. 1st Lt 1 Jul 1808. 2nd Capt 21 Jul 1813.

Served in the Peninsula 1808 – Jan 1809. Also served at Walcheren 1809 and Sicily 1810–1814. Took the name of Staveley in later life. Resigned his commission 20 Jul 1815. MP for Ripon 1832 and local benefactor, building the church and school at North Stainley.

HUTTON, George
Captain. 1st (Royal) Regiment of Dragoons.
Memorial: Near to village of Rendinas, Pyrenees, Spain. (M.I.)

"IN MEMORIAM / GEORGE HUTTON / MILITIS FORTISSIMI / DE PRIMA LEGIONE / EQUITATUS BRITANNICI / COHORTIS, / QUI OBIIT / 26 CALENDAS FEBRUARES, / ANNO DOMINI 1814, / ÆTATIS SUÆ 36, / HIC TUMULUS / SACRIETUR."

Capt 3rd Norfolk Militia. Cornet 1st Dragoons 26 Nov 1799. Capt 21 May 1807.

Served in the Peninsula Sep 1809 – Feb 1814. Present at Maguilla, Fuentes d'Onoro and Vittoria. Died of a fever 26 Feb 1814 and buried at a village near Rendinas.

IMPETT, John
Ensign. 71st (Highland Light Infantry) Regiment of Foot.
Memorial: St Mary's Church, Fort St George, Madras, India. (Photograph)

SACRED TO THE MEMORY OF / COLONEL JOHN IMPETT. / HE SERVED AT WATERLOO AT THE / AGE OF 15, AND DIED SHE-/ RIFF OF MADRAS IN THE 68TH YEAR / OF HIS AGE, ON THE 3RD OF DECEM- / BER A.D. 1866. THIS TABLET IS / ERECTED BY HIS MANY FRIENDS / TO WHOM HE HAD LONG ENDEA- / RED HIMSELF BY HIS URBANITY, / KINDLINESS AND SIMPLICITY OF / HIS CHARACTER.

Ensign 71st Foot 14 Apr 1814. Lt 5 Oct 1820. Capt 1st West India Regt 30 Jan 1835. Bt Major 9 Nov 1846. Capt 25th Foot 1852. Bt Lt Colonel 20 Jun 1854. Capt 74th Foot 25 May 1859. Bt Colonel 25 May 1859.

Present at Waterloo at the age of 15. Half pay 1841. Also served in India. Died in Madras 3 Dec 1866 where he was Sheriff. In 1865 a dinner was given in Madras in his honour in celebration of the 50th anniversary of Waterloo.

IMPETT, Thomas Rawstorne Senhouse
Lieutenant. 53rd (Shropshire) Regiment of Foot.
Memorial tablet: Quebec Cathedral, Quebec, Canada. (North gallery). (M.I)

"SACRED TO THE MEMORY / OF / CAPTAIN THOMAS IMPETT / LATE OF THE 32ND REGIMENT, / WHO DIED AT QUEBEC, / ON THE 15TH FEBRUARY, 1833, / AGED 40 YEARS, 5 MONTHS. / THIS MONUMENT WAS ERECTED BY HIS / BROTHER OFFICERS AS A TOKEN / OF THEIR ESTEEM AND REGARD."

Ensign 53rd Foot 28 May 1809. Lt 26 Jul 1810. Capt 32nd Foot 12 Jun 1828.

Served in the Peninsula Aug 1811 – Apr 1814. Present at the siege of Salamanca Forts, Salamanca, Burgos, Vittoria, Pyrenees, San Marcial, Nivelle and Toulouse where he was severely wounded. Also served in Ireland 1828–1830 and Canada 1830–1833.

IMPEY, Benjamin

Captain. 86th (Royal County Down) Regiment of Foot.
Memorial: Vellore Old Cemetery, Vellore, India. (M.I.)

"BT MAJOR BENJAMIN IMPEY 86TH REGT DIED 17 MAY 1813 AGED 38 YEARS."

Lt Loyal Irish Fencibles. Ensign 31st Foot 6 May 1797. Lt 12 Nov 1799. Capt 30 Dec 1800. Capt 6th Foot 12 Aug 1803. Capt 4th Garrison Battalion 3 Nov 1808. Capt 86th Foot 26 Jul 1810. Bt Major 1 Jan 1812.
    Served in the Peninsula Aug 1808 – Jan 1809. Present at Rolica, Vimeiro and Corunna with 6th Foot. Also served in India 1812 where he died 17 May 1813.

INCE, William

Captain. 38th (1st Staffordshire) Regiment of Foot.
Family Memorial tablet: St Mary's Church, Hadley, London. (Photograph)

.... / ALSO TO THE MEMORY OF / WILLIAM INCE ESQUIRE / THEIR FOURTH SON / LATE CAPTAIN IN THE 38TH REGIMENT / WHO DIED AT BROADWATER HERTS / ON THE 19TH OF MARCH 1818 AGED 37. / HE SERVED THROUGH THE GREATER PART OF THE PENIN-SULAR WAR / FROM THE COMMENCEMENT OF THE OPERATIONS / IN PORTUGAL IN 1808, / UNTIL THE TERMINATION OF HOSTILITIES / IN THE SOUTH OF FRANCE IN 1814. / HE SERVED ALSO IN THE EXPEDITION TO WALCHEREN IN 1809.

Ensign 8th Foot. Lt 7th Garrison Battalion 6 Dec 1806. Lt 38th Foot 6 Aug 1807. Capt 22 Sep 1813.
    Served in the Peninsula with 1/38th Aug 1808 – Jan 1809 and Jun 1812 – Apr 1814. Present at Rolica, Vimeiro, Corunna, Castrejon, Salamanca (wounded), Burgos, Villa Muriel, Osma, Vittoria, San Sebastian, Bidassoa, Nivelle, Nive and Bayonne. Also served at Walcheren 1809. Half pay 1814. Died in 1818 having never recovered from Walcheren fever.
REFERENCE: *Gentleman's Magazine, May 1818, pp. 466–7.*

INGHAM, Christopher

Private. 95th Regiment of Foot.
Ledger stone: Utley Cemetery, Keighley, Yorkshire. (Photograph)

IN MEMORY OF / THE LATE / CHRISTOPHER / INGHAM, / LANDLORD OF THE RESERVOIR / TAVERN, KEIGHLEY, WHO DIED ON SEPTEMBER / 9TH 1866 IN THE 80TH YEAR OF HIS AGE. / HE WAS ONE OF THE HEROES OF THE / PENINSULAR WAR, HAVING SERVED / IN THE 95TH REGIMENT OF FOOT, FOR WHICH HE RECEIVED THE SILVER / MEDAL WITH 9 CLASPS, FOR THE / ENGAGEMENTS AT TOULOUSE, ORTHES, / PYRENEES, VITTORIA, SALAMANCA, / BADAJOZ, CUIDAD RODRIGO, FUENTES / 'D' ONOR, AND BUSACO. HE ALSO RECEIVED / THE WELLINGTON MEDAL, / DATED JUNE 18TH 1815.

Pte 25 Mar 1809.
    Served in the Peninsula Jun 1809 – Apr 1814. Present at Coa, Busaco (wounded), Sabugal, Fuentes d'Onoro, Ciudad Rodrigo, Badajoz, Salamanca, Vittoria, Pyrenees, Orthes and Toulouse. Present at Waterloo. Also served in Ireland 1819–1825 and Nova Scotia 1825–1828. Discharged 21 Sep 1828. Chelsea Out Pensioner with a pension after 22 years service of one shilling and one half penny a day. Ingham's trade was that of a weaver but in 1832 he married the widow of the owner of the Reservoir Tavern in Keighley, so until his death in 1866 he was the landlord of this inn. MGS medal for Busaco, Fuentes d'Onoro, Ciudad Rodrigo, Badajoz, Salamanca, Vittoria, Pyrenees, Orthes and Toulouse.
REFERENCE: *Rowbotham, Ian, Story of Private Christopher Ingham, Waterloo Journal, Apr 1984, pp. 19–23.*

INGILBY, William Bates

1st Lieutenant. Royal Artillery.
Pedestal monument: Kensal Green Cemetery, London. (14364/112 – 125/3). (Monument collapsed – Inscription illegible. (Photograph)

2nd Lt 1 Apr 1809. 1st Lt 9 Apr 1812. 2nd Capt 22 Jul 1830. Capt 19 Jun 1840. Bt Major 9 Nov 1846. Lt Colonel 7 May 1847. Colonel 6 Nov 1854. Major General 22 Jun 1860. Lt General 1 Jan 1868. General 1 Oct 1877.

Served in the Peninsula 1810–1813. Present at Busaco, Miranda de Corvo, Foz d'Arouce, Sabugal, Fuentes d'Onoro, Ciudad Rodrigo, siege of Salamanca Forts (wounded), Salamanca, Burgos, Canizal, and Llerena. Present at Waterloo in Sir Robert Gardiner's Troop (wounded) and with the Army of Occupation. MGS medal for Busaco, Fuentes d'Onoro, Ciudad Rodrigo and Salamanca. Also served in the West Indies 1831–1832, Cape of Good Hope 1850–1856 (commandant at Capetown at the time of the sinking of the *Birkenhead 1852*). Colonel Commandant of Artillery 24 Aug 1866. KCB. Retired 1 Oct 1877. Died in London 6 Aug 1879.

REFERENCE: Ingilby, William Bates, *Diary of Lieutenant William Bates Ingilby, RA in the Peninsular War*, *Royal Artillery Journal, Sep 1981, pp. 140–55. Waterloo Diary of Lieutenant William Bates Ingilby, RHA, Royal Artillery Institution Proceedings, Vol 20, 1893, pp. 241–62.*

INGLIS, Sir William

Lieutenant Colonel. 57th (West Middlesex) Regiment of Foot.
Memorial tablet: Canterbury Cathedral, Kent. (Photograph)

WITHIN THE CHAPTER HOUSE / OF THIS CATHEDRAL, REST THE REMAINS OF / LIEUTENANT GENERAL SIR WILLIAM INGLIS, K.C.B. / GOVERNOR OF CORK: AND COLONEL OF THE / 57TH REGIMENT. / DURING MANY YEARS OF ACTIVE SERVICE IN THIS GALLANT CORPS, / HE ROSE THROUGH ALL THE VARIOUS RANKS, TO THAT OF ITS / LIEUTENANT COLONEL, AND WAS AT LENGTH APPOINTED ITS COLONEL, / AS A JUST TRIBUTE TO THE GALLANTRY WHICH HE HAD DISPLAYED, / AT ITS HEAD, IN THE SANGUINARY BATTLE OF / ALBUHERA, / (WHERE HE WAS SEVERELY WOUNDED,) / AND TO HIS SUBSEQUENT SERVICES AS A GENERAL OFFICER, / DURING THE PENINSULAR WAR. / HE DIED AT RAMSGATE THE 29TH OF NOVEMBER 1835, / IN THE 72ND YEAR OF HIS AGE, AND THE / 57TH OF HIS SERVICE.

Floor slab: Canterbury Cathedral, Kent. (Photograph)

W. I. / 1835

Ensign 57th Foot 11 Oct 1779. Lt 3 May 1782. Capt-Lieut 11 Jul 1785. Capt 26 Aug 1788. Bt Major 6 May 1795. Major 1 Sep 1795. Bt Lt Colonel 1 Jan 1801. Lt Colonel 16 Aug 1804. Bt Colonel 25 Jul 1810. Brigadier General 21 Jan 1813. Major General 4 Jun 1813. Lt General 27 May 1825.

Served in the Peninsula Jul 1809 – Jun 1811, Jan 1812 – Apr 1814 (Commanded 2 Brigade 2nd Division Sep 1809 – Jun 1811. Commanded 1 Brigade 7th Division Jul 1813 – Apr 1814). Present at Busaco, Pombal, first siege of Badajoz, Albuera (wounded and Mentioned in Despatches and awarded pension of £300 per annum), Pyrenees (Mentioned in Despatches), San Marcial (Mentioned in Despatches), Nivelle (Mentioned in Despatches) and Orthes. Gold Cross for Albuera, Pyrenees, Nivelle and Orthes. KCB Apr 1815. When Major General Hoghton was killed at Albuera, Inglis took command of the brigade. This hard fought battle showed the worth of the 57th and other regiments. It was there that Inglis uttered the words 'Die hard 57th, die hard', as he lay wounded. On that day 23 officers and 415 other ranks were among the killed and wounded from the brigade, and not a man missing. 'It was observed', wrote Marshal Beresford, 'that our dead, particularly the 57th were lying as they fought in ranks and every wound was in front. Nothing could exceed the conduct and gallantry of Colonel Inglis at the head of his regiment'. After Albuera he was sent home to recover from his wound.

Also served in North America 1781–1791, Flanders 1793–1795 (present at Nimwegen), West Indies 1795–1802 (present at St Lucia and Grenada), and Gibraltar 1802 – Jul 1809. Colonel 57th Foot 16 Apr 1830. Lt Governor of Kinsale 1827. Governor of Cork 1829.

REFERENCE: *Dictionary of National Biography. Royal Military Calendar, Vol 3, pp. 231–4. Gentleman's Magazine, Apr 1836, pp. 433–5. United Service Journal, Feb 1836, pp. 237–40.*

INGRAM, George
Lieutenant. 28th (North Gloucestershire) Regiment of Foot.
Family Memorial tablet: St Michael's Church, Owermoigne, Dorset. (Photograph)

IN MEMORY OF / THE INGRAM FAMILY / FORMERLY OF GALTON & HAZLEBURY / GEORGE, NICHOLAS, ROBERT & JOHN, / IN SUCCESSION BESIDES OTHERS / 2 OF WHOM WERE WOUNDED AT WATERLOO / ONE AT ABUKIR BAY UNDER NELSON.

Ensign 29 Jan 1810. Lt 6 Aug 1812.
Served in the Peninsula with 2/28th Jun 1810 – Jul 1811 and 1/28th Aug 1811 – Feb 1812. Present at Busaco, first siege of Badajoz and Albuera (wounded). Present at Waterloo (severely wounded, had his leg amputated, but bled to death when his tourniquet moved in the night). Brother of Lt John Nelson Ingram 1st Foot who was also wounded at Waterloo.

INGRAM, John Nelson
Lieutenant. 1st (Royal Scots) Regiment of Foot.
Family Memorial tablet: St Michael's Church, Owermoigne, Dorset. (Photograph)

IN MEMORY OF / THE INGRAM FAMILY / FORMERLY OF GALTON & HAZLEBURY / GEORGE, NICHOLAS, ROBERT & JOHN, / IN SUCCESSION BESIDES OTHERS / 2 OF WHOM WERE WOUNDED AT WATERLOO / ONE AT ABUKIR BAY UNDER NELSON.

Ensign 15th Foot 25 Feb 1806. Lt 18 Oct 1808. Lt 1st Foot 12 Jul 1809. Capt 7 Apr 1825.
Served in the Peninsula with 3/1st Apr 1810 – Nov 1812 and Sep 1813 – Apr 1814. Present at Fuentes d'Onoro, Badajoz, Castrejon, Salamanca, Burgos, Villa Muriel, Bidassoa, Nivelle, Nive and Bayonne. Present at Quatre Bras and Waterloo where he was wounded. Half pay 2 Sep 1836. Brother of Lt George Ingram 28th Foot who died of wounds at Waterloo.

INKERSOLE, James
Private. 40th (2nd Somersetshire) Regiment of Foot.
Headstone: St Mary and St Helena Churchyard, Elstow, Bedfordshire. Seriously eroded. (Photograph)

IN MEMORY OF / JAMES INKERSOLE / OF THE 40TH / REGIMENT OF FOOT / WHO LOST HIS ARM AT WATERLOO / WHICH CAUSED HIS DEATH AUGUST 17TH 1827 / AGED 34 YEARS

Present at Waterloo in Captain J. Lowry's Company where he was wounded and his arm amputated.

INNES, Alexander
Lieutenant. 42nd (Royal Highland) Regiment of Foot.
Headstone: Old Churchyard, Spital, Windsor, Berkshire. (Photograph)

IN / LOVING MEMORY OF / ALEXANDER INNES M. K. W. / LATE 42ND ROYAL HIGHLANDERS

BLACK WATCH / AND 94TH FOOT. / WOUNDED IN THE PENINSULA AND WATERLOO. / DIED 23RD SEPTEMBER 1875 / AGED 83 YEARS. / ....

Ensign 10 Jul 1810. Lt 15 Oct 1812. Lt 94th Foot 1 Dec 1823.
    Served in the Peninsula Mar – Apr 1814. Present at Toulouse (severely wounded). MGS medal for Toulouse. Present at Waterloo where he was wounded. Also served in the Netherlands 1814–1815. Half pay 25 Nov 1828. Military Knight of Windsor Oct 1867.

INNES, Gordon C.
Lieutenant. 94th Regiment of Foot
Family Memorial: Old Parish Burial Ground, Wick, Caithness, Scotland. (M.I.)

See inscription for Major John Innes 94th Foot below.

Ensign 12 May 1808. Lt 31 Aug 1809.
    Served in the Peninsula Feb 1810 – Jul 1812. Present at Cadiz, Redinha, Casal Nova, Foz d'Arouce, Sabugal, Fuentes d'Onoro, second siege of Badajoz, El Bodon, Ciudad Rodrigo, Badajoz and Salamanca where he was killed 22 Jul 1812. Brother of Lt William Innes 94th Foot, nephew of Capt Peter Innes, 79th Foot and nephew of Major John Innes 94th Foot.

INNES, John
Major 94th Regiment of Foot.
Family Memorial: Old Parish Burial Ground, Wick, Caithness, Scotland. (M.I.)

"HIS BROTHER MAJOR JAMES INNES OF THRUMSTER, 94TH REGT .... TWO OF THEIR SONS DIED IN THE PENINSULAR CAMPAIGN AS DID THEIR UNCLE JOHN, MAJOR 94TH REGT."

Ensign 73rd Foot 3 Aug 1781. Lt 94th Foot 27 Jul 1794. Capt 10 Jul 1799. Major 27 Sep 1804.
    Served in the Peninsula Feb – Jul 1810. Present at the defence of Cadiz. Also served in India 1799, the Mahratta War (present at Seringapatam where he was wounded) and the Polygar War 1801. Died at Portsmouth on his return from Lisbon from a liver complaint 27 Aug 1810. Uncle of Lt Gordon and Lt William Innes, both of 94th Foot and brother of Capt Peter Innes, 79th Foot.

INNES, John White
Lieutenant and Adjutant. 42nd (Royal Highland) Regiment of Foot.
Family Memorial tablet: Montrose Parish Church, Montrose, Angus, Scotland. (M.I.)

".................JOHN INNES, LT AND ADJUTANT, 42ND ROYAL HIGHLANDERS, FELL AT THE BATTLE OF ORTHES, 27.2.1814. ...."

Named on the Memorial: St Andrew's Church, (now Musée Historique), Biarritz, France. (Photograph)

Ensign 13 Sep 1804. Lt 2 Jul 1806. Adjutant 8 Dec 1808.
    Served in the Peninsula Jul 1809 – May 1812 and May 1813 – Feb 1814. Present at Busaco, Fuentes d' Onoro, Ciudad Rodrigo, Pyrenees, Nivelle, Nive and Orthes where he was killed 27 Feb 1814.

INNES, Peter
Captain. 79th (Cameron Highlanders) Regiment of Foot.
Tombstone in railed enclosure: Old Parish Burial Ground, Wick, Caithness, Scotland. (M.I.)

"IN MEMORY OF PETER INNES, 79™ REGT OF FOOT, DIED TANNACH, 29 APRIL 1822 AGED 66."

Caithness Legion. Ensign 42ⁿᵈ Foot 22 Jan 1801. Lt 4 Mar 1802. Capt 79ᵗʰ Foot 4 Sep 1805.
 Served in the Peninsula May 1812 – Apr 1814. Present at Salamanca, Burgos, Pyrenees, Nivelle, Nive and Toulouse (wounded). Present at Quatre Bras and Waterloo (one of nine officers of the 79ᵗʰ Foot out of forty one not killed or wounded at Waterloo). Innes fought a duel 9 Feb 1807 with Asst Surgeon Wood and severely wounded him. Fortunately Wood recovered. Half pay 20 Nov 1816. Brother of Major John Innes 94ᵗʰ Foot and uncle of Lt Gordon and Lt William Innes, both of 94ᵗʰ Foot.

INNES, William
Lieutenant. 94ᵗʰ Regiment of Foot
Family Memorial: Old Parish Burial Ground, Wick, Caithness, Scotland. (M.I.)

See inscription for Major John Innes 94ᵗʰ Foot above.

Ensign 3 Feb 1804. Lt 13 May 1805.
 Served in the Peninsula Apr – Jul 1810. Present at the defence of Cadiz where he died 11 Jul 1810. Brother of Lt Gordon Innes, 94ᵗʰ Foot, nephew of Major John Innes, 94ᵗʰ Foot and Capt Peter Innes, 79ᵗʰ Foot.

IRBY, Hon Edward Methuen
Ensign. 3ʳᵈ Regiment of Foot Guards.
Memorial tablet: St Mary's Church, Whiston, Northamptonshire. (Photograph)

SACRED TO THE MEMORY OF / THE HONᴮᴸᴱ EDWARD METHUEN IRBY, / SIXTH SON OF / FREDERICK AND CHRISTIAN, LORD AND LADY BOSTON, / AND ENSIGN IN THE 3ᴿᴰ REGT OF FOOT GUARDS. / HE WAS BORN MARCH 21ˢᵀ 1788 / HE WAS KILLED AT THE BATTLE OF TALAVERA, JULY 28ᵀᴴ 1809, / ON THE DAY OF THE SPLENDID VICTORY GAINED BY / THE BRITISH ARMS. / AS A SON, HE WAS MOST EXEMPLARY AND DUTIFUL; / AS A BROTHER, KIND AND AFFECTIONATE; / AS A FRIEND, SINCERE AND FAITHFUL; / TO HIS GOD, AND KING, MOST TRUE; / IN HIS PERSON GRACEFUL AND ELEGANT; / IN MANNERS, COURTEOUS AND ENGAGING, / ZEALOUSLY ATTACHED TO, AND INDEFATIGABLE IN HIS PROFESSION; / BY HIS REGIMENT UNIVERSALLY BELOVED, AND AS DEEPLY LAMENTED. / HIS CONDUCT WAS SUCH / AS TO OBTAIN THE HIGH APPROBATION OF / HIS SOVEREIGN, / TO WHOM HE HAD FORMALLY BEEN / ONE OF THE PAGES OF HONOUR. / HE WAS BURIED WITH HIS BRAVE COMPANIONS / WHO FELL IN THE FIELD OF BATTLE.

Named on Memorial Panel VI for Talavera: Royal Military Chapel, Wellington Barracks, London. (M.I.) (Destroyed by a Flying Bomb 1944)

Ensign 14 May 1804. Adjutant 26 Jan 1809.
 Served in the Peninsula Mar – Jul 1809. Present at Douro and Talavera where he was killed 28 Jul 1809. Educated at Eton.

IRONSIDE, George Edward
Lieutenant. 74ᵗʰ (Highland) Regiment of Foot.
Grave: British Cemetery, Lisbon, Portugal. (Grave number A 26). (M.I.)

"SACRED TO THE MEMORY OF GEORGE EDWARD IRONSIDE, LIEUT IN HIS MAJESTY'S 74ᵀᴴ REGT WHO DEPARTED THIS LIFE 25ᵀᴴ APRIL 1817. AGED 26. BELOVED AND REGRETTED."

Ensign 29th Foot 8 Jun 1809. Lt 74th Foot 31 Jan 1811.

Served in the Peninsula with 29th Foot Nov 1809 – Apr 1811 and 74th Foot Jun 1811 – Apr 1814. Present at Busaco, El Bodon, Ciudad Rodrigo, Badajoz (wounded), Salamanca, Vittoria, Pyrenees, Nivelle, Orthes (wounded) and Vic Bigorre.

IRVING, Jacob Aemilius
Lieutenant. 13th Regiment of Light Dragoons.
Memorial: St John's Anglican Church, Stamford, Niagara, Canada. (Photograph)

IN MEMORY OF / JACOB AEMILIUS IRVING / OF IRONSHORE, JAMAICA / A MEMBER OF THE LEGISLATIVE COUNCIL IN / THE PROVINCE OF CANADA / AND FORMERLY IN THE 13TH LIGHT DRAGOONS / BORN 29 JANUARY 1797 / DIED AT DRUMMONDVILLE / 7 OCTOBER 1856

Cornet 24 Mar 1814. Lt 18 May 1815.

Present at Waterloo where he was wounded. Half pay 5 May 1818. Emigrated to Canada 1834 and settled near Lundy's Lane. Became Magistrate, reformer, Legislative Councillor and First Warden of the Simcoe District, Niagara 1843.

IRVING, James
Private. 42nd (Royal Highland) Regiment of Foot.
Headstone: Old Parish Churchyard, Annan, Dumfriesshire, Scotland. (Photograph)

.... / JAMES IRVING, SON OF JAMES IRVING OF NEWBIE / MILL, WHO DIED AT WATERLOO OF HIS WOUNDS, / WHICH HE RECEIVED ON THE 18TH JUNE, 1815, AGED 24 YEARS.

Pte 42nd Foot.

Served at Waterloo in Capt Murdoch Maclaine's Company where he was killed.

IRWIN, Frederick Chidley
Lieutenant. 83rd Regiment of Foot.
Memorial tablet: Holy Trinity Church, Eckington, Worcestershire. (Photograph)

IN MEMORY OF / REV. JAMES IRWIN. M. A. / FOR 13 YEARS VICAR OF THIS CHURCH / WHO DIED FEB 20TH 1866, AGED 78 YEARS / .... / AND OF HIS BROTHER, / COLONEL FREDERICK CHIDLEY IRWIN, K.H. / FORMERLY OF THE 83RD REGT / AND FOR MANY YEARS COMMANDANT OF THE TROOPS / IN WESTERN AUSTRALIA. / HE ENTERED THE ARMY IN 1808, AND RETIRED IN 1856; / HAVING RECEIVING THE WAR MEDAL AND NINE CLASPS. / HE DIED AT CHELTENHAM / MARCH 31ST, 1860, AGED 66 YEARS. / ....

Ensign 83rd Foot 25 Mar 1808. Lt 17 Aug 1809. Capt 63rd Foot 27 Mar 1827. Bt Major 28 Jun 1836. Bt Lt Colonel 9 Nov 1846.

Served in the Peninsula Apr 1809 – Feb 1814. Present at Douro, Talavera (wounded), Redinha, Casal Nova, Foz d'Arouce, Sabugal, Fuentes d' Onoro, first siege of Badajoz, El Bodon, Ciudad Rodrigo, Badajoz, Salamanca, Vittoria, Pyrenees, Nivelle and Nive. Also served in Ceylon (present in the Kandian campaign 1817–1818), Australia with 63rd Foot to give military protection to the colony at Swan River 1828–1832. KH. MGS medal for Talavera, Fuentes d' Onoro, Ciudad Rodrigo, Badajoz, Salamanca, Vittoria, Pyrenees, Nivelle and Nive.

Returned to Australia 1837–1852 and became Commandant of Troops in Western Australia. Not always popular with the troops, very stern, very religious and organised prayer meetings for them. Wrote *The State and Position of Western Australia, commonly called the Swan River Settlement*, 1835.

Established the Church of England in the settlement of Western Australia and General Board of Education to found schools based on Christian principles. Half pay 1842. Returned to England 1854.
REFERENCE: *Australian Dictionary of Biography*.

IRWIN, William
Lieutenant. 28th (North Gloucestershire) Regiment of Foot.
Low monument: St John's Anglican Cemetery, Parramatta, New South Wales, Australia. (Photograph)

SACRED / TO THE MEMORY OF / WILLIAM IRWIN / BORN AT MOORFIELD COUNTY / SLIGO, IRELAND / DIED AT PARRAMATTA / NEW SOUTH WALES / ON THE 12TH OF NOVEMBER 1840 / AGED 57 YEARS

Memorial tablet: St John's Anglican Church, Parramatta, New South Wales, Australia. (Photograph)

SACRED TO THE MEMORY OF / BREVET MAJOR WILLIAM IRWIN, / OF HM 28TH REGIMENT, / WHO DIED AT PARRAMATTA / THE 12TH OF NOVEMBER 1840 / AGED 56 YEARS. / THIS TABLET WAS ERECTED BY HIS BROTHER OFFICERS / AS A TOKEN OF THEIR ESTEEM AND ADMIRATION / OF HIS LONG AND GALLANT SERVICE / OF 33 YEARS IN THE CORPS.

Ensign 10 Dec 1807. Lt 20 Jul 1809. Capt 9 May 1816. Bt Major 10 Jun 1837.
Served in the Peninsula with 1/28th Aug 1808 – Jan 1809, 2/28th Sep 1809 – Jul 1811 and 1/28th Aug 1811 – Apr 1814. Present in the Corunna campaign, Talavera, Busaco, first siege of Badajoz, Albuera, Arroyo dos Molinos, Almarez, retreat from Burgos, Vittoria (severely wounded), Pyrenees, Nivelle, Nive, Garris, Orthes, Aire and Toulouse. Present at Quatre Bras (severely wounded), but still fought at Waterloo. He was known as the strongest man in the regiment. Also served in Australia 1835–1840 to escort convicts and provide guards in New South Wales. Appointed Asst Engineer and Superintendent of the convict stockade.

IRWINE, Henry Bury
Captain. 68th (Durham) Regiment of Foot.
Named on the Memorial: St Andrew's Church, (now Musée Historique), Biarritz, France. (Photograph)

Ensign 20 Mar 1804. Lt 23 Jun 1804. Capt 4 Jun 1812.
Served in the Peninsula Oct 1811 – Nov 1813. Present at the siege of Salamanca Forts, Moriscos, Salamanca, Vittoria, Pyrenees (severely wounded) and Nivelle where he was killed 10 Nov 1813. Also served at Walcheren, 1809.

IVEY, William
Deputy Purveyor. Army Ordnance Medical Department.
Grave: Nunhead Cemetery. (Grave number 275 Sq52)

Served in the Peninsula 1810–1814. Present at Salamanca. Also served at Walcheren 1809. Died in Dublin and buried there 11 Nov 1848 aged 57. Exhumed and buried at Nunhead 7 Oct 1852.

JACK, John
Private. 52nd (Oxfordshire) Light Infantry Regiment of Foot.
Headstone: Parish Church, Turriff, Aberdeenshire. Inscription not recorded

Pte Militia 1803. Pte 52nd Foot 4 Apr 1805.
Served in the Peninsula 1808-1809 and 1810-1814. Present at the retreat and battle of Corunna, Busaco, Fuentes d'Onoro, Ciudad Rodrigo (volunteered for the storming party where he was wounded), Badajoz,

Salamanca, Vittoria, Pyrenees, Nivelle, Nive, Orthes and Toulouse. Present at Waterloo. Discharged 11 Nov 1826 'a good soldier and an honest man' after serving 23 years and eight months. Awarded a pension of one shilling and one penny a day. Returned to Scotland to New Blyth and took up his trade of shoe-making. MGS medal for Corunna, Busaco, Fuentes d'Onoro, Ciudad Rodrigo, Badajoz, Salamanca, Vittoria, Pyrenees, Nivelle, Nive, Orthes and Toulouse. Died 1870 at the age of 91.

REFERENCE: *Oxfordshire and Buckinghamshire Light Infantry Chronicle, 1905, pp. 204-6. Webster, David, Standing proud against Napoleon, Your Family Tree, Jan 2008, pp. 42-4. (Genealogical research in the Jack family).*

JACKSON, Basil

Lieutenant. Royal Staff Corps.
Low monument with cross: St Paul and St Peter Churchyard, Goodrich, Herefordshire. (Photograph)

BASIL JACKSON COLONEL ROYAL STAFF CORPS BORN JUNE 25 1795 DIED OCTOBER 22 1889

Memorial tablet: St Mary's Church, Ross-on-Wye, Herefordshire. (Photograph)

IN MEMORY OF / LIEUT. COLONEL BASIL JACKSON, ROYAL STAFF CORPS, / WHO SERVED ON THE QUARTERMASTER-GENERAL'S STAFF, / AT WATERLOO. / HE LIVED 15 YEARS AT HILLSBOROUGH, ROSS, / WHERE HE DIED OCTOBER 22ND 1889, / IN THE 95TH YEAR OF HIS AGE; / AND WAS BURIED AT GOODRICH. / "FAITHFUL UNTO DEATH."

Memorial window: St Paul and St Peter Church, Goodrich, Herefordshire. (Photograph)

TO THE MEMORY OF / LIEUT COL. BASIL JACKSON, ROYAL STAFF CORPS, / WHO SERVED ON THE QUARTERMASTER – GENERAL'S STAFF AT WATERLOO, / AND WAS ONE OF THOSE IN CHARGE OF NAPOLEON AT ST HELENA. / HE LIVED FOR 16 YEARS AT GLEWSTONE COURT IN THIS PARISH, AND IS / BURIED IN THE CHURCHYARD. / HE DIED AT ROSS, OCT 22 1889, AGED 94 YEARS. / "WELL DONE THOU GOOD AND FAITHFUL SERVANT." / THIS WINDOW WAS ERECTED BY FRIENDS AND OFFICERS OF THE ARMY.

Ensign 11 Jul 1811. Lt 6 May 1813. Capt 17 Sep 1825. Major 7 Feb 1834. Lt Colonel 9 Nov 1846.

Served at Waterloo (attached to QMG Department, where he used his engineering skills, learnt at the Military College, to clear roads), with the Army of Occupation and St Helena with Napoleon until 1819. Also served in the Netherlands 1814, Nova Scotia and Canada (helped build the Rideau Canal). Professor of Military Surveying in the East India Company's Military College at Addiscombe 1836–1857. Author of *A course of military surveying* 1838 which became a standard text. Retired from the Army 1849. When he died at the age of 94 he was one of four surviving officers from Waterloo. His father Basil also served at Waterloo in the Royal Waggon Train.

REFERENCE: *Jackson, Basil, Notes and reminiscences of a staff officer, chiefly relating to the Waterloo campaign and to St Helena matters during the captivity of Napoleon, 1903. Dictionary of National Biography. Annual Register, 1889, Appx, p. 162.*

JACKSON, John Napper

Captain. 94th Regiment of Foot.
Buried in Mont l'Abbaye Cemetery, St Helier, Jersey, Channel Islands. (No longer extant: Grave number E8). (Photograph of plot)

Ensign 1 Jul 1805. Lt 1 Jan 1806. Capt 28 Feb 1812. Capt 43rd Foot 30 Mar 1820. Capt 99th Foot 25 Mar 1824. Major 11 Jun 1829. Bt Lt Colonel 23 Nov 1841. Bt Colonel 20 Jun 1854. Major General 26 Oct 1858.

Served in the Peninsula Feb 1810 – Apr 1814. Present at Cadiz, Pombal, Redinha, Casal Nova, Foz d'Arouce, Sabugal, Fuentes d'Onoro, second siege of Badajoz, El Bodon, Ciudad Rodrigo, Badajoz, Salamanca, Madrid, Vittoria, Pyrenees, Nivelle, Nive, Orthes, Vic Bigorre, Tarbes and Toulouse. Colonel 3rd West India Regt 13 Aug 1862. Colonel 99th Foot 8 Jun 1863. MGS medal for Fuentes d'Onoro, Ciudad Rodrigo, Badajoz, Salamanca, Vittoria, Pyrenees, Nivelle, Nive, Orthes and Toulouse. Died at St Helier 25 Jan 1866.

JACOB, George Thomson
Ensign. 1st Regiment of Foot Guards.
Headstone: St Mary's Churchyard, Ambleside, Cumbria. (Photograph)

TO THE / MEMORY OF / GEORGE THOMSON JACOB ESQR / OF SHILLINGSTONE IN THE / COUNTY OF DORSET. / LIEUT COLONEL OF THE DORSET / REGIMENT OF MILITIA. / HE DIED AT RAYRIGG IN THIS / PARISH ON THE 13TH OF MAY 1858. / AGED 61.

Ensign 3 Feb 1814. Cornet 4th Dragoon Guards 11 Jun 1818. Cornet 2nd Dragoons 10 May 1839.
   Present at Waterloo and with the Army of Occupation. Half pay 24 Sep 1818. Retired 11 May 1839. Lt Colonel Dorset Militia 8 Feb 1846.

JAGO, Darell
2nd Lieutenant. Royal Artillery.
Ledger stone: Ford Park Cemetery, Plymouth, Devon. (Section CC 2/3 15). (Photograph)

SACRED / TO THE / MEMORY / OF / DARELL JAGO / CAPTAIN IN THE ROYAL ARTILLERY / WHO DIED 22ND DECEMBER 1850 / AGED 55. / ....

2nd Lt 5 Jul 1813. 1st Lt 26 Oct 1815. 2nd Capt 20 Nov 1834.
   Served at Quatre Bras and Waterloo in Capt. Sandham's Brigade, and with the Army of Occupation. Also served in Portugal 1826–1828 in the expedition under Sir William Clinton. Placed on temporary half pay 1 Feb 1819, but rejoined 1 Apr 1821. Retired on half pay 6 Jan 1836.

JAMES, Francis
Captain. 81st Regiment of Foot.
Memorial tablet: St Mary's Church, Hampstead Norrey's, Berkshire. (M.I.)

"TO THE MEMORY OF FRANCIS JAMES ESQR ELDEST SON OF SIR WALTER JAMES BART AND LADY JANE JAMES OF LANGLEY HALL IN THIS PARISH, CAPTAIN IN THE 81ST REGIMENT AND ASSISTANT ADJUTANT GENERAL IN MAJOR COLVILLE'S BRIGADE OF HIS MAJESTY'S FORCES IN PORTUGAL SERVING UNDER THE COMMAND OF THE MARQUESS OF WELLINGTON. THIS PROMISING YOUNG OFFICER DIED ON THE 11TH OF APRIL 1812 OF THE WOUNDS HE RECEIVED IN THE ASSAULT AT THE BREACH OF THE WALLS OF BADAJOS. ALTHOUGH BORN TO AFFLUENCE HE CHOSE THE MILITARY PROFESSION AND ALTHOUGH NOT MORE THAN 24 YEARS OF AGE HAD SEEN SERVICE IN THE WEST INDIES IN DENMARK IN EGYPT AT THE BATTLE OF MAIDA AND IN SPAIN AND PORTUGAL. THE REMAINS OF THIS GALLANT OFFICER WERE INTERRED BY THE LEAVE OF THE GOVERNOR OF BADAJOS IN THE BASTION CLOSE TO THE BREACH WHICH HE HAD BEEN ONE OF THE FIRST TO ASCEND. HIS AFFLICTED PARENTS HAVE CAUSED THIS RECORD TO BE PLACED IN THIS CHURCH AS A LASTING MEMORIAL OF THEIR IRREPARABLE LOSS AND OF THE DISTIN-GUISHED WORTH AND GALLANTRY OF THEIR SON."

Ensign Coldstream Guards 7 Sep 1804. Capt 81st Foot 3 Mar 1808.

Served in the Peninsula May – Jul 1811 (extra ADC to Lord Wellington), Aug – Nov 1811 (DAAG 5th Division) and Dec 1811 – Apr 1812 (DAAG 4th Division). Present at Badajoz where he was severely wounded at the assault 6 Apr and died of his wounds 14 Apr 1812. Also served in the West Indies, Sicily 1806 (present at Maida), Copenhagen 1807 and Egypt 1807.

JAMES, John
Ensign. 30th (Cambridgeshire) Regiment of Foot.
Named on the Regimental Memorial: St Joseph's Church, Waterloo, Belgium. (Photograph)

Ensign 2 Sep 1813.
    Present at Waterloo where he was killed.

JAMES, John Haddy
Assistant Surgeon. 1st Life Guards.
Cross on pedestal: St Mary's Churchyard, Lympstone, Devon. (Photograph)

IN MEMORY OF / JOHN HADDY JAMES / OF EXETER. / WHO DIED MARCH 17 1869 / AGED 80 YEARS.

Asst Surgeon. 27 Oct 1812.
    Present at Waterloo and in the Army of Occupation. Kept a journal of the Waterloo campaign. Half pay 30 Jul 1816. Returned to Exeter 1816 as Surgeon to Devon and Exeter Hospital and in general practice. In favour of medical students being trained in the provinces rather than in large cities such as London and Edinburgh. One of the original 300 members of the Royal College of Surgeons 1843 and of the Provincial and Surgical Association which became the British Medical Association. Influential in local affairs in Exeter. Town Councillor 1820, Sheriff 1826, Mayor 1828.
REFERENCE: *Dictionary of National Biography. James, John Haddy, Surgeon James's Journal 1815, edited by Jane Vansittart, 1964.*

JAMES, William
Ensign. 3rd Regiment of Foot Guards.
Headstone with a Cross: St Vincent's Churchyard, Littlebourne, Kent. (Photograph)

SACRED / TO THE MEMORY OF / CAPT. WILLIAM JAMES / LATE OF THE SCOTS / FUSILIER GUARDS / WHO DEPARTED THIS LIFE / 13TH OCTOBER / AD 1854 / AGED 58 YEARS

Ensign 4 Mar 1813. Lt and Capt 8 May 1817.
    Served at Waterloo and with the Army of Occupation. Half pay 25 Feb 1819.

JAMESON, James
Captain. 4th (King's Own) Regiment of Foot.
Chest tomb: Holy Trinity Churchyard, Berwick-on-Tweed, Northumberland. (Photograph)

SACRED TO THE MEMORY OF / MAJOR JOHN JAMESON, / LATE OF THE 64TH REGIMENT / WHO DIED 26TH OF JULY 1826 / AGED 47 YEARS. / MAJOR JAMES JAMESON, / LATE OF THE 4TH KING'S OWN INFANTRY / BORN AT BERWICK THE 27TH JANUARY 1785, / DIED IN LONDON 25TH APRIL 1851 / WHERE HIS REMAINS ARE INTERRED.

Interred in Kensal Green Cemetery, London. (No longer extant: Grave number 9529/106/RS).

Ensign 16 Aug 1801. Lt 17 Dec 1803. Capt 31 Oct 1810. Bt Major 22 Jul 1830.

Served in the Peninsula with 1/4th Aug 1808 – Jan 1809 and 2/4th May 1812 – Jan 1813. Present at Corunna, Salamanca, retreat from Burgos and Villa Muriel. Also served at Walcheren 1809. Retired on half pay 25 Feb 1816. MGS medal for Corunna and Salamanca.

JANSSEN, Georg
Captain. 3rd Regiment of Hussars, King's German Legion.
Named on the Regimental Memorial: La Haye Sainte, Waterloo, Belgium. (Photograph)

Lt 23 Dec 1805. Capt 25 Oct 1810.
    Served in the Peninsula Aug 1808 – Jan 1809. Present at Benevente. Present at Waterloo where he was killed. Also served in the Baltic 1807–1808 (wounded at Kiöge), North Germany 1813–1814 and the Netherlands 1814.

JARVIS, George Ralph Payne
Major. 36th (Herefordshire) Regiment of Foot.
Memorial tablet: St Peter's Church, Doddington, Lincolnshire. (Photograph)

IN MEMORY OF / COLONEL GEORGE RALPH PAYNE JARVIS / OF DODDINGTON HALL, / BORN 1774 – DIED 1851. / ....
Ensign 8 Feb 1792. Lt 19 Dec 1793. Capt 14 Nov 1799. Major 20 Dec 1810. Bt Lt Colonel 12 Aug 1819.

Served in the Peninsula Aug 1808 – Jan 1809 (on staff as DAAG). Present at Rolica, Vimeiro and Corunna. Retired on half pay 1811. MGS medals for Rolica, Vimeiro and Corunna. Later Deputy Lieutenant for Lincolnshire and Magistrate. Died 14 Jun 1851.

JEBB, Richard
Captain. 40th (2nd Somersetshire) Regiment of Foot.
Ledger stone: St Michael the Archangel Churchyard, Lyme Regis, Dorset. (Photograph)

SACRED / TO THE MEMORY OF / RICHARD JEBB ESQ. / WHO DIED DEC 28TH 1840.

Cornet 10th Lt Dragoons 12 Sep 1805. Lt 4 Aug 1808. Capt 9 May 1811. Capt 16th Lt Dragoons 6 May 1813. Capt 40th Foot 12 May 1814. Bt Major 22 Jul 1830. Major 1 May 1835.
    Served in the Peninsula Nov 1808 – Jan 1809. Present at Sahagun, Benevente and the Corunna campaign. Also served in Australia 1823–1829.

JEINSEN, Friedrich von
Lieutenant. 3rd Line Battalion, King's German Legion.
Named on the Regimental Memorial: La Haye Sainte, Waterloo, Belgium. (Photograph)

Commissioned from the ranks. Ensign 27 Oct 1807. Lt 19 Mar 1812.
    Served in the Peninsula 1812 – 1813. Present at Waterloo where he was severely wounded and died of his wounds 28 Jun at Brussels. Also served in Hanover 1805, the Baltic 1807, Mediterranean 1808–1812 and the Netherlands 1814.

JENKIN, James
Captain. 84th (York and Lancaster) Regiment of Foot.
Ledger stone: St Andrew's Churchyard, Clifton, Bristol, Somerset. (Photograph)

.... / ALSO OF / LT COL^L JAMES JENKIN / (LATE 84TH REG^{MT}) / DIED JANUARY 24TH 1850, / AGED 71 YEARS. / ....

Ensign 19 Oct 1799. Adjt 20 Oct 1801. Lt 3 Nov 1804. Capt 11 Jun 1808. Bt Major 26 Dec 1813. Bt Lt Colonel 1 Jan 1826. Major 47th Foot 21 Jun 1831.

Served in the Peninsula Jul 1813 – Apr 1814. Present at Bidassoa, Nivelle, Nive (wounded and awarded Bt Majority) and Bayonne. Gold Medal for Nive and MGS medal for Nivelle. Also served at Walcheren 1809. Retired Aug 1831.

JENKINS, George
Chaplain to the Forces. Chaplains Department.
Family box tomb: St Cadoc's Churchyard, Llancarfan, Glamorgan, Wales. (Photograph)

.... / ALSO OF GEORGE JENKINS / SECOND SON OF THE SAID / WILLIAM AND MARY JENKINS / CHAPLAIN TO THE FORCES / WHO DIED ON THE 26TH DAY OF APRIL / 1821 AGED 46 YEARS /AND WAS BURIED AT MONTREAL / CANADA N. A.

Chaplain to the Forces 5 Apr 1810.
Served in the Peninsula Sep 1810 – Apr 1814 (attached to 4th Division). Present at Bidassoa.

JENKINS, John
Captain. 11th Regiment of Light Dragoons.
Ledger stone: St Nicholas Churchyard, Brighton, Sussex. (M.I.)

"SACRED TO THE MEMORY OF MAJOR JOHN JENKINS / WHO DIED 31ST OCTOBER 1840 / ...."

Cornet 29 Jun 1807. Lt 31 Dec 1807. Capt 22 Dec 1814. Major 13 Nov 1834.
Served in the Peninsula Jun 1811 – Jun 1813. Present at El Bodon, Badajoz (wounded), Monestero, Castrejon, Salamanca and Venta del Poza. Covered the retreat of the infantry from Quatre Bras and present at Waterloo. Also served in India for 20 years (present at the siege of Bhurtpore 1825–1826 in command of two squadrons). Achieved his Cornetcy in 1807 by raising sufficient men for the regiment. Died 31 Oct 1840 aged 52.
REFERENCE: *Gentleman's Magazine, Dec 1840, p. 674.*

JENKINS, John
Quartermaster. 4th (King's Own) Regiment of Foot.
Ledger stone: St Thomas's Churchyard, Neath, Glamorgan, Wales. Seriously eroded. (Photograph)

SACRED / TO THE MEMORY OF / ELLEN GREY JENKINS / DAUGHTER OF QUARTER MASTER / JENKINS LATE OF KING'S / (OWN) ROYAL REGIMENT / DIED 2 APRIL 1817 AGED 1 YEAR / ALSO QUARTER MASTER JOHN JENKINS / DIED 20 MAY 1829 AGED 56 YEARS / ....

Quartermaster 15 Aug 1811.
Served in the Peninsula with 1/4th Sep 1811 – Apr 1814. Present at Badajoz, Salamanca, retreat from Burgos, Villa Muriel, Bidassoa, Nivelle, Nive and Bayonne.

JENKINSON, F. Edward
Lieutenant and Captain. Coldstream Regiment of Foot Guards.
Named on Memorial Panel VI for Fuentes D'Onoro: Royal Military Chapel, Wellington Barracks, London. (M.I.) (Destroyed by a Flying Bomb 1944)

Ensign 26 May 1803. Lt and Capt 29 May 1806.

Served in the Peninsula Mar – Aug 1809. Present at Douro and Talavera where he was severely wounded 28 Jul and died of his wounds 24 Aug 1809.

JENKS, George Samuel
Assistant Surgeon. 10ᵗʰ (Prince of Wales's Own) Regiment of Light Dragoons.
Buried in Locksbrook Cemetery, Bath, Somerset. (No longer extant: Grave number EE16). (Photograph of location).

Hospital Mate General Service 14 Aug 1812. Asst Surgeon 10ᵗʰ Lt Dragoons 22 Oct 1812.
   Present at Waterloo. Retired 25 Dec 1818.

JENNINGS, Joshua
Lieutenant and Adjutant. 51ˢᵗ (2ⁿᵈ Yorkshire West Riding) Light Infantry.
Named on the Regimental Memorial: KOYLI Chapel, York Minster, Yorkshire. (Photograph)

Sgt Major Coldstream Guards. Commissioned from the ranks. Ensign and Adjt 51ˢᵗ Foot 9 May 1805. Lt 29 Apr 1807.
   Served in the Peninsula Oct 1808 – Jan 1809. Present at Corunna. Also served at Walcheren 1809 where he died from fever 11 Sep 1809.

JERVOIS, William
Captain. 57ᵗʰ (West Middlesex) Regiment of Foot.
Low monument: Walcot Cemetery, Bath, Somerset. (Photograph)

IN MEMORY OF / GENERAL JERVOIS K.H. / COLONEL OF THE 76ᵀᴴ REGᵀ / DIED NOVEMBER 5ᵀᴴ 1862 / AGED 79 YEARS.

Ensign 89ᵗʰ Foot 7 Apr 1804. Lt 8 Aug 1804. Capt 14 Jul 1808. Capt 57ᵗʰ Foot 25 Mar 1813. Bt Major 4 Jun 1814. Bt Lt Colonel 22 Sep 1814. Capt 8ᵗʰ Foot 23 Dec 1817. Bt Colonel 10 Jan 1837. Major General 9 Nov 1846. Lt General 20 Jun 1854. General 3 Aug 1860.
   Served in the Peninsula Oct 1810. Present at Malaga (wounded at the Fort of Fuengirola). Also served in Hanover 1805, North America 1813–1815 (appointed to staff of Sir Gordon Drummond in 1813, went to Canada and fought in all the actions of 1814 (present at Niagara, Black Rock, Buffalo where he was awarded a Bt Majority and Lundy's Lane where he was awarded a Bt Lt Colonelcy). Half pay 17 Sep 1823. Colonel 76ᵗʰ Foot 10 May 1853.

JESSIMAN, Alexander
Ensign. 24ᵗʰ (Warwickshire) Regiment of Foot.
Headstone: Old Kirkyard, Dunbennan, Aberdeenshire, Scotland. (Photograph)

SACRED / TO THE MEMORY OF / JOHN JESSIMAN LATE FARMER IN / WESTERTOWN OF BOTRIPHNIE / .... / AND ALEXANDER / AN OFFICER IN THE BRITISH ARMY / WHO WAS WOUNDED AT TALAVERA / IN SPAIN IN 1809 / AND DIED SOON AFTER.

Ensign Aug 1808.
   Served in the Peninsula Apr – Aug 1809. Present at Talavera 28 Jul 1809 where he was wounded and taken prisoner. He escaped but was recaptured and shot.

JESSOP, John
Major. 44ᵗʰ (East Essex) Regiment of Foot.
Memorial tablet: St Matthew's Church, Pentrich, Derbyshire. (Photograph)

SACRED / TO THE MEMORY OF / MAJOR JOHN JESSOP, C.B. / OF BUTTERLEY HALL, IN THIS COUNTY. / LATE OF H.M. 44TH REGIMENT, / IN WHICH HE SERVED DURING THE PENINSULAR WAR. / HE WAS ALSO SEVERELY WOUNDED / AT THE EVER MEMORABLE BATTLE OF WATERLOO. / HE WAS BORN SEPTEMBER 8TH 1779, / AND DIED SEPTEMBER 13TH 1869.

Ensign 44th Foot 31 Oct 1798. Lt 20 Dec 1799. Capt 15 Jun 1804. Bt Major 4 Jun 1814.

Served in the Peninsula Apr 1810 – Apr 1812 and Dec 1812 – Jun 1813 (ADC to Major General Dunlop Aug – Oct 1811). Present at Cadiz, Coa, Fuentes d'Onoro, and Barba del Puerco. Present at Waterloo where he was wounded (AQMG). Also served in Egypt 1801 (present at Aboukir and Alexandria) and the Netherlands (present at Bergen-op-Zoom on the staff of Lord Lynedoch). MGS medal for Egypt and Fuentes d'Onoro. CB. Half pay 1821.

JODDRELL, Henry Edmund
Captain and Lieutenant Colonel. 1st Regiment of Foot Guards.
Interred in Catacomb B (v150 c13) Kensal Green Cemetery, London.

Ensign 29 Dec 1803. Lt and Capt 7 Apr 1808. Capt and Lt Colonel 25 Jul 1814. Bt Major 10 Jan 1837.

Served in the Peninsula with 2nd Battalion May 1810 – May 1811 (Brigade Major) and Sep 1812 – Apr 1814. Present at Cadiz, Barrosa, Bidassoa, Nivelle, Nive, Adour and Bayonne. MGS medal for Barrosa, Nivelle and Nive. Also served in Sicily 1806–1807 and Ireland 1809 (ADC to General H. Wynyard). Died 1868.

JOHN, Thomas
Sergeant. 43rd (Monmouthshire) Light Infantry Regiment of Foot.
Headstone: St Margaret's Churchyard, Roath, Cardiff, Glamorgan, Wales. (Photograph)

TO THE MEMORY OF / THOMAS JOHN / SERGEANT 43RD REGIMENT OF FOOT. / HE FOUGHT UNDER GENERAL MOORE / AND WELLINGTON THROUGH ALL THE / LATE WAR IN THE SPANISH PENINSULA. / HE WAS ALSO ENGAGED AT WATERLOO. / DIED 1864 AGED 82. / ALSO MARY HIS WIFE / DIED 1864 AGED 99. / SHE ACCOMPANIED HER HUSBAND / THROUGH THE PENINSULAR WAR AS ABOVE.

Pte 17 Dec 1800. Cpl 1808. Sgt 1812.

Served in the Peninsula Oct 1808 – Jan 1809 and Jul 1809 – Apr 1814. Present at the retreat to Corunna, Busaco, Fuentes d'Onoro, Ciudad Rodrigo, Badajoz (twice wounded), Vittoria, Pyrenees and Toulouse. Discharged 27 Dec 1818. MGS medal for Busaco, Fuentes d'Onoro, Ciudad Rodrigo, Badajoz, Vittoria, Pyrenees and Toulouse. His wife Mary was with him throughout the Peninsular campaign.

JOHNSON, Arthur
Lieutenant. 85th (Buckinghamshire Volunteers) Light Infantry Regiment of Foot.
Family Memorial tablet: St Mary the Virgin, Little Baddow, Essex. (M.I.)

".................... / AND OF ARTHUR JOHNSON / LIEUT OF HM 85TH REGT / WHO WAS KILLED IN ACTION ON THE 10TH OF NOV 1813 / THIS TABLET IS ERECTED BY CAPTAIN / R W JOHNSON RA / THE ONLY SURVIVING SON AND BROTHER"

Named on the Memorial: St Andrew's Church, (now Musée Historique), Biarritz, France. (Photograph)

Buried in the Churchyard of Urogne near St Jean de Luz, France. (No longer extant. Churchyard has been cleared)

Ensign Warwick Militia. Ensign 24th Foot 18 Aug 1808. Ensign 81st 11 Jul 1811. Lt 85th 27 May 1813.

Served in the Peninsula with 24th Foot Apr 1809 – Mar 1811 and 85th Foot Aug 1813 – Nov 1813. Present at Talavera (severely wounded, aged 15), Busaco, San Sebastian and Nivelle where he was killed aged 19 years. Also served in Guernsey and Jersey.

JOHNSON, David England
Captain. 5th (Northumberland) Regiment of Foot.
Buried in St Saviour's Churchyard, St Helier, Jersey, Channel Islands. (Burial register)

Ensign 9 Feb 1804. Lt 29 Dec 1804. Capt 12 Mar 1812. Bt Major 22 Jul 1830. Major 29 Dec 1837. Bt Lt Colonel 9 Nov 1846.

Served in the Peninsula with 1/5th Jul 1808 – Jan 1809 and 2/5th Jul 1809 – Dec 1812. Present at Rolica, Vimeiro, Lugo, Corunna, Busaco, Redinha, Casal Nova, Foz d'Arouce, Sabugal (wounded), Fuentes d'Onoro, El Bodon, second siege of Badajoz, Ciudad Rodrigo (severely wounded), Badajoz and Salamanca. Also served at Hanover 1805 (shipwrecked on the way and taken prisoner), South America 1806–1807 (present at Buenos Ayres) and West Indies 1819–1826. MGS medal for Rolica, Vimeiro, Corunna, Busaco, Fuentes d'Onoro, Ciudad Rodrigo, Badajoz and Salamanca. Died in Jersey 23 Jun 1853.
REFERENCE: *Gentleman's Magazine, Dec 1853, p. 637. Annual Register, 1853, Appx, p. 234.*

JOHNSON, Hugh
Lieutenant. 74th (Highland) Regiment of Foot.
Named on the Regimental Memorial: St Giles's Cathedral, Edinburgh, Scotland. (Photograph)

Ensign 25 May 1809. Lt 29 Dec 1810.

Served in the Peninsula Feb 1810 – May 1811. Present at Busaco, Casal Nova, Foz D'Aronce and Fuentes d'Onoro where he was wounded and died of his wounds 8 May 1811.

JOHNSON, Samuel
Captain. Royal Waggon Train.
Gravestone: St John's Churchyard, Croydon, Surrey. (M.I.)

"CAPTAIN SAMUEL JOHNSON / LATE OF HER MAJESTY'S ROYAL WAGGON TRAIN / DIED JULY 10 1828, AGED 44."

Lt 10 Jan 1804. Capt 3 Oct 1811.

Served in the Peninsula Apr 1810 – Sep 1812 and Sep 1813 – Apr 1814.

JOHNSON, William Augustus
Lieutenant Colonel. 32nd (Cornwall) Regiment of Foot.
Memorial tablet: St Andrew's Church, Witham-on-the-Hill, Lincolnshire. (In Chancel). (Photograph)

WILLIAM AUGUSTUS JOHNSON ESQUIRE / LIEUT GENERAL IN THE ARMY A LORD / LIEUTENANT AND MAGISTRATE OF THIS / COUNTY, AND FOR 32 YEARS CHAIRMAN / OF THE KESTEVEN QUARTER SESSIONS / OF THE PEACE. HE WAS ALSO J.P. FOR THE / LIBERTY OF PETERBOROUGH. SUCCESSIVELY / M.P. FOR THE BOROUGHS OF BOSTON AND / OLDHAM, AND PATRON BY THE STATUTES / OF THE GRAMMAR SCHOOLS OF OKEHAM & / UPPINGHAM FOUNDED BY HIS ANCESTOR / ARCHDN ROBERT JOHNSON IN THE TIME / OF QUEEN ELIZABETH. / HE WAS THE ELDEST SURVIVING SON OF / THE REV. ROBERT A. JOHNSON, RECTOR / OF WISTANSTOW, COUNTY SALOP, AND OF / ANNE REBECCA HIS WIFE, SISTER OF WILLIAM / 6TH BARON CRAVEN. HE MARRIED LUCY / DAUGHTER OF THE REVD. KINGSMAN FOSTER / J.P. RECTOR OF DOWSBY, IN THIS COUNTY. / BORN 15TH

OCTOBER 1777. / DIED 26TH OCTOBER 1863 AGED 86. / ………………..

Buried in St Andrew's Churchyard, Witham-on-the-Hill, Lincolnshire. (Photograph of burial plot and ringed cross containing only the inscription to his wife Lucy)

Ensign 2nd Foot 18 Sep 1793. Lt 2 Jan 1794. Capt 23 Apr 1794. Capt 32nd Foot 7 Jan 1795. Major 2 Apr 1803. Lt Colonel 17 May 1810. Bt Colonel 12 Aug 1819. Major General 22 Jul 1830. Lt General 23 Nov 1841.
    Served in the Peninsula Aug 1808 – Jan 1809 and Jul – Aug 1811. Present at Rolica, Vimeiro and Corunna. Also served at Walcheren 1809. Retired on half pay 18 Aug 1814. At the age of 16 in 1794 he obtained his Captaincy in 2nd Foot by raising sufficient men for the regiment. MGS medal for Rolica, Vimeiro and Corunna. Later served as a County Magistrate and MP for Boston 1821–1826 and Oldham 1837–1847.
REFERENCE: *Gentleman's Magazine, Oct 1858, p. 424.*

JOHNSON, William Yates
Captain. 84th (York and Lancaster) Regiment of Foot.
Named on the Memorial: St Andrew's Church, (now Musée Historique), Biarritz, France. (Photograph)

Lt 60th Foot 24 Oct 1800. Capt 9th Garrison Battalion 28 Nov 1806. Capt 84th Foot 20 Aug 1808.
    Served in the Peninsula Jul – Dec 1813. Present at Bidassoa and Nive where he was killed 11 Dec 1813. Also served at Walcheren 1809.

JOHNSTON, Archibald
Sergeant Major. 2nd (Queen's Royal) Regiment of Foot.
Memorial tablet: St Michael's Cathedral, Bridgetown, Barbados, West Indies. (West door). (Photograph)

SACRED / TO THE MEMORY OF / SERJEANT MAJOR / ARCHIBALD JOHNSTON / OF THE / SECOND OR QUEEN'S / ROYAL REGIMENT OF FOOT / WHO / AFTER HAVING FAITHFULLY & HONOURABLY / SERVED HIS KING AND COUNTRY FOR THE / SPACE OF 18 YEARS; WITH HIS REGIMENT / IN THE CAMPAIGNS, IN PORTUGAL, SPAIN, / AND FRANCE, UNDER HIS GRACE THE / DUKE OF WELLINGTON, / DISCHARGING HIS DUTIES WITH / ADVANTAGE TO THE SERVICE AND / CREDIT TO HIMSELF, DIED AFTER / A SHORT ILLNESS AT ST ANN'S / BARRACKS BARBADOES ON THE / 14TH SEPTEMBER 1816 / AGED 36 YEARS. / THIS STONE IS ERECTED AS A TRIBUTE / OF RESPECT TO HIS MEMORY, BY THE / NON-COMMISSIONED OFFICERS AND / PRIVATES OF THE REGIMENT.

Served in the Peninsula Aug 1808 – Jan 1809 and Mar 1811 – Apr 1814. Present at Vimeiro, Corunna, siege of Salamanca Forts, Salamanca, Burgos and retreat from Burgos, Vittoria, Pyrenees, Nivelle, Orthes, Bordeaux and Toulouse. Also served in the West Indies where he died in the yellow fever epidemic 1816.

JOHNSTON, Archibald
Sergeant. 2nd (Royal North British) Regiment of Dragoons.
Memorial monument: St Mary's Churchyard, Dumfries, Dumfriesshire, Scotland. (Photograph)

IN MEMORY OF / ARCHIBALD JOHNSTON / LATE SERGEANT MAJOR OF HER / MAJESTY'S ROYAL REGIMENT / OF SCOTS GREYS WHO SERVED IN / THE ABOVE CORPS FOR A PERIOD OF / 24 YEARS AND WAS PRESENT WITH / THIS REGIMENT AT THE EVER / MEMORABLE BATTLE OF WATERLOO / WHO DEPARTED THIS LIFE / ON THE 11TH OF NOVEMBER 1847 / AGED 66 YEARS. / ………………..

Pte 3 Apr 1800. Cpl 11 May 1808. Sgt 1817. Sgt Major 1819.

Served at Waterloo in Captain Poole's troop where he was wounded. Served from 3 Apr 1800 – 10 Jun 1824 for a total of 24 years and 66 days with 2 years service added for Waterloo. Discharged aged 42 with a pension of 1 shilling and eleven pence per day. Retired to Dumfries where he was landlord of the Black Horse and later the Ewe and Lamb Inn.

REFERENCE: *Carlisle Journal, 27 Nov 1847, p. 2.*

JOHNSTON, George

Surgeon. 88th (Connaught Rangers) Regiment of Foot.
Chest tomb: British Cemetery, Corfu, Greece. (Photograph)

SACRED TO THE MEMORY OF / GEORGE JOHNSTON ESQ. / LATE / SURGEON OF THE 88TH REGIMENT OF CONNAUGHT RANGERS / WHO DEPARTED THIS LIFE ON THE 8TH SEPTEMBER 1833 / AGED 53 YEARS / ERECTED BY THE ********** OFFICERS **********

Hospital Mate 25 Feb 1804. Asst Surgeon 51st Foot 2 Oct 1804. Surgeon 88th Foot 22 Aug 1811.

Served in the Peninsula Oct 1808 – Jan 1809 and Feb – Sep 1811. Present at Corunna.

JOHNSTON, Henry

Private. 3rd Regiment of Foot Guards.
Headstone: All Saints Churchyard, Fordham, Essex. (Photograph)

UNDERNEATH / REST THE REMAINS OF HENRY JOHNSTON / SERVED IN THE 2ND BATTALION OF THE 3RD / REGIMENT OF THE GUARDS AND FOUGHT AT THE GREAT / BATTLE OF WATERLOO ON THE 18TH JUNE 1815 / AFTER WHICH HE LIVED IN THIS HIS NATIVE VILLAGE / TO ENJOY THE BLESSINGS OF PEACE IN 41 YEARS / AND DIED MARCH 9th 1856 / AGED 64 YEARS

Served at Waterloo in Lt Colonel C. Dashwood's Company.

JOHNSTON, James

Captain. 40th (2nd Somersetshire) Regiment of Foot.
Mural Memorial tablet: Old Parish Churchyard, Portobello, Edinburgh, Scotland. (Photograph)

SACRED / TO THE MEMORY OF / LIEUT. COLONEL JAMES JOHNSTON / LATE 99TH REGIMENT, / DIED 12TH NOVEMBER 1861 / AGED 75 YEARS. / PROCEEDED WITH THE 40TH REGT / TO SOUTH AMERICA IN 1806 AND WAS / SEVERELY WOUNDED AT THE ASSAULT OF / MONTE VIDEO. / SERVED IN THE PENINSULA FROM / 1808 TO 1814 WHERE HE WAS AGAIN / SEVERELY WOUNDED AT ALBUERA / OBTAINED THE WAR MEDAL / AND CLASPS FOR ROLEICA / ALBUERA, BADAJOS, / VIMIERA, TALAVARA, / SALAMANCA, VITTORIA, / PYRE- NEES, & NIVELLE. / ALSO THE PORTUGUESE COMMAND MEDAL FOR / VITTORIA, PYRENEES, & NIVELLE, / THE CROSS FOR / THREE CAMPAIGNS, AND THE CROSS OF / THE TOWER AND SWORD.

Ensign Aug 1805. Lt 21 Aug 1806. Capt 24 Feb 1814. Bt Major 4 Sep 1817. Lt Colonel 99th Foot 11 Jun 1829. Portuguese Army: Capt 5th Line 7 May 1810. Major 1 Jul 1813.

Served in the Peninsula with 40th Foot Aug 1808 – Apr 1810 and Portuguese Army May 1810 – Dec 1813 (ADC to Major General Sir Manley Power from Dec 1811). Present at Rolica, Vimeiro, Talavera, Campo Mayor, Olivencia, Albuera (wounded), Badajoz, Salamanca, Vittoria, (awarded Majority in Portuguese Army for his conduct at Vittoria), Pyrenees and Nivelle. Also served in South America 1807 (present at Montevideo where he was severely wounded).

When he joined the Portuguese Army as Captain of the 5th Line of Infantry, he found they were totally disorganised, but by Dec 1810 had re-organised them to be able to take the field a few months later. Portuguese Command medal for Vittoria, Pyrenees, and Nivelle. KTS. MGS medal for Rolica, Vimeiro, Talavera, Albuera, Badajoz, Salamanca, Vittoria, Pyrenees and Nivelle.
REFERENCE: *Royal Military Calendar, Vol 5, pp. 345–6. Gentleman's Magazine, Dec 1861, p. 697. Annual Register, 1861, Appx, p. 459.*

JOHNSTON, William
Lieutenant Colonel. 68th (Durham) Regiment of Foot.
Grave: St James's Churchyard, Shirley, Southampton, Hampshire. (M.I.)

"SIR WILLIAM JOHNSTON, LIEUT GENERAL KCB, COLONEL 68TH REGIMENT OF LIGHT INFANTRY, 23 JANUARY 1844, AGED 71."

Ensign 18th Foot 3 Jun 1791. Lt 7 Jan 1794. Capt Smith's Corsican Regt 4 Apr 1795. Major 68th Foot 27 Feb 1800. Lt Colonel 13 Jul 1809. Bt Colonel 4 Jun 1814. Major General 27 May 1825. Lt General 28 Jun 1838.
 Served in the Peninsula Jun 1811 – Apr 1814. Present at siege of Salamanca Forts, Moriscos, Salamanca, Burgos, Vittoria (severely wounded and awarded pension of £300 per annum), Adour and Orthes. Gold Medal for Salamanca, Vittoria and Orthes. KCB 1837. Also served at Toulon 1793, Corsica 1794 (present at Bastia and Calvi where he was wounded), Irish Rebellion 1798, West Indies 1801 and Walcheren 1809 (present at the siege of Flushing). Colonel 68th Foot 6 Apr 1838.
REFERENCE: *Dictionary of National Biography. Gentleman's Magazine, Mar 1844, pp. 319–20. Annual Register, 1844, Appx, pp. 199–200. United Service Magazine, Feb 1844, p. 320.*

JOHNSTONE, James
Captain. 7th (Royal Fusiliers) Regiment of Foot.
Memorial: St Mary the Virgin Churchyard, Torquay, Devon. No longer extant: Plot 4 Grave number 32). (M.I.)

"SACRED TO THE MEMORY OF / JAMES JOHNSTONE / CAPTAIN 7TH ROYAL FUSILIERS / DEPARTED THIS LIFE / DECEMBER 17TH 1852 / AGED 61 YEARS."

Ensign 50th Foot 29 Dec 1808. Lt 30 Aug 1810. Capt 60th Foot 10 Jun 1813. Capt 7th Foot 16 Dec 1813.
 Served in the Peninsula Oct 1811 – Aug 1812, Jul 1813 – Dec 1813 (on Staff as ADC to General Walker) and 7th Foot Jan – Apr 1814 (ADC to General Walker). Present at Ciudad Rodrigo, Badajoz (wounded), Nivelle and Orthes. Also served at Walcheren 1809. MGS medal for Ciudad Rodrigo, Badajoz, Nivelle and Orthes. Half pay 25 Feb 1816.

JOHNSTONE, John
Captain. 3rd (King's Own) Regiment of Dragoons.
Memorial tablet: All Saints Church, Culmington, Shropshire. (Photograph)

SACRED TO THE MEMORY OF / CAPTN. JOHN JOHNSTONE, / OF MAINSTONE COURT HERE-FORDSHIRE; / THIRD SON OF CHARLES JOHNSTONE ESQRE. OF LUDLOW; / & GRANDSON OF COL. JOHN JOHNSTONE OF NETHERWOOD, / AND CHARLOTTE, MARCHIONESS OF ANNANDALE. / BORN 1783: DIED 1870. / HE SERVED IN THE PENINSULAR WAR AS A CAPTAIN IN THE / 3RD LIGHT DRAGOONS, AND WAS ADC TO THE DUKE OF WELLINGTON. / ....

Low monument: All Saints Churchyard, Culmington, Shropshire. (Photograph)

IN LOVING MEMORY OF / CAPT^N. JOHN JOHNSTONE, / OF MAINSTONE COURT, HERE-FORDSHIRE / BORN 1783 DIED 1870 / ....

Cornet North East Hants Cavalry 4 Dec 1804. Lt 5th Dragoon Guards. Capt 21 Aug 1806. Capt 21st Lt Dragoons 9 Mar 1809. Capt 3rd Dragoons 25 Oct 1810.
   Served in the Peninsula Aug 1811 – Mar 1813. Present at Salamanca (on Staff, Secretary to Board of Claims Salamanca May – Aug 1812). Resigned from army 20 Oct 1813. MGS medal for Salamanca. Educated at Charterhouse.

JOHNSTONE, Thomas
Major. 27th (Inniskilling) Regiment of Foot.
Named on the Memorial: St Andrew's Church, (now Musée Historique), Biarritz, France. (Photograph)

Ensign 64th Foot 14 Feb 1804. Lt 70th Foot 25 Sep 1804. Capt Bradshaw's Levy. Major 27th Foot 21 Jan 1813.
   Served in the Peninsula with 3/27th Aug – Nov 1813. Present at Nivelle where he was killed 10 Nov 1813. Also served in West Indies 1807–1812 (present at the capture of Guadaloupe 1810).

JOHNSTONE, William
Ensign. 57th (West Middlesex) Regiment of Foot.
Named on the Memorial: St Andrew's Church, (now Musée Historique), Biarritz, France. (Photograph)

Sgt Major 7th Foot. Commissioned from the ranks. Ensign 57th Foot 18 Jul 1811.
   Served in the Peninsula as Sergeant Major in the 7th (Royal Fusilier) Regiment. He fought so bravely at Albuera that he was promoted from the ranks and became Ensign in the 57th Foot. Present at Albuera, Pyrenees, Nivelle and the Nive where he was killed Dec 1813.

JOHNSTONE, William Frederick
Lieutenant and Captain. 1st Regiment of Foot Guards.
Monumental Cross: Kensal Green Cemetery, London. Inscription illegible. (2606/66/3). (Photograph)

Ensign 12 Dec 1811. Lt and Capt 16 Mar 1814. Capt and Lt Colonel 10 Jan 1837.
   Served in the Peninsula with 1st Battalion Apr 1813 – Apr 1814. Present at Bidassoa, Nivelle, Nive, Adour and Bayonne. MGS medal for Nivelle and Nive. Present at Waterloo. Retired 30 Oct 1840. Died 1877.

JOLLIFFE, Charles
Captain. 23rd (Royal Welch Fusiliers) Regiment of Foot.
Memorial tablet: St Peter and St Paul, Kilmersdon, Somerset. (Photograph)

THIS TABLET IS INSCRIBED / TO THE MEMORY / OF / CHARLES JOLLIFFE, CAPTAIN IN H. M. 23^D REG^T OF INFANTRY / ROYAL WELCH FUZILIERS. / WHO WAS SLAIN IN THE TREMEN-DOUS & DECISIVE BATTLE / OF WATERLOO. / AFTER BEING CONSTANTLY ENGAGED IN ACTIVE SERVICE / AT THE SIEGE OF COPENHAGEN / THE REDUCTION OF MARTINIQUE / IN NORTH AMERICA & DURING SEVERAL CAMPAIGNS IN THE / PENINSULA OF EUROPE / HE RECEIVED A SEVERE WOUND IN THE BRILLIANT ACTION OF ORTHES / FROM WHICH HE WAS SCARCELY RECOVERED / WHEN HE ACCOMPANIED HIS BATTALION TO BELGIUM; / WHERE, / BEING STRUCK BY A SHELL ON THE 18TH JUNE 1815, / HE MET A GLORIOUS DEATH! / DYING LAMENTED AS HE LIVED BELOVED, / ALTHOUGH THUS CUT OFF IN THE BLOOM OF MANHOOD, / FROM THE FAIREST PROSPECT OF ATTAINING / TO THE SUMMIT OF HIS PROFESSION, / HIS WELL EARNED FAME AND THAT OF HIS GALLANT COMRADES / WILL BE

RECORDED IN THE BRIGHTEST PAGE OF HISTORY / HIS REMAINS WERE INTERRED ON THE FIELD OF BATTLE. / HOW SLEEP THE BRAVE WHO SINK TO REST / BY ALL THEIR COUNTRY'S WISHES BLEST.

2nd Lt 11 Sep 1805. Lt 5 Jun 1806. Capt 18 Jun 1811.

Served in the Peninsula with 1/23rd Dec 1810 – Oct 1811 and Aug 1813 – Apr 1814. Present at Redinha, Olivencia, first siege of Badajoz, Albuera, Aldea da Ponte, Pyrenees, Nivelle, Nive, Orthes (severely wounded) and Toulouse. Present at Waterloo where he was killed. Also served at Copenhagen 1807 and Martinique 1809.

JONES, Arthur
Ensign. 83rd Regiment of Foot.
Named on the Memorial: St Andrew's Church, (now Musée Historique), Biarritz, France. (Photograph)

Ensign 5 May 1813.

Served in the Peninsula Sep – Dec 1813. Present at the Nive where he was killed Dec 1813.

JONES, Arthur R.
Major. 71st (Highland Light Infantry) Regiment of Foot.
Headstone: St Paul's Anglican Churchyard, Fort Erie, Ontario, Canada. (Photograph)

SACRED / TO THE MEMORY OF / LIEUT.-COLONEL / ARTHUR R. JONES C.B. / OF THE 71ST REGIMENT / WHO DIED NOVEMBER 15, 1836 / AGED 57 YEARS / ....

Ensign 36th Foot 1 Jan 1795. Lt 71st Foot 5 Oct 1795. Capt 24 Mar 1803. Major 22 Jun 1809. Bt Lt Colonel 4 Jun 1814. Lt Colonel 2 Jun 1825.

Served in the Peninsula Aug 1808 – Jan 1809 and Mar – Apr 1814. Present at Rolica, Vimeiro (wounded), Corunna, Tarbes and Toulouse. Present at Waterloo where he was severely wounded. CB. Served with the Army of Occupation until 1818. Also served in India 1795–1797, Cape of Good Hope 1806, South America 1807 (present at Buenos Ayres), Walcheren 1809 (present at the siege of Flushing) and Ireland 1822–1824. Took command of the regiment May 1824 and went to North America where he was in command until Jun 1831.
REFERENCE: *Royal Military Calendar, Vol 5, p. 63. United Service Journal, Feb 1837, pp. 285–6.*

JONES, Edward
Lieutenant. 77th (East Middlesex) Regiment of Foot.
Box tomb: St Bride's Churchyard, Llansantffraed-Cwmdeuddwr, Rhayader, Radnorshire, Wales. (Photograph)

UNDERNEATH LIES THE BODY OF / MAJOR EDWARD JONES OF THE 77TH FOOT, A NATIVE / OF THIS PARISH: WHO DIED MARCH 28TH 1857 A. 78. / ENSIGN 1807: LIEUTENANT 1810: CAPTAIN 1822: MAJOR 1826: / UNATTACHED 1832. / HIS PROMOTION WAS THE REWARD OF VALOUR AND GOOD CONDUCT. / MADEIRA IN 1807, WALCHEREN IN 1809, PENINSULAR AND FRANCE FROM / 1811 TO THE END OF THE WAR. / DISTINGUISHED FOR PERSONAL PROWESS AND USE OF THE SWORD HE WAS / ONE OF THE CHOSEN 500 WHO, AT BADAJOZ, TOOK FORT PICARINA. WHEN / WITH LADDERS 4 FEET SHORT THE ENTIRE DIVISION (PICTON'S) AMID GREAT / SLAUGHTER GAINED POSSESSION OF THE CASTLE. / NO AGE, NO NATION EVER SENT FORTH BRAVER TROOPS TO BATTLE THAN / THOSE WHO STORMED BADAJOZ. NAPIER.

Ensign 26 Aug 1807. Adjutant 2 Feb 1809. Lt 15 Oct 1810. Capt 7 Feb 1822. Major 10 Jun 1826.

Served in the Peninsula Jul 1811 – Apr 1813 and Oct 1813 – Apr 1814. Present at El Bodon, Ciudad Rodrigo (severely wounded), Badajoz (wounded) and Bayonne. Also served in Madeira 1807 and Walcheren 1809. Retired on half pay 28 Dec 1832.

JONES, Griffith
Surgeon. 44th (East Essex) Regiment of Foot.
Ledger stone: Walcot Cemetery, Bath, Somerset. (Photograph)

TO THE MEMORY OF / GRIFFITH JONES MD / LATE DEPUTY INSPECTOR / OF ARMY HOSPI-TALS / WHO DEPARTED THIS LIFE / ON THE 8TH OF MARCH 1850 / AGED 63 YEARS

Regimental Mate in Fencible Regiment Oct 1800 – Jul 1802. Asst Surgeon 44th Foot 20 Aug 1803. Surgeon Sicilian Regt 28 Mar 1811. Surgeon 44th Foot 5 Nov 1812. Surgeon 58th Foot 10 Jun 1824. Staff Surgeon 19 Nov 1830. Asst Inspector of Hospitals 9 Dec 1836.
    Served in the Peninsula Aug 1813 – Apr 1814. Present at Tarragona. Also served in North America 1814–1815 (present at Bladensburg). Retired on half pay 21 Jul 1839.

JONES, Harry David
2nd Captain. Royal Engineers.
Headstone with Cross: Royal Military College, Sandhurst, Surrey. (Photograph)

RESTS BENEATH / AFTER 58 YEARS OF ACTIVE SERVICE / LT GEN SIR HARRY JONES, G.C.B. R.E. / HE WAS APPOINTED GOVERNOR OF THIS COLLEGE / MAY 1856, AND DIED AUGUST 2 1866 / .... / SEVASTOPOL / BOMARSUND / NIVE / NIVELLE / SEBASTIAN / VITTORIA / BADAJOS / TARRAGONA / CADIZ / WALCHEREN

Memorial tablet: Beverley Minster, Beverley, Yorkshire. (Photograph)

WALCHEREN. PENINSULA. CADIZ. BOMARSUND. BIDASSOA, BAYONNE. ST SEBASTIAN. BADAJOS. TARRAGONA. VITTORIA. NIVELLE. NIVE. CRIMEA. SEBASTOPOL. / SACRED TO THE MEMORY OF / LIEUT GENERAL SIR HARRY DAVID JONES G.C.B. / THIS BRAVE OFFICER, WHO ENTERED THE CORPS OF ROYAL ENGINEERS IN 1808 / SERVED WITH GREAT DISTINC-TION DURING THE WAR WITH FRANCE, UNDER THE DUKE / OF WELLINGTON, IN THE YEARS 1809–10–11–12–13 AND 14, AND TOOK PART IN THE / FOLLOWING SIEGES AND BATTLES:- THE SIEGE AND CAPTURE OF FLUSHING, IN THE / ISLE OF WALCHEREN; THE DEFENCE OF CADIZ AND ISLAND OF MATAGORDA; THE RELIEF / OF TARRAGONA; THE SIEGE OF BADAJOS; THE BATTLE OF VITTORIA, WHERE HE WAS / RECOMMENDED FOR HIS DISTINGUISHED CONDUCT BY GENERAL OSWALD, COMMANDING / THE 5TH DIVISION; THE SIEGE OF S. SEBASTIAN, WHERE, AS RECORDED IN THE ADJOINING / TABLET, HE LED A STORMING PARTY, AND WAS LEFT WOUNDED WITHIN THE BREACH, WHERE / ALL HIS PARTY WERE KILLED; THE BATTLE OF NIVELLE AND IN THE OPERATIONS BEFORE / BAYONNE WITH THE 5TH DIVISION: THE PASSAGE OF THE BIDASOA AND NIVE, UNDER SIR / THOMAS GRAHAM, WHEN HE WAS AGAIN RECOMMENDED FOR PROMOTION BY GENERAL HAY / COMMANDING THE DIVISION, FOR DISTINGUISHED CONDUCT, AND RECEIVED THE THANKS / OF THE MASTER-GENERAL OF THE ORDNANCE, WHICH WAS PUBLICLY CONVEYED / TO HIM BY A CIRCULAR TO HIS CORPS. HE ALSO SERVED AT NEW ORLEANS DURING / THE AMERICAN WAR; THE CAPTURE OF PARIS BY THE ALLIED ARMIES IN 1815: / AND SERVED AS A COMMISSIONER WITH THE PRUSSIAN ARMY OF OCCUPATION / UNDER GENERAL ZIETEN, UNTIL 1818. / DURING THE PEACE HE OCCUPIED MANY CIVIL AND MILITARY POSITIONS OF / IMPORTANCE AT HOME AND ABROAD, AMONG WHICH WAS THAT CONNECTED WITH / THE RELIEF OF THE POOR IN IRELAND IN 1846. / DURING

THE RUSSIAN WAR HE COMMANDED IN 1854, AS A BRIGADIER GENERAL, / THE BRITISH TROOPS AT THE SIEGE AND CAPTURE OF THE FORTRESS OF BOMARSUND / IN THE BALTIC, AND IN 1855 WAS APPOINTED TO THE COMMAND OF THE ROYAL ENGINEERS / AT THE SIEGE OF SEBASTOPOL; DURING WHICH HE WAS CREATED A KNIGHT COMMANDER / OF THE BATH. IN THIS POSITION HE SERVED WITH GREAT DISTINCTION TO THE END OF / THAT LONG AND EVENTFUL SIEGE. HE WAS SEVERELY WOUNDED AT THE ASSAULT / OF THE GREAT REDAN, BUT WAS ABLE TO CONTINUE HIS DUTIES, AND AT THE LAST, / WHEN MUCH EXHAUSTED BY HIS WOUND AND THE EFFECTS OF EXPOSURE HE WAS / CARRIED TO HIS POST AT THE FINAL ASSAULT OF THE FORTRESS ON THE 8TH SEPTEMBER 1855. / IN 1856 HE WAS APPOINTED GOVERNOR OF THE ROYAL MILITARY STAFF COLLEGE / AT SAND-HURST, WHERE HE DIED ON 2ND AUGUST 1866, IN THE 74TH YEAR OF HIS AGE. / HIS NOBLE SENSE OF DUTY AND DEVOTION TO HIS COUNTRY, HIS CALM COURAGE / AND GENEROSITY OF CHARACTER, ENDEARED HIM TO ALL

Memorial tablet: Beverley Minster, Beverley, Yorkshire. (Extract from the memorial tablet to Lancelot Machell and Engineers at assault on San Sebastian). (Photograph)

.... / "THE THREE OFFICERS OF THE ENGINEERS EMPLOYED / TO CONDUCT THE DIFFERENT PARTS OF THE COLUMNS / OF ATTACK, BEHAVED ADMIRABLY, BUT SUFFER'D SEVERELY / CAPTN. LEWIS LOST HIS LEG. LIEUT. JONES WAS WOUNDED / AND TAKEN, AND LIEUT MACHELL ON HIS RETURN WAS / KILLED IN THE TRENCHES." / LIEUT. GENL. SR T. GRAHAM'S / REPORT 26TH JULY.

Named on the Regimental Memorial: Rochester Cathedral, Rochester, Kent. (Photograph)

Brass Memorial tablet: Royal Garrison Church, Portsmouth, Hampshire. (Back of a choir stall).

GENERAL SIR HARRY / D. JONES G.C.B. DIED / AUG 2 1866 AGE 75 / DD: FRIENDS.

2nd Lt 17 Sep 1808. 1st Lt 24 Jun 1809. 2nd Capt 12 Nov 1813. Capt 29 Jul 1825. Bt Major 10 Jan 1837. Lt Colonel 7 Sep 1840. Bt Colonel 11 Nov 1851. Colonel 7 Jul 1853. Brigadier General 10 Jul 1854. Major General 12 Dec 1854. Lt General 6 Jul 1860.
Served in the Peninsula May 1810 – Apr 1814. Present at Cadiz, Tarragona, Badajoz, Vittoria, San Sebastian (Mentioned in Despatches at the first assault, wounded and taken prisoner but was returned to the Engineers), Bidassoa, Nivelle, Nive (Mentioned in Despatches) and Bayonne. MGS medal for Badajoz, Vittoria, San Sebastian, Nivelle and Nive. On return from America landed at Ostend on 18 Jun 1815. Present at the Capture of Paris and with the Army of Occupation. Commissioner to the Prussian Army 1816. Also served at Walcheren 1809 and North America 1814 (present at New Orleans and Fort Bowyer), Baltic 1854 (Brigadier General commanded the siege of Bomarsund), Crimea 1855 (appointed to command the Royal Engineers Feb 1855 where he remained until the fall of Sebastopol (wounded on 18 Jun). Succeeded Sir George Scovell as Governor of the Royal Military College Sandhurst 1856. Colonel Commandant of the Royal Engineers 2 Aug 1860. GCB 1861. Died at Sandhurst 2 Aug 1866. Brother of Capt John Thomas Jones Royal Engineers.
REFERENCE: *Dictionary of National Biography. Gentleman's Magazine, Sept 1866, p. 420. Annual Register, 1866, Appx, pp. 215–6. United Service Journal, Sep 1866, pp. 131–2.*

JONES, John Thomas
Captain. Royal Engineers.
Memorial tablet: Church of St Philip and St James, Leckhampton, Gloucestershire. (Photograph)

SACRED / TO THE MEMORY OF / MAJOR GENERAL / SIR JOHN THOMAS JONES, / BARONET

K.C.B. / OF CRANMER HALL, NORFOLK. / HE SERVED WITH DISTINCTION / IN THE CORPS OF ROYAL ENGINEERS / THROUGHOUT THE CAMPAIGNS OF / CALABRIA, WALCHEREN, AND THE PENINSULAR, / THE LINES OF TORRES VEDRAS. / THE BELGIAN FORTRESSES CONSTRUCTED AFTER 1815 / ARE LASTING MEMORIALS OF / HIS GENIUS AND SCIENCE. / HE DIED AT CHELTENHAM / ON THE 26TH OF FEBRUARY A.D. 1843 / AGED 80 YEARS / A STATUE HAS BEEN ERECTED TO HIS MEMORY / IN ST PAUL'S CATHEDRAL / BY THE OFFI-CERS OF THE CORPS / OF ROYAL ENGINEERS.

Statue: St Paul's Cathedral, London. (South transept). (Photograph)

STATUE / OF THE LATE / MAJOR GENERAL / JOHN THOMAS JONES BART., K. C. B. / ERECTED / BY HIS SURVIVING BROTHER OFFICERS OF THE ROYAL ENGINEERS / IN TESTIMONY / OF THEIR SENSE OF HIS HIGH PROFESSIONAL ATTAINMENTS / AND OF HIS IMPORTANT MILI-TARY SERVICES / HIS HONORABLE CAREER / EXTENDED FROM / A.D. 1797 TO A.D. 1843.

Named on the Regimental Memorial: Rochester Cathedral, Rochester, Kent. (Photograph)

2nd Lt Aug 30 Aug 1798. 1st Lt Sep 14 Sep 1800. 2nd Capt 1 Mar 1805. Capt 24 Jun 1809. Bt Major 6 Feb 1812. Bt Lt Colonel 27 Apr 1812. Lt Colonel 11 Nov 1816. Bt Colonel 27 May 1825. Major General 10 Jan 1837.

Served in the Peninsula 1808 – Jan 1809 and Apr 1810 – Mar 1813. Present in the Corunna campaign, Torres Vedras, first and second sieges of Badajoz, Ciudad Rodrigo (Mentioned in Despatches and awarded Bt Majority), Badajoz (awarded Bt Lt Colonelcy) and Burgos (severely wounded, had to return to England and was unable to use his leg for 18 months). Gold Medal for Badajoz. CB. Also served in Gibraltar 1798 (Adjutant – devoted his spare time studying the military books in the excellent library in the garrison and learning Spanish), Malta 1805 (was able to study the fortifications of the island), Calabria 1806, Maida 1807 and Walcheren 1809 (present at the reduction of Flushing), Ionian Islands 1823 and Gibraltar 1840–1841.

The first officer to join the Corps of Royal Engineers without first serving in the Royal Artillery. Employed under General Leith to report on the state of the country and condition of Spanish armies in the north 1808. Became Leith's ADC but rejoined the Royal Engineers at Lugo and the rest of the retreat to Corunna. Responsible for fortresses in Belgium 1815 (the Duke of Wellington inspected these twice a year, always accompanied by Col Jones). Appointed to command the Royal Engineers and Royal Sappers at Woolwich 1818. Also served in the Ionian Islands 1823 (to review their fortifications). Took Command at Woolwich, improved the Arsenal, built a canal with a link to the Thames and improved the entrance gate 1825–1834. Toured the fortification of Gibraltar 42 years after he first went there Oct 1840–1841. He was the finest Military Engineer of his day, with sound judgement and mathematical knowledge, which he applied to all his opinions. He said that he would rather serve at one siege than six general actions; such was his devotion to his profession. Author of *Journal of Sieges carried on by the Army under the Duke of Wellington in Spain, between the years 1811 and 1814*, 3 vols, 1827. Brother of 2nd Capt Harry David Jones Royal Engineers.

REFERENCE: *Dictionary of National Biography. Gentleman's Magazine, Apr 1843, p. 428. United Service Magazine, 2, 1843, pp. 109–15. Annual Register, 1844, Appx, p. 428. Jones, W. editor, Jones, John Thomas, The military autobiography of Major General J. T. Jones, 1853. (Only 12 copies privately printed. Copy in British Library, Shelf mark C.40.i.8)*

JONES, Joseph Allingham
Captain. 39th (Dorsetshire) Regiment of Foot
Monument: Kensal Green Cemetery, London. (8910/75/IR). Inscription largely illegible. (Photograph)

SACRED / TO THE MEMORY OF / CAPTAIN JOSEPH JONES / ....

Ensign 4 Oct 1804. Lt 9 Oct 1806. Capt 3 Jun 1813.

Served in the Peninsula with 2/39ᵗʰ Jul 1808 – Dec 1811 and 1/39ᵗʰ Jan 1812 – Sep 1813. Present at Busaco, first siege of Badajoz, Albuera, Arroyo dos Molinos, Vittoria and Pyrenees where he was severely wounded at Maya 25 Jul 1813. Half pay 25 Feb 1816. Buried in Kensal Green 28 May 1850.

JONES, Leslie Grove
Captain and Lieutenant Colonel. 1ˢᵗ Regiment of Foot Guards.
Interred in Catacomb A (v30 c1) Kensal Green Cemetery, London.

Midshipman Royal Navy 1794. Ensign 1ˢᵗ Foot Guards 25 Nov 1796. Lt and Capt 25 Nov 1799. Capt and Lt Colonel 21 Jan 1813. Bt Major 4 Jun 1811. Major 25 Jul 1821.

Served in the Peninsula with 3ʳᵈ Battalion Oct 1808 – Jan 1809 and Jul 1811 – Nov 1812. Present at Corunna and Cadiz. Also served in the Netherlands 1814. Commandant at Brussels before Waterloo. Served in France with the Army of Occupation. After his retirement from the army became interested in politics, writing letters to *The Times* signed 'Radical' during the movement for Reform. Wanted to stand for Parliament but did not have the financial means to do so. Died 12 Mar 1839. Named Leslie George in Regimental records.
REFERENCE: *Dictionary of National Biography. Gentleman's Magazine, May 1839, pp. 541–2.*

JONES, Oliver Thomas
Lieutenant Colonel. 18ᵗʰ Regiment of Light Dragoons.
Memorial tablet: St Mary's Church, Penmark, Glamorgan, Wales. (Photograph)

IN / MEMORY OF / MAJOR GENERAL OLIVER THOMAS JONES / SECOND SON OF / ROBERT JONES OF FONMAN CASTLE ESQ / AND JOANNA HIS WIFE AND DAUGHTER AND HEIRESS / OF EDMUND LLOYD OF CARDIFF ESQUIRE. / HE WAS BORN THE 9ᵀᴴ DAY OF SEPTEMBER 1776. HE ENTERED / THE CAVALRY AT AN EARLY AGE AND PROVED HIMSELF AN / ABLE AND ZEALOUS OFFICER. HE SERVED IN THE LOW / COUNTRIES, IN THE WEST INDIES AND UNDER / SIR JOHN MOORE IN SPAIN IN THE COMMAND OF THE / 18ᵀᴴ HUSSARS AND FOR HIS DISTINGUISHED SERVICES / IN THAT CAMPAIGN HE WAS AWARDED THE GOLD MEDAL. / HE MARRIED FIRST LOUISA THE DAUGHTER AND / HEIRESS OF COLONEL HENRY STANLEY AND SECONDLY / MARIA ANTONIA THE YOUNGEST DAUGHTER OF / HENRY SWINBURNE OF HAMSTERLY IN THE COUNTY / OF DURHAM ESQUIRE. / HE DIED AT BATH ON THE 15ᵀᴴ OF NOVEMBER 1815 / AGED 39. / AND LEFT TWO SONS AND THREE DAUGHTERS. / HE IS BURIED UNDERNEATH. / .... / THIS MONUMENT IS ERECTED BY / ROBERT OLIVER JONES OF FONMAN CASTLE ESQUIRE.

Cornet 1ˢᵗ Dragoons 10 Nov 1792. Lt 8 Jun 1793. Major 20ᵗʰ Lt Dragoons 29 Nov 1798. Lt Colonel 18ᵗʰ Lt Dragoons 29 Jan 1801. Bt Colonel 25 Oct 1809. Major General 1 Jan 1812.

Served in the Peninsula Sep 1808 – Jan 1809. Present in the Corunna campaign (present at Benevente where he was awarded a Gold Medal). Also served in Flanders 1794–1795 (with his brother Robert), and West Indies 1795–1798.

JONES, Rice
Captain. Royal Engineers.
Headstone: Sandpits Cemetery, Gibraltar. (M.I.)

"COL. RICE JONES, K. H., R. E., / D. 20 MAR 1854, A. 65."

Named on the Regimental Memorial: Rochester Cathedral, Rochester, Kent. (Photograph)

2nd Lt 1 Feb 1806. 1st Lt 1 Jul 1806. 2nd Capt 1May 1811. Bt Major 21 Jun 1817. Lt Colonel 8 Jun 1830.
　　Served in the Peninsula Apr 1809 – Feb 1812 (Brigade Major Dec 1810 – Feb 1812). Present at Douro, Talavera, Torres Vedras, Busaco, first siege of Badajoz, Albuera, second siege of Badajoz and Ciudad Rodrigo. Also served in South America 1807. KH. MGS medal for Talavera, Busaco, Albuera and Ciudad Rodrigo.
REFERENCE: *Shore, E. editor, An Engineer Officer under Wellington in the Peninsula: diary and correspondence of Lieutenant Rice Jones, R.E., 1986.*

JONES, Richard Haynes
Captain. 11th (North Devonshire) Regiment of Foot.
Gravestone: St James's Churchyard, Piccadilly, London. (M.I.)

"SACRED TO THE MEMORY OF / RICHARD HAYNES JONES ESQRE / OF BISHOPS CASTLE, SHROPSHIRE / LATE SENIOR CAPTAIN OF / THE 11TH REGT OF FOOT, / IN WHICH HE SERVED DURING THE WHOLE / OF THE PENINSULAR WAR: / HE DEPARTED THIS LIFE / ON THE 6TH DAY OF FEBRUARY, 1830, / AGED 44 YEARS."

Ensign 2nd Garrison Battalion 26 Apr 1806. Lt 11th Foot 17 Aug 1808. Capt 1 Apr 1813.
　　Served in the Peninsula Oct 1810 – Apr 1814. Present at the siege of Salamanca Forts, Salamanca, Burgos and the retreat from Burgos, Pyrenees, Bidassoa, Nivelle, Nive, Bayonne, Orthes and Toulouse. Also served at Walcheren 1809.

JONES, William
Major. 52nd (Oxfordshire) Light Infantry Regiment of Foot.
Memorial tablet: St Baglan's Church, Llanfaglan, Caernarvonshire, Wales. (Redundant church under the care of the Friends of Friendless Churches, located about two miles from Llanfaglan on the coast). (Photograph)

.... / ALSO / TO THE MEMORY OF / WILLIAM JONES / THEIR FIFTH SON, MAJOR IN THE 52ND REGT / WHO GLORIOUSLY FELL ON THE 7TH OF APRIL 1812 / WHILE LEADING THE FORLORN HOPE AT THE EVER / MEMORABLE SIEGE OF BADAJOZ, AGED 35. / ....

Lt 2 Dec 1799. Adjutant 20 Nov 1800. Capt 15 Aug 1804. Major 6 Apr 1812.
　　Served in the Peninsula with 1/52nd Aug 1808 – Jan 1809 and Jul 1809 – Apr 1812. Present at Corunna, Coa, Busaco, Pombal, Redinha, Casal Nova (severely wounded), Ciudad Rodrigo and Badajoz where he was severely wounded in the storming party and died shortly afterwards. Promoted to a Majority on his death bed. Also known as Jack Jones.

JONES, William
Surgeon. 40th (2nd Somersetshire) Regiment of Foot.
Ledger stone: St Modwen's Churchyard, Burton-on-Trent, Staffordshire. (Photograph)

.... / ALSO OF / WILLIAM JONES, M.D. / OF BURTON ON TRENT, / BORN OCTOBER 21 1782. / DIED AUGUST 8 1862.

Hospital Mate 12 Nov 1805. Asst Surgeon 95th Foot 21 Nov 1805. Surgeon 40th Foot 3 Sep 1812.
　　Served in the Peninsula with 1/95th Aug 1808 – Jan 1809 and Jun 1809 – Sep 1812 and with 40th Foot Oct 1812 – Apr 1814. Present at Cacabellos, Corunna, Busaco, Pombal, Redinha, Casal Nova, Foz d'Arouce, Sabugal, Fuentes d'Onoro, Ciudad Rodrigo, Badajoz, Salamanca, Vittoria, Pyrenees, Bidassoa, Nivelle, Nive, Orthes and Toulouse. Also served in South America 1807 (present at Buenos Ayres where he was taken prisoner), and North America 1814–1815. Present at Waterloo. MD Glasgow 1818. Retired

10 May 1831. MGS medal for Corunna, Busaco, Fuentes d'Onoro, Ciudad Rodrigo, Badajoz, Salamanca, Vittoria, Pyrenees, Nivelle, Nive, Orthes and Toulouse.

JONQUIÈRE, J. W. E.
2nd Lieutenant. 7th National Militia Battalion, Dutch Infantry.
Named on the Memorial to Dutch officers killed at Waterloo: St Joseph's Church, Waterloo, Belgium. (Photograph)

JUDGE, John William
Sapper. Royal Engineers.
Grave: All Saints Churchyard, West Bromwich, Staffordshire. (No longer extant).

Served at Waterloo where he was wounded. Died Sep 1878 and was buried with military honours by the side of Elijah Paget who had died a few days earlier, both having served at Waterloo.
REFERENCE: *West Bromwich Weekly News, 7 Sep 1878.*

KAY, Arthur
Lieutenant. Royal Engineers.
Named on the Regimental Memorial: Rochester Cathedral, Rochester, Kent. (Photograph)

2nd Lt 20 Jul 1813. Lt 15 Dec 1813. 2nd Capt 10 Dec 1832. Capt 15 Aug 1840.
    Served in the Netherlands 1814–1815 and in France with the Army of Occupation 1815–1818. Retired on full pay 24 Oct 1842. Died at Yealmpton, Devon 2 Feb 1847.

KAY, Samuel
Sergeant. 3rd Regiment of Foot Guards.
Headstone: St Michael and All Angels Churchyard, Beetham, Cumbria. (Photograph)

IN MEMORY OF / SAMUEL KAY / WHO DEPARTED THIS LIFE ON THE 25TH OF / JULY 1857, AGED 78 YEARS. / DECEASED SERVED HIS KING AND COUNTRY / UPWARDS OF 20 YEARS: 11 YEARS PRIVATE, 4½ / CORPORAL, AND 5 YEARS SARGEANT, IN THE / 3RD REGIMENT OF FOOT GUARDS. / A TEAR THERE IS FOR ALL WHO DIE /A MOURNER OËR THE HUMBLEST GRAVE: / BUT NATIONS SWELL THE FUNERAL CRY /AND TRIUMPH WEEPS ABOVE THE BRAVE.

Pte 1796. Cpl 1807. Sgt 1812.
    Served in the Peninsula 1809–1814. Present at Talavera, Busaco, Fuentes d'Onoro, Ciudad Rodrigo, Salamanca and Vittoria. MGS Medal for Talavera, Busaco, Fuentes d'Onoro, Ciudad Rodrigo, Salamanca and Vittoria. Discharged 1817 aged 39.

KEANE, Sir John
Lieutenant Colonel. 60th (Royal American) Regiment of Foot.
Sarcophagus: St Michael's Churchyard, Sopley, Hampshire. (Photograph)

SACRED / TO THE MEMORY OF / LIEUTENANT GENERAL / LORD KEANE. G.C.B. AND G.C.H. / WHO SERVED AND FOUGHT FOR HIS COUNTRY / IN THE FOUR QUARTERS OF THE GLOBE. / DIED AUGUST 26 1844. AGED 63 YEARS.

Ensign 17th Foot 31 Jul 1793. Lt Independent Company 29 Apr 1793. Capt 124th Foot 12 Nov 1794. Capt 44th Foot 7 Nov 1799. Major 60th Foot 27 May 1802. Lt Colonel 13th Foot 20 Aug 1803. Bt Colonel 1 Jan 1812. Lt Colonel 60th Foot 25 Jun 1812. Major General 4 Jun 1814. Lt General 22 Jul 1830.

Served in the Peninsula Oct 1812 – Apr 1814 (Commanded 2 Brigade 3rd Division Aug 1813 – Apr 1814). Present at Vittoria, Pyrenees, Nivelle, Nive, Orthes, Vic Bigorre, Tarbes and Toulouse. Present in France with the Army of Occupation Jul 1815 – 1817. Also served in Egypt 1801, Martinique 1809 (present at Fort Desaix), North America 1814–1815 (in command of the Army until the arrival of Sir Edward Pakenham. Present at New Orleans where he was severely wounded 8 Jan 1815), West Indies 1823–1830 and India (Commander in Chief Bombay 1834 – Oct 1839, when he took over command of the Army of India from Sir Henry Fane and advanced into Afghanistan Apr 1839. Present at the assault and capture of Ghuznee Jul 1839 and occupation of Kabul Aug 1839. Awarded medal for Ghuznee). Gold Cross for Martinique, Vittoria, Pyrenees, Nivelle, Orthes and Toulouse. GCB. Colonel 94th Foot 18 Apr 1829. Colonel 68th Foot 13 Apr 1831. Colonel 46th Foot 6 Apr 1838 and Colonel 43rd Foot 1 Aug 1839. REFERENCE: *Dictionary of National Biography. Royal Military Calendar, Vol 3, p. 376. Gentleman's Magazine, Oct 1844, pp. 426–8. Annual Register, 1844, Appx, pp. 263–4. United Service Magazine, Oct 1844, pp. 318–9.*

KEDDLE, Robert
Lieutenant. 50th (West Kent) Regiment of Foot.
Ledger stone: St Macartin's Cathedral, Enniskillen, County Fermanagh, Northern Ireland. (Photograph)

ROBERT KEDDLE, / LIEUT. 50TH REGT, / DEPARTED THIS LIFE 30TH JUNE / 1815, AGED 28 YEARS. / HIS DEATH WAS OCCASIONED / BY A WOUND RECEIVED IN / ACTION WITH THE FRENCH, / ON THE 13TH DECR 1813 / AT ST PIERRE, NEAR BAYONNE. / THIS STONE IS ERECTED BY / HIS BROTHER OFFICERS, / TO PERPETUATE THE MEMORY / OF A / GALLANT OFFICER. / ....

Ensign Dorset Regiment of Militia 1 Oct 1806. Lt 50th Foot 7 Jan 1808.
    Served in the Peninsula Sep 1810 – Mar 1814. Present at Fuentes d'Onoro, Almarez, Alba de Tormes, Vittoria, Pyrenees, Nivelle, and Nive where he was severely wounded 13 Dec 1813. Also served at Walcheren 1809.

KEEVERS, William
Private. 18th Regiment of Light Dragoons.
Headstone: Anglican Cemetery, Whyalla Road, Jamberoo, New South Wales, Australia. (Photograph)

SACRED / TO THE / MEMORY OF / JOHN KEEVERS / .... / AND HIS FATHER / WILLIAM KEEVERS, / WHO WAS PRESENT AT / THE BATTLE OF WATERLOO, 1815. / DIED NOVR 14TH 1871 / AGED 84 YEARS. / ....

Pte 3 Dec 1810. Pte 3rd Foot 12 Jun 1822. Cpl 25 Dec 1826. Cpl 57th Foot 25 Oct 1827. Cpl 17th Foot 1 Jan 1831.
    Served in the Peninsula Feb 1813 - Apr 1814 with 18th Lt Dragoons. Present at Vittoria, Nivelle and Toulouse. Present at Waterloo in Capt J. R. L. Lloyd's Troop. Discharged 10 Sep 1821 but owing to lack of employment re-enlisted in 3rd Foot. The Regiment was escorting convicts to Australia. He left England 13 Mar 1823 with his wife and son. In 1825 Governor Sir Thomas Brisbane formed the Mounted Police Force to restore order to large areas of the country. Keevers was appointed Drill Inspector because of his cavalry experience. Discharged after 24 years of military service 30 Sep 1833. Bought 100 acres of Crown Land, calling it 'Hussars Farm' which he farmed successfully. Died in Jamberoo 14 Nov 1871.

KEITH, Henry Duncan
Ensign. 69th (South Lincolnshire) Regiment of Foot.
Named on the memorial tablet to 2nd (Queen's Royal) Regiment of Foot: Afghan Memorial Church, St John the Evangelist, Colaba, Bombay, India. (M.I.)

"CAPTAIN H. D. KEITH"

Ensign 21 Apr 1814. Lt 14 Aug 1815. Lt 89th Foot 21 Dec 1820. Lt 23rd Foot 12 Apr 1821. Lt 2nd Foot 25 Jan 1825. Capt 29 Jun 1837.
    Served at Quatre Bras and Waterloo. Also served in the Netherlands 1814–1815 and India. Died in Bombay 4 Mar 1839.

KELK, Edward
Private. 52nd (Oxfordshire) Light Infantry Regiment of Foot.
Buried in Hamilton Municipal Cemetery, Hamilton, Ontario, Canada. (No longer extant: Grave number Section CC-A, Lot 103)

Served in the Peninsula Jul 1809 – Apr 1814.
    Present at Talavera (possibly served with a Battalion of Detachments made up of men left behind sick in Lisbon when regiment went to Corunna), Busaco, Fuentes d'Onoro, Ciudad Rodrigo, Badajoz, Salamanca, Vittoria, Pyrenees, Nivelle, Nive, Orthes and Toulouse. Served at Waterloo in Capt John Shedden's Company. Discharged Sep 1830 with pension aged 42. Emigrated to Canada and served during the Rebellion of 1837–1838. MGS medal for Talavera, Busaco, Fuentes d'Onoro, Ciudad Rodrigo, Badajoz, Salamanca, Vittoria, Pyrenees, Nivelle, Nive, Orthes and Toulouse. Buried 12 Dec 1879 aged 85.

KELLETT, Christopher
Lieutenant. 61st (South Gloucestershire) Regiment of Foot.
Named on the Memorial: St Andrew's Church, (now Musée Historique), Biarritz, France. (Photograph)

Ensign 18 Jul 1811. Lt 4 Mar 1813.
    Served in the Peninsula Apr – Nov 1813. Present at Pyrenees and Nivelle where he was killed 10 Nov 1813.

KELLETT, Robert Napier
Volunteer. 95th Regiment of Foot.
Monument in railed enclosure: English Cemetery, Florence, Italy. (Grave number B121I). (Photograph)

SACRED / TO THE MEMORY OF ROBERT / NAPIER KELLETT LATE CAPTAIN / ROYAL HIGH-LANDERS OF RENFREWSHIRE / SCOTLAND, NEPHEW OF SIR RICHARD / KELLETT BART / DIED AT FLORENCE NOVEMBER 2ND 1853 / AGED 56 YEARS / REQUIESCAT IN PACE.

Volunteer 95th Foot. 2nd Lt 18 Jul 1815. Ensign 77th Foot 19 Jun 1823. Ensign 48th Foot 25 Mar 1824. Lt 80th Foot 19 Jun 1827. Capt 42nd Foot 3 Sep 1829.
    Served with 2/95th as a volunteer at Waterloo. Commissioned for his services at Waterloo. Present with the Army of Occupation 1815–1818. Retired 19 Oct 1838.

KELLY, Allan
Major. 54th (West Norfolk) Regiment of Foot.
Gravestone: Parish of Lea (Leig) Old Graveyard, County Laois, Ireland. (M.I.)

"SACRED TO ALLAN KELLY, LT COL 54TH REGT, DIED 11 SEP 1828, AGED 68 YEARS."

Lt 17 Aug 1798. Capt 21 Feb 1805. Major 31 Oct 1811. Bt Lt Colonel 12 Aug 1819.
Present at Waterloo in reserve at Hal, siege of Cambrai and with the Army of Occupation. Also served in Ireland 1799, Ferrol 1800, Egypt 1801 (present at Aboukir and Alexandria), South America 1807 (present at Montevideo and Buenos Ayres) and the Netherlands 1814.

KELLY, Dawson
Major. 73rd (Highland) Regiment of Foot.
Memorial tablet: St Patrick's Cathedral, Armagh, Northern Ireland. (South wall of nave). (Photograph)

TO THE MEMORY OF / COLONEL DAWSON KELLY, C. B, / LIEU^T COL^L, OF THE LXXIII REG^T, / OF FOOT. / AFTER HAVING MERITORIOUSLY SERVED / IN THE EARLY PART OF THE REVO-LUTION – / ARY WAR IN THE WEST INDIES AND IN / THE MEDITERRANEAN HE WAS APPOINTED / IN MDCCCIX, TO THE STAFF OF HIS GRACE / THE DUKE OF WELLINGTON, AS ASSISTANT / QUARTER MASTER GENERAL, IN WHICH SITUA – / TION HE CONTINUED WITH SHORT INTERMISSION / UNTIL THE DEFEAT OF THE FRENCH FORCES / AT THE BATTLE OF WATERLOO. / HE WAS PRESENT AT NEARLY ALL THE CONS – / IDERABLE ACTIONS IN SPAIN & PORTUGAL, / AND REPEATEDLY RECEIVED THE PUBLIC THANKS / FROM HIS ILLUSTRIOUS COMMANDER. / HE DIED AT DUNGANNON THE RES – / IDENCE OF HIS BROTHER IN LAW / EDWARD EVANS, ESQUIRE, MARCH / XXVII MDCCCXXXVII.

Ensign 47th Foot 25 Jun 1800. Lt 15 Jan 1801. Capt York Lt Infantry 26 Jan 1804. Capt 27th Foot 18 Sep 1806. Major 73rd Foot 31 Oct 1811. Bt Lt Colonel 18 Jun 1815. Bt Colonel 10 Jun 1837.
    Served in the Peninsula Nov 1808 – Nov 1811 (DAQMG) and Dec 1811 – Mar 1812 (AQMG). Present at the Douro, Talavera, Busaco, Fuentes d'Onoro, Fuente Guinaldo, Ciudad Rodrigo and Badajoz. Served at Waterloo (on staff as AQMG, but on being told by a sergeant from the 73rd Regt that 22 officers of the regiment were killed or wounded, immediately returned to his regiment and took command). Awarded Bt Lt Colonelcy and CB. Also served in the West Indies 1800–1807 (present at Dominica), Sicily 1807, Dantzig 1813 and Netherlands 1814 (present at Merxem). Died 27 Mar 1837. Brother of Lt Colonel William Kelly 24th Foot.
REFERENCE: *Lagden, Alan and John Sly, The 2/73rd at Waterloo, 2nd ed. 1998, pp. 194–6.*

KELLY, Edward
Captain. 1st Life Guards.
Memorial: Mullye Cemetery, Mullye, Bengal, India. (M.I.)

"SACRED TO THE MEMORY OF / LIEUTENANT-COLONEL EDWARD KELLY / OF HIS MAJESTY'S SERVICE, / WHO DIED ON THE 6TH AUGUST, ANNO DOMINI / ONE THOUSAND EIGHT HUNDRED AND TWENTY EIGHT, / IN THE FIFTY-FOURTH YEAR OF HIS AGE. / THIS GALLANT OFFICER SERVED HIS MAJESTY WITH / DISTINCTION IN FLANDERS, SPAIN AND AT WATERLOO, / WHERE HE WAS SEVERELY WOUNDED. HE WAS PRESENT / AT THE CAPTURE OF THE FORTRESS OF / BHURTPORE, AND SUBSEQUENTLY SERVED IN AVA, / WHERE HE CONTRACTED THE DISEASE WHICH / PROVED FATAL TO HIM. / AS A LAST MARK OF REGARD AND ESTEEM THE RIGHT / HONOURABLE THE VISCOUNT COMBERMERE, G. C. B. / COMMANDER-IN-CHIEF, IN WHOSE STAFF / LIEUT-COL. E. KELLY CAME TO INDIA, AND HIS / BROTHER OFFICERS OF THE STAFF HAVE / ERECTED THIS MONUMENT."

Cornet 2nd Life Guards 1801. Capt 1st Dragoons 12 May 1808. Capt 1st Life Guards 2 Aug 1810. Bt Major 18 Jun 1815. Bt Lt Colonel 1828.
    Served in the Peninsula Sep 1809 – Jun 1810, Aug – Sep 1813 and Jan – Apr 1814 (on staff as DAQMG Nov 1809 – Apr 1810, Aug – Sep 1813 and Jan – Apr 1814). Present on 17th June covering the retreat of the infantry from Quatre Bras. Kelly's troop charged the French at Genappe to save the 7th Lt Dragoons. He fought bravely at Waterloo although wounded, claiming eleven French dead including Colonel Hubert of 4th Cuirassiers. He never thought he had been given adequate reward for his conduct. Awarded Bt Majority and Knight of St Anne of Russia. Sold his commission and transferred to 23rd Lt Dragoons who were going to India, but debts and a large family in London made him move to the 6th Foot. Served in India 1824 (ADC to Lord Combermere at Bhurtpore 1825–1826). Died in India 6 Aug 1828.

REFERENCE: McGuffie, T. H., *Kelly of Waterloo*, Journal of the Society for Army Historical Research, Vol 33, No 135, Autumn 1955, pp. 97–109.

KELLY, Richard

Major. 4th Ceylon Regiment.
Memorial: Duleek Church of Ireland, County Meath, Ireland. (M.I.)

"SACRED TO THE MEMORY OF RICHARD KELLY LATE COLONEL IN THE 34TH REGT WHO DEPARTED THIS LIFE ON THE 7TH OF JANUARY 1840 AT WESTON IN CO. MEATH IN THE 68TH YEAR OF HIS AGE. THIS STONE WAS PLACED HERE BY HIS SORROWING FRIENDS AS A SMALL TRIBUTE OF AFFECTION AND TO RECORD THEIR LOSS."

Ensign 41st Foot 1 Aug 1797. Lt 12 Jan 1799. Capt 66th Foot 6 Mar 1806. Major 4th Ceylon Regt 6 Dec 1810. Bt Lt Colonel 3 Aug 1815. Major 83rd Foot 1 Jan 1818. Lt Colonel 34th Foot 8 Oct 1830.

Served in the Peninsula Apr 1809 – Dec 1810. Present at Douro, Talavera (wounded), Busaco and Torres Vedras. Took command of the 66th Foot at the Douro when Major Murray was severely wounded and continued in command for the next two years. Gold Medal for Talavera and was recommended for a Majority in 4th Ceylon Regiment, but did not leave the 66th until later the following year so Kelly was present at Busaco and Torres Vedras. Also served in the Kandian Wars 1814–1818.

His younger brother Ensign William Kelly was also in the 66th Foot at Talavera and carried the Regimental colour. He fell ill after the battle and was left in the hospital where he was taken prisoner Aug 1809 and died in captivity Sep 1809.

KELLY, Robert

Captain. 60th (Royal American) Regiment of Foot.
Ledger stone: Kensal Green Cemetery, London. Inscription illegible. (12316/112/2). (Photograph)

Volunteer 87th Foot. Ensign 60th Foot 30 Apr 1799. Lt 17 Oct 1800. Capt 16 Aug 1810. Major 22 Jul 1830.

Served in the Peninsula with 5/60th Feb 1813 – Apr 1814 (attached to 3rd Division). Present at Vittoria, Pyrenees, Nivelle, Nive, Orthes and Vic Bigorre (severely wounded 19 Mar 1814 and awarded pension of £100 per annum). MGS medal for Vittoria, Pyrenees, Nivelle, Nive and Orthes. Fort Major at Dartmouth. Half pay 15 Jan 1829. Died in 1855.

KELLY, Robert

Private. 12th (Prince of Wales's) Regiment of Light Dragoons.
Named on the Regimental Memorial tablet: St Joseph's Church, Waterloo, Belgium. (Photograph)
Killed at Waterloo.

KELLY, William

Lieutenant Colonel. 24th (Warwickshire) Regiment of Foot.
Memorial tablet: Armagh Cathedral, Armagh, Northern Ireland. (South wall of nave). (Photograph)

TO THE MEMORY OF / COLONEL WILLIAM KELLY, C.B. / LIEUT COLL OF HIS MAJESTY'S / XXIV REGT OF FOOT. / THE SERVICES OF THIS BRAVE OFFICER / WERE EXTENDED TO THE FOUR QUARTERS / OF THE GLOBE. / IN THE PENINSULAR WAR HE RECEIVED THE / PUBLIC THANKS OF HIS GRACE THE DUKE / OF WELLINGTON FOR HIS CONDUCT IN COM – / MAND OF THE XXIV REGT AT THE BATTLES OF / FUENTES D'ONORE, BADAJOS, SALA – / MANCA, VITTORIA – THE PYRENEES. / BEING OBLIGED TO RETURN HOME IN CONSE – / QUENCE OF A SEVERE WOUND RECEIVED AT THE / BATTLE OF THE PYRENEES, HE AFTERWARDS / JOINED THE BRITISH FORCES IN INDIA AND / WAS AGAIN HONOURED WITH THE GRATEFUL / THANKS

OF THE COMMANDER IN CHIEF FOR / HIS SERVICES AS THE COMMANDER OF A BRI – / GADE IN THE NEPAUL WAR. / THE EFFECTS OF HIS WOUND COMPELLING / HIM AGAIN TO QUIT ACTIVE SERVICE, HE DIED / SHORTLY AFTER REACHING ENGLAND AT / LITTLECOTT WILT-SHIRE, THE SEAT OF HIS / FRIEND LIEUT GENL SIR HORACE / POPHAM, IN MDCCCXVIII.

Memorial tablet: St Mary's Church, Chilton Foliat, Wiltshire. (Photograph)

SACRED TO THE MEMORY OF / COLONEL WILLIAM KELLY C. B. / LIEUT COL^L OF HIS MAJESTY'S 24TH REG^T OF FOOT, / WHO DEPARTED THIS LIFE AT LITTLECOTT, / THE 21ST OF AUGUST 1818. / COLONEL KELLY'S SERVICES WERE EXTENDED TO THE / FOUR QUARTERS OF THE GLOBE: / HE WAS SEVERELY WOUNDED AT THE BATTLE OF THE PYRENEES, / AND EXHAUSTED AFTERWARDS BY HIS SUCCESSFUL EXERTIONS / IN THE NEPAUL WAR IN INDIA. / HE RETURNED ONLY TO BREATHE HIS LAST WITH HIS FRIENDS / ADMIRED IN HIS PROFESSION AS A SOLDIER, / AND ESTEEMED BY ALL AS A MAN.

Ensign 28th Foot 17 Dec 1785. Lt 24th Foot 30 Jun 1792. Capt 31 Oct 1795. Major 24th Foot 5 Apr 1799. Bt Lt Colonel 1 Jan 1805. Lt Colonel 22 Feb 1810.
    Served in the Peninsula May 1811 – Aug 1813. (Commanded 3 Provisional Brigade from Dec 1812). Present at Fuentes d'Onoro, Ciudad Rodrigo, Salamanca, Burgos and retreat from Burgos, Vittoria and Pyrenees (severely wounded 2 Aug 1813). Gold Cross for Fuentes d'Onoro, Salamanca, Vittoria and Pyrenees. CB. Also served in Egypt 1801, Cape of Good Hope 1801–1806, India 1814–1817 (present in Nepaul at action on River Baghmati and hill fort of Hariharpur). Brother of Major Dawson Kelly 73rd Foot.

KELLY, William Waldron
Lieutenant. 40th (2nd Somersetshire) Regiment of Foot.
Buried in Cornwall Churchyard, Hanover, Jamaica, West Indies. (Burial register)

Ensign 3 Jun 1806. Lt 13 Aug 1807.
    Served in the Peninsula Nov 1809 – Apr 1814. Present at Busaco, Redinha, first siege of Badajoz (wounded), Ciudad Rodrigo, Badajoz, Castrejon (wounded), Salamanca, Vittoria, Pyrenees (wounded), Bidassoa, Nivelle, Nive and Orthes. Also served in the West Indies 1828 where he became Barrack Master in Jamaica and died 12 Nov 1836.

KEMPT, Sir James
Colonel. 60th (Royal American) Regiment of Foot.
Interred in Catacomb B (v57 c10) Kensal Green Cemetery, London.

Ensign 101st Foot 31 Mar 1783. Lt 18 Aug 1784. Capt 113th Foot 30 May 1794. Major 18 Sep 1794. Lt Colonel 81st Foot 23 Jul 1803. Bt Colonel 9 Mar 1809. Major General 1 Jan 1812. Colonel 60th Foot 4 Nov 1813. Lt General 27 May 1825. General 23 Nov 1841.
    Served in the Peninsula Jan – Jul 1812 (Commanded 1 Brigade 3rd Division) and Jan 1813 – Apr 1814 (Commanded 1 Brigade Lt Division). Present at Badajoz (wounded and Mentioned in Despatches), Vittoria, Pyrenees (Mentioned in Despatches), Vera (Mentioned in Despatches), Bidassoa (Mentioned in Despatches), Nivelle (wounded), Nive, Orthes, Tarbes and Toulouse. Present at Quatre Bras and Waterloo commanding 8th Brigade (28th, 32nd and 79th) – part of Picton's division. On the death of Picton at Waterloo he took command.
    When 101st Foot disbanded in 1785 Kempt went on half pay for nine years and worked as a clerk at the firm of Greenwood and Cox, Army agents. Also served at the Helder 1799, Egypt 1801, Sicily 1806 (present at Maida) and North America 1807–1811 (QMG). Lt Governor of Fort William 1813–1818, Lt Governor of Portsmouth 1819, Governor of Nova Scotia 1820–1828, Governor General of Canada 1828–1830, Master General of Ordnance 1834–1838. Colonel 3rd West India Regt 1819. Colonel 40th

Foot 8 Jun 1829. Colonel 2nd Foot 23 Dec 1834. Colonel 1st Foot 7 Aug 1846. Gold Cross for Maida, Badajoz, Vittoria, Nivelle, Nive, Orthes and Toulouse. MGS medal for Egypt and Pyrenees. GCB. GCH. Died 20 Dec 1854 aged 90.

REFERENCE: *Dictionary of National Biography. Gentleman's Magazine, Feb 1855, pp. 188–9. Annual Register, 1854, Appx, pp. 375–6.*

KENNEDY, Alexander Kennedy Clark see CLARK, Alexander Kennedy

KENNEDY, Andrew
Private. 79th (Cameron Highlanders) Regiment of Foot.
Headstone: Dunnottar Churchyard, Kincardineshire, Scotland. (M.I.)

"ERECTED BY ANDREW KENNEDY LATE OF 79TH OR CAMERON HIGHLANDERS IN MEMORY OF HIS WIFE REBECCA FERGUSON, WHO ACCOMPANIED HIM TO THE BATTLE OF WATERLOO AND DIED IN PEACE AT STONEHAVEN 25 NOV 1861 AGED 68; SAID ANDREW KENNEDY DIED 28 JUN 1865 AGED 83 YEARS."

Pte Canadian Fencibles 23 Dec 1803. Pte 79th Foot 1 May 1805.
    Served in the Peninsula 1808-1809 and Mar 1810 - Apr 1814. Present at Corunna, Busaco, Cadiz, Fuentes d'Onoro, Salamanca. Burgos (severely wounded), Nivelle, Nive and Toulouse. Present at Waterloo in Captain J. Campbell's Company No 7. Also served at Copenhagen 1807 and Walcheren 1809 (present at the siege of Flushing). Discharged 31 Dec 1823. MGS medal for Corunna, Busaco, Fuentes d'Onoro and Salamanca. His wife Rebecca Ferguson was present with him at Waterloo.

KENNEDY, Ewen
Lieutenant. 79th (Cameron Highlanders) Regiment of Foot.
Named on the Regimental Memorial: St Joseph's Church, Waterloo, Belgium. (Photograph)

Promoted from the ranks. Ensign 3 Oct 1811. Lt 25 Feb 1813.
    Served in the Peninsula Dec 1812 – Apr 1813. Present at Quatre Bras and Waterloo where he was killed.

KENNEDY, James Grant
Ensign. 1st (Royal Scots) Regiment of Foot.
Named on the Regimental Memorial: St Joseph's Church, Waterloo, Belgium. (Photograph)

Ensign 12 Apr 1814.
    Served at Quatre Bras aged 16 where he was killed while carrying the colours. 'He was carrying a Colour in advance of the Battalion and was shot in the arm but continued to advance. He was again shot and this time he was killed. A Sergeant, then attempted to take the colour from him, but could not disengage his grip. So he threw the body over his shoulder and rejoined the ranks. The officer commanding the French battalion ordered his men not to fire on the Sergeant and his burden – a chivalrous action'. (Records of the Royal Scots).

KENNEDY, Sir James Shaw see SHAW, James

KENNEDY, Simson
Captain. 68th (Durham) Regiment of Foot.
Grave: Mount Jerome Cemetery, Dublin, Ireland. (No longer extant: Grave number B46–166).)

Ensign 16 Aug 1804. Lt 25 Dec 1804. Capt 8 Oct 1812. Bt Major 22 Jul 1830.
    Served at Walcheren 1809 (present at Flushing). Half pay 14 Dec 1832. Died 16 Jul 1844 aged 74.

KENNEDY, Thomas
Captain. 96th Regiment of Foot.
Low monument: Candie Cemetery, St Peter Port, Guernsey, Channel Islands. (Grave number. D3Y).
(Photograph)

COLONEL THOMAS KENNEDY / DEPUTY QUARTER MASTER GENERAL / UNDER GENERAL
SIR JOHN DOYLE / WHO DIED ON THE 18TH DECEMBER 1849.

Westminster Middlesex Militia 1795. Temporary rank of Capt 36th Foot 1799. Ensign 7th Foot 1803. Lt
4 Dec 1805. Capt Sicilian Regiment 18 Feb 1808. Capt 96th Foot 3 Mar 1808. Bt Major 3 Dec 1812. Bt
Lt Colonel 27 May 1825. Bt Colonel 28 Jun 1838.
    Served in the Peninsula Nov 1808 – Jan 1809. Present at Corunna (DAQMG). Joined the 36th Foot
from the militia with temporary rank of Captain as he brought 100 men with him. All temporary officers
went on half pay in 1802. When war was declared again he became an Ensign in the 7th Foot. Went to
Spain to organise the Spanish troops 1808. Also served at Copenhagen 1807. MGS medal for Corunna.

KENNELLY, James
Lieutenant. 87th (Prince of Wales's Own) Irish Regiment.
Named on the Regimental Memorial tablet: Port Louis Protestant Church, Mauritius. (Photograph)

Ensign 103rd Foot 11 Jan 1809. Ensign 87th Foot 19 Mar 1812. Lt 18 Nov 1813. Capt 12 Apr 1826. Bt
Major 23 Nov 1841.
    Served in the Peninsula Sep 1812 – Apr 1814. Present at Vittoria, Pyrenees, Nivelle (severely wounded)
and Toulouse. Also served in India Dec 1815 – Jun 1827 (present in the Pindari War, siege of Hattrass
and Ava campaign 1824–1826) and Mauritius 1831–1843. Died in Mauritius 5 Mar 1843.

KENNERDELL, James
Sergeant Major. 31st (Huntingdonshire) Regiment of Foot.
Tombstone: Cemetery No 2, Dinapore, India. (M.I.)

"SACRED TO THE MEMORY / OF / JAMES KENNERDELL / LATE SERGT MAJOR H. M. 31ST REGT
/ WHO DEPARTED THIS LIFE MAY / 7TH 1826 / AGED 42 YEARS. / AND FOR UPWARDS OF
TWENTY ONE YEARS / HAD SERVED HIS KING AND COUNTRY WITH / ZEAL AND DEVOTION
AND BY / THE STRICT AND IMPARTIAL DISCHARGE / OF THOSE DUTIES TO HIS SIT –/ UATION
/ SPECIALLY IN THE COURSE OF THE / GLORIOUS WAR OF THE PENINSULA / IN WHICH HIS
REGIMENT WAS ACTIVE / LY ENGAGED / OBTAINED THE ESTEEM / APPROBATION OF HIS
SUPERIORS / AND THE GOOD WILL OF ALL THOSE WHO WERE / ACQUAINTED WITH HIM."

Served in the Peninsula Nov 1808 – Apr 1814. Also served in India 1824.

KENNY, Courtenay Crowe
Captain. 9th (East Norfolk) Regiment of Foot.
Family Memorial tablet: Cardross Churchyard, Dumbartonshire, Scotland. (Photograph)

.... / AND OF / COURTENAY CROWE KENNY, / CAP^T H. M. 9TH FOOT, / KILLED AT
BURGOS 1812.

Ensign 74th Foot 29 Apr 1797. Lt 33rd Foot 31 May 1800. Capt 9th Foot 28 Aug 1804.
    Served in the Peninsula with 2/9th Aug – Nov 1808 and 1/9th Mar 1810 – Sep 1812. Present at Vimeiro,
Busaco, Fuentes d'Onoro, Castrejon, Salamanca and Burgos where he was killed at the siege 30 Sep 1812
acting as an Engineer. Also served at Walcheren 1809. Father in law of Ensign Edward Kenny 89th Foot.

KENNY, Edward
Ensign. 89th Regiment of Foot.
Family Memorial tablet: Cardross Churchyard, Dumbartonshire, Scotland. (Photograph)

SACRED / TO THE MEMORY OF / ………………. / L^T COL EDWARD E. KENNY, / 89TH REG^T, / DIED AT LIVERPOOL 12TH JAN 1879. / ………………..

Volunteer 9th Foot. Ensign 17 Jun 1813. Ensign 89th Foot 3 Mar 1814. Lt 1 Nov 1819. Capt 4 Dec 1832. Major 26 Feb 1845. Lt Colonel 28 Nov 1854.
    Served in the Peninsula with 1/9th May 1813 – Mar 1814. Present at Osma, Vittoria, San Sebastian, Bidassoa (wounded), Nivelle, Nive and Bayonne. Also served in Burma 1824–1826. (Medal for Ava). MGS medal for Vittoria, San Sebastian, Nivelle and Nive. Son in law of Capt Courtney Crowe Kenny 9th Foot.

KEOWN, William
Ensign. 14th (Buckinghamshire) Regiment of Foot.
Family Mural Memorial: Kilmegan Parish Churchyard, Kilmegan, County Down, Northern Ireland. (Photograph)

SACRED / TO THE MEMORY OF JOHN KEOWN / ……………….. / HIS BROTHER WILLIAM LIEU-TENANT / IN THE 14TH REGIMENT OF FOOT WHO DIED / IN CALCUTTA IN THE YEAR 1822 / IN THE 30TH YEAR OF HIS AGE.

Ensign 21 Apr 1814. Lt 11 Nov 1820.
    Present at Waterloo. Also served in India 1817 (present in the Pindari War – capture of Hattrass Fort).

KERR, John
Lieutenant. Royal Engineers.
Named on the Regimental Memorial: Rochester Cathedral, Rochester, Kent. (Photograph)

2nd Lt 20 Jul 1813. Lt 15 Dec 1813.
    Served in the Netherlands and in France with the Army of Occupation 1814–1816. Also served in the West Indies where he died at Government House, Dominica 1 Oct 1826.

KERR, Robert
Lieutenant. Royal Waggon Train.
Ledger stone: Kensal Green Cemetery, London. (13953/74/3). (Photograph)

SACRED / TO THE MEMORY OF / ROBERT KERR ESQ^RE / LATE OF THE 60TH RIFLES, / WHO DIED THE 10TH JULY 1857.

Ensign 11 Feb 1811. Lt 25 May 1815. Lt 60th Rifles 28 Nov 1816.
    Served at Waterloo with the Royal Waggon Train (attached to QMG department). Half pay 25 Mar 1817.

KERR, William
Private. 12th (Prince of Wales's) Regiment of Light Dragoons.
Headstone: St Nicholas Churchyard, Portslade, Sussex. (Photograph)

IN MEMORY OF / WILLIAM KERR / WHO DIED MARCH 25TH 1854. AGED 75. / WILLIAM KERR WAS FOR EIGHTEEN YEARS / A PRIVATE IN THE 12TH LIGHT DRAGOONS AND / SERVED IN EGYPT SPAIN FLANDERS / UNDER ABERCROMBIE AND WELLINGTON / HE WAS PRESENT AT

THE BATTLES OF / ALEXANDRIA SALAMANCA VITTORIA / AND WATERLOO. / HE RESIDED
THIRTY SIX YEARS IN THIS PARISH / AND WAS REMARKABLE DURING THE LATTER / PART
OF HIS LIFE FOR HIS GENTLENESS OF / DISPOSITION AND GENERAL GOOD CONDUCT. / HE
DIED HOPING AND PRAYING FOR MERCY / IN THE NAME OF HIS REDEEMER.

Pte 1801.
    Served in the Peninsula Jun 1811 – Apr 1814. Present at Salamanca and Vittoria. Served at Waterloo
in Capt Henry Andrew's Troop. Also served in Egypt 1801 (present at Alexandria). MGS medal for Egypt
and Vittoria. Granted a pension in 1819.

KERRISON, Sir Edward
Lieutenant Colonel. 7th (Queen's Own) Regiment of Light Dragoons.
Memorial tablet: St Peter and St Paul Church, Hoxne, Suffolk. (Photograph)

IN / MEMORY OF / GENERAL SIR EDWARD KERRISON,/ BART K.C.B. G.C.H. / OF OAKLEY PARK,
IN THIS PARISH, / WHOSE REMAINS ARE HERE INTERRED. / HE SERVED MANY YEARS IN THE
VIITH HUSSARS, / COMMANDING HIS REGIMENT AT THE BATTLES OF / ORTHES, AND
WATERLOO, / AND WAS MORE THAN ONCE SEVERELY WOUNDED. / HE REPRESENTED THE
BOROUGH OF EYE IN PARLIAMENT / FROM MDCCCXXIV TO MDCCCLII. / HE WAS BORN IN
MDCCLXXIV AND DIED MARCH IX MDCCCLIII. / HELD IN HONOUR BY ALL WHO KNEW
HIM. / ....

Cornet 6th Dragoons 23 Jun 1796. Lt 1 Feb 1798. Capt 47th Foot 18 Oct 1798. Capt 7th Lt Dragoons 8
Nov 1798. Major 12 May 1803. Lt Colonel 4 Apr 1805. Bt Colonel 4 Jun 1813. Major General 12 Aug
1819. Lt General 10 Jan 1837. General 11 Nov 1851.
    Served in the Peninsula Nov 1808 – Jan 1809 and Aug 1813 – Apr 1814 (Commanded Brigade Nov –
Dec 1813). Present at Benevente Dec 1808 (severely wounded at Carrion, arm broken in two places during
the cavalry action), Nive, Sauveterre, Orthes (severely wounded) and Toulouse. Present at Waterloo in
command of the 7th Lt Dragoons (wounded), siege of Cambrai, Capture of Paris and with the Army of
Occupation. Also served at the Helder 1799.
    Knighted 5 Jan 1815. Baronet 27 Jul 1821. Gold Medal for Orthes. 'The 7th Hussars distinguished them-
selves upon this occasion and made many prisoners; their charges were highly meritorious' – Lord
Wellington's *Dispatch* on the battle of Orthes. MGS medal for Benevente, Nive and Toulouse. GCH. KCB.
MP for Shaftesbury 1812–1818, Northampton 1818–1824 and Eye 1824–1852. Colonel 14th Lt Dragoons
18 Jun 1830. Captain Commandant Suffolk Borderers Yeomanry Cavalry 18 Jul 1831.
    There is also a memorial plaque at Hoxne to Kerrison's three horses – Blake and Harlequin, both ridden
in the Peninsula and Gilt, killed under him at Waterloo. Blake was lost in the shipwreck of the *Dispatch*
transport returning from Corunna.
REFERENCE: *Dictionary of National Biography. Royal Military Calendar, Vol 4, p. 44. Gentleman's
Magazine, May 1853, pp. 542–3. Annual Register, 1853, Appx, p. 219.*

KERSSENBRUCH. Agatz von
Captain. 3rd Regiment of Hussars, King's German Legion.
Named on the Regimental Memorial: La Haye Sainte, Waterloo, Belgium. (Photograph)

Capt 9 Jun 1807.
    Served in the Peninsula Aug 1808 – Jan 1809. Present at Benevente. Served at Waterloo where he was
killed. Also present in Hanover 1805, the Baltic 1807–1808, North Germany 1813–1814 and the
Netherlands 1814.

KERSTEMAN, William Brewse

Captain. 10th (North Lincolnshire) Regiment of Foot.
Chest tomb: St Andrew's Churchyard, Bristol, Somerset. (Grave number 0588). (Photograph)

SACRED / TO THE MEMORY OF / LIEUT. COLONEL / WILLIAM BREWSE KERSTEMAN / OF HER MAJESTY'S 10TH REGIMENT OF FOOT / AND LATE OF MILVERTON / SOMERSETSHIRE / WHO DIED AT 22 THE LOWER CRESCENT / IN THIS PARISH / ON THE 27TH DAY OF JANUARY 1840 / AGED 54 YEARS. / HE WAS THE ELDEST SON OF THE LATE / MAJOR GENERAL KERSTEMAN, / ....

Ensign 46th Foot 31 Dec 1800. Lt 24 Jul 1802. Lt 67th Foot 9 Jul 1803. Capt 10th Foot 17 Oct 1805. Bt Major 18 Aug 1814. Bt Lt Col 10 Jan 1837.

Served in the Peninsula Aug 1812 – Apr 1814 (on Staff and AAG from Mar 1813). Present at Alicante. Half pay 25 Jun 1816.

KETT, Charles George

2nd Lieutenant. Royal Artillery.
Grave: Kensal Green Cemetery, London. Inscription not recorded. (3140 Section 108/RS)

2nd Lt 13 Dec 1813. 1st Lt 30 Sep 1816.

Present at Waterloo, siege of Cambrai and with the Army of Occupation until Feb 1817. Also served in Canada Jul 1823 – Aug 1829. Half pay at reduction of 10th Battalion 1 Apr 1817. Rejoined 4 Sep 1817. Retired on full pay 4 Mar 1835. Died 14 Sep 1841.

KIBBLE, William Thomas

Corporal 1st (King's) Dragoon Guards.
Headstone: St John's Churchyard, Knutsford, Cheshire. (Right of central path). (Photograph)

WILLIAM THOMAS KIBBLE / REGIMENTAL SERGEANT MAJOR / KINGS DRAGOON GUARDS, / EARL OF CHESTER'S YEOMANRY CAVALRY, / BORN NOVEMBER 5TH 1791. / DIED JULY 4TH 1878. / GENAPPE, QUATRE BRAS, WATERLOO.

Pte 9 Sep 1807. Cpl 25 Feb 1812. Sgt 11 Feb 1816. Troop Sgt Major 1 Aug 1827.

Enlisted aged 16. Served at Quatre Bras and Waterloo (severely wounded with gun shot wounds and sabre cuts). Discharged 5 Aug 1837 after 30 years service owing to the wounds he received at Waterloo. Joined the Earl of Chester's Yeomanry Cavalry.

KILPATRICK, John William

Conductor of Stores. Field Train Department of Ordnance.
Headstone: Maughold Churchyard, Isle of Man. (Photograph)

IN MEMORY OF / JOHN WILLIAM KILPATRICK ESQ. / LATE OF THE FIELD TRAIN / ROYAL ARTILLERY / FORMERLY OF WREXHAM NORTH WALES / WHO DIED AT RAMSEY / ON THE 8TH JUNE 1865 / IN THE 74TH YEAR OF HIS AGE. / HE WAS AT THE TAKING OF FLUSHING / UNDER LORD CHATHAM / AT THE BATTLE OF CORUNNA / UNDER SIR JOHN MOORE / AT CADIZ DURING THE SIEGE / BY THE FRENCH / AT TARIFA WHEN SUCCESSFULLY / DEFENDED BY THE BRITISH / AGAINST THE FRENCH / AND WITH THE ARMY OF OCCUPATION / DURING THEIR PERIOD OF SERVICE / IN FRANCE AT THE CLOSE OF / THE PENINSULAR WAR. / HE DIED TRUSTING IN THE MERITS / OF HIS REDEEMER.

Served in the Peninsula 1808 – Jan 1809 and 1811–1814. Present at Corunna, Cadiz and Eastern coast of

Spain (present at Tarifa). Served in France with the Army of Occupation 1815–1818. Also served at Walcheren 1809 (present at the siege of Flushing). MGS medal for Corunna.

KINCAID, John
1st Lieutenant and Adjutant. 95th Regiment of Foot.
Ledger stone: Borough Cemetery, Hastings, Sussex. (Grave: Division A, Section H, Row B23). (Photograph)

IN / MEMORY OF / A MOST GALLANT SOLDIER / SIR JOHN KINCAID / FORMERLY A CAPTAIN IN / THE RIFLE BRIGADE, / BORN 1789 DIED 1862 / SENIOR EXON OF / HER MAJESTY'S / YEOMAN OF THE GUARD.

Memorial tablet: Camelon Churchyard, Falkirk, Stirlingshire, Scotland. (M.I.)

"JOHN KINCAID .... 2ND SON JOHN DIED IN HASTINGS 23 APRIL 1862 AGED 76. ENTERED THE ARMY IN 1809 AND SERVED THROUGHOUT THE PENINSULAR WAR WITH RIFLE BRIGADE, KNIGHTED 1852 DIED SENIOR EXON OF H. M. ROYAL BODYGUARD AND FOR MANY YEARS GOVERNMENT INSPECTOR OF PRISONS AND FACTORIES IN SCOTLAND."

Named on the Regimental Memorial: Winchester Cathedral, Winchester, Hampshire. (Photograph)

Lt North Yorkshire Militia. 2nd Lt 95th Foot 27 Apr 1809. 1st Lt 23 May 1811. Capt 25 Nov 1826.
    Served in the Peninsula with 1/95th Oct 1810 – Apr 1814. Present at Pombal, Redinha, Casal Nova, Foz d'Arouce (wounded), Sabugal, Fuentes d'Onoro, Ciudad Rodrigo (present in the storming party), Badajoz, Castrejon, Salamanca, San Munos, San Millan, Vittoria, Pyrenees, Vera, Bidassoa, Nivelle, Nive, Tarbes and Toulouse. Present with 1/95th at Waterloo. Also served at Walcheren 1809. Retired 21 Jun 1831. MGS medal for Fuentes d'Onoro. Ciudad Rodrigo, Badajoz, Salamanca, Vittoria, Pyrenees, Nivelle, Nive and Toulouse. Exon of the Yeoman of the Guard 1844. Inspector of Prisons in Scotland. Knighted 1852.
REFERENCE: *Dictionary of National Biography. Fortescue, J. W. editor, Adventures in the rifle brigade in the Peninsula, France and the Netherlands from 1809 to 1815, by J. Kincaid, 1830, reprint 1981. Kincaid, John, Random shots of a rifleman, 1835, reprint 1981.*

KINCHANT, Francis Charlton
Cornet. 2nd (Royal North British) Regiment of Dragoons.
Memorial tablet: St Mary's Church, Middleton-on-the-Hill, Herefordshire. (Photograph)

SACRED TO THE MEMORY OF / FRANCIS CHARLTON KINCHANT / CORNET IN THE SCOTS GREYS / ONLY SON OF THE REV. F. KINCHANT AND MARY, HIS WIFE, OF EASTON IN THIS PARISH. / THIS YOUNG MAN HAD ONLY JOINED HIS REGIMENT LONG ENOUGH TO GAIN THE GOOD OPINION AND REGARD BOTH OF HIS BROTHER OFFICERS AND HIS MEN, AND TO GIVE GREAT PROMISE OF BECOMING AN ORNAMENT TO HIS PROFESSION WHEN HE WAS CUT-OFF AT THE BATTLE OF WATERLOO, THE 18TH OF JUNE 1815, IN THE 21ST YEAR OF HIS AGE. BEFORE HE FELL HE GAVE DECISIVE PROOFS OF HIS GREAT ZEAL, HUMANITY AND COURAGE. HIS SISTER, WHO ERECTS THIS SMALL MEMORIAL OF HER REGRET AND LOVE, ENDEAVOURS TO CONSOLE HERSELF IN REMEMBERING THAT HIS CAREER, THOUGH SHORT, WAS MOST HONOURABLE TO HIMSELF AND USEFUL TO HIS COUNTRY.

Cornet 18 Jan 1815.
    Present at Waterloo where he was killed in the charge of the Scots Greys. Sgt Ewart was covering Cornet Kinchant and Ewart quickly disarmed a French officer and was about to cut him down, but the Frenchman

pleaded for mercy and dropped his sabre as though surrendering. Hearing his cry Kinchant called upon Ewart to spare him and take him prisoner. Ewart obeyed orders and then heard a pistol shot behind him. He saw Kinchant falling backwards over his horse and the Frenchman holding a pistol under his coat. Seeing that Ewart had seen the pistol he cried for mercy again but with one mighty sweep Ewart cut off his head.

KING, Charles
Captain. 16th (Queen's) Regiment of Light Dragoons.
Pedestal tomb: Mount Jerome Cemetery, Dublin, Ireland. (Grave number C116–775). (Photograph)

UNDERNEATH / THIS MEMORIAL REPOSE / THE MORTAL REMAINS / OF / COLONEL CHARLES KING K.H / MANY YEARS ON THE STAFF / OF IRELAND / WHO DEPARTED THIS LIFE / JULY THE 5TH 1844 / AGED 58 YEARS

Cornet 11th Lt Dragoons 9 May 1805. Lt 30 Jan 1806. Capt 16th Lt Dragoons 18 Feb 1813. Major 2 Jun 1825. Lt Colonel 18 Oct 1827 (unattached). Bt Colonel 23 Nov 1841.
 Served in the Peninsula Jun – Oct 1811 and Apr 1814. Present at El Bodon (severely wounded, lost an arm and awarded pension of £100 per annum) and Bayonne. Present at Waterloo. After the battle made Brigade Major 4th Brigade. Also served in India 1823 (present at the siege of Bhurtpore 1825–1826). Army of India medal for Bhurtpore. KH. Inspecting Field Officer of Recruiting in Southern District of Ireland. REFERENCE: *Gentleman's Magazine, Sep 1844, pp. 320–1. Annual Register, 1844, Appx, pp. 252–3. United Service Magazine, Aug 1844, p. 640.*

KING, Charles
Captain. 74th (Highland) Regiment of Foot.
Table tomb: St Michan's Churchyard, Dublin, Ireland. (Photograph)

UNDERNEATH LIE THE REMAINS / OF CAP. CHARLES KING LATE 74TH / REGIMENT, WHO DIED IN KINGSTOWN / JAN 28TH 1843, / IN THE 57TH YEAR OF HIS AGE. / THIS STONE HAS BEEN ERECTED / TO HIS MEMORY BY HIS DISCONSOLATE WIDOW. / ....

Ensign 16 Jun 1808. Lt 27 Dec 1810. Capt 27 Apr 1827.
 Served in the Peninsula Feb 1810 – May 1813 and Nov 1813 – Apr 1814. Present at Busaco, Casal Nova, Foz d'Arouce, Fuentes d'Onoro, second siege of Badajoz, El Bodon, Badajoz (severely wounded), Vic Bigorre, Tarbes and Toulouse. Retired on half pay 27 Apr 1827.

KING, Henry
Lieutenant Colonel. 82nd (Prince of Wales's Volunteers) Regiment of Foot.
Monument: Kensal Green Cemetery, London. Inscription illegible. (11663/84/RS). (Photograph)

Cornet 24th Lt Dragoons 25 Mar 1794. Lt 26th Lt Dragoons 12 Aug 1795. Capt 3 May 1800. Major 82nd Foot 30 Apr 1807. Bt Lt Colonel 31 Dec 1811. Lt Colonel 4 Jun 1813. Bt Colonel 27 May 1825.
 Served in the Peninsula Jul 1811 – Jul 1813. Present at Tarifa (Commandant of garrison and awarded Bt Lt Colonelcy for its defence), Burgos and Vittoria (commanded 82nd Foot). Gold Medal for Vittoria. CB and KCH. MGS medal for Egypt. Also served in the West Indies 1797, Martinique 1798, Egypt 1801 (present at Aboukir and the action at Rahmanie where he commanded a squadron of the 26th Lt Dragoons, was severely wounded, lost his right leg and awarded pension of £300 per annum), Walcheren 1809 (present at Flushing). Later Lieutenant Governor of Heligoland. Knighted 1834. Colonel 3rd Foot 18 Mar 1845. Died 24 Jul 1854.
REFERENCE: *Gentleman's Magazine, Sep 1854, pp. 300–1. Annual Register, 1854, Appx, p. 318.*

KING, John
Private. 12th (Prince of Wales's) Regiment of Light Dragoons.
Named on the Regimental Memorial: St Joseph's Church, Waterloo, Belgium. (Photograph)
   Killed at Waterloo.

KING, William James
Captain. Royal Staff Corps.
Headstone with Cross: St Leonard's Churchyard, Hythe, Kent. (Photograph)

WILLIAM JAMES KING / MAJOR GENERAL: / LATE ROYAL STAFF CORPS. / BORN XI DEC. A.D. / MDCCLXXXIII. / DIED XXIV MARCH A.D. / MDCCCLXIV.

Ensign 16 May 1805. Lt Staff Corps 29 May 1809. Capt 17 Feb 1814. Major 25 Jun 1830. Bt Lt Colonel 9 Nov 1846. Bt Colonel 20 Jun 1854. Major General 1 May 1861.
   Served in the Peninsula 1812 – Apr 1814. Half pay 25 Jun 1830. Magistrate in Hythe.
REFERENCE: *Gentleman's Magazine, May 1864, p. 673.*

KINGSBURY, John
Major. 2nd (Queen's Royal) Regiment of Foot.
Memorial tablet: St Mary the Virgin Church, Battle, Sussex. (Photograph)

THIS MONUMENT IS ERECTED / BY THE / OFFICERS OF THE QUEEN'S ROYAL REGIMENT, / AS A TRIBUTE OF RESPECT / TO THE MEMORY OF / THE LATE LIEUTENANT COLONEL KINGSBURY / WHO DEPARTED THIS LIFE ON THE 14TH OF AUGUST 1813 / AGED 46 YEARS, / AFTER HAVING SERVED HIS COUNTRY / THIRTY THREE YEARS, TWENTY SIX OF WHICH WERE / IN THE ABOVE REGIMENT. / HE WAS WOUNDED / AT THE MEMORABLE SIEGE OF GIBRALTAR, / WAS IN THE ACTION OF THE 1ST OF JUNE, 1794, / AND SERVED IN THE CAMPAIGNS, / OF EGYPT, PORTUGAL AND SPAIN IN 1808 AND 1809, / AND WALCHEREN, / AND LATTERLY UNDER / THE MARQUIS OF WELLINGTON, / IN SPAIN AND PORTUGAL, / AND AT THE BATTLE OF / SALAMANCA, / WAS SEVERELY WOUNDED / AND HIS HORSE KILLED UNDER HIM.

Volunteer. Ensign 97th Foot 15 Dec 1781. Ensign 2nd Foot 7 May 1788. Lt 9 Apr 1793. Capt 16 Feb 1795. Major 5 May 1801. Bt Lt Colonel 7 May 1808.
   Served in the Peninsula Aug 1808 – Jan 1809 and Mar 1811 – Dec 1812. Present at Vimeiro, Corunna (led the regiment as the rear guard to cover the retreat of the Army during the embarkation to England), Almeida, siege of Salamanca Forts and Salamanca (led the regiment, severely wounded 22 Jul 1812). Gold Medal for Salamanca. Returned to England Feb 1813 owing to the wounds received at Salamanca, and commanded the six companies which had returned from 12 May – 14 Aug, when he died suddenly, probably from the effect of his wound. Also served at the siege of Gibraltar 1782 (wounded), on board HMS *Majestic* in Lord Howe's victory 1 Jun 1794, West Indies 1795, Ireland 1798, the Helder 1799, Egypt 1801 and Walcheren 1809.
REFERENCE: *Gentleman's Magazine, Nov 1813, p. 504.*

KINGSBURY, Robert
Lieutenant. 3rd (East Kent) Regiment of Foot.
Memorial tablet: Town Cemetery, Plattsburg, United States of America. (Photograph)

LT. R. KINGSBURY / 3RD REGT. BUFFS / B. ARMY / 6TH SEPT. 1814

Ensign 19 May 1812. Lt 25 Dec 1813.

Served in the Peninsula Sep 1813 – Apr 1814. Present at Nivelle, Nive, Garris, Orthes, Aire and Toulouse. Also served in North America 1814 where he was killed at the Battle of Plattsburg 6 Sep 1814.

KINGSMILL, Parr
Lieutenant. 88th (Connaught Rangers) Regiment of Foot.
Family Memorial tablet: St Mary's Church, Kilkenny, Ireland. (Photograph)

.... / PARR KINGSMILL BORN 1786 LIEUT. 88TH REG^T CONNAUGHT RANGERS, / WOUNDED IN THE PENINSULAR WAR, MAYOR OF KILKENNY 1835-6, / BURIED THERE 1840 LEAVING ISSUE IN ENGLAND AND A BRANCH IN / AUSTRALIA, DESCENDED FROM CHARLES KINGSMILL CANON OF GOULBURN N.S.W / ....

For full details of inscription see William Kingsmill, 66th Foot below

Ensign 14 Sep 1808. Lt 8 May 1811.
    Served in the Peninsula with 2/88th Jan – Dec 1810 and 1/88th Dec 1810 – Apr 1814. Present at Cadiz, Redinha, Casal Nova, Foz d'Arouce, Sabugal, Fuentes d'Onoro, second siege of Badajoz, El Bodon, Ciudad Rodrigo, Badajoz, Salamanca (wounded), Vittoria, Pyrenees, Nivelle, Nive, Orthes, Vic Bigorre and Toulouse. Retired on half pay 19 Apr 1817. Mayor of Kilkenny 1835–1836. Died 4 Mar 1840. Brother of Lt William Kingsmill 88th Foot.

KINGSMILL, William
Lieutenant. 66th (Berkshire) Regiment of Foot.
Family Memorial tablet: St Mary's Church, Kilkenny, Ireland. (Photograph)

TO THE MEMORY OF SOME MEMBERS OF THE KINGSMILL FAMILY BORN IN / KILKENNY WHOSE ANCESTORS' MONUMENTS STAND OUTSIDE ST MARY'S CHURCH / WILLIAM, BORN 1793 AN OFFICER OF THE 66TH REG^T, SERVED THROUGH THE PENINSULAR / WAR & AT ST HELENA GUARDING NAPOLEON. L^T. COLONEL CANADIAN MILITIA / FOR 21 YEARS SHERIFF OF NIAGARA AND BURIED THERE 1876. HIS GRANDSON / ADM^L. SIR CHARLES E. KINGSMILL R. N. FORMED AND COMMANDED THE / FIRST CANADIAN NAVAL FORCE IN WORLD-WAR 1; DIED 1935 AGED 80. / PARR KINGSMILL BORN 1786 LIEUT. 88TH REG^T CONNAUGHT RANGERS, / WOUNDED IN THE PENINSULAR WAR, MAYOR OF KILKENNY 1835–6, / BURIED THERE 1840 LEAVING ISSUE IN ENGLAND AND A BRANCH IN / AUSTRALIA, DESCENDED FROM CHARLES KINGSMILL CANON OF GOULBURN N.S.W / WILLIAM KINGSMILL BORN 1788 LIEUT 88TH REG^T. CONNAUGHT RANGERS, / CRIPPLED AT CIUDAD RODRIGO, LATER OF FRANKFORD, DIED 1854 BURIED AT BALLYBOY / KING'S CO. HIS SON WALTER, A PIONEER SETTLER S. AUSTRALIA HAD A YOUNGER SON / SIR WALTER KINGSMILL PRESIDENT OF THE COMMONWEALTH SENATE 1929–32 / THE EARLIER MONUMENTS WERE REPAIRED 1947-8 AND THIS TABLET ERECTED BY / MAJOR WALTER K. COOK KINGSMILL OF THE LATE INDIAN ARMY.

Memorial tablet: St Mark's Anglican Church, Niagara, Canada. (Photograph)

IN MEMORIAM, / LT COLONEL / WILLIAM KINGSMILL, / OF THE / INCORPORATED MILITIA, / OF CANADA. / FORMERLY CAPTAIN / H. M. 66TH REGIMENT OF FOOT, / AND / SHERIFF / OF THE / NIAGARA DISTRICT; / HE WAS THE SON OF / MAJOR KINGSMILL / OF H. M. 1ST ROYALS; / DIED IN TORONTO / 6TH MAY 1876. / AGED 82. / ....

Headstone: Relocated on wall of St Mark's Anglican Church, Niagara, Canada. (Photograph)

IN MEMORY OF / COLONEL WILLIAM KINGSMILL / SON OF THE LATE / MAJOR KINGSMILL H. M. 1ST ROYALS / DIED / IN TORONTO / 6TH MAY 1876 / AGED 82 / COL. KINGSMILL SERVED / IN H. M. 66TH REGT. / DURING THE PENINSULAR / WAR AND AFTERWARDS / AT ST HELENA DURING / NAPOLEON'S CAPTIVITY. / SUBSEQUENTLY COM – / MANDED 3RD INF. CORPS / BATT. OF UPPER CANADIAN / MILITIA AND WAS / FOR MANY YEARS / SHERIFF OF THE NIAGARA / DISTRICT / HE WAS A GALLANT SOLDIER / R.I.P.

Replacement Family Stone: St Mark's Anglican Churchyard, Niagara, Canada. (Photograph)

HERE LIES / CAPT. KINGSMILL / WHO DIED / 6TH MAY 1876 / AGED 82.

Ensign 23 Nov 1809. Lt 17 Sep 1812. Capt 21 Feb 1822.
    Served in the Peninsula Apr 1810 – Apr 1814. Present at Busaco, Arroyo dos Molinos and Nive. MGS medal for Busaco and Nive. Also served in St Helena during Napoleon's captivity. Afterwards went to Canada and became Lt Colonel of Militia and Sheriff of Niagara district.

KINGSMILL, William
Lieutenant. 88th (Connaught Rangers) Regiment of Foot.
Family Memorial tablet: St Mary's Church, Kilkenny, Ireland. (Photograph)

.... / WILLIAM KINGSMILL BORN 1788 LIEUT. 88TH REGT. CONNAUGHT RANGERS, / CRIPPLED AT CIUDAD RODRIGO, LATER OF FRANKFORD, DIED 1854 BURIED AT BALLYBOY / KING'S CO. HIS SON WALTER, A PIONEER SETTLER S AUSTRALIA HAD A YOUNGER SON / SIR WALTER KINGSMILL PRESIDENT OF THE COMMONWEALTH SENATE 1929–32. / ....

For full details of inscription for Kingsmill family see William Kingsmill 66th Foot above.

Ensign 15 Sep 1808. Lt 30 May 1811.
    Served in the Peninsula with 2/88th Jan – Dec 1810 and 1/88th Dec 1810 – May 1812. Present at Cadiz, Redinha, Casal Nova, Foz d'Arouce, Sabugal, Fuentes d'Onoro, second siege of Badajoz, El Bodon and Ciudad Rodrigo (severely wounded, lost a leg and awarded pension of £70 per annum). Retired on full pay in 10th Royal Veteran Battalion. MGS medal for Fuentes d'Onoro and Ciudad Rodrigo. Brother of Lt Parr Kingsmill 88th Foot.

KINLOCH, Charles
Captain. 52nd (Oxfordshire) Light Infantry Regiment of Foot.
Family Memorial: Clunie Churchyard, Perthshire, Scotland. (Photograph)

IN / MEMORY OF / CHARLES KINLOCH / OF GOURDIE / BORN 19TH OCTOBER 1788 / DIED 22 OCTOBER 1828 AGED 40 YEARS / ....

Ensign 52nd Foot 5 Jan 1806. Lt 12 Feb 1808. Capt 99th Foot 18 Mar 1813. Capt 52nd Foot 22 Jul 1813.
    Served in the Peninsula with 2/52nd Aug 1808 – Jan 1809, 1/52nd Sep 1810 – May 1812 and Dec 1813 – Apr 1814 (extra ADC to Lt General Sir John Hope). Present at Vimeiro, Vigo, Pombal, Redinha, Casal Nova, Foz d'Arouce, Sabugal, Fuentes d'Onoro, Ciudad Rodrigo, Badajoz (wounded), Nive, Adour and Bayonne. Present in France with the Army of Occupation 1815. Also served at Copenhagen 1807 and Walcheren 1809. Retired on half pay Jul 1816.
REFERENCE: Glover, Gareth ed., A hellish business: the letters of Captain Charles Kinloch, 52nd Foot 1806–1816, 2007.

KIRBY, James
Sergeant. 12th (Prince of Wales's) Regiment of Light Dragoons.
Named on the Regimental Memorial: St Joseph's Church, Waterloo, Belgium. (Photograph)
 Killed at Waterloo.

KIRK, George
Private. 45th (Nottinghamshire) Regiment of Foot.
Headstone: Nottingham Road Cemetery, Nottingham, Nottinghamshire. (Photograph)

.... / ALSO TO GEORGE KIRK, HER HUSBAND / WHO DIED OCTOBER 25TH 1868, / AGED 79 YEARS / HE WAS FOR A NUMBER OF YEARS IN THE 45TH / FOOT NOTTINGHAMSHIRE REGIMENT, AND WAS / ENGAGED IN ACTIVE SERVICE UNDER THE DUKE OF / WELLINGTON IN THE PENINSULAR WAR AT THE / FOLLOWING PLACES: TOULOUSE, ORTHES, NIVE, / NIVELLE PYRENEES, VITORIA, SALAMANCA AND / BADAJOZ. / ....

Served in the Peninsula 1812 – Apr 1814. Present at Badajoz (wounded), Salamanca, Vittoria, Pyrenees, Nivelle, Nive, Orthes, Vic Bigorre and Toulouse. MGS medal for Badajoz, Salamanca, Vittoria, Pyrenees, Nivelle, Nive, Orthes and Toulouse.

KIRKLAND, Joseph
Private. 3rd Regiment of Foot Guards.
Headstone: St Michael's Churchyard, Kirk Langley, Derbyshire. (Alongside boundary wall). (Photograph)

TO THE MEMORY OF / JOSEPH KIRKLAND, COLDSTREAM / GUARDS, PENINSULA VETERAN. / WHO DIED FEB 24TH 1853, AGED 80 YEARS. / MEDAL WITH SEVEN CLASPS / NIVE VITTORIA / SALAMANCA TALAVERA / CUIDAD–RODRIGO EGYPT / FUENTES D'ONORO / SOLDIER REST! THE WAR IS DONE. / THIS MONUMENT WAS PUT UP IN 1896 / BY G. F. MEYNELL

Pte 4 Sep 1795.
 Served in the Peninsula Mar 1809 – Apr 1814. Present at Talavera, Fuentes d'Onoro, Ciudad Rodrigo, Salamanca, Vittoria and Nive. Also served in Egypt 1801. MGS Medal for Egypt, Talavera, Fuentes d'Onoro, Ciudad Rodrigo, Salamanca, Vittoria and Nive. Discharged 6 Oct 1814 aged 39.
Note: Inscription incorrectly records him serving in the Coldstream Guards.

KLEJIN, P. R.
2nd Lieutenant, 5th National Militia Battalion, Dutch Infantry.
Named on the Memorial to Dutch officers killed at Quatre Bras: St Joseph's Church, Waterloo, Belgium. (Photograph)

KLENCK, Frederick von
Lieutenant. 1st Battalion Light Infantry, King's German Legion.
Named on the Memorial: St Andrew's Church, (now Musée Historique), Biarritz, France. (Photograph)

Ensign 1 Mar 1806. Lt 18 Jan 1811.
 Served in the Peninsula Aug 1808 – Jan 1809 and Mar 1811 – Oct 1813. Present at Vigo, Albuera, second siege of Badajoz, siege of Salamanca Forts, Moriscos, Salamanca, Venta del Poza, San Munos, Vittoria, Tolosa and Bidassoa where he was killed at the crossing of the Bidassoa Oct 1813. Also served in the Baltic 1807–1808 and Walcheren 1809. Named as Klanck on memorial.

KNATCHBULL, Wyndham
Ensign. 1st Regiment of Foot Guards.
Named on Memorial Panel VII: Royal Military Chapel, Wellington Barracks, London. (M.I.) (Destroyed by a Flying Bomb 1944)

Ensign 12 Sep 1811.

Served in the Peninsula with 3rd Battalion Apr – Oct 1813. Died aged 18 owing to ill health 14 Oct 1813 on the day the ship bringing him back to England arrived at Spithead. Buried in the Garrison Burying Ground at Portsmouth.
REFERENCE: *Gentleman's Magazine, Oct 1813, p. 406.*

KNEEBONE, Thomas
Volunteer 29th (Worcestershire) Regiment of Foot.
Headstone: New Burial Ground, Circular Road, Calcutta, India. (M.I.)

"SACRED TO THE MEMORY OF QUARTER MASTER THOMAS KNEEBONE OF H. M. 29TH REGT WHO DEPARTED THIS LIFE 4TH SEPTEMBER 1847 AGED 55 YEARS."

Volunteer from Royal Cornwall Militia 4 May 1812. Quartermaster 15 Jul 1824.

Served in the Peninsula. Also served in India in Sikh Wars (present at Sobraon 1846).

KNIGHT, Charles
Captain. 33rd (1st Yorkshire West Riding) Regiment of Foot.
Memorial tablet: St Thomas's Church, St Thomas's Island, Barbados, West Indies. (Photograph)

SACRED / TO THE MEMORY OF / LIEUTENANT COLONEL / CHARLES KNIGHT, / OF HER BRITANNIC MAJESTY'S / THIRTY THIRD REGIMENT: / WHO DEPARTED THIS LIFE / AT ST THOMAS, / ON HIS PASSAGE / FROM BARBADOS TO ENGLAND / ON THE 21. JULY 1841, / IN THE 51 YEAR OF HIS AGE. / LIEUTENANT COLONEL KNIGHT, / SERVED HIS COUNTRY WITH DISTINCTION IN THE FOUR / QUARTERS OF THE GLOBE, FOR THE PERIOD OF THIRTY / FIVE YEARS, AND WAS THE OFFICER IN COMMAND OF / THE THIRTY THIRD REGIMENT AT THE FINAL CLOSE OF / THE BATTLE OF / WATERLOO. / THE OFFICERS OF HIS REGIMENT HAVE CAUSED THIS TABLET TO BE / ERECTED AS A MEMORIAL OF THE ESTEEM AND REGARD FOR / THEIR LATE COMMANDING OFFICER AND FRIEND.

Ensign 4th Foot 14 Feb 1805. Lt 56th Foot 25 Jan 1807. Capt 30 Aug 1810. Capt 33rd Foot 26 Dec 1811. Bt Major 21 Jan 1819. Major 25 Nov 1821. Lt Colonel 10 Sep 1830.

Present at Quatre Bras and Waterloo where he was wounded. Also served at the Capture of Bourbon and Isle de France 1810, Netherlands 1814 (present at Antwerp and Merxem), Jamaica 1821–1822, 1825–1828 and 1831–1832, (on each occasion he returned home due to ill health but still returned to Jamaica), Gibraltar 1836–1840, and Jamaica 1841 (again had to return home owing to ill health). Died on the way home on 21 Jul 1841 and is buried on the island of St Thomas in Barbados.
REFERENCE: *United Service Journal, Oct 1841, p. 287. Gentleman's Magazine, Dec 1841, p. 668.*

KNIGHT, Edward
Captain. 63rd (West Suffolk) Regiment of Foot.
Memorial: Mount Jerome Cemetery, Dublin, Ireland. (Grave number C103–409). (Photograph)

TO THE MEMORY / OF / ANNA SOPHIE / WIFE OF / LIEU COL EDWARD KNIGHT / WHO DIED ON 31 MAY 1811 / AGED 17 YEARS / ALSO OF / EDWARD KNIGHT / HUSBAND OF THE ABOVE / DIED JULY 23RD 1847 / AGED 61 YEARS.

Cornet 15 Lt Dragoons 22 Dec 1804. Lt 18 Sep 1806. Capt 21 Jun 1810. Capt 63rd Foot 19 Sep 1811. Bt Major 4 Sep 1817. Bt Lt Colonel 10 Jan 1837. Portuguese Army: Major 12th Cavalry 23 May 1812. Major 11th Caçadores 1812.

Served in the Peninsula with 15th Lt Dragoons Nov 1808 – Jan 1809 and Portuguese Army May 1812 – Apr 1814. Present at Sahagun, Corunna, Vittoria, Pyrenees, Nivelle, Nive, Vic Bigorre and Toulouse. Commanded the 11th Caçadores at Vittoria (Awarded Gold Medal). Half pay 26 Dec 1816.

KNIGHT, William Home see ERSKINE, William Home Knight

KNIPE, Robert
Captain. 14th (Duchess of York's Own) Regiment of Light Dragoons.
Memorial tablet: Westminster Abbey, London. (South wall of south choir aisle). (Photograph)

IN MEMORY / OF TWO BROTHERS / WHO BOTH DIED IN THE SERVICE OF THEIR COUNTRY. / CAPTN JOHN KNIPE, 90TH REGT / AT GIBRALTAR: / OCTOBER 25TH 1798, IN THE 22ND YEAR OF HIS AGE. / CAPTN ROBERT KNIPE, 4TH LT DRAGOONS / AT VILLA FORMOSA, / MAY 17TH 1811, AGED 32. / TO THE FORMER AS A SMALL TRIBUTE TO HIS HIGH MILITARY / CHARACTER, AND MANY AMIABLE VIRTUES, HIS BROTHER / OFFICERS HAVE LONG SINCE AT THAT GARRISON, ERECTED / A MONUMENT AT THEIR PRIVATE / EXPENSE. / THE LATTER HAVING SIGNALLY DISTINGUISHED HIMSELF / AND SEVERELY SUFFERED IN MANY PRECEDING ACTIONS, WAS / MORTALLY WOUNDED AT THE BATTLE OF FUENTES DE MORA / IN PORTUGAL, ON THE 5TH OF MAY, AND TO THE DEEP REGRET / OF HIS BROTHER SOLDIERS, HIS FAMILY, AND MANY FRIENDS / EXPIRED ON THE 17TH FOLLOWING.

Cornet 26 Jul 1803. Lt 5 Jan 1805. Capt 28 Dec 1809.

Served in the Peninsula Jan 1809 – May 1811. Present at Douro (wounded), Talavera, Sexmiro, Coa, Busaco, Sobral, Pombal, Redinha, Casal Nova, Foz d'Arouce, Sabugal, Fuentes d'Onoro (severely wounded 5 May and died of his wounds 17 May 1811). Robert Knipe is buried in the same grave as Colonel Phillips Cameron of the 79th Foot, also killed at Fuentes d'Onoro. His elder brother who died at Gibraltar in 1798 is also commemorated on the tablet.

KNOLLYS, William Thomas
Ensign. 3rd Regiment of Foot Guards.
Grave: Highgate Cemetery, London. (Section East X). (Photograph)

GENERAL / THE RIGHT HONOURABLE / SIR WILLIAM KNOLLYS KC / COLONEL OF THE SCOTS GUARDS / 23RD JUNE 1883.

Ensign 9 Dec 1813. Lt and Capt 25 Sep 1817. Adjutant 1st Battalion 6 Sep 1821. Capt and Lt Colonel 31 Dec 1827. Bt Colonel 23 Nov 1841. Major 6 Dec 1844. Lt Colonel 28 Jun 1850. Major General 20 Jun 1854. Lt General 11 Jan 1860. General 17 Jun 1876.

Served in the Peninsula Mar – Apr 1814. Present at Bidassoa, Adour, Bayonne and Sortie from Bayonne where he commanded a picket. Present at the Capture of Paris and with Army of Occupation. Governor of Guernsey 1854–1855. Appointed Head of a commission in 1855 to investigate the system of internal administration in the French Army, especially the Commissariat and Transport departments which had been more efficient in the Crimea than the British. Took command of the newly created camp at Aldershot 1855–1860. When he left it was efficiently organised. Treasurer and Comptroller of Prince of Wales's household 1862–1877. This proved a difficult position as Queen Victoria held Knollys responsible for any of the Prince's misdemeanours. KCB 1867. Colonel Scots Guards 26 May 1883. Translated from the French *Journal of the Russian campaign of 1812*, by Duc de Fezensac, London, 1852 and also translated a *Selection of Odes of Horace*. Died 23 Jun 1883 and was carried to his grave in Highgate by the Sergeants of his Regiment.

REFERENCE: *Dictionary of National Biography. Annual Register, 1883, Appx, pp. 154–5.*

KNOWLES, Robert
Lieutenant. 7th (Royal Fusiliers) Regiment of Foot.
Memorial tablet: St Peter's Church, Bolton, Lancashire. (Photograph)

TO THE MEMORY OF / LIEUTENANT ROBERT KNOWLES, A NATIVE OF THIS / PARISH, WHO VOLUNTEERED MAY 6TH 1811, FROM THE 1ST / ROYAL LANCASHIRE MILITIA INTO THE 7TH REGIMENT OF / FUSILEERS, THEN UNITED WITH THE BRITISH ARMY IN THE / EXPULSION OF THE FRENCH FROM SPAIN. HE DISTINGUISHED / HIMSELF AT THE TAKING OF CIUDAD RODRIGO & AT / BADAJOS WHERE HE COMMANDED PART OF A DETACHMENT. / APPOINTED TO STORM FORT ST ROQUE – SUCH WAS HIS / INTREPIDITY, THAT HAVING FIRST MOUNTED THE WALL & / SUCCEEDED IN HIS ENTERPRISE HE OPENED THE GATES / TO THE REMAINDER OF THE DETACHMENT AND RECEIVED THE / COMMAND OF THE FORT – HE BEHAVED WITH MUCH COURAGE AT / SALAMANCA & VITTORIA AT THE FORMER OF WHICH PLACES / HE WAS SEVERELY WOUNDED – THIS BRAVE YOUNG MAN / FELL IN THE HARD CONTESTED ACTION AT THE PASS OF / RONCESVALLES IN THE PYRE-NEES JULY 25TH 1813 IN THE / 24TH YEAR OF HIS AGE. / THIS MONUMENT IS ERECTED AS A JUST TRIBUTE TO SO / MUCH HEROISM AND WORTH BY HIS FELLOW TOWNSMEN. / A.D. 1816.

Memorial tablet: Union Jack Club, Waterloo Road, London. (M.I.)

"TO THE ROYAL FUSILIERS IN MEMORY OF LT ROBERT KNOWLES WHO FELL AT RONCES-VALLES JULY 25 1813. DEDICATED BY HIS RELATIVE SIR LEES KNOWLES BART, CVO, JULY 25TH 1913."

Ensign Lancashire Militia. Lt 7th Foot 8 May 1811.
    Served in the Peninsula with 1/7th Sep 1811 – Jul 1813. Present at Aldea da Ponte, Badajoz (wounded), Castrejon, Salamanca (severely wounded), Vittoria and Pyrenees where he was killed at Roncesvalles 25 Jul 1813.
REFERENCE: *Knowles, Robert, The war in the Peninsula: some letters of Lieut Robert Knowles of the 7th or Royal Fusiliers, a Lancashire officer, arranged and annotated by his great-great-nephew Sir Lees Knowles, 1913, reprint 2004.*

KNOX, Edward
Captain. 31st (Huntingdonshire) Regiment of Foot.
Memorial tablet: Holy Trinity Church, Cheltenham, Gloucestershire. (Photograph)

IN MEMORY OF / LIEUT COLONEL EDWARD KNOX / WHOSE REMAINS ARE DEPOSITED / IN THE VAULTS OF THIS CHURCH / BORN, NOVBR 2D 1786. / DIED MARCH 3D 1849.

Ensign 26 Oct 1804. Lt 14 Mar 1805. Capt 5 Nov 1807. Bt Major 21 Jun 1817. Bt Lt Colonel 10 Jan 1837.
    Served in the Peninsula Nov 1808 – Mar 1814. Present at Talavera, Busaco, first siege of Badajoz, Albuera (wounded), Vittoria, Pyrenees, Nivelle, Nive and Garris (severely wounded 15 Feb 1814, lost an arm and awarded pension of £200 per annum). MGS medal for Talavera, Busaco, Albuera, Vittoria, Pyrenees, Nivelle and Nive. Retired on half pay 10 Apr 1823.

KNOX, Francis
Captain. Royal Artillery.
Celtic Cross: Greyfriars Churchyard, (Division 8), Edinburgh, Scotland. (Photograph)

SACRED / TO THE MEMORY OF / MAJOR / FRANCIS A. S. KNOX, / ROYAL ARTILLERY. / DIED 22 DEC^R 1832 / AGED 51 YEARS. / ………………..

2nd Lt 20 Dec 1798. 1st Lt 3 Dec 1800. 2nd Capt 1 Jun 1806. Capt 4 Oct 1814. Bt Major 12 Aug 1819.
 Served in the Peninsula Oct 1808 – Feb 1809 in Capt Holcombe's Company. Present in the Corunna campaign. Also served at the Helder 1799. Retired on half pay 1 Feb 1819.

KNOX, George
Lieutenant. 57th (West Middlesex) Regiment of Foot.
Named on the Memorial: St Andrew's Church, (now Musée Historique), Biarritz, France. (Photograph)

Ensign 18 Oct 1806. Lt 13 Feb 1808.
 Served in the Peninsula Aug 1811 – Nov 1813. Present at Vittoria, Pyrenees and Nivelle where he was killed 10 Nov 1813.

KNOX, Hon. John James
Captain. 85th (Buckinghamshire Volunteers) Light Infantry Regiment of Foot.
Headstone with Ringed Cross: Brighton Extra Mural Cemetery, Brighton, Sussex. (Photograph)

THE HON / JAMES KNOX / 9 JULY 1856 / AGED 66 YEARS

Ensign 52nd Foot 17 Aug 1808. Lt 19th Foot 16 Mar 1809. Lt 52nd Foot 15 May 1809. Capt 40th Foot 8 Oct 1812. Capt 85th Foot 25 Jan 1813. Major 27 May 1817. Bt Lt Colonel 24 Jun 1819.
 Served in the Peninsula with 2/52nd Aug 1808 – Jan 1809 and Mar 1811 – Mar 1812 and 85th Foot Aug 1813 – Apr 1814. Present at Vimeiro, Vigo, Sabugal, Fuentes d'Onoro, Ciudad Rodrigo, San Sebastian, Nivelle, Nive and Bayonne. Also served at Walcheren 1809 and North America 1814 (present at New Orleans where he was wounded). Retired 24 Aug 1832. MGS medal for Vimeiro, Fuentes d'Onoro, Ciudad Rodrigo, San Sebastian, Nivelle and Nive.

KÖHLER, Charles
Lieutenant. 5th Line Battalion, King's German Legion.
Named on the Memorial: St Andrew's Church, (now Musée Historique), Biarritz, France. (Photograph)

Ensign 15 Feb 1809. Lt 21 Sep 1810.
 Served in the Peninsula Apr 1809 – Apr 1814. Present at Douro, Talavera (severely wounded), Busaco, Fuentes d'Onoro, Ciudad Rodrigo, Moriscos, Salamanca, Burgos, Vittoria, Tolosa, San Sebastian, Bidassoa, Nivelle, Nive, St Etienne and Bayonne where he was killed at the Sortie from Bayonne 14 Apr 1814. Also served in Hanover 1805 and the Baltic 1807–1808.

KOSCHENBAR, Ernst von
Lieutenant. Duke of Brunswick's Oels' Corps.
Named on the Memorial: St Andrew's Church, (now Musée Historique), Biarritz, France. (Photograph)

Lt 25 Sep 1809.
 Served in the Peninsula Sep 1810 – Feb 1814 (attached to 5th Division Dec 1810 – Dec 1812). Present at Badajoz, Salamanca, Vittoria, Pyrenees (severely wounded 2 Aug 1813), Nivelle, Nive and Orthes where he was killed Feb 1814.

KREIJSIG, C. S.
Captain. 4th Dragoons, Dutch Cavalry.
Named on the Memorial to Dutch officers killed at Waterloo: St Joseph's Church, Waterloo, Belgium. (Photograph)

KUHLMANN, Otto
Lieutenant. 1st Regiment of Dragoons, King's German Legion.
Named on the Regimental Memorial: La Haye Sainte, Waterloo, Belgium. (Photograph)

Cornet 11 Apr 1812. Lt 15 Jun 1813.
   Served in the Peninsula Apr 1814. Present at Waterloo where he was killed. Also served in the Netherlands 1814–1815.

KYNOCK, John
Lieutenant and Adjutant. 79th (Cameron Highlanders) Regiment of Foot.
Named on the Regimental Memorial: St Joseph's Church, Waterloo, Belgium. (Photograph)
Grave: Dean Cemetery, Edinburgh, Scotland. (Section E Grave number 404). (M.I.)

"MARGARET LOGAN DIED 26 MARCH 1858. SISTER CHRISTIAN DIED 23 MAY 1868. HUSBAND LT AND ADJT KYNOCK. HM 79TH HIGHLANDERS".

Ensign 15 Nov 1810. Lt 13 Jun 1813. Adjt 19 May 1814.
   Served in the Peninsula Apr 1813 - Apr 1814. Present at Pyrenees (severely wounded) and Toulouse (Severely wounded). Present at Quatre Bras where he was killed 16 Jun 1815.

LACY, Richard John James
Major. Royal Artillery.
Family Memorial: Old Common Cemetery, Southampton, Hampshire. (HO55 030). (Photograph)

.... / ALSO OF / MAJOR GENL R. J. J. LACY, / DIRECTOR GENERAL OF ARTILLERY, / DIED AT WOOLWICH ARSENAL, / MARCH 9 1852 AGED 72 / AND WAS BURIED AT ST THOMAS. / ....

2nd Lt 8 Aug 1796. 1st Lt 17 Mar 1798. 2nd Capt 20 Jul 1804. Capt 24 Mar 1809. Major 4 Jun 1814. Lt Colonel 31 Dec 1827. Colonel 23 Jun 1837. Major General 9 Nov 1846.
   Served in the Peninsula Jul 1812 – Apr 1814. Present at Castalla (Mentioned in Despatches), Tarragona and Bayonne. Also served at the Helder 1799, Sicily 1811–1812, Gibraltar 1821–1822, Ionian Islands 1822–1827, West Indies 1832–1836, Spain 1837–1841 (Commissioner with the Army of the Allies in Valencia and Aragon). Inspector Royal Carriage Department Woolwich 1841. Colonel Commandant 30 Jun 1851. Buried at St Thomas's Church, Woolwich.
REFERENCE: *Gentleman's Magazine, Apr 1852, p. 430. Annual Register, 1852, Appx, p. 265.*

LAIDLEY, James
Deputy Assistant Commissary General. Commissariat Department.
Memorial tablet: St James's Church, Sydney, New South Wales, Australia. (Photograph)

SACRED / TO THE MEMORY OF / JAMES LAIDLEY ESQUIRE, / DEPUTY COMMISSARY GENERAL, / WHO DEPARTED THIS LIFE AT SYDNEY, / ON THE 30TH AUGUST 1835 / AGED 49 YEARS. / THIS TABLET IS ERECTED BY THE COMMISSARIAT / DEPARTMENT SERVING IN NEW SOUTH WALES / AS A TOKEN OF THEIR ESTEEM AND REGARD.

Dep Asst Comm Gen 5 Oct 1810.

Served in the Peninsula Oct 1810 – Apr 1814 (attached to 1st Division Aug 1810 – Sep 1811, Light Division May 1812 – Oct 1812 and 2nd Division May 1813 – Apr 1814). Also served in the West Indies 1814, Canada, Mauritius 1825 (Dep Comm Gen) and New South Wales 1827 (Dep Comm Gen where he remained until his death in 1835).
REFERENCE: *Australian Dictionary of Biography.*

LAIDLEY, John
Deputy Assistant Commissary General. Commissariat Department.
Headstone: St George's Cemetery, Lisbon, Portugal. (Grave number B2 25). (Photograph)

……………….. / ALSO OF / JOHN LAIDLEY / COMMISSARY GENERAL IN THE BRITISH ARMY / WHO DEPARTED THIS LIFE, DECEMBER 3RD 1874 / AGED 85 YEARS.

Dep Asst Comm Gen 11 Jan 1812. Dep Comm Gen 20 Jan 1837. Comm Gen 2 Jan 1856.

Served in the Peninsula Jan 1811 – Apr 1814 (attached to the Royal Waggon Train). Present at Fuentes d'Onoro, Ciudad Rodrigo and San Sebastian. MGS medal for Fuentes d'Onoro, Ciudad Rodrigo and San Sebastian.

LAING, Thomas
Major. 94th Regiment of Foot.
Memorial tablet in walled enclosure: East Preston Street Burial Ground, Edinburgh, Scotland. Seriously eroded. (Photograph)

SACRED / TO THE MEMORY / OF / MAJOR THOMAS LAING, / WHO AFTER SERVING MEMO-RABLY FOR 20 YEARS / IN HIS MAJESTY'S 94TH REGT OR SCOTCH BRIGADE, / DURING THE CAMPAIGNS, IN INDIA, AND / THE PENINSULA, WHERE HE DISTINGUISHED HIM- / SELF AT THE CAPTURE OF CIUDAD RODRIGO, / AND COMMANDED THE REGT AT THE BATTLES / OF NIVE, AND ORTHES. RETIRED FROM / THE SERVICE IN 1815 AND DIED ON THE 19TH DECR / 1826. REGRETTED BY ALL WHO KNEW HIM. / A LOVING HUSBAND, A TENDER PARENT, / A TRUE FRIEND, A BRAVE SOLDIER. / AN HONEST MAN.

Ensign 3 Jun 1795. Lt 10 Feb 1796. Capt 24 Dec 1804. Major 6 Jan 1814.

Served in the Peninsula Feb 1810 – Mar 1812 and Nov 1813 – Apr 1814. Present at Cadiz, Redinha, Casal Nova, Foz d'Arouce, Sabugal, Fuentes d'Onoro, second siege of Badajoz, El Bodon, Ciudad Rodrigo (severely wounded), Nivelle (in command of 94th Foot), Nive, Orthes (in command of 94th Foot), Vic Bigorre and Toulouse. Gold Medal for Nivelle and Orthes. Also served in India 1799 (present in the Mysore campaign, Malavelly and Seringapatam). Retired 16 Feb 1815.

LAKE, Charles
Ensign. 3rd Regiment of Foot Guards.
Memorial window: Durham Cathedral, County Durham. (M.I.)

IN LOVING MEMORY OF CHARLES LAKE, CAPTAIN IN THE SCOTS FUSILIER GUARDS. THIS WINDOW IS DEDICATED BY HIS SON WILLIAM CHARLES LAKE DEAN OF DURHAM, 1875.

Ensign 31 Oct 1811. Lt and Capt 2 Jul 1815.

Present at Waterloo where he was severely wounded in the head in the defence of Hougoumont in Lt Colonel Sir Alexander Gordon's Company. Also served in the Netherlands 1814–1815 (present at Merxem, Antwerp and Bergen-op-Zoom). Barrack Master at Weedon 1852.

LAKE, Hon. George Augustus Frederick
Lieutenant Colonel. 29th (Worcestershire) Regiment of Foot.
Cross on pedestal in railed enclosure: Columberia Heights, Rolica, Portugal. (Photograph)

SACRED / TO THE MEMORY OF THE HON / LIEUT COL G.A.F. LAKE OF THE / 29 REG WHO
FELL AT THE HEAD / OF THE CORPS IN DRIVING THE / ENEMY FROM THE HEIGHTS OF /
COLUMBERIA ON 17 AUG 1808 / THIS MONUMENT ERECTED BY HIS / BROTHER OFFICERS,
AS A TESTIMONY / OF HIGH REGARD AND ESTEEM

On the reverse is the inscription:

RESTORED BY THE / OFFICERS OF THE 29 FIRST BATT / WORCESTER REG / IN 1903

Side elevation:

RESTAURADO / ELOS OFFICIES / REG 29 / BAT. WORCESTERESEXXE / EM 1903

Restored again in 2008 by the Worcestershire Regiment.

Memorial tablet: Westminster Abbey, London. (North West Tower). (Photograph)

SACRED TO THE MEMORY / OF THE HON^BLE GEORGE AUGUSTUS FREDERICK LAKE / LATE
LIEU^T. COLONEL IN HIS MAJESTY'S 29TH REGIMENT OF FOOT / WHO FELL AT THE HEAD OF
HIS GRENADIERS IN DRIVING THE ENEMY / FROM THE HEIGHTS OF ROLEIA IN PORTUGAL
/ ON THE 17TH AUGUST 1808. / THIS STONE IS ERECTED TO HIS MEMORY BY THE OFFICERS
/ NON COMMISSIONED OFFICERS DRUMMERS / AND PRIVATES OF THE CORPS AS A TESTI-
MONY / OF THEIR HIGH REGARD AND ESTEEM. / AD 1816.

Cornet 8th Lt Dragoons 20 Aug 1796. Capt 4th Foot 5 Sep 1799. Bt Lt Colonel 12 Nov 1803. Lt Colonel
29th Foot 5 Nov 1804.
   Served in the Peninsula Jul – Aug 1808. Present at Rolica where he was killed 17 Aug 1808. Gold Medal
for Rolica. Also served in the Irish Rebellion 1798 (ADC to his father General Lake. Present at Castlebar,
Vinegar Hill and Ballynahinch), India 1801 (AAG to King's Forces and Military Secretary to Commander
in Chief India), the Mahratta War (present at Laswaree Nov 1803 where he was severely wounded).
DQMG to King's Troops in India 1804. Returned to England 1807.

LALLY, Edward
Captain. 4th (Royal Irish) Dragoon Guards.
Obelisk: Kensal Green Cemetery, London. Inscription illegible. (10945/49/RS). (Photograph)

Cornet Jan 1806. Lt Sep 1807. Capt 16 Feb 1809.
   Served in the Peninsula May – Aug 1812. Resigned 1812. Buried in Kensal Green 1 Aug 1853.

LAMB, John
Ensign. 5th Royal Veteran Battalion.
Buried in St George's Chapel, Windsor, Berkshire. (Burial record)

Ensign 5 Jan 1805.
   Served in the Peninsula 1808 – Dec 1809. Present at Rolica, Vimeiro and Talavera. Left behind sick in
Vimeiro so did not go to Corunna. Joined the provisional detachments and fought at Talavera. MGS medal
for Rolica, Vimeiro and Talavera. Military Knight of Windsor 28 Apr 1841. Died at Windsor 13 Aug 1853.

LAMBE, Peter K.
Assistant Surgeon. 59th (2nd Nottinghamshire) Regiment of Foot.
Named on the Regimental Memorial monument: Christ Church Churchyard, Tramore, County Waterford, Ireland. (Photograph)

Hospital Mate General Service 1 Feb 1810. Asst Surgeon 59th Foot 8 Feb 1810.
    Served at Waterloo with 2/59th in reserve at Hal, siege of Cambrai and Capture of Paris. Drowned when the *Sea Horse* transport was wrecked in a storm in Tramore Bay, 30 Jan 1816.

LAMBERT, Sir John
Captain and Lieutenant Colonel. 1st Regiment of Foot Guards.
Chest tomb: Holy Trinity Churchyard, Claygate, Surrey. (North side of church). (Photograph)

SACRED / TO THE MEMORY OF / SIR JOHN LAMBERT GCB / GENERAL IN THE ARMY / DIED SEPT^R 14TH 1847 / AGED 75 YEARS.

Ensign 27 Jan 1791. Lt and Capt 9 Oct 1793. Adjutant 14 May 1794. Capt and Lt Colonel 14 May 1801. Bt Colonel 25 Jul 1810. Major General 1 Jun 1813. Lt General 27 May 1825. General 23 Nov 1841.
    Served in the Peninsula with 1st Battalion Oct 1808 – Jan 1809 and 3rd Battalion Jul 1811 – Apr 1814 (Commanded Brigade Eastern Spain Oct 1811 – Apr 1812, Commanded a Brigade Cadiz May – Jun 1812 and Commanded 2 Brigade 6th Divison Jun 1813 – Apr 1814). Present at Corunna, Cadiz, Carthagena, Seville, Nivelle (Mentioned in Despatches), Nive, Orthes, Tarbes and Toulouse. Gold Cross for Nivelle, Nive, Orthes and Toulouse.
    Present at Waterloo (Commanded 10th British Brigade. Also acting GOC 6th Division Commander as Sir Lowry Cole was on his honeymoon). He marched his brigade from Ostend to Waterloo and arrived in time for the battle. He had a strong brigade comprised of the first battalions of 4th, 27th, 40th and 81st Foot. At first in reserve in the afternoon, they were called forward and lost many casualties from cannon fire. The first battalion 27th Foot remained in the same spot and had 66% casualties.
    Also served in Flanders 1793–1795 (present at Valenciennes, Lincelles and Dunkirk), Irish Rebellion 1798, the Helder 1799, Walcheren 1809, North America 1814–1815 (present at New Orleans, where he was sent out with reinforcements to help Pakenham and Gibbs who were both killed. Lambert took control of the English forces after the defeat at New Orleans and retreated successfully to Fort Bowyer which he had already taken). GCB. Knight 3rd Class of St Wladimir of Russia. Commander of Order of Maximilian Joseph of Bavaria. Colonel 10th Regiment 18 Jan 1824. Educated at Winchester. Brother of Capt and Lt Colonel Samuel Lambert 1st Foot Guards.
REFERENCE: *Royal Military Calendar, Vol 3, p. 307. Gentleman's Magazine, Nov 1847, p. 539. Annual Register, 1847, Appx, p. 251.*

LAMBERT, Samuel
Captain and Lieutenant Colonel. 1st Regiment of Foot Guards.
Box tomb: St Andrew's Churchyard, Kingston, Jamaica, West Indies. (Photograph)

TO THE MEMORY OF / MAJOR GENERAL SAMUEL LAMBERT / DIED 4TH JANUARY 1848 / AGED 62 YEARS / WHILE IN COMMAND OF H. M. FORCES / IN THIS ISLAND

Ensign 5 Nov 1803. Lt and Capt 27 Aug 1807. Adjt 21 Feb 1811. Capt and Lt Col 16 Mar 1814. Major with rank of Colonel 22 Jul 1830. Bt Lt Colonel 23 Jun 1838. Major General Mar 23 Nov 1841.
    Served in the Peninsula Oct 1808 – Jan 1814. (with 2nd Battalion Jan – May 1811 and 1st Battalion Sep 1812 – Mar 1814). Present at Corunna, Cadiz, Barrosa, Bidassoa, Nivelle, Nive, Adour and Bayonne.

Brigade Major 1ˢᵗ Brigade of Guards from Mar 1814. Also served at Walcheren 1809 and West Indies (commanded the forces in Jamaica). Brother of Capt and Lt Colonel John Lambert 1ˢᵗ Foot Guards.
REFERENCE: *Gentleman's Magazine, May 1848, pp. 546–7. Annual Register, 1848, Appx, p. 201.*

LAMBOURNE, James

Private. 14ᵗʰ (Buckinghamshire) Regiment of Foot.
Obelisk: Nunhead Cemetery, London. Inscription illegible. (Grave number 16888). (M.I.)

Served at Waterloo where he was wounded in Capt John Maxwell's Company. Later resident in St Saviour's workhouse, Southwark. Buried in Nunhead Cemetery 12 Dec 1885 aged 90, above the body of his old friend Peter Sandell (another Waterloo veteran) who was buried 22 Jul 1882, aged 97 years. The obelisk was found toppled over in a survey by the Friends of Nunhead Cemetery in 1996. Inscription illegible, but words 'Peter Sendells, (sic) Waterloo Veteran' and a reference to the interest of Queen Victoria who was one of the contributors to the public appeal for the erection of a memorial.
REFERENCE: *Lagden, Alan and John Sly, The 2/73ʳᵈ at Waterloo, 2ⁿᵈ ed. 1998, pp. 201–3.*

LAMONT, Daniel

Private. 71ˢᵗ (Highland Light Infantry) Regiment of Foot.
Headstone: Kirkyard of Kirkton, near Fort George, Invernesshire, Scotland. (Photograph)

IN MEMORY OF / DANIEL LAMONT LATE PIPER 71ˢᵀ / HIGHᴰ Lᵀ INF ʸ WHO DIED ON THE 12ᵀᴴ / JUNE 1833 AGED 44. HE SERVED IN / THAT CORPS 27 YEARS, WAS FIELD BUGLER / TO LIEUᵀ. COLᴸ THE HONᴮᴸᴱ H. CADOGAN / AT VITTORIA, WHEN THAT GALLANT / OFFICER FELL, AT THE HEAD OF HIS REGᵀ. / HE WAS PRESENT AT THE FOLLOWING BATTLES / ROLEIA VITTORIA / VIMIERA PYRENEES / SOBRAL BAYONNE / CORUNNA AYRE / WALCHEREN NIVE / ALMAREZ NIVELLE / FUENTES D'ONORO ORTHES / ARROYA DE MOLENIS TOULOUSE / WATERLOO. / ERECTED BY HIS COMRADES AS A / MARK OF ESTEEM.

Enlisted 1806 aged 17, and served as a piper for 27 years. Present at Rolica, Vimeiro, Corunna, Almarez, Fuentes d'Onoro, Arroyo dos Molinos, Vittoria, Pyrenees, Nivelle, Nive, Orthes, Aire and Toulouse. At Vittoria he was field bugler for Lt. Col. Cadogan. Present at Waterloo. Remained in the regiment and died while in a recruiting party at Fort George. Buried with full military honours.

LAMOTTE, James

Captain. 1ˢᵗ (Royal) Regiment of Dragoons.
Memorial tablet: Canterbury Cathedral, Kent. (South wall of Chapter House). (Photograph)

NEAR / THIS SPOT / ARE / INTERRED / THE REMAINS OF / CAPTᴺ JAMES LAMOTTE, / OF THE 1ˢᵀ OR ROYAL / REGIMENT OF DRAGOONS, / WHO DIED / ON THE 11ᵀᴴ OF JANUARY 1812 / IN THE 32ᴺᴰ YEAR OF HIS AGE, OF / A DISORDER BROUGHT ON BY FATIGUE / WHILE SERVING WITH THE BRITISH ARMY / UNDER LORD WELLINGTON IN SPAIN AND PORTUGAL. / TO THIS YOUNG OFFICER, / NO LESS DISTINGUISHED FOR / ACTION AND INTELLIGENT ZEAL, IN THE DISCHARGE / OF HIS PROFESSIONAL DUTIES, / THAN FOR EXEMPLARY CONDUCT / AND AMIABLE MANNERS IN ALL THE RELATIONS / OF DOMESTIC LIFE. / HIS AFFLICTED WIDOW / RAISES THIS MELANCHOLY TRIBUTE OF HER AFFECTION / AND AFFORDS THIS SINCERE TESTIMONY OF / HIS WORTH.

Cornet 14 Jul 1798. Lt 10 May 1800. Capt 21 Apr 1804.
    Served in the Peninsula Sep 1809 – Oct 1810.

LANCEY, Thomas Furber
Lieutenant. Royal Engineers.
Named on the Regimental Memorial: Rochester Cathedral, Rochester, Kent. (Photograph)

2nd Lt 14 Dec 1811. Lt 1 Jul 1812. 2nd Capt 10 Apr 1825. Capt 11 Jun 1836.
 Served in the Netherlands and in France with the Army of Occupation 1815–1818. Retired on full pay 28 Mar 1837. Died at Harwich 23 May 1843.

LANDMANN, George
Lieutenant Colonel. Royal Engineers.
Mural Memorial tablet: Highgate Cemetery, London. (No 6017 Plot L1. Terrace Catacomb, Arch 40.) (Photograph)

SACRED / TO THE MEMORY OF / LIEUT COL^L GEORGE LANDMANN, / LATE OF THE / CORPS OF ROYAL ENGINEERS, / WHO DEPARTED THIS LIFE AUGUST 27TH 1854. / AGED 74 YEARS. / ……………..

2nd Lt 1 May 1795. 1st Lt 3 Jun 1797. Capt-Lieut 13 Jul 1802. 2nd Capt 19 Jul 1804. Capt 1 Jul 1806. Lt Colonel (Spanish Corps of Engineers) 22 Feb 1809. Colonel of Infantry in Spanish Army 25 Mar 1810. Bt Major 4 Jun 1813. Lt Colonel Royal Engineers 16 May 1814.
 Served in the Peninsula Aug 1808 – Mar 1812. Present at Obidos, Rolica, Vimeiro (in command of the Royal Engineers at Rolica and Vimeiro), Cadiz (present at siege of Matagorda) and Barrosa. Gold Medal for Vimeiro. MGS medal for Rolica and Barrosa. Also served in Canada 1797–1802 (responsible for several engineering feats including the Fort on Lake Huron and the canal between the Cascades and St Lawrence river), Gibraltar 1805–1808 and Ireland 1813–1815.
REFERENCE: *Dictionary of National Biography. Royal Military Calendar, Vol 5, pp. 26–9. Landmann, George T., Adventures and recollections of Colonel Landmann, 2 volumes, 1854, reprint 2005. Gentleman's Magazine, Apr 1855, pp. 422–3. Annual Register, 1855, Appx, pp. 422–3.*

LANE, Daniel
Sergeant. 51st (2nd Yorkshire West Riding) Light Infantry.
Named on the Regimental Memorial: KOYLI Chapel, York Minster, Yorkshire. (Photograph)
 Killed in the Peninsula.

LANG, Francis
Private. 12th (Prince of Wales's) Regiment of Light Dragoons.
Named on the Regimental Memorial: St Joseph's Church, Waterloo, Belgium. (Photograph)
 Killed at Waterloo.

LANG, John Sibbald
Ensign. 94th Regiment of Foot.
Family Mural memorial: Kirk of the Forest Churchyard, Selkirk, Selkirkshire, Scotland. (In walled enclosure). (Photograph)

JOHN SIBBALD / SECOND SON OF JOHN LANG / SHERIFF CLERK OF SELKIRKSHIRE / AND OF JOAN SIBBALD HIS WIFE / ENSIGN 94TH REGIMENT OF FOOT / BORN NOV^{BR} 7 1787 KILLED WHILE / TAKING PART IN THE FINAL STORMING / ASSAULT OF BADAJOS APRIL 6 1812 / DULCE ET DECORUM EST / PRO PATRIA MORI

Ensign 9 Nov 1809.

Served in the Peninsula Feb 1810 – Apr 1812. Present at Cadiz, El Bodon, Ciudad Rodrigo, and Badajoz where he was killed in a storming party.

LANGLANDS, George
Major. 13th Royal Veteran Battalion.
Interred in Catacomb B (v201 c9) Kensal Green Cemetery, London.

Ensign 86th Foot 2 Feb 1796. Lt 19 Dec 1802. Capt 74th Foot 28 Sep 1803. Bt Major 27 Apr 1812. Major 13th Royal Veteran Battalion 25 Jan 1813.
    Served in the Peninsula Feb 1810 – Oct 1812. Present at Busaco, second siege of Badajoz, El Bodon, Ciudad Rodrigo (wounded) and Badajoz (severely wounded and awarded pension of £200 per annum). Gold Medal for Ciudad Rodrigo and Badajoz. Also served in India 1803–1806 (present at Assaye, Gawilghur and Argaum where he was wounded). Army of India medal for Assaye, Argaum and Gawilghur. MGS medal for Busaco. Died 22 Aug 1851.

LANGLEY, Frederick
Captain. 82nd (Prince of Wales's Volunteers) Regiment of Foot.
Ledger stone: Kensal Green Cemetery, London. Inscription illegible. (4836/43/3). Photograph)

Lt 74th Foot 24 May 1806. Capt 11 Mar 1808. Capt 82nd Foot 1 Nov 1809.
    Served in the Peninsula Dec 1812 – Apr 1814. Present at Vittoria, Pyrenees, San Marcial, Nivelle and Orthes. Buried in Kensal Green 1847.

LANGTON, Edward Gore
Captain. 52nd (Oxfordshire) Light Infantry Regiment of Foot.
Obelisk: Holy Trinity Churchyard, Newton St Loe, Somerset. (Photograph)

SACRED / TO THE MEMORY OF / EDWARD / GORE LANGTON / SECOND SON OF THE LATE / COLONEL WILLIAM / GORE LANGTON / OF NEWTON PARK / AND OF BRIDGET HIS WIFE. / THE DECEASED WAS A CAPTAIN IN HER MAJESTY'S / 52ND REGIMENT OF INFANTRY AND WAS PRESENT AT / THE BATTLES OF CORUNNA, FUENTES D'ONOR, / CUIADA-RODRIGO AND SALAMANCA / AND AT THE LAST DECISIVE BATTLE OF WATERLOO. / HE RECEIVED IN CONSIDERATION OF HIS SERVICES THE / WATERLOO MEDAL AND THE WAR MEDAL WITH FOUR CLASPS. / HE WAS BORN DECR 5TH 1788 AND DEPARTED THIS LIFE MARCH 3RD 1860 / BELOVED AND REGRETTED BY ALL WHO KNEW HIM. / THIS MONUMENT IS ERECTED TO HIS MEMORY / BY HIS SORROWING WIDOW AS A TRIBUTE OF HER AFFECTION

Memorial tablet and Stained glass window: Holy Trinity Church, Stapleton, Bristol, Somerset. (Photograph).
The inscription on the memorial tablet is the same as that on the obelisk in Newton St Loe churchyard.

Ensign 23 May 1805. Lt 27 Jul 1805. Capt 12 May 1812.
    Served in the Peninsula with 2/52nd Aug 1808 – Jan 1809 and Jul 1809 – Dec 1812. Present at Corunna, Coa, Pombal, Redinha, Casal Nova, Foz d'Arouce, Sabugal, Fuentes d'Onoro, Ciudad Rodrigo, Salamanca and San Munos. Present at Waterloo. MGS medal for Corunna, Fuentes d'Onoro, Ciudad Rodrigo and Salamanca. Also served in the Netherlands 1814. Half pay 8 Apr 1817.

LANGWERTH, Ernest Eberhard Kuno von
Colonel Commandant. 4th Line Battalion, King's German Legion.
Memorial tablet: St Paul's Cathedral, London. (North transept). Joint memorial with Major General Mackenzie.

NATIONAL MONUMENT / TO MAJOR GENERAL / J. R. MACKENZIE / AND BRIGADIER GENERAL / E. LANGWERTH / WHO FELL AT / TALAVERA. / JULY 28TH / MDCCCIX

Colonel Commandant 4th Line KGL 1804.
    Served in the Peninsula Sep 1808 – Jul 1809. (Commanded 3 Brigade 1st Division Jun – Jul 1809). Present at Douro and Talavera where he was killed 28 Jul 1809. Gold Medal for Talavera. Also served at Hanover 1805 and Copenhagen 1807.

LASCELLES, Charles Francis Rowley
Lieutenant and Captain. 1st Regiment of Foot Guards.
Interred in Catacomb B (v68 c12) Kensal Green Cemetery, London.
Memorial tablet: Grosvenor Chapel, South Audley Street, London. (Photograph)

SACRED TO THE MEMORY OF / COLONEL CHARLES FRANCIS ROWLEY LASCELLES, / LATE OF THE GRENADIER GUARDS: / SON OF ROWLEY LASCELLES, ESQRE / OF 33, UPPER GROSVENOR STREET / WHO DIED ON THE 8TH NOVEMBER 1860. / ………………..

Ensign 10 Sep 1812. Lt and Capt 9 Jun 1814. Capt and Lt Colonel 21 Feb 1828. Major 4 Jul 1843. Lt Colonel 10 Apr 1849.
    Served in the Peninsula Aug 1813 – Apr 1814. Present at Bidassoa, Nivelle, Nive, Adour and Bayonne. MGS medal for Nivelle and Nive. Present at Quatre Bras and Waterloo where he was wounded, the siege of Peronne and with the Army of Occupation. Retired 27 Dec 1850.

LASCELLES, Hon. Henry
Ensign. 1st Regiment of Foot Guards.
Buried in the Family vault, All Saints Churchyard, Harewood House, Harewood, Yorkshire.

Ensign 7 Apr 1814.
    Present at Waterloo where he was wounded. Half pay 24 Aug 1820. Later became 3rd Earl of Harewood. MP for Northallerton 1826–1837. Lord Lieutenant West Riding of Yorkshire 1846–1857. Died 22 Feb 1857.
REFERENCE: *Gentleman's Magazine, Apr 1857, pp. 490–1 (Under Harewood). Annual Register, 1857, Appx, pp. 293–4 (Under Harewood).*

LASCELLES, Thomas
Lieutenant. Royal Engineers.
Named on the Regimental Memorial: Rochester Cathedral, Rochester, Kent. (Photograph)

2nd Lt 5 May 1807. 1st Lt 18 Nov 1807.
    Served in the Peninsula Jul 1811 – Apr 1812. Present at Ciudad Rodrigo and Badajoz where he was killed 6 Apr 1812 leading the 5th Division in the assault on No 1 bastion. Also served at Walcheren 1809.

LATHAM, Matthew
Captain. 3rd (East Kent) Regiment of Foot.
Pedestal tomb: Blingel Churchyard, Blingel, Pays de Calais, France. (Photograph)

CAPITAINE LATHAM / 3 FOOT FOR THE BUFFS / AS A TESTIMONIAL / FROM HIS BROTHER OFFICERS / OF THEIR HIGH OPINION OF HIS DISTINGUISHED CONDUCT / IN DEFENDING THE COLOURS OF THE REGIMENT / IN THE BATTLE OF ALBUERA / IN WHICH HE LOST AN ARM AND PART OF HIS FACE. / A LA MÉMOIRE DE CE BRAVE MILITAIRE / DÉCÉDÉ DANS SA 79 ANNÉE LE 27 AVRIL 1865· / PRIEZ DIEU POUR LUI.

Ensign 15 Nov 1805. Lt 8 Apr 1807. Bt Capt 11 Feb 1813. Capt 3rd Foot 13 May 1813.

Served in the Peninsula Nov 1809 – Jul 1811. Present at Busaco and Albuera where he was severely wounded whilst saving the King's colour and awarded a pension of £170 per annum. He was surrounded by French cavalry trying to take the colour from him. His arm was cut off and his face badly disfigured by sword cuts. He managed to hide the flag in his jacket and was left for dead. However he lived, was promoted to Captain and awarded a Gold Medal by his regiment. The Prince Regent paid for his medical expenses to try to repair his face. Retired in 1820. MGS medal for Busaco and Albuera. Went to live in France and died there 27 Apr 1865.

LATTA, John
Ensign. 42nd (Royal Highland) Regiment of Foot.
Named on the Memorial: St Andrew's Church, (now Musée Historique), Biarritz, France. (Photograph)

Ensign 11 Feb 1813.
Served in the Peninsula Apr 1814. Present at Toulouse where he was killed 10 Apr 1814.

LAUTOUR, James Oliver
Ensign. 1st Regiment of Foot Guards.
Family Memorial tablet: St Faith's Church, Hexton, Hertfordshire. (Photograph)

……………….. / THIS TABLET / ALSO RECORDS THE DEATH OF THEIR YOUNGEST SON, / JAMES OLIVER, AN OFFICER IN THE GUARDS, / WHO DIED OF HIS WOUNDS RECEIVED IN ACTION AT BAYONNE, / 24TH DECEMBER 1813, AGED 24 YEARS.

Named on Memorial Panel VII for Nive: Royal Military Chapel, Wellington Barracks, London. (M.I.) (Destroyed by a Flying Bomb 1944)
Named on the Memorial: St Andrew's Church, (now Musée Historique), Biarritz, France. (Photograph)

Ensign 3 Oct 1811.
Served in the Peninsula with 3rd Battalion Apr – Dec 1813. Present at Bidassoa, Nivelle and Nive where he was severely wounded 11 Dec 1813 and died of his wounds at St Jean de Luz 24 Dec 1813. Younger brother of Lt and Capt Joseph Lautour 1st Foot Guards and Major Peter Augustus Lautour 23rd Lt Dragoons.

LAUTOUR, Joseph Andrew de
Lieutenant and Captain. 1st Regiment of Foot Guards.
Memorial tablet: St Faith's Church, Hexton, Hertfordshire. (Photograph)

TO THE MEMORY OF HER HUSBAND / JOSEPH ANDREW DE LAUTOUR / ELDEST SON OF FRANCIS JOSEPH LOUIS DE LAUTOUR / BORN AT MADRAS APRIL 17TH 1785, DECEASED AT PARIS MARCH 28TH 1845. / BURIED AT HEXTON APRIL 12TH 1845 / THIS TABLET / IS ERECTED BY CAROLINE, HIS WIDOW. / AS AN OFFICER OF THE GUARDS / HE SERVED HIS COUNTRY IN SICILY, HOLLAND, SPAIN AND PORTUGAL / RETIRING FROM THE ARMY IN 1814. / ALIKE DISTINGUISHED AS A SOLDIER AND A GENTLEMAN / HE DEVOTED HIS LEISURE HOURS AND HIS FORTUNE / TO THE NOT LESS HONOURABLE PURSUITS OF PEACE. / AND AMONGST MANY OTHER WORKS AT HEXTON, / REBUILT THIS CHURCH. / (VERSE)

Family Memorial tablet: St Faith's Church, Hexton, Hertfordshire. (Photograph)

……………… / THEIR ELDEST SON JOSEPH ANDREW, MARRIED CAROLINE, / SOLE SURVIVING DAUGHTER AND HEIRESS OF WILLIAM YOUNG, ESQRE / THROUGH WHOM BE

BECAME POSSESSED FOR HIS LIFE, / OF THE HERTFORDSHIRE, BEDFORDSHIRE AND HAMP-
SHIRE ESTATES.

Ensign 21 Jan 1802. Lt and Capt 22 Aug 1805.
    Served in the Peninsula with 1st Battalion, Oct 1808 – Jan 1809 and Sep 1812 – Jan 1813. Present at
Corunna. Also served in Sicily 1805. Resigned Feb 1813. Elder brother of Ensign James Lautour 1st Foot
Guards and Major Peter Augustus Lautour 23rd Lt Dragoons.

LAUTOUR, Peter Augustus
Major. 23rd Regiment of Light Dragoons.
Low monument with railings: Holy Trinity Churchyard, Bromley, Kent. (Photograph)

SACRED TO THE MEMORY OF / GENERAL PETER AUGUSTUS LAUTOUR C.B. K.H. / COLONEL
3RD KINGS OWN HUSSARS / BORN 26 MAY 1787. DIED 11 JANUARY 1866.

Cornet 11th Lt Dragoons 31 Mar 1804. Lt 4 Jul 1805. Capt 8 May 1806. Major 40th Foot 20 May 1813.
Major 23rd Lt Dragoons 6 Jan 1814. Bt Lt Colonel 18 Jun 1815. Bt Colonel 10 Jan 1837. Major General
9 Nov 1846. Lt General 20 Jun 1854. General 9 Mar 1861.
    Served in the Peninsula Jun 1811 – Dec 1812 with 11th Lt Dragoons. Present at El Bodon (attacked
French cavalry regiment which had captured the baggage of the Light Division), Moriscos, Castrejon,
Salamanca, Venta del Poza, Valladolid (captured a company of French artillery 1812) and retreat from
Burgos where he was wounded. Most of his time was spent on outpost duty and dealing with enemy
skirmishers.
    Present at Waterloo with 23rd Lt Dragoons where he commanded the regiment early in the day, and a
brigade later in the battle, the Capture of Paris and with the Army of Occupation. CB, KH and Bt Lt
Colonelcy for Waterloo. MGS medal for Salamanca. Colonel 3rd Lt Dragoons 26 May 1855. Brother of
Ensign James Latour and Lt and Capt Joseph Lautour both of 1st Foot Guards.
REFERENCE: *United Service Magazine, 1866, p. 488. Gentleman's Magazine, Feb 1866, p. 298.*

LAVERTON, James
Private. 71st (Highland Light Infantry) Regiment of Foot.
Headstone: Cumbrae Churchyard, Cumbrae, Buteshire, Scotland. (M.I.)

"JAMES LAVERTON DIED 24TH SEPT 1854 AGED 69 YEARS. HE SERVED IN THE 71ST REGT OF
FOOT 1799–1822."

Private 20 Mar 1799.
    Served in the Peninsula 1808–1809 and Sep 1810 – Apr 1814. Present at Rolica, Vimeiro, Corunna,
Vittoria, Pyrenees, Orthes and Toulouse. Served at Waterloo in Capt Archibald Armstrong's Company.
MGS medal for Rolica, Vimeiro, Corunna, Vittoria, Pyrenees, Orthes and Toulouse. Discharged 29 Oct
1822.

LAW, William Henry
Ensign. 62nd (Wiltshire) Regiment of Foot.
Headstone: Kensal Green Cemetery, London. Inscription illegible. (15693/32/4). (Photograph)

Ensign Wiltshire Regiment of Militia 5 Des 1812. Ensign 62nd Foot 29 Apr 1813. Lt 28 Nov 1816. Capt
83rd Foot 14 Jul 1825. Bt Major 28 Jun 1838. Major 2 Apr 1841. Lt Colonel 22 Dec 1845. Bt Colonel 28
Nov 1854. Major General 16 May 1856.
    Served in the Peninsula Oct 1813 – Apr 1814. Present at Nivelle, Nive and Bayonne. MGS medal for
Nivelle and Nive. Died 1860.

LAWDER, Rhynd
Assistant Surgeon. 32nd (Cornwall) Regiment of Foot.
Memorial tablet: St Ann's Church, Dublin, Ireland. (Photograph)

RHYND LAWDER ESQR M .D. / LATE SURGEON 7TH HUSSARS, / DIED 11TH JULY, 1836 / AGED 51 YEARS. / THIS TABLET / IS ERECTED BY / HIS BROTHER OFFICERS / AS A MARK OF RESPECT / TO HIS MEMORY.

Asst Surgeon 32nd Foot 25 May 1809. Asst Surgeon 2nd Royal Veteran Battalion 25 Oct 1823. Asst Surgeon 98th Foot 25 May 1826. Surgeon 59th Foot 21 Nov 1828. Surgeon 7th Hussars 12 Aug 1834.
    Served in the Peninsula Jul 1810 – Dec 1811 and Feb 1813 – Apr 1814. Present at Pyrenees, Bidassoa, Nivelle and Nive. Present at Waterloo with 32nd Foot. MD Edinburgh 1821. Died at Hounslow 1836.

LAWRENCE, Alexander William
Lieutenant Colonel. 2nd Garrison Battalion.
Family Memorial tablet: St Martin's Church, North Stoke, Bath, Somerset. (Photograph)

IN MEMORY OF / LT COL ALEXANDER WILLIAM LAWRENCE / BORN CO. LONDONDERRY 7 NOVEMBER 1764 D. AT CLIFTON 7 MAY 1855 / WHO LED THE FORLORN HOPE AT SERINGA-PATAM 1799 / AND COMMANDED THE GARRISON AT OSTEND DURING THE WATERLOO CAMPAIGN. /....................

Capt 19th Foot 17 Apr 1800. Major 21 Sep 1809. Lt Colonel 2nd Garrison Battalion 28 May 1812.
    Served in the Waterloo campaign where he commanded the Ostend Garrison. Also served in India (present at the storming of Seringapatam 1799 where he led the Forlorn Hope). Father of the Lawrence brothers who were so influential during the unrest in India before and during the Mutiny in 1857. Governor of Upnor Castle 1818.

LAWRENCE, William
Sergeant. 40th (2nd Somersetshire) Regiment of Foot.
Headstone: St Nicholas Churchyard, Studland, Dorset. (Photograph)

TO THE HONOURED MEMORY / OF / SERJEANT WILLIAM LAWRENCE / (OF THE 40TH REGI-MENT FOOT) / WHO AFTER A LONG AND EVENTFUL LIFE / IN THE SERVICE OF HIS COUNTRY / PEACEFULLY ENDED HIS DAYS AT STUDLAND / NOVEMBER 11TH 1869 / HE SERVED WITH HIS DISTINGUISHED REGIMENT / IN THE WAR IN SOUTH AMERICA 1805 / AND THROUGH THE WHOLE OF THE PENINSULAR WAR 1808 – 13 / HE RECEIVED A SILVER MEDAL AND NO LESS THAN TEN CLASPS / FOR THE BATTLES IN WHICH HE WAS ENGAGED / ROLEIA VIMIERA TALAVERA / CIUDAD RODRIGO / BADAJOZ / (IN WHICH DESPERATE ASSAULT BEING ONE OF THE VOLUNTEERS / FOR THE FORLORN HOPE HE WAS MOST SEVERELY WOUNDED) / VITTORIA PYRENEES NIVELLES / ORTHES TOULOUSE / HE ALSO FOUGHT AT THE GLORIOUS VICTORY OF / WATERLOO / JUNE 18TH 1815 / WHILE HE SERVED WITH HIS REGIMENT DURING THE / OCCUPATION OF PARIS BY THE ALLIED ARMIES / SERJEANT LAWRENCE MARRIED CLOTILDE CLAIRET / AT ST GERMAIN-EN-LAYE WHO DIED SEPT 26TH 1853 / AND WAS BURIED BENEATH THIS SPOT.

Pte 19 Feb 1805. Cpl 1812. Sgt 1813. Sgt 3rd Veteran Battalion 5 Nov 1819.
    Served in the Peninsula Jul 1808 – Apr 1814. Present at Rolica, Vimeiro, Talavera, Ciudad Rodrigo, Badajoz (severely wounded), Vittoria, Pyrenees, Nivelle, Orthes and Toulouse. Present at Waterloo where he was nearly killed by a French shell. By 4pm on 18 June he was ordered to defend the colours, after an

officer and 14 Sergeants had already died in their defence, but he survived. Served with the Army of Occupation and while in Paris met his future French wife.

Also served in South America 1807 (present at Montevideo) and Ireland 1819. MGS medal for Rolica, Vimeiro, Talavera, Ciudad Rodrigo, Badajoz, Vittoria, Pyrenees, Nivelle, Orthes and Toulouse. Discharged Jun 1821 on a pension of nine pence per day.

REFERENCE: *Lawrence, William, The autobiography of Sergeant William Lawrence: a hero of the Peninsular and Waterloo campaigns, edited by George Nugent Banks, 1886, reprint, 1987. Also reprinted as: A Dorset soldier, edited by Eileen Hathaway, 1993.*

LAWRENCE, William Hudson
1st Lieutenant. Royal Artillery.
Low monument: Locksbrook Cemetery, Bath, Somerset. (Photograph)

MAJOR / WILLIAM HUDSON LAWRENCE / R. A. / BORN JAN 21st 1793 / DIED MARCH 13TH 1884.

2nd Lt 28 Apr 1810. 1st Lt 17 Dec 1813. 2nd Capt 2 Feb 1832.

Served in the Peninsula Mar 1813 – Apr 1814. Present at the siege of Tarragona. Remained in Lisbon until Dec 1822. Also served in the Ionian Islands Aug 1823 – Jan 1828 and Leeward Islands Jan 1833 – May 1839. Retired on half pay 31 Jul 1840.

LAWRIE, Andrew
Major. 79th (Cameron Highlanders) Regiment of Foot.
Memorial tablet: St Bartholomew Church, Sydenham, London. (Photograph)

IN MEMORY OF / MAJOR ANDREW LAWRIE, 79th HIGHLANDERS / WHO FELL AT BURGOS 22ND SEPTEMBER 1812 / ………………..

Ensign 4th Foot 3 Jul 1801. Lt 61st Foot 9 Jul 1803. Capt 19 Apr 1804. Capt 79th Foot 25 Mar 1805. Major 4 Oct 1810.

Served in the Peninsula Aug 1808 – Jan 1809, Jan – Nov 1810 and Jan 1812 – Sep 1812 (ADC to Major General Alan Cameron May – Nov 1810). Present at Corunna, Cadiz, Busaco, Salamanca, Burgos (Mentioned in Despatches and killed leading an attack on the outward wall of citadel 22 Sep 1812). Also served in the Baltic 1807–1808 and Walcheren 1809.

LAWSON, Douglas
1st Lieutenant. Royal Artillery.
Grave: St Peter and St Paul Churchyard, Fareham, Hampshire. (M.I.)

"UNDERNEATH ARE DEPOSITED THE REMAINS OF DOUGLAS LAWSON. ESQ. LIEUT R. A. WHO DIED AT WOOLWICH 19 AUG 1823 AGED 31."

2nd Lt 17 Dec 1807. 1st Lt 28 Oct 1808.

Served at Waterloo with Major George Unett's brigade attached to 6th Division, siege of Cambrai and with the Army of Occupation.

LEACH, Jonathan
Captain. 95th Regiment of Foot.
Gravestone: Christ Church, Worthing, Sussex. (Grave 257). (M.I.)

"LIEUTENANT COLONEL JONATHAN LEACH, C. B. FORMERLY OF THE RIFLE / BRIGADE, DIED AT WORTHING 14TH JANUARY 1855, AGED 70 YEARS."

Ensign 70th Foot 7 Aug 1801. Lt 15 Oct 1801. Capt 7 Apr 1804. Capt 95th Foot 1 May 1806. Bt Major 21 Jun 1813. Bt Lt Colonel 18 Jun1815. Major 95th Foot 9 Sep 1819.

Served in the Peninsula with 2/95th Aug 1808 – Jan 1809 and 1/95th Jul 1809 – Apr 1814. Present at Obidos, Rolica, Vimeiro, Vigo, Coa, Busaco, Pombal, Redinha, Casal Nova, Fuentes d'Onoro, Ciudad Rodrigo, Badajoz, Salamanca, San Millan, Vittoria (awarded Bt Majority), Pyrenees, Vera, Bidassoa, Nivelle, Nive, Tarbes and Toulouse. Present at Waterloo where he took command of the battalion when his two senior officers were wounded and was himself wounded later and served with the Army of Occupation 1815–1818. CB and Bt Lt Colonelcy for Waterloo. MGS medal for Rolica, Vimeiro, Busaco, Fuentes d'Onoro, Ciudad Rodrigo, Badajoz, Salamanca, Vittoria, Pyrenees, Nivelle, Nive and Toulouse. Also served in the West Indies 1803–1805 and Copenhagen 1807. Retired 24 Oct 1821.

REFERENCE: *Leach Jonathan, Rough sketches of the life of an old soldier, … 1831. Reprint 2005 under title Captain of the 95th Rifles, 2005. Leach, J., Rambles along the Styx, 1847. Gentleman's Magazine, Mar 1855, pp. 311–2. Annual Register, 1855, Appx, pp. 242–3.*

LEATHES, Henry Mussendon
1st Lieutenant. Royal Artillery.
Memorial tablet: St Margaret's Church, Lowestoft, Suffolk. (North Chancel wall). Inscription not recorded.

2nd Lt 12 Jul 1805. 1st Lt 1 Jun 1806.

Served in the Peninsula Sep 1808 – Jan 1809. Present in the Corunna campaign in Capt. Skyring's 6th Company. MGS medal for Corunna. Present at Waterloo in Captain Mercer's 'G' Troop. Resigned his commission 1819. Known for his benevolence and philanthropy, was much loved by everyone who came in contact with him, especially French fishermen who came to the Port of Lowestoft. For his kindness and generosity he was awarded a Gold Medal by Napoleon III. Died at Lowestoft 16 Dec 1864.

REFERENCE: *Glover, Gareth, ed., Reminiscences of Waterloo: the correspondence between Henry Leathes and Alexander Mercer of G Troop RHA, reprint, 2004. Gentleman's Magazine, Feb 1865, p. 254.*

LE BLANC, Francis
Captain. 95th Regiment of Foot.
Memorial: Holy Trinity with St Columba Churchyard, Fareham, Hampshire. (No longer extant). (M.I.)

"………………. ELIZABETH HARRIET LE BLANC WIFE OF COL FRANCIS LE BLANC OF BLACK-BROOK HOUSE BORN 4TH JUNE 1794 DIED 17TH MARCH 1867. COL FRANCIS LE BLANC BORN 14TH MARCH 1790 DIED 7TH JANUARY 1880."

Ensign 4th Foot 30 May 1807. Lt 16 Mar 1809. Capt 4th Garrison Battalion 28 Sep 1813. Capt 95th Foot 1 Dec 1814. Capt 43rd Foot 17 Dec 1818. Major 31 Dec 1822. Lt Colonel (unattached) 11 Jul 1826. Lt Colonel 53rd Foot 9 Aug 1827. Bt Colonel 23 Nov 1841.

Served in the Peninsula Aug 1808 – Jan 1809 and Feb 1811 – Sep 1813. Present at Corunna, Barba del Puerco, Fuentes d'Onoro, Badajoz, Salamanca, retreat from Burgos, Vittoria and San Sebastian (commanded the storming party at the second assault, severely wounded and promoted Captain in 4th Garrison Battalion). Present at Waterloo. Half pay 28 Feb 1828. MGS medal for Corunna, Fuentes d'Onoro, Badajoz, Salamanca, Vittoria and San Sebastian. Colonel 46th Foot 16 May 1845 and retired the same day.

LECHLEITNER, C. M.
Lieutenant Colonel. 3rd Carabineers Regiment, Dutch Cavalry.
Named on the Memorial to Dutch officers killed at Waterloo: St Joseph's Church, Waterloo, Belgium. (Photograph)

LECKY, David
Major. 45th (Nottinghamshire) Regiment of Foot.
Family ledger stone within railed enclosure: St Columb's Cathedral Burial ground, Londonderry, Northern Ireland. (M.I.)

" .... AND THEIR SON LIEUT COL. DAVID LECKY, WHO DIED THE 27TH DAY OF MARCH 1821 AGED 47 YEARS."

Ensign Lt Colonel Ogle's Regt. Lt in Lt Colonel Talbot's Regt 15 Nov 1794. Capt 27 Aug 1804. Bt Major 1 Jan 1805. Major 28 Feb 1811. Bt Lt Colonel 1 Jan 1812.
    Served in the Peninsula Aug 1808 – Oct 1811. Present at Rolica, Vimeiro, Talavera, Redinha, Casal Nova, Foz d'Arouce, Sabugal, Fuentes d'Onoro, second siege of Badajoz and El Bodon.

LEDSAM, John
Sergeant. 7th (Royal Fusiliers) Regiment of Foot.
Memorial tablet: St George's Chapel, Windsor, Berkshire. (West wall of Deanery Cloisters). (Photograph)

SACRED TO THE MEMORY OF / JOHN LEDSAM, ESQRE / MILITARY KNIGHT OF WINDSOR, / AND FOR UPWARDS OF 21 YEARS / QUARTERMASTER / OF THE 7TH ROYAL FUSILIERS. / DIED AT WINDSOR DEC 1ST 1855, / IN THE 72ND YEAR OF HIS AGE.

Quartermaster 20 Apr 1826.
    Served in the Peninsula Jul 1810 – Apr 1814. Present at Busaco, Albuera, Ciudad Rodrigo, Badajoz, Salamanca, Vittoria, Pamplona, Orthes and Toulouse. Served in France with the Army of Occupation. Also served at Copenhagen 1807 and North America 1814 (present at New Orleans). MGS medal for Busaco, Albuera, Salamanca, Vittoria, Pyrenees, Orthes and Toulouse. Retired on half pay 1 Oct 1847. Military Knight of Windsor 18 Dec 1847.

LEECH, Samuel
Private. Royal Artillery.
Headstone: St Luke's Churchyard, Hodnet, Shropshire. (Photograph)

.... / ALSO / SAMUEL LEECH OF THE ABOVE / WHO DIED FEBRUARY 27TH 1877 / AGED 90 YEARS. / HE STOOD THE PENINSULAR WAR.

Pte 25 May 1806.
    Served in the Peninsula 1811 – Apr 1814. MGS medal for Badajoz, Salamanca, Vittoria and Toulouse. Discharged 30 Jun 1816 due to loss of his right eye. Awarded pension of one shilling per day.

LEEKE, William
Ensign. 52nd (Oxfordshire) Light Infantry Regiment of Foot.
Headstone: St Michael's Churchyard, Holbrooke, Derbyshire. (Photograph)

IN / LOVING MEMORY / OF THE / REV. WILLIAM LEEKE, M.A. / FOR 37 YEARS / THE BELOVED INCUMBENT / OF THIS PARISH. / HE CARRIED THE REGIMENTAL COLOURS OF THE / 52ND LIGHT INFANTRY AT THE BATTLE OF WATERLOO, / JUNE 18TH 1815. / HE ENTERED INTO REST / JUNE 6TH 1879, / AGED 81 YEARS / "A GOOD SOLDIER OF CHRIST". / ....

Stained glass window: St Michael's Church, Holbrooke, Derbyshire. (Photograph)

Ensign 4 May 1815. Lt 20 Nov 1823.

Present at Waterloo where he carried the regimental colours. Retired 1824. After attending Cambridge University he entered the church and was ordained 1829. Became Vicar of Holbrooke, Derbyshire 1840, and remained there until his death in 1879. While at Holbrooke wrote a history of the 52nd Regiment. REFERENCE: *Leeke, William, The History of Lord Seaton's Regiment (the 52nd Light Infantry) at the Battle of Waterloo … to which are added, many of the author's reminiscences of his military and clerical careers … 2 vols, 1866, Supplement 1871. Mansfield, Clifford, Ensign William Leeke: soldier and cleric, Derbyshire Life and Countryside, Jun 2008, pp. 98–9.*

LEES, John
Private. Royal Artillery.
Grave: St Mary's Churchyard, Oldham, Lancashire. (No longer extant). (M.I.)

"SACRED TO THE MEMORY OF ROBERT LEES, OF BENT-GREEN: WHO DIED FEB^Y. 29TH 1820 IN THE 55TH YEAR OF HIS AGE. ALSO JOHN LEES, HIS SON WHO DIED SEP^R 7TH 1819, IN THE 22ND YEAR OF HIS AGE".

Served at Waterloo in Lt Colonel R. Bull's Troop.

LEFEBURE, Charles
Captain. Royal Engineers.
Memorial tablet: St Mary's Church, Wareham, Dorset. (Photograph)

SACRED TO THE MEMORY OF / MAJOR CHARLES LEFEBURE, / OF THE ROYAL ENGINEERS, / WHO WAS KILLED AT FORT MATAGORDA / ON THE 22ND DAY OF APRIL 1810, / AGED 35 YEARS.

Named on the Regimental Memorial: Rochester Cathedral, Rochester, Kent. (Photograph)

2nd Lt Royal Artillery. 24 Apr 1793. 2nd Lt Royal Engineers. 25 Sep 1793. Lt 8 Jun 1795. Capt-Lt 11 Jun 1800. 2nd Capt 19 Jul 1804. Capt 1 Mar 1805. Bt Major 8 Mar 1810.
    Served in the Peninsula Aug 1808 – Jan 1809 and Mar – Apr 1810. Present in the Corunna campaign where he was wounded in the retreat. One of the military agents employed at the beginning of the campaign. Lefebure and J. T. Jones were employed to report to Major General Leith on the state of the roads and topography of northern Spain. Present at Cadiz (Mentioned in Despatches) where he arrived on 3 Mar and took command of the Royal Engineers in Cadiz and prepared the defences. Nearly killed by a shot which passed through his tent on 22 April, but on the same day was killed at Fort Matagorda by one of the last cannon shots from the French batteries as the fort was being evacuated.
    Also served in Flanders 1793–1794, West Indies (present at St Lucia 1796 and Trinidad 1797), Calabria 1806 and Sicily 1806–1807 (present at Maida where he was awarded a medal for his bravery). It was agreed to erect a monument to him in Westminster Abbey, but these plans did not come to fruition. Brother of Capt George Lefebure Royal Horse Artillery.

LEFEBURE, George
Captain. Royal Artillery.
Memorial tablet: St Mary's Church, Wareham, Dorset. (Photograph)

SACRED TO THE MEMORY OF / CAPTAIN GEORGE LEFEBURE, / OF THE ROYAL HORSE ARTILLERY, / WHO DIED AT MADRID / ON THE 22ND DAY OF OCTOBER 1812 / AGED 35 YEARS. / THAT THE BRAVERY, SKILL AND ZEAL WITH / WHICH THESE GALLANT MEN SERVED THEIR / COUNTRY, MAY NOT ENTIRELY BE UNRECORDED. / THESE MONUMENTS ARE RAISED / BY THEIR AFFECTIONATE BROTHER.

1st Lt 6 Mar 1795. Capt-Lieut 25 Jul 1802. Capt 1 Jun 1806.

Served in the Peninsula Mar 1810 – Oct 1812 (OC 'D' Troop RHA). Present at Albuera (Mentioned in Despatches), Usagre (Mentioned in Despatches), Fuente Guinaldo, Aldea da Ponte and Ribera (Mentioned in Despatches). Also served in Flanders 1794. Died of fever in Madrid 22 Oct 1812. Brother of Capt Charles Lefebure Royal Engineers.

LEGGATT, Samuel
Chaplain to the Forces. Chaplain's Department.
Memorial tablet: St Andrew's Church, Norwich, Norfolk. (Photograph)

SACRED / TO THE MEMORY OF / THE REVᴰ SAMUEL LEGGATT, A.M. / LATE CHAPLAIN / TO THE GARRISON FORCES / AT PORTSMOUTH: / DIED MARCH 7ᵀᴴ 1848.

Memorial tablet: Royal Garrison Church, Portsmouth, Hampshire. (North transept obscured behind organ). (M.I.)

"TO THE MEMORY OF THE REV SAMUEL LEGGATT A.M. UPWARDS OF 28 YEARS CHAPLAIN TO THE FORCES IN THIS GARRISON. OBIIT MARCH 7ᵀᴴ 1848 AETAT 74."

Chaplain to the Forces 31 Jul 1811.

Served in the Peninsula Sep 1811 – Apr 1814 at Lisbon. Later Chaplain to the Garrison at Portsmouth. Died 7 Mar 1848 aged 74.

LEIGH, George
Lieutenant Colonel. 10ᵗʰ (Prince of Wales's Own) Regiment of Light Dragoons.
Interred in Catacomb B (Pub v29 1/1) Kensal Green Cemetery, London.

Cornet 30 Oct 1790. Lt 30 Apr 1793. Capt 5 Apr 1794. Major 1 Jun 1797. Lt Colonel 19 Oct 1799.

Served in the Peninsula Nov 1808 – Jan 1809. Present at Sahagun and Benevente – awarded Gold Medal. Retired from the Army 3 May 1810. Equerry to the Prince of Wales 29 Jan 1800 who promoted Lt Colonel Slade out of the 10ᵗʰ Lt Dragoons to make way for Leigh who was invaluable to the Prince because of his knowledge of race horses and betting. Married Augusta, half sister of Lord Byron. Died 1850.

LEIGHTON, Burgh
Major. 4ᵗʰ (Queen's Own) Regiment of Dragoons.
Low monument: St Alkmund's Churchyard, Shrewsbury, Shropshire. (Photograph)

.... / ALSO OF LT COLONEL BURGH LEIGHTON / 4ᵀᴴ DRAGOONS. SON OF BALDWIN LEIGHTON. / BORN FEBRUARY 11ᵀᴴ 1761. DIED MAY 3ᴿᴰ 1833.

Cornet 11 Feb 1783. Capt-Lieut 6 Jun 1789. Capt 5 Jan 1798. Bt Lt Colonel 29 Apr 1802. Major 25 Nov 1808.

Served in the Peninsula Apr 1809 – Aug 1811. Present at Talavera, Busaco, Albuera and Usagre. Gold Medal for Albuera. Retired in 1811.

LEITH, Sir Alexander
Lieutenant Colonel. 31ˢᵗ (Huntingdonshire) Regiment of Foot.
Obelisk: Towie Kirkyard, Starthdon, Aberdeenshire, Scotland. (Photograph)

SACRED / TO THE MEMORY OF / GENERAL SIR ALEXANDER LEITH K.C.B. / OF FREEFIELD AND GLENKINDIE / WHO DIED 19ᵀᴴ FEBRUARY 1859, / AGED 84. / ....

Ensign 42nd Foot 8 Aug 1792. Lt Independent Company of Infantry 29 Nov 1794. Capt 109th Foot 27 Nov 1794. Capt 31st Foot 5 Sep 1795. Major 1 Aug 1804. Lt Colonel 7 Feb 1811. Bt Colonel 19 Jul 1821. Major General 22 Jul 1830. Lt General 23 Nov 1841. General 20 Jun 1854.

Served in the Peninsula Apr 1812 – Apr 1814. Present at Vittoria, Pyrenees, Nivelle, Nive (wounded), Garris, Orthes, Aire and Toulouse. Gold Cross for Vittoria, Pyrenees, Nivelle, Nive and Orthes. KCB. Also served in Flanders 1793 (present at Nieuport), West Indies 1796 (present at St Lucia), the Helder 1799 (severely wounded and lost an eye at Alkmaar) and Egypt 1807 (present at Rosetta). Half pay May 1815. Colonel 90th Foot 2 Sep 1841. Colonel 31st Foot 14 Jun 1858.

LEITH, Sir James
Colonel. 4th West India Regiment of Foot.
Memorial tablet: Formerly in Kennethmont Church Aberdeenshire, Scotland, now converted into a dwelling house. The tablet has been removed for safe keeping and is now in the care of a family member). (Photograph)

SACRED TO THE MEMORY OF / LIEUT.-GENERAL SIR JAMES LEITH, / KNIGHT GRAND CROSS OF THE MOST HONORABLE MILITARY ORDER OF THE BATH, / HONORARY KNIGHT COMMANDER / OF THE PORTUGUESE ORDER OF THE TOWER AND SWORD, / GRAND CORDON OF THE ORDER OF MILITARY MERIT OF FRANCE, / COMMANDER OF THE FORCES IN THE WEST INDIES, / COLONEL OF THE 4TH WEST INDIA REGIMENT, / AND CAPTAIN GENERAL AND GOVERNOR OF BARBADOES, &C. / HE WAS A NATIVE OF THIS PARISH, / BORN AT LEITH-HALL, AUGUST 8TH, 1763: / AND, AFTER A SERIES OF DISTINGUISHED SERVICES DIED AT BARBADOES, / OCTOBER 16TH, 1816, DEEPLY LAMENTED.

2nd Lt 21st Foot 1780. Lt 81st Foot 1781. Capt 3 Dec 1782. Capt 50th Foot 1784. Bt Major 1793. Colonel 4th West India Regt 19 Jul 1811. Major General 25 Apr 1806. Lt General 4 Jun 1813.

Served in the Peninsula on Staff Oct 1808 – Sep 1813 (Commanded 1 Brigade 2nd Division Oct 1808 – Jan 1809 and Jun – Jul 1810, Commanded 1 Brigade 2nd Division Jul 1810 – Feb 1811 and GOC 5th Division Dec 1811 – Jul 1812 and Aug – Sep 1813). Present at Corunna (led the charge of 59th at Lugo), Busaco, Badajoz, Salamanca (severely wounded) and San Sebastian (wounded). Gold Cross for Corunna, Busaco, Badajoz, Salamanca and San Sebastian. Also served in Gibraltar 1784, Toulon 1793, Ireland 1798 and Walcheren 1809. After his injury at San Sebastian he returned to England and in 1814, was appointed Commander of Forces in the West Indies and Governor of the Leeward Islands. Secured French West Indian islands for Louis XVIII. GCB. KTS. Died of yellow fever in Barbados 16 Oct 1816. Uncle of Capt Andrew Leith Hay 11th Foot.
REFERENCE: *Dictionary of National Biography. Gentleman's Magazine, Dec 1816, p. 566. Leith, Sir James, Memoirs of the late Lieutenant-General Sir James Leith, by a British Officer (Sir Andrew Leith Hay), 1818.*

LEITH, James William
Captain. 68th (Durham) Regiment of Foot.
Named on the Memorial: St Andrew's Church, (now Musée Historique), Biarritz, France. (Photograph)

Ensign 3 Feb 1804. Lt 24 Jul 1804. Capt 7 Oct 1812.
Served in the Peninsula Jun – Nov 1811 and Nov 1812 – Feb 1814. Present at Vittoria, Pyrenees (wounded at the second battle of Sorauren 30 Jul 1813 when 500 men of the 7th Division defeated 2,000 Frenchmen), Nivelle and Adour. Killed at the action at Gave d'Oleron, 23 Feb 1814.
REFERENCE: *Obit: Aberdeen Journal. 30 Mar 1814.*

LE MARCHANT, Carey

Lieutenant and Captain. 1st Regiment of Foot Guards.
Memorial tablet: St Andrew's Church, (now Musée Historique), Biarritz, France. (Photograph)

CAREY LE MARCHANT, / SON OF / MAJOR GENERAL JOHN GASPARD LE MARCHANT. / LIEU-
TENANT AND CAPTAIN / IN THE 1ST REGT. OF FOOT GUARDS. / AIDE DE CAMP TO / LIEUT.
GEN. THE HON. SIR WM STEWART K.C.B. / WAS MORTALLY WOUNDED / AT THE BATTLE OF
THE NIVE, / AND DIED AT ST JEAN DE LUZ, / ON THE 12TH MARCH 1814, / IN THE 23RD YEAR
OF HIS AGE.

Named on the Memorial: St Andrew's Church, (now Musée Historique), Biarritz, France. (Photograph)
Named on Memorial Panel VII for Nive: Royal Military Chapel, Wellington Barracks, London. (M.I.)
(Destroyed by a Flying Bomb 1944)

Cornet 7th Lt Dragoons 28 May 1807. Ensign 1st Foot Guards 15 Sep 1808. Lt and Capt 25 Mar 1813.
   Served in the Peninsula Aug 1811 – Mar 1814 (ADC to Major General Le Marchant May – Jul 1812,
ADC to Major General Long Oct 1812 – Jan 1813 and ADC to Lt General W. Stewart Feb 1813 – Mar
1814). Present at Cadiz, Salamanca, Vittoria, Pyrenees, Nivelle and Nive (severely wounded 13 Dec 1813
and died of his wounds 12 Mar 1814). Educated at Eton. Eldest son of Lt Colonel Sir J. Gaspard Le
Marchant who was killed at Salamanca in 1812.

LE MARCHANT, Sir John Gaspard

Lieutenant Colonel. 6th Dragoon Guards.
Memorial: St Paul's Cathedral, London. (North transept). (Photograph)

ERECTED / AT THE PUBLIC EXPENSE / TO THE MEMORY OF / MAJOR GENERAL / JOHN
GASPARD LE MARCHANT / WHO GLORIOUSLY FELL / IN THE BATTLE OF / SALAMANCA, /
JUNE THE 22ND 1812.

Named on the Memorial tablet to his son: St Peter's Church, St Peter Port, Guernsey. Channel Islands.
(Photograph)

SACRED TO THE MEMORY OF / GENERAL SIR J. GASPARD LE MARCHANT, / ....
GENERAL LE MARCHANT, / WHO FELL AT THE BATTLE OF SALAMANCA, 1812, / WHILE
GALLANTLY LEADING A BRILLIANT CHARGE OF CAVALRY, / WHICH VICTORIOUSLY
BROKE THE FRENCH LINES. / ....

Ensign Wiltshire Militia 25 Sep 1781. Ensign 1st Foot 18 Feb 1783. Cornet 6th Dragons 30 May 1787. Lt
2nd Dragoon Guards 18 Nov 1789. Capt 31 Dec 1791. Major 16th Lt Dragoons 11 Mar 1794. Lt Colonel
Hompesch's Hussars 6 Apr 1797. Lt Colonel 29th Lt Dragoons 29 May 1797. Lt Colonel 7th Lt Dragoons
1 Jun 1797. Bt Colonel 30 Oct 1805. Major General 4 Jun 1811. Lt Colonel 6th Dragoon Guards 25 Jul
1811.
   Served in the Peninsula Aug 1811 – Jul 1812 (GOC 'E' Cavalry Brigade). Present at Ciudad Rodrigo,
Llerena, Castrejon and Salamanca where he was killed 22 Jul 1812. Gold Medal for Salamanca. Also
served in Flanders 1793–1794 where he thought the British cavalry had not fought well. He designed a
lighter curved sabre for their use and drew up a more effective system of cavalry sword exercise. Began
plans for a national military college 1798–1799. Became first Lt Governor of the Royal Military College
at High Wycombe Jun 1801. By 1811 200 staff officers and 1,500 regimental officers had been through
the College, a tremendous benefit to Wellington's Peninsular Army.
   On being promoted Major General, Le Marchant was told he had to resume active service. Commanded
the heavy Cavalry in the Peninsula Jul 1811. His successful campaign ended with his death in a cavalry

charge at Salamanca 1812. Wellington said Le Marchant was a very able officer and his death would be a great loss to the Army. His son Lt and Capt Carey Le Marchant, 1st Regiment of Foot Guards died of wounds from the battle of the Nive 1813.

Le Marchant's works include *Cavalry Sword Exercise*, 1796. *Elucidation of Certain Points in H. M. Regulations for Cavalry*, 1797–1798, *Instructions for the Movements and Discipline of the Provisional Cavalry*, 1797–1798 and *Duty of Cavalry Officers on Outposts* – based on Prussian practice, knowledge acquired when his regiment was temporarily attached to the Prussians at the siege of Valenciennes.

REFERENCE: *Dictionary of National Biography. Gentleman's Magazine, Oct 1812, pp. 398–9. Le Marchant, Denis, Memoirs of the late Major General Le Marchant, 1841, reprint 2006. Thoumine, R., Scientific soldier: a life of General Le Marchant 1766 – 1812, 1968. Cole, John William, Memoirs of British Generals, Vol 2, 1856, pp. 225–93.*

LE MESURIER, Peter
Lieutenant. 9th (East Norfolk) Regiment of Foot.
Named on the Memorial: St Andrew's Church, (now Musée Historique), Biarritz, France. (Photograph)

Ensign 13 Aug 1808. Lt 23 Nov 1809.
    Served in the Peninsula with 1/9th Sep 1811 – Dec 1813. Present at Castrejon, Salamanca, Villa Muriel, Osma, Vittoria, San Sebastian, Bidassoa (wounded), Nivelle and Nive where he was killed 10 Dec 1813. Also served at Walcheren, 1809.

LEROUX, George Wilson
Lieutenant. 48th (Northamptonshire) Regiment of Foot.
Ledger stone in railed enclosure: St Mary the Virgin Churchyard, Carisbrooke, Isle of Wight. (Grave number 179). Seriously eroded and inscription recorded from memorial inscription. (Photograph)

"GEORGE WILSON LEROUX ESQ., LATE OF H.M. 48TH REGT, / SON OF REV JOHN LEROUX, LATE RECTOR OF LONG MELFORD / IN SUFFOLK, DIED 18 OCTOBER 1822, AGED 37."

Ensign Suffolk Militia 7 Sep 1804. Ensign 48th Foot 1806. Lt 3 Feb 1808.
    Served in the Peninsula Apr 1809 – Apr 1813. Present at Douro, Talavera, Busaco, Ciudad Rodrigo, Badajoz and Salamanca where he was severely wounded.

LESCHEN, Friedrich
Lieutenant. 3rd Line Battalion, King's German Legion.
Named on the Regimental Memorial: La Haye Sainte, Waterloo, Belgium. (Photograph)

Lt 29 Aug 1812.
    Present at Waterloo where he was severely wounded and died of his wounds at Brussels 28 Jun 1815. Also served in the Mediterranean 1808–1814 and Netherlands 1814.

L'ESTRANGE, George Guy Carleton
Lieutenant Colonel. 31st (Huntingdonshire) Regiment of Foot.
Memorial tablet: St Paul and St Margaret's Church, Nidd, Yorkshire. (Photograph)

IN THE VAULT BENEATH THIS TOWER REST THE REMAINS OF / BENJAMIN RAWSON / .... / ALSO OF / GEORGE GUY CARLETON L'ESTRANGE, MAJOR GENERAL, C.B. / BORN SEPT 18TH 1780, DIED AUG 26TH 1848. / ....

Ensign 6th Foot 1 Apr 1798. Lt 24 Nov 1798. Capt 60th Foot 13 Mar 1802. Capt 73rd Foot 26 May 1803. Major 98th Foot 22 May 1804. Major 31st Foot 21 Apr 1808. Bt Lt Colonel 30 May 1811. Lt Colonel 26th

Foot 10 Dec 1812. Lt Colonel 31st Foot 8 Jun 1815. Bt Colonel 19 Jul 1821. Major General 22 Jul 1830. Lt General 23 Nov 1841.

Served in the Peninsula Nov 1808 – May 1812. Present at Busaco, Torres Vedras, pursuit of Massena, Olivencia, first siege of Badajoz, Albuera (Mentioned in Despatches), Arroyo dos Molinos and Badajoz.

Sailed for Portugal with 31st Foot to join Sir John Moore but did not land in Lisbon until November 1808 and found that Moore was retreating to Corunna. So he and his cousin Edmund joined Benjamin D'Urban on the QMG's staff and went to join Sir Robert Wilson who was with the Spanish Army, observing the movements of the French between Spain and Portugal. This resulted in Edmund's capture and imprisonment in Verdun. Guy returned to the 31st Foot. At Albuera L'Estrange and the regiment distinguished themselves. Awarded a Bt Lt Colonelcy and Gold Medal. Wellington said of him 'there is one officer, Major L'Estrange of the 31st whom I must recommend in the strongest possible manner for some promotion or other. After the other parts of the same brigade were swept off by the cavalry the little battalion alone held its ground against all the columns en masse.'

Also served in Gibraltar 1812 (with 26th Foot), Manchester 1819 (in command of the 31st Foot at Peterloo), and Isle de France 1826 (DAG). CB. Colonel 59th Foot 12 Jun 1843. Colonel 61st Foot 29 Mar 1848.
REFERENCE: *United Service Journal, Sep 1848, p. 160. Gentleman's Magazine, Oct 1848, p. 424. Annual Register, 1848, Appx, p. 246.*

LEUE, Georg Ludwig
Major. 4th Line Battalion, King's German Legion.
Named on the Regimental Memorial: La Haye Sainte, Waterloo, Belgium. (Photograph)

Capt 15 Nov 1804. Major 4 Jun 1814.
Served in the Peninsula Aug 1812 – Apr 1814. Present at Castalla and Tarragona. Present at Waterloo where he was severely wounded and died of his wounds 23 Jun 1815. Also served in Hanover 1805, Baltic 1807, Mediterranean 1808–1812 and Netherlands 1814.

LEVETZOW, Friedrich Carl Ludwig von
Lieutenant. 1st Regiment of Dragoons, King's German Legion.
Named on the Regimental Memorial: La Haye Sainte, Waterloo, Belgium. (Photograph)

Cornet 22 Sep 1811. Lt 13 Mar 1812.
Present in the Peninsula Jan 1812 – Apr 1814. Present at Salamanca, Garcia Hernandez, Majalahonda, Vittoria, Tarbes and Toulouse. Present at Waterloo where he was killed. Also served in the Netherlands 1814–1815.

LEWIS, Charles
Sergeant. 66th (Berkshire) Regiment of Foot.
Buried in St James Churchyard, Cowley, Oxfordshire. (Burial record)

Pte 4 Aug 1802. Cpl 1806. Sgt 1809.
Served in the Peninsula Apr 1809 – Apr 1814. Present at Talavera, Busaco, Albuera (wounded), Vittoria, Pyrenees and Toulouse. Discharged 24 Jun 1817. Returned home to be an agricultural labourer. MGS medal for Talavera, Busaco, Albuera, Vittoria, Pyrenees and Toulouse. Died 26 Sep 1845 aged 65. Buried in an unmarked grave.
REFERENCE: *Waterloo Journal, Spring 2010, pp. 14–21.*

LEWIS, Griffith George
Captain. Royal Engineers.
Memorial tablet: Beverley Minster, Beverley, Yorkshire. (Extract from the memorial tablet to Lancelot Machell and Engineers at assault on San Sebastian). (Photograph)

.... / "THE THREE OFFICERS OF THE ENGINEERS EMPLOYED / TO CONDUCT THE DIFFERENT PARTS OF THE COLUMNS / OF ATTACK, BEHAVED ADMIRABLY, BUT SUFFER'D SEVERELY / CAP^{TN}. LEWIS LOST HIS LEG. LIEU^T. JONES WAS WOUNDED / AND TAKEN, AND LIEU^T MACHELL ON HIS RETURN WAS / KILLED IN THE TRENCHES." / LIEU^T. GEN^L. S^R T. GRAHAM'S / REPORT 26TH JULY.

Named on the Regimental Memorial: Rochester Cathedral, Rochester, Kent. (Photograph)

2nd Lt 15 Mar 1803. Lt 2 Jul 1803. 2nd Capt 18 Nov 1807. Capt 21 Jul 1813. Bt Major 21 Sep 1813. Lt Colonel 29 Jul 1825. Bt Colonel 28 Jun 1838. Colonel 23 Nov 1841. Major General 11 Nov 1851. Lt General 12 Aug 1858. Colonel Commandant 23 Nov 1858.
    Served in the Peninsula Feb – Aug 1813. Present at San Sebastian (severely wounded and Mentioned in Despatches 25 Jul 1813. Awarded Bt Majority). Served in France 1817. Also served in Calabria 1805–1806 (present at Maida, Scylla, Ischia, Procida) and St Maura 1810. MGS medal for Maida and San Sebastian. CB. Died at Brighton 24 Oct 1859.

LEWIS, Richard
Private. 23rd (Royal Welch Fusiliers) Regiment of Foot.
Headstone: All Saints Churchyard, Baschurch, Shropshire. (Left of pathway from main doors). (Photograph)

IN / AFFECTIONATE / REMEMBRANCE OF / RICHARD LEWIS, / WALFORD HEATH, / WHO DIED 5TH JUNE 1875 / AGED 83 YEARS.

Served in the Peninsula with 1/23rd 1812 – Apr 1814. Present at Vittoria, Nive, Orthes and Toulouse. Served at Waterloo. MGS medal for Vittoria, Nive, Orthes and Toulouse.
REFERENCE: *Shrewsbury Chronicle, May 1875.*

LIGHT, Henry
Captain. Royal Artillery.
Ledger stone: King Charles the Martyr Churchyard, Falmouth, Cornwall. (Photograph)

SIR HENRY LIGHT K.C.B. / FORMERLY OF THE ROYAL ARTILLERY / LATE GOVERNOR AND COMMANDER-IN-CHIEF / OF BRITISH GUINEA. / BORN THE 7TH OF FEBRUARY 1783. / DIED THE 3RD OF MARCH 1870. / ....

2nd Lt 1 Aug 1799. 1st Lt 18 Aug 1801. 2nd Capt 1 Jun 1806. Capt 20 Dec 1814. Bt Major 12 Aug 1819.
    Served in the Peninsula Apr – May 1810. Present at Cadiz, whilst serving at Gibraltar. Also served at Walcheren 1809. Retired 10 Jul 1824. Lt Governor of Antigua 1836. Governor and Commander-in-Chief of British Guiana 1838–1848. Retired 1848. KCB. One of the early explorers of Egypt and Nubia. Author of *Travels in Egypt, Nubia, Holy Land, Mount Libanon and Cyprus,* 1818 and *Sicilian Scenery,* which was illustrated with sketches by William Light 1823. Brother of Capt William Light 3rd Foot.
REFERENCE: *Light, Henry, The expedition to Walcheren 1809, reprint edited by Gareth Glover, 2005.*

LIGHT, John
Lieutenant. 28th (North Gloucestershire) Regiment of Foot.
Memorial tablet: King's Chapel, Gibraltar, (North wall). (Photograph)

TO THE MEMORY OF / LIEUTENANTS JOSEPH BENNETT & JOHN LIGHT / OF THE LIGHT INFANTRY & GRENADIER COMPANIES / OF THE 28TH REGIMENT, / COMMANDED BY LIEU-TENANT COLONEL BELSON, / WHICH, TOGETHER WITH THE FLANK COMPANIES OF THIS GARRISON / WERE DETACHED TO TARIFA, WHERE A FORCE WAS ASSEMBLED BY / LIEU-TENANT GENERAL GRAHAM / TO ATTACK, IN CONJUNCTION WITH THE SPANISH ARMY; / THE FRENCH BEFORE CADIZ. / AT THE MEMORABLE BATTLE OF BARROSA, / FOUGHT ON THE 5TH MARCH 1811, THOSE TWO PROMISING YOUNG OFFICERS, / AT THE HEAD OF THEIR RESPECTIVE COMPANIES, (THEIR / CAPTAINS HAVING BOTH QUITTED THE FIELD FROM SHOTS EARLY / IN THE ACTION) RECEIVED THEIR MORTAL WOUNDS. / THIS TABLET IS ERECTED BY THEIR BROTHER OFFICERS / IN TESTIMONY OF THEIR ESTEEM FOR THEM.

Ensign 2 Feb 1805. Lt 1 Apr 1806.
  Served in the Peninsula with 2/28th Jul 1809 – Jul 1810 and 1/28th Sep 1810 – Mar 1811. Present at Tarifa and Barrosa where he was killed.

LIGHT, William
Captain. 3rd (East Kent) Regiment of Foot.
Obelisk: Light Square, Currie Street, Adelaide, Australia. (Photograph)

Side 1:

IN MEMORY / OF / COLONEL WILLIAM LIGHT, / FIRST SURVEYOR-GENERAL, / BY WHOM / THE SITE OF ADELAIDE WAS FIXED / ON DECEMBER 29TH 1836. / DIED OCTOBER 5, 1839, / AGED 53 YEARS. / BURIED HERE OCTOBER 10, 1839. / ERECTED BY THE PEOPLE OF ADELAIDE, / ASSISTED BY THE GOVERNMENT OF THE STATE.

Side 2:

A TRIBUTE TO / COLONEL WILLIAM LIGHT / FIRST SURVEYOR-GENERAL AND FOUNDER OF THE CITY / OF ADELAIDE, WHO DIED 150 YEARS AGO ON / 5TH OCTOBER 1839. / "THE REASONS THAT LED ME TO FIX ADELAIDE / WHERE IT IS I DO NOT EXPECT TO BE GENER-ALLY / UNDERSTOOD OR CALMLY JUDGED OF AT THE PRESENT / . . . . I LEAVE IT TO POSTERITY . . . . TO DECIDE / WHETHER I AM ENTITLED TO PRAISE OR BLAME." / THIS PLAQUE WAS PLACED BY MEMBERS OF THE INSTITUTION / OF SURVEYORS, AUSTRALIA, THE S.A. / DEPARTMENT OF LANDS, / AND THE PIONEERS ASSOCIATION.

Statue: Montefiore Hill, Adelaide, Australia. (Photograph)

Side 1:

COLONEL WILLIAM LIGHT / FIRST SURVEYOR GENERAL / FIXED THE SITE AND LAID / OUT THE CITY OF ADELAIDE / IN 1836 / ERECTED BY CITIZENS 1906

Side 2:

EXTRACTS FROM COLONEL LIGHT'S JOURNAL, 1839 / "THE REASONS THAT LED ME TO FIX ADELAIDE WHERE IT IS I DO NOT EXPECT TO BE GENERALLY / UNDERSTOOD OR CALMLY

JUDGED OF AT THE PRESENT. MY ENEMIES, HOWEVER, BY DISPUTING THEIR / VALIDITY IN EVERY PARTICULAR, HAVE DONE ME THE GOOD SERVICE OF FIXING THE WHOLE OF THE / RESPONSIBILITY UPON ME. I AM PERFECTLY WILLING TO BEAR IT, / AND I LEAVE TO POSTERITY, AND NOT TO THEM, TO DECIDE WHETHER I AM ENTITLED TO PRAISE OR TO BLAME."

Cornet 4th Dragoons 5 May 1808. Lt 13 Aug 1809. Capt 3rd Foot 25 Nov 1814. Bt Major 21 Jun 1817. Capt 13th Foot 20 Aug 1818.

Served in the Peninsula May 1809 – Apr 1814 (attached to the Spanish Army May 1811 – Oct 1812 and on Staff as DAQMG Oct 1812 – Apr 1814). Present at Talavera, Busaco, Albuera, Usagre, Aldea da Ponte, Llerena and Salamanca. Served on the Staff as an intelligence officer (fluent in French and Spanish, he was also an artist). Retired on half pay and left the army in 1821. Went to Spain with Sir Robert Wilson in Apr 1823, who had raised a volunteer force to help the revolution. Light was appointed Lt Colonel in the Spanish Revolutionary Army and was severely wounded at the action at Corunna. The revolution was a failure and he returned to England in November 1823.

Travelled to Europe to continue sketching. His sketches were used in Henry Light's *Sicilian Scenery,* published in 1823, and *Views of Pompeii* in 1828. In Egypt he was commander of a paddle steamer on the River Nile with Captain John Hindmarch 1834–1835. Captain Hindmarch became Governor of South Australia Nov 1835 and he appointed William Light as Surveyor-General. Site of the new settlement was left to Light and in two months he had laid out 1,042 acres of Adelaide. By 1837 60,000 acres of the country around Adelaide had been surveyed. Despite some opposition to the site of Adelaide, Light had his way and truly became the 'founder of Adelaide'. Ill health prevented him from more work and he died 6 Oct 1839 and was buried in the square that bears his name. A new memorial was raised on 21 Jun 1905. Brother of Capt Henry Light Royal Artillery.

REFERENCE: *Australian Dictionary of Biography. Dutton, Geoffrey, Colonel William Light: founder of a city, 1991. Gill, Thomas, A bibliographical sketch of Colonel William Light, the founder of Adelaide, 1911.*

LILLEY, Samuel
Sergeant. 24th (Warwickshire) Regiment of Foot.
Headstone: St Mary the Virgin Churchyard, Fordwich, Kent. (Photograph)

SACRED TO THE MEMORY OF / SAMUEL LILLEY / SERJEANT OF THE 24TH REGT OF FOOT / WHO DEPARTED THIS LIFE DEC 17TH 1856 / IN THE 80TH YEAR OF HIS AGE. / BENEATH THIS TURF SLUMBERS ONE WHO LIVED / A SOLDIERS LIFE AS SOLDIERS LIFE SHOULD BE / TRUE TO HIS GOD HIS COUNTRY & HIS HOME / AND LOVED BY ALL, / HE DIED MOST PEACEFULLY.

Pte 1 Mar 1808. Cpl 25 Jul 1809. Sgt 1 May 1811.

Served in the Peninsula with 2/24th Apr 1809 – Dec 1812. Present at Busaco, Fuentes d'Onoro, Salamanca and Burgos (wounded). MGS medal for Busaco, Fuentes d'Onoro and Salamanca. Also served in India 1819–1823. Discharged 29 Nov 1826 aged 42. Died 17 Dec 1856.

LILLIE, Thomas
2nd Lieutenant. 23rd (Royal Welch Fusiliers) Regiment of Foot.
Cross on base: St Mary's Catholic Cemetery, Kensal Green, London. (6304 PS). Inscription largely illegible. (Photograph)

.... ONE OF THE HEROES OF WATERLOO / ....

2nd Lt 1 Oct 1812. Lt 17 Jul 1815. Capt Ceylon Rifles 7 Dec 1838. Bt Major 11 Nov 1851. Major 29 Aug 1856. Bt Lt Colonel 10 Oct 1858.

Served in the Peninsula with 1/23rd Mar 1813 – Apr 1814. Present at Subijana de Moullos, Vittoria, Pyrenees, Nivelle, Nive, Orthes (severely wounded) and Toulouse. Present at Waterloo, siege of Cambrai and with the Army of Occupation. MGS medal for Vittoria, Pyrenees, Nivelle, Nive, Orthes and Toulouse. Also served in Ceylon in command of the Ceylon Rifles from 1838. Took part in the Kandian War of 1848 and commanded the only European troops to take part. Received the thanks from the Governor of Ceylon for his gallantry. Died 24 Apr 1862.
REFERENCE: *Gentleman's Magazine, Jun 1862, p. 792. Annual Register, 1862, Appx, p. 369.*

LIND, Robert
Lieutenant. 71st (Highland Light Infantry) Regiment of Foot.
Ledger stone in Family railed enclosure: Derryloran Old Churchyard, Cookstown, County Tyrone, Northern Ireland. (Photograph)

SACRED / TO THE MEMORY OF / LIEUT ROBERT LIND WHO SERVED IN THE / GALLANT 71ST REGIMENT DURING THE PENINSULAR WAR / AND WHO WAS SEVERELY AND DANGER-OUSLY / WOUNDED AT THE EVER MEMORABLE BATTLE / OF WATERLOO AND WHOSE LONG AND / MERITORIOUS SERVICES WERE AMPLY / ACKNOWLEDGED AND REWARDED BY HIS COUNTRY. / HE DIED AT HIS RESIDENCE WATERLOO / COTTAGE COOKSTOWN ON THE 30TH JUNE 1851 / IN THE 71ST YEAR OF HIS AGE.

Ensign 11 Feb 1808. Lt 10 Oct 1809.
Served in the Peninsula Aug 1808 – Jan 1809 and Sep 1813 – Apr 1814. Present at Rolica, Vimeiro, Corunna and Nive. Present at Waterloo (severely wounded by a grape shot, weighing 10 ounces which entered his chest and was cut out of his shoulder three days later. Lind kept the shot and had it hooped in silver. Awarded pension of £70 per annum). Also served at Walcheren 1809. MGS medal for Rolica, Vimeiro, Corunna and Nive.

LINDSAY, James
Lieutenant and Captain. 1st Regiment of Foot Guards.
Memorial: Royal Military Chapel, Wellington Barracks, London. (M.I.) (Destroyed by a Flying Bomb in 1944)

"IN MEMORY OF LIEUT.-GENERAL JAMES LINDSAY OF BELCARRES. SERVED IN THE 1ST GUARDS IN THE WALCHEREN EXPEDITION, 1809. THE PENINSULAR WAR, 1811; HOLLAND, 1813; WOUNDED AT BERGEN-OP-ZOOM. DIED 1856. / THIS WINDOW IS GIVEN BY HIS WIDOW, ANNE LINDSAY, AND HIS FOUR CHILDREN, COUTTS LINDSAY, BART., LATE CAPTAIN GRENADIER GUARDS, ROBERT JAMES LOYD LINDSAY, V.C., LIEUT.-COLONEL LATE SCOTS FUSILIER GUARDS, MARGARET COUNTESS OF CRAWFORD, AND MARY ANNE HOLFORD."

Ensign 16 Dec 1807. Lt and Capt 10 Dec 1812. Capt and Lt Colonel 20 Nov 1823. Bt Colonel 28 Jun 1838. Major General 11 Nov 1851. Lt General 18 May 1855.
Served in the Peninsula with 3rd Battalion Apr 1811 – Apr 1813. Present at Cadiz. Also served at Walcheren 1809, Netherlands 1814 (present at Bergen-op-Zoom where he was severely wounded and awarded pension of £100 per annum). Half pay 19 Nov 1830. MP for County of Fife. Died at Genoa, Italy 5 Dec 1855.
REFERENCE: *Gentleman's Magazine, Jan 1856, p. 83. Annual Register, 1855, Appx, p. 323.*

LINDSAY, Martin
Lieutenant Colonel. 78th (Highland) Regiment of Foot.
Memorial tablet: St Paul's Church, Kandy, Ceylon. (Photograph)

SACRED / TO THE MEMORY OF / COL. MARTIN LINDSAY C.B. / 78TH HIGHLANDERS, / DIED HERE 28TH OF JANUARY 1847, / IN HIS 66TH YEAR. / ESTEEMED AND REGRETTED / BY ALL WHO KNEW HIM.

Ensign Jul 1794 (aged 13). Lt 46th Foot 29 Nov 1800. Capt 22 Nov 1801. Capt 78th Foot 25 May 1803. Major 4 Jan 1810. Lt Colonel 25 Nov 1813. Reduced to half pay Dec 1818. Reappointed Lt Colonel 78th Foot 12 Aug 1819. Bt Colonel 22 Jul 1830.

    Served in the Netherlands 1814–1815 (present at Merxem and Antwerp). Also served in the attack and capture of Java 1811 (on 16 Sep he commanded eight companies of the 78th Highlanders) and Ceylon 1819–1837 (Commandant at Trincomalee 1833). Gold Medal for Java. CB.
REFERENCE: *Gentleman's Magazine, Sep 1847, pp. 316–7. Lewis, J. Penry, List of inscriptions on tombstones and monuments in Ceylon, 1913, reprint 1994, pp. 324–5.*

LINDSAY, Patrick
Major. 39th (Dorsetshire) Regiment of Foot.
Memorial monument: St Michael's Churchyard, Inveresk, Edinburgh, Scotland. (Between two yew trees at west end of the churchyard). (Photograph)

SACRED TO THE MEMORY / OF MAJOR GENERAL SIR PATRICK LINDSAY / KCB / WHO AFTER A DISTINGUISHED SERVICE OF MORE THAN XLIV / YEARS IN ALMOST EVERY QUARTER OF THE GLOBE ACQUIRED A REPUTATION / OF THE HIGHEST ORDER / AN AFFECTIONATE RELATION A STEADFAST FRIEND / A BRAVE AND ACCOMPLISHED SOLDIER / MAY THE MEMORY OF HIS WORTH LONG SURVIVE THIS SIMPLE RECORD / OF HIS NAME AND AT THE LAST MAY HE BE FOUND ACCEPTED TO HIM / THROUGH WHOSE MERITS ALONE WE CAN BE RECEIVED INTO ETERNAL LIFE / NAT 21 FEBRUARY 1778 OBIT MARCH 1839

Capt 78 Foot 1 Sep 1795. Capt 39th Foot 20 Oct 1796. Major 1 Oct 1807. Bt Lt Colonel 20 Jun 1811. Lt Colonel 12 Aug 1824. Bt Colonel 27 May 1825. Major General 10 Jan 1837.

    Served in the Peninsula with 2/39th Jul 1809 – Jan 1812 and 1/39th Oct 1813 – Apr 1814. Present at Busaco, first siege of Badajoz, Albuera, Arroyo dos Molinos, Nivelle, Nive, Garris and Toulouse. Gold Medal for Albuera. KCB. Also served in Flanders 1794–1795, West Indies 1796, Sicily 1805, North America 1814–1815 and India (present in Burmese campaign 1824–1826).
REFERENCE: *Gentleman's Magazine, Jul 1839, p. 90.*

LINDSEY, Owen
Staff Surgeon. Medical Department.
Memorial tablet: Holy Trinity Church, Cheltenham, Gloucestershire. (Photograph)

IN MEMORY OF / OWEN LINDSEY ESQR M. D. / DEPUTY INSPECTOR GENL OF / ARMY HOSPITALS, / WHO DIED / AT BUDLEIGH SALTERTON DEVON, / MARCH 17TH 1851 / AGED 65. /
....

Asst Surgeon 2nd Dragoon Guards 31 Dec 1803. Surgeon 72nd Foot 2 Nov 1809. Surgeon 74th Foot 28 Dec 1809. Surgeon 5th Dragoon Guards 16 Jan 1812. Staff Surgeon 5 Nov 1812. Deputy Inspector General of Hospitals 22 Jul 1830.

    Served in the Peninsula Feb 1810 – Jan 1812 and May 1812 – Apr 1814 (attached to 4th Division from Mar 1813). Present at Busaco, Redinha, Casal Nova, Foz d'Arouce, Sabugal, Fuentes d'Onoro, second siege of Badajoz, El Bodon, Salamanca, Vittoria, Pyrenees, Nivelle, Nive, Orthes and Toulouse. Also served at Walcheren 1809. MD Glasgow 1827. MGS medal for Busaco, Fuentes d'Onoro, Salamanca, Vittoria, Pyrenees, Nivelle, Nive, Orthes and Toulouse.

LINTOTT, John
Lieutenant. 51ˢᵗ (2ⁿᵈ Yorkshire West Riding) Light Infantry.
Gravestone: Cemetery No 1, Dinapore, India. (M.I.)

"CAPTAIN JOHN LINTOTT, H M'S 13ᵀᴴ LT INFᵞ REGT., DIED 9ᵀᴴ AUGUST 1829, AGED 35 YEARS."

Ensign 101ˢᵗ Foot 22 Apr 1812. Ensign 50ᵗʰ Foot 16 Jul 1812. Lt 36ᵗʰ Foot 22 Apr 1813. Lt 51ˢᵗ Foot 25 Dec 1814. Capt 29 May 1817. Capt 13ᵗʰ Foot 9 Apr 1825.
    Present at Waterloo with 51ˢᵗ Foot. Also served in India with 13ᵗʰ Foot 1823 (present in the First Burmese War 1824–1826).

LITCHFIELD, Richard
1ˢᵗ Lieutenant. Royal Artillery.
Headstone: St Peter's Churchyard, Leckhampton, Gloucestershire. (Photograph)

IN / MEMORY OF / SARAH ELIZABETH / WIFE OF / CAPTAIN RICHARD LITCHFIELD R. A. / DIED FEB 17 1863 / AGED 68 YEARS / RICHARD LITCHFIELD / DIED SEPT 14 1865 / AGED 73 / HE SERVED IN THE PENINSULA / 1812 – 1814

2ⁿᵈ Lt 26 Nov 1808. 1ˢᵗ Lt 5 Sep 1811. 2ⁿᵈ Capt 6 Nov 1827.
    Served in the Peninsula Jan 1812 – Apr 1814. Present at Almarez, Vittoria, Orthes and Toulouse. Also served at Walcheren 1809 and North America 1814 (present at Plattsburg). MGS medal for Vittoria, Orthes and Toulouse.

LITTLE, George
Lieutenant. 45ᵗʰ (Nottinghamshire) Regiment of Foot.
Named on the Memorial: St Andrew's Church, (now Musée Historique), Biarritz, France. (Photograph)

Ensign 28 Sep 1809. Lt 7 Nov 1811.
    Served in the Peninsula Sep 1811 – Apr 1814. Present at Ciudad Rodrigo, Badajoz, Salamanca, Vittoria, (severely wounded), Pyrenees, Nivelle, Nive, Orthes, Vic Bigorre and Toulouse where he was severely wounded and died of his wounds 11 Apr 1814.

LITTLE, William
Captain. 92ⁿᵈ Regiment of Foot.
Family Memorial: Langholm Old Churchyard, Langholm, Dumfriesshire, Scotland. (No longer extant). (M.I.)

"SACRED TO THE MEMORY OF JOHN LITTLE .... AND OF HIS 3ᴿᴰ SON WILLIAM LITTLE, CAPTAIN IN THE 92ᴺᴰ REGIMENT, WHO WAS KILLED AT QUATRE BRAS 16ᵀᴴ JUNE, 1815 AGED 27."

Ensign 1807. Lt 24 May 1810. Capt 7 Jan 1813.
    Present at Quatre Bras where he was killed.

LIVINGSTONE, Francis
Captain. 90ᵗʰ (Perthshire Volunteers) Regiment of Foot.
Pedestal tomb: St George's Cemetery, Lisbon. (Grave number E 12). (Photograph)

SACRED / TO THE MEMORY / OF / CAPTAIN FRANCIS LIVINGSTONE / OF THE 90ᵀᴴ REGIMENT

BRITISH INFANTRY, / SON OF SIR ALEXANDER LIVINGSTONE. BARᵀ. / OF THE KINGDOM OF SCOTLAND. / HE DIED ON THE 11ᵀᴴ OCTᴿ 1812 / AGED 27 YEARS.

Ensign Glengarry Fencible Infantry 7 Oct 1797. Lt 2ⁿᵈ Foot 2 May 1801. Lt 26 Foot 19 Jun 1803. Capt 90ᵗʰ Foot 16 Oct 1806.
    Died in Lisbon 11 Oct 1812 after arriving from Spain to recover his health.

LLEWELLYN, Richard

Captain. 28th (North Gloucestershire) Regiment of Foot.
Monument: Kensal Green Cemetery, London. (20437/127/RS). (Photograph)

TO THE MEMORY OF / GENERAL SIR RICHARD LLEWELLYN / KNIGHT COMMANDER OF THE BATH / COLONEL IN CHIEF OF THE 39ᵀᴴ FOOT / DIED 7 DECEMBER 1867 / ....

Capt 52ⁿᵈ Foot Temporary rank 1799 – 1802. Ensign 24 Jul 1802. Lt 7 Apr 1804. Capt 28ᵗʰ Foot 28 Feb 1805. Bt Major 23 Apr 1812. Bt Lt Colonel 18 Jun 1815. Bt Colonel 10 Jan 1837. Major General 9 Nov 1846. Lt General 20 Jun 1854. General 18 Jan 1861
    Served in the Peninsula with 2/28ᵗʰ Jul 1809 – Jul 1811 and 1/28ᵗʰ Aug 1811 – Apr 1813. Present at Busaco, first siege of Badajoz, Albuera, Arroyo dos Molinos, Almarez, retreat from Burgos and Bordeaux. MGS medal for Busaco and Albuera. Present at Quatre Bras and Waterloo (severely wounded, awarded Bt Lt Colonelcy and a pension of £300 per annum). Also served at Ferrol with 52ⁿᵈ Foot 1800, Cadiz and Mediterranean 1800–1801. KCB 1862. Colonel 39ᵗʰ Foot 17 Jan 1853.
REFERENCE: *Gentleman's Magazine, Jan 1868, p. 119.*

LLOYD, Richard

Lieutenant Colonel. 84ᵗʰ (York and Lancaster) Regiment of Foot.
Pedestal tomb in railed enclosure: Bidart Churchyard, near St Jean de Luz, France. (Photograph)

A LA MÉMOIRE / DU LIEUᵀ COLONEL RICKARD LLOYD, / TUÉ AU COMBAT DE LA NIVE, LE 10ᴱ / DECEMBRE 1813, / A LA TÊTE DU 84ᴱ REGIMENT D'INFANTERIE ANGLAISE, / AGE 37 ANS. / ADMIRE ET RESPECTE PAR SA PATRIE RECONNAISSANTE, / HONORE ET ESTIME PAR SES OFFICIERS, ET SES SOLDATS, / CHERI ET REGRETTE PAR SES NOMBREUX AMIS. / RESTAURE PAR SOUSCRIPTION EN JULI, 1904 LA LISTE DES / SOUSCRIPTEURS EST DEPOSEE A LA MARIE ET AU PRESBYTERE. LECTEUR! / A QUELQUES NATIONS QUE TU APPARTIENNES, / RÉFLÉCHIS / ON CONTEMPLAIT CE TRIBUT D L'AFFECTION CONJUGALE, / AVEC L'AMOUR DE LA PATRIE, L'HONNEUR, LA PHILANTHROPIE, / LE RESPECT POUR LES RESTES DES MERITE DE LA VALEUR, / SONT NATURELS DANS TOUS LES CLIMATS.

Named on the Memorial: St Andrew's Church, (now Musée Historique), Biarritz, France. (Photograph)

Ensign 66ᵗʰ Foot 16 Oct 1792. Lt 15 Mar 1794. Capt in Lt Colonel's Fraser's Corps of Infantry 2 Oct 1800. Major Royal African Corps 25 Dec 1803. Lt Colonel Royal York Rangers 13 Nov 1806. Lt Colonel 84ᵗʰ Foot 24 Dec 1808.
    Served in the Peninsula Jul – Dec 1813. Present at Bidassoa and Nive where he was Mentioned in Despatches and killed 11 Dec 1813. Gold Medal for Nive. Also served at Walcheren 1809. An unusual feature of his grave is that he was buried standing upright.

LLOYD, Thomas

Major. 94ᵗʰ Regiment of Foot.
Named on the Memorial: St Andrew's Church, (now Musée Historique), Biarritz, France. (Photograph)

Ensign 54th Foot 1 Aug 1797. Lt 6 May 1799. Capt 6th Reserve Battalion 8 Oct 1803. Capt 43rd Foot 10 Aug 1804. Major 94th Foot 4 Oct 1810. Bt Lt Colonel 17 Aug 1812.

Served in the Peninsula with 1/43rd Oct 1808 – Jan 1809, Jul 1809 – Dec 1810 and with 94th Foot Jan – Jun 1811 and May 1812 – Nov 1813. Present at Vigo, Coa (wounded), Busaco, Salamanca, Vittoria, Pyrenees and Nivelle where he was killed 10 Nov 1813 and Mentioned in Despatches. Gold Medal for Salamanca, Vittoria and Nivelle. Also served at Copenhagen 1807. The oldest friend of Sir William Napier. 'this Lloyd, a Captain of the 43rd, was known throughout the Army for his genius, wit and bravery, his happy temper and magnificent person. He fell gloriously at the Battle of Nivelle in 1813.'

LLOYD, William John
Major. Royal Artillery.
Named on the Regimental Memorial: St Joseph's Church, Waterloo, Belgium. (Photograph)
Memorial tablet: Inside Mausoleum, Evere Cemetery, Brussels, Belgium. (Photograph)

MAJOR / WILLIAM JOHN / LLOYD / ROYAL ARTILLERY / AGED 35

2nd Lt 1 Jun 1795. 1st Lt 1 Apr 1797. Capt-Lieut 12 Sep 1803. Capt 1 Feb 1808. Major 4 Jun 1814.

Present at Quatre Bras and Waterloo in command of a brigade of Artillery where he was severely wounded and died of his wounds at Brussels 29 Jul 1815. One of the select band of soldiers buried in the Mausoleum at Evere. Also served at Walcheren 1809.

LLUELLYN, Richard, see LLEWELLYN, Richard

LOCK, Henry
Ensign. 51st (2nd Yorkshire West Riding) Light Infantry.
Tombstone: Mominabad Cemetery, Bihar District, India. (M.I.)

"SACRED TO THE MEMORY OF THE LATE LIEUT HENRY LOCK OF 26TH BENGAL NATIVE INFANTRY AND BRIGADE MAJOR OF H. H. THE NIZAM'S CAVALRY BRIGADE. SON OF REAR ADMIRAL LOCK OF THE ISLE OF WIGHT. DIED OF CHOLERA ON THE 16TH MAY 1824. AGED 26 YEARS."

Ensign 51st Foot 13 Oct 1814. Ensign 24th Bengal Native Infantry 7 Jan 1820. Lt 16 Apr 1822. Lt 26th Bengal Native Infantry Sep 1823. Lt 52nd Native Infantry May 1824.

Served at Waterloo with 51st Foot. Joined the Bengal Native Infantry in 1820 and served in India until his death from cholera in 1824.

LOCKE, John
Major. 84th (York and Lancaster) Regiment of Foot.
Cross on base: English Cemetery, Florence, Italy. (Grave number F2N-O). (Photograph)

SACRED TO THE MEMORY OF LIEUT GENERAL JOHN LOCKE / OF NEWCASTLE IRELAND / WHO DEPARTED THIS LIFE THE 28 FEBRUARY 1837 / AGED 67. / (VERSE)

Cornet 10th Lt Dragoons 21 Feb 1793. Lt 18 Jun 1794. Capt 26th Lt Dragoons 25 Mar 1795. Major 27th Lt Dragoons 22 Jan 1801. Major 87th Foot 1802. Bt Lt Colonel 1 Jan 1805. Major 84th Foot 25 Aug 1808. Bt Colonel 4 Jun 1813. Major General 12 Aug 1819. Lt General 10 Jan 1837.

Served in the Peninsula Sep 1813 – Jan 1814. Present at Bayonne. Also served in the West Indies 1793 – 1798 (present at Martinique, St Lucia, Guadeloupe – siege of Fort Bourbon and St Vincent 1795 in the Charib Wars) and Walcheren 1809. Died at Florence 28 Feb 1837.
REFERENCE: *Royal Military Calendar, Vol 4, p. 31. Gentleman's Magazine, Jun 1837, p. 659.*

LOCKHART, John Elliott
Cornet. 12th (Prince of Wales's) Regiment of Light Dragoons.
Named on the Regimental Memorial: St Joseph's Church, Waterloo, Belgium. (Photograph)

Cornet 28 Apr 1814.
  Killed at Waterloo.

LOFFT, Henry Capel
Lieutenant. 48th (Northamptonshire) Regiment of Foot.
Memorial tablet: St Mary's Church, Troston, Suffolk. (West wall). (Photograph)

FIDE & FORTITUDINE / TO / THE MEMORY / OF / HENRY CAPEL LOFFT / LIEUT: IN THE 48 REG: OF FOOT, / WHO WAS BORN AT TROSTON HALL, / 9 NOV 1783. / HE WAS LINEALLY DESCENDED FROM SIR ARTHUR CAPEL; / GRANDFATHER OF ARTHUR LORD CAPEL: / WHOSE MILITARY VIRTUE HE EMULATED: / AND WITH LIEUT. COL. DUCKWORTH, / AND MANY OTHER BRAVE OFFICERS AND MEN, / HONOURABLY FELL, / IN A MOST GALLANT CHARGE ON THE FRENCH LINE, / IN THE GREAT BATTLE OF ALBUHERA / NEAR BADAJOZ IN SPAIN, / EVER MEMORABLE FOR THE UNITED SUCCESSFUL HEROISM, / IN THE CAUSE OF NATIONAL INDEPENDENCE, / OF SPAIN, PORTUGAL, & BRITAIN. / 16TH MAY 1811; / IN HIS 28 YEAR. / QUANTUM NOVA GLORIA IN ARMIS, / ET PRÆDULEE DECUS, MAGNO IN CERTAMINE, POSSUNT. / V. EID. SEPT MDCCCXI. C. L. POSUIT.

Ensign 21 Nov 1805. Lt 29 May 1809.
  Served in the Peninsula Sep 1809 – May 1811. Present at Busaco and Albuera where he was killed 16 May 1811.

LOGAN, Joseph
Captain. 95th Regiment of Foot.
Low monument on base: St Mary's New Burial Ground, Cowgate Cemetery, (Plot 3 Grave BG260). Dover, Kent. (Photograph)

BENEATH THIS STONE / ARE BURIED THE REMAINS OF / COLONEL JOSEPH LOGAN

Ensign 62nd Foot 20 Dec 1799. Lt 8 Aug 1801. Lt 6th Battalion of Reserve 25 Sep 1803. Lt 95th Foot 9 Jun 1804. Capt 2 Feb 1809. Bt Major 18 Jun 1815. Major 10 Oct 1826. Lt Colonel 63rd 17 Dec 1829. Bt Colonel 23 Nov 1841.
  Served in the Peninsula with 1/95th Aug 1808 – Jan 1809 and 2/95th May 1812 – Apr 1814. Present at Cacabellos, Corunna, Salamanca, San Millan, Vittoria, Pyrenees, Vera, Bidassoa, Nivelle, Nive, Orthes, Tarbes and Toulouse. Present at Waterloo where he took command of the 2nd Battalion when his three senior officers were all wounded, for which he was awarded a Bt Majority and with the Army of Occupation. Also served in Hanover 1805, Copenhagen 1807, Walcheren 1809, Ireland 1818 with 95th Foot (Military Magistrate in Southern Counties), Australia 1830 with 63rd Foot and India with 63rd Foot. (Commander of Fort George 1834. In command of Tenasserim Provinces 1841 and had to defend them against the Burmese, but it did not come to war as the Burmese withdrew with 100,000 troops). Logan fell ill, returned to England and died in Dover 1 Sep 1844.
REFERENCE: *United Service Magazine, Oct 1844, pp. 319–20.*

LOGAN, Patrick
Lieutenant. 57th (West Middlesex) Regiment of Foot.
Mural Family Memorial tablet: Mordington Old Graveyard, Lamberton Farm, Berwickshire, Scotland. (Photograph)

ERECTED / IN MEMORY OF ABRAHAM LOGAN ESQ^R OF BURNHOUSE / .... / AND OF / HIS SON / PATRICK LOGAN. CAPTAIN OF THE 57 REG^T OF FOOT / WHO DIED IN AUSTRALIA IN 1831. AGED 39 YEARS.

Ensign 13 Dec 1810. Lt 25 Mar 1813. Capt 3 Apr 1825.

   Served in the Peninsula Aug 1811 - Apr 1814. Present at Vittoria, Pyrenees, Nivelle, Nive, Aire and Toulouse. Present in France with the Army of Occupation 1815-Nov 1817. Also served in North America 1814-1815, Australia 1823-1831. (Commandant of Moreton Bay Penal Settlement 1826). Led expeditions to explore regions of Queensland. Discovered rivers and was the first white man to climb Mount Barney. Murdered by Aborigines 28 Oct 1831 on one of his expeditions.
REFERENCE: *United Service Magazine, 1831, Part 2, p. 253. Australian Dictionary of Biography.*

LOGAN, Thomas Galbraith
Surgeon. 13th Regiment of Light Dragoons.
Low monument on base: St Margaret's Churchyard, Restalrig, Edinburgh, Scotland. (Photograph)

SACRED / TO THE MEMORY OF / THOMAS GALBRAITH LOGAN, M.D. / LATE SURGEON OF THE 5TH DRAGOON GUARDS / WHO DEPARTED THIS LIFE / THE 6TH MARCH 1836 AGED 56 YEARS. / THIS TOMB IS ERECTED BY HIS / BROTHER OFFICERS / AS A MARK OF THE ESTEEM AND REGARD / FOR THE DEPARTED WORTH. / REQUIESCAT IN PACE.

Asst Surgeon 48th Foot 31 Jan 1805. Asst Surgeon 7th Dragoon Guards 18 Sep 1806. Surgeon 71st Foot 24 Dec 1812. Surgeon 13th Lt Dragoons 9 Sep 1813. Surgeon 5th Dragoon Guards 25 Nov 1818.

   Served in the Peninsula May 1813 – Apr 1814. Present at Vittoria, Pyrenees, Nivelle, Nive, Garris, Orthes, Aire, St Gaudens and Toulouse. Present at Waterloo. MD Glasgow 1823. Father of Sir Thomas Galbraith Logan who served in the Sutlej campaign and Crimea where he was Principal Medical Officer to the Highland Division.

LOGGAN, George
Captain. 7th (Royal Fusiliers) Regiment of Foot.
Buried in Old Spital Churchyard, Windsor, Berkshire. (Grave number V 139)

Ensign 47th Foot 8 May 1806. Lt 14 Jun 1808. Lt 7th Foot 5 Apr 1809. Capt 21 Apr 1814. Capt 92nd Foot 9 Dec 1819.

   Served in the Peninsula with 2/7th Sep 1809 – Jun 1811 and 1/7th Jul 1811 – Oct 1813. Present at Busaco, Aldea da Ponte, Castrejon, Salamanca, Vittoria and Pyrenees (severely wounded at Sorauren 27 Jul 1813 and awarded pension of £100 per annum). MGS medal for Busaco, Salamanca, Vittoria and Pyrenees. Retired 13 Jun 1822. Military Knight of Windsor 13 Feb 1856. Died at Windsor 1 Mar 1860.

LOMAX, Thomas
Private. 2nd Life Guards.
Ledger stone: St John's Churchyard, Great Harwood, Lancashire. (Photograph)

SACRED / TO THE MEMORY OF / THOMAS LOMAX OF HARWOOD / WHO DIED ON THE 5TH DAY OF JUNE 1845, / AGED 51 YEARS. / HE SERVED IN HER MAJESTY'S SECOND / REGIMENT OF LIFE GUARDS FOR UPWARDS / OF SIX AND TWENTY YEARS. / HE WAS IN THE PENINSULA, AND ON THE / CONTINENT DURING THE YEARS 1813, 1814, / 1815 & 1816, AND WAS PRESENT AT THE GREAT / BATTLE OF WATERLOO, JUNE THE 18TH 1815, / WHERE HE WAS WOUNDED ON THE LEFT / SHOULDER, SIDE AND HEAD. / ON OBTAINING HIS DISCHARGE, HE WAS / PRESENTED, IN ADDITION TO HIS PENSION, WITH / A GRATUITY, AND A SILVER MEDAL FOR HIS / GOOD CONDUCT. / HE DEPARTED THIS LIFE, AFTER A LONG AND /

PAINFUL ILLNESS, IN PERFECT PEACE, RELYING / ON THE MERITS AND MEDIATION OF OUR / LORD AND SAVIOUR JESUS CHRIST.

Served in the Peninsula Nov 1812 – Apr 1814. Present at Vittoria and Toulouse. Present at Waterloo where he was wounded and with the Army of Occupation until 1816. MGS medal for Vittoria and Toulouse and Good Conduct medal.

LONDONDERRY, Marquis of see STEWART, Hon. Charles William

LONG, Edward Noel
Ensign. Coldstream Regiment of Foot Guards.
Memorial tablet: St Lawrence's Church, Seale, Surrey. (Photograph)

THIS STONE IS ERECTED IN MEMORY OF / EDWARD NOEL LONG, / ENSIGN IN THE COLD-STREAM REGIMENT OF FOOT GUARDS, / ELDEST SON OF EDWARD BEESTON LONG, / OF THIS PARISH, / HE WAS BORN MARCH 22ND 1788, / AND ON HIS VOYAGE TO JOIN THE BRITISH FORCES IN SPAIN, / HE, WITH OTHERS OF THE REGIMENT, / PERISHED IN THE OCEAN NEAR CAPE ST VINCENT, / DURING THE CONFUSION OF A FATAL ACCIDENT, / OCCA-SIONED BY THE ISIS MAN OF WAR / FALLING ON BOARD THE TRANSPORT WHEREIN HE WAS EMBARKED / THE NIGHT OF THE 8TH OF MARCH / 1809. / THE EXCELLENT QUALITIES OF HIS HEAD AND HEART, / WHICH SO DEEPLY ENDEARED HIM TO HIS RELATIONS, / AND TO HIS MANY YOUTHFUL COMPANIONS, / HAVE BEEN THUS COMMEMORATED / BY HIS EARLY FRIEND AND SCHOOLFELLOW. / NOW LAST, BUT NEAREST, OF THE SOCIAL BAND, / SEE, HONEST, OPEN, GENEROUS, CLEON STAND: / WITH SCARCE ONE SPECK, TO CLOUD THE PLEASING SCENE, / NO VICE DEGRADES THAT PUREST SOUL SERENE, / ON THE SAME DAY OUR STUDIOUS RACE WAS RUN, / THUS, SIDE BY SIDE, WE STROVE FOR MANY A YEAR / AT LAST, CONCLUDED IN SCHOLASTIC LIFE, / WE NEITHER CONQUER'D IN THE CLASSIC STRIFE, / AS SPEAKERS, EACH SUPPORTS AN EQUAL NAME; / AND CROUDS ALLOW TO BOTH A PARTIAL FAME; / TO SOOTHE A YOUTHFUL RIVAL'S EARLY PRIDE / THOUGH CLEONS CANDOUR WOULD THE PALM DIVIDE; / YET CANDOUR'S SELF COMPELS ME NOW TO OWN, / JUSTICE AWARDS IT TO MY FRIEND ALONE.

Named on Memorial Panel VI: Royal Military Chapel, Wellington Barracks, London. (M.I.) (Destroyed by a Flying Bomb 1944)

Ensign 4 Dec 1806.
   Present at Copenhagen 1807. Drowned on passage to the Peninsula 8 Mar 1809. The regiment was on board the transport ship *Prince George* which ran into the *Isis* late at night. Several of the officers and men jumped on board the *Isis* but Ensign Long failed in his jump to reach the *Isis* and was drowned. Verse on his memorial written by Lord Byron who was his friend and fellow scholar at Harrow and Cambridge. Nephew of Lt Colonel Robert Ballard Long 15th Lt Dragoons.

LONG, Robert Ballard
Lieutenant Colonel. 15th (King's) Regiment of Light Dragoons.
Memorial tablet: St Laurence's Church, Seale, Surrey. (Photograph)

IN MEMORY OF / LIEUTENANT GENERAL / ROBERT BALLARD LONG, / LIEUT: COLONEL OF THE 15TH HUSSARS, / SECOND SON OF / EDWARD LONG AND MARY HIS WIFE, / DAUGHTER AND HEIR OF THOMAS BECKFORD. / ON ENTERING THE ARMY, / HE SERVED HIS COUNTRY UNREMITTINGLY: / IN THE NETHERLANDS AND HOLLAND, / UNDER H.R.H. THE DUKE OF YORK: / IN IRELAND, / DURING THE UNHAPPY DISTURBANCES: / AT THE CAPTURE OF

WALCHEREN, / WHERE HE WAS ADJUTANT GENERAL OF THE FORCES: / AND IN SPAIN AND PORTUGAL, / WHERE HE WAS PRESENT AT THE / BATTLE OF CORUNNA, / AND HELD A HIGH COMMAND IN / THE GLORIOUS CONFLICTS / OF ALBUERA AND VITTORIA. / BORN APRIL 4TH 1771, DIED MARCH 2ND 1825. / ....

Cornet 1st Dragoon Guards 4 May 1791. Lt 8 Jun 1793. Capt 22 Nov 1794. Major Royal York Rangers 26 Jul 1797. Lt Colonel Hompesch's Mounted Riflemen 8 Mar 1798. Lt Colonel York Hussars 18 May 1800. Lt Colonel 2nd Dragoon Guards 3 Dec 1803. Lt Colonel 16th Lt Dragoons 22 Aug 1805. Lt Colonel 15th Lt Dragoons 17 Dec 1805. Bt Colonel 25 Apr 1808. Major General 4 Jun 1811. Lt General 19 Jul 1821.

Served in the Peninsula Nov 1808 – Jan 1809 and Mar 1811 – Aug 1813 (Commanded a Cavalry Brigade under General Hill Mar – Jun 1811, Commanded 2 Brigade Cavalry 2nd Division Jun 1811 – Mar 1813 and Commanded 7 Brigade Cavalry Apr – Aug 1813). Present at Corunna, Campo Mayor (Mentioned in Despatches), Los Santos (Mentioned in Despatches), Usagre (Mentioned in Despatches), Albuera, Arroyo dos Molinos (Mentioned in Despatches), Ribera (Mentioned in Despatches), Hormanza (Mentioned in Despatches) and Vittoria. Gold Medal for Vittoria. Wellington considered him incompetent and had him recalled Dec 1813.

Also served in Flanders 1793–1795, Irish Rebellion 1798 and Walcheren 1809 (Adjutant General, present at Flushing). After his death his nephew Charles Edward Long published articles to clear his uncle's name especially over Campo Mayor after criticism of his conduct in Napier's *History of the war in the Peninsula* and *Letter to General Lord Beresford*. Uncle of Ensign Edward Noel Long Coldstream Guards. REFERENCE: McGuffie, T. H., *Peninsular Cavalry General (1811–13): the correspondence of Lieutenant-General Robert Ballard Long*, 1951. Dictionary of National Biography. Royal Military Calendar, Vol 3, p. 165. Gentleman's Magazine, Apr 1825, pp. 373–4.

LONG, William
Lieutenant. 71st (Highland Light Infantry) Regiment of Foot.
Ledger stone: St Mary's Churchyard, Charlton Kings, Cheltenham, Gloucestershire. (Photograph)

SACRED / TO THE MEMORY OF / COLONEL WILLIAM LONG / LATE 71ST LIGHT INFANTRY / WHO DIED 19TH MARCH 1860 / HE SERVED WITH GREAT / DISTINCTION THROUGHOUT THE / PENINSULAR WAR AND AT WATERLOO / FOR WHICH HE RECEIVED / TWO MEDALS WITH FOUR CLASPS.

Ensign 6 Oct 1808. Lt 14 Jun 1810. Capt 31 Oct 1822. Major 10 Jun 1837. Bt Lt Colonel 11 Nov 1851. Bt Colonel 28 Nov 1854.

Served in the Peninsula Sep 1813 – Apr 1814. Present at Nivelle, Nive (wounded), Garris, Orthes, Aire, Tarbes and Toulouse. Present at Waterloo where he was wounded. MGS medal for Nivelle, Nive, Orthes and Toulouse. Retired on half pay 1838.

LONGLEY, Joseph
Lieutenant. Royal Engineers.
Memorial tablet: King's Chapel, Gibraltar. (South aisle). (Photograph)

LIEUTENANT JOSEPH LONGLEY / OF THE ROYAL ENGINEERS, / FELL / IN THE UNSUCCESSFUL ASSAULT / OF THE ENEMY UPON THE TOWN OF / TARIFA, / 31ST DECR 1811 IN HIS 22ND YEAR. / THIS STONE IS ERECTED BY THE CAPTAIN OF / ENGINEERS UNDER WHOSE ORDERS HE SERVED, / AS A TRIBUTE OF REGARD TO THE MEMORY OF A / SOLDIER.

Named on the Regimental Memorial: Rochester Cathedral, Rochester, Kent. (Photograph)

2nd Lt 11 Jul 1808. 1st Lt 24 Jun 1809.
    Served in the Peninsula Mar 1810 – Dec 1811. Present at Cadiz, Tarifa where he was Mentioned in Despatches and killed taking part in the defence. Also served at Walcheren 1809.

LONSDALE, William
Lieutenant. 4th (King's Own) Regiment of Foot.
Headstone: Arnos Vale Cemetery, Bristol, Somerset. (Photograph)

IN MEMORY OF / WILLIAM LONSDALE ESQR / AS LIEUTENANT IN THE 4TH KINGS OWN REGIMENT / HE SERVED AT WATERLOO AND DIED AT BRISTOL 10TH NOVR 1871 / AGED 77 YEARS

Ensign 1 Feb 1810. Lt 15 May 1812.
    Served in the Peninsula with 1/4th Jun 1812 and 2/4th Aug 1812 – Jan 1813. Present at Salamanca, retreat from Burgos and Villa Muriel. MGS medal for Salamanca. Present at Waterloo. Retired on half pay 25 Mar 1817.

LORIMER, Charles Hunt
Lieutenant. 1st (Royal Scots) Regiment of Foot.
Memorial tablet: St George's Chapel, Windsor, Berkshire. (Photograph)

TO THE MEMORY OF / LIEUTENANT CHARLES HUNT LORIMER; / ONE OF THE MILITARY KNIGHTS OF WINDSOR AND FORMERLY OF THE 1ST ROYALS / IN WHICH REGIMENT HE SERVED UNDER GENERAL SR JOHN MOORE / AT THE BATTLE OF CORUNNA. / WHERE HE WAS SEVERELY WOUNDED AND AFTER MANY YEARS OF INTENSE SUFFERING / DEPARTED THIS LIFE ON NOVEMBER 20TH 1850; AGED 70 YEARS.

Ensign 91st Foot 4 Sep 1804. Ensign 8th West India Regt 12 Jan 1805. Lt 6th West India Regt 1806. Lt 1st Foot 16 Jan 1808. Lt 19th Foot 29 Mar 1810. Lt 8th Royal Veteran Battalion Nov 1815.
    Served with 3/1st in Sir David Baird's Army in the north of Spain 1808–1809. Present at Corunna (saved a convoy of provisions with which he was entrusted on the retreat when closely followed by the enemy. Severely wounded. Awarded pension of £70 per annum). Also served at Walcheren 1809 with 3/1st (present at the siege of Flushing (severely wounded in both legs). MGS medal for Corunna. Military Knight of Windsor 5 Apr 1827.
REFERENCE: *Gentleman's Magazine, May 1851, p. 567. Annual Register, 1850, Appx, p. 282. United Service Magazine, Jan 1851, p. 167.*

LOVE, James Frederick
Captain. 52nd (Oxfordshire) Light Infantry Regiment of Foot.
Ledger stone: Brompton Cemetery, London. (BR 43645). (Photograph)

IN MEMORY OF / GENERAL / SIR JAMES FREDERICK LOVE / G.C.B. K.H. / COLONEL 43RD LIGHT INFANTRY / DIED 13TH JANUARY 1866.

Memorial tablet: St Saviour's Church, St Helier, Jersey, Channel Islands. (Photograph)

IN / GRATEFUL REMEMBRANCE / OF / .GENL SIR FREDERICK LOVE / G.C.B. K.H. / FORMERLY LT COLONEL 73RD REGT / LIEUTENANT GOVERNOR OF THE ISLAND / AND COLONEL 43RD REGIMENT, / AND OF MARY HIS WIDOW / WHO ARE BOTH BURIED IN / BROMPTON CEMETERY / THIS TABLET IS ERECTED BY / TAMZEN COMBE

Ensign 26 Oct 1804. Lt 5 Jun 1805. Capt 11 Jul 1811. Bt Major 16 Mar 1815. Bt Lt Colonel 5 May 1825.

Major 9 Jul 1830. Lt Colonel 73rd Foot 6 Sep 1834. Colonel 28 Jun 1838. Major General 11 Nov 1851. Lt General 26 Sep 1857.

Served in the Peninsula with 1/52nd Aug 1808 – Jan 1809, Jul 1809 – Jul 1811 and 2/52nd Aug 1811 – Mar 1812. Present at Corunna, Coa, Busaco, Pombal, Redinha, Casal Nova, Foz d'Arouce, Sabugal, Fuentes d'Onoro and Ciudad Rodrigo. Present at Waterloo where he was severely wounded. Also served in the Baltic 1808, Netherlands 1814 (present at Merxem and Antwerp). North America 1814–1815 (present at New Orleans where he was wounded). Commanded the 73rd Foot in the Mediterranean, Gibraltar, Nova Scotia and Canada in the Rebellion of 1838–1839. MGS medal for Corunna, Busaco, Fuentes d'Onoro and Ciudad Rodrigo. GCB. KH. Lieutenant Governor of Jersey 1852. Inspector General of Infantry 1857 – 1862. Colonel 57th Foot 24 Sep 1856.

REFERENCE: *Dictionary of National Biography. Gentleman's Magazine, Mar 1866, p. 442.*

LOWE, Sir Hudson
Colonel. Royal Corsican Rangers.
Memorial tablet: St Mary's Church, North Audley Street, London. (Photograph)

SACRED TO THE MEMORY OF / LIEUT. GENERAL SIR HUDSON LOWE / K.C.B. G.C.M.G. / KNIGHT OF THE RED EAGLE AND MILITARY ORDER OF MERIT OF PRUSSIA / ST GEORGE OF RUSSIA, AND CRESCENT OF TURKEY. / COLONEL OF THE 50TH QUEENS OWN REGIMENT. / AFTER HAVING SERVED HIS COUNTRY UNINTERRUPTED FROM 1787 TO 1815 / INCLUDING ACTIVE SERVICE IN CORSICA, EGYPT, DEFENCE OF CAPRI, / CAPTURE OF THE IONIAN ISLES, AND THE CAMPAIGNS OF 1813, 1814 / WITH THE ALLIED ARMY UNDER MARSHAL BLUCHER, / HE WAS SELECTED FOR THE ONEROUS POST OF GOVERNOR OF ST HELENA, / DURING THE CAPTIVITY OF / NAPOLEON. / HIS OBEDIENCE TO THE ORDERS OF GOVERNMENT / IN THE FULFILMENT OF THIS HARASSING DUTY, / EARNED FOR HIM THE APPROBATION OF HIS SOVEREIGN, / BUT EXPOSED HIM EVER AFTERWARDS TO PERSECUTION AND CALUMNY; / AND MORE THAN ONCE CAUSED HIS LIFE TO BE ENDANGERED. / HISTORY WILL DO JUSTICE TO A BRAVE AND ZEALOUS OFFICER. / A TRUE AND GENEROUS FRIEND / AND AN UPRIGHT AND FAITHFUL SERVANT OF HIS COUNTRY. / BORN 28TH JULY 1769, DIED 10TH JANUARY 1844. / ALSO TO SUSAN, WIFE OF THE ABOVE, / AND SISTER TO COLONEL SIR WILLIAM DE LANCEY, WHO FELL AT WATERLOO / BORN 22ND AUGUST, 1782, DIED 22ND AUGUST, 1832. / BOTH BURIED BENEATH THIS CHURCH.

Volunteer 50th Foot 1785–1786. Ensign 50th Foot 25 Sep 1787. Lt 16 Nov 1791. Capt 6 Sep 1795. Major Corsican Rangers 5 Jul 1800. Major 7th Foot 19 Apr 1803. Major Corsican Rangers 15 Oct 1803. Lt Colonel 23 Feb 1805. Bt Colonel 1 Jan 1812. Major General 4 Jun 1814. Lt General 22 Jul 1830.

Served in the Netherlands (QMG of the Army) for a few weeks before Waterloo, but Wellington did not like him and had him replaced with Colonel Sir William Howe de Lancey, Hudson Lowe's brother in law. In charge of Napoleon at St Helena Aug 1815 but they were hostile to each other. Napoleon did not like Lowe's connection with the Corsican Rangers as Napoleon regarded them as traitors. Napoleon died in May 1821 and Lowe left St Helena in July but was dogged by controversy over his time in St Helena.

Also served at Toulon 1793, Corsica 1794, Minorca 1799 (established the Corps of Corsican Rangers from anti-republican Corsicans), Egypt 1801 (present at Alexandria – awarded Turkish Gold Medal), Malta 1803, Ischia 1809 and Ionian Islands 1809–1810 (present at the capture of Cephalonia and Zante), with the Russian Army 1813 (present at Bautzen and Würschen) and with Blucher and Prussian Army Jan 1814. Deputy Governor of Ceylon 1825–1828. Colonel 93rd Foot 1822. Colonel 56th Foot 23 Jul 1832. Colonel 50th Foot 17 Nov 1842. KCB. GCMG. Prussian order of Red Eagle.

REFERENCE: *Dictionary of National Biography. Royal Military Calendar, Vol 3, pp. 383–4. Gentleman's Magazine, Mar 1844, p. 320. Annual Review, 1844, Appx, p. 193. United Service Magazine, Mar 1844, pp. 417–23.*

LOWTHER, Hon. Henry Cecil

Major. 10th (Prince of Wales's Own) Regiment of Light Dragoons.
Memorial brass: St Michael's Church, Lowther, Cumbria. (Photograph)

TO THE MEMORY OF / COLONEL THE HONOURABLE HENRY CECIL LOWTHER / SECOND SON OF / WILLIAM FIRST EARL OF LONSDALE. / BORN 27 JULY 1790. DIED 6 DEC^R 1867. / HE SERVED IN THE 7TH LIGHT DRAGOONS IN THE / PENINSULAR WAR UNDER SIR JOHN MOORE, AND IN THE ARMY OF / OCCUPATION IN FRANCE UNDER THE DUKE OF WELLINGTON. / HE WAS COLONEL OF THE ROYAL CUMBERLAND MILITIA / AND REPRESENTED THE COUNTY OF WESTMORELAND IN / PARLIAMENT 55 YEARS, DYING "FATHER OF THE HOUSE / OF COMMONS".

Memorial tablet: St Michael's Church, Lowther, Cumbria. (Photograph)

IN MEMORY / OF / COLONEL THE HONOURABLE HENRY / CECIL LOWTHER SECOND SON OF / WILLIAM EARL OF LONSDALE K.G. / BORN XXVII JULY MDCCXC / DIED VI DECEMBER MDCCCLXVII / ....

Stained glass window: All Saints Church, Oakham, Rutland.

Cornet 7th Lt Dragoons 16 Jul 1807. Lt 21 Jul 1808. Capt 4 Oct 1810. Major 14 Apr 1814. Major 10th Lt Dragoons 12 Nov 1814. Lt Colonel 12th Foot 20 Apr 1817.

   Served in the Peninsula Nov 1808 – Jan 1809 and Aug 1813 – Apr 1814. Present at Mayorga, Sahagun, Benevente and retreat to Corunna. Returned to England and was elected MP for Westmoreland Oct 1812. After his first session in the House of Commons he returned to the Peninsula in Aug 1813 and served until the end of the war. Present at Orthes and Toulouse. MGS medal for Sahagun and Benevente, Orthes and Toulouse. Arrived in France after Waterloo to join his regiment, the 10th Lt Dragoons and was present at the Capture of Paris and with the Army of Occupation. Half pay 1818. Commanded the Westmoreland Yeomanry Cavalry until his retirement from the regular army in 1830. Colonel Royal Cumberland Militia 1830. MP for Westmorland for 55 years from 1812–1867, becoming the Father of the House of Commons 1862. Played first class cricket for Hampshire and Surrey.
REFERENCE: *Gentleman's Magazine, Jan 1868, pp. 108–9.*

LUARD, John

Lieutenant. 16th (Queen's) Regiment of Light Dragoons.
Buried in St Andrew's Churchyard, Farnham, Surrey. (Burial register number 1543)

Served in Royal Navy 1802–1807. Cornet 4th Lt Dragoons 25 May 1809. Lt 30 May 1811. Lt 16th Lt Dragoons 2 Mar 1815. Capt 13 Dec 1821. Capt 30th Foot 16 Nov 1832. Major 21st Foot 17 Oct 1834. Bt Lt Colonel 28 Jun 1838.

   Served in the Peninsula Feb 1811 – Apr 1814. Present at Albuera, Usagre, Aldea da Ponte, Llerena, Salamanca and Toulouse. Present at Waterloo with 16th Lt Dragoons. MGS medal for Albuera, Salamanca and Toulouse. Also served in India (present at the siege of Bhurtpore 1825–1826 for which he received Army of India medal). Having studied the Polish Lancers at Waterloo he was able to instruct his regiment in the use of the lance. Luard is credited with being the first person in the Army to use the weapon at the siege of Bhurtpore. Retired on half pay Jun 1838. Like the rest of his family he was an excellent draughtsman. His *History of the dress of the British soldier*, published in 1852 contains his sketches of costumes from the Peninsular War. Published *Views of India, St Helena and Car Nicobar* in 1835. On retirement became a director of the London and South Western Railway. Died at Farnham 24 Oct 1875 aged 85.
REFERENCE: *Lunt, James, Scarlet Lancer, 1964, (biography of John Luard). Obit: Surrey Advertiser, 30 Oct 1875.*

LÜCKEN, Hartwig von

Ensign. 1st Line Battalion, King's German Legion.
Named on the Regimental Memorial: La Haye Sainte, Waterloo, Belgium. (Photograph)

Ensign 1 Feb 1814.
    Present at Waterloo where he was killed. Also served in the Netherlands 1814.

LUMLEY, Hon. Sir William

Colonel. Royal West India Rangers.
Interred in Catacomb B (v128 c2) Kensal Green Cemetery, London.

Cornet 10th Lt Dragoons 24 Oct 1787. Lt 19 Mar 1790. Capt 4 Dec 1793. Major in Colonel Warde's Regiment 10 Mar 1795. Lt Colonel 22nd Lt Dragoons 25 May 1795. Bt Colonel 29 Apr 1802. Major General 25 Oct 1809. Colonel Royal West India Rangers 7 Nov 1812. Lt General 4 Jun 1814. General 10 Jan 1837.
    Served in the Peninsula on Staff Sep 1810 – Aug 1811 (Commanded 3 Brigade, 2nd Division and GOC Cavalry Brigade at Albuera May 1811). Present at first siege of Badajoz, Albuera and Usagre. Also served during the Irish Rebellion 1798 (severely wounded at Antrim and awarded pension of £400 per annum), Egypt 1801 (commanded 22nd Dragoons), Cape of Good Hope 1805, South America 1807 (present at Montevideo and Buenos Ayres where he was second in command to General Sir Samuel Auchmuty) and Ischia 1809. Gold Medal for Albuera. MGS medal for Egypt. Colonel 6th Dragoons 3 Nov 1827. Colonel 1st Dragoons Guards 30 Apr 1840. GCB. Died 15 Dec 1850.
REFERENCE: *Dictionary of National Biography. Royal Military Calendar, Vol 2, pp. 352–4. Gentleman's Magazine, Mar 1851, p. 312. Annual Register, 1850, Appx, p. 287. United Service Magazine, Jan 1851, p 168.*

LUTMAN, John

Captain. 4th Royal Veteran Battalion.
Memorial tablet: St John's Wood Chapel, London. (M.I.)

"CAPTAIN JOHN LUTMAN, LATE OF THE ROYAL VETERAN BATTALION, AND FORMERLY OF THE 81ST REGIMENT; WHO AFTER PAINFULLY LINGERING FROM A SEVERE WOUND RECEIVED ON THE 16TH OF JANUARY 1809, IN THE BATTLE OF CORUNNA, WHEN SERVING IN THE LATTER CORPS, DIED JAN. 20. 1821."

Adjt/Lt 81st Foot 9 Jun 1803. Lt 4 Apr 1804. Capt 2 Feb 1809. Capt 4th Royal Veteran Battalion 13 May 1813.
    Served in the Peninsula 1808 – Jan 1809. Present at Corunna (severely wounded). Retired on full pay 1814. There is also a Lt John Lutman in the 81st Foot who was also wounded at Corunna.

LUTTRELL, Francis Fownes

Lieutenant and Captain. 1st Regiment of Foot Guards.
Stained glass window: St George's Church, Dunster, Somerset. (Photograph)

FRANCIS FOWNES LUTTRELL. DIED JANUARY 4 1862. AGED 69.

Buried in the Family plot: St George's Churchyard, Dunster, Somerset.

Memorial: Royal Military Chapel, Wellington Barracks, London. (M.I.) (Destroyed by a Flying Bomb in 1944)

"LIEUT.-COLONEL FRANCIS FOWNES LUTTRELL. / 1ˢᵀ GUARDS, 1811–25. "PENINSULA." "WATERLOO." / D.D. HIS SON, GEORGE FOWNES LUTTRELL, OF DUNSTER CASTLE."

Ensign 26 Dec 1811. Lt and Capt 17 Mar 1814.
    Served in the Peninsula with 1ˢᵗ Battalion Apr 1813 – Apr 1814. Present at Bidassoa, Nivelle, Nive, Adour and Bayonne. Present at Waterloo where he was wounded. Retired 28 Apr 1825. MGS medal for Nivelle and Nive.

LUTYENS, Benjamin
Captain. 11ᵗʰ Regiment of Light Dragoons.
Low monument: Kensal Green Cemetery, London. (17550/157/IR). (Photograph)

IN MEMORY OF A BELOVED FATHER / MAJOR BENJAMIN LUTYENS, LATE 11ᵀᴴ LIGHT DRAGOONS, /WHO DIED AT KENSINGTON DECᴿ 23ᴿᴰ 1862, AGED 85. / ………………

Family Memorial tablet: St Augustine's Church, Broxbourne, Hertfordshire. (Photograph)

……………….. BENJAMIN. / LATE OF THE 11ᵀᴴ LIGHT DRAGOONS: / DIED AT KENSINGTON, 23ᴿᴰ DECEMBER 1862, AGED 85 YEARS. / ………………..

Memorial tablet: St Mary Abbots Church, Kensington, London. (Over North porch). (Photograph)

SACRED TO THE MEMORY OF / CHRISTIANA, WIFE OF MAJOR BENJAMIN LUTYENS, / LATE 11ᵀᴴ LIGHT DRAGOONS, / DIED NOVEMBER 4ᵀᴴ 1844, AGED 67. / SHE WAS THE DAUGHTER OF WILLIAM MAIR, OF COLBY HOUSE. / MAJOR BENJAMIN SERVED IN EGYPT 1801, SPAIN 1808 (UNDER SIR JOHN MOORE), / DIED HERE DECEMBER 23ᴿᴰ 1862, AGED 85, BURIED AT KENSAL GREEN. / ALSO OF THE ABOVE NAMED / MAJOR BENJAMIN LUTYENS. / HE SERVED AT THE LANDING IN EGYPT AND AT / THE BATTLE OF ALEXANDRIA IN 1801 / AND AS A DEP: ASS: ADJ: GEN THROUGHOUT THE / CAMPAIGN IN SPAIN IN 1808–9 UNDER / THE COMMAND OF LIEUT GENERAL SIR JOHN MOORE KB / AND DEPARTED THIS LIFE AT KENS-INGTON / DECEMBER 23ᴿᴰ 1862 AGED 85 YEARS. / HIS MORTAL REMAINS ARE DEPOSITED AT / KENSAL GREEN CEMETERY. THE VAULTS UNDER THIS CHURCH / HAVING BEEN CLEARED BY PUBLIC AUTHORITY. / THIS TABLET IS ERECTED IN FOND REMEMBRANCE OF / VALUED PARENTS BY THEIR TWO DAUGHTERS.

Cornet 18ᵗʰ Lt Dragoons 28 Oct 1795. Cornet 16ᵗʰ Lt Dragoons 27 Feb 1796. Lieutenant 18 Jul 1799. Capt 11ᵗʰ Lt Dragoons 4 Aug 1804. Bt Major 4 Jun 1814.
    Served in the Peninsula Sep 1808 – Jan 1809 (DAAG) and Jun 1811 – Apr 1814. Present at Corunna. Returned to the Peninsula Jun 1811 and was immediately in action near Elvas on 22 June. While on picket duty he found that his troop was cut off from Elvas by French cavalry who had encircled them. Lutyens thought his only chance to escape was a speedy charge. He broke through the first rank but his whole troop was either killed or taken prisoner by the second charge. Lutyens was taken prisoner and spent the rest of the war until Apr 1814 in prison. Wellington blamed General Long for not issuing clear directions for picket duty and for the fact that their troop had been used even though they had only just arrived in the Peninsula. 'This tends to show the difference between old and new troops. However we must make the new as good as the old' (Despatch to Lord Liverpool). Present at Waterloo.
    MGS medal for Egypt and Corunna. Also served at the Helder 1799 and Egypt 1801 (served under Abercromby and was one of the last survivors of the campaign. Awarded Sultan's Gold Medal presented to British regimental officers in the campaign). Brother of Deputy Commissary General Charles Lutyens Paymaster Daniel Lutyens 11ᵗʰ Lt Dragoons and Lt Engelbert Lutyens 20ᵗʰ Foot.

LUTYENS, Charles
Deputy Commissary General. Commissariat Department.
Family Memorial tablet: St Augustine's Church, Broxbourne, Hertfordshire. (Photograph)

.... CHARLES. / DEPUTY COMMISSARY GENERAL OF HER MAJESTY'S FORCES, / DIED 13TH DECEMBER 1848, AGED 75 YEARS / ....

Dep Comm Gen 26 Jun 1809.
    Served in the Peninsula Sep 1808 – Feb 1811 and Feb 1813 – Apr 1814. Present at Lisbon. Brother of Capt Benjamin Lutyens 11th Lt Dragoons, Paymaster Daniel Lutyens 11th Lt Dragoons and Lt Engelbert Lutyens 20th Foot.

LUTYENS, Daniel
Paymaster. 11th Regiment of Light Dragoons.
Family Memorial tablet: St Augustine's Church, Broxbourne, Hertfordshire. (Photograph)

.... / DANIEL, / FORMERLY PAYMASTER OF THE 11TH LIGHT DRAGOONS, / AND LATE OF THE 3RD DRAGOON GUARDS: / DIED 6TH JUNE 1841, AGED 60 YEARS.

Paymaster 11 Dragoons 19 Oct 1804. Paymaster 3rd Dragoon Guards 30 Jun 1820.
Served in the Peninsula Jun 1811 – Jun 1813. Present at El Bodon, Morales, Castrejon, Salamanca and Venta del Pozo. Present at Waterloo. Half pay 19 Oct 1838. Brother of Capt Benjamin Lutyens 11th Lt Dragoons, Deputy Commissary General Charles Lutyens and Lt Engelbert Lutyens 20th Foot.

LUTYENS, Engelbert
Lieutenant. 20th (East Devonshire) Regiment of Foot.
Family Memorial tablet: St Augustine's Church, Broxbourne, Hertfordshire. (Photograph)

.... / ENGELBERT. / MAJOR OF THE 20TH REGIMENT OF FOOT: / DIED ON HIS PASSAGE TO INDIA 26TH JANUARY 1830, / AGED 45 YEARS. / ....

Lt 21 Mar 1805. Capt 25 Aug 1813. Bt Major 5 Jul 1821.
    Served in the Peninsula Aug 1808 – Jan 1809 and Nov 1812 – Apr 1814. Present at Vimeiro, Corunna, Vittoria, Pyrenees (wounded at Echellar 2 Aug 1813), Nivelle, Nive, Orthes and Toulouse. Also served at St Helena with 20th Foot guarding Napoleon (awarded Brevet Majority). Brother of Capt Benjamin Lutyens 11th Lt Dragoons, Deputy Commissary General Charles Lutyens and Paymaster Daniel Lutyens 11th Lt Dragoons.
REFERENCE: *Knowles, Sir Lees, Letters of Captain Engelbert Lutyens, orderly officer at Longwood, St Helena, Feb 1820 to Nov 1823, 1915.*

LUXMOORE, Thomas Coryndon
Lieutenant. Royal Engineers.
Named on the Regimental Memorial: Rochester Cathedral, Rochester, Kent. (Photograph)

2nd Lt 1 Jan 1814. Lt 1 Aug 1814. 2nd Capt 6 Nov 1834. Capt 11 Sep 1841. Bt Major 9 Nov 1846. Lt Colonel 1 Jul 1849. Bt Colonel 28 Nov 1854. Major General 2 Aug 1860. Lt General 7 Sep 1867. General 8 Jun 1871.
    Served in the Netherlands and in France with the Army of Occupation 1815–1816. Retired on full pay 1 Apr 1852. Died at Tunbridge Wells 26 Nov 1878.

LYE, Benjamin Leigh
Lieutenant. 11th Regiment of Light Dragoons.
Ledger stone: Abbey Cemetery, Bath, Somerset. (Photograph)

.... / BENJAMIN LEIGH LYE. / DIED DECEMBER 9TH 1855 AGED 71 /. ....

Cornet 4 Aug 1808. Lt 30 Jul 1811.
   Served in the Peninsula Feb 1812 – Apr 1813. Present at Moriscos, Castrejon, Salamanca, and Venta del Poza (wounded). Present at Waterloo. MGS medal for Salamanca. Half pay 5 Jun 1817. Later Adjutant, North Somerset Yeomanry Cavalry 1821. Secretary Bath and West Society 1818–1849.

LYGON, Hon. Edward Pyndar
Major and Lieutenant Colonel. 2nd Life Guards.
Buried in St Mary the Virgin Churchyard, Madresfield, Worcestershire. (Burial record)

Cornet 1 Jun 1803. Lt 7 Nov 1805. Capt 15 Feb 1808. Major and Lt Colonel 27 Apr 1815. Lt Colonel 14 Apr 1818. Colonel 27 Apr 1822. Major General 10 Jan 1837. Lt General 9 Nov 1846. General 20 Jun 1854.
   Served in the Peninsula Nov 1812 – Mar 1814. Present at Vittoria. Present at Waterloo in command of 2nd Life Guards. CB and 4th Class of St Vladimir of Russia. MGS medal for Vittoria. Colonel 13th Lt Dragoons 29 Jan 1845. Inspector General of Cavalry. Educated at Winchester. Died 11 Nov 1860. Brother of Major Hon. Henry Beauchamp Lygon 16th Lt Dragoons.
REFERENCE: *Annual Register, 1860, Appx, p. 459.*

LYGON, Hon. Henry Beauchamp
Major. 16th (Queen's) Regiment of Light Dragoons.
Memorial tablet: St Mary the Virgin Church, Madresfield, Worcestershire. (Photograph)

TO THE MEMORY / OF / HENRY BEAUCHAMP LYGON / 4TH EARL BEAUCHAMP / COLONEL OF HER MAJESTY'S SECOND / REGIMENT OF LIFE GUARDS / BORN JANUARY 6TH 1785 / DIED SEPTEMBER 8TH 1863. / HE WAS ELEVEN TIMES CHOSEN / KNIGHT OF THE SHIRE / FOR THE COUNTRY OF WORCESTER.

Cornet 13th Lt Dragoons 9 Jul 1803. Lt 24 May 1804. Capt 15 Jan 1807. Capt 16th Lt Dragoons 12 Feb 1807. Major 7 May 1812. Major and Lt Col 1st Life Guards 18 Jun 1815. Colonel 24 Mar 1822. Major General 10 Jan 1837. Lt General 9 Nov 1846. General 20 Jun 1854.
   Served in the Peninsula Apr 1809 – Aug 1810 and Feb – Apr 1814. Present at Douro, Talavera, the Coa (severely wounded in the neck in Massena's advance to Busaco, near Almeida 28 Aug 1810) and Bayonne. MGS medal for Talavera. MP for West Worcestershire for 20 years from 1816. Colonel 10th Hussars Jun 1843. Colonel 2nd Life Guards 1852. Educated at Winchester. Brother of Major and Lt Colonel Edward Pyndar Lygon 2nd Life Guards.
REFERENCE: *Gentleman's Magazine, Oct 1863, pp. 506–7.*

LYNAM, Joseph
1st Lieutenant. 95th Regiment of Foot.
Gravestone: Templemore Parish Churchyard, County Tipperary, Ireland. (M.I.)

"LIEUT JOSEPH LYNAM, 3RD ROYAL VETERAN BATTALION, DIED MARCH 22ND 1821, AGED 29."

2nd Lt 25 Jun 1812. Lt 22 Mar 1815. Lt 3rd Veteran Battalion 24 Feb 1820.

Served in the Peninsula Feb – Sep 1813. Present at Waterloo where he was wounded and awarded pension of £70 per annum. Half pay Dec 1818 on reduction of the regiment. Died 1821, probably due to his wound from Waterloo.

LYNCH, David
Private. 83rd Regiment of Foot.
Headstone: Philips Park Cemetery, Hulme, Manchester, Lancashire. (Photograph)

OF YOUR CHARITY PRAY FOR THE SOUL OF / DAVID LYNCH / BORN APRIL 16TH 1794. / DIED FEBRUARY 27TH 1871. / HE PASSED THROUGH THE PENINSULAR CAMPAIGN / AS A PRIVATE IN THE 83RD REGIMENT OF FOOT / AND WAS PRESENT AT THE FOLLOWING / ENGAGEMENTS / TORRES VEDRAS. SALAMANCA. / ALMEIDA. VITTORIA. / FUENTES D' OR. PYRENEES. / TALAVERA. SAN SEBASTIAN / CUIDAD RODRIGO. ORTHES. / BADAJOZ. TOULOUSE.

Served in the Peninsula Apr 1809 – Apr 1814. Present at Talavera, Torres Vedras, Fuentes d'Onoro, Almeida, Ciudad Rodrigo, Badajoz, Salamanca, Vittoria, Pyrenees, San Sebastian, Orthes and Toulouse. MGS medal for Ciudad Rodrigo, Badajoz, Salamanca, Vittoria, Pyrenees, Nivelle, Orthes and Toulouse.

LYNCH, Henry Blois
Captain. Royal York Rangers.
Monument: Partree Private Cemetery, Partree, County Mayo, Ireland. (Photograph)

SACRED / TO THE MEMORY OF / MAJOR HENRY BLOIS LYNCH. 73 REGT / BORN AT PARTREE. HE SERVED WITH THE ARMY / UNDER THE DUKE OF WELLINGTON DURING THE / WHOLE OF THE PENINSULAR WAR. HIS GALLANTRY / AT THE SIEGE OF CIUDAD RODRIGO WAS / MENTIONED IN THE DISPATCHES OF THE DUKE. / HE DIED AT PARTREE ON THE 1ST OF JUNE, 1823.

Ensign 20th Foot 25 Mar 1795. Lt 29th Foot 6 May 1795. Lt 95th Foot 12th Aug 1800. Capt 25 Jun 1803. Bt Major 1 Jan 1814. Capt 73rd Foot 25 Jun 1815. Portuguese Army: Major 16th Line 13 Sep 1811.
   Served in the Peninsula with Portuguese Army Sep 1811 – Dec 1812 and Mar – Dec 1813. Present at Ciudad Rodrigo (Mentioned in Despatches), Salamanca, Burgos, Vittoria, Bidassoa and Nivelle. Also served at Copenhagen 1807.

LYNCH, James Stewart
Major. 1st (Royal Scots) Regiment of Foot.
Gravestone: Wallajabad, Chingleput District, India. (M.I.)

MAJOR JAMES STEWART LYNCH / OF H. M. 1ST REGIMENT OF FOOT. / DIED 5 JULY 1819, AGED 44 YEARS.

Ensign 83rd Foot 13 Dec 1794. Capt 1st Foot 16 Jul 1803. Major 6 Dec 1810.
   Served in the Peninsula Apr 1812 – Sep 1812. Present at Castrejon and Salamanca. Later served in India 1816–1819 (present in the Mahratta War, Nagpore and Mehidpur).

LYNCH, Martin Crean
Captain. 27th (Inniskilling) Regiment of Foot.
Low monument: St Mary's Catholic Cemetery, Kensal Green, London. (6707). (Photograph)

TO THE MEMORY OF / COLONEL MARTIN CREAN LYNCH / FORMERLY OF THE 14TH REGT OF FOOT / WHO DIED ON 21ST JUNE 1853 AGED 71 / THIS MONUMENT IS ERECTED BY HIS WIDOW.

Ensign 11 Feb 1808. Lt 31 May 1809. Capt 24 Dec 1812. Capt 14th Regt 22 Jun 1826.

Served in the Peninsula with 1/27th Nov 1812 – Jan 1813, 2/27th Feb – May 1813 and 3/27th Jun 1813 – Apr 1814. Present on the East Coast of Spain, Pyrenees, Nivelle, Nive, Orthes and Toulouse. Also served at Maida 1806, North America 1814 and India (present at the siege and assault of Bhurtpore 1825–1826 where he was wounded). MGS medal for Maida, Pyrenees, Nivelle, Nive, Orthes and Toulouse.

LYNEDOCH see GRAHAM, Sir Thomas

LYON, William John
Lieutenant. 14th (Duchess of York's Own) Regiment of Light Dragoons.
Pedestal monument with Cross: Cimetière de Cadillon, France. (Photograph)

A / GUILLAUME – JEAN LYON / LIEUT AU 14ME REGT DES DRAGONS / BRITANNIQUES QUI FUT TUE / LE 18 MARS 1814 – PRÈS / CADILLON A LA RETRAITE / DE L'ARMÈE – FRANCAISE / VERS – TOULOUSE.

Memorial tablet: All Saints Parish Church, Horstead, Norfolk. (North wall). (Photograph)

TO THE MEMORY OF / LIEUTENANT WILLIAM JOHN LYON, / OF THE 14TH REGIMENT OF DRAGOONS, / HE WAS KILLED IN ACTION IN FRANCE, / ON THE 18TH DAY OF MARCH, / IN THE YEAR 1814; / IN THE 23RD YEAR OF HIS AGE. / HIS REMAINS WERE INTERRED / BY THE HUMANE PERMISSION OF THE PRIEST / OF THE PARISH, / IN THE CHURCHYARD OF CADILLON / IN THE DEPARTMENT OF THE LOWER PYRENEES / NEAR THE SPOT WHERE HE FELL.

Named on the Memorial: St Andrew's Church, (now Musée Historique), Biarritz, France. (Photograph)

Cornet 23 Apr 1812. Lt 10 Jun 1813.

Served in the Peninsula Jan 1813 – Mar 1814. Present at Vittoria, Pyrenees, Nivelle, Nive, Orthes and Vic de Bigorre where he was killed Mar 1814.

Place Index

ENGLAND

Bedfordshire
Bedford: Ainslie, George Simon Harcourt
Bedford: Amos, John Greene
Bedford: Clay, Matthew
Carlton: Horne, James
Elstow: Inkersole, James
Pulloxhill: Gudgin, George

Berkshire
Hampstead Norrey's: James, Francis
Windsor: Allen, John
Windsor: Beatty, John Walwyn
Windsor: Blacklin, Richard
Windsor: Boyes, Robert Nairne
Windsor: Buckeridge, John Charles
Windsor: Campbell, Adam Gordon
Windsor: Clarke, John
Windsor: Cochrane, Robert (47th Foot)
Windsor: Cochrane, Robert (95th Foot)
Windsor: Copeland, George
Windsor: Douglas, Joseph
Windsor: Doyle, Sir John Milley
Windsor: Elley, Sir John
Windsor: Fitzgibbon, James
Windsor: Fleming, Hugh
Windsor: Gee, Francis
Windsor: Gillespie, William
Windsor: Griffith, Joseph
Windsor: Hollinsworth, Henry
Windsor: Holmes, Samuel
Windsor: Hopkins, John Paul
Windsor: Innes, Alexander
Windsor: Lamb, John
Windsor: Ledsam, John
Windsor: Loggan, George
Windsor: Lorimer, Charles Hunt
Wokingham: Dukinfield, Samuel George

Buckinghamshire
Amersham: Drake, William Tyrwhitt
Amersham: Eeles, Charles
Amersham: Eeles, William

Chalfont St Peter: Hibbert, John Nembhard
Chicheley: Chester, John
Marlow: Clayton, William Robert
Soulbury: Hanmer, Henry
Wavendon: Fisher, William

Cambridgeshire
Comberton: Chapman, Thomas
Pampisford: Freeman, William
Swaffham Prior: Allix, Charles
Swaffham Prior: Allix, William
Woodston: Bringhurst, John Dorset

Cheshire
Chester: Buchanan, John Philips
Chester: Cochrane, Robert
Chester: Cotton, Sir Stapleton
Chester: Currie, Edward
Chester: Gould, Thomas
Chester: Hilton, Thomas
Combermere: Cotton, Sir Stapleton
Holmes Chapel: Harrison, Charles
Holmes Chapel: Hodges, William Arthur
Knutsford: Barra, Joseph
Knutsford: Hill, Henry
Knutsford: Kibble, William Thomas
Mobberley: Blakiston, John
Nantwich: Hall, Charles
Stockport: Briscall, Samuel
Stockport: Fouracres, Thomas
Tarporley: Egerton, Richard
Winwick: Ashcroft, Timothy
Wrenbury: Cotton, Sir Stapleton

Cornwall
Falmouth: Boase, John
Falmouth: Coope, William Jesser
Falmouth: Duperier, Henry
Falmouth: Falck, Neil
Falmouth: Fenwick, William
Falmouth: Hodge, Peter
Falmouth: Light, Henry
Mylor: Daniel, Catherine
Veryan: Clear, Philip

Cumbria
Ambleside: Jacob, George T.
Appleby: Armstrong, Andrew
Beetham: Kay, Samuel
Bowness-on-Windermere: Beaufoy, Mark
Carlisle: Graham, James Reginald Torin
Carlisle: Grant, James
Cockermouth: Hagger, John
Great Urswick: Gardner, Thomas
Haverthwaite: Fell, William
Hayton: Eves, John
Kendal: Gibson, John
Kirkbride: Clark, Joseph Taylor
Kirkby Lonsdale: Brady, John James
Lowther: Lowther, Hon. Henry Cecil
Penrith: Grisedale, Levi

Derbyshire
Church Gresley: Craufurd, Alexander C. G.
Derby: Frost, George
Derby: Hall, William
Eyam: Holmes, Adam
Great Longstone: Heathcote, Joseph
Holbrooke: Leeke, William
Kedleston: Curzon, Hon. William
Kirk Langley: Kirkland, James
Matlock: Cumming, William G.
Melbourne: Gooch, Henry Edmund
Pentrich: Jessop, John
Spondon: Gell, Thomas
Wirksworth: Gratton, Charles

Devon
Appledore: Blyth, John Willes
Barnstaple: Harding, William
Bideford: Bishop, William Bradshaw
Bideford: Crowe, John
Bradworthy: Cann, John
Brixham: Hackett, John
Chittlehampton: Facey, Peter
Exeter: Allen, George Augustus
Exeter: Guard, William
Georgeham: Hill, John
Lympstone: James, John Haddy
Lynton: Herries, William Lewis
Newton Ferrars: Colborne, Sir John
Plymouth: Campbell, Archibald Argyle
Plymouth: Campbell, John
Plymouth: Gammell, William
Plymouth: Holloway, William C. E.
Plymouth: Jago, Darell

Plymtree: Dornford, Joseph
Salcombe Regis: Grey, John
Sidmouth: Brine, James
Sidmouth: Floyd, Henry
Sidmouth: Gray, Loftus
Topsham: Duckworth, George Henry
Topsham: Follett, George
Torquay: Bouchier, Thomas
Torquay: Johnstone, James

Dorset
Chardstock: Brine, James
Frampton: Grant, Sir Colquhoun
Langton Long: Fraser, James John
Lyme Regis: Jebb, Richard
Owermoigne: Ingram, George
Owermoigne: Ingram, John N.
Studland: Lawrence, William
Thorncombe: Bragge, William
Wareham: Calcraft, Sir Granby Thomas
Wareham: Lefebure, Charles
Wareham: Lefebure, George
Warmwell: Foster, Augustus
Weymouth: Howard, Thomas Phipps
Wimborne Minster: Fraser, James John
Winterbourne Came: Dawson Hon. George L.

Durham
Barnard Castle: Crampton, James
Durham: Lake, Charles
Houghton-Le-Spring: Beckwith, William
Hurworth: Dryden, James

Essex
Boreham: Haselfoot, William H.
Chelmsford: Allen, Thomas
Colchester: Burrows, John
Fordham: Johnston, Henry
Great Bromley: Hanson, William
Harwich: Donaldson, Gordon Graham
Hempstead: Harvey, Edward
Little Baddow: Johnson, Arthur
North Benfleet: Cole, John
Theydon Bois: Boulcott, Joseph
Upminster: Branfill, Champion E.
Upminster: Cox, Philip Z.
Warley: Harcourt, John

Gloucestershire
Charlton Kings: Long, William
Cheltenham: Allen, James

Cheltenham: Birtwhistle, John
Cheltenham: Blackwell, Nathaniel S. F.
Cheltenham: Buckley, James Ogden
Cheltenham: Capel, Daniel
Cheltenham: Cox, John
Cheltenham: Crowder, John
Cheltenham: Cuppage, Stephen
Cheltenham: Elliot, William Rowley
Cheltenham: Ellis, Richard Rogers
Cheltenham: Everest, Henry Bennett
Cheltenham: Framingham, Sir Haylett
Cheltenham: Houghton, Richard Rollo
Cheltenham: Knox, Edward
Cheltenham: Lindsey, Owen
Chipping Sodbury: Blathwayt, George
Cirencester: Bathurst, Hon. Thomas Seymour
Doynton: Davy, William G.
Dyrham: Blathwayt, George
Elmore: Guise, John Wright
Gloucester: Davy, William G.
Kemerton: Burke, James
Leckhampton: Diggle, Charles
Leckhampton: Jones, John Thomas.
Leckhampton: Litchfield, Richard
Leigh: Faulkner, Sir Arthur B.
Minsterworth: Hawkins, John Pauncefoot
Newland: Adair, Walter William
Pitchcombe: Fletcher, Sir Richard
Southam: Hardinge, Sir Henry
Southam: Campbell, Colin (Lord Clyde)
Tidenham: Fenton, Thomas C.

Guernsey
St. Andrew: Bainbrigge, John Hankey
St Peter Port: Barry, Philip
St Peter Port: Baynes, George Macleod
St Peter Port: Baynes, Henry
St Peter Port: Brock, Saumarez
St Peter Port: Cameron, Sir John
St Peter Port: Carey, Octavius
St Peter Port: Dalgairnes, William
St Peter Port: Harding, George Judd
St Peter Port: Kennedy, Thomas
St Peter Port: Le Marchant, Sir J. Gaspard

Hampshire
Boldre: Douglas, Sir Howard
Bramdean: Gomm, Richard Stonier
Buriton: Hugonin, James
Fareham: Borlase, Charles
Fareham: Lawson, Douglas

Fareham: Le Blanc, Francis
Fawley: Bradby, Joseph
Fordingbridge: Hay, Andrew
Fordingbridge: Hay, George
Havant: Arabin, Frederick
Lymington: Burrard, Sir Harry
Lymington: Burrard, Paul Harry Durrell
Lyndhurst: Breton, John Frederick
Lyndhurst: Hogge, Fountain
Minstead: Buckley, George Richard
Nateley Scures: Carleton, Hon. Dudley
Nateley Scures: Carleton, Hon. George
Portsmouth: Butler, Hon. Henry Edward
Portsmouth: Cathcart, Hon George
Portsmouth: D'Aguilar, George Charles
Portsmouth: Dickson, Sir Alexander
Portsmouth: Elliott, Robert T.
Portsmouth: Gawler, George
Portsmouth: Hill, Lord Rowland
Portsmouth: Hovenden, Nicholas
Portsmouth: Jones, Harry David
Portsmouth: Leggatt, Samuel
Sopley: Keane, Sir John
Southampton: Blunt, Richard
Southampton: Browne, Thomas Gore
Southampton: Byam, William
Southampton: Cairnes, George
Southampton: Campbell, Patrick
Southampton: Doherty, George
Southampton: Goldie, George Leigh
Southampton: Hall, Lewis Alexander
Southampton: Henderson, George
Southampton: Hewett, William
Southampton: Johnston, William
Southampton: Lacy, Richard John J.
Titchfield: Bainbrigge, Philip
Titchfield: Bogue, Richard
Upton Grey: Beaufoy, John Henry
Winchester: Barnard, Andrew Francis
Winchester: Beckwith, Sir Thomas Sidney
Winchester: Cameron, Alexander
Winchester: Colborne, Sir John
Winchester: Costello, Edward
Winchester: Green, William
Winchester: Hartley, William
Winchester: Himbury, John
Winchester: Kincaid, John
Wonston: Dallas, Alexander Richard Charles

Herefordshire
Eastnor: Cocks, Edward Charles

Goodrich: Jackson, Basil
Leintwardine: Clerke, William Henry
Middleton-on-the-Hill: Kinchant, Francis C.
Ross-on-Wye: Jackson, Basil
Walford: Evans, Kingsmill

Hertfordshire
Aldenham: Burne, Robert
Aldenham: Dalrymple, Adolphus John
Aldenham: Dalrymple, Sir Hew Whitford
Aldenham: Dalrymple, Leighton C.
Aldenham: Fanshawe, Edward
Barkway: Clinton, Sir Henry
Barkway: Clinton, Sir William Henry
Broxbourne: Lutyens, Benjamin
Broxbourne: Lutyens, Charles
Broxbourne: Lutyens, Daniel
Broxbourne: Lutyens, Engelbert
Elstree: Burton, Francis
Essendon: Clitherow, William Henry
Harpenden: Hadden, James
Harpenden: Hadden, William Frederick
Hexton: Lautour, James Oliver
Hexton: Lautour, Joseph Andrew de
Hitchin: Hinde, Samuel Venables

Huntingdonshire
Eynesbury: Humbley, Philip
Eynesbury: Humbley, William

Isle of Man
Malew: Creighton, Thomas
Malew: Raynes, William Augustus
Maughold: Kilpatrick, John William

Isle of Wight
Arreton: Anwyl, Robert
Bonchurch: Arbuthnot, Sir Robert
Bonchurch: Hamilton, William F.
Carisbrooke: Blomer, Charles
Carisbrooke: Cheek, Edward
Carisbrooke: Leroux, George Wilson
Gatcombe: Geary, Henry
Newport: Denecke, George
Newport: Evelegh, Henry
Whippingham; Butcher, George Kear

Jersey
St Brelade: Henegan, Richard D.
St Helier: Archdall, Richard
St Helier: Aubin, Phillip

St Helier: Barrington, Edward George
St Helier: Budgen, John Robert
St Helier: Buttery, William
St Helier: Cadell, Charles
St Helier: Campbell, Archibald
St Helier: Campbell, Norman
St Helier: Cleary, Richard Stanton
St Helier: Crawford, Adam Fife
St Helier: Day, James
St Helier: Dixon, Francis
St Helier: Don, George
St Helier: Gibbs, Edward
St Helier: Gossett, John Noel
St Helier: Hibbert, John Gray
St Helier: Jackson, John Napper
St Helier: Johnson, David England
St Helier: Love, James Frederick

Kent
Beckenham: Alexander, Henry
Beckenham: Hodge, Edward
Bidborough: Hardinge, Richard
Boughton Monchelsea: Archer, Clement
Broadstairs: Clarke, Isaac Blake
Bromley: Lautour, Peter Augustus
Canterbury: Cairnes, Robert Macpherson.
Canterbury: Delmar, John
Canterbury: Fraser, Erskine Alexander
Canterbury: Fraser, George
Canterbury: Gipps, George
Canterbury: Inglis, Sir William
Canterbury: Lamotte, James
Charlton: Bentham, William
Charlton: Clark, John
Charlton: Eeles, William
Charlton: English, Frederick
Charlton: Fisher, George Bulteel
Charlton: Frazer, Sir Augustus Simon
Charlton: Fyers, Peter
Charlton: Hamilton, Alexander
Charlton: Harding, John
Charlton: Hoste, Sir George Charles
Deal: Backhouse, John William
Dover: Girardot, Charles Andrew
Dover: Hart, James
Dover: Hutchesson, Thomas
Dover: Logan, Joseph
Eastry: Boteler, Richard
Faversham: Harris, Hon. Charles
Faversham: Harris, Lord William George
Fordcombe: Hardinge, Sir Henry

Fordwich: Lilley, Samuel
Goudhurst: Beresford, Sir William Carr
Ham: Harris, Thomas Noel
Harbledown: Cockburn, Francis
Hayes: Fraser, Alexander Mackenzie
Hythe: King, William James
Igtham: Chapman, Thomas
Littlebourne: James, William
Maidstone: Crump, Ely
Maidstone: Havelock, William
Maidstone: Hill, Sir Thomas Noel
Margate: Coghlan, John Robert
Penshurst: Hardinge, Sir Henry
Plumstead: Bredin, Andrew
Plumstead: Dickson, Sir A.
Plumstead: Drummond, Percy
Plumstead: Dyer, Sir John
Plumstead: Fead, George
Plumstead: Glubb, Frederick
Plumstead: Grueber, Daniel
Plumstead: Hall, Edward S.
Plumstead: Hawker, James
Plumstead: Hunt, Arthur
Ramsgate: Garrett, Robert
Ramsgate: Harris, Thomas Noel.
Rochester: Baddeley, Frederick Henry
Rochester: Barou, Richard John
Rochester: Birch, James
Rochester: Birch, John Francis
Rochester: Blakiston, John
Rochester: Blanshard, Thomas
Rochester: Bolton, Daniel
Rochester: Boteler, Richard
Rochester: Bryce, Alexander
Rochester: Buckeridge, Henry Mark
Rochester: By, John
Rochester: Chapman, Stephen Remnant
Rochester: Cheyne, Alexander
Rochester: Cole, Pennel
Rochester: Collyer, George
Rochester: Cooper, Robert Henry Spencer
Rochester: Covey, Edward
Rochester: Cuyler, Henry
Rochester: Dalton, George
Rochester: Davy, Henry
Rochester: Dawson, William Francis
Rochester: De Salaberry, Edward A.
Rochester: Dickens, Thomas Mark
Rochester: Dickenson, Sebastian
Rochester: Ellicombe, Charles Grene
Rochester: Elphinstone, Howard

Rochester: Elton, Isaac Marmaduke
Rochester: Emmett, Anthony
Rochester: Eyre, James William
Rochester: Faris, William
Rochester: Fletcher, Sir Richard
Rochester: Forbes, James
Rochester: Ford, William Henry
Rochester: Forster, William Frederick
Rochester: Fyers, Edward
Rochester: Fyers, Thomas
Rochester: Gilbert, Francis Yarde
Rochester: Grierson, Crighton
Rochester: Hall, Lewis Alexander
Rochester: Hamilton, George Augustus
Rochester: Harris, John Brenchley
Rochester: Head, Francis Bond
Rochester: Henderson, Alexander
Rochester: Henderson, George
Rochester: Hulme, John Lyon
Rochester: Hunt, Richard
Rochester: Hustler, Robert Samuel
Rochester: Jones, Harry David
Rochester: Jones, John Thomas
Rochester: Jones, Rice
Rochester: Kay, Arthur
Rochester: Kerr, John
Rochester: Lancey, Thomas Furber
Rochester: Lascelles, Thomas
Rochester: Lefebure, Charles
Rochester: Luxmoore, Thomas Coryndon
Sandwich: Harvey, William Maundy
Shorncliffe: Barnard, Andrew Francis
Shorncliffe: Beckwith, Sir Thomas Sidney
Shorncliffe: Craufurd, Robert
Tunbridge Wells: Dallas, Robert William
Tunbridge Wells: D'Oyley, Henry
Upper Walmer: Hunt, John Philip
West Malling: Downman, Thomas
Woolwich: Adye, Stephen Galway
Woolwich: Colquhoun, James Nesbit
Woolwich: Dickson, Sir Alexander
Woolwich: Fensham, George
Woolwich: Forbes, James Staats

Lancashire
Bolton: Adams, John
Bolton: Knowles, Robert
Eccles: Floyd, Thomas
Great Harwood: Lomax, Thomas
Heywood: Bentinck, Richard
Hindley: Eckersley, Nathaniel

Kirkham: Buck, Henry Rishton
Leigh: Baddeley, Benjamin
Manchester: Bradbury, Emmanuel
Manchester: Ferriar, Thomas Ilderton
Manchester: Lynch, David
Oldham: Lees, John
Oswaldtwistle: Grimshaw, John
Preston: Cross, Richard
Preston: Dixon, Robert
Preston: Hardman, Job
Rochdale: Butterworth, Henry
Rochdale: Grindrod, Timothy
Rochdale: Hopwood, John
Salford: Arbuthnot, Sir Thomas
Walton-le-Dale: Hoghton, Daniel

Leicestershire
Birstall: Gomersall, John
Gaddesby: Cheney, Edward Hawkins
Gilmorton: Burbidge, Frederick
Leicester: Green, William

Lincolnshire
Algarkirk: Boothby, Charles
Bassingham: Campion, William
Belton: Cust, Hon. Edward
Belton: Cust, Hon. Peregrine Francis
Corringham: Beckett, Richard
Doddington: Jarvis, George Ralph Payne
Fulbeck: Fane, Charles
Fulbeck: Fane, Sir Henry
Fulbeck: Fane, Mildmay
Fulbeck: Horton, Pickwick Baxter Posthumus
Lincoln: Armstrong, Richard
Lincoln: Bromhead, John
Sleaford: Handley, Benjamin
Thurlby: Bromhead, Edmund de G.
Witham-on-the-Hill: Johnson, William A.

London
Arranged under: Brompton, Royal Military Chapel
Kensal Green and Other London locations

Brompton
Baller, George
Bruce, William
Burgoyne, John Fox
Carr, James
Chadwick, William
Elliott, William Henry
Este, Michael Lambton

Forester, Francis
Freeth, James
Gore, Hon. Sir Charles Stephen
Graham, James Reginald Torin
Hennis, William Howe
Herries, William Lewis
Love, James Frederick

Royal Military Chapel
Adair, Robert
Aitchison, Sir John
Allen, George
Anstruther, Robert
Ashburnham, Hon. John
Ashton, John
Askew, Henry
Barnett, Charles John
Barrington, Hon. Samuel Shute P.
Bathurst, Hon. Thomas Seymour
Beckett, Richard
Beckford, Francis Love
Bentinck, Charles Anthony Frederick
Blackman, John Lucie
Blane, Hugh Seymour
Bowater, Edward
Bowles, George
Bradford, Sir Henry Hollis
Bradford, Keating James
Bridgeman, Orlando
Brown, Thomas
Bryan, George
Buchanan, James
Buckeridge, John Charles
Buckley, George Richard
Bulteel, John
Burgess, Wentworth Noel
Burnaby, John Dick
Burrard, Sir Harry
Burrard, Paul Henry Durrell
Burrard, William
Burroughs, William
Byng, Sir John.
Canning, Charles Fox
Campbell, Sir Henry Frederick
Chambers, Newton
Chaplin, Thomas
Cheney, Robert
Clifton, George
Clinton, Sir Henry
Clinton, Sir William Henry
Clitherow, John

Clitherow, Robert
Clitherow, William Henry
Clive, Edward
Cocks, Hon. Philip James
Collier, William George
Colquitt, John Scrope
Commerell, William Henry
Cooke, George
Cookson, George Parker
Cowell, John Stepney
Crauford, Thomas
Croft, Sir Thomas Elmsley
Crofton, Hon. William George
Dalling, Edward
Dalrymple, Robert
Dalzell, Robert Alexander
Davies, Francis John
Davies, Thomas Henry Hastings
Dawkins, Francis Henry
De Courcy, Hon. John
Dilkes, William Thomas
Disbrowe, George
Donaldson, George Gordon
D'Oyley, Sir Francis
D'Oyley, Henry
Ellison, Robert
Elrington, John Hamilton
Eyre, Gervase Anthony
Fludyer, George
Forbes, Hon. Hastings Brudenel
Forbes, Hon. James
Forbes, Walter
Fox, William Augustus Lane
Fraser, Charles Mackenzie
Fremantle, John
Gascoigne, Ernest Frederick
Gomm, Sir William Maynard
Gordon, Sir Alexander
Gunthorpe, James
Hardinge, Sir Henry
Harrison, John
Harvey, Edward
Hay, James Lord
Hepburn, Francis Ker
Higginson, Alexander
Higginson, George Powell
Holburne, Francis R Thomas
Hood, Hon. Francis Wheler
Hornby, Charles
Howard, Sir Kenneth Alexander
Hulse, Richard

Hutchinson, John Hely
Irby, Hon. Edward Methuen
Jenkinson, F. Edward
Knatchbull, Wyndham
Lautour, James Oliver
Le Marchant, Carey
Lindsay, James
Long, Edmund Noel
Luttrell, Francis Fownes

Kensal Green
Aitchison, Sir John
Algeo, James
Anson, Sir George (23rd Lt Dragoons)
Anson, Hon. George (3rd Foot Guards)
Anson, Sir William
Anstruther, Windham Carmichael
Bacon, Anthony
Balfour, William
Barnes, James Stevenson
Bathurst, James
Baxter, Alexander
Bell, George
Bell, John
Bolton, John
Bowles, George
Bradshawe, George Paris
Brereton, William
Bridges, Edward Jacob
Broke, Horatio George
Brooke, Sir Arthur
Brooke, Thomas
Broughton, Samuel Daniel
Buchan, John
Bunbury, Thomas
Burton, John Curzon
Butler, Pierce
Callender, Alexander James
Campbell, Sir James
Campbell, Sir John
Campbell, Thomas Dundas
Campbell, William
Capel, Hon. Thomas Edward
Cater, Thomas Orlando
Chadwick, Nicholas
Charretie, Thomas
Chowne, Christopher Tilson
Cochrane, Andrew Coutts
Cochrane, William George
Cole, John
Colville, Hon. Sir Charles

Cooper, Samuel
Couper, George
Cowell, John Stepney
Cradock, Sir John Francis
Crewe, John Frederick
Cumming, Henry John
Daniel, Robert
Dansey, Charles Cornwallis
Darley, Edward
De Bathe, William Plunkett
Dent, Thomas
De Renzy, George Webb
Des Voeux, Benfield
Disney, Sir Moore
Dowling, Joseph
Doyle, Carlo Joseph
Drake, Thomas
Duffy, John
Elliot, Theodore Henry
Ellison, Robert
Elrington, James Hamilton
Erskine, William Howe Knight
Evans, Sir George de Lacy
Ewart, John Frederick
Ferguson, Sir Ronald Crauford
Fleming, Edward
Floyd, Henry
Forbes, Charles Ferguson
Fraser, William
French, Henry John
Fry, William Dowell
Fugion, Edward
Fuller, Sir Joseph
Gardiner, John
Gascoigne, Ernest Frederick
Gibbs, John
Gillkrest, James
Gloster, Thomas
Gubbins, Richard
Gunthorpe, James
Guthrie, George James
Halpin, William
Hamilton, Sir John
Hammersley, Frederick
Hart, Henry
Hawker, Peter
Hawker Samuel
Hawkins, Henry
Head, George
Hill, John Montgomery
Holland, Thomas Edward

Hope, James
Hope, John Charles
Hume, John Robert
Hutchinson, Scroop
Ingilby, William Bates
Jameson, James
Joddrell, Henry Edmund
Johnstone, William Frederick
Jones, Joseph Allingham
Jones, Leslie Grove
Kelly, Robert
Kempt, Sir James
Kerr, Robert
Kett, Charles George
King, Henry
Lally, Edward
Langlands, George
Langley, Frederick
Lascelles, Charles Frederick Rowley
Law, William Henry
Leigh, George
Lillie, Thomas
Llewellyn, Richard
Lumley, Hon. Sir William
Lutyens, Benjamin
Lynch, Martin Crean

Other London locations
Camden : Batty, Robert
Charterhouse: Havelock, William
Chelsea: Cadogan, Hon. Henry
Chelsea: R. Hospital: Barnard, Andrew F.
Chelsea: R. Hospital: Gleig, George Robert
Chelsea: R. Hospital: Gore, Hon. Sir Charles
Chelsea: R. Hospital: Halkett, Sir Colin
Covent Garden: Cameron, Hector
Cranford: Cozens, Benjamin H.
Edmonton: Elwin, Fountain
Hadley: Dickens, James
Hadley: Harman, George
Hadley: Ince, William
Hampton-on-Thames: Cumberland, R. F. G.
Hampton-on-Thames: Fitzclarence, George
Hampton-on-Thames: Fitzroy, Lord Charles
Harefield: Cooke, George
Harefield: Cooke, Henry Frederick
Harefield: Crespigny, George Champion
Harrow: Graham, Henry
Hendon: Crichton, Nathanial Day
Highgate: Babington, John
Highgate: Collier, Charles

Highgate: Cooke, John Henry
Highgate: Fergusson, William
Highgate: Haly, William A.
Highgate: Knollys, William Thomas
Highgate: Landmann, George
Hillingdon: Dalton, George
Holborn: Ellison, John Montague
Hyde Park Place: Clavering, James
Institute of Directors: Graham, Sir Thomas
Isleworth: Goldsmid, Albert
Kensington: Hutchins, Thomas
Kensington: Lutyens, Benjamin
Kew Green: Haverfield, John
Lambeth: Buckley, Henry
Marylebone: Bentinck, Lord William H. C.
Marylebone: Cameron, Sir Alan
Marylebone: Fitzgerald, Richard
North Audley St: Lowe, Sir Hudson
Nunhead: Costello, Edward Nunhead
Nunhead: Davies, David
Nunhead: Dickson, John
Nunhead: Fuller, Francis
Nunhead: Gomm, Sir William
Nunhead: Ivey, William
Nunhead: Lambourne, James
Piccadilly: Brookes, Robert
Piccadilly: Campbell, Sir Colin
Piccadilly: Chambers, Courtney
Piccadilly: Chambers, Newton
Piccadilly: Hamilton, Digby
Piccadilly: Jones, Richard Haynes
St John's Wood: Gibbons, Frederick
St John's Wood: Godley, Samuel
St John's Wood: Lutman, John
St Mary-Abchurch: Carey, Octavius
St. Pancras: Hilditch, Neil
St. Paul's: Bowes, Barnard Foord
St. Paul's: Cadogan, Hon. Henry
St. Paul's: Craufurd, Robert
St. Paul's: Gibbs, Sir Samuel
St. Paul's: Gore, Arthur
St. Paul's: Gurwood, John
St. Paul's: Hay, Andrew
St. Paul's: Hoghton, Daniel
St. Paul's: Jones, John Thomas
St. Paul's: Langwerth, Ernest E. K. von
St. Paul's: Le Marchant, Sir John Gaspard
Soho: Arnold, Edward John Richard
South Audley St: Lascelles, Charles F. R.
Southgate: Goulburn, Frederick
Sydenham: Lawrie, Andrew

Teddington: Borland, James
Teddington: Bridgeman, Orlando
Teddington: Hedding, William Levitt
Tower of London: Burgoyne, John Fox
Tower of London: Gomm, Sir William
Tower of London: Gurwood, John
Twickenham: Blakeney, Sir Edward
Union Jack Club: Knowles, Robert
Waterloo Place: Burgoyne, Sir John Fox
Waterloo Place: Campbell, Colin (Lord Clyde)
Westminster Abbey: Beresford, John T.
Westminster Abbey: Bryan, George
Westminster Abbey: Campbell, Colin (Lord Clyde)
Westminster Abbey: Fletcher, Sir Richard
Westminster Abbey: Knipe, Robert
Westminster Abbey: Lake, Hon. George A. F.
Westminster St John's Burial Ground: Colquhoun, Robert
West Norwood: Enoch, John

Middlesex see London

Norfolk
Buxton: Bourchier, James Claud
Catfield: Cubitt, Thomas
Cawston: Baker, James Harrison
Holt: Girling, Thomas Andrews
Honing: Cubitt, Edward George
Horstead: Lyon, William John
King's Lynn: Hawes, Thomas
Norwich: Hankin, Thomas Pate
Norwich: Leggatt, Samuel
Snettisham: Herring, Robert
Tharston: Harvey, Robert John
Wroxham: Blake, Robert
Wroxham: Collyer, George

Northamptonshire
Aynho: Cartwright, William
Flore: Cartwright, William
Hardingstone: Bouverie, Everard William
Horton: Gunning, George Orlando
Weedon Beck: Fry, John
Whiston: Irby, Hon. Edward Methuen
Wicken: Fitzroy, Lord Charles

Northumberland
Alnwick: Doyle, James
Berwick-on-Tweed: Cairns, John
Berwick-on-Tweed: Calder, Thomas
Berwick-on-Tweed: Jameson, James

Chillingham: Gough, Hugh
Hartburn: Bradford, Sir Henry Hollis
Hartburn: Bradford, Sir Thomas
Heddon on the Wall: Akenside, William
Newcastle: Cave, James
Newcastle: Greenwell, Leonard
Norham: Gourlay, Alexander
Warkworth: Crawford, William
Warkworth: Grey, Sir John

Nottinghamshire
Bingham: Holt, Richard
Nottingham: Chetham, Isaac
Nottingham: Hill, Robert
Nottingham: Kirk, George
Selston: Green, William
Tuxford: Holburne, Francis Ralph Thomas

Oxfordshire
Chipping Norton: Dawkins, George A. F.
Chipping Norton: Dawkins, Henry
Clifton Hampden: Dyke, William
Cowley: Lewis, Charles
Great Tew: Dayman, Charles
Harpsden: Hall, Henry Gallopine
Iffley: Dudley, Samuel
Kidlington: Dashwood, Charles
Little Tew: Bowers, Charles Robert
Sandford St Martin: Cox, Samuel Fortnam

Rutland
Oakham: Lowther, Hon. Henry Cecil
Oakham: Bullivant, John
Oakham: Freer, Edward Gardner
Oakham: Freer, William Gardner

Shropshire
Baschurch: Lewis, Richard
Cleobury Mortimer: Cocks, Hon. Philip James
Culmington: Johnstone, John
Hadnall: Hill, Lord Rowland
Hodnet: Leech, Samuel
Prees: Hill, Clement Delves
Prees: Hill, Sir Robert Chambré
Shrewsbury: Betton, John
Shrewsbury: Cureton, Charles Robert
Shrewsbury: Davies, Thomas
Shrewsbury: Hill, Lord Rowland
Shrewsbury: Leighton, Burgh
Whitchurch: Day, Thomas

Somerset
Banwell: Blachley, Charles
Banwell: Blachley, Henry
Banwell: Emery, Henry Gresley
Banwell: Day, Richard
Bath: Acland, Sir Wroth Palmer
Bath: Anderson, Paul
Bath: Austin, John
Bath: Austin, William
Bath: Barry, William
Bath: Bayly, Frederick
Bath: Black, John Lewis
Bath: Blood, John Aylward
Bath: Browne, Barton Parker
Bath: Brunton, Richard
Bath: Bull, Robert
Bath: Caldecot, Henry
Bath: Campbell, Archibald
Bath: Campbell, Charles
Bath: Clark, Joseph
Bath: Coffin, Edward Pine
Bath: Coghlan, Andrew
Bath: Crosse, Robert Noble
Bath: Cumin, William
Bath: Dampier, Lud Westley
Bath: Daubeney, Henry
Bath: Doherty, Patrick
Bath: Drawater, Augustus Charles
Bath: Drummond, George Duncan
Bath: Edwards, Benjamin Hutchins
Bath: Evans, John Blewitt
Bath: Fenton, John James
Bath: Fergusson, James
Bath: Gammell, James
Bath: Gomm, Sir William Maynard
Bath: Grieve, Patrick
Bath: Grove, Henry
Bath: Gun, William
Bath: Hamilton, John Potter
Bath: Haverfield, William
Bath: Holburne, Francis Ralph Thomas
Bath: Jenks, George Samuel
Bath: Jervois, William
Bath: Jones, Griffith
Bath: Lawrence, William Hudson
Bath: Lye, Benjamin Leigh
Bathford: Cochrane, James Johnston
Bristol: Austin, Thomas
Bristol: Faunce, Alured Dodsworth
Bristol: Fothergill, Joshua
Bristol: Gordon, Charles John

Bristol: Gore, George
Bristol: Hood, George
Bristol: Jenkin, James
Bristol: Kersteman, William Brewse
Bristol: Lonsdale, William
Charlton Musgrave: Bailey, Morris William
Clevedon: Ellis, Charles Parker
Dunster: Luttrell, Francis Fownes
Farleigh-Hungerford: Houlton, Sir George
Freshford: Edwards, Benjamin Hutchins
Kilmersdon: Jollife, Charles
Kingston St Mary: Chapman, Stephen R.
Minehead: Gifford, George St James
Newton St. Loe: Langton, Edward Gore
North Stoke: Lawrence, Alexander W.
South Stoke: Crookshank, Arthur C. W.
Stapleton: Langton, Edward Gore
Taunton: Collis, Charles
Taunton: Dance, Charles Webb
Wells: Foster, Charles Edward
Wiveliscombe: Bale, John

Staffordshire
Barton-under-Needwood: Fowler, Richard
Burton-on-Trent: Jones, William
Cheadle: Blood, Thomas
Handsworth: Devey, Henry Fryer
Lichfield: Bunbury, Thomas
Lichfield: Dyott, William
West Bromwich: Judge, John William

Suffolk
Bury St Edmunds: Baker, James Harrison:
Bury St Edmunds: Baxter, Robert
Bury St Edmunds: Collier, William George
Fornham All Saints: Cowsell, John
Hengrave: Craufurd, Alexander Charles G.
Hengrave: Craufurd, Thomas Gage
Hoxne: Kerrison, Sir Edward
Ipswich: Booth, Charles
Ipswich: Heise, Gabriel Wilhelm
Lowestoft: Chambers, Thomas Walker
Lowestoft: Leathes, Henry Mussendon
Nacton: Broke, Sir Charles
Nacton: Broke, Horatio George
Santon Downham: Cadogan, Hon. Henry
Troston: Lofft, Henry Capel
Wissett: Freestone, Anthony
Yaxley: Bond, Robert

Surrey
Bletchingley: Clayton, William Robert
Brookwood: Chatterton, Sir James Charles
Brookwood: Goldfinch, Henry
Carshalton: Houstoun, William
Claygate: Douglas, Robert
Claygate: Lambert, Sir John
Cobham: Brotherton, Thomas William
Croydon: Johnson, Samuel
Egham: Hervey, Felton Elwill Bathurst
Esher: Cookson, George
Esher: Cookson, George Parker
Farncombe: Dallas, Charles Robert King
Farnham: Luard, John
Hersham: Frederick, Edward Henry
Hersham: Frederick, Roger
Mortlake: Geary, Henry
Nutfield: Eligé, John Peter
Richmond: Bean, George
Sandhurst: Jones, Harry David
Seale: Long, Edward Noel
Seale: Long, Robert Ballard
Shalford: Godwin, Henry Thomas
South Holmwood: Arnold, Robert
West Molesley: Berkeley, Sir George H. F.
Wooton: Barclay, Delancy
Wooton: Evelyn, George

Sussex
Battle: Kingsbury, John
Brighton: Jenkins, Robert
Brighton: Knox, Hon. John James
Buxted: D'Oyly, Sir Francis
Chailey: Hepburn, Francis Ker
Chichester: Buckner, Richard
Fletching: Hattrell, Daniel
Frant: By, John
Hastings: Kincaid, John
Hollington: Greenock, Hon. Charles Murray
Hove: Blake, William Williams
Hove: Campbell, Patrick
Hove: Clark, John
Hove: Darling, Ralph
Hove: Gardiner, James Ballard
Lower Beeding: Boldero, Lonsdale
Nuthurst: Boldero, Lonsdale
Nuthurst: Boldero, Henry
Portslade: Kerr, William
South Berstead: Egerton, Thomas
Storrington: Bishopp, Cecil
Storrington: Bradford, Sir Henry Hollis

Storrington: Bradford, William
Storrington: Dalzell, Robert Alexander
Tillington: Ayling, John
Woolbeding: Bouverie, Sir Henry Frederick
Worthing: Berford, Richard
Worthing: Leach, Jonathan

Warwickshire
Coventry: Gardner, David
Coventry: Gregory, Arthur Francis
Coventry: Hood, Hon, Francis Wheler
Kenilworth: Champ, Thomas
Warwick: Greville, Hon. Sir Charles James
Wootton Wawen: Houghton, Henry

Wiltshire
Alton Barnes: Crowe, George William
Chilton Foliat: Kelly, William
Potterne: Grubbe, William Hunt

Worcestershire
Eckington: Irwin, Francis Chidley
Elmley Castle: Davies, Thomas Henry H.
Kempsey: Bell, Edward Wells
Madresfield: Lygon, Hon. Edward Pyndar
Madresfield: Lygon, Hon. Henry Beauchamp
Malvern: Annesley, Marcus
Malvern: Davy, Charles William
Malvern: Hardwick, William
Ombersley: Hill, Lord Arthur Moyse William
Worcester: Ellis, Sir Henry Walton

Yorkshire
Bedale: Hincks, John
Beverley: Barnard, Charles Lewyns
Beverley: Bowes, Barnard Foord
Beverley: Cheney, Robert
Beverley: Ditmas, John
Beverley: Jones, Harry David
Beverley: Lewis, Griffith G.
Bradford: Barwick, Thomas
Castle Howard: Howard, Hon. Frederick
Copgrove: Duncombe, Slingsby
Doncaster: Higgins, Thomas
Elloughton: Deighton, William
Gilling West: Hildreth, William
Harewood: Lascelles, Hon. Henry
Harrogate: Gray, John Walker
Hedon: Heron, John
Honley: Drawbridge, Charles
Keighley: Ingham, Christopher

Kirkheaton: Broadbent, William
Kirkheaton: Cliffe, Stephen
Kirkheaton: Filton, John
Kirkleatham: Brunton, Thomas
Kirklington: Dalbiac, James Charles
Kirklington: Dalbiac, Susanna Isabelle
Leeds: Beckett, Richard
Leeds: Gray, Frederick
Marske-by-the Sea: Dundas, Hon. Sir Robert
Middleton Tyas: Healey, John
Nidd: L'Estrange, George Guy Carleton
Northallerton: Booth, Henry
North Stainley: Hutchinson, Thomas K.
Pickering: Fothergill, John
Pontefract: Blanco, Thomas
Richmond: Blythman, Augustus
Rotherham: Howard, Sir Kenneth Alexander
Sand Hutton: Acomb, John
Sand Hutton: Childers, Michael
Sedbergh: Buck, Henry Rishton
Selby: Cleeves, Andrew
Sheffield: Briggs, William
Sheffield: Hird, John
Skelton: Hodgson, Ellis
South Dalton: Hotham, Beaumont Lord
Stanhope: Brumwell, John
Thirkleby: Frankland, Frederick William
West Tanfield: Bell, William
York: Ball, James
York: Beecham, Joseph
York: Bloomfield, James Henry
York: Braund, John
York: Bussey, John
York: Butcher, Thomas
York: Curson, Andrew
York: Dodd, Robert
York: Douglas, Charles Aytoyne W.
York: Downs, James
York: Doyle, Thomas
York: Drew, J. H.
York: Fitton, John
York: Forrester, Richard
York: Graves, Anthony
York: Hamilton, Robert
York: Hanger, John
York: Hanks, William
York: Hoare, Henry
York: Honey, Henry
York: Jennings, Joshua
York: Lane, Daniel

SCOTLAND
Aberdeenshire
Aberdeen: Emslie, John
Aberdeen: Fraser, William
Aberdeen: Hay, Lord James
Aberdeen: Huntly, George (Marquess of)
Aberdour: Gordon, Alexander (C. Guards)
Ellon: Gordon, Hon. Sir Alexander (3 Ft Gds)
Dunbennan: Jessiman, Alexander
Huntly: Davidson, James
Kennethmont: Hay, Andrew Leith
Kennethmont: Leith, Sir James
Maryculter: Boswell, John Irvine
Migvie: Anderson, James
Starthdon: Leith, Sir Alexander
Turriff: Jack, John

Angus
Aberelliot: Goodall, George
Arbroath: Cumming, William
Brechin: Cairncross, John
Brechin: Glenn, James
Dundee: Chalmers, Sir William
Dundee: Clayhills, James Menzies
Forfar: Douglas, Sir William
Friockheim: Croall, James
Kirriemuir: Cruikshank, William
Monifieth: Bowman, David
Montrose: Innes, John White

Argyllshire
Campbell Town: Campbell, Frederick
Lismore: Gregorson, Donald

Ayrshire
Ayr: Campbell, Dugald
Colmonell: Barton, Alexander
Irvine: Forbes, Duncan
Kilmarnock: Findlay, William
Kirkmichael: Hutchinson, John
Largs: Brisbane, Sir Thomas Makdougall
Largs, Hunter, William
Maybole: Aird, Thomas

Banffshire See Morayshire

Berwickshire
Coldingham: Fair, David
Duns: Gillies, John
Earlston: Hewat, Richard
Edrom: Houstoun, Sir William

Fogo: Alcorn, William
Mordington: Logan, Patrick

Buteshire
Cumbrae: Laverton, James

Caithness
Bower: Henderson, David
Olrig: Andrew, Donald
Thurso: Davidson, Benjamin
Thurso: Davidson, James
Thurso: Davidson, Sinclair
Wick: Innes, Gordon C.
Wick: Innes, John
Wick: Innes, Peter
Wick: Innes, William

Clackmannanshire
Clackmannan: Bruce, Robert

Dumbartonshire
Cardross: Kenny, Courtenay Crowe
Cardross: Kenny, Edward
Dumbarton: Connolly, James

Dumfriesshire and Galloway
Annan: Dirom, John Pasley
Annan: Irving, James
Annan: Forrest, George William
Cummertrees: Douglas, Sholto
Dumfries: Adair, James
Dumfries: Cannon, William
Dumfries: Clark, Alexander Kennedy
Dumfries: Gornall, John
Dumfries: Gracie, James
Dumfries: Halliday, Andrew
Dumfries: Hinde, William
Dumfries: Johnston, Archibald
Ecclefechan: Arnott, Archibald
Kirkton: Bramwell, John
Langholm: Fletcher, Simon
Langholm: Little, William
Sanquhar: Barker, Robert
Sanquhar: Hair, Archibald
Wauchope: Fogo, James

East Lothian
Bolton: Blantyre, Robert
Dunglass: De Lancey, Sir William Howe
Haddington: Hope, Sir John

Edinburgh see Midlothian

Elginshire see Morayshire

Fife
Abercrombie: Anstruther, Robert
Cupar: Hope, Sir John
Largo: Briggs, James
Largo: Briggs, John Falconer

Galloway see Dumfriesshire and Galloway

Invernesshire
Ardersier Findlay, Alexander:
Boleskine: Fraser, James John
Boleskine: Fraser, Thomas
Corpach: Cameron, Alexander
Corpach: Cameron, Dugald
Corpach: Cameron, John
Corpach: Cameron, William
Duthil: Grant, Sir Maxwell
Eskadale: Chisholm, Stuart
Fort William: Cameron, Robert
Glen Convinth: Fraser, James
Glen Nevis: Cameron, Ewen
Inverness: Chisholm, Harold
Kirkton: Lamont, Daniel

Kincardineshire
Dunnottar: Kennedy, Andrew
Fetteresso: Duthie, William

Lanarkshire
Glasgow: Cadogan, Hon. Henry
Glasgow: Campbell, Colin (Lord Clyde)
Glasgow: Carmichael, Thomas
Glasgow: Cruikshank, Alexander
Glasgow: Cruikshank, James
Govan: Gwyn, William
Shotts: Hamilton, James Inglis

Midlothian
Abercorn: Hope, Sir John (92nd Foot)
Edinburgh: Abercromby, Hon. Alexander
Edinburgh: Anderson, Alexander
Edinburgh: Anderson, Andrew
Edinburgh: Andrews, Thomas
Edinburgh: Ansell, Francis Hutchings
Edinburgh: Bain, William
Edinburgh: Blair, Thomas Hunter
Edinburgh: Bone, Hugh

Edinburgh: Brown, Thomas
Edinburgh: Campbell, Sir Archibald
Edinburgh: Campbell, Archibald Argyle
Edinburgh: Canch, Thomas
Edinburgh: Collins, Bassett
Edinburgh: Coulter, William
Edinburgh: Crokat, William
Edinburgh: Cruikshank, Alexander
Edinburgh: Custance, Holman
Edinburgh: Deuchar, David
Edinburgh: Dick, Robert Henry
Edinburgh: Drysdale, Alexander
Edinburgh: Dudgeon, Peter
Edinburgh: Dundas, William Bolden
Edinburgh: Ewart, Charles
Edinburgh: Ewing, Daniel
Edinburgh: Falconer, Chesborough Grant
Edinburgh: Farquharson, John
Edinburgh: Ferguson, Adam
Edinburgh: Forbes, Duncan
Edinburgh: Geddes, John
Edinburgh: Gilmour, Dugald Little
Edinburgh: Gordon, John
Edinburgh: Gordon, Thomas
Edinburgh: Grant, Alexander
Edinburgh: Hamilton, Henry Stewart
Edinburgh: Harrison, John
Edinburgh: Hope, John (60th Foot)
Edinburgh: Hope, Sir John (92nd Foot)
Edinburgh: Johnson, Hugh
Edinburgh: Johnston, James
Edinburgh: Knox, Francis
Edinburgh: Kynock, John
Edinburgh: Laing, Thomas
Edinburgh: Logan, Thomas Galbraith
Inveresk: Elphinstone, James Drummond F.
Inveresk: Elphinstone, William Keith
Inveresk: Home, John
Inveresk: Lindsay, Patrick

Morayshire
Cromdale: Blair, William
Cromdale: Carmichael, Lewis
Cromdale: Grant, John
Elgin: Brown, George
Elgin: Huntly, George (Marquess of)
Fochabers: Briggs, James
Forres: Grant, Colquhoun
Garmouth: Dunbar, George
Inveraven: Grant, Lewis
Kinrara: Cameron, John

Kirkmichael: Gordon, James
Kirkmichael: Gordon, William A.
Speymouth Essil: Fyfe, William

Perthshire
Abernyte: Gardiner, David
Abernyte: Gardiner, John
Clunie: Kinloch, Charles
Crieff: Baird, Sir David
Dunkeld: Dick, Robert Henry
Dunkeld: Holcombe, Harcourt Forde
Dunkeld: Fisher, Henry
Errol: Gardiner, John
Fortingall: Campbell, Duncan
Longforgan: Hedderwick, David
Methven: Graham, Sir Thomas
North Inches: Graham, Sir Thomas
Perth: Campbell, Archibald
Perth: Forbes, Walter
Tibbermore: Balvaird, William

Renfrewshire
Bishopton: Blantyre, Robert
Greenock: Crawfurd, Henry
Paisley: Fulton, Robert

Roxburghshire
Hawick: Douglas, Robert
Kelso: De Bourgh, Anthony Philip
St Boswell: Fairfax, Henry

Selkirkshire
Selkirk: Anderson, Andrew
Selkirk: Lang, John Sibbald

Stirlingshire
Bridge of Allan: Drummond, Peter
Falkirk: Kincaid, John
Inchmahome: Grahame, Duncan
Larbert: Dundas, Thomas
Stirling: Baird, James
Stirling: Baird, Patrick
Stirling: Forbes, Alexander

Sutherland
Dornoch: Campbell, Donald
Kildonan: Gordon, John
Kildonan: Gordon, William

WALES
Abergele: Hesketh, Robert H. Bamford
Aberystwyth: Cranston, Thomas
Bangor: Heyland, Arthur Rowley
Bettws Cedewain: Griffiths, Richard
Brecon: Ekins, Clement
Cardiff: Donovan, Henry Douglas
Carmarthen: Ellis, Sir Henry Walton
Conway: Foulkes, Thomas
Erbistock: Boates, Henry Ellis
Goytre: Bird, Henry
Llancarfan: Jenkins, George
Llanelly: Griffiths, Thomas
Llanfaglan: Jones, William
Llanfair: Gregory, Adam
Llanfrynach: Douglas, Archibald Murray
Llanllwch: Davies, John
Llanllwch: Edwardes, David John
Llanllwch: Gwynne, Henry Lewis Edwardes
Llansantffraed-Cwmdeuddwr: Jones, Edward
Llanwenarth: Bubb, Anthony
Mold: Griffith, Edwin
Montgomery: Humphreys, Charles Gardiner
Neath: Grant, Turner
Neath: Jenkins, John
Newport: Carr, Stephen
Newton: Davies, Edward
Newtown: Howe, John
Penmark: Jones, Oliver Thomas
Presteigne: Burch, Thomas
Roath: John, Thomas
St Asaph: Browne, Thomas Henry
St Maughan: Brownrigg, Sir Robert
St Nicholas: Camac, Burges
Saundersfoot: Craig, Phillip
Tenby: Ferrior, Samuel
Welshpool: Cart, Richard

NORTHERN IRELAND
Aghalurcher: Brooke, Francis (1st Dgn Gds)
Aghalurcher: Brooke, Francis (4th Foot)
Armagh: Kelly, Dawson
Armagh: Kelly, William
Ballymena: Dyas, Joseph
Belfast: Hardcastle, William A.
Bellaghy: Downing, Adam G.
Clogher: Bloomfield, David
Cookstown: Lind, Robert
Donaghadee: De La Cherois, Nicholas
Downhill: Bruce, John Robertson
Enniskillen: Betty, Christopher S.

Enniskillen: Cole, Sir Galbraith Lowry
Enniskillen: Fawcett, John James
Enniskillen: Keddle, Robert
Killyleagh: Blackwood, Robert T.
Kilmegan: Keown, William
Larne: Dobbs, John
Londonderry: Lecky, David
Newry: Browne, Richard Jebb
Newry: Buchanan, John
Newry: Dowdall, Patrick
Newry: Falls, Thomas
Waringstown: Atkinson, Abraham

IRELAND, REPUBLIC OF
Ballingarry: Faddy, Peter
Bandon: Bernard, Hon. Francis
Bandon: Bernard, Hon. Henry Boyle
Bannow: Boyce, Shapland
Cahir: Hickman, Charles
Castlebar: Browne, John
Castlebellingham: Bellingham Henry T.
Castlebridge: Huson, Charles
Castleconnell: Bourke, Richard
Castletown: Faulkner, Sir Arthur Brooke
Clifden: Dallas, Alexander R. C.
Clonmacnoise: Frazer, John W.
Cork: Chatterton, James Charles
Cork: Gillan, Martin
Dublin: Barlow, James
Dublin: Birch, Robert Henry
Dublin: Birnes, Joseph
Dublin: Bury, George
Dublin: Butler, Theobald
Dublin: Campbell, Sir Guy
Dublin: Coote, Robert
Dublin: Cosgrove, John
Dublin: Cuyler, Augustus
Dublin: D'Arcey, Edward
Dublin: Dallas, Alexander R. C.
Dublin: Doherty, George
Dublin: Elkington, James Goodall
Dublin: Feltom, Thomas
Dublin: Freeman, Thomas
Dublin: Freeman, Robert
Dublin: Fyers, William
Dublin: Gough, Hugh
Dublin: Haines, Gregory
Dublin: Hall, Charles
Dublin: Hamilton, Nicholas
Dublin: Hay, James
Dublin: Holmes, Stephen

Dublin: Hughes, Richard
Dublin: Hutchinson, John Hely
Dublin: Kennedy, Simson
Dublin: King, Charles (16 Lt Dgs)
Dublin: King, Charles (74 Foot)
Dublin: Knight, Edward
Dublin: Lawder, Rhynd
Duleek: Kelly, Richard
Dundalk: Battersby, James
Dundrum: Cowell, William
Dunganstown: Hoey, William
Enniscorthy: Collins, George
Fiddown: Briscoe, Edward
Galway: Davis, George Lenox
Goresbridge: Gore, Arthur
Kildangan: Hoysted, Frederick William
Kilkeary: Carrol, Sir William Parker
Kilkenny: Anderson, James
Kilkenny: Gore, Arthur
Kilkenny: Kingsmill, Parr
Kilkenny: Kingsmill, William (66 Foot)
Kilkenny: Kingsmill, William (88 Foot)
Kilmore: Carrol, Sir William Parker
Kinsale: Arbuthnot, Sir Thomas
Kinsale: Cochrane, Thomas
Kinsale: Davenport, Edmund
Kinsale: Harding, Edwin
Lea (Leig): Kelly, Allan
Littleton: Beere, Henry
Littleton: Beere, Hercules
Loughcrew: Battersby, George
Monkstown: Cox, William
Monkstown: Drewe, Edward Ward
Newton-Fertullagh: Grey, George
Orchardstown: Hamerton, John Millett
Partree: Lynch, Henry Blois
Rathaspeck: Brunker, James
Rathaspeck: Elgee, William
Sligo: Elliot, Gilbert
Stradbally: Evans, George
Taghmon: Cox, William
Templemore: Cameron, Ewen
Templemore: Faris, James Fleming
Templemore: Lynam, Joseph
Tramore: Baird, William
Tramore: Dent, Abraham
Tramore: Douglas, Charles
Tramore: Hagan, James
Tramore: Hill, Rowland F.
Tramore: Lambe, Peter K.
Tuam: Fairfoot, Robert

Tullamore: Grant, James
Turlough: Fitzgerald, Edward Thomas
Wexford: Cavenagh, George Walter
Whitechurch: Burnett, John

OVERSEAS MEMORIALS

AUSTRALIA
Adelaide: Baye, Benjamin
Adelaide: Davis, William
Adelaide: Light, William
Beechworth: Drummond, John
Cobbity: Dunk, Jesse
Goulburn: Forster, Henry
Hobart: Ashton, Henry
Hobart: Cheyne, Alexander
Hobart: De Gillern, William
Ipswich: Gray, Charles George
Jamberoo: Keevers, William
Maitland: Hall, William
Melbourne: Anderson, Joseph
Morpeth: Close, Edward C.
Mount Barker: Barker, Collet
Muswellbrook: Dumaresq, Henry
One Tree Hill: Garlick, Moses Bendle
Parramatta: D'Arcy, George Pitt
Parramatta: Irwin, William
Port Macquarie: Crummer, James Henry
Singleton: Cooke, William
Sydney: Barker, Collet
Sydney: Barney, George
Sydney: Blomfield, Thomas Valentine
Sydney: Bourke, Richard
Sydney: Campbell, John
Sydney: Dumaresq, William John
Sydney: Laidley, James
Yass: Allman, Francis

BELGIUM
Evere
Barrington, Hon. Samuel S. P.
Blackman, John Lucie
Brown, Thomas
Clyde, James
Cotton, Edward
Cromie, Michael Thomas
De Lancy, Sir William Howe
Forbes, Hon. Hastings Brudenel
Gordon, Hon. Sir Alexander
Grose, Edward
Hay, James Lord

Lloyd, William John

Waterloo

St Joseph's Church
Adair, Robert
Anderson, William
Armstrong, John
Ashton, John
Baird, William
Barrington, Samuel Shute P.
Battersby, George
Baxter, John
Bean, George
Beere, Henry
Bertie, Lindsay James
Bisdom, D. R.
Bishop, Isaac
Boeltjes, K.
Bolton, Samuel
Boyce, John
Breda, Cornelius
Bringhurst, John D.
Brown, Thomas
Buck, Henry Rishton
Buckley, Henry
Buckley, William
Bullen, James
Burley, William
Cairnes, Robert Macpherson
Cameron, Donald
Cameron, John (33rd Foot)
Cameron, John (79th Foot)
Campbell, Neil
Canning, Charles Fox
Carondel, J. C.
Chambers, Newton
Chambers, Thomas Walker
Clare, Charles
Clarke, Thomas
Cochrane, Charles
Coenegracht, L. P.
Cox, Wilson
Craufurd, Thomas Gage
Cromie, Michael Thomas
Daey, H. A.
Daxter, William
De Berlaere, A. J. L. P.
De Collaert, Baron J. A.
De Haan, J.
De La Howarderie, Graaf D.

De Nave, B. D. J.
De Schulzen, Detlef
De Villers, C. N. J. F. M.
Devitt, Guy
Donnegan, Hugh
D'Oyly, Sir Francis
Eadie, Edward
Early, John
Ellis, Sir Henry Walton
Engel
Finley, Thomas
Fisher, James
Fitzgerald, Richard
Forbes, Hon. Hastings Brudenel
Foster, Francis
Fuller, William
Glass, John
Gordon, Hon. Sir Alexander
Gore, Arthur
Griffith, Edwin
Grose, Edward
Growcock, Edward
Gunning, George Orlando
Haigh, John
Haigh, Thomas D.
Halford, Thomas
Hardt, A.
Haren, Baron C. F. S. van
Hart, James
Hay, Alexander
Hay, James Lord
Hechmann, G.
Heiden, F. M. von
Heil, P.
Henry, J. J.
Hickey, Jeremiah
Hodge, Edward
Horston, William
Howard, Hon. Frederick
Hurst, George
James, John
Jonquière, J. W. E.
Kelly, Robert
Kennedy, Ewen
Kennedy, James Grant
King, John
Kirby, James
Klejin, P. R.
Kreijsig, C. S.
Kynock, John
Lang, Francis

Lechleitner, C. M.
Lloyd, William John.
Lockhart, John Elliott

Hougoumont
Blackman, John Lucie
Cotton, Edward
Craufurd, Thomas Gage

La Haye Sainte
Gordon, Hon. Sir Alexander

KGL Memorial – (La Haye Sainte)
Albert, Anton
Bobers, Carl von
Bösewiel, Adolph
Brüggemann, Heinrich
Bülow, Friedrick von
Chüden, George Wilhelm C.
Cronhelm, Theodor von
Deichmann, Wilhelm
Diedel, Friederich
Drangmeister, Heinrich
Du Plat, Georg Carl August
Goeben, August A. von
Heiden, F. M. von
Heise, Georg
Holle, Carl von
Holzerman, Philipp
Janssen, Georg
Jeinsen, Friedrich von
Kerssenbruch, Agatz von
Kuhlmann, Otto
Leschen, Friederich
Leue, Georg Ludwig
Levetzow, Friedrick C. L
Lücken, Hartwig von

Mont St Jean
Gunning, John

Quatre Bras
Brunswick, Frederick William, Duke of

Waterloo Museum
Ellis, Sir Henry Walton
Fitzgerald, Richard
Heyland, Arthur Rowley

CANADA

Beaverton-Thorah: Cameron, Kenneth
Fort Erie: Jones, Arthur R.
Halifax: Fullerton, James
Hamilton: Kelk, Edward
Kingston: Bonnycastle, Richard Henry
Lake Francis Island: Colborne, Sir John
Montreal: D'Urban, Sir Benjamin
Montreal: Gordon, John
Niagara: Bishopp, Cecil
Niagara: Claus, William
Niagara: Currie, Lachlan
Niagara: Elliot, William R.
Niagara: Gordon, John
Niagara: Hemphill, William
Niagara: Hiscott, Richard
Niagara: Irving, Jacob Aemilius
Niagara: Kingsmill, William
Quebec: Impett, Thomas R. S.
Toronto: Colborne, Sir John

CEYLON (SRI LANKA)

Colombo: Abell, Charles
Colombo: Haddock, Robert
Kandy: Dawson, William Francis
Kandy: Fletcher, Thomas
Kandy: Fraser, John
Kandy: Lindsay, Martin

FRANCE

Biarritz

Ackland, Dudley
Andrews, Thomas
Angrove, John George
Arden, Henry
Baillie, Mackay Hugh
Baker, James Harrison
Bent, James
Bignall, Francis
Blumenbach, Carl Edward
Bolton, George
Bolton, Robert Dawson
Bone, Peter Joseph
Boyd, George
Bright, Henry
Burroughs, William
Butler, John O'Bryan
Cameron, Duncan
Cameron, Ewen
Cameron, John
Campbell, Alexander
Campbell, William M.
Capel, Thomas
Carroll, John
Clitherow, William Henry
Chüden, Paul Gotlieb
Coghlan, John Robert
Collier, William George
Crofton, Hon. William George
Cromie, James
De Braxion, Ernst
Dobbin, Robert Brown
Dobbyn, Alexander
Douglas, John Graham
Doyle, John
Drechsell, Baron Frederick von
Duncan, John
Dunkley William
Eccles, Thomas
Ewing, Daniel
Farquharson, Donald
Favell, William Anthony
Fearon, Peter
Fitzgerald, James
Forbes, Thomas
Fraser, Alexander John
Fraser, John
Freer, Edward Gardner
Furnace, William H.
Gale, Arthur
Gibbons, George
Gordon, Charles John
Gordon, Stephen
Gordon, William
Gough, Hugh
Hamilton, Henry Stewart
Hamilton, John
Hardy, James
Hay, Andrew
Henderson, Charles
Henderson, John
Hill, John
Hilliard, Morgan
Holburne, Francis Ralph Thomas
Hood, Hon. Francis Wheler
Hopkins, Henry Lewis
Hopwood, John
Innes, John White
Irwine, Henry Bury
Johnson, Arthur
Johnson, William Yates
Johnstone, Thomas

Johnstone, William
Jones, Arthur
Kellett, Christopher
Klenck, Frederick von
Knox, George
Köhler, Charles
Koschenbar, Ernst von
Latta, John
Lautour, James Oliver
Leith, James William
Le Marchant, Carey
Le Mesurier, Peter
Little, George
Lloyd, Richard
Lloyd Thomas
Lyon, William John

Other French Locations
Aix-la-Chapelle: Grant, Colquhoun
Bidart: Lloyd, Richard
Blingel: Latham, Matthew
Cadillon: Lyon, William J.
Lyon: Gordon, Thomas William
Pau: Auchmuty, Samuel
Bayonne: Burroughs, William
Bayonne: Collier, William G.
Bayonne: Crofton, Hon. William George
Bayonne: Hamilton, John
Bayonne: Hay, Andrew
Bayonne: Holburne, Francis Ralph Thomas
Toulouse: Bright, Henry
Toulouse: Forbes, Thomas
Toulouse: Gordon, Charles John
Toulouse: Hood, Hon. Francis Wheler
Toulouse: Hunter, John
Urogne: Johnson, Arthur
Valenciennes: Douglas, Sir William
Verdun: Butler, Theodore

GERMANY
Brunswick: Brunswick, F. W. Duke of
Hanover: Alten, Count Charles von
Hanover: Baring, Baron George von
Paunsdorf: Bogue, Richard
Taucha: Bogue, Richard

GIBRALTAR
Holy Trinity: Don, George
Holy Trinity: Frankland, Frederick William
King's Chapel: Bennett, Joseph
King's Chapel: Haden, Francis Wastie

King's Chapel: Hall, Richard
King's Chapel: Hennen, John
King's Chapel: Light, John
King's Chapel: Longley, Joseph
Sandpits Cemetery: Browne, Thomas Gore
Sandpits Cemetery: Buckeridge, Henry Mark
Sandpits Cemetery: Casey, Bartholomew
Sandpits Cemetery: Erskine, Robert
Sandpits Cemetery: Hacket, William
Sandpits Cemetery: Haden, Francis Wastie
Sandpits Cemetery: Heron, Basil Robinson
Sandpits Cemetery: Jones, Rice
Trafalgar Cemetery: Connell, John
Trafalgar Cemetery: Grant, John

GREECE
Corfu: Adam, Frederick William
Corfu: Freer, William Gardner
Corfu: Hackett, Richard
Corfu: Johnston, George

INDIA
Agra: Churchill, Chatham H.
Ambala: Cormick, Edward
Ambala: Hill, Dudley St Leger
Bangalore: Doherty, Joseph
Bangalore: Hill, Clement Delves
Barrackpore: Churchill, Chatham H.
Bombay: Arnold, Robert
Bombay: Beckwith, Sir Thomas Sidney
Bombay: Cochrane, Christopher Irwin
Bombay: Elphinstone, William Keith
Bombay: Girdlestone, Charles
Bombay: Keith, Henry Duncan
Calcutta: Bentinck, Lord William Henry C.
Calcutta: Cavenagh, George Walter
Calcutta: Guthrie, John Cleland
Calcutta: Hardinge, Sir Henry
Calcutta: Hillier, George
Calcutta: Kneebone, Thomas
Cannamore: Giles, John
Cawnpore: Higginson, Philip Talbot
Chinsurah: Cameron, Charles
Dinapore: Beggs, John
Dinapore: Kennerdell, James
Dinapore: Lintott, John
Ferozepore: Baldwin, George
Ferozepore: Bolton, Samuel
Ferozepore: Dick, Robert H.
Gujerat: Brookes, Robert
Karnal: Eager, Francis Russell

Madras: Brown, Ebenezer
Madras: Campbell, Sir Alexander
Madras: Dick, Robert H.
Madras: Elder, Sir George
Madras: Fehrszen, Oliver George
Madras: Hay, Patrick
Madras: Impett, John
Meerut: Armstrong, Henry Bruere
Meerut: Arnold, Edward John Richard
Meerut: Arnold, Robert
Meerut: Byrom, Ashton Johnson
Meerut: Considine, James
Meerut: Coxen, Edward
Mullye: Hay, Charles Peter
Mullye: Kelly, Edward
Mominabad: Lock, Henry
Neembolah: Fraser, Thomas
Ramnagar: Cureton, Charles Robert
Ramnagar: Havelock, William
Ranipet: Blankley, Henry Stanyford
Secunderabad: Evans, John
Simla: Godwin, Henry Thomas
Sitabaldi: Bell, Thomas
Vellore: Impey, Benjamin
Wallajabad: Lynch, James S.

ITALY
Florence: De Courcy, Gerard
Florence: Gordon, Arthur Helsham
Florence: Gregorie, Charles
Florence: Hughes, James
Florence: Kellett, Robert Napier
Florence: Locke, John
Leghorn: Forbes, Hon. James
Leghorn: Forrest, George William
Messina: Buxton, James William
Naples: Ansley, Benjamin
Naples: Carmichael, Alexander
Naples: Clark, John
Naples: Fleming, Pierre Edward
Rome: Daubeney, Henry
Rome: Gilmour, Dugald Little.

MALTA
Floriana: Bowman, William Flockhart
Garrison Cemetery: Colcroft, John
Ta Braxia: Bowen, Robert
Valetta: Bouverie, Henry F.

MAURITIUS
Port Louis: Kennelly, James

NEW ZEALAND
Auckland: Dean, George
Dunedin: Cargill, William

PORTUGAL
Almeida: Beresford, John Theophilus
Elvas: Bevan, Charles
Elvas: Hoghton, Daniel
Gouveia: Collins, Richard
Lisbon: Ainslie, George
Lisbon: Bradnock, George
Lisbon: Clubb, Robert
Lisbon: Crompton, Richard
Lisbon: Curby, Edward
Lisbon: Fletcher, Sir Richard
Lisbon: Hamilton, George Augustus
Lisbon: Handley, Benjamin
Lisbon: Ironside, George Edward
Lisbon: Laidley, John
Lisbon: Livingstone, Francis
Rolica: Lake, Hon. George Augustus F.
Villa Formosa: Cameron, Phillips

ST HELENA
James Town: Hare, John

SOUTH AFRICA
Bathurst: Brown, Stephen
Grahamstown: Bambrick, Robert

SPAIN
Alcala de Guadaira: Colquitt, John Scrope
Ciudad Rodrigo: Craufurd, Robert
Corunna: Anstruther, Robert
Rendinas: Hutton, George
San Sebastian: Collyer, George
San Sebastian: Fletcher, Sir Richard
Sorauren: Craufurd, George Douglas
Vera: Cadoux, Daniel
Vera: Hill, John
Villa Franca: Hanson, William

SWITZERLAND
Geneva: Felix, Orlando
Geneva: Gomm, Henry

UKRAINE
Cathcart's Hill Cemetery: Cathcart, Hon George

UNITED STATES OF AMERICA
Asheville: Brown, James
New York: Granger, Early
Plattsburg: Kingsbury, Robert

VENEZUELA
Carabobo: Ferriar, Thomas Ilderton

WEST INDIES
Antigua: Burrows, Charles Montagu
Barbados: Adams, John
Barbados: Clutterbuck, William
Barbados: Crosse, Robert Noble
Barbados: De Wendt, Edward Michael
Barbados: Dow, Edward
Barbados: Edgell, Charles James
Barbados: Ekins, Clement
Barbados: Fletcher, John Wynne
Barbados: Gordon, John
Barbados: Grant, Charles
Barbados: Gray, William
Barbados: Johnston, Archibald
Barbados: Knight, Charles
British Guiana: Goodman, Stephen Arthur
British Guiana: Doyle, Charles Simon
Dominica: Emes, Thomas
Grenada: Clarke, Joseph
Jamaica: Campbell, Dugald
Jamaica: Charleton, Andrew Robert
Jamaica: Eppes, William Randolph
Jamaica: Fullerton, Alexander
Jamaica: Hill, Charles
Jamaica: Kelly, William Waldron
Jamaica: Lambert, Samuel
Montserrat: France, Harold

Regimental Index

1st Life Guards

Bishop, William B.	Cpl Major
Brunton, Thomas	Pte
Camac, Burges	Capt
Cliffe, Stephen	Pte
Cox, Samuel Fortnam	Cornet
Este, Michael Lambton	Surgeon
Ferrior, Samuel	Major and Lt Col
Gardner, Thomas	Pte
James, John Haddy	Asst Surgeon
Kelly, Edward	Capt

2nd Life Guards

Acomb, John	Cpl
Barwick, Thomas	Pte
Broughton, Samuel D.	Surgeon
Charretie, Thomas	Capt
Fitzgerald, Richard	Capt
Godley, Samuel	Pte
Gray, Frederick	Pte
Hird, John	Pte
Lomax, Thomas	Pte
Lygon, Hon Edward P.	Major and Lt Col

Royal Regiment of Horse Guards

Boates, Henry Ellis	Lt
Bouverie, Everard W.	Lt
Cart, Richard	Cpl
Clayton, William Robert	Capt
Drake, William Tyrwhitt	Capt
Elley, Sir John	Lt Colonel
Grubbe, William Hunt	Lt
Hanmer, Henry	Capt
Hill, Clement Delves	Capt
Hill, Sir Robert Chambré	Lt Colonel

1st (King's) Dragoon Guards

Adams, John	Sgt
Battersby, George	Capt
Bernard, Hon. Henry B.	Cornet
Bradbury, Emanuel	Sgt
Bringhurst, John Dorset	Capt
Brooke, Francis	Lt
Dawson Hon. George L.	Capt

Fuller, William	Lt Colonel
Graham, Henry	Capt
Hibbert, John Nembhard	Lt
Kibble, William Thomas	Cpl

3rd (Prince of Wales's) Dragoon Guards

Betton, John	Capt
Calcraft, Sir Granby T.	Lt Colonel
Clark, Joseph	Sgt
Cust, Hon. Peregrine	Capt
Dudley, Samuel	Capt
Gray, John Walker	Lt
Hadden, James	Lt

4th (Royal Irish) Dragoon Guards

Fane, Sir Henry	Colonel
Lally, Edward	Capt

5th (Princess Charlotte of Wales's) Dragoon Guards

Barrington, Edward G.	Lt
Brunker, James	Paymaster
Byrom, Ashton Johnson	Lt
Gordon, Arthur Helsham	Major
Hammersley, Frederick	Lt

6th Regiment of Dragoon Guards

Cathcart, Hon. George	Lt
Le Marchant, Sir John G.	Lt Colonel

1st (Royal) Regiment of Dragoons

Clark, Alexander K.	Capt
Eckersley, Nathanial	Capt
Fletcher, Simon	Pte
Foster, Charles E.	Lt
Gornall, John	Pte
Heathcote, Joseph	Sgt
Hutton, George	Capt
Lamotte, James	Capt

2nd (Royal North British) Regiment of Dragoons

Alcorn, William	Pte
Barnard, Charles L.	Capt
Brown, James	Pte

Cheney, Edward H.	Capt	
Clarke, Isaac Blake	Major	
Crawford, William	R S M	
Dickson, John	Cpl	
Ewart, Charles	Sgt	
Fenton, Thomas Charles	Capt	
Forbes, Duncan	Pte	
Gillies, John	Sgt	
Graham, James R. T.	Lt	
Hamilton, James Inglis	Lt Colonel	
Hankin, Thomas P.	Major	
Johnston, Archibald	Sgt	
Kinchant, Francis C.	Cornet	

3rd (King's Own) Regiment of Dragoons
Bragge, William	Capt
Branfill, Champion E.	Capt
Hugonin, James	Major
Hunter, John	Capt
Hutchins, Thomas	Major
Johnstone, John	Capt

4th (Queen's Own) Regiment of Dragoons
Carleton, Hon. Dudley	Capt
Cubitt, Edward George	Lt
Dalbiac, James Charles	Lt Colonel
Gregory, Arthur Francis	Lt
Hugonin, James	Major
Leighton, Burgh	Major

6th (Inniskilling) Regiment of Dragoons
Bolton, John	Surgeon
Hadden, William F.	Capt
Heron, John	Pte

7th (Queens Own) Regiment of Light Dragoons
Brown, Stephen	Pte
Campbell, Sir John	Capt
Cave, James	Pte
Cotton, Edward	Pte
Dukinfield, Samuel G.	Capt
Elphinstone, James D. F.	Capt
Feltom, Thomas	Paymaster
Fraser, James John	Capt
Hodge, Edward	Major
Kerrison, Sir Edward	Lt Colonel

9th Regiment of Light Dragoons
Bernard, Hon. Francis	Lt
Gore, George	Major
Handley, Benjamin	Lt

10th (Prince of Wales's Own) Regiment of Light Dragoons
Arnold, Robert	Lt
Bacon, Anthony	Lt
Cartwright, William	Lt
Cozens, Benjamin H.	Pte
Floyd, Henry	Capt
Gordon, Charles John	Capt
Grey, John	Capt
Grisedale, Levi	Sgt
Gunning, George W.	Lt
Gurwood, John	Capt
Hill, Lord Arthur M. W.	Capt
Hodgson, Ellis	Lt
Howard, Hon. Frederick	Major
Jenks, George Samuel	Asst Surgeon
Leigh, George	Lt Colonel
Lowther, Hon. Henry C.	Major

11th Regiment of Light Dragoons
Bambrick, Robert	Pte
Bentinck, Lord William	Colonel
Bourchier, James C.	Capt
Browne, Barton Parker	Cornet
Butcher, George Kear	Sgt Major
Childers, Michael	Capt
Crampton, James	Pte
Cumming, Henry John	Lt Colonel
Des Voeux, Benfield	Lt
Grindrod, Timothy	Cornet and Adjt
Jenkins, John	Capt
Lutyens, Benjamin	Capt
Lutyens, Daniel	Paymaster
Lye, Benjamin Leigh	Lt

12th (Prince of Wales's) Regiment of Light Dragoons
Arnold, Edward John R.	Lt
Baird, William	Sgt
Barton, Alexander	Capt
Baxter, John	Pte
Bertie, Lindsay James	Lt
Bishop, Isaac	Pte
Burley, William	Pte
Chatterton, Sir James C.	Lt
Clare, Charles	Pte
Clarke, Thomas	Pte
Cochrane, Charles	Pte
Cox, Wilson	Sgt
Craufurd, Alexander C.	Capt
Daxter, William	Pte

Devitt, Guy	Pte
Donnegan, Hugh	Pte
Eadie, Edward	Pte
Early, John	Pte
Finley, Thomas	Sgt
Fisher, James	Pte
Foster, Francis	Pte
Glass, John	Pte
Goldsmid, Albert	Lt
Growcock, Edward	Pte
Halford, Thomas	Pte
Hickey, Jeremiah	Pte
Horston, William	Cpl
Hurst, George	Pte
Kelly, Robert	Pte
Kerr, William	Pte
King, John	Pte
Kirby, James	Sgt
Lang, Francis	Pte
Lockhart, John Elliott	Cornet

13th Regiment of Light Dragoons

Bowers, Charles Robert	Lt
Boyce, Shapland	Major
Doherty, George	Lt
Doherty, Joseph	Capt
Doherty, Patrick	Lt Colonel
Goulburn, Frederick	Capt
Gregorie, Charles	Capt
Holmes, Samuel	Capt
Irving, Jacob Clemilius	Lt
Logan, Thomas Galbraith	Surgeon

14th (Duchess of York's Own) Regiment of Light Dragoons

Armstrong, Henry B.	Lt
Babington, John	Capt
Brotherton, Thomas W.	Major
Capel, Daniel	Capt
Clavering, James	Lt
Foster, Augustus	Capt
Hawker, Peter	Capt
Hawker, Samuel	Lt Colonel
Hervey, Felton E. B.	Lt Colonel
Humphreys, Charles G.	Lt
Knipe, Robert	Capt
Lyon, William John	Lt

15th (King's) Regiment of Light Dragoons

Buckley, Henry	Lt
Buckley, James Ogden	Capt

Byam, William	Lt
Dalrymple, Leighton C.	Lt Colonel
Dawkins, George A. F.	Lt
Dundas, Thomas	Capt
Forester, Francis	Major
Grant, Sir Colquhoun	Lt Colonel
Griffith, Edwin	Major
Griffith, Joseph	Lt
Hickman, Charles	R S M
Hoare, Henry	Pte
Long, Robert Ballard	Lt Colonel

16th (Queen's) Regiment of Light Dragoons

Archer, Clement	Lt Colonel
Barra, Joseph	Lt and Adjutant
Beckwith, William	Cornet
Blood, Thomas	Sgt Major
Buchanan, John Phillips	Capt
Crichton, Nathaniel Day	Lt
Floyd, Thomas	Sgt
Hay, Alexander	Cornet
King, Charles	Capt
Luard, John	Lt
Lygon, Hon. Henry B.	Major

18th Regiment of Light Dragoons

Bolton, Robert Dawson	Capt
Duperier, Henry	Lt
Ellis, Richard Rogers	Capt
Harrison, John	Sgt Major
Hay, Charles Peter	Capt
Hughes, James	Major
Jones, Oliver Thomas	Lt Colonel
Keevers, William	Pte

20th Regiment of Light Dragoons

Blake, William Williams	Major
Cormick, Edward	Capt
Cotton, Sir Stapleton	Colonel
Cureton, Charles Robert	Cornet
Hanson, William	Capt

23rd Regiment of Light Dragoons

Allen, James	Capt
Anson, Sir George	Colonel
Blathwayt, George W.	Lt
Cox, Philip Zachariah	Capt
Dance, Charles Webb	Capt
Grove, Henry	Capt
Hall, William	Cpl
Hill, Henry	Lt

Howard, Thomas Phipps	Capt	Cole, John	Pte
Howe, John	Pte	Colquhoun, Robert	Quartermaster
Lautour, Peter Augustus	Major	Colquitt, John Scrope	Capt and Lt Col
		Commerell, William H.	Ensign

24th Regiment of Light Dragoons

Fitzclarence, George	Capt	Cooke, George	Capt and Lt Col
		Cranston, Thomas	Pte

Staff Corps of Cavalry

Dryden, James	Capt	Croft, Sir Thomas E.	Ensign
		Davies, Edward	Pte

Royal Waggon Train

Aird, Thomas	Lt Colonel	Davies, Francis John	Lt and Capt
Hamilton, Digby	Colonel	Davies, Thomas H. H.	Lt and Capt
Hibbert, John Gray	Asst Surgeon	Dawkins, Francis H.	Lt and Capt
Johnson, Samuel	Capt	De Courcy, Hon. John	Lt and Capt
Kerr, Robert	Lt	Dirom, John Pasley	Ensign
		Disbrowe, George	Lt and Capt
		Donaldson, Gordon	Capt and Lt Col

1st Regiment of Foot Guards

Adair, Robert	Lt and Capt	D'Oyly, Sir Francis	Capt and Lt Col
Allen, George Augustus	Ensign	D'Oyly, Henry	Capt and Lt Col
Allix, Charles	Lt and Capt	Dunbar, George	Pte
Anson, Sir William	Capt and Lt Col	Duncombe, Slingsby	Ensign
Armstrong, Andrew	Asst Surgeon	Dyke, William	Pte
Ashcroft, Timothy	Pte	Ellis, Charles Parker	Lt and Capt
Askew, Henry	2nd Major	Ellison, Robert	Lt and Capt
Barclay, Delancey	Capt and Lt Col	Evans, Joseph Blewitt	Lt and Capt
Barrington, Hon. Samuel	Ensign	Evans, Kingsmill	Lt and Capt
Bathurst, Hon. Thomas S.	Ensign	Eyre, Gervase Anthony	Ensign
Batty, Robert	Ensign	Fead, George	Capt and Lt Col
Boldero, Lonsdale	Lt and Capt	Fitzroy, Lord Charles	Lt and Capt
Boulcott, Joseph	Sgt	Fludyer, George	Ensign
Bradford, Sir Henry H.	Capt and Lt Col	Fox, William A. L.	Lt and Capt
Bridgman, Orlando	Lt and Capt	Grant, Turner	Lt and Capt
Brooke, Thomas	Lt and Capt	Griffiths, Richard	Pte
Brown, Thomas	Lt and Capt	Grose, Edward	Lt and Capt
Bruce, Robert	Ensign	Gunthorpe, James	Lt and Capt
Bulteel, John	Lt and Capt	Hardinge, Sir Henry	Capt and Lt Col
Burnaby, John Dick	Capt and Lt Col	Harrison, John	Asst Surgeon
Burrard, Sir Harry	Lt Colonel	Hay, James Lord	Ensign
Burrard, Paul Harry D.	Ensign	Hay, Lord James	Lt and Capt
Burrard, William	Ensign	Higginson, Alexander	Lt and Capt
Campbell, Sir Henry F.	Third Major	Higginson, George P.	Lt and Capt
Capel, Hon. Thomas E.	Capt and Lt Col	Hill, Sir Thomas Noel	Capt and Lt Col
Chambers Courtney	Ensign	Hutchinson, John Hely	Lt and Capt
Chambers, Newton	Lt and Capt	Jacob, George Thomson	Ensign
Cheney, Robert	Capt and Lt Col	Joddrell, Henry Esmund	Capt and Lt Col
Churchill, Chatham H.	Lt and Capt	Johnstone, William F.	Lt and Capt
Clifton, George	Capt and Lt Col	Jones, Leslie Grove	Capt and Lt Col
Clitherow, Robert	Capt and Lt Col	Knatchbull, Wyndham	Ensign
Clive, Edward	Lt and Capt	Lambert, Sir John	Capt and Lt Col
Cocks, Hon. Philip James	Capt and Lt Col	Lambert, Samuel	Capt and Lt Col
		Lascelles, Charles F. R.	Lt and Capt
		Lascelles, Hon. Henry	Ensign
		Lautour, James Oliver	Ensign

Lautour, Joseph Andrew	Lt and Capt
Le Marchant, Carey	Lt and Capt
Lindsay, James	Lt and Capt
Luttrell, Francis Fownes	Lt and Capt

Coldstream Regiment of Foot Guards

Abercromby, Hon. A.	Capt and Lt Col
Acland, Sir Wroth P.	Capt and Lt Col
Anstruther, Windham C.	Lt and Capt
Arbuthnot, Sir Robert	Capt and Lt Col
Ashburnham, Hon. John	Ensign
Beaufoy, Mark	Ensign
Beckett, Richard	Lt and Capt
Beckford, Francis Love	Ensign
Bentinck, Charles A. F.	Lt and Capt
Blackman, John Lucie	Lt and Capt
Boswell, John Irvine	Lt and Capt
Bouverie, Sir Henry F.	Capt and Lt Col
Bowen, Robert	Ensign
Bowles, George	Lt and Capt
Bryan, George	Lt and Capt
Buckeridge, John C.	Ensign
Buckley, George R.	Ensign
Burgess, Wentworth N.	Ensign
Burroughs, William	Lt and Capt
Campbell, Sir Colin	Capt and Lt Col
Chaplin, Thomas	Lt and Capt
Collier, William George	Capt and Lt Col
Cowell, John Stepney	Lt and Capt
Crofton, Hon. William G.	Lt and Capt
Cuyler, Augustus	Ensign
Dalling, Edward	Lt and Capt
Dawkins, Henry	Capt and Lt Col
Forbes, Hon. James	Ensign
Forbes, Walter	Ensign
Fraser, Charles M.	Lt and Capt
Freeman, William	Pte
Fremantle, John	Lt and Capt
Fuller, Sir Joseph	Capt and Lt Col
Girardot, Charles A.	Lt and Capt
Gomm, Sir William	Capt and Lt Col
Gooch, Henry Edward	Ensign
Gordon, Alexander	Ensign
Grimshaw, John	Pte
Harvey, Edward	Lt and Capt
Hotham, Beaumont Lord	Lt and Capt
Howard, Sir Kenneth A.	2nd Major
Hulse, Richard	Capt and Lt Col
Hunter, William	Asst Surgeon
Jenkinson, F. Edward	Lt and Capt
Long, Edward Noel	Ensign

3rd Regiment of Foot Guards

Aitchison, Sir John	Capt and Lt Col
Anson, Hon. George	Ensign
Anstruther, Robert	Capt and Lt Col
Ashton, John	Lt and Capt
Barnett, Charles John	Lt and Capt
Blane, Hugh Seymour	Ensign
Bowater, Edward	Capt and Lt Col
Bradford, Keating James	Lt and Capt
Buchanan, James	Lt and Capt
Byng, Sir John	Capt and Lt Col
Campion, William	Pte
Canning, Charles Fox	Capt and Lt Col
Clay, Matthew	Pte
Clitherow, John	Capt and Lt Col
Clitherow, William H.	Lt and Capt
Cochrane, Andrew C.	Ensign
Cochrane, James J.	Capt and Lt Col
Cookson, George Parker	Ensign
Copeland, George	Cpl
Craufurd, Thomas Gage	Lt and Capt
Cumberland, Richard F.	Lt and Capt
Dalrymple, Robert	Lt and Capt
Dashwood, Charles	Capt and Lt Col
Dilkes, William Thomas	Capt and Lt Col
Drummond, Peter	Pte
Elrington, John Hamilton	Lt and Capt
Evelyn, George	Lt and Capt
Forbes, Hon. Hastings	Lt and Capt
Gordon, Hon. Sir A.	Capt and Lt Col
Gordon, Thomas William	Capt and Lt Col
Guise, John Wright	First Major
Hamilton, John Potter	Capt and Lt Col
Hamilton, William F.	Ensign
Hattrell, Daniel	Pte
Hawkins, Henry	Lt and Capt
Hepburn, Francis Ker	2nd Major
Hesketh, Robert H. B.	Lt and Capt
Holbourne, Francis R. T.	Lt and Capt
Hood, Hon. Francis W.	Capt and Lt Col
Hornby, Charles	Lt and Capt
Irby, Hon. Edward M.	Ensign
James, William	Ensign
Johnston, Henry	Pte
Kay, Samuel	Sgt
Kirkland, Joseph	Pte
Knollys, William Thomas	Ensign
Lake, Charles	Ensign

1st (Royal Scots) Regiment of Foot

Allen, John	Ensign

Anderson, William	Ensign
Armstrong, John	Lt
Barnes, James Stevenson	Lt Col
Bell, Thomas	Lt
Black, John Lewis	Lt
Blacklin, Richard	Volunteer
Buckley, William	Capt
Clayhills, James Menzies	Capt
Deuchar, David	Capt
Dixon, Robert	Pte
Falck, Neil	Lt
Fraser, Thomas	Lt Colonel
Gordon, John	Major
Gordon, Thomas	Lt
Gordon, William	Capt
Hardman, Job	Pte
Hay, Andrew	Lt Colonel
Hay, George	Capt
Hemphill, William	Lt
Hildreth, William	Pte
Hughes, Richard	Pte
Ingram, John Nelson	Lt
Kennedy, James Grant	Ensign
Lorimer, Charles Hunt	Lt
Lynch, James Stewart	Major

2nd (Queen's Royal) Regiment of Foot

Adams, John	Lt
Berford, Richard	Lt
Borlase, Charles	Capt
Clutterbuck, William	Lt
Frankland, Frederick W.	Lt
Girdlestone, Charles	Lt
Gordon, John (1)	Capt
Gordon, John (2)	Capt
Grant, Charles	Lt
Gray, William	Lt
Johnston, Archibald	Sgt Major
Kingsbury, John	Major

3rd (East Kent) Regiment of Foot

Blake, Robert	Lt
Blunt, Richard	Lt Colonel
Cameron, Charles	Captain
Fergusson, James	Lt Colonel
Fleming, Pierre Edward	Capt
Gardiner, John	Lt and Adjt
Haselfoot, William Henry	Capt
Houghton, Richard Rollo	Capt
Kingsbury, Robert	Lt
Latham, Matthew	Capt

Light, William	Capt

4th (King's Own) Regiment of Foot

Anwyl, Robert	Capt
Bell, John	Capt
Bellingham, Henry T.	Capt
Bevan, Charles	Lt Colonel
Bond, Robert	Pte
Brooke, Francis	Lt Colonel
Browne, John	Capt
Burton, Francis	Surgeon
Edgell, Charles James	Capt
Erskine, Robert	Capt
Faunce, Alured D.	Major
Fletcher, John Wynne	Capt
Fraser, John	Lt
Green, William	Pte
Holland, Thomas Edward	Ensign
Jameson, James	Capt
Jenkins, John	Quartermaster
Lonsdale, William	Lt

5th (Northumberland) Regiment of Foot

Baxter, Robert	Pte
Baye, Benjamin	Pte
Bird, Henry	Major
Campbell, Archibald	Lt
Canch, Thomas	Lt
Emes, Thomas	Major
Girling, Thomas Andrews	Capt
Grey, John	Major
Harding, William	Lt
Higgins, Thomas	Lt
Hopkins, Henry Lewis	Lt
Johnson, David England	Capt

6th (1st Warwickshire) Regiment of Foot

Bowes, Barnard Foord	Lt Colonel
Campbell, Archibald	Lt Colonel
Campbell, Sir Guy	Major
Everest, Henry Bennett	Lt
Gardiner, John	Major
Gomm, Henry	Major
Grahame, Duncan	Capt

7th (Royal Fusiliers) Regiment of Foot

Auchmuty, Samuel B.	Major
Beatty, John Walwyn	Major
Beaufoy, John Henry	Lt
Bell, Edward Wells	Lt
Blakeney, Sir Edward	Lt Colonel

Bussey, John	Pte
Chapman, Thomas	Pte
Crowder, John	Major
Devey, Henry Fryer	Capt
Fisher, Henry	Asst Surgeon
Hackett, Richard	Capt
Hay, James	Lt
Healey, John	Lt
Johnstone, James	Capt
Knowles, Robert	Lt
Ledsam, John	Sgt
Loggan, George	Capt

8th (King's) Regiment of Foot
Hoghton, Daniel	Lt Colonel

9th (East Norfolk) Regiment of Foot
Bolton, George	Ensign
Brookes, Robert	Lt
Brownrigg, Sir Robert	Colonel
Cameron, Hector	Capt
Cameron, Sir John	Lt Colonel
Crawfurd, Henry	Major
Davis, George Lennox	Lt
Dumaresq, Henry	Capt
Fraser, Erskine A.	Lt
Fraser, George	Paymaster
Garlick, Moses Bendle	Pte
Kenny, Courtenay Crowe	Capt
Le Mesurier, Peter	Lt

10th (North Lincolnshire) Regiment of Foot
Carey, Octavius	Major
Dent, Thomas	Capt
Grieve, Patrick	Capt
Henderson, David	Capt
Kersteman, William B.	Capt

11th (North Devonshire) Regiment of Foot
Dunkley, William	Lt
Grant, Colquhoun	Major
Hay, Andrew L.	Capt
Jones, Richard H.	Capt

12th (East Suffolk) Regiment of Foot
Cooke, Henry Frederick	Lt Colonel

14th (Buckinghamshire) Regiment of Foot
Akenside, William	Lt
Armstrong, Henry B.	Lt
Baldwin, George	Lt

Boldero, Henry	Lt
Burrows, Charles M.	Volunteer
Davis, William	Pte
Gudgin, George	Pte
Hewett, William	Capt
Hill, Robert	Pte
Keown, William	Ensign
Lambourne, James	Pte

15th (Yorkshire East Riding) Regiment of Foot
Disney, Sir Moore	Colonel

20th (East Devonshire) Regiment of Foot
Arnott, Archibald	Surgeon
Battersby, James	Lt
Bent, James	Major
Burrows, John	Sgt
Cheek, Edward	Lt
Crockat, William	Capt
Falls, Thomas	Capt
Hollinsworth, Henry	Sgt Major
Houstoun, Sir William	Colonel
Lutyens, Engelbert	Lt

21st (Royal North British Fusiliers) Regiment of Foot
Adam, Frederick William	Lt Colonel
Gracie, James	1st Lt
Gubbins, Richard	Major

23rd (Royal Welch Fusiliers) Regt of Foot
Baddeley, Benjamin	Pte
Bentinck, Richard	Drummer
Blanckley, Henry S.	Capt
Browne, Thomas Henry	Capt
Campbell, William	Capt
Clyde, John	1st Lt
Davies, Thomas	Colour Sgt
Day, Richard	Pte
Ellis, Sir Henry Walton	Lt Colonel
Enoch, John	1st Lt
Fensham, George	1st Lt
Foulkes, Thomas	Pte
Griffiths, Thomas	Drum Major
Jolliffe, Charles	Capt
Lewis, Richard	Pte
Lillie, Thomas	2nd Lt

24th (Warwickshire) Regiment of Foot
Baird, Sir David	Colonel
Collis, Charles	Capt

Croall, James	Sgt		Light, John	Lt
Fleming, Hugh	Lt		Llewellyn, Richard	Capt
Jessiman, Alexander	Ensign			
Kelly, William	Lt Colonel			

29th (Worcestershire) Regiment of Foot

Lilley, Samuel	Sgt

Davidson, James	Pte
Davy, Charles William	Capt

25th (King's Own Borderer's) Regiment of Foot

Egerton, Thomas	Major

Dyott, William	Lt Colonel
Fitzgerald, Edward T.	Capt

Elliot, William Rowley	Capt
Gell, Thomas	Capt
Gillespie, William	Quartermaster

26th (Cameronian) Regiment of Foot

Gregory, Adam	Capt

Campbell, Adam Gordon	Capt
Connell, John	Quartermaster
Hogge, Fountain	Lt Colonel

Hodge, Peter	Major
Kneebone, Thomas	Volunteer
Lake, Hon. George A. F.	Lt Colonel

27th (Inniskilling) Regiment of Foot

30th (Cambridgeshire) Regiment of Foot

Adair, James	Capt		Bailey, Morris William	Major
Betty, Christopher S.	Ensign		Beere, Henry	Lt
Bignall, Francis	Capt		Bullen, James	Ensign
Blakiston, John	Capt		Chambers, Thomas W.	Major
Crewe, John Frederick	Capt		Daniel, Robert	Lt
Crowe, George William	Paymaster		Elkington, James Goodall	Surgeon
Davidson, James	Lt and Adjt		Evans, John	Asst Surgeon
Ditmas, John	Ensign		Grey, George	Major
Drewe, Edward Ward	Lt		Hamilton, Alexander	Lt Colonel
Drysdale, Alexander	Capt		James, John	Ensign
Erskine, William H. K.	Major			
Geddes, John	Capt			

31st (Huntingdonshire) Regiment of Foot

Gough, Hugh	Lt		Beggs, John	Pte
Harcourt, John	Asst Surgeon		Blomer, Charles	Capt
Hare, John	Capt		Bolton, Samuel	Lt
Johnstone, Thomas	Major		Dowdall, Patrick	Major
Lynch, Martin Crean	Capt		Eager, Francis Russell	Capt
			Fearon, Peter	Capt

28th (North Gloucestershire) Regiment of Foot

Hardcastle, William A.	Ensign

Alexander, Henry	Lt		Hardy, James	Ensign
Bennett, Joseph	Lt		Kennerdell, James	Sgt Major
Bradby, Joseph	Capt		Knox, Edward	Capt
Briggs, John Falconer	Major		Leith, Sir Alexander	Lt Colonel
Cadell, Charles	Capt		L'Estrange, Guy G. C.	Lt Colonel
Cann, John	Pte			
Carroll, John	Capt			

32nd (Cornwall) Regiment of Foot

Clark, Joseph Taylor	Lt		Barlow, James	Surgeon
Crummer, John Henry	Lt		Birtwhistle, John	Ensign
Delmar, John	Ensign		Bloomfield, David	Sgt
Facey, Peter	Sgt		Boase, John	Lt
Forster, Henry	Sgt		Butler, John O'Bryan	Ensign
Gale, Arthur	Capt		Butler, Theobald	Lt
Gordon, Stephen	Lt		Butterworth, Henry	Lt
Ingram, George	Lt		Clear, Philip	Pte
Irwin, William	Lt		Coote, Robert	Major

Crowe, John	Capt
Dallas, Charles Robert K.	Ensign
Davies, David	Lt and Adjt
Graves, Anthony	Capt
Hall, Charles	Pte
Hawes, Thomas	Pte
Hinde, Samuel Venables	Lt Colonel
Horne, James	Pte
Johnson, William A.	Lt Colonel
Lawder, Rhynd	Asst Surgeon

33rd (1st Yorkshire West Riding) Regiment of Foot

Bain, William	Ensign
Boyce, John	Lt
Briggs, William	Pte
Buck, Henry Rishton	Lt
Cameron, John	Lt
Elphinstone, William K.	Lt Colonel
Fry, William Dowell	Asst Surgeon
Gibson, John	Sgt
Gore, Arthur	Lt Colonel
Gore, Arthur	Lt
Haigh, John	Capt
Haigh, Thomas B.	Lt
Hart, James	Lt
Knight, Charles	Lt Colonel

34th (Cumberland) Regiment of Foot

Baker, James H.	Capt
Bell, George	Lt
Chadwick, William	Capt
Egerton, Richard	Capt
Fenwick, William	Lt Colonel

35th (Sussex) Regiment of Foot

Austin, Thomas	Lt
Berkeley, Sir George H. F.	Lt Colonel
Cameron, Robert	Capt
Doyle, Charles S.	Surgeon
Hedding, William L.	Ensign

36th (Herefordshire) Regiment of Foot

Bone, Peter Joseph	Lt
Burne, Robert	Colonel
Cairnes, George	Lt
Colcroft, John	Lt
Cromie, James	Ensign
Crosse, Robert Noble	Capt
Forbes, Duncan	Capt
Harris, Thomas Noel	Capt
Jarvis, George R. Payne	Major

37th (North Hampshire) Regiment of Foot

Dow, Edward	Surgeon

38th (1st Staffordshire) Regiment of Foot

Crookshank, Arthur C.	Major
Cross, Richard	Lt
Ekins, Clement	Asst Surgeon
Greville, Hon. Sir Charles	Lt Colonel
Hall, Charles	Ensign
Ince, William	Capt

39th (Dorsetshire) Regiment of Foot

Barker, Collet	Lt
Brine, James	Capt
Caldecot, Henry	Lt
Cosgrove, John	Pte
Cuppage, Stephen	Capt
D'Arcy, George Pitt	Capt
Dunk, Jesse	Pte
Gee, Francis	Pte
Grueber, Daniel	Lt
Jones, Joseph A.	Capt
Lindsay, Patrick	Major

40th (2nd Somersetshire) Regiment of Foot

Amos, John Greene	Capt
Ayling, John	Lt
Bale, John	Pte
Balfour, William	Major
Barry, William	Asst Surgeon
Chetham, Isaac	Lt
Cooke, William	Pte
Dampier, Lud Westley	Capt
Dobbyn, Alexander	Ensign
Doyle, James	Drummer
Fisher, William	Capt
Heyland, Arthur Rowley	Major
Hill, John	Sgt
Holt, Richard	Pte
Inkersole, James	Pte
Jebb, Richard	Capt
Johnston, James	Capt
Jones, William	Surgeon
Kelly, William Waldron	Lt
Lawrence, William	Sgt

41st Regiment of Foot

Bainbrigge, John Hankey	Capt

42nd (Royal Highland) Regiment of Foot

Anderson, Alexander	Capt

Blantyre, Lord Robert	Lt Colonel
Campbell, Archibald A.	Major
Connolly, James	Sgt
Cowell, William	Major
Dick, Robert Henry	Major
Farquharson, Donald	Lt
Farquharson, John	Lt Colonel
Fraser, William	Ensign
Gordon, William	Lt
Grant, Maxwell	Major
Henderson, John	Capt
Home, John	Paymaster
Huntly, George Marquess of	Colonel
Innes, Alexander	Lt
Innes, John White	Lt and Adjt
Irving, James	Pte
Latta, John	Ensign

43rd (Monmouthshire) Light Infantry Regt of Foot

Angrove, John George	Lt
Baillie, Mackay Hugh	Lt
Booth, Henry	Capt
Brock, Saumarez	Capt
Brumwell, John	Lt
Buchanan, John	Lt
Capel, Thomas	Capt
Casey, Bartholomew	Lt
Champ, Thomas	Capt
Considine, James	Lt
Cooke, John Henry	Lt
Cradock, Sir John F.	Colonel
Craig, Phillip	Sgt
D'Arcey, Edward	Lt
Duffy, John	Major
Edwards, Benjamin H.	Lt
Ferriar, Thomas I.	Lt
Follett, George	Lt
Freer, Edward G.	Lt
Freer, William G.	Capt
Freestone, Anthony	Pte
Gardner, David	Capt
Gifford, George St John	Capt
Gillkrest, James	Surgeon
Hair, Archibald	Asst Surgeon
Havelock, William	Lt
Haverfield, William	Major
Hill, John Montgomery	Lt
Hood, George	Lt
Hopkins, John Paul	Capt
Houlton, Sir George	Lt
John, Thomas	Sgt

44th (East Essex) Regiment of Foot

Brooke, Sir Arthur	Lt Colonel
Burke, James	Lt
Campbell, John	Lt
Carleton, Hon. George	Lt Colonel
Elwin, Fountain	Major
Fane, Mildmay	Capt
Fenton, John James	Lt
Guthrie, John Cleland	Capt
Hamerton, John Millet	Lt Colonel
Jessop, John	Major
Jones, Griffith	Surgeon

45th (Nottinghamshire) Regiment of Foot

Cole, John	Capt
Douglas, Joseph	Lt
Forbes, Thomas	Lt Colonel
Greenwell, Leonard	Lt Colonel
Guard, William	Lt Colonel
Hardwick, William	Capt
Hilton, Thomas	Capt
Huson, Charles	Capt
Kirk, George	Pte
Lecky, David	Major
Little, George	Lt

46th (South Devonshire) Regiment of Foot

Cuyler, Henry	Lt Colonel

47th (Lancashire) Regiment of Foot

Carmichael, Thomas	Ensign
Cochrane, Christopher I.	Lt
Cochrane, Robert	Lt
De La Cherois, Nicholas	Ensign
Hall, Richard	Lt
Hodges, William Arthur	Capt

48th (Northamptonshire) Regiment of Foot

Allman, Francis	Capt
Blomfield, Thomas V.	Lt
Campbell, John	Lt
Clarke, Joseph	Lt
Close, Edward Charles	Lt
Donovan, Henry D.	Ensign
Duckworth, George H.	Lt Colonel
Goodman, Stephen A.	Major
Herring, Robert	Capt
Lecky, David	Major
Leroux, George Wilson	Lt
Lofft, Henry Capel	Lt

50th (West Kent) Regiment of Foot

Campbell, Thomas D.	Major
Custance, Holman	Capt
Douglas, Sholto	Lt
Gardiner, James Ballard	Capt
Gordon, William A.	Capt
Hill, Charles	Lt Colonel
Keddle, Robert	Lt

51st (2nd Yorkshire West Riding) Light Infantry

Ball, James	Sgt
Beecham, Joseph	Sgt
Blanco, Thomas	Pte
Bloomfield, James H.	Capt
Braund, John	Sgt
Butcher, Thomas	Sgt
Curson, Andrew	Sgt
Darling, Ralph	Lt Colonel
Dodd, Robert	Lt
Douglas, Charles A. W.	Capt
Downs, James	Sgt
Doyle, Thomas	Sgt
Drew, J. H.	Lt
Dyas, Joseph	Lt
Elliott, William H.	Lt
Filton, John	Pte
Fitton, John	Sgt
Forrester, Richard	Sgt
Frederick, Edward Henry	Capt
Gibbs, John	Paymaster
Hamilton, Robert	Asst Surgeon
Hanger, John	Sgt
Hanks, William	Sgt
Honey, Henry	Lt
Jennings, Joshua	Lt and Adjt
Lane, Daniel	Sgt
Lintott, John	Lt
Lock, Henry	Ensign

52nd (Oxfordshire) Light Infantry Regt of Foot

Austin, William	Lt
Booth, Charles	Lt
Burnett, John	Lt
Butler, Pierce	Paymaster
Campbell, Patrick	Capt
Chalmers, William	Capt
Clerke, William Henry	Lt
Colborne, Sir John	Lt Colonel
Davies, John	Pte
Diggle, Charles	Capt
Dobbs, John	Lt

Douglas, Archibald M.	Capt
Douglas, John G.	Capt
Fell, William	Pte
Fraser, Alexander J.	Ensign
Freeman, Robert	Cpl
Freeman, Thomas	Cpl
Gawler, George	Lt
Gibbs, Edward	Lt Colonel
Gould, Thomas	Pte
Hedderwick, David	Cpl
Holmes, Adam	Pte
Hutchinson, Scroop	Surgeon
Jack, John	Pte
Jones, William	Major
Kelk, Edward	Pte
Kinloch, Charles	Capt
Langton, Edward Gore	Capt
Leeke, William	Ensign
Love, James Frederick	Capt

53rd (Shropshire) Regiment of Foot

Fehrszen, Oliver G.	Major
Giles, John	Capt
Haly, William A.	Capt
Harrison, Charles	Capt
Impett, Thomas R. S.	Lt

54th (West Norfolk) Regiment of Foot

Bromhead, Edmund de G.	Lt
Clark, John	Ensign
Claus, William	Lt
Granger, Early	Pte
Kelly, Allan	Major

55th (Westmoreland) Regiment of Foot

Clinton, Sir William H.	Colonel
Dalgairnes, William	Lt
Goodall, George	Ensign

56th (West Essex) Regiment of Foot

Gibbons, Frederick	Capt

57th (West Middlesex) Regiment of Foot

Ackland, Dudley	Major
Arbuthnot, Sir Thomas	Lt Colonel
Aubin, Phillip	Lt
Bouchier, Thomas	Surgeon
Dalrymple, Sir Hew W.	Colonel
Inglis, Sir William	Lt Colonel
Jervois, William	Capt
Johnstone, William	Ensign

Knox, George — Lt
Logan, Patrick — Lt

58th (Rutlandshire) Regiment of Foot
Austin, John — Capt
Broke, Horatio George — Capt
Collins, George — Lt
Dudgeon, Peter — Capt
Ferguson, Adam — Capt
Fugion, Edward — Lt
Gomersall, John — Capt

59th (2nd Nottinghamshire) Regiment of Foot
Baird, William — Quartermaster
Carmichael, Lewis — Lt
Chadwick, Nicholas — Lt
Dent, Abraham — Lt and Adjt
Douglas, Charles — Major
Fane, Charles — Lt Colonel
Forrest, George William — Capt
Fothergill, John — Capt
Fuller, Francis — Capt
Gibbs, Sir Samuel — Lt Colonel
Hagan, James — Surgeon
Hill, Rowland F. — Ensign
Hovenden, Nicholas — Lt
Hoysted, Frederick W. — Major
Lambe, Peter K. — Asst Surgeon

60th (Royal American) Regiment of Foot
Anderson, Paul — Lt Colonel
Archdall, Richard — Lt
Bathurst, James — Major
Brunton, Richard — Capt
Campbell, Colin — Capt
Clinton, Sir Henry — Colonel
Craufurd, Robert — Lt Colonel
Cust, Hon. Edward — Capt
Dalrymple, Adolphus J. — Lt Colonel
Dalzell, Robert A. — Capt
De Bourgh, Anthony P. — Lt
De Wendt, Edward M. — Capt
Eccles, Thomas — Lt
Hamilton, John — Lt
Hope, John — Lt Colonel
Hunt, John Philip — Lt Colonel
Keane, Sir John — Lt Colonel
Kelly, Robert — Capt
Kempt, Sir James — Colonel

61st (South Gloucestershire) Regiment of Foot
Anderson, Andrew — Surgeon
Annesley, Marcus — Capt
Arden, Henry — Lt
Beere, Hercules — Ensign
Bubb, Anthony — Lt
Coghlan, Charles — Lt Colonel
Coghlan, John Robert — Lt Colonel
Cox, William — Major
Ellison, John M. — Lt
Favell, William A. — Ensign
Furnace, William H — Capt
Gammell, James — Lt
Gloster, Thomas — Lt
Horton, Pickwick B. P. — Lt
Kellett, Christopher — Lt

62nd (Wiltshire) Regiment of Foot
Blackwell, Nathaniel S. F. — Lt Colonel
Darley, Edward — Major
Drawater, Augustus C. — Capt
Fawcett, John J. — Asst Surgeon
Gwynne, Henry L. — Capt
Hartley, William — Capt
Law, William Henry — Ensign

63rd (West Suffolk) Regiment of Foot
Knight, Edward — Capt

66th (Berkshire) Regiment of Foot
Baird, James — Capt
Clarke, John — Lt
Coulter, William — Ensign
Dobbin, Robert Brown — Lt
Findlay, William — Col Sgt
Goldie, George Leigh — Capt
Humbley, Philip — Lt
Kingsmill, William — Lt
Lewis, Charles — Sgt

67th (South Hampshire) Regiment of Foot
Blair, William — Ensign

68th (Durham) Regiment of Foot
Blood, John Aylward — Ensign
Crespigny, George C. — Major
Currie, Lachlan — Sgt
Hawkins, John P. — Major
Irwine, Henry Bury — Capt
Johnston, William — Lt Colonel
Kennedy, Simson — Capt

Leith, James William   Capt

69th (South Lincolnshire) Regiment of Foot
Ainslie, George S. H.   Ensign
Blackwood, Robert T.   Capt
Curzon, Hon. William   Capt
Deighton, William   Pte
Fouracres, Thomas   Pte
Keith, Henry Duncan   Ensign

70th (Glasgow Lowland) Regiment of Foot
Cole, Sir Galbraith Lowry   Colonel
De Courcy, Hon. Gerard   Major

71st (Highland Light Infantry) Regiment of Foot
Anderson, James   Lt
Cadogan, Hon. Henry   Lt Colonel
Campbell, Sir Archibald   Lt Colonel
Campbell, Norman   Lt
Campbell, William M.   Lt
Cowsell, John   Lt
Creighton, Thomas   Sgt
Drummond, John   Pte
Grant, Lewis   Capt
Hall, Henry Gallopine   Capt
Henderson, Charles   Lt
Impett, John   Ensign
Jones, Arthur R.   Major
Lamont, Daniel   Pte
Laverton, James   Pte
Lind, Robert   Lt
Long, William   Lt

72nd (Highland) Regiment of Foot
Hill, Lord Rowland   Colonel

73rd (Highland) Regiment of Foot
Cochrane, William G.   Capt
Dowling, Joseph   Lt
Harris, William George   Lt Colonel
Hay, Patrick   Ensign & Adjt
Houghton, Henry   Pte
Kelly, Dawson   Major

74th (Highland) Regiment of Foot
Andrews, Thomas   Capt
Ansell, Francis H.   Capt
Atkinson, Abraham   Lt
Cargill, William   Capt
Collins, Bassett   Capt
Ewing, Daniel   Lt

Grant, Alexander   Lt
Hamilton, Henry Stewart   Lt
Hillier, George   Capt
Ironside, George Edward   Lt
Johnson, Hugh   Lt
King, Charles   Capt

76th Regiment of Foot
Bullivant, John   Lt
Carr, James   Major
Chowne, Christopher T.   Colonel
Cleary, Richard Stanton   Lt
Hiscott, Richard   Pte

77th (East Middlesex) Regiment of Foot
Algeo, James   Lt
Baird, Patrick   Capt
Bradshawe, George Paris   Lt
Bromhead, John   Lt Colonel
Campbell, Archibald   Lt
Jones, Edward   Lt

78th (Highland) Regiment of Foot
Falconer, Chesborough G.   Capt
Fraser, Alexander M.   Colonel
Holmes, Stephen   Capt
Lindsay, Martin   Lt Colonel

79th (Cameron Highlanders) Regiment of Foot
Andrew, Donald   Pte
Brown, Thomas   Lt
Bruce, William   Capt
Burch, Thomas   Cpl
Cameron, Sir Alan   Colonel
Cameron, Donald   Lt
Cameron, Duncan   Lt
Cameron, Ewen (1)   Lt
Cameron, Ewen (2)   Lt
Cameron, John (1)   Capt
Cameron, John (2)   Capt
Cameron, Kenneth   Lieut and Adjt
Cameron, Phillips   Lt Colonel
Cameron, William   Capt
Campbell, Donald   Major
Campbell, James   Capt
Campbell, Neil   Capt
Cocks, Hon. Edward C.   Major
Cruikshank, Alexander   Pte
Davidson, Benjamin   Pte
Davidson, Sinclair   Capt
Forbes, Alexander   Lt

Fraser, James	Lt
Fulton, Robert	Lt Colonel
Harvey, William Maundy	Lt Colonel
Innes, Peter	Capt
Kennedy, Andrew	Pte
Kennedy, Ewen	Lt
Kynock, John	Lt and Adjt
Lawrie, Andrew	Major

81st Regiment of Foot

Buttery, William	Pte
Downing, Adam G.	Capt
Fair, David	Lt
James, Francis	Capt

82nd (Prince of Wales's Volunteers) Regt of Foot

Bradford, Sir Thomas	Lt Colonel
Davenport, Edmund	Lt
Day, Thomas	Sgt
De Renzy, George W.	Capt
Elliott, Robert T.	Ensign
Harding, Edwin	Lt
Harman, George	Lt
King, Henry	Lt Colonel
Langley, Frederick	Capt

83rd Regiment of Foot

Abell, Charles	Lt
Collins, Richard	Lt Colonel
Cumming, William G.	Capt
Elliot, Gilbert	Capt
Emslie, John	Lt
Irwin, Frederick Chidley	Lt
Jones, Arthur	Ensign
Lynch, David	Pte

84th (York and Lancaster) Regiment of Foot

Daubeney, Henry	Lt Colonel
Jenkin, James	Capt
Johnson, William Yates	Capt
Lloyd, Richard	Lt Colonel
Locke, John	Major

85th (Buckinghamshire) Regiment of Foot

Boyes, Robert Nairne	Ensign
Brown, George	Major
Charleton, Andrew R.	Lt
De Bathe, William P.	Capt
Fairfax, Henry	Capt
French, Henry John	Lt
Gascoigne, Ernest F.	Lt

Gleig, George Robert	Lt
Gore, Hon. Sir Charles S.	Capt
Harris, Hon. Charles	Capt
Johnson, Arthur	Lt
Knox, Hon. John J.	Capt

86th (Royal County Down) Regiment of Foot

Impey, Benjamin	Capt

87th (Prince of Wales's Own Irish) Regt of Foot

Bright, Henry	Capt
Butler, Theodore	Ensign
Carr, Stephen	Quartermaster
Cavenagh, George W.	Capt
Doyle, Sir John Milley	Capt
Fitzgerald, Joseph	Lt
Gough, Hugh	Lt Colonel
Haddock, Robert	Lt
Higginson, Philip T.	Lt
Hilliard, Morgan	Ensign
Kennelly, James	Lt

88th (Connaught Rangers) Regiment of Foot

Adair, Walter W.	Capt
Beresford, John T.	Lt
Beresford, Sir William C.	Colonel
Campbell, Duncan	Paymaster
Cumin, William	Surgeon
Faris, James Fleming	Lt
Gardiner, David	Lt
Gillan, Martin	Pte
Hackett, John	Ensign
Johnston, George	Surgeon
Kingsmill, Parr	Lt
Kingsmill, William	Lt

89th Regiment of Foot

Grant, John	Major
Gwyn, William	Lt Colonel
Kenny, Edward	Ensign

90th (Perthshire Volunteers) Regiment of Foot

Currie, Edward	Lt Colonel
Graham, Sir Thomas	Colonel
Livingstone, Francis	Capt

91st Regiment of Foot

Blair, Thomas H.	Capt
Bowman, David	Capt
Briggs, James	Lt
Bunbury, Thomas	Lt

Callender, Alexander J.	Capt	Budgen, John Robert	1st Lt
Campbell, Dugald	Capt	Burbidge, Frederick	Pte
Craufurd, George D.	Lt	Cadoux, Daniel	Capt
Douglas, Robert	Surgeon	Cairns, James	Sgt
Douglas, Sir William	Lt Colonel	Cameron, Alexander	Major
Gibson, James	Pte	Cameron, Dugald	1st Lt
Gregorson, Donald	Major	Campbell, Alexander	2nd Lt
Gun, William	Capt	Chapman, Thomas	Pte
		Cochrane, Robert	1st Lt

92nd Regiment of Foot

Bramwell, John	Ensign	Cochrane, Thomas	1st Lt
Cameron, Ewen	Lt	Costello, Edward	Pte
Cameron, John	Lt Colonel	Cox, John	1st Lt
Campbell, Dugald	Capt	Coxen, Edward	1st Lt
Chisholm, Harold	Pte	Dixon, Francis	1st Lt
Couper, George	Capt	Dornford, Joseph	Volunteer
Cruikshank, James	Pte	Doyle, John	1st Lt
Cruikshank, William	Pte	Drake, Thomas	Capt
Fyfe, William	Capt	Drummond, George D.	1st Lt
Gordon, James	Paymaster	Duncan, John	Capt
Hope, James	Lt	Eeles, Charles	Capt
Hope, Sir John	Colonel	Eeles, William	Capt
Little, William	Capt	Fairfoot, Robert	Sgt
		Felix, Orlando	1st Lt

93rd Regiment of Foot

Fraser, William	Lt	Fowler, Richard	2nd Lt
		Fry, John	1st Lt

94th Regiment of Foot

Campbell, Charles	Major	Fullerton, James	Capt
Campbell, Frederick	Capt	Gammell, William	1st Lt
Cannon, William	Lt	Gardiner, John	1st Lt
Colville, Hon. Sir Charles	Colonel	Gibbons, George	Capt
Hutchinson, John	Capt	Gilmour, Dugald Little	Lt Colonel
Innes, Gordon C.	Lt	Gossett, John Noah	1st Lt
Innes, John	Major	Gray, Charles George	Capt
Innes, William	Lt	Gray, Loftus	Capt
Jackson, John Napper	Capt	Green, William	Pte
Laing, Thomas	Major	Hall, William	Sgt
Lang, John Sibbald	Ensign	Hill, John	2nd Lt
Lloyd, Thomas	Major	Himbury, John	Pte
		Hinde, William	Sgt
		Hope, John Charles	1st Lt

95th Regiment of Foot

Allix, William	1st Lt	Hopwood, John	1st Lt
Backhouse, John William	1st Lt	Humbley, William	1st Lt
Baller, George	Sgt	Ingham, Christopher	Pte
Balvaird, William	Major	Kellett, Robert Napier	Volunteer
Barker, Robert	2nd Lt	Kincaid, John	1st Lt and Adjt
Barnard, Sir Andrew F.	Lt Colonel	Leach, Jonathan	Capt
Beckwith, Sir Thomas S.	Lt Colonel	Le Blanc, Francis	Capt
Blythman, Augustus	Pte	Logan, Joseph	Capt
Briggs, James	Pte	Lynam, Joseph	1st Lt

96th Regiment of Foot

Don, George	Colonel

Kennedy, Thomas	Capt	Lynch, Henry Blois	Capt

97th (Queen's Own) Regiment of Foot

		Royal West India Rangers	
Briscoe, Edward	Lt	Dean, George	Capt
Garrett, Robert	Capt	Hill, Dudley St Leger	Capt
Grant, James	Lt	Lumley, Hon. Sir William	Colonel

98th Regiment of Foot

		York Chasseurs	
Bishopp, Cecil	Major	Anderson, Joseph	Capt
Fothergill, Joshua	Lt	Coghlan, Andrew	Lt Colonel
		Dallas, Robert William	Capt

99th (Prince of Wales's Tipperary) Regiment of Foot

		Ewart, John Frederick	Lt Colonel
Hoey, William R.	Capt	**1st Ceylon Regiment**	
		Fraser, John	Capt

Permanent Assistant Quartermaster Generals

		2nd Ceylon Regiment	
Bainbrigge, Philip	Major	Hamilton, Sir John	Colonel
Broke, Sir Charles	Major		
Greenock, Hon. Charles	Lt Colonel	**4th Ceylon Regiment**	
Haverfield, John	Lt Colonel	Fletcher, Thomas	Capt
Herries, William Lewis	Major	Kelly, Richard	Major

Staff Appointments in Spain and Portugal Employed upon a Particular Service

		2nd Garrison Battalion	
Armstrong, Richard	Major	Lawrence, Alexander	Lt Colonel
Bourke, Richard	Major		
Carrol, William Parker	Major	**3rd Garrison Battalion**	
Elder, Sir George	Major	Evans, George	Lt
Harvey, Sir Robert John	Major		

		4th Garrison Battalion	
Royal Staff Corps		Butler, Hon. Henry E.	Major
Dumaresq, William John	Lt	Doyle, Carlo Joseph	Major
Dundas, Sir Robert L.	Major		
Freeth, James	Lt	**5th Garrison Battalion**	
King, William James	Capt	Hart, Henry	Asst Surgeon

		7th Garrison Battalion	
2nd West India Regiment of Foot		Davy, William G.	Lt Colonel
D'Urban, Sir Benjamin	Lt Colonel		
Findlay, Alexander	Ensign	**4th Royal Veteran Battalion**	
Fleming, Edward	Major	Lutman, John	Capt

		5th Royal Veteran Battalion	
4th West India Regiment of Foot		Lamb, John	Ensign
Buchan, John	Lt Colonel		
Leith, Sir James	Colonel	**7th Royal Veteran Battalion**	
		Frederick, Roger	Capt

		13th Royal Veteran Battalion	
5th West India Regiment of Foot		Gourlay, Alexander	Capt
Evans, George de Lacy	Capt	Hagger, John	Lt

Royal York Rangers

Brisbane, Sir Thomas M.	Lt Colonel
Douglas, Sir Howard	Major

Langlands, George	Major

Glengarry Lt Infantry Fencibles

Fitzgibbon, James	Capt

New Brunswick Fencibles

Cockburn, Francis	Lt Colonel

King's German Legion
Staff

Bobers, Carl von	Capt and B Major
Drechsell, Frederick von	Capt and B Major

1ˢᵗ Regiment of Dragoons

Halpin, William	Paymaster
Kuhlmann, Otto	Lt
Levetzow, Friedrich von	Lt

2ⁿᵈ Regiment of Dragoons

Bulow, Friedrich von	Capt
Drangmeister, Henrich	Cornet

3ʳᵈ Regiment of Hussars

Brüggemann, Heinrich	Lt and Adjutant
Deichmann, Wilhelm	Cornet
Heise, Gabriel Wilhelm	Capt
Janssen, Georg	Capt
Kerssenbruch, Agatz von	Capt

1ˢᵗ Battalion Light Infantry

Albert, Anton	Lt
Alten, Charles von	Colonel
Goeben, August A. von	Capt
Klenck, Friedrich von	Lt

2ⁿᵈ Battalion Light Infantry

Baring, George Baron	Major
Bösewiel, Adolph	Major
Halkett, Sir Colin	Colonel

1ˢᵗ Line Battalion

Allen, Thomas	Lt
Boyd, George	Lt
Carmichael, Alexander	Lt
Holle, Carl von	Capt
Holzerman, Philipp	Capt
Lücken, Hartwig von	Ensign

2ⁿᵈ Line Battalion

Chüden, Paul G.	Major

3ʳᵈ Line Battalion

Diedel, Friedrich	Capt
Jeinsen, Friedrich von	Lt
Leschen, Friedrich	Lt

4ᵗʰ Line Battalion

Chüden, Georg W. C.	Major
Cronhelm, Theodor von	Ensign
Du Plat, Georg Carl A.	Lt Colonel
Heise, Georg	Capt
Langwerth, Ernest E. K.	Col Commandant
Leue, Georg Ludwig	Major

5ᵗʰ Line Battalion

Köhler, Carl	Lt

KGL Artillery

Blumenbach, Carl E.	Lt
Cleeves, Andrew	2ⁿᵈ Capt
De Schulzen, Detlef	Lt

Duke of Brunswick Oels' Corps

Brunswick, F.W. Duke of	Colonel in Chief

Duke of Brunswick Oels' Corps (Infantry)

De Braxion, Ernst	Capt
De Gillern, William	Capt
Heinemann, Rudolf von	Lt Colonel
Koschenbar, Ernst von	Lt

York Light Infantry Volunteers

Campbell, Sir Alexander	Colonel
Crompton, Richard	Capt

Royal Corsican Rangers

Ansley, Benjamin	Lt Colonel
Lowe, Sir Hudson	Colonel

Sicilian Regiment of Foot

Ferguson, Sir Ronald C.	Colonel

1ˢᵗ (Duke of York's) Greek Lt Inf Regt

D'Aguilar, George C.	Major

Royal Artillery

Adye, Stephen Galway	Lt Colonel
Arabin, Frederick	2ⁿᵈ Capt
Bayly, Frederick	1ˢᵗ Lt
Baynes, George M.	1ˢᵗ Lt
Baynes, Henry	2ⁿᵈ Capt
Bean, George	Capt

Bell, William	Lt		Glubb, Frederick	Capt
Bentham, William	2nd Capt		Hall, Edward S.	2nd Lt
Birch, Robert Henry	Capt		Harding, John	Colonel
Blachley, Charles	2nd Capt		Hardinge, Richard	1st Lt
Blachley, Henry	2nd Capt		Hawker, James	Lt Colonel
Bogue, Richard	Capt		Hennis, William Howe	2nd Lt
Bolton, Samuel	Capt		Heron, Basil R.	1st Lt
Bredin, Andrew	Capt		Hincks, John	1st Lt
Brereton, William	1st Lt		Holcombe, Harcourt F.	Capt
Breton, John F.	1st Lt		Hunt, Arthur	Capt
Bridges, Edward J.	1st Lt		Hutchesson, Thomas	Capt
Broadbent, William	Pte		Ingilby, William	1st Lt
Browne, Thomas G.	2nd Capt		Jago, Darell	2nd Lt
Bruce, John R.	1st Lt		Kett, Charles George	2nd Lt
Buckner, Richard	Lt Colonel		Knox, Francis	Capt
Bull, Robert	Capt		Lacy, Richard John J.	Major
Burton, John Curzon	1st Lt		Lawrence, William H.	1st Lt
Cairncross, John	Bombardier		Lawson, Douglas	1st Lt
Cairnes, Robert M.	2nd Capt		Leathes, Henry M.	1st Lt
Campbell, Patrick	Capt		Leech, Samuel	Pte
Cater, Thomas O.	1st Lt		Lees, John	Pte
Chester, John	Capt		Lefebure, George	Capt
Colquhoun, James Nesbit	1st Lt		Light, Henry	Capt
Cookson, George	Colonel		Litchfield, Richard	1st Lt
Crawford, Adam F.	2nd Capt		Lloyd, William John	Major
Cromie, Michael Thomas	1st Lt			

Ordnance Medical Department

Buxton, James William	2nd Asst Surgeon
Chisholm, Stuart	2nd Asst Surgeon
Frazer, John Whitley	Asst Surgeon
Ivey, William	Deputy Purveyor

Cubitt, Thomas	2nd Capt
Dansey, Charles C.	2nd Capt
Day, James	1st Lt
Dickson, Sir Alexander	Capt
Douglas, Robert	Capt
Downman, Thomas	Lt Colonel
Drawbridge, Charles	1st Lt
Drummond, Percy	Major
Dundas, William B.	2nd Capt
Duthie, William	Bombardier
Dyer, Sir John	Lt Colonel
Edwardes, David J.	1st Lt
Elgee, William	1st Lt
Eligé, John Peter	Capt
Evelegh, Henry	Lt Colonel
Eves, John	Gunner
Faddy, Peter	2nd Capt
Fisher, George B.	Lt Colonel
Fogo, James	2nd Capt
Forbes, James Staats	Gunner
Framingham, Sir Haylett	Colonel
Frazer, Sir Augustus S.	Lt Colonel
Frost, George	Bombardier
Fyers, Peter	Lt Colonel
Geary, Henry	Capt

Royal Artillery Drivers

Anderson, James	Pte
Blyth, John Willes	1st Lt Commissary
Calder, Thomas	Sgt
Glen, James	Driver

Field Train Department of Ordnance

Bradnock, George	Paymaster
Clubb, Robert	Clerk of the Stores
Fullerton, Alexander	Conductor/Stores
Henegan, Richard Drake	Commissary
Kilpatrick, John William	Conductor/Stores

Royal Engineers

Baddeley, Frederick H.	Lt
Barney, George	2nd Capt
Barou, Richard J.	Lt
Barry, Philip	Lt
Birch, James	2nd Capt

Birch, John Francis	Lt Colonel
Blanshard, Thomas	2nd Capt
Bolton, Daniel	Lt
Bonnycastle, Richard H.	2nd Capt
Boothby, Charles	Capt
Boteler, Richard	Capt
Bryce, Alexander	Colonel
Buckeridge, Henry Mark	Lt
Burgoyne, John Fox	Lt Colonel
By, John	Capt
Chapman, Stephen R.	Lt Colonel
Cheyne, Alexander	2nd Capt
Cole, Pennel	Lt
Collyer, George	2nd Capt
Cooper, Robert H. S.	Lt
Covey, Edward	Lt
Dalton, George	Lt
Davy, Henry	Lt
Dawson, William F.	2nd Capt
De Salaberry, Edward A.	Lt
Dickens, Thomas Mark	Capt
Dickenson, Sebastian	2nd Capt
Ellicombe, Charles G.	Capt
Elliott, Theodore Henry	Lt
Elphinstone, Howard	Lt Colonel
Elton, Isaac M.	Lt
Emmett, Anthony	2nd Capt
English, Frederick	Capt
Eyre, James William	Lt
Fanshawe, Edward	Capt
Faris, William	Lt
Fletcher, Sir Richard	Lt Colonel
Ford, William Henry	Lt Colonel
Forster, William F.	Lt
Fyers, Edward	2nd Capt
Fyers, Peter	Lt Colonel
Fyers, Thomas	Capt
Fyers, William	Colonel
Gilbert, Francis Yarde	Lt
Gipps, George	2nd Capt
Goldfinch, Henry	Lt Colonel
Grierson, Crighton	Lt
Hall, Lewis Alexander	Lt
Hamilton, George A.	2nd Capt
Harding, George Judd	Capt
Harris, John B.	2nd Capt
Head, Francis Bond	Lt
Henderson, Alexander	Lt
Henderson, George	Capt
Holloway, William C. E.	Capt
Hoste, Sir George C.	Capt

Hulme, John Lyon	2nd Capt
Hunt, Richard	Lt
Hustler, Robert S.	Capt
Hutchinson, Thomas K.	2nd Capt
Jones, Harry David	Capt
Jones, John Thomas	Capt
Jones, Rice	Capt
Judge, William	Sapper
Kay, Arthur	Lt
Kerr, John	Lt
Lancey, Thomas Furber	Lt
Landmann, George G.	Lt Colonel
Lascelles, Thomas	Lt
Lefebure, Charles	Capt
Lewis, Griffith George	Capt
Longley, Joseph	Lt
Luxmoore, Thomas C.	Lt

Royal Sappers and Miners

Birnes, Joseph	Pte
Gratton, Charles	Sub Lt

Recruiting Districts

Hamilton, Nicholas	Major

Commissariat Department

Ainslie, George	Asst Com Gen
Ashton, Henry	Clerk
Bowman, William F.	DACG
Coffin, Edward Pine	Dep Com Gen
Coope, William Jesser	Dep Com Gen
Cumming, William	Asst Com Gen
Dallas, Alexander R. C.	Asst Com Gen
Dickens, James	Dep Com Gen
Eppes, William R.	Treasury Clerk
France, Harold	Asst Com Gen
Gomm, Richard S.	Asst Com Gen
Haden, Francis Wastie	Asst Com Gen
Haines, Gregory	Dep Com Gen
Head, George	DACG
Laidley, James	DACG
Laidley, John	DACG
Lutyens, Charles	Dep Com Gen

Medical Department

Baxter, Alexander	Staff Surgeon
Bone, Hugh	Staff Surgeon
Borland, James	Insp Gen of Hosp
Brady, John James	Hospital Assistant
Brown, Ebenezer	Dep Insp Gen
Browne, Richard Jebb	Staff Surgeon

Clark, John	Staff Surgeon	**8th Hussars**	
Collier, Charles	Staff Surgeon	De La Howarderie, Graaf	Capt
Cooper, Samuel	Staff Surgeon	De Villers, C. N. J. F. M.	Major
Crump, Ely	Staff Surgeon		
Curby, Edward	Asst Surgeon	**Infantry – Staff**	
Denecke, George	Physician	Haren, Baron C. F. S. van	1st Lt and Adjt
Emery, Henry Gresley	Staff Surgeon		
Faulkner, Sir Arthur B.	Physician	**27th Jager Battalion**	
Fergusson, William	Insp of Mil Hosp	De Nave, B. D. J.	Capt
Forbes, Charles F.	Dep Insp Gen		
Forbes, James	Physician	**7th Infantry Battalion**	
Grant, James Robert	Insp Gen of Hosp	Carondel, J. C.	1st Lt
Gunning, John	Dep Insp Gen	De Berlaere, A. J. L. P.	1st Lt
Guthrie, George J.	Dep Insp Gen		
Hacket, William	Staff Surgeon	**5th National Militia Battalion**	
Halliday, Andrew	Staff Surgeon	Boeltjes, K.	1st Lt
Hennen, John	Staff Surgeon	De Haan, J.	1st Lt
Hilditch, Neil	Apothecary	Klejin, P. R.	2nd Lt
Hume, John Robert	Dep Insp Gen		
Lindsey, Owen	Staff Surgeon	**7th National Militia Battalion**	
		Heil, P.	2nd Lt
Chaplains Department		Jonquière, J. W. E.	2nd Lt
Bradford, William	Chaplain to Forces		
Briscall, Samuel	Chaplain to Forces	**2nd Nassau Regiment**	
Dayman, Charles	Chaplain to Forces	Hardt, A.	1st Lt
Jenkins, George	Chaplain to Forces	Hechmann, G.	Major
Leggatt, Samuel	Chaplain to Forces		
		28th Orange-Nassau Regiment	
Dutch Officers		Engel.	1st Lt
Cavalry – Staff			
De Collaert, Baron J.	Lt Gen		

1st Carabineers Regiment
Bisdom, D. R. — Major
Coenegracht, L. P. — Lt Colonel

2nd Carabineers Regiment
Henry, J. J. — 2nd Lt

3rd Carabineers Regiment
Lechleitner, C. M. — Lt Colonel

4th Dragoons
Daey, H. A. — 2nd Lt
Kreijsig, C. S. — Capt

6th Hussars
Breda, C. — Cornet
Heiden, F. M. van — Capt